WINN L. ROSCH
HARDWARE BIBLE, FIFTH EDITION

A Division of Macmillan Computer Publishing, USA
201 W. 103rd Street
Indianapolis, Indiana 46290

Winn L. Rosch Hardware Bible, Fifth Edition

International Standard Book Number: 0-7897-1743-3

Library of Congress Catalog Card Number: 98-85585

Printed in the United States of America

First Printing: August 1999

00   99   98   4   3   2   1

Trademarks

Warning and Disclaimer

Executive Editor
Jim Minatel

Acquisitions Editor
Jenny Watson

Development Editor
Tom Dinse

Managing Editor
Lisa Wilson

Project Editor
Sara Bosin

Copy Editor
Kristine Simmons

Indexer
Bruce Clingaman

Proofreader
Billy Fields

Technical Editor
Matthew Rainoff

Software Development Specialist
Aaron Price

Interior Design
Gary Adair

Cover Designer
Maureen McCarty

Copy Writer
Eric Bogert

Layout Technicians
Brian Borders
Susan Geiselman
Mark Walchle

Contents at a Glance

Table of Contents

About the Author

An accomplished photojournalist, for ten years **Winn L. Rosch** wrote regular columns in the *Cleveland Plain Dealer*, Ohio's largest daily newspaper, about stereo and video equipment. Occasionally he contributes features to that paper, often illustrated with photographs he has taken. Topics have varied from various local festivals to ice boating, hot air ballooning, and curling.

Rosch started writing about personal computers in 1981, when IBM introduced its first PC. Since then he has contributed over 1,000 articles to a number of magazines. At present, he is a contributing editor to *PC Magazine*. He has also been a contributing editor to *PC World*, *PC Week*, *PC Sources*, *PC Computing*, *Computer Shopper*, and *MacUser*. The Computer Press Association has given him its award for Best Feature.

Rosch has also written a dozen books about PCs, the best known being this one, the *Winn L. Rosch Hardware Bible*. He has also written the *Winn L. Rosch Printer Bible*, the *Winn L. Rosch Multimedia Bible*, and several others. He has moderated symposia at NetWorld and PC Expo personal computer conventions and often speaks before computer user groups.

Rosch holds a Doctor of Jurisprudence degree, is licensed to practice law in the State of Ohio, and has served several years on the Ohio State Bar Association's committee on computer law. In what he considers other lifetimes, he worked as a broadcast engineer, serving as chief engineer for several Cleveland radio stations, and building a television station in that city. He has also worked on electronic journalism projects for NBC and CBS.

In his off-hours, Rosch enjoys photography, oil painting, and occasionally torturing an old harpsichord. A local church recently recommended him for canonization, but he declined when he discovered its pastor's intent to propel him through the air with a black-powder charge. He lives quietly in a suburb of Cleveland, and chooses not to be more specific lest creditors, process-servers, and other ne'er-do-wells locate him.

Dedication

For Granny

Tell Us What You Think!

As the reader of this book, *you* are our most important critic and commentator. We value your opinion and want to know what we're doing right, what we could do better, what areas you'd like to see us publish in, and any other words of wisdom you're willing to pass our way.

As an *Associate Publisher* for *Que*, I welcome your comments. You can fax, email, or write me directly to let me know what you did or didn't like about this book—as well as what we can do to make our books stronger.

Please note that I cannot help you with technical problems related to the topic of this book, and that due to the high volume of mail I receive, I might not be able to reply to every message.

When you write, please be sure to include this book's title and author as well as your name and phone or fax number. I will carefully review your comments and share them with the author and editors who worked on the book.

Fax: 317.581.4666

Email: hardware@mcp.com

Mail: *Associate Publisher*
Que
201 West 103rd Street
Indianapolis, IN 46290 USA

Preface to the Fifth Edition

A mere two years have passed since the previous edition of the *Hardware Bible*, and yet PCs and the industry that created them have changed in unanticipated ways. Most dramatic has been the plummet in PC prices. Who would have expected PCs for free even two years ago? Today bargains are the norm rather than exception. Now PCs are cheap enough to be promotional giveaways. You can walk out of a retail store with a system for under $300 or keep the tab under $2000 even if you hold out for the latest and greatest microprocessor. Although notebook systems are persistently expensive—a temporary shortage of display screens in early 1999 helps assure that—their prices, too, have retreated. Any way you tally it up, the PC is closer to a toaster than ever before—the long-awaited information appliance, the computing commodity, but still a digital delight.

Technological developments, of course, underlie those low prices, just as they do the existence of the PC at all. Today, however, the PC represents a mature technology. Unlike a decade ago, you can buy any PC off the shelf and expect to work exactly the same as the rest—racing through your programs with such speed your head will spin as you try to justify buying an even faster PC. Of course Windows will, as always, crash in the middle of the afternoon, but it won't be from compatibility problems or foolish product selection. Nearly all the old bugaboos of matching components are gone, so price can be your primary guide—and a tempting one at that.

Two factors have led the way in making PCs cheaper—mass marketing and miniaturization. Shrinking the essential electronics of a computer onto a handful of cheap chips helps make the entire system cheap. The mass market—mass demand and mass sales—has provided the economic muscle underwriting the miniaturization and economy of scale. Neither of these factors changes the underlying technology—smaller, more numerous PCs still work the way they used to. Why then would anyone need a new edition of a book about those empowering technologies?

Because the turn of the millennium marks a turning point for PCs, too. Two decades into the PC revolution, PC technology is poised to make the most dramatic change since its inception. Finally the industry is about to break free from its roots. Much of the design of the first PC, which has for 20 years been the heart of every computer, will soon be cast aside to make way for new ideas and technologies. Tomorrow's PCs will be new and noble machines free from the shackles of the original PC design. Today, however, systems slide in between and combine the new and the old—the new to pave the way for the millennium and beyond and the old to keep your vintage peripherals and software working. That last bit of backward compatibility will remain only until you can see how pointless it is to cling to the slow old devices that hold no new profit potential for the PC industry. In other words, this edition is about PCs in transition.

Most of the technologies underlying the big changes are not truly news, at least if you've labored through earlier editions of this book. For example, you'll find FireWire and USB—the new interfaces that help empower the revolution—discussed in earlier editions (as well as here). PCI goes back a full *two* editions. The problem has been that the hardware and standards have outrun the software. Support for FireWire and USB has run ahead of operating system software. The first operating system with native support for both new interface standards will be Windows 2000. (The second edition of Windows 98 might arrive a bit earlier with similar support spliced on.) With the new software will come the long anticipated change—and the reason for a new edition.

Other changes also demand the attention of a new edition. PCI has nearly supplanted ISA as the bus standard. Not only has the quantity of memory you expect in a PC grown but the technology under it has changed as well. Instead of the Synchronous DRAM that now dominates new PCs, you'll soon want (and need) Rambus and its promise of 133MHz and higher speeds to push performance into new territories. Disk capacities are shooting up, too, breaking old barriers. Newer, high-speed connection systems are ready to link ever-faster disks to your PC—connection standards with names like UDMA/66. DVDs will soon be standard in every system. Flat-panel monitors are sprouting on desktops. Analog modems are singing their swan songs. Digital cameras have become the hottest new peripheral for PCs, if just to put pictures on your eBay offerings.

The sharks in the PC technology industry know they must keep moving to stay alive. And *you* need an edge to stay a couple strokes ahead of the sharks. That's what this book is for.

From my perspective, this has been one of the happier revisions to the *Hardware Bible*. Not that it was easy. Keeping up to date is never simple, and this time around it involved gutting a few chapters, reorganizing others (and to some extent, the book). But it has been among the most enlightened revisions, too. Instead of tearing material out to keep the size manageable, the book is written to keep things in check. The goal has been readability, keeping blocks of detail—both textual and tabular—out of the flow and reserving it for electronic reference.

With the freedom and storage space of the accompanying compact disc, nothing from previous editions and few new-but esoteric-details needed to be left out. Instead you can easily dig deeper by checking any of the more than 30 electronic appendixes, each specifically referenced in the text. In addition to the familiar hard disk parameter table, I've extracted the microprocessor quick reference from the *Hardware Bible* Web site and added a new, quick reference, Connectorama. With a couple of clicks, you can now find the pin-out for almost any connector in a PC as well as the wiring for the most important adapter cables.

Did I mention the *Hardware Bible* Web site (appropriately enough at www.hardwarebible.com)? Thanks to the cooperation of the publisher, the full text of the book can now appear on-line at a special password-protected location on the site that allows access to book owners only. You can reference all the book text and appendixes that are on the CD without the CD. Better still, as chapters get updated and revised throughout the life of the book, the changes will appear on-line so you can keep up to date. As long as you have the hardcopy of the book handy, you'll have access to the site—at least until a new edition comes out (incorporating all those changes and probably more).

So what are the changes? I could say you'll have to read the book to find out, but that's hardly an incentive. So in the spirit of television news, here's a tease to make you stick it out.

A guide to the Fifth Edition:

- Chapter 1 remains a basic introduction to PCs but has changed dramatically. To make the explanation more logical, I start this hardware book backward with a discussion of software. Then I work my way through the links between software and hardware to the hardware itself.

- Chapter 2, "System Boards," now looks at both mother and daughter—all the printed circuit boards in your PC. The emphasis in this chapter is the physical construction of modern electronics, how the motherboard holds the PC together, and how expansion boards add to the mix.

- Chapter 3, "Microprocessors," is, as always, an update including the latest microprocessors from Intel, AMD, Cyrix, and Centaur. In addition, I've reorganized the chapter to make it more readable, downplaying legacy microprocessors while preserving their history to help explain why today's chip designs are they way they are.

- Chapter 4, "Memory," shifts emphasis to new technologies and from chips to modules. You'll find discussion of more memories than at a 50th class reunion, including the latest RIMMs (that's Rambus In-line Memory Modules, if you can't wait to read the chapter).

- Chapter 5, "The BIOS," admits itself to be an exercise in irrelevance, given the rise of operating systems that steal both its thunder and lightning. Of course, you'll still find an explanation of how your PC starts up and what it does until the operating system takes over. Trends in BIOS design are all covered, up through Plug-and-Play and a pointer to ACPI, later in the book.

- Chapter 6, "Chipsets," concentrates on the products of today and casts aside the less-relevant aspects of PC history. The focus is the PCI-based architecture that serves as the foundation of the modern PC. I've also cleaned up some of the confusing issues regarding interrupt sharing, eliminating a mistake from the earlier edition.

- Chapter 7, "The Expansion Bus," puts more emphasis on PCI and CardBus, ready to move ISA to the legacy bin. Despite the changes, you'll still find a complete explanation of how the expansion bus actually works.

- Chapter 8, "Mass Storage Technology," builds on its foundation in previous editions, adding multiples to the discussions of gigabytes and updating topics like RAID.

- Chapter 9, "Storage Interfaces," now covers new modes brought by the ATA-5 and SPI-2 standards and corrects some inaccuracies in the earlier edition—chiefly which standards included specific features—caused by that edition covering standards before their approval. And I still look at standards before their approval, such as 66MHz ATA and Ultra 160m SCSI.

- Chapter 10, "Hard Disks," has been streamlined to shed issues irrelevant to the modern PC (I've moved them to appendixes).

- Chapter 11, "Floppy Disks," moves 5.25-inch to an appendix and adds coverage of the latest high-capacity drives including the 120MB SuperDisk, the Fuji/Sony 200MB HiFD system, and 250MB ZIP disks.

- Chapter 12, "Compact Disks," has been entirely rewritten to give a more cohesive view of the two technologies. It includes the latest information available on recordable and rewriteable DVDs and their drives. I've also included a first look at the new and competing DVD-Audio and Super Audio CD standards.

- Chapter 13, "Tape," still tips its hat at old technologies but notes the new and all the efforts that are keeping this ancient medium alive. I've added information about the Linear Tape Open formats (Accelis and Ultrium) as well as Advanced Intelligent Tape while preserving historic background on older tape formats that remain available.

- Chapter 14, "Input Devices," says good-bye to vintage technologies (like capacitive keyboards) and adds in USB support. Also new is improved covered of notebook PC pointing devices.

- Chapter 15, "Graphic Input Devices," is brand new, adding coverage of digital cameras to an updated view of scanners (extracted from the previous chapter).

- Chapter 16, "The Display System," still covers the basics of image-making but approaches new issues arising from 3D accelerators and multimedia needs and takes a more comprehensive look at video.

- Chapter 17, "Display Adapters," minimizes coverage of legacy display systems and focuses in on modern graphics adapters.

- Chapter 18, "Displays," illustrates more issues involved with CRTs but puts more emphasis on LCDs and a new technology called FED that holds a promise of someday replacing both CRTs and LCDs. And it hopes to have the final word on the new connection systems for desktop digital LCD monitors.

- Chapter 19, "Audio," looks at everything you'll want to hear from your PC, from microphones to speakers with more emphasis on compression technologies like the ubiquitous MP3. MIDI moves to an appendix.

- Chapter 20, "Peripheral Ports," examines the ports slated to be standard in the next generation of PCs—USB and FireWire—as well as IrDA. The old port designs, both serial and parallel move to...

- Chapter 21, "Legacy Ports," which covers the long-familiar RS-232C and parallel (Centronics through ECP) designs. Although the latest PC standards call for the elimination of these ports, with millions in service I couldn't ignore them, so here they are.

- Chapter 22, "Telecommunications," has streamlined analog modem coverage through V.90 technology and adds depth in its treatment of digital standards (say DSL).

- Chapter 23, "Networking," outlines the basics you need to know to build a small office or home network. In addition, you'll find hardware buying guidance and step-by-step setup instruction in Appendix N.

- Chapter 24, "Hard Copy," reflects the changes in printer technology over the last couple of years—many incremental improvements but few breakthroughs.

- Chapter 25, "Power," updates the previous edition and includes discussions of the latest standards from APM and ACPI to Smart Battery as well as familiar power-protection materials.

- Chapter 26, "Cases," gets physical and discusses the physical aspects of PC packaging including a look at the nascent Device Bay standard. Hands-on installation moves to Appendixes Y and Z.

Reflecting all those promises made for the appendixes, you'll find them in profusion on the Hardware Bible CD. I ran out of letters of the alphabet to identify them. Last count I had 32, not including the new Connectorama.

In addition, I've captured a couple features from the Hardware Bible Web site for faster access (though not as up to the minute) including the Microprocessor Quick Reference and the venerable Disk Parameter Reference for older drives.

As always, my publisher and I have done our best to assure the accuracy of what you find in here. Most of the material is drawn from the minds of industry experts who work with these technologies every day as well as from official standards (or proposals for standards-to-be). It has been at least double-checked and verified by other experts. And if that's not enough for you, I've included means to contact the organizations controlling the major standards so you can dig further into the details yourself. Admittedly the book falls short of a true scholarly text, missing the apparatus—footnotes, endnotes, and the like—but makes up for it in readability. After all, information you can understand is more valuable than detail you cannot fathom.

As always, you can depend on the names and dates given here. No date is mentioned lightly. It reflects when a given standard or technology was developed or released, specifically stated as such. Where names are too often forgotten, I've made an effort to put credit where it is due for many of the minor inventions that have made PCs as successful as they are. Where possible, I've made references to the Web using URLs current (and tested) when the book was written.

This book has always served two purposes: It's an introductory text to help anyone get up to speed on PCs and how they work. But once you know what's going on inside, it continues to serve as the ultimate PC reference. I've tried to update both as well as keep it relevant in today's vastly changed world of computing. As in previous editions, if you need an answer about PCs, how they work, how to make them work, or when they began to work, you will find it answered here, definitively.

Introduction

You don't need anyone, especially a pretentious book, to tell you what a PC is. You know. A PC is how you surf the Web. How you get and send your email. How you write newsletters or papers for school, memos and reports for work. How you analyze stocks for your retirement portfolio or that multi-million dollar business your company wants to acquire. How you clean up photographs, edit videos, collect MP3 music, and while away whatever hours you have left blasting aliens back where they came from—more likely invading out of a box you bought in a software store rather than from some distant planet. Distilled to its essence, a PC is something you need to carry on with your life in the modern world. You may even carry it around with you.

Although your PC truly is all of those things to you—and more—it's something else, too. More than just a means to an end, a PC is a physical thing. It's a chunk of metal, plastic, paint, and silicon that sits on your desk or next to it, nestles in your lap, or takes over the kitchen table after you clear away the remains of dinner. It has a bright colorful screen to mesmerize you and, to trip up your fingers, a set of spring-loaded traps called a keyboard. Inside it's filled with circuits sprouting more transistor junctions than you could count in half a lifetime, a work of technical sophistication arguably more complex than the Saturn V rockets that sent human aspirations and astronauts to the moon and back. (For the record, the astronauts made their valiant journeys to the moon without benefit of PCs—or even microprocessors. Things *were* simpler back then.)

As with any of humankind's other great inventions, the PC and the technologies developed around it not only stand to alter the course of civilization but already have. For two decades PCs have changed the way people work and play. Like some insidious silicon-based life form, they have wormed their way into our daily lives. Even people with myopic hindsight admit that PCs have changed how we see the world, the how we communicate, and even how we think. Most dramatic of all, PCs are even changing how we *shop*.

Indeed, the mystery is gone from the PC, and it's probably time we move beyond the classic clichés. You know the ones. Today the PC you can hold in the palm of your hand is as more powerful than a 1950's computer the size of a battleship (they had battleships in the Fifties) that consumed as much power as all the factories in North America combined—which probably wouldn't be much because they'd get pretty jumbled in the combining process. You don't go to the guru to buy a computer any more. You can shop for a PC in the same store you look for fishing tackle, panty hose, or dishwashers. Your children—maybe even you— probably don't know what a world *without* computers would be like.

One of the most important reasons for this popularity is how easy to use PCs have become. Whir your mouse around and you can edit a video or email the Emir of Bahrain. Learn one program, and you have a good idea how *all* the rest operate.

But that ease of use is all a big front. Behind the scenes, both the software and the computer you need to run it are immensely more complicated than the already complex products of just a few years ago. Programs have grown a thousandfold in the last decade and, fortunately, computers are about a thousand times more powerful. It's a wonderful if not miraculous situation—providing, of course, you already have the computer that's perfectly suited to your software.

If, however, you want to buy a new computer for the first time, replace the geriatric machine you already have, or add new capabilities to a new or old PC, that increased complexity can only make an analgesic manufacturer happy. Your headaches will multiply faster than rabbits bumbling into a warehouse full of Viagra. You'll confront terminology seemingly created with no other purpose than to confuse you and technologies more baffling than quantum mechanics—some, in fact, based on quantum principles.

Try to buy a PC without knowing what you're doing, and you might as well post your credit card number on the Web. A journey into the computer store or electronics department becomes something akin a trek through Antarctica—with your only guide, the salesperson, more intent on raiding your provisions than assuring your survival. Work on adding an accessory to your system without understanding how it works and connects to your PC, and you won't have to worry about what to do on your free evenings for the next few months.

Moreover, if you don't understand your system and the technologies behind it, you probably won't tap all the power of the PC. You won't be able to add to it and make it more powerful. You may not even know how to use everything that's there. You definitely won't know whether you have got the best computer for your purposes or some overpriced machine that cannot do what simpler models excel at.

The purpose of this book is to help you understand your present or future personal computer so that you can use rather than fear it. So that you can buy wisely and add to it intelligently. So that you can master the modern tool that's become part of nearly every occupation and avocation. So that you know not only what to do but why you have to do it that way.

This text is designed to give you an overview of what makes up a computer system. It will give you enough grounding in how the machine works so that you can understand what you're doing if you want to dig in and customize, expand, or upgrade your system. More importantly, you'll be able to buy a new PC more intelligently and select the best peripherals to add to it match your computer to your exact needs.

In addition, the charts and tables provide you with the reference materials you need to put that knowledge in perspective and to put it to work. Not only can you pin down the basic dates of achievements in technology, find the connections you need to link a printer or modem, and learn the meaning of every buzz word, this book will help you understand the general concept of your personal computer and give you the information you need to choose a computer and its peripherals. As you become more familiar with your system, this book will serve as a guide. It will even help you craft your own adapters and cables, if you choose to get your hands dirty.

The computer is nothing to fear and it need not be a mystery. It is a machine, and a straightforward one at that. One that you can master in the few hours it takes to read this book.

Basics

Putting a PC in its place is more than a matter of dropping it on your desk or lap. You need to understand what it does and what it can do—its purpose. What a PC does is run software, and that software carries out the tasks for which you bought your PC. This chapter gives you an overview of what a PC is from the purposeful perspective of what it does. First, we'll look at software, then how software and hardware work together; the various hardware components of a PC, and the technologies that underlie their construction. The goal is perspective so you have an overview of how the various parts of a PC work together. The rest of this book fills in the details.

What Is a PC and What Isn't—Definitions of Related Devices

Personal Computer	A computer designed to be used by one person. Five characteristics define the PC. It is *interactive* and responds immediately to your commands. It is *dedicated* to one individual rather than sharing its power simultaneously among several users. It is *programmable*, allowing software to define how it works and what it does. It is *connectable*, allowing you to link with other PCs and the World Wide Web. It is *accessible*, allowing anyone to quickly learn to use it and take control.
Workstation	In some circles, the term "workstation" is reserved for a PC that is connected to a network server. The other application of the term "workstation" refers to powerful, specialized computers still meant to be worked on by a single individual. For instance, a graphic workstation typically is a powerful computer designed to manipulate technical drawings or video images at high speed.
Server	A function rather than a particular PC technology or design. A server is a computer that provides resources that can be shared by other computers. These resources include files such as programs, databases, and libraries; output devices such as printers, plotters, and film recorders; and communications devices such as modems and Internet access facilities.
Simply Interactive	In early 1996, Microsoft coined the term SIPC to stand for *Simply Interactive Personal Computer*—the software giant's vision of what the home computer will eventually become. The idea was that the SIPC would become a home entertainment device, and part of, if not the complete home entertainment system.
Network Computer	Sometimes abbreviated as NC, the network computer was conceived as a scaled-down PC aimed primarily at making Internet connections. The NC is related to the *set-top box* that was meant to be an Internet link that used your television as the display, although the NC retained more computer features.
NetPC	An effort by industry leaders Intel and Microsoft (assisted by Compaq Computer Corporation, Dell Computer Corporation, and Hewlett-Packard Company) to create a specialized *business* computer that lowers the overall cost of using and maintaining small computers. The NetPC definition adds easy upgrading through a network and shaves off such things as floppy disks and the ISA expansion bus.
Numerical Control System	An NCS is a PC designed for harsh environments such as factories and machine shops. One favored term for the construction of the NCS is *ruggedized*, which essentially means made darned near indestructible with a thick steel or aluminum case that's sealed against oil, shavings, dust, and dirt.
Notebook	A PC repackaged for portability that includes all processing power and memory, the display system, the keyboard, and a stored energy supply (batteries).
Sub-notebook	A portable PC weighing less than five pounds, it is a specialized device meant to supplement rather than replace a desktop system.
Personal Digital Assistant	A general term for small devices that don't quite rise to being full PCs that come in two types. The *palmtop computer* fits in your hand and is dominated by a touch-sensitive screen that accepts pen input. The *handheld PC* looks more like a miniature PC with keyboard and screen, both reduced in size. The handheld is both an input and output device, truly a complete computer.

If anything puts people off from trying to understand PCs, it is the computer mystique. It's the smokescreen supposed computer gurus blow in your face to cover their own awe and lack of understanding.

Long ago, these self-proclaimed gurus conjured up images of the computer as the thinking machine, something both smarter than you and beyond your understanding. They have convinced most people that a computer of any kind is a machine with an electronic brain inside; with this logic, it quickly follows that working on such a machine is a job as delicate, demanding, and daunting as brain surgery.

Those gurus want you to believe that their thinking machine is inherently unknowable, something that operates as unfathomably as the human mind—something you cannot master because you, after all, are nothing but a mere mortal, not a computer guru. They want you to believe that you must consult an expert before buying one of these mysterious contraptions, pay someone to feed and care for it, and consult with someone before you make the least change or even think about using it. Hardly surprisingly, the someone they have in mind is like the guru who fills your own organic brain with such thoughts and empties your pockets.

Don't believe a word of it. A computer of any kind no more thinks like you than does a toaster. Computers think only in the way a filing cabinet or adding machine thinks—hardly in the same way as you do or Albert Einstein did. The computer has no emotions or motivations. It does nothing on its own, without explicit instructions that specify each step it must take. Moreover, the PC has no brain waves. The impulses traveling through the computer are no odd mixture of chemicals and electrical activity or of activation and repression. The computer deals in simple pulses of electricity, well understood and carefully controlled. The intimate workings of the computer are probably better understood than the seemingly simple flame that inhabits the internal combustion engine inside your car. Nothing mysterious lurks inside the thinking machine called the computer.

Nevertheless, with all the ways that PCs make your work and life easier and, sometimes, more fun, they are wonderful. And as they have become increasingly powerful in the last few years, they have become even more wonderful, taking on new jobs such as video editing and Web surfing and playing games that are quickly becoming more realistic than reality itself.

But PCs are not wonderful because they are so powerful. They are remarkable because they are so *useful*. All of the power in the PC is important to your life because it lets you do so many things. And that's the essence of it. A PC is a tool, a way of getting things done. And not just work.

What makes a PC useful is not the hardware. Left to itself, a PC is lazier than a hot summer day in the country. It won't do anything unless you tell it to. Far from using its vast intelligence to plot to take over the world, your spaceship, or even your free time, a PC is not the least bit imaginative. It simply waits for your orders and obeys them as your slave. Not one of all the PCs in the world has ever had an original thought. Everything they do originates in the human mind.

Instead of creating ideas, the PC helps bring ideas to life—capturing words, rendering images, controlling other machines. Your PC lets you extend your human abilities and reach beyond your limitations. To sum that up in a word, a PC is a tool. Like any tool from a stone ax to a Cuisinart, the PC assists you in achieving some goal. It makes your work easier—keeping your books, organizing your inventory, tracking your recipes, or honing your wordplay. It makes otherwise impossible tasks—for example, logging onto the Internet—manageable, often even enjoyable.

Before you can understand what makes a PC, how you make it work, and how you can make yours work better, you need to know what a PC is. That's where this chapter comes in. We'll start out in the traditional way, stepping tentatively at first, and then surely, from what we know into the dark jungle of the unknown. We begin with what you actually see and do with your PC, what makes the machine so useful: the jobs that it does, its *software*. Then, we'll dig into how the PC gets its work done, what makes the PC work, the physical embodiment required to carry out the computer's tasks—*hardware*. Next, we'll bring those two together, combining the goals and ideas with the hard reality, the link between software and hardware that makes the PC both viable and useful. Finally, we'll finish by examining the PC for what it is, a system, a tool, a thing that you can buy and use.

Software

Now, that's a surprise—a book on computer hardware and long before it mentions the minutiae of all that electronic stuff in the hard metal box, it digs into software. It wasn't always that way (look at the last edition of this book!), but today, the world is different. The days of buying a computer for the sake of having a computer are long gone. No longer do hobbyists salivate over megahertz and wait states. No longer is a system a status symbol and microprocessor power another gauge of virility. The personal computer has fallen from its pedestal and into your lap. For many people, the biggest question about computer hardware is whether the machine can run Netscape or the latest version of some favorite game such as *Cyberpunk Christmas*. The computer is not an end in itself but a means to an end—and that end is software.

The word doesn't describe a singular thing. Software is more than the box you buy and the little silver disc that comes inside it. Software is an entire technology that embraces not only what you see when you run your PC, but also a multitude of invisible happenings hiding beneath the surface. A modern PC runs several software programs simultaneously even when you think you're using just one—even when you don't think anything is running at all. These programs operate at different levels, each one taking care of its own specific job, invisibly linking to the others to give you the illusion you're working with a single, smooth-running machine.

What shows on your monitor are only the most obvious of all this software, the *applications*, the programs such as Myst or Office that you actually buy and load onto your PC, the ones that boldly emblazon their names on your screen every time you launch them. But there's more. Related to applications are the *utilities* you use to keep your PC in top running order, protect yourself from disasters, and automate repetitive chores. Down deeper, the *operating system* links your applications and utilities together and to the actual hardware of your PC. At or below the operating system level, you use *programming languages* to tell your PC what to do. You can write applications, utilities, or even your own operating system with the right programming language.

Definitions

Software earns its name for what it is not. It is not hardware. Whatever is not hard is soft and thus the derivation of the name. Hardware came first—simply because the hard reality of machines and tools existed long before anyone thought of computers or of the concept of programming. Hardware happily resides on page 551 of the 1965 dictionary I keep in my office. Software is nowhere to be found. (Why I keep a 1965 dictionary in my office is another matter entirely.)

Software comprises abstract ideas. In computers, the term embraces not only the application programs you buy and the other kinds of software (such as that in Table 1.1, below), but also the information or data used by those programs.

Programs are the more useful part of software because they do the actual work. The program tells your PC what to do—how to act, how to use the data it has, how to react to your commands, how to be a computer at all. Data just slows things down.

"Data," by the way, is the plural form of the Latin word "datum" and thus should take a plural verb—if you are writing in Latin. I've attempted to write this book in English, so I'll leave the pedantic "data are" constructions to the purists who'll celebrate the new millennium a year late.

Although important, a program is actually a simple thing. Broken down to its constituent parts, a computer program is nothing but a list of commands to tell your hardware what to do. Like a recipe, the program is a step-by-step procedure that, to the uninitiated, seems to be written in a secret code. In fact, the program *is* written in a code called the *programming language*, and the resultant list of instructions is usually called *code* by its programmers.

Everything that the computer does consists of nothing more than a series of these step-by-step instructions. The most elaborate computer program you can buy is simply a list of computer instructions together with some of the data on which the instructions act. The instructions are simple, but long and complex computer programs are built from them just as epics and novels are built from the words of the English language.

As with recipes that call for other recipes—a particular dish may require a sauce with its own recipe—computer programs may depend on or work with other programs. Think of the application as the dish and the operating system as the sauce. In modern systems, however, computer programs get stacked upon one another deeper than the most complex recipe. When it's running, a PC today is gorged with a feast of software. Too much software in the wrong form or place can make it choke and die, just as analogies can go too far.

Applications

The programs you buy in the box off your dealer's shelves, in person or through the Web, the ones you run to do actual work on your PC, are its *applications*. The word is actually short for *application software*. These are programs with a purpose, programs you apply to get something done. They are the dominant beasts of computing, the top of the food chain, the software you actually pay for. Everything else in your computer system, hardware and software alike, exists merely to make your applications work. Your applications determine what you need in your PC simply because they won't run—or run well—if you don't supply them with what they want.

Today's typical application comes on one or more CDs (compact discs, for the uninitiated) and comprises megabytes, even hundreds of megabytes, of digital stuff that you dutifully copy to your hard disk during the installation process. Hidden inside these megabytes is the actual function of the program, the part of the code that does what you buy the software for—be it to translate keystrokes into documents, calculate your bank balance, brighten your photographs, or turn MP3 files into music. The part of the program that actually works on the data you want to process is called an *algorithm*, the mathematical formula of the task converted into program code. An algorithm is just a way for doing something, written down as instructions, so you can do it again.

The hard-core computing work performed by major applications—the work of the algorithms inside them—is typically both simple and repetitive. For example, a tough statistical analysis may involve but a few lines of calculations, although the simple calculations will often be repeated again and again. Changing the color of a photo is no more than a simple algorithm executed over and over for each dot in the image.

That's why computers exist at all. They are simply good at—or at least patient enough—to repeatedly carry out the simple mathematical operations of the algorithms without complaining.

If you were to tear apart a program to see how it works—what computer scientists call *disassembling* the program—you'd make a shocking discovery. The algorithm makes up little of the code of a program. Most of the multi-megabyte bulk you buy is meant to hide the algorithm from you, like the fillers and flavoring added to some potent but noxious medicine.

Before the days of graphical operating systems, as exemplified by Microsoft's ubiquitous Windows family, the bulk of the code of most software applications was devoted to making the rigorous requirements of the computer hardware more palatable to your human ideas, aspirations, and whims. The part of the software that serves as the bridge between your human understanding and the computer's needs is called the *user interface*. It can be anything from a typewritten question mark that demands you type some response to a Technicolor graphic menu luring your mouse to point and click. Windows simplifies the programmer's task by providing most of the user-interface functions for your applications. Now, most of the bulk of an application is devoted to mating not with you, but with Windows. The effect is the same. It just takes more megabytes to get there.

No matter whether your application must build its own user interface or relies on that provided by Windows, the most important job of most modern software is simply translation. The program converts your commands, instructions, and desires into a form digestible by your operating system and PC. In particular, the user interface translates the words you type and the motion of your arm pointing your mouse into computer code.

This translation function, like the Windows user interface, is consistent across most applications. All programs work with the same kind of human input and produce the same kind of computer codes. The big differences between modern applications are the algorithms central to the tasks to be carried out. Application software often is divided into several broad classes based upon these tasks. Table 1.1 lists the traditional division of functions or major classifications of PC application software.

TABLE 1.1   Basic Types of PC Application Software

Class of Software	Function
Web browsers	Entering and interacting with Web sites and servers to buy, sell, and research your favorite interests and just while away evenings, afternoons, and the rest of your life
Email programs	Sending and receiving instant messages from friends, associates, and solicitors from your neighborhood and around the world

Class of Software	Function
Word processors	Getting your words ready for print or electronic publishing
Spreadsheets	Making the accountant's ledger automatic to calculate arrays of numbers
Databases	Filing with instant access and the ability to automatically sort itself
Drawing and painting programs	Creating and editing images such as blueprints and cartoon cells that can be filed and edited with electronic ease
Multimedia software	Playing MP3 and WAV files for music, showing AVI or MOV video files, playing games, or displaying images and sound like a movie theatre under the control of an absolute dictator (you)

The lines between many of these applications are blurry. For example, many people find that spreadsheets serve all their database needs, and most spreadsheets now incorporate their own graphics for charting results.

Several software publishers completely confound the distinctions by combining most of these applications' functions into a single package that includes a database, graphics, a spreadsheet, and word processing. These combinations are termed *application suites.* Ideally, they offer several advantages. Because many functions (and particularly the user interface) are shared between applications, large portions of code need not be duplicated as would be the case with standalone applications. Because the programs work together, they better know and understand one another's resource requirements, which means you should encounter fewer conflicts and memory shortfalls. Because they are all packaged together, you stand to get a better price from the publisher.

Although application suites have vastly improved since their early years, they sometimes show their old weaknesses. Even the best sometimes fall short of the ideal. They are often comprised of parts that don't perfectly mesh together because the individual parts are created by different design teams over long periods. Even the savings can be elusive because you may end up buying several applications you rarely use among the ones you want. Nevertheless, packages such as Microsoft Office or Lotus Smart Suite have become popular because they are single-box solutions that fill the needs of most people, handling more tasks with more depth than they ordinarily need. In other words, the suite is an easy way to ensure you'll have the software you need for almost whatever you do.

Utilities

Even when you're working toward a specific goal, you often have to make some side trips. Although they seem unrelated to where you're going, they are as much a necessary part of the journey as any other. You may run a billion-dollar pickle packing empire from your office, but you might never get your business negotiations done were it not for the regular housekeeping that keeps the place clean enough for visiting dignitaries to walk around without slipping on pickle juice on the floor.

The situation is the same with software. Although you need applications to get your work done, you need to take care of basic housekeeping functions to keep your system running in top condition and working most efficiently. The programs that handle the necessary auxiliary functions are called *utility software*.

From the name alone, you know that utilities do something useful, which in itself sets them apart from much of the software on today's market. Of course, the usefulness of any tool depends on the job you have to do—a pastry chef has little need for the hammer that so well serves the carpenter or PC technician—and most utilities are crafted for some similar, specific need. For example, common PC utilities keep your disk organized and running at top speed, prevent disasters by detecting disk problems and viruses, and save your sanity should you accidentally erase a file.

The most important of these functions are included with today's PC operating systems, either integrated into the operating system itself or as individual programs that are part of the operating system package. Others you buy separately, at least until Microsoft buys out the company that offers them.

Common utilities include backup, disk defragmenters, font management, file compression, and scheduling—all of which were once individual programs from different publishers, now all of which come packed in Windows. Antivirus and version-tracking programs are utilities available separately from Windows.

Modern utilities are essentially individual programs that load like ordinary applications when you call upon them. The only difference between them and other applications is what they do. Utilities are meant to maintain your system rather than come up with answers or generate output.

Applets

An *applet* is a small software application that's usually dedicated to a single simple purpose. It may function as a standalone program you launch like an ordinary application, or it may run from within another application. Typically, the applet performs a housekeeping function much like a utility, but the function of an applet is devoted to supporting an overriding application rather than your PC in general. That said, some system utilities may take the form of applets, too. Applets are mostly distinguished from other software by their size and the scope of their functions.

Applets are often included with or as part of application software packages. Some are included with operating systems such as Windows. In addition, the Java code routines that your web browser downloads to add action to your screen or perform simple tasks are often considered applets. The chief distinction between an applet and a full application may be little more than that you don't buy applets separately and never have.

Operating Systems

The basic level of software with which you will work on your PC is the operating system. It's what you see when you don't have an application or utility program running. But an operating system is much more than what you see on the screen.

As the name implies, the operating system tells your PC how to operate, how to carry on its most basic functions. Early operating systems were designed simply to control how you read from and wrote to files on disks and were hence termed *disk operating systems*, (which is why the original PC operating system, DOS, was called DOS). Today's operating systems add a wealth of functions for controlling every possible PC peripheral from the keyboard (and mouse) to the monitor screen.

The operating system in today's PCs has evolved from simply providing a means of controlling disk storage into a complex web of interacting programs that perform several functions. The most important of these is linking the various elements of your computer system together. These linked elements include your PC hardware, your programs, and you. In computer language, the operating system is said to provide a common hardware interface, a common programming interface, and a common user interface.

An *interface*, by the way, is the point at which two things connect together; for example, the human interface is where you, the human being, interact with your PC. The hardware interface is where your computer hardware links to its software. The programming interface is where programs link to the operating system. And the user interface is where you, as the user, link to the operating system. Interfaces can combine and blend together. For example, the user interface of your operating system is part of the human interface of your PC.

Of the operating system's many interfaces, only one, the user interface, is visible to you. The user interface is the place at which you interact with your computer at its most basic level. Sometimes, this part of the operating system is called the *user shell*. In today's operating systems, the shell is simply another program and you can substitute one shell for another. Although with Windows most people stick with the shell that Microsoft gives them, you don't have to. People who use UNIX or Linux often pick their own favorite shell.

In effect, the shell is the starting point to get your applications running and the home base that you return to between applications. The shell is the program that paints the desktop on the screen and lets you choose the applications you want to run.

Behind the shell, the *Application Program Interface*, or API, of the operating system gives programmers a uniform set of *calls*, key words that instruct the operating system to execute a built-in program routine that carries out some predefined function. For example, the API of Windows allows programmers to link their applications to the operating system to take advantage of its user interface. A program can call a routine from the operating system that draws a menu box on the screen.

Using the API offers programmers the benefit of having the complicated aspects of common program procedures already written and ready to go. Programmers don't have to waste their time on the minutiae of moving every bit on your monitor screen or other common operations. The use of a common base of code also eliminates duplication, which makes today's overweight applications a bit more svelte. Moreover, because all applications use basically the same code, they have a consistent look and work in a consistent manner. This prevents your PC from looking like the accidental amalgamation of the late-night work of thousands of slightly aberrant engineers that it is.

As new technologies, hardware, and features get added to the repertory you expect from your PC, the operating system maker must expand the API to match. Old operating systems required complete upgrades or replacements to accommodate the required changes. Modern operating systems are more modular and accept extensions of their APIs with relatively simple installations of new code. For example, one of the most important additions to the collection of APIs used by Windows 95 was set of multimedia controls called *DirectX*. Although now considered part of all versions of Windows, this collection of four individual APIs, later expanded to six, didn't become available until two months after the initial release of Windows 95. The DirectX upgrade APIs supplemented the original API multimedia control program code in the original release with full 32-bit versions.

At the other side of the API, the operating system links your applications to the underlying computer hardware through the hardware interface. Once we take a look at what that hardware might be, we'll take a look how the operating system makes the connection in the section "Linking Software and Hardware," later in this chapter.

Outside of the shell of the user interface, you see and directly interact with little of an operating system. The bulk of the operating system program code works invisibly (and continuously). And that's the way it's designed to be.

Programming Languages

A computer program—whether applet, utility, application, or operating system—is nothing more than a list of instructions for the brain inside your computer, the microprocessor, to carry out. A microprocessor instruction, in turn, is a specific pattern of bits, a digital code. Your computer sends the list of instructions making up a program to its microprocessor one at a time. Upon receiving each instruction, the microprocessor looks up what function the code says to do, and then it carries out the appropriate action.

Microprocessors by themselves only react to patterns of electrical signals. Reduced to its purest form, the computer program is information that finds its final representation as the ever-changing pattern of signals applied to the pins of the microprocessor. That electrical pattern is difficult for most people to think about, so the ideas in the program are traditionally represented in a form more meaningful to human beings. That representation of instructions in human-recognizable form is called a *programming language.*

As with a human language, a programming language is a set of symbols and the syntax for putting them together. Instead of human words or letters, the symbols of the programming language correspond to patterns of bits that signal a microprocessor exactly as letters of the alphabet represent sounds that you might speak. Of course, with the same back-to-the-real-basics reasoning, an orange is a collection of quarks squatting together with reasonable stability in the center of your fruit bowl. The metaphor is apt. The primary constituents of an orange—whether you consider them quarks, atoms, or molecules—are essentially interchangeable, even indistinguishable. By itself, each one is meaningless. Only when they are taken together do they make something worthwhile (at least from a human perspective), the orange. The overall pattern, not the individual pieces, is what's important.

Letters and words work the same way. A box full of vowels wouldn't mean anything to anyone not engaged in a heated game of *Wheel of Fortune*. Match the vowels with consonants and arrange them properly, and you might make words of irreplaceable value to humanity: the works of Shakespeare, Einstein's expression of general relativity, or the formula for Coca-Cola. The meaning is not in the pieces but their patterns.

The same holds true for computer programs. The individual commands are not as important as the pattern they make when they are put together. Only the pattern is truly meaningful.

You make the pattern of a computer program by writing a list of commands for a microprocessor to carry out. At this level, programming is like writing reminder notes for yourself after a morning when you know you'll still be too groggy to think straight—first socks, then shoes.

This step-by-step command system is perfect for control freaks but otherwise is more than most people want to tangle with. Even simple computer operations require dozens of microprocessor operations, so writing complete lists of commands in this form can be more than many programmers—let alone normal human beings—want to deal with. To make life and writing programs more understandable, engineers developed *higher-level programming languages.*

A higher-level language uses a vocabulary that's more familiar to people than patterns of bits, often commands that look something like ordinary words. A special program translates each higher-level command into a sequence of bit-patterns that tells the microprocessor what to do.

Machine Language

Every microprocessor understands its own repertoire of instructions just as a dog might understand a few spoken commands. Where your pooch might sit down and roll over when you ask it to, your processor can add, subtract, move bit-patterns around, and change them. Every family of microprocessor has a set of instructions that it can recognize and carry out, the necessary understanding designed into the internal circuitry of each microprocessor chip.

The entire group of commands that a given model of microprocessor understands and can react to is called that microprocessor's *instruction set* or its *command set*. Different microprocessor families recognize different instruction sets, so the commands meant for one chip family would be gibberish to another. For example, the Intel family of microprocessors understands one command set; the IBM/Motorola PowerPC family of chips recognizes an entirely different command set. That's the basic reason why programs written for the Apple Macintosh (which is based on PowerPC microprocessors) won't work on PCs (which use Intel microprocessors).

That native language that a microprocessor understands, its instruction set and the rules for using it, is called *machine language*. The bit-patterns of electrical signals in machine language can be expressed directly as a series of ones and zeros, such as 0010110. Note that this pattern directly corresponds to a binary (or base-two) number. As with any binary number, the machine language code of an instruction can be translated into other numerical systems as well. Most commonly, machine language instructions are expressed in hexadecimal form (base-16 number system). For example, the 0010110 subtraction instruction becomes 16 (Hex).

Assembly Language

Machine language is great if you're a machine. People, however, don't usually think in terms of bit-patterns or pure numbers. Although some otherwise normal human beings can and do program in machine language, the rigors of dealing with the obscure codes takes more than a little getting used to. After weeks, months, or years of machine language programming, you begin to learn which numbers do what. That's great if you want to dedicate your life to talking to machines but not so good if you have better things to do with your time.

For human beings, a better representation of machine language codes involves mnemonics rather than strictly numerical codes. Descriptive word fragments can be assigned to each machine language code so that 16(Hex) might translate into SUB (for subtraction).

Assembly language takes this additional step, enabling programmers to write in more memorable symbols.

Once a program is written in assembly language, it must be converted into the machine language code understood by the microprocessor. A special program called an *assembler* handles the necessary conversion. Most assemblers do even more to make the programmer's life more manageable. For example, they enable blocks of instructions to be linked together into a block called a *subroutine*, which can later be called into action by using its name instead of repeating the same block of instructions again and again.

Most of assembly language involves directly operating the microprocessor using the mnemonic equivalents of its machine language instructions. Consequently, programmers must be able to think in the same step-by-step manner as the microprocessor. Every action that the microprocessor does must be handled in its lowest terms. Assembly language is consequently known as a low-level language because programmers write at the most basic level.

High-Level Languages

Just as an assembler can convert the mnemonics and subroutines of assembly language into machine language, a computer program can go one step further, translating more human-like instructions into multiple machine language instructions that would be needed to carry them out. In effect, each language instruction becomes a subroutine in itself.

The breaking of the one-to-one correspondence between language instruction and machine language code puts this kind of programming one level of abstraction further from the microprocessor. That's the job of the high-level languages. Instead of dealing with each movement of a byte of information, high-level languages enable the programmer to deal with problems as decimal numbers, words, or graphic elements. The language program takes each of these high-level instructions and converts it into a long series of digital code microprocessor commands in machine language.

High-level languages can be classified into two types: interpreted and compiled. Batch languages are a special kind of interpreted language.

Interpreted Languages

An interpreted language is translated from human to machine form each time it is run by a program called an *interpreter*. People who need immediate gratification like interpreted programs because they can be run immediately, without intervening steps. If the computer encounters a programming error, it can be fixed, and the program can be tested again immediately. On the other hand, the computer must make its interpretation each time the program is run, performing the same act again and again. This repetition wastes the computer's time. More importantly, because the computer is doing two things at once, both executing the program and interpreting it at the same time, it runs more slowly.

Today, the most important interpreted computer language is Java, the tongue of the Web created by Sun Microsystems. Your PC downloads a list of Java commands and converts them into executable form inside your PC. Your PC then runs the Java code to make some obnoxious advertisement dance and flash across your screen.

The interpreted design of Java helps make it universal. The Java code contains instructions that any PC can carry out regardless of its operating system. The Java interpreter inside your PC converts the universal code into the specific machine language instructions your PC and its operating system understands.

Before Java, the most popular interpreted language was BASIC, an acronym for the Beginner's All-purpose Symbolic Instruction Code. BASIC was the first language for personal computers and was the foundation upon which Microsoft Corporation was built. (See Appendix A, "PC History.") It got a boost in the PC realm when IBM hardwired BASIC into the first several generations of its personal computers.

In classic form, using an interpreted language involved two steps. First, you would start the language interpreter program, which gave you a new environment to work in, complete with its own system of commands and prompts. Once in that environment, you then executed your program, typically starting it with a "Run" instruction. More modern interpreted systems such as Java hide the actual interpreter from you. The Java program appears to run automatically by itself, although in reality the interpreter is hidden in your Internet browser or operating system. Microsoft's Visual Basic gets its interpreter support from a *runtime module*, which must be available to your PC's operating system for Visual Basic programs to run.

Compiled Languages

Compiled languages execute like a program written in assembler, but the code is written in a more human-like form. A program written with a compiled language gets translated from high-level symbols into machine language just once. The resulting machine language is then stored and called into action each time you run the program. The act of converting the program from the English-like compiled language into machine language is called *compiling* the program; to do this, you use a language program called a *compiler*. The original, English-like version of the program, the words and symbols actually written by the programmer, is called the *source code*. The resulting machine language makes up the program's *object code*.

Compiling a complex program can be a long operation, taking minutes, even hours. Once the program is compiled, however, it runs quickly because the computer needs only to run the resulting machine language instructions instead of having to run a program interpreter at the same time. Most of the time, you run a compiled program directly from the DOS prompt or by clicking on an icon. The operating system loads and executes the program without further ado. Examples of compiled languages include today's most popular PC programming language, C++, as well as other tongues left over from earlier days of programming—COBOL, FORTRAN, and Pascal.

Object-oriented languages are special compiled languages designed so that programmers can write complex programs as separate modules termed *objects*. A programmer writes an object for a specific, common task and gives it a name. To carry out the function assigned to an object, the programmer needs only to put its name in the program without reiterating all the object's code. A program may use the same object in many places and at many different times. Moreover, a programmer can put a copy of an object into different programs without the need to rewrite and test the basic code, which speeds up the creation of complex programs. C++ is object-oriented.

Because of the speed and efficiency of compiled languages, compilers have been written that convert interpreted language source code into code that can be run like any compiled program. A BASIC compiler, for example, will produce object code that will run from the DOS prompt without the need for running the BASIC interpreter. Some languages, such as Microsoft QuickBasic, incorporate both interpreter and compiler in the same package.

When PCs were young, getting the best performance required using a low-level language. High-level languages typically included error routines and other overhead that bloated the size of programs and slowed their performance. Assembly language enabled programmers to minimize the number of instructions they needed and ensured that they were used as efficiently as possible.

Optimizing compilers do the same thing as ordinary compilers but do it better. By adding an extra step (or more) to the program compiling process, the optimizing compiler checks to ensure that program instructions are arranged in the most efficient order possible to take advantage of all the capabilities of the computer's processor. In effect, the optimizing compiler does the work that would otherwise require the concentration of an assembly language programmer.

In the end, the result of using any language is the same. No matter how high the level of the programming language, no matter what you see on your computer screen, no matter what you type to make your machine do its daily work, everything that your computer does results from following a pattern of digital code to which it reacts in knee-jerk fashion. Not exactly smart on the level of an Albert Einstein or even the trouble-making kid next door, but it's the results that count. Your computer can carry out complex tasks quickly and efficiently as if it were actually thinking.

Libraries

Inventing the wheel was difficult and probably took human beings something like a million years—a long time to have your car sitting up on blocks. Reinventing the wheel is easier because you can steal your design from a pattern you already know. But it's far, far easier to simply go out and buy a wheel.

Writing program code for a specific but common task often is equivalent to reinventing your own wheel. You're stuck with stringing together a long list of program commands just like all the other people writing programs have to do. Your biggest consolation is that you need to do it only once. You can then re-use the same set of instructions the next time you have to write a program that needs the same function.

For really common functions, you don't have to do that. Rather than reinvent the wheel, you can buy one. Today's programming languages include collections of common functions called *libraries* so you don't have to bother with reinventing anything. You only need pick the prepackaged code you want from the library and incorporate it into your program. The language compiler links the appropriate libraries to your program so that you only need to refer to a function by a code name. The functions in the library become an extension to the language, a *meta-language*.

Development Environments

Even when using libraries, you're still stuck with writing a program in the old-fashioned way—a list of instructions. That's an effective but tedious way of building a program. The PC's strength is taking over tedious tasks, so you'd think you could use some of that power to help you write programs more easily.

In fact, you can. A *development environment* lets you program the way you run modern software. You drag and drop items from menus to build the interface. The software remembers what you do and what you accomplish, and then operating as a *code generator*, it creates the series of programming language commands that achieves the same end.

Working with a development environment is a breeze compared to traditional programming. For example, instead of writing all the commands to pop a dialog box on the screen, you click on a menu and choose the kind of box you want. After it obediently pops on the screen, you can choose the elements you want inside it from another menu, using your mouse to drag buttons and labels around inside the box. When you're happy with the results, the program grinds out the code. In a few minutes, you can accomplish what it might have taken you days to write by hand.

Batch Languages

A *batch language* allows you to submit a program directly to your operating system for execution. That is, the batch language is a set of operating system commands that your PC executes sequentially as a program. The resulting batch program works like an interpreted language in that each step gets evaluated and executed only as it appears in the program.

Applications often include their own batch languages. These, too, are merely lists of commands for the application to carry out in the order that you've listed them to perform some common, everyday function. Communications programs use this type of programming to automatically log into the service of your choice and even retrieve files. Databases use their own sort of programming to automatically generate reports that you regularly need. The process of transcribing your list of commands is usually termed *scripting*. The commands that you can put in your program scripts are sometimes called the *scripting language*.

Scripting actually *is* programming. The only difference is the language. Because you use commands that are second nature to you (at least after you've learned to use the program) and follow the syntax that you've already learned running the program, the process seems more natural than writing in a programming language. That means if you've ever written a script to log onto the Internet or modified an existing script, you're a programmer already. Give yourself a gold star.

Hardware

Hardware is what puts your software into action. From the standpoint of running a program, hardware is your entire PC. You require everything that's in the box to make an application work; otherwise, it wouldn't be in the box and you shouldn't have to pay for it. In other words, your PC is a comprehensive hardware whole aimed specifically at running your software.

Every PC is built from an array of components, each of which serves a specific function in making the overall machine work. As with the world of physical reality, a PC is built from fundamental elements combined together. Each of these elements adds a necessary quality or feature to the final PC. These building blocks are *hardware components*, built of electronic circuits and mechanical parts to carry out a defined function. Although all of the components work together, they are best understood by examining them and their functions individually.

The major functions of a modern PC in running its software are five: thinking, remembering, listening, monitoring, and communicating. Each of these functions requires one or more hardware components to carry out. For example, thinking is not merely a matter of microprocessors. It requires memory in which to execute programs, a chipset to link its circuits to the rest of the PC, and some semi-permanent software in the form of the BIOS to bring it all to life.

Over the years of the development of the PC, the distinctions between many of these individual components have turned out not to be hard and fast. In the early days of PCs, most manufacturers followed the same basic game plan using the same components in the same arrangement, but today greater creativity and diversity rules. What once were separate components have merged together; others have been separated out. Their functions, however, remain untouched. For example, although modern PCs may lack the separate timer chips of early machines, the function of the timer has been incorporated into the support circuitry chipsets, all of which remain part of its "thinking" function.

For purposes of this book and discussion, we'll divide the PC into several major functional areas, each of which can be subdivided into the major components required to make a complete PC. These include the thinking part (the system unit), the remembering part (mass storage), the listening part (the keyboard-and-mouse control system and various input devices), the monitoring part (the display system), and the communicating part (various ports and external devices).

Thinking

The entire PC is a thinking machine, and the part of a PC that most people usually think of as the computer—the box that holds all the essential components except, in the case of desktop machines, the keyboard and monitor—is the *system unit*. Sometimes called CPU—for Central Processing Unit, a term also used to describe microprocessors as well as mainframe computers—the system unit is the basic computer component. It houses the main circuitry of the computer and provides the jacks (or outlets) that link the computer to the rest of its accouterments, including the keyboard, monitor, and peripherals. A notebook computer combines all of these external components into one but is usually called simply the computer rather than system unit or CPU.

One of the primary functions of the system unit is physical. It gives everything in your computer a place to be. It provides the mechanical mounting for all the internal components that make up your computer, including the motherboard, disk drives, and expansion boards. The system unit is the case of the computer that you see and everything that is inside it. The system unit supplies power to operate the PC and its internal expansion, disk drives, and peripherals.

Motherboard

The centerpiece of the system unit is the motherboard. All the other circuitry of the system unit is usually part of the motherboard or plugs directly into it.

The electronic components on the motherboard carry out most of the functions of the machine, running programs, making calculations, even arranging the bits that will display on the screen.

Because the motherboard defines each computer's functions and capabilities and because every computer is different, it only stands to reason that every motherboard is different, too. Not exactly. Many different computers have the same motherboard designs inside. And oftentimes, a single computer model might have any of several different motherboards depending on when it came down the production line (and what motherboard the manufacturer got the best deal on).

The motherboard holds the most important elements of your PC, those that define its function and expandability. These include the microprocessor, BIOS, memory, mass storage, expansion slots, and ports.

Microprocessor

The most important of the electronic components on the motherboard is the *microprocessor*. It does the actual thinking inside the computer. Which microprocessor of the dozens currently available determines not only the processing power of the computer but also what software language it understands (and thus what programs it can run).

Many older computers also had a *coprocessor* that added more performance to the computer on some complex mathematical problems such as trigonometric functions. Modern microprocessors generally internally incorporate all the functions of the coprocessor.

Memory

Just as you need your hands and workbench to hold tools and raw materials to make things, your PC's microprocessor needs a place to hold the data it works on and the tools to do its work. *Memory*, which is often described by the more specific term *RAM* (which means Random Access Memory), serves as the microprocessor's workbench. Usually located on the motherboard, your PC's microprocessor needs memory to carry out its calculations. The amount and architecture of the memory of a system determines how it can be programmed and, to some extent, the level of complexity of the problems that it can work on. Modern software often requires that you install a specific minimum of memory—a minimum measured in megabytes—to execute properly. With modern operating systems, more memory often equates to faster overall system performance.

BIOS

A computer needs a software program to work. It even needs a simple program just to turn itself on and be able to load software. The *Basic Input/Output System* (BIOS) of a computer is a set of permanently recorded program routines that give the system its fundamental operational characteristics, including instructions telling the computer how to test itself every time it is turned on. Using today's plug-and-play technology, the BIOS cooperates with your operating system to configure all the peripherals you plug into your PC. The operating system then replaces most of the BIOS code with its own software. In other words, after the BIOS boots and tests your PC, it steps out of the way so that your software can get the real work done.

Chipsets

The *support circuitry* on your PC's motherboard links its microprocessor to the rest of the PC. A microprocessor, although the essence of a computer, is not a computer in itself. (If it were, it would be called something else, such as a computer.) The microprocessor requires additional circuits to bring it to life: clocks, controllers, and signal converters. Each of these support circuits has its own way of reacting to programs and thus helps determine how the computer works.

In today's PCs, all of the traditional functions of the support circuitry have been squeezed into *chipsets*, relatively large integrated circuits. In that most PCs now use one of a small range of microprocessors, their chipsets distinguish their motherboards and performance as much as do their microprocessors. In fact, for some folks the choice of chipset is a major purchasing criterion.

Expansion Slots

Exactly as the name implies, the *expansion slots* of a PC allow you to expand its capabilities by sliding in accessory boards, cleverly termed expansion boards. The slots are spaces inside the system unit of the PC that provide special sockets or connectors to plug in your expansion boards. The expansion slots of notebook PCs accept modules the size of credit cards that deliver the same functions as expansion boards.

Remembering

A PC must remember huge amounts of program code and data to carry out your programs. The components of your PC that do this remembering are called *mass storage* devices. They deal with data in bulk.

In nearly all of today's computers, the primary repository for this information is a hard disk drive. Floppy disks, CD ROM, and DVD drives give you a way of transferring programs and data to (and from) your PC. One or more mass storage interfaces link the various storage systems to the rest of your PC. In modern systems, these interfaces are often part of the circuitry of the motherboard.

Hard Disk Drives

The basic requirements of any mass storage system are speed, capacity, and low price. No technology delivers as favorable a combination of these virtues as the hard disk drive, now a standard part of nearly every PC. The hard disk drive stores all of your programs and other software so that they can be loaded into your PC's memory almost without waiting. In addition, the hard disk also holds all the data you generate with your PC so that you can recall and reuse it whenever you want. In general, the faster the hard disk and the more it can hold, the better.

Floppy Disk Drives

Inexpensive, exchangeable, and technically unchallenging, the floppy disk was the first, and at one time only, mass storage system of many PCs. Based on well-proven technologies and mass produced by the millions, the floppy disk provided the first PCs with a place to keep programs and data and, over the years, served well as a distribution system through which software publishers could make their products available.

In the race with progress, however, the simple technology of the floppy disk has been hard-pressed to keep pace. The needs of modern programs far exceed what floppy disks can deliver, and other technologies (such as those CD ROM drives) provide less expensive distribution. New incarnations of floppy disk technology that pack 50 to 100 times more data per disk hold promise but at the penalty of a price that will make you look more than twice at other alternatives.

All that said, the floppy disk drive remains a standard part of all but a few highly specialized PCs, typically those willing to sacrifice everything to save a few ounces (sub-notebooks) and those that need to operate in smoky, dusty environments that would make Superman cringe and Wonder Woman cough.

CD and DVD Drives

Getting data into your PC requires a distribution medium, and when you need to move megabytes, the medium of choice today is the CD ROM or DVD drive. Any new PC requires one or the other of this specialized kind of disc drive.

Software publishers have made the CD ROM their preferred means of getting their products to you. A single CD that costs about the same as a floppy disk holds hundreds of times more information and keeps it more secure. CDs are vulnerable to neither random magnetic fields nor casual software pirates. CD ROM drives are a necessary part of all multimedia PCs, which means just about any PC you'd want to buy today.

The initials stand for Compact Disc Read-Only Memory and Digital Versatile Disc, technologies that allow manufacturers to stamp out megabytes or gigabytes of code and data about as easily as you cut out sugar cookies. DVDs hold more but are not yet as universal as CDs. Although DVDs have room enough to pack a whole movie (and more) on a five-inch disk, few applications and suites require so much capacity—at least today.

Tape Drives

Tape is for backup, pure and simple. It provides an inexpensive place to put your data just in case—just in case some light-fingered freelancer decides to separate your PC from your desktop; just in case the fire department hoses to death everything in your office that the fire and smoke failed to destroy; just in case you empty your recycling bin moments before discovering you accidentally deleted all of your exculpatory tax records; just in case that nagging head cold turns out to be a virus that infects your PC and formats your hard disk; just in case your next-door neighbor bewitches your PC and turns it into a golden chariot pulled by a silver charger that once was your mouse; just in case an errant asteroid ambles through your roof. Having an extra copy of your important data helps you recover from such disasters and those that are even less likely.

Listening

If you want your PC to do anything useful, you have to be able to tell it what to do. Although some PCs actually do listen to you speak using *voice recognition* technology, most systems depend on traditional control systems—input devices such as the keyboard and mouse—to put you in control.

In addition, many applications require that you fill your PC with data—keystrokes, images, and sounds. Your PC acquires this information by electronically listening to any of several *input devices*. Graphic devices such as scanners and digital cameras grab real world images. Video capture cards and sound boards grab multimedia pictures and sound.

Control

The keyboard remains the most efficient way to enter text into applications, faster than even the most advanced voice recognition systems that let you talk to your PC. The mouse—more correctly termed a *pointing device* to include mouse-derived devices such as trackballs and the proprietary devices used by notebook PCs—relays graphic instructions to your computer, letting you point to your choices or sketch, draw, and paint.

Input

The variety of input devices is as wide, even wider, than the types of information you want your PC to collect. They are key to letting your PC capture data in bulk. Although an ordinary keyboard suffices if you only need to acquire words and numbers, other kinds of data demand more powerful input devices. Scanners collect both images and printed text. Digital cameras let you capture images from real life. A video camera helps make a PC into a multimedia production system.

Monitoring

Your window into the mind of your PC that lets you monitor what it does is its display system, itself a combination of a graphics adapter or video board and a monitor or flat-panel display. The display system gives your PC the means to tell you what it is thinking, to show you your data in the form that you best understand, be it numbers, words, or pictures.

The two halves of the display system work hand-in-hand. The graphics adapter uses the digital signals inside your PC to built an electronic map of what the final image should look like, storing the data for every dot on your monitor in memory. Electronics generate the image that appears on your monitor screen.

Graphics Adapters

Your PC's graphics adapter forms the image that you will see on your monitor screen. It converts digital code into a bit-pattern that maps each dot that you'll see. Because it makes the actual conversion, the graphics adapter determines the number of colors that can appear on your monitor as well as the ultimate resolution of the image. In other words, the graphics adapter sets the limit on the quality of the images your PC can produce. Your monitor cannot make an image any better than what comes out of the graphics adapter. The graphics adapter also determines the speed of your PC's video system; a faster board will make smoother video displays.

Many PCs now include at least a rudimentary form of graphics adapter in the form of display electronics on their motherboards; others put the display electronics on an expansion board.

Monitors

The monitor is the basic display system that's attached to most PCs. Monitors are television sets built to Bill Gates' budget. Although a 21-inch TV might cost $300 in your local appliance store, the same size monitor will likely cost $1500 and still not show the movies you rent as well. Opt for those inches in a new flat-screen LCD display, and you might as well buy a new car.

Certainly any monitor (sometimes called a *display*) will let you work with your PC, but the quality of the monitor attached to your PC determines the quality of the image you see and, often, the work you do. Although no monitor can make anything look better than what's in the signals from your graphics adapter, a bad monitor can make them look much worse and limit both the range of colors and the resolution (or sharpness) of the images.

Communicating

The real useful work that PCs do involves not just you but also the outside world. Your PC must be able to communicate to put its intelligence to work.

The ability of a PC to send and receive data to different devices and computers is called *connectivity*. Your PC can link to any of a number of hardware peripherals through its input/output ports. Better still, through modems, networks, and related technologies, it can connect with nearly any PC in the world.

Input/Output Ports

Your PC links to its peripherals through its input and output ports. Every PC needs some way of acquiring information and putting it to work. Input/output ports are the primary route for this information exchange.

In the past, the standard equipment of most PCs was simple and almost pre-ordained—one serial port and one parallel port, typically as part of their motherboard circuitry. Modern standards are phasing out these ports, so we'll consider them (for purposes of this book) *legacy ports*.

Today, new and wonderful port standards are proliferating faster than dandelions in a new lawn. Hardwired serial connections are moving to the new Universal Serial Bus (USB), whereas the Infrared Data Association (IrDA) system provides wireless links. Similarly, the simple parallel port has become an external expansion bus capable of linking dozens of devices to a single jack.

Printers

The electronic thoughts of a PC are notoriously evanescent. Pull the plug and your work disappears. Moreover, monitors are frustratingly difficult to pass around and post through the mail when you want to show off your latest digital art creation. *Hard copy*, the printout on paper, solves the problem. And the printer makes your hard copy.

Modems

To connect with other PCs and information sources such as the Internet through the international telephone system, you need a modem. Essentially a signal converter, the modem adapts your PC's data to a form compatible with the telephone system.

In a quest for faster transfers than the ancient technology of the classic telephone circuit can provide, however, data communications are shifting to newer systems such as digital telephone services (like ISDN), high-speed cable connections, and direct digital links with satellites. Each of these requires its own variety of connecting device, not strictly speaking a modem but called that for consistency's sake. Which one you need depends on the speed you want and the connections available to you.

Networks

Any time you link two or more PCs together, you've made a network. Keep the machines all in one place—one home, one business, one site in today's jargon—and you have a Local Area Network (LAN). Spread them across the country, world, or universe with telephone, cable, or satellite links and you get a Wide Area Network (WAN).

Once you link up to the World Wide Web, your computer is no longer merely the box on your desk. Your PC becomes part of a single, massive international computer system. Even so, it retains all the features and abilities you expect from a PC; it only becomes even more powerful.

Linking Software and Hardware

The subtitle for this section might read "Why you need a fast Pentium III to do what your parents did with PCs dumber than today's pocket calculators." Then again, you could go back and ask why you need a PC today to do what your grandparents did with a box of index cards, a pencil, and a string tied around one finger, but that's a marketing rather than a hardware question.) The answer is that the various interfaces that are part of the modern operating system—and the hardware interface in particular—swallow up so much of your computer's power that only a fraction of it is left for carrying out actual work. Clearly, the hardware-software link deserves a bit of scrutiny.

Linking hardware to software has always been one of the biggest challenges facing those charged with designing computer systems—not just individual PCs but whole families of computers, those able to run the same programs. The solution has almost invariably been to wed the two together by layering on software, so much so that the fastest processors struggle when confronted by relatively simple tasks. An almost unbelievable amount of computer power gets devoted to moving bytes from software to hardware through a maze of program code, all in the name of making the widest variety of hardware imaginable work with a universal (at least if Microsoft has its way) operating system.

The underlying problem is the same as in any mating ritual. Software is from Venus. Hardware is from Mars—or, to ruin the allusion for sake of accuracy, Vulcan. Software is the programmer's labor of love, an ephemeral spirit that can only be represented. Hardware is the physical reality, the stuff pounded out in Vulcan's forge—enduring, unchanging, and often priced like gold. (And, yes, for all you Trekkers out there, it *is* always logical.) Bringing the two together is a challenge that even self-help books would find hard to manage. Yet every PC not only faces that formidable task but also tackles it with aplomb, though maybe not as fast as you'd like.

Here's the challenge: In the basic PC, every instruction in a program gets targeted on the microprocessor. Consequently, the instructions can control only the microprocessor and don't themselves reach beyond. The circuitry of the rest of the computer and all of the peripherals connected to it all must get their commands and data relayed to them by the microprocessor. Somehow, the microprocessor must be able to send signals to these devices. Today, the pathway of a command is rarely direct. Rather, the chain of command is a hierarchy, one that often takes on aspects of a bureaucracy.

Control Hierarchy

Perhaps the best way to get to know how software controls hardware is to look at how your system executes a simple command. Let's start with a common situation.

Because your patience is so sorely tested by reading the electronic version of this book using your Web browser, *Internet Scapegoat*, you decide to quit and go on to do something really useful—such as play FreeCell. Your hand wraps around your mouse, you scoot it up to the big black "X" at the upper-right corner of the screen, and you click your left mouse button. Your hardware has made a link with software.

Your click actually closes the contacts of a switch inside the mouse, squirting a brief pulse of electricity through its circuitry. The mouse hardware reacts by sending a message out the mouse wire to your PC. The mouse port of your PC detects the message and warns your PC by sending a special attention signal called a *hardware interrupt* (see Chapter 6, "Chipsets") squarely at your microprocessor.

At the same time, the mouse driver has been counting pulses sent out by your mouse that indicate its motion. The mouse driver counts each pulse and puts the results into the memory of your PC.

The interrupt causes your PC to run a software interrupt routine contained in the mouse *driver software*, and the driver in turn signals to Windows that you've pressed the button. Windows checks in memory to find the value the mouse driver has stored there. This value tells Windows where the mouse pointer is to determine how to react to your button press. When it discovers you've targeted the "X," Windows sends a message to the program associated with it, your browser.

The browser reacts, muttering to itself the digital equivalent of, "He must be insane," and immediately decides to pop up a dialog box that asks you whether your really, really want to quit such a quality program as the browser. The dialog box routine is part of the program itself, but it builds the box and its contents from graphics subroutines that are part of the Windows operating system. The browser activates the subroutines through the Windows application interface.

Windows itself does not draw the box. Rather it acts as a translator, converting the box request into a series of commands to draw it. It then sends these commands to its graphics *driver*. The driver determines what commands to use so that the video board will understand what to do. The driver then passes those commands to another drive, the one associated with the video board.

The video board's driver routes the command to the proper hardware ports through which the video board accepts instructions. The driver sends a series of commands, which causes the processor on the video board (a graphics accelerator) to compute where it must change pixels to make the lines constituting the box. Once the graphic accelerator finishes the computations, it changes the bytes that correspond to the areas on the screen where the line will appear in a special memory area on the video board called the *frame buffer*.

Another part of the video board, the *rasterizer*, scans through the frame buffer and sends the data it finds there to the port leading to your monitor, converting it into a serial data stream for the journey. Using synchronizing signals sent from the video board as a guide, the monitor takes the data from the data stream and illuminates the proper pixels on the screen to form the pattern of the dialog box.

When you awake from your boredom-inspired daze, you finally see the warning box pop up on the screen and react.

The journey is tortuous, but when all goes right, it takes a smaller fraction of a second than it does for you to become aware of what you've done. And when all doesn't go right, another tortuous chain of events will likely result—often one involving flying PCs, picture windows, and shards of glass on the front lawn.

Key to making this chain of command function are the application program interface, the driver software, and the device interfaces of the hardware itself. Sometimes, a special part of your PC, the *BIOS*, also gets involved. Let's take a deeper look at each of these links.

Application Program Interface

A quick recap: An interface is where two distinct entities come together. The most important of the software interfaces in the Windows environment is the *application program interface*, or API.

Rather than a physical thing, the API is a standard set of rules for exchanging commands and data. The Windows API comprises a set of word-like commands termed *program calls*. Each of these causes Windows to take a particular action. For example, the command DrawBox could tell Windows to draw a box on the screen, as in the preceding example.

To pass along data associated with the command—in the example, how large the box should be and where to put it on the screen—many calls require your program to send along *parameters*. Each parameter is ordinary data that is strictly formatted to meet the expectation of Windows. That is, the order of the parameters is predefined and the range permitted for the data is similarly constrained.

Each software interface in the Windows system uses a similar system of calls and parameter passing. Gaining familiarity with the full repertory of the API is one of the biggest challenges facing programmers.

Device Drivers

Device drivers are matchmakers. They take a set of standardized commands from the operating system and match them to the capabilities of the device that the driver controls. Typically, the device that gets controlled is a piece of hardware, but as our example shows, one driver may control another driver that controls the hardware.

Just about every class of peripheral has some special function shared with no other device. Printers need to switch ribbon colors; graphics boards need to put dots on screen at high resolution; sound boards need to blast fortissimo arpeggios; video capture boards must grab frames; and mice have to do whatever mice do. Different manufacturers often have widely different ideas about the best way to handle even the most fundamental functions. No programmer or even collaborative program can ever hope to know all the possibilities. It's even unlikely that you could fit all the possibilities into an operating system written in code that would fit onto a stack of disks you could carry. There are just too many possibilities.

Drivers make the connection, translating generalized commands made for any hardware for the specific device in your PC. Instead of packing every control or command you might potentially need, the driver implements only those that are appropriate for a specific type, brand, and model of product that you actually connect to your PC. Without the driver, your operating system could not communicate with your PC.

Device drivers give you a further advantage. You can change them almost as often as you change your mind. If you discover a bug in one driver—say sending an uppercase F to your printer causes it to form feed through a full ream of paper before coming to a panting stop—you can slide in an updated driver that fixes the problem. You don't have to replace the device or alter your software. In some cases, new drivers extend the features of your existing peripherals because the programmer didn't have enough time or inspiration to add everything to the initial release.

The way you and your system handles drivers depends on your operating system. Older operating systems (such as DOS and old versions of Windows) load all of their drivers when they start and stick with them all the while you use your PC. Windows 95 and newer versions treat drivers dynamically, loading them only when they are needed. Not only does this design save memory because you only need to load the drivers that are actually in use, but it also lets you add and remove devices while you're using your PC. For example, when you plug in a USB scanner, Windows can determine what make and model of scanner you have and then load the driver appropriate for it.

Although today drivers load invisibly and automatically, things were not always so easy. The driver needs to know what system resources your hardware uses for its communications. These resources are the values you set through the Windows Add Hardware Wizard. (Click on the Resources tab in Device Manager to see them.) With old-fashioned drivers, hardware, and operating systems, you had to physically adjust settings on the hardware to assign resources and then configure the driver to match what you configured. It wasn't pretty, often wasn't easy, and was the most common reason people could not get hardware to work—usually because you created the problem yourself. Now, Windows creates the problems automatically.

BIOS

The *Basic Input/Output System*, or BIOS, of a PC has many functions, as discussed in Chapter 5, "The BIOS." One of these is to help match your PC's hardware to software. In effect, the BIOS acts as special driver software that's included with your PC so that it can boot up right after you take it out of the box.

Part of the BIOS is program code for drivers that's permanently recorded (or semi-permanently, in the case of Flash BIOS systems) in special memory chips. The code acts like the hardware interface of an operating system but at a lower level; it is a hardware interface that's independent of the operating system.

Programs or operating systems send commands to the BIOS, and the BIOS sends out the instructions to the hardware using the proper resource values. It lies waiting in your PC, ready for use.

The original goal of the BIOS was to make PC software platform-independent. That is, programs would not care what kind of PC they were running on. Although that seems a trivial concern in these days of dynamic-loading drivers, it was only a dream a couple of decades ago when PCs were invented. In those dark old days, programmers had to write commands aimed specifically at the hardware of the PC. Change the hardware—plug in a different printer—and the software wouldn't work. The BIOS, like today's driver software, was meant to wallpaper over the difference in hardware. (The idea, although a good one, didn't work. As with today's drivers, the BIOS robbed some of the performance of PCs. PCs were so slow as it was that programmers opted to skip the BIOS in favor of speed.)

The BIOS persists as a common means of accessing hardware before the operating system loads. The BIOS code of every PC today still includes the equivalent of driver software to handle accessing floppy disk drives, the keyboard, printers, video, and parallel and serial port operation.

Device Interfaces

No matter whether software uses device drivers, looks through the BIOS, or accesses hardware directly, the final link to hardware may be made in one of two ways set by the hardware design—input/output mapping and memory mapping. *Input/output mapping* relies on sending instructions and data through ports. *Memory mapping* requires passing data through memory addresses. Ports and addresses are similar in concept but different in operation.

Input/Output Mapping

A *port* is an address but not a physical location. The port is a logical construct that operates as an addressing system separate from the address bus of the microprocessor even though it uses the same address lines. If you imagine normal memory addresses as a set of pigeon holes for holding bytes, input/output ports act like a second set of pigeon holes on the other side of the room. To distinguish which set of holes to use, the microprocessor controls a flag signal on its bus called memory-I/O. In one condition, it tells the rest of the computer the signals on the address bus indicate a memory location; in its other state, the signals indicate an input/output port.

The microprocessor's internal mechanism for sending data to a port also differs from memory access. One instruction, move, allows the microprocessor to move bytes from any of its registers to any memory location. Some microprocessor operations can even be performed in immediate mode, directly on the values stored at memory locations.

Ports, however, use a pair of instructions, *In* to read from a port and *Out* to write to a port. The values read can only be transferred into one specific register of the microprocessor (called the accumulator) and can only be written from that register. The accumulator has other functions as well. Immediate operations on values held at port locations are impossible—which means a value stored in a port cannot be changed by the microprocessor. It must load the port value into the accumulator, alter it, and then reload the new value back into the port.

Memory Mapping

The essence of memory mapping is sharing. The microprocessor and the hardware device it controls share access to a specific range of memory addresses. To send data to the device, your microprocessor simply moves the information into the memory locations exactly as if it were storing something for later recall. The hardware device can then read those same locations to obtain the data.

Memory-mapped devices of course need direct access to your PC's memory bus. Through this connection, they can gain speed and operate as fast as the memory system and its bus connection allows. In addition, the microprocessor can directly manipulate the data at the memory location used by the connection, eliminating the multi-step load/change/reload process required by I/O mapping.

The most familiar memory-mapped device is your PC's display. Most graphic systems allow the microprocessor to directly address the frame buffer that holds the image that appears on your monitor screen. This design allows the video system to operate at the highest possible speed.

The addresses used for memory mapping must be off limits to the range in which the operating system loads your programs. If a program should transgress on the area used for the hardware connection, it can inadvertently change the data there—nearly always with bad results. Moreover, the addresses used by the interface cannot serve any other function, so they take away from the maximum memory addressable by a PC. Although such deductions are insignificant with today's PCs, it was a significant shortcoming for old systems that were limited to a maximum of 1 to 16 megabytes.

Addressing

To the microprocessor, the difference between ports and memory is one of perception: Memory is a direct extension of the chip. Ports are the external world. Writing to I/O ports is consequently more cumbersome and usually requires more time and microprocessor cycles.

I/O ports give the microprocessor and computer designer greater flexibility. And they give you a headache when you want to install multimedia accessories.

Implicit in the concept of addressing, whether memory or port addresses, is proper delivery. You expect a letter carrier to bring your mail to your address and not deliver it to someone else's mailbox. Similarly, PCs and their software assume that deliveries of data and instructions will always go where they are supposed to. To assure proper delivery, addresses must be correct and unambiguous. If someone types a wrong digit on a mailing label, it will likely get lost in the postal system.

To use port or memory addresses properly, your software needs to know the proper addresses used by your peripherals. Many hardware functions have fixed or standardized addresses that are the same in every PC. For example, the memory addresses used by video boards are standardized (at least in basic operating modes), and the ports used by most hard disk drives are similarly standardized. Programmers can write the addresses used by this fixed-address hardware into their programs and not worry whether their data will get where it's going.

The layered BIOS approach was originally designed to eliminate the need for writing explicit hardware addresses in programs. Drivers accomplish a similar function. They are written with the necessary hardware addresses built in.

Resource Allocation

The basic hardware devices got assigned addresses and memory ranges early in the history of the PC and for compatibility reasons have never changed. These fixed values include those of serial and parallel ports, keyboards, disk drives, and the frame buffer that stores the monitor image. Add-in devices and more recent enhancements to the traditional devices require their own assignments of system resources. Unfortunately, beyond the original hardware assignments, there are no standards for the rest of the resources. Manufacturers consequently pick values of their own choices for new products. More often than you'd like, several products may use the same address values.

Manufacturers attempt to avoid conflicts by allowing a number of options for the addresses used by their equipment. In days gone by, you had to select among the choices offered by manufacturers using switches or jumpers. Modern expansion products still require resource allocation but use a software-controlled scheme called *plug and play* to set the values, usually without your intervention or knowledge.

Although a useful PC requires all three—software, hardware, and the glue to hold them together—hardware plays the enabling role. Without it, the PC doesn't exist. It *is* the PC. The rest of this book will individually examine the individual components of that hardware and related technologies that enable your PC to be the powerful tool that it is.

CHAPTER

2

System Boards

The basic technology underlying all personal computers is the printed circuit board. Traditionally, the centerpiece of most personal computers is a special printed circuit board called the motherboard. It is the physical and logical backbone of the entire system. In many PCs, the motherboard may be the entire system. Most machines, however, are augmented by auxiliary printed circuit boards usually termed expansion boards. The circuitry located on these circuit boards— the motherboard particularly—defines the computer, its capabilities, its limitations, and its personality. Where once motherboard design was a free-for-all, new standards define the size, shape, and connections you can expect. This chapter examines the physical aspects of motherboards and expansion boards that provide a home for your PC's electrical circuitry.

Microprocessor (see Chapter 3)	The motherboard is the home of the microprocessor, and which chip it accommodates determines the power of your PC.
Memory (see Chapter 4)	In a modern PC, the motherboard provides the physical space for memory, and its capacity determines the total memory you can install in your PC. Expect room for at least 384MB in a modern PC.
Expansion Slots (See Chapter 7)	Expansion slots give your PC room to grow. A desktop PC needs to follow the PCI standard and have three (in a low-profile system) to six PCI slots. A single ISA slots should be all your need to accommodate legacy expansion boards. In notebook systems, look for two CardBus slots. A notebook system should have two type 2 CardBus slots.
Video (see Chapters 16 and 17)	Desktop systems should have an AGP slot (with a video board installed) for your display system. Some motherboards (particularly those in low-cost desktops and notebook PCs) include video circuitry, which sets (and constrains) the resolution and color potential of your PC. You'll want a minimum of 1024×768 in a desktop system, 800×600 in a budget notebook.
Audio (see Chapter 19)	New motherboards avoid the need for a separate sound card by incorporating all the necessary audio circuitry.
Network Adapter (see Chapter 23)	PCs meant for business applications should have a 10/100Base-T port built into their motherboards. It's a handy option for home systems too.
Ports (see Chapters 20 and 21)	Most PCs get all the ports they need on their motherboards. A modern PC should have two USB jacks. Look for a parallel (printer) and serial port to accommodate legacy peripherals. If you plan on working with digital video, look for a PC with a built-in FireWire (IEEE-1394) port.

You don't need to understand electricity to run a program on your PC. In fact, you could build a computer that doesn't need electricity at all, as any visit to Stonehenge will prove. If you're patient, you can heave rocks about and compute the motion of the sun. You'll also soon discover the reason neolithic sages wore long grey beards.

Today's computers are somewhat quicker because they use electricity, a medium not favored by Merlin and his kin because of control issues. You can't do much planning—or computing—when your chief supply of power doesn't strike twice in the same place.

The essence of modern computer technology, modern electronics, and even modern appliances is that we have learned the secret of controlling the flow of electricity. We make parcels of passing electrons do our bidding, our housework, and our thinking.

Although you can use your PC without knowing the least about electricity or its control—you can run Doom even if switching on an electric light isn't within your ken—truly understanding how a PC works as well as all the ins and outs of connecting, maintaining, and expanding it requires that you learn a few fundamentals.

In this chapter, we'll start with the physical side of using electricity to make a computer—what the circuits do and how they are fabricated. After those basics, we'll see what those circuits make, the boards from which a modern PC gets built.

The *motherboard* is the electrical foundation of the computer. It gives the system its life and holds it all together, just like Mom. *Expansion boards* give your PC its flexibility, allowing you to customize and adapt it to suit your precise needs. Although different in size and function, both kinds of boards operate under the same electrical principles and are fabricated with the same technology.

Technologies

Personal computers could not exist, at least in their current, wildly successful form, were it not for two concepts: binary logic and digital circuitry. The binary approach reduced data to its most minimalist form, essentially an information quantum. A binary data bit simply indicates whether something is or is not. Binary logic provides rules for manipulating those bits to allow them to represent and act like real-world information we care about, things such as numbers, names, and images. The binary approach involves both *digitization*, using binary data to represent information, and *Boolean algebra*, the rules for carrying out the manipulations of the binary data.

The primary logic element in all modern PCs is a device called the *microprocessor*, important enough to earn not only its own chapter in this book but also to empower the personal computer revolution. The microprocessor is today's pre-eminent manipulator of binary logic, and current devices rank among the most complex of all human creations.

Digital electronic circuitry makes the microprocessor's fast, error-free manipulation of binary data possible.

Despite the complexity of the microprocessor, the technology that makes it work is quite basic. The microprocessor simply controls the flow of electrical signals. It is an electronic circuit, a special kind called a *digital logic circuit*. The only thing remarkable about the microprocessor is the significance we apply to the signals it controls.

Digital Logic Circuitry

The essence of the digital logic that underlies the operation of the microprocessor and motherboard is the ability to use one electrical signal to control another.

Certainly, there are myriad ways to use one electrical signal to control another, as any student of Rube Goldberg can attest. As interesting and amusing as interspersing cats, bellows, and bowling balls in the flow of control may be, most engineers have opted for a more direct system that uses a more direct means based on time-proven electrical technologies.

In modern digital logic circuitry, the basis of this control is *amplification*, the process of using a small current to control a larger current (or a small voltage to control a larger voltage). The large current (or voltage) exactly mimics the controlling current (or voltage) but is stronger or amplified. In that every change in the large signal is exactly analogous to each one in the small signal, devices that amplify in this way are called *analog*. The intensity of the control signal can represent continuously variable information—for example, a sound level in stereo equipment. The electrical signal in this kind of equipment thus is an analogy to the sound that it represents.

In the early years of the evolution of electronic technology, improving this analog amplification process was the primary goal of engineers. After all, without amplification, signals eventually deteriorated into nothingness. The advent of digital information and the earliest computers made them use the power of amplification differently.

The limiting case of amplification occurs when the control signal causes the larger signal to go from its lowest value, typically zero, to its highest value. In other words, the large signal goes off and on—switches—under control of the smaller signal. The two states of the output signal (on and off) can be used as part of a binary code that represents information. For example, the switch could be used to produce a series of seven pulses to represent the number 7. Because information can be coded as groups of such numbers (digits), electrical devices that use this switching technology are described as *digital*. Note that this switching directly corresponds to other, more direct control of on-off information such as pounding on a telegraph key, a concept we'll return to in later chapters.

Strictly speaking, a electronic digital system works with signals called *high* and *low*, corresponding to a digital one and zero. In formal logic systems, these same values are often termed true and false. In general, a digital one or logical true corresponds to an electronic high. Sometimes, however, special digital codes reverse this relationship.

In practical electrical circuits, the high and low signals only roughly correspond to on and off. Standard digital logic systems define both the high and low signals as *ranges* of voltages. High is a voltage range near the maximum voltage accepted by the system, and low is a voltage range near (but not necessarily exactly at or including) zero. A wide range of undefined voltages spreads between the two, lower than the lowest edge of high but higher than the highest edge of low. The digital system ignores the voltages in the undefined range. Figure 2.1 shows the ranges of voltages interrelate.

FIGURE 2.1

Significance of TTL voltage levels.

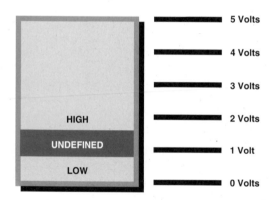

Perhaps the most widely known standard is called TTL (for transistor-transistor logic). In the TTL system, which is still common inside PC equipment, a logical low is any voltage below 0.8 volts. A logical high is any level above 2.0 volts. The range between 0.8 and 2.0 volts is undefined.

As modern PCs shift to lower voltages, the top level of the logical high shifts downward—for example, from the old standard of 5.0 volts to the 3.3 volts of the latest computer equipment (and even lower voltages of new power-conserving microprocessors)—but their relationship along with the undefined range in between remains the same. Modern systems usually retain the same low and undefined ranges; just lop the top off the figure showing the TTL voltage levels.

When applied to the operating voltage of a microprocessor, Intel calls the 3.3 voltage level *STD*. Under Intel's microprocessor specification, the STD level specifies that the operating voltage will actually fall in the range of 3.135 to 3.6 volts. To increase the reliability of some higher speed chips, Intel specifies operation at a higher voltage level called *VRE* that is nominally 3.5 volts but may fall anywhere in the range 3.4 to 3.6 volts. Because the

VRE range allows a greater difference between high and low, it helps the higher speed microprocessors better avoid noise that might impair their operation.

Digital systems are equally apt to pick up noise as analog systems. However, an analog signaling system cannot distinguish the noise from the subtle variations of the desired signal. The noise becomes part of the signal. It gets transmitted and amplified with the signal. The further the signal goes or the more it is amplified, the more noise—and thus, degradation—it will suffer. If too much noise gets mixed in with an analog signal, the signal becomes unusable. Digital systems, however, ignore traces of noise that get added into the signal. Typically even when it is added to the digital signal, the noise will not be enough to move the signal from low to undefined. Because the digital system accepts the entire range of low voltages as having the same meaning, small changes added by noise within a given range are simply ignored. Moreover, because the noise is ignored, every time the digital signal goes through logic circuitry (the digital equivalent of analog amplification), the noise is left behind, removed from the signal entirely. With each pass through a logic circuit, the signal starts out fresh and noise free. Where noise continuously adds into analog signals, it gets continually cleansed away in digital systems.

Electronics

The essence of any digital logic system is that one electrical current (or voltage) can control another one. No matter whether a microprocessor understands a few instructions or many, no matter whether it operates as fast as lightning or as slow as your in-bred in-laws, it depends on this principle of electrical control. Over the years, improving technology has steadily refined the mechanisms for carrying out this action, allowing electronic circuits to become denser (more functions in smaller packages) and faster.

The first approach to electrical control of electrical flow evolved from the rattling telegraph key. Instead of just making noise, the solenoid of the telegraph sounder was adapted to closing electrical contacts, making a mechanism now called the *relay*. In operation, a relay is just a switch that's controlled by an electromagnet. Activating the electromagnet with a small current moves a set of contacts that switch the flow of a larger current. The relay doesn't care if the control current starts off in the same box as the relay or a continent away. The basis of Bell Lab's 1946 Mark V computer, the relay is a component that's still used in modern electrical equipment.

Vacuum Tubes

The vacuum tube improved on the relay design by eliminating the mechanical part of the remote-action switch. Vacuum tubes developed out of Edison's 1880 invention of the incandescent light bulb. In 1904, John Ambrose Fleming discovered electrons would flow from the negatively charged hot filament of the light bulb to a positively charged cold collector plate but not in the other direction, creating the diode tube. In 1907, Lee De

Forest created the Audion, now known as the triode tube, which interposed a control grid between the hot filament (the cathode) and the cold plate (the anode). The grid allowed the Audion to harness the power of the attraction of unlike electrical charges and repulsion of like charges, enabling a small charge to control the flow of electrons through the vacuum inside the tube.

The advantage of the vacuum tube over the relay in controlling signals is speed. The relay operates at mechanical rates, perhaps a few thousand operations per second. The vacuum tube can switch millions of times per second. The first recognizable computers (such as Eniac) were built from thousands of tubes, each configured as a digital logic gate.

Semiconductors

Using tube-based electronics in computers is fraught with problems. First is the space-heater effect: Tubes have to glow like light bulbs to work and they generate heat along the way, enough to smelt rather than process data. And, like light bulbs, tubes burn out. Large tube-based computers required daily shut-down and maintenance and several technicians on the payroll. In addition, tube circuits are big. The house-sized computers of 1950s vintage science fiction would easily be outclassed in computing power by today's desktop machines. In the typical tube-based computer design, one logic gate required one tube that took up considerably more space than a single microprocessor with tens of millions of logic gates. Moreover, physical size isn't only a matter of housing. The bigger the computer, the longer it takes its thoughts to travel through its circuits—even at the speed of light—and the more slowly it thinks.

Making today's practical PCs took another true breakthrough in electronics: the *transistor*, first created at Bell Laboratories in 1947 and announced in 1948, developed by the team of John Bardeen, Walter Brattain, and William Shockley. A tiny fleck of germanium (later, silicon) formed into three layers, the transistor was endowed with the capability to let one electrical current applied to one layer alter the flow of another, larger current between the other two layers. Unlike the vacuum tube, the transistor needed no hot electrons because the current flowed entirely through a solid material—the germanium or silicon—hence, the common name for tubeless technology, *solid-state electronics*.

Germanium and silicon are special materials (actually, metals) called semiconductors. The term describes how these materials resist the flow of electrical currents. They resist more than conductors (like the copper in wires) but not as much as insulators (like the plastic wrapped around the wires).

By itself, being a poor but not awful electrical conductor is as remarkable as lukewarm water. Infusing atoms of impurities into the semiconductor's microscopic lattice structure dramatically alters the electrical characteristics of the material and makes solid-state electronics possible. The process of adding impurities is called doping. Some impurities add extra electrons (carriers of negative charges) to the crystal; others leave holes in the lattice where electrons would ordinarily be, and these holes act as positive charge carriers. Electricity easily flows across the junction between the two materials when passed by the extra electrons to the holes on the other side because the holes willingly accept the electrons, passing them on to the rest of the circuitry. The electrical flow in the other direction is severely impeded because the electron-rich side won't accept more electrons carried to the junction by the holes. In other words, electricity flows only in one direction through the semiconductor junction just as it flows only one way through a vacuum tube diode.

The original transistor incorporated three layers with two junctions between dissimilar materials. Ordinarily, no electricity could pass through such an arrangement because the two junctions would be oriented in opposite directions, one blocking electrical flow one way and the second blocking flow in the other direction. The neat trick that makes a transistor work is draining away some of the electrons at the junction that prevents the electrical flow. A small current drains away the excess electrons and allows a large current to move through the junction. By this means, the transistor can amplify and switch currents.

A semiconductor is often described by the type of impurity that has been added to its structure: N-type for those with extra electrons (negative charge carriers) and P-type for those with holes (positive charge carriers). Ordinary three-layer transistors, for example, come in two configurations, NPN and PNP, depending on which type of semiconductor is in the middle.

Modern computer circuits mostly rely on a kind of transistor in which the current flow through a narrow channel of semiconductor material is controlled by a voltage applied to a gate (which surrounds the channel) made from metal oxide. The most common variety of these transistors is made from N-type material and results in a technology called NMOS, an acronym for N-channel Metal Oxide Semiconductor. A related technology combines both N-channel and P-channel devices and is called CMOS (Complementary Metal Oxide Semiconductor) because the N- and P-type materials are complements (opposites) of one another.

The typical microprocessor once was built from NMOS technology. Although NMOS designs are distinguished by their design simplicity and small size (even on a microchip level), they have a severe shortcoming: They constantly use electricity whenever their gates are turned on. Because about half of the tens or hundreds of thousands of gates in a microprocessor are switched on at any given time, an NMOS chip can draw a lot of current. This current flow creates heat and wastes power, making NMOS unsuitable for miniaturized computers (which can be difficult to cool) and battery-operated equipment, such as notebook computers.

Some earlier and most contemporary microprocessors now use CMOS designs. CMOS is inherently more complex than NMOS because each gate requires more transistors, at least a pair per gate. But this complexity brings a benefit. When one transistor in a CMOS gate is turned on, its complementary partner is switched off, minimizing the current flow through the complementary pair that make up the circuit. When a CMOS gate is idle, just maintaining its state, it requires almost no power. During a state change, the current flow is large but brief. Consequently, the faster the CMOS gate changes state, the more current that flows through it and the more heat it generates. In other words, the faster a CMOS circuit operates, the hotter it becomes. This speed-induced temperature rise is one of the limits on the operating speed of many microprocessors.

CMOS technology can duplicate every logic function made with NMOS but with a substantial saving of electricity. On the other hand, manufacturing costs are somewhat more because of the added circuit complexity.

Integrated Circuits

The transistor overcomes several of the problems with using tubes to make a computer. Transistors are smaller than tubes and give off less heat because they don't need to glow to work. But every logic gate still requires one or more transistors (as well as several other electronic components) to build. If you allocated a mere square inch to every logic gate, the number of logic gates in a personal computer microprocessor such as the Pentium Pro would require a circuit board on the order of 200 feet square.

At the very end of the 1950s, Robert N. Noyce at Fairchild Instrument and Jack S. Kilby independently came up with the same brilliant idea of putting multiple semiconductor devices into a single package. Transistors are typically grown as crystals from thin-cut slices of silicon called *wafers*. Typically, thousands of transistors are grown at the same time on the same wafer. Instead of carving the wafer into separate transistors, the engineer linked them together (integrated them) to create a complete electronic circuit all on one wafer. Kilby linked the devices with micro wires; Noyce envisioned fabricating the interconnecting circuits between devices on the silicon itself. The resulting electronic device, for which Noyce applied for a patent on July 30, 1959, became known as the *integrated circuit* or IC. Such devices now are often called chips because of their construction from a single small piece of silicon, a chip off the old crystal. Integrated circuit technology has been adapted to both analog and digital circuitry. Their grandest development, however, is the microprocessor.

Partly because of the Noyce invention, Fairchild flourished as a semiconductor manufacturer throughout the 1960s. The company was acquired by Schlumberger Ltd. in 1979, which sold it to National Semiconductor in 1987.

The IC has several advantages over circuits built from individual (or discrete) transistors, most resulting from miniaturization. Most importantly, integration reduces the amount of packaging. Instead of one metal or plastic transistor case per logic gate, multiple gates (even millions of them) can be combined into one chip package.

Because the current inside of the chip need not interact with external circuits, the chips can be made arbitrarily small, enabling the circuits to be made smaller, too. In fact, today the limit on the size of elements inside an integrated circuit is mostly determined by fabrication technology; internal circuitry is as small as today's manufacturing equipment can make it affordably. The latest Intel microprocessors, which use integrated circuit technology, incorporate the equivalent of nearly ten million transistors using interconnections that measure less than four-tenths of a micron (millionths of a meter) across.

In the past, a hierarchy of names was given to ICs depending on the size of circuit elements. Ordinary ICs were the coarsest in construction. Large-scale integration (LSI) put between 500 and 20,000 circuit elements together; very large scale integration (VLSI) puts more than 20,000 circuit elements onto a single chip. All microprocessors use VLSI technology, although the most recent products have become so complex (Intel's Pentium Pro, for example, has the equivalent of about 5.5 million transistors inside) that a new term has been coined for them, ultra large scale integration (ULSI).

Printed Circuits

An integrated circuit is like a gear of a complex machine. By itself, it does nothing. It must be connected to the rest of the mechanism to perform its appointed task. The integrated circuit needs a means to acquire and send out the logic and electrical signals it manipulates. In other words, each integrated circuit in a PC must be logically and electrically connected; essentially, that means linked by wires.

In early electrical devices, wires in fact provided the necessary link. Each wire carried one signal from one point to another, creating a technology called *point-to-point wiring*. Because people routinely soldered together these point-to-point connections by hand using a soldering iron, they were sometimes called *hand wiring*. This was a workable if not particularly cost-effective technology in the days of tubes when even a simple circuit spanned a few inches of physical space. Today, point-to-point wiring is virtually inconceivable because a PC crams the equivalent of half a million tube circuits into a few square inches of space. Connecting them with old-fashioned wiring would take a careful hand and some very fine wire. The time required to cut, strip, and solder in place each wire would make building a single PC a lifetime endeavor.

Long before the introduction of the first PC, engineers found a better way of wiring together electrical devices, the *printed circuit board*. The term is sometimes confusingly shortened to "PC board" even when the board is part of some other, non-computer device. Today, printed circuit boards are the standard from which nearly all electronic devices are made. The "board" in the name "motherboard" results from the assembly being a printed circuit board.

Fabrication

Printed circuit board technology allows all the wiring for an entire circuit assembly to be fabricated together in a quick process that can be entirely mechanized. The wires themselves are reduced to copper traces, a pattern of copper foil bonded to the substrate that makes up the support structure of the printed circuit board. In computers, this substrate is usually green composite material called *glass-epoxy* because it has a woven glass fiber base that's filled and reinforced with an epoxy plastic. Less critical electronic devices (read "cheap") substitute a simple brownish substrate of phenolic plastic for the glass-epoxy.

The simplest printed circuit boards start life as a sheet of thin copper foil bonded to a substrate. The copper is coated with a compound called photo-resist, a light-sensitive material. When exposed to light, the photo-resist becomes resistant to the effects of compounds, such as nitric acid, which strongly react with copper. A negative image of the desired final circuit pattern is placed over the photo-resist covered copper and exposed to a strong light source. This process is akin to making a print of a photograph. The exposed board is then immersed in an *etchant*, one of those nasty compounds that etch or eat away the copper that is not protected by the light-exposed photo-resist. The result is a pattern of copper on the substrate corresponding to the photographic original. The copper traces can then be used to connect the various electronic components that will make up the final circuit. All the wiring on a circuit board is thus fabricated in a single step.

When the electronic design on a printed circuit board is too complex to be successfully fabricated on one side of the substrate, engineers can switch to a slightly more complex technology to make two-sided boards. The traces on each side are separately exposed but etched during the same bath in etchant. In general, the circuit traces on one side of the board run parallel in one direction, and the traces on the other side run generally perpendicular. The two sides get connected together by components inserted through the board or through *plated-through holes*, holes drilled through the board then filled with solder to provide an electrical connection.

To accommodate even more complex designs, engineers have designed *multilayer circuit boards*. These are essentially two or more thin, double-sided boards tightly glued together into a single assembly. Most PC system boards use multilayer technology, both to accommodate complex designs and to improve signals characteristics. Sometimes, a layer is left nearly covered with copper to shield the signal in the layers from interacting with one another. These shields are typically held at ground potential and are consequently called *ground planes*.

One of the biggest problems with the multilayer design (besides the difficulty in fabrication) is difficulty in repair. Abnormally flexing a multilayer board can break one of the traces hidden in the center of the board. No reasonable amount of work can repair such damage.

Pin-in-Hole Technology

Two technologies are in wide use for attaching components to the printed circuit board. The older technology is called *pin-in-hole*. Electric drills bore holes in the circuit board at the points where the electronic components are to attach. Machines (usually) push the leads (wires that come out of the electronic components) into and through the circuit board holes and bend them slightly so that they hold firmly in place. The components are then permanently fixed in place with solder, which forms both a physical and electrical connection. Figure 2.2 shows the installation of a pin-in-hole electronic component.

FIGURE 2.2

Pin-in-hole compo-nent technology.

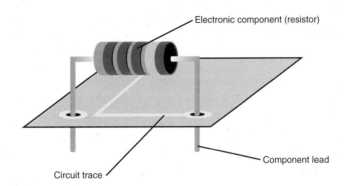

Electronic component (resistor)

Component lead

Circuit trace

Most mass-produced pin-in-hole boards use *wave soldering* to attach pin-in-hole components. A conveyer belt slides the entire board over a pool of molten solder (a tin and lead alloy), and a wave on the solder pool extends up to the board, coating the leads and the circuit traces. When cool, the solder holds all the components firmly in place.

Workers can also push pin-in-hole components into circuit boards and solder them individually in place by hand. Although hand fabrication is time-consuming and expensive, it can be effective when a manufacturer requires only a small number of boards. Automatic machinery cuts labor costs and speeds production on long runs; assembly workers typically make prototypes and small production runs or provide the sole means of assembly for tiny companies that can afford neither automatic machinery or farming out their circuit board work.

Surface-Mount Technology

The newer method of attaching components, *surface-mount technology*, promises greater miniaturization and lower costs than pin-in-hole. Instead of holes to secure them, surface-mount components are glued to circuit boards using solder flux or paste, which temporarily holds them in place. After all the components are affixed to a circuit board in their proper places, the entire board assembly runs through a temperature-controlled oven, which melts the solder paste and firmly solders each component to the board. Figure 2.3 illustrates surface-mount construction.

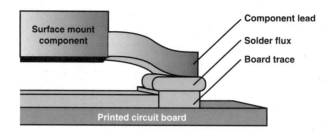

FIGURE 2.3
*Surface-mount circuit
board construction.*

Surface-mount components are smaller than their pin-in-hole kin because they don't need leads. Manufacturing is simpler because there's no need to drill holes in the circuit boards. Without the need for large leads, the packages of the surface-mount components can be smaller, so more components will fit in a given space with surface-mount technology.

On the downside, surface-mount fabrication doesn't lend itself to small production runs or prototyping. It can also be a headache for repair workers. They have to squint and peer at components that are often too small to be handled without tweezers and a lot of luck. Moreover, many surface-mount boards also incorporate some pin-in-hole components, so they still need drilling and wave soldering.

Motherboards

Nearly all PCs and compatible computers share one common feature: They are built with a single, large printed circuit board as their foundation. In many cases, the big board—usually called the *motherboard*—essentially is the entire computer. Almost completely self-contained, the one board holds the most vital electronic components that define the PC: its microprocessor, support circuitry, memory, and often video and audio functions. Anything you want to add to your PC plugs into the expansion bus that's part of the motherboard. As such a basic element, the motherboard defines both the PC and its capabilities. The circuitry it contains determines the overall performance of your system. Without the motherboard, you wouldn't have a PC.

In a modern PC, the motherboard is the big green centerpiece inside the case. Each computer maker essentially builds the rest of its PCs around the motherboard. On the motherboard, the PC makers put all the most important electrical circuits that make up the computer. The expansion bus on the motherboard provides a foundation for future expansion, adding new features and capabilities to your PC.

Open your PC and you'll see the motherboard inside. It usually lines the bottom of desktop systems or one side of tower and mini-tower systems. It's the biggest circuit board inside the PC, likely the biggest circuit board in any electronic device you have around your home or office. Typically, it takes the form of a thick green sheet about the size of a piece of notebook paper and decorated with an array of electronic components.

Although all motherboards look much the same, that similarity belies many differences in technologies and approaches to PC design. Some computer makers strive to cram as much circuitry as possible on the motherboard. Others put as little as possible there. The difference affects both the initial cost of your PC and its future use and expansion.

Design Approaches

Nothing about computers requires a motherboard. You could build a PC without one—at least if you had sufficient knowledge of digital circuits and electronic fabrication, not to mention patience that would make Job seem a member of the television generation. Building a PC around a single centralized circuit board seems obvious, even natural, only because of its nearly universal use. Engineers designed the very first mass-market PCs around a big green motherboard layout, and this design persists to this day.

Motherboards exist from more than force of habit, however. For the PC manufacturer, the motherboard design approach has immediate allure. Building a PC with a single large motherboard is often the most economical way to go, at least if your aim is soldering together systems and pushing them out the loading dock. There are alternatives, however, which can be more versatile and are suited to some applications. The more modular approach used in some of these alternatives allows you more freedom in putting together or upgrading a system to try to keep up with the race of technology.

The motherboard-centered design of most PCs is actually a compromise approach. Basic PC design is a combination of two diametrically opposed design philosophies. One approach aims at diversity, adaptability, and expandability by putting the individual functional elements (microprocessor, memory, and input/output circuitry) on separate boards that plugged into connectors that linked them together through a circuit bus. Such machines are known as bus-oriented computers. The alternative concentrates on economy and simplicity by uniting all the essential components of the computer on a single large board. Each of these designs has its strengths.

Bus-Oriented Computers

At the time the PC was developed, the bus-oriented design was the conservative approach. A true bus-oriented design seems the exact opposite of the motherboard. Instead of centralizing all circuitry, the bus-oriented design spreads it among multiple circuit boards. It's sort of the Los Angeles approach to computer design; it sprawls out all over without a distinct downtown. Only a freeway system links everything together to make a working community. In the bus-oriented computer, that freeway system is the *bus*.

A bus gets its name because, like a Greyhound, all the signals of the bus travel together and make the same stops at the same connectors along the way. The most popular small business computers of that pre-PC era were built around the *S-100* bus standard. The name was mostly descriptive, indicating that the complete bus comprised 100 connections.

Most larger computers made at the time the PC was introduced used the bus-oriented design as well.

The bus approach enabled each computer to be custom configured for its particular purpose and business. You attached whatever components the computer application required to the bus. When you needed them, you could plug larger, more powerful processors, even multiple processors, into the bus. This modular design enabled the system to expand as business needs expanded. It also allowed for easier service. Any individual board that failed could be quickly removed and replaced without circuit-level surgery.

Actually, among smaller computers that preceded the PC, the bus-oriented design originated as a matter of necessity simply because all the components required to make a computer would not fit on a circuit board of practical size. The overflowing circuitry had to be spread among multiple boards, and the bus was the easiest way to link them all. Although miniaturization has nearly eliminated such needs for board space, the bus-oriented design still occasionally resurfaces. You'll sometimes find special purpose PCs such as numerical control systems and network servers that use the bus-oriented approach for sake of its modularity.

Single-Board Computers

The advent of integrated circuits, microprocessors, and miniaturized assemblies that put multiple electronic circuit components into a single package often as small as a fingernail greatly reduced the amount of circuit boards required for building a computer. By the end of the 1970s, putting an entire digital computer on a single circuit board became practical.

Reducing a computer to a single circuit board was also desirable for a number of reasons. Primary among them was cost. Fewer boards means less fabrication expense and lower materials cost. Not only can the board be made smaller, but also the circuitry that's necessary to match each board to the bus can be eliminated. Moreover, single-board computers have an advantage in reliability. Connectors are the most failure-prone part of any computer system. The single-board design eliminates the bus connectors as a potential source for system failure.

On the downside, however, the single-board computer design is decidedly less flexible than the bus-oriented approach. The single board has its capabilities forever fixed the moment it is soldered together at the factory. It can never become more powerful or transcend its original design. It cannot adapt to new technologic developments.

Although the shortcomings of the single-board computer make it an undesirable (but not unused) approach for desktop computers, the design works well for many laptop and notebook computers. The compactness of the single-board approach is a perfect match for the space- and weight-conscious notebook PC design, and the lack of expansion is tolerated for sake of a compact, tote-able design.

Notebooks computers show the essence of the single-board design. Created to be completely self-contained while minimizing mass and volume, notebook machines cram as much as possible onto their circuit boards. In a quest for compactness, some of the biggest savings come from shaving away the connectors required by an expansion bus.

Notebook machines also illustrate the shortcomings of the pure single-board design. Computer technology changes fast, but innovations in different areas arrive independently. A notebook PC that's otherwise in tune with the times might fall short in one particular area of operation. You might, for example, buy a fast notebook PC only to find that a new kind of high-speed modem becomes affordable a few months later. A single-board system with a built-in modem would be forever stuck with older, slower modem designs. With the ability to add circuitry to your PC, however, you can adapt your system to new standards and technologies as they arrive.

All better notebook computers now amend the single-board computer approach with a specialized, miniature expansion bus such as PC Card or CardBus. (See Chapter 7, "The Expansion Bus.")

Compromise Designs

Rather than strictly follow either the single-board or bus-oriented approach, the companies that made the first mass-market small computers brought the two philosophies together, mixing the best features of the single-board computer and the bus-oriented design in one box. In IBM's initial implementation of this design, the first PC model, one large board hosts the essential circuitry that defines the computer and spaces that are available for expansion and adaptability.

Throughout the history of the PC, functions have migrated from auxiliary circuit boards to the motherboard. Early PCs required extra circuit boards for their serial and parallel ports. Modern PCs pack those ports and USB (and even FireWire) ports on the motherboard. At one time, most system memory, mass storage interfaces, high-quality sound circuitry, network adapters, and video circuitry all required additional boards. Now, many systems incorporate all of these functions on their motherboards.

At least three motivations underlie this migration: expectations, cost, and capability. As the power and potential of personal computers have increased, people expect more from their PCs. The basic requirements for a personal computer have risen so that features that were once options and afterthoughts are now required. To broaden the market for personal computers, manufacturers have striven to push prices down. Putting the basics required in a computer on the main circuit board lowers the overall cost of the system for exactly the same reasons that a single-board computer is cheaper to make than the equivalent bus-oriented machine. Moreover, using the most modern technologies, manufacturers simply can fit more features on a single circuit board. The original PC had hardly a spare square inch for additional functions. Today, all the features of a PC hundreds of times more powerful than that original will fit into a couple of chips.

As with any trend, however, aberrant counter-trends in PC design appear and disappear occasionally. Some system designers have chosen to complicate their systems to make them explicitly upgradable by pulling essential features, such as the microprocessor, off the main board. The rationale underlying this more modular design is that it gives the manufacturer (and your dealer) more flexibility. The PC maker can introduce new models as fast as he can slide a new expansion board into a box; motherboard support circuitry need not be re-engineered. Dealers can minimize their inventories. Instead of stocking several models, the dealer (and manufacturer) need only keep a single box on the shelf, shuffling the appropriate microprocessor module into it as the demand arises. For you, as the computer purchaser, these modular systems also promise upgradability, which is a concept that's desirable in the abstract (your PC need never become obsolete) but often impractical (upgrading is rarely a cost-effective strategy).

The compromise of a big board and slots will continue to be popular as long as PCs need to be expandable and adaptable. In the long term, however, you can expect single-board systems to appear again in the form of products dedicated to a purpose, for example, a dedicated multimedia playback machine (an intelligent entertainment engine, essentially a VCR with a college education) or a set-top box to connect your television to the World Wide Web (essentially a PC with a learning disability).

Nomenclature

You say "tomato," and I say "pomme d'amour." Let's call the whole thing off. If we don't talk the same language, making a pot of chili or PC may be more of a challenge than it needs to be. Even with something as unambiguous as a motherboard, however, the terminology can easily trip you up. That term alone sports several synonyms, each with subtle, often unacknowledged, differences.

Other terms you may commonly encounter that mean "motherboard" or something similar include system board, planar board, main board, baseboard, logic board, and backplane.

> **System boards.** This term is little more than a de-sexed version of motherboard introduced to the realm of personal computers by IBM when it introduced its first machine. At the time, America was preoccupied with issues of sexual equality, and well-meaning but linguistically naïve people confused issues of gender with sex. The term "system board" stands in its own right, however, because it indicates the role of the board as the centerpiece of the entire computer system. IBM continues to use the term to mean "motherboard."

Planar boards. Although *planar board* may seem simply another de-sexed word for "motherboard," it bears a distinction. Although all modern circuit boards are planar in the sense they take the form of a flat plane, the planar board in a PC forms the mounting plane of the entire system.

Baseboards. Intel often refers to the "motherboard" as the *baseboard* in many of its technical manuals. The company is not consistent about its usage; for example, the manual dated May 1996 for Intel VS440FX lists the product as a "motherboard," whereas the manual for the Performance/AU dated December 1995 terms the product a "baseboard." Again, there is a subtle distinction. A motherboard goes into a PC; a baseboard decorates the junction of a wall and a floor.

Main board. Apparently contributed by off-shore motherboard makers, the term *main board* may be a result of translation, but it is actually a particularly appropriate term. The "main board" is the largest circuit board inside and the foundation for the computer system and, hence, it *is* the main board in a PC's case.

Logic board. In the realm of the Apple Macintosh, the term *logic board* often refers to the equivalent of a PC's motherboard—notwithstanding every printed circuit board inside a computer contains digital logic.

Backplane. Another name sometimes used to describe the motherboard in PCs is *backplane*. The term is a carry-over from bus-oriented computers. In early bus-oriented design, all the expansion connectors in the machine were linked by a single circuit board. The expansion boards slid through the front panel of the computer and plugged into the expansion connectors in the motherboard at the rear. Because the board was necessarily planar and at the rear of the computer, the term "backplane" was perfectly descriptive. With later designs, the backplane found itself lining the bottom of the computer case.

Backplanes are described as active if, as in the PC design, they hold active logic circuitry. A passive backplane is nothing more than expansion connectors linked by wires or printed circuitry. The system boards of most personal computers could be described as active backplanes, although most engineers reserve the term "backplane" for bus-oriented computers in which the microprocessor plugs into the backplane rather than reside on it. The active circuitry on an active backplane under such a limited definition would comprise bus control logic that facilitates the communication between boards.

Physical Requirements

Besides holding the essential circuitry of a PC, the motherboard of a PC must accommodate some form of expansion. In desktop PCs, the motherboard is home to special electrical jacks called *expansion connectors* that allow you to plug in additional printed circuit boards. The space potentially occupied by an expansion board is an expansion *slot*, usually referred to simply as a slot.

Notebook PCs and their ilk also incorporate expansion boards but in a different form. A protective shell, usually sheathed with aluminum, encases their circuit boards to make a near monolithic assembly that's termed a PCMCIA card or PC Card. PCMCIA stands for the organization that sets the standard for these cards, the Personal Computer Memory Card International Association. PC Card is actually a term of art that more particularly describes one of the interface standards used by these cards. Most people call the space potentially occupied by the cards a PCMCIA slot or simply a card slot.

Manufacturers cannot designate expansion areas on their motherboards willy-nilly. There is order and reason behind their designs—all backed by standards.

Beyond standardization, other concerns include the number, size, and arrangement of the slots. These considerations determine how expandable a given PC really is. In addition, the spacing of the bus connectors in the slots is a concern. Put them too close together, and you'll limit the designer's choice of circuit components to those that are short or force the designer to put the components flat against the board, wasting its expensive space. Even the number of expansion connectors may be set or limited by the bus standard.

Bus Standard

The basic characterization of motherboards is by the standard they follow for the physical and electrical characteristics of their expansion slots. The choice dictates which boards plug into the motherboard—in other words, which products you can use to upgrade your PC. Although the choice is no longer wide, variations remain.

Expansion standards for desktop PC motherboards have gone through a lengthy evolution with a number of interesting but now essentially irrelevant side trips. Today, however, one standard (PCI) dominates and the only option is whether a given motherboard or PC condescends to accommodate legacy (old) expansion boards that follow the ISA standard. The situation is simpler among notebook PCs because their evolution has been shorter and they missed the chaotic early days of PC development. You'll find a complete discussion about the history of expansion standards in Chapter 7.

Slot Number

The number of expansion slots in a given PC is a compromise with multiple considerations. More is better, but a PC with an infinite number of slots would be infinitely wide. The practical dimensions of motherboard and case limit the space available for slots.

Electrical considerations also keep the slot count modest. The high-speed signals used by today's expansion buses are hard to control. The higher the speed, the fewer slots that are practical. Even at 33MHz, today's most popular expansion bus standard allows for only three slots per controller.

Adding more slots requires additional control circuitry, which adds to the price of the PC (as does the cost of the expansion connectors themselves). With manufacturers slugging it out over every penny of their prices, the tendency is to constrain costs and slot count.

How many expansion slots you need on a motherboard depends on how many functions the motherboard-maker has integrated into the board. Most practical PCs fill one or more of their slots with standard equipment (such as a video board and modem). Over the three- to five-year life of the typical PC, you're likely to add more than one new accessory to your PC, likely something you might not have conceived when you bought the machine. You need to plan in advance for the need for expansion.

Notebook PCs get away with two or fewer slots because they do encapsulate all the normal functions of a PC on their motherboards. Nevertheless, two is still better than one, and you're likely to use what's available. Note, too, that super-thin PCs, which are most likely to have single slots, are the ones that will more likely need two. For example, these machines may require a slot to run a CD drive that would otherwise be built into a thicker system.

Slot Spacing

Expansion boards are three-dimensional objects (as is everything else in the real world). In addition to length and width, they also have thickness. PCMCIA explicitly gives all three dimensions of conforming cards. The thickness of desktop computer expansion is more implicit, determined by the spacing of the expansion slots. If slot spacing is too narrow, boards simply won't fit. Worse, one board might touch another and short-circuit a computer signal, leading to erratic operation or complete non-operation of the PC. If slots spacing is too wide, fewer will fit in a PC of reasonable size, limiting your expansion options.

A printed circuit board itself is quite thin, about one-eighth inch, and can be made even thinner when board dimensions become small. The thickness of most expansion boards and the requirement for adequate slot spacing arises from the components installed on the board—which may include another printed circuit board clinging to the first like a remora.

Surface-mount components make thinner boards practical, but taller components remain prevalent enough that the spacing of slots has remained the same since 1982. On all motherboards, expansion connectors are located on 0.8-inch centers.

Not only does this standard set the maximum thickness of any expansion board, but it also dictates the number of slots that may be available for a given size of motherboard. The board must be as least wide enough to accommodate all the slots it is to hold. Some motherboards are hardly wider than that.

In any case, the spacing of expansion slots was originally set arbitrarily. It represents what the developers of the first PCs thought was the optimum compromise between compact layout and adequate allowances for the height of circuit components. The choice was wise enough that it still reigns today.

Slot Layout

In desktop PCs, the layout of the slots is mostly a concern of the system designer. As long as your boards fit, you shouldn't have to worry. The designer, however, must fret about the electrical characteristics of signals that are close to invading the territory of microwave ovens. Some are purely electronic issues that cause high-speed buses to operate erratically and detrimentally interact with other electronic circuits by generating interference.

Expansion buses pose more engineering problems than other circuits because they require the balancing of several conflicting needs. The expansion bus must operate as fast as possible to achieve the highest possible transfer rate. The expansion bus also must provide a number of connectors for attaching peripherals, and these connectors must be spread apart to allow a reasonable thickness for each peripheral. In other words, the bus itself must stretch over several inches. The common solution is to use several short buses instead of one long one. Although the connectors on the motherboard may appear to link all expansion boards into a single bus, if your system has more than three high-speed expansion slots, it likely has multiple buses, each with its own controller, powering the slots.

There's another design consideration in desktop and tower PCs—whether expansion boards slide into their slots vertically or horizontally. In full-size systems, expansion boards plug into the motherboard perpendicularly. The result is that the main plane of each expansion board is vertical in desktop computers and horizontal in tower-style machines. A few compact desktop PCs termed *low-profile* designs align expansion boards parallel to the motherboard, horizontal in desktop systems.

Although alignment of the expansion slots appears to be only an aesthetic consideration, it also has a practical importance. Vertical boards cool naturally through convection. Air currents can rise across each board and cool its innermost components. Horizontal boards defeat convective cooling because the boards themselves block vertical air currents. In general, PCs with horizontal expansion boards should have some kind of active cooling system; translated from bureaucratic language, that means they need a fan to blow a cooling breeze across them.

Slot layout is more complicated in notebook computers in which the layout of PCMCIA slots may determine what cards you can plug into your PC. Most notebook PCs have two slots, and they are arranged like the barrels of a shotgun—either side-by-side or over-and-under. These options are not functionally equivalent. PC Cards come in any of three thicknesses (discussed later), and most slots accommodate the two slimmer sorts of cards.

An over-and-under arrangement of two slots will hold either two slim cards or one of the thickest sort. Although the over-and-under configuration gives you the largest number of expansion options, many of today's ultra-thin notebooks can only accommodate side-by-side slot mounting.

Standards

Modern motherboards can be any size or shape that suits the design of the PC. Only the need for standard-size expansion slot connectors limits the freedom of design. Many PCs, however, are built around motherboards of a few standard sizes. This standardization is a matter of convenience. It allows a PC manufacturer flexibility in the choice of suppliers; standardized dimensions make motherboards interchangeable.

For you as the purchaser of a new computer, motherboard standardization has its downside. You face the problem of the PC manufacturer selling systems equipped with a motherboard *du jour*, whatever OEM motherboard was available cheapest on the day the PC was put together. On the other hand, a PC built around a standard-sized motherboard gives you upgrade freedom. Should you become dissatisfied in the performance of your PC, you can replace a standard-size motherboard with a more powerful one.

The earliest motherboard standards followed the leads set by IBM. They duplicated the physical dimensions of the motherboards used by the most popular IBM machines. Even when they lopped off vast areas of board to trim costs, most manufacturers retained compatibility with IBM's designs, keeping mounting holes in the same locations so that one board could be substituted for another. This heritage continues even in some of the latest designs.

After IBM ceded its influence as the setter of the standard dimensions of motherboards, the industry was essentially adrift. Major manufacturers developed their own designs without regard to older products, although smaller manufacturers clung to the old board layouts. The situation is changing, however, with new motherboards standards now promulgated by Intel. These most recent of these, the *ATX motherboard* design, goes further than ever before and specifies not only dimensions and mounting holes but also connector placement and even connector designs. To standardize the motherboards of more powerful computer workstations, the PC industry recently developed the *WTX specification*.

Motherboard design divergence first arose among makers of small-footprint PCs, machines designed with smaller dimensions to cover less of your desktop. These machines compromised expansion by reducing the number of expansion slots and drive bays to gain their more modest measurements. Many manufacturers developed *low-profile PCs* that reduced system height by turning expansion boards on their sides. These designs necessitated changes from the more standardized motherboard layout. The PC industry has rallied around the low-profile design and produced two standards that support the concept.

First came the *LPX motherboard* and a smaller derivative (*mini-LPX*). To accommodate the needs of new microprocessor and memory technologies (and add a wealth of other features), the industry adopted the *NLX motherboard*.

In general, smaller manufacturers are more likely to use standard-size motherboards. Larger manufacturers are better able to afford the price of custom-designing cases and motherboards to match. Even large PC makers have moved to standard-size boards at least for their offerings that take advantage of the latest microprocessors. In truth, systems that use the latest microprocessors often all have exactly the same motherboard design inside, using a motherboard designed and manufactured by Intel. Even large manufacturers may rely on Intel motherboards until their engineers develop a familiarity with new chips. For example, all but a handful of the first Pentium Pro computer models uniformly used standard-size Intel-manufactured motherboards.

Early Motherboards

The first motherboard to be used in PCs was that of IBM's original Personal Computer. These measured about 8.5 by 11 inches and had five expansion slots spaced one inch apart in the left-rear corner of the board. This spacing proved overly generous and was abandoned for new systems within a year. IBM's second iteration of PC design back in 1982 set an enduring standard for slot spacing that endures today in nearly all PCs. With the XT motherboard, IBM squeezed the slots to 0.8-inch spacing. The dimensions of this board, 8.5 by 12 inches, soon became the *de facto* standard throughout the PC industry. Some motherboards are still designed to these dimensions, as shown in Figure 2.4.

FIGURE 2.4

The XT motherboard dimensions and layout.

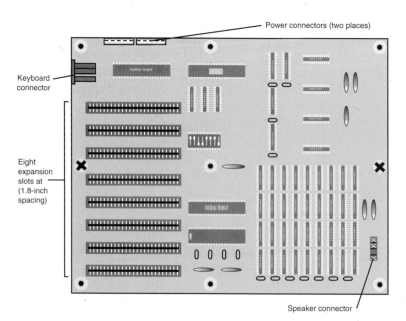

As manufacturers attempted to make more powerful PCs, the chief shortcoming of the XT design prove to be its size—too small to accommodate all the circuit components required in early systems. IBM extended the board space to the XT motherboard to 13.5 by 12 inches to create its AT motherboard design, as shown in Figure 2.5.

FIGURE 2.5

AT motherboard dimensions and screw placement.

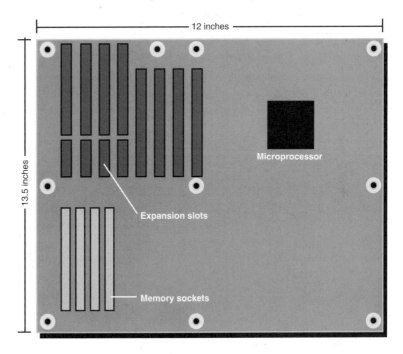

This form factor became another *de facto* industry standard through the 1980s and early 1990s. Some motherboard makers still use it today.

The primary way PC manufacturers reduce the cost of their products is by taking advantage of increased circuit integration. Once a given class of microprocessor has been on the market for a while, typically a year or two, chip-makers develop the technology to reduce the number of chips required on a motherboard. Instead of several dozen, the principal circuitry of the motherboard may be reduced to three or four chips. Fewer chips require less circuit board space. By making the motherboard physically smaller, manufacturers can reduce the cost of the materials to produce the motherboard. This gives manufacturers incentive to make miniaturized motherboards.

Because the placement of mounting holes and the spacing of expansion slots of the AT motherboard have become essentially industry standards over the years, engineers have crafted smaller motherboard designs that retain these features. These smaller AT-compatible designs are termed *mini-AT motherboards.*

Although the exact dimensions vary with the board maker, a typical mini-AT motherboard measures about 13 inches by 8.7 inches (330 by 220 millimeters) with the expansion slots running parallel to the long axis of the board. Figure 2.6 illustrates the general layout of a mini-AT motherboard.

FIGURE 2.6

A typical mini-AT system board.

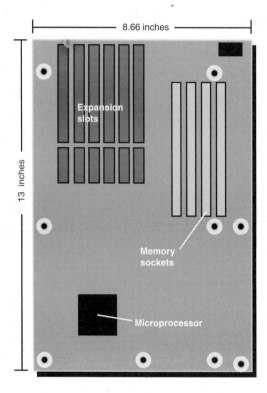

Although this form factor is not a true standard, many motherboard makers still offer products described as "mini-AT." In coming years, however, truly standardized designs will likely replace it as well as the other early motherboard designs.

ATX

To bring a degree of uniformity to motherboard design, the PC industry created a new motherboard standard that roughly conforms to the mini-AT board size but with a few design twists that result in lower-cost engineering. Called *ATX*, the standard is promulgated by Intel but is openly published. Intel released the most recent version, 1.1, in February 1996, fine-tuning the design based on industry feedback.

The principal design twist of the ATX board is that it gives a 90-degree turn to the mini-AT design, putting the long axis of the board parallel to the rear panel of the host PC chassis. The ATX standard defines the number and position of the motherboard mounting holes and offers recommendations as to component, expansion board, and port connector placement. Although the standard does not demand any particular slot type or configuration, it's aimed primarily at ISA, PCI, and ISA/PCI combination designs. It also allows for both 5.0 and 3.3 volt system operation (or both simultaneously).

The odd orientation of the board facilitates port placement. It provides the maximum space for expansion boards and port connectors at the rear of the host PC chassis. The design also envisions that the microprocessor will be located near the right edge of the board where it will be in close proximity to both the power supply and cooling fan. In the recommended configuration, memory sockets can be readily accessed between the microprocessor and expansion slots.

The ATX board itself measures a maximum of 12 by 9.6 inches (305 by 244 millimeters). This size is not a random choice but, according to Intel, was selected to allow manufacturers to cut two boards from a standard-size 18 by 24-inch raw printed circuit panel. It provides sufficient space for about seven expansion slots, which are spaced at the conventional 0.8 inches apart. It incorporates nine mandatory and one optional mounting hole, most of which are in the same positions as the holes in a mini-AT motherboard. Figure 2.7 shows the dimensions and mounting hole placement for an ATX motherboard.

FIGURE 2.7
Dimensions and hole placement of an ATX motherboard.

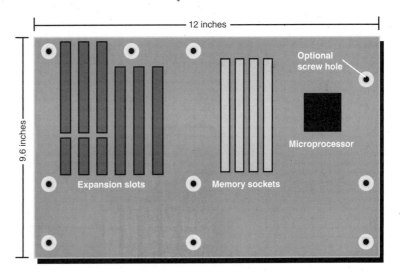

The ATX specification goes further than simply indicating mechanical board dimensions. The standard also embraces the PS/2 size of power supply and specifies a new motherboard power connector. (See Chapter 25, "Power.")

Besides uniformity, the ATX design aims at trimming costs for PC makers. Putting port connectors on the motherboard, even in multiple layers, eliminates the cost of connecting cables as well as the labor required for assembly. Eliminating cables also helps minimize potential radio frequency interference. In its recommended configuration, the ATX layout also allows the use of shorter floppy and hard disk connecting cables, with similar benefits. The power supply choice and location also trims cost for the PC manufacturer and helps the PC run cooler and even quieter.

Mini-ATX

The designers of the ATX board realized that the one certainty in PC circuit design is that functions get combined and made more compact. Just as all the circuitry on the AT-size board was shrunk to fit the mini-AT board, the ATX designers imagined that soon much of the ATX real estate would be superfluous. In that one of the primary goals in the design of ATX was trimming costs, it figured that trimming motherboards to a size smaller than ATX as the technology permitted it would reap savings in materials cost. Consequently, they included a standard size for mini-ATX motherboards in the ATX specification.

The mini-ATX design chops the ATX motherboard down to 11.2 by 8.2 inches (284 by 208 millimeters). When installed in a PC, the mini-ATX motherboard still sits at the rear edge of the chassis so that port connectors can be mounted directly to it without cables. In most chassis, the left edge still aligns with the left side of the case to allow space for a full complement of expansion boards. Because of this placement, the smaller size of the mini-ATX board cuts off one row of mounting ATX mounting holes. As a result, the lower row of mounting holes are displaced on the mini-ATX design, as shown in Figure 2.8.

FIGURE 2.8

Mini-ATX mother-board dimensions and layout.

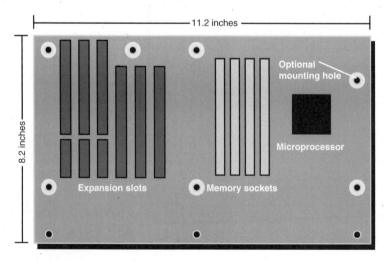

The mini-ATX design has one chief benefit. It reduces the materials costs for a motherboard by about 30 percent when compared to a full-size ATX board.

LPX

One thing stands in the way of making a low-profile PC—the height of the expansion boards. You can't make a system shorter than the height of an expansion board, at least if you have hopes of installing standard expansion boards into it.

Shorter PCs have their allure. Compact systems are less intimidating and more stylish and even make good monitor stands. To push down the top of the case of their systems, most manufacturers resorted to turning the expansion boards (and, of course, their mating connectors) on their sides inside the system chassis. The result was a profusion of odd-shaped motherboards with a number of different arrangements of their expansion provisions.

Bringing sense to this chaos and helping you find a replacement motherboard that fits most systems, the PC industry has developed a standard form factor for low-profile motherboards. Called *LPX*, the standard low-profile board measures 8.66 by 13 inches (or 220 by 330 millimeters), essentially the same dimensions as a mini-AT board. The short dimension of the board runs parallel to the rear of the PC chassis and hosts the connectors for input and output ports. In fact, the chief difference between an LPX motherboard and a mini-AT design is the form and placement of the expansion connectors, as shown in Figure 2.9.

FIGURE 2.9

Basic layout of an LPX motherboard.

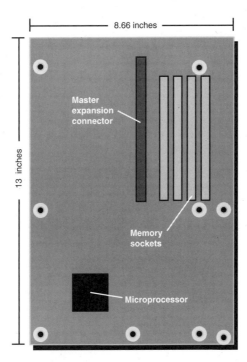

In place of expansion slots, the LPX motherboard has a single master expansion connector near the rear of the board, just right of its centerline. A small daughter card plugs into this slot and holds one or more standard expansion connectors that follow the ISA or PCI standard (or both). Guides in the chassis secure the boards in the slots so that they are parallel to the motherboard.

The keyboard connector on an LPX motherboard keeps to the same location as that of the mini-AT design. I/O connector placement is not part of the LPX layout, so different manufacturers locate port connectors wherever they see fit.

Mini-LPX

To save both cabinet space and the cost of materials, some manufacturers trim the LPX size motherboard to even smaller dimensions to create a *mini-LPX* board. In all other ways much the same as a full-size LPX board, the miniaturized design lops about three inches from the long axis of the board. The result measures about 10 inches by 8.66 inches, as shown in Figure 2.10.

FIGURE 2.10

Basic layout of a mini-LPX motherboard.

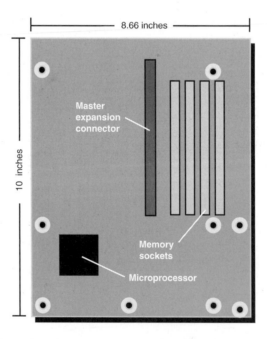

One example of the mini-AT motherboard is Intel's Advanced/MN design that is found in some low-profile Pentium PCs.

NLX

Announced in September 1996 by Intel, the NLX motherboard design was a cooperative effort among several manufacturers, including IBM. At the time of its introduction, twelve PC makers and one motherboard-only manufacturer (ASUStek) had announced support of the specification. The PC makers included AST, Digital Equipment Corporation (now part of Compaq), Fujitsu, Gateway 2000, Hewlett-Packard, IBM, ICL Personal Computers, Micron Electronics, NEC Computer Systems, Sony, Toshiba, and Tulip Computers.

NLX is an improved low-profile layout. It was created specifically to overcome some shortcomings of the LPX design that interfered with its adaptation to the latest technologies. NLX is meant to support all current Intel microprocessor designs and memory technologies as well as the Accelerated Graphics Port (AGP) for high-speed interconnections with video boards. In addition, the NLX design enhances the physical packaging of systems to allow greater mechanical integrity, better cooling, and more space for peripheral ports.

Key to the NLX design is the *riser* board. Although similar to the riser boards of LPX systems because you plug expansion boards into it, under the NLX design the riser takes on a greater role. In effect, it operates as a backplane and the NLX motherboard itself is a glorified processor board. The riser board attaches permanently to the chassis of its host computer, while the NLX motherboard readily slides in and out of the case like a steroid-enhanced expansion board. In purest form of the NLX implementation, all cables in the system—including the power supply—attach to the riser and none to the motherboard. Typically, the cables for the floppy disk and hard disk drives in a PC will plug into the riser.

Although the design of the NLX motherboard is fixed by the specification, the riser board is not. PC makers can customize its design to accommodate different system designs. Although the typical riser board has four expansion connectors, the NLX specification allows a great deal of freedom to accommodate not only low-profile PCs but also tower-style systems. The specification describes signals for up to five PCI expansion slots and an unlimited number of ISA slots on a single riser. All boards slide into the riser parallel to the motherboard.

The one aberration in the NLX motherboard/riser design is its accommodation for AGP video boards. The specification reserves a special area on the left side of the motherboard, opposite the riser board, for a single AGP slot. The AGP board slides into the motherboard slot parallel to the riser board. Microprocessors (the NLX design accommodates up to two) and memory reside on the right side of the motherboard so that they do not interfere with expansion boards. Figure 2.11 shows the basic layout of this two-board system.

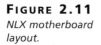

FIGURE 2.11
NLX motherboard layout.

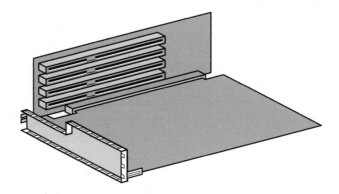

An L-shaped integral rear panel of the board provides space for peripheral connectors. The higher part of the panel allows designers to stack multiple connectors one over the other on the right side of the chassis, away from expansion boards. The NLX design envisions the motherboard to be readily removable without removing expansion board (except the AGP board) from inside the PC case. In a typical PC, the motherboard slides out the side of the chassis guided by rails at the bottom of the chassis. Four screws inside the PC secure the board to the chassis and electrically ground the two together. A latch that's part of the chassis and under the motherboard holds the board horizontally in place and also serves as a board ejector to aid in removing the motherboard. Spring-like contact fingers around the periphery of the rear panel shield electrically integrate the board with the rest of the chassis.

The mechanical specification of NLX motherboards allows a small degree of freedom in the size of the board. The specs allow any width between 8 and 9 inches (inclusive) except for systems integrating AGP video boards. These must be 9 inches wide because the space reserved for the AGP connector is on the last inch of the board. NLX motherboards may be between 10.0 and 13.6 inches long. The smallest NLX motherboard is approximately the size of a mini-LPX motherboard; the largest about the size of a LPX board.

The NLX specifications provide for three different mounting screw patterns depending on the length of the board. An NLX motherboard may use any of the three patterns, but each NLX chassis design must accommodate all three.

NLX uses a 340-pin connector between the motherboard and riser. This single connector carries signals for the ISA and PCI buses, IDE drives, and miscellaneous system functions. The pin-out is available in the electronic version of this book. In addition, the specification reserves space for a larger connector to accommodate future, wider expansion buses and an optional connector for other system features.

WTX

Workstations require greater power and design flexibility from ordinary general-purpose PCs, so in September 1998, Intel introduced a new specification aimed at standardizing many aspects of workstation design. Although ostensibly a motherboard standard, the WTX specification is so flexible as to be a non-standard. The chief aim of the design appears to guide fabricators of PC chassis and motherboard makers to match their products so generic boards will fit generic cases. WTX includes not only the motherboard itself but also the form factor of the case to house it. Additionally, the standard defines how areas within the case are to be used.

WTX anticipates a classic single-board design and provides a huge parcel of glass-epoxy real estate for building upon. Under the specification, motherboards can be up to 14 by 16.75 inches or any size smaller. The standard prescribes no minimum dimensions.

The magic of WTX—the way it mates the diverse motherboard size possibilities to generic chassis—is its *adapter plate*. This flat sheet of metal serves as a mount custom made for the particular size of motherboard chosen by the manufacturer. It mates with a standardized set of mounting holes in the WTX chassis using five hooks to latch to the chassis. The chassis has five matching slots, one for each hook, which are raised to provide clearance below the adapter plate and prevent the hooks from dipping below the outside plane of the chassis. Two brackets on the rear of the adapter plate allow it to be screwed to the rear of the chassis and secure it in place. What goes on between the motherboard and adapter plate is left to the motherboard maker; the board could attach to the adapter plate with baling wire and still comply with the standard. Figure 2.12 shows a typical adapter plate.

FIGURE 2.12
A typical WTX adapter plate.

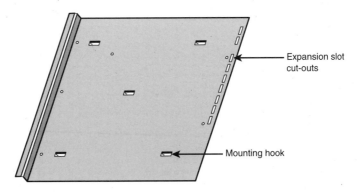

Expansion slot cut-outs

Mounting hook

The WTX standard dictates only a few features of the motherboard. It precisely defines the location and alignment of the expansion connectors so that boards will properly install in the chassis. Although the standard does not compel any number or arrangement of peripheral ports, it does specify a cut-out on the chassis where motherboard-mounted connectors project through. In addition, the WTX specification recommends against placing motherboard-to-adapter plate mounts in the locations at which the adapter screws to the chassis.

WTX contemplates but does not compel the use of PCI expansion slots and an AGP port. It also introduces a new type of slot, the *Flex Slot*. Although classed as a single slot and assigned a single predefined location on the WTX motherboard and chassis, the Flex Slot actually accommodates two standard PCI-size expansion boards. The WTX specification anticipates the Flex Slot will be used for peripheral ports but defines no specific purpose for it. Even the expansion connectors on the motherboard for the Flex Slot are left to the motherboard designer. Only the volume occupied by contents of the slot and the opening in the rear panel of the PC to accommodate the port connectors installed in the slot are defined in the standard. As its name implies, the intention is to give system designers added flexibility in creating workstations.

Expansion Boards

Although a motherboard *could* hold all the circuitry necessary for making a complete PC—in fact, most notebook and smaller computers use such a strategy effectively—the ability to add to or enhance the motherboard extends the power of the PC concept. The ability to expand a PC makes the PC-as-tool into a platform of almost unlimited opportunities. Expansion capabilities allow you to customize your PC to your exact purposes.

In this chapter, we'll consider the physical issues involved in mating expansion boards with your PC and its motherboard. In Chapter 7, we'll consider the electrical and logical operation of the expansion bus.

Nomenclature

Is it a card or a board? The PC industry uses the two terms indiscriminately. This confused usage has good precedent; long before PCs, the electronics industry used the same terms for printed circuit assemblies. If there was any distinction, board was the generalized term (as in printed circuit board). Cards typically were smaller and usually plugged into a connector. Boards were usually screwed or bolted in place. No one cared because both terms were generally understood.

The PC Card and CardBus *cards* used in the external slots of notebook computers complicate the matter. They are cards through their similarity to credit cards. That similarity and the name were not accidental.

> **Expansion boards**. The smaller printed circuit boards that plug into your PC's motherboard are most often termed *expansion boards* because they provide you with

the means of expanding the capabilities of your PC. As noted before, the expansion board is distinct from the expansion slot, the space inside the computer chassis the board occupies (or potentially occupies), and the expansion connector into which you plug the board.

Expansion boards are often distinguished by the standard followed by their interface or the connector at the bottom of the board. For example, an *ISA board* follows the Industry Standard Architecture bus standard, and a *PCI board* follows the Peripheral Component Interconnect standard. We'll discuss these standards in the "Standards" section later in this chapter.

Option boards. Some PC makers prefer to describe expansion boards as *option boards*. You plug them into your system to add an optional feature. Strictly speaking, then, a standard equipment expansion board—for example, a graphics adapter—would not be an option board, but for consistency's sake (or maybe inconsistency), most of these manufacturers include such standard equipment among their options boards, perhaps to give you the idea you're getting options for free—just like that lunch.

Daughter boards. Strictly speaking, any board that plugs into a motherboard should be a daughter board, but in the realm of the PC, the family relationship is not so straightforward. Many boards that plug into the motherboard of a PC have special names of their own; memory modules, microprocessor cartridges, and expansion boards are all daughter boards. Most PC hardware makers reserve the term "daughter board" for add-on circuit boards that attach as a second layer to their expansion boards.

This two-story form of packaging was prevalent when all the circuitry needed to build an expansion board just wouldn't fit in the space available in a single slot. The daughter board bought added square inches for circuitry. Today's circuits are so compact that this form of construction is rarely used. Most manufacturers don't even use the entire allowable size for their expansion board products.

Riser boards. As noted earlier, low-profile PCs reduce their size by providing horizontal slots for their expansion boards. To connect these boards to the motherboard, most use a special board called a *riser board*. As with an ordinary expansion board, the riser board plugs into the motherboard, but its circuit endowment comprises little more than a set of connectors to accommodate your expansion boards.

Although PC expansion boards can all be considered daughter boards, not all daughter boards are expansion boards. For example, some PC expansion boards can themselves be expanded by plugging a daughter board onto them. Because such boards plug only into their host board, they are not true PC expansion boards. Most people call the circuit boards that plug into the motherboard the system's expansion boards. Circuit boards that plug into expansion boards are daughter boards. That convention at least relieves us of adding another generation and creating the granddaughter board.

Construction

Several components define the physical reality of the standard PC expansion board. The board proper is an ordinary printed circuit board fabricated with pin-in-hole or surface-mount technology or a combination of both. An expansion connector connects the board to the electronic circuitry of your PC. A retaining bracket secures the board inside your computer and provides a place to put peripheral connectors.

Substrate

The substrate is the board itself, a slice of glass-epoxy upon which the various circuit components and connection traces are bonded. PC makers fabricate expansion boards using exactly the same technologies as motherboards.

The original design for expansion boards envisioned one end of each board sliding into a *card guide*, a thin slot at one end of the expansion slot, to stabilize the board inside the PC and keep it from bending or flapping in the breeze. These expansion boards that stretch from one end of the slot to the other are often called *full-length* expansion boards.

Most modern expansion board designs don't require all of area allowed for the substrate in the PC and are classed as *short cards*. Because of their diminutive dimensions and low mass, they are adequately secured in your PC by the expansion connector and their retaining brackets.

Retaining Bracket

Nearly all expansion boards have an L-shaped bracket attached at one end. Manufacturers use a *number* of terms for this bracket, perhaps the most colorful being ORB, an acronym for *Option Retaining Bracket*. The current trend is to refer to this bracket as the *bracket*.

In a PC, the bracket serves two functions. It secures and stabilizes the expansion board in its slot. It provides a mounting space for port connectors that may be required for connecting peripherals to the expansion board. And it helps shield your PC, keeping electrical interference inside your PC's case by plugging up the hole at the end of the expansion slot.

In most PCs, a screw secures the bracket to the computer's chassis. When installing an expansion board, you should always ensure that this screw tightly holds each expansion board in place. Properly installing each board with a screw will prevent your accidentally pushing the board out of the expansion connector when you plug into the connector on the board. (Tilting the expansion board can cause the contacts on its edge connector to bridge across several pins of the expansion connector—shorting them out—and possibly crashing or even damaging your PC.) In addition, firmly screw-mounting the bracket assures electrical continuity between the bracket and PC chassis.

Connector

The card-edge connector on each expansion board is little more than an extension of the etched copper traces of the printed circuits on the board substrate. The chief difference is that the connector pads are gold plated during the fabrication of the expansion board. The gold does not tarnish or oxidize, so it assures that the edge connector will make a clean contact with the expansion connector on the motherboard.

The chief current expansion board standard uses the placement of pad areas and slots to key the board so that expansion boards fit only in slots designed for them.

Nearly all expansion standards for desktop PCs use *edge connectors* for one very good reason: They are cheap. The connector contacts get etched onto the board at the same time as the rest of its circuit traces. The only extra expense is the thin gold plating on the contact area to stave off the oxidation of the copper or lead-and-tin coated traces.

After the pragmatic choice of an edge connector, the creator of an expansion standard still has a variety of choices. Most important is the spacing between contacts in the connector. The spacing along with the number of contacts determines the size. In a dream world—the one in which many designers operate—the size of the connector is no concern. In the real world, however, it has two dramatic effects. It determines how much space must be given up to connectors on the motherboard, and it governs the insertion force of an expansion board into the connector.

In true bus-style computers, the board space given up to the expansion bus is immaterial. The computer chassis is nothing but the bus, so there is no problem in devoting the whole back or bottom of the machine to the expansion bus. In the traditional PC design, however, the bus takes up space on the motherboard, which also has to provide the basic circuitry of the computer. The more motherboard space taken up by the bus, the less space available for building the basic PC. Consequently, the bus area must be as compact as possible to yield the largest possible circuit space on the motherboard.

The larger the connector, the more area of the expansion board that rubs against the contacts inside the socket when you plug in the board. To assure a reliable electrical connection, the socket contacts must press forcefully against the contact tabs on the circuit board. Sliding an expansion board into a socket requires enough force to squeeze the board contacts between the socket contacts. The more area devoted to contacts, the greater the required *insertion force*. When a connector is too long, the insertion force may be greater than some people can comfortably apply, even greater than the automatic insertion machinery used by PC manufacturers can apply. Worse, if the insertion force is high enough, sliding in an expansion board may overly stress the motherboard, potentially cracking it or one of the conductive traces and putting it out of action.

Making the contact smaller shortens the connector, cutting down on the motherboard space required for the bus and reducing insertion force. It also requires greater precision in the manufacture of expansion boards. Nevertheless, newer expansion board standards are marked by closer spacing of their edge connector contacts; just compare an ISA board to a PCI board inside your PC.

More specialized bus standards such as those for notebook PCs and industrial computers rely on *pin connectors*. These necessarily cost more because they add another part that must be soldered to each expansion board. But because the connector is a separate part, it can be manufactured with greater precision, and the greater precision allows smaller, more compact connectors. Moreover, pin connectors can use more than two contact rows to further reduce the space that must be devoted to the bus. Pin connectors are also more reliable because they allow their contacts to mate on multiple sides. Pin connectors are also easier to shield, making them more desirable as concerns about emissions increase along with bus speeds.

Standards

Standardization is key to the success of PC expansion. The slots, connectors, mounting, signals, and logical interface are all rigidly defined, allowing you to install nearly any PC expansion board in nearly any PC.

Standardization is not a single issue. Expansion boards must be physically, electrically, and logically compatible with the motherboards with which they mate.

First of all, a board must fit into the computer for which it is designed. Consequently, today's expansion board standards dictate the physical size of expansion boards. In addition, the board must be able to send its signals to the motherboard and listen to those that the motherboard sends it. It must have some kind of electrical connection with the motherboard. Consequently, the physical standardization of expansion boards extends to their electrical connectors. Before signals can hope to get from one board to another, the connectors must mate together. They must match as to size, style, and placement so that they can properly fit together.

Although the physical size of an expansion board has no effect on its electrical compatibility, it is a major issue in compatibility. After all, an expansion board has to fit in the PC it is meant to expand. All expansion standards define the size of the circuit boards they use either as exact dimensions or as a set of maximum and, often, minimum dimensions.

Given his druthers—or even someone else's druthers—a circuit board designer would rather have more board space, acres upon acres of it stretching from here to the horizon to the limits of time and the universe. More space to work with makes the job easier. Unfortunately for the designer, practical concerns such as keeping the size of the PC manageable restrain his ambitions and board space. After all, an expansion board has to fit inside the PC in which it is meant to operate.

On the other hand, smaller boards help manufacturers cut costs, at least after the price for developing new designs is paid. They require less in the way of the glass-epoxy base materials from which the boards are built. Consequently, setting the dimensions for an expansion board standard is always a compromise.

The prototype of all expansion boards was the card that fit into the original IBM PC of 1981. The bus and physical form of this board lurks behind all PC expansion to this day. Until the day when manufacturers finally get up enough nerve to leave legacy sockets out of their computer products, PCs will have at least one slot capable of accommodating a circuit board from the original PC—and holding the possibility the board might actually work.

Even the newest, all-PCI computer owes a debt to the original PC design and still shows its heritage in several of its physical characteristics. The maximum board length and thickness all go back to the first days of the PC. The multi-part basic design, too, harks back to the first PC expansion cards. Even the latest CardBus cards for notebook PCs hold the electrical and logical legacy of the original PC expansion slot.

Legacy (ISA) boards
Only three dimensions of ISA boards are critical: maximum board length, substrate height, and connector placement.

Dimensions
The maximum substrate length is a simple physical limit set by the size of the expansion slot itself. Boards can be no longer because they won't fit into the confines of the PC chassis. Because of the overwhelming desire for backward compatibility that has guided chassis design since the days of the first PC, modern ISA expansion boards are limited to a maximum length of 13.415 inches (340.7 millimeters), from the back edge of the mounting bracket to the far edge mating with the card guide. The substrate itself is a bit shorter to allow for a physical gap between it and the bracket that measures at least 0.04 inches (1.02 millimeter).

Full-length boards are uncommon today because of the miniaturization of components. The term *short board* refers to any board that does not reach to the card guides. Short boards may be any length, ungoverned by any standard.

Compatibility also rules when it comes to the height of ISA expansion boards. Modern boards conform to the pattern set by the first PCs; the plural is important because the standard is twofold.

Most ISA boards conform to the height limit set by the first PC, 4.2 inches (or 106.68 millimeters). Boards of this size are described as *XT height* because they fit the IBM Personal Computer XT, successor to the original PC. Figure 2.13 shows the maximum dimensions of an XT-size expansion board.

FIGURE 2.13

Dimensions of an XT-height ISA expansion board.

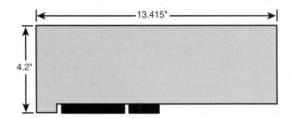

The need for more board space at a time when computers demanded more power but had not reaped the full benefits of circuit miniaturization led to the adoption of taller cases to accommodate taller expansion boards in the IBM Personal Computer AT. For these systems, designers increased the maximum board height to 4.8 inches (121.92 millimeters). Boards of this size are consequently termed *AT height*. The EISA standard (see Chapter 7) accepted these dimensions as the maximum for expansion boards conforming with its specifications as well. These were the largest expansion boards to be used in PC, as shown in Figure 2.14.

FIGURE 2.14

Dimensions of an AT-height ISA expansion board.

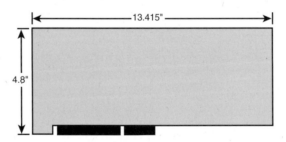

Although combining the added height of these boards with shorter length is somewhat contradictory—the height gives more board space but reducing the length takes it away—some manufacturers did make products in the form of short AT-height boards.

Board height is important. Cases made to accommodate only XT-height boards will not accept AT-height boards. Most modern PCI-based computers are tall enough to accept only XT-height expansion boards, so AT-height boards cannot be used in these systems (at least if you want to put the top back on the case). The presence of ISA slots does not guarantee that all ISA expansion boards will fit into a given system. As the importance of ISA diminishes, so will this issue of compatibility. However, if you're hoping to use an old board in a new PC, you must take into account ISA board height.

PC/104

Makers of industrial computers and numerical control systems adapted the electrical design of ISA into a more robust format termed PC/104. The expansion boards of PC/104 differ from ordinary ISA boards chiefly in their mechanical aspects. Besides being smaller than ordinary ISA cards, PC/104 boards use a different connector. As with ISA, boards may use either an 8- or 16-bit interface. The wider-bus boards have an auxiliary connector to handle their additional signals. The connectors are ordinary pin-style headers with the pins uniformly spaced 0.1 inch apart in two rows similarly spaced. The 8-bit connector comprises 64 pins; the 16-bit connector, 40 pins. The name of the technology merely states the total pin count—104 pins. Figure 2.15 shows the layout and dimensions of a PC/104 board.

FIGURE 2.15

Layout and dimensions of a PC/104 card.

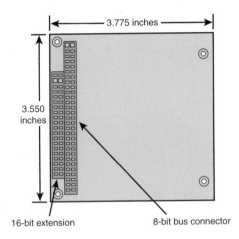

3.775 inches

3.550 inches

16-bit extension   8-bit bus connector

Instead of plugging into a bus, PC/104 cards make their own bus by stacking connectors. Each board has both male and female contacts, one set above, one below. One board plugs atop another and provides a new jack to plug in the next board. When stacked, four metal or plastic spacers between each pair of cards keep them a uniform 0.6 inches apart.

PCI Boards

PCI defines several variations on the basic expansion board. The specification defines two sizes of board, each with three connector arrangements (5 volt, 3.3 volt, and dual voltage). The two board sizes are based on traditional ISA expansion boards.

Dimensions

A full-size PCI expansion board measures 12.283 inches (312 mm) long. The main body of the board is about 3.875 inches high, although the expansion edge connector and a short skirt extend the width of the board to 4.2 inches (106.68 mm). The critical reference dimension is the centerline of the notch in the expansion connector, which is displaced

4.113 inches (104.47 mm) from the back edge (retaining bracket side) of the board. Figure 2.16 shows the dimensions of a full-size PCI board in 5-volt configuration. Cards designed for 3.3 volts or universal operation will differ in contact number and placement but not overall size.

FIGURE 2.16

Primary dimensions of a full-size five-volt PCI expansion board.

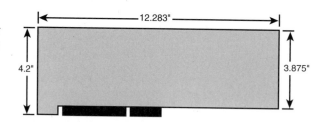

PCI also defines a short board, about half the length of a full-size board at 6.875 inches (174.63 mm) front to back. All other vital dimensions, including the distance from rear edge to the registration notch in the expansion connector, are identical to a full-size board. Figure 2.17 shows the dimensions of a PCI short card.

FIGURE 2.17

Primary dimensions of a five-volt PCI short card.

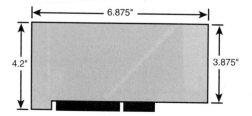

No matter the length of the board, PCI specifies a maximum thickness. The components on a PCI board can rise no more than 0.570 inches above the substrate. On the other side of the board, components can protrude no more than 0.105 inches. Add those heights to the nominal 0.100-inch thickness of the substrate, and PCI provides for a 0.025 inches of safety gap between board components with standard slot spacing of 0.800 inches.

Connectors

To accommodate the development of low-voltage "green" PCs, PCI specifies two connector types and three different connector regimes—a 5-volt connector for today's prevailing circuit designs; a 3.3-volt connector for low-power designs; and the capability to combine both connectors on a single expansion board for a smooth transition between designs. A key on 5-volt sockets (blocking pins 50 and 51) prevents the insertion of 3.3-volt boards. (Five-volt boards have a slot corresponding to the key.) A key on 3.3-volt sockets (at pins 12 and 13) restricts the insertion to correspondingly slotted 3.3 volt boards. Boards capable of discriminating the two voltage regimes have slots in both places, as shown in Figure 2.18.

FIGURE 2.18

Edge connectors for 5 and 3.3 volt PCI cards (32-bit).

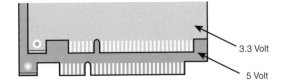

3.3 Volt

5 Volt

The 64-bit implementation of PCI extends the edge connector to accommodate the additional required signals. Figure 2.19 shows this extended connector and the full implementation of all of its options.

FIGURE 2.19

The 64-bit universal PCI edge connector.

64-BIT UNIVERSAL PCI CONNECTOR

3.3 volt   Base 32-bit connector   5 volt   64-bit expansion

CompactPCI

Derived from rather than a subset of the Peripheral Component Interconnect 2.1 standard, CompactPCI adapts the signals and control system to a smaller but more robust form. The physical design of CompactPCI cards makes them fit the well-proven Eurocard standard. The basic card has a 3U form factor, which measures 100 by 160 millimeters (3.9 by 6.3 inches). The standard also allows cards of the extra-height 6U size measuring 233.35 by 160 millimeters (9.2 by 6.3 inches). CompactPCI slots are spaced at 20.32 millimeter (0.8 inch) increments. Figure 2.20 shows the layout and dimensions of a CompactPCI board.

FIGURE 2.20

Layout and dimensions of a CompactPCI board.

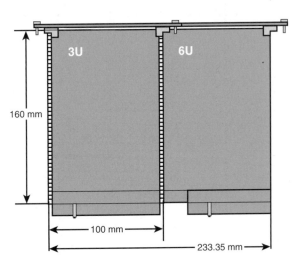

3U

6U

160 mm

100 mm

233.35 mm

The CompactPCI standard provides for up to eight slots in a given system. The bus between the slots is a passive backplane. One slot, called the *system slot*, is reserved for a card that provides system management functions, including arbitration, clocking, and reset. The system slot can be at either end of the backplane. The remaining slots are called *peripheral slots* and provide normal system expansion.

Key to the extensive expansion abilities of CompactPCI is its connector, a shielded design that has seven rows of 57 pins each spaced on 2 millimeter (0.08 inch) centers. The system provides guide lugs to ensure proper insertion of the connector as well as keying for 3.3- or 5-volt operation. The CompactPCI specification envisions hot-swapping expansion cards, although support for this feature was incomplete in the first release of the standard.

PC Cards

PC Cards come in three sizes, differing only in thickness. The basic unit of measurement—the size of the typical card slot—is based on the medium-thickness card, designated Type II, measuring 54 by 85 millimeters (2.126 by 3.37 inches) and 5 mm (about three-sixteenths of an inch) thick.

The PC Card physically follows the form factor of earlier memory cards (including the IC Card) standardized by JEIDA (the Japan Electronic Industry Design Association). The first release of the PCMCIA specification paired this single-size card with a Fujitsu-style 68-pin connector. Under the current PCMCIA 2.1 specification, this form factor is designated as the Type I PC Card.

The thinness of the Type I card proved an unacceptable limitation. Even without allowing for the PC Card packaging, some solid-state devices are themselves thicker than 3.3 mm. Most important among these "fat" devices are the EPROMs used for nonvolatile storage. (Most PCs use EPROMs to store their system BIOS, for example.) Unlike ordinary, thin ROMS, EPROMs can be reprogrammed, but this requires a transparent window to admit the ultraviolet radiation used to erase the programming of the chip. The windowed packaging makes most EPROMs themselves 3.3 mm or thicker.

Fujitsu faced this problem when developing the firmware to be encoded on memory cards and so developed a somewhat thicker card that could be plugged into the same sockets as could standard memory cards. Modem and other peripheral makers found the Fujitsu fat card more suited to their purposes. To accommodate them, PCMCIA 2.0 standardized an alternative, Type II PC Card. Essentially based on the old Fujitsu developmental EPROM form factor, Type II PC Cards are 5.0 millimeters thick but otherwise conform to the same dimensions as Type I cards.

The PCMCIA 2.0 standard puts the extra thickness in a planar bulge, called the substrate area, in the middle of the card. This thicker area measures 48 mm wide and 75 mm long. Three millimeters along each side of the Type II PC Card are kept to the thinness of the

Type I standard so that the same card guides can be used for either card type. Similarly, the front 10 mm of a Type II card maintain the 3.3 mm thickness of the Type I standard so that the same connector can be used for either card type. Naturally, the actual card slot for a Type II PC Card must be wide enough to accommodate the maximum thickness of the card.

In September 1992, PCMCIA approved a third, Type III form factor for PC Cards. These still-thicker cards expand the bulge of Type II from 5 mm to 10.5 mm and are designed to accommodate miniaturized hard disks and similar mechanical components. As with Type II cards, Type III PC Cards remain thin at the edges to fit standard card guides and standard connectors.

In practical terms, a Type I card comes closest to being a truly flat, credit-card style card. Type II have small bulges top and bottom to accommodate circuitry. Type III cards have thick lumps to hold a disk drive. Figure 2.21 illustrates the apparent differences between the three card types.

FIGURE 2.21
The three PC Card types vary in thickness from 3.3 to 10.5 mm.

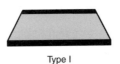
Type I

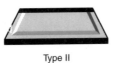
Type II

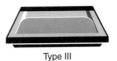
Type III

Under Release 2.0, both Type I and Type II cards can be implemented in extended form. That is, their depth can be increased by an additional 50 mm (to 135 mm) to hold additional componentry. Such extended cards project about two inches more from standard PCMCIA slots.

To ensure that all cards easily and securely mate with their connectors, the PC Card standard requires that card guides be at least 40 mm long and that the PC Card connector must engage and guide the connector pins for 10 mm before the connector bottoms out.

The layout of a PC Card is essentially symmetrical, meaning that it could inadvertently be inserted upside down. The PC Card design allows for such cases of brain fade by eliminating the risk of damage. Although the cards do not work while inverted, neither they nor the computers into which they are plugged will suffer damage.

Because the size and placement of labels on the cards is part of the standard, when you are familiar with the layout of one PC Card, you will know the proper orientation of them all. Moreover, other physical aspects of the cards—the position of the write-protect switch (if any) and battery (if needed)—are standardized as well. The PCMCIA standard also recommends that the batteries in all cards be oriented in the same direction (positive terminal up).

In addition to the physical measures that facilitate getting the cards into their sockets, two pins—one on each side of the connector—allow the PC host to determine whether the card is properly seated. If the signal (ground) from one is present and the other is not, the system knows that the card is skewed or otherwise improperly inserted in the connector.

The one part of the PC Card that has not yet been standardized is the rear edge, where connections are made to communications products such as modems. PCMCIA is currently working on this area and hopes to develop specifications for the connectors and their placement.

Connector

All types of PC Cards use the same 68-pin connector, whose contacts are arranged in two parallel rows of 34 pins. The lines are spaced at 1.27 mm (0.050 inch) intervals between rows and between adjacent pins in the same row. Male pins on the card engage a single molded socket on the host.

To ensure proper powering up of the card, the pins are arranged so that the power and ground connections are longer (3.6 mm) than the signal leads (3.2 mm). Because of their greater length, therefore, power leads engage first so that potentially damaging signals are not applied to unpowered circuits. The two pins (36 and 67) that signal that the card has been inserted all the way are shorter (2.6 mm) than the signal leads.

Microprocessors

The microprocessor is the heart and brain inside every personal computer. This tiny chip of silicon determines the speed and power of the entire computer by handling most, if not all, of the data processing in the machine. The microprocessor determines the ultimate power of any PC. Relentless development has made chip and systems ever more powerful.

Every new PC should have a fifth-generation (or better) microprocessor, distinguished by the following characteristics:

32-to-36-bit Address Bus	Allows addressing 4 to 64 GB of memory
64-bit data bus	Stores and retrieves data in eight-byte (quad-word) chunks
Integral floating-point unit graphic performance	Speeds processing of complex numbers for better statistical and
Integral secondary cache	128K to 2MB (more is better, particularly in servers and work-stations) to match the chip to memory
Multiple pipelines	Lets the processor carry out two or more instructions at once
Enhanced instruction set	MMX, SSE, or 3DNow! accelerates multimedia performance

Your top choices for a microprocessor include:

Celeron	Intel's entry-level microprocessor with a smaller but fast cache
Mobile Celeron	Intel's low-power bargain chip for notebook systems with surprisingly fast performance
Mobile Pentium II	Intel's current high-end notebook processor. Look for it to be replaced by a Mobile Pentium III with superior multimedia performance
Pentium III users	Intel's current top-of-the line microprocessor for individual
Pentium II	Intel's old flagship chip, still competitive as a desktop processor, lagging only in multimedia performance
Xeon	Intel's premier processor aimed at servers
K6-2	Once AMD's top processor, now their price leader that's popular on the desk and in notebook systems.
K6-3 cache	Currently AMD's best chip with a unique three-level integral
MII	A processor comparable to the Pentium II from Cyrix

The microprocessor made the PC possible. Today, one or more of these modern miracles serves as the brain in not only personal computers but also nearly all systems up to the latest supercomputers. At the same time, the PC changed and guided the history of the microprocessor and microprocessor architectures. The most successful microprocessor maker, Intel Corporation, tailors its more lucrative products to the PC market.

Despite this strong synergistic relationship, the PC is only the most visible application of microprocessor technology and computers represent only a fraction of the total number of microprocessors made and sold. Nearly every consumer electronic device now has a microprocessor inside. Nearly every new automobile relies on one or more microprocessors to control its engine. Every VCR runs under control of a microprocessor. Even many children's toys gain their appeal through microprocessor technology: Think Furby.

Microprocessors are so commonplace today that you probably take them for granted, never thinking about them—perhaps because they do so much of your thinking for you. For the most part, the vast majority of these microprocessors are invisible, hidden by design.

In PCs, on the other hand, the microprocessor is the centerpiece. Chip choice is one of the chief guides in selecting a computer. Nowhere are microprocessors more visible. You buy a PC based on the type and speed of microprocessor it contains. You know that if a system doesn't hold a fifth- or sixth-generation microprocessor running at a speed of *at least* 300MHz, it isn't even suitable for running children's games.

No matter its application, however, every microprocessor works the same way. Each one is based on the same electronic technologies and relies on the same principles of logic to guide its operation. This chapter is a guide to those technologies and the successful products based on them that make today's PCs possible.

Background

Technically, today's microprocessor is a masterpiece of high-tech black magic. It starts as silicon that has been carefully grown as an extremely pure crystal. The silicon is sliced thin with great precision, and then the chips are heinously polluted by baking in hot ovens containing gaseous mixtures of highly purified poisons (such as arsenic without the old lace) that defuse into the silicon as impurities and change its electrical properties. This alchemy turns sand to gold, making huge profits for the chip makers and creating electronic brains as capable as that of, say, your average arthropod.

The comparison is apt. As with insects and crustaceans, your PC can react, learn, and remember. Unlike higher organisms bordering on true consciousness (for example, your next door neighbors with the plastic fauna in their front yard), the microprocessor doesn't reason. Nor is it self-aware. Clearly, although computers are often labeled as "thinking machines," what goes through their microprocessor minds is far from your thought processes and stream of consciousness. Or maybe not. Some theoreticians believe your mind and a computer work fundamentally the same way, although no one knows exactly how the human mind actually works. Let's hope they know more about microprocessors.

They do. The operating principles of the microprocessor are well understood. After all, despite its revolutionary design and construction, the operating principle of the microprocessor is exactly the same as a bread-making machine or dishwasher. As we'll see, all these contrivances carry out their jobs as a series of steps under some guiding mechanism, be it a timing motor or software program. You dump raw materials in and expect to get out the desired result, although if you're not careful you're apt to face a pile of gooey powder, broken pots, or data as meaningless as the quantum wave function of *Gilligan's Island*.

As with your home appliances, microprocessor hardware was designed to carry out a specific function, and silicon semiconductor technology was simply harnessed to implement those functions. Nothing about what the microprocessor does is true mystical magic that might be practiced by a shaman, charlatan, or accountant.

In fact, a microprocessor need not be made from silicon (scientists are toying with advanced semiconducting materials that promise higher speeds), nor need it be based on electronics. A series of gears, cams, and levers or a series of pipes, valves, and pans could carry out all the logical functions to achieve exactly the same results as your PC. Mechanical and hydraulic computers have, in fact, been built, although you'd never mistake one for a PC.

The advantage of electronics and the microprocessor is speed. Electrical signals travel at nearly the speed of light; microprocessors carry out their instructions at rates of a hundred to two million per second. Without that speed, the elaborate programs on your dealer's shelves would never have been written. Executing such a program with a steam-driven computing engine might have taken lifetimes. The speed of the microprocessor makes it into the miracle that it is.

The advantage of the silicon-based form of electronics is familiarity. An entire industry has arisen to work with silicon. The technology is mature. Fabricating silicon circuits is routine and the results are predictable. Familiarity also breeds economy. Billions of silicon chips are made each year. Although the processes involved are precise and exotic, the needed equipment and materials are readily available. In other words, silicon is used a lot because it is used a lot.

Circuit Design

Reduced to its fundamental principles, the workings of a modern silicon-based micro-processor are not difficult to understand. They are simply the electronic equivalent of a knee-jerk. Every time you hit the microprocessor with an electronic hammer blow (the proper digital input), it reacts by doing a specific something, always the same thing for the same input and conditions, kicking out the same function.

The complexity of the microprocessor and what it does arises from the wealth of inputs it can react to and the interaction between successive inputs. Although the microprocessor's function is precisely defined by its input, the output from that function varies with what the microprocessor had to work on, and that depends on previous inputs. For example, the result of you carrying out a specific command—"Simon says lift your left leg"—will differ dramatically depending on whether the previous command was "Simon says sit down" or "Simon says lift your right leg."

Getting an electrical device to respond in knee-jerk fashion rates as one of the greatest breakthroughs in technology. The first application was to extend the human reach beyond what you could immediately touch, beyond the span of the proverbial 10-foot pole. The simple telegraph is one of the earliest and perhaps the best examples. Closing a switch (pressing down on the telegraph key) sends a current down the wire that activates an elec-tromagnet at the distant end of the wire, causing the rattle at the other end that yields a message to a distant telegrapher. This grand electro-mechanical invention underlies all of modern computer technology. It puts one electrical circuit in control of another circuit a great or small distance away.

From these simple beginnings, from the telegraph technology of the 1850s, you can build a computer. Everything that a computer does involves one of two operations: decision-making and memory, or in other words, reacting and remembering. Telegraph technology can do both. Silicon semiconductor does likewise because it, too, allows you to control one signal with another.

The electrical circuit that makes decisions is called a logic gate. One that remembers is termed a latch or simply memory.

Logic Gates

Giving an electrical circuit the power to make a decision isn't as hard as you might think. Start with that same remote mechanical telegraph but add a mechanical arm that links it to a light switch on your wall so as the telegraph pounds, the light flashes on and off. Certainly, you'll have done a lot of work for a little return in that the electricity could be used to directly light the bulb. There are other possibilities, however, that produce intriguing results. You could, for example, pair two weak telegraph arms so that their joint effort would be required to throw the switch to turn on the light. Or you could link the two telegraphs so that a signal on either one would switch on the light. Or you could install the switch backwards so that when the telegraph activated, the light would go out instead of on.

These three telegraph-based design examples actually provide the basis for three different types of computer circuits called logic gates (the AND, OR, and NOT gates, respectively). As electrical circuits, they are called "gates" because they regulate the flow of electricity, allowing it to pass through or cutting it off, much as a gate in a fence allows or impedes your own progress. These logic gates endow the electrical assembly with decision-making power. In the light example, the decision is necessarily simple: when to switch on the light. But these same simple gates can be formed into elaborate combinations that make up a computer that can make complex logical decisions.

The concept of applying the rigorous approach of algebra to logical decision-making was first proposed by English mathematician George Boole. In 1847, Boole founded the system of modern symbolic logic that we now term *Boolean logic* (alternately, Boolean algebra). In his system, Boole reduced propositions to symbols and formal operators that followed the strict rules of mathematics. Using his rigorous approach, logical propositions could be proved with the same certainty as mathematical equations.

The three logic gates can perform the function of all of the operators in Boolean logic. They form the basis of the decision-making capabilities of the computer as well as other logic circuitry. You'll encounter other kinds of gates such as NAND (short for "Not AND"), NOR (short for "Not OR"), and exclusive OR, but you can build any one of the others from the basic three, AND, OR, and NOT.

In computer circuits, each gate requires at least one transistor. A microprocessor with ten million transistors may have nearly that many gates.

Memory

These same gates also can be arranged to form memory. Start with the familiar telegraph. Instead of operating the current for a light bulb, however, reroute the wires from the switch so that they, too, link to the telegraph's electromagnet. In other words, when the telegraph moves, it throws a switch that supplies itself with electricity. Once the telegraph is supplying itself with electricity, it will stay on using that power even if you switch off the original power that first made the switch. In effect, this simple system *remembers* whether it has once been activated. You can go back at any time and see if someone has ever sent a signal to the telegraph memory system.

This basic form of memory has one shortcoming: It's elephantine and never forgets. Resetting this memory system requires manually switching off both the control voltage and the main voltage source.

A more useful form of memory takes two control signals; one switches it on, the other switches it off. In simplest form, each cell of this kind of memory is made from two latches connected at cross purposes so that switching one latch on cuts the other off. Because one signal sets this memory to hold data and the other one resets it, this circuit is sometimes called *set-reset memory*. A more common term is *flip-flop* because it alternately flips between its two states. In computer circuits, this kind of memory is often simply called a *latch*. Although the main memory of your PC uses a memory that works on a different electrical principal, latch memory remains important in circuit design.

Instructions

Although the millions of gates in a microprocessor are so tiny that you can't even discern them with an optical microscope (you need at least an electron microscope), they act exactly like elemental, telegraph-based circuits. They use electrical signals to control other signals. The signals are just more complicated, reflecting the more elaborate nature of the computer.

Today's microprocessors don't use a single signal to control their operations. Rather they use complex combinations of signals. Each microprocessor command is coded as a pattern of signals, the presence or absence of an electrical signal at one of the pins of the microprocessor's package. The signal at each pin represents one bit of digital information.

The designers of a microprocessor give certain patterns of these bit-signals specific meanings. Each pattern is a command called a *microprocessor instruction* that tells the microprocessor to carry out a specific operation. The bit pattern 0010110, for example, is the instruction that tells an Intel 8086-family microprocessor to subtract in a very explicit manner. Other instructions tell the microprocessor to add, multiply, divide, move bits or bytes around, change individual bits, or just wait around for another instruction.

Microprocessor designers can add instructions to do just about anything from matrix calculations to back flips—that is, if the designers wanted to, if the instruction actually did something useful, and if they had unlimited time and resources to engineer the chip. Practical concerns such as keeping the design work and the chip manageable constrain the range of commands given to a microprocessor.

The entire repertoire of commands that a given microprocessor model understands and can react to is called that microprocessor's *instruction set* or its command set. The designer of the microprocessor chooses which pattern to assign to a given function. As a result, different microprocessor designs recognize different instruction sets just as different board games have different rules.

Despite their pragmatic limits, microprocessor instruction sets can be incredibly rich and diverse and the individual instructions incredibly specific. The designers of the original 8086-style microprocessor, for example, felt that a simple command to subtract was not enough by itself. They believed that the microprocessor also needed to know what to subtract from what and what it should do with the result. Consequently, they added a rich variety of subtraction instructions to the 8086 family of chips that persists into today's Pentium IIIs. Each different subtraction instruction tells the microprocessor to take numbers from different places and find the difference in a slightly different manner.

Some microprocessor instructions require a series of steps to be carried out. These multi-step commands are sometimes called complex instructions because of their composite nature. Although the complex instruction looks like a simple command, it may involve much work. A simple instruction would be something like "pound a nail"; a complex instruction may be as far ranging as "frame a house." Simple subtraction or addition of two numbers may actually involve dozens of steps, including the conversion of the numbers from decimal to binary (1s and 0s) notation that the microprocessor understands. For instance, the previous sample subtraction instruction tells one kind of microprocessor that it should subtract a number in memory from another number in the microprocessor's accumulator, a place that's favored for calculations in today's most popular microprocessors.

Everything that the microprocessor does consists of nothing more than a series of these step-by-step instructions. A computer program is simply a list of microprocessor instructions. The instructions are simple, but long and complex computer programs are built from them just as epics and novels are built from the words of the English language. Although writing in English seems natural, programming feels foreign because it requires you think in a different way, in a different language. You even have to think of jobs, such as adding numbers, typing a letter, or moving a block of graphics, as a long series of tiny steps. In other words, programming is just a different way of looking at problems and expressing the process of solving them.

Registers

Before the microprocessor can work on numbers or any other data, it first must know what numbers to work on. The most straightforward method of giving the chip the variables it needs would seem to be supplying more coded signals at the same time the instruction is given. You could dump in the numbers 6 and 3 along with the subtract instruction, just as you would load laundry detergent along with shirts and sheets into your washing machine. This simple method has its shortcomings, however. Somehow the proper numbers must be routed to the right microprocessor inputs. The microprocessor needs to know whether to subtract 6 from 3 or 3 from 6. (The difference could be significant, particularly when you're balancing your checkbook.)

Just as you distinguish the numbers in a subtraction problem by where you put them in the equation (6–3 versus 3–6), a microprocessor distinguishes the numbers on which it works by their position (where they are found). Two memory addresses might suffice were it not for the way most microprocessors are designed. They have only one pathway to memory, so they can effectively "see" only one memory value at a time. So instead, a microprocessor loads at least one number to an internal storage area called a register. It can then simultaneously reach both the number in memory and the value in its internal register. Alternately (and more commonly today), both values on which the microprocessor is to work are loaded into separate internal registers.

Part of the function of each microprocessor instruction is to tell the chip which registers to use for data and where to put the answers it comes up with. Other instructions tell the chip to load numbers into its registers to be worked on later or to move information from a register someplace else, for instance, to memory or an output port.

A register functions both as memory and a workbench. It holds bit patterns until they can be worked on or sent out of the chip. The register is also connected with the processing circuits of the microprocessor so that the changes ordered by instructions actually appear in the register. Most microprocessors typically have several registers, some dedicated to specific functions (such as remembering which step in a function the chip is currently carrying out; this register is called a counter or *instruction pointer*) and some designed for general purposes. At one time, the *accumulator* was the only register in a microprocessor that could manage calculations. In modern microprocessors, all registers are more nearly equal (in some of the latest designs, all registers are equal, even interchangeable), so the accumulator is now little more than a colorful term left over from a bygone era.

Not only do microprocessors have differing numbers of registers, but also the registers may be of different sizes. Registers are measured by the number of bits that they can work with at one time. A 16-bit microprocessor, for example, should have one or more registers that each holds 16 bits of data at a time. Today's microprocessors have 32- or 64-bit registers.

Adding more registers to a microprocessor does not make it inherently faster. When a microprocessor lacks advanced features such as pipelining or superscalar technology (discussed later), it can perform only one operation at a time. More than two registers would seem superfluous. After all, most math operations involve only two numbers at a time (or can be reduced to a series of two-number operations). Even with old-technology microprocessors, however, having more registers helps the software writer create more efficient programs. With more places to put data, a program needs to move information in and out of the microprocessor less often, which can potentially save several program steps and clock cycles.

Modern microprocessor designs, particularly those influenced by the latest research into design efficiency, demand more registers. Because microprocessors run much faster than memory, every time the microprocessor has to go to memory, it must slow down.

Therefore, minimizing memory accessing helps improve performance. Keeping data in registers instead of memory speeds things up.

On the other hand, having many registers is the equivalent of moving main memory into the microprocessor with all the inherent complexities and shortcomings of memory technology. Research has determined that about 32 registers for microprocessors using current technologies works best. Consequently, nearly all of today's most advanced microprocessors, the RISC chips discussed later, have 32 registers.

The *width* of the registers does, however, have a substantial effect on the performance of a microprocessor. The more bits assigned to each register, the more information that the microprocessor can process in every cycle. Consequently, a 64-bit register in one of today's top RISC chips holds the potential of calculating eight times as fast as an 8-bit register of a first generation microprocessor—all else being equal.

The performance advantage of using wider registers depends on the software being run, however. If, for example, a computer program tells the microprocessor to work on data 16 bits at a time, the full power of 32-bit registers will not be tapped. For this reason, DOS, a 16-bit operating system written with 16-bit instructions, does not take full advantage of the today's powerful 32-bit microprocessors. Nor do most programs written to run under DOS or advanced operating systems that have inherited substantial 16-bit code (such as Windows 95). Modern 32-bit operating systems are a better match and consequently deliver better performance with the latest microprocessors such as the Pentium Pro.

You might notice one problem with really wide registers: Most data isn't all that wide. Text normally comes in byte-wide (8-bit) blocks. Sound usually takes the form of two-byte units. Image data may be one, two, three, or four bytes wide but almost never needs to be the eight bytes wide that many modern microprocessors prefer. Microprocessors using Intel's MMX technology are designed to more efficiently use their wide registers by processing multiple narrow data types simultaneously in a single register. The special MMX instructions tell the microprocessor how to process all the short data blocks at once. SSE—Intel's new Streaming SIMD Extensions—further elaborate on this design.

Clocked Logic

Microprocessors do not carry out instructions as soon as the instruction code signals reach the pins that connect the microprocessor to your computer's circuitry. If chips did react immediately, they would quickly become confused. Electrical signals cannot change state instantly; they always go through a brief, though measurable, transition period—a period of indeterminate level during which the signals would probably perplex a microprocessor into a crash. Moreover, all signals do not necessarily change at the same rate, so when some signals reach the right values, others may still be at odd values. As a result, a microprocessor must live through long periods of confusion during which its signals are at best meaningless, at worst dangerous.

To prevent the microprocessor from reacting to these invalid signals, the chip waits for an indication that it has a valid command to carry out. It waits until it gets a "Simon says" signal. In today's PCs, this indication is provided by the system clock. The clock sends out regular voltage pulses, the electronic equivalent of the ticking of a grandfather's clock. The microprocessor checks the instructions given to it each time it receives a clock pulse—providing it is not already busy carrying out another instruction.

Early microprocessors were unable to carry out even one instruction every clock cycle. Vintage microprocessors may require as many as 100 discrete steps (and clock pulses) to carry out a single instruction. The number of cycles required to carry out instructions varies with the instruction and the microprocessor design. Some instructions take a few cycles, others dozens. Moreover, some microprocessors are more efficient than others in carrying out their instructions. The trend today is to minimize and equalize the number of clock cycles needed to carry out a typical instruction.

Today's microprocessors go even further in breaking the correspondence between the system clock and the number of instructions that are executed. They deliberately change the external system clock speed before it is used internally by the microprocessor circuitry. In most cases, the system clock frequency is increased by some discrete factor (typically two or three, although some Pentium chips use non-integral factors such as 1.5 as their clock multipliers) so that operations inside the chip run faster than the external clock would permit. Despite the different frequencies inside and outside the chip, the system clock is still used to synchronize logic operations. The microprocessors' logic makes the necessary allowances.

The lack of correspondence between cycles and instruction execution means that clock speed (typically a frequency given in megahertz, or MHz) alone does not indicate the relative performance of two microprocessors. If, for example, one microprocessor requires an average of six clock cycles to execute every instruction and another chip needs only two, the first chip will be slower (by 50 percent) than the second even when its clock speed is twice as fast. The only time that clock speed gives a reliable indication of relative performance is when you compare two identical chip designs that operate at different frequencies, say Pentium III chips running at 450 and 500MHz. (The latter Pentium III would calculate about 10 percent faster.)

Functional Parts

Most microprocessor designs divide their internal clocked logic circuitry into three function parts: the input/output unit (or I/O unit), the control unit, and the arithmetic/logic unit (or ALU). The last two are sometimes jointly called the central processing unit (or CPU), although the same term often is used as a synonym for the entire microprocessor. Some chip makers further subdivide these units, give them other names, or include more than one of each in a particular microprocessor. In any case, the functions of these three units are an inherent part of any chip.

All three parts of the microprocessor interact together. In all but the simplest microprocessor designs, the I/O unit is under control of the control unit, and the operation of the control unit may be determined by the results of calculations of the arithmetic/logic unit CPU. The combination of the three parts determines the power and performance of the microprocessor.

Each part of the microprocessor also has its own effect on the processing speed of the system. The control unit operates the microprocessor's internal clock, which determines the rate at which the chip operates. The I/O unit determines the bus width of the microprocessor, which influences how quickly data and instructions can be moved in and out of the microprocessor. And the registers in the arithmetic/logic unit determine how much data the microprocessor can operate on at one time.

Input/Output Unit

The input/output unit links the microprocessor to the rest of the circuitry of the computer, passing along program instructions and data to the registers of the control unit and arithmetic/logic unit. The I/O unit matches the signal levels and timing of the microprocessor's internal solid-state circuitry to the requirements of the other components inside the PC. The internal circuits of a microprocessor, for example, are designed to be stingy with electricity so that they can operate faster and cooler. These delicate internal circuits cannot handle the higher currents needed to link to external components. Consequently, each signal leaving the microprocessor goes through a signal buffer in the I/O unit that boosts its current capacity.

The input/output unit can be as simple as a few buffers or it may involve many complex functions. In the latest Intel microprocessors used in some of the most powerful PCs, the I/O unit includes cache memory and clock-doubling or -tripling logic to match the high operating speed of the microprocessor to slower external memory.

The microprocessors used in PCs have two kinds of external connections to their input/output units: those connections that indicate the address of memory locations to or from which the microprocessor will send or receive data or instructions and those connections that convey the meaning of the data or instructions. The former is called the *address bus* of the microprocessor; the latter, the *data bus*.

The number of bits in the data bus of a microprocessor directly influences how quickly it can move information. The more bits that a chip can use at a time, the faster it is.

Microprocessors with 8-, 16-, and 32-bit data buses are all used in various ages of PCs. The latest Pentium and Pentium Pro microprocessors go all the way to 64 bits.

The number of bits available on the address bus influences how much memory that a microprocessor can address. A microprocessor with 16 address lines, for example, can directly work with 2^{16} addresses; that's 65,536 (or 64KB) different memory locations. The different microprocessors used in various PCs span a range of address bus widths from 20 to 32 bits. Although the Pentium and Pentium Pro stick with a 32-bit address bus, other chip makers have extended the reach of some of their products to 64 bits.

Control Unit

The control unit of a microprocessor is a clocked logic circuit that, as its name implies, controls the operation of the entire chip. Unlike more common integrated circuits, whose function is fixed by hardware design, the control unit is more flexible. The control unit follows the instructions contained in an external program and tells the arithmetic/logic unit what to do. The control unit receives instructions from the I/O unit, translates them into a form that can be understood by the arithmetic/logic unit, and keeps track of which step of the program is being executed.

With the increasing complexity of microprocessors, the control unit has become more sophisticated. In the Pentium, for example, the control unit must decide how to route signals between what amounts to two separate processing units. In other advanced microprocessors, the function of the control unit is split among other functional blocks, such as those that specialize in evaluating and handling branches in the stream of instructions.

Arithmetic/Logic Unit

The arithmetic/logic unit handles all the decision making (the mathematical computations and logic functions) that is performed by the microprocessor. The unit takes the instructions decoded by the control unit and either carries them out directly or executes the appropriate microcode to modify the data contained in its registers. The results are passed back out of the microprocessor through the I/O unit.

The first microprocessors had but one ALU. Modern chips may have several, which commonly are classed into two types. The basic form is the *integer unit*, one that carries out only the simplest mathematical operations. More powerful microprocessors also include *floating-point units*, which handle advanced math operations (such as trigonometric and transcendental functions) typically at greater precision. Early Intel microprocessors made the floating-point unit a separate optional chip sometimes called a numeric or *math coprocessor*, discussed later.

Even chips equipped solely with integer units can carry out advanced mathematical operations with suitable programs that break the problems into discrete simple steps.

Floating-point units use separate, dedicated instructions for their advanced functions and carry out the operations more quickly.

Floating-Point Unit

A floating-point unit differs from an integer unit in the form of the numbers it handles. As the name implies, the floating-point unit works best on *floating-point numbers*.

Floating-point describes a way of expressing values, not a mathematically defined type of number such as an integer, rational, or real number. The essence of a floating-point number is that its decimal point "floats" between a predefined number of significant digits rather than remaining fixed in place the way dollar values always have two decimal places.

Mathematically speaking, a floating-point number has three parts: a *sign*, which indicates whether the number is greater or less than zero; a *significant*—sometimes called a mantissa—which comprises all the digits that are mathematically meaningful; and an *exponent*, which determines the order of magnitude of the significant, essentially the location to which the decimal point floats. Think of a floating-point number as being like those represented by scientific notation. But where scientists are apt to deal in base ten—the exponents in scientific notation are powers of ten—math coprocessors think of floating-point numbers digitally in base two, all ones and zeros in powers of two.

Intel Architecture

As a practical matter, the form of floating-point numbers used in computer calculations follows standards laid down by the Institute of Electrical and Electronic Engineers. The IEEE formats take values that can be represented in binary form using 80 bits. Although 80 bits seems somewhat arbitrary in a computer world that's based on powers of two and a steady doubling of register size from 8 to 16 to 32 to 64 bits, it's exactly the right size to accommodate 64 bits of significant value with 15 bits leftover to hold an exponent value and an extra bit for the sign of the number held in the register. Although the IEEE standard allows for 32-bit and 64-bit floating-point values, most floating-point units are designed to accommodate the full 80-bit values.

The floating-point units of Intel processors have eight of these 80-bit registers in which to perform their calculations. Instructions in your programs tell the math chip what format of numbers to work on and how. The only real difference is the form in which the math chip delivers its results to the microprocessor when it's done. All calculations are carried out using the full 80 bits of the chip's registers, unlike the integer units, which can independently manipulate its registers in byte-wide pieces.

The eight 80-bit registers in Intel floating-point units also differ from integer units in the way they are addressed. Commands for integer unit registers are directly routed to the appropriate register as if sent by a switchboard. Floating-point unit registers are arranged in a stack, sort of an elevator system. Values are pushed onto the stack, and with each new number, the old one goes down one level. *Stack machines* are generally regarded as lean and mean computers. Their design is austere and streamlined, which helps them run more quickly. The same holds true for stack-oriented floating-point units.

External Math Coprocessors

Until the advent of the Pentium, a floating-point unit was not a guaranteed part of a microprocessor. Some 486 and all previous chips omitted floating-point circuitry. The floating-point circuitry simply added too much to the complexity of the chip, at least for the state of fabrication technology at that time. Although a few hundred thousand extra transistors adds little to the budget (and adds immensely to the performance) of a chip with 5.5 million transistors, it can double the size and cost of a lesser chip. To cut costs, chip makers simply left the floating-point unit as an option.

When it was necessary to accelerate numeric operations, the earliest microprocessors used in PCs allowed you to add an additional, optional chip to your computer to accelerate the calculation of floating-point values. These external floating-point units were termed *math coprocessors.*

The math coprocessor is a special case of a general circuit type called the *coprocessor*. A coprocessor is simply something that works in cooperation with your PC's microprocessor. The goal is performance won by greater efficiency through specialization and division of labor—the electronic equivalent of a miniature Industrial Revolution. To divide the labor, the coprocessor takes charge of some particular task normally relegated the general purpose microprocessor, relieving the main chip of some of its load. At the same time, the coprocessor is a specialist, designed to handle one particular task—and one task only—with the greatest possible efficiency. In sacrificing the need to be all things to all software, the specialist coprocessor can be trimmed down to the bare essentials required to perform its task most efficiently. The math coprocessor specializes in processing floating-point numbers.

Each Intel chip before the Pentium had its own matching math coprocessor. Table 3.1 lists Intel processors and the coprocessors designed to match them. Several companies also made coprocessors compatible with 386 chips. All external coprocessors are now essentially obsolete.

TABLE 3.1   Coprocessors for Intel Microprocessors

Microprocessor	Coprocessor
8086	8087
8088	8087
80286	80287

Microprocessor	Coprocessor
386DX	387DX*
386SX	387SX*
486DX	None required
486SX	487

Many early PCs with 386DX or 386SX processors accommodated 80287 coprocessors in addition to or in lieu of the matching 387 chip.

Advanced Technologies

Because higher clock speeds make circuit boards and integrated circuits more difficult to design and manufacture, engineers have a strong incentive to get their microprocessors to process more instructions at a given speed. Most modern microprocessor design techniques are aimed at exactly that.

One way to speed up the execution of instructions is to reduce the number of internal steps the microprocessor must take for execution. Step reduction can take two forms: making the microprocessor more complex so that steps can be combined or making the instructions simpler so that fewer steps are required. Both approaches have been used successfully by microprocessor designers—the former as CISC microprocessors, the latter as RISC.

Another way of trimming cycles required by programs is to operate on more than one instruction simultaneously. Two approaches to processing more instructions at once are pipelining and superscalar architecture. Both CISC and RISC chips take advantage of these technologies as well as several design techniques that help them operate more efficiently. Differences in the two classes of microprocessor are easier to understand if you first know the underlying technologies.

Pipelining

In older microprocessor designs, a chip works single-mindedly. It reads an instruction from memory, carries it out step by step, and then advances to the next instruction. Each step requires at least one tick of the microprocessor's clock. Pipelining enables a microprocessor to read an instruction, start to process it, and then, before finishing with the first instruction, read another instruction. Because every instruction requires several steps each in a different part of the chip, several instructions can be worked on at once and passed along through the chip like a bucket brigade or its more efficient alternative, the pipeline. Intel's Pentium chips, for example, have four levels of pipelining. Up to four different instructions may be undergoing different phases of execution at the same time inside the chip. When operating at its best, pipelining reduces the multiple step/multiple clock cycle processing of an instruction to a single clock cycle.

Pipelining is powerful, but it is also demanding. The pipeline must be carefully organized and the parallel paths kept carefully in step. It's sort of like a chorus singing a canon like "Frere Jacques"—one missed beat and the harmony falls apart. If one of the execution stages delays, all the rest delay as well. The demands of pipelining are one factor pushing microprocessor designers to make all instructions execute in the same number of clock cycles. That way, keeping the pipeline in step is easier.

In general the more stages to a pipeline, the greater acceleration it can offer. Super-pipelining breaks the steps of the basic pipelining themselves into multiple steps. Today's fastest Intel microprocessor, the Pentium Pro, uses 12 stages in its super-pipeline.

Real-world programs conspire against lengthy pipelines, however. Nearly all programs branch. That is, their execution can take alternate paths down different instruction streams, depending on the results of calculations and decision-making. A pipeline can load up with instructions of one program branch before it discovers that another branch is the one the program is supposed to follow. In that case, the entire contents of the pipeline must be dumped, and the whole thing loaded up again. The result is a lot of logical wheel-spinning and wasted time. The bigger the pipeline, the more time wasted. The waste resulting from branching begins to outweigh the benefits of bigger pipelines in the vicinity of five stages.

Branch Prediction

Today's most powerful microprocessors are adopting a technology called *branch prediction logic* to deal with this problem. The microprocessor makes its best guess at which branch a program will take as it is filling up the pipeline; it then executes these most likely instructions. Because the chip is guessing at what to do, this technology is sometimes called *speculative execution.*

When the microprocessor's guesses turn out to be correct, the chip benefits from the multiple pipeline stages and is able to run through more instructions than clock cycles. When the chip's guess turns out wrong, however, it must discard the results obtained under speculation and execute the correct code. The chip marks the data in later pipeline stages as invalid and discards it. Although the chip doesn't lose time—the program would have executed in the same order anyway—it does lose the extra boost bequeathed by the pipeline.

Superscalar Architectures

The steps in a program normally are listed sequentially, but they don't always need to be carried out exactly in order. Just as tough problems can be broken into easier pieces, program code can be divided as well. If, for example, you want to know the larger of two rooms, you have to compute the volume of each and then make your comparison. If you had two brains, you could compute the two volumes simultaneously. A superscalar micro-processor design does essentially that. By providing two or more execution paths for pro-grams, it can process two or more program parts simultaneously. Of course, the chip needs enough innate intelligence to determine which problems can be split up and how to do it. The Pentium, for example, has two parallel, pipelined execution paths.

The first superscalar computer design was the Control Data Corporation 6600 main-frame, introduced in 1964. Designed specifically for intense scientific applications, the ini-tial 6600 machines were built from eight functional units and were the fastest computers in the world at the time of their introduction.

Superscalar architecture gets its name because it goes beyond the incremental increase in speed made possible by scaling down microprocessor technology. An improvement to the scale of a microprocessor design would reduce the size of the microcircuitry on the silicon chip. The size reduction shortens the distance signals must travel and lowers the amount of heat generated by the circuit (because the elements are smaller and need less current to effect changes). Some microprocessor designs lend themselves to scaling down. Superscalar designs get a more substantial performance increase by incorporating a more dramatic change in circuit complexity.

Using pipelining and superscalar architecture cycle-saving techniques has dramatically cut the number of clock cycles required for the execution of a typical microprocessor instruc-tion. Early microprocessors needed, on average, several cycles for each instruction. Many of today's chips (both CISC and RISC) actually have average instruction throughputs of fewer than one cycle per instruction.

Out-of-Order Execution

No matter how well the logic of a superscalar microprocessor divides up a program, each pipeline is unlikely to get an equal share of the work. One or another pipeline will grind away while another finishes in an instant. Certainly, the chip logic can shove another instruction down the free pipeline—if another instruction is ready. But if the next instruc-tion depends on the results of the one before it and that instruction is the one stuck grind-ing away in the other pipeline, the free pipeline stalls. It is available for work but can do no work. Potential processor power gets wasted.

Like a good Type A employee who always looks for something to do, microprocessors can do the same thing. They can check the program for the next instruction that doesn't depend on previous work that's not finished and work on the new instructions. This sort of ambitious approach to programs is termed *out-of-order execution*, and it helps micro-processors take full advantage of superscalar designs.

This sort of ambitious microprocessor faces a problem, however. It is no longer running the program in the order that it was written, and the results might be other than the programmer had intended. Consequently, microprocessors capable of out-of-order execution don't immediately post the results from their processing into their registers. The work gets carried out invisibly and the results of the instructions that are processed out of order are held in a buffer until the chip has finished processing all the previous instructions. The chip puts the results back into the proper order, checking to be sure that the out-of-order execution has not caused any anomalies, before posting the results to its registers. To the program and the rest of the outside world, the results appear in the microprocessor's registers as if they had been processed in normal order, only faster.

Register Renaming

Out-of-order execution often runs into its own problems. Two independently executable instructions may refer to or change the same register. In the original program, one would carry out its operation, and then the other would do its work later. During superscalar out-of-order execution, the two instructions may want to work on the register simultaneously. Because that conflict would inevitably lead to confusing results and errors, an ordinary superscalar microprocessor would have to ensure the two instructions referencing the same register executed sequentially instead of in parallel, eliminating the advantage of its superscalar design.

To avoid such problems, advanced microprocessors use *register renaming*. Instead of a small number of registers with fixed names, they use a larger bank of registers that can be named dynamically. The circuitry in each chip converts the references made by an instruction to a specific register name to point instead to its choice of physical register. In effect, the program asks for the EAX register, and the chip says, "Sure," and gives the program a register it calls EAX. If another part of the program asks for EAX, the chip pulls out a different register and tells the program that this one is EAX, too. The program takes the microprocessor's word for it, and the microprocessor doesn't worry because it has several million transistors to sort things out in the end.

And it takes several million registers because the chip must track all references to registers. It must ensure that when one program instruction depends on the result in a given register, it has the right register and results dished up to it.

Instruction Sets

Instructions are the basic units for telling a microprocessor what to do. Internally, the circuitry of the microprocessor has to carry out hundreds, thousands, or even millions of logic operations to carry out one instruction. The instruction in effect triggers a cascade of logical operations. How this cascade is controlled marks the great divide in microprocessor and computer design.

The first electronic computers used a *hardwired* design. An instruction simply activated the circuits appropriate for carrying out all the steps required. This design has its advantages. It optimizes the speed of the system because the direct hardwire connection adds nothing to slow down the system. Simplicity means speed, and the hardwired approach is the simplest. Moreover, the hardwired design was the practical and obvious choice. After all, computers were so new that no one had thought up any alternative.

But the hardwired computer design has a significant drawback. It ties the hardware and software together into a single unit. Any change in the hardware must be reflected in the software. A modification to the computer means that programs have to be modified. A new computer design may require that programs be entirely rewritten from the ground up.

Microcode

The inspiration for breaking away from the hardwired approach was the need for flexibility in instruction sets. Throughout most of the history of computing, determining exactly what instructions should make up a machine's instruction set was more an art than a science. IBM's first commercial computers, the 701 and 702, were designed more from intuition than from any study of which instructions programmers would need to use. Each machine was custom tailored to a specific application. The 701 ran instructions thought to serve scientific users; the 702 had instructions aimed at business and commercial applications.

When IBM tried to unite its many application-specific computers into a single, more general-purpose line, these instruction sets were combined so that one machine could satisfy all needs. The result was, of course, a wide, varied, and complex set of instructions. The new machine, the IBM 360 (introduced in 1964), was unlike previous computers in that it was created not as hardware but as an *architecture*. IBM developed specifications and rules for how the machine would operate but enabled the actual machine to be created from any hardware implementation designers found most expedient. In other words, IBM defined the instructions that the 360 would use but not the circuitry that would carry them out. Previous computers used instructions that directly controlled the underlying hardware. To adapt the instructions defined by the architecture to the actual hardware that made up the machine, IBM adopted an idea called *microcode*, originally conceived by Maurice Wilkes at Cambridge University.

Using this technology, an instruction causes a computer to execute a small program to carry out the logic instructions required by the instruction. The collection of small programs for all the instructions the computer understands is its microcode.

Although the additional layer of microcode made machines more complex, it added a great deal of design flexibility. Engineers could incorporate whatever new technologies they wanted inside the computer yet still run the same software with the same instructions originally written for older designs. In other words, microcode enabled new hardware designs and computer systems to have backward compatibility with earlier machines.

Since the introduction of the 360, nearly all mainframe computers have used microcode. When the microprocessors that enabled PCs were created, they followed the same design philosophy as the 360 by using microcode to match instructions to hardware. In effect, the microcode in a microprocessor is a secondary set of instructions that run invisibly inside the chip on a nanoprocessor—essentially a microprocessor within a microprocessor.

This microcode-and-nanoprocessor approach makes creating a complex microprocessor easier. The powerful data processing circuitry of the chip can be designed independently of the instructions it must carry out. The manner in which the chip handles its complex instructions can be fine-tuned even after the architecture of the main circuits are laid into place. Bugs in the design can be fixed relatively quickly by altering the microcode, which is an easy operation compared to the alternative of developing a new design for the whole chip, a task that's not trivial when millions of transistors are involved. The rich instruction set fostered by microcode also makes writing software for the microprocessor (and computers built from it) easier, reducing the number of instructions needed for each operation.

Microcode has a big disadvantage, however. It makes computers and microprocessors more complicated. In a microprocessor, the nanoprocessor must go through several of its own microcode instructions to carry out every instruction you send to the microprocessor. More steps means more processing time taken for each instruction. Extra processing time means slower operation. Engineers found that microcode had its own way to compensate for its performance penalty—complex instructions.

Using microcode, computer designers could easily give an architecture a rich repertoire of instructions that carry out elaborate functions. A single complex instruction might do the job of half a dozen or more simpler instructions. Although each instruction would take longer to execute because of the microcode, programs would need fewer instructions overall. Moreover, adding more instructions could boost speed. One result of this microcode "more is merrier" instruction approach is that typical PC microprocessors have seven different subtraction commands.

RISC

Although long the mainstream of computer and microprocessor design, microcode is not necessary. While system architects were staying up nights concocting ever more powerful and obscure instructions, a counter force was gathering. Starting in the 1970s, the

Advanced Technologies

microcode approach came under attack by researchers who claimed it takes a greater toll on performance than its benefits justify.

By eliminating microcode, this design camp believed, simpler instructions could be executed at speeds so much higher that no degree of instruction complexity could compensate. By necessity, such hardwired machines would offer only a few instructions because the complexity of their hardwired circuitry would increase dramatically with every additional instruction added. Practical designs are best made with small instruction sets.

John Cocke at IBM's Yorktown Research Laboratory analyzed the usage of instructions by computers and discovered that most of the work done by computers involves relatively few instructions. Given a computer with a set of 200 instructions, for example, two thirds of its processing involves using as few as 10 of the total instructions. Cocke went on to design a computer that was based on a few instructions that could be executed quickly. He is credited with inventing the *Reduced Instruction Set Computer*, or RISC, in 1974. In 1987, Cocke's work on RISC won him the Turing Award (named for computer pioneer Alan M. Turing, known best for this Turing Test definition of artificial intelligence), given by the Association for Computing Machinery as its highest honor for technical contributions to computing.

Note that the RISC concept predated the term, however. The term RISC is credited to David Peterson, who used it in a course in microprocessor design at the University of California at Berkeley in 1980. The first chip to bear the label and to take advantage of Cocke's discoveries was RISC-I, a laboratory design that was completed in 1982. To distinguish this new design approach from traditional microprocessors, microcode-based systems with large instruction sets have come to be known as *Complex Instruction Set Computers*, or CISC, designs.

Cocke's research showed that most of the computing was done by basic instructions, not by the more powerful, complex, and specialized instructions. Further research at Berkeley and Stanford Universities demonstrated that there were even instances in which a sequence of simple instructions could perform a complex task faster than a single complex instruction could. The result of this research is often summarized as the *80/20 rule*: About 20 percent of a computer's instructions do about 80 percent of the work. The aim of the RISC design is to optimize a computer's performance for that 20 percent of instructions, speeding up their execution as much as possible. The remaining 80 percent of the commands could be duplicated, when necessary, by combinations of the quick 20 percent. Analysis and practical experience has shown that the 20 percent could be made so much faster that the overhead required to emulate the remaining 80 percent was no handicap at all.

In 1979, IBM introduced its model 801, the first machine to take advantage of Cocke's findings. It is credited as the first computer intentionally designed with a reduced instruction set. The 801 was a 32-bit minicomputer with 32 registers that could execute its simple instructions in a single processor cycle. The 801 led to the development of IBM's Personal Computer/RT in 1986, which was refined into the RISC System/6000. The multi-chip processor in the RS/6000 was consolidated into a single chip that formed the basis of IBM's PowerPC microprocessors (now being jointly developed with Motorola).

The Berkeley line of RISC research led to the RISC-II microprocessor (in 1984) and SOAR. Together, these laboratory designs inspired Sun Microsystems to develop the SPARC line of microprocessors.

RISC philosophy also inspired John Hennesey at Stanford University to found the MIPS project there. Although the MIPS group once said that the acronym was derived from a description of their design goal (Microprocessor without Interlocked Pipeline Stages), more commonly it is held to stand for Millions of Instructions Per Second, a rudimentary yardstick of microprocessor performance. The MIPS project eventually spawned RISC-chip developer MIPS Computer Systems (known as MIPS Technologies since its merger with Silicon Graphics in 1992). The Silicon Graphics MIPS chips trace their heritage back to the Stanford line of development.

No sharp edge demarcates the boundaries of what constitutes a reduced or complex instruction set. The DEC Alpha, for example, one of the most recent RISC designs, has a very full repertoire of 160 instructions. In contrast, Intel's Pentium, generally considered to be a CISC microprocessor, features about 150 instructions (depending on how you count). In light of such incongruities, some RISC developers now contend the RISC term has stood not for Reduced Instruction Set but rather for Restricted Instruction Set Computer all along.

More important than the nomenclature or number of instructions that a computer or microprocessor understands in characterizing RISC and CISC is how those instructions are realized. Slimming down a computer's instruction set is just one way that engineers go about streamlining its processing. As the instructions are trimmed, all the ragged edges that interfere with its performance are trimmed off, and all that remains is honed and smoothed to offer the least possible resistance to the passage of data. Consequently, RISC designs are best distinguished from CISC not by a single to-be-or-not-to-be rule but whether (and how well) they incorporate a number of characteristics. Some of the important characteristics of RISC include

> **Single-cycle or better execution of instructions.** Most instructions on a RISC computer will be carried out in a single clock cycle, if not faster, because of pipelining. The chip doesn't process a single instruction in a fraction of a cycle but instead works on multiple instructions simultaneously as they move down the pipeline. For example, a chip may work on four instructions simultaneously, each of which

requires three cycles to execute. The net result is that the chip would require three fourths of a clock cycle for each instruction.

Uniformity of instructions. The RISC pipeline operates best if all instructions are the same length (number of bits), require the same syntax, and execute in the same number of cycles. Most RISC systems have instruction sets made up solely of 32-bit commands. In contrast, the CISC command set used by the Intel-standard micro-processors in PCs use instructions 8, 16, or 32 bits long.

Lack of microcode. RISC computers either entirely lack microcode or have very little of it, relying instead on hardwired logic. Operations handled by microcode in CISC microprocessors require sequences of simple RISC instructions. Note that if these complex operations are performed repeatedly, the series of RISC instructions will lodge in the high-speed memory cache of the microprocessor. The cache contents then act like microcode that's automatically customized for the running program.

Load-store design. Accessing memory during the execution of an instruction often imposes delays because RAM cannot be accessed as quickly as the microprocessor runs. Consequently, most RISC machines lack immediate instructions (those that work on data in memory rather than in registers) and minimize the number of instructions that affect memory. Data must be explicitly loaded into a register before it can be worked on using a separate load instruction. The sequence of instructions in program code can then be organized (by an optimizing compiler) so that the delay on the pipeline is minimized.

The hard work is in the software. The RISC design shifts most of the work in achieving top performance to the software that runs on the system. RISC performance depends on how efficiently the instructions for running the system are arranged. Processing multiple instructions in a single clock cycle requires that the program pipeline be kept full of instructions that are constantly moving. If the pipeline harmony breaks down, the system stalls.

RISC systems depend on special language programs called optimizing compilers that analyze the instruction steps they generate to see whether rearranging the instructions will better match the needs of the microprocessor pipeline. In effect, RISC programs are analyzed and rewritten for optimum speed before they are used. The extra time spent on preparing the program pays off in increased performance every time it runs. Commercial programs are already compiled when you get them, so you normally don't see the extra effort exerted by the optimizing compiler. You just get quicker results.

Design simplicity. Above all, simplicity is the key to the design of a RISC machine or microprocessors. Although, for example, the Intel 80486 microprocessor has the equivalent of about one million transistors inside its package, the RISC-based MIPS M/2000 has only about 120,000, yet the two are comparable in performance. Fewer transistors mean fewer things to go wrong. RISC chips aren't necessarily more reliable, but making them without fabrication errors is easier than with more complex chips.

More important than the number of transistors is the amount of space on the silicon chip that needs to be used to make a microprocessor. As the area of a chip increases, the likelihood of fabrication errors increases. During the fabrication process, errors are inevitable. A speck of dust or a bit of semiconductor that doesn't grow or etch properly can prevent the finished circuit from working. A number of such defects are inevitable on any single silicon matrix. The larger and more complex the circuits on the matrix, the more likely any one (or all of them) will be plagued by a defect. Consequently, the yield of usable circuits from a matrix plummets as the circuits become more complex and larger. Moreover, the bigger the design of a chip, the fewer patterns that will fit on a die. That is, the fewer chips that can be grown at a time with given fabrication equipment. Overall, the yield of RISC chips can thus be greater. In more practical terms, it costs more to build more complex microprocessors.

Because they are simpler, RISC chips are easier to design. Fewer transistors means less circuitry to lay out, test, and give engineers nightmares. Just as the blueprints of an igloo would be more manageable than those for a Gothic cathedral, RISC chip designs take less work and can be readied faster. Although Intel chips retain their complex instruction sets—which have become increasingly complex with the addition of MMX and Streaming SIMD Extensions—the logic core of the company's current chips relies on many RISC techniques.

Micro-Ops

Many microprocessors that look like CISC chips and execute the classic Intel CISC instruction set are actually RISC chips inside. Although chip makers seeking to clone Intel's microprocessors were first to use such designs, Intel adopted the same strategy for its Pentium Pro microprocessor and all of its later designs.

The basic technique involves converting the classic Intel instructions into RISC-style instructions to be processed by the internal chip circuitry. Intel calls the internal RISC-like instructions *micro-ops*. The term is often abbreviated as uops (strictly speaking, the initial "u" should be the Greek letter mu, an abbreviation for micro) and pronounced *you-ops*. Other companies use slightly different terminology. NexGen (now part of Advanced Micro Devices) used the term *RISC86 instructions*. AMD itself prefers the term *R-ops* or ROPs.

By design, the micro-ops sidestep the primary shortcomings of the Intel instruction set by making the encoding of all commands more uniform, converting all instructions to the same length for processing, and eliminating arithmetic operations that directly change memory by loading memory data into registers before processing.

The translation to RISC-like instructions allows the microprocessor to function internally as a RISC engine. The code conversion occurs in hardware, completely invisible to your applications and out of the control of programmers. They are just another way that the modern microprocessor functions as a magical black box; you simply dump in any old code, and answers pop out at amazing speed.

Very Long Instruction Words (VLIW)

Just as RISC is flowing into the product mainstream, a new idea is sharpening the leading edge. Very Long Instruction Word technology at first appears to run against the RISC stream by using long, complex instructions. In reality, VLIW is a refinement of RISC meant to better take advantage of superscalar microprocessors. Each very long instruction word is made from several RISC instructions. In a typical implementation, eight 32-bit RISC instructions combine to make one instruction word.

Ordinarily, combining RISC instructions would add little to overall speed. As with RISC, the secret of VLIW technology is in the software—the compiler that produces the final program code. The instructions in the long word are chosen so that they execute at the same time (or as close to it as possible) in parallel processing units in the superscalar microprocessor. The compiler chooses and arranges instructions to match the needs of the superscalar processor as best as possible, essentially taking the optimizing compiler one step further. In essence, the VLIW system takes advantage of preprocessing in the compiler to make the final code and microprocessor more efficient.

VLIW technology also takes advantage of the wider bus connections of the latest generations of microprocessors. Existing chips link to their support circuitry with 64-bit buses. Many have 128-bit internal buses. The 256-bit very long instruction words push little further yet allow a microprocessor load several cycles of work in a single memory cycle.

No VLIW microprocessor systems are currently available. In fact, the only existing VLIW command sets remain experimental. The next generation of microprocessors very likely will see the integration of VLIW concepts.

Single Instruction, Multiple Data

In a quest to improve the performance of Intel microprocessors on common multimedia tasks, Intel's hardware and software engineers analyzed the operations multimedia programs most often required. They then sought the most efficient way to enable their chips to carry out these operations. They essentially worked to enhance the signal processing abilities of their general purpose microprocessors so that they would be competitive with dedicated processors such as digital signal processor (DSP) chips. They called the technology they developed *Single Instruction, Multiple Data*. SIMD was the enabling element of Intel's Multimedia Extensions (MMX) to its microprocessor command set. Intel further developed this technology to add its Streaming SIMD Extensions, once known as the Katmai New Instructions, to its Pentium III microprocessors to enhance their 3D processing power.

As the name implies, SIMD allows one microprocessor instruction to operate across several bytes or words (or even larger blocks of data). In the MMX scheme of things, the SIMD instructions are matched to the 64-bit data buses of Intel's Pentium and newer microprocessors. All data, whether it originates as byte, words, or 16-bit double-words, gets packed into 64-bit form. Eight bytes, four words, or two double-words get packed into a single 64-bit package that gets loaded into a 64-bit register in the microprocessor. One microprocessor instruction then manipulates the entire 64-bit block.

Although the approach at first appears counter-intuitive, it improves the handling of common graphic and audio data. In video processor applications, for example, it can trim the number of microprocessor clock cycles for some operations by 50 percent or more.

Operating Modes

As Intel Corporation developed its microprocessors, it kept in mind the commendable goal of compatibility. Each new microprocessor maintained some degree of compatibility with its predecessors. For example, the commands of one generation were carried over to the next. A new generation chip can use its registers as if they were in an older chip, for instance, addressing half of a 32-bit register as a 16-bit register.

Some of these quests for compatibility have led to the odd structure or operation of modern microprocessors. For example, Intel's use of segmented memory for its first generation of microprocessors was an effort at backward compatibility. So that the one megabyte address range would look like sixteen 64KB ranges of memory compatible with the earlier generation of chip, addressing became convoluted and program writing was complicated. The chips treated memory as 16 separate blocks instead of a single broad range.

With later generations, Intel's attempts at a solution to the backward compatibility and memory problems was to create different operating modes. As a result, modern Intel microprocessors have three chief operating modes: real mode, protected mode, and virtual 8086 mode.

Each of the modes plays a role in the operation of a modern PC and its software. All have been available in Intel-architecture microprocessors since the introduction of the 80386 in 1987.

Real Mode

The basic operating mode of Intel architecture microprocessors is *real mode*, the native and only operating mode available to the first generation of Intel microprocessors. Intel's engineers elected to carry this operating mode forward to all subsequent chips for compatibility purposes. Even in the most advanced Intel-architecture microprocessors, real mode mimics the 8086 microprocessor and all of its limitations.

Real mode earns its name from its exact correspondence between physical memory—the hard reality of it—and the logical addresses used by the microprocessor. The logical addresses specified in programs that operate in real mode indicate physical addresses in memory determined by the design of the computer hardware.

In real mode, the microprocessor can directly address up to one megabyte of memory, the limit imposed by the 20-bit memory addresses generated by first generation microprocessors. To achieve backward compatibility with earlier microprocessors, Intel elected to *segment* the memory accessed in real mode. Instead of a single wide range of addresses, the microprocessor locates memory in 64KB segments. To specify a location, the microprocessor indicates a segment as an *offset* and the location in the memory as a *base* address.

Modern microprocessors extend the reach of real mode through a design quirk. In addition to the 20-bit address values, these chips also track a *carry bit*, which the chip can use to indicate an additional memory segment for a total of 1088KB of real-mode memory. (Well, not quite. Another quirk puts 16 bytes of this extra segment off limits.) Transitional operating system enhancements between DOS and modern Windows exploited this real-mode feature to create the High Memory Area discussed in Chapter 4, "Memory."

All Intel-architecture microprocessors (at least since the 8086) boot up in real mode. Software, typically an operating system like Windows or Linux, then switches the microprocessor to a more advanced mode to take advantage of features such as greater addressability and memory protection.

Protected Mode

Intel introduced Protected Virtual Address Mode in 1982 to give the 80286 microprocessor the ability to reach all 16MB of its addressing range. The new mode, more commonly called simply *protected mode*, is more than a matter of addressability, however. As the name implies, protected mode operation allows microprocessors to protect ranges of memory so that when multiple tasks run simultaneously, they do not interfere with each other's memory. In addition, when operating in protected mode, Intel microprocessors have an added repertory of instructions, most of which are aimed at multitasking.

To safeguard the operation of your software and PC, protected mode doesn't build walls around applications. Rather, it allows programmers to give their software one of four priority levels and prevents applications with lower priority from reaching the memory assigned to higher priority. For example, the operating system would be assigned the highest priority so the crash of a program with lower priority would not affect it. Before a microprocessor references memory in protected mode, it checks the protection level. If the access is not allowed, the chip refuses to carry out the instruction and signals an error (an *exception* in programming terminology).

In protected mode, memory remains segmented, but Intel turned the disadvantage into a feature. In protected mode, segments become a means of managing memory and tasks rather than a constraint on addressing. Segments can be any size, each defined by a special descriptor block that tracks how much memory there is, where in the address range of the microprocessor it is located, and what level of protection the segment is afforded.

Intel's protected mode architecture also supports a *flat memory model*, which means treating memory as a single, continuous expanse, for software (such as UNIX) that assumes it has a large, linear range of addresses. In the Intel scheme of things, however, flat memory is simply a special case of segmented memory with one segment defined for data and another for code.

The protected mode of Intel microprocessors also supports *demand paging*, a technique that allows a microprocessor to run programs requiring a lot of memory to run with a lesser amount of physical memory. Demand paging works by slicing memory into small sections called *pages*, which it manages individually. Intel microprocessors fix the page size at 4KB. The microprocessor simulates larger memory endowment by swapping pages of code and data into physical memory as it is needed (on demand).

Although the 80286 microprocessor that introduced protected-mode memory could address only 16MB, protected mode itself is constrained by no such limit. Protected mode makes the full power of modern processors available to your programs.

Virtual 8086 Mode

To accommodate the old DOS operating system in the protected mode environment, Intel added *virtual 8086 mode* to the third and all subsequent generations of its microprocessors; that is, all chips since the 386 recognize this mode. More commonly called *virtual mode* or *virtual x86 mode*, this mode earns its name by dividing the operation of a single microprocessor into several virtual microprocessors, each capable of running a separate DOS task as if it were a dedicated 8086 chip. Each virtual microprocessor running under virtual 8086 mode can access up to the full 1MB addressing limit of real mode and can use the same microprocessor instructions and facilities as would be available with a dedicated 8086 chip.

Unlike real mode, virtual 8086 mode operates as part of protected mode and affords the same isolation between programs. One or more protected-mode applications can run at the same time as one or more virtual 8086 mode programs. An operating system running under protected mode typically manages the applications running in virtual 8086 mode.

Each of the virtual machines running in virtual 8086 mode can run its own program, totally isolated from the rest of the virtual computers. That means you can simultaneously run several DOS programs on one computer. Although this kind of multitasking was possible without the exotic architecture of the 80386 chip that first implemented virtual 8086 mode, most such systems were either complex or shaky, and most required that software be specially written to proprietary standards to effect multitasking operation. Virtual 8086 mode, on the other hand, makes multitasking control software simple because all the hard work is done in hardware. Off-the-shelf DOS programs work without modification in virtual 8086 mode using any Intel microprocessor from the 386 onward.

As the number of real-mode applications, such as those written for DOS, steadily diminishes, the importance of virtual 8086 mode similarly diminishes. Nevertheless, it remains part of the Intel microprocessor repertory and probably will remain so until Intel discards its conventional architecture.

Electrical Characteristics

At its heart, a microprocessor is an electronic device. No matter what logical design it uses—CISC, RISC, VLIW, SIMD, or whatever—it uses logic gates made from semiconductor circuitry to carry out its operations. The electronic basis of the microprocessor has important ramifications in the construction and operation of chips.

The free lunch principle (that is, there is none) tells us that every operation has its cost. Even the quick electronic thinking of a microprocessor takes a toll. The thinking involves the switching of state of tiny transistors, and each state change consumes a bit of electrical power, converting it to heat. The transistors are so small that the process generates a minuscule amount of heat, but with millions of them in a single chip, the heat adds up. Modern microprocessors generate so much heat that keeping them cool is a major concern in their design.

Heat is wasted power, and power is a premium in notebook computers. Consequently, microprocessor designers, with an eye to prolong battery life, have adopted a number of strategies to cut power consumption in portable applications.

Thermal Constraints

The tight packing of circuits on chips makes heat a major issue in their design and operation. Heat is the enemy of the semiconductor because it can destroy the delicate crystal structure of a chip. If a chip gets too hot, it will be irrevocably destroyed. Packing circuits tightly concentrates the heat they generate, and the small size of the individual circuit components makes them more vulnerable to damage.

Heat can cause problems more subtle than simple destruction. Because the conductivity of semiconductor circuits also varies with temperature, the effective switching speed of transistors and logic gates also changes when chips get too hot or too cold. Although this temperature-induced speed change does not alter how fast a microprocessor can compute (the chip must stay locked to the system clock at all times), it can affect the relative timing between signals inside the microprocessor. Should the timing get too far off, a microprocessor might make a mistake, with the inevitable result of crashing your system. All chips have rated temperature ranges within which they are guaranteed to operate without such timing errors.

Because chips generate more heat as speed increases, they can produce heat faster than it can radiate away. This heat build-up can alter the timing of the internal signals of the chip so drastically that the microprocessor will stop working and—as if you couldn't guess—cause your system to crash. To avoid such problems, computer manufacturers often attach heatsinks to microprocessors and other semiconductor components to aid in their cooling.

A *heatsink* is simply a metal extrusion that increases the surface area from which heat can radiate from a microprocessor or other heat-generating circuit element. Most heatsinks have several fins, rows of pins, or some geometry that increases its surface area. Heatsinks are usually made from aluminum because that metal is one of the better thermal conductors, enabling the heat from the microprocessor to quickly spread across the heatsink.

Heatsinks provide *passive cooling*, called that because it requires no power-using mechanism to perform its cooling. Heatsinks work by convection, transferring heat to the air that circulates past the heatsink. Air circulates around the heatsink because the warmed air rises away from the heatsink and cooler air flows in to replace it.

In contrast, *active cooling* involves some kind of mechanical or electrical assistance in removing heat. The most common form of active cooling is a fan, which blows a greater volume of air past the heatsink than would be possible with convection alone.

As a byproduct of a microprocessor's thinking, heat is waste. The energy that raises the temperature of the microprocessor does no useful work. But it does drain the energy source that's supplying the microprocessor.

Some chips run so hot that their manufacturers integrate active cooling with the chip itself. For example, Intel's Pentium Overdrive upgrade chips have a small, built-in plastic fan. The problem with such integrated active cooling is that the fan can fail and the chip overheat. Intel's solution to this problem is to slow the chip to a modest speed (typically about 25MHz) upon the failure of the fan, cutting heat production and helping preserve the chip against thermal damage. Unfortunately, the chip does not warn when it slows down, and the response of your PC may slow noticeably for no apparent reason.

The makers of notebook PCs face another challenge in efficiently managing the cooling of their computers. Using a fan to cool a notebook system is problematic. The fan consumes substantial energy, which trims battery life. Moreover, the heat generated by the fan motor itself can be a significant part of the thermal load of the system. Most designers of notebook machines have turned to more innovative passive thermal controls such as heat pipes and using the entire chassis of the computer as a heatsink.

Operating Voltages

In desktop computers, overheating rather than excess electrical consumption is the major power concern. Even the most wasteful of microprocessors use far less power than an ordinary light bulb. The most that any PC-compatible microprocessor consumes is about nine watts, hardly more than a night light and of little concern when the power grid supplying your PC has megawatts at its disposal.

If you switch to battery power, however, every last milliwatt is important. The more power used by a PC, the shorter the time its battery can power the system or the heavier the batteries it will need to achieve a given life between charges. Every degree a microprocessor raises its case temperature clips minutes from its battery runtime.

Battery-powered notebooks and sub-notebook computers consequently caused microprocessor engineers to do a quick about-face. Where once they were content to use bigger and bigger heatsinks, fans, and refrigerators to keep their chips cool, today they focus on reducing temperatures and wasted power at the source.

One way to cut power requirements is to make the design elements of a chip smaller. Smaller digital circuits require less power. But shrinking chips is not an option; microprocessors are invariably designed to be as small as possible with the prevailing technology.

To further trim the power required by microprocessors to make them more amenable to battery operation, engineers have come up with two new design twists: low-voltage operation and system management mode. Although founded on separate ideas, both are often used together to minimize microprocessor power consumption. Most new microprocessor designs will likely incorporate both technologies. In fact, some older microprocessor designs have been retrofitted with such power-saving technologies (for example, the SL-Enhanced series of Intel 486 chips and the portable versions of the Pentium).

Since the very beginning of the transistor-transistor logic family of digital circuits—the design technology that later blossomed into the microprocessor—digital logic has operated with a supply voltage of five volts. That level is essentially arbitrary. Almost any voltage would work. But five-volt technology offers some practical advantages. It's low enough to be both safe and frugal with power needs but high enough to avoid noise and allow for several diode drops, the inevitable reduction of voltage that occurs when a current flows across a semiconductor junction.

Every semiconductor junction, which essentially forms a diode, reduces or drops the voltage flowing through it. Silicon junctions impose a diode drop of about 0.7 volts, and there may be one or more such junctions in a logic gate. Other materials impose smaller drops—that of germanium, for example, is 0.4 volts—but the drop is unavoidable.

There's nothing magical about five volts. Reducing the voltage used by logic circuits dramatically reduces power consumption because power consumption in electrical circuits increases by the square of the voltage. That is, doubling the voltage of a circuit increases the power it uses by fourfold. Reducing the voltage by one half reduces power consumption by three quarters—providing, of course, that the circuit will continue to operate at the lower voltage.

All current microprocessor designs operate at 3.3 volts or less. The latest Pentium II and III designs operate around 2.0 volts. To minimize power consumption, Intel sets the operating voltage of the core logic of its chips as low as possible, as low as 1.8 volts. The integral secondary caches of these chips (which are fabricated separately from the core logic) usually require their own, often higher, voltage supply. In fact, operating voltage has become so critical that Intel devotes several pins of its Pentium II and later microprocessors to encoding the voltage needs of the chip, and the host PC must adjust its supply to the chip to precisely meet those needs.

Most bus architectures and most of today's memory modules operate at the 3.3 volt level. Future designs will push that level lower. Rambus memory systems, for example, operate at 2.5 volts. (See Chapter 4.)

Extremely Low Voltage Semiconductors

Even 1.8 volts is not near the minimum for working semiconductors. In February 1996 at the International Solid State Circuits Conference in San Francisco, Toshiba America Electronic Components Inc. showed a circuit technology it termed *Extremely Low Voltage Semiconductors*. According to Toshiba, the new design allows integrated circuits to operate at a level of only 0.5 volt. This factor of ten reduction effectively reduces power requirements to one hundredth of what would be needed at the old 5.0 volt TTL level or about one fifteenth of current Pentium II chips. The design achieves its low voltage capabilities by allowing the chip maker to individually control the threshold voltage of each transistor in a chip. The threshold voltage is the level at which a transistor switches from off to on, and current circuit designs require all transistors in a chip to operate at a common threshold voltage.

Currently, no commercial products use Extremely Low Voltage Semiconductor technology, although chips like the Pentium III come close. Noise and interference concerns make applying it to overall PC architectures and circuits outside the safe confines of chip packaging problematic. Internally, however, today's designs are reaching down to extremely low voltage operation that promises dramatic reductions in the power needs of notebook PCs.

Power Management

Most microprocessors have been designed to be like the Coast Guard, always prepared. (The U.S. Coast Guard motto is *semper paratus*.) They kept all of their circuits not only constantly ready but also operating at full potential, whether they were being used or not. From an energy usage viewpoint, that's like burning all the lights in your entire house while you sit quietly in the living room reading a book. You might venture into some other room, so you keep those lights burning—and keep the local electric company in business.

Most people (at least, most frugally minded people) switch on the lights only in the rooms in which they are roaming, keeping other lights off to minimize the waste of electricity. Newer microprocessors are designed to do the same thing; switch off portions of their circuitry and even some of the circuits in your PC external to the microprocessor when they are unneeded. When, for example, you're running a program that's just waiting around for you to press a key, the microprocessor could switch most of its calculating circuits off until it receives an interrupt from the keyboard controller. This use-only-what's-needed feature is called system management mode. It was pioneered by Intel's 386SL microprocessor and has become a standard feature of most newer chips.

In addition, many microprocessors are able to operate at a variety of speeds. Slowing a chip down reduces its power consumption (and also reduces performance). Many current chips enable their host computers to force a speed reduction by lowering the clock speed. Microprocessors that use static logic designs are able to stop operating entirely without risking their register contents, enabling a complete system shutdown to save power. Later, they can be reactivated without losing a beat (or byte). The electrical charges in ordinary, dynamic designs drain off faster than they get restored if the dynamic circuit slows too much.

Overclocking

In the old days when operating a PC was a sport akin to bronco busting for venturesome souls or those a bit short of cash and common sense, one common method of eking more speed from a PC was to alter the system clock frequency and run the microprocessor at a frequency beyond its ratings, a technique called *overclocking*. In that the master clock derives its frequency from a single clock controlled by a single crystal, the change was too tempting. After all, you can buy clock crystals at most electronic parts stores for a few dollars. You can easily pull out the 66MHz crystal and slide in one rated at 100MHz.

Modifying clock frequencies is both easier and more complicated than ever before. New motherboard designs make altering frequencies easier. But you have more than one frequency to dicker with and more chances for making your system go sour.

Modern motherboards often make the operating speed of their master oscillators programmable. Instead of ordinary oscillators, they use *frequency synthesizers*, special chips that can create nearly any necessary frequency from any other. They use a crystal to keep their operating frequency rock-stable but are electrically programmed to generate the frequencies needed to run the system. So that the motherboard can accommodate the widest range of microprocessors, manufacturers often let you adjust the operating frequency of the synthesizer using a jumper or switch. A few motherboards even make the external bus an advanced setup option that you can change from your keyboard when configuring its CMOS. Depending on your PC, you may be able to change the microprocessor clock directly or alter it indirectly by changing the external microprocessor bus speed and the microprocessor's internal multiplier. In any case, you simply make the setting that best matches the chip you want to plug in. If you want to experiment and push the envelope, just change the synthesizer settings. You'll also want to have handy a bucket of water to cool things down and a big enough credit limit to buy a new microprocessor should your best laid schemes go astray as they often can.

Sources that advocate overclocking note that altering the internal microprocessor speed often makes less of an improvement than changing the external microprocessor bus speed that's used by the memory system. And when you alter the external bus speed, with most modern motherboards you'll also be changing the speed of the PCI bus. You have to take all three speeds into consideration and make the proper match between them.

Some microprocessors are more amenable to overclocking than others. Most sources agree that Intel chips (with a few exceptions) are conservatively rated and can be successfully overclocked. Microprocessors from other makers are more likely to have pushed their manufacturing technology to its limits. With them, chip reliability may be severely compromised at speeds higher than their ratings. These chips run close to their thermal limits already. Pushing the envelope might make it catch on fire.

Overclocking also takes a more insidious form. Unscrupulous semiconductor dealers sometimes buy microprocessors (or memory chips or other speed-rated devices) and change their labels to reflect higher speed potentials; for example, buying a 300MHz Pentium II and altering its markings to say 400MHz. A little white paint increases the market value of some chips by hundreds of dollars. It also creates a product that is likely to be operated out of its reliable range. Intel introduced internal chip serial numbers with the Pentium III to help prevent this form of fraud. From the unalterable serial number of the chip, you can determine its factory-issue speed rating.

Physical Matters

The working part of a microprocessor is exactly what the nickname "chip" implies: a small flake of a silicon crystal no larger than a postage stamp. Although silicon is a fairly robust material with moderate physical strength, it is sensitive to chemical contamination. After all, semiconductors are grown in precisely controlled atmospheres, the chemical content of which affects the operating properties of the final chip. To prevent oxygen and contaminants in the atmosphere from adversely affecting the precision-engineered silicon, the chip itself must be sealed away. The first semiconductors, transistors, were hermetically sealed in tiny metal cans.

The art and science of semiconductor packaging has advanced since those early days. Modern ICs are often surrounded in epoxy plastic, an inexpensive material that can be easily molded to the proper shape. Unfortunately, microprocessors can get very hot, sometimes too hot for plastics to safely contain. Most powerful modern microprocessors are consequently cased in ceramic materials that are fused together at high temperatures. Older, cooler chips reside in plastic. The most recent trend in chip packaging is the development of inexpensive tape-based packages optimized for automated assembly of circuit boards.

Packaging

The most primitive of microprocessors—that is, those of the early generation that had neither substantial signal nor power requirements—fit in the same style housing popular for other integrated circuits, the infamous dual inline pin or DIP package. The only problem chips in DIPs face is getting signals in and out. Even ancient 8-bit chips require more connections than the 14 to 20 that fit on normal-size DIP packages. Consequently, most DIP microprocessors have housings with 40 or more pins.

The typical microprocessor DIP is a black epoxy plastic rectangle about two inches long and half an inch wide. Some more powerful DIP chips use ceramic cases with metal seals over the location where the silicon itself fits. A row of connecting pins line both of the long sides of the chip package like the legs of a centipede.

The most important of these legs is pin number one, which helps determine the proper orientation for putting the chip in its socket. The number-one pin of the two rows terminates the row of pins that's on the same end of the chip as its orientation notch, on the left row when viewed from the top of the chip (see Figure 3.1).

The DIP package is far from ideal for a number of reasons. Adding more connections, for example, makes for an ungainly chip. A centipede microprocessor would be a beast measuring a full five inches long. Not only would such a critter be hard to fit onto a reasonably sized circuit board, but also it would require that signals travel substantially farther to reach the end pins than those in the center. At modern operating frequencies, that difference in distance can amount to a substantial fraction of a clock cycle, potentially putting the pins out of sync.

FIGURE 3.1

*An 80286 DIP chip
showing pin one at
the lower left.*

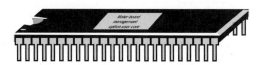

Modern chip packages are compact squares that avoid these problems. At least four separate styles of package have been developed to accommodate the needs of the latest microprocessors.

Today, the most common is the Pin Grid Array, or PGA, a square package that varies in size with the number of pins that it must accommodate. Recent microprocessors are about two inches square. Sixteen-bit chips typically have two rows of pins parallel to each edge of the chip and dropping down from its bottom, a total of about 68 pins. Processors with 32-bit bus connections have between 112 and 168 pins arranged similarly but in three rows. Chips with 64-bit connection potential may have up to 321 pins in four rows arrayed as one square inside another.

In any case, the pins are spaced as if they were laid out on a checkerboard, all evenly spaced, with the central block of pins (and sometimes those at each of the four corners) eliminated. Again, pin number one is specially marked for orientation purposes. The ferrule through which the pin leaves the ceramic case is often square for pin one and round for the others. In addition, the corner of the chip that corresponds to the location of pin one is typically chopped off (see Figure 3.2).

FIGURE 3.2

*Pin-grid array socket
(with PGA chip).*

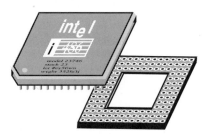

To fit the larger number of pins used by the latest Pentium and Pentium Pro chips into a reasonable space, Intel rearranged the pins, staggering them so that they can fit closer together. The result is a *staggered pin grid array* package.

Each of these PGA and SPGA packages have their own matching sockets. Some chips fit different sockets. For example, a chip without a keying pin fits into a socket with a keying pin. The socket used for the microprocessor on your PC's motherboard determines which upgrades you can use in your PC. These issues are addressed in the section "Sockets and Slots," later in this chapter.

The Pentium Pro adds another twist to the classic PGA package. Its twofold design—separate CPU and cache chips—uses a unique package that offers a separate chamber for each chip. The result is called a *Multi-Cavity Module*, or MCM. Although the Pentium Pro's MCM uses pins in parallel rows much like a normal PGA package, the MCM is rectangular and the number of pin rows on the long and short sides are different (four on the long, two on the short). In addition, on one side of the module, an extra pin sprouts between each square of four. The ceramic-based MCM used by the Pentium Pro provides suitable packaging for the chip and enough space for the 387 pins needed by the complex processor, but on the downside, it is expensive (reputedly as much as $30 each). Figure 3.3 illustrates a Pentium Pro MCM.

FIGURE 3.3
Multi-cavity module SPGA package.

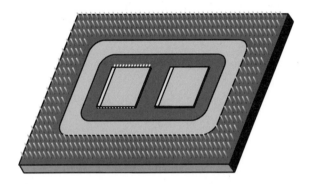

Pins such as those used by the PGA, SPGA, and MCM packages are prone to damage and relatively expensive to fabricate, so chip makers have developed pinless packages for microprocessors. The first of these to find general use was the Leadless Chip Carrier, or LCC, socket. Instead of pins, this style of package has contact pads on one of its surfaces. The pads are plated with gold to avoid corrosion or oxidation that would impede the flow of the minute electrical signals used by the chip (see Figure 3.4). The pads are designed to contact special springy mating contacts in a special socket. Once installed, the chip itself may be hidden in the socket or under a heatsink, or perhaps only the top of the chip may be visible, framed by the four sides of the socket.

FIGURE 3.4
Leadless Chip Carrier microprocessor, top and bottom views.

In an LCC socket, the chip is held in place by a pivoting metal wire. You pull the wire off the chip, and the chip pops up. Hold an LCC chip in your hand and it resembles a small ceramic tile. Its bottom edge is dotted with bright flecks of gold—the chip's contact pads.

BGA, PGA, and LCC packages are usually made from a ceramic material because the rigid material provides structural strength needed by the chip. To avoid the higher cost of ceramics, chip makers created an alternate design that could be fabricated from plastic. Called the Plastic Leaded Chip Carrier, or PLCC, this package has another advantage besides cost: a special versatility. It can be soldered directly to a printed circuit board using surface-mount techniques. Using this package, the computer manufacturer can save the cost of a socket while improving the reliability of the system. (Remember, connections like those in chip sockets are the least reliable part of a computer system.)

The PLCC chip can also be used in a socket. In this case, the socket surrounds the chip. The leads from the chip are bent down around its perimeter and slide against mating contacts inside the inner edge of the socket's perimeter. A PLCC chip is rather easy to press into its socket but difficult to pop out; you must carefully wedge underneath the chip and lever it out.

Some microprocessors with low thermal output sometimes use a housing designed to be soldered down, the Plastic Quad Flat Package, or PQFP, sometimes called simply the "quad flat pack" because the chips are flat (they fit flat against the circuit board) and they have four sides (making them a quadrilateral, as shown in Figure 3.5).

FIGURE 3.5
Plastic Quad Flat Package microprocessor.

Manufacturers like this package because of its low cost and because chips using it can be installed in exactly the same manner as other modern surface-mount components. However, the quad flat pack is suitable only for lower power chips because soldered connections can be stressed by microprocessors that get too hot. As with other chip packages, proper orientation of a quad flat pack is indicated by a notch or depression near pin number one.

Another new package design takes the advantage of the quad flat pack a step further. Called the *Tape Carrier Package*, it looks like a piece of photographic film with a square pregnant bulge in the middle once it's stripped of its shipping protection. Thin, gold-plated leads project from each edge of the compact package that measures just over one inch wide (26 mm) and thinner than a dime (1 mm). Perfect for weight-conscious portable PCs, a Pentium processor in a TCP package weighs less than a gram compared to about 50 grams for its PGA equivalent. Figure 3.6 shows a tape carrier package.

FIGURE 3.6

Tape Carrier Package microprocessor.

The TCP package starts with a substrate of polyimide film laminated to copper foil. The foil is etched to form two contact patterns, one that will engage with tabs on the silicon chip of the microprocessor and others that engage with the system board of a PC. After etching, the traces are gold plated as are matching tabs on the silicon chip. The chip is placed on the film and the gold-plated tabs and traces bonded together. The silicon chip is then encapsulated with polyimide siloxane resin to protect it. Multiple microprocessors can be encapsulated individually or at regular intervals along a long length of tape, which is delivered to PC makers on a spool. This fabrication process is called *tape automated bonding* and is regularly used to make a variety of electronic components, including most LCD panels.

TCP microprocessors must be installed using special tools. During automated assembly of a circuit board, the assembly machine cuts the individual TCP microprocessors from the individual protective carrier or tape spool. It then shapes the etched leads from sticking straight out from the sides of the package into a Z-shape that extended below the bottom of the package so that they can contact the circuit board. A special paste applied to the circuit board physically and thermally bonds the chip to the predefined mounting area (which may include a built-in heatsink), and a hot bar clamps down on the leads to solder them to the contacts on the board.

The latest chip package uses the PGA layout but eliminates the most vulnerable and expensive part of the design, the pins themselves. Instead, it substitutes precision-formed globs of solder that can mate with socket contacts or be soldered directly to a circuit board using surface-mount technology. Because the solder contacts start out as tiny balls but use a variation on the PGA layout, the package is termed *solder-ball grid array.* (The "solder" is often omitted from the name, yielding the abbreviation BGA.) The process of forming the solder balls is so precise that chip manufacturers can space the resulting contacts more closely than when using pins. Consequently, SBGA is winning favor for the latest chips that have 300 or more contacts. Among the first chips to use the BGA package design is the Cyrix MediaGX. Some Celeron chips have adopted this kind of package as well.

Intel's latest innovation in microprocessor packaging is to pre-install chips on modules that slide into sockets like ordinary expansion boards. As with expansion boards, the modules have an edge connector with a single row of contacts. Consequently, Intel calls this package, first introduced with the Pentium II, the *Single Edge Contact cartridge* or SEC cartridge (which Intel often abbreviates SECC). This modular design has several important benefits. It allows you to easily install or upgrade microprocessors, which in turn means lower support cost for Intel and a larger potential upgrade market. It also allows Intel to use any kind of chip packaging it wants inside the cartridge; for example, inexpensive tape-carrier designs. Although the SEC cartridge adds a second set of connections (one between chip and module, one between the module and your PC), edge connectors are substantially less expensive to fabricate than chip packages with multiple pins so the overall cost of manufacturing can be lower. Figure 3.7 shows the Pentium II microprocessor SEC cartridge.

FIGURE 3.7

The SEC cartridge as used by the Intel Pentium II.

The SEC cartridge comprises several essential elements. The *cover* is the metal shell that covers the top of the entire cartridge assembly. The back of the cartridge is called the *thermal plate*. It acts as a heatsink, although for most microprocessors, it does not offer sufficient cooling of itself. Rather it serves as a channel to route heat from the circuit elements of the microprocessor to the outside where it can be more effectively removed by auxiliary heatsinks or an active cooling system.

Inside the SEC is a printed circuit board called the *substrate* that links together the electronic circuits (which Intel calls the *internal components*) that make up the entire microprocessor. These circuits include the *processor core*, which is the execution engine of the microprocessor, the part that actually acts upon program instructions; the level-two (L2) cache, which buffers the high-speed circuits of the microprocessor from the lower performance memory bus; and *bus termination circuits*, which match the internal components of the microprocessor to the circuits of its computer host. An *edge connector* extends from the bottom of the substrate to electrically link the microprocessor to the socket in its host computer.

The Intel Pentium II Xeon microprocessors also use an SEC cartridge, but the implementation differs substantially from the Pentium II design. At the heart of the difference is a new socket design used by the Xeon. The result is that although both the plain Pentium II and Xeon use the same *technology* for their packages, the physical embodiments of the two chips differ substantially—the Xeon is about twice as tall and just as long as the standard Pentium II, measuring 6 inches long, 4.84 inches tall, and about 0.75 inch thick—and the two are not at all interchangeable. Figure 3.8 shows the Xeon implementation of the SEC cartridge.

FIGURE 3.8

SEC cartridge as used by the Pentium II Xeon.

Closely related to the SEC cartridge is the Single-Edge Processor package, or SEP. In effect, the SEP package is the SEC cartridge without the cover. This design lowers the cost of the assembly. Understandably, then, its initial (and so far, only) application has been in Intel's low-cost Celeron series of microprocessors. Note that the shell is not the only difference between the Celeron and Pentium II processor line; the memory cache design of the two chips is substantially different. The Pentium II makes the cache a separate circuit element external to the main processor, but the more recent Celeron integrates a smaller cache with the main processor. (The earliest Celerons entirely lacked a memory cache.) Despite these differences, the pin out used for sockets for the SEP and SEC cartridges is the same. Figure 3.9 shows the SEP package as used by the Celeron microprocessor.

The package that the chip is housed in has no effect on its performance. It can, however, be important when you want to replace or upgrade your microprocessor with a new chip or upgrade card. Many of these enhancement products require that you replace your system's microprocessor with a new chip or adapter cable that links to a circuit board. If you want the upgrade or a replacement part to fit on your motherboard, you may have to specify which package your PC uses for its microprocessor.

FIGURE 3.9

The SEP package as used by the Intel Celeron microprocessor.

Location

Ordinarily, you should have no need to see or touch the microprocessor in your PC. As long as your computer works (and considering the reliability that most have demonstrated, that should be a long, long time), you really need not concern yourself about your microprocessor except to know that it's inside your computer doing its job. However, some modern system upgrades require that you plug a new microprocessor into your system or even replace the one that you have.

Before you can replace your microprocessor, you have to identify which chip it is. That's easy. As a general rule, all you have to look for is the largest integrated circuit chip on your computer's motherboard. Almost invariably, it will be the microprocessor. That's only fitting because the microprocessor is also the most important chip in the computer. In modern PCs, the microprocessor uses a large, square package.

If you find several large chips on your system board, odds are that one of them is the microprocessor. Others may be equally big because they have elaborate functions and need to make many connections with the system board, which means they need relatively large packages to accommodate their many leads.

Almost universally, the microprocessor chip will be installed in a socket (which may or may not be visible); most support chips will be soldered directly to the system board. Sometimes, the microprocessor will be hidden under a heatsink, which you can identify by its heat-radiating fins.

The appearance of each different microprocessor depends on the package it uses, but all can be identified by their model number emblazoned on top. You'll have to sort through a few lines of numbers to find the key identifying signature, but the model designations of most chips are readily sorted out.

Sockets and Slots

Ordinarily, you don't have to deal with microprocessor sockets unless you're curious and want to pull out the chip, hold it in your hand, and watch a static discharge turn a $300 circuit into epoxy-encapsulated sand. Choose to upgrade your PC to a new and better microprocessor, and you'll tangle with the details of socketry, particularly if you want to improve your Pentium.

Intel recognizes nine different microprocessor sockets for its processors from the 486 to the Pentium Pro. In 1999, it added a new socket for some incarnations of the Pentium II Celeron. Other Pentium II and Pentium III chips, packaged as modules or cartridges, mate with slots instead of sockets. Table 3.2 summarizes these socket types, the chips that use them, and the upgrades appropriate to them.

TABLE 3.2 Sockets and Slots for Intel Microprocessors and Upgrades

Socket or Slot Number	Pins	Layout	Voltage	Microprocessor	OverDrives
Sockets					
0	168	Inline	5V	486DX	DX2, DX4
1	169	Inline	5V	486DX, 486SX	DX2, DX4
2	238	Inline	5V	486DX, 486SX, DX2	DX2, DX4, Pentium
3	237	Inline	3V or 5V	486DX, 486SX, DX2, DX4	DX2, DX4, Pentium
4	273	Inline	5V	60 or 66MHz Pentium	Pentium
5	320	Staggered	3V	Other Pentium	Pentium
6	235	Inline	3V	DX4	Pentium
7	321	Staggered	3V	Other Pentium	Pentium
8	387	Staggered	3V	Pentium Pro	Pentium Pro
Slots					
1	242	Inline	3V	Pentium II, Celeron	
2	330	Inline	3V	Xeon	
A (EV6)	NA	Inline	3V	AMD K7	
M	NA	Inline	3V	Merced	
SC242	242	Inline	3V	Pentium III, Celeron	

Socket 0. The first 486-based PCs used a standard PGA socket with 168 pins arranged in the shape of three concentric squares. Although Intel does not officially designate it, for consistency we will call this ground-level socket by the designation *Socket 0*.

Socket 1. Intel's original plans made *Socket 1* the official 486 upgrade socket, distinguishing it by the addition of an extra pin hole (to make 169). The design intention was to use the socket exclusively for the chip upgrades—math processors to enhance 486SX-based PCs and OverDrive chips. The extra pin prevented unknowing users from putting the upgrade chip in the wrong socket. Intel short-circuited its own strategy when, seeking to maximize its upgrade market, it developed chips lacking the extra pin to fit Socket 0. Figure 3.10 shows Socket 1.

FIGURE 3.10
Socket 1 with 169 pins for 486 upgrades.

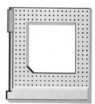

Socket 2. To smooth the transition to Pentium technology, Intel developed Socket 2 as an upgrade socket for 486-based PCs. Socket 2 is a superset of Socket 1. The inner 169 pins (of 238) match the Socket 1 standard, so a 486 microprocessor simply plugs into the center of the socket, leaving the outermost row of pin holes open. 486-level OverDrives plug into this socket in exactly the same way. The outer row of pinholes accommodates the wider bus of the Pentium OverDrive (P24T) upgrade.

Socket 3. When Intel developed lower-voltage microprocessors, it also created a new socket so that low-voltage chips could not be inadvertently inserted into sockets supporting only higher (and thus damaging) voltages. Socket 3 follows the pattern set by Socket 2 but rearranges the keying pins, omitting one (leaving 237 pins). The pin rearrangement helps key the socket so that 3V microprocessors cannot accidentally (and fatally) get plugged into 5 volt PCs. The socket accommodates all the same upgrades as Socket 2 in addition to 3.3-volt chips.

Socket 4. Intel introduced *Socket 4* to accommodate the needs of the wider interface of the initial Pentium release, code-named P5. No other Intel original equipment processors use this 273-pin socket, although Intel has designed Pentium OverDrive chips to fit it.

Socket 5. The second generation Pentiums, those operating at speed of 75MHz and higher, adopted an entirely new socket design, *Socket 5*, based on Staggered Pin Grid Array technology. Unlike earlier sockets in which the holes that accept microprocessor pins are arranged in a strict square matrix, the staggered design squeezes them closer together by shifting alternate rows half a space over. In addition, Socket 5 requires a ZIF (zero insertion force) design that allows a chip to drip into place without resistance and then is locked down by a lever on the side of the socket. The Socket 5 design used 320 pins.

Socket 6. Because the 486DX4 chip had different power needs than previous designs, Intel created a special socket design for the chip. The socket matched a pin-out on the chip design to preclude the use of the chip in older PCs. The result, *Socket 6*, followed the same basic design as Socket 3 but used only 235 pins.

Socket 7. The last of Intel's Pentium sockets, *Socket 7*, added another keying pin to the staggered pin-grid arrangement of Socket 5. Socket 7 is the company's preferred socket for all new Pentium systems and has become the choice for Pentium-level chips from compatible microprocessor makers. Socket 7 allows the most OverDrive upgrade options, although OverDrive chips are available to match both Sockets 5 and 7. Figure 3.11 shows Socket 7.

FIGURE 3.11

Microprocessor Socket 7 for the Pentium and related chips.

Socket 8. The large Pentium Pro chip required an entirely new socket for its Pentium Pro microprocessor. The design, now known as *Socket 8*, matches the chip in shape—an elongated rectangle—with two distinct arrays of pins, part staggered, part in line. Socket 8 is the largest pin-type socket in common use, with 387 pins. Figure 3.12 shows Socket 8.

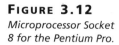

FIGURE 3.12
Microprocessor Socket 8 for the Pentium Pro.

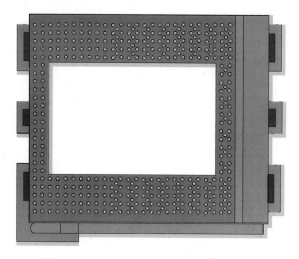

Super 7. Although Intel has essentially abandoned all of these sockets for its new microprocessor designs, compatible chip makers continue to use and develop Socket 7. In its ultimate form, called *Super 7*, the signals remain essentially the same as the basic Socket 7, but a higher, 100MHz speed is supported for the bus interface. This simple expedient gives the old design the same performance potential as Intel's new designs, although the socket lacks some of the advanced system support features found in Intel's new designs.

Socket PGA370. When Intel introduced its higher speed (366 and 400MHz) Celeron chips, it opted for less expensive packaging than used by earlier chips, one that uses a socket similar to the Socket 7 design but with two important differences: an increased pin count and a different type of signals. The new socket has 370 pins arranged in a staggered grid array, so the design is termed Socket PGA370. In addition, it uses the GTL+ signaling system introduced with the Pentium II that makes the connection less susceptible to noise. Figure 3.13 shows a PGA370 socket.

FIGURE 3.13
Microprocessor Socket PGA370 for some versions of the Celeron microprocessor.

As this is written, Cyrix was reportedly designing its next generation of microprocessors to use the PGA370 socket design, moving up from the Super 7 design. The company cites the superiority of the 370-pin socket for chips with integral secondary caches, which Cyrix will likely adopt. Because of cross-licensing agreements between Intel and Cyrix-parent National Semiconductor, the company is entitled to use the design for its products.

The shift from sockets to slots with the Pentium II occurred for two primary reasons. The new ranges of microprocessors proved much more complex and large, thus requiring larger packages and providing the physical foundation for a new (and less expensive) type of connector. In addition, the choice of a new connector with a proprietary design gives Intel an additional tool in its competition with other chip makers. Intel has protected its slot designs with patents, leading Advanced Micro Devices to look elsewhere for slots for its next-generation processors.

The new slots take the form of dual inline edge connectors, the same type of printed circuit board connectors used in expansion slots. Rather than pins, the male connector (the microprocessor end) of the slot design uses pads on a printed circuit board substrate much like ISA or PCI boards. Because of the number of connections required and the limited available space, however, the pads of the slot connectors are interleaved, squeezing them about 50 percent tighter together.

The first of these was *Slot 1*, designed for the Pentium II and used by it as well as the similar Celeron and Pentium III chips. With the introduction of the Pentium III, Intel renamed Slot 1 as SC242.

Because the Pentium II Xeon has different interconnection needs because of its newer cache and multiprocessor support designs, Intel created a second slot type for it, *Slot 2*, with 330 contacts.

Although the Intel slots work like edge connectors, they are more delicate than expansion boards. Their specifications call for only 50 removal/insertion cycles. The electronics of the microprocessor are not guaranteed to function after hot-swapping. In other words, you should always switch off the power to a PC before removing or inserting a microprocessor cartridge into an Intel-style slot.

Although compatible chip makers have stuck with the Socket 7 design in the face of Slots 1 and 2, the limitations of that socket put severe constraints on the design of new microprocessors. For its next generation of microprocessors, the K7 series, AMD has elected to use a microprocessor slot. For various reasons, including patents on the Intel design, AMD has opted for an alternate design that Digital Equipment (DEC, now part of Compaq) designed for its Alpha series of microprocessors and called the *Alpha EV6 bus*. Although the same design is shared by two companies, it remains private and proprietary, controlled by Compaq.

History

The history of the microprocessor can be summed up in quoting Moore's Law, a bit of dogma propounded by Gordon Moore, long-time chairman of Intel Corporation: Microprocessor power doubles every 18 months. Indeed, since the inception of the microprocessor concept, processing power has continually increased at about the rate Moore claimed; over the 18-year history of the PC, the predicted power increase is a factor of 4,096, a reasonable reflection of the difference between the 8088 microprocessor of the original PC and a Pentium III. (By my calculation, Moore was off by only about 10 percent on the optimistic side.)

The story of the microprocessor is hardly so simple, however. Achieving the dramatic increase in processor power required a confluence of factors, including innovative designs, great technical advances, and the motivation of constant competitive pressure.

Design innovations started with the basics. With each new generation of microprocessor, manufacturers increased the number and size of its registers, broadening the data and address buses to match. When that strategy stalled, they moved to superscalar designs with multiple pipelines. Inevitably, each new microprocessor was more complex than the previous one as transistor counts grew from thousands into the millions, from 2,300 in the first microprocessor to 7,500,000 in current models.

Improvements in semiconductor fabrication technology made the increasing complexity of modern microprocessor designs both practical and affordable. In the three decades since the introduction of the first microprocessor, the linear dimensions of semiconductor circuits have decreased to one fiftieth their original size, from 10 micron design rules to 0.18 micron—which means microprocessor makers can squeeze 2,500 transistors where only one fit originally. This size reduction also facilitates higher speeds. Today's microprocessors run nearly 5,000 times faster than the first chip out of the Intel foundry, 500MHz in comparison to the 108KHz of the first chip.

Competition drives the need for speed. Chip makers struggle to make their products the most desirable by giving the most processor power—or the most power for the money. Staying ahead—or just keeping up—requires constant innovation.

That competition has shifted through the three decades of microprocessor evolution. At first, chip makers struggled to prove the superiority of their individual architectures. As the PC flourished, the competition shifted to a rivalry between almost identical and interchangeable products. With the advent of the Pentium and Intel's abandonment of its policy of licensing other chip makers, the competition has swung back to architectural rivalries again.

For the sake of brevity and forestry, this book puts early microprocessors in historical perspective and discusses only current chips in detail. You'll find more detail about chips no longer useful in modern computers in Appendix G, "Microprocessors of the Past."

Industry Competition

Thanks to the ascendance of the PC, Intel Corporation is now the largest maker of microprocessors and the largest independent maker of semiconductors in the world. Depending on your viewpoint, you could credit its dominance of the industry to hard work, astute planning, corporate predation, or cosmic coincidence. But the root of the success is undeniable. Credit for the invention of the microprocessor goes to Intel.

Years of research and development go into the design of every integrated circuit, and microprocessors are among the most complicated (and expensive to design) of ICs. But most of the design and development work can be avoided by simply copying someone else's effort by reverse-engineering, deducing the design from the product. More reputable firms start with the specifications of the chip and its instructions set and design from the ground up a chip that mimics the function of the original. Less reputable sources may merely x-ray a chip to determine the layout of the various silicon layers. To prevent other companies from copying their chip designs, most makers of integrated circuits refuse to disclose any of the inner workings of their products. Moreover, they use patents, copyrights, and secrecy to prevent predatory copying.

On the other hand, when a design is unproved and a company struggling, chip makers will sometimes license other makers to use the masks they have designed to lay down the silicon circuitry of a chip to provide a second source for a product. This licensing or "second-sourcing" earns the original designer a royalty and, often, greater acceptance of the chip because buyers of integrated circuits look askance at any product with a single source of supply. Second sources insulate against labor or manufacturing troubles and can sometimes reduce costs through competition.

Before the success of the PC was proven, Intel licensed its designs to other chip makers. Both the 8086 family and 286 families were offered by second sources. Starting with the 386 series, however, Intel has staunchly refused to license other chip makers, with the exception of IBM. With its fifth-generation designs, Intel stopped licensing even IBM (which, at the time, had become an important Intel competitor with its PowerPC chips, jointly developed with Motorola).

The success of Intel microprocessors has attracted a number of companies to do their best to copy Intel's designs while skirting the company's legal protections. Today, three major cloners (AMD, Cyrix, and IDT) offer fifth- and sixth-generation products. Other manufacturers are reputedly working on their own designs.

Whether licensed or cloned, a number of Intel-compatible chips have found their way to market in various processor generations. Table 3.3 summarizes the essential characteristics of some of the earlier Intel-compatible microprocessors. Current products are discussed in depth later.

TABLE 3.3   Modern Pre-Pentium Intel-Compatible Microprocessors

Chip	Manufacturer	Data Bus Width	Address Bus Width	Internal Clock	Integral Cache	Integral FPU
386SX	Intel	16	24	1x	No	No
	AMD	16	24	1x	No	No
38600SX	C&T	16	24	1x	No	No
386SLC	IBM	16	24	1x	8KB	No
38605SX	C&T	16	24	1x	0.5KB	No
386DX	Intel	32	32	1x	No	No
	AMD	32	32	1x	No	No
38600DX	C&T	32	32	1x	No	No
38605DX	C&T	32	32	1x	0.5KB	No
486SL	Intel	32	32	1x	8KB	Yes
486SLC	Cyrix	16	24	1x	1KB	No
486SLC/E	TI	16	24	1x	1KB	No
486SLC2	IBM	32	32	2x	16KB	No
486SX	Intel	32	32	1x	8KB	No
	AMD	32	32	1x	8KB	No
486SXLV	AMD	32	32	1x	8KB	No
486SX2	Intel	32	32	2x	8KB	No
486DLC	Cyrix	32	32	1x	1KB	No
486DLC/E	TI	32	32	1x	1KB	No
486DX	Intel	32	32	1x	8KB	Yes
	AMD	32	32	1x	8KB	Yes
486DXLV	AMD	32	32	1x	8KB	Yes
486DX2	Intel	32	32	2x	8KB	Yes
486DX4	Intel	32	32	3x	16KB	Yes

Manufacturer Chip	Bus Bus	Data Clock Width	Address Width	Integral Internal	Cache	Integral FPU
486BL	IBM	32	32	3x	16KB	No
5x86	Cyrix/IBM	32	32	3x	16KB	Yes
5x86	AMD	32	32	4x	16KB	Yes

Designing and manufacturing microprocessors is an expensive business. Only a handful of companies have chosen to develop Intel-compatible microprocessors. None have come close to Intel's success, although a few rate as survivors. The most notable of these competitors include the following.

Advanced Micro Devices

AMD was founded in 1969 and first got into the microprocessor business in 1975 when it released a reversed-engineered version of the Intel 8080 chip. Although that product put AMD and Intel into direct competition, the two companies entered into a patent cross-licensing agreement in 1977 so that each could take advantage of the other's designs, giving each company a better chance of success in the then-unproved microprocessor market. The two companies became more closely involved when IBM demanded a second source for Intel's 8088 microprocessor before they would put the chip into its first PCs. IBM wasn't sure that Intel would stay in business and was afraid to build a product with the possibility of not having a chip supplier. Consequently, Intel allowed AMD to second-source the 8088. For much the same reason of giving microprocessor purchasers a greater sense of security, Intel also granted AMD the right to make its 286.

By the time the 386 had been rolled out, however, Intel had a secure place in the semiconductor industry, and the company figured it could cash in on a monopoly on the 386. Consequently, it never directly granted AMD the right to make the 386.

AMD nevertheless developed its own version of the 386 chip using its own hardware design and Intel's microcode. The circuit design underlying the AMD chips is slightly more efficient and uses less power than the Intel chips. Intel promptly sued. According to AMD, contracts between the two companies enabled AMD to use all of Intel's designs and patents through 1995, a right for which AMD paid Intel approximately $350,000 (about 35 percent of its profits in the year the agreement was signed). In the dispute, Intel claimed the 1975 agreement gave AMD the right only to copy Intel's microcode, not to distribute it. (Intel had also claimed the designation "386" as a trademark, but the numbers were ruled generic on March 1, 1991, enabling AMD and other companies to call their clone chips 386s.) Finally, on February 24, 1992, an arbitrator awarded AMD the right to use Intel's 386 microcode without royalty or disputes, but AMD got no more rights to Intel's technology. Recent developments in the case have turned the matter more in Intel's favor.

Chips and Technologies

First and foremost a designer of chipsets for PC motherboards, Chips & Technologies elected to expand its product line by entering the microprocessor market in 1991 with its F8680 chip. Shortly thereafter, it introduced a line of third-generation processors of its own design. None of these proved successful, and C&T left the microprocessor business in 1992. It continued to develop motherboard chipsets until 1997 when the company was acquired by Intel Corporation into which it has been integrated as the Graphics Component Division (GCD).

Cyrix Corporation

Cyrix Corporation was founded with the intention of developing compatible chips. It entered the market with several series of math coprocessors compatible with Intel's third-generation microprocessors. When Intel shifted to integral floating-point units, Cyrix shifted to designing Intel-compatible microprocessors using its own core logic.

Cyrix was a design and marketing organization. It did not have its own fabrication facilities and instead contracted with other companies—notably IBM and Texas Instruments—to manufacture microprocessors to its specifications. In November 1997, the company was acquired by National Semiconductor as a wholly owned subsidiary.

IBM

The corporate history begins on June 15, 1911 when the company was first incorporated at the Computing-Tabulating-Recording Company through the merger of the Tabulating Machine Company with the Computing Scale Company of America and International Time Recording Company. The company's roots stretch back to 1890 when German immigrant Herman Hollerith won a competition to win a Census Department contract for tabulating the census data using punch cards with an electrical sensor, leading to Hollerith forming the Tabulating Machine Company in 1896. In 1914, the merged company hired Thomas J. Watson as general manager. He became its president within the year.

In 1924, the company name was changed to International Business Machines. It entered the computer market in 1952 with a machine it called the "Defense Calculator." Later renamed the 701, the machine proved capable of about 2,200 multiplications per second. From there, it went on to be the world's largest computer manufacturer. Along the way, it developed its own microprocessors for some of the machines it sold. When it introduced the Personal Computer upon which today's PC industry is based in August 1981, it chose to use Intel microprocessors. It has made Intel-compatible microprocessors using Intel's designs under license and using its own designs. In addition, it co-developed the PowerPC line of processors used by Apple Power Macintosh computers. For a period, IBM produced microprocessors for Cyrix in its foundry and sold some chips designed by Cyrix under the IBM name.

IDT/Centaur

Centaur Technology Inc. was founded in 1995 by IBM fellow Glenn Henry in Austin, Texas, and introduced its first Intel-compatible microprocessor, the WinChip C6, in May 1997. Centaur is now a wholly owned subsidiary of Integrated Device Technology (IDT), a Santa Clara company that designs and manufactures a variety of semiconductor products, including memory and microprocessor chips. More information on both companies and their products appears on the www.idt.com and www.winchip.com Web sites.

Texas Instruments

Texas Instruments began business in the 1930s as Geophysical Service, Inc., which provided geological data to aid Texas wildcatters in finding oil. Its official date of incorporation was December 23, 1938. In 1939, it changed its name to Coronado Corporation, with GSI becoming a division of the new parent company. In 1941, Coronado sold GSI to a group of insiders, and the company began to make electronic gear during World War II. In 1951, the company changed its name again, to Texas Instruments, and again made GSI a subsidiary.

As Texas Instruments, the company was first to commercially produce silicon transistors, and in 1958, one of its engineers, Jack Kilby, was credited as co-inventor of the integrated circuit. TI developed its own line of highly regarded microprocessors and small computers, thought by many to be more powerful than those available at the time from Intel. Unfortunately, TI's computers did not win the business acceptance of the IBM PC. For a few years, Texas Instruments marketed chips derived from Cyrix designs as its own. Under contract, Texas Instruments also fabricated chips for Cyrix in its foundries.

TI remains a major semiconductor manufacturer and technology developer.

Microprocessor Generations

Many writers divide up microprocessors and their technology by generations, roughly demarcated by chip model numbers. The general consensus is that the current generation is the sixth, although some people and organizations see an additional generation among modern microprocessors.

During the first decade of personal computing, microprocessor generations were of great importance. The generation level of a chip determined what software it could run; an old chip couldn't handle the newest software. Since the introduction of Intel's third generation of PC microprocessors, however, the basic microprocessor features required by today's software have been locked in place if by nothing else but the pressures of the industry.

Speed is now the thing that determines whether a given chip can handle a specific program or operating system. Although the earliest third-generation Intel processor could run Windows 2000, you wouldn't want to prove it. Performance would be so slow you might wait all day for the operating system to simply boot up.

Generational differences between processors now mark how the chips achieve their ever-higher levels of performance. Each ensuing generation has brought at least one new technology or concept that has notched up performance, typically from 50 to 100 percent over the previous generation processor at the same clock speed. Table 3.4 lists the distinguishing characteristics of the various generations of Intel microprocessors.

Intel's naming system complicates attempts at drawing lines between microprocessor generations. Clearly Intel believed that the Pentium was a fifth-generation processor. The concept is inherent in the name. As that name became a valuable trademark, however, Intel was loathe to discard it for the simple reason of releasing a new generation of microprocessors; hence, we have the Pentium II and the Pentium III.

The real guidance is the design of the core logic. The Pentium Pro marks Intel's move to a newer core design, markedly different from the Pentium. In fact, Intel developed the Pentium Pro under the code name P6. The Pentium II and Pentium III have the same core, so by rights all three—Pro, II, and III—are sixth-generation chips.

Generational lines become fuzzier still when considering manufacturers competing with Intel. Throughout the early generations, their products paralleled those made by Intel; they were essentially identical because of licensing or reverse engineering. After the fourth generation, however, competing manufacturers veered off in their own directions, often adding new technologies before Intel. Competitors started building their chips from RISC cores a generation before Intel. AMD added extended 3D graphics to its chip's command sets before Intel released the Pentium III. The generational lines have been so useful in describing the chip industry, however, that most writers follow the Intel generation timeline and peg competing chips to it based on their match with the performance of Intel products. This book follows that arbitrary convention.

TABLE 3.4 Intel Microprocessor Time Line

Chip	Intro Date	MIPS (est.)	Int. Bus width	Ext. Bus Width	Transistors	Design Rules	Memory	Ext. Clock	Int. Clock	Int. FPU?
4004	15 Nov 71	0.06	4	4	2300	10.0	640 bytes	0.108	0.108	No
8008	Apr 72	0.06	8	8	3500	10.0	16KB	0.2	0.2	No
8080	Apr 74	0.64	8	8	6000	6.0	64KB	2	2	No
8085	Mar 76	0.37	8	8	6500	3.0	64KB	5	5	No
8086	Jun 78	0.33	16	16	29,000	3.0	1MB	5	5	No
		0.66	16	16	29,000	3.0	1MB	8	8	No
		0.75	16	16	29,000	3.0	1MB	10	10	No
8088	Jun 79	0.33	16	8	29,000	3.0	1MB	5	5	No
		0.75	16	8	29,000	3.0	1MB	8	8	No
80286	Feb 82	1.2	16	16	134,000	1.5	16MB	8	8	No
		1.5	16	16	134,000	1.5	16MB	10	10	No
		1.66	16	16	134,000	1.5	16MB	12	12	No
386DX	Oct 85	5.5	32	32	275,000	1.5	4GB	16	16	No
	Feb 87	6.5	32	32	275,000	1.5	4GB	20	20	No
	Apr 88	8.5	3290	32	275,000	1.5	4GB	25	25	No
	Apr 89	11.4	32	32	275,000	1.5	4GB	33	33	No

continues

TABLE 3.4   Continued

Chip	Intro Date	MIPS (est.)	Int. Bus width	Ext. Bus Width	Transistors	Design Rules	Memory	Ext. Clock	Int. Clock	Int. FPU?
386SX	Jun 88	2.5	32	16	275,000	1.5	4GB	16	16	No
	Jan 89	2.5	32	16	275,000	1.5	4GB	20	20	No
		2.7	32	16	275,000	1.5	4GB	25	25	No
	Oct 92	2.9	32	16	275,000	1.5	4GB	33	33	No
386SL	Oct 90	4.2	32	16	855,000	1.0	32MB	20	20	No
	Sep 91	5.3	32	16	855,000	1.0	32MB	25	25	No
486DX	Apr 89	20	32	32	1,200,000	1.0	4GB	25	25	Yes
	May 90	27	32	32	1,200,000	1.0	4GB	33	33	Yes
	Jun 91	41	32	32	1,200,000	0.8	4GB	50	50	Yes
486SX	Sep 91	13	32	32	1,185,000	1.0	4GB	16	16	No
	Sep 91	16.5	32	32	1,185,000	1.0	4GB	20	20	No
	Sep 91	20	32	32	1,185,000	1.0	4GB	25	25	No
	Sep 92	27	32	32	900,000	0.8	4GB	33	33	No
486DX2	Mar 92	41	32	32	1,200,000	0.8	4GB	25	50	Yes
	Aug 92	54	32	32	1,200,000	0.8	4GB	33	66	Yes
486SL	Nov 92	15.4	32	32	1,400,000	0.8	64MB	20	20	Yes
		19	32	32	1,400,000	0.8	64MB	25	25	Yes
		25	32	32	1,400,000	0.8	64MB	33	33	Yes
486DX4	Mar 94	53	32	32	1,600,000	0.6	4GB	25	75	Yes
		70	32	32	1,600,000	0.6	4GB	33	100	Yes

Chip	Intro Date	MIPS (est.)	Int. Bus width	Ext. Bus Width	Transistors	Design Rules	Memory	Ext. Clock	Int. Clock	Int. FPU?
Pentium P5	Mar 93	100	64	32	3,100,000	0.8	4GB	60	60	Yes
		112	64	32	3,100,000	0.8	4GB	66	66	Yes
	Oct 94	126	64	32	3,200,000	0.6	4GB	50	75	Yes
Pentium P54C	Mar 94	150	64	32	3,200,000	0.6	4GB	60	90	Yes
		166	64	32	3,200,000	0.6	4GB	66	100	Yes
	Mar 95	203	64	32	3,200,000	0.6	4GB	60	120	Yes
	Jun 95	219	64	32	3,300,000	0.35	4GB	66	133	Yes
	Jan 96	255	64	32	3,300,000	0.35	4GB	60	150	Yes
		278	64	32	3,300,000	0.35	4GB	66	166	Yes
	Jun 96	336	64	32	3,300,000	0.35	4GB	66	200	Yes
Pentium P55C	Jan 97	278	64	32	4,500,000	0.35	4GB	661	66	MMX
	Jan 97	336	64	32	4,500,000	0.35	4GB	66	200	MMX
Pentium Pro	Nov 95	337	64	32	5,500,000	0.6	64GB		60	150	Yes
		373	64	32	5,500,000	0.35	64GB	66	166	Yes
		404	64	32	5,500,000	0.35	64GB	60	180	Yes
		450	64	32	5,500,000	0.35	64GB	66	200	Yes

Processors Before the PC

No matter the designation or origin, all microprocessors in today's PCs share a unique characteristic and heritage. All are direct descendents of the very first microprocessor, the Intel 4004. The instruction set used by all current PC microprocessors is rooted in the instructions selected for the 4004, with enough elaboration over the years that you'd never suspect the link to today's Pentiums without a history lesson.

This view of microprocessors is necessarily historic. Today's fastest chips must abide by design decisions made more than a quarter century ago. The history of Intel microprocessors has been one of adding new features, each of which is a combination Band-Aid and bridge: a Band-Aid to patch problems inherent in the historic design and a bridge between that history and the latest (and most powerful) microprocessor design ideals. The steady progress in the power of Intel microprocessors is a testament to the tremendous resources Intel has devoted to the development of its products.

The history of the microprocessor stretches back to a 1969 request to Intel by a now-defunct Japanese calculator company, Busicom. The original plan was to build a series of calculators, each one different and each requiring a custom integrated circuit. Using conventional IC technology, the project would have required the design of 12 different chips. The small volumes of each design would have made development costs prohibitive.

Intel engineer Mercian E. (Ted) Hoff had a better idea, one that could slash the necessary design work. Instead of a collection of individually tailored circuits, he envisioned creating one general-purpose device that would satisfy the needs of all the calculators. His approach worked. The result was the first general-purpose microprocessor, the Intel 4004.

The chip was a success. Not only did it usher in the age of the low-cost calculator, but it also gave designers a single solid-state programmable device for the first time. Instead of designing the digital decision-making circuits in products from scratch, developers could buy an off-the-shelf component and tailor it to their needs simply by writing the appropriate program.

The 4004 was first introduced to the marketplace in 1971. As might be deduced from its manufacturer's designation 4004, this ground-breaking chip had registers capable of handling four bits at a time through a four-bit bus. The emergence of the eight-bit byte as the standard measure of digital data resulted in it being chosen as the register size of the next generation of microprocessor, Intel's 8008 introduced in 1972.

Intel continued development (as did other integrated circuit manufacturers) and, in 1974, created a rather more drastic revision, the 8080. Unlike the 8008, it was planned from the start for byte-size data. Intel gave the 8080 a richer command set, one that embraced all the commands of the 8008 but went further. This set a pattern for Intel microprocessors: Every increase in power and range of command set enlarged on what had gone before rather than replace it, assuring backward compatibility (at least to some degree) of the software.

First-Generation Processors

Although PC history begins in 1981, the chips that armed the revolution date back to 1978. In that year, Intel released the 8086, the first of the first generation of PC microprocessors. The design was a marked improvement over earlier chips. Intel doubled the size of the registers in its 8080 to create a chip with 16-bit registers and about 10 times the performance. The 16-bit design carried through completely, also doubling the size of the data bus of earlier chips to 16 bits to move information in and out twice as fast.

In addition, Intel broadened the address bus from 16-bit to 20-bits to allow the 8086 to directly address up to one megabyte of RAM. Intel divided this memory into 64KB segments to make programming and the transition to the new chip easier. A single 16-bit register could address any byte in a given segment. Another, separate register indicated which of the segments that address was in.

A year after the introduction of the 8086, Intel introduced the 8088. The new chip was identical to the 8086 in every way—16-bit registers, 20 address lines, the same command set—except one. Its data bus was reduced to 8 bits, enabling the 8088 to exploit readily available 8-bit support hardware. At that, the 8088 broke no new ground and should have been little more than a footnote in the history of the microprocessor. However, its compromised design that mated 16-bit power with cheap 8-bit support chips made the 8088 IBM's choice for its first Personal Computer. With that, the 8088 entered history as the second most important product in the development of the microprocessor after the ground-breaking 4004.

Both the 8086 and 8088 used NMOS (N-channel Metal Oxide Semiconductor) circuitry, an early fabrication technique that yielded fast but power-hungry chips. Intel later introduced lower-power versions crafted from CMOS (Complementary Metal Oxide Semiconductor) silicon as the Intel 80C86 and 80C88. (All modern microprocessors use refinements on CMOS technology.) Later, the company integrated most of the support circuitry needed for building a small computer along with the core logic of the 8086 and 8088 to make the 80186 and 80188 chips, rounding out the first generation.

Second-Generation Processors

Following the dictate of Moore's Law, Intel's engineers were hard at work for a new, more powerful microprocessor even as the 8088 was released onto the market. This designated successor was to be the 80286, the first and only major chip of the second generation. With several times the speed and 16 times more addressable memory than its predecessors, the 80286 was destined for great things. Inherent in its design was the capability of multitasking with new instructions for managing tasks and a new operating mode, protected mode, that made its full 16MB of memory fodder for advanced operating systems. Despite all that going for it, the most memorable aspect of the 80286 is the epithet bestowed on it by the PC industry, "brain dead."

Missing from Intel's design equation for the 80286 was just one thing, consideration of DOS, the operating system that drove the PC marketplace. DOS could not take advantage of all the power of the new chip. It was restricted to real mode and its one megabyte of RAM. In retrospect, it's probably more charitable to call DOS "brain dead" and the 80286 misunderstood, but such judgment will probably cheer only the 80286 developers and their mothers. In fact, the 80286 proved to be the dominant microprocessor in PCs for about three years, from 1984 to 1987, actually somewhat longer than its "brain alive" successor, the 386.

Although introduced in 1982, the world only took notice of the 80286 in 1984 with the introduction of IBM's Personal Computer AT. With a full 16-bit data bus with 16-bit internal registers, the chip powered the AT to the top of the market and established its design as an industry standard that would survive for two more microprocessor generations. Initially released running at 6MHz, PCs powered by the 80286 quickly climbed to 8MHz and then 10MHz. Versions operating at 12.5, 16, 20, and ultimately 24MHz were eventually marketed.

Although the 80286 was designed by Intel, the company licensed the design to several manufacturers including AMD, Harris Semiconductor, IBM, and Siemens. All of these chips were designated 286 in one way or another and used the same Intel design for their core logic. Except for clock speed, they are interchangeable.

The second generation dead-ended with the 80286 because of its mismatch with DOS. Although it launched millions of PCs and served well in other applications, few people lamented the passing of the 80286.

Third-Generation Processors

As with most human endeavors, getting the design of the microprocessor for today's PCs took three tries to get right. Intel hit upon the gold that made the company's fortune and serves at the foundation for all microprocessors used in today's Windows-based systems with the third generation, the 386. No single factor made this third try magical. With the combination, however, Intel developed a winner.

Part of the reason for the success of the 386 generation is the power of hindsight. Intel's engineers got a good look at what was wrong with the 286 generation. They could see the importance that the PC's primeval operating system had in the computer industry, so they designed to it instead of to some vaguely conceived successor. In addition, they gave the 386 power, enough to make the chip a fearsome competitor.

The actual innovations of the third generation take the form of two distinguishing features: a full 32-bit design for both data and addressing and the new virtual 8086 mode. The first gave the third generation unprecedented power. The second made that power useful.

The principal chip of the third generation was the 386, later renamed the 386DX to distinguish it from Intel's entry-level model, the 386SX, identical except for an external 16-bit data bus. Internally, the 386SX incorporated 32-bit registers and full 32-bit addressing. The origin of the D/S nomenclature is easily explained. The external bus of the 386DX handled double words (32 bits); that of the 386SX, single words (16 bits).

At the time Intel introduced the 386DX, neither its 32-bit power nor its 4GB address range mattered much to the PC marketplace. All existing PC software used 16-bit code. Moreover, memory was expensive, and it was a rare machine that came equipped with more than a megabyte. The stodgy second generation was more than sufficient on both counts. Consequently, the 386 didn't find wide application in PCs until 1987 despite its original introduction in 1985. Once ensconced in PCs and operating system software that caught up to it, however, the 386 took off.

Virtual 8086 mode made the difference. New operating systems used the new mode to run multiple DOS applications simultaneously. The oft-promised multitasking systems became reality. Ordinary second-generation processors could not handle it, but even the lowly 386SX chip could. Virtual 8086 mode marked the great divide: Microprocessors with it could run all of the latest software. Older chips that lacked it were stuck struggling along with DOS. The microprocessor in your PC became a vital consideration in buying applications, and the 386 family was the top choice.

Intel knew it had a winner and severely restricted its licensing of the 386 design. IBM (Intel's biggest customer at the time) got a license only by promising not to sell chips. It could only market the 386-based microprocessors it built inside complete PCs or on fully assembled motherboards. AMD won its license to duplicate the 386 in court based on technology-sharing agreements with Intel dating before even the 80286 had been announced. Another company, Chip & Technologies, reverse-engineered the 386 to build clones, but these were introduced too late—well after Intel advanced to its fourth generation of chips—to see much market success.

For its own part, Intel turned the 386 into a full family of microprocessors: the full-power 386DX, the economy model 386SX (introduced in 1988), and the low-power, highly integrated portable chip, the 386SL (introduced in 1990).

Fourth-Generation Processors

In contrast to the transitions between previous generations of Intel's PC microprocessors, the move to the fourth generation was marked by no fundamental operational differences: no new modes. The 386 design had proven itself and had become the foundation for a multi-billion dollar software industry. The one area for improvement was performance, and even here, Intel's microprocessor technology was pushing ahead of the rest of the PC industry. The chips had already passed the performance level of many other components used in building computers.

In response to this situation, Intel added to the new generation three features that could boost processing speed by working *around* handicaps in external circuitry. These innovations included an integral level-one cache that helped compensate for slow memory systems, pipelining within the microprocessor to get more processing power from low clock speeds, and an integral floating-point unit that eliminated the handicap of an external connection. As this generation matured, Intel added one further refinement that let the microprocessor race ahead of laggardly support circuits—splitting the chip so that its core logic and external bus interface could operate at different speeds.

Intel introduced the first of this new generation in 1989 in the form of a chip then designated 80486, continuing with its traditional nomenclature. When the company added other models derived from this basic design, it renamed the then-flagship chip the 486DX and distinguished lower-priced models by substituting the -SX suffix and low-power designs for portable computers using the -SL designation as it had with the third generation. Other manufacturers followed suit, using the 486 designation for their similar products and often the D/S indicators for top-of-the-line and economy models.

In the 486 family, however, the D/S split does not distinguish the width of the data bus. The designations had become disconnected from their origins. In the 486 family, Intel economized on the SX version by eliminating the integral floating-point unit. The savings from this strategy can be substantial; without the floating-point circuitry, the 486SX required only about half the silicon of the full-fledged chip, making it cheaper to make. In the first runs of 486SX, however, the difference was more marketing. The SX chips were identical to the DX chips except that their floating-point circuitry was either defective or deliberately disabled to make a less capable processor.

As far as hardware basics are concerned, the 486 series retained the principal features of the earlier generation of processors. Chips in both the third and fourth generations have three operating modes (real, protected, and virtual 8086), full 32-bit registers, and a 32-bit address bus enabling up to 4GB of memory to be directly addressed. Both support virtual memory that extends their addressing to 64TB. Both have built-in memory management units that can remap memory in 4KB pages.

But the hardware of the 486 also differs substantially from the 386 (or any previous Intel microprocessor). The pipelining in the core logic allowed the chip to work on parts of several instructions at the same time. At times, the 486 could carry out one instruction every clock cycle. Tighter silicon design rules (smaller details etched into the actual silicon that makes up the chip) gave the 486 more speed potential than preceding chips. The small but robust 8KB integral primary cache helped the 486 work around the memory wait states that plagued faster 386-based PCs.

The streamlined hardware design (particularly pipelining) meant that the 486-level microprocessors could think faster than 386 chips when the two operated at the same clock speed. On most applications, the 486 proved about twice as fast as a 386 at the same clock rate, so a 20MHz 486 delivered about the same program throughput as a 40MHz 386.

By 1992, Intel's sub-micron fabrication technology had developed more speed potential than could be exploited at practical external bus speeds. Chips could run faster than then-current (and affordable) circuit designs. Intel's astute response to this situation was to break the lock between the bus speed and core logic speed. Using an internal multiplier, Intel designed the core logic to operate at twice, then at three times, the external bus speed in the DX2 (introduced in 1992) and DX4 (introduced in 1994) series of 486 microprocessors.

These innovations aside, the 486 generation rated as simply an improved 386. The entire 486 series ran all 386 software. Although the 486 could be distinguished from the 386 by one flag, one exception, two page-table entry bits, six instructions, and nine control-register bits, few consumer-level programs exploited these features. The commands and controls of the 486 represent nothing more than a superset of the 386; that is, the 486 does everything the 386 does and a little more.

Also in 1992, Intel introduced its portable 486 alternative, an altogether formidable chip called the 486SL. Unlike the 386SL (which was essentially a 386SX engineered for power saving), the 486SL doesn't slight on performance. Moreover, it integrates a substantial number of system functions into its silicon.

Instead of special low-power microprocessors for portable applications, other chip makers elected to make their entire product lines more energy frugal. In 1993, Intel changed directions and followed suit, announcing that it would cease further development of the 486SL line and instead move its features into the main 486 series. The process involved a gradual phase-in that produced what Intel calls its SL Enhanced Intel 486 Microprocessor Family. The SL-enhanced family included equivalents to the 486DX, 486DX2, 486SX, and 486SX2 chips.

Intel had become so successful making microprocessors that other companies tried to elbow their way onto the market to share the wealth.

AMD, by doggedly fighting Intel through the courts to gain rights to Intel's microcode, was able to precisely duplicate the 486. AMD actually improved on the Intel design and eked more speed from its 486 line, getting 40MHz from its plain 486DX, where Intel topped out at 33MHz. AMD kept the same percentage edge with clock-doubling and clock-tripling chips (all the way to 120MHz core speed in its top-of-the-line chip).

IBM, working with a license like that for the 386, derived two chips from the basic Intel design. IBM's 486SLC2 took the venerable 386SX to the extreme, giving it the 486 command set and integral cache and pushing its performance into 486 territory despite retaining the 16-bit data bus of the 386SX. By expanding the core logic and external bus to 32 bits, IBM created its Blue Lightning, sometimes termed the 486BL. Neither IBM chip included an integral floating-point unit.

Cyrix Corporation started making microprocessors from its own designs in the fourth generation, starting with OEM products that required new motherboards, then with 486-level chips that used the same pin-outs as the Intel 386 line, and then those that fit 486 sockets. Cyrix developed them all with its own core logic design. Although early chips were handicapped by a small, 1KB integral cache, later chips had 8KB caches and could hold their own with early fifth-generation chips.

Texas Instruments also entered the 486 fray with both DX and SX clones, neither of which achieved notable market share.

When Intel jumped to its fifth generation, its competitors could not keep up. Instead, they developed new fourth-generation processors that they gave fifth-generation names. AMD developed its own $Am5_x86$, a 486-based design fully able to keep up with Intel's first fifth-generation chips. Despite aggressive pricing, the $Am5_x86$ did not find great market acceptance.

Cyrix developed a different 5x86, also a fourth-generation chip, although its core logic was based on a RISC design that evolved into Cyrix's fifth generation. IBM also offered a chip wearing the same 5x86 designation. Except for the label, it was identical to the Cyrix product.

Fifth-Generation Processors

Separating the first four generations of PC microprocessors from those powering new PCs today is a huge technological advance—superscalar architecture. All of the current microprocessors from Intel have multiple pipelines enhanced with other features borrowed from the RISC design. In fact, all of the latest chips from all PC microprocessor manufacturers *are* RISC chips with internal translators that understand the old Intel architecture command set. The sole holdout that uses the Intel CISC command set in its native mode is the Cyrix (and IBM) 6x86 series, including the M II.

Although RISC processors started the trend, the Intel Pentium was the first microprocessor to put superscalar technology inside the PC.

All current Intel chips have "Pentium" somewhere in their official names; even the top-of-the-line Xeon is officially the Pentium II Xeon. The names serve only to obscure the differences between the chips. Its function is to give a brand identity to Intel's products in that the name is an Intel trademark.

Even plain Pentium chips are not all the same. Intel has released three distinct varieties of Pentium. The most useful way to distinguish them is by code name. The original Pentium was termed the P5 during development. It was followed by the P54. The Pentium II shows a similar development hierarchy. The original Pentium II was code-named Klamath. An improved version, Deschutes, is now the dominant chip in the line.

What exactly is Pentium-level performance or a Pentium-compatible chip is hard to define, especially for chip makers. Those other than Intel want you to believe that any microprocessor quicker than the slowest Pentium fits the bill. Consequently, both AMD and Cyrix class two chips in the Pentium category, calling them "fifth generation" and giving them designations beginning with the number "5," even though they are little more than fast 486 clones. Similarly, these companies move the sixth generation—which means little more than chips with the number "6" in their designations—down to a level meaning something that works better than their own ordinary Pentium clones. These sixth-generation chips are not true clones of the Pentium Pro but rather improved basic Pentiums—which is not necessarily bad. The latest of these, the AMD K6 and Cyrix M II, include MMX abilities, putting them on par with the capabilities if not performance of Intel's own offerings.

If there is a general rule, it is that a fifth-level chip will deliver performance about on par with a Pentium with the same megahertz speed rating. Although some manufacturers (for example, AMD and NexGen) claimed their chips to be faster than the basic Pentium, they adjusted their speed ratings to reflect the equivalent Pentium performance instead of the actual operating rate of the microprocessor. You can expect chips with the sixth-level designation to be faster than Pentiums with the same rating.

Sixth-Generation Processors

The Pentium Pro was the first sixth-generation PC microprocessor. It featured a radically new core logic design, termed "P6" during development, that was based on a RISC design. The more noticeable difference, however, was greater integration. With the Pentium Pro, Intel integrated not only the primary but also the secondary cache as part of the microprocessor. In addition, Intel expanded the addressing of its sixth generation, enabling the new chips to directly reach to 64GB of RAM. All current Intel sixth-generation processors—the Pentium Pro, Pentium II, Celeron, Xeon, and Pentium III—share these characteristics.

Current Products

Except for a few notebook computers, any new PC will come equipped with a sixth-generation microprocessor—a Celeron, Pentium II, Pentium III, or Xeon chip from Intel or a chip from another manufacturer with similar performance (for example, AMD K6-3 or Cyrix M II).

Intel

Because Intel has invested heavily in developing brand recognition for its Pentium trademark, all current Intel PC microprocessors wear that name despite using two different generations of core logic. The Pentium, Pentium with MMX Technology, and mobile and OverDrive variations of these chips fit into the fifth generation of Intel processors. The Pentium Pro, Pentium II, and Pentium III all share essentially the same sixth-generation core logic.

Intel Pentium

In March 1993, Intel introduced its first superscalar microprocessor. At the time, the computer industry expected Intel to continue its naming tradition and label the new chip the 80586. In fact, the competition was banking on it. Many had already decided to use that numerical designation for their next generation of products. Intel, however, wanted to distinguish its new chip from any potential clones and establish its own recognizable brand on the marketplace. Getting trademark protection for the 586 designation was unlikely. A federal court had earlier ruled that the 386 numeric designation was generic—that is, it describes a type of product rather than something exclusive to a particular manufacturer—so trademark status was not allowed for it. Intel coined the word *Pentium* because it could get trademark protection. It also implied the number "5," signifying fifth-generation much as "586" would have.

Competing manufacturers did use the 586 designation or variations on it for their own products. (Cyrix even upped the ante to 6x86.) Soon they, too, learned the value of brand recognition and bestowed their own made-up model designations on the market (the AMD K series, for example).

The singular Pentium name belies a diversity of microprocessors. Two very different chips wear the plain designation "Pentium." Later, Intel further capitalized on its brand name by introducing new models with elaborations clumsily appended to the Pentium name: the Pentium with MMX technology and Mobile Pentium. It even carried the Pentium name into the sixth generation and appended it to other brand names. Clearly, Intel sees "Pentium" both as a product and a brand name as a valuable asset.

The original Pentium began its life under the code name of *P5* and was designated successor to the 486DX. Although it was fabricated using essentially the same process and technology as the earlier chip, the superscalar design was a radical departure from previous Intel products.

Basic Design

Intel's design engineers faced a significant problem as the company sought to push past the performance of its 486 chip design. Thanks to pipelining, that chip was already executing almost one instruction every clock cycle. The chief opportunity for squeezing out more performance was increasing clock speed, a strategy the company had already adopted for its 486DX2 clock-doubling processors and would later use in its 486DX4. The 0.8 micron fabrication technology then current would not allow reliable operation in excess of the 66MHz achieved by the 486DX2.

The Intel solution was to borrow the superscalar technology then popular in RISC systems. Instead of speeding up the pipeline, Intel added a second pipeline to the Pentium. Although taking advantage of superscalar designs usually requires an optimizing compiler to prepare the program code for such parallel processing, Intel developed a way of handling existing programs. Through a bit of hardware mastery, Intel built preprocessing logic that could slice up programs and send the pieces through the two parallel pipelines simultaneously (or nearly so). Although not as effective as recompiling programs through an optimizing compiler (which remains an option for programs designed specifically to run on the Pentium), the Intel hardware design boosted Pentium performance to a level about 30 percent faster than the single pipeline 486 running at the same clock speed.

As Intel's engineers increased the speed of the Pentium, they faced another problem: getting program code and data into the chip fast enough to feed its twin pipelines. Again, they came up with a double-barreled solution. They doubled the width of the external data bus. Although the original Pentium (and all current chips wearing the Pentium name) are true 32-bit chips with 32-bit registers in their integer units, they connect to the rest of the computer through a 64-bit data bus and swallow data in quad-world gulps. In addition, Intel doubled the clock speed of the data bus nominally, from 33MHz to 66MHz. (The 60MHz Pentium chips had a matching 60MHz data bus.)

As had long been the case, memory still could not keep up with the Pentium despite the higher clock speeds. To help match the Pentium to PC memory systems, Intel built a 16KB internal cache into the chip. Unlike cache of the 486 chips, which lumped both instructions and data together, Intel gave the Pentium a more efficient cache that separated the two functions, allocating 8KB for data and 8KB for instructions.

Combined caches can stall when program requirements don't match cache contents. For example, the cache may fill with program data while executing a loop. When it needs the next instruction, it must reach out of the cache to slow main memory. Separate caches for program instructions and data assure that neither will stall the system.

As with the 486 series, the Pentium integrates a floating-point unit as part of the main processor. In fact, the Pentium uses the same essential circuitry as the 486 for its floating-point operations using 80-bit registers. Unlike RISC designs, however, the Pentium does not give the floating-point unit its own pipeline. In fact, only one of the integer pipelines in the Pentium can access the floating-point unit.

Development History

Even without an engineering degree, you should be able to figure out that the Pentium would produce about twice as much heat as a 486 and would be a devil to keep cool. It was. Consequently, Intel introduced the Pentium at two closely spaced speed levels, 66MHz and a slower but easier-to-make and easier-to-cool 60MHz.

After the P5 staked Intel's claim to the high end of the microprocessor market, the company's engineers worked feverishly to make the chip faster, cheaper, and more reliable. Key to their efforts was a new production line that allowed fabricating the chip with tighter design rules, 0.6 microns. In addition, they shifted to lower voltage operation, 3.3 volts instead of 5.0 volts. Together, those innovations were enough to push the speed of the Pentium's core up 50 percent, from 66 to 100MHz (and from 60 to 90MHz), in March 1994. In October that year, Intel added a budget-priced Pentium running at 75MHz.

Memory and support chips were already straining at 66MHz, so Intel kept the external bus of the fastest of the then-new Pentiums locked there. As a result, the second release of Pentium chips used Intel's first non-integral clock multiplier, 1.5x.

The 90 and 100MHz Pentiums were only an interim effort. The real Pentium push came in June 1995, when Intel shifted to a new Pentium design code-named the P54C. This radical revision capitalized on Intel's new 0.35 micron fabrication process to push Pentium speed up to 133MHz at first and eventually to 200MHz.

Intel continued development of the Pentium through 1998, producing a number of chips with various improvements on the same basic design. These include the Pentium OverDrive and the Pentium with MMX technology, Mobile Pentium, and Mobile Pentium with MMX technology, each discussed separately later.

Bus Speed Multipliers

Operationally, the P54C was the same as the older chip. The only significant difference was the clock multiplier. In general, Pentiums used clock multipliers consistent with not exceeding the 66MHz limit on the external bus, including half-step non-integral rates. Typically, the lower speeds used in practical computers are 60 and 50MHz, and factional multipliers are common. Table 3.5 lists the multipliers and bus speeds for the most common Pentium internal speeds.

TABLE 3.5 Bus Speeds and Multipliers of Pentium Chips

Chip Speed	Multiplier	Bus Speed
60	1x	60
66	1x	66
75	1.5x	50
90	1.5x	60
100	1.5x	66
120	2x	60
150	2.5x	60
166	2.5x	66
200	3x	66

Note that other multipliers besides these values are possible. For example, a Pentium with a 150MHz internal speed may operate with a 2.5x or 3x multiplier for bus speeds of 60 or 50MHz. The higher bus speed will yield somewhat better performance on tasks that involve substantial memory access and input/output operations.

The effects of the bus speed multiplier have an even more dramatic effect on input/output operation across the PCI expansion bus. The PCI bus typically operates at half the external memory bus speed of the microprocessor. For example, with a 66MHz memory bus speed, the PCI bus operates optimally at 33MHz. Consequently, microprocessors that use 50MHz external buses run their PCI buses at 25MHz, multiplying the low-speed penalty. Because of such penalties in synchronizing all the buses attached to a Pentium, many people shun chip speed because the overall performance improvement they deliver is not commensurate with the increase in megahertz—and the increase in the price that Intel charges.

Physical Matters

Pentium chips come in unassuming packages, small in comparison to today's slot-mounted cartridges but huge when seen next to its predecessors. The basic Pentium package is an expanded ceramic PGA socket nominally measuring 2.16 inches square and 1.10 inches thick. Depending on the Pentium model, the chip has between 273 and 320 pins.

The Pentium began a major preoccupation with socket design that has percolated through the microprocessor industry. In fact, one of the sockets designed for the Pentium has led to an industry standard and supporting organization.

The original P5 came with its own socket requirements because of its 64-bit data bus, which could not be accommodated by previous sockets. Its 273 pins fit Socket 4. The P54C brought a new socket requirement, Socket 5, to accommodate its 320 connections.

The revised socket requirement reflects a fundamental difference between the two Pentium breeds. The older chips operated solely from a 5-volt power supply; new chips wanted 3.3 volts. Making the two chips require specific socket designs—although physically differing by a single pin—assures that you won't succeed at the potentially destructive mistake of sliding a low voltage chip into a high voltage socket.

Pentium OverDrive

Intel provided an OverDrive upgrade for many of its slower Pentium processors. Table 3.6 lists the OverDrive speed Intel offers for various original Pentium processors.

TABLE 3.6   Pentium OverDrive Upgrade Speeds

Original Pentium Speed (MHz)	OverDrive Pentium Speed (MHz)	Socket Required
60	120	4
66	133	4
75	125	5 or 7
90	150	5 or 7
100	166	5 or 7
120	180	5 or 7
133	200	5 or 7
150	180	5 or 7
166	200	5 or 7

The internal logic of the Pentium OverDrive chips matches that of the P54C chips and is built using 0.35 micron technology. They differed in subtle ways so that they better match existing systems. Their clock multipliers are hardwired to match the bus speed of the Pentiums they are meant to replace, so you need not alter the jumpers or other configuration settings of your PC when plugging in a Pentium OverDrive. To ensure proper cooling of the faster, more energy-hungry logic, Intel packages its Pentium OverDrives with built-in active cooling fans and heatsinks. In addition, the OverDrive chips include voltage reduction or filtering to match the power supplied by older host PCs. The upgrade chips for 60 and 66MHz Pentiums include a regulator to reduce the 5 volts supplied the older Pentium socket to the 3.3 volts used by the OverDrive. The filtering incorporated into other OverDrive chips matches the internal logic to the standard 3.3 volt or reduced voltage systems.

Not all Pentium PCs can be upgraded with OverDrive chips. In particular, multiprocessor systems are *not* upgradable. Multiprocessor PCs with two Pentiums will not operate properly even if you replace both of their existing Pentium chips with OverDrives.

Pentium Processor with MMX Technology

In January 1997, Intel introduced its first MMX-enhanced Pentiums, which when under development had been termed the *P55C* chip. The first of the chips, which Intel officially calls the *Pentium Processor with MMX Technology,* operated at 166 or 200MHz with external bus clocks of 66MHz. The basic design of the Pentium MMX is identical to that of the earlier P54C Pentium with two important differences. As fits the name, the new chips recognize the MMX instruction set, handling them much like coprocessor instructions. In addition, Intel enlarged the on-chip primary memory cache, doubling its size to 32KB.

By processing several blocks of data at one time, the MMX chips can improve the performance of suitable applications by up to 60 percent, according to Intel. Except for the edge gained by the larger cache, however, the Pentium MMX chips will *not* accelerate the performance of conventional software. To gain its full speed, the chips require a diet of MMX instructions, which requires software specifically written using the instructions. Intel has introduced a labeling program (described in Chapter 1, "Basics") to identify software products using MMX instructions so you can easily recognize applications that MMX technology will benefit.

Mobile Pentium Processors

To put the latest in Pentium power in the field, Intel re-engineered the Pentium with MMX Technology chip for low-power operation to create the Mobile Pentium with MMX Technology. Unlike its deskbound predecessor, the addressing ability of the Mobile chip was enhanced by four more lines to allow direct access to 64GB of physical memory.

The Pentium with MMX Technology was initially introduced with 150 and 166MHz operating speeds. A year later, the introduction of the 0.25 micron fabrication process allowed a reduction in operating voltage to reduce the power needs of the 166MHz as well as bump the top speed of the chip to 266MHz. Later in 1998, Intel introduced intermediate versions.

Pentium Pro

Once code-named the *P6*, the Pentium Pro marked the beginning of Intel's sixth generation of PC microprocessors. The design was revolutionary for the company, an abandonment of its traditional CISC architecture in favor of a true RISC core. Using its own internal circuits, it translates classic Intel instructions into micro-ops that can be processed in a RISC-based core using all the RISC design tricks to massage extra processing speed from the code. Intel continued to develop this same core logic for its Pentium II and Pentium III processors, and it is expected to be the last design to implement classic Intel architecture.

The Pentium Pro introduced another technology standard on all Intel processors (except, briefly, the first few Celerons), the integral secondary cache. In the case of the Pentium Pro, this is a 256KB cache.

Although a primary cache had been standard on Intel processors since the introduction of the 486DX in 1989, the secondary cache had remained an external option left to motherboard designers to implement. The same reasoning that makes the integral primary cache such a good idea applies to an integral secondary cache: The local connection permits wider, higher-speed links and more efficient protocols. The chief drawback is complexity. Microprocessor cores have always pushed the limits of silicon fabrication, the largest chips that can be affordably manufactured. Secondary caches involve simple circuits but so many of them that they require huge chunks of silicon, on par with the processor core logic. Combining the two on a single substrate has never been (and still is not) technically nor practically feasible. Intel's Pentium Pro solution was to use two distinct substrates and package them together with a high-speed connection between them.

The RISC core and cache endowed the Pentium Pro with speed, but its 32-bit design and translation logic proved a handicap. Although the Pentium Pro raced through 32-bit software such as Windows NT, it limped along when running 16-bit code, including the popular Windows 95 operating system. As a result, the Pentium Pro was well received as a server processor, where it served well, but never found wide application on the desktop.

Overview

The Pentium Pro introduces a technology, new only for Intel, that the company calls *dynamic execution*. In the standard language of RISC processors, dynamic execution merely indicates a combination of out-of-order instruction execution and the underlying technologies that enable its operation (branch prediction, register renaming, and so on). Building on the Pentium, the Pentium Pro is both superscalar and super-pipelined.

At the software level, the Pentium Pro is nearly identical to the Pentium. It uses the same instruction set—basically that of the 386—with one addition. Intel added a *conditional move* instruction that copies the contents of one register to another only for a given condition (that is, the condition flag is set). This new instruction will help programmers avoid branches in their software. Although the branch-prediction logic of the Pentium Pro is accurate about 90 percent of the time, bad branch predictions can significantly slow the performance of the chip. Minimizing branches helps avoid the problem. Of course, programs using the new instruction will execute properly only on the Pentium Pro and its successors.

Strictly speaking, the P6 itself is a RISC chip, one that features extensive translation logic that converts classic Intel microprocessor instructions into a form more palatable for RISC processing. It takes some of the function of a RISC chip's optimizing compiler and puts it in the chip silicon.

The hardware design of the Pentium Pro takes many of the technologies used in the original Pentium a step further. Equipped with 11 individual execution units, the Pentium Pro can send instructions to up to 5 of them every clock cycle, thanks to its dynamic execution. In executing normal programs, the Pentium Pro averages three instructions per clock. Its pipeline has 12 stages, divided into three sections: an in-order fetch/decode stage, an out-of-order execution/dispatch stage, and an in-order retirement stage.

Perhaps the most notable feature of the Pentium Pro is that it is a forward- rather than backward-looking chip. When Intel's engineers laid out the basic design of the Pentium Pro in 1990, they envisioned that the world would have shifted to full 32-bit applications and operating systems by the time of the chip's release in 1995. One consequence of this design choice was that the Pentium Pro suffers a substantial performance handicap when running 16-bit (and, heaven forbid, 8-bit) instructions. For these older instructions, the Pentium Pro abandons its dynamic execution design and processes strictly in order with consequential delays. On 16-bit code, the Pentium Pro may be no better (and even sometimes worse) than an ordinary Pentium.

Design

One look and there's no mistaking the Pentium Pro. Instead of a neat square chip, it's a rectangular giant. Intel gives this package the name *multi-chip module* (MCM). It is also termed a *dual-cavity PGA* (pin-grid array) package because it holds two distinct slices of silicon, the microprocessor core and secondary cache memory. Notably, this design results in more pins than any previous Intel microprocessor and a new socket requirement, Socket 8 (discussed earlier).

The main processor chip of the Pentium Pro uses the equivalent of 5.5 million transistors. About 4.5 million of them are devoted to the actual processor itself. The other million provide the circuitry of the chip's primary cache, which provides a total of 16KB storage bifurcated into separate 8KB sections for program instructions and data. Compared to true RISC processors, the Pentium Pro uses about twice as many transistors. The circuitry that translates instructions into RISC-compatible micro-ops requires the additional transistor logic.

The integral secondary RAM cache fits onto a separate slice of silicon in the other cavity of the MCM. Its circuitry involves another 15.5 million transistors and operates at the same speed as the core logic of the rest of the Pentium Pro.

The secondary cache connects with the microprocessor core logic through a dedicated 64-bit bus, termed a *back-side bus*, that is separate and distinct from the 64-bit *front-side* bus that connects to main memory. The back-side bus operates at the full internal speed of the microprocessor, but the front-side bus operates at a fraction of the internal speed of the microprocessor.

The Pentium Pro bus design superficially appears identical to that of the Pentium with 32-bit addressing, a 64-bit data path, and a maximum clock rate of 66MHz. Below the surface, however, Intel enhanced the design by shifting to a *split-transaction protocol*. Where the Pentium (and, indeed, all previous Intel processors) handled memory accessing as a two-step process—on one clock cycle, the chip sends an address out the bus, reading the data at the next clock cycle—the Pentium Pro can put an address on the bus at the same time it reads data from a previously posted address. Because the address and data buses use separate lines, these two operations can occur simultaneously. In effect, the through-put of the bus can nearly double without an increase in its clock speed.

The internal bus interface logic of the Pentium Pro is designed for multiprocessor systems. Up to four Pentium Pro chips can be directly connected together pin-for-pin without any additional support circuitry. The PC's chipset arbitrates the combination.

Operation

Processing in the Pentium Pro begins with its 8KB instruction buffer, loading code into one of these *instruction decoders*, which translate the classic Intel x86 instruction set into micro-ops for processing by the rest of the chip. These decoders are not identical. Two of them, called *restricted decoders* or simple decoders, only tackle simple instructions that each directly translate into a single micro-op. The other, the *general decoder* or complex decoder, can handle more complex x86 instructions that translate into four or fewer micro-ops. Complex instructions and, in particular, those that directly reference memory, must be processed by the general decoder. Programs that make many direct memory references (such as a lot of old DOS applications) frustrate the multi-part decoder design of the Pentium Pro. Some x86 instructions are too complex even for the general decoder and are routed to a special *microcode instruction sequencer*. Operating at maximum capacity with code that perfectly fits their needs, the three decoders can generate six micro-ops per clock system (one from each restricted decoder, four from the general decoder). Less than perfect code—the typical instruction stream—results in the generation of about three micro-ops per clock cycle.

As with the instructions of true RISC processors, Pentium Pro micro-ops are all the same length, 118 bits, and are structured to include both the source and destination of the data as 32-bit values. According to Intel, on the average, each classic x86 instruction translates into 1.5 to 2.0 micro-ops.

As micro-ops get generated by the decoders, they are passed to the *re-order buffer*. Besides providing a reservoir of micro-ops to keep instructions smoothly flowing through the Pentium Pro's pipelines, the re-order buffer also logs the exact sequence in which each instruction occurs. Later, after the out-of-order processing further down the pipeline, the Pentium Pro uses this log to reconstruct the correct sequence of instructions before posting the results in its visible registers. In current Pentium Pro chips, the re-order buffer can store up to 40 entries of 254 bits each. Each entry can store a micro-op along with two operands, the results of the operation of each micro-op, and information about other changes that execution of the micro-op might make (status bits). The re-order buffer can prepare up to three micro-ops for processing per clock tick and accepts up to three more as they complete to be put back into the proper order.

The re-order buffer also manages the Pentium Pro's register renaming process. It determines which register the Pentium Pro uses to execute a given micro-op, drawing as necessary on the hidden internal registers of the chip to prevent the processing flow from stalling when the register needs of out-of-order instructions conflict. The Pentium Pro provides 40 registers for the renaming process.

As the instruction decoders pass micro-ops to the re-order buffer, they also send them to the *reservation station*. This section of the Pentium Pro has two primary functions. Foremost, it is a conduit that passes micro-ops along to a suitable execution unit as one becomes available. In addition, it acts as yet another buffer, storing up to 20 micro-ops and their data. It prevents slowdowns in the decoders from starving the processors and prevents the decoders from stalling when the processors are fully engaged.

The reservation station connects to five ports linking to six *execution units* that carry out the actual data manipulations. These six units include two integer units, one floating-point unit, one jump unit, and two address generation units (one load, one store). The ports are necessarily divided unequally among the units: the store units get two ports, the load unit gets one, and the other four share two ports in pairs. Through the various ports, the reservation station can pass along up to five micro-ops every clock cycle. On typical program code, it will actually dispatch about three micro-ops.

Once a micro-op has been carried out in an execution unit, it is passed back to the re-order buffer. The results get filled into the entry corresponding to the original micro-op that was sent out for execution. The 40 buffer entries can be updated in any order; the first executed are the first written to the buffer.

To bring the instruction stream back into program sequence, the Pentium Pro reads through the re-order buffer in sequence as if it were a loop. When the chip logic finds an instruction that has been properly executed, it passes the results down to the next pipeline stage and frees the entry in the re-order buffer. That entry is immediately recycled, filled with the next instruction to emerge from the decoders (which is actually about 40 instructions later in the code stream). If, as the Pentium Pro reads through the re-order buffer, the next entry has not fully executed, the system waits for its completion before going on because at this point, instructions must be in order. In other words, the processor stalls. When the executed micro-op is finally written to the buffer, it is immediately emptied out and sent for refilling.

As the micro-ops are retired, the results are written to the x86-compatible-registers expected by the program. They can then be passed along to the rest of the system and memory through the primary and secondary caches.

Pentium II

The Intel Pentium II starts with the same essential core logic as the Pentium Pro (Intel classes both chips in its P6 processor family), making it officially a sixth-generation processor based on a RISC core. Atop that foundation, the Pentium II adds several enhancements to give the chip an edge in running today's application software.

The P6 design does not require major changes in the RISC core logic of the processor. Instead, the enhancements in moving from Pentium Pro to Pentium II (and eventually Pentium III) require only alterations in the front end that translates old Intel architecture instructions into RISC code.

The chief distinctions of the Pentium II is its addition of MMX technology and a new package called the Single Edge Contact cartridge or SEC cartridge. The socket it plugs into is termed Slot 1.

As with the earlier Pentium Pro, the Pentium II has both a 32KB primary cache (16KB data, 16KB instruction) operating at the microprocessor's clock speed along with a secondary cache (512KB for the Pentium II) built into the microprocessor package and coupled with a dedicated 64-bit bus. Unlike the Pentium Pro, the Pentium II module actually contains a circuit board with separate component packages mounted on it, including a separate processor core (incorporating the primary cache) and individual secondary cache chips. Because of this arrangement, the secondary cache of the Pentium II operates at one half the core speed of the microprocessor. This reduced speed is, of course, a handicap. It was a design expediency. It lowers the cost of the technology, allowing Intel to use off-the-shelf cache memory (from another manufacturer, at least initially) in a lower cost package.

The Pentium II incorporates many RISC concepts to increase its performance. These include dynamic execution (which includes out-of-order execution and speculative execution) and the ability to decode up to three instructions per clock cycle and execute up to four. The sixth-generation core of the Pentium II can execute two MMX instructions simultaneously through its separate pipelines, each of which has 12 stages. That capability should give it a distinct advantage over all other microprocessors on multimedia applications that take advantage of MMX. Because both MMX and the 32-bit power of the Pentium Pro require new programs to gain their fullest advantage, most software writers will undoubtedly exploit both in their new creations. Once such programs become available, you won't care about looking back to the 16-bit world, and the laggardly 16-bit performance of the Pentium Pro will be like disco, something of historical interest with little relevance to your life (or wardrobe) today.

Although the Pentium II can address up to 64GB of memory, its cache can track only 512MB. Fortunately, that size is large enough to be beyond the useful capacity of current PCs because most are limited to 384MB by their chipsets.

Mobile Pentium II

To bring the power of the Pentium II processor to notebook computers, Intel re-engineered the desktop chip to reduce its power consumption and altered its packaging to fit slim systems. The resulting chip preserves the full power of the Pentium II while sacrificing only its multiprocessor support. The power savings come from two changes. The core logic of the Mobile Pentium II is specifically designed for low-voltage operation and has been engineered to work well with higher external voltages. It also incorporates an enriched set of power management modes, including a new Quick Start mode that essentially shuts down the chip except for logic that monitors for bus activity by the PCI bridge chip and allows the chip to wake up when it's needed. This design, because it does not monitor for other processor activity, prevents the Mobile Pentium II from being used in multiprocessor applications. The Mobil Pentium II can also switch off its cache clock during its sleep or Quick Start states.

The Mobile Pentium II shares the same P6 core logic design with the rest of the Pentium II family and includes the ability to process two MMX instructions simultaneously. To match slower memory systems, the Mobile Pentium II has both a 32KB primary cache (16KB data, 16KB instruction) operating at the microprocessor's clock speed along with a 512KB secondary cache operating at half clock speed incorporated into its mini-cartridge package.

As with the Pentium II, the Mobile Pentium II incorporates many RISC concepts to increase its performance. These include dynamic execution (which includes out-of-order execution and speculative execution) and the ability to decode up to three instructions per clock cycle and execute up to four. The Mobile Pentium II has two 12-stage pipelines, both of which are capable of executing MMX instructions, and an integral 80-bit floating-point unit.

Unlike the Pentium II, the mobile chip has the ratio between its core and bus clocks fixed at the factory. Current Mobile Pentium II models operate with a 66MHz front-side bus.

Although the Mobile Pentium II can address up to 64GB of memory, its 512KB integral secondary cache can track only 512MB.

Pentium II Celeron

Introduced in 1998, the Celeron was Intel's entry-level processor derived from the Pentium II. Although it had the same processor core as what was at the time Intel's premier chip (the second-generation Pentium II with 0.45 micron design rules), Intel trimmed the cost of building the chip by eliminating the integral 512KB secondary (level two) memory cache installed in the Pentium II cartridge.

The company also opted to lower the packaging cost of the chip by omitting the metal outer shell of the full Pentium II and instead leaving the Celeron's circuit board substrate bare. In addition, the cartridge-based Celeron package lacks the thermal plate of the Pentium II and the latches that secure it to the slot. Intel terms the Celeron a Single-Edge Processor Package to distinguish it from the Single-Edge Cartridge used by the Pentium II.

In 1999, Intel introduced a new, lower-cost package for the Celeron, a plastic pin-grid array (PPGA) shell that looks like a first-generation Pentium on steroids. It has 370 pins and mates with Intel's PGA370 socket. The chip itself measures just under two inches square (nominally 49.5 millimeters) and about three millimeters thick not counting the pins, which hang down another three millimeters or so (the actual specification is 3.05 to 3.30 millimeters).

When the Celeron chip was initially introduced, the absence of a cache made such a hit on the performance that Intel was forced by market pressure to revise its design. In 1998, the company added a 128KB cache operating at one-half core speed to the Celeron. At the same time, Intel upgraded the core logic of the chip to its latest 0.25 micron process technology.

Distinguishing these early Celerons is both a matter of speed and nomenclature. The initial Celerons ran at 266MHz and all lacked an integral secondary cache. The first generation of 300MHz chips did likewise. The slowest chips of the revised design operate at 300MHz. To distinguish them from their cache-less forebears, Intel gave them the designation 300A. All Celerons faster than 300MHz have a secondary cache.

People in the know sometimes call the initial cache-less Celerons by its code name, *Covington*. The revised chip was code-named Mendocino. Both chips recognize the MMX command set, but neither has built-in facilities for Intel's Streaming SIMD Extensions.

All Celerons include the same 32KB primary cache of the Pentium II line, devoting half that memory to program code and half to data. Unlike in the Pentium II design, however, Intel has integrated the 12 million transistors of the secondary cache on the silicon die of the Celeron itself. According to Intel, the speed of the secondary cache "scales" with the speed of the core logic. Outside sources report that the clock speed of the secondary cache of the Celeron is the same as the core logic speed.

Intel also distinguishes the Celeron from its more expensive processor lines by limiting its front-side bus speed to 66MHz. This lowers the cost of memory in keeping with the design goal of the chip but compromises performance. The bus speed multipliers of the Celeron is fixed. Table 3.7 lists the bus multipliers used by various speeds of Celeron chip.

TABLE 3.7   Celeron Bus Speed Multipliers

Core Speed	Front-Side Bus Speed	Multiplier
266MHz	66MHz	4
300MHz	66MHz	4.5
333MHz	66MHz	5
366MHz	66MHz	5.5
400MHz	66MHz	6
433MHz	66MHz	6.5
466MHz	66MHz	7

Intel limits the memory addressing of the Celeron to 4GB of physical RAM. The four highest address bus signals used by the Pentiums II and III for addressing up to 64GB are omitted from the Celeron pin-out. This is not a grave limitation as no available chipset for any Pentium II or Pentium III allows the direct addressing of more than 1GB of RAM.

In addition, the Celeron does not support multiprocessor operation. Again, this is not a major limitation in desktop PCs, although it eliminates the Celeron from consideration in high-end servers.

The Pentium III has a threefold performance advantage over the Celeron: larger secondary cache, higher front-side bus speed, and Streaming SIMD Extensions. (The Pentium II has the first two of these.) At the same clock speed, the Pentium III (and Pentium II) will deliver somewhat greater performance, but most of the difference typically is masked by other aspects of real-world computers.

Pentium II Xeon

In 1998, Intel sought to distinguish its higher performance microprocessors from its economy line. In the process, the company created the Xeon, a refined Pentium II microprocessor core enhanced by a higher-speed memory cache, one that operated at the same clock rate as the core logic of the chip.

At heart, the Xeon is a full 32-bit microprocessor with a 64-bit data bus, as with all Pentium-series processors. Its address bus provides for direct access to up to 64GB of RAM. The internal logic of the chip allows for up to four Xeons to be linked together without external circuitry to form powerful multiprocessor systems.

A sixth-generation processor, the Xeon is a Pentium Pro derivative by way of the standard Pentium II. It incorporates two 12-stage pipelines and dynamic execution microarchitecture.

The Xeon incorporates two levels of caching. One is integral to the logic core itself, a primary 32KB cache split 16KB for instructions, 16K for data. In addition, a separate secondary cache is part of the Xeon processor module but mounted separately from the core logic on the cartridge substrate. This integral-but-separate design allows flexibility in configuring the Xeon. Current chips are available equipped with either 512KB or 1MB of L2 cache, and the architecture and slot design allow for secondary caches of up to 2MB. This integral cache runs at the full core speed of the microprocessor.

This design required a new interface, tagged Slot 2 by Intel.

Initially, the core operating speed of the Xeon started where the Pentium II left off (at the time) at 400MHz and followed the Pentium II up to 450MHz.

The front-side bus of the Xeon was initially designed for 100MHz operation, although higher speeds are possible and expected. A set of contacts on the SEC cartridge allows the motherboard to adjust the multiplier that determines the ratio between front-side bus and core logic speed.

The independence of the logic core and cache is emphasized by the power requirements of the Xeon. Each section requires its own voltage level. The design of the Xeon allows Intel flexibility in the power requirements of the chip through a special coding scheme. A set of pins indicates the core voltage and the cache voltage required by the chip, and the chip expects the motherboard to determine the requirements of the board and deliver the required voltages. The Xeon design allows for core voltages as low as 1.8 volts or as high as 2.1 (the level required by the first chips). Cache voltage requirements may reach as high as 2.8 volts. Nominally, the Xeon is a 2-volt chip.

Overall, the Xeon is optimized for workstations and servers and features built-in support for up to four identical chips in a single computer.

Pentium II OverDrive

To give an upgrade path for systems originally equipped with the Pentium Pro processor, Intel developed a new OverDrive line of direct-replacement upgrades. These *Pentium II OverDrive* chips fit the same zero-insertion force Socket 8 used by the Pentium Pro, so you can slide one chip out and put the other in. Dual processor systems can use two

OverDrive upgrades. Intel warns that some systems may require a BIOS upgrade to accommodate the OverDrive upgrade.

The upgrade offers the revised design of the Pentium II (which means better 16-bit operation) as well as higher clock speeds. The chip also earns an edge over ordinary Pentium II's operating at the same speeds; the 512KB secondary cache in the OverDrive chip operates at full core logic speed, not half speed as in the Pentium II.

Intel offers two models of Pentium II OverDrive to upgrade four speeds of Pentium Pros. These include replacements for 150 and 180MHz Pentium Pros (that is, those having a 60MHz data bus speed) to a 300MHz Pentium II OverDrive. Pentium Pros operating at 166 or 200MHz (with a 66MHz bus speed) upgrade to a 333MHz Pentium II OverDrive.

Pentium III

Announced in January 1999 and officially released on February 26, 1999, the Pentium III was the first of Intel's newest generation of microprocessors. Code-named *Katmai* during its development, the new chip is most notable for adding SSE to the Intel microprocessor repertory. SSE is a compound acronym for Streaming SIMD Extensions, SIMD itself being an acronym for Single Instruction, Multiple Data. SIMD technology allows one microprocessor instruction to operate across several bytes or words (or even larger blocks of data). In the Pentium III, SSE (formerly known as the Katmai New Instructions, or KNI) is a set of 70 new SIMD codes for microprocessor instructions that allow programs to specify elaborate three-dimensional processing functions with a single command.

Unlike the MMX extensions, which added no new registers to the basic Pentium design and instead simply redesignated the floating-point unit registers for multimedia functions, Intel's Streaming SIMD Extensions add new registers to Intel architecture, pushing the total number of transistors inside the core logic of the chip above 9.5 million.

At heart, the Pentium III uses the same core logic as its Pentium II forebears. Its initial fabrication will use the same 0.25 micron technology as the earlier chip, although Intel plans a rapid shift to newer 0.18 micron technology for the chip. The first commercial releases of the Pentium III are expected at the 450 and 500MHz speed levels; the shift in fabrication technology will likely take the chip to 600MHz and beyond. The chip plugs into the same Slot 1 as the Pentium II.

The most controversial aspect of the Pentium III was its internal serial number. Hard-coded into the chip, this number is unique to each individual microprocessor. Originally, Intel foresaw that a single command—including a query from a distant Web site—would cause the chip to send out its serial number for positive identification (of the chip, of the computer it is in, of the person owning or using the computer). Intel believed the feature would improve Internet security, not to mention allow the company to track its products and detect counterfeits. Consumer groups saw the "feature" as in invasion of privacy, and under threat of boycott, Intel changed its policy. Where formerly the Pentium III would default to making the identification information available, after the first production run of the new chip, the identification would default off and require a specific software command to make the serial number accessible. Whether the chip serial number is available will likely become a setup feature of the BIOS in PCs using the Pentium III chip.

Pentium III Xeon

To add its Streaming SIMD Extensions to its server products, on March 17, 1999, Intel introduced the Pentium III Xeon. As with the Pentium III itself, the new instructions are the chief change, but they are complemented by a shift to finer technology. As a result, the initial new Xeons start with a speed of 500MHz. At this speed, Intel offers the chip with either a 512KB, 1MB, or 2MB integral secondary cache operating at core speed. A 550MHz version with a 512KB cache was promised for April with 1MB- and 2MB-cache versions due around September. The new Slot 2 chips also incorporate the hardware serial number feature of the Pentium III chip.

Advanced Micro Devices

For years, AMD microprocessors have been, at best, an undercurrent in the PC marketplace. With the advent of budget PCs, however, AMD chips have come into prominence. Computer prices dipping below $500 make every dollar of microprocessor price important. The lower cost of AMD chips and growing acceptance in the market have made the K6 line of chips a top choice in entry-level computers. AMD hopes to maintain or even increase its market presence with the introduction of a new processor design, the K7, which promises to go head-to-head with the Pentium III.

K5

Unlike the 5_x86, which is built using a traditional CISC core, AMD adopted the same tack used by Intel for its Pentium Pro in designing its own Pentium-level product, the K5. The chip is built around a RISC core and uses translation logic to convert Intel instructions into the necessary RISC operations. It was called the K5 during its development but was initially released on the market as the AMD K5. In late 1996, the product was rechristened the K5, now its official moniker.

Although the idea behind the AMD effort resembles that of Intel and NexGen, the implementation is very much different. Unlike the other RISC-based Pentium level chips from NexGen and Intel, the K5 is socket compatible with today's Pentium. Consequently, control for the secondary cache is left to external circuitry, and a floating-point unit is integrated into the K5 silicon. The core logic of the K5 FPU is the same as was developed for the highly regarded AMD 29000 RISC processor.

Program processing in the K5 begins with an instruction decoder that translates Intel instructions into fixed-length RISC commands, which can be processed more efficiently, each one in a single cycle. The uniformity of instructions helps the K5 load a six-stage pipeline that can process four instructions simultaneously. The six stages include two integer processors, the floating-point processor, two load/store units, and a branch unit.

Although AMD originally expected its design to allow the K5 to run through programs about 30 percent faster than a Pentium operating at the same clock speed, performance of commercial chips has proven disappointing. The AMD chips have only been able to match 133MHz Pentiums, keeping the out of the profitable high end of the market.

As with the Pentium, the external bus speed of the K5 is programmable to run at a fraction (one half, two thirds, or unity) of the internal clock. Current models of the K5 operate internally at either 1.5 or 2.0 times the external bus speed. Two pins allow for the programming of the clock multiplier. Table 3.8 lists the possible K5 speed relationships.

TABLE 3.8   AMD K5 Microprocessor Speed Relations

Model Code	Chip Speed	Multiplier	Bus Speed	P-Rating
0	75	1.5	50	P75
0	90	1.5	60	P90
0	100	1.5	66	P100
1	90	1.5	60	P120
1	100	1.5	66	P133
1	120	2.0	60	P150
1	133	2.0	66	P166

To match with slower external memory, the K5 uses a four-way set-associative cache split like that of the Pentium between a separate instruction and data cache. The instruction cache doubled the size of that of the initial Pentiums, 16KB versus 8KB, and the data cache holds 8KB. (The latest Pentiums offer both 16KB instruction and data caches.) Making up for the smaller size of the data cache, it is four-way set-associative and dual ported, allowing simultaneous loading and storing within a single clock cycle.

K6

AMD dubbed its next generation of microprocessor the AMD K6, again harking back to a developmental name—after briefly flirting with the 6_K86 designation. The K6 actually beats Intel to the draw by introducing Intel's MMX technology before its developer. The K6 is the first available microprocessor to understand MMX instructions. Don't feel sorry for Intel, however, because Intel licenses its MMX technology to AMD.

The K6 fits into Intel's standard Socket 7. The AMD K6 was probably the prime motivation behind AMD acquiring NexGen. The prize of the acquisition was the NexGen Nx686, which forms the foundation of the AMD K6. AMD refined the NexGen design to increase the size of the level-one cache while sacrificing the on-chip level-two cache controller. AMD also altered the pin-out to match Intel's Pentium and grafted on the MMX compatibility.

Although the core of the K6 was developed by NexGen as the successor to the Nx586, it is a ground-up design. Where its predecessor had but a single pipeline, the K6 has two that are fed by a group of four instruction decoders, which translate Intel x86 instructions into RISC instructions to match the chip's core logic. Although the K6 design cannot process 32-bit instructions quite as quickly as Intel's Pentium Pro, it suffers none of that chip's disadvantages when using 16-bit code. The pipelines are purposely short (six stages) but are blessed with branch prediction and speculative execution.

The caches distinguish the K6 from Intel's Pentium chips. As with the Pentium, the K6 has separate instruction and data caches. Those of the K6 are four times larger, a full 32KB each. Both are two-way set-associative and use a 32-byte line size. The data cache uses a dual-ported write-back design that allows it to load and store data simultaneously in a single clock cycle.

AMD has made large investments in its chip fabrication facilities, resulting in the ability to built the initial K6 chips with design rules of 0.35 micron. Industry experts expect that even in its first generation, those design rules will allow the K6 to run at speeds of 180MHz and match the performance of a 200MHz Pentium. Potential future improvements in fabrication technology and reductions in design rules may permit the manufacture of K6 chips running at 300MHz, which should enable them to equal or surpass the performance of today's 200MHz Pentium Pro.

K6-2

In 1998, AMD introduced an improved version of its K6 chip, one enhanced by a broadened instruction set aimed specifically at speeding the execution of three-dimensional graphics routines popular in computer games. AMD gave these additional instructions the name *3D Now!* The K6-2 also supports the full MMX instruction set.

The K6-2 uses the AMD P-rating system, which specifies not the actual operating speed of the microprocessor but the speed of a Pentium chip that would deliver similar performance. The actual clock speed of a K6-2 is thus substantially lower than its P-rating, as noted in Table 3.9.

TABLE 3.9   AMD K6-2 Clock Speed Relationships

Rated clock speed (MHz)	300	333	350
Actual clock speed (MHz)	90	100	117

K6-3

Code-named *Sharptooth* before its introduction on February 22, 1999, the AMD K6-3 extends the life of the company's K6 core with performance enhancements brought by improved semiconductor technology. The most important move is to a new cache design that AMD calls "TriLevel Cache." The name reflects its three stages: a 64KB level-one cache, a 256KB level-two cache integrated into the chip silicon, and integral support for up to 1MB of external level-three cache. Both the level-one and level-two caches operate at the full speed of the core logic. The optional external level-three cache couples through a 100MHz front-side bus. It also incorporates a 192-byte translation look-aside buffer, a four-way design that's twice the size of that used by Intel's competitive chips.

The caches feed the K6-3's seven-stage pipelines and a core logic design essentially the same as the K6-2. As with the K6-2, the newer chip incorporates all of AMD's instruction set enhancements, including both MMX and 3D Now!. According to AMD, the chip performs on the level of an Intel Pentium III rated one speed higher—that is, the 400MHz K6-3 will deliver performance much the same as a 450MHz Pentium III.

The large on-chip cache results in the K6-3 design requiring 21.3 million transistors. Initial chips follow 0.25 micron design rules and were offered at speed of 400 and 450MHz.

Although the K6-3 continues to use a PGA package compatible with Socket 7, it adds features that motivated Intel to adopt its slotted-processor strategy.

K7

Advanced Micro Devices announced its first seventh-generation microprocessor in October 1998 as the K7. Based on new core logic, the chip promises a quantum boost in performance based on a nine-issue superscalar design. That is, when operating optimally, the chip can handle nine different instructions simultaneously.

These nine instructions are divided into three classes. The chip has three parallel instruction decoders that recognize the standard x86 instruction set. These feed three superscalar out-of-order integer pipelines and three superscalar out-of-order multimedia pipelines—essentially floating-point processors that recognize the MMX and 3D Now! instruction sets.

To interface with its system host, the K7 design incorporates 128KB of level-one cache, split 64KB for instructions and 64KB for data. Through a dedicated 64-bit back-side bus, it supports level-two caches from 512KB to 8MB. Its front-side bus (system interface) can operate at speeds up to 200MHz through the Alpha EV6 bus slot.

Initial K7 chips use 0.25 micron design rules that allow the core logic to run at 500MHz. Improved fabrication technology will allow higher speeds.

Centaur Technology

The market impact of processors from Centaur Technology has been small. No major PC maker has yet offered a system based on the company's chips, although the chips are compatible with a wide number of Socket 7-style motherboards. (The company maintains a list of compatible products on its Web site at www.winchip.com.) The company philosophy is to put transistors to work where they are most effective, and thus far, it has scorned speculative and out-of-order execution for simpler logic designs. Although its designs are compact, it faces price competition that may continue to limit its market penetration.

WinChip C6

The first microprocessor to be released from Centaur Technologies, a subsidiary of Integrated Device Technology, the WinChip C6 is aimed at powering computers at the low-priced end of the market. Based on a RISC core, the C6 uses a relatively small slice of silicon (88 millimeter square using 0.35 micron technology) to keep costs down and is electrically frugal. Nevertheless, it incorporates a larger primary cache than other microprocessors in its range (32KB) as well as the full MMX instruction set in its 5.4 million transistors.

Despite the differences in design, a WinChip C6 delivers nearly identical performance to an Intel Pentium with MMX technology operating at the same clock speed. Introduced at 200MHz, the C6 topped out at 240MHz, so it can no longer be considered for serious computers. According to Centaur, the company sold about half a million C6 chips since their December 1997 introduction. Announced May 20, 1997, sampling began on June 4, 1997.

WinChip 2 3D

The WinChip 2 uses the same core logic as the C6 but takes it to higher speed—although not high enough. The chip is competitive with AMD, Cyrix, and Intel chips at its speed rating, but it does not reach up to the same megahertz as its competition. Sampling of the chip began on May 19, 1998, and actual shipments of the chip began in September 1998, with chips speed rated at 200, 225, and 240MHz built using 0.25 micron technology.

Centaur believes it achieves an edge through the use of a large, fast primary cache, 128KB in the WinChip 3D design, double the primary cache of the Pentium series. The company believes that a larger level-one cache is more important than the combination of a smaller level-one cache and a level-two cache. The WinChip 2 3D lacks an integral secondary cache. On the other hand, the chip takes advantage of the 100MHz front-side bus made possible by following the Super 7 socket standard. At 300MHz, the WinChip lags about 5 percent behind a Pentium II on application tests.

One major advantage of the WinChip design is size. It uses substantially less silicon than other Pentium level chips (about 58 millimeters square versus 81 for AMD's K6-2, 88 for the Cyrix M II, and 135 for the Pentium II), potentially allowing Centaur to produce it less expensively. One reason for the smaller die size is the simplified execution unit of the WinChip. It does not support out-of-order execution but does use a six-stage pipeline.

The "3D" in the name tells the story: With the WinChip 2 3D, IDT was the first outside chip maker to adopt AMD's 3D Now! instruction set. A second generation processor from IDT, the WinChip 2 3D refines the company's compact RISC core logic to increase clock speeds while keeping power consumption low. As with the company's other products, the WinChip 2 3D is aimed at bringing down the price of entry-level systems, keeping pace with Intel's introductions.

The second-generation WinChip 2 3D offers performance comparable to an Intel Celeron running at the same clock speeds.

WinChip 4

Centaur calls its planned next generation chip the WinChip 4. It expects to offer the new product at speeds of 450 and 500MHz.

The WinChip 4 uses a new core logic design that incorporates an 11-stage pipeline with what the company claims is advanced branch-prediction logic superior to that used by other chip makers.

It follows the same caching philosophy as its predecessor, with 128KB of primary cache split 64KB for programs and 64KB for data. It also uses a split 256-byte translation lookaside buffer (TLB).

Initially, the chip is to be fabricated with 0.25 micron technology and a die size of about 100 mm square. These chips should be available in the last half of 1999 with speed ratings from 400 to 500MHz. As the company pushes into 0.18 micron fabrication (expected in the first half of 1999), the die size should shrink to about 60 mm and speed potential increase to 700MHz.

Cyrix Corporation

Cyrix has had mixed success selling its microprocessors. In the Pentium generation, its 6x86 is hailed for its excellent performance but, at least initially, lambasted for running hot. Its MediaGX won favor in the first round of low-cost PCs and in some budget-priced notebook systems. Its current main thrust is with its M II (or M II) processor, which has found a strong following as a budget-priced alternative to Intel's Celeron products.

6x86

Having proven its ability to duplicate the function of Intel's older microprocessors, Cyrix has pushed ahead by combining classical designs with new technologies to go the Pentium one better—at least in Cyrix's own humble view. Where the Pentium requires a new generation of software or at least recompiled applications to take advantage of its superscalar design, Cyrix has shifted the job of matching today's software to tomorrow's microprocessors to hardware. The result was its M1 architecture, not a single chip but a plan for a new family of high-performance processors. The first of these was the 6x86, a chip aimed at competing with Intel's Pentium. Indeed, the competition is rather direct: the 6x86 is designed to be socket-compatible with the P54C Pentium. The 6x86 is also offered under the IBM name.

At its heart, the M1 architecture of the 6x86 is superscalar like the Pentium with two somewhat asymmetrical integer arithmetic units capable of operating in parallel. Each integer unit has its own pipeline, the pair known as the X pipeline and the Y pipeline. Where the Pentium is pipelined with four stages, Cyrix calls its design super-pipelined because it features a full seven stages. These stages are termed prefetch, decode 1, decode 2, address calculation 1, address calculation 2, execute, and write-back.

Processing in each of the pipelines begins with the prefetch stage. At this point, the pipeline gathers up to 16 bytes of instructions (typically about four instructions) from an on-chip cache. At this stage, the instructions are first evaluated to determine whether they code any branches in the program code. If a branch is detected, the chip attempts to predict the course the branch will take at this preliminary stage.

Next, processing moves to the decode 1 stage, which is primarily charged with determining the length of the instruction. The actual decoding of each instruction occurs in the decode 2 stage. At this point, the chip determines whether a given instruction will travel through the X or Y pipeline. Most instructions can take either path, and the one chosen will be that which best keeps the twin pipelines full and flowing. Certain instructions, however, must take the X pipeline. These include protected-mode segment loads, string instructions, multiply or divide instructions, input and output instructions, far branches, instructions that may require multiple memory accesses, and certain push and pop instructions.

Processing then progresses to the address calculation 1 stage in which up to two addresses are calculated per clock cycle. This stage also determines which of the chip's registers will be used for carrying out the instruction.

The address calculation 2 stage performs the actual memory access, checking the translation look-aside buffer, cache, and register files.

The execute stage then carries out any arithmetic or logical instructions, including multiply and divide commands.

The write-back stage finishes the execution by writing the resulting data to the register file and write buffers (whence they go to the cache and memory).

The biggest challenges of the 6x86's M1 design are twofold: dividing the work between two processing chains and making the additional pipeline stages pay off. Cyrix uses a number of technologies to pull off these tricks. Branch prediction and speculative execution help keep the pipelines full without stalling. According to Cyrix, its four-state branch prediction algorithm achieves 90 percent accuracy. Its speculative execution abilities handles up to four conditional branches or floating-point operations.

To eliminate problems that might arise in parallel execution, the 6x86 takes advantage of several novel techniques. Register renaming allows each pipeline to work with what it thinks is the same register. The architecture includes 32 registers and allows each physical register to be assigned a logical name equivalent to any of the registers in an Intel microprocessor. For example, two instructions can execute simultaneously even though they both call for manipulating the EAX register. The M1 chip assigns a different hardware register the EAX name in each pipeline. Later, it consolidates the results. Data forwarding allows the M1 chip to route the results of execution in one pipeline to the other when the operation of one instruction is dependent on the other. Further, the M1 design allows for out-of-order execution so no problem arises when one pipeline completes execution of a simple instruction before the other pipeline finishes a more complex instruction that appears earlier in the program. Out-of-order execution only occurs at the execute stage or later so that memory control (which takes place in the address calculation stages) and faults always occur in the proper order.

As with the Pentium, the 6x86 design incorporates an integral floating-point unit in addition to its two integer units. The Cyrix floating-point unit operates fully in parallel with the integer units when the instruction stream permits. Floating-point instructions can be executed out-of-order with related integer instructions, and a set of four write buffers permit speculative execution of floating-point instructions. The floating-point unit itself links to the rest of the 6x86 processor through a 64-bit internal bus and follows the IEEE 754 standard. It recognizes and executes all standard Intel coprocessor instructions.

The cache design of 6x86's M1 architecture is unlike that of any other current microprocessor. Its cache has a two layer structure. To speed loading of instructions, the M1 design used a special 256-byte primary instruction cache, which Cyrix calls the microcache. Another cache, much larger, combines the functions of primary data cache and secondary instruction cache. Although the size of this large unified cache is not set by the architecture's specifications, in initial implementations it will likely be on the order of the 16KB cache of the Pentium. The unified cache uses a four-way set-associative design.

Other elements of the hardware design of the M1 are much like the Pentium. It is a full 32-bit chip—all registers are 32 bits wide—that connects to its support circuitry with a 64-bit data path. It uses 32-bit addressing to support up to 4GB of physical memory. The internal hardware design is optimized for high-speed operation at 100MHz or higher.

According to Cyrix, the design of the 6x86 gives it a performance edge over the Pentium. A 6x86 operating at 133MHz internally delivers performance equivalent to a Pentium running at 166MHz. Cyrix identifies its parts with the performance level the chip delivers as related to an equivalent Pentium rather than the actual internal speed of the chip. Table 3.10 lists the Cyrix part designations and the actual operating speed of the various available 6x86 models.

TABLE 3.10   Cyrix 6x86 Microprocessor Specifications

Designation	Pentium Equivalent	Bus Speed	Actual Internal Speed
6x86-P166+GP	P166+	66MHz	133MHz
6x86-P150+GP	P150+	60MHz	120MHz
6x86-P133+GP	P133+	55MHz	110MHz
6x86-P120+GP	P120+	50MHz	100MHz

Initial 6x86 chips were welcomed on the market for their performance. They outperform Pentium chips operating at the same speed by 10 to 30 percent. The penalty for this performance was heat. The chips produced prodigious amounts of it, making system cooling critical. PCs with poor airflow were apt to overheat and shut down. Some experimenters even reported the chips self-destructing. Improvements in fabrication have tamed the power requirements of the 6x86, and overheating of new chips (stepping—Intel's term for revision level—2.7 or later) should no longer be a problem.

In 1998, Cyrix revised the 6x86 design to add recognition of the Intel MMX instruction set. The new version of the chip is designated 6x86MX, and the company offered it with four speed ratings: 6x86MX-PR266, 6x86MX-PR233, 6x86MX-PR200, and 6x86MX-PR166.

MediaGX

Designed chiefly for low-cost multimedia computers, the Cyrix MediaGX combines an Intel-compatible microprocessor core that operates at the Pentium level with a variety of system and multimedia support functions. More than a mere microprocessor, the

MediaGX is akin an entire PC on a chip—actually two chips, the microprocessor itself and the special support chip, the Cx5510.

The core logic of the MediaGX achieves similar performance to a standard Intel Pentium microprocessor operating at the same clock speed. Initial MediaGX chips, introduced in March 1997, were rated at 120 and 133MHz, putting them at the lower end of today's performance spectrum. Compensating somewhat for the slow clock speeds is an integrated display control system, which can speed up some graphic functions.

The Cyrix core logic design uses six pipeline stages and includes a floating-point processor. Integral to the MediaGX chip is a 16KB unified data/instruction cache that uses a four-way set associative design with write-back capabilities. As with Intel's Pentium chips, the MediaGX has 32-bit internal registers and a 64-bit connection with its external data bus.

The MediaGX chip also includes a built-in graphics system with its own pipeline. Because the microprocessor itself handles all graphic functions, it lends itself to a Unified Memory Architecture (UMA) design, segmenting out part of main memory to serve as a frame buffer. The support circuitry in the MediaGX can directly interface to many LCD display systems or to ordinary computer monitors using an external RAMDAC (a digital-to-analog converter chip). The MediaGX chip itself emulates all VGA and VESA display modes at resolutions as high as 1,280 × 1,024 pixels in 256 colors (or 1,024 × 768 in 256K colors). Although it incorporates many accelerated graphics functions, it does not support Intel's MMX architecture.

The Cx5510 support chip provides several additional functions. For audio, it adds SoundBlaster-compatible audio support along with a MIDI interface and digital audio processing. To augment the PCI bus control logic built into the MediaGX chip, the Cx5510 incorporates the bridge logic to add an ISA bus to the system along with four ATA ports for disk drives all with bus-mastering EIDE support. The Cx5510 also supplies the basic support functions required in any PC, such as an AT-compatible timer, an interrupt controller, and a DMA system. The Cx5510 also handles system power management.

M II

Today, the Cyrix flagship processor is its M II. Although it's an outgrowth of the 6x86 (M1) core logic design with twin seven-stage pipelines, Cyrix made numerous improvements throughout the chip to optimize its performance. The chip recognizes all of the instructions used by Intel's Pentium II microprocessor generation, including the full range of MMX instructions and identifies itself as a sixth-generation chip.

Rather than license MMX from Intel, however, Cyrix developed its own implementation based on the public disclosures Intel has made regarding the MMX instructions. MMX instructions add additional stages to the pipeline, stretching it to 9 or 10 stages, depending on the processing. Unlike the MMX-enhanced Pentium Pro that can simultaneously process two MMX instructions, the M II can tackle only one at a time (the same as the MMX-enhanced Pentium).

Perhaps the most noticeable improvement in the M II is its enlarged primary data/secondary instruction cache, now 64KB instead of 16KB. The microcache (the primary instruction cache) remains 256 bytes. As in the M1 design, the cache is four-way set-associative, uses a 32-byte line size, and can handle two accesses every clock cycle.

Inside the pipeline, Cyrix redesigned the translation look-aside buffer, giving it a two-level structure. A small (16 entries) high-speed direct-mapped buffer eliminate the need for an extra pipeline stage in most operations; it has about a 92 percent hit rate. When it misses, the second level, a six-way set-associative buffer with 384 entries, takes over, imposing only a one-cycle penalty (instead of stalling the pipeline).

In the M II, Cyrix has blessed the floating-point unit with its own bus leading directly to the cache. This allows both the integer and floating-point units to access the cache concurrently. In the M1, the floating-point unit stalled if the integer units were accessing the cache.

The M II uses a silicon substrate that's smaller than Intel's competitive Pentium II and Celeron chips but operates at a somewhat higher voltage, 2.9 volts for the core logic and 3.3 for input/output circuitry. Cyrix released its first M II chips operating at 233MHz using a 66MHz memory bus. As this is written, the M II is offered in 300, 333, and 350MHz versions. The internal multiplier that sets the relationship between bus and core speed is programmable for ratios of 2x, 2.5x, 3x, and 3.5x. Using the Super 7 socket, it supports memory bus speeds up to 100MHz and delivers performance within a few percentage points of competitive Intel products.

Jalapeno

On October 13, 1998, Cyrix announced the design of a new architecture for its next generation of microprocessors under the code name *Jalapeno*. The design adds a 3D graphics engine to an 11-stage pipeline and new floating-point unit. The floating-point unit is actually two units in one, with two execution units each capable of running standard floating-point or MMX instructions. The graphic section, designed for the 3D Now! instruction set, is tightly coupled to the floating-point unit and also incorporates hardware-based DVD playback.

Showing that Cyrix recognizes where its growth will come from, the company has optimized the design for minimal die size to keep manufacturing costs down. It also incorporates a 256KB on-chip level-two cache in an 8-way associated design that operates at full core speed. The graphics engine shares the cache to accelerate complex 3D tasks.

Current Products

Jalapeno's deep pipeline and on-chip L2 cache are designed to overcome bottlenecks typically associated with high-speed processors. By using an 11-stage pipeline, the design provides for scalability to beyond one gigahertz clock speeds. The 256KB on-chip L2 cache is 8-way associative, 8-way interleaved, and fully pipelined to operate at the core frequency. To further enhance memory performance, Cyrix has integrated a memory controller with a 3.2GB per second bandwidth.

The chip, expected to debut at about 600MHz, has a goal of topping one gigahertz. The chip will begin life with tight 0.18 micron design rules, fabricated at parent company National Semiconductor Facilities.

Memory

Memory is mandatory to make a microprocessor and your PC work. Moreover, the memory in your PC in part determines what programs you can run and how fast. Memory is vital. It's where all the bytes must be in order for your PC's microprocessor to operate. Memory holds both the raw data that needs to be processed and the results of the processing. Memory can even be a channel of communication between the microprocessor and its peripherals. Memory comes in many types, described and delimited by function and technology. Each has its role in the proper function of your PC.

Issues to consider in adding memory to your PC (or when judging between two PCs you are considering buying):

Issue	In short
Speed	Describes how quickly your memory passes data to your microprocessor. Today's fast PCs need memory that's faster than ever before. Today's quickest memory is ready within eight nanoseconds.
Front Side Bus	The channel through which data moves from memory to your microprocessor. The faster the bus, the faster your PC runs. Modern PCs have front side buses that run from 66 to 133 MHz.
Technology	Tells how the memory is fabricated and used. Today's PCs require synchronous memory, but soon a new technology called Rambus will be the top choice.
Capacity	Describes how many bytes (usually in millions) a module of memory can store. Although Windows 98 works with as little as 16 MB, for Windows 2000 you'll need at least 64MB. Even more is better.
Package	The physical form of memory that determines whether it will fit into your PC. Most desktop and notebook PCs use standard-size modules, but the two applications often observe different standards.
Module addressing	Tells how many address lines reach into a module and how many modules you need to make a single bank of memory. Today's modules are mostly four-byte or eight-bytes wide, requiring two (for four-byte) or one per 64-bit bank.
Cache memory	Special high-speed memory that matches microprocessor speed to slower memory systems. Most microprocessors have built in memory caches although some still use external secondary (or tertiary) cache memory. Cache memory uses an entirely different technology from the main memory in your PC.

The difference between genius and mere intelligence is storage. The quick-witted react fast, but the true genius can call upon memories, experiences, and knowledge to find real answers—the difference between pressing a button fast and having the insight to know which button to press.

PCs are no different. Without memory, a PC is nothing more than a switchboard. All of its reactions would have to be hard-wired. The machine could not read through programs or retain data. It would be stuck in a persistent vegetative state, kept alive by electricity but able to react only autonomously.

A fast microprocessor is meaningless without a place instantly at hand to store programs and data for current and future use. Its internal registers can only hold a handful of bytes (and they can be slippery critters, as you know if you've tried to grab hold of one), hardly enough for a program that accomplishes anything truly useful. Memory puts hundreds, thousands, even millions of bytes at the microprocessor's disposal, enough to hold huge lists of program instructions or broad blocks of data. Without memory, your PC's microprocessor is worthless. It can't even function as a doorstop; most microprocessors are too thin. Moreover, without enough memory your favorite applications will run slowly, if at all.

With today's huge applications and operating systems, memory can be one of the most important influences on the overall performance of your PC. Both the quantity and quality of the memory in your system have their effects on speed. Installing more memory helps your PC work its quickest. Memory technologies also influence the speed at which your PC's microprocessor can work. The same chip can be a speed demon when linked to an optimum memory system or a slug when chained to memory constrained by yesterday's technologies.

Background

The term "memory" covers a lot of territory even when confined to the computer field. Strictly speaking, memory is anything that holds data, even a single bit. That memory can take a variety of forms. A binary storage system, the kind used by today's PCs, can be built from marbles, marzipan, or metal-oxide semiconductors. Not all forms of memory work with equal efficacy (as you'll soon see), but the concept is the same with all of them—preserving bits of information in recognizable and usable form. Some forms of memory are just easier for an electronic microprocessor to recognize and manipulate. On the other hand, other sorts of memory may roll or taste better.

True old timers who ratcheted themselves down into PCs from mainframe computers sometimes speak of a computer's memory system as *core*. The term doesn't derive from the centrality of memory to the operation of the computer but rather from one of the first memory technologies used by ancient computers—a fabric of wires with a ferrite dough-nut, called a core, woven into (literally) each intersection of the warp and woof.

Although today core is but a memory, all current memory technologies share with it one important characteristic, that electricity be able to alter it. After all, today's computers think with electricity. They are made from electronic integrated circuits. Little wonder that the most practical memory for computers is also made from integrated circuits. But the memory that's available in IC form comes in a variety of ways, differing, for example, in function, accessibility, technology, capacity, and speed. Before we can get into the inti-mate details, we need to understand the broad concepts underlying computer memory.

Primary and Secondary Storage

A variety of devices and technologies can store digital information in a form that's electri-cally accessible. Function distinguishes what is generally termed computer memory from the kind of data storage kept by disks and tapes. Both normal memory and disk storage preserve information that the computer needs, but for different purposes.

What most people consider as computer memory in a specific sense functions as your PC's *primary storage*. That is, the contents of the storage system are in a form that your PC's microprocessor can immediately access, ready to be used. In fact, the direct instruc-tions used by some microprocessors can alter the values held in primary storage without the need to transfer the data into the chip's registers. For this reason, primary storage is sometimes called *working memory*.

The immediacy of primary memory requires that your microprocessor be able to find any given value without poring through huge blocks of data. The microprocessor must access any value at random. Consequently, most people refer to the working memory in their PCs as *Random Access Memory*, or RAM, although RAM has a more specific definition when applied to memory technologies.

No matter the name you use for it, primary storage is in effect the short-term memory of your PC. It's easy to get at but tends to be limited in capacity—at least compared to other kinds of storage.

The alternate kind of storage is termed *secondary storage*. In most PCs, disks and tape sys-tems serve as the secondary storage system. They function as the machine's long-term memory. Not only does disk and tape memory maintain information that must be kept for a long time, but also it holds the bulk of the information that the computer deals with. Secondary storage may be tens, hundreds, or thousands of times larger than primary stor-age. Secondary storage is often termed *mass storage* because of its voluminous capacity: It stores a huge mass of data.

Secondary storage is one extra step away from your PC's microprocessor. Your PC must transfer the information in secondary storage into its primary storage system in order to work on it. Secondary storage also adds a complication to the hardware. Most secondary storage is electromechanical. In addition to moving electrical signals, it also involves physically moving a disk or tape to provide access to information. Because mechanical things generally move more slowly than electrical signals—except in science fiction—secondary storage is slower than primary storage, typically by a factor of a thousand or more.

In other words, the most important aspect of primary storage system in your PC is access speed, although you want to have as much of it as possible. The most important aspect of secondary storage is capacity, although you want it to be as fast as possible.

Volatility

In all all-too-human memories, one characteristic separates out short-term and long-term memories. The former are fleeting. If a given fact or observation doesn't make it into your long-term memory, you'll quickly forget whatever it was—for example, the name that went with the face so quickly introduced to you at a party.

Computer memories are similar. The contents of some are fleeting. With computers, however, technology rather than attention determines what gets remembered and what is forgotten. For computers, the reaction to an interruption in electrical supply defines the difference between short- and long-term memory. The technical term used to describe the difference is memory *volatility*. Computer memory is classed either as non-volatile or volatile:

> **Volatile memory** is, like worldly glory, transitory. It lasts not the 3 score years and 10 of human existence or the 15 minutes of fame. It survives only as long as does its source of power. Remove power from volatile memory, and its contents evaporate in microseconds. The main memory system in nearly every PC is volatile.

> **Non-volatile memory** is exactly what you expect memory to be, forever. Once you store something in non-volatile memory, it stays there until you change it. Neither rain, nor sleet, nor dark of night, nor a power failure affects non-volatile memory. Types of non-volatile memory include magnetic storage (tape and disk drives) and special forms of memory chips (read-only memory and flash memory). Non-volatile memory can be simulated by providing backup power to volatile memory systems—a technology commonly used in the CMOS configuration memory systems used in most PCs—but this memory remains vulnerable to the vagaries of the battery. Should the battery die or should it slip from its connection even momentarily, the contents of this simulated non-volatile memory may be lost.

Given the choice, you'd of course want the memory of your PC to be non-volatile. The problem is that nearly all memory systems based solely on electricity and electronic storage are volatile. Electricity is notorious for its intransigence. Given the slightest opportunity, it will race off or drain away. On the other hand, electronic memory systems are fast: All non-volatile systems are slower, often substantially so.

Electronic memory systems can be made to simulate non-volatile memories by assuring a steady stream of power with a battery backup system. To prolong the period through which battery power can protect memory contents, these systems are also designed to minimize power drain. But technologies that consume the least power also tend to be more expensive. Consequently, the bulk of PC memory systems is volatile, prone to memory loss from power failures. PCs with memories innately immune to power loss would be prohibitively expensive and excruciatingly slow.

Measurement

In digital computer systems, memory operates on a very simple concept. In principle, all that computer memory needs to do is preserve a single bit of information so that it can later be recalled. Bit, an abbreviation for binary digit, is the smallest possible piece of information. A bit doesn't hold much intelligence—it only indicates whether something is or isn't—on or off, up or down, something (one) or nothing (zero). It's like the legal system: Everything is in black and white, and there are no shades of gray (at least when the gavel comes down).

When enough bits are taken collectively, they can code meaningful information. A pattern of bits can encode more complex information. In their most elementary form, for example, five bits could store the number 5. Making the position of each bit in the code significant increases the amount of information a pattern with a given number of bits can identify. (The increase follows the exponential increase of powers of two; for n bits, 22 unique patterns can be identified.) By storing many bit patterns in duplicative memory units, any amount of information can be retained.

Measuring Units

People don't remember the same way computers do. For us human beings, remembering a complex symbol can be as easy as storing a single bit. Although two choices may be enough for a machine, we prefer a multitude of selections. Our selection of symbols is as broad as the imagination. Fortunately for typewriter makers, however, we've reserved just a few characters as the symbol set for our language—26 uppercase letters, a matching number of lowercase letters, 10 numerals, and enough punctuation marks to keep grammar teachers preoccupied for entire careers. Representing these characters in binary form makes computers wonderfully useful, so computer engineers tried to develop the most efficient bit patterns for storing the diversity of symbols we finicky humans prefer. If you add together all those letters, numbers, and punctuation marks, you'll find that the lowest power of two that could code them all is 128 (or 2^7). Computer engineers went one better—by using an 8-bit code yielding a capacity of 256 symbols, they found that all the odd diacritical marks of foreign languages and similar nonsense (at least to English speakers) could be represented by the same code. The usefulness of this 8-bit code has made 8 bits the standard unit of computer storage, the ubiquitous byte.

Half a byte—a four-bit storage unit—is called a nibble because, at least in the beginning of the personal computer revolution, engineers had senses of humor. Four bits can encode 16 symbols—enough for 10 numerals and 6 operators (addition, subtraction, multiplication, division, exponents, and square roots), making the unit useful for numbers-only devices such as handheld calculators.

The generalized term for a package of bits is the digital word, which can comprise any number of bits that a computer might use as a group. The term "word" has developed a more specific meaning in the field of PCs, however, because Intel defines a word as 2 bytes of data, 16 bits. According to Intel, a double-word comprises 2 words, 32 bits; a quad-word is 4 words, 8 bytes, or 64 bits.

The most recent Intel microprocessors are designed to handle data in larger gulps. To improve performance, they feature wider internal buses between their integral caches and processing circuitry. In the case of the 486, this bus is 128 bits wide. Intel calls a single bus-width gulp a *line* of memory. Table 4.1 summarizes the common names for the sizes of primary storage units.

TABLE 4.1   Primary Intel Memory Storage Unit Designations

Unit	Bits	Bytes
Bit	1	0.125
Nibble	4	0.5
Byte	8	1
Word	16	2
Double-word	32	4
Quad-word	64	8
Line (486)	128	16

The Multimedia Extensions (MMX) used by all the latest PC microprocessors introduced four additional data types into PC parlance. These repackage groups of smaller data units into the 64-bit registers used by the new microprocessors. The new units are all termed *packed* because they fit or pack as many smaller units as possible into the larger registers. These new units are named after the smaller units comprising them. For example, when 8 bytes are bunched together into one 64-bit block to fit an MMX microprocessor register, the data is in *packed byte* form. Table 4.2 lists the names of these new data types.

TABLE 4.2   New 64-Bit MMX Data Types

Name	Basic Units	Number of Units
Packed byte	Byte (8 bits)	8
Packed word	Word (16 bits)	4
Packed double-word	Double-word (32 bits)	2
Quad-word	64 bits	1

To remember a single bit—whether alone or as part of a nibble, byte, word, or double-word—computer memory needs only to preserve a single state, that is, whether something is true or false, positive or negative, a binary one or zero. Almost anything can suffice to remember a single state—whether a marble is in one pile or another, whether a dab of marzipan is eaten or molding on the shelf, whether an electrical charge is present or absent. The only need is that the memory unit has two possible states and that it will maintain itself in one of them once it is put there. Should a memory element change on its own, randomly, it would be useless because it does not preserve the information that it's supposed to keep.

Although possibilities of what can be used for remembering a single state are nearly endless, how the bits are to be used makes some forms of memory more practical than others. The two states must be both readily changeable and readily recognizable by whatever mechanism is to use them. For example, a string tied around your finger will help you remember a bit state but would be inconvenient to store information for a machine. Whatever the machine, it would need a mechanical hand to tie the knot and some means of detecting its presence on your finger—a video camera, precision radar set, or even a gas chromatography system.

Today's applications demand thousands and millions of bytes of memory. The basic measuring units for memory are consequently large multiples of the byte. Although they wear common Greek prefixes shared by units of the metric system, the computer world has adopted a slightly different measuring system. Although the Greek prefix "kilo" means thousand, computer people assign a value of 1,024 to it, the closest round number in binary, 2^{10} (two to the tenth power). Larger units increase by a similar factor so that a megabyte is actually 2^{20} bytes and a gigabyte is 2^{30} bytes. Table 4.3 summarizes the names and values of these larger measuring units.

TABLE 4.3   Names and Abbreviations of Large Storage Units

Unit	Abbreviation	Size in Units	Size in Bytes
Kilobyte	KB or K	1,024 bytes	1,024
Megabyte	MB or M	1,024 kilobytes	1,048,576
Gigabyte	GB	1,024 megabytes	1,073,741,824
Terabyte	TB	1,024 gigabytes	1,099,511,627,776
Petabyte	PB	1,024 terabytes	1,125,899,906,843,624
Exabyte	EB	1,024 petabytes	1,152,921,504,607,870,976
Zettabyte	ZB	1,024 exabytes	1,180,591,620,718,458,879,424
Yottabyte	YB	1,024 zettabytes	1,208,925,819,615,701,892,530,176

Another term tossed into conversations about memory is "bank." The word indicates not a quantity but an arrangement of memory. A *bank* of memory is nothing more than a block of storage considered a single unit for some specific purpose. For example, a bank-switching system connects and disconnects banks or blocks of memory with your microprocessor.

When discussing the primary storage of PCs, "bank" has a more specific definition. In this context, a *bank* of memory is any size block of memory that is arranged with its bits matching the number of data connections to your microprocessor. That is, a bank of memory for a Pentium is a block of memory arranged 64 bits wide.

Although memory often comes in byte-width units, modern PCs have 32- or 64-bit memory buses. They require banks that are addressed four to eight bytes at a time. Consequently, each bank in such a machine may comprise four or eight memory modules, each unit having the same capacity.

Granularity

When system designers speak about memory granularity, they mean the smallest increments in which you can add memory to your PC. The granularity depends on three factors: the data bus width of your PC, the bus width of the memory, and the minimum size of the available memory units. When the bus width of your PC matches that of the memory modules it uses, the granularity is the minimum capacity module your PC will accommodate. When your PC data bus width exceeds the width of the modules it uses, you must add multiple modules for each memory increase. The granularity is then the total capacity of all the modules you must add for the minimum increase.

For example, if you have a Pentium computer that uses four-byte wide modules (called 72-pins SIMMs, discussed later), you need a minimum of two modules to expand the memory of your machine. In that the current smallest size of 72-bit module is 4MB, your machine has a memory granularity of 8MB. Most modern PCs have a granularity of 8MB.

The data bus of a PC depends on its processor. PCs with 486 microprocessors have data buses four bytes (32 bits) wide. Pentium and Pentium Pro PCs have eight-byte (64-bit) data buses.

Most modern PCs use memory modules that have bus widths from one to eight bytes wide. Your PC determines the memory module bus width that you must use because the width is fixed by the memory sockets on your PC's motherboard. Although memory modules with 8-bit bus widths remain available, few Pentium level computers use them. Early Pentium-class PCs used four-byte modules. Modern Pentium II, Celeron, Xeon, and Pentium III machines use 8-byte modules with a 168-pin interface.

Module capacities depend on the technology available and the price you're willing to pay. The earliest modules held only 256KB, and as technology permitted, capacities expanded to 1, 2, 4, 8, and 16MB per module. Today, high memory needs make the minimal module size 32MB. Capacities of 128MB are readily available.

New memory technologies are creating a counter-current in memory technology. Rambus memory, which many computer manufacturers have embraced for new and future machines because of its higher bandwidth and faster performance, comes packaged in modules with a two-byte granularity—that is, a 16-bit memory bus interface. Because of the radical design of Rambus memory, however, each bank of a 64-bit Pentium-class PC needs only a single module. The Rambus memory controller sorts out the difference.

Requirements

How much memory you actually need in a PC depends on what you want to do. Even the first PCs, which came equipped with only 16KB of memory, did what was expected of them. Today, even a thousand times more is not enough. Today's software simply demands megabytes of memory. A modern operating system requires 16 to 64MB just to get started. Getting optimum performance from your system may require substantially more. The minimum you need and the most you can reasonably use depends on the operating system you choose. Each of today's most popular operating systems—Windows 95, Windows 98, Windows NT, or Windows 2000—has its own particular need and limitations when it comes to memory.

Windows 95

Windows 95 is not a single entity. In its earliest form, its memory requirements were modest. After OSR 2, however, its needs increased substantially. To get the initial release of Windows 95 started, you needed only 4MB—if you were patient. With that little memory, you had to spend most of your time waiting while Windows tried to fill its memory needs with bytes from your hard disk. In other words, with 4MB the initial release of Windows 95 was functional but frustratingly slow. Its performance became tolerable—you were not apt to fall asleep when switching between applications—at about 8MB. But for full functionality, multitasking or loading several applications simultaneously, the early Windows 95 required about 16MB. The later release of Windows 95 *required* 16MB and came into its own at about 32MB. With any version, more memory is better, although the point of diminishing returns comes quickly, at about 64MB.

Windows 98

The memory needs of Windows 98 are akin to the later releases of Windows 95. It will work, albeit clumsily, with 16MB. Most computer makers equip their systems with 32MB to get acceptable performance. The point of diminishing returns appears at about 128MB.

Windows NT

The various versions of NT each have its own memory requirements. The current release (and final release—the change of nomenclature that makes Windows 2000 the successor to NT) version 4.00 requires 32MB to get started. NT is better than 16-bit Windows versions in handling memory and benefits more from larger endowments. Most NT users prefer about 128MB. From there, your wallet is the limit. NT makes memory up to the physical capacities of most PCs (that is, from 256MB to 512MB) useful, particularly if your application handles such tasks as audio or video editing, which involves large amounts of data.

Windows 2000

Microsoft asks for 64MB as the minimum requirement for Windows 2000, and the operating system will perform acceptably at this equipment level. As with other versions of NT, Windows 2000 can take advantage of memory to the limit of the physical capacity of most PCs. If the past is any guide, you won't want to stick with 64MB forever, however. Even for starting out, 128MB appears to be the preferred amount, and by the time Windows 2000 gives way to Windows 2002 (or whatever), you should expect 256MB to be the optimum level (if not the starting point for many PCs).

Access

Memory works like an elaborate set of pigeon holes used by post office workers to sort local mail. A memory location called an address is assigned to each piece of information to be stored. Each address corresponds to one pigeon hole, unambiguously identifying the location of each unit of storage. The address is a label, not the storage location itself (which is actually one of those tiny electronic capacitors, latches, or fuses).

Because the address is most often in binary code, the number of bits available in the code determines how many such unambiguous addresses can be directly accessed in a memory system. As noted before, an 8-bit address code permits 256 distinct memory locations (2^8 = 256). A 16-bit address code can unambiguously define 65,536 locations (2^{16} = 65,536). The available address codes generally correspond to the number of address lines of the microprocessor in the computer, although strictly speaking they need not do so.

The amount of data stored at each memory location depends on the basic storage unit, which varies with the design of the computer system. Generally, each location contains the same number of bits that the computer processes at one time—so an 8-bit computer (like the original PC) stores a byte at each address and a 32-bit machine keeps a full double-word at each address.

Although today's Pentium-class microprocessors have 32-bit registers and 64-bit data buses, the smallest unit of memory they can individually address is actually four double-words, 16 bytes. Smaller memory units cannot be individually retrieved because the four least significant address lines are absent from these microprocessors. Because the chips prefer to deal with data one line at a time, greater precision in addressing is unnecessary.

In writing to memory, where the chip might need to change an individual byte, the chips use a technology termed *masking*. Although they address the byte by the chunk it lies within, the mask prevents overwriting the bytes of memory that do not need to change.

Memory chips do not connect directly to the microprocessor's address lines. Instead, special circuits that compose the memory controller translate the binary data sent to the memory address register into the form necessary to identify the memory location requested and retrieve the data there. The memory controller can be as simple as address-decoding logic circuitry or an elaborate application-specific integrated circuit that combines several memory-enhancing functions.

To read memory, the microprocessor activates the address lines corresponding to the address code of the wanted memory unit during one clock cycle. This action acts as a request to the memory controller to find the needed data. During the next clock cycle, the memory controller puts the bits of code contained in the desired storage unit on the microprocessor's data bus. This operation takes two cycles because the memory controller can't be sure that the address code is valid until the end of a clock cycle. Likewise, the microprocessor cannot be sure the data is valid until the end of the next clock cycle. Consequently, all memory operations take at least two clock cycles.

Writing to memory works similarly: the microprocessor first sends off the address to write to, the memory controller finds the proper pigeon hole, and then the microprocessor sends out the data to be written. Again, the minimum time required is two cycles of the microprocessor clock.

Reading or writing can take substantially longer than two cycles, however, because micro-processor technology has pushed into performance territory far beyond the capabilities of today's affordable DRAM chips. Slower system memory can make the system micro-processor—and the rest of the PC—stop while it catches up, extending the memory read/write time by one or more clock cycles.

Constraints

All else being equal, more memory is better. Unfortunately, the last time all else was equal was before chaos split into darkness and light. You may want an unlimited amount of memory in your PC, but some higher authority may mitigate against it—simple physics for one. The Pauli exclusion principle made practical: You can't stuff your system with more RAM than will fit into its case.

Long before you reach any such physical limit, however, you'll face a more steadfast bar-rier. (After all, you can always buy a bigger case for your PC.) Many aspects of the design of real-world PCs limit the amount of memory that the system can actually use. Important factors include the addressing limits of microprocessors, the design limits of systems, and the requirement that program memory be contiguous.

Microprocessor Addressing

Every Intel microprocessor has explicit memory handling limits dictated by its design. Specifically, the amount of memory that a particular microprocessor can address is con-strained by the number of address lines assigned to that microprocessor and internal design features. Ordinarily, a microprocessor can directly address no more memory than its address lines will permit. Although modern microprocessors make this constraint pretty much irrelevant, for older chips these limits are very real.

A microprocessor needs some way of uniquely identifying each memory location it can access. The address lines permit this by assigning a memory location to each different pat-tern that can be coded by the chip's address lines. The number of available patterns then determines how much memory can be addressed. These patterns are, of course, simply a digital code.

The number of bits in the address code constrains the memory the microprocessor can use. The number of address lines used by the chip imposes a limit. For example, the on/off patterns of the 20 address lines of the PC's original 8088 microprocessor prevented PCs from using more than 1MB of memory. With today's microprocessors, however, the constraints of 32-bit (Pentium) or 36-bit addressing (Pentium Pro and newer) do affect the practical memory that can be used in a PC. Instead, the design of the overall system imposes substantially more modest limits.

System Capacity

No PCs take advantage of the full address range that their microprocessors can access. Although your system may have a Pentium or Pentium III chip that can address 4 or 64GB, no system makes any provision for installing that much memory.

As a practical matter, physically fitting that much memory inside a PC would be difficult with today's packaging technologies—unless, perhaps, your PC's case unfolded accordion-style. Moreover, although the price of memory is at an all-time low (as it usually is), adding a few gigabytes costs more than most of us want to spend.

It's doubtful you'd want a few gigabytes, anyway. Only a few specialized applications have regular need for a gigabyte of memory; you're likely not to notice any difference between 128MB and double that when you use your PC for normal home or office applications.

PC makers are not free to install any number of sockets for memory on their mother-boards. All of the various chipsets that make up the basic motherboard circuitry have their own addressing limits. Some allow as little as 256MB; others reach to 768MB or a full gigabyte. These limits cannot be exceeded no matter how many sockets are installed on the motherboard. The chipset simply doesn't generate the signals needed to address more memory.

Note, too, that plain Pentium chips have their own limit on useful memory. These chips allow DMA addressing to only 1GB of memory. Although they can perform some operations on higher addresses, many applications will be limited to the gigabyte that falls under DMA control.

Older PCs faced other limits on memory capacity, none of which you need to worry about in Pentium-class PCs. For example, many 386-based PCs that use the class AT bus for expansion generally permit the direct addressing of only 16MB. The reason for this memory-addressing shortfall is that the AT bus was designed with only 24 addressing lines rather than the full 32 of the microprocessor. A few systems built a similar limit into their motherboard memory because designing and building PCs with such limits was easier and cheaper. Some other systems restrict you to 32MB or so because of constraints built into their support chips.

As designers were breaking through the 16MB limit, many machines demonstrated contiguity problems because of early ROM shadowing designs and the memory apertures used by some dated video boards. These systems reserved one or more blocks of memory near the 16MB boundary for a specialized purpose. Unfortunately, many applications assumed they had contiguous memory and could not use the bytes beyond the shadowing area or aperture. Modern PCs move shadowing and apertures—should they have any—near the top of the 4GB address range of modern microprocessors, eliminating contiguity concerns.

Cacheability

Although the memory size that can be cached does not limit the total memory size of a PC, the amount of memory that is cacheable does constrain the amount of useful memory. Memory that is beyond the reach of the cache controller suffers a severe handicap in comparison to cached memory.

The limit on the amount of memory that can be cached depends on the microprocessor and chipset in your PC. For example, although the Pentium III microprocessor can directly address 64GB of RAM, only 4GB of that is cacheable.

With some chipsets, the amount of system memory that can be cached depends on the size of the secondary cache installed in the system. A larger cache can handle larger memory endowments.

Most PCs are designed so that their maximum memory endowment will be within the reach of the cache. Some systems in which the secondary cache is not integrated into the microprocessor may, however, require cache upgrades when you exceed a given size of memory.

In nearly every current Pentium or better PC, the cache can reach at least 128MB of system memory. If you're planning to dramatically increase the total memory installed in your PC, check to be sure that you will not exceed the limit that the secondary cache can address.

Technologies

In digital computers, it is helpful to store a state electrically so the machine doesn't need eyes or hands to check for the string, marble, or marzipan. Possible candidates for electrical state-saving systems include those that depend on whether an electrical charge is present or whether a current will flow. Both of these techniques are used in computer memories for primary storage systems.

The analog of electricity, magnetism, can also be readily manipulated by electrical circuits and computers. In fact, a form of magnetic memory called core was the chief form of primary storage for the first generation of mainframe computers. Some old timers still call primary storage "core memory" because of this history. Today, however, magnetic storage is today mostly reserved for mass storage because magnetism is one step removed from electricity. Storage devices have to convert electricity to magnetism to store bits and magnetic fields to electrical pulses to read them. The conversion process takes time, energy, and effort—all of which pay off for long-term storage, at which magnetism excels, but are unnecessary for the many uses inside the computer.

Using electrical circuits endows primary storage with the one thing it needs most—speed. Only part of its swiftness is attributable to electricity, however. More important is the way in which the bits of storage are arranged. Bits are plugged into memory cells that are arranged like the pigeon holes used for sorting mail—and for the same reason. Using this arrangement, any letter or bit of memory can be instantly retrieved when it is needed. The microprocessor does not have to read through a huge string of data to find what it needs. Instead, it can zero in on any storage unit at random. Consequently, this kind of memory is termed Random Access Memory, more commonly known by its acronym, RAM.

Random Access Memory

The vast majority of memory used in PCs is based on storing electrical charges rather than magnetic fields. Because all the other signals inside a PC are normally electronics, the use of electronic memory is only natural. It can operate at electronic speed without the need to convert technologies. Chip makers can fabricate electronic memory components exactly as they do other circuits, even on the same assembly lines. Best of all, electronic memory is cheap, the most affordable of all direct-access technologies.

Dynamic Memory

The most common electronic memory inside today's personal computers brings RAM to life using minute electrical charges to remember memory states. Charges are stored in small capacitors. The archetypal capacitor comprises two metal plates separated by a small distance that's filled with an electrical insulator. A positive charge can be applied to one plate, and because opposite charges attract, it draws a negative charge to the other nearby plate. The insulator separating the plates prevents the charges from mingling and neutralizing each other.

The capacitor can function as memory because a computer can control whether the charge is applied to or removed from one of the capacitor plates. The charge on the plates can thus store a single state and a single bit of digital information.

In a perfect world, the charges on the two plates of a capacitor would forever hold themselves in place. One of the imperfections in the real world results in no insulator being perfect. There's always some possibility that a charge will sneak through any material; although better insulators lower the likelihood, they cannot eliminate it entirely. Think of a perfect capacitor as being like a glass of water, holding whatever you put inside it. A real-world capacitor inevitably has a tiny leak through which the water (or electrical charge) drains out. The leaky nature of capacitors themselves is made worse by the circuitry that charges and discharges the capacitor because it, too, allows some of the charge to leak off.

This system seems to violate the primary principal of memory; it won't reliably retain information for very long. Fortunately, this capacitor-based system can remember long enough to be useful—a few or few dozen milliseconds—before the disappearing charges make the memory unreliable. Those few milliseconds are sufficient that practical circuits can be designed to periodically recharge the capacitor and refresh the memory. For example, some Motorola 1MB SIMMs require memory refreshing every 8 milliseconds. Some 8MB SIMMs need a refresh only every 32 ms.

Refreshing memory is akin to pouring extra water into a glass from which it is leaking out. Of course, you have to be quick to pour the water while there's a little left so you know which glass needs to be refilled and which is supposed to be empty.

To assure the integrity of its memory, PCs periodically refresh memory automatically. During the refresh period, the memory is not available for normal operation. Accessing memory also refreshes the memory cell. Depending on how a chip maker has designed its products, accessing a single cell also may refresh the entire row or column containing the accessed memory cell.

Because of the changing nature of this form of capacitor-based memory and its need to be actively maintained by refreshing, it is termed *dynamic memory*. Integrated circuits that provide this kind of memory are termed dynamic RAM or DRAM chips.

In personal computer memories, special semiconductor circuits that act like capacitors are used instead of actual capacitors with metal plates. A large number of these circuits are combined together to make a dynamic memory integrated circuit chip. As with true capacitors, however, dynamic memory of this type must be periodically refreshed.

Static Memory

Although dynamic memory tries to trap evanescent electricity and hold it in place, static memory allows the current flow to continue on its way. Instead, it alters the path taken by the power, using one of two possible courses of travel to mark the state being remembered. Static memory operates as a switch that potentially allows or halts the flow of electricity.

A simple mechanical switch will, in fact, suffice as a form of static memory. It has the handicap that it must be manually toggled from one position to another by a human or robotic hand.

A switch that can be itself controlled by electricity is called a relay, and this technology was one of the first used for computer memories. The typical relay circuit provided a latch. Applying a voltage to the relay energizes it, causing it to snap (from not permitting electricity to flow to allowing it). Part of the electrical flow could be used to keep the relay itself energized, which would in turn maintain the electrical flow. Like a door latch, this kind of relay circuit stays locked until some force or signal causes it to change, opening the door or the circuit.

Transistors, which can behave as switches, can also be wired to act as latches. In electronics, a circuit that acts as a latch is sometimes called a flip-flop because its state (which stores a bit of data) switches like a political candidate who flip-flops between the supporting and opposing views on sensitive topics. A large number of these transistor flip-flop circuits, when miniaturized and properly arranged, together make a static memory chip. Static RAM is often shortened to SRAM by computer professionals. Note that the principal operational difference between static and dynamic memory is that static RAM does not need to be periodically refreshed.

Read-Only Memory

Both the relay and the transistor latch must have a constant source of electricity to maintain their latched state. If the current supplying them falters, the latch will relax and the circuit forgets. Even static memory requires a constant source of electricity to keep it operating. Similarly, if dynamic memory is not constantly refreshed, it also forgets. When the electricity is removed from either type of memory circuit, the information that it held simply evaporates, leaving nothing behind. Consequently, these electrically dependent memory systems are called volatile. A constant supply of electricity is necessary for them to maintain their integrity. Lose the electricity, and the memory loses its contents.

Not all memory must be endowed with the ability to be changed. Just as there are many memories that you would like to retain—your first love, the names of all the constellations in the Zodiac, the answers to the chemistry exam—a computer is better off when it can remember some particularly important things without regard to the vagaries of the power line. Perhaps the most important of these more permanent rememberings is the program code that tells a microprocessor that it's actually part of a computer and how it should carry out its duties.

In the old-fashioned world of relays, you could permanently set memory in one position or another by carefully applying a hammer. With enough assurance and impact, you could guarantee that the system would never forget. In the world of solid state, the principal is the same but the programming instrument is somewhat different. All that you need are switches that don't switch—or, more accurately, that switch once and jam. This permanent kind of memory is so valuable in computers that a whole family of devices called read-only memory, or ROM, chips has been developed to implement it. These devices are called read-only because the computer that they are installed in cannot store new code in them. Only what is already there can be read from the memory.

In contrast, the other kind of memory, to which the microprocessor can write as well as read, is logically termed read/write memory. That term is, however, rarely used. Instead, read/write memory goes by the name RAM even though ROM also allows random access to its contents.

Mask ROM

If ROM chips cannot be written by the computer, the information inside must come from somewhere. In one kind of chip, the mask ROM, the information is built into the memory chip at the time it is fabricated. The mask is a master pattern that's used to draw the various circuit elements on the chip during fabrication. When the circuit elements of the chip are grown on the silicon substrate, the pattern includes the information that will be read in the final device. Nothing, other than a hammer blow or its equivalent in destruction, can alter what is contained in this sort of memory.

Mask ROMs are not common in personal computers because they require their programming be carried out when the chips are manufactured; changes are not easy to make and the quantities that must be made to make things affordable are daunting.

PROM

One alternative is the programmable read-only memory chip, or PROM. This style of circuit consists of an array of elements that work like fuses. Too much current flowing through a fuse causes the fuse element to overheat, melt, and interrupt the current flow, protecting equipment and wiring from overloads. The PROM uses fuses as memory elements. Normally, the fuses in a PROM conduct electricity just like the fuses that protect your home from an electrical disaster. Like ordinary fuses, the fuses in a PROM can be blown to stop the electrical flow. All it takes is a strong enough electrical current, supplied by a special machine called a PROM programmer or PROM burner.

PROM chips are manufactured and delivered with all of their fuses intact. The PROM is then customized for its given application using a PROM programmer to blow the fuses one-by-one according to the needs of the software to be coded inside the chip. This process is usually termed "burning" the PROM.

As with most conflagrations, the effects of burning a PROM are permanent. The chip cannot be changed to update or revise the program inside. PROMs are definitely not something for people who can't make up their minds—or for a fast changing industry.

EPROM

Fortunately, technology has brought an alternative, the erasable programmable read-only memory chip, or EPROM. Sort of self-healing semiconductors, the data inside an EPROM can be erased and the chip re-used for other data or programs.

EPROM chips are easy to spot because they have a clear window in the center of the top of their packages. Invariably, this window is covered with a label of some kind and with good reason. The chip is erased by shining high-intensity ultraviolet light through the window. If stray light should leak through the window, the chip could inadvertently be erased. (Normal room light won't erase the chip because it contains very little ultraviolet. Bright sunshine does, however, and can erase EPROMs.) Because of their versatility, permanent memory, and easy reprogrammability, EPROMs are ubiquitous inside personal computers.

EEPROM

A related chip is called electrically erasable programmable read-only memory, or EEP-ROM (usually pronounced double-E PROM). Instead of requiring a strong source of ultraviolet light, EEPROMs need only a higher than normal voltage (and current) to erase their contents. This electrical erasability brings an important benefit: EEPROMs can be erased and reprogrammed without popping them out of their sockets. EEPROMs give electrical devices such as computers and their peripherals a means of storing data without the need for a constant supply of electricity. Note that although EPROMs must be erased all at once, each byte in EEPROM is independently erasable and writable. You can change an individual byte if you want. Consequently, EEPROMs have won favor for storing setup parameters for printers and other peripherals. You can easily change individual settings yet still be assured the values you set will survive switching the power off.

EEPROMs have one chief shortcoming: they can be erased only a finite number of times. Although most EEPROM chips will withstand tens or hundreds of thousands of erase-and-reprogram cycles, that's not good enough for general storage in a PC that might be changed thousands of times each second you use your machine. This problem is exacerbated by the manner in which EEPROM chips are erased; unlike ordinary RAM chips in which you can alter any bit whenever you like, erasing an EEPROM means eliminating its entire contents and reprogramming every bit all over again. Change any one bit in an EEPROM, and the life of every bit of storage is shortened.

Flash Memory

A new twist to EEPROM is *flash ROM*, sometimes called flash RAM (as in the previous edition of this book—we've altered our designation to better fit usage and continuity in our discussion of ROM technology) or just flash memory. Instead of requiring special, higher voltages to be erased, flash ROM can be erased and reprogrammed using the normal voltages inside a PC. Normal read and write operations use the standard five-volt power that is used by most PC logic circuits. (Three-volt flash ROM is not yet available.) An erase operation requires a *super-voltage*, a voltage in excess of the normal operating supply for computer circuitry, typically 12 volts.

For system designers, the electrical reprogrammability of flash ROM makes it easy to use. Unfortunately, flash ROM is handicapped by the same limitation as EEPROM; its life is finite (although longer than ordinary EEPROM) and it must be erased and reprogrammed as one or more blocks instead of individual bytes.

The first generation of flash ROM made the entire memory chip a single block, so the entire chip had to be erased to reprogram it. Newer flash ROMs have multiple, independently erasable blocks that may range in size from 4KB to 128KB. The old, all-at-once style of flash ROM is now termed *bulk erase* flash memory because of the need to erase it entirely at once.

New multiple-block flash ROM is offered in two styles. *Sectored-erase* flash ROM is simply divided into multiple sectors. *Boot block* flash ROM specially protects one or more blocks from normal erase operations so that special data in it—such as the firmware that defines the operation of the memory—will survive ordinary erase procedures. Altering the boot block typically requires applying the super-voltage to the reset pin of the chip at the same time as performing an ordinary write to the book block.

Although modern flash ROMs can be erased only in blocks, most support random reading and writing. Once a block is erased, it will contain no information. Each cell will contain a value of zero. Your system can read these blank cells, although without learning much. Standard write operations can change the cell values from zero to one but cannot change them back. Once a given cell has been changed to a logical one with a write operation, it will maintain that value until the flash ROM gets erased once again, even if the power to your system or the flash ROM chip fails.

Flash memory is an evolving technology. The first generation of chips required that your PC or other device using the chips handle all the minutiae of the erase and write operations. Current generation chips have their own on-board logic to automate these operations, making flash ROM act more like ordinary memory. The logic controls the timing of all the pulses used to erase and write to the chip, ensures that the proper voltages reach the memory cells, and even verifies that each write operation was carried out successfully.

On the other hand, the convenience of using flash ROM has led many developers to create disk emulators from it. For the most effective operation and longest life, however, these require special operating systems (or modified versions of familiar operating systems) that minimize the number of erase-and-reprogramming cycles.

Virtual Memory

Even before anyone conceived the idea of the first PC, computer designers faced the same tradeoff between memory and mass storage. Mass storage was plentiful and cheap; memory was expensive, so much so that not even large corporations could afford as much as they wanted. In the early years of PCs, engineers tried to sidestep the high cost of memory by faking it, making computers think they had more memory that they actually did. With some fancy footwork and a lot of shuffling around of bytes, they substituted mass storage for memory. The engineers called the memory the computer thought it had but that really didn't exist in reality *virtual memory*. Although the cost of memory has fallen by a millionfold, memory use has followed suit. Programs' need for memory still outpaces what any reasonable person or organization can afford (or wants to pay for), so virtual memory not only exists but is flourishing.

Microprocessors cannot ordinarily use disk storage to hold the data they work on. Even if they could, it would severely degrade the performance of the system because the access time for disk storage is thousands of times longer than for solid-state memory. To prevent performance problems and keep active programs in solid-state memory where your PC's microprocessor cannot hold them, virtual memory systems swap blocks of code and data between solid-state and disk storage.

Demand Paging

Most modern PCs take advantage of a feature called *demand paging* that has been part of all Intel microprocessors since the 386. These chips are able to track memory contents as it is moved between disk and solid state memory in 4KB blocks. The microprocessor assigns an address to the data in the block, and the address stays constant regardless of where the data actually gets stored.

Once solid-state memory reaches its capacity, the virtual memory system copies the contents of one or more pages of memory to disk as the memory space is required. When the system needs data that has been copied to disk, it copies the least recently used pages to disk and refills their space with the disk-based pages it needs. When your system attempts to read from a page with an address that's not available in solid-state memory, it creates a *page fault*. The fault causes a virtual memory manager routine to handle the details of exchanging data between solid-state and disk storage.

This reactive kind of control is called *demand paging* because it swaps data only when the microprocessor demands unavailable addresses. It makes no attempt to anticipate the needs of the microprocessor.

Virtual memory technology allows your PC to run more programs than would be otherwise possible given the amount of solid-state memory in your system. The effective memory of your system approaches the spare capacity of your disk. The downside is that it takes away from the capacity of your hard disk (although disk storage is substantially less expensive than solid-state memory by about two orders of magnitude). In addition, performance slows substantially when your system must swap memory.

Virtual memory is an old technology, harking back to the days of mainframe computers when, as now, disk storage was cheaper than physical memory. Many DOS applications took advantage of the technology, and it has been part of every version of Windows since Windows 386.

Windows uses a demand-paging system that's based on a least-recently used algorithm. That is, the Windows virtual memory manager decides which data to swap to disk based on when it was last used by your system. The Windows VMM also maintains the virtual memory page table, which serves as a key to which pages are used by each application, which are kept in solid-state storage, and which are on disk.

Windows decides which pages to swap to disk using two flags for each page. The *accessed* flag indicates that the page has been read from or written to since the time it was loaded into memory. The *dirty* flag indicates the page has been written to.

When Windows needs more pages in solid-state memory, it scans through its page table looking for pages showing neither the accessed nor dirty flags. As it makes its scan, it resets the accessed but not the dirty flags. If it does not find sufficient unflagged pages, it scans through the page table again. This time, more pages should be unflagged because of the previous resetting of the accessed flags. If it still cannot find enough available pages, the Windows virtual memory manager then swaps pages regardless of the flags.

Swap Files

The disk space used by a virtual memory system usually takes the form of an ordinary file, although one reserved for its special purpose. Engineers call the virtual memory file a swap file because the memory system swaps data to and from the file as the operating system requires it. Although earlier versions of Windows had several options you could choose for swap files—primarily the choice between a temporary file that swelled as you used it and a permanent file that forever stole disk space—Windows 95 erased such complications.

Under Windows 95 as well as Windows 98, the swap file mixes together features of temporary and permanent swap files. Like a temporary swap file, the current Windows swap file is dynamic, expanding as your system demands virtual memory and contracting when it does not. In addition, it can shuffle itself into the scatter clusters of a fragmented hard disk. It can even run on a compressed hard disk.

Windows gives you full menu control of its swap file. You can start the virtual memory control system by clicking the Virtual Memory button you'll find in the Performance tab of Device Manager. (You start the Device Manager by clicking the System icon in Control Panel.) Once you click the Virtual Memory button, you should see a screen like that shown in Figure 4.1.

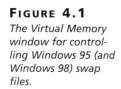

FIGURE 4.1

The Virtual Memory window for controlling Windows 95 (and Windows 98) swap files.

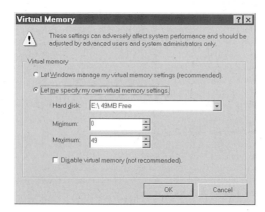

You can choose to let Windows choose the size and place of your swap file or take direct control. By default, Windows puts your swap file in the Windows directory of your C: drive. By selecting the appropriate box, you can tell Windows the disk and directory in which to put your swap file and set minimum and maximum limits for its size.

Logical Organization

Although it may be made from the same kind of chips, not all memory in a PC works in the same way. Some programs are restricted to using only a fraction of the available capacity; some memory is off limits to all programs.

Memory handling is, of course, determined by the microprocessor used to build a computer. Through the years, however, the Intel microprocessors used in PCs have dramatically improved their memory capabilities. In less than seven years, the microprocessor-mediated memory limitation was pushed upward by a factor of 4,000, far beyond the needs of any program written or even conceived of—at least today.

Neither PCs nor applications have kept up with the memory capabilities of microprocessors. Part of the reason for this divergence has to do with some arbitrary design decisions made by IBM when creating the original PC. But the true underlying explanation is your own expectations. You expect new PCs to be compatible with the old, run the same programs, and use most of the same expansion hardware. To achieve that expected degree of compatibility, the defects and limitations of the original PC's memory system have been carried forward for ensuing generations to enjoy. A patchwork of improvements adds new capabilities without sacrificing (much of) this backward compatibility, but they further confuse the PC's past memories.

The result is that PCs are stuck with a hierarchy of memory types, each with different abilities and compatibilities, some useful to some applications, some useless to all but a few. Rather than improve with age, every advance adds more to the memory mix-up.

The classification of memory depends, in part, on the operating system that you run. Part of modern operating systems is memory management software that smoothes over the differences in memory type.

Hardware

At the hardware level, your PC divides its memory into several classes that cannot be altered except by adjusting your hardware. The electrical wiring of your PC determines the function of these memory types. Although your PC's setup procedure may give you the option of adjusting the amount of memory assigned to some of these functions, the settings are made in the hardware circuitry of your PC. They cannot ordinarily be adjusted while programs are running because the change you make will overrule anything the program does. Moreover, the alterations will likely surprise your programs. For example, the program may expect an address range in the memory to be available for its use that the hardware setting reappropriates for another purpose. The effect is like pulling a carpet out from under a well-meaning grandmother—a crash from which she might not be able to get up.

Real-Mode Memory

Memory that can be addressed in real mode is the foundation of modern PC architecture—the system starts with and builds upon real-mode memory.

For today's microprocessors based on the Intel design to be backward compatible, they must mimic the memory design of the original 8086 family. The hallmark of this design is the real operating mode in which they must begin their operation. Because of the original Intel 8086 microprocessor design, real mode only allows for 1MB of memory. Because it serves the host microprocessor operating in its real mode, this starting memory is termed *real-mode memory*.

The address range used by real-mode memory starts at the very beginning of the address range of Intel microprocessors, zero. The last address is one shy of a megabyte (because counting starts at zero instead of one), that is, 1,048,575 in decimal, expressed in hexadecimal as 0FFFFF(Hex). Because this memory occurs at the base or bottom of the microprocessor address range, it is also called *base memory*.

When real mode was supplemented by protected mode with the introduction of the 80286 microprocessor, a new, wider, more exotic address range opened up in protected mode. Because this range was off limits to microprocessors and programs of the then status quo, the real-mode range also earned the epithet *conventional memory*, hinting that there was something unconventional, even suspicious, about using addresses beyond the megabyte limit. Today, of course, the most conventional new PCs sold have many times the old "conventional" memory limit.

Protected-Mode Memory

The rest of the memory that can be addressed by modern microprocessors is termed *protected-mode memory*. As the name implies, this memory can be addressed only when the microprocessor is running in its protected mode. The address range of protected-mode memory stretches from the top of real-mode memory to the addressing limit of your microprocessor. In other words, it starts at 1MB—1,048,576 or 100000(Hex)—and extends to 16MB for 286 microprocessors, to 4GB for 386 through Pentium Pro and Celeron microprocessors, and to 64GB with the Pentiums II and III (including the Xeon offshoots).

To contrast it with base memory, protected-mode memory is sometimes called *extended memory*.

Lower Memory

When IBM's engineers created the PC, they reserved half of the basic 1MB addressing range of the 8088 microprocessor, 512KB bytes, for the system's BIOS code and direct microprocessor access to the memory used by the video system. The lower half was left for running programs.

Even though 512KB seemed generous in the days when 64KB was the most memory other popular computers could use, the wastefulness of the original limit soon became apparent. Less than a year after the original PC was introduced, IBM engineers rethought their memory division and decided that an extra 128KB could safely be reassigned to program access. That change left 384KB at the upper end of the address range for use by video memory and BIOS routines.

This division persists, leaving us with the lower 640KB addressing range assigned for program use. Because it appears at the lower end of the real-mode range, this memory is commonly called *lower memory*.

The "lower memory" designation is rather recent and reflects the breaking away of PCs from any one operation system. Lower memory once was called *DOS memory* because the programs written using DOS could only run in lower memory and DOS was the only significant operating system available.

BIOS Data Area

IBM also reserved the first kilobyte of lower memory for specific hardware and operating system functions, to provide space for remembering information about the system and the location of certain sections of code that are executed when specific software interrupts are made. Among other functions, this memory range holds data used by BIOS functions, and it is consequently called the *BIOS data area*.

Included among the bytes at the bottom of the addressing range are interrupt vectors, pointers that tell the microprocessor the addresses used by each interrupt it needs to service. Also kept in these bottom bytes is the keyboard buffer—16 bytes of storage that hold the code of the last 16 characters you pressed on the keyboard. This temporary storage allows the computer to accept your typing while it's temporarily busy on other tasks. It can then go back and process your characters when it's not as busy. The angry beeping your PC makes sometimes when you hold down one key for too long is the machine's way of complaining that the keyboard buffer is full and that it has no place to put the latest characters, which it steadfastly refuses to accept until it can free up some buffer space. In addition, various system flags, indicators of internal system conditions that can be equated to the code of semaphore flags, are stored in this low memory range.

Upper Memory

The real-mode addressing range above lower memory is called, logically enough, *upper memory*. Unlike the address range of lower memory that is, in most PCs, completely filled with physical RAM, upper memory is an amalgam of RAM, ROM, and holes. Not all addresses in upper memory have physical memory assigned to them. Instead, a few ranges of addresses are given over to specific system support functions and other ranges are left undefined. The expansion boards you slide into your PC take over some of these unused ranges to give your microprocessor access to the BIOS code stored in the ROM chips on the boards.

In most PCs, the top 32KB of upper memory addresses are occupied by the ROM holding the BIOS code of the system. Until recently, all IBM computers filled the next lower 32KB with the program code of its Cassette BASIC language.

The memory mapping abilities of 386 and later microprocessors allow software designers to remap physical memory to some of the unused addresses in the upper memory range. Using memory management software, DOS can run some utility programs in upper memory addresses. Consequently, this memory range is sometimes called *high DOS memory*, but that term is misleading. Because of the design of DOS, however, the program code in normal DOS applications must fit into a contiguous block of addresses. System functions assigned to address ranges in upper memory interrupt the contiguity of upper memory and prevent DOS applications from running in the address space there.

High Memory Area

Microprocessors with protected mode memory capabilities have an interesting quirk: They can address more than one megabyte of memory in real mode. When a program running on an 8088 or 8086 microprocessor tries to access memory addresses higher than 1MB, the addresses "wrap" around and start back at zero. However, with a 286 or more recent microprocessor, including the 486 and Pentiums, if the 21st address line (which 8088s and their kin lack) is activated, the first segment's worth of addresses in excess of 1MB will reach into extended memory. This address line (A20) can be activated during real mode using a program instruction. As a result, one segment of additional memory is accessible by 286 and better microprocessors in real mode.

This extra memory, a total of 64KB minus 16 bytes, is called the *high memory area*. Because it is not contiguous with the address range of lower memory, it cannot be used as extra memory by ordinary DOS applications. However, memory managers can relocate driver and small utility programs into its address range much as they do the addresses in upper memory. Only one driver or utility, no matter its size (at least as long as it fits—that means it must be less than 65,520 bytes), can be loaded into the high memory area under DOS.

Frame Buffer Memory

PC video systems are memory-mapped, which means that the color of every pixel on your monitor gets stored in a memory location that your PC's microprocessor can directly alter the same way it writes data into memory. Your PC holds a complete image frame in memory. Your video system scans the memory address by address to draw an image frame on your monitor screen. The memory that holds a complete image frame is termed a *frame buffer*.

Because your PC's microprocessor needs direct access to the frame buffer to change the data (and hence pixels or dots) in the image, the memory used by the frame buffer must fit within the addressing range of your PC's microprocessor. In the early years of PCs, IBM reserved several address ranges in upper memory for the frame buffers used by the different video standards it developed. The frame buffer of the VGA system begins immediately after the 640KB top boundary of lower memory. The memory assigned to the original monochrome display system and still used in VGA text modes starts 64KB higher.

Video systems more recent than VGA often place frame buffers in the protected-mode addressing range. Even these still use the VGA frame buffer range for compatibility purposes.

The physical memory of the frame buffer is usually separate and distinct from the main memory of your PC. In most PCs, the frame buffer is part of the video board installed in an expansion slot. Even PCs that incorporate their video circuitry on the motherboard separate the frame buffer from main memory (although this design is changing in Unified Memory Architecture systems, noted later). Because of this separation and because the frame buffer cannot be used for running programs, the amount of memory in the frame buffer is usually *not* counted in totaling up the amount of RAM installed in a PC.

A *memory aperture* is the address range used by PC peripherals for memory-mapped input/output operation and control, one of the most common uses being to reach the frame buffer. That is, your PC sends data to the frame buffer by writing to the range of addresses in the aperture. The video controller picks up the data there, converts it to video, and passes it along to your monitor.

Because most display adapters include their own video memory, these memory apertures don't steal any of the RAM you install in your PC. Moreover, because the frame buffer memory is not used by your programs for execution, it need not be contiguous with the rest of your system's memory. The exception appears in systems with Unified Memory Architecture (discussed later) that reserve a block of system memory for use as the frame buffer.

Shadow Memory

The latest 32-bit and 64-bit computers provide a means to access memory through 8-, 16-, 32-, or 64-bit data buses. It's often most convenient to use a 16-bit data path for ROM BIOS memory (so only two expensive EPROM chips are needed instead of the four required by a 32-bit path or eight by a 64-bit path). Many expansion cards that may have on-board BIOS extensions connect to their computer hosts through 8-bit data buses. As a result, these memory areas cannot be accessed nearly as fast as the host system's 32-bit or 64-bit RAM. This problem is compounded because BIOS routines, particularly those used by the display adapter, once were the most often used code in the computer.

To break through this speed barrier, many PC designers started to shadow memory. That is, they copied the slot 8- or 16-bit ROM routines into fast 32-bit or 64-bit RAM and used the memory mapping abilities of 386 and newer microprocessors to switch the RAM into the address range used by the ROM. Execution of BIOS routines sped up by a factor of four or more—more because a greater wait states often are imposed when accessing slower ROM memory. Of course, these shadow memory routines are volatile and must be loaded with the BIOS routines every time the computer is booted up.

Windows has changed all of that. It uses its own protected-mode drivers to handle the functions once left to the BIOS. These drivers typically execute using 32-bit code in protected mode (hence the name) and make BIOS code look like it's running on an abacus. In fact, the only time that BIOS code comes into play in a modern PC is when it's booting up, before Windows loads. From that perspective, there's no reason to use ROM shadowing on a modern PC.

Most modern PCs make shadowing an option that can be switched on or off during their advanced setup procedures. Switching shadowing off prevents the relocated ROM from interfering with normal RAM addressing.

In modern systems, you have little incentive to tangle with shadowing issues. It doesn't hurt performance because most of what your PC does ignores it entirely. Its impact on the memory available in most PCs is trivial. And although shadowing often caused trouble in early systems that used it, the technology is so commonplace and widely understood that few problems arise from it today.

Shadowing persists because some users expect it. After all, you never know when you'll want to torch the cobwebs off your copy of DOS 2.1 and run VisiCalc on your PC.

Cache Memory

The cache memory, used by most of today's PCs to match their microprocessors to main memory, operates as a separate and distinct system, one beyond the control of your programs. Its function is determined by your PC's hardware, and the cache is addressed solely by your PC's cache controller memory locations. To your microprocessor, the cache appears to have the addresses of the data that's replicated in the cache.

Cache adds speed but not capacity to your PC's memory system. The bytes devoted to the cache are not counted when totaling the memory in a given PC.

Bank-Switched Memory

Running out of addresses is not limited only to computer memory systems but can be a more common problem. For example, the telephone company long ago—back when there was but one telephone company—faced its own addressing shortage when the number of phones in use exceeded the 10 million distinct 7-digit telephone numbers. The telephone company solution was to break the nation (and the world) into separate ranges, what we know now as area codes. Each area code has the full 10 million phone numbers available to it, expanding the range of available telephone numbers by a factor equal to the number of area codes.

When PCs were limited to a few dozen kilobytes by the addressing range of their micro-processors, clever engineers developed their own version of the area code. They divided memory into *banks*, each of which individually fit into the address range of the micro-processor. Using the computer equivalent of a giant channel selector knob, they enabled the PC to switch any one of the banks into the addressing range of the microprocessor while removing the rest from the chip's control. The maximum addressable memory of the system becomes the product of the addressing range of the chip and the number of banks available. Because the various banks get switched in and out of the system's limited addressing range, this address extension technique is usually called *bank switching*.

Originally used in computers that predated IBM's PC, innovative manufacturers adapted bank switching to the early models of the PC to create expanded memory. Bank switching is also used to squeeze a wider address range for video memory into the 64KB range allowed in high DOS memory area.

The memory banks on the motherboards of most modern PCs have nothing to do with bank switching. Rather, true bank switching requires a special memory board that incor-porates data registers that serve as the actual bank switches. In addition, programmers must specifically write their applications to use bank-switched memory. The program (or operating system that it runs under) must know how to track every switch and turn of memory to be sure that the correct banks is in use at any given moment.

The large address ranges of modern microprocessors have made bank switching unneces-sary except for the special case of video memory. In fact, modern chips can simulate bank switched memory (specifically EMS memory, discussed Appendix M, "Legacy Memory") using their internal memory management facilities.

Unified Memory Architecture

A continuing design trend in PCs, particularly lower cost models, is *Unified Memory Architecture*, sometimes abbreviated as UMA. This design unifies the memory in a PC by moving the video frame buffer from its privileged position connected through a bus to the video controller to part of the main memory of the PC. In other words, part of the memory of the system gets allocated for storing video images. Because both the microprocessor and video controller have access to this memory, it is sometimes called *shared memory architecture*.

The chief attraction of this design is that it cuts the cost of a PC. Manufacturers no longer need pay for video board memory. It can also improve the performance of a PC because the frame buffer, as part of main memory, operates at the same speed as main memory rather than at the lower rate associated with the expansion bus or local bus.

The UMA design can be misleading. Because some of the memory in a UMA system must be given over to the video buffer, it is not available to your applications. Hence, a UMA system acts as if it has less memory than the specification sheet implies.

To the digital logic of your PC's microprocessor, the UMA design appears no different from a conventional video system. The frame buffer appears in the same logical location as always. If it did not, your applications would not be able to access it. On the other hand, the hardware implementation of UMA is radically different and, if poorly carried out, can have dramatic effects on the performance of the overall PC.

The conventional memory design makes video memory a self-contained subsystem. It handles its own housekeeping and provides its own, dedicated access channel for the video controller, which operates independent of the host microprocessor. The UMA design makes video memory part of the main memory system where it is treated as ordinary DRAM. The graphics chip, should the system have one, must share access to the frame buffer with the rest of the system. Or the microprocessor may manage video operations itself, taking over the function of the graphics chip (which again, helps to trim costs). Either way, performance suffers. The multitasking aspect of having a graphics accelerator is lost. Moreover, because video memory in UMA designs is drawn from the PC's main memory, it cannot benefit from high-speed memory designs (such as Video RAM) without forcing the entire system to use the more costly technology.

Software

For PC programs, the vast amount of memory in today's computers is like the Wild West—a seemingly unlimited romping ground under a forever-blue sky. When two butt head-to-head, however, the odds of survival are worse than at the O.K. Corral. Everybody ends up dead. Multiple programs cannot be turned loose in memory lest they collide and kill one another. Memory must be managed and allocated to each application, and modern PCs give that management job to the operating system.

Windows uses prodigious amounts of memory but makes up for its profligacy by managing the memory that you have. Moreover, by requiring programs to be written without reference to absolute memory locations, Windows and particularly Windows 95 and its successors erase many of the old concerns of DOS memory management—at least when you run Windows applications. Windows 95, for example, uses a flat memory model, which eliminates the penalties involved with Intel's segmented memory architecture. On the downside, however, every version of Windows adds its own memory terminology and a whole new set of concerns.

Although the latest versions of Windows can address all of the memory in your PC and treat it as a single large block, it allocates memory into functional ranges. Each of these ranges has its own limitations, although their constraints only appear when you try to run old applications designed before the acceptance of Windows 95.

DOS Memory Under Windows

Old DOS applications don't follow the Windows rules and don't benefit from the wide Windows address space. They must still abide by the restrictions of their own memory addressing—which means they can step beyond real mode's megabyte. When you run an old DOS application under a current Windows version, however, you can often use more memory than DOS yielded you. Windows 95 (and newer versions) allows most DOS applications to access devices through its virtual device drivers, so you don't need to clutter the real-mode address range in your DOS sessions with drivers. This design keeps more memory free for your DOS applications.

Some old DOS applications require *expanded memory*. Although Windows itself uses extended rather than expanded memory, it can emulate expanded memory for DOS applications that need it. You can control this feature through the MS DOS properties sheet, as shown in Figure 4.2.

FIGURE 4.2

The Windows MS DOS properties sheet.

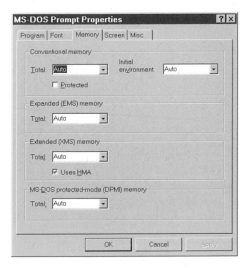

System Resource Memory

Although Windows sees the memory in your PC as one vast expanse, it internally allocates blocks of memory to specific purposes. Windows calls these blocks *heaps*, and together they make up *system resource memory*. For reasons reaching back into the history of the Windows environment, these blocks are fixed in size and can impose severe limits on the operation of your PC. You may have dozens of megabytes available in your PC, but Windows will issue an "out of memory" error when one of these heaps approaches its capacity. It may also tell you to unload some of your applications to free up memory, although this rarely helps. Windows just doesn't deal with depleted resources well, and the best cure is usually a reboot.

For example, if you try to put too many icons on the screen at once, you may run out of memory in a heap. Windows will report too little memory and fail to rasterize the icons, leaving them black boxes, even though you have multiple megabytes of free memory in your system. Free up some memory, and the icons will come back, but whatever problem caused the shortfall—typically a poorly designed program—will still nibble away at your resources, often even after you unload the errant application.

You can check the available system resources in a Window 95 or 98 system by choosing the System icon from the Control Panel window. Select the Performance tab, and Windows will list its memory and system resource usage, as shown in Figure 4.3.

FIGURE 4.3

The Windows Performance tab.

Application Memory

The amount of memory you have installed in your PC and the amount of memory available to your applications are not directly related because of Windows' use of virtual memory. Your programs get both more and less than the physical memory installed in your PC. Virtual memory gives them more. Windows gives them less—less because it needs space for its own files and that need is big. About half the memory noted as the minimal requirement for running Windows is typically given over to operating system overhead. The balance is shared between your applications.

By design, Windows can address all of the memory you install in your PC. Microsoft targeted Windows 95 to reach the 4GB capacity of Intel microprocessors like the Pentium and Celeron. However, the operating system imposes one limit on this memory it makes available to your Windows applications: Half of the 4GB address range is reserved for Windows' own purposes. The reserve includes addresses, not physical memory, and has little effect on practical PCs. No available system can handle as much as 2GB of physical memory, so at least half the address range of every PC is otherwise unused.

Although the physical memory in your PC does not affect how many applications you can load, it does affect performance by reducing Windows' reliance on virtual memory. The less often Windows must resort to virtual memory, the less disk access will affect performance. Your PC will run fastest when you have sufficient physical memory that Windows can load all of your applications into it.

Performance

Besides quantity—the amount of memory you have stuffed into your PC—the other important issue is the performance. The rate at which your PC's microprocessor can push data into memory and pull information out is one of the major determinants of the overall performance of the system. Even the fastest microprocessor dawdles along when its memory cannot respond quickly enough.

Memory performance is not a single issue, however. Although the bottom line is a single factor—speed—achieving a given level of performance may involve exotic combinations of semiconductor technology, the logical and electrical interconnection of memory chips, chip design, and even system architecture. These issues aren't just the concern of the system designer, however. When you select a new PC or want to upgrade your existing machine, you'll confront all of these issues.

Memory Speed

Memory speed is one of the most important limitations on the performance of PCs. Affordable memory chips simply cannot keep up with the processing speed of today's Pentium processors.

In fact, speed deficiencies are nothing new, having first occurred in computers based on the lowly 286 microprocessor. Ordinary memory chips could not keep pace with the speed of such a fast (by the standards of 1984, remember) microprocessor; the chip would request bytes in such short order that memory was unable to respond. Consequently, engineers added what has become the bane of every memory system in PCs to this day, *wait states*. Although you don't hear about wait states often any more, your PC probably suffers them with every access. They are now as common, and as taken for granted as air—and noticed and discussed nearly as often.

A wait state is exactly what it sounds like; the microprocessor suspends whatever it's doing for one or more clock cycles to give the memory circuits a chance to catch up. The number of wait states required in a system depends on the speed of the microprocessor in relation to the speed of memory.

Microprocessor speeds are usually expressed as a frequency in megahertz—millions of cycles per second—and memory chips are rated by time in nanoseconds—billionths of a second. The two measurements are reciprocal. At a speed of 1MHz, one clock cycle is 1,000 nanoseconds long; 8MHz (ISA bus speed) equals 125; 33MHz (PCI bus speed), 33 nanoseconds; 66MHz (memory bus speed), 17 nanoseconds; 100MHz (the new front-side bus speed), 10 nanoseconds; and so on.

Dynamic memory chips are speed-rated, usually with a number emblazoned on the chip following its model designation. This number reflects the access time of the chip given in nanoseconds. A chip with a –60 has a 60-nanosecond access time, typical for EDO memory. (See "Extended Data Out Memory" later in this chapter.) Today's SDRAM has ratings of 10 or 12 nanoseconds.

The computer industry has shifted from this raw rating system to one that more directly reflects the needs of your PC. Today, you're more likely to select memory based on the speed of the bus to which it connects, such as the front-side bus (discussed in the following section) at 66MHz.

When you select memory for your PC, you only need to look for the front-side bus speed at which it was designed to operate. Faster 100MHz memory usually has no problem in systems designed for slower 66MHz memory, but the reverse is not true. Properly designed systems can sense the speed of the memory that you have installed and adjust themselves to run at its speed. The net result is that plugging slow memory into a fast system makes a slow system. If you mix memory speeds—which is never a recommended procedure—your system will slow down to the speed required to accommodate the most laggardly memory.

Front-Side Bus

The speed of the memory bus in a PC—which, in regard to Pentium microprocessors, Intel calls the *front-side bus*—affects overall performance because of two factors: the absolute speed of the memory bus and its relative speed in comparison to microprocessor speed. The best of both makes a faster system.

Two speeds of the front-side bus are most common: 66MHz and 100MHz. The numbers alone should make it obvious that the higher-speed memory systems are about 50 percent faster.

In addition to these speeds, others are possible. The latest AMD K6-2 microprocessors also have an option for an intermediate 95MHz memory bus speed. Some chipsets make other speeds selectable, often offering rates of up to 112MHz.

In the past, some Pentium-class chips operated at other rates, notably 50 and 60MHz. You'll still find some systems based on these chips running at these lower speeds. No current systems are slower. In any case, you'll want the memory bus of your PC to run as quickly as possible with 100MHz today's target to aim for. By the end of 1999, the computer industry fully expects Intel Corporation to unveil chip designs meant for 133MHz front-side bus operation.

The memory speed is a fraction of the microprocessor speed, or from the other perspective, the microprocessor speed is a multiple of memory speed. Different chips operate at different multiples. Table 4.4 lists current chips and their front-side bus speeds.

TABLE 4.4   Speed Multipliers

Microprocessor Speed	Multiplier	Memory Speed
133	2	66
150	3	50
166	2.5	66
180	3	60
200	3	66
233	3.5	66
266	4	66
300	4.5	66
300	3	100

continues

TABLE 4.4   Continued

Microprocessor Speed	Multiplier	Memory Speed
333	5	66
350	3.5	100
400	4	100
450	4.5	100

As you'll see from the table, the only place for concern in selecting a system is with 300MHz processors where some Pentium II systems have 66MHz buses and other, newer systems have 100MHz buses. The latter is, of course, the better choice.

In any case, the new 100MHz speed (or the closest one available) is the best option in a new PC. It is a feature you'll want to look for. Today's Celeron processors do not operate with 100MHz front-side buses. The most recent Pentium II and all Pentium III chips readily handle 100MHz front-side bus speeds.

In general, a smaller multiplier is better because it better matches memory and microprocessor speed. Of course, for best performance you want faster memory and not a slower microprocessor to achieve the low ratio. In addition, some sources report that non-integral multipliers—the 2.5, 3.5, or 4.5 ratios—pose timing problems for your data and are not as good as a strict mathematical comparison would lead you to believe. In that you usually have no choice (except at 300MHz), the issue is not important.

Interleaving

Before the advent of the Pentium microprocessor, engineers often used *interleaved memory* to help match slow chips to fast processors. Interleaved memory works by dividing the total RAM of a system into two or more banks. Sequential bits are held in alternate banks, so the microprocessor goes back and forth between banks when it reads sequential bytes. While one bank is being read, the other is cycling, so the microprocessor does not have to wait. Of course, if the microprocessor must read logically noncontiguous bits, whether or not it encounters wait states is governed by the laws of probability.

In a typical interleaved memory system, system RAM is divided into two banks, so the probability of encountering a wait state is about 50 percent. A four-way interleave can reduce wait states by 75 percent.

Because interleaved memory does not require special memory chips, it was perhaps the most affordable method of speeding up system operation. On the downside, you need an even number of memory banks to achieve a two-way interleave. The wide, 64-bit bus of the Pentium made interleaving less practical, and the technology was soon eclipsed by other means of coping with slow memory—in particular, caching.

Caching

With today's highest-performance microprocessors, the most popular memory-matching technique is memory caching. A memory cache interposes a block of fast memory—typically high-speed static RAM—between the microprocessor and the bulk of primary storage. A special circuit called a cache controller attempts to keep the cache filled with the data or instructions that the microprocessor is most likely to need next. If the information the microprocessor requests next is held within the static RAM of the cache, it can be retrieved without wait states. This fastest possible operation is called a cache hit. If the needed data is not in the cache memory, it is retrieved from ordinary RAM at ordinary RAM speed. The result is called a cache miss.

Not all memory caches are created equal. Memory caches differ in many ways: size, logical arrangement, location, and operation.

Cache Size

A major factor that determines how successful the cache will be is how much information it contains. The larger the cache, the more data that is in it, and the more likely any needed byte will be there when your system calls for it. Obviously, the best cache is one that's as large as and that duplicates the entirety of system memory. Of course, a cache that big is also absurd. You could use the cache as primary memory and forget the rest. The smallest cache would be a byte, also an absurd situation because it guarantees the next read is not in the cache. Practical cache sizes range from 1KB (as used internally by some Cyrix microprocessors) to several megabytes. With today's multitasking operating systems, a cache size of about 256KB is most favored.

The disadvantage of a larger cache is cost. Faster SRAM chips inevitably cost more, pushing up the overall cost of the system. Some manufacturers give you an option—scaleable caches. These allow you to start small and add more SRAM as you can afford it. If you expect to find the end of a rainbow sometime after buying your new PC, such a system deserves consideration.

Cache Level

Caches are sometimes described by their logical and electrical proximity to the microprocessor's core logic. At one time, there was only one level of caching. New microprocessors such as the AMD K6-3 chips now offer the potential of three levels of caching.

The level-one cache is often called the primary cache. It is usually the smallest cache and the one electrically closest to the microprocessor's core logic, built into the microprocessor itself. It almost always operates at the same clock speed as the core logic. All current microprocessors have primary caches ranging from 16KB to 64KB in size.

The level-two cache is often called the secondary cache. At one time, the secondary cache was separate from the microprocessor and linked the chip to the memory system. Modern microprocessor design has subsumed the secondary cache function. Starting with the Pentium Pro, the secondary cache has been part of the microprocessor assembly. In the case of the Pentium II, Pentium III, and Xeon microprocessors from Intel Corporation, the secondary cache comprises several separate chips external to the core logic but mounted on the same cartridge substrate as the core. The Pentium Pro puts the cache in the same ceramic housing as the core logic, as do Celeron chips that use PGA packaging.

Level-two caches may operate anywhere from core logic speed to memory speed with faster, of course, being better. The Pentium II, for example, operates its secondary cache at one-half core logic speed. Level-two caches typically range from 128KB (most Celeron chips) to 2MB (some Xeon chips).

The level-three cache is—so far in its only implementation—external to the microprocessor. It operates at memory speed but, unlike memory, is fast enough not to impose wait states.

Describing Cache Performance

Quantifying cache performance is difficult because it varies with the demands of your software. For example, an entire small DOS utility can fit inside the internal cache of many microprocessors so that you'd never face a cache miss while the program runs. The same cache system might generate misses with every other access when multitasking half a dozen Windows applications.

The most common means of designating the performance of a PC memory system is by listing the number of clock cycles required for each access to transfer a line of memory. For example, the 486 requires four transfers to acquire or store a single line, so engineers list the performance of their 486 memory systems as a series of four numbers. Usually, the figures represent the best-case performance (continual cache hits), although the same system is sometimes used to show performance degradation with cache misses. Pentium caching usually is described in the same way.

The best possible memory performance would be 1-1-1-1, requiring one cycle for each double-word transfer. The burst mode of Pentium microprocessors requires two cycles for the first transfer (one to set the address, one to read or write data), so the best performance in practice is 2-1-1-1. Many systems are substantially slower, some operating at rates of 6-4-4-4. Because modern microprocessors require a line of memory at a time, the total rather than individual numerical values is the most important. Peak performance would be five cycles per line. Some systems may require 20 or more cycles for each line transferred.

Cache Mapping

The logical configuration of a cache involves how the memory in the cache is arranged and how it is addressed, that is, how the microprocessor determines whether needed information is available inside the cache. The major choices are three: direct mapped, full associative, and set associative.

The direct-mapped cache divides the fast memory of the cache into small units, call lines (corresponding to the lines of storage used by Intel 32-bit microprocessors, which allow addressing in 16-byte multiples, blocks of 128 bits), each of which is identified by an index bit. Main memory is divided into blocks the size of the cache, and the lines in the cache correspond to the locations within such a memory block. Each line can be drawn from a different memory block, but only from the location corresponding to the location in the cache. Which block the line is drawn from is identified by a tag. For the cache controller—the electronics that ride herd on the cache—determining whether a given byte is stored in a direct-mapped cache is easy; just check the tag for a given index value.

The problem with the direct-mapped cache is that if a program regularly moves between addresses with the same indexes in different blocks of memory, the cache needs to be continually refreshed—which means cache misses. Although such operation is uncommon in single-tasking systems, it can occur often during multitasking and slow down the direct-mapped cache.

The opposite design approach is the full-associative cache. In this design, each line of the cache can correspond to (or be associated with) any part of main memory. Lines of bytes from diverse locations throughout main memory can be piled cheek-by-jowl in the cache. The major shortcoming of the full-associative approach is that the cache controller must check the addresses of every line in the cache to determine whether a memory request from the microprocessor is a hit or miss. The more lines to check, the more time it takes. A lot of checking can make cache memory respond more slowly than main memory.

A compromise between direct-mapped and full-associative caches is the set-associative cache, which essentially divides up the total cache memory into several smaller direct-mapped areas. The cache is described as the number of "ways" into which it is divided. A four-way set-associative cache, therefore, resembles four smaller direct-mapped caches. This arrangement overcomes the problem of moving between blocks with the same indexes. Consequently, the set-associative cache has more performance potential than a direct-mapped cache. Unfortunately, it is also more complex, making the technology more expensive to implement. Moreover, the more "ways" there are to a cache, the longer the cache controller must search to determine whether needed information is in the cache. This ultimately slows down the cache, mitigating the advantage of splitting it into sets. Most PC makers find a four-way set-associative cache to be the optimum compromise between performance and complexity.

Burst-Mode Caches

Pentium processors require the fastest possible cache. One way to speed up cache designs is to shift to burst mode. As with main memory, bursting in a cache eliminates the need to send a separate address for each memory read or write operation. Instead, the cache memory system reads or writes a contiguous sequence of addresses in a quick burst.

Depending on whether the system is reading or writing, a burst-mode cache can trim access time by up to about 54 percent. The improvement offered by bursting varies with the memory operation. The greatest improvement occurs when writing a burst. On the other hand, burst cache technology offers no improvement in reading individual cache addresses. Table 4.5 summarizes the performance improvements possible with a burst-mode cache.

TABLE 4.5   Non-Burst and Burst Cache Performance

Cycle Type	Non-Burst Cache	Burst Cache	Improvement
Burst read	3-2-2-2	3-1-1-1	33%
Burst write	4-3-3-3	3-1-1-1	54%
Single read	3	3	None
Single write	4	3	25%
Back-to-back burst read	3-2-2-2-3-2-2-2...	3-1-1-1-3-1-1-1...	33%

Ordinary static memory chips do not respond quickly enough to support cache bursting. Two memory technologies make high-speed memory bursts possible, shifting from asynchronous to synchronous designs and pipelining within memory chips.

Synchronous Burst SRAM

To eliminate the need to send an address for every memory access, synchronous burst SRAM uses an internal clock to count up to each new address after each memory operation. Because the chip automatically increments the address, it doesn't need your system to send a new address for the next operation—as long as the addresses are in sequence.

The "synchronous" name comes from the inherent requirement of this technology to keep the clock in the memory to stay in lock-step with the rest of your PC by internally synchonizing it with the external memory system. The timing constraints on the memory module are critical for fast, error-free operation, making the construction of synchronous burst SRAM inherently more expensive than conventional (asynchronous) cache designs.

Pipelined Burst SRAM

The tight timing required by synchronous caches makes its manufacture more difficult. Using a somewhat different design, *pipelined burst SRAM* achieves the same level of performance without the need for a synchronous internal clock. A pipelined burst SRAM module includes an extra register that holds the next piece of data in the sequence to be read. While the register holds data ready to be read, internally the chip continues to run, accessing the next address to load the pipeline. As soon as the host reads the output register, the pipeline can unload the data from the next address, holding it in the register ready for the next read operation. Because the pipeline in the chip keeps a supply of data always ready, this form of memory can run as fast as the host system requests data, limited only by the access time of the pipeline register.

Internal and External Caches

Caches can be either internal or external to the microprocessor they serve. In general, internal caches are better because they can deliver the best performance.

Internal caches do not suffer the design restrictions imposed by external circuitry. Wiring can be kept short if wiring is necessary at all. Signals need not traverse connectors with all of their vagaries. Bus width need not be artificially limited by signal or packaging concerns. For example, the internal level-one caches of Pentium-level microprocessors operate at the same speed as the core logic, a practical impossibility with current external circuit designs. The cache connects to the core with at least a 128-bit bus width.

Moving the level-two cache inside the chip or cartridge offers the same speed-up potentials. In addition, it simplifies the design of the rest of the system. Engineers don't have to worry about the details of the cache when it comes fully armed inside the microprocessor.

Separate Versus Combined Caching

When a cache is used for storing any kind of information, be it instructions or data bytes, it is termed a combined cache or an I+D (instructions plus data) cache. Sometimes, primary caches are divided functionally into separate instruction caches and data caches. The instruction cache solely stores microprocessor instructions and the data cache holds only data. This segregation can yield improvements in overall performance and is used effectively by Intel's Pentium and Pentium Pro, some Motorola microprocessors, and most RISC chips, including the PowerPC. The Intel 486 series of microprocessors uses a single, combined cache for data and instructions. Older Intel chips have no integral memory caches.

Write-Through and Write-Back Caches

Caches also differ in the way they treat writing to memory. Most caches make no attempt to speed up write operations. Instead, they push write commands through the cache immediately, writing to cache and main memory (with normal wait-state delays) at the same time. This *write-through cache* design is the safe approach because it guarantees that main memory and cache are constantly in agreement. Most Intel microprocessors through the current versions of the Pentium use write-through technology.

The faster alternative is the *write-back cache*, which allows the microprocessor to write changes to its cache memory and then immediately go back about its work. The cache controller eventually writes the changed data back to main memory as time allows.

The chief problem with the write-back cache is that there are times when main memory and the cache have different contents assigned to the same memory locations—for example, when a hard disk is read and information is transferred into memory through a control system (the DMA system) that does not involve the microprocessor. The cache controller must constantly check the changes made in main memory and ensure that the contents of the cache properly track such alteration. This "snooping" ability makes the design of a controller more complex—and, therefore, expensive. For the utmost in performance, however, the write-back cache is the best design.

One preferred solution is to delegate all responsibilities for supervising the cache to dedicated circuits designed for that purpose. In the PC environment, a number of cache controller chips are available. Some chipsets also incorporate memory caching into their circuitry. (See Chapter 6, "Chipsets.")

DRAM Technology

The obvious way to make memory faster is to make the memory chips themselves faster. Like shedding weight, stopping smoking, or achieving world peace, making chips faster is a lot easier said than done. By carefully designing chips to trim internal delays and taking advantage of the latest fabrication technologies, chip makers can squeeze out some degree of speed improvement. The fastest standard DRAM chips generally available allow access as fast as 45 to 50 nanoseconds. Such small gains are hard won and expensive.

By altering the underlying design of the chips, engineers can wring out much greater performance increases, often with little increase in fabrication cost. In a quest for quicker response, designers have developed a number of new memory chip technologies. To understand how they work and gain their edge, you first need to know a bit about the design of standard memory chips.

The best place to begin a discussion of the speed limits and improvements in DRAM is with the chips themselves. The critical issue is how they arrange their bits of storage and allow it to be accessed.

The traditional metaphor for memory as the electronic equivalent of pigeon holes is apt. As with the mail sorter's pigeon holes, memory chips arrange their storage in a rectangular matrix of cells. A newer, better metaphor is the spreadsheet because each memory cell is like a spreadsheet cell, uniquely identified by its position, expressed as the horizontal row and vertical column of the matrix in which it appears. To read or write a specific memory cell, you send the chip the row and column address, and the chip sends out the data.

In actual operation, chips are somewhat more complex. To keep the number of connections (and thus, cost) low, the addressing lines of most memory chips are *multiplexed*. That is, the same set of lines serve for sending both the row and column addresses to the chip. To distinguish whether the signals on the address lines mean a row or column, chips use two signals. The Row Address Strobe signal indicates that the address is a row, and the Column Address Strobe signal indicates the address is a column. These signals are most often abbreviated as RAS and CAS, each acronym crowned with a horizontal line indicating the signals are inverse (logical complements), meaning that they indicate "on" when they are "off." Just to give engineering purists nightmares (and to make things typographically easier and more understandable), this book uses a slightly different convention, putting a minus sign in front of the acronyms for the same effect. Multiplexing allows 12 address lines plus the –CAS and –RAS signals to encode every possible memory cell address in a 4 Mbit chip (or 4MB memory module).

In operation, the memory controller in your PC first tells the memory chip the row in which to look for a memory cell and then the column the cell is in. In other words, the address lines accompanied by the –RAS signal select a memory bank, and then a new set of signals on the address lines accompanied by the –CAS signal selects the desired storage cell.

Even though electricity travels at close to the speed of light, signals cannot change instantly. Changing all the circuits in a chip from row to column addressing takes a substantial time, at least in the nanosecond context of computer operations. This delay, together with the need for refreshing, are the chief limits on the performance of conventional memory chips. To speed up memory performance, chip designers have developed a number clever schemes to sneak around these limits.

These memory technologies have steadily evolved. Ordinary DRAM chips proved too slow to accommodate the needs of the 386 microprocessor. Manufacturers first tried static column memory before hitting on fast page-mode DRAM chips, which proved the industry stalwart through 1995. By then, a newer technology, extended data out (EDO) memory, was taking over industry dominance. Burst EDO stands next in line.

All of these technologies from page mode to burst EDO hold in common the same way of addressing their cells and the same basic underlying technology, differing only in a few signals and timing. These technologies require few alterations in PCs to work and add small cost to the price of memory. Another group of technologies follows alternate avenues for acceleration. Enhanced DRAM, cached DRAM, and synchronous DRAM all integrate high-speed caches into individual chips. Rambus DRAM alters the memory arrangement and data channel inside the chip. Video RAM and Windows RAM aim for a different goal with a different expedient, helping your PC and its memory save time by doing two things at once. You're sure to find one or more of these technologies in any new PC you buy.

Static Column RAM

The first of the speed-up tricks to be used in personal computers was *static column RAM*. With a redesign in the circuitry, these chips allowed reading from within a single memory column without wait states. They operate by putting an address on the chips' address lines and then sending the –CAS signal. Once the column was registered, you could then send a new set of addresses and indicate a valid row by activating –RAS all the while holding the –CAS signal on to indicate the column stayed constant.

Page-Mode RAM

Today's most popular memory technology uses a variant of the column-addressing strategy. The memory controller first sends out a row address and then activates the –RAS signal. While holding the –RAS signal active, it sends out a new address and the –CAS signal to indicate a specific cell. If the –RAS signal is kept active, the controller can then send out one or more additional new addresses, each followed by a pulse of the –CAS, to indicate additional cells within the same row.

In memory parlance, the row is termed a *page* and the kinds of memory chips that permit this sort of operation are called *page-mode* RAM.

The chief benefit of this design is that your PC can rapidly access multiple cells in a single memory page. With typical chips, the access time within a page can be trimmed to 25 or 30 nanoseconds, fast enough to eliminate wait states in many PCs. Of course, when your PC needs to shift pages, it must change both the row and column addresses with the consequent speed penalty.

Extended Data Out Memory

The most popular of the memory technologies for PCs with 66 MHz front-side buses is called *Extended Data Out*, or EDO, memory. Computer makers particularly like EDO memory because it delivers enough speed that they can forego putting secondary caches into their PCs entirely. Although EDO memory does, in fact, perform measurably better than ordinary page-mode memory, it works best in combination with a cache.

Rather than a radical new development, EDO is a variation on fast page-mode memory (which allows waitless repeated access to bits within a single page of memory). The trick behind EDO is elegant. Where conventional memory discharges after each read operation and requires recharging time before it can be read again, EDO keeps its data valid until it receives an additional signal. EDO memory modifies the allowed timing for the –CAS signal. The data line remains valid for a short period after the –CAS line switches off (by going high). As a result, your system need not wait for a separate read cycle but can read (or write) data as fast as the chip will allow address access. It doesn't have to wait for the data to appear before starting the next access but can read it immediately. In most chips, a 10 nanosecond wait period is normally required between issuing the column addresses. The EDO design eliminates this wait, allowing the memory to deliver data to your system faster. Standard page-mode chips turn off the data when the –CAS line switches off. For this system to work, however, your PC has to indicate when it has finished reading the data. In the EDO design, the memory controller signals with the Output Enable signal.

In effect, EDO can remove additional wait states, thereby boosting memory performance. In theory, EDO could give a performance boost as high as 50 to 60 percent. In reality, and in the latest PCs, the best EDO implementations boost performance by 10 to 20 percent compared to older systems that use memory caches.

Physically, EDO chips and SIMMs appear identical to conventional memory. Both use the same packaging. You can't tell a difference just by looking—unless you're intimately familiar with the part numbers. Telling the difference is important, however. You can't just plug EDO into any PC and expect it to work. It requires a completely different management system, which means the system (or at least its BIOS) must match the memory technology. Although you can install EDO SIMMs in most PCs, they will work, if at all, as ordinary memory and deliver no performance advantage.

In multimedia applications, the difference between a large cache and EDO memory probably won't be noticeable. In other words, you'll want to consider EDO to be an alternative to a secondary cache—at least for the time being.

The primary application of EDO was to replace fast page-mode DRAM as performance demands increased. Then, with the advent of 100 MHz front-side buses, EDO technology was outpaced. Manufacturers built millions of machines using EDO, and many remain on the market.

When confronting an older PC, you'll find little difference between the fast-page mode and EDO memory. The chips and modules made from them appear identical except for the part numbers. In fact, the difference between the two is so small that many PCs designed for fast page-mode memory will accept EDO memory as well, although they will gain no performance benefit from EDO technology. Although fast page-mode memory can't mimic EDO, newer PCs can sense which kind of memory you have installed and operate it appropriately.

Note that the speed ratings of EDO chips are given in nanoseconds much like page-mode chips. For a given nanosecond rating, however, EDO memory will act as if it is about 30 percent faster. For example, where a 70 ns page-mode chip can deliver zero wait-state operation to a 25MHz memory bus, a 70 ns EDO chip can operate at zero wait states on a 33MHz bus.

Burst EDO DRAM

To gain more speed from EDO memory, Micron Technology added circuitry to the chip to make it match the burst mode used by Intel microprocessors since the 486. The new chips, called *burst EDO* (BEDO) DRAM, perform all read and write operations in four-cycle bursts. The same technology also goes by the more generic name *pipeline nibble mode DRAM* because it uses a data pipeline to retrieve and send out the data in a burst.

The chips work like ordinary EDO or page-mode DRAM in that they send out data when the –CAS line goes active. However, instead of sending a single nibble or byte of data (depending on the width of the chip), a two-bit counter pulses the chip internally four times, each pulse dealing out one byte or nibble of data.

BEDO is relatively easy and inexpensive to fabricate because it requires a minimum of changes from ordinary EDO or page-mode DRAM. In fact, there's no difference at all between the mask used to make ordinary current EDO and BEDO chips. The silicon of the chip holds a fuse that determines whether the chip functions as EDO or BEDO. The chip can change from one personality to the other (irreversibly) by blowing the fuse after the chip has been manufactured.

As with EDO chips, BEDO chips are given nanosecond ratings, but BEDO with a given rating can operate with zero wait states in buses at about twice the speed as similarly rated page-mode chips. Current BEDO technology is capable of operating at a true 66MHz bus speed with zero wait states using chips rated at 52 ns. The same rating in a page-mode chip could operate at zero wait states only as fast as 33MHz. The BEDO design shows potential for even higher zero wait-state speeds.

Synchronous DRAM

Because of their multiplex operation, ordinary memory chips cannot operate in lock-step with their host microprocessors. Normal addressing requires alternating cycles. With a redesign of the basic chip interface, however, memory chips can make data available every clock cycle. Because these resulting chips can (and should) operate in sync with their computer hosts, they are termed *synchronous DRAM*.

Although altering the interface of the chip may remove system bottlenecks, it does nothing in itself to make it perform faster. To help SDRAM chips keep up with their quicker interface, they also use a pipelined design. As with pipelined microprocessors, SDRAM chips are built with multiple, independently operating stages so that the chip can start to access a second address before it finishes processing the first. This pipelining extends only across column addresses within a given page.

SDRAM chips are rated with very high speeds (low numbers of nanoseconds). The interface and pipelining help SDRAM chips achieve speed ratings as fast as 10 ns, which allows them to serve 100MHz memory buses. Current chips have other timing constraints, so today's 100 MHz systems often use memory with even faster ratings. Despite such higher ratings, SDRAM is unlikely to operate at speeds higher than 100MHz because ordinary SIMM sockets become unreliable at higher frequencies. That's one reason Intel opted for the entirely new interface used by Rambus for its 133 MHz front-side bus design.

Note that for a given speed of memory bus operation, the rating of a SDRAM chip must be radically different from that of chips based on a more conventional design. Table 4.6

summarizes the speed ratings required of competitive memory technologies for several common memory bus speeds.

TABLE 4.6   Speed Rating Required for Zero Wait-State Operation Using Various Memory Technologies

Memory Bus Speed	Fast Page Mode	EDO	Burst EDO	SDRAM
25	70 ns	*70 ns	*70 ns	*12 ns
33	52 ns	70 ns	*70 ns	15 ns
50	N/A	52 ns	70 ns	12 ns
66	N/A	N/A	52 ns	10 ns
100	N/A	N/A	N/A	8 ns
133	N/A	N/A	N/A	N/A

Slower memory will work, but the speed listed represents the slowest commercially available speed.

One of the chief drawbacks to any design that foregoes multiplexing is that it will need more pins and thus use larger packages than more conventional multiplexed chips. By itself, this constraint requires a redesign of the host system. Of course, the faster, information-every-cycle operation also requires special support. Many chipset makers have already added SDRAM support to their products.

Enhanced DRAM

Enhanced DRAM makes ordinary dynamic random access memory perform much faster by adding a small block of static cache memory to each chip. The cache operates at high speed—typically, it is rated at about 15 nanoseconds—so it can supply data requests made by your PC's microprocessor without adding wait states while the balance of the RAM in the chip gets refreshed. The cache layout in EDRAM uses a direct-mapped design. The developer and promoter of EDRAM technology was Ramtron, and the company cites four chief advantages for the design:

- Intimately linking the SRAM cache with the DRAM on the same slab of silicon allows the use of a wide bus to connect the two. The Ramtron design uses a 16,384-bit wide bus link. This design results in a potential cache fill rate of about 60 GB/sec compared to the 110 MB/sec rate achieved by standard cached page-mode DRAM. As a result, filling the on-chip secondary cache requires only 35 nanoseconds, about 7 times better than cached non-interleaved page-mode memory, which takes about 250 nanoseconds for similar results.

- The Ramtron chip design also uses a different control structure from conventional DRAM chips, which allow the DRAM to be precharged at the same time your system makes burst-mode reads from the on-chip cache. This precharging helps prepare the DRAM for cache misses, minimizing memory access time. Conventional DRAM must perform both the precharge and ordinary access upon the occurrence of a cache miss.

- Although the EDRAM cache uses a write-through design, the direct writes to main memory can be made with zero wait states. Because memory writes get sent to the DRAM with no write-back or snooping overhead, the first write operation requires only 7 nanoseconds, and the normal page write cycle is 15 nanoseconds.

- The EDRAM design spreads the cache memory through every memory bank. In multitasking systems, this distribution of the cache improves the odds of obtaining a cache hit in each thread.

Cached DRAM

Cached DRAM, pioneered by Mitsubishi, also adds a dash of cache memory into each chip, but it uses a set-associative design. In addition, the initial 4MB chips offered by the company incorporate more cache than the Ramtron product, 2KB instead of 256 bytes.

In addition, the CDRAM chips use two nibble-wide 16-word buffers between its cache and external circuitry. This small buffer cuts the penalty of a cache miss to a single line.

Unlike EDRAM chips, the CDRAM parts give their cache and main DRAM their own address port so they can operate independently as well as an integrated system. The cache is quick enough to deliver a 16-nibble burst at a 100MHz clock speed. The chip also allows its two buffers to operate independently so that they can alternately output data to provide a continuous stream. In addition, the chip can operate synchronously to deliver true 100MHz performance.

Rambus DRAM

The next step up in memory speed comes from revising the interface between memory chips and the rest of the system. The leading choice is the Rambus design, developed by the company with the same name. Intel chose Rambus technology for its fastest system designs. An earlier incarnation of the technology is used in the Nintendo-64 game system.

The Rambus design uses a 2,048-byte static RAM cache that links to the dynamic memory on the chip through a very wide bus that allows the transfer of an entire page of memory into the cache in a single cycle. The cache is fast enough that it can supply data at a 15-ns rate during hits. When the cache misses, the chip retrieves the request data from its main memory and, at the same time, transfers the page containing it into the cache so that it is ready for the next memory operation. Because subsequent memory operations will likely come from the cache, the dynamic portion of the chip is free to be refreshed without stealing system time or adding wait states.

Rambus memory doesn't link to a computer system like standard memory. Instead, the design uses a special high-speed bus (hence the origin of the Rambus name). No matter the connection with the host microprocessor, the bus between the memory controller and Rambus chips is just one byte wide. Compensating for its narrow width is high speed. The Rambus operates at 250MHz, and the overall system design allows two bytes to move each clock cycle, one on the leading edge and a second on the trailing edge of each clock pulse. The Rambus speed is isolated from the host microprocessor and remains constant no matter the microprocessor speed. Its peak 500 MB/sec transfer rate approaches the speed of all but the fastest of today's microprocessors and exceeds the bandwidth of most conventional memory systems.

Rambus memory is subdivided into three types: Base Rambus, Concurrent Rambus, and Direct Rambus. The last of these is the choice for PCs. The chief practical difference is speed. Base Rambus operates at 600MHz and offers a bandwidth of 600 MB/sec; Concurrent Rambus operates at 700MHz with a bandwidth of 700 MB/sec; and Direct Rambus operates at 800MHz with a bandwidth of 1.6 GB/sec. To achieve its higher bandwidth, Direct Rambus also uses a two-byte wide data bus and a more efficient internal transfer protocol, one that achieves about 95 percent efficiency compared to the 60 to 80 percent of older Rambus designs.

Practical Rambus memory for PCs uses a special module design termed a *RIMM* (for Rambus Inline Memory Module, discussed later) that uses a narrow, 16-bit interface but compensates with high-speed operation. Current products operate at 800MHz and yield a module-level throughput of 1.6 GB/sec.

The Rambus operates like a small network, sending data in packets that can be up to 256 bytes long. The system uses its own control language to control memory and steer bytes around. The overhead from this system saps about 10 percent of the bandwidth from the peak transfer rate of the system.

The Rambus design is radical and requires an equally radical reworking of its computer host's design so you can install Rambus memory in place of other memory types.

Multibank DRAM

Instead of an overall block of cells, each of which can be addressed by its own row and column number, Multibank DRAM, developed by MoSys Incorporated, splits the storage of each chip into a number of separate banks. In the initial 4-Mbit Multibank DRAM chip design, each of the 16 banks holds 256 kilobits. The banks are connected together through a central data bus that accesses each bank individually.

This design allows one bank to send or receive a burst of data and then, in a single clock cycle, switch to another bank for another burst. Because each bank has its own 32-bit interface that works much like that of SDRAM, the Multibank DRAM chips operate quickly. MoSys claims transfer speeds peaking at 1 GB/sec.

Video Memory

Memory access problems are particularly prone to appear in video systems. Memory is used in display systems as a frame buffer, where the onscreen image is stored in digital form with one unit of memory (be it a bit, byte, or several bytes) assigned to each element of the picture. The entire contents of the frame buffer are read from 44 to 75 times a second as the stored image is displayed on the monitor screen. All the while, your PC may be attempting to write new picture information into the buffer to appear on the screen.

With normal DRAM chips, these read and write operations cannot occur simultaneously. One has to wait for another. The waiting negatively affects video performance, your system's speed, and your patience.

The wait can be avoided with special memory chips that have a novel design twist—two paths for accessing each storage location. With two access paths, this memory acts like a warehouse with two doors; your processor can push bytes into the warehouse through one door while the video system pulls them out through another. Strictly speaking, this memory can take two forms: True dual-ported memory allows simultaneous reading and writing; video memory chips (often called VRAM for Video Random Access Memory) gives one access port full read and write random access while the other port only allows sequential reading (which corresponds to the needs of scanning a video image).

The chief disadvantage of VRAM technology is that it is more expensive because it requires more silicon (about 20 percent more area on the chip die). It more than makes up for its higher cost with its speed advantage. Using VRAM can speed up video systems by as much as 40 percent.

Windows RAM

The latest twist on the dual-ported VRAM design is Windows RAM, developed by Samsung. As the name implies, chips using the technology serve well in video systems designed to accommodate a graphic interface like Windows.

The basic WRAM chip holds eight megabits arranged as 32 bit-planes, each of which is a 512-by-512 matrix of cells. Four chips supply the necessary memory for a display system with 1,024-by-768 resolution on a 1,024-by-1,024 desktop with a bit depth of 32, enough for TrueColor 24-bit operation with an extra 8-bit alpha channel.

Internally, a 256-bit data bus links each bit-plane to the chip's internal control logic, which multiplexes the data down to a 32-bit data width that's compatible with today's PC circuitry. To provide a smooth stream of data suitable for feeding a video scan, the chip incorporates two serial data registers in its output. The chip fills one register as the other sends out data, switching between them once the sending register empties. The chip also contains four 32-bit registers, two for storing the foreground and background colors and two more for control and masking.

With a transfer rate peaking at 640 MB/sec, the WRAM design can speed video systems by 50 percent compared to VRAM. Because WRAM uses a smaller amount of silicon, Samsung estimates it will eventually cost about 20 percent less than VRAM.

Errors

No memory system is perfect. Certainly, your PC won't mislay its gloves or forget your birthday, but it can suffer little slips, an errant bit here and there. Although one bit in a few million might not seem like a big deal, it's enough to send your system into a tailspin or, worse, alter the answer to some important calculation, jogging the decimal point a few places to the left.

Causes

The memory errors that your PC is likely to suffer fall into two broad classes, soft errors and hard errors. Either can leave you staring at an unflinching screen, sometimes but not always emblazoned with a cryptic message that does nothing to help you regain the hours of work irrevocably lost. The difference between them is transience. Soft errors are little more than disabling glitches that disappear as fast as they come. Hard errors linger until you take a trip to the repair shop.

Soft Errors

For your PC, a soft memory error is an unexpected and unwanted change. Something in memory turns up different from what it is supposed to be. One bit in a memory chip may suddenly, randomly change state. Or a glitch of noise inside your system may get stored as if it were valid data. In either case, one bit becomes something other than what it's supposed to be, possibly changing an instruction in a program or a data value.

With a soft error, the change appears in your data rather than hardware. Replace or restore the erroneous data or program code, and your system will operate exactly as it always has. In general, your system needs nothing more than a reboot; a cold boot is best to gain the assurance of your PC's self-test of its circuits (including memory). The only damage is the time you waste retracing your steps to get back to the place in your processing at which the error occurred. Soft errors are the best justification for the sage advice, "Save often."

Most soft errors result from problems either within memory chips themselves or in the overall circuitry of your PC. The mechanisms behind these two types of soft errors is entirely different.

Chip-Level Errors

The errors inside memory chips are almost always a result of radioactive decay. The problem is not nuclear waste (although nuclear waste *is* a problem) but something even more devious. The culprit is the epoxy of the plastic chip package, which like most materials may contain a few radioactive atoms. Typically, one of these minutely radioactive atoms will spontaneously decay and shoot out an *alpha particle* into the chip. (There are a number of radioactive atoms in just about everything; they don't amount to very much but they are there. And by definition, a radioactive particle will spontaneously decay sometime.) An alpha particle is a helium nucleus, two protons and two neutrons, having a small positive charge and a lot of kinetic energy. If such a charged particle hits a memory cell in the chip, the charge and energy of the particle can cause the cell to change state, blasting the memory bit it contains to a new and different value. This miniature atomic blast is not enough to damage the silicon structure of the chip itself, however.

Whether a given memory cell will suffer this kind of soft error is unpredictable, just as predicting whether a given radioactive atom will decay is impossible. When you deal with enough atoms, however, this unpredictability becomes a probability, and engineers can predict that one of the memory cells in a chip will suffer such an error. They just can't predict which one.

In the early days of PCs, radioactive decay inside memory chips was the most likely cause of soft errors in computers. Thanks to improved designs and technology, each generation of memory chip has become more reliable no matter whether you measure per bit or per chip. For example, any given bit in 16KB might suffer a decay-caused soft error every billion or so hours. The likelihood that any given bit in a modern 16MB chip will suffer an error is on the order of once in two trillion hours. In other words, modern memory chips are about 5,000 times more reliable than those of first-generation PCs, and the contents of each cell is about 5 *million* times more reliable once you take into account that chip capacities have increased a thousand-fold. Although conditions of use influence the occurrence of soft errors, the error rate of modern memory is such that a typical PC with 8MB of RAM would suffer a decay-caused soft error once in 10 to 30 years. The probability is so small that many computer makers now ignore it.

System-Level Errors

Sometimes, the data traveling though your PC gets hit by a noise glitch. If a pulse of noise is strong enough and occurs at an especially inopportune instant, it can be misinterpreted by your PC as a data bit. Such a system-level error will have the same effect on your PC as a soft error in memory. In fact, some system-level errors may be reported as memory errors, for example, when the glitch appears in the circuitry between your PC's memory chips and the memory controller.

The most likely place for system-level soft errors to occur is on your PC's buses. A glitch on a data line can cause your PC to try to use or execute a bad bit of data or program code, causing an error. Or your PC could load the bad value into memory, saving it to relish (and crash from) at some later time. A glitch on the address bus will make your PC similarly find the wrong bit or byte, and the unexpected value may have exactly the same effects as a data bus error.

The probability of a system-level error occurring depends on the design of your PC. A careless designer can leave your system not only susceptible to system-level errors but even prone to generating the glitches that cause them. Pushing a PC design to run too fast is particularly likely to cause problems. You can do nothing to prevent system-level soft errors other than to choose your PC wisely.

Hard Errors

When some part of a memory chip actually fails, the result is a hard error. For instance, a jolt of static electricity can wipe out one or more memory cells. As a result, the initial symptom is that same as a soft error—a memory error that may cause an error in the results you get or a total crash of your system. The operative difference is that the hard error doesn't go away when you reboot your system. In fact, your machine may not pass its memory test when you try to start it up again. Alternately, you may encounter repeated, random errors when a memory cell hovers between life and death.

Hard errors require attention. The chip or module in which the error originates needs to be replaced.

Note, however, that operating memory beyond its speed capability often causes the same problem as hard errors. In fact, operating memory beyond its ratings causes hard errors. You can sometimes clear up such problems by adding wait states to your system's memory cycles, a setting many PCs allow you to control as part of their advanced setup procedure. This will, of course, slow down the operation of your PC so that it can accommodate the failing memory. The better cure is to replace the too-slow memory with some that can handle the speed.

Detection and Prevention

Most PCs check every bit of their memory for hard errors every time you switch on your system or perform a cold boot, although some PCs give you to option of bypassing this initial memory check to save time. Soft errors are another matter entirely. They rarely show up at boot time. Rather, they are likely to occur at the worst possible moment— which means just about any time you're running your PC.

PC makers use two strategies to combat memory errors, parity and detection/correction. Either one will assure the integrity of your system's memory. Which is best—or whether you need any error compensation at all—is a personal choice.

Parity

When memory chips were of dubious reliability, PC manufacturers followed the lead of the first PC and added an extra bit of storage to every byte of memory. The extra bit was called a *parity check bit*, and it allowed the computer to verify the integrity of the data stored in memory. Using a simple algorithm, the parity check bit permits a PC to determine that a given byte of memory has the right number of binary 0s and 1s in it. If the count changes, your PC knows an error occurred.

When a microprocessor writes a byte to memory, the value stored in the parity check bit is set either to a logical 1 or 0 in such a way that the total of all nine bits storing the byte is always odd. Every time your PC reads a given portion of memory, the memory controller totals up the nine bits storing each byte, verifying that the overall total (including the parity check bit) remains odd. Should the system detect a total that's even, it immediately knows that something has happened to cause one bit of the byte to change, making the stored data invalid.

The philosophy behind the parity design of the original IBM PC was that having bad data is worse than losing information through a system crash. After all, wrong data can result in erroneous paychecks, abstruse inventory reports, and bridges collapsing, but a crash immediately notifies you that something is wrong. Consequently, most early PCs were designed to shut down when incorrect parity is discovered. When these systems discovered a wrong parity total in its memory, it automatically blasts a Parity Check error message on your monitor screen. Some systems went so far as to display the message "Parity Check 1" to indicate motherboard memory problems and "Parity Check 2" to indicate a problem with memory on an expansion board (an unlikely occurrence in a modern PC).

Many manufacturers have abandoned parity checking in their PCs. They cite several reasons for the change. The biggest is probably cost. Parity adds 10 to 15 percent to the cost of memory in a PC, and in today's highly competitive market, that savings can mean the difference between profit and loss for a manufacturer. Parity can also steal circuit board space, which may be an issue in compact systems. Although parity and non-parity memory modules for desktop systems are generally the same size, omitting parity chips allows for more compact proprietary modules for notebook PCs. Manufacturers believe that the improved reliability of modern memory makes parity checking superfluous. The reliability of memory from reputable chip makers is such that a PC with 16MB of RAM is not likely to see a soft error during its useful life.

Note, too, that the purpose of parity it to ensure the reliability of your data. It does not in itself improve the reliability of your PC. If an error occurs, the parity system will shut down your PC as surely (actually even more so) as a system crash. The parity chip merely guarantees you don't compute with bad data.

Fake Parity

Fake parity memory is a means of cutting the cost of memory modules for PCs with built-in parity checking. Instead of actually performing a parity check of the memory on the module, the fake parity system always sends out a signal indicating that memory parity is good.

To your PC, a memory module with fake parity appears exactly like one that has true parity detection. The technology serves as a design expedient that allows memory module makers to sell non-parity memory that will work in PCs that accept only parity memory. Because the chips that generate fake parity are less expensive than memory chips (particularly as capacities grow larger), using them allows the module maker to save about 10 percent in the cost of a memory module.

Fake parity has two downsides. The cost savings often are not passed down to you, at least explicitly. The fake parity modules are often sold as ordinary parity modules with no indication of the underlying shortchange on technology. Moreover, a fake parity module does not offer protection against parity errors causing erroneous data in your PC. One fake parity module defeats the operation and purpose of the parity memory system in your PC.

If you want to add a lower cost non-parity memory to a machine that requires parity, fake parity gives you one alternative. A better alternative is simply to switch off parity detection in your PC (many newer PCs allow you to do this; check your instruction manual for specific directions) and simply plug in non-parity modules.

Unfortunately, some vendors do not identify fake parity memory modules as such, passing them off as standard parity modules and pocketing extra profits. In general, fake parity memory modules appear identical to those with actual parity memory. The only way to positively identify them is by testing them with a SIMM tester. Because fake parity memory modules work at the hardware level, ordinary memory testing software cannot detect them.

You can sometimes identify fake parity memory modules by the part numbers on the chips used for generating the false positive readings. These look like ordinary memory chips and wear the same chip identification markings. According to memory vendor Kingston Technology, however, fake parity chips often are often marked with one of the following designations: BP, GSM, MPEC, or VT.

Detection/Correction

Parity checking can only locate an error of one bit in a byte. More elaborate error-detection schemes can detect larger errors. Better still, when properly implemented, these schemes can fix single-bit errors without crashing your system. Called Error Correction Code, or ECC, this scheme in its most efficient form requires three extra bits per byte of storage. The additional bits allow your system not only to determine the occurrence of a memory error but also to locate any single bit that changed so that the error can be reversed. Some people call this technology Error Detection and Correction, or EDAC.

IBM uses ECC on its larger computers and some high-end PCs designed to be used as network file servers. Memories in PCs were small and reliable enough that IBM's engineers did not think the additional expense of ECC bits were justified. As total system capacities stretch beyond 16MB, however, ECC may become a standard part of the memory systems of some PCs. When the integrity of the data on a PC is a paramount concern—for example, in a file server—you should choose a PC with ECC memory. For this reason, a growing number of more powerful PCs use ECC memory.

PC makers have another reason for shifting from parity to ECC memory. As the width of the data bus increases, error correction memory become less expensive to implement. In fact, with today's Pentium PCs—which have 64-bit data buses—the cost of extra memory for parity checking and full error correction are the same. Table 4.7 summarizes the penalty required by parity and ECC technology for various bus widths.

TABLE 4.7   Comparison of Parity and ECC Memory

	Extra Bits Required		Cost Increase	
Bus width	Parity	ECC	Parity	ECC
8	1	5	12.5%	62%
16	2	6	12.5%	38%
32	4	8	12.5%	25%
64	8	8	12.5%	12.5%

Parity and ECC memory are technologies for people who want or need to take every possible precaution. They are the kind of people who check the weather report and then put on their galoshes and carry an umbrella even when the predictions are 100 percent in favor of sun. They are the folks who get the last laugh when they are warm and dry after a once-in-a-century freak thunderstorm rumbles through, people who know that the best solution to computer and memory problems is prevention.

Repair

If your PC suffers a hard memory error, the only cure is to replace the ailing chip or memory module. The mechanics of the repair are essentially the same as artificial resuscitation—out with the bad and in with the good. The biggest problem you face is finding the bad chip in order to replace it.

When PCs had dozens of memory chips in every bank, finding the one chip that went bad was a challenge. Trial-and-error chip swapping was out of the question unless you had time on your hands and a chip puller in them. You had to rely on diagnostics to locate the bad chip. Ultimately, this meant consulting a look-up table or deciphering a complex formula to find the bad chip from the obscure numerical message reported by the diagnostic.

With modern SIMM-based PCs, however, the math of the chip-finding formula is probably more bothersome than simply swapping a few modules. Most PCs have only one to four memory modules, so you can usually locate the bad module in a few minutes simply by swapping modules. If you want the most efficient means of locating a bad module, you can use a formula similar to the one for calculating the Tower of Hanoi puzzle. For example, you could shift a couple modules around and look for changes in the diagnostic error message, but the limited access in most PCs makes you remove the outermost modules to get to the inner ones. You ultimately end up pulling out most of the modules anyway. If you ever do encounter a hard error in one of your system's SIMMs, you'll probably find repair easier if you just exchange one module from your PC for a known good module (the replacement) and work your way through a memory bank.

Packaging

An actual memory chip is a sliver of silicon smaller than a fingernail and so delicate that exposure to ordinary air will cause it to self-destruct. To make it easier to handle, memory chips (like all semiconductors) are hermetically sealed in a larger case that both protects the silicon and provides a convenient means of handling the chip and attaching it to circuit assemblies. This case is called the chip's packaging.

Almost universally, memory chips are individually packaged as integrated circuits that are commonly called discrete chips. Early PCs were designed to accept these discrete chips in their memory sockets, normally nine chips per memory bank. With the advent of 32-bit microprocessors, however, memory needs have become so large that discrete chips are inconvenient or impractical for memory. One bank typically would comprise 36 chips, and multiple banks would quickly consume more board space than is available in most PCs.

The modern alternative package is the memory module, which simply puts several discrete chips on a single small plug-in circuit board. Memory modules are more compact than discrete chips for two reasons. Chips are soldered to memory modules, eliminating space-wasting sockets and allowing the chips to be installed closer together (because no individual access is required). Moreover, because the discrete chips that are installed in the memory module never need to be individually manipulated except by machine, they can use more compact surface-mount packages. A single memory module just a few inches long can thus accommodate a full bank of memory.

Nearly all new PCs use memory modules of some type, so you rarely have to deal with individual memory chips. Only very old PCs and video boards still use discrete chips for expansion.

Memory modules are the large, economy-size RAM in a bigger package to better suit the dietary needs of today's PCs. Besides the more convenient package that allows you to deftly install a number of chips in one operation, the memory module also better matches the way your PC uses memory. Unlike most chips, which are addressed at the bit level, memory modules usually operate in bytes. Where chip capacities are measured in kilobits and megabits, memory modules are measured in megabytes.

The construction of a memory module is straightforward, simply a second level of integration above the basic memory chip. Several chips are brought together on a small glass-epoxy circuit board with their leads soldered down to the circuit traces and the entire assembly terminated in an external connector suitable for plugging into a socket or soldering to another circuit board.

Memory modules come in a variety of types. Most have CELP (Card Edge Low Profile) connectors with from 30 to 83 contacts on each side of the module. Single Inline Memory Modules connect the contacts on the opposite sides of the board together so each pair provides a single signal contact. Dual Inline Memory Modules put separate signals on each contact so that the contacts on each side of the board serve different purposes. Single Inline Pin Package modules have a row of pins projecting from the bottom of the module instead of edge connectors. As with the edge connectors on expansion boards, those on SIMMs and DIMMs are designed solely to plug into matching edge-connector sockets. The design allows these modules to be repeatedly added or removed without tools or damage. SIPPs, on the other hand, are more often soldered in place, although they are sometimes made removable through the use of special sockets.

The number of connections on each module further defines it. Four types of modules are currently popular: 30-pin and 72-pin SIMMs, 72-pin Small Outline DIMMs (SODIMMs), and 168-bit DIMMs. SIPPs usually have 30 pins. Each of the module types is discussed in the following sections.

30-Pin SIMMs

The original SIMM design to appear on the marketplace came as a convenience as PC memories expanded. Because PCs deal with memory in bytes, packaging memory in byte-wide containers made sense, as did eliminating the handling of individual chips. The first SIMMs provided both benefits, hundreds of thousands of bytes of storage in a single plug-in package. Instead of dealing with nine individual memory chips, you only needed to slide in a single SIMM.

The SIMM was little more than the normal addressing connections for individual memory chips, ganged together on the SIMM itself, and sufficient extra connections to provide the necessary bus width. In that most memory chips at that time used multiplexed row/column addressing on 20 pins, adding an extra 8 pins for the additional bus width made 30 pins a compelling package. The original 30-pin SIMM was, in fact, little more than 9 chips tied together on a single small board, as shown in Figure 4.4.

FIGURE 4.4

30-pin SIMM package.

The chips themselves dictated the minimal size of the basic SIMM package. Little larger than 9 side-by-side discrete memory chips, the 30-pin SIMM measures about 3.5 inches wide and an inch tall. The 30-pin package proved compelling, and many PC manufacturers adopted it. Although the standard sockets dictate the width of SIMMs, height is not constrained, and some SIMMs may be taller than others. Figure 4.5 shows the dimensions of a typical 30-pin SIMM.

FIGURE 4.5

Dimensions of a typical 30-pin SIMM.

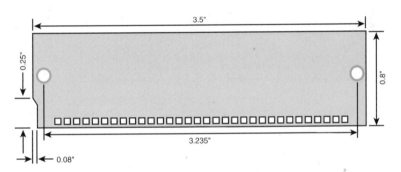

As with other memory products, the 30-pin package must be properly aligned with its socket. A notch on one edge of the package prevents you from inadvertently inserting a SIMM with an improper orientation. The two holes on either side of the SIMM allow sockets to latch the module securely in place.

As with PCs at the time, the first 30-pin SIMMs allowed 9 bits of storage for each byte, using the extra bit for parity checking. Consequently, 30-pin SIMM are sometimes called 9-bit SIMMs. Parity SIMMs only store an additional bit of data. The error detection circuitry is external to the SIMM itself, part of the overall memory system that's usually located on your PC's motherboard.

As improving memory technology allowed PC designers to craft reliable systems without parity checking, 8-bit SIMMs became popular. These use a package identical to 9-bit SIMMs, differing only in the presence of the parity bit and its associated signals. The pin-out of 8- and 9-bit SIMMs is identical except for the three signals used in the parity-check system—pins 26, 28, and 29. Table 4.8 lists the pin-outs of both 8- and 9-bit 30-pin SIMMs.

TABLE 4.8 · 30-Pin SIMM Pin-Outs

	8-Bit SIMM (Non-Parity)		9-Bit SIMM	
Pin	Mnemonic	Function	Mnemonic	Function
1	VCC	Supply voltage	VCC	Supply voltage
2	–CAS	Column address strobe	–CAS	Column address strobe
3	DQ0	Data line 0	DQ0	Data line 0
4	A0	Address line 0	A0	Address line 0
5	A1	Address line 1	A1	Address line 1
6	DQ1	Data line 1	DQ1	Data line 1
7	A2	Address line 2	A2	Address line 2
8	A3	Address line 3	A3	Address line 3
9	VSS	Ground	VSS	Ground
10	DQ2	Data line 2	DQ2	Data line 2
11	A4	Address line 4	A4	Address line 4
12	A5	Address line 5	A5	Address line 5
13	DQ3	Data line 3	DQ3	Data line 3
14	A6	Address line 6	A6	Address line 6
15	A7	Address line 7	A7	Address line 7
16	DQ4	Data line 4	DQ4	Data line 4
17	A8	Address line 8	A8	Address line 8
18	A9	Address line 9	A9	Address line 9
19	A10	Address line 10	A10	Address line 10
20	DQ5	Data line 5	DQ5	Data line 5
21	–WE	Read/write input	–WE	Read/write input
22	VSS	Ground	VSS	Ground
23	DQ6	Data line 6	DQ6	Data line 6
24	NC	No connection	NC	No connection
25	DQ7	Data line 7	DQ7	Data line 7
26	NC	No connection	Q8	Parity data out
27	–RAS	Row address strobe	–RAS	Row address strobe
28	NC	No connection	–CS8	Parity column strobe
29	NC	No connection	D8	Parity data in
30	VCC	Supply voltage	VCC	Supply voltage

Because non-parity systems ignore the parity signals on a 9-bit SIMM, you can usually substitute a 9-bit SIMM for an 8-bit SIMM in a non-parity PC or printer. On the other hand, you cannot simply substitute an 8-bit SIMM for a 9-bit SIMM because most parity PCs will immediately register a parity error because of the lack of the extra bit. Some systems allow you to switch off parity checking. Indeed, some do it automatically when they detect a non-parity SIMM. In such machines, you can use an 8-bit SIMM in place of a 9-bit one, providing you set up the system accordingly. Note, too, that adjustments to parity checking are system wide. By adding a non-parity SIMM, you will defeat parity checking throughout the entire memory system.

You'll find one more interesting difference in SIMMs—three-chip versus nine-chip parity-checked models and two-chip versus eight-chip non-parity SIMMs. The three-chip variety is like a three-chip memory bank. It links two nibble-wide chips for data storage and a bit-wide chip for parity. Nine-chip SIMMs put each bit of every byte of storage in a separate chip. Functionally, these two types of SIMMs should be interchangeable, and in most PCs, they are. Two-chip SIMMs provide byte-wide memory without parity checking so they do away with the parity chip. Otherwise, a two-chip SIMM should function identically to an eight-chip module. Alas, a few PCs are more particular about SIMM configuration because their system timing specifications are tuned to a particular SIMM type. Such PCs prefer one type of SIMM to the other. (For example, a handful of systems simply won't work with three-chip SIMMs.) Moreover, to avoid difficulties, you should never mix three- and nine-chip SIMMs in the same memory bank.

Because 30-pin SIMMs use byte-wide data buses, you need multiple SIMMs to make a single memory bank with most microprocessors. PCs with 16-bit data buses (such as those based on the 286 and 386SX microprocessors) will require two 30-pin SIMMs per bank. PCs with 32-bit data buses (such as 386DX and 486 PCs) require four 30-pin SIMMs per memory bank. PCs with 64-bit data buses (such as the Pentium series) would require eight 30-pin SIMMs per memory bank. Of course, that number is almost as ungainly as using discrete memory chips. Consequently, 30-pin SIMMs have fallen from favor in more advanced computer systems.

72-Pin SIMMs

Although the byte-wide addressing of 30-pin SIMMs marked an improvement over using discrete chips, it fell short of the needs of more modern PCs, which used wider data buses. In response to the needs for simplified expansion, in 1987 PC manufacturers led by IBM created SIMMs with more pins to accommodate wider data buses. The result was the 72-pin SIMM that packs 4 byte-wide banks on a single module.

The standard 72-pin SIMM design incorporate several interlocks that prevent you from plugging in the wrong style of SIMM or sliding in an improperly oriented SIMM. The notch in the center of the SIMM edge connector prevents you from accidentally sliding a

30-pin SIMM into a 72-pin socket. Because of their greater width, a 72-pin SIMM won't fit a 30-pin socket. In addition, the notch on the left side of every 72-pin SIMM (when viewed from the component side) prevents improper orientation of the SIMM. As with 30-pin SIMMs, the holes at either side of the SIMM latch in the socket to prevent the SIMM from wriggling loose. Figure 4.6 shows a typical 72-pin SIMM.

FIGURE 4.6

72-pin SIMM package.

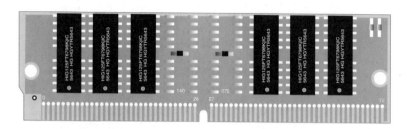

To accommodate their larger capacities, 72-pin SIMMs are somewhat larger than their 30-pin kin. All share the same width, about 4.25 inches, so they can fit the same sockets. The critical dimension is the width between the two keying holes that latch into their connectors. A notch at one end of the SIMM assures that you won't inadvertently insert a SIMM backward.

The height and thickness of 72-pin SIMMs varies. A typical module is about one inch high. Modules may have components on either one or two sides. The latter are thicker. A typical two-sided SIMM is about 0.38 inches thick. Figure 4.7 shows the dimensions of a typical 72-pin SIMM.

FIGURE 4.7

Dimensions of a typical 72-pin SIMM.

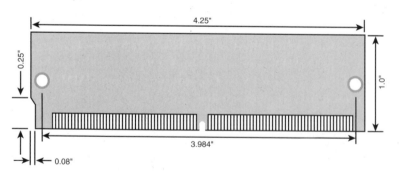

To achieve higher capacities, 72-pin SIMMs are often double-sided. That is, they spread chips on both sides of their glass-epoxy substrate. Double-sided SIMMs are necessarily thicker.

Four pins of a 72-pin SIMM are used for indicating the speed rating of the module. Table 4.9 lists the coding used for common module speeds.

TABLE 4.9   Speed Codes for 72-Pin SIMMs

Speed	Signal			
	PD0	PD1	PD2	PD3
50 ns	VSS	NC	VSS	VSS
60 ns	VSS	NC	NC	NC
70 ns	VSS	NC	VSS	NC
80 ns	VSS	NC	NC	VSS

Both parity and non-parity 72-pin SIMMs are available. The former are often termed 36-bit SIMMs and the latter, 32-bit.

An abbreviated nomenclature has become common for describing the different capacities and bit arrangements of 72-pin SIMMs. The general form of this description lists the total SIMM capacity in megabytes followed by the width of the module's data bus. For example, a 2×36 SIMM would store 2MB of 36-bit wide storage, that is, parity-checked memory. A 16×32 SIMM would offer 16MB of non-parity memory using a 32-bit wide bus.

Dual Inline Memory Modules

Even 72-pin SIMMs fall short when it comes to Pentium and Pentium Pro PCs. With their 64-bit data buses, these chips would call for two 72-pin SIMMs per bank, just as 486 machines required four 30-pin SIMMs. To provide easier expansion for newer 64-bit machines, memory makers developed modules with more connections to permit wider addressing. The resulting modules have 168 separate connections, arrayed across two sides of the module, a design that created the first Dual Inline Memory Modules. Figure 4.8 illustrates a typical 168-pin DIMM.

FIGURE 4.8
168-pin Dual Inline Memory Module package.

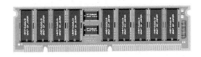

As with other DIMMs, the two rows of edge connectors, one on each side of the module, are independent. These contacts are divided into three groups with short gaps between. The first group runs from pin 1 to pin 10; the second group from pin 11 to pin 40; and the third group from pin 41 to pin 84. Pin 85 is opposite pin 1.

As with previous designs, notches in the edge connector of the DIMM prevent your sliding smaller SIMMs with fewer connections into a DIMM socket. Instead of a notch on the side of the DIMM, the asymmetrical arrangement of the notches on the DIMM prevent its inadvertent improper insertion into its socket. Some DIMMs have holes to allow you to latch the modules into their sockets, although some DIMMs lack these holes.

To accommodate the larger edge connectors and provide greater storage capacity, DIMMs are physically large, about 5.25 inches wide and typically one inch tall. Figure 4.9 shows the dimensions of a typical 168-pin DIMM.

FIGURE 4.9

Dimensions of a typical 168-pin DIMM.

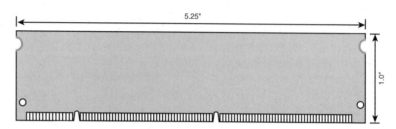

As with 72-pin SIMMs, 168-pin DIMMs include electrical provisions for telling your PC the speed rating of the module. The module connector provides eight pins for signaling this information. Table 4.10 lists the signal codes used to indicate the available speed ratings. Note that for current chips, only the PD6 and PD7 signals carry significant information; the other six pins are the same for all practical speed ratings.

TABLE 4.10	168-Pin DIMM Speed Codes			
Signal	*Pin*	*60 ns*	*70 ns*	*80 ns*
PD1	79	L	L	L
PD2	163	L	L	L
PD3	80	H	H	H
PD4	164	L	L	L
PD5	81	L	L	L
PD6	165	H	L	H
PD7	82	H	H	L
PD8	166	H	H	H

Table 4.11 lists some of the part numbers of current 168-pin DIMMs used by various manufacturers.

TABLE 4.11 Sampling of 66MHz DIMM Part Numbers

Manufacturer	Model	Type	Capacity	Speed
Vanguard	VG26V17805BJ6	EDO	16MB	66MHz
Toshiba	TC51V17805BNTS-60	EDO	16MB	66MHz
Vanguard	VG26V17405CJ-6	EDO	32MB	66MHz
Hyundai	HYM5V64804FG	EDO	64MB	66MHz
SEC	KM44V4104BS-L6	EDO	64MB	66MHz
LG	GM72V16821BT10K	SDRAM	16MB	66MHz
Fujitsu	81117822A-100	SDRAM	16MB	66MHz
SEC	KM416S1120AT-G10	SDRAM	16MB	66MHz
SEC	KM48S2020AT-G10	SDRAM	16MB	66MHz
Hitachi	HM5216805TT10	SDRAM	32MB	66MHz
LG	GM72V16821BT10K	SDRAM	32MB	66MHz
NEC	D4516821AG5-A10-7JF	SDRAM	32MB	66MHz
SEC	KM48S2020AT-G10	SDRAM/ECC	32MB	66MHz
Mitsubishi	M5M4V64S40ATP-10	SDRAM	32MB	66MHz
Mitsubishi	M5M4V16S30BTP	SDRAM	32MB	66MHz
Fujitsu	81117822E-100FN	SDRAM	32MB	66MHz
Micton	MT48LC2M8A1TG-10	SDRAM	32MB	66MHz
Hyundai	HYM7072A801-TFG	SDRAM	64MB	66MHz
Mitsubishi	M5M4V64S40APT-10	SDRAM	64MB	66MHz
Mitsubishi	M5M4V64S30APT-10	SDRAM/ECC	128MB	66MHz

Rambus Inline Memory Modules

Because of the radical interface required by Rambus memory, memory makers redesigned individual modules to create a special RIMM to accommodate the technology. The basic module appears similar to a standard DIMM with individual memory chips soldered to a printed circuit board substrate that links to a socket using a conventional edge connector. Despite the relatively narrow bus interface used by the Rambus systems (16 bits), the RIMM package pushes its pin count to 184, partly because alternate pins are held to ground potential as a form of shielding to improve stability and decrease interference at the high clock frequency for which the modules are designed (800MHz).

RIMMs also differ in their operating voltage. The Rambus standard calls for 2.5 volt operation, as opposed to the 3.3 volts standard with DIMMs. Future RIMMs may operate at 1.8 volts.

The standard 184-pin design supports both non-parity and error-correction RIMMs with bus widths of 16 and 18 bits, respectively. Figure 4.10 shows a RIMM package.

FIGURE 4.10
A RIMM package.

Small Outline DIMMs

Although convenient for desktop computers, SIMMs are unnecessarily large for notebook machines. Consequently, the makers of miniaturized PCs trimmed the size of 72-pin SIMMs while retaining the same number of connections with a simple expedient. Instead of linking together the edge connector tabs on the two sides of the module, they let the tabs on each side of the module carry a separate signal. This expedient cuts the length of the required connector and the potential size of the module in half. The result is called a Small Outline Dual Inline Memory Module—small because of the reduced size of the module and dual inline because of twin rows of independent connector tabs, one on each side of the module. Figure 4.11 illustrates a typical Small Outline Dual Inline Memory Module.

FIGURE 4.11
72-pin Small Outline Dual Inline Memory Module package.

As you would expect, a 72-pin SODIMM is about half the length of a 72-pin SIMM, measuring about 2.35 inches long. As with other module styles, a notch at one end of a 72-pin SODIMM prevents you from latching it into its socket with the wrong orientation. The notch is on your left when you look at the chip side of the SODIMM. Figure 4.12 show the dimensions of a typical SODIMM.

Electrically, a 72-pin SODIMM is the equivalent of a 72-pin SIMM with the connections moved to both sides of the module. Each SODIMM provides four separate banks of memory that allow their use in PCs with data buses either one, two, or four bytes wide.

FIGURE 4.12
Dimensions of a typical Small Outline Dual Inline Memory Module.

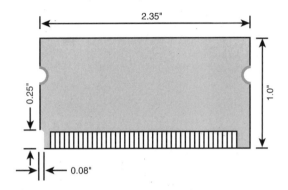

Using the same strategy of shrinking module size for portable applications, a new SoDIMM has become popular in notebook systems. The 144-pin SoDIMM uses a similar 64-bit interface as 168-pin DIMMs but packs the memory into a smaller package.

SIPPs

Single Inline Pin Package Modules, often shortened to SIPPs, use pin connectors. Like SIP chip packages, the connections of a SIPP module are brought out as wire-like pins that hang down from the basic board in a single collinear row. The leads on a SIPP are designed for soldering in place, although sometimes they are installed in special sockets much like SIP chips. A SIPP socket often is nothing more than a line of holes reinforced by contact cups in the circuit board to which the SIPP mates. Figure 4.13 shows a typical SIPP package.

FIGURE 4.13
30-pin SIPP memory.

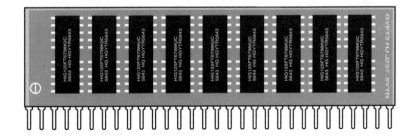

Although SIPPs are electrically identical to 30-pin SIMMs, they are physically somewhat smaller. Moreover, because their edges are not bound in a connector, their width may vary. Only the spacing between their pins—one-tenth inch—is fixed. Figure 4.14 illustrates a typical SIPP.

FIGURE 4.14

Dimensions of a standard height 30-pin SIPP.

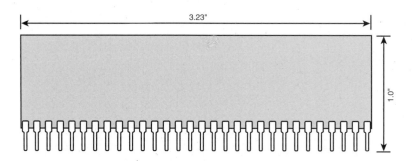

Some manufacturers offer low-profile SIPPs that require less headroom, allowing them to neatly fit between expansion bus connectors in PCs or similar spaces where part height is restricted. Figure 4.15 shows the dimensions of a typical low-profile SIPP.

FIGURE 4.15

Dimensions of a low-height 30-pin SIPP.

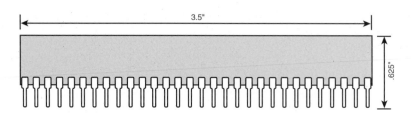

Functionally, SIMMs and SIPPs can carry the same memory chips, technologies, and capacities. However, their differing mounting schemes make them mutually incompatible. When you want to add memory to your PC or replace a defective module, you'll have to specify whether it uses SIMMs or SIPPs.

Installation

In general, the memory of your PC will work throughout the life of the machine without requiring any attention. Memory has no moving parts that require service or lubrication. The only time you're likely to tangle with memory is when you decide to add to your PC's native endowment, either of its main memory on the motherboard or on an expansion board to enhance the size of a disk cache or video frame buffer.

Memory installation is a process that requires care but does not demand expertise or extreme precision. You can usually add a few megabytes in a few minutes without worrying about damaging the memory, your PC, or yourself.

The care required is that of taking simple precautions. Avoid static electricity, which can damage *any* solid-state circuitry, including memory chips. The most cautious sources usually recommend that you ground yourself on a cold water pipe before you dig into the circuitry of your PC. Most people just plug in chips or modules without giving a thought to static. Unless you draw sparks when you touch things on your workbench, you're probably safe to install memory modules.

In that one of the primary design goals of memory modules is simplified installation, modules make expanding the memory of your PC easy—or at least easier than it would be with a box full of discrete chips. Modules do not, however, make memory installation or expansion trouble-free. You still must match modules with your PC and insert them in their sockets properly.

Mixing Modules

Because memory modules are made from discrete chips, they use the same underlying technologies. SIMMs made using static, dynamic, video, and page-mode RAM technologies are available. As with discrete chips, different module technologies are not completely interchangeable, so you need to specify the correct type when ordering memory for your PC.

Current PCs may use fast page-mode, EDO, Fast EDO, or SDRAM memory on their SIMMs. In general, a PC designed for fast page-mode SIMMs can use other SIMM technologies but derives no benefit from doing so. The higher speed of the more advanced memories will be wasted. Similarly, you can usually slide a fast page-mode SIMM into an EDO socket—at the price of slowing down your entire system to the fast page-mode speed.

SDRAM demands entirely different system timings than page-mode or EDO memory. In other words, SDRAM and its PCs must be made for each other. When they are, you get the fastest DRAM now available, but your upgrades must be SDRAM. Don't even think about loading SDRAM in a PC not designed for it.

You also need to match the speed ratings of your modules, both to the requirements of your PC and, often, to other modules that are already installed. New PCs—those that use 72-pin or 168-pin SIMMs—are quite accommodating when it comes to memory speed. They sense the speed rating of the SIMMs you install and adjust themselves accordingly. Note that they lower their memory speed to match the *slowest* SIMMs you've installed, so you won't want to install anything more laggardly than what you've already got.

Older PCs, particularly those that use 30-pin SIMMs, can't sense speed, so you must match the speed of the memory you install to your system's explicit requirements. Some systems allow you to adjust memory wait states so you can install faster memory and adjust the speed upward (by selecting fewer wait states). Again, the fastest setting you can make must match that of the *slowest* SIMM in the system, so you'll have to toss your older, slower memory to ratchet up the performance ladder.

Note that some older PCs won't tolerate mixing SIMMs with different speed ratings. The least expensive—and most cost-effective—solution is to match the speed rating of the SIMMs you already have. If you don't know what speed your PC uses, look at the chips on its SIMM modules. The last two digits in the designation indicate its speed. As the gulf between technologies broadens, the likelihood of successfully accommodating different memory systems declines and the performance penalty for a mismatch becomes ever more draconian. The best memory to use is that which matches your PC. A match helps assure optimum performance and prevents you from paying for more than will benefit your PC.

In systems that use 30-pin SIMMs and 64-bit PCs using 72-pin SIMMs, memory modules follow the same mixing rules as chips: All the modules in a given bank of memory must have the same capacity. For example, in a 32-bit computer, the four modules that comprise one bank must have the same capacity. In PCs that use a single SIMM or DIMM for a memory bank, you can generally mix speed ratings as you see fit. The sensing connections on the modules allow your PC to adjust its operation to accommodate the available memory performances. Note, however, that in such mixed-speed systems, the entire memory system will slow to the rate of the slowest module that has been installed.

Contact Material

You'll find another subtle variation among SIMMs, the material that the manufacturer uses to plate the edge connector contacts of the module. In general, they choose one of two materials for this plating, gold or tin.

The purpose of this plating is to prevent oxidation or corrosion that would increase the resistance of the contact and lower the reliability of the connection. In the abstract, gold is the preferred material because it oxidizes less readily. Gold also costs substantially more, encouraging manufacturers to opt for tin.

One manufacturer of electronic component sockets, AMP, points out that the material is not so important as the match. You should choose SIMMs with contacts plated with the same material as used in the SIMM sockets in your PC. The explanation goes deeper than the plating.

According to AMP, putting tin in contact with gold and exerting pressure on the contact results in a problem called *fretting*. Part of the tin rubs off, attaches to the gold, and oxidizes there, building up a thin layer of tin oxide. The longer the two materials contact one another, the thicker the oxide builds up.

Gold is not the only material susceptible to this oxide build-up. It can develop when tin contacts nearly any dissimilar metal. The problem does not arise when tin-plated contacts press against other tin-plated contacts. Of course, the tin surface will naturally oxidize on the tin-plated contacts, but when you insert a tin-plated edge connector into a tin-plated socket, the soft tin gives way. Pushing the contacts together squeezes or wipes the tin oxide away from the contact area so that tin presses against tin.

Although the fretting problem takes time to develop—perhaps longer than the useful life of your PC—the best strategy is to use SIMMs with contacts plated with the same material as the SIMM sockets on your motherboard. Some motherboard makers—in particular, Intel—use tin-plated contacts on their SIMM sockets and recommend *against* the use of gold-plated SIMMs.

SIMM Adapters

If you still have a stack of 30-pin SIMMs left over from that old 386 you converted into a planter for your begonias and you want to recycle them with one of those clever little adapters that takes four 30-pin SIMMs and makes them work as one 72-pin jobbie, think again. With modern memory prices, recycling 4MB of SIMMs for the price of a $50 adapter doesn't make sense—particularly considering your old modules are likely to have a rickety speed rating.

When you use an adapter, you also face the problem of matching SIMMs. Most adapters and PCs work best when all the SIMMs are matched. If you're upgrading a Pentium, that means a 64-bit bank of eight matching SIMMs spread across two matching adapters. Don't expect to match an adapter on one bank and a standard 72-pin SIMM on the other and have your PC work reliably.

Identifying Modules

The only way to properly identify memory modules is by part number. The manufacturer's part number given to a memory module is often stenciled on the side of the board opposite that carrying the individual memory chips. If you cannot find a part number on the module itself, you can often determine the capacity and technology of the module from the marking on the individual discrete chips installed on the module. For example, a module made from nine 4-megabit chips rated at 60 nanoseconds is a 4MB, 60 nanosecond memory module.

For a better look when attempting to identify memory modules, you may want to pop the module from its socket. Just be careful because memory modules are made from discrete chips and consequently have the same sensitivity to static electricity. If you take the proper precautions, however, the removal process for SIPPs is easy; just pull each one out, applying even pressure to the two ends of the SIPP.

SIMMs and DIMMs are more difficult. Normally, both SIMMs and DIMMs are latched into place by plastic fingers at either end of the slot in their connectors. Look closely and you'll see that the plastic of the socket has two latching fingers at each end. You must carefully pry these away from the memory module before you can put it out. You can then lean the SIMM over a bit and pull it out. When you re-insert the module, you must press it firmly in place until the fingers lock it down again and little round tabs appear in the latching holes in the module near the fingers.

Orientation

When installing DIMMs, SIMMs or SIPPs, remember that their orientation is important. In general, all memory modules in a PC will face in the same direction. With SIMMs in modern, slanted sockets, that generally means the chips on the DIMM or SIMM circuit board will be on the top of the module once you lean it down into the socket. Most memory module sockets have keying tabs on them to prevent your putting a module in backwards. Should you try to insert a memory module and discover that it refuses to fit, you probably have it in the wrong orientation or improperly seated.

CHAPTER

5

The BIOS

At one time, a set of built-in program routines called the Basic Input/Output System, or BIOS, defined the "personality" of a PC, defining what the machine could do and how it was done. Today's software and operating systems make the BIOS something to be avoided yet a thing still necessary for making your PC work—sort of like a big-city freeway system. Although only a fraction of the size of a typical application program—often less than 32KB of code—the BIOS is the default control for many of the most important functions of your PC—how it interprets keystrokes, how it puts characters on the screen, how it communicates through its ports. It defines the compatibility of your PC with expansion hardware. As with that freeway system, you cannot avoid the BIOS. Without it, your PC couldn't even boot up.

The BIOS is critical to many aspects of the operation of your PC. The most important of these include:

Boot up	Tests your PC for proper operation and assures that the microprocessor, memory and most peripherals are functioning.
Drive parameters	Retains values that match your hard and floppy disk to your PC. Older PCs often require a BIOS update to address the full capacity of today's larger hard disk drives.
Time of day	Memory that's part of the BIOS system tracks the time and day while your PC is switched off.
Keyboard and video	Before your operating system loads, the BIOS handles input from the keyboard and output to your display so you can control and monitor your PC's operation.
Program calls	Before your operating system loads (and even afterward with old operating systems) the BIOS provides the primary link between your PC's hardware and the software that you want to run.
Advanced setup	The BIOSs of most PCs provide a portal for controlling performance and compatibility features of your PC including memory speed and boot-up options.
Security	Most modern PC BIOSs give your PC password protection prevent to unauthorized people from using your PC, even to the extent of making your notebook PC useless to a thief.

Think of the Basic Input/Output System of your PC as its crazy Aunt Maud, locked away from public eyes in a cobwebby garret. Except for the occasional deranged laughter that rings through the halls, you might never know she was there, and you don't think about her again until the next reel of the B-movie that makes up your life.

As with your own old Aunt Maud, your PC's BIOS is something that you want to forget but is always there, lingering in the background, popping into sight only at the least convenient times. Despite its idiosyncrasies and age, despite the embarrassment it causes, your PC can't live without its BIOS. It defines what your PC is and keeps it in line, just as Aunt Maud defines what your family really is and her antics keep you in line (or at least tangled up in obscure legal proceedings). You'd really like to be rid of Aunt Maud, but only she knows the secret of your family's jewels, a secret someday you hope you'll wrest from her.

The BIOS of your PC lingers around like that unwelcome relative, but it also holds the secrets of your PC. You can lock it up, even build a wall around it, but it will always be there. When you switch on your PC, it laughs at you from the monitor screen, appearing in the rags and tatters of text mode before your system jumps off into modern high-resolution color. Most of what you do on your PC now sidesteps the BIOS, so you'd think you could do without it. You might never suspect that behind the scenes the BIOS of your PC tests your system, assures you that everything is okay when you start your system, helps you set up your PC so that it runs at its best, and gracefully steps out of the way when you no longer need it.

Although modern operating systems such as Windows do their best to hide the BIOS and take its place, it always lurks in the background like crazy old Aunt Maud locked in the garret. Just as Aunt Maud may ruin a dinner party when she suddenly pops up babbling about a talking moose, your BIOS bursts onto the scene when you least expect it and ruins your fun—for example, by hiding half of your new hard disk.

Your Aunt Maud might just be not as crazy as she seems, watching over you quietly from her garret, hiding in the background but working in her own mysterious ways to make sure your life goes well.

Background

Although mostly invisible and oft forgotten, your PC's BIOS is nevertheless one of its most important and enabling parts. The BIOS is, in fact, the one essential constituent that distinguishes one PC from another even when they both share the same microprocessor, motherboard, and support hardware.

Firmware

Strictly speaking, however, the BIOS isn't hardware at all even though it is an essential part of your PC's hardware. The BIOS is special program code—in a word, software—that's permanently (or nearly so) encapsulated in ROM chips or, as is most often the case with newer PCs, flash memory. Because of the two-sided aspects of the BIOS, existing in the netherworld between hardware and software, it and other pieces of program code encapsulated in ROM or flash memory are often termed *firmware*.

The importance of the BIOS arises from its function. The BIOS tests your PC computer every time you turn it on. It may even allocate your system's resources for you automatically, making all the adjustments necessary to accommodate new hardware. The BIOS also determines the compatibility of your PC with both hardware and software and can even determine how flexible your PC is in setup and use.

Firmware can do more. If some enterprising PC maker wanted to, it could put the entire operating system and application software into firmware. Some portable computers actually came close; early Hewlett-Packard Omnibook sub-notebook PCs packed Windows and part of Microsoft Office into their ROMs. Of course, these machines are not very useful any more. The Windows inside is version 3.0, which points out the disadvantage of putting too much into firmware; updates are cumbersome and the code storage requirements of today's software would fill more chips than you could comfortably carry. The storage available in a PC's ROM gives engineers kilobytes to work with, not the gigabytes today's systems demand for storage of their software.

Today, firmware plays only a subsidiary role in most PCs. All modern operating systems enhance the basic BIOS firmware with additional instructions loaded from disk like ordinary software; typically such enhancements totally replace the BIOS firmware. This new code supplied by the operating system performs some of the same functions as the traditional BIOS firmware, linking your PC's hardware to the software programs that you run. But every PC still requires at least a vestigial piece of BIOS firmware, if just to enable enough of your system to run so that it can load the operating system. Although the BIOS plays a less active role in every operation of your PC, it is essential to getting your PC going, and it remains an essential part of every new PC and future machines still waiting on the engineer's drawing board.

Functions

The BIOS code of most PCs has a number of separate and distinct functions. The BIOS of a typical PC contains routines that test the computer, blocks of data that give the machine its personality, special program routines that allow software to take control of the PC's hardware so that it can more smoothly mesh with the electronics of the system, and even a complete system (in some PCs) for determining which expansion boards and peripherals you have installed and ensuring that they do not conflict in their requests for input/output ports and memory assignments. Although all of these functions get stored in the same memory chips, the program code of each function is essentially independent of the rest. Each function is a separate module, and the name BIOS refers to the entire group of modules.

This list of functions is not an exhaustive list of what a BIOS *could* do. It represents only what the makers of current PCs use the BIOS for. In fact, there's little limit on what BIOS code can do. Apple has put most of the graphics its Macintosh systems in its BIOS (since 1984), and IBM for years encapsulated a small programming language in the BIOSs for the first PCs.

The classic definition of the PC BIOS is the firmware that gives the PC its *personality*. This definition refers only to one functional module of the PC, the one that's invariably replaced by operating system code. The nebulous term "personality" described how the computer performed its basic functions, those necessary to make it a real computer. Although this definition includes a number of different factors, including how quickly and smoothly various operations were completed, the term "personality" mostly distinguished PCs from Apple Macintoshes.

Most of the personality of the PC has moved from its BIOS to the operating system, loaded entirely from disk storage into RAM, and the BIOS now plays a subsidiary role. Chiefly, it is in charge of getting your PC going and running things until your hard disk can disgorge the hundreds of megabytes of operating system code and that software takes over control of your PC.

In most PCs, the first thing the BIOS tells the microprocessor to do is to run through all the known components of the system—the microprocessor, memory, keyboard, and so on—and to test to determine whether they are operating properly. After the system is sure of its own integrity, it checks to see whether you have installed any expansion boards that hold additional BIOS code. If you have, the microprocessor checks the code and carries out any instructions that it finds. A modern PC may even check to see if any new expansion boards are plugged in without being set up properly. The BIOS code might then configure the expansion board so that it functions properly in your PC.

When the microprocessor runs out of add-in peripherals, it begins the actual boot-up process, which engineers call the Initial Program Load, or IPL. The BIOS code tells the microprocessor to jump to a section of code that tells the chip how to read the first sector of your floppy or hard disk. Program code then takes over from the BIOS and tells the microprocessor how to load the operating system from the disk to start the computer running.

Exactly what the BIOS does after the operating system loads depends on the operating system. The first PC operating system, DOS, worked in conjunction with the BIOS. DOS relied on the BIOS firmware, which includes several sets of routines that programs can call to carry out everyday functions—typing characters on the screen or to a printer, reading keystrokes, timing events. Because of this basic library, programmers writing for DOS could create their grand designs without worrying about the tiny details.

With Windows, however, the BIOS gets pushed out of the way. After the BIOS has assured the operating integrity of your system, Windows takes over. First, the operating system starts loading its own boot code, and then, it installs drivers that take over the various interface functions of the BIOS one by one.

The operating system replaces the BIOS interface routines for several reasons. Because software drivers load into RAM, they are not limited in the amount of space available for their code. Software drivers also extend the capabilities, whereas the BIOS limits them. Using only the BIOS, your PC cannot do anything that the BIOS does not know about, so relying on the BIOS alone you won't be able to use the wide variety of peripherals you're apt to connect to your PC. Moreover, because the BIOS is designed to run at boot-up when your PC is in real mode, it uses only real-mode code with all of the limitations that implies—in particular, a total address space of one megabyte. Software drivers can (and nowadays invariably do) run in protected mode. Not only can they access more memory, but also protected mode drivers can be written in 32-bit code that executes faster on modern microprocessors.

Initialization Functions

The BIOS starts to work as soon as you switch on your system. When all modern Intel microprocessors start to work, they immediately set themselves up in real mode and look at a special memory location that is exactly 16 bytes short of the top of the one-megabyte real-mode addressing range, absolute address 0FFFF0(Hex). This location holds a special program instruction, a jump that points to another address where the BIOS code actually begins—the starting point for the boot process, which can occur in the following ways:

- **Cold boot** describes the process of starting your PC and loading its operating system by turning the power on. If your PC is running, you cold boot by first switching it off and then back on.

- **Warm boot** describes the process of restarting your PC and loading its operating system anew after it has already been running and has booted up at least once before. You start a warm boot by giving the infamous "three finger salute" by pressing the Ctrl, Alt, and Del keys at the same time.

- **Hot boot** describes what you get when you slide a piece of footwear into your oven in a mistaken attempt at the preparation of filet of sole. The term is not used to describe the PC boot-up process.

At the operating system level, a cold boot and a warm boot are essentially the same. Your PC starts from the beginning and loads the operating system from scratch. A warm boot or switching your PC off for a cold boot signals the microprocessor to reset itself to its turn-on condition, erasing the contents of its registers. The microprocessor then loads or reloads the operating system.

The important difference between a cold and warm boot is not what happens to your operating system but the effect on your PC's internal circuits. A cold boot automatically restores all the circuits in your PC to their original, default condition whether they are on the motherboard or expansion boards because it cuts off their electrical supply. It also wipes away everything in its memory for a fresh start. A warm boot does not affect the supply of electricity to your PC's circuitry, so memory and the boards installed in your PC are not wiped clean, although some of its contents get overwritten as your operating system reloads.

Because a warm boot does not automatically restore all the expansion boards in your PC to their initial conditions, it sometimes does not solve software problems. For example, your modem may not release the telephone line (hang-up) at the end of your Internet session. A warm boot may leave the modem connected, but a cold boot will assure the modem disconnects and releases your telephone line.

Unless the boards in your PC follow the plug-and-play standard that specifies a standard reset condition, your PC has no way of telling the state of each board in your PC after a warm boot. It makes no attempt to find out and just takes what it gets. Ordinarily, such blind acceptance is not a problem. If, however, some odd state of an expansion board caused your PC to crash, a warm boot will not solve the problem. For example, sometimes video boards will come up in odd states with strange screen displays after a crash that's followed by a warm boot. Cold booting your PC again usually eliminates such problems.

Your PC also behaves differently during the cold and warm booting process. During a cold boot, your PC runs through its Power-On Self Test (POST) procedure to test all its circuitry. During a warm boot, your PC sidesteps POST under the assumption that your PC has already booted up once so its circuitry must be working properly.

Your PC must somehow distinguish between a cold and warm boot to decide whether to run its POST diagnostics. To sort things out, your PC uses its normal memory, which it does not wipe out during a warm boot. Each time your PC boots up, it plants a special two-byte signature in memory. When your system boots, it looks for the signature. If it finds the signature, it knows it has been booted at least once before because you turned on the power, so it does not need to run through POST. When it fails to find the signature, it runs its diagnostics as part of the cold boot process. Note that if something in your system changes the signature bytes—as crashing programs sometimes do—your PC will run through a cold boot even though you haven't turned it off.

The signature bytes have the value 1234(Hex). Because they are stored in Intel *little endian format* (that is, the least significant byte comes first), they appear in memory as the sequence 3412.

Programs can also initiate a warm or cold boot simply by jumping to the appropriate section of BIOS code. However, because some expansion boards don't automatically reset when your PC runs through the cold boot BIOS code, anomalies may persist after such a program-initiated cold boot. For example, your video board may latch itself into an odd state, and a complete reset may not unlock it. For this reason, some programs instruct you to turn your PC off and back on during the installation process to guarantee all the hardware in your system properly resets.

Power-On Self Test

Every time your PC switches on, the BIOS immediately takes command. Its first duty is to run through a series of diagnostic routines—system checks—called the Power-On Self Test routine, or POST, which ensures every part of your PC's hardware is functioning properly before you trust your time and data to it. One by one, the POST routine checks the circuits of your system board and memory, the keyboard, your disks, and each expansion board. After the BIOS makes sure that the system is operating properly, it initializes the electronics so that they are ready for the first program to load.

Error Codes

The BIOS tests are relatively simple. The BIOS sends data to a port or register and then looks to see the results. If it receives expected results, the BIOS assumes all is well. If it finds a problem, however, it reports the failure as well as it can. If the display system is working, it posts an *error code* number on your monitor screen. (The limited amount of memory available prevents the BIOS from storing an elaborate—that is, understandable—message for all the hundreds of possible error conditions.) If your PC is so ill that the display system will not even work, the BIOS sends a coded series of beeps through your system's loudspeaker.

Many BIOSs also write the code numbers of the ongoing tests to input/output port 80(Hex). Special *diagnostic boards* that plug into a vacant expansion slot can monitor this test procedure and show the test progress and failure. Repair technicians often use such diagnostic boards when servicing systems.

Beep Codes

Displaying an error code on your monitor screen presupposes that at least part of your PC—and a major part at that—is operating properly: the display system. If your video board or monitor is not functioning and you don't have a diagnostic board, the error code display is useless. Consequently, most BIOSs also generate error identifications that are independent of the display system.

Instead of visual displays, they use audible error codes played through the small speaker system that is standard equipment in all PCs. Because the speaker system links to your PC at a rudimentary level—only a single amplifier chip stands between the speaker and its associated input/output port—the basic PC speaker will always function except during the most dire failures, such as a non-working microprocessor. (Note that this basic PC speaker is separate from the sound board or multimedia sound system present in most new PCs.) These audible error messages take the form of beeps from the system speaker. Consequently, they are usually termed *beep codes*.

As PCs have become more complex, the systems of beep codes have become correspondingly elaborate. Some sound more elaborate than a mayday call from a sinking ocean liner. Every BIOS maker uses its own coding scheme for these aural error warnings. Usually, a single short beep means your PC is okay; anything else warns of an error. (See Appendix J, "Error Codes" on the CD-ROM.)

Should your PC start with a continuous beep that won't stop until you switch off the power, your PC has a major problem most likely with its power or logic system. Oftentimes, a defective expansion board or an improperly inserted expansion board will elicit such an unending beep. It can also result from a bad microprocessor or other motherboard problem. If you encounter a beep that won't end, check your expansion boards first. Ensure that all are seated properly, and then remove them one by one or *en masse* until the beep quiets down. (Be sure to switch off your PC before you add or remove an expansion board.)

BIOS Extensions

After the actual testing of your PC and its associated circuitry is complete, its BIOS begins to execute initialization routines that configure the various options inside your PC. Exactly what happens next depends on the design of the BIOS. A conventional BIOS merely looks for add-in BIOS routines, initializes devices using the routines already in the BIOS, and starts the disk boot-up.

Every PC assumes that many of its peripherals are loaded with specific data values when it starts up. That is, all the default operating values are loaded by the BIOS so your timer knows what to time and the speaker knows the frequency at which to beep. The serial ports are set to their default speed. A plug-and-play system such as those of nearly all new PCs runs through a more structured initialization process that amounts to completely setting up system resources each time the computer boots. The section "Plug and Play" later in this chapter gives a step-by-step outline of this BIOS boot procedure.

By design, the basic PC BIOS knows how to search beyond the confines of the system board. It knows how to locate the extra instructions and data that get added in with some expansion boards. Where some computers require you to replace the BIOS firmware with new chips to add new features, the PC BIOS was designed to be extendible. That is, the full extent of the BIOS is not forever cast in the silicon of the firmware. The extendible BIOS is capable of accepting additional code as its own into one integrated whole. Rather than replace the BIOS chips, this extendibility means that you can add more firmware containing their own BIOS routines to your PC. The BIOS incorporates the new routines into itself.

The key to making the BIOS extendible is itself an extra firmware routine that enables the BIOS to look for add-in code. During the initialization process, the BIOS code reads through the address range looking for code stored on add-in boards. If it finds a valid section of code, it adds those instructions to the BIOS repertory. New interrupt routines may be added, for instance, or the function of existing routines may be changed.

The routine to extend the BIOS works as follows: Following the actual testing portion of the Power-On Self Test, after basic system board functions have been initialized (for example, the interrupt vectors have been loaded into RAM), the resident BIOS code instructs the computer to check through its ROM memory for the occurrence of the special preamble bytes that mark the beginning of add-in BIOS routines. The original IBM BIOS searches for these preamble bytes in the absolute address range 0C8000(Hex) to 0F4000(Hex); newer BIOSs check the range from 0C0000(Hex) to 0EFFFF(Hex). Either of these subsets of the full, reserved, high memory range—that is, 0A0000(Hex) to 0FFFFF(Hex)—exclude the areas used by video memory and the BIOS itself to prevent confusing data with preamble bytes.

If the BIOS finds the special preamble bytes, it verifies that the subsequent section of code is a legitimate BIOS extension by performing a form of cyclical redundancy check on the specified number of 512 byte blocks. The values of each byte in the block are totaled using Modulo 0100(Hex) addition; the effect is the same as dividing the sum of all the bytes by 4,096. A remainder of zero indicates that the extension BIOS contains valid code.

The preamble bytes take a specific form. Two bytes indicate the beginning of an extension code section—055(Hex) followed by 0AA(Hex). Immediately following the two-byte preamble bytes is a third byte that quantifies the length of the additional BIOS. The number represents the number of blocks 512 bytes long needed to hold the extra code. Plug and Play peripherals have a more structured header that follows the preamble bytes.

After a valid section of code is identified, system control (BIOS program execution) jumps to the fourth byte in the extension BIOS and performs any functions specified there in machine language. Typically, these instructions tell the BIOS how to install the extra code. Finally, when the instructions in the extension BIOS are completed, control returns to the resident BIOS. The system then continues to search for additional blocks of extension BIOS. When it finally completes its search by reaching the absolute address 0F4000(Hex), it starts the process of booting up your computer from disk.

The ROM or flash memory chips containing this extra BIOS code do not have to be present on the system board. The memory locations used also are accessible on the expansion bus. This feature allows new chips that add to the BIOS to be part of expansion boards that can be slid into the computer. The code necessary to control the expansion accessory loads automatically whenever the system boots up.

Multiple sections of this add-in code fit into any computer, limited only by the address range available. One complication is that no two sections of code can occupy the same memory area. As a result, the makers of conventional ISA expansion boards typically incorporate jumpers, DIP switches, or EPROM memory on their products to allow you to reassign the addresses used by their BIOS extensions and avoid conflicts. Plug-and-play designs have made this conflict resolution automatic during the setup process.

Initial Program Load

Once the BIOS of your PC has completed all of its tests, checked for additional BIOS code, and set up all the devices it knows about, it yields control over to your operating system. In older PCs, the operating system simply takes over and brings your PC to life. In a plug-and-play system, the operating system continues the initialization of the devices inside and connected to your PC. In effect, the plug-and-play system completes the BIOS configuration process.

In either case, whether your BIOS completes the initialization of your system or it transfers control to the operating system to complete the process, somehow your operating system must load. Your PC must know enough about your disks—floppy, hard, and CD— to be able to find the operating system and get its code running. The process of getting the operating system started is called the *initial program load*.

The IPL procedure is quite simple and understandably so. When the first PC was created, ROM chips, like all other parts of computers, were expensive. The PC's designers opted to use as little ROM as possible to get the system started. They added a short code routine at the end of the BIOS test procedure that told the BIOS to read the first sector from your floppy disk. This first sector is sometimes called the *boot sector* because of its function. (In newer PCs, the BIOS is smart enough to look to your hard disk as well as floppy and sometimes even to your CD-ROM drive to find a boot sector. Many BIOSs allow you to select which of these it searches for and in what order it makes its search.) If the BIOS finds executable code there, it loads it into memory and executes it. If it finds no executable code or no available disk, the BIOS complains and does nothing because it doesn't know how to do anything else.

The small amount of code used by the IPL routine is unforgiving. It searches only the first physical sector on your disks. It looks for sectors rather than clusters or allocation units because at this point, it doesn't know what operating system you have and how it organizes disk storage. The BIOS must know how to find the first physical sector on the disk; consequently, it requires a BIOS extension associated with the disk to tell it how to make the required access. A disk drive that uses only a software device driver will be invisible to the BIOS and the IPL routines, and consequently, such a disk cannot boot the system.

The code in the boot sector is also short and to the point because it has to fit into the confines of a single sector. Its code tells your PC how to find the rest of the operating system. Once it locates the main operating system, the boot sector code starts loading that code into memory and yields control to it. The operating system takes command and completes the process of booting your PC.

Plug and Play

One of the gravest shortcomings of legacy PCs—old PCs built in pre-Pentium days—was their ISA expansion bus that lacked automatic configuration procedures. You were left to adjust settings and configure software yourself. And each of the dozens of settings you had to make brought its own potential for error. Putting even one jumper in the wrong place or throwing the wrong switch was often sufficient to turn $2000 of PC into a noisy desk ornament.

To eliminate such setup problems and shift the tedious job of system configuration to someone (or something) better equipped to deal with it, the PC industry developed the *plug-and-play initiative*. The idea was to make your PC responsible for configuring itself. After all, PCs specialize in taking over jobs that you find tedious. The goal was to create PCs with no switches, no jumpers, and no headaches. So far, they've achieve two out of three, a pretty good average.

The straightforward goal belies the arduous journey in reaching today's reasonably successful automatic configuration systems. Making Plug and Play work required changes in every PC's BIOS, expansion bus, expansion boards, and the operating system. The universal adoption of Plug and Play was a lengthy transition, one that dragged on as compliant products slowly coursed into the market, one that continues today.

Background

The first stab at a plug-and-play specification appeared with the original Intel-Microsoft specification for ISA on May 28, 1993. That effort inspired other companies to join in, and related standards are being developed to extend Plug and Play to other troubling configuration processes, particularly SCSI expansion. Compaq Computer Corporation and Phoenix Technologies joined Intel to develop a BIOS specification for Plug and Play, first released November 1, 1993.

Today's plug-and-play system works by shifting the responsibility for remembering and assigning setup options from you to your computer system. After all, your PC likely has a better memory than you do, and it doesn't mind running through a check-up procedure however many times as is needed.

Plug and Play requires all three elements of the system written to its standards—the PC and its BIOS, the operating system, and the expansion boards and peripherals attached to the PC. Any older device that does not conform to the plug-and-play standard is considered to be a *legacy* device. The plug-and-play system attempts to accommodate legacy devices, but it cannot resolve all conflicts between them. The developers see the ultimate solution as attrition. As time goes by, old non-compliant products will fade from the market. To accelerate the demise of legacy products, Intel and Microsoft have written support for ISA out of their most recent system standards, although many people still insist on at least one ISA slot in their newest PCs.

If you've bought a PC in the last five years, you are almost certain to have plug-and-play support. All BIOSs created in the last half decade incorporate plug-and-play abilities. All Microsoft operating systems since Windows 95 have been plug-and-play savvy. Nearly all PCI expansion boards have been built to plug-and-play standards (as have many recent ISA boards).

Expansion Board Support

The basic plug-and-play procedure is a three-step process that lends itself to automation: First, your system checks what resources each expansion device needs. Next, it coordinates the assignments to avoid conflicts. Finally, it tells your system and software which choices it has made.

The plug-and-play configuration process calls upon specific hardware features of plug-and-play expansion boards. Most importantly, each plug-and-play board is able to inactivate itself so that it does not respond to the normal control signals inside your PC. The board disconnects itself from all system resources so that when it is inactive, it cannot possibly cause conflicts.

In addition, each plug-and-play board has several new on-board registers that are reached through a standardized set of three I/O port addresses so that the BIOS or operating system can control the configuration of the board. These ports are designated Address, Write Data, and Read Data.

The Address port functions as a pointer that expands the number of control registers directly accessible to your system without stealing more system resources. Loading a register number in the Address port makes that register available for reading or writing through the Write Data and Read Data ports.

The plug-and-play specification explicitly defines eight card control registers and reserves two large ranges, one of 24 registers for future elaboration of the standard and a second 16-port range that board makers can assign to their own purposes. In addition, the plug-and-play specification allows cards to be configured as multiple logical devices, and it assigns ports for their control. The Address port allows the Write Data port to select which of the logical devices is active and the resources used by each.

Plug-and-play expansion boards act in one of two ways, depending on whether they are needed for booting the system. Boards that are required for boot-up—that is, display adapters and disk controllers—start up active. That is, they come online exactly like conventional expansion boards using the resources assigned them as power-on defaults. They will grab the resources that they need, participate in the normal POST procedure, and let you operate your PC normally. They may also cause the same old resource allocation problems, as will any conventional expansion boards that don't support Plug and Play. The other plug-and-play devices (those not needed in booting your PC) automatically inactivate themselves when your system comes on, waiting to be told what configuration to use by your operating system.

Plug-and-play boards not required during boot-up normally start up inactive. They do nothing until specifically activated, typically by the plug-and-play operating system.

Every plug-and-play board has specific circuitry for managing its configuration. This circuitry operates independently from the normal functions of the board. Unlike the functional circuits on the board that can be disconnected from the bus interface, the plug-and-play circuits always monitor the signals on the bus. However, the plug-and-play circuitry operates in one of four states—Wait for Key, Isolation, Configuration, and Sleep—without regard to whether the functional circuitry is active or inactive.

Boot Operation

All plug-and-play boards, whether active or inactive, boot up in their Wait for Key state. In this condition, the boards refuse to respond to any signal on the ISA bus until they receive an explicit command called an Initiation Key. The Initiation Key is actually a precisely defined 32-step interaction between the host plug-and-play system and circuitry on each expansion board.

All 32 comparisons must be correct for the Initiation Key to be successful. Upon properly receiving the Initiation Key, plug-and-play expansion boards shift into Sleep mode.

Because a legacy PC BIOS does not know how to carry out the Initiation Key process, it cannot remove plug-and-play boards from the Wait for Key state. The configuration circuitry of the plug-and-play boards does not activate (if at all) until the plug-and-play operating system loads.

In a fully plug-and-play PC, the BIOS automatically sends out the Initiation Key. It can then take control of individual boards, interrogate each plug-and-play device about the system resources it requires, and resolve conflicts between boot-up devices. The BIOS ordinarily does not, however, make resource assignments or activate the boards not involved in boot-up. Instead, it leaves that decision-making to the operating system.

To configure each expansion board, the plug-and-play BIOS or operating system must be able to individually communicate with each board to independently instruct each what to do. Ordinarily, that's difficult in the ISA system because all signals are broadcast in common to all expansion boards. The creators of Plug and Play envisioned that ISA bus being modified to include slot-specific signals to unambiguously identify each expansion board. Knowing such changes would take years to creep onto desktops, however, they also developed a board-identification system compatible with the existing ISA bus that allows individual addressing except when multiple identical boards are installed in a single PC. In this plug-and-play system, a Card Select Number (CSN) identifies each board. Each board is dynamically assigned its CSN by the plug-and-play BIOS (if your PC has one) or the plug-and-play operating system.

The CSN is actually a convenience that works as a handle, much like the file handles used by the operating system. The ROM on each plug-and-play board model includes a serial identifier, an eight-byte code coupled with a one-byte checksum. Two bytes store a three-letter manufacturer identification in compressed ASCII code (five bits per character). Two more store the model number of the board, and four more bytes code a board-specific serial number.

In contrast, the CSN is an individual byte value that are more convenient to store and manipulate than all the information in the on-board ROM. Moreover, CSN numbers allow you to install multiple copies of a given board model in one PC without conflict—providing your PC has a means of individually addressing each expansion slot.

All plug-and-play boards boot up with a CSN of zero (0). To assign a unique CSN to a plug-and-play board, the plug-and-play BIOS or operating system must isolate individual boards from the bus. It does this by first arousing all boards from the Sleep state into their Isolation state by broadcasting a Wake command that specifies the default CSN of zero to the Write Data ports of all boards.

In the Isolation state, each board interacts with your PC (and the plug-and-play BIOS or operating system) in a precisely defined manner called the isolation sequence. The plug-and-play BIOS or operating system uses the serial identifier to uniquely locate each board. The system merely compares the bit patterns of the serial identifiers, ignoring their information content.

The isolation sequence involves simultaneously scanning all serial identifiers one bit at a time in the Lineral Feedback Shift Register. The host system sends out 72 consecutive one-bit read operations (one operation for each of the 64 bits in the code plus its 8-bit checksum). At every step, each plug-and-play board compares one bit in its LFSR to that of the other boards by observing bus signals.

When the board has a high bit (digital 1) in its LFSR, it asserts a data signal across the bus; boards with low bits (digital 0) at that position in their serial identifiers do not. When a board with a low bit detects the signal from one or more boards with high bits in a given position in their ID codes, it drops out of the isolation sequence by slipping back into its Sleep state. This bit-comparison process continues until, at the end of 72 evaluations, only one board has not dropped off to sleep.

Once a single board is thus uniquely identified, the operating system then assigns that board its unique CSN number. The board then stores the CSN for future reference in a special CSN register and it, too, goes into its Sleep state. Then, the plug-and-play BIOS or operating system initiates another isolation sequence to assign the next CSN and so on until all boards have been assigned their CSNs. Only the boards with a CSN of zero participate in later isolation sequences because only they respond to the Wake command that starts the sequence.

After all plug-and-play boards have been isolated and assigned CSNs, the BIOS or operating system then checks the resource needs of each one. To do this, the BIOS or operating system individually switches each board into its Configuration mode to read its resource needs from the data stored on the board.

A board with a valid CSN switches into Configuration mode when it detects a Wake command specifying its CSN. Only one board is permitted in Configuration mode at a time, so other boards automatically switch to Sleep mode when they detect the Wake command meant for another board.

In PCs with a plug-and-play BIOS, the BIOS checks each board by reading registers through its Read Data port to compile a list of resource requirements and then finishes the boot-up process. The plug-and-play operating system takes over at that point. In PCs without plug-and-play BIOSs, the operating system merely jumps from the isolation to the configuration process.

After a given expansion board has been configured, the operating system can activate it by writing to the appropriate register on the board. A single expansion board may have several functions, each called a virtual device, which the operating system can separately activate.

After the configuration process is completed (or at any other necessary time), the operating system can switch the designated expansion board out of its Sleep state and back to its Configuration state to activate it, deactivate it, or change its configuration. It controls each board individually using the Wake command and specifying a CSN. This process allows the operating system to dynamically modify the resource usage of any board in the system as applications require.

Structure

Besides introducing several new steps to the standard BIOS-mediated POST procedure, Plug and Play adds a new structure to add-in BIOS code. It allows a given expansion board to include code targeted to specific operating systems so that a given expansion board can take on different personalities depending upon the operating system that's in control.

The plug-and-play BIOS swings into action mimicking the BIOS convention originated by IBM in 1981 by scanning through the memory address range used for BIOS code to look for add-in code held on expansion boards. As with the standard ISA POST procedure, the plug-and-play BIOS looks for a special add-in ROM signature—the two-byte 055(Hex), 0AA(Hex) code—which indicates a block of add-in BIOS code follows.

The plug-and-play system adds additional information to this signature—a pointer that immediately follows it to indicate the location of an expansion header in the BIOS code or a chain of several headers. Each header is identified by a special four-byte preamble—024(Hex), 050(Hex), 06E(Hex), 050(Hex)—which corresponds to the ASCII characters $PnP. Each header can be keyed to an individual operating system using additional codes. Unlike conventional expansion boards, the operating system and not the PC's own BIOS reads through this add-in code on plug-and-play boards because the boards are inactive and effectively decoupled from the bus during a normal BIOS scan.

Using the CSNs given by the BIOS (or the operating system itself), the operating system can identify each plug-and-play board, read through its BIOS area, and find each header. Information encoded in each expansion header includes the types of devices on the board and the location of program code to boot the PC (if a device on the board can boot the computer). A Device Indicator byte in the header indicates whether the ROM on the board initializes as a device driver, may be shadowed, can be cached, and operates as a boot, display, or input device. A Device Type code helps the system BIOS figure out which devices should be used for booting the system if none is overtly specified. It identifies exactly what kind of peripheral is connected through the expansion slot. The serial identifier is also included in the header.

The plug-and-play specification allows each board maker a generous apportionment of the available memory and port addresses. Each board can use up to four non-contiguous ranges of memory base addresses for BIOS code and up to eight non-contiguous base addresses for input/output ports. In addition, a board can use from zero to two separate interrupt levels and up to two DMA channels. Each manufacturer determines the number of resources that a given board can use. Which it uses, however, is a matter left to the board maker.

Resource requirements need not be configurable. A board with minimal plug-and-play support merely tells what resources it wants and stodgily sticks there. Most plug-and-play products will, however, allow for several options in their resource requirements. Even when irresolvable conflicts arise between boards, the plug-and-play system can keep a PC operating by inactivating one of the conflicting boards.

The plug-and-play scheme allows the ROM on each expansion board to hold interface and driver code for multiple operating systems, each coded by its own expansion header. An operating system can identify the code that applies specifically to it by reading the headers.

Accommodating Legacy Boards

Despite its antiquity and severe limitations, people have been reluctant to give up the old ISA bus. It's like an old friend who knows only three jokes that he repeats all the time; you're tired hearing those jokes over and over again, but darn, you like those jokes. ISA is as familiar as *Seinfield* reruns on television, and no one wants to give it up. Consequently, the plug-and-play players designed the new system to accommodate old ISA and allow a gradual phase-in of its improved technology. Although a completely hassle-free system will require your PC to be equipped with a new BIOS and nothing but plug-and-play expansion boards, setup headaches will nevertheless fade away as you add new operating systems and expansion boards to your current PC. Eventually, they believe, ISA will be nothing but a bad joke.

With old PCs that were built before Plug and Play was conceived and that lack explicit code for it in their BIOSs, the automatic configuration system divides the task of sorting through resource conflicts between you and the operating system. Although the plug-and-play operating system manages plug-and-play expansion boards, you have to configure your legacy expansion boards.

Updating an aged PC to one with a plug-and-play BIOS won't help resolving conflicts between conventional expansion boards because the hardware-mediated resource allocation on conventional boards can't be changed by software alone. Once you've eliminated non-plug-and-play products from your veteran PC or—better still—replaced your PC entirely, your setup headaches will disappear.

Implementing the basic plug-and-play procedure is complicated by the shortcomings of the legacy ISA design. For example, the ISA bus provides no way of singling out an individual expansion board to determine exactly what resources it might require. Boards can be used individually only after they are configured and your software notified which resources they use.

ISA expansion boards, too, lack the facilities required for automatic configuration. They need some means to allow their resource needs to be set automatically. Instead of jumpers and switches, they must have software latches. And they must understand a common command set for making their adjustments.

In addition, an automatic configuration procedure itself needs its own control system. That is, it needs a program to step through the configuration procedure. And it requires some method for communicating the addresses and assignment it makes to your software so your applications can reach your PC's peripherals.

These shortcomings show that building an automatic configuration system will involve changes in nearly every aspect of a PC. To individually address expansion boards, the ISA expansion bus needs revision. To permit automatic configuration, ISA expansion board design must change. The setup procedure needs to be built into your PC's test procedure, which requires changes to the system BIOS. And linking with software is best implemented by redesigning the overall operating system.

Interface Functions

Although the primary role for the BIOS today is to get your PC started, it retains its BIOS name it earned from its function as the software-to-hardware interface of your machine. It is a control system that operates at the lowest possible level—the most basic—at which the input and output of your computer are designed to link to programs. In effect, it is like a remote control for a television set. The BIOS allows your software to press buttons at a distance from the hardware, just as you control the channel of your TV from your easy chair—and without prying open the set and ratcheting its tuning circuits. In operation, the BIOS is a universal remote control. It lets you push the same buttons, no matter what model or brand of television at which you point it.

The original purpose of this one-step removed BIOS design is to allow PC hardware to be revised and updated without the need to change software correspondingly. It helps guarantee the backward compatibility of PCs. The extra BIOS step is needed because all computers have many hardware elements that are located at specific addresses in memory or within the range of certain input/output ports. Other computer components may have registers of their own, used in their control, that also are addressed at specific locations. Because of the number of separate components inside any computer, the potential number of possible variations in the location of these features is limitless. Software that attempts to control any of this hardware must properly reach out to these registers. As long as all computers are crafted exactly the same, with the same ports used for exactly the same hardware with exactly the same registers, no problems should occur. But if a computer designer wants to change the hardware to a technology that delivers better performance or greater reliability, he may be stymied by the old addresses. Software may expect to reach the old design at one set of ports, whereas the new, improved design may be memory-mapped and not use ports at all. The old software would not know how to reach the new hardware, and the new design simply would not work.

The BIOS gives the software a link. The software reaches into the BIOS for the hardware function it wants. Then, the BIOS dips down into the hardware. If the design of a computer system is changed radically, only the BIOS needs to be changed to reflect the new way of getting at the features of the PC. The changed BIOS still works the same way to the software, so all older programs run exactly as they did before the change. In effect, the new system design requires a new route to get to an old destination—a detour. The new BIOS is an updated road map that shows only the detour.

Certainly, today's driver software easily accomplishes this function of the BIOS. Back in the days when the PC was first created, however, there were no drivers. The original PC BIOS didn't even have provisions for adding extra hardware, and the first operating system had no intrinsic provisions for adding drivers. Not knowing what was to come of the personal computer, IBM put its reliance on BIOS technology in its first PCs and reserved the right to alter the hardware at will. The company made no guarantee that any of the ports or registers of the PC would be the same in any later computer. In effect, IBM created the PC in a well-ordered dream world in which programs would never need to directly address hardware. Instead, each program would call up a software routine in the BIOS, which would have the addressing part of the instruction permanently set in its code. Later computers with different hardware arrangements would use BIOS routines that worked like the old ones and were indistinguishable from the old ones when used by application software. The addresses inside the routines would be changed, however, to match the updated hardware. The same software could work, then, with a wide variety of hardware designs, giving the designer and manufacturer the flexibility to upgrade the entirety of system hardware, if necessary.

Compatibility

In the days when your PC's operating system worked cooperatively with the BIOS instead of co-opting its function, BIOS compatibility was a major issue in buying a new PC. A PC had to have a BIOS functionally equivalent to that of an IBM Personal Computer to work reliably with the software of the day. Consequently after the IBM BIOS made its debut, it became the most copied set of software routines in the world. The PC BIOS laid out all the entry points used by subsequent IBM BIOS and most compatible BIOSs as well. It also defined the functions that could—and must—be expected in any BIOS. And it established the way that the BIOS works. The BIOS that IBM developed for its 1984 PC-AT still defines the minimum level of compatibility for *all* PCs.

Today, PC makers can buy a compatible BIOS off the shelf from any of several sources. It wasn't always that easy. Achieving off-the-shelf BIOS compatibility was one of the great sagas of PC history.

BIOS Development

Because the copyright laws forbade any copying of someone else's work, compatible BIOSs had to be written "clean." That is, the programmers were kept from ever viewing the source code or having any knowledge of the routines it contains. Instead, they worked from a list of instructions and the functions that the BIOS carries out when given each specific instruction. In other words, they looked at the BIOS they wanted to copy as a black box that takes an input and gives an output. The programmers then deduced the instructions for the inside of the box that would give the desired results.

Working in this way was time-consuming and expensive. Few computer companies had the resources to do it all themselves. Compaq was first to successfully tackle the job. The vast majority of compatible PC manufacturers bought the necessary BIOS firmware from specialist firms. The first to offer compatible BIOSs was Phoenix Technologies. Now, computer makers also select BIOS chips from American Megatrends, Inc, Award Software, or MR BIOS.

Because each BIOS vendor must develop its own product separately, the exact code used by each BIOS version is different. Functionally, however, they all look the same to your software (including your operating system).

Hardware Compatibility

At the other side of the interface—where the BIOS links to your PC's hardware—BIOSs can be quite different. By design, every BIOS is created to match the specific hardware in the PC in which it operates. That is part of its job—uniting different hardware designs so that they work interchangeably with all software. Every BIOS is customized for the PC it controls. Typically, computer motherboard manufacturers modify a generic BIOS from one of the BIOS makers to suit their own purposes.

Because each BIOS is customized for a particular model of PC, no generic BIOS can hope to work properly in a given PC. BIOSs are not interchangeable. Moreover, should you want to change or upgrade your PC's BIOS for any reason—either through buying new chips or downloading code for flash memory—you need to get one that matches the exact model of computer that you own.

Advanced BIOS

For several years, BIOS makers faced another compatibility issue, support of IBM's Advanced BIOS, added in 1987 to accommodate IBM's attempt at a protected-mode operating system, OS/2. Instead of integrating the new code into the existing BIOS, IBM chose to make the new routines a separate entity so that the 1987 BIOS comprised two sections—the old BIOS renamed as the Compatibility BIOS, or CBIOS, and the Advanced BIOS code, or ABIOS.

Most manufacturers of BIOSs for compatible PCs choose simply to ignore the ABIOS. After all, Windows essentially sidesteps the entire BIOS, so ABIOS support is unnecessary. Today, the ABIOS is just a historical footnote.

Software Interrupts

The BIOS design created for the first PCs does its linking through a system of software interrupts. To gain access to the underlying hardware, a program sends out an interrupt, a special instruction to the microprocessor. The software interrupt causes the microprocessor to stop what it is doing and start a new routine. It does this by suspending the execution of the code on which it is working, saving its place, and then executing the program code of the BIOS routine.

The various functions the BIOS carries out are termed *interrupt service routines* or *interrupt handlers*. To call a given interrupt handler, a calling program needs to be able to find the program code that carries out the function. The design of the PC BIOS allows the system to put these interrupt handlers at any convenient address. So that a calling program can find the proper routine, the BIOS reserves part of your PC's memory for a map called a *BIOS interrupt vector table*. This map consists of a long list of 32-bit addresses with one address corresponding to each interrupt handler. These addresses point to the first byte of the program code for carrying out the interrupt and are called *interrupt vectors*. The microprocessor reads the value of the vector and starts executing the code located at the value stored in the vector.

The table of interrupt vectors begins at the very start of the microprocessor's memory, address 00000(Hex). Each vector comprises four bytes, and all vectors are stored in increasing order. Table 5.1 summarizes the principal BIOS interrupt vectors and the associated functions.

TABLE 5.1   BIOS Interrupt Vector Table

Absolute Address (Hex)	Interrupt Value	Function	Hardware Interrupt
0000:0000	00H	Divide by zero interrupt header	
0000:0004	01H	Single step interrupt handler	
0000:0008	02H	Non-maskable interrupt	
0000:000C	03H	Breakpoint	
0000:0010	04H	Arithmetic overflow handler	
0000:0014	05H	Print screen	

continues

TABLE 5.1 Continued

Absolute Address (Hex)	Interrupt Value	Function	Hardware Interrupt
0000:0018	06H	Reserved	
0000:001C	07H	Reserved	
0000:0020	08H	Timer interrupt (18.21590 /sec)	
0000:0024	09H	Keyboard service	
0000:0028	0AH	VGA retrace (AT slave)	IRQ2
0000:002C	0BH	Serial port 2	IRQ3
0000:0030	0CH	Serial port 1	IRQ4
0000:0034	0DH	Hard disk	IRQ5
0000:0038	0EH	Floppy disk	IRQ6
0000:003C	0FH	Parallel port	IRQ7
0000:0040	10H	Video services	
0000:0044	11H	Equipment check	
0000:0048	12H	Memory size check	
0000:004C	13H	Floppy and hard disk I/O	
0000:0050	14H	RS-232 service	
0000:0054	15H	System services	
0000:0058	16H	Keyboard	
0000:005C	17H	Printer I/O	
0000:0060	18H	Basic ROM entry point (startup)	
0000:0064	19H	Initial program load (IPL)	
0000:0068	1AH	Time of day	
0000:006C	1BH	Keyboard break	
0000:0070	1CH	User timer	
0000:0074	1DH	Monitor ROM pointer	
0000:0078	1EH	Disk control table pointer	
0000:007C	1FH	Character generator pattern table pointer	
0000:0080	20H	DOS terminate program	
0000:0084	21H	DOS function calls	

Interface Functions

Absolute Address (Hex)	Interrupt Value	Function	Hardware Interrupt
0000:0088	22H	DOS terminate address	
0000:008C	23H	DOS Ctrl+Break exit address	
0000:0090	24H	DOS fatal error exit address	
0000:0094	25H	DOS absolute disk read	
0000:0098	26H	DOS absolute disk write	
0000:009C	27H	DOS terminate and stay resident	
0000:00A0	28H	DOS idle loop	
0000:00A4	29H	DOS console device raw output handler	
0000:00A8	2AH	DOS network communications	
0000:00AC	2BH-2DH	Reserved	
0000:00B8	2EH	DOS execute command	
0000:00BC	2FH	DOS print spool control	
0000:00C0	30H-31H	DOS internal use	
0000:00C8	32H	Reserved	
0000:00CC	33H	Mouse driver calls	
0000:00D0	34H-3EH	Reserved	
0000:00FC	3FH	LINK (internal use)	
0000:0100	40H	Floppy and hard disk handler	
0000:0104	41H	Pointer to hard disk parameters	
0000:0108	42H	EGA video vector screen BIOS entry	
0000:010C	43H	EGA initialization parameters	
0000:0100	44H	EGA graphics character patterns	
0000:0114	45H	Reserved	
0000:0118	46H	Pointer to second fixed disk parameters	
i0000:011C	47H	Reserved	
0000:0120	48H	PCjr cordless keyboard	
0000:0124	49H	PCjr non-keyboard scan code table	
0000:0128	4AH	Alarm routine	

continues

TABLE 5.1   Continued

Absolute Address (Hex)	Interrupt Value	Function	Hardware Interrupt
0000:012C	4BH-4FH	Reserved	
0000:0140	50H	Periodic alarm from timer	
0000:0144	51H-59H	Reserved	
0000:0168	5AH	Cluster adapter BIOS-entry address	
0000:016C	5BH	Cluster boot	
0000:0170	5CH	NetBIOS entry point	
0000:0174	5DH-5FH	Reserved	
0000:0180	60H-66H	User program interrupts	
0000:019C	67H	Expanded memory manager routines	
0000:01A0	68H-6BH	Unused	
0000:01B0	6CH	System resume vector	
0000:01B4	6DH-6FH	Unused	
0000:01C0	70H	Real-time clock	IRQ8
0000:01C4	71H	LAN adapter (IRQ2 replacement)	IRQ9
0000:01C8	72H	Reserved	IRQ10
0000:01CC	73H	Reserved	IRQ11
0000:01D0	74H	Mouse	IRQ12
0000:01D4	75H	80287 NMI error	IRQ13
0000:01D8	76H	Hard disk controller	IRQ14
0000:01DC	77H	Reserved	IRQ15
0000:01E0	78H-7FH	Unused	
0000:0200	80H-85H	BASIC	
0000:0218	86H	NetBIOS	
0000:021C	87H-F0H	BASIC	
0000:03C4	F1H-FFH	Reserved for program interrupts	

The interrupt vectors are stored in the RAM of your PC so that the values in the table can be changed. For example, a program or software driver may want to alter or update a BIOS routine to take advantage of a special feature of new hardware you install in your

PC. The BIOS code itself loads default values for many of these interrupt vectors into the appropriate RAM locations with the vectors pointing at the routines stored in your PC's ROM.

Sometimes, programs add extra routines to a given BIOS function, a process called *chaining interrupts*. To chain an interrupt, a program looks at the interrupt vector it wants to chain to and remembers its value. It then substitutes the starting location of the program code that it wants to add to the old routine. It then modifies its own code to make the execution of its routines jump to the old interrupt when the processing of the new code finishes. In this way, the new routine added in the interrupt chain executes first and then starts the original interrupt handler.

Parameter Passing

Because fewer interrupts are available than things one would want to do with the BIOS, different functions are available for many of the interrupts. These separate functions are identified through a technique called *parameter passing*. A program needing service from the BIOS—the calling program—passes a number identifying the command to be carried out to the BIOS as a *parameter*, a value held in one or more of the registers at the time the software interrupt is issued.

The calling program decides what function it wants the BIOS to carry out, loads the parameter value into the proper register, and issues the interrupt. The BIOS code examines the register to determine what function the programs wants.

This same technique may be used to pass information between the calling program and the BIOS. The data to be passed along is simply loaded into one register and the parameter identifying the command into another register. To pass new data back to the calling program, the BIOS loads the data into a register, which the calling program can then read.

Using registers to move data into a BIOS routine has its shortcomings. The functions and parameters are limited to those that are common among PCs. There's little room for programs to add their own interrupts. Moreover, the scant number of registers in Intel microprocessors limits the number of parameters that can be passed to and from a function. Most routines use a single byte of data.

To move larger blocks of data, some BIOS routines and most programs use memory. A calling program stores the values it wants to pass to a subroutine in a block of RAM addresses. It then passes to the subroutine the location of the data, and the subroutine digs into the data, changing what it requires, and leaves the block for later access by the program. Although programs and subroutines identify the block of memory by its address, programming languages let you use names for the data. The program chooses the block of addresses to associate with the name and looks to those addresses whenever the programmer uses that name. Similarly, program subroutines may be named, and the program uses the names to find the block of memory holding to microprocessor instructions making up the subroutine.

Entry Points

The various code routines in each BIOS start and end at addresses assigned to the BIOS function in the PC memory map. The address at which each routine starts is called that routine's entry point. The entry point of a BIOS function is completely different from the interrupt that calls that function. When the BIOS in your PC sets itself up—either before or during the actual boot-up—it loads the addresses of the entry points into a table in memory that becomes the interrupt vectors. In theory, an entry point can be at any location for any BIOS function; it needs only to be loaded into the slot in the BIOS interrupt vector table to be properly recognized. Unfortunately, some program writers decided to call BIOS routines by their entry points instead of using interrupts because the direct approach is faster. Consequently, a few applications require that some entry points be at specific physical BIOS addresses. If the entry point of a BIOS differs from that which the program expects, the result is likely to be a system crash.

IBM has maintained the same entry points with all of its BIOSs, and many compatible BIOSs use exactly the same addresses. A few do not, however. In general, the BIOSs with varying entry points have been written as programming modules that can be combined in various ways to suit the needs of a PC designer. What these modular BIOSs add in flexibility, they lose in compatibility.

Unlike programs that write directly to system hardware, however, programs that require specific BIOS entry points are rare. With the popularity of compatible computers and modular BIOSs, they are sure to become rarer. Modern software, nevertheless, is getting away from a dependency on complete compatibility down to the level of specific entry points. In fact, many programs avoid the BIOS entirely.

The chief beneficiaries of the BIOS are individual programmers who need to create code quickly. In many cases, using BIOS routines can simplify the writing of a program. Certain system operations always are available and can be accessed easily through software. They are reasonably well-documented and well-understood, removing many of the programmer's concerns.

Linking to Hardware

Controlling the hardware of your PC requires that your system be able to pass commands and data to that hardware. For example, if you have a modem, you need to send the modem commands to dial numbers and change speeds. Once you're communicating, you have to send bytes, even megabytes, of data to the modem and receive more bytes in return.

The BIOS routines may use memory or I/O ports to pass the commands and data to hardware devices. When a device uses a block of memory to exchange information, it is termed *memory mapped*. When it uses I/O ports, it is termed *I/O mapped.*

Memory mapping works exactly as described in the section "Parameter Passing" earlier in this chapter. The BIOS routine and hardware device share a common range of memory addresses they use for passing bytes back and forth. Programs use BIOS routines instead of physical addresses to reach memory-mapped devices to give the hardware designer the freedom of moving the memory window used by a given device. The designer needs only change the interrupt handler to match the address he chooses.

I/O mapping uses input/output ports to exchange data. An input/output port of a microprocessor is a special range of addresses that are isolated from main memory and have special access instructions.

In the Intel scheme of things, microprocessors have a range of 65,536 input/output ports (compared to more than four billion discrete memory addresses). However, due to an aberration in the design of the first expansion boards for PCs, only 1,024 are commonly assigned to devices that plug into standard PC expansion slots. To cut the costs of the first expansion boards, engineers designed boards to decode only 10 of the 16 address lines.

Although newer buses can take advantage of the full range of input/output ports, expansion boards can quickly consume the available ports or two boards may attempt to use the same port. Such conflicts between boards is the most common reason why expansion boards fail to operate properly. Sometimes, installing an expansion board creates a port conflict that prevents the rest of the system from working at all. Table 5.2 lists some of the common conflicts that arise in I/O port assignments.

TABLE 5.2   Common I/O Port Assignments and Potential Conflicts

Device	Range Used	Conflict
Color video boards	3D0–3DF	3C0
COM1	3F8–3FF	3E0
COM2	2F8–2FF	2E0
COM3	3E8–3EF	3E0
COM4	2E8–2EF	2E0
Expansion unit	210–217	200

continues

TABLE 5.2   Continued

Device	Range Used	Conflict
Floppy controller	3F0–3F7	3E0
Game controller	200–20F	200
LPT1	3BC–3BF	3A0
LPT2	378–37F	360
LPT3	278–27F	260
MDA, monochrome video	3B0–3BF	3A0
Microsoft bus mouse, primary	23C–23F	
Microsoft bus mouse, alt.	238–23B	
Primary bi-sync card	3A0–3A9	3A0
Secondary bi-sync card	380–38C	380
SoundBlaster speaker default	220–223	220
SoundBlaster control	388–389	
VGA	3C0–3CF	3C0

If you're running Windows on your PC, you can view the actual I/O port assignments used by your PC. To view these assignments, consult Device Manager by selecting the System icon in Control Panel. Select your Computer on the device menu, and click on the Properties button. From the View Resources menu that pops on your screen, select the Input/Output (I/O) radio button. You'll see a screen akin Figure 5.1 listing all the input/output ports in use and the hardware using them.

Through Plug and Play and the manual options of the Add Hardware process, Windows generally will make the proper assignments of I/O ports. If you want to reserve one or more I/O ports so that devices that you install later cannot steal them, click on the Reserve Resources tab and enter the ports you want to reserve.

New expansion buses such as PCI provide access to the full range of I/O ports, reducing the chance of conflicts. Plug-and-play expansion boards are supposed to automatically resolve port conflicts entirely. Eventually, worries about I/O conflicts should disappear. For most PCs, however, eventually has not yet arrived.

FIGURE 5.1

Windows' Device Manager showing I/O port usage.

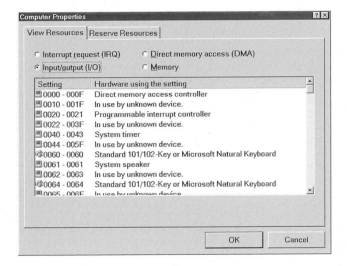

Performance Penalties

Although the BIOS held many advantages for programmers, it also brought an array of penalties. Most of these involve performance. BIOS routines add extra steps to every function. Worse, the code used by most BIOS routines fails to take advantage of the power of modern microprocessors.

The steps added by the routines can slow many computer functions. BIOS performance problems are most evident in the video display. All the original PC BIOS routines, for example, were designed for putting information on the video display one character at a time using dozens of microprocessor instructions to place each one. Text can be blasted onto the screen much faster by directly manipulating the hardware.

Using BIOS routines, software first has to load particular registers with the character to display its attribute (color or underlining or the like), perhaps even its location on the screen. Then, the program issues a software interrupt to give the BIOS control to do its job. The BIOS then runs through a dozen or more assembly language instructions to move the character onto the screen.

Taking direct control—avoiding the BIOS—means writing directly to the display memory on the video card. A program can write directly to the screen simply by loading the appropriate address and moving the needed byte value to that address in one assembly language step. The dozens of steps saved in writing each character add up to real performance gains, the difference between watching changes slowly scroll down the screen and instant updates.

Bypassing the BIOS with programs that directly address the system hardware is not difficult, even if at heart such a concept is forbidden by the original IBM dream. In fact, so many software writers have taken their liberties with direct hardware control that many of the hardware features of personal computers are more standardized than the BIOS. Writing directly to video memory and avoiding the BIOS eventually became the preferred way to handle video—at least until the advent of today's complex video systems.

BIOS-mediated access also imposes performance penalties because most PC BIOSs use only 8-bit or 16-bit code in this age of 32-bit and 64-bit PCs. Modern operating systems sidestep these performance shortcomings by using software routines instead of firmware for accessing hardware. These software routines are the familiar drivers that you have to install and worry about. Software drivers replace the BIOS routines for their associated functions. Certainly, this extra layer of software imposes performance penalties despite the quicker code, but the power and speed of today's microprocessors mask this handicap.

Storage Functions

Because the BIOS comes in the physical form of ROM chips, its storage functions should not be surprising. For example, the BIOS stores its own name and the date it was written inside its own code. But the BIOS also incorporates storage functions that go beyond the bytes encapsulated in its ROM silicon. Although physically separate from the BIOS chips themselves, the setup memory of your PC is controlled by BIOS functions and is often consider with, even as part of, the BIOS. This memory records vital details about your PC hardware so that you don't have to set up each expansion board and disk drive every time you switch on your computer. In addition, the BIOS tells your PC to reserve several small block of memory for dynamic data that your PC and its operating system use for tracking several system functions.

Legacy Data

As with any computer program, the BIOS code uses data for its operations and produces data as its result. The BIOS stores some of this data to be used as a reference by your programs. The BIOS acquires some of this information as it sets up the system. By storing it all in one place, it eliminates the need for every program to waste its time looking up common features. Other data is encoded as part of the BIOS itself so that programs can determine what kind of computer—and what kind of BIOS—with which they have to work.

Much of the information the BIOS stores is a carryover from the early days of PCs and is useful to programs that rely on the BIOS but irrelevant to those that do not. Some of it, however, is critical to the operation of your system. All of this storage is grouped below, classed here as *legacy data* because of its carryover status.

BIOS Data Area

During the initialization process, the BIOS searches through the system for specific features. It checks the number and kinds of ports installed, the type of display adapter (monochrome or color), and other options. Included among the data that it stores are equipment flags, the base addresses of input/output adapters, keyboard characters, and operating modes. The BIOS then stores this information in specific memory locations so that your programs can check to see which features are available or being used. For example, the BIOS looks for serial ports at specific addresses (see Chapter 19, "Peripheral Ports"). As it finds them, the BIOS records the base address that each serial port uses.

All of this self-descriptive information about your system is stored in a special part of RAM called the BIOS data area. Located just above the interrupt vectors, the BIOS data area comprises 256 bytes of memory, starting at absolute memory location 000400(Hex) and running to 0004FF(Hex).

Date

Nearly every BIOS identifies itself with a copyright message and (usually) a version number so that you can determine who made it. (More specifically, the copyright message protects the writers of the BIOS from other people copying their work.) This identification information may appear anywhere within the BIOS code range.

In addition, the revision date of your BIOS helps you identify how recently its code was updated. As PCs have expanded their abilities, BIOSs have been revised to enable new operations. Sometimes, older BIOSs will not work with new peripherals. For example, many BIOSs from before 1998 don't let you use all the space on hard disks larger than eight gigabytes. Older BIOSs may impose even more severe limits.

You can determine the date of your BIOS in several ways. The most convenient are catching the boot-up screen of your PC, which usually displays the date and revision number of the BIOS, and using a diagnostic utility. Microsoft Diagnostics, supplied with most versions of Windows, will show you the detail of your PC's BIOS—its date and manufacturer. This program is located in the Command subfolder of your Windows folder as MSD.EXE. You can either click on its icon or run it from the MS DOS prompt by typing MSD and then pressing Enter. Click on the Computer button, and it will list some of the BIOS details of your PC, as shown in Figure 5.2.

Note that Microsoft has not updated the diagnostic program for years, so the most recent microprocessor it will recognize is a 486DX! The System Information program found under System Tools in Accessories from the Programs choice at the Start button is Microsoft's preferred tool; it shows your system in exquisite, even painful, detail. But it offers no direct display of your system's BIOS date.

Figure 5.2

Microsoft Diagnostics showing system details.

System Identification Bytes

The original PC BIOS included a byte of data to identify what kind of computer in which the BIOS was installed. Programs that might react differently depending on the processor or other aspect of the computer could use this byte to identify the hardware and adjust themselves accordingly. At least, that was the idea of the IBM engineers who came up with the idea in 1981.

The scheme had its problems, however. Allowing for a single byte soon seemed short-sighted, so this memory area was expanded to two bytes starting with the IBM XT Model 286, introduced in 1985. The overall storage area was termed the *system identification bytes*, and in IBM nomenclature, it was divided into the *model byte* and the *submodel byte*. A third byte was reserved to indicate any major revision to the system.

IBM created an elaborate table of designations for the various models of PC it offered. Unfortunately, the company made no provision to coordinate the use of this storage area for other manufacturers. Consequently, the rest of the industry used designations marking their IBM equivalent. Because all systems since 1984 follow the architecture of the IBM AT system, nearly all PCs now define themselves as using the AT code. In other words, the system identification bytes store essentially meaningless data.

The model byte is located at absolute memory address 0FFFFE(Hex) and is FC(Hex) in nearly all current PCs. The submodel byte follows it with a value of 01(Hex). The revision byte follows and is usually zero.

Although the these bytes are meaningless, they are retained in current PCs for compatibility—just in case a program check to see what kind of computer it is running on. That is itself a meaningless task because modern software won't run on anything but an AT-compatible PC.

BIOS Identification

Today's BIOSs are so robust and stable that most people take them for granted. Knowing which BIOS is installed in your PC is about as significant as knowing the number of molecules in a given glass of water. When you need to upgrade your BIOS—for example, because you encounter compatibility difficulties with a new feature or peripheral you add to your PC—you may need to know the BIOS maker and version installed inside your PC.

You can usually find this information two places: on a label affixed to the BIOS memory chips and encoded electronically in the BIOS code itself. This identification is for more than merely your information. It serves as a notification of the BIOS maker's copyright in the BIOS code.

To check the BIOS label, open your PC and search for ROM chips with white or metallic stick-on labels. Most modern PCs have a matched pair of two chips bearing legends that typically vary by a single character. The ROM chips usually take the form of a 40-pin DIP.

The electronic identification of the BIOS takes the form of ASCII characters embedded in the BIOS code. System probing and reporting software such as Microsoft Diagnostics will usually display the BIOS data. Or you can search through the bytes of BIOS code looking for the key word "copyright" or some variation.

You can often ascertain quite a bit of detail about a given BIOS from its manufacturer's identification. The coding used by manufacturers is usually consistent, but it varies between BIOS makers.

AMI BIOS

BIOSs written by AMI take the form of an alphanumeric string divided into four blocks, some of which are further subdivided. These strings take the form of a reference number with the form *ABBB-NNNN-MMDDYY-KX*.

The first character (*A* in the example) indicates whether setup or diagnostics are included in the BIOS. A leading "D" indicates that the BIOS includes diagnostics. An "S" indicates a built-in setup program; an "E" indicates an extended setup program is built in. The next three digits of the first block (*BBB* in the example) indicate the motherboard manufacturer and model for which the BIOS is intended. Table 5.3 summarizes some of the more common codes for these digits.

TABLE 5.3   AMI BIOS Application Codes

Character Code	Intended Application
286	Generic 286 motherboards, including VLSI and G2
AMI	AMI motherboards
C&T	Chips & Technologies 386 chipset

continues

TABLE 5.3   Continued

Character Code	Intended Application
G23	G2 386 motherboards
INT	Intel motherboards
NET	Chips & Technologies NEAT chipset
PAQ	COMPAQ-compatible 386 motherboards
SUN	SUNTAC 286 motherboards

The next block of four digits (*NNNN* in the example) is the PC or motherboard maker's identification of the BIOS. The third block encodes the last revision data of the BIOS, devoting two digits each to the month, day, and year of the revision. And the final block (*KX* in the example) indicates the AMI version number of the BIOS.

Award BIOS

Award Software uses a different scheme for identifying its BIOSs. The first five digits of the BIOS identification usually indicate the chipset maker and the chipset part number for which the BIOS was designed. Table 5.4 summarizes some of the common Award BIOS model numbers.

TABLE 5.4   Award BIOS Identification Chart

Award BIOS Model	Chipset Maker	Chipset Part Number
2A5KB*xxx*	Ali	1449/61/51
2A4KC*xxx*	Ali	1439/45/31
2ARKD*xxx*	Ali	1489
2A5KE000	Ali	1511
2A4H2*xxx*	Contaq	82C596-9
2A499*xxx*	Intel	Aries
2A597*xxx*	Intel	Mercury
2A59A*xxx*	Intel	Neptune ISA
2B59A*xxx*	Intel	Neptune EISA
2B69D*xxx*	Intel	Orion
2A498*xxx*	Intel	Saturn II
2A59C*xxx*	Intel	Triton
2A59F*xxx*	Intel	Triton II

Award BIOS Model	Chipset Maker	Chipset Part Number
2A5UL*xxx*	Opti	82C822/596/597
22A5UM*xxx*	Opti	82C822/546/547
2A5UL*xxx*	Opti	82C822/571/572
2A5UN*xxx*	Opti	Viper 82C556/557/558
2C4I8*xxx*	SiS	471B/E
2A5IA*xxx*	SiS	501/02/03
2A5Id*xxx*	SiS	5511/12/13
2A4IB*xxx*	SiS	496/497
2A4X5*xxx*	UMC	8881/8886
2A5X7*xxx*	UMC	82C890
2A4L6*xxx*	VIA	496/406/505
2C4L2*xxx*	VIA	82C486A

Disk Parameter Tables

One of the more important entries in the BIOS data area is the *disk parameter table*. Most PCs store the parameters used by user-defined hard disks, typically reflected as hard disk type 47 in the setup program, in the BIOS data area. The most common memory location for this information is absolute address 0000:0300. Some BIOSs give you the option of locating the disk parameter table in an alternate location, typically DOS memory. In any case, interrupt vector 41(Hex) points to the location of the disk parameter table for the first hard disk in a PC. Interrupt vector 46(Hex) points to the location of the parameters of the second hard disk.

In general, the best location for your disk parameter table is absolute address 0000:0300. However, some peripherals such as older sound cards and network adapters use this address for their own purposes. Conflicts between the peripheral and your hard disk may render either or both inoperable. Relocating the disk parameter table through a BIOS setting solves the problem.

You may encounter two kinds of disk parameter tables. A standard *Fixed Disk Parameter Table*, or FDPT, contains a single description of the vital parameters of the associated hard disk, listing the number of cylinders, heads, and sectors used by the disk. An *Enhanced Fixed Disk Parameter Table*, or EDPT, has two entries, the logical cylinder-head-sector values and the physical cylinder-head-sector values. The logical values reflect the way your PC sees and accesses the disk. The physical values reflect the actual number of cylinders, heads, and sectors used by the disk.

The standard FDPT is sufficient only for smaller disks, those with both fewer than 1,024 cylinders and a capacity less than 504MB. Due to the design of the standard FDPT, only 10 bits are allowed for storing the number of cylinders, so numbers larger than 1,024 cannot be encoded. The EDPT defaults to 16 heads for all disks, allowing 4 more bits for storing the number of cylinders.

Your PC deals with any disk by the logical values in the EDPT. Programmers check the value stored here using software interrupt 13(Hex).

DOS Tables

DOS stores many of the parameters it uses for managing your PC and its programs in a series of tables. To achieve the utmost in compatibility, DOS locates these tables at the lowest available reaches of conventional memory. Among the data stored here are file handle identifications (FILES), the last referenced disk data (BUFFERS), file control information (FCBS), drive tables (LASTDRIVE), and system operating information (STACK).

Most memory managers allow you to relocate this data into XMS memory to free up more space in the conventional area. Although this technique is commonplace and well-tested, you will sometimes encounter compatibility problems such as a crash of your system. For example, early incarnations of most network operating systems expect to find this data in conventional memory (along with COMMAND.COM itself). The only way to avoid this problem is to avoid the network, avoid DOS, or refrain from relocating this data with your memory manager—the last usually being the most viable option. You'll want to avoid relocating any of these DOS tables if your system exhibits compatibility problems or its network redirector behaves oddly.

System Configuration

To properly test a computer, the BIOS needs to know exactly what it is testing—what peripherals are installed, how much memory it must look through, and whether you have installed a coprocessor. To boot a computer, the BIOS needs to know exactly what kind of disk is connected to it. For you to see what is going on when your system boots up, the BIOS needs to know what kind of display system you have.

In some cases, the BIOS code itself can be written to search out and find the vital information it needs to get your system going. Such a search is not always accurate. Nor is it easy to write the proper search method into a few kilobytes of BIOS code. Even if the proper program could be written and packed into ROM, you probably do not want to sit around and wait—and wait—while the BIOS probes into every nook and cranny to see if something is there.

Nearly every PC requires that you or some other human being tell it some of this information. For example, most PCs demand you tell them what type of disk drives you have installed. You must use the PC's setup or BIOS configuration process to load this data into your PC.

When this setup process was first conceived, PC makers relied on software programs on special *Reference Diskettes* to give you a way to interact with your PC and enter the needed data. So many people lost their diskettes that PC makers were forced to find a better way, and they did. They incorporated the setup program in the BIOS and allowed you to run it by pressing a couple of keys while your system boots up.

The particular keys to press and the time at which to press them varies with each BIOS maker. Table 5.5 lists some of the more common combinations for entering the setup programs of various BIOSs.

To let the BIOS (and the rest of the PC) know what options are installed in a given system, all PCs record vital setup information that can be referenced quickly. The storage system for this data—that is, system setup memory—has one requirement: It must be non-volatile. Other than that, the storage format and method are flexible because the BIOS isolates them from the rest of your software. The BIOS looks up this system data and transfers it to the BIOS data area for reference by your programs.

TABLE 5.5   Common BIOS Setup Entry Points

BIOS Maker	Entry Keys	When
AMI	Del	During POST
Award	Ctrl+Alt+Esc	Anytime
DTK	Esc	During POST
IBM PS/2	Ctrl+Alt+Ins	After Ctrl+Alt+Del
Phoenix	Ctrl+Alt+Esc or Ctrl+Alt+S	Anytime

This flexibility has given designers freedom to use a number of storage technologies for this setup information. Among the most popular have been physical memory (switches), non-volatile electronic memory, and magnetic (disk) memory. Since the AT was introduced a decade and a half ago, however, the basic form of this setup memory used by most PCs has been the same—a few bytes of CMOS memory kept fresh—continuously operating—by battery power.

CMOS

When the world and PCs were young, all the differences between PCs could be coded by one or two banks of DIP switches. But as the options began to pile up, the switch proved to be more a problem than a panacea. A reasonable number of switches couldn't allow for the number of options possible in a modern PC. Another problem with switches is that they are prone to mechanical problems—both of their own making and otherwise. Switch contacts naturally go bad, and they can be helped along the path of their own destruction by people who attempt to adjust them with pencils. (The graphite that scrapes off the point is conductive and can short out the switches.) People often set switches wrong and wonder what is awry.

Background

IBM developed a better scheme for the AT. Vital system parameters would be stored in a special, small block of battery-backed CMOS memory, a total of 64 bytes, in the form of a special chip, a Motorola MC146818, which also held a real-time clock. The lower 14 of those bytes are used by the real-time clock to hold the current time and an alarm time, leaving 50 bytes for storage of setup information. Locations were assigned for storing information about floppy and hard disks, the presence of a coprocessor, the amount of installed memory, and the type of display system (monochrome or color). Because CMOS memory is volatile, every system has a battery of some kind to keep this memory fresh and the real-time clock running (see Chapter 24, "Power").

Most PCs follow the basic IBM scheme, minimally augmenting it to reflect the increasing capabilities of their systems. Although the MC146818 chip rarely appears in PCs anymore, its functions are carried over into new support chips. For example, clock modules from Dallas Semiconductor incorporate all the functions of the Motorola chip, a built-in lithium battery, and more. The only major change in CMOS storage that's been made is the almost universal adoption (at the aegis of Microsoft) of the plug-and-play system.

Basic Memory Assignments

The basic CMOS data remains the same no matter the manufacturer of the PC, and the various bytes of data are stored in the same rigidly structured format. Table 5.6 summarizes the basic storage assignments that are common across nearly all modern PCs.

TABLE 5.6　　CMOS Memory Byte Assignments

Byte	Assignment	Purpose
00	Seconds	Real-time clock
01	Second alarm	Real-time clock
02	Minutes	Real-time clock
03	Minute alarm	Real-time clock
04	Hours	Real-time clock
05	Hours alarm	Real-time clock
06	Day of the week	Real-time clock
07	Date of the month	Real-time clock

Byte	Assignment	Purpose
08	Month	Real-time clock
09	Year	Real-time clock
0A	Status register A	Real-time clock
0B	Status register B	Real-time clock
0C	Status register C	Real-time clock
0D	Status register D	Real-time clock
0F	Shutdown status	
10	Diskette drive type	
11	Reserved	
12	Hard disk type	
13	Reserved	
14	Equipment type	
15	Low base memory	
16	High base memory	
17	Low expansion memory	
18	High expansion memory	
19	Reserved	
1A	Reserved	
1B	Reserved	
1C	Reserved	
1D	Reserved	
1E	Reserved	
20	Reserved	
21	Reserved	
22	Reserved	
23	Reserved	
24	Reserved	
25	Reserved	

continues

TABLE 5.6   Continued

Byte	Assignment	Purpose
26	Reserved	
27	Reserved	
28	Reserved	
29	Reserved	
2A	Reserved	
2B	Reserved	
2C	Reserved	
2D	CMOS checksum	
2E	CMOS checksum	
30	Low expansion memory	
31	High expansion memory	
32	Date century	
33	Information flags	
34	Reserved	
35	Reserved	
36	Reserved	
37	Reserved	
38	Reserved	
39	Reserved	
3A	Reserved	
3B	Reserved	
3C	Reserved	
3D	Reserved	
3E	Reserved	
3F	Reserved	

Although the CMOS that holds this data is conventional memory, it is not in the direct reach of your PC's microprocessor. Unlike normal system memory, this CMOS setup memory was I/O mapped. That is, its contents were accessed through two input/output ports. Port 070(Hex) indicates the memory byte you want to access, and port 071(Hex) provides the pathway to the indicated byte. Reading or writing a byte of CMOS setup memory requires two steps. First, you write to port 070(hex) with the byte location in the CMOS range you want to read or write. Reading port 071(hex) tells you the value stored at the location you have chosen. Writing to port 071(Hex) changes the byte value at the appointed location.

The contents of most of the storage locations in this CMOS setup memory are monitored by storing a checksum in bytes 02E and 02F(Hex). If the checksum does not agree with the modular total of the monitored bytes, your system reports a CMOS memory error. The diagnostic status byte—00E(Hex)—indicates the gross nature of the error and additionally reports whether battery power has failed. If all systems are go, this byte has a zero value; any bit set indicates a specific error (with two bits reserved).

Newer PCs have elaborated on this CMOS storage scheme, adding more bytes to hold the status of other system features. In function and operation, however, all follow the pattern set by the AT.

Resetting CMOS

The chief reason you're advised not to tinker with the advanced settings of your PC's BIOS is that the control they afford allows you to set up your PC so that it does not work. For example, if you err by setting too few wait states for the memory you have installed in your PC, you may encounter a memory error as soon as your PC switches on and checks its BIOS settings. You won't have an opportunity to jump back into setup to fix the problem. You'll be stuck with a dead computer and have no way of bringing it back to life.

Well, not quite. Most PC BIOSs have factory defaults that are set conservatively enough that the machine will operate with whatever you've installed. The only trick is to restore the factory defaults.

Switch or Jumper Reset

Many PCs have jumpers or a DIP switch that force the reset. Check the documentation of your PC or motherboard to see if this option is available to you. Typically, you'll find this information using the index of your instruction manual and looking under "factory defaults" or "BIOS defaults."

The exact procedure usually takes one of two forms, depending on the design of your PC. The easiest requires only that you move a jumper or slide a DIP switch and then turn your PC back on. The position of the switch or jumper doesn't matter. All that counts is that you move it. The most complicated procedure isn't much more difficult. You move the jumper or slide the switch, wait a few minutes, and then move it back. The delay allows the tiny amount of power that's lock in the CMOS circuitry to drain away.

Power Deprivation

The alternate procedure for resetting your CMOS works for nearly every PC and is based on the same power depravation principle. You only need to deprive your PC's CMOS of its battery power so that the contents of its memory evaporate. Exactly how to deprive your CMOS of its lifeblood electricity depends on the design of your system.

If your PC's motherboard uses an external battery, simply unplug it from the motherboard. If your PC uses a replaceable disc-style battery in a matching battery holder, pop out the battery. In either case, allow 10 minutes for the residual power in the CMOS to drain away before reconnecting or reinstalling the battery.

Some motherboards use permanently installed rechargeable nickel-cadmium batteries instead of replaceable cells. Usually, these PCs have some provision for electrically disconnecting the battery power from the CMOS (a jumper or switch as noted in the previous section). A few PC motherboards make no provision for disconnecting their ni-cads. If you have such a PC and have put your BIOS in a non-functional configuration, as a last resort you can sometimes force a reset to the factory defaults by discharging the battery. The battery will recharge the next time you operate your PC.

Never short out a nickel-cadmium battery to discharge it. The low resistance of ni-cad cells produces high currents (even with small batteries), sufficient to melt circuit board traces and even start your PC on fire. Instead of shorting out the battery, discharge it through a resistor. A half-watt, 39 ohm resistor will safely discharge a ni-cad cell in about half an hour without danger to you or your PC. Alternately, you can use a six-volt lamp, such as one designed for battery-powered lanterns, as a battery load. The lamp will show you the progress of the discharge, glowing brightly at first and dimming as the battery's charge gets drained away. Connect either the resistor or the lamp directly between the terminals of the battery using clip leads.

Advanced Setup

After you press the right combination of keys to bring up your PC's setup menu, you are usually allowed to jump to advanced setup. This extension of setup allows you to alter vital system operating parameters that are controlled by the motherboard chipset. The advanced setup procedure alters additional, often proprietary, storage in CMOS and, sometimes, in other parts of your PC. Typically, advanced setup is a second menu (or series of menus) accessed through the initial setup menu.

Altering the options can have a dramatic effect on the performance of your PC. Importune tinkering often can lead to a machine that will not work. Performance becomes zero. On the other hand, you can sometimes optimize your system to take best advantage of the options you've installed, for example, to coax the best possible performance from the memory system or highest transfer rate from your expansion bus.

The range of features controlled by advanced setup varies with both the BIOS and the chipset inside your PC. Most chipsets give you a wide range of options to wade through. Some of the options available with different chipsets and BIOSs include the following:

Parity Check

Some systems permit you to switch off memory parity checking, disabling error detection. Taking this option prevents your system from halting when memory parity errors are detected. You are well-advised to leave parity checking enabled except when attempting to find elusive memory problems. Because this option is meaningful only for PCs that have parity-checked memory, it offers you no savings as would a system that used 8-bit SIMMs instead of parity-checked 9-bit SIMMs. Your system is likely to halt when a parity-error occurs in program code, but the crash is less controlled than an error-warning message. Files may be destroyed. If the error occurs within data, you may never know when your information is inaccurate.

Memory Testing

Testing the prodigious amounts of RAM in a modern PC can take a long time, indeed, adding a minute or more to the cold boot sequence. To minimize the wear and tear on your patience, many BIOSs allow you to defeat the entire memory test sequence or specific portions of it. With the claims of extreme reliability for today's memory systems, you may want to consider switching off your PC's memory test.

Commonly, you'll find an option termed *Above 1MB Memory Check* that allows you to switch off memory testing beyond the base megabyte in your PC. Selecting this option will cut your boot-up time from a few minutes to a few dozen seconds. Checking the base megabyte of memory in your PC usually is not an option because your PC needs error-free real-mode memory for running the setup program.

Some systems give you the option of adding an audible click or beep each time they test a block of megabyte or so of memory. The sound is simply reassurance that your PC is successfully coursing through its lengthy memory test. Some people find this sound obnoxious rather than reassuring, and the *Memory Test Click Sound* setup option allows them to silence their systems.

Numeric Processor Testing

The BIOSs of some older PCs offered the option of defeating the *Numeric Processor Test*. Although you might be tempted to forgo this test to accelerate the boot process, you may be surprised at its effect. Many BIOSs assume that if you tell them not to test the numeric processor, you don't have one. They set a flag that tells your applications you don't have a coprocessor installed so your software won't use the coprocessor even if one is installed, even as part of your microprocessor.

PCs based on the 386 and 486 microprocessors may also give you the option of selecting a Weitek coprocessor. You must select this option to enable your software to take advantage of the Weitek chip.

Cache Operation

Some systems require that you set the size of the secondary (external) memory cache you have installed. You'll want to change this setting only if you install additional SRAM chips to increase the size of your PC's memory cache.

Some BIOSs allow you to switch on or off the cache. Some allow the individual control of the internal (that is, primary) cache inside your microprocessor and the external (secondary) cache. The only time you should switch off your system's caches is when you want to pin down software problems or diagnose hardware errors.

Wait States

This setting controls the number of wait states injected during memory accesses. Typically, you have a choice of 0, 1, 2, and possibly 3 wait states. Some systems allow the separate setting of read and write wait states. Choosing fewer wait states makes your PC faster, but choosing too few to accommodate the speed of your system's memory leads to memory errors..Set this value too low, and your PC may not boot at all. If you are a diehard tinkerer and want to explore the potentials of this setting, adjust it downward one step at a time. Then, run your PC for a while to check its reliability. Toying with this setting may also familiarize you with the location of the CMOS reset jumper.

Bus Clock

Many ISA systems allow you to adjust the clock speed of their expansion buses so you can eke the most performance from your old expansion boards. Some systems give you a choice of clock speeds in megahertz; others express the speed in terms of the microprocessor clock. (For example, CLOCKIN/4 implies one quarter the microprocessor clock speed, 8.25MHz with a 33MHz system.) Higher speeds (lower divisors) can deliver more performance, but rates above about 12MHz may sacrifice reliability. In VL Bus and PCI systems, the bus clock setting has less effect on overall performance because the devices that need the most bus bandwidth (that is, a faster bus speed) will be connected to the higher speed local bus. The clock speed of the local bus is not affected by the bus clock setting.

ROM Shadowing

Manufacturers may provide any of a number of options to enable or disable the shadowing of ROM code in fast RAM memory. Some merely allow the simple enable/disable choice. Others allow you to control ROM elements separately. One variety of BIOS lets you individually enable and disable system ROM and expansion ROM. System ROM means the BIOS code on your motherboard; expansion ROM is the code on expansion boards, which typically includes your video card and hard disk host adapter. Another variety of BIOS gives the choice of system, video, and adapter. A fourth BIOS type lets you choose whether to shadow ROM memory by address range, letting you select enabling or disabling by 16KB, 32KB, or 64KB blocks.

In general, you should shadow only those memory ranges actually in use by ROM. Shadowing unused ranges wastes memory. Shadowing memory ranges used for buffers by network adapters or ancient expanded memory (EMS) boards may actually degrade system performance or cause compatibility problems.

Remember, shadowing only helps the performance of applications that use BIOS code in ROM, which for the most part means only DOS. If you primarily run any version of Windows or OS/2, which make little use of the BIOS, shadowing yields no performance improvement and may cause compatibility problems. You will probably want to switch off shadowing when using any modern operating system.

Experimenting with shadowing can also lead to a system that does not boot. It is best to enable one block of shadowing at a time and then run your system to observe the result.

Concurrent Refresh

Most early PCs must devote 10 percent or more of their active time to refreshing memory. Newer systems are able to refresh memory concurrently—that is, while they are performing normal tasks. Concurrent refreshing ekes more performance from your system, so it is the preferred operating mode. Some BIOS makers call this kind of memory refresh *hidden refresh*. Normally, your PC will deliver better performance with concurrent refresh. Some older RAM designs (used mostly in 386 and older PCs) cannot handle concurrent refreshing and may cause memory errors when this feature is enabled.

Page Interleave

Some systems with two or four identical banks of RAM chips or memory modules can operate in an interleaved fashion, that is, alternating banks in back-to-back memory requests. Statistically, interleaving can cut wait states by nearly half. Although the effect is less pronounced in modern cached systems, enabling page interleave (when supported with sufficient memory) can improve performance.

Page Mode

Page-mode memory chips and modules also can trim wait states. Page-mode SIMMs can make repeated accesses to one memory page without wait states. If you equip your system with page-mode memory and enable this option, you should get better performance.

Virus Protection

With all the concern in the industry about computer viruses, some BIOS makers have added their own form of protection, a warning message that appears when software attempts to write to the boot sector of your hard disk. When the protection is switched on, you're given the option of canceling the write operation to prevent infection. Because some operating systems such as the OS/2 Boot Manager rewrite boot sector data when you switch between boot modes, you can't simply obstruct all boot sector write operations.

The protection afforded by this system is limited in two ways. It potentially stops only boot sector viruses. It does not stop those that afflict the active operating system files. And it protects only hard disks controlled through the PC BIOS. SCSI disks that rely on separate BIOS code in your SCSI host adapter are not protected.

Typematic Rate

Many BIOSs allow you to alter the way the keyboard reacts to your keystrokes, repeating them if you hold a key down. This feature, called *typematic*, is fully discussed in Chapter 14, "Input Devices."

Many BIOSs have an overall toggle, typically termed *typematic programming*, that enables or disables the settings for the typematic feature. You must enable typematic programming to alter other typematic settings. In addition, your keyboard must allow its typematic feature to be programmed. You can control the typematic feature through Windows 95 or 98 no matter what kind of keyboard you have or the BIOS typematic settings.

If a BIOS and keyboard support typematic programming, you can generally alter two aspects of this feature. *Typematic rate delay* specifies how long you must hold down a key before the typematic feature kicks in and characters start repeating. This setting is generally specified in milliseconds. *Typematic rate* controls how quickly the characters repeat after the initial delay. This value is usually specified as a number of character per second that will appear on your screen and in your text.

Num Lock

Some BIOSs let you configure the toggle state of some keyboard keys. The most common option is the setting of the Num Lock key. Most systems default to booting up with Num Lock switched off. This option lets you have your system boot with Num Lock on so you can go right to work crunching numbers. This option is an aid primarily for systems with old 84-key keyboards that lack a separate cursor pad. MS DOS 6.0 and later allow you to accomplish the same effect as setting this option by adding the line NUMLOCK=ON to your CONFIG.SYS file.

Boot Device or Sequence

By design, PCs normally try to boot from floppy disk first, and only if they find no disk in the floppy drive do they attempt to boot from the hard disk. This strategy helps you get going when something happens to your hard disk so that it's no longer bootable. On the downside, it slows the boot process and forces you to wait for the buzz of the first floppy drive access. It also requires you to keep disks out of your floppy drive until after your PC boots up.

Although neither of these shortcomings is fatal, they can be bothersome. Consequently, some BIOS makers give you the option of setting the order that the BIOS searches for a bootable disk drive. Depending on the PC and BIOS maker, several options are possible.

Some BIOS makers allow you to directly specify the *boot order* of your PC's disk drives. Typically, your options will be listed as A:, C: or C:, A:. Sometimes, only the first drive letter will be listed. Specify A: to make your system attempt first to boot from floppy or C: to skip the floppy and try your hard disk first.

Most new BIOSs now also give you an option for booting from a CD drive and even let you select where in the boot order your PC will try the CD drive.

Many new BIOSs even let you select which of your hard disk drives (when you have more than one) to first try booting from. This option is handy if you want to choose between several operating systems. Just put one on each drive, and use the BIOS setup to choose which drive and operating system to use.

Other BIOSs have an option for *Floppy Seek at Bootup* that lets you toggle between yes or no. If you select "No," the BIOS will ignore the floppy disk drive when attempting to boot your PC even if it has a valid system disk in it. You can take advantage of this option to prevent inexperienced users from booting your PC from their own, possibly virus-infected, floppy disks.

Recent systems also give you the option for *Auto Boot Sequence* or *Smart Boot*. This option attempts the best of both worlds. Most of the time, the intelligence of this technique is limited to sampling the floppy disk drive to determine whether it contains a disk, booting from it if the disk is a system disk, and ignoring the drive and booting from hard disk if the disk in the floppy drive is not a system disk or no disk is there at all.

Passwords

Many BIOSs have built-in password protection so that you can limit who uses your PC. The setup program typically gives you the option to enable or disable password protection. When you enable protection, the system stores your password in its CMOS memory. If the battery that backs up your CMOS gets low, you'll lose password protection until you replace the battery.

Upgrades

There are two very good reasons to upgrade the BIOS of a particular PC—fixing and features.

Because a BIOS is basically software set in stone, it can suffer the same plague of bugs as any software product. As with any program, sometimes subtle problems crop up long after the manufacturer unleashes the product on an unsuspecting public. The manufacturer may issue a new BIOS to fix such problems.

The race of technology being as it is, a PC maker cannot anticipate what features you will expect from a computer a year—or even six months—after its manufacture. New standards can arise that quickly and unexpectedly. For example, before IBM introduced the 2.88MB floppy disk, other PC makers had no idea that they would need new disk controllers and BIOSs to enable their systems to use the new technology. Older systems are often unable to support new hardware that you want to use or to exploit its full capabilities because of BIOS shortcomings. For example, older PCs often cannot use the full speed or capacity potentials of EIDE hard disk drives. Although a new BIOS cannot patch up all of these shortcomings by itself, it often is necessary to make the real fix work properly.

When it is possible, upgrading a BIOS can take one of two forms, a new set of BIOS chips for your PC or an update to a flash BIOS system. Which of these your PC requires depends on the choice made by the engineers who designed it.

Replacement Chips

BIOS code is invariably stored in ROM chips of one form or another. The straightforward way to update the BIOS code consequently is directly replacing the ROM chips.

Although every BIOS has the same functions, the BIOS of every PC is different. They are not interchangeable. Consequently, you normally cannot buy a generic replacement BIOS, plug it in, and expect your PC to burst forth with new capabilities. Because every BIOS is intimately linked with motherboard hardware, nearly every PC model has a different BIOS. BIOS makers customize each BIOS for a specific product, if just to add the appropriate copyright message. More often, the BIOS maker tailors the BIOS code to suit the particular requirements of the PC maker. The result is that the BIOS code for two PCs— even when they use the same chipsets and even motherboards—can be minutely different. As a result, you cannot exchange BIOS chips between PCs unless they are exactly the same make and model (and in the case of some PC makers, equipped with the same motherboard). You must get BIOS chips tailored to your PC and motherboard.

The biggest problem with replacement chips is that finding the chips themselves is often impossible. Because each BIOS is custom-created for a given PC model, hundreds or thousands of subtly different BIOSs are currently in use. No one vendor can hope to stock replacements for them all. Moreover, the agreements between BIOS makers and PC manufacturers may preclude the BIOS maker from selling the same BIOS code to anyone else—including you.

The general rule is that the first place to look for a BIOS upgrade for a given PC is the manufacturer of that PC. If the manufacturer will not deal with you directly, the proper channel is through the dealer who sold your PC to you.

A few independent companies offer BIOS upgrade chips for some more popular PC models. In general, however, the cost of a set of loose BIOS chips is a substantial fraction (often more than half) of the price of an entirely new motherboard completely equipped with BIOS, though lacking microprocessor and memory. If your PC is more than a year or so old, replacing the entire motherboard is a better option than simply upgrading an old BIOS.

In addition, buying a single copy of a BIOS can be expensive. Bought in bulk (that is, the way a PC maker would buy BIOSs to be installed in a full production run of PCs), the rights to use a BIOS can be quite inexpensive—only a few dollars per copy. Buying an individual BIOS for your personal PC costs much more because you do not get the benefit of a manufacturer's mass-order bargaining power. Moreover, you must buy the physical chip that holds the code, whereas computer makers often buy the code on disk or tape and make the copies they need (and have paid for) themselves. Consequently, a single copy of a BIOS can cost you $20 to $50, depending on what you buy and from whom.

Flash BIOS

To facilitate BIOS upgrades, many PC makers have shifted to using flash ROM chips for their BIOS code instead of EPROM. You can upgrade a system equipped with such a *flash BIOS* as easily as running a single program that writes updated code to the flash ROM chips.

Most of today's PC makers use flash ROM chips to store their BIOS simply because they can encode the BIOS program more quickly into flash ROM than EPROM. To make the BIOS flash-upgradable, however, your PC's motherboard requires special circuitry to apply the programming voltages to flash ROM chips. Not all PCs using flash ROM for BIOS storage have the necessary circuitry. You should check your PC's owner's manual to determine whether the flash ROM in your system is software upgradable.

Updating a flash BIOS usually involves two files, a binary file that contains the actual BIOS code and a special program called a *loader*. The loader activates the motherboard circuitry required to write to the BIOS chips and then transfers the contents of the binary BIOS file to the chips. The loader's job is one of the most delicate in the operation of a PC because if it makes a mistake, your system may be rendered inoperable. It might not be able to boot up and re-run the loader. Consequently for your security, some system makers require that you take elaborate precautions before you try making a BIOS upgrade. For example, the manufacturer may require you to use both the battery and AC power supplies of a notebook PC to make a BIOS update.

To prevent a BIOS upgrade from accidentally rendering your PC inoperable, many PCs include *boot block protection*. This feature simply protects or prevents the block of the flash

ROM used for the essential boot-up code—the code necessary to read a floppy disk but not necessarily any other support or even diagnostics—from being erased during the upgrade. The protected code is sufficient to get your floppy going so that you can try upgrading your BIOS once again—or if the new BIOS itself is the problem, restore your old BIOS.

Because motherboard circuitry varies among different computer brands and models, the BIOS loader made for one system may not work with another. Unless you're advised otherwise by your PC's manufacturer or a BIOS maker, you should assume that you need a matched pair of files—the BIOS code and loader—to make a BIOS upgrade. In general, a loader will warn if it is not meant for your particular system, but don't depend on such a warning to avoid incompatibilities. A loader that makes a mistake can mean your PC must go back to the factory for new BIOS chips before it will boot again.

Along with fixing problems, upgrading a flash BIOS can sometimes cause them, too. BIOS makers usually design their flash BIOS loaders to reset your PC's setup parameters to the factory defaults so your system gets a fresh start with its new BIOS. If you've customized your system before making the upgrade (for example, adjusting the energy conservation options of a notebook machine), you'll have to re-establish your settings after the upgrade. Sometimes, you may find that the load process has altered the date set in CMOS. Operating your system without checking and resetting the date can cause problems with programs sensitive to the relationship between the current time and file date codes. For example, your backup system or disk maintenance program may not work properly after you've upgrade your BIOS if you don't properly restore your system clock.

Suppliers

Nearly all PCs manufactured in the last five years use flash memory for storing their BIOSs, so you can readily upgrade them in a few minutes without opening up your PC. But first, of course, you need the BIOS upgrade code. *All* major PC manufacturers post BIOS upgrades on their Web sites, usually under the support page. You only need to find the particular model of your PC, select the appropriate upgrade, and settle in for the half hour or so it will take to download.

The availability of BIOS upgrades—or lack of same—is one of the better reasons for avoiding PCs that lack name brands. If you do not have a ready source for a new BIOS, the future usefulness of your PC may be handicapped. For example, I bought a new system in 1997 and wanted to install a 10GB hard disk drive upgrade a year later. Surprise! The machine's BIOS would not recognize more than 8GB of the new disk. The PC maker, however, had a BIOS upgrade that solved the problem.

You'll want to check to be sure the maker of any computer you're considering buying has a Web site and posts BIOS upgrades. If you opt to get a "custom" system from a local garage-based PC manufacturer, make sure you have an upgrade source, either through the motherboard maker or the BIOS maker. Note that Intel motherboards are some of the more popular products in today's market, and Intel does offer upgrades for some of its motherboard BIOSs on its Web site, although you may have to search for them. In other words, when you buy a PC from a manufacturer with doubtful support, check the motherboard maker for additional support.

Some manufacturers regularly post BIOS upgrades. (My laptop was up to revision "O.") You don't need to install them all. In fact, because any revision opens the chance for adding new bugs along with new features, you might want to stick with what you have until you encounter a problem or deficiency. In other words, let sleeping dogs lie in the bed they've made for themselves. But when you do encounter a new version of your BIOS, download it immediately and save it for future use. You never know when it may disappear from the Web.

If you can't find a Web site for your PC's maker or if you cannot find a BIOS upgrade on the manufacturer's site, you still have hope. Although the number of PC manufacturers is only slightly less than the total count of garages in North America, the number of different BIOSs is relatively small. A few computer companies write their own BIOSs (or contract others to write BIOSs for them). The BIOSs of most PCs, however, come from one of a handful of companies. Award Software International makes the Award BIOS. American Megatrends International manufacturers the AMI BIOS. Microid Research offers the MR BIOS, which is often called Mister BIOS because of its abbreviation. Phoenix Technologies created the Phoenix BIOS. Older systems may also have a BIOS made by Quadtel. You may be able to get support for your BIOS or even an upgrade from one of these publishers.

All BIOS manufacturers offer a wealth of information about their products and how to troubleshoot problems with them. The most convenient way to get this information is from the Web site of the BIOS manufacturer. Most BIOS makers do not, however, sell BIOSs—either new or upgrades—to end users.

Determining who wrote your PC's BIOS is easy. When your PC boots up, check the copyright message that displays on your screen. The message will list the copyright holder, which is the publisher of the BIOS. Once you know that, you can easily contact the publisher.

The following list includes the addresses and Web sites maintained by the most popular BIOS companies:

Award Software International, Inc.

777 East Middlefield Rd.

Mountain View, CA 94043

`http://www.award.com`

American Megatrends International

6145-F Northbelt Pkwy.

Norcross, GA 30071

`http://www.megatrends.com`

Microid Research, Inc.

2336-D Walsh Ave.

Santa Clara, CA 95051

`http://www.mrbios.com`

Quadtel

At one time a major player in the BIOS market, Quadtel merged with Phoenix Technologies in early 1992. It is now a wholly owned subsidiary of Phoenix. Information and support for Quadtel products are available from Phoenix and its authorized distributor, Micro Firmware.

Phoenix Technologies Ltd.

2770 De La Cruz

Santa Clara, CA 95050

`http://www.ptltd.com`

Although Phoenix Technologies supplies a wealth of information at its Web site, you'll find more troubleshooting information and get better end-user upgrade support though its authorized distributor, Micro Firmware. That company's address is as follows:

Micro Firmware

330 West Gray St.

Norman, OK 73069

`http://www.firmware.com`

WINN L. ROSCH
HARDWARE BIBLE,
FIFTH EDITION

CHAPTER

6

Chipsets

Chipsets and other support circuits are the glue that holds a PC together, providing the signals that the microprocessor needs to operate as well as those that link the PC and its peripherals. Over the years of development, the form and nature of those support circuits have changed but their function has remained consistent, part of the definition of a PC. Today's chipsets essentially define the PC, serve as the foundation of the motherboard, and determine the basic features of the overall PC.

Support circuits do more than keep your microprocessor running. They perform functions that your PC would not be a computer without. Some of these include:

Function	In short
Timing circuits	Control and coordinate the operation of your PC as well as setting its speed
Interrupt control	Lets applications and devices gain the immediate attention of your PC's microprocessor to carry out time-critical tasks
Direct memory access	Provides an alternate route for data from disk and other devices to memory that bypasses your microprocessor and lets it use its time more wisely
Bus interface	Links the circuitry of your PC to that of expansion boards and insures that they can safely (and quickly) interchange information
Power management	Minimizes the power use of your PC with the least sacrifice in performance; most helpful in prolonging operating time when running from batteries
Memory control	Guides data to and from memory and assures that the contents of memory stay alive and accurate
Disk control	Insures your PC gets the right data from your disk and stores information where it can be quickly retrieved.
Keyboard control	Routes the signals from your keystrokes to your microprocessor and assures they get the attention they need
Port control	Links your PC with peripheral devices including printers, modems, and the Internet

Just as you can't build a house without nails, you can't put together a computer without support chips. A PC needs a wealth of circuits to hold together all its functions, coordinate its operation, and control the signals inside it. After all, you need more than a microprocessor to make a computer; otherwise, a microprocessor *would be* a computer. Although some systems come close to being little more than microprocessors and some microprocessors come close to being complete computers, today most personal computers require a number of support functions to make their microprocessors useful—and make the microprocessors work.

PC *chipsets* package these electrical and logical functions into a handful of integrated circuits, often the largest chips inside your PC except for the microprocessor. The chipset is the foundation of the motherboard, and a PC maker's choice of chipsets determines the overall functionality of the PC. How well the manufacturer puts the chips to work can determine the overall performance of the system.

Although the chipset used by a PC is rarely mentioned in advertisements and specification sheets, its influence is pervasive. Among other issues, the chipset determines the type and number of microprocessors that can be installed in the system; the maximum memory a system can address; the memory technology used by the system (EDO, Burst EDO, SDRAM, or Rambus); whether the system can detect memory errors; the speed of the memory bus; the size and kind of secondary memory cache; the type, speed, and operating mode of the expansion bus; whether you can plug a video board into an Accelerated Graphics Port in your PC; the mass storage interfaces available on the motherboard; the ports available on your motherboard; and whether your PC has a built-in network adapter. That's a lot of power packed into a few chips—and a good reason for wondering what you have in your PC.

Background

Beyond simply having a microprocessor, every PC needs a handful of electrical functions to make it work. These include a clock or oscillator to generate the signals that lock the circuits together; a memory controller to ensure each byte goes to the proper place and stays there; bus-control logic to command the flow of data in and out of the chip and the rest of the system; direct memory access control to assist in moving data; and interrupt control to meet the needs of interactive computing. In addition, some functions that aren't strictly necessary are usually part of a complete PC—such things as a controller for the expansion bus, an interface for the mass storage system, and the various ports that connect your PC to its peripherals.

Every PC manufactured since the first amphibians crawled from the primeval swamp has had these circuits inside it. The first of these ancient computers lacked chipsets. No one had yet invented the chipset; the technology was nascent and the need was negligible.

Instead, PC engineers built the required functions from a variety of discrete circuits—small, general purpose integrated circuits such as logic gates—and a few functional blocks, larger integrated circuits designed to a particular purpose but not necessarily one that had anything to do with computers. These garden-variety circuits, together termed *support chips*, were combined to build all the necessary computer functions into the first PC.

Today, only the form of these circuit elements has changed magically into the chipset. The motivation is the same as guides all the innovations in personal computing—profits. Circuits are more compact in combination and more affordable, too. As PCs became increasingly popular, enterprising semiconductor firms combined dozens of the related computer functions together into a few packages individually termed Application-Specific Integrated Circuits, or *ASIC*s, collectively making up the chipset.

Of course, you do gain some benefits. PCs can be smaller, cheaper, and more reliable using chipsets. One look at a circuit board, and the size advantage is obvious. Everything is compact these days, and the motherboard looks nearly bare with only the few big black circuits of the chipset decorating it. Eliminating the discrete circuits and all their inter-connections reduces the number of failure-prone connections, and the circuits themselves are more dependable. Moreover, because a multitude of circuits could be grown together at the same time, this integrated approach made the PC support circuitry less expensive.

History

You can trace the genealogy all the way back to the first PC. All of the most basic func-tions of the modern chipset lie within its circuits. The history of the chipset is little more than combining and elaborating on these original functions. This heritage results from the simple need for compatibility. PCs mimic the function of the earliest PCs—and IBM's original Personal Computer of 1981 in particular—so that they can all run the same soft-ware. Although seemingly anachronistic in an age when those who can remember the first PC also harbor memories of Desotos and Dinosaurs, even the most current chipsets must precisely mimic the actions of early PCs so that the oldest software will still operate prop-erly in new PCs—providing, of course, all the other required support is also present. After all, some Neanderthal will set switchboards glowing from I-95 to the Silicon Valley with threats of lawsuits and aspersions about the parenthood of chipset designers when the DOS utilities he downloaded in 1982 won't run on his new Pentium III.

Large, multifunction chips have been present in PCs since the beginning (for example, the video controller in the first PCs), but they have seen continuing elaboration. IBM intro-duced the term "ASIC" with its Personal System/2 line, starting in 1987. This marked the coming of age of the PC. The market for the machines had finally grown large enough to support designing chips specifically for it. Soon, semiconductor design houses began turn-ing out their own ASICs for building computers. Among the first was Chips and Technologies, since 1997 part of Intel Corporation.

Not only did the advent of the chipset create a new branch of the semiconductor industry, but it also changed the face of the PC industry. With discrete support circuitry, designing a PC motherboard was a true engineering challenge because it required a deep understanding of the electronic function of all the elements of a PC. Using a chipset, a PC engineer need only be concerned with the signals going in and out of a few components. The chipset might be a magical black box for all the designer cares. In fact, in many cases the only skill required to design a PC from a chipset is the ability to navigate from a roadmap. Most chipset manufacturers provide circuit designs for motherboards to aid in the evaluation of their products. Many motherboard manufacturers (all too many, perhaps) simply take the chipset maker's evaluation design and turn it into a commercial product.

Taken to the extreme, a chipset becomes a single-chip PC. In fact, not only is a single integrated circuit sufficient to hold all the support circuitry of an entire PC, but also chip-makers have tried integrating support circuitry with a microprocessor. One of the best examples remains Intel's 486SL, a full-fledged 486DX microprocessor designed for low power and total system control, a single chip with a whole computer inside. Although Intel hasn't pushed its Pentium technology to this level of integration—yet—other manufacturers now offer high-powered PCs-on-chips, such as the PowerPC MPC821 (which, alas, is not compatible with today's Windows-based PCs). Every couple of years, a "computer on a chip" makes it into the headlines of trade journals, although rarely into a product as wildly successful as the ordinary chipset-based PC.

Functions

Because chipsets control specific hardware features, they are typically designed to match a given type of microprocessor and, often, expansion bus. Today's most popular chipsets link to the Pentium microprocessor and PCI expansion bus and include all the high-tech functions you expect from a computer.

No matter how simple or elaborate the chipset in a modern PC, it has three chief functions. It must act as a *system controller* that holds together the entire PC, giving all the support the microprocessor needs to be a true computer system. As a *memory controller*, it links the microprocessor to the memory system, establishes the main memory and cache architectures, and assures the reliability of the data stashed away in RAM chips. And to extend the reach of the microprocessor to other system components, it must act as a *peripheral controller* and operate input/output ports and disk interfaces.

The chipset industry often lumps the system and memory functions together as a unit they call the *north bridge*. The north bridge circuits are the essential elements of the PC. Without their system and memory control functions, there could be no PC.

In the same parlance, the peripheral control functions make up the *south bridge*, which is often a single, separate chip. Although its functions are sometimes classed as nonessential, you wouldn't want a PC that lacked them; your PC would have neither the means for communicating with the outside world nor a way of storing your programs and data.

One chipset function, bus control, is now usually included as part of the north bridge, although in earlier chipsets its functions were often part of the peripheral controller. Many chipsets leave their bus controller in a separate chip they call the *PCI bridge*. In earlier editions of this book, the bus controller was described in conjunction with the peripheral controller. That's because at the time, the ISA bus *was* considered a peripheral; it operated like a peripheral, and it performed like a peripheral (that is, slowly). The modern PCI bus is more tightly integrated with the microprocessor, one reason it was at one time termed a "local bus" and part of the reason it delivers much better performance.

System Controller

The basic function of a chipset is to turn a chip into a PC, to add what a microprocessor needs to be an entire computer system. The basic functions required by a modern PC are several:

- **Timers and oscillators**, which create the timebases required for the microprocessor, memory, and the rest of the computer to operate
- **Interrupt controller**, which manages the hardware interrupts that give priority to important functions
- **DMA controller**, which governs data transfers to and from memory independently of the microprocessor to free the chip up for more important duties (such as thinking)
- **Power manager**, which watches over the overall electrical use of the computer to save power and, in notebook machines, conserve battery reserves

The *system controller* in the north bridge of a modern chipset handles all of these functions. Nearly all of the functions of the system controller in a PC chipset are well defined and for the most part standardized. In nearly all PCs, the most basic of these functions use the same means of access and control; the ports and memory locations match those used by the very first PCs. In fact, the access to these functions determines the fundamental PC compatibility of a computer.

That said, designers didn't think of some of the system control functions required by a modern PC when they crafted the first computers. The most important of these is power management, which was never an issue until PCs started running from—and running through—batteries. Consequently, the "Power Management" functions of chipsets vary in hardware design, although most now share common software control systems (discussed in the "Power Management" section of Chapter 25, "Power"). Moreover, some chipsets may omit some of these less standard functions.

Designers match the system controller in most chipsets to a particular microprocessor. Some, however, are more versatile and will work with microprocessors of a given class (for example, all fifth-generation chips such as the original Intel Pentium and its "586" competitors from AMD, Cyrix, and others), whereas others may even have broader application. Because the functions of the system controller are so basic and well-defined, you can expect any chipset to handle them well.

Memory Controller

You can't just toss the memory every PC needs into a computer's case like broadcasting grass seed and hope to have everything (or anything!) work. The memory must be logically and electronically linked to the rest of the system. Moreover, memory chips and modules have their own maintenance needs that your PC must manage to keep its electronic storage intact. The simple memory systems of early PCs needed little more than a simple decoder chip to link memory to the microprocessor. Modern memory architectures are substantially more complex, incorporating layers of caching, error correction, and automatic configuration processes. Today's chipsets handle all the interconnection and support that the most complicated memory system requires.

In addition to handling main memory, the memory controller in the typical chipset may also act as the cache controller for your PC's secondary memory cache. This function varies with the design of the host microprocessor, however. The sixth-generation Pentium Pro shifted basic cache control from the chipset into the microprocessor itself, and the Pentiums II and III continue with this design.

The design of the memory controller in a chipset has dramatic ramifications on the configuration of your PC. It determines how much RAM you can plug into your PC, what kind of RAM your PC can use (for example, parity, non-parity, or error-corrected), the operating speed and rating of the memory modules you install, and the size and technology of the secondary cache.

Peripheral Controller

The system controller of the chipset makes your PC operate. The *peripheral controller* lets it connect. The peripheral controller creates the interfaces needed for other devices to link to your microprocessor. The primary functions of the peripheral controller include

- **Floppy disk interface**, which puts one or two floppy disk drives under the control of the system
- **Hard disk interface**, which links your hard disk drives to the system
- **Keyboard controller**, which translates codes from the keyboard into a form readily understood by your PC and its programs
- **I/O port controller**, which gives access to the input and output ports of your PC so you can make serial and parallel connections with your peripherals

As with the system control functions, most of the peripheral interface functions are well-defined standards that have been in use for years. The time-proved functions usually cause few problems in the design, selection, or operation of a chipset. Some interfaces have a more recent ancestry, and if anything will cause a problem with a chipset, they will. For example, the PCI bus and UDMA disk interface are newcomers when compared to the decade-old keyboard interface or an even older ISA bus. When a chipset shows teething pains, they usually arise in the circuits relating to these newer functions.

Some chipset designs break out one or more of the peripheral control functions and put them in dedicated chips. This expedient allows independent development and permits the chip maker to revise the design of one section of the chipset without affecting the circuits of the other functions or their manufacturer. For example, Intel put the PCI bridge controller of its Pentium Pro Orion chipset in a separate package, as do most current Intel chipsets.

System Control

Crack open one of the latest chipsets, and you'll find three system control functions so essential that they would have to be incorporated into modern PCs even if perfect backward compatibility were not an issue: timing circuits, interrupt control, and direct memory access control. The following sections take a closer look at each one.

Timing Circuits

Although anarchy has much to recommend it, should you believe in individual freedom or sell firearms, anarchy is an anathema to computer circuits. Today's data processing designs depend on organization and controlled cooperation—factors that make timing critical. The meaning of each pulse passing through a PC depends to a large degree on time relationships. Signals must be passed between circuits at just the right moment for the entire system to work properly.

Timing is critical in PCs because their circuits are designed using a technology known as *clocked logic*. All the logic elements in the computer operate *synchronously*. They carry out their designated operations one step at a time, and each circuit makes one step at the same time as all the rest of the circuits in the computer. This synchronous operation helps the machine keep track of every bit that it processes, assuring that nothing slips between the cracks.

The circuit element that sends out timing pulses to keep everything synchronized is called a *clock*. PCs don't have just one clock, however. They have several, each for a specific purpose. Among these are the system clock, the bus clock, the video clock, and even a time-of-day clock.

The *system clock* is the conductor who beats the time that all the circuits follow, sending out special timing pulses at precisely controlled intervals. The clock, however, must get its cues from somewhere, either its own internal sense of timing or some kind of metronome. Most clocks in electronic circuits derive their beats from oscillators.

Oscillators

An electronic circuit that accurately and continuously beats time is termed an oscillator. Most oscillators work on a simple feedback principal. Like the microphone that picks up its own sounds from public address speakers too near or turned up too high, the oscillator, too, listens to what it says. As with the acoustic-feedback squeal that the public address system complains with, the oscillator, too, generates it own howl. Because the feedback circuit is much shorter, however, the signal need not travel as far and their frequency is higher, perhaps by several thousandfold.

The oscillator takes its output as its input, amplifies the signal, and sends it to its output, where it goes back to the input again in an endless—and out of control—loop. By taming the oscillator by adding impediments to the feedback loop, by adding special electronic components between the oscillator's output and its input, the feedback and its frequency can be brought under control.

In nearly all PCs, a carefully crafted crystal of quartz is used as this frequency control element. Quartz is one of many piezoelectric compounds. Piezoelectric materials have an interesting property; if you bend a piezoelectric crystal, it generates a tiny voltage. Or if you apply a voltage to it in the right way, the piezoelectric material bends.

Quartz crystals do exactly that. But beyond this simple stimulus/response relationship, quartz crystals offer another important property. By stringently controlling the size and shape of a quartz crystal, it can be made to resonate at a specific frequency. The frequency of this resonance is extremely stable and very reliable—so much so that it can help an electric watch keep time to within seconds a month. Although PCs don't need the absolute precision of a quartz watch to operate their logic circuits properly, the fundamental stability of the quartz oscillator guarantees that the PC operates at a clock frequency within its design limits always available to it.

The various clocks in a PC can operate separately or they may be locked together. Most PCs link these frequencies together, synchronizing them. They may all originate in a single oscillator and use special circuits such as *frequency dividers* that reduce the oscillation rate by a selectable factor or *frequency multipliers* that increase it. For example, a PC may have a 100MHz oscillator that directly controls the memory system. A frequency divider may reduce that to one third that rate to run the PCI bus, and another divider may reduce it by 12 to produce the clock for the ISA legacy bus. A frequency multiplier inside the microprocessor may boost the 100MHz outside clock to 450 or 600MHz for operating the core circuitry of the chip. Because all of these frequencies originate in a single clock signal, they are automatically synchronized. Even the most minute variations in the original clock are reflected in all those frequencies derived from it.

Some sections of PCs operate asynchronously using their own clocks. For example, the scan rate used by your PC's video system usually is derived from a separate oscillator on the video board. In fact, some video boards have multiple oscillators for different scan rates. Some PCs may even have separate clocks for their basic system board functions and run their buses asynchronously from their memory and microprocessor. For keeping track of the date, most PCs have dedicated time-of-day clocks that are essentially a digital Timex grafted onto the motherboard.

System Clocks

Although today's preferred bus frequency of 100MHz is a nice, round number, a lot of the oscillators inside PCs run at some pretty strange values—say 14.31818MHz. Many of these values are entirely arbitrary but have historic roots.

In the beginning (to crib from *Genesis*), IBM crafted the very first Personal Computer around a single oscillator running at that odd-sounding 14.31818 megahertz rate. The odd frequency was chosen for a particular reason; it's exactly four times the subcarrier frequency used in color television signals (3.58MHz). The engineers who created the original PC thought compatibility with televisions would be an important design element of the PC. Rather than anticipating multimedia, they were looking for a cheap way of putting PC images onscreen. When the PC was released, no inexpensive color computer monitors were available (or necessary for almost nonexistent color graphic software). Making PCs work with color televisions seemed an expedient way of creating computer graphics.

The TV-as-monitor never really caught on, but the 14.31818MHz frequency persists, but not for motherboard television circuits. The video part of PCs, even when meant to display on an ordinary television or monitor, has its own oscillator separate from the 14.31818MHz system on the motherboard. Instead, the motherboard oscillator gets sliced down to 1.19MHz to serve as the timebase for the PC's timer/counter circuit.

Examined overall, the goal in the oscillator/clock design of the early PC seems to have been frugality rather than flexibility, versatility, or usability. In those early systems, one master frequency was cut, chopped, minced, and diced into whatever else was needed inside the computer. Besides the video frequency and timer/counter timebase, the PC divided the same oscillator by three to produce a frequency of 4.77MHz (the actual clock signal used by the microprocessor in the PC), determining the operating speed of the system microprocessor. This same clock signal also synchronized all the logic operations inside the PC and related eight-bit bus computers.

The one-for-all oscillator design has a fundamental weakness. Try to change any frequency by tinkering with the oscillator, and *everything* changes. Try to speed up the microprocessor, for example, and the bus goes faster and time whizzes by at a rate that makes amphetamines seem tame. Avoiding such side effects requires coming up with alternative timebases—more oscillators—and PC makers quickly shifted to designs with multiple clocks.

By the time manufacturers unleashed the second generation of PCs, designers had separated the 14.131818MHz timer from the system clock, running each from its own separate oscillator so you could alter one without affecting the other. This design led to all sorts of mischief—overclocking being the chief culprit—and became the cornerstone of modern system design.

At this stage of development, the bus clock and microprocessor clock still ran in lockstep together, although the basic system timer/counter had been cut free to run with its own clock and crystal. The linked bus and microprocessor clocks inevitably lead to technological trouble. As microprocessors got faster, so did the bus. Unfortunately, few expansion boards could keep up with such exciting speeds as *12* megahertz. For this reason, when Compaq introduced its first DeskPro 386 in 1987, it broke the link between the bus and the microprocessor clocks. The first of these machines, which ran at 16MHz, sliced the microprocessor and memory clock in two to run the bus. Once the microprocessor and expansion bus clocks were separated, they almost never came together again.

IBM experimented with asynchronous buses, most notably its 1987 Micro Channel design. These asynchronous buses had no fixed mathematical relationship between the two clocks and relied on handshaking to pass data back and forth.

For technical and legal reasons, however, other designers found it easier to synchronize the microprocessor bus and expansion bus clocks. Although today's PCI bus can operate asynchronously, most PC makers synchronize it at a frequency that is a submultiple of the microprocessor's clock.

When microprocessors began to outrun memory, microprocessors again introduced another clock, the internal clock of the chip. These internal clocks do not have their own oscillators but instead multiply the external clock supplied to the microprocessors. They are thus guaranteed to be synchronized with the rest of the computer.

Consequently in modern PCs, the memory and expansion buses operate at different speeds, but those speeds are synchronized. For example, the 33MHz PCI bus in a 500MHz PC actually operates at exactly one third the speed of the memory bus and one fifteenth the internal clock speed of the microprocessor.

Despite all these changes and innovations, you'll still find a 14.31818MHz oscillator in modern PCs. This oscillator drives the *system timer*, which runs at 1.19MHz. All PCs incorporate a system timer at this frequency for compatibility reasons.

In all, you'll find at least five different clock frequencies inside your PC, each of which someone will likely call a "clock":

- Microprocessor speed
- Front-side bus (memory bus) speed
- Expansion bus speed
- System timer
- Video system clock

And, of course, your PC also has its real-time clock running from its own oscillator—yet another clock.

Timers

The system timer serves three important functions. It maintains the time of day for your PC separately from the dedicated time-of-day clock, signals the time to refresh memory, and generates the sounds that come from the tiny speakers of PCs that lack multimedia pretensions. The design of the timer system makes these functions available for programmers, which at one time meant not only the folks writing applications but also ordinary people like you who wanted to tinker with their PCs.

The original PC used a simple timer chip for these functions, specifically chip type 8253. Although this chip would be as foreign in a modern PC as a smudge pot or buggy whip, its exact functions are still there, locked inside some nondescript chipset. The system timer counts pulses from the 1.19MHz system clock and divides them down to the actual frequencies it needs, for example, to make a beep of the right pitch.

The timer works simply. You load one of its registers with a number, and it counts to that number. When it reaches it, it outputs a pulse and starts all over again. Load the 8253 register with 2, and it sends out a pulse at half the frequency of the input. Load it with 1,000, and the output becomes 1/1000th the input. In this mode, the chip can generate an interrupt at any of a wide range of user-defined intervals. Because the highest value you can load into its 16-bit register is 216 or 65,536, the longest single interval it can count is about .055 second—that is, the 1.19MHz input signal divided by 65,536.

The 8253 timer/counter actually had six operating modes, all of which are carried through on modern PCs. Table 6.1 lists these modes.

TABLE 6.1   Operating Modes of 8253 Timer/Counter Chip

Mode	Name	Operation
0	Interrupt on Terminal Count	Timer is loaded with a value and counts down from that value to zero, one counter per clock pulse.
1	Hardware Retriggerable One-Shot	A trigger pulse causes timer output to go low; when the counter reaches zero, the output goes high and stays high until reset. The process repeats every time it's triggered. Pulse length is set by writing a control word and initial count to the chip before the first cycle.
2	Rate Generator	Timer divides incoming frequency by the value of the initial count loaded into it.
3	Square Wave	Produces a series of square waves with a period (measured in clock pulses) equal to the value loaded into the timer.
4	Software Retriggerable Strobe	Timer counts down the number of clock cycles loaded into it and then pulses its output. Software starts the next cycle.
5	Hardware Retriggerable Strobe	Timer counts down the number of clock cycles loaded into it and then pulses its output. Hardware-generated pulse initiates the next cycle.

The time-of-day signal in the original PC used the 8253 timer/counter to count out its longest possible increment, generating pulses at a rate of 18.2 per second. The pulses cause the time-of-day interrupt, which the PC counts to keep track of the time. These interrupts can also be used by programs that need to regularly investigate what the computer is doing—for instance, checking the hour to see whether it's time to dial up a distant computer.

The speaker section of the timer system works the same way, but it generates a square wave that is routed through an amplifier to the internal speaker of the PC to make primitive sounds. Programs can modify any of its settings to change the pitch of the tone and, with clever programming, its timbre.

In modern PCs, the memory controller in the chipset rather than the system timer handles refresh operations. Otherwise, the timer functions are much the same as they were with the first PCs.

Real-Time Clock

The first PCs tracked time only when they were awake and running, simply counting the ticks of their timers. Every time you booted up, your PC asked you the time to set its clock. To lift that heavy chore from your shoulders, all new PCs since about 1984 have a built-in real-time clock among their support circuits. All of these built-in time-of-day clocks trace their heritage back to a specific clock circuit, the Motorola MC146818 that IBM choose for its Personal Computer in that year. In addition to tracking time around the clock, this chip also held the CMOS memory that stored system setup information.

The clocks in today's PCs are either built into their chipsets or patterned after a dedicated module patterned after the MC146818, although today's PCs have increased CMOS storage. For example, the Dallas 12887A module or one of its derivatives is popular on modern motherboards.

Usually based on low-power CMOS circuitry that's kept powered up by a battery even when your PC is shut down, the time-of-day clock circuitry in your PC runs constantly whether power to your PC is on or off.

The time-of-day clocks have their own timebases, typically an oscillator built into the chip, one that's independent from the other clocks in a PC. The time-of-day clock needs its own timebase because none of the other oscillators in your PC are running when you shut down your system.

Although the time-of-day clock should be as accurate as a digital watch (its circuitry is nothing more than a digital watch in a different form), many tell time as imaginatively as a four-year-old child. One reason is that although a quartz oscillator is excellent at maintaining a constant frequency, that frequency may not be the one required to keep time correctly. Some PCs have trimmers for adjusting the frequency of their time-of-day clocks, but their manufacturers sometimes don't think to adjust them properly.

In many PCs, a trimmer (an adjustable capacitor) in series with their quartz crystal allows the manufacturer—or anyone with a screwdriver—to alter the resonate frequency of the oscillator. Giving the trimmer a tweak can bring the real-time clock closer to reality—or further into the twilight zone. (You can find the trimmer by looking for the short cylinder with a slotted shaft in the center near the clock crystal, which is usually the only one in a PC with a kilohertz rather than megahertz rating.)

The time-of-day clocks in many PCs are also sensitive to the battery voltage. When the CMOS backup battery is nearing failure, the time-of-day clock may go wildly awry. If your PC keeps good time for a while (months or years) and then suddenly wakes up hours or days off, try replacing your PC's CMOS backup battery.

A built-in bug also assures that your PC's clock can screw up, skipping an entire day or two if you or your software does not access the system clock for several days, say if you leave your PC on over the weekend. To indicate to your PC's operating system that the date has changed, the BIOS sets a flag bit that programs or the operating systems check when they read the clock. If they see the flag, they move on to the next date. A single flag bit can only indicate a change of one day, and if two or more days elapse between the time your operating system checks the clock, your software will increment by only one day instead of the number that actually elapsed. This was a problem with operating systems before Windows that just sat around doing nothing when you didn't do anything with your PC. With today's Windows, however, the clock gets checked many times a day so the problem won't arise.

The real-time clock chip first installed in early PCs also had a built-in alarm function, which has been carried into the time-of-day clocks of new PCs. As with the rest of the time-of-day clock, the alarm function runs from the battery supply so it can operate while your PC is switched off. This alarm can thus generate an interrupt at the appropriate time to start or stop a program or process. In some systems, it can even cause your PC to switch on at a preset time. Throw a WAV file of the national anthem in your startup folder, and you'll have a truly patriotic alarm clock.

Reading the time-of-day clock inside your PC requires the same two-step process as reading or writing BIOS configuration information. The clock is addressed through the same two I/O ports as setup memory: one port—070(Hex)—to set the location to read or write and a second port—071(Hex)—to read or write the value.

Interrupt Control

Intel microprocessors understand two kinds of interrupts—software and hardware.

A *software interrupt* is simply a special instruction in a program that's controlling the microprocessor. Instead of addition, subtraction, or whatever, the software interrupt causes program execution to temporarily shift to another section of code in memory.

A *hardware interrupt* causes the same effect but is controlled by special signals outside of the normal data stream. The only problem is that the microprocessors recognize far fewer interrupts that would be useful; only two interrupt signal lines are provided. One of these is a special case, the non-maskable interrupt. The other line is shared by all system interrupts.

To extend the capabilities of the interrupt system, PCs use an *interrupt controller chip* that manages several interrupt signals and sets the priority determining which gets serviced first. Although a separate chip in early PCs, specifically a type 8259A, the functions of the interrupt controller have long been integrated into PC chipsets.

The first interrupt controller had one grave limitation: It recognized only eight interrupts. The needs of even basic PCs quickly overran those available. In its second generation of PCs, IBM added a second interrupt controller, a second 8259A chip, to double the number of interrupts. IBM's engineers grafted in the second controller by cascading it with the first. That is, all of the interrupts of the second chip funneled into a single interrupt of the first.

The PCI bus does not use this interrupt structure, substituting a newer design. However, all PCs that maintain an ISA legacy bus—which currently include nearly all PCs—mimic this design for compatibility reasons.

Assignments and Priority

Each interrupt is assigned a priority, the more important one getting attention before those of lesser importance. In the original PC scheme of things with eight interrupts, the lower the number assigned to an interrupt, the more priority it got. The two-stage design in current systems, however, abridges the rule.

In the current cascade design, the second interrupt controller links to the input of the first controller that was assigned to interrupt two. Consequently, *every* interrupt on the second controller (that is, numbers 8 through 15) has a higher priority than those on the first controller that are numbered higher than 2. The hardware-based priorities of interrupts in current PCs thus range as listed in Table 6.2.

TABLE 6.2 Hardware Interrupt Priorities

0 (most priority)
1
8
9
10
11
12
13
14
15
3
4
5
6
7 (least priority)

To take the place of interrupt number two, its functions were reassigned to one of the new interrupt channels, number nine. This interrupt works the same with its new connection; the signal only needs to traverse two controllers instead of one before the interrupt swings into action. Despite its new number, the new interrupt nine functions just like PC interrupt two, with the same priority activated by the same control line on the expansion bus.

Although within some hardware limitations (discussed in the following sections) any interrupt can be assigned to any device, a degree of standardization has developed over the history of the PC. For the most part, the PC industry followed the interrupt assignments IBM made for its Personal Computer AT in 1984. Table 6.3 lists these original AT interrupt assignments.

TABLE 6.3 AT Interrupt Assignments

Interrupt Number	Function
IRQ0	Timer output 0
IRQ1	Keyboard (buffer full)
IRQ2	Cascade from IRQ9
IRQ3	Serial port 2; serial port 4; SDLC communications; BSC communications; cluster adapter; network (alternate); 3278/79 (alternate)
IRQ4	Serial port 1; serial port 3; SDLC communications; BSC communications; voice communications adapter
IRQ5	Parallel port 2, audio
IRQ6	Floppy disk controller
IRQ7	Parallel port 1; cluster adapter (alternate)
IRQ8	Real-time clock
IRQ9	Software redirected to INT 0A(Hex); video; network; 3278/79 adapter
IRQ10	Reserved
IRQ11	Reserved
IRQ12	Reserved, built-in mouse
IRQ13	Coprocessor
IRQ14	Primary hard disk controller (IDE)
IRQ15	Secondary hard disk controller

The advent of the PCI expansion bus and the plug-and-play configuration system has altered how PCs and their software treat interrupts, however. The plug-and-play system can make the required assignments automatically without regard to the traditional values. In these systems, interrupt values and the resulting priorities get assigned dynamically when the PC configures itself. The values depend on the combination of hardware devices installed in such systems. Although the standardized step-by-step nature of the plug-and-play system usually assigns the same interrupt value to the same devices in a given PC each time it boots up, it doesn't have to. Interrupt values *could* (but usually do not) change day to day. The traditional interrupt assignment chart—or any other fixed list of interrupt assignments—is consequently meaningless in a plug-and-play world.

If you want to know what's what, the only way to be sure is to check your system right there and then. If you're running Windows 95 or 98, you can easily take a look. To view the actual interrupt usage of your PC, you need to consult Device Manager by selecting the System icon in Control Panel. Select your Computer on the device menu and click on the Properties button. Select the Interrupt request (IRQ) radio button in the View Resources tab—which is the default screen that pops up—and you'll see a list of the actual interrupt assignments in use in your PC, akin to that shown in Figure 6.1.

FIGURE 6.1

Windows 95 and 98 Device Manager showing actual interrupt assignments.

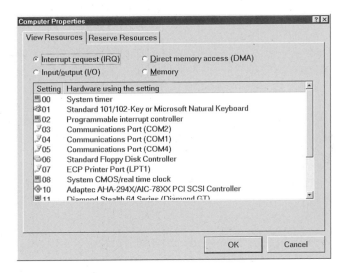

In the days of hardware configuration when you could select which interrupt a given product used by setting jumpers, you could assign a lower interrupt value to a device you wanted to have a higher priority. Automatic configuration through plug-and-play deprives you of that option. In general, however, interrupt priorities don't make much difference in the operation of your PC because interrupts rarely occur simultaneously and most interrupt service routines don't last long enough to make a difference.

A few interrupt assignments are inviolable. In all systems, four interrupts can never be used for expansion devices. These include IRQ0, used by the timer/counter; IRQ1, used by the keyboard controller; IRQ2, the cascade point for the upper interrupts (which is redirected to IRQ9); and IRQ8, used by the real-time clock. In addition, all modern PCs have microprocessors with integral floating-point units or accept external FPUs, both of which use IRQ13.

Interrupt Sharing

Not all PC devices require interrupts, but in the early days of PCs, those that did need one got a dedicated interrupt. That device and only that device would use the interrupt assigned to it. Although 15 interrupts seem like a lot, it is nowhere near enough to give every device in a modern PC its own interrupt. As early as 1987, the sharing of interrupts consequently became a major issue for PC designers. At first, PCs didn't share interrupts very well. Modern PCs are better at it, but problems still arise.

When an interrupt is shared, each device that's sharing a given interrupt uses the same hardware interrupt request line to signal to the microprocessor. The interrupt-handling software or firmware then directs the microprocessor for the action to take to service the device making the interrupt. The interrupt-handler distinguishes between the various devices sharing the interrupt to assure only the right routine gets carried out.

Although software or firmware actually sorts out the sharing of interrupts, a PC expansion bus needs to be properly designed to make the sharing reliable. Old bus designs such as the ISA legacy bus use *edge-triggered* interrupts, a technique that is particularly prone to sharing problems. Modern systems used a different technology, *level-sensitive* interrupts, which avoid some of the pitfalls of the older technique.

An edge-triggered interrupt signals the interrupt condition as the transition of the voltage on the interrupt line from one state to another. Only the change—the edge of the waveform—is significant. The interrupt signal needs only to be a pulse, after which the interrupt line returns to its idle state. A problem arises if a second device sends another pulse down the interrupt line before the first has been fully processed. The system may lose track of the interrupts it is serving.

A level-sensitive interrupt signals the interrupt condition by shifting the voltage on the interrupt request line, for example, from low to high. It then maintains that shifted condition throughout the processing of the interrupt. It effectively ties up the interrupt line during the processing of the interrupt so no other device can get attention through that interrupt line. Although it would seem that one device would hog the interrupt line and not share with anyone, the presence of the signal on the line effectively warns other devices to wait before sending out their own interrupt requests. Interrupts are less likely to be confused.

Serialized Interrupts

PCI changed the traditional interrupt structure entirely, finally breaking the nearly 20-year-old tie with the first PC. The PCI bus does not use the old AT-compatible interrupt controller but instead integrates its own interrupt control circuitry in its host bridge in the PCI chipset.

The PCI system uses four interrupt lines, and the function of each is left up to the designer of each individual expansion board. The PCI specification puts no limits on how these interrupt signals are used (the software driver that services the board determines that) but specifies level-sensitive interrupts so that the four signals can be reliably shared.

Because of the design of the PCI system, the lack of the old IRQ signals poses a problem. Under standard PCI architecture, the compatibility expansion bus (ISA) links to the host microprocessor through the PCI bus and its host bridge. The IRQ signals cannot be passed directly through this channel because the PCI specification does not define them. To accommodate the old IRQ system under PCI architecture, several chipset and PC makers, including Compaq, Cirrus Logic, National Semiconductor, OPTi, Standard Microsystems, Texas Instruments, and VLSI Technology, developed a standard they called *serialized IRQ support for PCI systems.*

The serialized IRQ system relies on a special signal called *IRQSER*, which encodes all available interrupts as pulses in a series. One long series of pulses called an *IRQSER cycle* sends data about the state of all interrupts in the system across the PCI channel.

The IRQSER cycle begins with an extended pulse of the IRQSER signal lasting from four to eight cycles of the PCI clock (each of which is nominally 33MHz but may be slower in systems with slower bus clocks). After a delay of two PCI clock cycles, the IRQSER cycle is divided into frames, each of which is three PCI clock cycles long. Each frame encodes the state of one interrupt; if the IRQSER signal pulses during the first third of the frame, it indicates the interrupt assigned to that frame is active. Table 6.4 lists which interrupts are assigned to each frame position.

TABLE 6.4   PCI Serialized Interrupt Frame Encoding

Interrupt Encoded	Frame Position	Clocks Past Start
IRQ0	1	2
IRQ1	2	5
SMI#	3	8
IRQ3	4	11
IRQ4	5	14

continues

TABLE 6.4   Continued

Interrupt Encoded	Frame Position	Clocks Past Start
IRQ5	6	17
IRQ6	7	20
IRQ7	8	23
IRQ8	9	26
IRQ9	10	29
IRQ10	11	32
IRQ11	12	35
IRQ12	13	38
IRQ13	14	41
IRQ14	15	44
IRQ15	16	47
IOCHCK#	17	50
INTA#	18	53
INTB#	19	56
INTC#	20	59
INTD#	21	62
Unassigned	22 to 32	65 to 95

In addition to the 16 IRQ signals used by the old interrupt system, the PCI serialized interrupt scheme also carries data about the state of the system management interrupt (SMI#) and the I/O check (IOCHCK#) signals as well as the 4 native PCI interrupts and 10 unassigned values that may be used by system designers. According to the serialized interrupt scheme, support for the last 14 frames is optional.

The IRQSER cycle ends with a stop signal, a pulse of the IRQSER signal that lasts two or three PCI clocks, depending on the operating mode of the serialized interrupt system.

The PCI serialized interrupt system is only a means of data transportation. It carries the information across the PCI bus and delivers it to the microprocessor and its support circuitry. The information about the old IRQ signals gets delivered to a conventional 8259A interrupt controller or its equivalent in the microprocessor support chipset. Once at the controller, the interrupts are handled conventionally.

Although the PCI interrupt-sharing scheme helps eliminate setup problems, some systems demonstrate their own difficulties. For example, some PCs force the video and audio systems to share interrupts. Any video routine that generates an interrupt, such as scrolling a window, will briefly halt the playing of audio. The audio effects can be unlistenable. The cure is to reassign one of the interrupts, if your system allows it.

Direct Memory Access

The best way to speed up system performance is to relieve the host microprocessor of all its housekeeping chores. Among the more time-consuming is moving blocks of memory around inside the computer—for instance, shifting bytes from a hard disk (where they are stored) through its controller into main memory (where the microprocessor can use it). Today's system designs allow PCs to delegate this chore to support chips and expansion boards (for example, through bus mastering). Before such innovations, when the microprocessor was in total control of the PC, engineers developed Direct Memory Access technology, or DMA, to relieve the load on the microprocessor by allowing a special device called the *DMA controller* to manage some device-to-memory transfers. DMA was an integral part of the ISA bus design. Even though PCI lacks DMA features and soon PCs will entirely lack ISA slots, DMA technology survives in motherboard circuitry and the ATA disk interface. Consequently, the DMA function has been carried through into modern chipsets.

DMA functions through the DMA controller. This specialized chip only needs to know the base location of where bytes are to be moved from, the address to where they should go, and the number of bytes to move. Once it has received that information from the microprocessor, the DMA controller takes command and does all the dirty work itself. DMA operations can be used to move data between I/O devices and memory. Although DMA operations could in theory also expedite the transfer of data between memory locations, this mode of operation was not implemented in PCs.

Assignments

As with other aspects of circuit design, the model for the DMA systems for modern PCs dates back to the first IBM design, carried forward for compatibility reasons. The basic design affords four separate DMA channels, each one eight bits wide, which could be used independently for memory moves. The original design reserved one of these channels for refreshing system memory. The other three channels were made available on the ISA bus.

The current DMA system offers seven channels, based on the design IBM adopted for its Personal Computer AT in 1984. As with the interrupt system, IBM essentially doubled the available DMA channels by grafting in a second DMA controller cascaded through one of the channels of the original controller. In addition, IBM increased the bus width of the DMA system to 16 bits, although it maintained compatibility with 8-bit operation of the original channels.

Over the years, various system designs have suffered quirks that have limited the usefulness of the DMA system. For example, many early machines limited the reach of the DMA system to the lowest 16 megabytes of system memory. Moreover, the implementation of DMA in many systems (such as the prototypical IBM AT) proved marginal, so slow that many systems abandoned DMA for disk transfers. Today, however, DMA technology gives ATA interface hard disk drives their faster transfer modes.

Modern PCs use chipset circuits to emulate the function of the two DMA chips used in classic system architecture, although they often implement all 7 channels with 16-bit capabilities. Table 6.5 summarizes the functions that are commonly assigned to the seven DMA channels.

TABLE 6.5 DMA Assignments of a Modern Motherboard

DMA Channel	Data Width	Function
0	8 or 16 bits	Audio
1	8 or 16 bits	Audio or LAN
2	8 or 16 bits	Floppy disk
3	8 or 16 bits	ECP/EPP port
4	16 bits	Cascade channel
5	16 bits	Not assigned
6	16 bits	Not assigned
7	16 bits	ISA IDE

If you are curious, Windows 95 or 98 will show you the DMA channel assignments in actual use by your PC. To determine your PC's assignments, check with Device Manager by selecting the System icon in Control Panel. Select your Computer on the Device Manager tab and then click on the Properties button. From the View Resources screen that pops up, select the Direct Memory Access (DMA) radio button and you'll see your PC's current DMA assignments listed (see Figure 6.2).

In general, individual tasks use only one DMA channel at a time. When you run multiple tasks at the same time, nothing changes under Windows 95 or 98. Because they used serialized I/O, those operating systems handle only one I/O task at a time and then go on to the next. In effect, only a single path for data is available. Only in rare instances will that path have a DMA channel at both ends (which puts two channels into operation simultaneously). Windows NT and 2000 know no such limits and can run multiple I/O tasks and use multiple DMA channels.

FIGURE 6.2

Windows 95 and 98 Device Manager showing DMA usage.

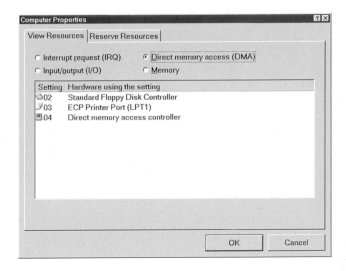

The DMA circuitry has long been plagued with minor problems. A few very early PCs had defective DMA chips (type 8237A) that only allowed one of their DMA channels to work at a time and would not run some backup programs properly. Modern PCs that emulate the 8237A in their chipsets don't suffer such problems. The NEC 765 floppy disk controller and some chipsets that use its design for integral floppy disk control without added data buffering can sometimes lose a byte of data because of a flaw in its DMA timing.

Distributed DMA Support

As with the lack of old-fashioned IRQ signals, the lack of dedicated DMA signals in the PCI design poses a problem for compatibility with devices that demand it. Consequently, the same companies that developed the serialized interrupt system also developed and published a means of implementing DMA in PCI systems called *distributed DMA support for PCI systems.*

The technique relies on circuitry built into the PCI bridge with the host microprocessor that functions as a *DMA master.* When a program or the operating system requests a DMA transfer, the DMA master intercepts the signal. It translates the commands bound for the 8237A DMA controller in older PCs into signals compatible with the PCI design. These signals are routed through the PCI bus to a DMA slave, which may in turn be connected to the ISA compatibility bus, PCMCIA bus, disk drives, or I/O ports in the system. The DMA slave interprets the instructions from the DMA master and carries them out as if it were an ordinary DMA controller.

In other words, to your software the DMA master looks like a pair of 8237A DMA controller chips. Your hardware sees the DMA slave as a 8237A that's in control. The signal translations to make this mimicry possible are built into the PCI bridges in the chipset.

Bus Interface

In early PCs, simple conversion circuitry—demultiplexing and buffering—linked the microprocessor to the expansion bus. As bus designs have become more sophisticated, however, managing the bus has become a full-time job, one that would substantially drain performance available to other tasks. Designers have consequently shifted the task to dedicated chips called *bus controllers* and from them to the integrated chipset. Chapter 7, "The Expansion Bus," covers the intimate details of bus operation.

The *PCI bridge* in the chipset handles all the functions of the PCI bus. Systems that retain ISA slots for compatibility purposes control them through their south bridge chip.

Power Management

To economize on power to meet Energy Star standards or prolong the period of operation on a single battery charge, most chipsets—especially those designed for notebook PCs—incorporate power management abilities. These include both manual power control that lets you slow your PC or suspend its operation and automatic control that reduces power similarly should you not actively work on your system for a predetermined period.

Typically, when a chipset switches to standby state, it will instruct the microprocessor to shift to its low-power mode, spin down the hard disk, and switch off the monitor. In standby mode, the chipset itself stays in operation to monitor for alarms, communications requests (answering the phone or receiving a fax), and network accesses. In suspend mode, the chipset itself shuts down until you reactivate it, and your PC goes into a vegetative state.

By design, most new chipsets conform to a variety of standards. They take advantage of the System Management Mode of recent Intel microprocessors and use interrupts to direct the power conservation. They should also conform to the latest version of the Advanced Power Management standard, version 1.1. (See "Advanced Power Management" in Chapter 24, "Power.")

Memory Control

At one time, attaching memory to a microprocessor required only the memory chips themselves and an address decoder to translate the microprocessor's addressing method into a form compatible with the chips. The memory system of a modern PC is more like a ShopMate or food processor with accessories sticking out all over. The chipset must handle not only addressing but also memory refreshing, cache updating, and whatever errors may pop up.

Because memory is one of the major determinants of the performance of a modern PC, the chipset choice has become critical. The better it handles memory—for example, the better its caching control and its interface with high-speed memory technologies—the more speed you'll get from your PC.

Again, some chipsets put all memory functions in one package, whereas others split them into two or more chips. In the Intel's first Pentium Pro chipsets, for example, one or more *Data Path* chips (abbreviated as TDP by Intel) such as the 82438FX provide most memory buffering functions, whereas the system controller (a TSC such as the 82437FX) handles multiplexing and cache management.

Addressing

To a microprocessor, accessing memory couldn't be simpler. It just needs to activate the proper combination of address lines to indicate a storage location and then read its contents or write a new value. The address is a simple binary code that uses the available address lines, essentially a 64-bit code with a Pentium-level microprocessor.

Unfortunately, the 64-bit code of the microprocessor is completely unintelligible to memory chips and modules. Semiconductor makers design their memory chips so that they will fit any application no matter the addressing of the microprocessor or even whether they link to a microprocessor. Chips, with a few megabytes of storage at most, have no need for gigabyte addressability. They need only a sufficient number of addresses to put their entire contents—and nothing more—on line.

Translating between the addresses and storage format used by a microprocessor and the format used by memory chips and modules is the job of the *memory decoder*. This chip or, in the case of chipsets, function determines not only the logical arrangement of memory but also how much and what kind of memory that a PC can use.

The memory functions of modern chipsets determine the basic timing of the memory system, controlling which signals in the memory system are active at each instant for any given function. The ability to adjust these timing values determines the memory technology that a PC can use. For example, early chipsets timed their signals to match page-mode memory chips. Modern chipsets can handle fast page mode, EDO, enhanced EDO, and often synchronous DRAM memory technologies.

The chipset also determines support of burst transfers between memory and the microprocessor, which can have a large effect on overall memory performance. Newer chipsets allow the microprocessor to take advantage of pipelined bursts, for example, reducing 8-3-3-3 page-hit burst reads (that's 17 clock cycles to read 32 bytes) to 2-2-2-2 pipelined reads (8 cycles for 32 bytes) with EDO memory.

Although the number of sockets for memory modules sets the practical limit for memory capacity in most PCs, the real upper limit is usually set by the memory function of the chipset. Although any Intel-architecture microprocessor from the 386 onward can address up to four gigabytes of physical memory, most chipsets constrain total system capacity to lower values. The typical limit of most modern chipsets is 512 megabytes, for example, at six 64-bit banks of 16MB memory modules. Fortunately, that's well above the amount of memory that's practical or affordable to install in a desktop PC—at least this month.

Refreshing

Housekeeping for dynamic RAM chips or modules means periodically refreshing each memory cell, rewriting the charges so that they can endure for a few more microseconds. The task is not difficult but necessary.

Getting the most from the latest new memory technologies requires some sophistication in refreshing. For example, a chipset that allows for hidden refresh operations (see Chapter 4, "Memory") can eke an extra few percent of performance from the memory system. Chipsets designed for suspend mode with DRAM chips must somehow continue to keep memory fresh. Many opt for *self-refresh* that allows the memory to be refreshed without intervention by the microprocessor.

Error Handling

One of the big differences between so-called home and business chipsets is the way they handle memory errors. Home machines don't need the utmost in reliability in their memory systems—or at least the chipset makers seem to believe—so they can get along with even basic parity checking. Not only does this simplify the design of the chipset, albeit trivially, but it more importantly saves on the cost of memory because there's no need for the extra parity bit or the memory to store it. For example, Intel's 430VX Pentium chipset designed for home use and other less demanding applications does not support parity. Business machines—which for many chipset makers means a PC that may act as a server—require the utmost in memory integrity, so chipsets for these machines accommodate error correction codes. Intel's high-end Pentium chipset, the 430HX, incorporates ECC.

Caching

Depending on the microprocessor, a chipset may be called upon to control the secondary memory cache. All Intel chips introduced before the Pentium Pro required a separate cache controller, which was often part of the chipset. Both the secondary cache and its controller are built into all current models of the Pentium Pro. The chipset in part determines the technologies used in the secondary cache, which can have a dramatic effect on performance. Ultimate control of technology is, however, in the hands of the system designer because he may choose not to use the most advanced features of a given chipset, for example, if he has qualms about the reliability of unfamiliar features or should he want to distinguish various models in a product line.

The chipset is one factor that can determine the ultimate size of the secondary cache. Most chipsets allow for caches in the range of 64KB to 512KB with the latest chips having capacities of 2MB or more of fast static RAM.

The chipset also determines the write policies available to the system designer. The latest chipsets make all the standard cache types—write-through, write-back, and adaptive write-back—programmable. Other factors controlled (or limited) by the chipset include the option of using burst, synchronous, or pipelined SRAM technologies for the secondary cache. The best chipsets make all of these options available to the system designer.

Peripheral Control

Communicating with other devices is an essential need of a PC. After all, if a PC has no way of getting information or sending it out, it would be no more help around your office than a rock or insurance salesman. Because of the need for making connections, even the earliest chipsets included some form of peripheral control. Their silicon included circuitry to link signals to an expansion bus. Some even went so far as to include port circuitry and floppy disk controllers. As PC makers have sought to better integrate their systems—to make them smaller and not incidentally cheaper—chipset makers have shoehorned an ever-increasing range of peripheral control functions into their products.

These peripheral control functions need not reside in a single chip. In the latest Intel chipsets, for example, a *PCI ISA/IDE accelerator* chip (abbreviated as PIIX by Intel) such as the 82371FX provides control of the expansion buses and hard disk interface. A separate ASIC, not part of the Intel PCI product line per se, takes care of the serial and parallel ports, keyboard, and floppy disk control functions. Many motherboards manufactured by Intel in fact use the National Semiconductor PC87306B super I/O controller for these functions as well as the system real-time clock and CMOS configuration memory. Intel essentially designed around the PC87306B chip when crafting its PIIX. Together, they encapsulate all the common peripheral control functions of a complete PC—the bus interface, hard and floppy disk controllers, keyboard interface, and I/O port circuitry.

Hard Disk Interface

Most modern chipsets include all the circuitry needed to connect a hard disk to a PC, typically following the enhancement of the AT Attachment standard such as UDMA. Although this interface is a straightforward extension of the classic ISA bus, it requires a host of control ports for its operation, all provided for in the chipset.

As the standard has developed, chipset makers have been hard-pressed to keep up. Only the newest chipsets support all of the advanced modes and highest potential performance levels of the interface. In general, the highest ATA mode number offers the best performance (see Chapter 9, "Storage Interfaces"), and the latest chipsets go as high as a 33MB/sec peak transfer rate in their UDMA modes. Better chipsets make the hard disk a bus master. (Look for an integrated bus master IDE controller in the chipset.)

Even when a PC designer puts SCSI support on a motherboard, the port design almost always relies on a dedicated SCSI control chip rather than direct chipset support. To take advantage of the highest speed SCSI options, however, the chipset must be capable of dealing with the most recent DMA standard. In particular, systems designed for heavy multimedia use should have Type F DMA support for highest speed audio and video data streaming.

Floppy Disk Controller

Chipsets often include a variety of other functions to make the PC designer's life easier. These can include everything from controls for indicator lights for the front panel to floppy disk controllers. Nearly all chipsets incorporate circuitry that mimics the NEC 765 floppy disk controller used by nearly all adapter boards. Newer chipsets should also include support for 2.88MB floppies.

In that the basic floppy disk interface dates back to the dark days of the first PCs, it is a technological dinosaur. PC makers desperately want to eliminate it in favor of more modern (and faster) interface alternatives. Some software, however, attempts to control the floppy disk by reaching deep into the hardware and manipulating the floppy controller directly through its powers. To maintain backward compatibility with new floppy interfaces, the chipset must still mimic this original controller and translate commands meant for it to the new interface.

Keyboard Controller

One additional support chip is necessary in every PC, a keyboard decoder. This special purpose chip, an Intel 8042 in most PCs, an equivalent chip, or part of a chipset that emulates an 8042, links the keyboard to the motherboard. The primary function of the keyboard decoder is to translate the serial data that the keyboard sends out into the parallel form that can be used by your PC. As it receives each character from the keyboard, the keyboard decoder generates an interrupt to make your PC aware you have typed a character. The keyboard decoder also verifies that the character was correctly received (by performing a parity check) and translates the scan code of each character. The keyboard decoder automatically requests the keyboard to retransmit characters that arrive with parity errors.

Each character in the serial data stream sent to the keyboard decoder comprises 11 bits—a start bit, 8 bits of data, a parity bit, and a stop bit. The bits are synchronized to a clock signal originating inside the keyboards. In AT and more recent keyboards, the keyboard decoder can also send data to the keyboard to program its internal microprocessor. (Keyboards and scan codes are discussed more completely in Chapter 14, "Input Devices.")

USB-based keyboards promise the elimination of the keyboard decoder or controller. These pass packets of predigested keyboard data through the USB port of your PC instead of through a dedicated keyboard controller. In modern system design, the keyboard controller is thus a legacy device and may be eliminated from new systems over the next few years.

Input/Output Ports

Most modern chipset makers offer full-featured products that include floppy disk control circuitry, input/output ports (parallel, serial, mouse, keyboard, and game ports), and a connector for an embedded controller (IDE) hard disk. Some chipset manufacturers incorporate video (VGA) circuitry into their products as well.

If you are buying rather than designing a PC, you may find no particular advantage in the extreme integration of today's single-chip PCs. Although a single-chip solution is, in theory, more reliable than a three-chip PC, the difference may be between whether the machine ultimately fails when your great-great grandchildren are playing with the system or when their children are reveling in the primitive glory of playing with an ancient PC. Probably the only important support circuit issue to ponder when purchasing a new PC is whether port, video, and floppy disk control circuitry on the motherboard can be defeated to eliminate I/O and interrupt conflicts with other expansion products. Most modern PCs let you setup or defeat these ports through their setup procedure. You may want to run through the system setup and configuration procedure when you're trying out a PC before you buy it. You'll get a good view of what's there and what you can do with it. (IDE ports don't need defeatability because an unused IDE port acts as an expansion connector with nothing plugged in.) Other support chip issues represent only different paths to the same destination.

If a system doesn't have the right combination of support circuitry, it simply won't work like a PC. And if it has the right support circuitry, all you need is exactly what you should expect—a trouble-free PC that runs your favorite programs.

CHAPTER

7

The Expansion Bus

Your PC's expansion bus allows your system to grow. It provides a high-speed connection for internal peripherals that enhance the capabilities of your PC. Standardized buses spawned an entire industry dedicated to making interchangeable PC expansion boards. Today, PC makers are cutting the last ties with the past and, after nearly 20 years, foregoing the original PC expansion bus called ISA for a faster, more versatile (and more complex) standard for today and the immediate future, termed PCI.

Expansion buses have followed many standards. The most important of these include (roughly in order of importance):

Bus-style Expansion

Standard	Also Known As	In short
PCI	Peripheral Component Interconnect	The main expansion bus in modern PCs. PCI slots allow you to slide in almost any expansion board into your PC.
AGP	Accelerated Graphics Port	Provides a higher speed link to your PC's graphic display system. AGP lets your PC display data up to eight times faster than through PCI.
ISA	Industry Standard Architecture	Slots that follow the old expansion standard and allow you to use legacy boards in your newer PC—for example, to accommodate old boards for which there is no modern high-speed alternative.
EISA	Enhanced Industry Standard Architecture	A faster, wider form of ISA that has been superceded by PCI but may still be found in older servers.
MCA	Micro Channel Architecture	IBM's proprietary improvement on ISA that paved the way for new bus designs but had little market impact.
VL Bus	VESA Local Bus	An extension of ISA designed to make video systems (primarily) faster but was quickly overtaken by industry acceptance of PCI as the high-speed standard.

Card-style Expansion

Standard	Also Known As	In Short
PC Card	PC Card	Puts ISA expansion on a credit-card size module that's chiefly used in older notebook PCs.
CardBus	CardBus	Puts PCI-style expansion on a credit-card size module that's the standard among modern notebook PCs.
CompactFlash	CompactFlash	A miniaturized version of PC Card optimized for flash memory that's popular in digital cameras.
SmartMedia	Solid State Floppy Disk	A tiny package that lets you interchange flash memory chips like expansion cards that's popular with some digital cameras.

PCs earn their versatility with their expansion slots. By sliding the appropriate board into a slot, you can make your PC into anything you want it to be—within reason, of course. You can't expect to turn your PC into a flying boat, but a video production system, international communications center, cryptographic analyzer, or medical instrument interface are all easily within the range of possibilities. Even if your aims are more modest, you'll need to become familiar with expansion slots. All of the most common options for customizing your PC—modems, network interface cards, and television tuners—easily slide into slots.

Nothing is magical about expansion slots. A slot is just a space for the board. The real power for pushing the capabilities of your system comes from the connections provided by the slot—the *expansion bus*, the electrical connector sitting at the bottom of the slot. The expansion bus is your PC's electrical umbilical, a direct connection with the PC's logical circulatory system that allows whatever expansion brainchild you have to link to your system.

The purpose of the expansion bus is straightforward: It enables you to plug things into the machine and enhance the PC's operation. The buses themselves, however, are not quite so simple. Buses are much more than simple electrical connections like you make when plugging in a lamp. Through the bus circuits, your PC transfers not only electricity but also information. Like all the data your PC must deal with, that information is defined by a special coding in the sequence and pattern of digital bits.

The bus connection must flawlessly transfer that data. To prevent mistakes, every bus design also includes extra signals to control the flow of that information. Adjust its rate to accommodate the speed limits of your PC and its expansion accessories, and adjust the digital pattern itself to match design variations.

Different buses each take their own approach to the signals required for control and translation, and these design variations govern how your computer can grow. Some use extra hardware signals to control transfers across the bus. Others use extensive signaling systems that package information into blocks or packets and route them across the bus by adding addresses and identification bytes to each block.

Bus standards define how your PC and its expansion board negotiate all the transfers across the bus. As a result, the standard that your PC's bus follows is a primary determinant of what enhancement products work with it—whether they are compatible. The design of the expansion bus also sets certain limits on how the system performs and what its ultimate capabilities can be.

Today's preferred computer configuration includes two expansion buses, a *high-speed* bus for expanding your system with modern peripherals and a *compatibility* bus that accommodates older add-in devices, such as those carried over from an old PC when you upgrade to a new system. Nearly all modern desktop PCs follow the Peripheral Component Interconnect, or PCI, standard for their high-speed expansion slots. Systems that retain a compatibility bus generally use slots designed to ISA, or Industry Standard Architecture. In addition, most new PCs have a special PCI slot designed for video boards called an Accelerated Graphics Port.

Major industry influences—Intel and Microsoft, for two—are working hard to exterminate the compatibility bus. Already PCs have shifted from a balance between high-speed and compatibility buses to systems with a single compatibility slot. Soon, new PCs will entirely lack a compatibility bus—and that's not necessarily a bad thing. Configuring boards that slide into compatibility slots has been the biggest bugaboo in customizing and upgrading PCs. Eliminating the old slots eliminates most PC setup problems.

Although the two major buses inside today's desktop PCs share basic similarities—the qualities that make them buses at all—they operate quite differently. The differences result from the major changes in technology and philosophy that have swept through the PC industry in the last couple of decades. ISA is a minimalist design, reflecting the state of technology in the age in which it was created. PCI incorporates all the advances made in the ensuing years, its complex circuit requirements made possible by modern semiconductor technology. We'll discuss the two separately, leading off with ISA because of its simpler, more easily understood design.

Notebooks PCs have their own style of expansion slots that use PC Cards rather than expansion boards. These slots follows the standards set by the Personal Computer Memory Card Industry Association (PCMCIA). The basic PC Card design allows for performance and operation patterned after the ISA design. CardBus slots expand on that basic design with PCI-style bus connections. Obsolescence is not an issue with card slots, however. CardBus slots are backward compatible: A CardBus slot will accept either a CardBus or PC Card expansion card (with one exception) so your old cards will happily work even in the newest of PCs.

Unlike those of desktop computers, the slots of notebook machines are externally accessible; you don't have to open up the PC to add an expansion board. External upgrades are, in fact, a necessity for notebook computers in that cracking open the case of a portable computer is about as messy as opening an egg and, for most people, is an equally irreversible process. In addition, both the PC Card and CardBus standards allow for hot-swapping. That is, you can plug in and unplug boards that follow either standard while the electricity is on to your PC and the machine is running. The expansion slots inside desktop PCs generally do not allow for hot-swapping.

CompactFlash cards shrink the PC Card design to less than half its size to fit miniaturized devices. Even so, CompactFlash cards are electrically and logically (though not physically) compatible with the PC Card standard. We'll examine the small alternatives after the basic buses—and after a short ramble through bus background and history.

Background

Although the concept of an expansion bus is simple—extend and link the signals of your system to new devices—practical expansion buses are not. Each one represents a complex set of design choices confined by practical constraints. Designers make many of the choices by necessity; others they pick pragmatically. The evolution of the modern expansion bus has been mostly a matter of building upon the ideas that came before (or stealing the best ideas of the predecessors). The result in today's PCs is a high-performance PCI upgrade system that minimizes (but has yet to eliminate) setup woes.

Not all buses share the same capabilities because they may be designed for different purposes and systems. Special applications have spawned bus alternatives—PCIX for servers, CompactPCI for rugged systems, and CompactFlash for digital cameras.

The range of bus functions and resources is wide. The most important of these is providing a data pathway that links the various components of your PC together. It must provide both the channel through which the data moves and a means of assuring the data gets where it is meant to go. In addition, the expansion bus must provide special signals to synchronize the thoughts of the add-in circuitry with those of the rest of the computer. Newer bus designs (for example, PCI but not ISA) also include means of delegating system control to add-in products and tricks for squeezing extra speed from data transfers.

Although not part of the electrical operation of the expansion bus, the physical dimensions of the boards and other components are also often governed by agreed-on expansion bus specifications. Moreover, today's bus standards go far beyond merely specifying signals. They also dictate transfer protocols and integrated, often automated, configuration systems.

How these various bus features work—and how well they work—depends on the specific features of each bus design. In turn, the expansion bus design exerts a major influence on the overall performance of the PC it serves. Bus characteristics also determine what you can add to your PC—how many expansion boards, how much memory, what other system components—and how easy your system is to set up. The following sections examine the features and functions of all expansion buses, the differences among them, and the effects of those differences in the performance and expandability of your PC.

Data Lines

The most important function of any expansion bus, indeed the defining characteristic of a bus, is the capability to share information between the computer host and the expansion accessories. The bus must provide the connections needed for moving data between the add-in circuits and the microprocessor and the rest of the computer.

The connections that carry data across the expansion bus are termed *data lines*. The fundamental factor in describing an expansion bus is thus the number of data lines it provides. More is always better, although adding more beyond the number of data connections on the host microprocessor adds little but undue complexity.

Although the information could be transferred either by serial or parallel means, the expansion buses inside PCs use parallel data transfers. The choice of the parallel design is a natural. All commercial microprocessors have parallel connections for their data transfers. The reason for this choice in microprocessors and buses is exactly the same: Parallel transfers are faster. Multiple connections means that the system can move multiple bits every clock cycle. The more bits that the bus can pass in a single cycle, the faster it will move information. Wider buses—those with more parallel connections—are faster, all else being equal.

Ideally, the expansion bus should provide a data path that matches that of the microprocessor. That way, an entire digital quad-word used by today's Pentium-class microprocessors—a full 64 bits—can stream across the bus without the need for data conversions. When the bus is narrower than a device that sends or receives the signals, the data must be repackaged for transmission; the PC might have to break a quad-word into four sequential words or eight bytes to fit an old 16- or 8-bit bus. Besides the obvious penalty of requiring multiple bus cycles to move the data the microprocessor needs, a narrow bus also makes system design more complex. Circuitry to handle the required data repackaging complicates both motherboards and expansion boards.

On the other hand, increasing the number of data connections also complicates the design of a PC if only because of the extra space and materials that are required. Finding the optimal number of connections for a given application consequently is a tradeoff between speed (which requires more connections) and complexity (which increases with connection count and thus speed).

In modern PCs with multiple expansion buses, each bus usually has a different number of data connections, reflecting the speed requirements of each bus. The bus with the highest performance demands—the memory bus—has the most connections. The bus with the least performance demands—the compatibility bus—has the fewest.

Address Lines

As long as a program knows what to do with data, a bus can transfer information without reference to memory addresses. Having address information available, however, increases the flexibility of the bus. For example, making addressing available on the bus enables you to add normal system memory on expansion boards. Addressing allows memory-mapped information transfers and random access to information. It allows data bytes to be routed to the exact location at which they will be used or stored. Imagine the delight of the dead letter office of the post office and the ever-increasing stack of stationery accumulating there if everyone decided that appending addresses to envelopes was superfluous. Similarly, expansion boards must be able to address origins and destinations for data. The easiest method of doing this is to provide address lines on the expansion bus corresponding to those of the microprocessor.

As with microprocessor address lines, those of the bus determine the maximum memory range addressable by the bus. Usually, a computer bus provides the full range of address lines used by a PC's host microprocessor. Some buses shortchange on the number of address lines. When the addresses not included are those at the top of the range (the most significant bits of each address), this strategy puts some addresses off limits to expansion boards. For example, the ISA compatibility bus has only 24 address lines, which allows it to address only 16MB of memory. Because of the lack of high-order address lines on the bus, a modern microprocessor with 32 or 36 address lines (which includes anything from an ancient 386DX to a Pentium III Xeon) still cannot access more than 16MB on the legacy bus. Any memory-mapped peripherals attached to the ISA bus must consequently locate their buffers within the lowest 16MB of the microprocessor, which can impose severe penalties on the host computer—such as the inability to use more than 16MB of memory for any purpose, effectively wasting 4,278,190,080 potential memory locations.

On the other hand, modern microprocessors have no need to address every individual byte. They swallow data in 32- or 64-bit chunks—that is, double-words or quad-words. They do not have to be able to address memory any more specifically than every fourth or eighth byte. When they do need to retrieve a single byte, they just grab a whole double-word or quad-word at once and sort out what they need internally. Consequently, most 32-bit expansion buses designed to accommodate these chips commonly delete the two least significant address bits. Although they have only 30 address lines, they can access the full 4GB range used by microprocessors with 32-bit addressing. Buses with 64 data lines can similarly omit the four least significant address lines, although most don't because they are simply extensions of 32-bit buses. Certainly, omitting two (or four) address lines limits how precisely memory can be identified, but that degree of precision is unnecessary with a wide bit data bus.

Even in writing to memory, the bus simply does not need to be more specific. Using a technique called *masking*, a wide chip can limit its writing to one or more bytes at one of the 32- or 64-bit locations it can address. It masks off all the bytes it doesn't want to change just as a painter lays masking tape over edges he wants to keep sharp.

Memory is not the only thing that needs to be addressed. Accessing input/output ports also requires the use of address lines for access. In that the Intel microprocessor design only allows for 65,536 I/O ports using 16-bit addressing, any modern expansion bus would seem to be able to handle the challenge with little difficulty. Back in the early days of PCs, however, engineers didn't think they needed to access all those ports. They saved a few cents by designing expansion boards to only decode 10 bits of I/O port addresses. As a result, each board was limited to 1,024 potential port addresses. Although all modern expansion bus specifications require the decoding of all 16 bits of I/O addresses, the ISA compatibility bus is stuck with the 10-bit limit. Longer addresses would be ambiguous to boards with 10-bit decoding, so they are off limits to ISA to maintain backward compatibility. After all, a compatibility bus that doesn't offer full compatibility doesn't have much of a reason for existence.

The number of data and address lines can become prodigious, and for technical and practical reasons, engineers prefer to minimize the number of physical connections on expansion buses. A common strategy for reducing the connection count is *multiplexing*. In bus design, multiplexing means giving a set of connections more than one function. Typically, the bus uses the same connections for data and address information. These designs use a special signal to indicate which kind of information the combined data-and-address connections carry. In one state, the signal says the computer and expansion boards should interpret the bus signals as addresses. In the other state, the signal says to treat the signals as data. With a typical system with 32 address lines and 32 data lines, this strategy can save 31 connections—adding one control signal while eliminating 32 others. The PCI bus uses multiplexing. ISA does not.

Power Distribution

Although all electrical devices need some source of electricity to operate, no immutable law requires an expansion bus to provide that power. For example, when you plug a printer into your PC, you also usually plug the printer into a wall outlet. Similarly, expansion boards could have their own sources of needed electricity. Providing that power on the expansion bus makes the lives of engineers much easier. They don't have to worry about the design requirements, metaphysics, or costs of adding power sources such as solar panels, magnetohydrodynamic generators, or cold fusion reactors to their products.

By today's conventions, most digital logic circuits require 5 or 3.3 volts of direct current to operate, so most expansion buses are designed to provide a copious flow at that potential. A few devices have more extensive requirements—for example, a negative 5-volt supply or 12 volts (positive and negative) for special functions—so some PC buses also make those voltages available. Some designs even make allowance for future voltage standards below 3.3 volts.

Older buses like ISA make no provision for the 3.3-volt logic used by low-power microprocessors and their associated circuitry. That omission doesn't make old buses totally incompatible with new logic because on-board voltage regulators can drop the off-board supply down to the right level.

All complete electrical circuits require two wires, one to send the power out from its source and a return line. For example, every battery has a positive and negative terminal, both of which must be connected to make electricity flow. In a personal computer, the return circuit for all power connections is the system *ground*, and all voltages on the expansion buses are referenced to ground. The positive 5-volt power conductor measures five volts higher than ground potential. The negative five-volt power conductor measures five volts lower than ground. Consequently, the difference between the plus 5 and minus 5-volt conductors on a personal computer expansion bus is 10 volts.

All circuits inside a personal computer—both logic signals and power—share a common return line, the system ground. Although ground signals may appear several places on a bus connector, all are the same and are electrically linked together. These additional grounds serve two purposes. The multiple connections allow greater current handling; two wires can carry more current than one. In addition, the arrangement of signals helps minimize the interaction of signals. A ground line interposed between two signal lines absorbs noise signals that attempt to cross it. This reduction of interference helps engineers increase bus speeds.

The reason ground is called "ground" dates back to the earliest days of electrical discovery. The earliest communication system—the telegraph—often used only one wire for its signal. The other side of the connection was connected to the earth—the ground—which served as the return path. Soil conducts electricity well enough for such designs to work. Although the ground signals used in computer circuits rarely get connected to the earth, the computer chassis is supposed to link to electrical ground through the third prong of the power plug (and this ground is connected with the actual earth *somewhere*).

Sometimes, expansion buses also have multiple power leads for a given voltage. Again, the multiple leads increase current capacity. Because they offer a low resistance signal pathway, power leads can also provide shielding similar to that of interposed ground lines.

Timing

Expansion cards are like children: They can be totally independent like the kids who go their own way and only choose to drop a card to the parents at the odd moments that financial need arises, or they can be completely committed like kids who live at home and keep their lives in lockstep with father and mother and their bank balance. Many tightly coupled expansion boards are designed to operate in lockstep with the circuitry of their computer hosts. Such a bus is synchronized to the clock of its host and is described as a *synchronous* expansion bus. To keep the circuitry on the expansion board synchronized with the rest of the system, the host provides a system clock signal on the expansion bus.

The purest example of a synchronous expansion bus is that of the original IBM PC. The clock that controls the PC bus operates at exactly the same speed as the one that operates the microprocessor. In fact, it is exactly the same clock, controlled by the same vibrating quartz crystal.

This design was short-lived because microprocessor speeds soon raced ahead of the capabilities of expansion bus and boards. To allow the bus to operate at a speed compatible with slower expansion boards in a system with a fast microprocessor, designers added a new synchronizing signal, the *bus clock*. This signal provides a reference frequency to expansion boards that may or may not be the same speed as the clock that runs the microprocessor.

In the original design using a separate bus clock—what has now become ISA—the bus was still synchronized with the microprocessor, but the bus speed was a sub-multiple of the microprocessor speed. Despite the different speeds, engineers retain the term "synchronous" for such designs because the signals remain locked together. Synchronous operation simplifies system design because all timing signals are automatically in alignment; they start together. No additional circuits or processing is required to match microprocessor cycles to bus cycles.

Most advanced expansion buses are designed with even greater speed flexibility. By incorporating special circuitry to negotiate data transfers, holding back data until the host system is at the right instant in its clock cycle to receive it, expansion boards can run any speed the system designer wants. Called *asynchronous* expansion buses because the system and bus clocks are not locked together, these designs still require bus clock signals, although the bus clock frequency need have no mathematical relationship to the system clock. The penalty for this flexibility is complexity. Asynchronous designs require more circuitry, for example, to hold data delivered by the system bus at the start of one of its cycles until the bus begins one of *its* cycles. Fortunately, modern technology has shrunk all the required circuit components onto a single ASIC (Application-Specific Integrated Circuit) and made asynchronous buses both practical and affordable. Microprocessor-independent expansion buses generally operate asynchronously to allow full flexibility in the choice host microprocessor.

Although modern expansion buses are designed to be able to operate asynchronously, they are often set to run at a sub-multiple of the microprocessor's speed. Although the PCI bus sometimes ran as 30MHz or even 25MHz in some systems with earlier microprocessors, in modern PCs it invariably runs at 33MHz, one half the front-side bus of a Celeron or Pentium II running slower than 400MHz or one third of a Pentium III or a Pentium II at 40MHz or quicker. This synchronous operation makes the best match between bus and microprocessor cycles and optimizes transfer rate.

Some bus specifications set a fixed operating frequency (and thus speed) for a bus. For example, the ISA standard specifies a bus speed within a small range around 8MHz. Modern bus designs have more flexibility. PCI allows operation anywhere in the range from 0 to 33MHz. Lowering the bus speed or stopping the bus entirely saves power in portable applications.

Flow Control

Even when the operation of an expansion board is synchronized with its host PC, the board might not be able to keep up with the speed needs of the computer. For example, a serial board might be able to accept data at 1,000 characters per second while the computer is generating information a thousand times faster. If the PC pushes out all the data it makes as fast as it can, the serial board would soon be swamped with information. Bailing itself out would mean throwing away the data it was supposed to send. To avoid such data losses when a speed disparity arises between an expansion board and its host, most expansion buses include flow control signals. In the simplest form, the board sends a special "not ready" signal across the bus, warning the host to wait until the board catches up. Switching off "not ready" signals the host to dump more data on the board.

The original expansion bus design follows the microprocessor pattern for making data transfers. (After all, the original PC bus was simply a direct extension of the microprocessor.) Each transfer requires at least two clock cycles even without flow-control slowdowns. First, the microprocessor uses one clock cycle to signal what memory location is being addressed. Moving the data requires a second clock cycle. As a result, actual data throughput is less than half what the bus clock speed implies. This two-cycle-per-transfer mode holds one great advantage. Because each data transfer includes an individual address, it allows full random access. Any transfer can be made to or from any valid memory location. On the other hand, its one-move-in-two-cycles speed is inefficient.

When random access is not required, modern buses can switch into higher speed modes. Most microprocessors—and buses derived from them—use burst modes during which several data transfers occur after a single address cycle. Bus designs differ in how they control bursts and the lengths of bursts that they allow. Longer bursts involve less overhead and thus speed data transfers.

The basic burst mode used in modern bus design is patterned after that of the 486 microprocessor. A burst of the 486 comprises a single address cycle that is followed by four data cycles. Moving one line of data—four 32-bit double-words (16 bytes), the basic unit with which the 486 preferred to work—thus requires five clock cycles rather than eight, a performance boost of over 60 percent. All Pentium, Pentium II, and Pentium III microprocessor support this same 486 burst mode.

Advanced expansion buses extend burst-like transfers to longer blocks of data and work independently from the design of the host microprocessor. For example, in some designs a single address cycle can be followed by as many data cycles as can be pushed across the bus before some other system function (such as memory refreshing) requires access.

When moving large blocks of bytes, this kind of bursting can nearly double bus through-put. Its primary drawback is its capability to shift only contiguous, sequential data. It sac-rifices random access for speed.

All modern expansion buses have burst modes of some sort, although they sometimes give it another name. For example, IBM called the burst mode of its Micro Channel bus *streaming data mode*.

System Control

In a modern PC, peripherals often do more than shift information around. Many of them need to communicate with the host microprocessor, for example, to break into a running program when they have "hot" data that needs to be processed immediately, such as a byte waiting at an unbuffered serial port. The peripheral needs to be able to send interrupt sig-nals to the microprocessor to get its attention. All PC expansion buses have provisions for one or more interrupt signals for this purpose.

Early bus designs allowed a dedicated control line for each hardware interrupt that could be used by the bus. Even when all of the hardware interrupt signals of an Intel micro-processor are available on the bus, however, they are insufficient for the needs of a PC loaded with expansion boards. Consequently, modern PCs and expansion buses make pro-visions for *interrupt sharing*.

Some PC buses also make provisions for giving expansion boards control over the Direct Memory Access (DMA) controllers in the computer host. More recent bus designs do away with the DMA signals and rely on transfer protocols to control the DMA system.

An expansion bus may also have a number of other control signals. Most buses have a *reset* signal that tells the expansion boards to initialize themselves and reset their circuits to the same state as they would have when initially powering up. Buses may also have special sig-nals that indicate the number of data lines containing valid data during a transfer. Another signal may indicate whether the address lines hold a memory address or an I/O port address.

Bus Mastering and Arbitration

In the early days of PCs, the entire operation of the expansion bus was controlled by the microprocessor in the host computer. The bus was directly connected to the microproces-sor; in fact, the bus was little more than an extension of the connections on the chip itself. A bus connected directly to the microprocessor data and address lines is termed a local bus because it is meant to service only the components in the close vicinity of the micro-processor itself. However, another technology has usurped the "local bus" term, and in common parlance a local bus computer is generally one that has both a local bus-style expansion interface as well as other bus technologies.

Using this direct-connection design, the microprocessor in the computer controls every byte that's transferred. The microprocessor first reads the byte from one device or memory location and then writes it to another device or location. This style of operation is not only time-consuming but also monopolizes the microprocessor's time. For example, when the microprocessor wants to put a byte from one of its registers into memory, on one bus cycle it sends out the address to which it wants to send the data. The memory system then prepares that address to receive the data. On the next cycle, the microprocessor puts the bit values of the data on the bus, and the memory subsystem collects the bits and stores them in DRAM chips. The speed of this simple bus-transfer operation is governed by the bus speed, which is directly linked to the microprocessor speed. Most bus operations are not so simple, however. The microprocessor must go through gyrations of machine language instructions for every byte it transfers. This load gets dropped on the microprocessor whether it is the source or target of the bus transfers and even when the chip should have no need to get involved at all—for example, when bytes must move from hard disk to video memory to put a stored image on the monitor screen.

With slow microprocessors, the power of the microprocessor can limit the performance of bus transfers. With fast microprocessors, the need for the microprocessor to wait for the bus can slow the performance of the entire computer system.

The microprocessor need not be burdened with controlling the expansion bus, however. Just as an executive delegates all his work to underlings, a computer's microprocessor can delegate the control of the bus to special circuitry dedicated to the task. A Direct Memory Access, or DMA, controller does exactly that. But even with a DMA chip controlling the actual movement of data, often the microprocessor must set up and oversee the DMA transfers, tying up the chip throughout the bus transfer.

Newer buses break the direct microprocessor connection by vesting the authority to control bus transfers in special logic circuits—typically called *bus controllers*—to make an arbitrated expansion bus. In the arbitrated bus design, the microprocessor abdicates its all-powerful position and takes a place as an equal to the expansion boards in the system. Although the microprocessor still controls the bus transfers that it originates or receives, it need not become involved in transfers between other devices in the system.

A device that takes control of the expansion bus to mediate its own transfers is called a *bus master*. The device that receives the data from the master is termed the *bus slave*. Some systems use the names *initiator* and *target* for these functions.

The bus controller determines when and which master can take control of the bus, a process called *bus arbitration*. Each bus design uses its own protocol for controlling the arbitration process. This protocol can be software, typically using a set of commands across the bus like data, or hardware, using special dedicated control lines in the bus. Most practical PC bus designs use a hardware signaling scheme.

In the typical hardware-based arbitration system, a potential master indicates its need to take control of the bus by sending an attention signal on a special bus line. If several devices want to take control at the same time, an algorithm determines which competing master is granted control, how long that control persists, and when after losing control it can be granted to the same master again.

In software-based systems, the potential bus-master device sends a request to its host bus control logic. The host grants control by sending a special software command in return.

The design of the arbitration system usually has two competing goals, fairness and priority. *Fairness* assures that one device cannot monopolize the bus, that within a given period every device is given a crack at bus control. For example, some designs require that once a master has gotten control of the bus, it will not get a grant of control again until all other masters also seeking control have been served. *Priority* allows the system to act somewhat unfairly, and to give more of the bus to devices that need it more. Some bus designs forever fix the priorities of certain devices; others allow priorities of some or all masters to be programmed.

In the typical PC, these issues are immaterial. Rarely do they see so many competing bus requests that prioritizing will affect performance. Bus mastering will help overall performance simply by removing the bus from the host microprocessor's responsibility. The exact type of arbitration is immaterial—except to the bus design engineers who take delight in arguing such things at length.

Slot-Specific Signals

Buses are so named because their signals are "bused" together—that is, directly connected to one another with wiring, traditionally called bus wires in the electrical industry. In other words, pin one in every connector on the bus is linked to pin one in every other connector on the bus, and the signal that appears on any given pin number appears in all slots on exactly the same pin number. This design makes every slot equal and enables you to slide any expansion board into every slot.

This straightforward, straight-through design has a significant drawback: Communicating to an expansion board individually is difficult. Typically, some elaborate protocol is called for. The host must send a signal that switches off all but the desired card using some form of identification system.

A number of newer PC expansion buses include slot-specific signals that connect individually and uniquely to each slot. The host computer can use this signal to switch on or off features on individual cards or entire cards.

Most systems use only a single slot-specific signal on a dedicated pin (the same pin in each slot, but a different slot-specific signal on the pin in each slot). This slot-specific signaling is used chiefly during testing and setup. Each board can be individually activated for testing, and the board (or separately controllable parts) can be switched off if defective. Slot-specific signals also are used to poll expansion boards individually about their resource usage so that port and memory conflicts can be automatically managed by the host system. This automatic configuration simplifies system setup by eliminating the need to adjust DIP switches or jumpers on individual expansion boards.

Bridges

The modern PC with multiple buses—often operating with different widths and speeds—poses a problem for the system designer: How to link those buses together. Make a poor link-up, and performance will suffer on *all* the buses.

The bus-linking problem rose in prominence with the introduction of PCI. Central to the PCI architecture design was the solution, the *bridge*. In the PCI scheme of things, a bridge is a system building block designed to transport data from one bus to another bus. The bridge takes care of all the details of the transfer, converting data formats and protocols automatically without the need for special programming or additional hardware. The bridge itself can take the form of a standalone hardware element such as an ASIC, or it may be part of the chipset that makes up the fundamental PC circuitry.

A bridge can span buses that are similar or different. A PCI-based PC can readily incorporate any bus for which bridge hardware is available. For example, in a typical PCI system, bridges will link three dissimilar buses—the microprocessor bus, the high-speed PCI bus, and an ISA compatibility bus—and may additionally tie in another similar PCI bus to yield a greater number of expansion opportunities.

When a PCI bridge links to another PCI bridge, the result is called a PCI-to-PCI bridge, or PPB. This form of bridge is common because the PCI specification limits a single PCI bus to 10 loads. The number of loads adds up quickly because each PCI bus connector with a plugged-in expansion board constitutes two loads and a single-chip device connected to the bus is a single load. Most PCI buses are consequently limited to three or four expansion slots. Putting more slots in a given PC automatically requires a PPB.

In PCI architecture, bridges can be connected to bridges up to a maximum of 256 PCI buses in a single PC. For example, a designer can put a PCI bridge on a PCI expansion card to accommodate multiple expansion functions on the card.

The interconnected buses logically link together in the form of a family tree, spreading out as it radiates downward. The buses closer to the single original bus at the top are termed *upstream*. Those in the lower generations more distant from the progenitor bus are termed *downstream*. Bridge design allows data to flow from any location on the family tree to any other. However, because each bridge imposes a delay for its internal processing called *latency*, a transfer that must pass across many bridges suffers performance penalties. The penalties increase the further downstream the bus is located.

To avoid latency problems, when PCs have multiple PCI buses, they are usually arranged in a *peer bus* configuration. That is, instead of one bridge being connected to another, the two or three bridges powering the expansion buses in the PC are connected to a common point, either the PCI controller or the most upstream bridge.

Compatibility

The only reason ISA slots persist in PCs today is to allow you to plug in old, even ancient, expansion boards you already have into your spanking new PC. That's sort of like GM adding a coal bin to all of its new cars on the off chance someone might want to add in a steam engine. Anything you can do with a vintage ISA expansion board you can do with a new PCI board—and probably several times better. Plugging an old board into a new PC is less a way of prolonging your investment than it is prolonging your agony. Not only are old boards condemned by the design of the ISA bus to be slow, but they are also likely to be more troublesome to set up.

That said, you might want to retain an old board that has no higher speed equivalent because its performance is held back by some speed limit other than the bus. For example, no modem is going to stress the capabilities of an expansion bus because even the quickest modems cannot move data faster than 56,000 bits per second.

On the other hand, unless you're trying to keep alive an old PC that would benefit more from a visit from Jack Kevorkian than an upgrade, you should avoid any new expansion board that uses the ISA interface. Although you might be able to plug an ISA board into your current PC, your next computer is another matter. A board using an old bus is condemned to a short, painful life—a short stay on this mortal coil before obsolescence fetches it away, painful not to its unfeeling electronics but to your fragile human patience.

History

Expansion board technology is mature, at least for now. The necessary standards are in place and stable. You can take it for granted that you can slide a PCI expansion board in a PCI slot and have it automatically configure itself and operate in your PC. Most ISA boards slide in just as easily. You can even select from a wealth of PC Card and CardBus modules for your notebook PC—all without any concern about compatibility. Although those statements sound so obvious as to be trivial, reaching this point has been a long and interesting journey. The way has been marked with pragmatism and insight, cooperation and argument, even a major war between industry giants. At least nine major standards for PC expansion have been the result, as summarized in Table 7.1.

TABLE 7.1   Expansion Bus Standards

Name	Date	Bus Width	Clock Speed	Addressing
PC bus	1981	8 bits	4.77MHz	1MB
ISA	1984	16 bits	8MHz	16MB
Micro Channel	1987	16/32 bits	10MHz	16MB/4GB
EISA	1988	32 bits	8MHz	4GB
VL Bus	1992	32/64 bits	50MHz	4GB
PCI	1992	32/64 bits	33MHz	4GB
PCIX	1998	32/64 bits	66 or 133MHz	4GB
PC Card	1990	16 bits	8MHz	64MB
CardBus	1994	32 bits	33MHz	4GB

Pinpointing the origins of computer bus technology depends on the definition you choose. Early mainframe computers were massive entities made from many racks of equipment connected by snarls of cables. Through the expedience of plugging and unplugging subassemblies, you could add extra capabilities to the computer. You could consider those cables as rudimentary buses, but in the context of today's machines, the wires were more like the circuit board traces connecting one integrated circuit to another. After all, one of today's ICs performs many more functions than a whole rack of tube-based computer gear. Nor did the cables of the first mainframe computers enable you to add off-the-shelf components because each early mainframe was a unique machine.

Buses Before the PC

As mainframe computers matured, they developed into assemblies of identical parts connected in a bus-like structure. But what's usually considered the first computer bus appeared in the first downsizing of computers from the traditional mainframe to the new minicomputer, essentially invented by Digital Equipment Corporation. The first products DEC offered were plug-in boards that held building block circuits that could be used in the design or testing of computers. As the DEC modules became more complex, they evolved into complex boards that could be combined to make a minicomputer. When DEC started selling minicomputers, they were based on this bus-oriented design. But the bus was proprietary, as were the bus designs of the products of competing minicomputer companies that came to the market.

When computers first moved to the next step, the initial designs were single-board machines. They were the work of experimenters, not commercial products, and expansion was as simple as grafting a new circuit onto a breadboard or strapping in another module with a ribbon cable much as the original mainframe assemblies were linked together. After all, experimenters had little motivation to add expansion buses when they had nothing to expand with.

The machine most people regard as the first personal computer, Altair, was originally put together as a single-board system by its creator, Ed Roberts. The machine was publicized in that form in the January 1975 issue of *Popular Electronics* magazine. But when the prototype disappeared in shipping, Roberts turned his setback into an opportunity; he redesigned the Altair to use a bus-oriented design. In the process, he laid the groundwork for the first personal computer expansion bus. Originally called the Altair bus after the name of the machine that introduced it to the world, its adoption by other manufacturers lead to a more neutral name, S-100, which first appeared in late 1976. Later, a standard based on the S-100 design was officially agreed upon by the Institute of Electrical and Electronic Engineers as IEEE 696. In this form, the bus is *still* used in obscure corners of the computer industry.

Roberts' original design choices set the pattern for today's most popular expansion buses. First, he chose edge connectors popular in electronic equipment at the time because they could be cheaply etched into circuit boards when the other interconnecting traces were formed. The off-the-shelf connectors had two rows of 50 contacts each spaced at 0.1-inch increments. The 100 contact total became the basis for the later S-100 name. Roberts' original Altair design only used 86 contacts, allowing future expansion to take over the remaining 14. This forethought allowed the Altair bus, originally created for 8-bit microprocessors, to be readily adapted to 16-bit technology.

Although the S-100 was popular, it suffered several flaws that prevented it from becoming the dominant standard when the popularity of personal computers took off. It was designed originally for true bus-oriented computers; the bus itself was passive, nothing more than a parallel set of wires. It had no official operating speed because that would be set by the boards attached to it (although most machines using S-100 operated at about 2.5MHz). Later computer designs were more like single-board systems with grafted-on expansion buses, which allowed much of the support circuitry to be held in common on the motherboard. The S-100 design required substantial duplication of circuitry. For example, S-100 boards had to devote space and cost to power-hungry voltage regulation circuitry on every expansion board.

By the late 70s, other manufacturers had developed their own expansion buses more suited to the needs of microcomputers. None was truly dominant. Designers of other early computers such as the Apple II simplified their expansion buses and lowered the cost and complication of expansion. But the Apple design added more complications because the slots were not equal; slots were individually addressed.

PC Bus

All PC expansion buses trace their roots to the bus built into IBM's original PC, introduced with the PC on August 1, 1981. The design of this prototype bus owed nothing to any great brain trust, research and development, or design innovation. It was nothing more than an extension of the connections of the 8088 microprocessor, buffered so that the signals would be strong enough to power external circuits; de-multiplexed so that the signals that shared pins on the chip would have their own connections on the bus; and arranged on an industry-standard connector in a way that easily matched available componentry.

The PC bus had all the virtues of the S-100 and other expansion buses popular at the time. It allowed the versatility of adding different options to the system (ports, memory, display adapters). Moreover, the bus approach was necessary in the first PC because all the circuitry to make a PC would not fit on the motherboard using the technology that existed at the time. The expansion bus gave engineers a chance to add more features and make substitutions as technology progressed.

Little attention was paid to the technical aspects of bus design because IBM never expected sales of the PC to exceed 100,000. Although technically on par with the Apple II and S-100 buses, today the layout of the original PC bus appears almost haphazard, having little regard for signal integrity or radio frequency emissions. Then again, at the low operating speed of the bus and with the lack of FCC regulation, none of those concerns was critical.

The starting point for the original PC bus was the local bus of the 8088 microprocessor. The addressing and width of the data path of the PC bus was exactly matched to the 8088 microprocessor, and the bus operated at the 8088's speed under the microprocessor's direct control. But to make this nearly pure local bus useful, IBM mixed in a few additional signals, among them five control lines to signal hardware interrupts. The control of input/output ports was achieved by a control line that toggled the address bus between memory and the I/O ports. However, IBM chose only to decode the 10 least significant bits of I/O port addresses in the circuitry of its first expansion boards. As a result, only 1,024 of the 65,536 possible I/O ports were usable by these early expansion boards.

A few electrical characteristics needed to be changed to allow system expansion and isolate the microprocessor from more nefarious expansion board designs. All the connections to the chip were not assigned separate pins on the chip package. A few were combined together—multiplexed—to give the 8088 more leg-room. These connections must be de-multiplexed before they can be used by the computer's other circuits. These de-multiplexed connections were then extended to the PC bus. In addition, the 8088 chip itself was not designed to supply enough power to run the numerous devices that might be plugged into an expansion slot. Consequently, the microprocessor connections were re-powered—run through a digital amplifier called a buffer that boosts the current available for running accessories.

The PC bus design put the microprocessor in direct contact and direct control of everything on the expansion bus. Because of its local connection, the operating frequency of the PC bus exactly matched the microprocessor in PCs. That means it operated at the same speed and bus width—4.77MHz and one byte wide. Because every bus cycle required two ticks of the system clock (on the first tick, an address was put on the bus; on the second, the data was actually moved), the maximum speed at which information could be transferred across the bus was 2.38 MB/sec. But even that speed was restricted to short periods between other system functions, such as refreshing memory. Nevertheless, the PC bus operated as fast as anything could in the PC. Not only was there no speed penalty for plugging into the bus, but also using the bus was the only way to attach memory beyond the first 64KB (or 256KB in later models) into a system.

Industry Standard Architecture

By 1984, the rudimentary design of the PC bus was already falling behind the times. As IBM's engineers were working on a revolutionary new product (for then) based on a fast 286 microprocessor designed to run at 8MHz (though initially limited to 6MHz), they confronted a bus unsuited for the performance level of the new machine. Because the 286 used a full 16-bit data bus, IBM decided to add more data signals (as well as address and control signals) to the PC bus to match the capabilities of the new and more powerful chip. The bus speed of the AT also was matched to the microprocessor, so again no performance penalty was incurred in connecting a peripheral—even expansion memory—to the bus.

Not only was the PC bus limited in its memory handling and the width of its data path to the capabilities of a microprocessor on the road to oblivion (the 8088), but many of the available system services were in too short supply for growth of the PC beyond a desktop platform for simple, single-minded jobs. For example, most systems ran out of hardware interrupts long before they ran out of expansion slots or clever ideas and expansion boards needing interrupts for control. At the same time, engineers were faced by the profusion of PC bus-based expansion products, many of those made by IBM, which would be rendered incompatible if the bus were radically changed. A complete redesign required creating an entirely new line of expansion products for IBM and the compatibles industry, probably creating an outcry loud enough to weaken the IBM standard.

As a result of balancing these conflicting needs, the new AT bus was born a hybrid. It retained compatibility with most earlier PC expansion products while adding functionality needed to push forward into full 16-bit technology. In addition, the AT bus contained a few new ideas (at least for PC-compatible computers) that hinted at—and perhaps even foretold—the bus-mastering abilities of the PCI bus. Inherent in the AT bus but almost entirely unused are provisions for cohabiting microprocessors inside the system, able to take control and share resources.

The big physical difference between the PC/XT bus and the AT bus was the addition of a second connector to carry more data and address lines—four more address lines and eight data lines—for a total of 16 data lines and 24 address lines, enough to handle 16MB, the physical addressing limit of the 80286 chip. To make up for some of the shortcomings of the PC, which limited its expandability, the new AT bus also included several new interrupts and DMA control lines. In addition, IBM added a few novel connections. One in particular helps make expansion boards compatible across the 8- and 16-bit lines of the IBM PC; it signals to the host that the card in the socket uses the PC or AT bus.

Maintaining physical compatibility with the earlier PC bus was accomplished with the simple but masterful stroke of adding the required new bus connections on a supplementary connector rather than redesigning the already entrenched 62-pin connector. Expansion cards that only required an 8-bit interface and needed no access to protected-mode memory locations or the advanced system services of the AT could be designed to be compatible with the full line of 8- and 16-bit IBM-standard computers. Those needing the speed or power of the AT could get it through the supplemental connector. The design even allowed cards to use either 8- or 16-bit expansion depending on the host in which they were installed.

Because of its initial speed and data-path match with the 286 microprocessor, the original AT bus substantially out-performed the PC bus; its 16-bit data path combined with its 8MHz clock (in its most popular form) yielded a potential peak transfer rate of 8 MB/sec. Its 24 address lines put 16MB of memory within reach. However, the number of useful I/O ports was still limited to 1,024 because of compatibility concerns with PC bus expansion boards.

The AT bus design incorporated one major structural difference over the original PC bus, however. Where the PC had a single oscillator to control all its timing signals, including bus and microprocessor, the AT used several separate oscillators. The microprocessor speed, time-of-day clock, system timer, and bus speed were separated and could be independently altered. As a result, separate clocks could be used for the microprocessor and the expansion bus (as well as the system timers). This change allowed expansion boards to operate at a lower speed from that of the microprocessor. Because of this change, the ultra-compatible AT bus could be used with higher performance PCs as they became available. Although expansion boards might not work at the 25MHz or 33MHz clock speed of 386 and new microprocessors, the bus could be held back to its 8MHz rate (or a slightly higher sub-multiple of the microprocessor clock frequency) to ensure backward compatibility with old expansion boards. At first, the lower speed of the bus was no problem because nothing anyone wanted to plug into the bus needed to transfer data faster than 8 MB/sec. For example, the fastest devices of the time—state-of-the-art ESDI drives—pushed data around at a 1.25 MB/sec rate, well within the peak of the 8 MB/sec limit of ISA. Eventually, however, the speed needs of peripherals (and memory) left the AT bus design far behind.

One glaring problem with the original PC and AT expansion buses was that they were designed not just for peripherals but also for the basic memory expansion of the host PC. This worked at first when both microprocessor and bus ran at the same speed but became bothersome as microprocessors raced ahead of bus capabilities—to such extreme rates as 16MHz! Adding memory for a fast microprocessor into a slow bus just doesn't make sense. Every time the PC would need to access its bus-mounted memory, it would have to slow down to bus speed.

In early 1987, Compaq Computer Corporation cleverly sidestepped this problem with the introduction of its first Deskpro 386, which operated at 16MHz. The first dual-bus PC, the Deskpro was the first machine to provide a separate bus for its memory, operating at microprocessor speed, and for input/output operations, operating at the lower speeds that expansion boards can tolerate. All modern PCs exploit this dual-bus concept, expanding on it with a third bus. The AT bus suffered another shortcoming. Although IBM documented the function of every pin on the AT bus, IBM never published a rigorous set of timing specifications for the signals on the bus. As a result, every manufacturer of AT expansion boards had to guess at timing and hope that their products would work in all systems. Although this empirical approach usually did not interfere with operation at 8MHz, compatibility problems arose when some PC makers pushed the AT bus beyond that speed. The timing specifications of the AT bus were not officially defined until 1987 when a committee of the IEEE (Institute of Electrical and Electronic Engineers) formally approved a bus standard that became known as Industry Standard Architecture or simply ISA. It also goes under several other names: ISA, classic bus, and its original name, AT bus.

The problem with holding the speed of the ISA bus at 8MHz for backward expansion board compatibility first became apparent when people wanted to add extra memory to their higher speed PCs. When the microprocessor clock speed exceeded the bus speed, the microprocessor had to slow down (by adding wait states) whenever it accessed memory connected through the expansion bus. System performance consequently suffered, sometimes severely.

System designers at Compaq solved the problem by devoting a special, second bus to memory in the company's 1987 Deskpro 386. All current ISA-based PCs follow this design—a separate bus for high-speed memory and another for I/O expansion.

Since the time the IEEE set the ISA specification, its bus signals have remained essentially unchanged. The introduction of the Plug and Play ISA specification on May 28, 1993, a joint development by Intel and Microsoft, alters the way expansion boards work in conjunction with the bus.

Plug and Play ISA is designed to give ISA systems the same if not better self-configuration capabilities enjoyed by more recent expansion bus designs. In fully compliant systems, you can plug in any combination of expansion boards and never have to worry about such things as DIP switch settings, jumper positions, interrupts, DMA channels, ports, or ROM ranges. Each Plug and Play ISA card can tell its computer host exactly what resource it requires. If the resource requests of two or more cards conflict, the Plug and Play system automatically straightens things out.

Instead of altering the bus, Plug and Play ISA substitutes an elaborate software-based isolation protocol. Effectively, it keeps an expansion board switched off until it can be uniquely addressed, so that one card can be queried at a time. The host system then can determine the resources the board needs, check to make sure that no other board requires the same resources, and reserve those resources for the target board.

Although Plug and Play ISA does not require them, it can make use of slot-specific address-enable signals. The use of such signals—which are now not part of the ISA specification—can eliminate the complex software-query system used for isolating cards. Although software-based Plug and Play configuration is possible with current systems, using the streamlined hardware-based scheme requires new motherboards.

Transitional Buses

Manufacturers and industry groups made several attempts at improving the performance of personal computer expansion buses with varying degrees of success. Although none of the efforts proved to be an enduring solution, each step helped define important features of the current bus standard.

First among these transitional buses was *Micro Channel Architecture*, developed as a proprietary product by IBM and first released in 1987. As the name implies, the Micro Channel was not simply a bus but a revision to the entire architecture of the PC. It introduced several new concepts, including automatic configuration, asynchronous operation, bus mastering and arbitration, and higher performance thanks to a combination of a more speed-friendly design and wider interface. The chief weakness of Micro Channel was not technical but IBM's marketing of it. PC makers saw it as an attempt by IBM to rein in control of their industry, and few other manufacturers adopted the design. Current PCs, however, benefit from many of the innovations that IBM developed for Micro Channel.

Enhanced ISA, better known as *EISA*, first appeared in 1988, promoted by a consortium of nine companies (termed by industry wags as the "Gang of Nine")—AST Research,

Compaq Computer Corporation, Epson, Hewlett-Packard, NEC, Olivetti, Tandy, Wyse, and Zenith Data Systems. Based on Micro Channel concepts but designed to be backward compatible with ISA expansion boards, EISA was essentially the designated successor to ISA. As with Micro Channel, EISA broadened the expansion bus to 32 bits and added bus mastering, arbitration, and automatic configuration. Many manufacturers adopted it for high-end systems and network servers, but it failed to win widespread support primarily because it added to the cost of computer systems (initially almost $1,000) and delivered little perceived performance improvement. At the time, the expansion bus was not a major constraint on overall system speed.

By 1991, however, high-performance PCs were suffering bus throughput problems, primarily in their video systems. The basic PC design forced all onscreen graphics through the standard input/output bus, ISA, even if the video circuitry was on the motherboard. The handicap was substantial: High-performance microprocessors could move screen data at speeds approaching 132 MB/sec, but the old ISA bus could only push bytes at a 8 MB/sec rate.

A twist to system design called the *local bus* promised to break through this bus speed barrier. The local bus grafted a second expansion bus onto the conventional PC, one more directly connected to the host microprocessor and operating at the same clock speed as the microprocessor. (Actually, the local bus was the *third* bus in such systems. By 1991, most PC designs included both an expansion bus and a separate, high-speed memory bus.)

The first machines to demonstrate the local bus concept—NEC's PowerMate desktop PCs introduced in 1991—used the design solely to accelerate display performance. The local bus linked the microprocessor to the motherboard-mounted display systems of these machines but provided no expansion slot connections.

Many PC makers copied the NEC design but longed for a standard that would allow putting high-speed video circuitry on an expansion board. Although early in 1992 OPTi, a maker of PC chipsets, proposed an open local bus standard based on its products, the proprietary design never found wide adoption.

Rather than a proprietary standard, the PC industry sought an open standard. In response to this need, the Video Electronics Standards Association (VESA), an industry consortium that had previously standardized monitor timing to improve the intercompatibility of PCs and their displays, developed the *VESA Local Bus*, or VL Bus. Formally announced on August 28, 1992, VL Bus was an instant success because it gave the PC industry what it wanted most: a standardized connector and protocol for a local bus expansion system for PCs. Although originally targeted at advanced video systems, the resulting specification was made broad enough to be equally adept at handling other peripherals requiring high-bandwidth transfers, such as mass storage and network interfaces.

Reflecting the introduction of the 64-bit Pentium in 1993, VESA developed a second generation VL Bus standard (version 2.0). This time, however, the new standard went nowhere. The PC industry had shifted its attention to PCI, where it remains today.

Peripheral Component Interconnect

In July 1992, Intel Corporation introduced Peripheral Component Interconnect. Long awaited as a local bus specification, the initial announcement proved to be more and less than the industry hoped for. The first PCI standard fully documented Intel's conception of what local bus should be—and it wasn't a local bus. Instead, Intel defined mandatory design rules, including hardware guidelines to help ensure proper circuit operation of motherboards at high speeds with a minimum of design complication. It showed how to link together PC circuits—including the expansion bus—for high-speed operation. But the initial PCI announcement fell short exactly where the industry wanted the most guidance: the pin-out of an expansion bus connector that allows the design of interchangeable expansion boards. In truth, PCI turned out not to be a local bus at all, but a high-speed interconnection system a step removed from the microprocessor—but one that runs more closely to microprocessor speed than does a traditional expansion bus.

Although in its initial form, PCI was not incompatible with VL Bus, Intel positioned its design more as a VL Bus alternative by introducing PCI release 2.0 in May 1993. The new specification extended the original document in two primary ways. It broadened the data path to 64 bits to match the new Pentium chip, and it gave a complete description of expansion connectors for both 32-bit and 64-bit implementations of a PCI expansion bus. That design, with minor revision, survives as today's PCI 2.1.

The design of PCI was unlike and incompatible with VL Bus. Foremost, PCI 2.0 was designed to be microprocessor-independent rather than limited to Intel's own chips. Instead of linking almost directly to the microprocessor, the PCI 2.0 specification provided a compatibility layer, making it what some industry insiders called a *mezzanine bus*.

Although PCI tolerates older buses and can cohabitate in PCs with other buses as it does with ISA in most of today's PCs, the underlying concept of the PCI design is to *replace* the other expansion buses. Machines that combine PCI with ISA amount to little more than an easing of the new technology into dominance of the marketplace.

On September 9, 1998, Compaq, Hewlett-Packard, and IBM announced their intention to expand on the PCI design to create a higher performance alternative aimed at server applications. Called *PCI-X*, the standard (still under development) promises a 64-bit wide bus operating at 133MHz, able to move data at a peak rate in excess of one gigabyte per second.

PCMCIA

All these bus standards presuppose one thing: They will be used in a desktop box that has room and power available for expansion. But this underlying assumption runs directly contrary to one of the strongest currents in the PC mainstream—machine miniaturization that has led to notebook, sub-notebook, and handheld computers. After all, an individual expansion board for one of these desktop standards likely stretches out longer than the largest dimension of most notebook machines. And a single board might draw more power than an entire notebook computer.

The world of movable computers has its own demands for expansion that were becoming apparent in 1987 by which time memory manufacturers were packing expansion RAM for notebook computers in slide-in credit card-size boards. In fact, memory cards of charge card dimension can trace their heritage back to the ROM cards used to store laser printer fonts as early as 1984.

Although such memory cards were becoming popular in 1987, no single standard existed. The industry leader at that time was Mitsubishi, whose memory cards used a proprietary 60-pin package. Fujitsu Microelectronics had a similar, competing line of memory cards and smart cards (Fujitsu's term for any small card with integrated circuits on it), but these were based on a 68-pin connector design.

John Reimer, upon being appointed marketing manager for microcomputer products at Fujitsu in 1987, quickly determined that he had inherited what amounted to a product looking for a purpose. It seemed to Reimer that card memory had the potential to serve as a data exchange medium that lacked the environmental vulnerability of floppy disks. A solid state card could withstand the traditional hazards to storage magnetic media such as dust, high (or low) temperatures, strong magnetic fields, shock, and impact.

While exploring marketing opportunities for his memory cards, Reimer discovered that the Poqet Computer Company was itself investigating the use of memory cards as an alternative to disk drives for a new product that was ultimately to become the first true sub-notebook PC. (Fujitsu had invested in the Poqet startup and has since acquired the company.) But Poqet was so concerned about the lack of standards among the various memory cards that it hesitated to select a memory card product because of uncertainty about which designs would succeed.

Sensible as was Poqet's desire to standardize memory cards throughout the industry, Reimer found that realizing the desire was a practical impossibility. No single standards organization was set up to rule on all the required aspects of such a design: physical card size, number and function of the connector pins, data file formats, and software interface. And to run all the different facets of a card design through the whole gamut of separate standards sanctioning organizations might take longer than the useful life of the product.

While promoting the idea that the personal computer industry should itself develop a memory card standard, Reimer discovered that Lotus Development was contemplating putting its software on ROM cards. Lotus had been among the first to embrace putting software on the larger cartridges of the ill-fated PCjr. But Lotus, too, balked at the prospect of a profusion of incompatible card designs and offered its support when Reimer proposed to bring parties interested in memory card standardization together. Reimer found enough initial support among other major suppliers of software, semiconductors, and personal computers to convene a meeting of representatives from about 25 manufacturers that took place at the Fairmont Hotel in San Jose in June 1988.

That first informal meeting pointed out the possibilities—including the potential for an antitrust suit. So with $10,000 contributed by Fujitsu, Reimer hired lawyers to draft guidelines that would avert legal tangles and organized the group that became the Personal Computer Memory Card Industry Association, or PCMCIA. At that early point, however, the role and future of the organization were uncertain. Early on, Reimer entertained the possibility that PCMCIA would craft a standard and quietly fade away, mission accomplished. But the organization gained its own momentum at its monthly meetings, and the standard expanded in scope from a PC enhancement to a universal digital data exchange mechanism.

Facing the rapid increases in peripheral performance brought by local bus interfaces, the original PCMCIA specifications look laggardly indeed. To keep in step with technology, the organization developed a new standard that incorporated the strengths of the local bus design. To distinguish the standards, PCMCIA now prefers to term its original, AT-bus based standard as *PC Card* and the local bus-based cards as *CardBus*. In addition, another industry group led by Intel developed a smaller version of PCMCIA cards using a subset of its signals and restricted it to memory operations. The resulting standard was termed *Miniature Card*. Although Miniature Card has not been widely adopted, it led to the *CompactFlash* card that is widely used by digital camera makers.

Industry Standard Architecture

If any one characteristic has defined a PC, it is Industry Standard Architecture. For many manufacturers, ISA is The One True Bus. If you want to add something to your PC, odds are it is available in ISA. It is the sine qua non of the personal computer. When poets need to note some unimaginably large number, they can add the installed base of ISA boards to classics like the grains of sand on the beach, the stars in the universe, and celebrity spouses. Greek philosophers would probably have ranked ISA as one of the grand ultimates—along with Truth, Beauty, Justice, and the five cent cigar. You get the idea. ISA is both the ultimate blessing for the PC and still something that's not quite perfect. But it's what we have—what we're stuck with—and we'll make do, even if we have to delude ourselves.

Like the rest of our universe, ISA did not spring fully formed from the head of Zeus but underwent a prolonged and painful birth. Its development parallels that of the entire PC industry. From pragmatic beginnings in the first PC, it grew to double its size, went through a troubled and troubling adolescence, and finally matured into the accepted standard known today. To know it isn't exactly to love it, but knowing it gives you valuable insight into why PCs are the way they are.

Initial Design

Historically and operationally, the classic PC bus is the best place to start examining how all the bus signals work together. It's both the oldest design you'll still find in PCs and the most primitive. Just as humans can trace the salt water in their cells back to the primordial ooze our ancestors first crawled from, the classic 8-bit bus marks where PC buses began. Its original constituents still echo through the latest bus incarnations.

Basic Signals

The expansion connector for each slot, located on the system board, had two rows of 31 pins each with center-to-center pin spacing of 0.1 inch. The mating contacts on each expansion board were simply etched in place when the board traces were etched. Most but not all boards had these board edge-connector contacts gold-plated for reliability.

Of the 62 pins used by the PC/XT bus, 3 are grounds; 5 are lines to supply the various voltages needed around the computer (two 5-volt direct current as well as one each at –5, 12, and –12 volts); 20 are address lines; 8 are data lines; 10 are devoted to interrupts; and several are special-purpose connections to bring it all to life. *Connectorama* lists the complete signal assignments of the PC/XT bus connector.

Although the list of bus functions is complicated by a wealth of specialized terminology that makes it look as forbidding as the list of ingredients on a candy bar, everything is completely straightforward.

The *oscillator* line supplies a signal derived directly from the crystal oscillator that runs all the clocks and timers inside the computer. Operating at 14.31818MHz, in the PC bus design, this oscillator is the single frequency standard of the entire computer.

The odd frequency on which PCs were based was actually derived from a very practical consideration. It's exactly three times the speed at which the microprocessor operates and four times the frequency that televisions (and inexpensive computer monitors) use to lock their color signals to. This one oscillator can serve multiple purposes through simple frequency dividers, running both the microprocessor and display system.

The *clock* line on the bus is one of those signals derived from the oscillator. It's the one electrically divided by four—to 4.77MHz—and supplied to the microprocessor and other system circuitry to time and synchronize all logical operations.

The I/O Channel Check line provides the microprocessor with an integrity check of the memory and devices connected to the PC bus. If the signal on this line is interrupted, it indicates to the microprocessor that a parity check error has occurred. Grounding this line effectively crashes the system.

Supplying a pulse to the reset driver line of the PC bus instructs the whole system to reset or initialize itself. A signal is generated on this line whenever the system is turned on or power is interrupted.

The data lines carry digital information in parallel form throughout the computer. These same lines are used to move information to and from both memory and input/output devices. Eight data lines are used in the PC, identified with numbers from zero to seven, with zero indicating the line carrying the least significant bit of each digital word of information.

The address lines are used for specifying locations in memory to and from which bytes of information are moved. The 20 total lines are identified with numbers 0 through 19, again with line 0 being the least significant.

Bus Control

To read or write memory, the microprocessor sends the memory address that it wants to use down the address lines and then pulses a special line called the Address Latch Enable to indicate to devices connected to the bus that it sent a valid address and that the devices should remember it (by "latching"—electronically locking their circuits to that address). Finally, the microprocessor sends a signal down the Memory Read Command, which tells the memory controller to put the data at the indicated address on the data lines. Alternatively, the microprocessor can send a signal down the Memory Write Command line, which indicates that the microprocessor itself has put a byte of information on the data lines and that the memory controller should store that information at the indicated addresses.

The same data lines are used for moving bytes to input/output devices through other special purpose lines on the bus. The I/O Read Command line tells a device to move information from an input port onto the data lines so that the microprocessor can read it into its registers. The I/O Write Command line instructs an input/output device to take the information on the data lines, put there by the microprocessor, and move it to its output port.

Because the microprocessor can generate or demand data quicker than an input/output device or even memory might be able to handle it, the PC bus also includes a provision for making the microprocessor wait while the other part of the system catches up. By removing the ready signal from the I/O Channel Ready line, the memory controller or input/output device tells the microprocessor to pause for one or more clock cycles.

If the microprocessor does not find a ready on this line at the beginning of a clock cycle when it tries to use the bus, it waits until the start of the next clock cycle before trying again—and continues to wait as long as the ready signal is not present. IBM specifications do not allow these delays to extend for longer than 10 clock cycles.

DMA Control

Information can be moved from one place in a PC to another much faster under DMA control than through the use of the microprocessor. To make those moves, however, the DMA controller must take command of both the address and data lines. In addition, devices connected to the bus must be able to signal to the DMA controller to make those moves, and the controller needs to be able to signal back to the system when it's done. Several bus lines are used for these functions.

The Address Enable line is used to tell the DMA controller that the microprocessor has disconnected itself from the bus to let the DMA controller take command. After this signal is asserted, the DMA controller has charge of the address and data lines in addition to the memory and input/output read and write control lines.

At the end of a DMA memory move, a pulse is sent down the Terminal Count line. It is called that because the pulse represents the termination (end) of a count of the number of bytes moved in the DMA transfer. (The number of bytes to be moved must be declared before the transfer begins so that they can be appropriately counted.)

Devices indicate to the DMA controller that they want to make DMA transfers by sending signals down one of the three DMA request lines. Each line is assigned a priority level corresponding to its numerical designation, with one having the highest priority, three the lowest.

To indicate that a request has been received by the DMA controller as well as provide the rest of the system with an acknowledgment of the DMA request, four DMA acknowledge lines are provided. Three are used to confirm the DMA requests across the bus itself, designated by numbers corresponding to the request acknowledged. The fourth, designated zero, acknowledges memory refreshing (which also deprives other devices access to the PC bus).

Finally, the PC bus provides for five interrupt request lines, which are used for hardware signals from various devices to the microprocessor to capture its attention and temporarily divert it to a different process. The interrupt request lines are designated with numbers two through seven, in order of decreasing priority.

Interrupts zero and one are not available on the bus but are used internally by the PC in its system board circuitry. The former is controlled by the system timer and generates a periodic interrupt at a rate of 18.2 per second. The other is devoted to servicing the keyboard, generating an interrupt with each key press. In addition, a special interrupt, called the non-maskable interrupt, or NMI, because it cannot be masked or switched off in the normal operation of the system through software, is used to signal the microprocessor about parity errors.

16-Bit Extension

To push the already aging 8-bit PC bus into the 16-bit world of the AT, IBM grafted on a second connector. The auxiliary edge connector, with the same pin spacing (0.1 inch center-to-center) but fewer pins (38 versus 62), was added in front of the old connector to give good backward compatibility. Because the 8-bit connector retained its normal position, 8-bit boards would readily slide into 16-bit slots by simply ignoring the extra connector. At the same time, 16-bit boards would fit into most 8-bit slots with their auxiliary connectors hanging free and unused. Bus signals (or lack of them) indicated to both board and computer that the auxiliary connector was unused.

Data Bus

The obvious addition required when moving from 8 to 16 data bits is 8 additional data lines. These 8 new lines, designated data 8 through 15, complete the sequence started with the first 8, increasing in significance with their designations.

Because both 8- and 16-bit devices may be present in one computer, some provision must be made to indicate how many bits are actually to be used for each memory and input/output operation. IBM uses several signals to facilitate such matters. One of these is called System Bus High Enable, and it must be active for 16-bit data transfers to take place. In addition, expansion cards indicate to the host system that the data transfer taking place is a 16-bit operation with the Memory 16-bit Chip Select and I/O 16-bit Chip Select signals, depending on whether the transfer is from or to memory or an input/output device.

Besides slowing down memory access with the I/O Channel Ready signal, the AT bus also provides for a speed-up signal. The Zero Wait State signal indicates that the current bus cycle can be completed without wait states.

Address Bus

To accommodate the full 16MB physical address range of the 80286 microprocessor used in the AT, IBM expanded the number of memory address lines to 24. Instead of adding just four new lines, however, IBM elected to add eight.

The new address lines differ from the old in that they do not latch; that is, their value is not held by the system board throughout the memory cycle. Instead, they are asserted only until the memory read or write command is given, at which point their value becomes undefined. The expansion board is charged with the responsibility for remembering the address for any longer period that it needs to. This technique can allow faster operation on the bus.

The memory read and memory write functions of the AT bus are shifted to the supplementary connector, whereas the bus connections at the positions used by the memory read and memory write functions of the original (8-bit) PC bus are devoted only to operation on real-mode memory.

Memory transfers within the 1MB real addressing range require that both the new and old memory read or write lines be activated. When a read or write request is made to the area above the 1MB limit of real memory, however, only the supplementary connector memory read or write lines are activated. An 8-bit card thus never receives a command (or be able to issue one) that it cannot act upon.

Added System Services

To make up for the shortages of interrupts and DMA channels that often occur in PCs and XTs when multiple serial ports, hard disks, tape systems, and other peripherals are installed, IBM virtually doubled the number of each. Two sets of DMA controllers are available—one that yields four 8-bit channels and one with four 16-bit channels of which one is reserved for use only on the system board. The operation and priorities assigned to DMA channels follow the pattern set with the PC. DMA channel 0 has the highest priority; DMA channel 7, the lowest.

The number of interrupts was also nearly doubled in the AT, from 8 to a total of 15. Not all these appear on the expansion bus, however. Five interrupts are reserved to the system board: Interrupts 0, 1, 2, 8, and 13. In addition, the AT makes provisions for interrupt sharing so that one interrupt can be used for several functions.

Bus Sharing

As with the XT's slot eight, IBM made a token effort toward adding more power on the PC bus. In the AT, however, IBM gave specific support to running more than one microprocessor on the bus, and this support was not restricted to a single slot.

The bus sharing of ISA works like a DMA cycle. The expansion card containing the visiting microprocessor first activates a DMA request and receives back an acknowledgment. After it has its acknowledgment, the visiting microprocessor activates the master line on the bus, which gives the chip complete control of all address, data, and control lines of the bus. For a short period, it is the master in charge of the computer.

The short period is delimited by memory refreshing, which requires host system access to RAM. If the visiting microprocessor tries to steal more than 15 microseconds at a time from the bus, the host may lose its memory and mind because the chip gets total control, and the host cannot even refresh its own memory.

To prevent unwanted interruptions during memory refresh cycles, the AT bus also provides for a refresh signal, which serves as a warning as to what is going on.

Plug and Play ISA

The ISA standard leaves issues of system setup to you. You have to ensure that every expansion board plugged into your system gets the interrupt service, memory address range, port addresses, and DMA access that it requires. You also must ensure that the needs of each board conflict with none of the others in the system. Before you slide each expansion board into your system, you have to check jumpers or DIP switch settings to ensure that they do not conflict with those of anything else in your system. Or should you be blessed with a board that includes its own software setup procedure, you get to wade through a program written by someone intent on creating a cipher the CIA cannot understand. When the inevitable conflict arises, you are left with the limitless joy of a computer or peripheral that absolutely refuses to work and will not say why. You, as the manager of the PC, are to blame, and your punishment is to devote a substantial fraction of your life to penance—that is, surrounding yourself with manuals, notepads, and a hexadecimal calculator to sort things out.

Plug and Play ISA gives all that brainwork to the electronic entity closest to the problem, your PC itself. Using the features specified by the standard, individual expansion boards can tell your system their needs and what substitutions they will accept, and your system then can make the necessary arrangements itself.

Plug and Play works without modification to the ISA bus, although it allows for advanced systems to streamline their configuration process by adding a single slot-specific signal to each bus connector. The main modification required by Plug and Play ISA is the addition of special registers to each expansion board and the capability for each card to deselect itself, essentially disconnecting itself from the bus so that it does not respond to commands and signals meant for other boards.

Isolation Sequence

The key to setting up individual boards in a Plug and Play ISA system is the capability to isolate each board from the rest. The Plug and Play ISA specification standardizes the isolation sequence used.

Whenever you switch on your system or give it a cold boot, all the Plug and Play ISA cards inside it come up in their Wait for Key state. In this condition, the expansion boards refuse to respond to any signal on the ISA bus until they receive their initiation key. When a board receives the initiation key code, it switches to its Sleep state. The card (and all the rest in the PC) then waits again for a Wake[Card Select Number] command. Upon receiving that command, all cards in the system shift to their Isolation state, which allows them to listen to bus signals.

The host computer then executes a series of 72 reads of consecutive read-only registers that store a board identification number. Every Plug and Play ISA expansion board (not merely every model) is assigned a number during manufacture that should be unique in every PC. After the number of a card is uniquely identified, all the other boards in the system are forced back into their Sleep state, and a unique number is written to the Card Select Number register on the board. Writing this number back to the card causes the designated card to enter its Config state. The board now can be configured independently from any other board in the system (all the others will be in the Sleep state), or the system can switch the selected card back to its Sleep state by sending a Wake[0] command to it. However, the uniquely assigned CSN number can be used any time thereafter to isolate and individually command the selected board.

When a board has a Card Select Number assigned to it, it drops out of the isolation sequence. The system continues to step through the process until each board in it has been assigned a unique Card Select Number.

Assigning Resources

Plug and Play ISA allows for any board to ask for up to four non-contiguous ranges of memory base addresses; up to eight non-contiguous base addresses for input/output ports; up to two separate interrupt levels; and up to two DMA channels. The system can query a board as to its needs only when the board is in its Config state. Only one board can be in Config state at a time; this state is selected either during the isolation sequence or by sending a Wake command using the board's unique Card Select Number (which must be assigned earlier during the isolation sequence).

Peripheral Component Interconnect

The bus of tomorrow today is perhaps the best way to characterize Intel's Peripheral Component Interconnect. Of all the expansion systems currently in use in desktop PCs, PCI holds the best promise of replacing the ancient ISA once and for all. Three characteristics back this promise. PCI is fast, an excellent match for the current generation of microprocessors. In addition, PCI is microprocessor-independent, so if the world of PCs does move away from the Intel microprocessor standard, PCI will still give machines expansion reach no matter what chip is inside. Finally, PCI has no real competition and solid backing. Unlike VL Bus, PCI is designed to replace rather than supplement conventional expansion buses, and it is supported (and was developed) by the largest microprocessor maker and standalone semiconductor firm in the world, arguably one of two companies powerful enough to steal the mantle from IBM as computer-industry standard setter. (The other? Microsoft, of course.)

Although PCI got off to a rocky start when the initial chipsets for empowering it proved flawed, computer makers have almost universally announced support. The first PCI machines will bridge the standards, offering both ISA and PCI expansion. As the new standard gains momentum, however, there will be less reason to ever look back. Finally, the PC may be able to break free from the chains imposed by the pragmatic design of the first PC.

Architectural Overview

The original explicit purpose of the PCI design was to make the lives of those who engineer chipsets and motherboards easier. It wasn't so much an expansion bus as an interconnection system, hence its pompous name; peripheral component is just a pompous way of saying chip, and interconnect means simply link. And that is what PCI is meant to be—a fast and easy chip link.

Even when PCI was without pretensions of being a bus standard, its streamlined linking capabilities held promise for revolutionizing PC designs. Where each new Intel microprocessor family required the makers of chipsets and motherboards to completely redesign their products with every new generation of microprocessor, PCI promised a common standard, one independent of the microprocessor generation or family. As originally envisioned, PCI would allow designers to link together entire universes of processors, coprocessors, and support chips without glue logic—the pesky profusion of chip needed to match the signals between different integrated circuits—with a connection the speed of which was unfettered by frequency (and clock) limits. All PC chips that follow the PCI standard can be connected together on a circuit board without the need for glue logic. In itself, that could lower PC prices by making designs more economical while increasing reliability by minimizing the number of circuit components.

As a chip link, PCI was designed to operate at the full clock speed of Intel's top-of-the-line microprocessors—33MHz and beyond. That high speed makes the layout of circuit traces on the motherboard itself critical. Consequently, the original PCI specification gave guidelines for the physical configuration of the chips to be connected on the motherboard. Intel believed that PCI devices should physically be arranged as close together as possible so that chip connections to the high-speed parallel circuit traces (an on-board bus that Intel called the PCI speedway) are spaced about one inch apart. The chips straddle the speedway, alternating sides of the speedway so that those located on a given side appear at two-inch increments. This staggered design minimizes the length of the bus and the capacitive effects that limit its operating frequency.

The published design was entirely open because Intel intended PCI to become the single industry standard to which chip makers would design their products. Such an open standard would foster third-party manufacturers creating a wide variety of chips with specialized functions that could easily attach to PCI—not just video but also SCSI controllers, LAN adapters, and audio and video products for multimedia systems.

PCI was initially released into a world clamoring for a local bus standard just before the VL Bus standard was officially ratified. The original PCI was a local bus, but one that stuck to the motherboard. Although the signals needed for an external expansion bus were noted in the specifications, the one thing the expansion industry clamored for was absent: a pin-out for an expansion connector. On the surface, motherboard-oriented PCI appeared to be compatible with VL Bus. That compatibility, however, was not to stay in Intel's long-range plans.

When Intel upgraded the PCI specifications to match the Pentium processor, it also tightly plugged the one hole in the original design. By specifying not only a connector pin-out but also an entire expansion board architecture, Intel's engineers pushed PCI into the forefront of expansion design.

As with VL Bus, the revised PCI was designed to work inside PCs based on the legacy ISA bus or one of the transitionary buses (Micro Channel or EISA). But PCI was designed as a full bus that did not need to affiliate with another bus as did VL Bus. The PCI bus standard envisioned PCI boards connecting only to the PCI bus and getting all the signals they need from the PCI connector. The new standard defined physical compatibility so that the same board can easily be adapted to fit the form factor of a legacy system.

A key tenet of the PCI design is processor independence; that is, its circuits and signals are not tied to the requirements of a specific microprocessor or family.

That alone removes PCI from being a true local bus. Even though the standard was developed by Intel, the PCI design is not limited to Intel microprocessors. In fact, some computers based on DEC's Alpha chip are expected to use PCI.

Although PCI can deliver performance on par with the host microprocessor's local bus, it is one step removed from the microprocessor. This intermediary position has given PCI the title mezzanine bus.

Bus Speed

PCI can operate synchronously or asynchronously. In the former case, the speed of operation of the PCI bus is dependent on the host microprocessor's clock and PCI components are synchronized with the host microprocessor. Typically, the PCI bus will operate at a fraction of the external interface of the host microprocessor. The most common arrangement runs the PCI bus at one half of the microprocessor external clock; a PCI runs at 33MHz while the microprocessor runs externally at 66MHz. The PCI standard allows operation at any frequency in the range from 20 to 33MHz to accommodate most microprocessor clocks at reasonable multiples.

When operating asynchronously, the PCI bus speed bears no relationship to the microprocessor speed. For example, the microprocessor's external frequency may be 50MHz while the PCI bus runs at 33MHz. Asynchronous operation keeps the bus frequency high, which can enhance expansion performance.

PCI is designed to maintain data integrity at operating speeds down to 0Hz, a dead stop. Although it won't pass data at 0Hz, the design allows notebook PCs to freely shift to standby mode or suspend mode.

Although all PCI peripherals should be able to operate at 33MHz, the PCI design allows you to connect slower peripherals. To accommodate PCI devices that cannot operate at the full speed of the PCI bus, the design incorporates three flow-control signals that indicate when a given peripheral or board is ready to send or receive data. One of these signals halts the current transaction. Consequently, PCI transactions can take place at a rate far lower than the maximum 33MHz bus speed implies.

The PCI design provides for expansion connectors extending the bus off the motherboard but limits such expansion to a maximum three connectors. (None are required by the standard.) As with VL Bus, this limit is imposed by the high operating frequency of the PCI bus. More connectors would increase bus capacitance and make full-speed operation less reliable.

To attain reliable operation at high speeds without the need for terminations (as required by the SCSI bus), Intel chose a reflected rather than direct signaling system for PCI. To activate a bus signal, a device raises (or lowers) the signal on the bus only to half its required activation level. As with any bus, the high-frequency signals meant for the slots propagate down the bus lines and are reflected back by the unterminated ends of the conductors. The reflected signal combines with the original signal, doubling its value up to the required activation voltage.

The basic PCI interface requires only 47 discrete connections for slave boards (or devices), with two more on bus-mastering boards. To accommodate multiple power supply and ground signals and blank spaces to key the connectors for proper insertion, the physical 32-bit PCI bus connector actually includes 124 pins. Every active signal on the PCI bus is adjacent to (either next to or on the opposite side of the board from) a power supply or ground signal to minimize extraneous radiation.

Multiplexing

Although the number of connections used by the PCI system sounds high, Intel actually had to resort to a powerful trick to keep the number of bus pins manageable. The address and data signals on the PCI bus are time multiplexed on the same 32 pins. That is, the address and data signals share the same bus connections (AD00 through AD31). On the one clock cycle, the combined address/data lines carry the address values and set up the location to move information to or from. On the next cycle, the same lines switch to carrying the actual data.

This address/data cycling of the bus does not slow the bus. Even in non-multiplexed designs, the address lines are used on one bus cycle and then the data lines are used on the next. Moreover, PCI has its own burst mode that eliminates the need for alteration between address and data cycles. PCI also can operate in its own burst mode. During burst-mode transfers, a single address cycle can be followed by multiple data cycles that access sequential memory locations.

PCI achieves its multiplexing using a special bus signal called Cycle Frame (FRAME#). The appearance of the Cycle Frame signal identifies the beginning of a transfer cycle and indicates the address/data bus holds a valid address. The Cycle Frame signal is then held active for the duration of the data transfer.

Burst Mode

Use of the Cycle Frame signal allows PCI to offer a burst mode that does not suffer the 4-cycle, 16-byte limit of the burst mode of VL Bus and today's 486 microprocessors. During burst-mode transfers, a single address cycle can be followed by multiple data cycles that access sequential memory locations, limited only by the needs of other devices to use the bus and other system functions (such as memory refresh). The burst can continue as long as the Cycle Frame signal remains active. With each clock cycle that Cycle Frame is high, new data is placed on the bus. If Cycle Frame is active only for one data cycle, an ordinary transfer takes place. When it stays active across multiple data cycles, a burst occurs. In effect, the PCI burst mode is equivalent to the streaming data modes of a transitionary bus.

This burst mode underlies the 132 MB/sec throughput claimed for the 32-bit PCI design. (With the 64-bit extension, PCI claims a peak transfer rate of 264 MB/sec.) Of course, PCI attains that rate only during the burst. The initial address cycle steals away a bit of time and lowers the data rate (the penalty for which declines with the increasing length of the burst). System overhead, however, holds down the ultimate throughput.

Even though PCI anticipates all devices following the standard will use its full 32-bit bus width, the standard allows for transfers of smaller widths. Four Byte Enable signals (C/BE0# through C/BE3#) are used to indicate which of four byte-wide blocks of PCI's 32-bit signals contain valid data. In 64-bit systems, another four signals (C/BE4# through C/BE7#) indicate the additional active byte lanes.

To accommodate devices that cannot operate at the full speed of the PCI bus, the design incorporates three flow-control signals: Initiator Ready (IRDY# at pin B35), Target Ready (TRDY# at pin A36), and Stop (STOP# at pin A38). Target Ready is activated to indicate that a bus device is ready to supply data during a read cycle or accept it during a write cycle. When Initiator Ready is activated, it signals that a bus master is ready to complete an ongoing transaction. A Stop signal is sent from a target device to a master to stop the current transaction.

Data Integrity Signals

To ensure the integrity of information traversing the bus, the PCI specification makes mandatory the parity checking of both the address and data cycles. One bit (signal PAR) is used to confirm parity across 32 address/data lines and the four associated Byte Enable signals. A second parity signal is used in 64-bit implementations. The parity signal lags the data it verifies by one cycle, and its state is set so that the sum of it, the address/data values, and the Byte Enable values is a logical high (1).

If a parity error is detected during a data transfer, the bus controller asserts the Parity Error signal (PERR#). The action taken on error detection—for example, re-sending data—depends on how the system is configured. Another signal, System Error (SERR#), handles address parity and other errors.

Parity checking of the data bus becomes particularly important as bus width and speed grow. Every increase in bus complexity also raises the chance of errors creeping in. Parity checking prevents such problems from affecting the information transferred across the bus.

Bus Mastering and Arbitration

The basic PCI design supports arbitrated bus mastering like that of other advanced expansion buses, but PCI has its own bus command language (a 4-bit code) and supports secondary cache memory.

In operation, a bus-master board sends a signal to its host to request control of the bus and starts to transfer when it receives a confirmation. Each PCI board gets its own slot-specific signals to request bus control and receive confirmation that control has been granted. This approach allows great flexibility in assigning the priorities, even the arbitration protocol, of the complete computer system. The designer of a PCI-based computer can adapt the arbitration procedure to suit his needs rather than have to adapt to the obscure ideas of the engineers who conceived the original bus specification.

Bus mastering across the PCI bus is achieved with two special signals, Request (REQ#) and Grant (GNT#). A master asserts its Request signal when it wants to take control of the bus. In return, the central resource (Intel's name for the circuitry shared by all bus devices on the motherboard, including the bus control logic) sends a Grant to the master to give permission to take control. Each PCI device gets its own dedicated Request and Grant signal.

As a self-contained expansion bus, PCI naturally provides for hardware interrupts. PCI includes four level-sensitive interrupts (INTA# through INTD# at pins A6, B7, A7, and B8) that enable interrupt sharing. The specification does not itself define what the interrupts are or how they are to be shared. Even the relationship between the four signals is left to the designer. (For example, each can indicate its own interrupt, or they can define up to 16 separate interrupts as binary values.) Typically, these details are implemented in a device driver for the PCI board. The interrupt lines are not synchronized to the other bus signals and may thus be activated at any time during a bus cycle.

Low-Voltage Evolution

The PCI specification also anticipates an eventual switchover from standard 5-volt logic to power-saving 3.3-volt operation. PCI uses a physical keying system, discussed in Chapter 2, "System Boards," to assure boards rated to operate a different voltages are not used inadvertently in incompatible systems.

Slot Limits

High frequencies, radiation, and other electrical effects also conspire to limit the number of expansion slots that can be attached in a given bus system. These limits become especially apparent with local bus systems that operate at high clock speeds. All current local bus standards limit the number of high-speed devices that can be connected to a single bus to three.

Note that the limit is measured in devices and not slots. Many local bus systems use a local bus connection for their motherboard-based display systems. These circuits count as one local bus device, so PCs with local bus video on the motherboard can offer at most two local bus expansion slots.

The three-device limit results from speed considerations. The larger the bus, the higher the capacitance between its circuits (because they have a longer distance over which to interact). Every connector adds more capacitance. As speed increases, circuit capacitance increasingly degrades its signals. The only way to overcome the capacitive losses is to start with more signals. To keep local bus signals at reasonable levels and yet maintain high speeds, the standards enforce the three-device limit.

As practical matter, the three-device limit brings no disadvantage. A single computer can accommodate multiple PCI expansion buses bridged together. Each of these sub-buses then uses its own bus-control circuitry. From an expansion standpoint—or from the standpoint of an expansion board—splitting the system into multiple buses makes no difference. The signals get where they are supposed to, and that's all that counts. The only worries are for the engineer who has to design the system to begin with—and even that is no big deal. The chipset takes care of most expansion bus issues.

Setup

PCI builds upon the plug-and-play system to automatically configure itself and the devices connected to it without the need to set jumpers or DIP switches. Under the PCI specification, expansion boards include plug-and-play registers to store configuration information that can be tapped for automatic configuration. The PCI setup system requires 256 registers. This configuration space is tightly defined by the PCI specification to ensure compatibility. A special signal, Initialization Device Select (IDSEL), dedicated to each slot, activates the configuration read and write operations as required by the plug-and-play system.

Standards and Coordination

The PCI standard is managed and maintained by the PCI Special Interest Group. The latest revision of the specification is available from the following address:

> PCI Special Interest Group
> 2575 NE Kathryn St. #17
> Hillsboro, OR 97124
> Fax: (503) 693-8344
> `http://www.pcisig.com`

PC Card

Although the desktop remains a battlefield for bus designers, notebook computer makers have selected a single standard to rally around: PC Card, promulgated by the Personal Computer Memory Card Industry Association. Moreover, the PC Card bus is flexible and cooperative. Because they are operating system and device independent, you can plug the same PC Card peripherals into a PC, Mac, Newton, or whatever the next generation holds in store. The PC Card expansion system can cohabitate in a PC with desktop buses like ISA or PCI. Or it will work in devices that aren't even computers—from calculators to hair curlers or CAD workstations to auto-everything cameras. Someday, you may even find a PC Card lurking in your toaster oven or your music synthesizer.

The PC Card system is self-configuring, so you do not have to deal with DIP switches, fiddle with jumpers, or search for a reference diskette. PC Card differs from other bus standards in that it allows for external expansion; you don't have to open your PC to add a PC Card.

The design is so robust that you can insert or remove a PC Card with the power on without worrying that you will damage it, your PC, or data stored on the card. That is, PC Cards are designed for *hot-swapping*. The system is designed to notify your operating system what you've done so it can reallocate its resources as you switch cards. The operating system sets up its own rules and may complain if you switch cards without first warning it, although the resulting damage accrues mostly to your pride.

The engineers who created the PC Card standard originally envisioned only a system that put memory in credit-card format—hence the name, Personal Computer *Memory Card* Industry Association. They saw PC Card as an easy way to put programs into portable PCs without the need for disk drives. Since then, the standard has grown to embrace nearly any expansion option—modems, network interface cards, SCSI host adapters, video subsystems, all the way to hard disk drives.

History

PC Card release 1.0, the first generation of the PCMCIA standard, was introduced in September 1990. It contemplated only the use of solid-state memory on the card as a means of data storage. But the PC Card intrigued both the makers of sub-notebook computers and peripheral developers, who believed that the standard could be expanded to incorporate I/O devices as well as memory.

As a result, the PC Card standard was updated in September 1991 to comprise a more generalized interface that would accommodate both storage and input/output devices. Additionally, the release 2.0 standard allowed the use of thicker cards, permitting the incorporation of a wider variety of semiconductor circuits. It also allowed programs stored on PC Cards to be executed in the card memory instead of requiring the code to be downloaded into standard RAM.

In keeping with good practice, backward compatibility was maintained: Cards designed under PCMCIA release 1.0 plug into and work in release 2.0 machines. Because release 2.0 adds a wealth of features that older hardware may not understand, however, all the functions of a new card may not work in an older system. Because normal thickness cards of both generations are physically the same, new cards will fit slots in old systems. No combination of card and system will result in damage at either end of the connection. These features have been maintained through all current versions of the standard.

Backward compatibility at that early stage was, of course, practically a non-issue. The only device limited solely to PCMCIA release 1.0 form factor slots was the Poqet sub-notebook. All modern PCs accommodate cards of whatever vintage.

The completed PC Card standard (as well as its 32-bit CardBus enhancement, below) are much more than simple sets of physical specifications for card dimensions and a bus pinout. The standard also describes file formats and data structures, a method through which a card can convey its configuration and capabilities to its host, a device-independent means of accessing card hardware and software links independent of operating systems.

Architectural Overview

At first glance, the basic PC Card standard looks a bit archaic as an expansion bus. It provides only a 16-bit interface; it lacks such advanced features as bus mastering; and it offers but a single interrupt request (IRQ) line. PCMCIA's expansion system is not a simple extension to the bus circuitry of a computer. Rather, it is a system that includes everything from a computer and host-independent socket for the PC Cards to program calls that link software into the PCMCIA system.

A hardware device supporting the PC Card standard can have from one to 255 PCMCIA adapters—that is, circuits that match the signals of PC Cards to the host. Up to 16 separate PC Card sockets can be connected to each adapter, much as you can connect two hard disks to an IDE controller or seven devices to a SCSI host adapter. Consequently, the standard allows for the possibility of plugging up to 4,080 PC Cards into one system.

The memory and I/O registers of each PC Card are individually mapped into the address range of the host device. Thus, the addresses on the card need not be identical with those of the host. The host accesses the PC Card resources through one or more windows, which are memory or register ranges that can be directly addressed by the host. The entire memory on a PC Card can be mapped into a single large window (for simple memory expansion, for example), or it can be paged (like EMS memory) through one or more windows. The PC Card itself determines the access method through configuration information it stores in its own memory.

Physical Characteristics

The centerpiece of PCMCIA expansion is the PC Card itself. Measuring 54 by 85 millimeters (2.126 by 3.37 inches) and 3.3mm (just over one-eighth inch) thick, the PC Card physically follows the form factor of earlier memory cards (including the IC Card) standardized by JEIDA (the Japan Electronic Industry Design Association). The first release of the PCMCIA specification paired this single-size card with a Fujitsu-style 68-pin connector. This form factor is designated as the Type I PC Card.

The thinness of the Type I card proved an unacceptable limitation. Even without allowing for the PC Card packaging, some solid-state devices are themselves thicker than 3.3mm. Most important among these "fat" devices are the EPROMs used for non-volatile storage. (Most PCs use EPROMs to store their system BIOS, for example.) Unlike ordinary, thin ROMS, EPROMs can be reprogrammed, but this requires a transparent window to admit the ultraviolet radiation used to erase the programming of the chip. The windowed packaging makes most EPROMs themselves 3.3mm or thicker.

Fujitsu faced this problem when developing the firmware to be encoded on memory cards and so developed a somewhat thicker card that could be plugged into the same sockets as could standard memory cards. Modem and other peripheral makers found the Fujitsu fat card more suited to their purposes. To accommodate them, PCMCIA 2.0 standardized an alternative, Type II PC Card. Essentially based on the old Fujitsu developmental EPROM form factor, Type II PC Cards are 5.0 millimeters thick but otherwise conform to the same dimensions as Type I cards.

The PC Card standard puts the extra thickness in a planar bulge, called the substrate area, in the middle of the card. This thicker area measures 48 mm wide and 75 mm long. Three millimeters along each side of the Type II PC Card are kept to the thinness of the Type I standard so that the same card guides can be used for either card type. Similarly, the front 10 mm of a Type II card maintain the 3.3mm thickness of the Type I standard so that the same connector can be used for either card type. Naturally, the actual card slot for a Type II PC Card must be wide enough to accommodate the maximum thickness of the card.

In September 1992, PCMCIA approved a third, Type III form factor for PC Cards. These still-thicker cards expand the bulge of Type II from 5 mm to 10.5 mm and are designed to accommodate miniaturized hard disks and similar mechanical components. As with Type II cards, Type III PC Cards remain thin at the edges to fit standard card guides and standard connectors.

In practical terms, a Type I card comes closest to being a truly flat, credit-card style card. Type II cards have small bulges top and bottom to accommodate circuitry. Type III cards have thick lumps to hold a disk drive. Figure 2.21 (in Chapter 2) illustrates the apparent differences between the three card types.

Both Type I and Type II cards can be implemented in extended form. That is, their depth can be increased by an additional 50 mm (to 135 mm) to hold additional componentry. Such extended cards project about two inches more from standard PCMCIA slots.

To ensure that all cards easily and securely mate with their connectors, the PC Card standard requires that card guides be at least 40 mm long and that the PC Card connector must engage and guide the connector pins for 10 mm before the connector bottoms out.

The layout of a PC Card is essentially symmetrical, meaning that it could inadvertently be inserted upside down. The PC Card design allows for such cases of brain fade by eliminating the risk of damage. Although the cards do not work while inverted, neither they nor the computers into which they are plugged will suffer damage.

Because the size and placement of labels on the cards is part of the standard, when you are familiar with the layout of one PC Card, you will know the proper orientation of them all. Moreover, other physical aspects of the cards—the position of the write-protect switch (if any) and battery (if needed)—are standardized as well. The PC Card standard also recommends that the batteries in all cards be oriented in the same direction (positive terminal up).

In addition to the physical measures that facilitate getting the cards into their sockets, two pins—one on each side of the connector—allow the PC host to determine whether the card is properly seated. If the signal (ground) from one is present and the other is not, the system knows that the card is skewed or otherwise improperly inserted in the connector.

Bus Connection

All types of PC Cards use the same 68-pin connector, whose contacts are arranged in two parallel rows of 34 pins. The lines are spaced at 1.27 mm (0.050 inch) intervals between rows and between adjacent pins in the same row. Male pins on the card engage a single molded socket on the host.

To ensure proper powering up of the card, the pins are arranged so that the power and ground connections are longer (3.6 mm) than the signal leads (3.2 mm). Because of their greater length, therefore, power leads engage first so that potentially damaging signals are not applied to unpowered circuits. The two pins (36 and 67) that signal that the card has been inserted all the way are shorter (2.6 mm) than the signal leads.

Signals and Operation

The standard PC Card connector itself allows for three variations: memory-only (which essentially conforms to the release 1.0 standard), I/O cards, and multimedia cards.

All but 10 pins of the standard 68 share common functions between the two card styles. Four memory card signals are differently defined for I/O cards (pins 16, 33, 62, and 63); three memory card signals are modified for I/O functions (pins 18, 52, and 61); and three pins reserved on memory cards are used by I/O cards (pins 44, 45, and 60).

The PC Card standard allows for card implementations that use either 8- or 16-bit data buses. In memory operations, two Card Enable signals (pins 7 and 42) set the bus width; pin 7 enables even-numbered address bytes; and pin 42 enables odd bytes. All bytes can be read by an 8-bit system by activating pin 7 but not pin 42 and toggling the lowest address line (A0, pin 29) to step to the next byte. The CardBus standard expands the bus to 32 bits.

Memory Control

Standard PC Cards use 26 address lines, allowing the direct addressing of up to 64MB of data. The memory areas on each card are independent. That is, each PC Card can define its own 64MB address range as its common memory. Not all this memory range is directly addressable by some hosts: 8088-based systems are limited by their microprocessors to 1MB of directly addressed memory, for example. The entire 64MB range can be addressed by such systems through a PCMCIA window, however.

In addition to common memory, each card has a second 64MB address space devoted to the attribute memory that holds the card's setup information. The entire range need not have physical memory associated with it. In fact, most PC Cards will likely devote only a few kilobytes of the available addressing range to CIS storage.

Activating the Register Select signal (pin 61) shifts the 26 address lines normally used to address common memory to specify locations in attribute memory instead. The address space assigned to attribute memory need not correspond to a block of memory separate from common memory. To avoid the need for two distinct memory systems, a PC Card can be designed so that activating the Register Select signal simply points to a block of common memory devoted to storing setup information. All PC Cards limit access to attribute memory to an 8-bit link using the eight least-significant data lines.

Memory cards that use EPROM memory often require higher than normal voltages to reprogram their chips. Pins 18 and 52 on the PCMCIA interface provide these voltages when needed.

Data Transfers

To open or close access to data read from a PC Card, the host computer activates a signal on the card's Output Enable line (pin 9). A Ready/Busy line (pin 16) on memory cards allows the card to signal when it is busy processing and cannot accept a data transfer operation. The same pin is used on I/O cards to make interrupt requests to the host system. During setup, however, an I/O card can redefine pin 16 back to its Ready/Busy function. Memory or I/O PC Cards also can delay the completion of an operation in progress—in effect, slowing the host to accommodate the time needs of the card—by activating an Extend Bus Cycle signal on pin 59.

The Write Protect pin (pin 33) relays the status of the write-protect switch on memory cards to the computer host. On I/O cards, this pin indicates that a given I/O port has a 16-bit width.

The same 26 lines used for addressing common and attribute memory serve as port selection addresses on I/O cards. Two pins, I/O read (44) and I/O write (45), signal that the address pins will be used for identifying ports and whether the operation is a read or a write.

Unlike memory addresses, however, the I/O facilities available to all PC Cards in a system share "only" one 67,108,864-byte (64MB) range of port addresses. Considering that the AT bus allows only 64KB of I/O ports, of which some systems recognize a mere 16KB, the shared port address space represents no real limitation. Even assigning 16KB ports to each of the 4,080 possible PC Cards in a system leaves a few port addresses unused. Whether ports are 8 or 16 bit is indicated by the signal on pin 33.

I/O PC Cards each have a single interrupt request signal. The signal is mapped to one of the PC interrupt lines by the computer host. In other words, the PC Card generates a generic interrupt, and it is the host computer's responsibility to route the interrupt to the appropriate channel.

The PCMCIA specification requires all PC Cards to be able to generate edge-triggered (PC and AT-style) interrupts and level-sensitive interrupts (as used by PCI). Every card conforms to the host's requirements.

Configuration

PC Card release 2.0 added a single Reset signal to all cards at pin 58. When the host computer activates this signal, the card returns to pre-initialization settings, with I/O cards returning to their power-on memory card emulation.

When a PC Card is plugged into a slot, the host computer's PCMCIA adapter circuitry initially assumes that it is a memory card. The card defines itself as an I/O card through its on-board CIS data, which the host computer reads upon initializing the PC Card. Multimedia cards similarly identify themselves through their software and automatically reconfigure the PC Card to accept their special signals.

Audio

An audio output line also is available from I/O PC Cards. This connection is not intended for high-quality sound, however, for it allows only binary digital (on/off) signals. The audio lines of all PC Cards in a system are linked together by an XOR (exclusive OR) logic gate fed to a single common loudspeaker, equivalent to the sound system of a primitive PC lacking a sound board.

Zoomed Video

For higher quality sound or video applications, the PC Card standard defines special multimedia cards. When the PC Card software in your PC recognizes a multimedia card, it redefines many of the connections in the card connector to switch it into operating as a *zoomed video* port.

Specifically in multimedia mode, 21 address signals and 3 control signals get replaced by 4 audio, 19 video signals, and a new control signal. The video signals are meant to write directly to the frame buffer of the host computer, allowing a PC Card to generate quick displays. In effect, whatever device is on the PC Card with zoomed video has direct access to your notebook PC's screen. It can push pixels without the delays inherent in bus transfers.

The PC Card connection is only part of the zoomed video system. The host PC must also be designed to give access to its frame buffer from the port connector.

Despite its appealing name, zoomed video does not make the ordinary displays on your PC screen any faster. The only time it helps display speed is when you have a graphics accelerator or other high-performance video device that installs on a PC Card or CardBus card.

Power

Pins 62 and 63 on memory cards output two battery status signals. Pin 63 indicates the status of the battery: When activated, the battery is in good condition; when not activated, it indicates that the battery needs to be replaced. Pin 62 refines this to indicate that the battery level is sufficient to maintain card memory without errors; if this signal is not activated, it indicates that the integrity of on-card memory may already be compromised by low battery power.

The PC Card standard allows operation at either the standard TTL 5-volt level or a power-saving reduced voltage level of 3.3. Early low-voltage cards initialized at 5 volts and then shifted to lower voltage operation under the direction of the card's configuration information. Card can operate solely at 3.3 volts.

Software Interface

PC Card requires layers of software to ensure its compatibility across device architectures. PCs, for example, require two layers of software drivers—socket services and card services—to match the card slots in addition to whatever drivers an individual card requires. (For example, a modem requires a modem driver.)

As with other hardware advances, Windows 95 helped out the PC Card. Support for the expansion standard is built into the operating system (as well as Windows 98). Although Windows NT (through version 4.0) lacks integral PC Card support, Windows 2000 embraces the standard. Most systems accept cards after you slide them in, automatically installing the required software. Unusual or obscure boards usually require only that you install drivers for their manufacturer-specific features using the built-in Windows installation process.

Socket Services

To link the PC Card to an Intel-architecture PC host, PCMCIA has defined a software interface called socket services. By using a set of function calls under Interrupt 1A (which socket services shares with the CMOS time-of-day clock), software can access PC Card features without specific knowledge of the underlying hardware. In other words, socket services make access to the PC Card hardware independent, much like the BIOS of a PC. In fact, socket services are designed so that they can be built into the PC BIOS. Socket services also can be implemented in the form of a device driver, however, so that PCMCIA functionality can be added to existing PCs.

Using socket services, the host establishes the windows used by the PC Card for access. Memory or registers then can be directly addressed by the host. Alternatively, individual or multiple bytes can be read or written through socket services function calls.

Card Services

In September 1992, PCMCIA approved a card services standard that defines a program interface for accessing PC Cards. This standard establishes a set of program calls that link to those socket services independent of the host operating system. Like the socket services associated with Interrupt 1A, card services can either be implemented as a driver or be built in as part of an operating system. (Protected-mode operating systems such as Windows require the latter implementation.)

Setup

For an advanced system to work effectively, each PC Card must be able to identify itself and its characteristics to its computer host. Specifically, it must be able to tell the computer how much storage it contains; the device type (solid-state memory, disk, I/O devices, or other peripherals); the format of the data; the speed capabilities of the card; and any of a multitude of other variables about how the card operates.

Card Identification Structure

Asking you to enter all the required data every time you install a PC Card would be both inconvenient and dangerous. Considerable typing would be required, and a single errant keystroke could forever erase the data off the card. Therefore, PCMCIA developed a self-contained system through which the basic card setup information can be passed to the host regardless of the data structure of the on-card storage or of the operating system of the host.

Called the Card Identification Structure (CIS) or metaformat of the card, the PCMCIA configuration system works through a succession of compatibility layers to establish the necessary link between the PC Card and its host. As with the hardware interface, each layer of CIS is increasingly device specific.

Only the first layer, the basic compatibility layer, is mandatory. This layer indicates how the card's storage is organized. Only two kinds of information are relevant here: The data structures used by the layer itself and such standard and physical device information as the number of heads, cylinders, and sectors of a physical or emulated disk.

Data Recording Format Layer

The next layer is the data recording format layer, which specifies how the stored data is organized at the block level. Four data formats have been supported since release 2.0: unchecked blocks, blocks with checksum error correction, blocks with cyclic redundancy error checking, and unblocked data that does not correspond to disk organization (for example, random access to the data, such as is permitted for memory).

Data Organization Layer

The third CIS layer, the data organization layer, specifies how information is logically organized on the card; that is, it specifies the operating system format to which the data conforms. PCMCIA recognizes four possibilities: DOS, Microsoft's flash file system for flash RAM, PCMCIA's own execute-in-place (or XIP) ROM image, and application-specific organization. Microsoft's flash file system is an operating system specifically designed for the constraints of flash memory. It minimizes rewriting specific memory areas to extend the limited life of the medium and to allow for speedy updates of required block writes.

System-Specific Standards

The fourth CIS layer is assigned to system-specific standards that comply with particular operating environments. For example, the execute-in-place or XIP standard defines how programs encoded on ROM cards are to be read and executed.

XIP is PCMCIA's own specification that allows program code in read-only memory to execute without being first loaded into main system (read/write) memory. Application-specific organization allows card developers to create data organizations unique to their products so as to implement special features.

Attribute Memory

The setup information for all these layers is stored in a reserved area on the PC Card called attribute memory. This area is isolated from the card's ordinary storage, which under PCMCIA 2.1 is called common memory. The CIS information is structured as a linked chain of data blocks called tuples, each of which can be up to 128 bytes long. To give all systems a common starting point to search for CIS data, the first tuple of the metaformat is located at the first address in attribute memory. This ensures that the data is within the addressing range of even those primitive microprocessors that can address only 1MB of RAM. Because the CIS system must work in any PC or other host, it assumes that memory can be accessed only in byte widths.

The first 2 bytes of each tuple, as well as the format of many predefined tuples, are strictly defined. The first byte encodes the function of the tuple and the parameters it describes. The second byte links to the next tuple in the chain (if any); it specifies the number of data bytes in the tuple, which, of course, indicates where the next tuple begins. The PCMCIA 2.1 specifications define the options available for many common tuples. PC Card manufacturers are free to add their own tuples to store data for setting up cards that contain proprietary features.

As the storage and expansion needs of PCs and other electronic devices continue to evolve, the PCMCIA PC Card standard will likely follow in lockstep. Undoubtedly, it is the PC expansion system of the future—and the first truly universal data interchange system.

CardBus

To bring the PC Card into the 32-bit world, PCMCIA adapted the highly regarded PCI expansion bus to the credit-card format in November 1994 to create the CardBus. Just as PC Card is a miniaturized version of ISA, CardBus shrinks down PCI while yielding the same high data transfer rates with one important exception: Due to limitations in the connector design, CardBus extends only to a 32-bit bus width, but the PCI standard allows for 64-bit buses. Although CardBus is not truly a PCI system—it is designed to be a platform-independent 32-bit system—it is functionally equivalent to PCI and uses PCI protocol for bus operations.

New Features

Besides a wider, faster bus and PCI-based protocol, CardBus adds several new features to the PC Card repertory. CardBus supports arbitration and bus mastering with multiple bus masters, again patterned after PCI. A CardBus device can take command of its own transfers to the host system and free the host PC's microprocessor from the chore. CardBus also incorporates a new pulse-width modulation audio mode. This mode allows a CardBus device to transfer audio in digital form across a single bus line. As with all digital audio, the PWM signals are a series of pulses, but the length of each pulse rather than a coded pattern determines its audio equivalent. (See Chapter 18, "Audio," for a discussion of how pulse width modulation works.) PWM mode allows the CardBus device to transfer multiple high-quality audio signals in real-time.

Power

All CardBus cards operate at 3.3 volts in keeping with the trend toward lower voltage operation in both desktop and notebook PCs. The CardBus cards take advantage of the PC Card voltage keying system so that you cannot insert a CardBus product into a PC Card slot that supports only 5-volt operation (and thereby damaging the card, your PC, or both).

The low operating voltage helps assure that minimal power drain on the computer host. The configuration system, too, was designed with power in mind. When a CardBus product starts, only a limited part of its circuitry gets powered up, only enough to allow the host computer to read the Card Identification Structure. The host can then determine what kind of card it is, how much power it requires, and whether it has enough resources to operate the card. Only when the host computer determines the compatibility of the CardBus product and accepts it does full power flow into the card. Besides allowing the host system to reject products that might otherwise drain its energy resources, the stepped start-up procedure also prevents a surge in power demand when the host PC boots up.

Compatibility

One primary design intention with CardBus was continuity with the PC Card standard. PCMCIA wanted CardBus and PC Cards to be as compatible with one another as possible.

One incompatibility cannot be breached. Because CardBus supports only 3.3-volt operation, its slots are off limits to 5-volt only PC Cards. The voltage key prevents you from inserting 5-volt PC Cards into CardBus slots. Except for the voltage issue, the two types of slots accept cards made to either standard. That is, all 3.3-volt PC Cards fit and work in CardBus slots.

The primary challenge in making CardBus backward compatible with PC Card was fitting all the necessary 32 bits of addressing and 32 bits of data signaling on to a 68-pin connector and still having enough connections for support functions. The simple design expedient was the same as used by PCI, multiplexing. CardBus connections do double-duty handling both address and data signals, cutting the number of pins required in half and making a 32-bit bus on a 68-pin card viable.

Standards and Coordination

One key to the PC Card's success is that it is not a proprietary standard foisted on the industry by a single company or small coterie. The design is the product of a group called the Personal Computer Memory Card International Association (PCMCIA), which has more than 220 members involved in all aspects of the computer and electronics industry. CardBus continues in that tradition and is similarly maintained. The various PCMCIA standards are completely open, and all specifications are available to anyone requesting them from the organization. Rather than operate completely independently, PCMCIA cooperates with other standard-setting organizations. For example, by working jointly with the Japan Electronic Industry Development Association (JEIDA) in December 1989, PCMCIA was able to ensure that the standards it developed would be truly international in scope. Today, each organization sends a delegation to the meetings of the other.

Besides the efforts at extending PCMCIA to future technologies such as 32-bit data paths and bus mastering, PCMCIA is also developing standards for incorporating specific device types into the system. Already the group has fully described the needs for XIP, which allows programs to execute from their storage locations on PC Cards instead of needing to be loaded as if from disk into normal system RAM. PCMCIA has also developed standards for linking AT Attachment-style IDE hard disks into PC Card sockets.

To obtain more information about PCMCIA products and standards, contact the following address:

Personal Computer Memory Card International Association
1030 East Duane Ave., Suite G
Sunnyvale, CA 94086
(408) 720-0107
Fax: (408) 720-9416
`http://www.pc-card.com`

CompactFlash

Sometimes, even a PC Card is too big, so in a quest for miniaturization the electronics industry led by Intel developed a yet-smaller standard. Appropriately called *Miniature Card*, it was designed as a reduced-size version of PC Card aimed particularly at memory devices. Although it never caught on, its heir, CompactFlash, has found wide application in digital cameras. Although engineers designed the Miniature Card to be a general-purpose expansion format, one application dominated the minds of designers eyeing the small cards: memory. A variety of electronic devices have a need for compact and removable memory, perhaps the most important of which initially was the digital camera.

Intel developed Miniature Card and released the initial version (logically enough, version 1.0) on February 29, 1996. Envisioned as the perfect memory solution for digital cameras and miniaturized digital audio recorders, Miniature Cards measured less than an inch and a half square but could store up to 64MB using any standard memory technology. The limited was imposed by the bus design, pure PC Card.

In 1994, PC Card maker SanDisk developed a new small card design as CompactFlash. As the name implies, the company aimed the product specifically at accommodating flash memory in a format small enough to fit into a digital camera that wouldn't require a mule team to transport. By 1998, the following camera makers had adopted the CompactFlash format for their products:

Canon

Casio

Chinon

Hewlett-Packard

Kodak

NEC

Nikon

Sharp

The CompactFlash specification is now governed by the CompactFlash Association, or CFA, founded in 1995 by Apple Computer, Canon, Eastman Kodak, Hewlett-Packard, LG Semicon, Matsushita, Motorola, NEC, Polaroid, SanDisk, Seagate, and Seiko Epson. The organization maintains a Web site at `www.compactflash.org`.

An early promoter of the various PCMCIA specifications, SanDisk patterned the signals used by CompactFlash cards on the PC Card bus design. Logically, the interface conforms to the AT Attachment specifications, and software accesses the memory on the card as if it were a disk drive.

Electrically, CompactFlash cards act much like full-size PC Cards. As a result, each card must include its own control logic and conform to the logical format standards promulgated by PCMCIA. This makes the cards more complex than the competing tiny-card format *SmartMedia*, discussed later. Although the larger amount of circuitry also adds to the cost of producing the cards, large-scale integration and high volumes hold the potential of minimizing any such handicap. In fact, the prices of the two media are comparable, although the edge usually goes to SmartMedia.

The added complexity of PC Card compatibility has one big benefit. It allows CompactFlash cards to be readily adapted to full-size PC Card slots. The required adapter card need contain no electronics—making it inexpensive—having only the need to make the small card physically fit into a larger socket and reroute its circuits to fit the larger connector used by the PC Card standard.

Standard CompactFlash cards measure 43 mm (1.7 inches) by 36 mm (1.4 inches) by 3.3mm (0.13 inch), the same thickness as a PC Card and about one quarter the size. To increase physical capacity, the CFA has designed a slightly thicker format, designated CompactFlash Type II. At 5 millimeters thick, the new format conforms to the thickness of Type II CardBus and PC Cards.

Unlike physical disk drives, however, CompactFlash cards can withstand more physical abuse (about 2000 Gs) and wider temperature ranges (–25 C to +75 C for CompactFlash compared to +5 C to +55 C for typical disk drives). The expected life of the medium is in excess of 100 years with data integrity protected by both built-in dynamic defect management and error correction.

CompactFlash capacities start at 2MB. Currently, the largest capacity per card is 32MB with intermediary capacities of 4, 8, 10, 15, and 20MB available. Systems can double the data storage of any card using compression software, although digital cameras use JPEG compression, which ordinarily cannot be further compressed by standard software compression algorithms.

The CompactFlash design requires dual-voltage operation. All cards are completely compatible with both 5- and 3.3-volt systems. Any card will work in any system regardless of its operating voltage.

Most operating systems support the PCMCIA logical interface used by CompactFlash cards through software drivers. CompactFlash cards can be used with DOS, Windows 95 and 98, OS/2, Apple Macintosh, and most flavors of UNIX.

SmartMedia

SmartMedia claims to be the thinnest and smallest type of removable flash memory card at about one third the size of a PC Card, measuring 45 mm by 37 mm by 0.76 mm. It appears like a monolithic slice of plastic, and that's almost what it is. Its "overmolded" thin package, or OMTP, simply encases one or more memory chips with a solid protective outer shell. Two rows of a total of 22 surface contacts provide the necessary connections for an 8-bit interface.

Originally developed under the name of the *Solid-State Floppy Disk Card*, or SSFDC, a name that still rules over its supporting body's Web site (http://www.ssfdc.or.jp/english/), its original creator (Toshiba) has trademarked the name SmartMedia for the format. The SmartMedia format is currently used by the makers of many digital cameras, including nearly all Japanese brands as well as Agfa and Apple. The following camera makers support the SmartMedia format:

    Agfa
    Apple
    Epson
    Fuji
    Minolta
    Olympus
    Toshiba
    Sega
    Sanyo

The small size of the SmartMedia cards does not stand in the way of large capacities. Although they were originally introduced only in sizes from 2MB to 8MB, Toshiba has developed a high-density connection and packaging system to increase the potential storage of the SmartMedia format. Current specifications allow cards storing up to 128MB.

The total capacity of each card is arrayed in blocks of about 16KB, each block comprising 32 pages of 528 bytes each. Because the memory is solid state, access time is brief, rated at only 7 microseconds. Transferring a bit through the serial interface requires only 50 nanoseconds, an effective clock speed of 20 Mbits/sec. In actual operation, transfer speeds of 0.5 to 1.0 MB/sec can be achieved. Writing is slower—about two milliseconds to erase a 16KB block of memory and 200 microseconds to write it again.

The heart of each SmartMedia card is NAND flash EEPROM (Electrically Erasable Programmable Read-Only Memory) chips embedded in the plastic shell. The NAND flash memory technology used by SmartMedia provides fast write and erase functions plus high-speed read with minimal power consumption. Toshiba's capacity-doubling break-through enables two chips to be assembled on a single printed circuit board (PCB) and pasted in the base card, connecting them electrically so they appear as a single chip. This simple electrical design is key to the low-cost potential of SmartMedia. Despite the name, the cards are not very intelligent. They contain only memory. The controller is in the host. To work in a PC Card slot, an adapter for SmartMedia cards must itself contain a controller. Adapters are consequently more expensive than slot adapters for PC Cards.

The SmartMedia logical data format is based on the AT Attachment and DOS file standards and is compatible with PCs running Windows 95, Windows 98, Windows NT, or OS/2 Warp. It also works in Apple Macintosh computers.

Both 5-volt and 3.3-volt cards are permitted under the SmartMedia specification. A notch codes the voltage used by each card to prevent your putting a board in a host supplying the wrong voltage. A right notch indicates 3.3-volt cards; a left notch, 5 volts.

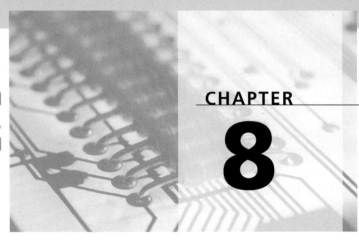

Mass Storage Technology

Mass storage is where you put the data that you need to keep at hand but that will not fit into memory. Designed to hold and retrieve megabytes at a moment's notice, mass storage traditionally has been the realm of magnetic disks, but other technologies and formats now serve specialized purposes and await their chances to move into the mainstream.

Mass storage is where you save your work. It's *mass* because it lets you save a lot; and its storage because it keeps your data secure even without power. Today's PCs use a number of mass storage devices, each with its own individual strength, including:

Device	Chief Function	In short
Floppy disks	Data exchange	Old floppies yield small capacities at tiny prices; new floppies have moderate capacities and moderate prices
Hard disks	Primary storage	Keep all your programs and data online and ready for instant access
Cartridge disks	Exchange and backup	Let you make copies of your data to share with others or retain against disasters
Magneto-optical disks	Exchange and backup	Let you make copies of your data to share with others or retain against disasters
CDs	Distribution	Give program publishers and musicians an inexpensive medium on which to deliver their software
DVDs	Distribution	Give program publishers and movie-makers an inexpensive medium on which to deliver their software
Tape	Backup	Lets you keep copies of your important data in secure locations to thwart disaster
Flash memory	Exchange	Provides temporary storage that you can move between locations and devices, for example between a digital camera and your PC

The difference between genius and mere intelligence is storage. The quick-witted react fast, but the true genius can call upon memories, experiences, and knowledge to find real answers. PCs are no different. Putting a fast microprocessor in your PC would be meaningless without a means to store programs and data for current and future use. Mass storage is the key to giving your PC the long-term memory that it needs.

Essentially an electronic closet, mass storage is where you put information that you don't want to constantly hold in your hands but that you don't want to throw away, either. As with the straw hats, squash rackets, wallpaper tailings, and all the rest of your dimly remembered possessions that pile up out of sight behind the closet door, retrieving a particular item from mass storage can take longer than when you have what you want at hand.

Mass storage can be online storage, instantly accessible by your microprocessor's commands, or offline storage, requiring some extra intervention (such as you sliding a cartridge into a drive) for your system to get the bytes that it needs. Sometimes, the term *near-line storage* is used to refer to systems in which information isn't instantly available but can be put into instant reach by microprocessor command. The jukebox—an automatic mechanism that selects CD ROM cartridges (sometimes tape cartridges)—is the most common example.

Moving bytes from mass storage to memory determines how quickly stored information can be accessed. In practical online systems, the time required for this access ranges from less than 0.01 second in the fastest hard disks to 1,000 seconds in some tape systems, spanning a range of 100,000 or five orders of magnitude.

By definition, the best offline storage systems have substantially longer access times than the quickest online systems. Even with fast-access disk cartridges, the minimum access time for offline data is measured in seconds because of the need to find and load a particular cartridge. The slowest online and the fastest offline storage system speeds, however, may overlap because the time to ready an offline cartridge can be substantially shorter than the period required to locate needed information written on a long online tape.

Various mass storage systems span other ranges as well as speeds. Storage capacity reaches from as little as the 160KB of the single-sided floppy disk to the multiple gigabytes accommodated by helical tape systems. Costs run from less than $100 to more than $10,000.

Personal computers use several varieties of mass storage. You can classify mass storage in several ways: the technology and material the storage system uses for its memory, the way (and often, speed) your PC accesses the data, and whether you can exchange the storage medium to increase storage, to exchange information, or provide security.

Another way of dividing up mass storage—and probably the most familiar—is by device type. Mass storage devices common among PCs include hard disks, floppy disks, PC Cards, magneto-optical (MO) drives, CD ROM drives (players and recorders), and tape drives. Although each of these devices gives your PC a unique kind of storage, they share technologies and media. For example, magnetic storage serves as the foundation for both hard disks and tape drives. The devices differ, however, in how they put magnetic technology to work. Hard disks give your PC nearly instant access to megabytes and gigabytes of data, but tape drives offer slower, even laggardly, access in exchange for an inexpensive cartridge medium that gives you a safe backup system.

All mass storage systems have four essential qualities: capacity, speed, convenience, and cost. The practical differences between mass storage devices are the tradeoffs they make in these qualities.

Today's mass storage systems use three basic technologies: magnetic, optical, and solid-state memory. Hard disks, floppy disks, and tape systems use magnetic storage. CD drives use optical storage. PC Cards use solid-state memory. (Of course, hard disk drives also come in PC Card format.) Magneto-optical drives combine magnetic and optical technologies.

Mass storage systems use one of two means of accessing data, random access and sequential access. Tape drives are the only sequential media devices in common use with PCs. New technologies are blurring the distinction between random and sequential storage, however. MO disks and CD ROMs began life as sequential devices with enhanced random-access capabilities. Special hard disks, called AV drives, are random access devices that have been specially designed to enhance their sequential storage abilities.

Most mass storage systems put their storage media in interchangeable cartridges. Only one kind of mass storage does not permit you to interchange cartridges, the hard disk drive. This inflexible technology is the most popular today chiefly because it scores highest in all other mass storage qualities: capacity, speed, and cost.

All of these media share the defining characteristics of mass storage. They deal with data *en masse* in that they store thousands and millions of bytes at a time. They also store that information online. To earn their huge capacities, the mass storage system moves the data out of the direct control of your PC's microprocessor. Instead of being held in your computer's memory where each byte can be accessed directly by your system's microprocessor, mass storage data requires two steps to use. First, the information must be moved from the mass storage device into your system's memory. Then, that information can be accessed by the microprocessor.

The best way to put these huge ranges into perspective is to examine the technologies that underlie them. All mass storage systems are unified by a singular principal: They use some kind of mechanical motion to separate and organize each bit of information they store. To retain each bit, these systems make some kind of physical change to the storage medium—burning holes in it, blasting bits into oblivion, changing its color, or altering a magnetic field.

Technologies

The key to mass storage is the medium. Mass storage relies on having a medium that can be readily changed from one state to another *and* retains those changes for a substantial period, usually measured in years, without the need for maintenance such as an external power source. Paper and ink have long been a successful storage medium for human thoughts; the ink readily changes the paper from white to black, and those changes can last centuries, providing the printer doesn't skimp on the quality of the paper or ink.

In fact, paper and ink have been used successfully for computer storage. Bar codes and even the Optical Character Recognition (OCR) of printed text allow PCs to work with this time-proven storage system. But paper and ink comes up short as a computer storage system. It lacks the speed, capacity, and convenience required for a truly effective PC mass storage system. You can't avoid the comparisons; whatever latest computer storage system some benighted manufacturer introduces has the capacity of several Libraries of Congress full of printed text and speed that makes Evelyn Woods look dyslexic. Perhaps a reverse metaphor is more apt. A single VGA screen image, if printed in its hexadecimal code as text characters, would fill an average book. Text characters of the code of a single Windows program would fill an encyclopedia. Your computer needs to read the entire VGA-image book in less than a blink of an eye and load the encyclopedic program in a few seconds.

Compared to what paper and ink delivers, the needs of a PC for mass storage capacity are prodigious indeed. The storage system must also allow the PC to sort through its storage and find what it wants faster than the speed of frustration, which typically runs neck-and-neck with light. And the medium must be convenient to work with, for you and your PC. The list of suitable technologies is amazingly short: magnetic and optical. All PC mass storage media are based on those two basic technologies or a combination of them.

Magnetic

Magnetic storage media have long been the favored choice for computer mass storage. The primary attraction of magnetic storage is non-volatility. That is, unlike most electronic or solid-state storage systems, magnetic fields require no periodic addition of energy to maintain their state once it is set. Over decades of development, the capacities of magnetic storage systems have increased by a factor in the thousands and their speed of access has shrunk similarly. Despite these differences, today's magnetic storage system relies on exactly the same principles as the first devices.

The original electronic mass storage system was magnetic tape—that thin strip of paper (in the United States) upon which a thin layer of refined rust had been glued. Later, the paper gave way to plastic, and the iron oxide coating gave way to a number of improved magnetic particles based on iron, chrome dioxide, and various mixtures of similar compounds.

The machine that recorded upon these rust-covered ribbons was the Magnetophon, the first practical tape recorder, created by the German division of the General Electric Company, Allgemeine Elektricitaets Gesellschaft (AEG), in 1934. Continually improved but essentially secret through the years of World War II despite its use at German radio stations, the Magnetophon was the first device to record and play back sound indistinguishable from live performances. After its introduction to the United States (in a demonstration by John T. Mullin to the Institute of Radio Engineers in San Francisco on May 16, 1946), tape recording quickly became the premiere recording medium and within a decade gained the ability to record video and digital data. Today, both data cassettes and streaming tape systems are based on the direct offspring of the first Magnetophon.

The principle is simple. Some materials become magnetized under the influence of a magnetic field. Once the material becomes magnetized, it retains its magnetic field. The magnetic field turns a suitable mixture or compound based on one of the magnetic materials into a permanent magnet with its own magnetic field. A galvanometer or similar device can later detect the resulting magnetic field and determine that the material has been magnetized. The magnet material remembers.

Magnetism

Key to the memory of magnetism is permanence. Magnetic fields have the wonderful property of being static and semi-permanent. On their own, they don't move or change. The electricity used by electronic circuits is just the opposite. It is constantly on the go and seeks to dissipate itself as quickly as possible. The difference is fundamental. Magnetic fields are set up by the spins of atoms physically locked in place. Electric charges are carried by mobile particles—mostly electrons—that not only refuse to stay in place but also are individually resistant to predictions of where they are or are going.

Given the right force in the right amount, however, magnetic spins can be upset, twisted from one orientation to another. Because magnetic fields are amenable to change rather than being entirely permanent, magnetism is useful for data storage. After all, if a magnetic field were permanent and unchangeable, it would present no means of recording information. If it couldn't be changed, nothing about it could be altered to reflect the addition of information.

At the elemental particle level, magnetic spins are eternal, but taken collectively, they can be made to come and go. A single spin can be oriented in only one direction, but in virtually any direction. If two adjacent particles spin on opposite directions, they cancel one another out when viewed from a larger, macroscopic perspective.

Altering those spin orientations takes a force of some kind, and that's the key to making magnetic storage work. That force can make an alteration to a magnetic field, and after the field has changed, it will keep its new state until some other force acts upon it.

The force that most readily changes one magnetic field is another magnetic field. (Yes, some permanent magnets can be demagnetized just by heating them sufficiently, but the demagnetization is actually an effect of the interaction of the many minute magnetic fields of the magnetic material.)

Despite their different behavior in electronics and storage systems, magnetism and electricity are manifestations of the same underlying elemental force. Both are electromagnetic phenomena. One result of that commonality makes magnetic storage particularly desirable to electronics designers; magnetic fields can be created by the flow of electrical energy. Consequently, evanescent electricity can be used to create and alter semipermanent magnetic fields.

When set up, magnetic fields are essentially self-sustaining. They require no energy to maintain because they are fundamentally a characteristic displayed by the minute particles that make up the entire universe (at least according to current physical theories). On the sub-microscopic scale of elemental particles, the spins that form magnetic fields are, for the most part, unchangeable and unchanging. Nothing is normally subtracted from them; they don't give up energy even when they are put to work. They can affect other electromagnetic phenomena, for example, used in mass to divert the flow of electricity. In such a case, however, all the energy in the system comes from the electrical flow; the magnetism is a gate, but the cattle that escape from the corral are solely electrons.

The magnetic fields that are useful in storage systems are those large enough to measure and effect changes on things that we can see. This magnetism is the macroscopic result of the sum of many microscopic magnetic fields, many elemental spins. Magnetism is a characteristic of sub-microscopic particles. (Strictly speaking, in modern science magnetism is made from particles itself, but we don't have to be quite so particular for the purpose of understanding magnetic computer storage.)

Magnetic Materials

Three chemical elements are magnetic—iron, nickel, and cobalt. The macroscopic strength as well as other properties of these magnetic materials can be improved by alloying them, together and with non-magnetic materials, particularly rare earths such as samarium.

Many particles at the molecular level have their own intrinsic magnetic fields. At the observable (macroscopic) level, they do not behave like magnets because their constituent particles are organized—or disorganized—randomly so that in bulk, the cumulative effects of all their magnetic fields tend to cancel out. In contrast, the majority of the minute magnetic particles of a permanent magnet are oriented in the same direction. The majority prevails, and the material has a net magnetic field.

Some materials can be magnetized. That is, their constituent microscopic magnetic fields can be realigned so that they reveal a net macroscopic magnetic field. For instance, by subjecting a piece of soft iron to a strong magnetic field, the iron will become magnetized.

Magnetic Storage

If that strong magnetic field is produced by an electromagnet, all the constituents of a magnetic storage system become available. Electrical energy can be used to alter a magnetic field, which can be later detected. Put a lump of soft iron within the confines of an electromagnet that has not been energized. Any time you return, you can determine whether the electromagnet has been energized in your absence by checking for the presence of a magnetic field in the iron. In effect, you have stored exactly one bit of information.

To store more, you need to be able to organize the information. You need to know the order of the bits. In magnetic storage systems, information is arranged physically by the way data travel serially in time. Instead of being electronic blips that flicker on and off as the milliseconds tick off, magnetic pulses are stored like a row of dots on a piece of paper—a long chain with a beginning and end. This physical arrangement can be directly translated to the temporal arrangement of data used in a serial transmission system just by scanning the dots across the paper. The first dot becomes the first pulse in the serial stream, and each subsequent dot follows neatly in the data stream as the paper is scanned.

Instead of paper, magnetic storage systems use one or another form of media—generally a disk or long ribbon of plastic tape—covered with a magnetically reactive mixture. The form of medium directly influences the speed at which information can be retrieved from the system.

In operation, the tape moves from left to right past a stationary read/write head. When a current is passed through an electromagnetic coil in this head, it creates the magnetic field needed to write data onto the tape. When the tape is later passed in front of this head, the moving magnetic field generated by the magnetized particles on the tape induces a minuscule current in the head. This current is then amplified and converted into digital data. The write current used in putting data on the tape overpowers whatever fields already exist on the tape, both erasing them and imposing a new magnetic orientation to the particles representing the information to be recorded.

No matter whether tape or disk, when a magnetic storage medium is blank from the factory, it contains no information. The various magnetic domains on it are randomly oriented. Recording on the medium reorients the magnetic domains into a pattern that represents the stored information, as shown in Figure 8.1.

FIGURE 8.1
Orientation of magnetic domains in blank and recorded media.

Blank magnetic medium

Digitally recorded magnetic medium

After you record on a magnetic medium, you can erase it by overwriting it with a strong magnetic field. In practice, you cannot reproduce the true random orientation of magnetic domains of the unused medium. However, by recording a pattern with a frequency out of the range of the reading or playback system—a very high or low frequency—you can obscure previously recorded data and make the medium act as if it were blank.

Digital Magnetic Systems

Computer mass storage systems differ in principle and operation from tape systems used for audio and video recording. Whereas audio and video cassettes record analog signals on tape, computers use digital signals.

In the next few years, this situation will likely change as digital audio and video tape recorders become increasingly available. Eventually, the analog audio and video tape will become historical footnotes, much as the analog vinyl phonograph record was replaced by the all-digital compact disc.

In analog systems, the strength of the magnetic field written on a tape varies in correspondence with the signal being recorded. The intensity of the recorded field can span a range of more than six orders of magnitude. Digital systems generally use a code that relies on patterns of pulses, and all the pulses have exactly the same intensity.

The technological shift from analog to digital is rooted in some of the characteristics of digital storage that make it the top choice where accuracy is concerned. Digital storage resists the intrusion of noise that inevitably pollutes and degrades analog storage. Every time a copy is made of an analog recording, the noise that accompanies the desired signal essentially doubles because the background noise of the original source is added to the background noise of the new recording medium; however, the desired signal does not change. This addition of noise is necessary to preserve the nuances of the analog recording; every twitch in the analog signal adds information to the whole. The analog system cannot distinguish between noise and nuance. In digital recording, however, there's a sharp line between noise and signal. Noise below the digital threshold can be ignored without losing the nuances of the signal. Consequently, a digital recording system can eliminate the noise built up in making copies. Moreover, noise can creep into analog recordings as the storage medium deteriorates, whereas the digital system can ignore most of the noise added by age. In fact, properly designed digital systems can even correct minor errors that get added to their signals.

Saturation

Digital recordings avoid noise because they ignore all strength variations of the magnetic field except the most dramatic. They just look for the unambiguous "it's either there or not" style of digital pulses of information. Analog systems achieve their varying strengths of field by aligning the tiny molecular magnets in the medium. A stronger electromagnetic field causes a greater percentage of the fields of these molecules to line up with the field, almost in direct proportion to the field strength, to produce an analog recording. Because digital systems need not worry about intermediate levels of signal, they can lay down the strongest possible field that the tape can hold. This level of signal is called saturation because much as a saturated sponge can suck up no more water, the particles on the tape cannot produce a stronger magnetic field.

Although going from no magnetic field to a saturated field would seem to be the widest discrepancy possible in magnetic recording—and therefore the least ambiguous and most suitable for digital information—this contrast is not the greatest possible or easiest to achieve. Magnetic systems attempt to store information as densely as possible, trying to cram the information in so that every magnetic particle holds one data bit. Magnetic particles are extremely difficult to demagnetize—but the polarity of their magnetic orientation is relatively easy to change. Digital magnetic systems exploit this capability to change polarity and record data as shifts between the orientations of the magnetic fields of the particles on the tape. The difference between the tape being saturated with a field in one direction and the tape being saturated with a field in the opposite direction is the greatest contrast possible in a magnetic system and is exploited by nearly all of today's digital magnetic storage systems.

Coercivity

One word that you may encounter in the description of a magnetic medium is *coercivity*, a term that describes how strongly a magnetic field resists change, which translates into how strong of a magnetic field a particular medium can store. Stronger stored fields are better because the more intense field stands out better against the random background noise that is present in any storage medium. Because a higher coercivity medium resists change better than a low coercivity material, it also is less likely to change or degrade because of the effects of external influences. Of course, a higher coercivity and its greater resistance to change means that a recording system requires a more powerful magnetic field to maximally magnetize the medium. Equipment must be particularly designed to take advantage of high-coercivity materials.

With hard disks, which characteristically mate the medium with the mechanisms for life, matching the coercivity of a medium with the recording equipment is permanently handled by the manufacturer. The two are matched permanently when a drive is made. Removable media devices—floppy disks, tape cartridges, cassettes, and so on—pose more of a problem. If media are interchangeable and have different coercivities, you face the possibility of using the wrong media in a particular drive. Such problems often occur with floppy disks, particularly when you want to skimp and use cheaper double-density media in high-density or extra-high density drives.

Moreover, the need for matching drive and medium makes upgrading a less-than-simple mater. Obtaining optimum performance requires that changes in media be matched by hardware upgrades. Even when better media are developed, they may not deliver better results with existing equipment.

The unit of measurement for coercivity is the *Oersted*. As storage media have been miniaturized, the coercivity of the magnetic materials as measured in Oersteds has generally increased. The greater intrinsic field strength makes up for the smaller area upon which data are recorded. With higher coercivities, more information can be squeezed into the tighter confines of the newer storage formats. For example, old 5.25-inch floppy disks had a coercivity of 300 Oersteds. Today's high-density 3.5-inch floppies have coercivities of 750 Oersteds. Similarly, the coercivities of the tapes used in today's high-capacity quarter-inch cartridges is greater than that of the last generation. Older standards used 550 Oersted media; data cartridges with capacities in excess of 1.5GB and minicartridges with capacities beyond 128MB require 900 Oersted tape. Although invisible to you, the coercivities of tiny modern hard disks drives are much higher than big old drives.

Coercivity is a temperature-dependent property. As the temperature of a medium increases, its resistance to magnetic change declines. That's one reason you can demagnetize an otherwise permanent magnet by heating it red hot. Magnetic media dramatically shift from being unchangeable to changeable—meaning a drop in coercivity—at a material-dependent temperature called the Curie temperature. Magneto-optical recording systems take advantage of this coercivity shift by using a laser beam to heat a small area of magnetic medium that is under the influence of a magnetic field otherwise not strong enough to affect the medium. At room temperature, the media used by magneto-optical systems have coercivities on the order of 6,000 Oersteds; when heated by a laser, that coercivity falls to a few hundred Oersteds. Because of this dramatic change in coercivity, the magnetic field applied to the magneto-optical medium changes only the area heated by the laser above its Curie temperature (rather than the whole area under the magnetic influence). Because a laser can be tightly focused to a much smaller spot than is possible with traditional disk read/write heads, using such a laser-boosted system allows data to be defined by tinier areas of recording medium. A disk of a given size thus can store more data when its magnetic storage is optically assisted. Such media are resistant to the effects of stray magnetic fields (which may change low coercivity fields) as long as they are kept at room temperature.

Retentivity

Another term that appears in the descriptions of magnetic media is *retentivity*, which measures how well a particular medium retains or remembers the field that it is subjected to. Although magnetic media are sometimes depended upon to last forever—think of the master tapes of phonograph records—the stored magnetic fields begin to degrade as soon as they have been recorded. A higher retentivity ensures a longer life for the signals recorded on the medium.

No practical magnetic material has perfect retentivity, however; the random element of modern physical theories ensures that. Even the best hard disks slowly deteriorate with age, showing an increasing number of errors as time passes after data has been written. To avoid such deterioration of so-called permanent records, many computer professionals believe that magnetically stored recordings should be periodically refreshed. For example, they exercise tapes stored in mainframe computer libraries periodically (in intervals from several months to several years, depending on the personal philosophy and paranoia of the person managing the storage). Although noticeable degradation may require several years (perhaps a decade or more), these tape caretakers do not want to stake their data—and their jobs—on media written long ago.

Disk makers view such precautions as verging on paranoia. The magnetic medium used in modern disk drives is nothing like that in the old, self-erasing tapes. Their plated media have much higher retentivities. Moreover, new technologies such as S.M.A.R.T. let drives detect any degradation in the magnetic medium and warn you before you stand a chance of losing your data.

Old floppy disks and backup tapes are another matter. They are likely to deteriorate with time, enough so that the data on decade-old disks and tapes may be at risk. If you have old records on old media, for safety's sake you should consider copying the records to fresher media or a newer technology, such as an optical disc.

Magneto-Optical

Magneto-optical technology uses an optical laser to enhance the capabilities of a conventional magnetic storage system. In an MO system, the recording medium is fundamentally a magnetic material (but one unlike anything you'll find on hard disks and floppies) that relies on magnetic fields to store information. The optical part is used only to assist the magnetic mechanism, to refine its perceptions. A tightly focused laser beam points out where the magnetic mechanism is to write data onto the disk and prepares the medium to make it recordable. In reading, however, MO drives are purely optical. The laser by itself reads the magnetically stored data from the disk.

The combination of magnetic and laser technologies allows MO drives to achieve high data densities. Several factors limit the data density that hard disks can achieve, for example the flying height of the read/write head. The underlying problem is that the magnetic fields from the read/write head inevitably spread out. The lasers used by optical drives are readily focused and can shoot great distances from the optical head to the substrate without spreading out. Figure 8.2 illustrates this difference.

FIGURE 8.2
Magnetic fields spread, but laser beams can be focused.

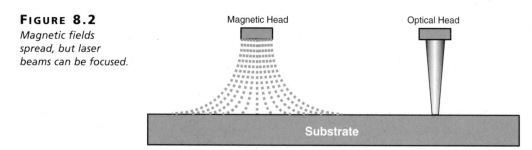

In typical applications, the laser of an optical drive reaches its sharpest focus *below* the surface of an optical disc. Newer systems vary the focus of the laser to allow storage to be arranged in independent layers, multiplying the capacity of the drive.

Certainly lasers can be used alone for purely optical drives. Compact disc technology, a purely optical system, has been used commercially for nearly two decades. But purely optical technology has a distinct disadvantage in rewritable media. Pure optical systems suffer from fatigue. All materials that change their reflectivity in response to light eventually wear out. The media in all purely optical rewritable systems (both CD-RW and all rewritable DVD formats) are rated for a limited number of read/write cycles. They can withstand hundreds of thousands or millions of write/read cycles but nevertheless decay with use.

Magnetic and magneto-optical systems, on the other hand, suffer no such degradation. They can be written and rewritten almost indefinitely. (Nothing is forever, remember.) Even though the fields of the particles in magnetic materials change, the particles themselves don't change. Because MO drives are based on this recyclable—and well understood—magnetic principle, they are generally considered to be capable of an unlimited number of write-rewrite cycles. There's no worry about stress, fatigue, failure, and data loss, yet they still can achieve the high storage densities of optical systems.

Write Operation

The writing process for a MO system relies on the combined effects of magnetic fields and laser-beam optics. The drives use a conventional magnetic field, called the *bias field*, to write data onto the disk. Of course, the nature of the field is limited by the same factors in traditional magnetic hard disks; the size of the magnetic domains that are written is limited by the distance between the read/write head and the medium and is, at any practical distance, much larger than the size of a spot created by a focused laser.

To get the size of a magnetic domain down to truly minuscule size, MO drives use the laser beam to assist magnetic writing. In effect, the laser illuminates a tiny area within a larger magnetic field, and only this area is affected by the field.

This optical-assist in magnetic recording works because of the particular magnetic medium chosen for use in MO disks. This medium differs from that of ordinary magnetic hard disk drives in having a higher coercivity, a resistance to changing its magnetic orientation. In fact, the coercivity of a MO disk is about an order of magnitude higher than the 600 or so Oersteds of coercivity of the typical magnetic hard disk.

This high coercivity alone gives MO disks one of their biggest advantages over traditional magnetic media; they are virtually immune to self-erasure. All magnetic media tend to self-erase; that is, with passing time their magnetic fields lose intensity because of the combined effects of all external and internal magnetic fields upon them. The fields just get weaker. The higher the coercivity, the better a medium resists self-erasure. Consequently, MO disks with their high coercivities are able to maintain data more reliably over a longer period than purely magnetic hard disks.

Along with such benefits, the higher coercivity of MO media brings another challenge: obtaining a high enough magnetic flux to change the magnetic orientation of the media while keeping the size of recorded domains small. Reducing this high coercivity is how the laser assists the bias magnet in a MO drive.

The coercivity of the magnetic medium used by MO disks, as with virtually all magnetic materials, decreases as its temperature increases and becomes zero at the media-dependent *Curie temperature*. By warming the MO disk medium sufficiently close to the Curie temperature, the necessary field strength to initiate a change can be reduced to a practical level. The magnetic medium used by MO disks is specifically engineered for a low Curie temperature, about 150 degrees Celsius.

The same laser that's used for reading the MO disk can simply be increased in intensity to heat up the recording medium to its Curie temperature. This laser beam can be tightly focused to achieve a tiny spot size. Although the magnetic field acting on the medium may cover a wide area, only the tiny spot heated by the laser actually changes its magnetic orientation because only that tiny spot is heated high enough to have a sufficiently low coercivity.

Practical mechanisms based on this design have one intrinsic drawback. The bias magnetic field must remain oriented in a single direction during the process of writing a large swath of a disk, a full sector or track. The field cannot change quickly because the high inductance of the electromagnet that forms the field prevents the rapid switching of the magnet's polarities. The field must be far larger and stronger than those of traditional magnetic disks because the magneto-optical head is substantially further from the disk; it doesn't fly but rides on a track.

Because of the inability of the magnetic field to change rapidly, the bias magnet in today's MO drives can align magnetic fields in a given area of a disk track only one direction each time that portion of a track passes beneath the read/write head. For example, when the bias field is polarized in the upward direction, it can change downward-oriented fields on the disk to upward polarity, but it cannot alter upward-oriented field to the downward direction.

Practical MO systems today therefore require a two-step rewriting process. Before an area can be rewritten on the disk, all fields in that area must be oriented in a single direction. In other words, a given disk area must be separately erased before it can be recorded. In conventional MO drive designs, this erasure process requires a separate pass under the bias magnet with the polarity of the magnet temporarily reversed. After one pass for erasing previously written material, the field of the magnetic head is reversed again to the writing orientation. The actual information is written to disk on a second pass under the head. The only areas that change magnetic polarity are those struck with and heated by the laser beam.

The penalty for this two-step process is an apparent increase in the average access time of MO drives when writing data. The extra time for a second pass is substantial. Although speeds vary, many MO drives spin their disks at a leisurely 2,400 revolutions per minute, roughly a third slower than even the oldest hard disk drives (which typically operated at about 3,600 RPM; current drives may spin up to twice as fast). Each turn of such an MO disk therefore requires 25 milliseconds. Even discounting head movement, the average access time for writing to an MO drive cannot possibly be faster than 37.5 milliseconds. (On the average, the data to be erased will be half a spin away from the read/write head, 12.5 milliseconds, and a second spin to write the data will take an additional 25 milliseconds.) Understandably, most manufacturers are working on "one-pass" MO drives and are speeding the spins of their disks. Some drives now spin faster, at the same 3,600 RPM rate as hard disks. The 3.5-inch MO drives typically operate at 3,000 RPM.

Read Operation

At the field strengths common to electronic gear, light beams are generally unreactive with magnetic fields. Fiber optic cables, for example, are impervious to the effects of normal electromagnetic noise that would pollute ordinary wires. Consequently, getting a laser to read the miniscule magnetic fields on an MO disk is a challenge.

The trick used in MO technology is polarization. The MO disk is read by a laser beam that is reflected from the disk surface as in other technologies, but in the MO drive the laser beam is polarized. That is, the plane of orientation of its photons in the laser beam are all aligned in one direction.

When the polarized beam strikes the magnetically aligned particles of the disk, the magnetic field of the media particles causes the plane of polarization of the light beam to rotate slightly, a phenomenon called the *Kerr effect*. Although small, as little as a 1 percent shift in early MO media but now reportedly up to 7 percent, this change in polarization can be detected as reliably as the direct magnetic reading of a conventional magnetic hard disk. A polarized beam passing through a second polarizing material diminishes in intensity depending on how closely the polarity of the beam is aligned with that of the second material. In effect, the polarity change becomes a readily detected intensity change.

Media

The medium used by magneto-optical disks differs substantially from their magnetic siblings. Moreover, all magneto-optical systems use cartridges. The MO medium is suited to cartridge design because it is relatively invulnerable to the environmental dangers that can damage magnetic media. Moreover, the storage densities of MO storage allow a single platter cartridge to hold useful amounts of data.

MO cartridge media come in two size, roughly corresponding to those of hard disks: 5.25 inches and 3.5 inches. Despite their common name, 5.25-inch MO cartridges are filled with optical disk platters that actually measure 130 millimeters (5.12 inches) in diameter. The cartridges themselves measure 0.43 by 5.31 by 6.02 inches (HWD) and somewhat resemble 3.5-inch floppy disks in that the disk itself is protected by a sliding metal shutter. So-called 3.5-inch magneto-optical disks have platters that are actually 90 millimeters across in a cartridge shell, about the same size and appearance as a 3.5-inch floppy disk—only the MO disks are thicker.

The magnetic medium on an MO disk is constructed from several layers. First, the plastic substrate of the disk is isolated with a dielectric coating. The actual magneto-optical compound—an alloy of terbium (a rare-earth element), iron, and cobalt—comes next, protected by another dielectric coating. A layer of aluminum atop this provides a reflective surface for the tracking mechanism. This sandwich is then covered by 0.30 millimeters inches of transparent plastic. Disks are made single-sided, and then two are glued together back-to-back to produce two-sided media.

Unlike conventional magnetic hard disks that store data on a number of concentric tracks or cylinders, under the ISO standard, MO drives use a single, continuous spiral track much like the groove on an old vinyl phonograph record. The spiral optimizes the data transfer of the drive because the read/write head does not need to be moved between tracks during extended data transfers. It instead smoothly scans across the disk.

Optical

Optical mass storage systems fall into three classes, read-only, write-once, and erasable (read/write). The basic CD and DVD formats through which software—be it computer programs or movies—is distributed are classic read-only media. WORM drives, used in archiving systems, and CD-R drives that let you make your own CDs at home are write-once media. Erasable systems include CD-RW, DVD-RW, DVD-RAM, DVD-RW, and DVD+RW as well as the proprietary PCD (Phase Change Disc) and PD (Phase Disc) formats. All erasable optical media use the same technology with minor variations.

The erasable optical technology is called *phase change*. It is based on exotic compounds that have two desirable properties. The materials have two markedly different reflectivities in two different phase states. They have an amorphous state in which their molecules are jumbled in such a way they form a rough surface that does not reflect light well. They also have a crystalline state in which their molecules form the perfect array of a crystal that has a smooth surface that reflects light well.

The other desirable quality is that a beam of light can change the material from one phase to another. The material starts off in its amorphous state. Upon heating it with a laser beam, the molecules align to the crystalline state. Further, stronger heating destroys the crystal and returns the material to the amorphous state.

The primary drawback of phase-change media is that the material eventually wears out and cannot reliably change its phases. Current compounds last between 500,000 and 1,000,000 erase cycles before the material deteriorates to a point it is unacceptable for data storage. To compensate for the limited life of phase-change media, the software drivers for the drives is designed to minimize the repeated erasing of sectors and spread sector usage across the disc.

Data Organization

Computer storage systems differ in the way they organize and allow access to the information that they store. Engineers class the storage systems in modern computers as either sequential or random access. From a practical standpoint, the difference is functional, how the computer system finds the information that it needs. But it also has a historic dimension; sequential computer mass storage pre-dates random access. You can also look at the difference topographically. Sequential storage is one dimensional and random access has two (or possibly more) dimensions.

Neither technology is inherently better. Both are used in modern PCs. For a given application, of course, one of the two is typically more suitable. But because each has its own strengths, both will likely persist as long as PCs populate desktops, if not longer.

Sequential Media

A fundamental characteristic of tape recording is that information is stored on tape one dimensionally—in a straight line across the length of the tape. This form of storage is called sequential because all of the bits of data are organized one after another in a strict sequence, like those paper-based dots. In digital systems, one bit follows after the other for the full length of the tape. Although the width of the tape may be put to use in multi-track, and the helical recording may be used by video systems, conceptually these, too, store information in one dimension only.

CD and DVDs for audio and video applications (that is, CD-DA, CD-Video, DVD-Video, and DVD-Audio) are designed to work best as one-dimensional media as well. They record data as a continuous stream meant to be displayed (or listened to) in the same sequential order it was recorded. However, the two-dimensional nature of the disc (a disc is a two-dimensional plane, after all) allows these media to transcend some of the limitations of sequential recording.

In the Newtonian universe (the only one that appears to make sense to the normal human mind), the shortest distance between two points is always a straight line. Alas, in magnetic tape systems, the shortest distance between two bits of data on a tape may also be a long time. To read two widely separated bits on a tape, all the tape between them must be passed over. Although all the bits in between are not to be used, they must be scanned in the journey from the first to second bits. If you want to retrieve information not stored in order on a tape, the tape must shuttle back and forth to find the data in the order that you want it. All that tape movement to find data means wasted time.

In theory, there's nothing wrong with sequential storage schemes; depending on the storage medium that's used, they can be very fast. For example, one form of solid-state computer memory, the all-electronic shift register, moves data sequentially at nearly the speed of light.

The sequential mass storage systems of today's computers are not so blessed with speed, however. Because of their mechanical foundations, most tape systems operate somewhat slower than the speed of light. For example, although light can zip across the vacuum of the universe at 186,000 miles per second (or so), cassette tape crawls along at one and seven-eighths inches per second. Although light can get from here to the moon and back in a few seconds, moving a cassette tape that distance would take about 10 billion times longer, several thousand years.

Although no tape stretches as long as the 238,000 mile distance to the moon, sequential data access can be irritatingly slow. Instead of delivering the near-instant response most of today's impatient power users demand, picking a file from a tape can take as long as 10 minutes. Even the best of today's tape systems require 30 seconds or more to find a file. If you had to load all your programs and data files from tape, you might as well take up crocheting to tide you through the times you're forced to wait.

Most sequential systems store data in blocks, sometimes called exactly that, sometimes called records. The storage system defines the structure and contents of each block. Typically, each block includes identifying information (such as a block number) and error-control information in addition to the actual data. Blocks are stored in order on tape. In some systems, they lay end to end, but others separate them with blank areas called inter-record gaps.

Most tape systems use multiple tracks to increase their storage. (Some systems spread as many as 144 tracks across tape just one-quarter inch wide.) The otherwise stationary read/write head in the tape machine moves up and down to select the correct track. This multi-track design also improves the access speed of the medium. With multiple tracks, the drive doesn't have to scan the whole tape to get at a particular block. With 144 tracks, a drive needs only to scan 1/144th the length of the tape to find a particular block. Sequential CDs and DVDs provide a greater speed-up because they can select among thousands of radial positions along the disc to read.

To take advantage of the speed-up afforded by multiple tracks, the drive needs to know on which track to find the block you're seeking. Old tape systems didn't keep track of location information; they would scan back and forth along the tape, one track after another, to find the blocks you wanted. New tape standards put a directory on the tape that holds the location of information on the tape. By consulting the directory, the drive can determine which track holds the information you want and zero in on the correct track to trim the response time of the tape system.

Random Access Media

On floppy and most hard computer disks as well as some CD and DVD formats, the recorded data are organized to take advantage of the two-dimensional aspect of the flat, wide disk surface to give even faster access than is possible with the directory system on tape. Instead of being arranged in a single straight line, disk-based data are spread across several concentric circles like lanes in a circular racetrack or the pattern of waves rolling away from a splash. Some optical drives follow this system, but many other optical systems modify this arrangement, changing the concentric circles into one tightly packed spiral that continuously winds from the edge to the center of the disk. But even these continuous data systems behave much as if they had concentric circles of information.

The mechanism for making this arrangement is quite elementary. The disk moves in one dimension under the read/write head, which scans the tape in a circle as it spins and defines a track, which runs across the surface of the disk much like one of the lanes of a racetrack. In most disk systems, the head, too, can move—else the read/write head would be stuck forever hovering over the same track and the same stored data, making it a sequential storage system that wastes most of the usable storage surface of the disk.

In most of today's disk systems, the read/write moves across a radius of the disk, perpendicular to a tangent of the tracks. The read/write head can quickly move between the different tracks on the disk. Although the shortest distance between two points (or two bytes) remains a straight line, to get from one byte to another, the read/write head can take shortcuts across the lanes of the racetrack. After the head reaches the correct track, it still must wait for the desired bit of information to cycle around under it. However, disks spin relatively quickly—300 revolutions per minute for most floppy disks and up to 7,200 RPM for some hard disks—so you only need to wait a fraction of a second for the right byte to reach your system.

Because the head can jump from byte to byte at widely separated locations on the disk surface and because data can be read and retrieved in any order or at random in the two-dimensional disk system, disk storage systems are often called *random access devices*, even though they fall a bit short of the mark with their need to wait while hovering over a track.

The random access capability of magnetic disk systems makes the combination much faster than sequential tape media for the mass storage of data. Disks are so superior and so much more convenient than tapes that tape is almost never used as a primary mass storage system. Usually, tape plays only a secondary role as a backup system. Disks are used to store programs and files that need to be loaded on a moment's notice.

Combination Technologies

Some PC applications involve long streams of data and only occasional random access. The most important of these is multimedia. For example, a video plays a long sequence of data bytes and requires random access only when you want to leap between scenes.

Although in theory random access storage should work for such applications, practical storage systems sometimes have problems. When a disk drive needs to gather together a number of random blocks of data to put together a data stream, its head may have to jump all over the disk to locate the blocks. Although the drive can read data within each block at a rate faster than the requirements of the data stream, the delay imposed by physically moving the drive's head to find the next block may interrupt the smooth flow of the data stream. As a result, a video played from an ordinary hard disk may drop frames or appear jumpy. Sequential devices don't suffer this problem and are eminently suited to playing video, as your home VCR ably demonstrates. What your VCR cannot do, however, is quickly shift from a scene at the beginning of a tape to one at the end of the tape.

Some PC mass storage devices consequently combine sequential and random access. DVD drives, for example, play sequential videos or retrieve random data from DVD-ROM, depending on the disc you slide in.

Most magneto-optical (MO) and pure optical (CD and DVD) drives organize their storage as a single continuous track spiral, essentially the topological equivalent of sequential tape. However, the read/write head of the drive is still capable of moving radially across the disk. It has to, if just to follow the long spiral. Because it still can leap from one part of the continuous track to another, the moving head also endows these systems with fast random access speeds. Because the head can follow the track inward without jogging and briefly skipping over an unreadable disk area, these continuous track systems can smoothly read long blocks of data at high speeds. Consequently, they offer excellent random access speeds and high continuous data transfer rates.

Data Coding

The goal of any data storage system is to pack as much information into as small a space as possible, at least with an acceptable level of security and reasonable hope of being able to recover it later. Long ago, archivists realized that the information content was paramount. The form in which they stored the information was negotiable. Instead of locking away sheaves and reams of paper, they could microfilm the images and store the data content in a fraction of the space.

In digital storage, more in less space has always been the credo. Again, one of the big secrets is having freedom to manipulate the form of the data without affecting its information content.

Flux Transitions

In magnetic storage systems, the 1s and 0s of digital information are not normally represented by the absolute direction in which the magnetic field is oriented, but by a change from one orientation to another so that they can take advantage of the most easily detected maximal magnetic change—from saturation in one direction to saturation in the other. These dramatic changes are termed flux transitions because the magnetic field or flux makes a transition between each of its two allowed states. In the very simplest magnetic recording systems, the occurrence of a flux transition would be the equivalent of a digital 1; no transition would be a digital 0.

The system must know when to expect a flux transition, or it would never know that it had missed one. Somehow, the magnetic medium and the recording system must be synchronized with one another so that the system knows the point at which a flux transition should occur or not. Instead of simple bit-for-bit recording, digital magnetic storage requires an elaborate coding system to keep the data straight.

Certainly, assigning a single flux transition the job of storing a digital bit could be made to work, but this obvious solution is hardly the optimal one. For instance, to prevent errors, a direct one-to-one correspondence of flux-to-data would require that the pulse train on the recording medium be exactly synchronized with the expectations of the circuitry reading the data, perhaps by carefully adjusting the speed of the medium to match the expected data rate. A mismatch would result in all of the data read or written being in error. It might take several spins of the disk—each spin lasting more than a dozen milliseconds—to get back in sync.

By including extra flux transitions on the disk to help define the meaning of each flux change on a magnetic medium, you could eliminate the need for exact speed control or other physical means of synchronizing the stored data. All popular magnetic recording systems use this expedient to store data asynchronously. However, all of these asynchronous recording schemes also impose a need for control information to help make sense from the unsynchronized flux transition pulse train.

Single-Density Recording

In one of the earliest magnetic digital recording schemes called Frequency Modulation, or FM, recording, the place in which a flux transition containing a digital bit was going to occur was marked by an extra transition called a clock bit. The clock bits form a periodic train of pulses that enables the system to be synchronized. The existence of a flux change between those corresponding to two clock bits indicated a digital 1, and no flux change between clocks indicated a digital 0.

The FM system requires a reasonably loose frequency tolerance. That is, the system could reliably detect the presence or absence of pulse bits between clock bits even if the clock frequency was not precise. In addition, the bandwidth of the system is quite narrow, so circuit tolerances are not critical. The disadvantage of the system is that two flux changes were needed to record each bit of data, the least-dense practical packing of data on disk.

Initial digital magnetic storage devices used the FM technique, and for years, it was the prevailing standard. After improvements in data packing were achieved, FM became the point of reference, often termed single-density recording.

Double-Density Recording

Modified Frequency Modulation (MFM) recording, or double-density recording, was once the most widely used coding system for PC hard disks and is still used by many PC floppy disk drives. Double-density recording eliminates the hard clock bits of single density to pack information on the magnetic medium twice as densely.

Instead of clock bits, digital 1s are stored as a flux transition and 0s as the lack of a transition within a given period. To prevent flux reversals from occurring too far apart, an extra flux reversal is always added between consecutive 0s.

Group Coded Recording

Even though double-density recording essentially packs every flux transition with a bit of data, it's not the densest way of packing information on the disk. Other data coding techniques can as much as double the information stored in a given system as compared to double-density recording.

FM and MFM share a common characteristic, a one-to-one correspondence between bits of data and the change recorded on the disk. Although such a correspondence is the obvious way to encode information, it is not the only way. Moreover, the strict correspondence does not always make the most efficient use of the storage medium.

The primary alternative way of encoding data is to map groups of bits to magnetic patterns on the magnetic storage medium. Encoding information in this way is called Group Coded Recording, or GCR.

On the surface, group coding appears like a binary cipher. Just as in the secret codes used by simplistic spies in which each letter of the alphabet corresponds to another, group coding reduced to an absurdity would make a pattern like 0101 record on a disk as a pattern of flux transitions like TTNT where T is a transition and N is no transition. Just as simple translations buy the spy little secrecy (such transpositional codes can be broken in minutes by anyone with a rudimentary knowledge of ciphering), they do little for the storage system. Where they become valuable is in using special easy-to-record patterns of flux transitions for each data groups, typically with more transitions than there are bits in the data group. This technique succeeds in achieving higher real densities because the real limit on data storage capacity is the spacing of flux transitions in the magnetic medium. The characteristics of the magnetic medium, the speed at which the disk spins, and the design of the disk read/write head together determine the minimum and maximum spacing of the flux changes in the medium. If the flux changes are too close together, the read/write head might not be able to distinguish between them; if they are too far apart, they cannot be reliably detected.

By tinkering with the artificial restraints on data storage, more information can be packed within the limits of flux transition spacing in the medium.

Run Length Limited, or RLL, is one special case of Group Coded Recording designed to use a complex form of data manipulation to fit more information in the storage medium without exceeding the range limits of its capability to handle flux transitions. In the most common form of RLL, termed 2,7, each byte of data is translated into a pattern of 16 flux transitions.

Although this manipulation requires double the number of flux transition bits to store a given amount of information, it has the virtue that only a tiny fraction of the total number of 16-bit codes is needed to unambiguously store all the possible 8-bit data codes. There are 256 eight-bit codes and 65,536 sixteen-bit codes. Consequently, the engineer designing the system has a great range of 16-bit codes to choose from for each byte of data. If he's particularly astute, he can find patterns of flux translations that are particularly easy to record on the disk. In the 2,7 RLL system, the 16-bit patterns are chosen so that between 2 and 7 digital zeroes are between each set of digital ones in the resulting 16-bit data stream of flux transitions. The 16-bit code patterns that do not enforce the 2,7 rule are made illegal and never appear in the data stream that goes to the magnetic storage device.

Although the coding scheme requires twice as many bits to encode its data, the pulses in the data stream better fit within the flux transition limits of the recording medium. In fact, the 2,7 RLL code ensures that flux transitions will be three times farther apart than in double-density recording because only the digital 1s cause flux changes, and they are always spaced at least three binary places apart. Although there are twice as many code bits in the data stream because of the 8-to-16 bit translation, their corresponding flux transitions will be three times closer together on the magnetic medium while still maintaining the same spacing as would be produced by MFM. The overall gain in storage density achieved by 2,7 RLL over MFM is 50 percent.

The disadvantage of the greater recording density is that much more complex control electronics and wider bandwidth electronics in the storage device are required to handle the higher data throughput.

Advanced RLL

A more advanced RLL coding system improves not only on the storage density that can be achieved on a disk but is also more tolerate of old-fashioned disks. This newer system differs from 2,7 RLL in that it uses a different code that changes the bit pattern so that the number of sequential zeros is between three and nine. This system, known for obvious reasons as 3,9 RLL or Advanced RLL still uses an 8-to-16 bit code translation, but it ensures that digital 1s will never be closer than every four bits. As a result, it allows data to be packed into flux transitions four times denser. The net gain, allowing for the loss in data translation, amounts to 100 percent. Information can be stored about twice as densely with 3,9 RLL as ordinary double-density recording techniques.

This seemingly extraordinary data packing capability is a result of the various artificial limits enforced in most data storage systems. Until recently, most storage devices were designed for double-density recording, and they followed tightly defined interface standards for the connections between themselves and their control electronics. However, new interfacing schemes for hard disks isolate the data coding from the stream of data sent to the computer host. Drive manufacturers are thus free to use whatever form of data coding they like, and neither you nor your PC ever know the difference. Consequently, with modern hard disk drives, the form of data coding used is rarely revealed (unless you take a critical look at the manufacturer's specification sheet). The information is irrelevant when you use an advanced disk interface.

Partial Response Maximum Likelihood

Although group recording techniques have served well through the evolution of the PC hard disk, another technique called *Partial Response Maximum Likelihood* technology works in the opposite direction. Instead of modifying the data—essentially expanding it to make it work better with existing hardware—it modifies the read electronics of the disk drive so they can better sort through densely recorded data. IBM first introduced PRML electronics in 1990, and the technology found its way into PC hard disk drives a few years later.

PRML works only during reading the disk. Its specific goal is to compensate for *inter-symbol interference*, a kind of distortion that appears when a drive packs data densely. As the read/write head scans the disk, it produces an analog signal. Conventional disk read electronics detect the peaks of the analog pulses and translate them into digital bits. At high bit rates, which occur when flux transitions are packed densely and disks spin rapidly, the peaks can blur together. The electronics can readily mistake two bits for one or make similar errors. PRML read electronics can better sort through the analog signals and more reliably translate the signals into data.

The first step in the PRML process is to filter the signal from the read/write head using digital techniques, shaping it with a partial response characteristic by altering its frequency response and timing characteristics. Using digital processing, the PRML system then detects where signals from flux transitions are most likely to occur. The PRML system uses a sequence-detection algorithm developed by Andrew Viterbi, which accurately sorts through the data.

The chief advantage of PRML is that it ensures data integrity with high bit densities and faster data rates between head and electronics. PRML does not require special coding during recording. In fact, one of its advantages is that it sidesteps the increase in bit count that arises with group coding techniques. Because fewer bits must be written to disk, PRML allows more data to fit on a given disk. Because PRML allows higher disk densities, it can increase the read rate of a disk without altering its mechanical rate of rotation.

Data Compression

Using group coding, the correspondence between each bit pattern in the input data and the flux transitions represented by it is independent of all the other bit patterns in the data stream. Each pattern directly corresponds to its own pattern of flux transitions. The group coding system can mindlessly match bit pattern for flux pattern to achieve the optimal storage density of each byte of data.

But group coding does not represent the most efficient way of squeezing information into a storage medium. Many of the bytes in a stream of data are redundant. Their information content could be represented in some other manner using many fewer bytes. Group coding seeks to represent the stream of individual bytes without regard to content, simply ensuring each pattern can be faithfully reproduced. It does nothing to guarantee the actual information is encoded in the data stream as efficiently as possible.

In contrast to the local view taken by the group-coding mechanism, data compression systems take a global view. By examining the patterns of bytes rather than the bit patterns inside each byte, the compression system seeks to find patterns that can be more efficiently represented. The goal of the data compression system is to eliminate redundancy, separating the bulk from the content. In effect, the compression system squeezes the air out of the data stream. Data compression can reduce fat files into their slimmest possible representation, which can later, through a decompression process, be reconstituted into their original form.

Most compression systems work by reducing recurrent patterns in the data stream into short tokens. For example, the two-byte pattern "at" could be coded as a single byte such as "@," cutting the storage requirement in half. Most compression systems don't permanently assign tokens to bit patterns but instead make the assignments on the fly. They work on individual blocks of data one at a time, starting afresh with each block. Consequently, the patterns stored by the tokens of one block may be entirely different from those used in the next block. The key to decoding the patterns from the tokens is included as part of the data stream.

Disk compression systems put data compression technology to work by increasing the apparent capacity of your disk drives. Generally, they work by creating a virtual drive with expanded capacity with which you can work as though it were a normal (but larger) disk drive. The compression system automatically takes care of compressing and decompressing your data as you work with it. The information is stored in compressed form on your physical disk drive, which is hidden from you.

The compression ratio compares the resultant storage requirements to those required by the uncompressed data. For example, a compression ratio of 90 percent would reduce storage requirements by 90 percent. The compressed data could be stored in 10 percent of the space required by its original form. Most data compression systems achieve about a 50 percent compression ratio on the mix of data found that most people use.

Because the compression ratio varies with the kind of data you store, the ultimate capacity of a disk that uses compression is impossible to predict. The available capacity reported by your operating system on a compressed drive is only an estimate based on the assumed compression ratio of the system. You can change this assumption to increase the reported remaining capacity of your disk drive, but the actual remaining capacity (which depends on the data you store, not the assumption) will not change.

Lossless Versus Lossy Compression

Most compression systems assume that you want to get back every byte and every bit that you store. You don't want numbers disappearing from your spreadsheets or commands from your programs. You assume that decompressing the compressed data will yield everything you started with—without losing a bit. The processes that deliver that result are called lossless compression systems.

Sometimes, however, your data may contain more detail than you need. For example, you might scan a photo with a true-color 24-bit scanner and display it on an ordinary VGA system with a color range of only 256 hues. All the precise color information in your scan is wasted on your display, and the substantial disk space you use for storing it could be put to better use.

Analog images converted to digital form and analog audio recordings digitized often contain subtle nuances beyond the perception of most people. Some data reduction schemes called lossy compression systems ignore these fine nuances. The reconstituted data does not exactly replicate the original. For viewing or listening, the restored data is often good enough. Because lossy compression systems work faster than lossless schemes and because their resulting compression ratios are higher, they are often used in time- and space-sensitive applications—digital image and sound storage.

Software Compression

Compression is a data transformation much like all the other manipulations made by a microprocessor. Consequently, an ordinary software program can convert your PC's microprocessor into an excellent data compressor.

The most popular software-based disk compression system today is DriveSpace, if only by virtue of being a standard part of Microsoft's operating system offerings. DriveSpace is in its third incarnation. Microsoft created the first version as an enhancement to DOS 6.22 to resolve patent litigation with Stac Electronics, the developers of Stacker. DriveSpace 2 was the standard compression software included with Windows 95. Microsoft offers the most recent version, DriveSpace 3, as a low-cost option with its Plus! utilities pack and as standard equipment with Windows 98.

The design of DriveSpace and DriveSpace 2 limited them to storing a maximum of 512MB of compressed data. DriveSpace 3 ups that maximum capacity to 2GB. DriveSpace 3 adds two advanced compression options: HiPack, which works on the fly and promises to squeeze an extra 10 to 15 percent (Microsoft's figures) from your hard disk; and UltraPack, which runs offline, typically at night as scheduled by Compression Agent (another utility in the Plus! package), and wrings out the last available byte. Files open more slowly once they've been ultra-packed, so much so that Microsoft recommends this level of compression not be used with 486 and slower systems. Once you open an ultra-packed file, it gets stored in a less compressed and faster-opening form until the next after-hours ultra-packing.

All three versions of DriveSpace use the same basic underlying mechanism. They create a virtual drive that appears to you and your programs as the actual hard disk you work with. The data on that virtual drive gets stored as a *compressed volume file* on your physical hard disk, which Microsoft terms the *host drive*. In the process of setting up your system each time you boot, the operating system usually makes the CVF appear as drive C: and the host drive is shifted from its normal drive letter (what typically *would have been* C:) to drive H:, although its drive letter may be hidden from normal listings. The CVF resides on the host drive in the form of a file with the name of DRVSPACE.000, which you normally won't see in directory listings because it has its read-only, hidden, and system attributes set on. These attributes also prevent you from altering the CVF. Although you can change the attributes of the CVF and view or edit it, making any change to the CVF may corrupt the entire file and can make *all* the data stored on the CVF unusable.

To squeeze just a bit more from your hard disk, DriveSpace allocates files in the CVF in units of 512 bytes instead of normal allocation units (which may contain up to 32KB on large drives with 16-bit file allocation tables). These smaller allocation units trim the amount used by each file because on average each file (which also includes subdirectories and shortcuts) wastes half an allocation unit of disk space. With DriveSpace 3, you can take advantage of this feature without using compression by specifying "No Compression" under the Settings selection from the Advanced menu when setting up a DriveSpace drive, as shown in Figure 8.3.

FIGURE 8.3

DriveSpace 3 No Compression option.

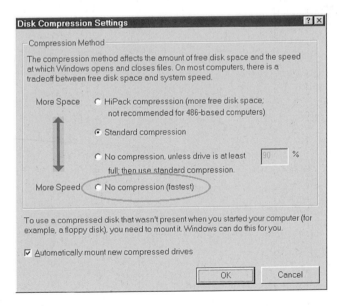

The Microsoft design of DriveSpace requires that your operating system read the disk compression driver from your boot disk before it can use compression. Consequently, the files that the operating system requires for the preliminary steps of booting up cannot be compressed; if they were, the operating system would not be able to decipher them. When DriveSpace sets itself up, it normally reserves space for the required files before allocating for the CVF.

Early versions of DriveSpace and Windows did not allow locating virtual memory or your swap file on the CVF. Additional space on the host drive had to be reserved to store such files in uncompressed form. Windows 95 and later versions allow you to locate both the Registry and swap file on the compressed drive, although locating the swap file there requires that your disk system use a protected-mode drive to access the host drive. The swap file is not actually compressed on the CVF. Primarily for performance reasons, it is marked uncompressable and stored in its native form. To minimize its fragmentation (and again improve performance), it is located as the last file in the sector heap.

Once you've created a CVF, its size is fixed by the space allocated to it on the host drive. Because the actual compression ratio any software can achieve varies with the type data you store, the actual storage capacity, like your mileage, may vary. DriveSpace uses a simple algorithm to calculate the free space that your operating system will report for the compressed drive; it simply multiplies the actually space remaining in the CVF on the host drive by a compression ratio, nominally two. You can change this compression ratio using the Change Ratio selection in the Advanced menu in DriveSpace. Changing this number will alter the apparent remaining capacity of your compressed drive; raise the ratio and the apparent capacity will increase commensurately. The actual storage space *does not* change. Setting the ratio too high will result in compressed disk space disappearing with amazing speed, perhaps leaving you with a full disk and no place to save files.

When your operating system reports the size of a file that's stored on a compressed drive, it give you the *uncompressed* size of the file.

DriveSpace gives you two options in creating a compressed drive. It can start with what you have and compress your existing files, or it can create a new compressed drive. The latter operation is faster because DriveSpace does not have to compress any data. If you choose to compress a drive with existing files on it, Microsoft rightly warns you to make a backup first. Although the compression process usually progresses flawlessly, errors can occur from which you may not be able to recover.

Hardware Compression

Some hard disk manufacturers have investigated device-level compression for some of their products. This technology moves the compression coprocessor from an expansion board to the disk drive. Such disks can store more information than their resources would otherwise allow. Because the compression circuitry is part of the drive and automatically fits in the middle of the data stream, there's no need for software drivers to make this form of compression work. Unlike ordinary software or hardware compression that requires driver software, limiting its use to a specific operating system, device-level compression will work with any operating system and is completely invisible. All it requires is basic hardware compatibility: an interface into which you can plug in the drive.

Such drives have one disadvantage. All compression systems—including software, coprocessor (board-level hardware), and disk device-level compression—use essentially the same compression methods, even the same algorithms. As a result, using more than one of these methods is counterproductive. After you have compressed data, you cannot squeeze it again (at least using the same algorithm). Layering multiple levels of compression won't yield more space, may in fact waste space, and definitely impacts performance.

Few, if any, hard disk drives with built-in device-level hardware compression have been marketed. With the great strides made in enhancing capacity with other technological improvements, the gains haven't been worth the pain. It does, of course, remain a possibility should a drive maker need a capacity edge.

File Compression and Archiving Systems

Compression has proven to be such a valuable technology that it is used in other ways besides increasing disk storage. For example, advanced modem protocols often include data compression to increase throughput levels. In addition, file archiving software such as the popular program PKZip also takes advantage of compression to more effectively use your disk's space.

File compression and archiving software differs from ordinary disk compression in several ways. It works on a file-by-file basis rather than across a complete disk. It is not automatic; you manually select the files you want to archive and compress. The archiving software does not work on the fly but instead executes upon your command. It compresses files individually but can package several files together into a single archive file. Archive files are stored as ordinary Windows files but can be read or executed only after they have been uncompressed.

Because these archiving systems do not compress on the fly, they can spend extra time to optimize their compression—for example, trying several compression algorithms to find the most successful one. They can often achieve higher compression ratios than standard disk compression software. (Because they are time insensitive, these programs can try more complex compression methods and avoid the rule that a compressed file can be compressed no further.) Your disk compression software, however, can't squeeze their contents any tighter.

Perhaps the most popular application for file compression software is preparing files for transmission by modem. It allows you to package together a group of related files, shrink them to the minimal possible size, and conveniently ship them off with a single send command. Of course, the resulting files will not be further compressible, so your modem will apparently operate at a slower speed, passing along the compressed data byte-for-byte.

Electronics and Interfaces

A mass storage system usually consists of three parts, which are sometimes combined together. The actual drive or transport (complete with its own internal electronics) handles the medium, spooling the tape or spinning the disk. The controller electronics generate the signals that control the transport from commands given by the host computer system. The host adapter converts the signals generated by the host computer—for our purposes, the signals that travel on the ISA or PCI bus—into those that are compatible with the controller.

The electronics on the drive itself take on a number of functions depending on the vintage of the drive. The electronics of the oldest drives were charged merely with governing the physical operation of the drive. They would monitor and control the speed of the recording medium—for example, assuring that the spin of a hard disk was the correct and constant rate. Otherwise, the electronics would merely buffer signals from an external controller, boosting their level so that they delivered power adequate for their physical function. The drive didn't care about what it recorded. It simply passed the bits it read directly to its host to deal with.

With these products, an external controller managed the data stream from the drive. A *data separator* took the raw signal and pulled the bits out. Other logic on the drive formatted the data to be compatible with the host computer, for example, taking the serial data stream and creating a parallel bus signal. The controller also translated high-level commands from the computer into the signals needed to physically operate the drive. This kind of controller is termed a *device-level controller* because its design and operation will vary with the device that's being controlled. A device-level controller for a hard disk must generate different signals than one for a tape drive.

As it became possible to shrink electronics down to a size that all the controller functions would fit onto the drive itself, engineers took a new tack in designing interfaces. They arranged that the interface would deliver the same signals regardless of the type of device connected to it. The interface would use a common electrical interface for all device types. Instead of using hardware signals to control the device, control came through software commands. The interface boasted a command set that embraced all the functions needed to operate any device type that could connect to the interface. The interface delivered data from the drive not in a raw serial bit stream but as a parallel data channel similar to a computer bus, with the data already formatted and ready to use. This kind of interface is described as *system level* because its signals are compatible with the host system rather than a particular device.

In contrast to device-level interfaces, system-level interfaces give the mass storage designer a great deal of freedom. The inner workings of the storage device are hidden from the interface; all that comes out is formatted data compatible with the host computer. Although conventional device-level designs push the raw data stream from the disk or other device through the interface (with the data goes device formatting information such as sector identifications), system-level interfaces transfer only active data. The system-level interfaces pass along only an executive summary of the device's information; device-level interfaces must include the footnotes, page numbers, and irrelevant digressions. Without all the chaff, the system-level interface can move more data even when operating at exactly the same clock rate as a device-level interface.

In addition, because the actual device is hidden from the interface signals, the system-level design allows technical innovation without altering compatibility. New technologies for higher capacities, greater security, or even faster throughput can be accommodated without violating the standard. All modern interfaces—in particular, AT Attachment and SCSI—are system level.

Caching

All mass storage devices—be they magnetic hard disks, floppies, or optical—face two primary performance constraints: access speed and transfer rate. Access speed is the inevitable delay between the instant your computer requests a particular byte or block of information from the disk drive and when that information is located on the disk. In specifications, access speed is represented by a number termed average access time, which describes the mean time (in milliseconds) required for the read/write head of a drive to move between disk tracks. Transfer rate describes the speed at which the information stored on the disk can be moved into the working memory of your PC. It is usually measured in megabytes per second.

Access speed and transfer rate are issues of design, but their ultimate limits arise from mechanical issues. Because of the mechanical nature of these speed limits, any miraculous improvement in disk performance is impossible. Because laws of motion involving inertia and other principles that scientists hold dear preclude instantaneous acceleration, access delays can never be eliminated from mechanical systems. More to the point, practical mechanisms can never lower the delays to the point that some people—likely including yourself—won't be bothered by them. Similarly, the rotation rates of disks are limited by such issues as mechanical integrity (spin a disk too fast and centrifugal force will tear it apart) and the fact that the packing of data is constrained by the capability of the read/write technology to resolve individual bits on the disk surface.

The big problem with these mechanical limits is that they are orders of magnitude lower than the electronic and logic limits of computers. A computer thinks in nanoseconds and microseconds but has to wait milliseconds when it needs data from a disk. The computer may need to wait longer when it needs to transfer a large block of information from a mass storage device.

The best way to hurdle these mechanical barriers is with caching. A read cache attempts to keeps the next data you'll need from disk in memory so that you can access it at electronic rather than mechanical speeds. A write cache grabs data you want to write to disk at electronic speed and then slowly, at mechanical speed, copies it into disk memory. All modern operating systems include caches of some kind, either integrated into the file system or as add-on programs. Caches are part of both the NTFS file system used by Windows NT and Windows 2000 and the VFAT system native to Windows 95 and Windows 98.

Caches are generally classified into two types—software and hardware—depending on the type of memory used to build the cache and where the cache is located in the system. Software caches use part of the main memory of your PC. Hardware caches use their own, dedicated memory supply. Most modern hard disks have built-in buffers that range in size from one track to a megabyte. High-performance disk host adapters often incorporate hardware caches that accommodate 16MB or more.

Software caches hold a performance advantage in that they work after the disk interface and expansion bus. They can operate faster than whatever performance limit is imposed by the interface and bus. Information from the hardware cache, even if instantly available, still may be throttled as it courses through the interface and expansion bus. As a practical matter, however, that difference amounts to little more than an interesting fact. Today's fast interfaces and buses make the connections with little constraint. Moreover, the two caching technologies benefit different applications, making the issue irrelevant as a practical matter.

Cache Operation

Disk caching systems differ in three principal ways: How they handle read operations, how (and whether) they cache disk-write operations, and their usage and management of system memory.

Read Buffering

The fundamental function of a disk cache is buffering read operations. The cache software fills its memory with what data it anticipates your system and software will need and supplies that information from its buffers on request at RAM speed when there is a cache hit. If there is a miss, the cache directs the software to retrieve data from disk at disk speed.

The design issues control how efficient that read cache operates—and thus how often it speeds up disk operations. These issues include how the memory of the cache is filled with data, how the contents of memory are updated, and how the cache recognizes whether needed information is contained in its memory.

The first issue appears simple. After all, before you can expect to read anything in a cache, there must be something there. But filling a cache is a task akin to seeing an omen; the cache-control software must make a stab at predicting your system's needs. Most caches take a straightforward approach, reading somewhat more disk than your application software requests of a given disk track or (less commonly) file. The underlying assumption is that you'll need more of what you're already looking at.

After a few read requests, the cache memory will fill up, and the control software is faced with the problem of what to save and what to discard to make room for new data. Several different algorithms are used by the writers of software caches. Most are variations of *Least Frequently Used* (LFU) and *Least Recently Used* (LRU) designs, in that order of popularity. The former discards the data in the cache that your system has asked least often. The latter throws away the data that was requested the longest time previously. The LFU technique is more complex and demands more from system resources, so LRU often performs better. Even so, in typical systems, the gain performance in using the two techniques falls within about 8 percent of one another, close enough to be a draw.

Keeping track of the data in the cache is a matter of minimizing the time required to determine whether needed data is held within the cache. In general, cache programs assign tags to associate data in memory with data on the disk. The exact handling of this information, like the other details of caching algorithms used by specific products, is a matter of great secrecy among most commercial cache publishers. For the most part, publishers treat their technology as if it were black magic—but even more mysterious.

Despite such proprietary miracles, most cache designers admit that the read performance among disk caching systems vary little. In cases where you can substitute or add other caching systems, you won't see a significant change in writing speed (although moving to another technology, the hardware cache discussed later in this chapter, is another matter). This inescapable fact coupled to the caches built into modern operating systems has virtually eliminated the market for third-party add-in caching software.

Write Buffering

Write caching is a complex issue. Many cache designers avoid it because it is inherently dangerous. Data you expect to be written to disk is temporarily caught in the limbo of solid-state memory. If you switch off your PC before the data gets written, it may be lost even though you thought it had been saved.

Early, aggressive add-in caching software was often designed to use a technique called *delayed writing*. The caching software held disk-bound data in memory if your system were busy, particularly if it were writing to disk. When it sensed a break—for example, you sitting there staring at the screen wondering what to do next—it immediately rushed everything to disk. The longer it waited, the longer your disk-bound data would be vulnerable to your whims and power failures. Most such add-in caches limited the maximum period to delay before writing; many let you decide how long to wait.

An alternative to delayed writing is *concurrent writing*. Instead of waiting for a break, the cache writes your data concurrent with whatever else you do next, making it appear your write operation executed immediately and instantly. The technique is simple in concept; the cache accepts data from your application and immediately begins writing it to disk. Instead of holding back your system while the data is doled out through the drive interface and drive mechanism, you never lose control of your software. The actual writing to disk continues for some time afterward, concurrent with the continuation of normal operation of your PC. Most modern operating systems use this approach to write caching, making the write operation a separate program thread. Although this technique might not be considered a true write cache—no special memory is reserved for the cache and no special algorithms are required—it achieves the same end.

Such concurrent writing technology is not risk-free. Switching off your PC before the disk write completes still results in lost data. However, there will be no unpredictable period of vulnerability as is the case with delayed writing systems. As soon as the drive-activity indicator extinguishes, you're safe to switch off or reboot your PC. If you follow the normal orderly shut-down procedure required by your operating system—clicking Shut Down before switching off your PC—you won't have anything to worry about (at least in regard to disk writing).

Memory Usage

Read caches and delay writing caches all require memory of some kind to temporarily hold your disk data before it is used or written. Read caches in particular can be heavy users of memory because of their speculative nature: They need to hold as much data as they can to better the chances what you want will be in the cache. In general, the more memory devoted to the cache, the faster it will appear to be.

Software Caches

This memory has to come from somewhere. If you rely on the cache built into your software (or an add-in software-based cache program), whatever is put to work as a buffer for the cache is stolen from your programs. A bigger cache buffer means less memory for applications. With modern operating systems that use virtual memory, with a big cache the operating system ends up shuffling more data into virtual memory (which uses disk space to emulate solid-state memory). As a result, a larger cache can slow down your system rather than speed it up.

Modern caches integrated into operating systems allocate their memory to avoid such problems. They seek to make the best compromise between the cache and application memory. Most will, however, let you tune the cache somewhat.

For example, Windows 95 lets you choose the amount of memory to devote to the cache, although its method is a bit backhanded. You select the cache size (and thus performance) by selecting the size of the blocks it reads ahead. Choosing larger blocks puts more data in the buffer and potentially yields higher performance.

You can tune the Windows 95 cache by opening the System folder in Control Panel and clicking to the Hard Disk tab in File System Properties. You will see a screen like that in Figure 8.4.

FIGURE 8.4

Windows 95 hard disk read-ahead optimization.

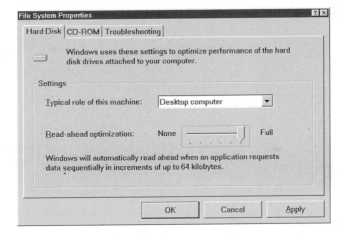

You can change the setting in two ways, by application or by directly setting the read-ahead block increment. Either way you make the change, you'll see it reflected in the size of the read-ahead block. The minimum is 0KB and the maximum is 64KB.

Hardware Caches

Hardware caches don't take memory away from your programs because they use their own, dedicated memory. Although a lot has been written about the advantage of hardware versus software caching, the issues all boil down to one: cost. To add hardware caching to a PC means buying a caching disk host adapter and filling it with memory. During the DRAM shortage a couple of years ago, the cost of memory imposed a severe penalty. Today, the price of RAM has fallen to such low levels that 16MB may be affordable. The caching host adapter may, however, cost $200 or more. Considering you get a software cache free, built into your operating system, you should expect to get a big benefit from your hardware caching investment. Whether you do depends on what your PC does.

A large hardware cache definitely improves the response of a disk server that's shared among many users. Because the data requests from different users likely involve different data but may be interwoven in time, the small buffers built into most of today's hard disks don't offer much help. Each time the disk serves a different user, it will dump much of the contents of its buffer, defeating its purpose. A large hardware cache can accommodate additional disk data from multiple users and deliver it at memory speed. Not only the user getting data from the cache but also the one next in line (and all those queued up for disk access) get faster response.

In a single-user system, dedicated hardware caching is a more dubious choice. It will speed up system operation, particularly when the operating system calls upon virtual memory. When the operating system needs to shift between applications and call on virtual memory, what it wants may be in the hardware cache. However, if the memory that's devoted to the hardware cache is instead used to augment the main memory of the PC, the operating system will have less need to use virtual memory. It will probably perform better than if it had the hardware cache.

Drive Arrays

When you need more capacity than a single hard disk can provide, you have two choices: trim your needs or plug in more disks. But changing your needs means changing your lifestyle—foregoing instant access to all of your files by deleting some from your disk, switching to data compression, or keeping a tighter watch on backup files and intermediary versions of projects under development. Of course, changing your lifestyle is about as easy as teaching a dog to change its spots. The one application with storage needs likely to exceed that capacity of today's individual hard disks—1.5GB and climbing—is a network server, and a total lifestyle change for a network server is about as probable as getting a platoon of toddlers to clean up a playroom littered with a near-infinite collection of toys.

Consequently, when the bytes run really low, you're left with the need for multiple disks. In most single-user PCs, each of these multiple drives acts independently and appears as a separate drive letter (or group of drive letters) under common Windows. Through software, such multiple drive systems can even be made to emulate one large disk with a total storage capacity equal to that of its constituent drives. Because Windows 95 and Windows 98 handle I/O serially—they can do only one I/O task at a time—such a solution is satisfactory, but it's hardly the optimum arrangement where reliability and providing dozens of users instant access is concerned. Instead of operating each disk independently, you can gain higher speeds, greater resistance to errors, and improved reliability by linking the drives through hardware to make a drive array—what has come to be known as a Redundant Array of Inexpensive Disks, or RAID.

Technologies

The premise of the drive array is elementary: Combine a number of individual hard disks to create a massive virtual system. But a drive array is more than several hard disks connected to a single controller. In an array, the drives are coordinated, and the controller specially allocates information between them using a program called Array Management Software. The AMS controls all the physical hard disks in the array and makes them appear to your PC as if they were one logical drive. For example, in some drive arrays, the AMS assures that the spin of each drive is synchronized and divides blocks of data to spread among several physical hard disks.

The obvious benefit of the drive array is the same as any multiple disk installation—capacity. Two disks can hold more than one, and four more than two. But drive array technology can also accelerate mass storage performance and increase reliability.

Data Striping

The secret to both of these innovations is the way the various hard disks in the drive array are combined. They are not arranged in a serial list where the second drive takes over once the capacity of the first is completely used up. Instead, data is split between drives at the bit, byte, or block level. For example, in a four drive system, two bits of every byte might come from the first hard disk, the next two bits from the second drive, and so on. The four drives could then pour a single byte into the data stream four times faster; moving all the information in the byte would only take as long as it would for a single drive to move two bits. Alternately, a four-byte storage cluster could be made from a sector from each of the four drives. This technique of splitting data between several drives is called data striping.

At this primitive level, data striping has a severe disadvantage: The failure of any drive in the system results in the complete failure of the entire system. The reliability of the entire array can be no greater than that of the least reliable drive in the array. The speed and capacity of such a system are greater but so are the risks involved in using it.

Redundancy and Reliability

By sacrificing part of its potential capacity, an array of drives can yield a more reliable, even fault tolerant, storage system. The key is redundancy. Instead of a straight division of the bits, bytes, and blocks each drive in the array stores, the information split between the drives can overlap.

For example, in the four-drive system instead of each drive getting two bits of each byte, each drive might store four. The first drive would take the first four bits of a given byte;

the second drive the third, fourth, fifth, and sixth bits; the third, the fifth, sixth, seventh, and eighth; the fourth, the seventh, eighth, first, and second. This digital overlap allows the correct information to be pulled from another drive when one encounters an error. Better yet, if any single hard disk should fail, all of the data it stored could be reconstituted from the other drives.

This kind of system is said to be fault tolerant. That is, a single fault—the failure of one hard disk—will be tolerated, meaning the system operates without the loss of any vital function. Fault tolerance is extremely valuable in network applications because the crash of a single hard disk does not bring down the network. A massive equipment failure therefore becomes a bother rather than a disaster.

The example array above represents the most primitive of drive array implementations, one that is particularly wasteful of the available storage resources. Advanced information coding methods allow higher efficiencies in storage, so a strict duplication of every bit is not required. Moreover, advanced drive arrays even allow *hot-swapping*, a feature that permits a failed drive to be replaced and the data that was stored upon it reconstructed without interrupting the normal operation of the array. A network server with such a drive array need not shut down even for disk repairs.

Implementations

Just connecting four drives to a SCSI controller won't create a drive array. An array requires special electronics to handle the digital coding and control of the individual drives. The electronics of these systems are proprietary to their manufacturers. The array controller connects to your PC through a proprietary or standard interface. SCSI is becoming the top choice. Currently, most drive arrays are assembled by computer manufacturers for their own systems, but a growing number are becoming available as plug-in additions to PCs.

In 1988, three researchers at the University of California at Berkeley—David A. Patterson, Garth Gibson, and Randy H. Katz—first outlined five disk array models in a paper entitled "A Case for Redundant Arrays of Inexpensive Disks." They called their models RAID levels and labeled them as RAID 1 through 5, appropriately enough. Their numerical designations were arbitrary and were not meant to indicate that RAID 1 is better or worse than RAID 5. The numbers simply provide a label for each technology that can be readily understood by the cognoscenti.

In 1993, these levels were formalized in the first edition of the *RAIDBook*, published by the RAID Advisory Board, an association of suppliers and consumers of RAID-related mass storage products. The book is part of one of the RAID Advisory Board's principle objectives, the standardization of the terminology of RAID-related technology. Although the board does not officially set standards, it does prepare them for submission to the recognized standards organizations. The board also tests the function and performance of RAID products and verifies that they perform a basic set of functions correctly.

The RAID Advisory Board currently recognizes nine RAID implementation levels. Five of these conform to the original Berkeley RAID definitions. Beyond the five array levels described by the Berkeley group, several other RAID terms are used and acknowledged by the RAID Advisory Board. These include RAID Level 0, RAID Level 6, RAID Level 10, and RAID Level 53.

The classification system is non-hierarchical; that is, a higher number does not imply a better or more advanced technology. The numbers are no more than labels for quickly identifying the technologies used. Because the common perception—really a misperception— is that the numbers *do* imply a ranking and that higher is better, some manufacturers have developed proprietary labels (RAID 7) or exploited non-Berkeley definitions (RAID 10 and 53) with high numbers that hint they are somewhat better than the lower numbered systems. Although each level has its unique advantages (and disadvantages), no one RAID technology is better than any of the others for all applications.

In an attempt to avoid such confusion, the RAID Advisory Board now classifies disk array products by what they accomplish in protecting data rather than by number alone. The board's Web site includes both a description and list of classified products.

RAID Level 0

Early workers used the term RAID Level 0 to refer to the absence of any array technology. According to the RAID Advisory Board, however, the term refers to an array that simply uses data striping to distribute data across several physical disks. Although this RAID Level 0 offers no greater reliability than the worst of the physical drives making up the array and no protection against data loss, it can improve the performance of the overall storage system. For example, reading data in parallel from two drives can effectively double throughput.

RAID Level 1

The simplest of drive arrays, RAID Level 1, consists of two equal-capacity disks that mirror one another. One disk duplicates all the files of the other, essentially serving as a backup copy. Should one of the drives fail, the other can serve in its stead.

This reliability is the chief advantage of RAID Level 1 technology. The entire system has the same capacity as one of its drive alone. In other words, the RAID Level 1 system yields only 50 percent of its potential storage capacity, making it the most expensive array implementation. Performance depends on the sophistication of the array controller. Simple systems deliver exactly the performance of one of the drives in the array. A more sophisticated controller could potentially double data throughput by simultaneously reading alternate sectors from both drives. Upon the failure of one of the drives, performance reverts to that of a single drive, but no information (and no network time) is lost.

RAID Level 2

The next step up in array sophistication is RAID Level 2, which interleaves bits or blocks of data as explained earlier in the description of drive arrays. The individual drives in the array operate in parallel, typically with their spindles synchronized.

To improve reliability, RAID Level 2 systems use redundant disks to correct single-bit errors and detect double-bit errors. The number of extra disks needed depends on the error-correction algorithm used. For example, an array of eight data drives may use three error correction drives. High-end arrays with 32 data drives may use 7 error correction drives. The data, complete with error-detection code, is delivered directly to the array controller. The controller can instantly recognize and correct for errors as they occur, without slowing the speed information is read and transferred to the host computer.

The RAID Level 2 design anticipates that disk errors occur often, almost regularly. At one time, mass storage devices might have been error-prone, but no longer. Consequently, RAID Level 2 can be overkill except in the most critical of circumstances.

The principal benefit of RAID Level 2 is performance; because of their pure parallel nature, it and RAID Level 3 are the best-performing array technologies, at least in systems that require a single, high-speed stream of data. In other words, it yields a high data transfer rate. Depending on the number of drives in the array, an entire byte or even 32-bit double-word could be read in the same period it would take a single drive to read one bit. Normal single-bit disk errors don't hinder this performance in any way because of RAID Level 2's on-the-fly error correction.

The primary defect in the RAID Level 2 design arises from its basic storage unit being multiple sectors. As with any hard disk, the smallest unit each drive in the array can store is one sector. File sizes must increase in units of multiple sectors—one drawn from each drive. In a 10-drive array, for example, even the tiniest 2-byte file would steal 10 sectors (5,120 bytes) of disk space. (Under the Windows VFAT system, which uses clusters of four sectors, the two-byte file would take a total of 20,480 bytes!) In actual applications, this drawback is not severe because systems that need the single-stream speed and instant error correction of RAID Level 2 also tend to be those using large files, for example, mainframes.

RAID Level 3

This level is one step down from RAID Level 2. Although RAID Level 3 still uses multiple drives operating in parallel interleaving bits or blocks of data, instead of full error correction it allows only for parity checking. That is, errors can be detected but without the guarantee of recovery.

Parity checking requires fewer extra drives in the array—typically only one per array—making it a less expensive alternative. When a parity error is detected, the RAID Level 3 controller reads the entire array again to get it right. This re-reading imposes a substantial performance penalty; the disks must spin entirely around again, yielding a 17 millisecond delay in reading the data. Of course, the delay appears only when disk errors are detected. Modern hard disks offer such high reliability that the delays are rare. In effect, RAID Level 3 compared to RAID Level 2 trades off fewer drives for a slight performance penalty that occurs only rarely.

RAID Level 4

This level interleaves not bits or blocks but sectors. The sectors are read serially, as if the drives in the array were functionally one large drive with more heads and platters. (Of course, for higher performance, a controller with adequate buffering could read two or more sectors at the same time, storing the later sectors in fast RAM and delivering them immediately after the preceding sector has been sent to the computer host.) For reliability, one drive in the array is dedicated to parity checking. RAID Level 4 earns favor because it permits small arrays of as few as two drives, although larger arrays make more efficient use of the available disk storage.

The dedicated parity drive is the biggest weakness of the RAID Level 4 scheme. In writing, RAID Level 4 maintains the parity drive by reading the data drives, updating the parity information, and then writing the update to the parity drive. This read-update-write cycle adds a performance penalty to every write, although read operations are unhindered.

RAID Level 4 offers an extra benefit for operating systems that can process multiple data requests simultaneously. An intelligent RAID Level 4 controller can process multiple input/output requests, reorganize them, and read its drives in the most efficient manner, perhaps even in parallel. For example, while a sector from one file is being read from one drive, a sector from another file can read from another drive. This parallel operation can improve the effective throughput of such operating systems.

RAID Level 5

This level eliminates the dedicated parity drive from the RAID Level 4 array and allows the parity-check function to rotate through the various drives in the array. Error checking is thus distributed across all disks in the array. In properly designed implementations, enough redundancy can be built in to make the system fault tolerant.

RAID Level 5 is probably the most popular drive-array technology currently in use because it works with almost any number of drives, including arrays as small as three, yet permits redundancy and fault tolerance to be built in.

RAID Level 6

To further improve the fault tolerance of RAID Level 5, the same Berkeley researchers who developed the initial five RAID levels proposed one more, now known as RAID Level 6. This level adds a second parity drive to the RAID Level 5 array. The chief benefit is that any two drives in the array can fail without the loss of data. This enables an array to remain in active service while an individual physical drive is being repaired yet still remain fault tolerant. In effect, a RAID Level 6 array with a single failed physical disk becomes a RAID Level 5 array. The drawback of the RAID Level 6 design is that it requires two parity blocks to be written during every write operation. Its write performance is extremely low, although read performance can achieve levels on par with RAID Level 5.

RAID Level 10

Some arrays employ multiple RAID technologies. RAID Level 10 represents a layering of RAID Levels 0 and 1 to combined the benefits of each. (Sometimes, RAID Level 10 is called RAID Level 0&1 to more specifically point at its origins.) To improve input/output performance, RAID Level 10 employs data striping, splitting data blocks between multiple drives. Moreover, the Array Management Software can further speed read operations by filling multiple operations simultaneously from the two mirrored arrays (at times when both halves of the mirror are functional, of course.) To improve reliability, the RAID level uses mirroring so that the striped arrays are exactly duplicated. This technology achieves the benefits of both of its individual layers. Its chief drawback is cost. As with simple mirroring, it doubles the amount of physical storage needed for a given amount of logical storage.

RAID Level 53

This level represents a layering of RAID Level 0 and RAID Level 3; the incoming data is striped between two RAID Level 3 arrays. The capacity of the RAID Level 53 array is the total of the capacity of the individual underlying RAID Level 3 arrays. Input/output performance is enhanced by the striping between multiple arrays. Throughput is improved by the underlying RAID Level 3 arrays. Because the simple striping of the top RAID Level 0 layer adds no redundant data, reliability falls. RAID Level 3 arrays, however, are inherently so fault tolerant that the overall reliability of the RAID Level 53 array far exceeds that of an individual hard disk drive. As with a RAID Level 3 array, the failure of a single drive will not adversely affect data integrity.

Which implementation is best depends on what you most want to achieve with a drive array: efficient use of drive capacity, fewest number of drives, greatest reliability, or quickest performance. For example, RAID 1 provides the greatest redundancy (thus reliability), and RAID 2 the best performance (followed closely by RAID 3).

Parallel Access Arrays

In parallel access arrays, all of the individual physical drives in the array participate in every input and output operation of the array. In other words, all of the drives operate in unison. Systems that correspond to the RAID 2 or RAID 3 design fit this definition. The drives in independent access arrays can operate independently. In advanced arrays, several individual drives may perform different input and output operations simultaneously, filling multiple input and output requests at the same time. Systems that follow the RAID 4 or RAID 5 designs fit this definition. Although RAID 1 drives may operate either as parallel access or independent access arrays, most practical systems operate RAID 1 drives independently.

You can reach the RAID Advisory Board at the following address:

RAID Advisory Board, affiliated with Technology Forums LTD
13 Marie Ln.
St. Peter, MN 56082-9423
Phone: (507) 931-0967
Fax: (507) 931-0976
www.raid-advisory.com

Storage Interfaces

An interface links two disparate devices together. The most important of these link your PC to its mass storage devices. The design of the interface not only determines how your PC controls the device but also sets the limits on the performance of the overall system. The two most widely used mass storage interfaces are AT Attachment (ATA) and SCSI, each of which has its own advantages and complications.

Any of a wide variety of interfaces may be used by a modern PC or peripheral device. The most important of these modern interfaces are:

Standard	Peak Transfer Rate	In Short
ATA	8Mbytes/sec	The original and obsolete PC-based disk-only interface
IDE	8Mbytes/sec	Another name for ATA
EIDE	16Mbytes/sec	Added speed, capacity, and flexibility to ATA extending its reach to CDs and tape
UDMA	33Mbytes/sec	Today's current minimum, doubling EIDE's speed
UDMA/66	66Mbytes/sec	The next step for PC disk drives, doubling UDMA
SCSI	5Mbytes/sec	The original standard for connecting hard disks as well as other peripherals to PCs
SCSI-2	5Mbytes/sec	A refinement on the original standard that serves as the foundation for all modern SCSI systems
Wide SCSI	10Mbytes/sec	Doubles the original 8-bit bus width of SCSI (to 16-bits, of course) to double peak transfer rate
Fast SCSI	10Mbytes/sec	Doubles the original 5MHz clock speed of SCSI to double peak transfer rate
Ultra SCSI	20Mbytes/sec	Pushes the bus speed of SCSI to 20MHz
Ultra Wide SCSI	40Mbytes/sec	Doubles the bus width of Ultra SCSI to again double the peak transfer rate
Ultra 2 SCSI	40Mbytes/sec	Pushes the SCSI bus clock to 40MHz but requires more complicated differential signaling
Ultra2 Wide SCSI	80Mbytes/sec	Doubles the bus width of Ultra 2 SCSI to again double the peak transfer rate
Ultra 160m SCSI	160Mbytes/sec	The next level up, doubling the SCSI clock speed and bus width once again to push up the transfer rate

"Interface" may just top more lists of jargon capable of reducing advocates of simpler speech to tears. To those who don't know better, it sounds erudite in a technical, over-educated way just right to elevate the speaker into intellectual incomprehensibility. Restricted to its use in computer technology, it fares little better. It remains misunderstood and, when bantered about, serves to separate those who know they don't know from those who don't know they don't know.

Interface is so slippery because it's hard to define. Strictly speaking, an interface is a coming together. In computers, it's where two disparate devices link up. The confusion starts with that link because transferring information requires several levels of connection. Plugs must mechanically fit into the appropriate jacks. The electrical signals must match. The definition of data bits must match, and the overall logical structure of the data must agree.

Ordinarily, you don't have to worry about interfaces. When you buy a PC, everything is connected together and works without your intervention. The mass storage interfaces available in your PC become important when you want to add to your storage or replace an ailing drive. You must match interfaces or be prepared for the expense and complication of adding a new one to your PC. To prevent future surprises, you should take into account the interfaces installed in any prospective new PC.

If performance is an issue, you also need to take a serious look at the mass storage interfaces in your PC. The interface used by a mass storage device has a definite influence on the performance of the device. A slow interface can hold back the best storage device.

When you want to improve the performance of your PC, you may also want to consider upgrading the interface used by your system's drives. Hard disk standards only two years old may deliver data throughput at a rate only one quarter that which can be achieved with new drives. To get the full benefit of this speed improvement, you have to upgrade not only your hard disk drive but also the interface circuitry (and software) inside your PC.

Mass storage interfaces come in great variety. The oldest and slowest one still in use is that used by floppy disk drives. Some tape backup systems also take advantage of this connection system because it's cheap; every desktop PC (so far) and most notebook systems have built-in floppy disk drives and the interface to match.

By far, the two most popular high-performance mass storage interfaces are AT Attachment and the SCSI. This chapter takes an in-depth look at both. Older interfaces no longer current in PC applications are covered in Appendix H1, Legacy Interfaces. Higher performance interfaces are also being developed with the hope that someday they will become as popular in PCs as today's interfaces are. Appendix H2, "Specialized Interfaces," covers these connection systems.

Background

A mass storage interface exists for one and only one reason—to allow you to connect a drive to your PC. Differences in interfaces arise in how well they accomplish that goal. Some interfaces are faster than others. Some let you link together more devices. Some specialize in keeping costs low. Unfortunately, no single interface combines *all* of the most desirable qualities in one.

Moreover, interfaces are constantly evolving. As technology permits storage devices to operate faster and store more information, designers struggle to make the interfaces keep pace. Current disk capacities, for example, are about 50 times the size engineers expected when they designed the original AT Attachment interface and they can read and write data nearly 10 times faster. In the last two years alone, the top speed of both of the major mass storage interfaces has doubled.

Designers must continually explore all possibilities for improving their interface designs to optimize for each of the three most important issues: performance, connectability, and cost. As designers reach ever higher in trying to achieve these three goals, they improve and refine the interface standards and the products based on them.

Performance

A mass storage interface does not speed up your system. It throttles it. All information in your storage system must pass through the interface on its way to your PC's microprocessor and memory. The speed at which the bytes move through the interface sets the ultimate limit on the performance of the storage system.

Engineers use two ways of expressing this speed. The term *peak transfer rate* usually describes the theoretical limit to the speed of the interface as determined by multiplying its clock frequency by the width of the data bus of the interface. The term *throughput* expresses a more realistic value of how many bytes can move through the interface in a given time in an actual installation. The throughput is often substantially less than the peak transfer rate because of the inherent requirements of the interface (such as the overhead required in addressing and acknowledging the transfer of data packets) and physical limitations of the interface and the storage devices themselves. Peak transfer rate is usually quoted for interface standards because they deal with the purely on-paper theoretic aspects of the interface.

Both the peak transfer rate and throughput are usually measured in units of bytes, kilobytes, or megabytes that pass through the interface in a second. The most common measure of modern interfaces consequently is megabytes per second, abbreviated MB/sec.

Sometimes, specifications list the peak transfer rates of older interfaces such as ST506 and ESDI (both covered in Appendix H1, "Legacy Interfaces") as the clocking frequency in megahertz (MHz). Because these older interfaces were serial designs, which means each had a single one-bit-wide data channel, the megahertz measure translated almost directly into mega*bits* per second. To get the equivalent of the MB/sec (mega*bytes* per second) quoted for most modern interface, you must divide the MHz or Mbits/sec figure of the serial interface by eight.

Modern mass storage interfaces use parallel connections that are able to pass 8, 16, or 32 bits during every cycle. The peak transfer rates of these interfaces thus can be a multiple of their clock frequency. The clock frequency of the interface bus, expressed in MHz, thus controls but does not completely define the performance of these parallel interfaces. In fact, clock speed is an issue of concern to designers but not you as a user or buyer of a device using the interface.

Moreover, the peak transfer rate does not in and of itself describe the throughput of an interface system even for brief periods. The most common interfaces for PC hard disk drives, AT Attachment and SCSI, typically involve disconcertingly different amounts of overhead. The command overhead of a typical SCSI host adapter is in the range from one to two milliseconds. The overhead in an AT Attachment host adapter often is 10 times less, typically in the range from 100 to 300 microseconds. This overhead eats into the actual throughput you can expect from a drive.

Remember, too, that the interface is only one factor in the performance of a mass storage system (and only a limitation at that). At one time, mass storage systems could outperform the ability of a computer to deal with the information transferred to it. All modern PC microprocessors easily outperform today's fastest disk interfaces, although some aspects of some systems lag behind interface performance. For example, the legacy ISA bus is no match for UltraSCSI or UDMA hard disk systems. Drive mechanisms typically lag behind interface transfer rates, although the caches in modern drives can push interfaces to their limits when your data needs allow.

That said, a faster interface *usually* leads to better performance from a mass storage system. Moreover, faster devices typically use faster interfaces.

Although the actual value of the peak transfer rate is close to meaningless, it is a good relative guide for comparing different interfaces. That is, the most straightforward way to compare speeds of drive systems is to look at their peak transfer rates.

Often, mass storage devices name the interface that they use rather than list a numerical figure. Table 9.1 compares the peak transfer rates of various mass storage interface standards—common and current as well as uncommon and obsolete.

TABLE 9.1 Interface Transfer Rates Compared

Interface	Peak transfer rate (in megabytes per second)
Floppy disk	0.125
ST506	0.625
ESDI	3.125
AT Attachment (IDE)	4
SCSI	5
Fast SCSI-2	10
ATA-2 (EIDE)	16
UltraDMA (ATA-4)	33
Ultra SCSI Wide	40
UltraDMA/66	66
Ultra2 SCSI Wide	80
Ultra160/m SCSI	160
P1394	800 (3200 proposed)
FC-AL	100

The interface of a given mass storage device is a characteristic that's fixed by its designer and manufacturer. In general, they match the interface to the drive mechanism to deliver the best performance that the mechanism can deliver under the rubric of the interface standard. To avoid performance constraints, you'll want to choose devices that use the fastest possible interface.

Connectability

The interface, through its design and cabling, also determines how you connect storage devices to your PC. This connectability determines how easy or difficult a challenge you'll face in adding more storage to your PC. It also determines how many storage devices you can connect to a given interface.

Connectability has several aspects, but all are defined by the specifications of the interface. Issues include the number of devices that can be connected to a single host adapter, the means by which the devices are cabled together, and the mechanism by which your PC recognizes the device once it is connected.

Most straightforward of these and the easiest to deal with is the maximum number of devices. Each interface standard sets its own limit, as listed in Table 9.2.

TABLE 9.2   Maximum Number of Drivers per Interface Port

Interface	Number of devices
Floppy disk	2
ST506	2
ESDI	2
AT Attachment (IDE)	2
SCSI	7
Fast SCSI-2	7
ATA-2 (EIDE)	4
UltraDMA (ATA-4)	4
Ultra SCSI Wide	15
UltraDMA/66	4
Ultra2 SCSI Wide	15
Ultra160/m SCSI	15
P1394	127
FC-AL	126

These limits are sometimes a bit slippery, however. In the case of SCSI drives, for example, you can violate its constraints within a single PC by installing more than one host adapter for a given interface. The AT Attachment interface, however, set a system limit both on the number of drives that can link to a single cable and the number of drives in a single system. Moreover, in some situations you can cascade interfaces. Some drive arrays, for example, connect to their computer hosts as if they were a single device even though they may comprise several drives.

Cost

Although drive manufacturers often offer the same basic mechanism with different interfaces, the drives of some interfaces tend to be costlier than others. In particular, when some manufacturers sell the same hard disk mechanism with SCSI and ATA interfaces, the SCSI-based drive is often more expensive. The difference may range from 10 to 25 percent.

This difference results not from the relative simplicity or complexity of the interfaces but from sheer volume. On the order of 85 percent of all hard disks manufactured today use the AT Attachment interface. Because of economies of scale—not to mention intense competition—AT Attachment drives are substantially less expensive.

This price differential alone often makes drives with the ATA interface the better choice for most desktop PCs that do not require the added expandability of the SCSI system.

ATA Versus SCSI

The interface market has sorted itself out with most individual PCs using AT Attachment drives—often described by one of the variations of the standard: IDE, EIDE, ATA-3, ATA-4, UDMA, or some such—and servers and workstations depending primarily on SCSI products.

Cost is the most important driving factor. AT Attachment drives are less expansive. Moreover, the circuitry to add the interface to a PC costs virtually nothing. Nearly all modern chipsets have AT Attachment circuitry built in.

Cost is not so much a factor with servers and workstations. These systems inherently cost more, and the higher prices mask much of the interface price differential. SCSI drives have been preferred for these more expensive computer systems because they are seen to offer better performance. Traditionally, SCSI hard disk drives have been seen as having a performance edge over ATA products. That edge only applies at the highest end, however. The fastest current ATA drives (those using the ATA/66 variation of the standard) are quicker than all SCSI drives except those using the Ultra2 Wide SCSI variation. SCSI will likely retain its overall performance edge; the fastest proposed implementation of the standard pushes its peak transfer rate to 160MB/sec.

SCSI earns its place in servers and workstations because of all the devices other than hard disks that connect through the interface. The best tape backup systems, for example, all use the SCSI interface. Moreover, the SCSI standard allows you to connect more devices to a given PC.

Although in the past ATA drives have been seen as easier to set up than SCSI products, as a practical matter the difference is negligible. Hard disks using either interface require that you set or check jumpers before you install them. After that, most modern controllers, PCs, and operating systems make the installation process essentially automatic.

Identifying a Drive Interface

One of the most common problems you may encounter when dealing with disk and tape drives is determining the interface used by a particular product when you cannot find a manual or other documentation for it. You can identify the interface or narrow down the possibilities by checking the connector on the drive itself. In some cases, this quick identification is sufficient to get the drive working.

With the exception of PC Card devices, the most popular of the newer drives use header-like pin connectors to plug into your system. You'll find the connector on the rear of the drive. With these header-style drives, the number of pins in the connector unambiguously identifies the interface. An AT Attachment drive uses a connector with 40 or, less often, 44 pins. A narrow-bus SCSI drive uses 50 pins arranged as two parallel rows or in a miniaturized D-shell.

Wide-bus SCSI drives use a similar miniaturized D-shell but one with 68 pins. SCSI drives designed for hot-swapping use miniaturized ribbon connectors with 80 contacts.

Note that knowing a device is a SCSI drive is not enough to get it working. You also need to know whether the drive uses single-ended or differential signaling. As noted later in the section "SCSI Parallel Interface," the SCSI standard allows both single-ended and differential drives to use the same connector. Connecting a drive to a controller using the wrong signals can damage both the controller and the drive. You'll find more specific details on each of these connectors in the appropriate interface section.

High performance disks may use one of the third-generation interfaces, either SSA or FC-AL. With them, the connector is again the give-away. An SSA drive has a unique molded connector with four projecting, oddly shaped tabs. Drives using the FC-AL interface have a 40-pin D-shell connector. Unlike the more familiar D-shells that have staggered rows of round pins, those of FC-AL are square and aligned in two rows.

Older drives that use the ST506 or ESDI interfaces use edge connectors rather than pin connectors. Because these two interfaces use exactly the same connectors, you cannot distinguish them from one another by examination (although a quick look will tell you that you have an old, slow drive that may not be worth dealing with). Any drive using edge connectors is too old (and of too small capacity) for use in a modern PC.

AT Attachment

The dominant hard disk interface for the PC has become the AT Attachment design—a natural outcome considering that the interface is based on the ISA expansion bus, still the most widely used computer bus. Despite its wide application, you still might never have heard of the AT Attachment name, however. It goes under more aliases than a candidate for the Ten Most Wanted list. The most familiar of its alternate monikers is IDE, which stands for *Integrated Drive Electronics* and is a term that correctly describes a technology rather than a specific interface. Nevertheless, the name IDE gets used indiscriminately by people in the PC industry for the AT Attachment design. Sometimes, engineers call ATA the *AT interface*, which strictly speaking it is not.

In modern PCs, the various progeny of AT Attachment are more popular than the original. Although AT Attachment started life as a single standard, the need for speed has motivated the industry to revise it several times, resulting in a number of variations on the AT theme. Today's ATA-2, ATAPI, EIDE, Fast ATA, Fast ATA-2, ATA-3, ATA-4, ATA-5, ATA/66, UDMA, and UDMA/66 interfaces are all elaborations on the original AT Attachment design.

Background

Although engineers created ATA in its original form for low-cost small-capacity drives, it has grown along with the needs of modern PCs, keeping in step with the need for both higher capacities and faster access to information. The standard hard disk drive in most PCs uses the AT Attachment interface. Most new CD ROM drives also use one of the more recent versions of ATA.

The popularity of AT Attachment has arisen for a very good reason. It offers something for everyone. The interface holds distinct advantages for disk-drive makers, computer makers, and computer buyers.

The hallmark of ATA is simplicity. You, as a computer buyer and user, gain a great deal of convenience from ATA interface drives. Connecting them is easy; they require only two cables: a signal cable and a power cable. No other mass storage interface poses as few cabling concerns. Unlike other interfaces, both the old designs that ATA replaced and its modern-day competitor SCSI, with ATA you have no need to fret about proper terminations or where and which drive gets plugged into the daisy-chain cable. Moreover, when matching a drive to your PC you don't have to worry about such bits of exotica as RLL data coding or modulation technique. All the esoteric and mind-numbing details of the inner working of the drive are hidden from you. This simplicity-by-design means that installing an ATA drive need be no more complex than plugging in a cable.

With the modern incarnations of the AT Attachment design, you don't have to give up mass storage performance to gain installation ease. ATA connections also offer some of the highest data-transfer rates of any hard disk interfacing scheme for personal computers. Nor do you lose capacity. Although the early incarnation of AT Attachment did limit the size of hard disks that it could accommodate, the revised interfaces of modern PCs pose no such restrictions. The current ATA design allows for hard disk capacities up to 8GB.

On the other side of the sales counter, ATA looks just as good. Computer makers benefit from AT-interface technology because they don't need to put separate hard disk controllers in their products. That results an immediate cost benefit; the manufacturer doesn't have to pay for the unneeded controller and can pass along the lower price to you. In addition, ATA interface drives can lower assembly cost because there's one less cable and one less expansion board to install in new PCs. Of course, building a special ATA interface connector to a system board adds to the manufacturer's cost of making a system. Moreover, although the interface is still called AT Attachment, its connection with the bus is mostly historic. ATA now includes protocol, advanced features, clock frequencies, and modes well out of the realm of the ISA bus. Nevertheless, it retains its price advantage because today's latest chipsets that form the basis for system board designs include integral AT Attachment support. From the computer maker's viewpoint, ATA is essentially free; the added system board connector may be the only cost added by including an ATA interface for hard disks and other peripherals.

Integrating control electronics on the drive to make an ATA interface may not at first seem to benefit the hard disk maker. After all, the integration makes a more complex product that should be more expensive to manufacture. But other benefits won by IDE and improvements in other areas of disk design have made the integration of control electronics a big plus for hard disk and other device manufacturers.

As with all electronics, the trend for the control circuitry on hard disk drives has been toward large-scale integration, combining all the needed functions into one large chip (or a small set of larger chips). Although engineering functions onto a Very Large Scale Integration (VLSI) chip is expensive, manufacturing is less so, and assembly can be cheaper; VLSI means fewer components so there is not as much to install. There's also less to fail, so ATA interface drives can cost less to warrant and maintain.

For disk manufacturers, the best part of any ATA interface is the freedom it gives hard disk designers in getting the most capacity possible from a given mechanism. Because the inner workings of the drive are hidden from you and your PC, ATA-interface drives can break traditional rules and limits with impunity. Your system never knows the difference. You get the gain without conventional hard disk pains.

History

The idea for using an ordinary AT interface for linking hard disks to PCs goes back to the primeval days when Compaq Computer Corporation was developing its long-discontinued Portable II computer. Work on designing the new interface started in 1985 as a means to minimize the number of slots required to integrate a hard drive into the computer. The Portable II would be short of slots, and eliminating a slot-mounted hard disk controller would free up one more slot. In this first design, the controller was still a separate board built by Western Digital Corporation to Compaq specifications but coupled directly to the drive.

The term "Integrated Drive Electronics" first appeared in early 1986, when Compaq worked with Western Digital and the Magnetic Peripherals division of Control Data Corporation (the division is now part of Seagate) to integrate the WD controller chip onto a CDC half-height, 5.25-inch, 40MB hard disk drive. In this implementation, the controller was grafted onto the hard disk assembly, but its circuitry was identifiable by a controller separate from the rest of the drive's electronics. This drive was first used in the Deskpro 386, in which it connected to a multifunction board in one of the machine's expansion slots. At this time, the specification was first expanded to handle two drives through one connection. If nothing else, this first use of the technology bequeath it the name that most people would use to describe the interface for years to come, *IDE*.

In the middle of 1986, in parallel with the CDC effort, Compaq and Conner Peripherals (which in late 1995 also became a part of Seagate) started a joint development effort to emulate the original IDE interface with a gate array that was integrated with the rest of the control electronics of the hard disk. At this point, the controller had truly become integrated in an effort to reduce the cost and complexity of the hard disk system while improving its reliability. The ATA interface connector was first moved to the system board with Compaq's Portable III.

Once the benefits of the AT-bus connection were proved, other disk makers adopted the design. But because no official standard or even unofficial guidelines had been declared, each drive maker added its own nuances and variations to the interface. Consequently, early drives based on the ATA interface from different manufacturers may suffer compatibility problems, principally when you try to connect two drives of different makes to a single ATA interface connector.

In October 1988, a group of companies that make and use hard disk drives formed the CAM (Common Access Method) Committee. Although its primary goal was to develop a common software interface for handling data transfers in SCSI systems, it also worked to create a standard for disk drives using the AT interface. The group formalized the specifications for the AT Attachment interface in March 1989 and submitted them as a proposed standard to the American National Standards Institute in November 1990. In 1991, a standard was finally and formally approved, and the CAM Committee disbanded shortly thereafter. Other organizations (principally the Small Form Factor Committee) now work on revising and expanding the original specification.

Along with the familiarity and power of the AT expansion bus, the AT Attachment interface also inherited its drawbacks. As high-performance PCs forsook the AT bus design (now termed ISA) for higher speed local buses, ATA was left behind. It soon became the chief restraint on the throughput of lower cost hard disk drives. The need for speed outpaced the ability of standard-making organizations to extend the limits of the design. As a consequence, disk drive makers improvised and developed their own, proprietary extensions to AT Attachment. The result was the growth of two camps within the PC industry, those with allegiance to EIDE and those promoting Fast ATA.

To help its disk drives keep up with the increased throughput possible with PCs using local bus connections for mass storage, Seagate Technology created its own set of extensions to the original AT Attachment standard, which the company called *Fast ATA*. Originally published in 1994, Fast ATA documents new, higher speed timing of the signals across the ATA interface. Beyond the performance increase and means to distinguish conforming drives, Fast ATA made no other changes or additions to the original ATA specification.

About the time Seagate developed Fast ATA, drive maker Western Digital sought to push up the transfer rate of its ATA hard disks, but it also wanted to strengthen other weaknesses in the original ATA standard. The company called its vision of the future Enhanced IDE or EIDE.

EIDE is a package of four improvements to the original ATA standard. To add faster throughput across the ATA bus, EIDE endorsed the same quicker transfer modes as Fast ATA. In addition, EIDE attempted to standardize the approach of the interface design to attaching a second pair of drives to a PC. To broach the Interrupt 13(Hex) addressing limit of 504MB per ATA drive, EIDE provided a standard for logical block addressing. And to extend the reach of ATA ports to tape and CD ROM drives, EIDE incorporated the ATA Packet Interface that was at the time in development.

These competing camps became united as new versions of the ATA standard have been developed and approved. All aspects of both Fast ATA and EIDE are now part of the official standard. Faster transfers became officially sanctioned by the 1996 ATA-2 standard. In 1997, ATA-3 added support for larger drives through logical block addressing (discussed later). In 1998, the packet interface that extended official ATA support to CD drives and other devices beyond hard disks was added under ATA-4.

That level of the ATA standard also added new high-speed modes known as variously as Ultra ATA and UDMA. This technology was developed jointly by Intel, Quantum, and Seagate and uses double-clocking and bus mastering to achieve a 33MB/sec data rate. The next generation of the standard, ATA-5, is nearing official approval as this is written in 1999. It will legitimize the 66MB/sec drives now entering the market.

Performance

Speed has always been an allure of the AT Attachment design. For most of its life, AT Attachment has kept ahead of the abilities of drive mechanisms to deliver data. The mechanism rather than the interface is usually the limit. Thanks to updates to the AT Attachment specifications, the interface still exceeds the performance limits of drive mechanisms.

That's not to say that every drive will deliver its optimum performance with every ATA host adapter. Since the inception of the AT Attachment design, speed at both ends of the connection have gone up several times. Although new devices are generally backward compatible with older modes and equipment, each step backward takes its toll on speed.

Moreover, if you don't properly match ATA equipment to your PC, you'll lose speed again.

A single number cannot describe the performance of ATA devices. The current standard recognizes 11 transfer modes, each with its own performance limit. Drives, host adapters, and software all differ in their support of these modes. The fastest modes work only with the most recent products, and all elements of the AT Attachment system—from operating system through host adapter to the drive itself—must support a specific mode for you to achieve its level of performance. Table 9.3 summarizes the principal transfer modes of the AT Attachment standard.

TABLE 9.3   AT Attachment Transfer Modes and Speeds

Transfer mode	Cycle time Nanoseconds	Speed Mbps	Standard
PIO Mode 0	600	1.67	ATA
PIO Mode 1	383	2.61	ATA
PIO Mode 2	240	4.17	ATA
PIO Mode 3	180	11.1	ATA-2
PIO Mode 4	120	16.7	ATA-3
PIO Mode 5	90	22	
DMA, Single Word, Mode 0	960	1.04	ATA
DMA, Single Word, Mode 1	480	2.08	ATA
DMA, Single Word, Mode 2	240	4.17	ATA
DMA, Multiple Word, Mode 0	480	4.17	ATA
DMA, Multiple Word, Mode 1	150	13.3	ATA-2
DMA, Multiple Word, Mode 2	120	16.7	ATA-3
Synchronous DMA, Mode 0	235	16	ATA-4
Synchronous DMA, Mode 1	160	24	ATA-4
Synchronous DMA, Mode 2	120	33.3	ATA-4
Synchronous DMA, Mode 3	90	45	ATA-5
Synchronous DMA, Mode 4	60	66.6	ATA-5

AT Attachment supports two broad classes of transfers, *Programmed Input/Output*, or PIO, and *Direct Memory Access*, or DMA. Under the more recent iterations of the ATA standard, DMA is further divided into Single-Word DMA, Multi-Word DMA, and UltraDMA modes. With today's PCs, UDMA modes are preferred for their higher performance, although nearly all drives support all lesser modes to the highest one they offer.

The difference between PIO and DMA modes regards how they use the resources in your PC. The DMA modes provide an opportunity for improved overall system performance through bus mastering, but the full potential of this benefit requires matching hardware and software in your PC. The fastest modes match only with the most recent PCs.

Programmed Input/Output puts your microprocessor to work. The microprocessor in your system directly controls every byte that moves through the interface. The microprocessor directly writes values from its registers or memory to a special I/O port, which transfers the data to the control circuitry of the interface. PIO transfers can of one of two types, blind and flow control.

Blind transfers don't give the AT Attachment drive full control of the transfers. It has no information about the ability of the microprocessor host to accept data. In effect, it is blind to the capabilities of the host. By design, any error the system makes will be on the conservative side to maximize the reliability of the system. Because sometimes only a part of the full bandwidth of your PC is available for making disk transfers, blind transfers throttle back to the worst case. Consequently, the AT Attachment operates blind transfers at a slow rate regardless of the host computer's ability to capture the data. It moves bytes at the lower, throttled rate even when 100 percent of the bandwidth is available.

Flow-control transfers use a form of handshaking to assure that disk transfers take advantage of all the available bandwidth. Specifically, controlled transfers use the I/O Channel Ready (or IORDY) line in the AT Attachment interface to signal to the computer host when the drive needs to make a high-speed transfer. Using the IORDY line, the drive can call for maximum drive bandwidth support and increase its transfer rate.

The current ATA specifications allow for five modes of PIO transfers, listed in Table 9.4. Modes 0, 1, and 2 use blind transfers. Modes 3 and 4 use flow control. Although the original ATA specification made provisions for this feature, called "Flow Control Using IORDY," its application was not standardized and required matching the features of the host adapter and drive.

TABLE 9.4   AT Attachment Programmed I/O Modes

Transfer mode	Cycle time Nanoseconds	Speed Mbps
PIO Mode 0	600	1.67
PIO Mode 1	383	2.61
PIO Mode 2	240	4.17

Transfer mode	Cycle time Nanoseconds	Speed Mbps
PIO Mode 3	180	11.1
PIO Mode 4	120	16.7
PIO Mode 5	90	22

Mode 3 PIO transfers were first officially sanctioned in ATA-2. The ATA-3 revision introduced Mode 4 using altered timing to increase the speed of flow-controlled transfers.

PIO Modes 3 and 4 require support from both the ATA device and host adapter to operate. Normally, all drives default to blind transfer mode. Gaining the increased speed of flow control requires the host adapter to send the device a Set Features command.

The AT Attachment standard allows for Direct Memory Access transfers that allow bypassing the host computer's microprocessor and moving data directly to memory. Because DMA transfers use their own handshaking, they are effectively as efficient as flow-controlled PIO transfers in maximizing data throughput. Moreover, when the host operating system does not serialize input/output functions, DMA transfers allow a degree of parallel processing. The host microprocessor can engage in other activities while the DMA transfer progresses. DOS and Windows 95 serialize their I/O functions so they do not gain this benefit. OS/2, UNIX, and Windows NT can achieve gains from this transfer strategy. The real gain comes from the reduced cycle times, bursting, and bus-mastering functions of the more advanced implementations of DMA in AT Attachment.

AT Attachment allows both single- and multi-word DMA transfers. *Single-word DMA transfers* move one word at a time. The host sets up the transfer, selects the data to be transferred, and then makes the transfer. The next word repeats the process. The ATA specifications acknowledge three single-word DMA modes, as listed in Table 9.5.

TABLE 9.5   AT Attachment Single-Word DMA Transfer Modes and Speeds

Transfer mode	Cycle time Nanoseconds	Speed Mbps
DMA, Single Word, Mode 0	960	1.04
DMA, Single Word, Mode 1	480	2.08
DMA, Single Word, Mode 2	240	4.17

Although single-word DMA could offer performance advantages over the PIO modes by lifting transfer overhead from your PC's microprocessor, the one-word-at-a-time transfers incur substantial unnecessary overhead. Under the ATA-3 specification, single-word transfers are classified as obsolete.

Multi-word DMA transfers take their place and deliver improved performance by operating as a burst mode. After the host sets up the transfer, it selects the starting and ending words for the transfer, and then the interface moves the entire block of data from start to end with no further intervention. During each step of the development of ATA, engineers added a new mode, bringing the total through ATA-3 to thee. Table 9.6 lists these ATA multi-word DMA Modes.

TABLE 9.6   AT Attachment Multi-Word DMA Transfer Modes and Speeds

Transfer mode	Cycle time Nanoseconds	Speed Mbps	Standard
DMA, Multiple Word, Mode 0	480	4.17	ATA
DMA, Multiple Word, Mode 1	150	13.3	ATA-2
DMA, Multiple Word, Mode 2	120	16.7	ATA-3

For ATA-4, engineers created three new double-clocked timings which they called synchronous DMA modes . Two more are slated under the proposed ATA-5 standard. Table 9.7 lists all of the UDMA modes.Table 9.7

TABLE 9.7   AT Attachment Synchronous DMA Transfer Modes and Speeds (UDMA)

Transfer mode	Cycle time Nanoseconds	Speed Mbps	Standard
Synchronous DMA, Mode 0	120	16.6	ATA-4
Synchronous DMA, Mode 1	80	25	ATA-4
Synchronous DMA, Mode 2	60	33.3	ATA-4
Synchronous DMA, Mode 3	45	44.4	ATA-5
Synchronous DMA, Mode 4	30	66.6	ATA-5

Two of these modes are particularly favored in new hard disks and have earned common names. Synchronous DMA Mode 2 is often called UDMA (for *UltraDMA*) or, more recently, UDMA/33. It is also called Ultra ATA. Although UDMA describes a technology that's also used by some SCSI drives, just as IDE describes a technology rather than a standard, the term has become the most popular designation of this speed class of hard disk drive.

Mode 4 is sometimes termed UDMA/66 or ATA/66. No matter the name, it is an extrapolation of UDMA.

The UltraDMA modes combine two performance-enhancing technologies. The most straightforward boost comes from quickening the clock or reducing cycle time and taking advantage of bus-mastering technology. By shifting control of the bus to the drive system, the UDMA modes can quicken the pace of transfers.

In addition, UltraDMA doubles up transfers. Normally, a DMA transfer is made on one edge of the clock cycle—typically on the leading or rising edge when the cycle begins—so one transfer occurs during each clock tick. An UltraDMA system can transfer data on both the rising and the falling edge of each clock cycle; that's two transfers for every clock tick, an effective doubling of throughput. To make this system work reliably, the ATA designers shifted from asynchronous transfers to synchronous transfers. The transmitting device (the PC when writing data; the disk drive when reading) generates the clock and synchronizes the data pulses to the clock. Because one device controls both the clock and the data, it can control it better.

For the disk drive to take control of the timing, it must act as a bus master, so this technology is sometimes termed *bus master DMA*. In addition, error protection is built into the transfer protocol using a Cyclical Redundancy Check algorithm. The CRC applies only to the cable transfer, not the data stored on disk.

Plain UltraDMA takes advantage of the 16.6MHz clocking speed available in ATA PIO Mode 4 but enhances it with double-clocking. UDMA/66 uses a faster clock, 33MHz, to further improve performance.

Ordinarily, you don't have to worry about the transfer mode used by an ATA drive system. Your PC should automatically use the fastest mode available without your intervention—or knowledge.

The issue stares you squarely in the face when you want to buy and connect a new drive to your PC or if you want to be sure you're getting all the performance out of your drive system that you can. Getting a drive that supports the highest speed mode is not enough. Your PC must also be able to handle the mode and speed of the drive.

With relatively recent drives and PCs, the major concern is the chipset used by your PC. Support for ATA-4 UDMA/33 is built into most Pentium II chipsets. Intel's 440BX, 440LX, and 440TX chipsets in Pentium systems also have the required support as do the VIA VPX and VP2/97 and SiS 5597/98, 5581/82, and 5601 chipsets. If your PC lacks integral support for UDMA/33, you can gain it by adding a host adapter that supports that transfer mode.

In addition, you may require driver software to take advantage of UDMA/33 with your operating system. Only Windows 98 and Windows 2000 have built-in support. Windows NT 4.0 or earlier and Windows 95 require special UDMA/33 drives (usually shipped with the disk drive) to bring the full-speed potential of this operating mode to life. DOS does not support UDMA/33.

As this is written, support for UDMA/66 is just appearing on the market. Chipsets released in 1999 are likely to include support for the fastest modes, but earlier chipsets are unlikely to. Of course, you can add in a host adapter to take advantage of ATA/66 in an older system. Older PCs will also need a BIOS upgrade to take full advantage of the fastest transfer modes.

Ordinarily, you need only be concerned with modes and transfer rates when you are selecting a hard disk drive to match with your PC. In operation, your PC's BIOS will automatically recognize the drive and set itself up for the fastest operating mode that it shares with your hard disk drive. Some BIOSs let you check the mode they have discovered and are using through the Advanced option within their disk setup procedure.

Of course, all of these speeds represent theoretical maximums. The actual performance of AT Attachment devices will always be less because real-world throughput is limited by the mechanical performance of the devices and system overhead. On the other hand, many devices that use an AT Attachment connection can approach the speed limit of the interface if they use large on-board buffers and those buffers are full of the data requested from the computer hosts.

Capacity

In itself, the hardware of an interface does not affect the capacity of a storage system. All it provides is a channel that, given long enough, can conduct as much information from one place to another. For example, a few zillion gigabytes of data lie on the other side of your serial port and modem. AT Attachment, like all PC disk interfaces, incorporates more than a transfer channel. It also includes a control system for the devices connected to it. In the case of AT Attachment, part of that control is an addressing system that allows your PC and its software to specify a given block of data on the ATA device for reading or writing.

The interface does limit storage, however. The issue is addressing. Although a drive may physically be able to store hundreds of gigabytes, that capacity may not be useful because the interface used by the drive does not allow all of the bytes to be addressed. In effect, the bytes on the drive beyond the addressing limit imposed by the interface have unlisted numbers, and no amount of begging or cajoling the operator will get you through to them.

Addressing limitations have constrained the usable capacity of AT Attachment drives almost since their inception. As the need for greater addressing reach has appeared, designers have added new addressing modes to the ATA standard. The latest move finally pushes the upper limit beyond any currently feasible drive capacity.

CHS Addressing

AT Attachment built its basic addressing system on the model of a hard disk. Data blocks get assigned addresses based on a scheme of heads, tracks, and sectors. This addressing system is sometimes called *CHS addressing* for Cylinder (the techie term for "track"), Head, Sector addressing.

The original ATA standard allowed for addressing 16 separate heads or disk surfaces, each of which may have up to 65,536 tracks spread across it. Each track can contain up to 255 sectors of 512 bytes each. Multiply it out, and the addressing limit of AT Attachment works out to be 136,902,082,560 bytes or 127.5GB. Most sources round those numbers to 128GB. (It does work out to an exact 128GB because of the limit of 255 rather than 256 sectors per track. For historical reasons, drive makers start numbering sectors with one rather than zero.)

That ultimate capacity requires that nothing else impose a limit on the AT Attachment interface. Unfortunately, in practical application, the BIOSs of older PCs severely constrained ATA addressing.

All software that relies on Interrupt 13(Hex) code routines in your PC's BIOS must abide by the BIOS's own disk addressing system. The BIOS routines originally developed in 1982 for the IBM Personal Computer XT allow for disks with up to 255 heads or disk surfaces (IBM started numbering heads with one so the limit is 255 rather than 256), each with up to 1,024 tracks on them. Each track can hold up to 63 sectors. Using standard 512-byte sectors, the BIOS addressing system allows for a much smaller ultimate disk capacity, 8,422,686,720 bytes or 7.8GB. Again, most sources round this figure upward to 8GB.

Taken by itself, that wasn't much of a limit. In 1982, a huge drive measured 33 *mega*bytes, and it would be 15 years before PC hard disks poked their noses past 8GB. The technical conspiracy between the ATA standard and IBM BIOS kept PCs from addressing anything but a fraction of the ATA limit, however. The largest value that the system can handle for any of the three drive parameters is the smaller of the limits set by the two standards. Most importantly, ATA permits addressing only 16 heads, not the 256 available through the BIOS, so the overall system cannot address more than 16 heads. Table 9.8 summarizes the interaction between the BIOS and ATA limits.

TABLE 9.8   ATA and Interrupt 13(Hex) Addressing Limits

Feature	ATA Limit	BIOS Limit	Combined Limit
Heads	16	255	16
Tracks	65,536	1024	1024
Sectors	255	63	63
Total sectors	267,386,880	16,450,560	1,032,192
Capacity	127.5GB	7.8GB	0.5GB

The result of the conflict between the two systems is that ATA disks that are addressed through the Interrupt 13 facilities of the BIOS of a PC cannot address more than 63 sectors per track (the BIOS limit), 16 heads (the ATA limit), and 1,024 tracks (the BIOS limit again). With 512-byte sectors, the top capacity is 528,482,304 bytes (about 504MB). Bytes beyond this limit simply cannot be addressed through the standard Interrupt 13(Hex) routines of the standard PC BIOS.

Because this addressing limit is imposed by the combination of the BIOS and ATA design, it comes into play only when software uses the BIOS Interrupt 13(Hex) routines to access your ATA devices. DOS is the chief culprit. Windows versions through 3.11, which operate through DOS, are also constrained by these limits. Software and operating systems that do not use Interrupt 13(Hex) do not face these constraints.

Most modern operating systems use software drivers that bypass the BIOS for their disk access, but this design does not entirely free them from the BIOS. To boot up, all PCs use code in their BIOSs to read their hard disk in order to load the operating system code from the disk. Consequently, the boot sectors of the drive must be addressable using the conventional Interrupt 13(Hex) system even when running an advanced operating system.

Although Windows 95 normally prefers to use 32-bit device drivers for disk access, much of the operating system is still bound by the DOS-imposed Interrupt 13(Hex) limits. Windows 95 and 98 boots through DOS and uses DOS functions for compatibility with DOS-based applications. Consequently, Windows 95 and 98 can butt squarely into the 504MB limit.

Fortunately, two methods of sidestepping this limit are in common use, CHS translation and logical block addressing. They enable both DOS and Windows 95 to take advantage of ATA storage devices with capacities well beyond 504MB.

CHS Translation

Because the AT Attachment design, as a system-level interface, allows the inner workings of the ATA device to be hidden from your PC, manufacturers are free to alter the geometry of the drive as long as they make it look like something recognizable to your PC. The number of physical heads, tracks, and sectors inside the drive are usually totally different from the number of heads, tracks, and sectors your PC uses to address the sectors on the disk. The drive *translates* the incoming addresses to its own, internal physical addresses when it seeks out a sector.

One way of breaking through the 504MB limit is by adding a similar form of translation to the BIOS in your PC called *CHS translation*. The BIOS accepts commands from your software and operating system based on its own CHS addressing system, the one that limits disk capacity to 7.8GB. Program code in the BIOS then translates those addresses into a form compatible with the addressing system used by the ATA device. For example, your BIOS might pretend that each block of 1,024 tracks (of the potential 65,536 tracks times 16 heads) on your disk were a separate logical head, thus easily accommodating the 255 heads your operating system refers to.

This translation mode has its own constraints. Because under this translation system your operating system still refers to addresses on your ATA devices using the Interrupt 13(Hex) system, its 7.8GB capacity limit applies. Because your BIOS carries out the translation, it must know how to do it. Not all BIOSs allow for this kind of translation. Moreover, the exact translation systems used by different BIOSs may be different. A disk formatted using one BIOS may not be compatible with another translating BIOS. Unless you are certain that two PCs use identical translation algorithms (for example, because both use the same BIOS version) you cannot move a hard disk between PCs and be certain you can recover all your data intact.

Although there is no surefire way of detecting whether your BIOS supports CHS translation other than calling its creator or your PC's manufacturer, you can sometimes determine support by checking your PC's advanced setup options. If the advanced setup options include ATA or IDE addressing modes, it likely supports CHS translation. Most BIOSs call CHS translation large disk support or simply "large."

Translating ATA host adapters include an on-board BIOS that provides the necessary CHS translation functions. In addition, disk management software can add CHS translation to your system. When your PC boots up, it loads the disk management software first using the Interrupt 13(Hex) routines, and then the disk management software takes over and activates its own CHS translation system.

Because the CHS translation takes place in your PC, it imposes some microprocessor overhead. Your PC must calculate the new addresses before they get sent along to your ATA device. Today's PCs are fast enough and the calculations are trivial enough that you probably won't notice the effect.

Logical Block Addressing

The official way of getting around the 504MB limit imposed on ATA devices by Interrupt 13(Hex) is *logical block addressing*, or LBA. This technology, introduced with EIDE and formalized in the ATA-2 specifications, substitutes 28-bit logical block addresses for CHS addressing used by Interrupt 13(Hex). Each sector on the drive is assigned a unique logical address that would be used by the BIOS to reach its contents. The full 28-bit addressing scheme allows for 268,435,456 sectors, a theoretic capacity of about 137.5GB.

To maintain compatibility with older operating systems such as DOS, however, your PC's BIOS must translate the CHS addresses generated by the software into the LBA values required by the ATA system. As a result, your PC needs a BIOS with built-in LBA addressing abilities to use this technology. Moreover, because your operating system still communicates to the BIOS—even if it is a new one—using the old Interrupt 13(Hex) head, track, and sector values, the 8GB BIOS limit still applies.

LBA requires support at both ends of the connection. In your PC, the BIOS (and whatever disk software drivers your operating system uses) must know how to send out logical block addresses. In addition, your ATA devices must understand LBA. In other words, to take advantage of the LBA system requires the Interrupt 13(Hex) firmware code of the host computer to be rewritten to accommodate the new addressing scheme. Getting full capacity from a drive using LBA (and having more than 504MB of storage) requires a PC with a BIOS that specifically supports LBA or an add-in host adapter card that has its own compatible BIOS. On the other end of the connection, nearly all ATA devices with capacities in excess of 504MB understand logical block addressing.

To help avoid attempts at using the LBA scheme with disks that do not support the feature, the ATA standard designates a flag bit in one of the drives registers (specifically bit 6 of the drive's SDH register) to indicate which form of addressing a drive uses.

The constraints of CHS translation also apply to logical block addressing. For a drive that uses LBA to boot up, your PC requires a BIOS that supports LBA operation. Because a drive cannot switch from head-track-sector addressing to LBA on the fly, the drive must boot in LBA mode. Consequently, your PC must have an LBA-compatible BIOS if you want to run an operating system that uses the LBA system.

Note that both Windows 95 and 98 include enhanced support for hard disk drives that use logical block addressing for capacities up to the 137.5GB limit. The protected-mode disk handler drivers of Windows extend Interrupt 13(Hex) functions to bring LBA to life automatically. However, the Windows disk handler doesn't come into play until after your PC loads the operating system using the BIOS, so you'll still need an LBA-compatible BIOS even with Windows.

New BIOS designs include full support for the entire LBA addressing range. However, some BIOSs written as recently as 1997 peg out at the old 8GB limit. These systems cannot recognize hard disk capacities in excess of 8GB. In most cases, however, you can upgrade your PCs BIOS to accommodate the full LBA limit. You'll know you need to make an upgrade as soon as you install a drive and cannot see its full capacity when you prepare it for your operating system.

Although a 137.5GB limit is sufficient to address any current hard disk drive (the largest available drive as this is written is 50GB), with the annual doubling of capacity the ATA addressing constraint may become confining in as little as two years. The ATA watchdogs are not asleep, however. The ATA-5 proposal breaks the practical limits of this LBA system by allowing additional storage for block addresses, increasing the ability of the ATA interface to handle drives of 16 mega-tera-bytes.

Other Features

Although speed and capacity issues highlight most discussions of disk interfaces, the AT Attachment standard covers other issues as well. Some of these are just as important as performance in making your PC work the way you want it to. Among these are the ATA Packet Interface that allows you to connect other devices such as CD ROM drives to an interface that was originally designed just to handle hard disks. Power management under the ATA rubric makes your PC more energy efficient—and lets you keep computing on your notebook PC even after a mixture of fog, terrorists, and pilots lost in the lounge leave you waiting at the airport gate long after any of your hopes of making your connection have departed. Built-in security features protect you from prying eyes and your data from errant erasures. And the automatic drive identification abilities of ATA makes setting up a PC a simpler chore, one that makes lengthy lists of drive parameters as happily behind you as a visit from in-laws who have finally finished an overly prolonged visit.

ATA Packet Interface

As originally propounded, the AT Attachment design was meant solely to link hard disk drives. The interface proved so popular—and so economical for equipment makers—that the manufacturers of tape drives and CD ROM players eyed it covetously. Unfortunately, it was unusable by non-disk storage devices because it did not provide the control they required. Although AT Attachment provides all the hardware signaling that is require to link these devices, the original standard provided no set of commands suitable for handling these devices. Although hard disks happily moved data any which way in the form of sectors or logical blocks, modern tape and CD drives work with data packets. To give a means of controlling such devices through the AT Attachment interface, the Small Form Factor committee developed the *ATA Packet Interface*, or ATAPI.

At the time ATAPI was conceived, most CD ROM players used SCSI interfaces, as did higher performance tape drives. Although SCSI yielded a fast, efficient interface, it also meant that the computer maker or user had to add yet another connector and its associated circuitry to its basic PC to make these peripherals work. As tight-fisted manufacturers and PC users plumbed the lowest ranges of prices that they can offer their PCs, they've eyed the ATA interface connector greedily. If the ATA interface will handle two drives, and most PCs need only one hard disk, why can't they plug the CD ROM player there, too?

The answer is as simple as ATA and SCSI not matching—different connectors—but it goes deeper. The ATA interface lacks the facilities to control everything that a CD ROM player needs to do. Hard disks merely absorb and disgorge data. When it comes to ordinary data, however, CD ROMs are simpler still; they only discharge data. They also usher audio around, though. The ATA interface provides no means of linking audio to your PC, nor does it give any means of controlling the audio signals or several other aspects of normal CD ROM operation.

The connection problem is easily solved. SCSI has no audio connection, either, but relies on an extra jack or two. Control is another matter—one for which the ATA-4 standard brought a solution: the ATA Packet Interface. An enhancement to the ordinary ATA interface, ATAPI gives the system a means of sending packets of commands to CD ROM players. The commands exactly match those used by SCSI, making the translation of SCSI CD ROM products to the new system easier. The hardware side of the ATAPI enhancement is nothing more than the standard 40-pin ATA connector augmented by two jacks for audio signals (one serial digital, one two-channel analog). The ATAPI specification is designed to be completely compatible with existing ATA hardware and drivers. It changes nothing on the computer side of the ATA connection, and it does not affect the design or operation of ATA hard disk drives. It just gives the makers of CD ROM players and programmers guidance as to how to link their products to PCs in a standard way.

Under ATAPI, a CD ROM player can replace the slave ATA interface drive in your PC. But the specification requires that CD ROM players be configurable as master or slave so that you can connect two CD ROM drives to a single ATA cable.

Normally, an ATA hard disk gets its commands through eight registers called the Task file, which passes along all the commands and parameters needed to operate the disk. Unfortunately, these eight registers are not sufficient for the needed CD ROM control. ATAPI adds one new command: the Packet command, which initiates a mode in which multiple writes to the Task file will send packets of commands to the CD ROM player. Most ATAPI command packets contain 12 bytes, although the standard also defines 16-byte packets for compatibility with future devices.

Although ATAPI uses many of the same block and command definitions described by SCSI, it does not use many of the other features of SCSI protocol such as messaging, bus sharing with multiple computers, disconnect/reconnect, and linking and queuing of commands.

The first of the 12 bytes in the ATAPI Packet command (byte 0) is an operation code that defines the command itself. The initial ATAPI specification defined 29 operation codes, two of which are reserved for CD ROM XT systems. The third through sixth bytes (bytes 2–5) of each packet hold the logical block address of the data to be used if the command involves the use of data. The CD ROM logical addresses start with zero as the first block and increase sequentially up to the last block. The eight and ninth bytes (bytes 7 and 8) of the packet define the length of the transfer, parameter list, or allocation involved in the command. Special extended commands add an extra byte for indicating this length. The remaining bytes in the packet are not defined by the specification but are reserved for future implementations.

Power Management

In PCs where electrical consumption is a critical issue—battery powered notebook machines—the hard disk is one of the major drains of power. Most disk drives meant for portable machines help conserve power by allowing their electrical use to be trimmed when the drive's fastest response is unnecessary.

The ATA-3 specification incorporates standards for power management. Part of that standardization is defining four power modes that allow frugal PCs to economize as the occasions arise: active, idle, standby, and sleep.

Active mode means normal operation for a disk drive. All functions of the drive are available, the drive electronics are fully operational, and the disk platters are spinning. The drive can react immediately to any command, including a seek to move its head to read or write data. The only delay is that imposed in normal disk access. The price for this fast access is that this mode consumes the most power, particularly during seeks.

Idle mode provides more for safety than power savings. The head may move away from the active data area of the disk, but otherwise the drive is fully operational. A seek command sends the head instantly scurrying to the appointed sector with little additional delay. Because the drive does not transfer data in idle mode, the part of its electronics associated with decoding, deserializing, and transferring data from (or to) the disk can be shut down. The part of the electronics that processes commands stays alive, ready to receive instructions from your PC and carry them out.

Standby mode saves power by stopping the spin of the platters, shutting down the spindle motor to eliminate that power drain. The electronics of the drive are left in essentially the same state as idle mode. Only as much of the circuitry is kept awake as is needed to receive commands and activate the rest of the drive when requested. Because the drive must spin up to its normal operating speed before it can read or write data, this mode imposes a delay on all data handling operations. Typically, this delay will be on the order of 10 seconds, although the ATA standard allows for a delay of up to 30 seconds.

Sleep mode totally shuts down the hard disk and its electronics. The drive does not listen for commands and cannot act on commands sent to it. The only way of leaving sleep mode is by sending a hardware or software reset command. The reset causes the drive to enter normal power-up mode as determined by its manufacturer. Sleep mode reduces the power consumption of a drive nearly to zero but incurs the longest delay in accessing data. Not only must the drive spin up its platter, but also the rest of the system must take its normal course through its reset action.

Table 9.9 summarizes and distinguishes the four power management modes of the ATA specification.

TABLE 9.9   AT Attachment Power Management Modes

Mode	Electronics	Motor (Spin)	Response	Power savings
Active	On	On	Instant	None
Idle	Partially off	On	Instant	Small
Standby	Partially off	Off	Delay	Substantial
Sleep	Off	Off	Delay	Complete

AT Attachment drives with the power management option also include a built-in *standby timer* that can shift the drive into its lower power standby mode after the drive has been inactive for a preset period. This changeover is a function of the drive and occurs automatically without the intervention of the host PC. The host PC can, however, switch off the standby timer so that the drive does not shift to standby automatically. The host PC can then take full command of the power mode of the drive.

To switch the drive from active mode to a lower power mode, the host PC sends the drive a power management command. Any drive access command automatically forces the drive back into active mode. In addition, the AT Attachment standard includes a Check Power Mode command that allows the host PC at any time to determine in which mode the drive is currently operating.

Security

The ATA-3 specification includes device-level password security allowing for a completely self-contained system to limit access to information on the drive. Although you set the drive access password through your PC, the drive stores the password on its own media and it uses the same password even if you unplug the drive from one PC and attach it to another. Consequently, if you activate its password security system and someone later steals your drive, they cannot access the data stored on the drive.

Depending on the secrecy of your data, you can set security to one of two levels, normal or maximum. The chief ramification of your choice is what happens should you forget your password. Choose normal security, and the drive maker can recover your data for you. When you set your drive for maximum security, even the drive maker cannot retrieve your data.

The AT Attachment standard allows for two kinds of passwords, User and Master:

User passwords are those you set yourself to limit access to your drive. The command structure used by the AT Attachment standard allows for passwords up to 32 bytes long. The standard provides a common means of setting these passwords and gaining access to the drive that operates at the interface level. Normally, you'll deal with a password through your BIOS, operating system, or application software, which links to the drive security system through the ATA interface.

Master passwords are set at the factory. They are not normally used in the everyday operation of the drive but allow for recovery of data by the drive maker should you forget your password. If you've set your drive for normal security, the drive maker can use its master password to access your data or inactivate the old password so you can change your password to something that you *can* remember. When you set security to maximum, the master password only allows the drive maker to *erase* your drive and restore it to its original condition: blank with no password set. Your files will be gone forever.

Under the ATA security system, your drive operates in one of three modes, locked, unlocked, and frozen:

Unlocked mode is the normal operating mode of the disk drive. The drive carries out all commands sent to it. It can read and write to any of the data areas on the disk. You can also add or change your password in unlocked mode.

A new drive will normally arrive in its unlocked mode. It will operate unlocked until you set a user password. Thereafter, the drive will always start operating in the locked mode and remain in locked mode until it receives a valid user or master password. Normally, the drive will accept five tries at sending it a password. It will then reject subsequent password attempts until it has been reset.

Locked mode prevents you from accessing or changing any data that's stored on the disk. In locked mode, the drive automatically aborts all read and write commands without executing them. The drive carries out normally all commands that do not access or alter the data stored on the disk, for example, to enter a low-power mode.

Frozen mode prevents the security features of the drive from being altered. The drive carries out all normal read and write operations but will not change its security level or password. If you value your data, frozen mode will be your standard operating mode so that no one can change your drive password should you leave your PC unattended.

Device Identification

Each device includes 512 bytes of storage for identifying information. Device makers are free to locate this storage anywhere they want. It can be stored on a non-removable storage medium such as a hard disk or in EEPROM or flash memory.

No matter its location, however, the AT Attachment standard includes a standard command for reading this identifying block. Using this command, your PC can interrogate the device to find out what it is and automatically configure itself for optimum operation, including maximizing its data transfer rate. Included are the device parameters, the features supported (including transfer modes and thus speeds), and the model number and serial number of the drive.

Because AT Attachment is basically a 16-bit interface, arranging this storage in 16-bit words is only natural. Table 9.10 lists the coding of the ATA device identification information.

TABLE 9.10   Coding of AT Attachment Device Identification Information

Start Word	End Word	Bits	Value	Function
0				General configuration information
		0		Reserved
		1-5		Vendor specific (obsolete)
		6	1	Not removable device
		7	1	Removable media device
		8-14	0	ATA device
	0		1	ATAPI device
1	1			Number of logical cylinders
2	2			Reserved
3	3			Number of logical heads
4	5			Vendor specific (obsolete)
6	6			Number of logical sectors per track
7	9			Vendor specific
10	19			Serial number in ASCII
20	21			Vendor specific (obsolete)
22	22			Bytes available in R/W Long commands
23	26			Firmware revision in ASCII

Start Word	End Word	Bits	Value	Function
27	46			Model number in ASCII
47	47	0-7		Maximum sectors in R/W Multiple command
48	48			Reserved
49				Capabilities
		0-7		Vendor specific
		8-9		Obsolete
		10	0	IORDY can be disabled
		11	0	IORDY may be supported
		11	1	IORDY is supported
		12		Reserved
		13	0	Vendor-specific standby timer
		13	1	Standard standby timer
	49	14-15		Reserved
50	50			Reserved
51		0-7		Vendor specific
	51	8-15		PIO transfer cycle timing mode
52		0-7		Vendor specific
	52	8-15		Obsolete
53		0	0	Fields in words 54-58 may be valid
		0	1	Fields in words 54-58 are valid
		1	0	Fields in words 64-70 are not valid
	53	1	1	Fields in words 64-70 are valid
54	54			Current number of logical cylinders
55	55			Current number of logical heads
56	56			Current number of sectors per track
57	58			Current capacity in sectors
59		0-7		Current sectors per R/W Multiple command
		8	1	Multiple sector setting is valid

continues

TABLE 9.10   Continued

Start Word	End Word	Bits	Value	Function
	59	9-15		Reserved
60	61			Total user addressable sectors in LBA mode
62	62			Obsolete
63	63	0-7		Multi-word DMA mode active
		8-15		Multi-word DMA modes supported
64		0-7		Advanced PIO modes supported
	64	8-15		Reserved
65	65			Minimum multi-word DMA cycle time per word
66	66			Drive-maker's recommended DMA cycle time
67	67			Minimum PIO cycle without flow control in ns
68	68			Minimum PIO cycle with flow control in ns
69	79			Reserved
80	80			Major version number (03 Hex for ATA-3)
81	81			Minor version number
82				Command set supported
		0	1	SMART feature set supported
		1	1	Supports security feature set
		2	1	Supports removable media feature set
		3	1	Supports power management feature set
	82	4-15		Reserved
83	83	0-13		Reserved
		14	1	Always set to one (except if no reporting)
		15	0	Always set to zero
84	127			Reserved
128				Security status

Start Word	End Word	Bits	Value	Function
		0	1	Security is supported
		1	1	Security is enabled
		2	1	Security locked
		3	1	Security frozen
		4	1	Security count expired
		5		Reserved
		8	0	Level set to High Security
		8	1	Level set to Maximum Security
	128	9-15		Reserved
129	159			Vendor specific
160	255			Reserved

S.M.A.R.T.

ATA now includes a formalized protocol for reporting S.M.A.R.T. data as described in Chapter 8, "Mass Storage Technology."

Standards

Officially, five incarnations of the ATA standard have been formalized and approved by the American National Standards Institute (or, in the case of ATA-5, will be shortly). These official standards follow.

ATA

The original AT Attachment interface was adopted by the American National Standards Institute as its standard X3.221-1994. The formal name for the standard is the AT Attachment Interface for Disk Drives.

ATA-2

The Small Form Factor committee formalized the major elements of Seagate's Fast ATA initiative together with those of Western Digital's EIDE proposal as ATA-2. Its official name became the AT Attachment Interface with Extensions (ATA-2) standard, ANSI X3.279-1996.

The important additions brought by ATA-2 included the higher speed transfer modes of Fast ATA and EIDE—specifically PIO Mode 3 and Multi-Word DMA Mode 1, which each approximately tripled the previous top transfer speeds of the original ATA standard. In addition, ATA-2 enhanced the Identify Drive command so that your PC's BIOS or operating system could query the drive to determine more of its features. In addition, ATA-2 added logical block addressing as an option for locating data on a drive.

ATA-3

Even before ATA-2 was formally approved as an official standard, work was progressing on pushing the AT Attachment standard to even higher speeds. Part of ATA-3 involves making ATA-2 more reliable. The electrical specifications of ATA-2 nudged the limits of reliability at its highest speeds because the characteristics in the interface cable were not completely taken into account. The cable acted like a transmission line, which requires termination for proper operation, but the ATA-2 standard avoided terminations to keep things simple for the user. ATA-3 described a compromise means of controlling the signal while retaining the user-friendly aspects of ATA wiring.

In addition, ATA-3 pushes speeds even higher with both a new PIO mode (Mode 4) and multi-word DMA mode (Mode 2). It also adds standards for optional power saving and security features that are described earlier. What ATA-3 does not change are the registers used, the commands, and protocols, so new drives, even if they require new connections, will work with existing software (operating systems and applications).

In addition, ATA-3 made logical block addressing mandatory for all compliant drives. It added S.M.A.R.T. technology to the standard and defined the reporting protocol. It also added security features to the standard. The standard was officially formalized by ANSI as ANSI X3.298-1997, AT Attachment-3 Interface.

ATA-4

The most important addition brought by ATA-4 was the addition of the packet interface that added official support for CD ROM drives. ATA-4 added three synchronous DMA transfer modes (0, 1, and 2) that permit transfers up to 33.3MB/sec across an ATA connection. The highest speed of these modes is sometimes termed Ultra ATA, UDMA, or most recently, UDMA/33. ATA-4 was officially adopted in 1998 as ANSI NCITS 317-1998 AT Attachment-4 with Packet Interface Extension.

ATA-5

As this is written, ATA-5 is still in draft stage. The most notable likely addition will be the adoption of Synchronous DMA Modes 3 and 4, the foundation for ATA/66 or UDMA/66 drives capable of transferring data at 66MB/sec. It also broadens the logical block addressing system to handle disks of any imaginable capacity up to 16 mega-tera-bytes.

32-Bit ATA

The next likely extension of the ATA interface standard will broaden its bus to a full 32 bits. One proposal takes advantage of the extra conductors in the 80-conductor ATA/66 cable. The doubling of the width of the bus instantly doubles the data rate of the interface to 132MB/sec.

Organization

The ATA standards are published and maintained by the American National Standards Institute, Inc., 11 West 42nd Street, New York, NY 10036. The more recent versions of the ATA standards have been prepared by the T13 technical committee of Accredited Standards Committee NCITS. The committee maintains a Web site that publishes the working documents and drafts of prospective standards at www.t13.org. The final approved standards are available in final form only from ANSI.

Compatibility

As a general rule, all ATA drives support the standard under which they were made as well as all earlier versions of the ATA standard. That is, you can plug the most recent ATA drive into the ATA connector of a vintage PC and have reasonable expectations that it will work. Similarly, you can blow the cobwebs out of drives that conform to earlier ATA standards, plug it into the newest PC, and have it work. (You may have to manually configure your system to accept old drives by entering parameters into its setup program.)

Plugging a fast drive into a slow system yields a slow drive, however. The interface is not magic and is constrained by the oldest technology in the system. Plug the latest ATA/66 drive into a old PC, and you may get a drive that works only in PIO modes. Worse, if your system doesn't recognize logical block addressing, only a fraction of the total capacity of the drive may be accessible.

Drives that conform to Fast ATA, EIDE, UDMA, and UDMA/66 are fully backward compatible with all AT Attachment host adapters. You can plug the latest drive into almost any old PC and get it to work. (Only the very earliest PCs—made before 1990— may demonstrate ATA idiosyncrasies. To take advantage of their higher speed potential, however, all the rest of the drive system must match the standard level of the drive. In other words, you'll have to be sure your PC's host adapter circuitry, its BIOS, and its driver software all match the highest speed standard you want to use.

In general, you can mix drives with different speed ratings on a single cable. Because ATA handles each transaction individually, the drives should operate at the highest speed at which they are individually capable in the given system. Note that UDMA/66 has its own cabling requirements. For operation at its highest speeds, you'll need a cable to match, although such drives will work at lower data rates with older cables, as noted in the next section.

Wiring

The AT Attachment scheme simplifies cabling in other ways. In the ATA-interface scheme, the drives and not the cable determine what drive letter is assigned to each drive. (Note that some BIOSs and the Windows NT family of operating systems let you override these device-determined drive assignments.) All the signals in the cable are extended to each of the two drives that potentially can be attached to a single host connector. Both drives that can be connected to a host AT Attachment port through the cable receive exactly the same signals on the same pins. No weird twists in the ribbon cable are used to distinguish the drives from one another, as is required in floppy disk connection arrangements. Instead, the signals to and from individual AT Attachment-interfaced drives are distinguished by control signals and timing.

The standard AT Attachment cable looks like that shown in Figure 9.1. It is a flat ribbon cable with 40 conductors and three connectors, all the same. The typical cable puts two connectors close together at one end and a single connector at the other. The paired connectors are for your disk drives; the solitary connector links to your PC's motherboard or hard disk host adapter. In fact, you can connect any plug on the cable to any device—after all, they all have exactly the same signals—but the physical placement of the connectors favors the popular usage.

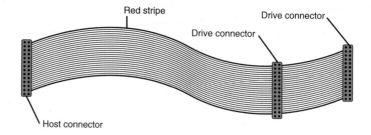

FIGURE 9.1

An AT Attachment cable.

The new UDMA Modes 3 and 4, however, require such high frequencies in their operation that the conventional ATA cable works marginally at best. To control signal quality in these high-speed modes, engineers developed a special 80-conductor cable. Every other conductor in this cable is held at ground potential so there is always a ground between two active signals on the cable. The ground effectively shields the two active signals from one another. The ground wires are all linked together in the cable connector.

Most AT Attachment cables have a red stripe on one edge. This stripe corresponds to the signal assigned to pin one on the ATA connector (see "40-Pin Connector" later in this chapter.) Although AT Attachment cables are often keyed by blocking out a single pin (number 20) and removing a pin from the corresponding jack on the hard disk or host adapter, this keying is often absent and you can inadvertently plug in a connector backwards. Using the red stripe as a guide, you can properly align the cable even without the key.

Single Drive

Although the logical signals are the same at the same positions on both drive connectors on an AT Attachment cable, the high frequency of the signals makes the cable dependent on loading. That is, the electrical characteristics of the signals on an AT Attachment cable vary depending upon which of the two connectors you plug in a single drive into. You can plug a single drive into either drive connector on an AT Attachment cable, but you'll get more reliable results by using the connector at the end of the cable, as shown in Figure 9.2. In this arrangement, the drive terminates the cable properly.

FIGURE 9.2

Recommended wiring of a single AT Attachment drive.

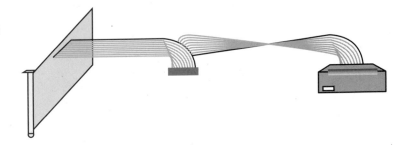

Using the middle connector leaves a stub of wire after the device as shown in Figure 9.3. This stub is called *unterminated* because it is connected to no circuitry that can absorb the signals that reach the connector. Because this arrangement can degrade the quality of the signals at the middle connector to which the drive is attached, connecting a single drive in this manner is not recommended.

FIGURE 9.3

Improper wiring of a single AT Attachment drive.

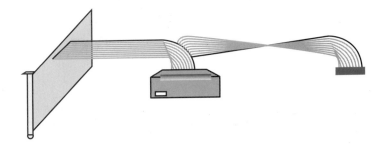

The problem arises because of the nature of electrical signals. The AT Attachment signal doesn't stop completely at the drive in the middle position. A fraction of the signal travels down the stub and reflects off the unterminated end. The reflected signal travels back and mixes with the signal at the middle drive connector. Because of the time it takes the signal to travel back and forth through the stub, the reflected signal is not a mirror image of the signal at the connector. The signal at the connector will have changed during the travel time. As a result, the combination of the new and reflected signals will be something unpredictable. The result is noise that can interfere with the desired signals at the drive connector.

Two Drives

Connecting two drives to an AT Attachment cable eliminates the electrical concerns. One drive necessarily will be at the end of the cable and terminate it properly, as shown in Figure 9.4.

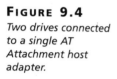

FIGURE 9.4

Two drives connected to a single AT Attachment host adapter.

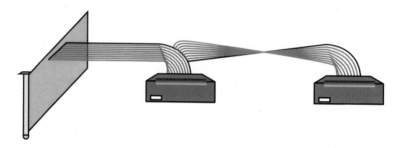

When two drives are connected to a single AT Attachment port, they do not behave as equals. One drive is designated as the master, and the other is the slave. However, the master is master only in nomenclature. The master drive does not control the slave. Its only superior function is to perform signal decoding for both drives in the two-drive system.

All AT Attachment drives have the potential for being masters or slaves. The function of each drive is determined by jumper settings on the drive. With a jumper in one position, a drive will act as the master. In another position, it will be a slave. The place at which the drive is connected to the AT Attachment cable makes no difference in whether the drive is a master or slave because the signals at all connectors in the cable are identical.

Only one master and one slave are permitted in a single AT Attachment connection, so each of the two drives in a single AT Attachment chain must have its master/slave jumpers properly set for the system to work. Most drives are shipped jumpered for operation as the master, so you only have to adjust the second AT Attachment drive you add to the short chain.

Three or Four Drives

Some ATA interface host adapters enable you to connect more than two drives. They add their own extra BIOS code to the system so that your PC can recognize more than two drives. Electrically, these host adapters provide two isolated ATA interface drive systems, each with its own master and slave drives, as shown in Figure 9.5.

FIGURE 9.5
Four drives attached to one ATA-2 host adapter.

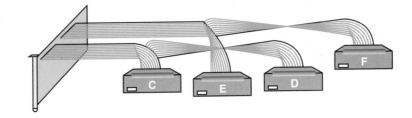

Note that the drive letters in the figure are only examples. Drive letters do not correspond to positions on a given cable, although the C and D drives must share one cable connected to the primary ATA port and the E and F drives share the cable attached to the secondary port.

Connectors

The AT Attachment standard allows two primary styles of connectors. In normal application, 3.5-inch and larger drives use a 40-pin connector and 2.5-inch and smaller drives use a 50-pin connector, the latter of which integrates power and master/slave designation as well as normal signal functions. AT Attachment drives that fit into PC Cards use another connector style that is governed by the PC Card standard.

40-Pin Connector

The standard ATA connector on the rear of most bay-mounted 3.5-inch disk drives is a simple 40-pin jack, basically a header with two rows of 20 pins each (and each pin spaced 0.10 inch from the next) surrounded by a plastic rim. This jack allows for two kinds of keying to prevent you from inadvertently plugging in the mating plug backwards. The ATA standard specifies that a key pin is actually a lack-of-pin key. Pin 20 is omitted on the jack and the matching hole on the plug is blocked, preventing the plug from sliding into the jack. In addition, most ATA connectors include a notch in the top of the shell around the jack mates with a tab on the plug providing a similar polarity fail-safe. Figure 9.6 illustrates these two forms of connector keying.

FIGURE 9.6
The 40-pin ATA connector found on 3.5-inch and larger drives.

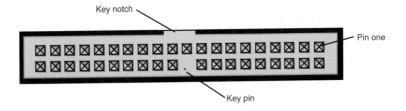

Unfortunately, both of the matching keys are often missing from AT Attachment cables and plugs. The key notch on the jack shell is not required by the ATA specification.

Moreover, many if not most ATA cables omit the plug on pin 20. The only surefire way of assuring you've properly plugged in an ATA drive is to match the color code on the cable with pin one on the jack. The red stripe, as always, should be oriented with the same side of the jack as pin one.

Devices using the 40-pin ATA connector use a supplementary power jack. Typically, it is a conventional four-wire drive power connector or a miniature power connector. Some drives include both styles of power connector.

44-Pin Connector

The 44-pin connector used by smaller drives is similar but smaller. The individual pins are spaced on 2-millimeter centers (that is, 0.079 inch apart). Pin 20 remains designated as a key. Pins 41 through 44 provide power for the drive. Most smaller drives actually use 50-pin connectors rather than those with 44 pins. At the other end of these larger connectors, six additional pins (designated A through F) do not plug into the drive cable. Instead, the first four of them accept jumpers to designate the drive as master or slave. The last two (E and F) are omitted as a key and allow space for the edge of the mating plug. Figure 9.7 shows the functional divisions of this connector.

FIGURE 9.7

The 50-pin ATA connector used in 2.5-inch and smaller drives.

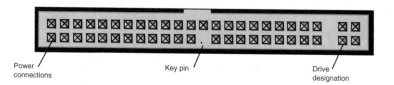

Power connections   Key pin   Drive designation

The shroud or shell around the connector is not part of the standard. Most drives omit it and use a simple 50-pin header.

68-Pin Connector

Hard disk drives built into PC Cards use the standard PC Card connector for all of their functions. This connector, discussed in Chapter 7, "The Expansion Bus," includes data, control, and power signals on its 68 pins.

The timing and bus width of the PC Card interface constrain the performance of today's tiny hard disk drives. Future implementations will likely follow the CardBus convention to match PCI bandwidth using the same 68-pin connector.

Signals and Operation

In purest form, an ATA interface drive would be one you could slide directly into an expansion slot inside your PC—a hard disk card. The drive would use exactly the same signals as any other expansion board and exactly the same connector. After all, the expansion bus is the real AT interface.

True ATA interface drives are different. Contrary to what you would expect from the interface name, drives that use the ATA interface specification do not use a direct connection to the standard ISA expansion bus. Instead, they attach to a special connector with signals somewhat different from those floating around on the ISA bus.

One reason for this difference is that the expansion buses inside computers are not designed to have cables plugged into them. Their circuitry is not optimized for transmitting signals beyond the back plane of the system board. Moreover, you wouldn't want to plug a full-height 5.25-inch hard disk directly into an expansion slot—at least if you wanted any hope of further expanding your system. The drive would be just too big and clumsy.

The ATA drive interface instead uses a special connector on the system board of PCs compatible with the standard. Alternately, a small host adapter board (which should never be called a controller card because the control electronics are on the drive) may be used, for example to implement special features (new transfer modes or RAID capabilities).

The ATA interface for hard disks doesn't aim for full-plug compatibility with the ISA bus. Instead, it modifies the bus signals somewhat to give it more reach and less complexity. You simply don't need all 98 connections of the ISA expansion bus to run a hard disk drive. Hard disk drives are not normally memory-mapped devices, for example, so there's no need to give a hard disk control of all 24 addressing lines of the AT bus.

Instead of direct access to bus addressing, in the ATA design, the cable going to the hard disk is connected to address-decoding logic circuitry. Thanks to this circuitry, only the signals sent to the addresses used in controlling the hard disk are sent to the drive. The address lines become superfluous. The actual addresses used by the AT interface connection are not part of the specification but are determined by the circuitry and BIOS of the host computer.

In addition to address-decoding logic, the ATA design adds buffering circuits to enable the connection to safely transverse the length of cable running to the disk drive. Because of the relatively high speed of these signals (corresponding to the 8MHz bus clock of the ISA expansion bus), the length of this connecting cable is severely constrained. Under the ATA specifications, signal cables are limited to 18 inches.

The initial ATA specification reduced the 98 pins used by the two ISA bus connectors to a single 40-pin connector. Table 9.11 lists the signal assignments for the various pins of this connector.

TABLE 9.11   AT Attachment (IDE) 40-pin Connector Pin Assignments

Pin	Function	Pin	Function
1	RESET-	2	Ground
3	Data line 7	4	Data line 8
5	Data line 6	6	Data line 9
7	Data line 5	8	Data line 10
9	Data line 4	10	Data line 11
11	Data line 3	12	Data line 12
13	Data line 2	14	Data line 13
15	Data line 1	16	Data line 14
17	Data line 0	18	Data line 15
19	Ground	20	(key pin)
21	DMARQ	22	Ground
23	DIOW-	24	Ground
25	DIOR-	26	Ground
27	IORDY	28	PSYNC:CSEL
29	DMACK-	30	Ground
31	INTRQ	32	IOCS16-
33	DA1	34	PDIAG-
35	DAO	36	DA2
37	CS1FX-	38	CS3FX-
39	DASP-	40	Ground

In addition to the 16 bits of data (some ATA interface drives and host adapter implementation may use just 8 bits exactly as some expansion boards have only 8-bit connectors), a variety of control signals are provided for. These signals manage the functions of the ATA interface drive through input/output registers in the control circuitry on the drive. Among these control signals are those to request reading or writing data, to make DMA transfers, to check the results of running diagnostics, and to indicate which of the two drives that can be connected to an AT interface port is to perform a given function. The interface also provides a "spindle sync" signal so that two drives can spin synchronously, as is required for some implementations of drive array.

The 44-pin connector used by 2.5-inch drives adds the three essential power connections as well as a coding pin. The 50-pin connectors actually used on most drives allow four vendor unique pin assignments, typically used for indicating master or slave status for a given drive. Table 9.12 lists the functions assigned to each pin on the 44- and 50-pin AT Attachment connectors.

TABLE 9.12   AT Attachment 44/50-Pin Connector Pin Assignments

Pin	Function	Pin	Function
A	Vendor Unique	B	Vendor Unique
C	Vendor Unique	D	Vendor Unique
E	(key pin)	F	(key pin)
1	RESET-	2	Ground
3	Data line 7	4	Data line 8
5	Data line 6	6	Data line 9
7	Data line 5	8	Data line 10
9	Data line 4	10	Data line 11
11	Data line 3	12	Data line 12
13	Data line 2	14	Data line 13
15	Data line 1	16	Data line 14
17	Data line 0	18	Data line 15
19	Ground	20	(key pin)
21	DMARQ	22	Ground
23	DIOW-	24	Ground
25	DIOR-	26	Ground
27	IORDY	28	PSYNC:CSEL
29	DMACK-	30	Ground
31	INTRQ	32	IOCS16-
33	DA1	34	PDIAG-
35	DAO	36	DA2
37	CS1FX-	38	CS3FX-
39	DASP-	40	Ground
41	+5V (Logic)	42	+5V (Motor)
43	Ground (Return)	44	Type- (0=ATA)

Regardless of the connector used by a drive, the function assigned each pin remains the same. Seven of the connections of the AT Attachment interface (numbers 2, 19, 22, 24, 26, 30, and 40) are grounds, scattered among the signals to provide some degree of isolation of one signal from another. Sixteen pins (3 through 18) are devoted to ATA's 16-bit data bus.

Beside the 16-bit connection system used by all of today's devices, the AT Attachment specification allows for 8-bit connections through the interface. Such narrow-bus system use only the odd-numbered 8 pins in the standard sequence.

The remaining 16 pins of the standard 40-pin connector are assigned various signal control functions such as those to manage reading or writing data, make DMA transfers, and coordinate the operation of two drives.

The AT Attachment signals primarily concerned with controlling the transfer of data across the interface are given their own dedicated connections. Commands to the drives and the responses from the drives (including error indications) are passed through 17 8-bit registers.

The two drives permitted under the AT Attachment standard share the connection and receive all signals across the interface indiscriminately. To signal which drive should act on a given command, the AT Attachment uses a special control register. The same register also determines the head, track, and sector that is to be used at any given time.

Seven signals are used to select among the registers. The registers are divided into two groups: control block registers and command registers, indicated by two interface signals. Activating the Drive Chip Select 0 signal (pin 37) selects the control block registers. Activating the Drive Chip Select 1 signal (pin 38) selects the command block registers. When the Drive I/O Write signal (pin 23) is active, the registers that accept commands from the host are accessible through the interface data lines. When the Drive I/O Read signal (pin 25) is active, the registers indicate drive status through the data lines.

Drive Address Bus 0 through 2, located on pins 35, 33, and 36 (with the other signals), control which register is currently selected and accessible through the data lines. The AT Attachment standard defines two read and one write control block register as well as seven read and seven write command block registers. Of these, one write command block register selects the active drive and head (up to 16 heads are allowed). Two registers select the drive track (allowing up to 65,536 tracks on a single drive), another register selects the sector to start reading from or writing to, and another register selects the number of the track to be read or written. The read registers indicate which drive and head is active and which track and head is being scanned. Other registers provide status information and define errors that occur during drive operation.

The number of register bits available sets the logical limits on device size: up to 16 heads, 65,536 tracks, and 256 sectors per track. Because many PCs are incapable of handling more than 1,024 tracks, the maximum practical capacity of an AT Attachment drive is 2,147,483,648 bytes (2GB).

During active data transfers, separate signals are used as strobes to indicate that the data going to or coming from the drive or values in the control registers are valid and can be used. The falling edge of the Drive I/O Read signal (pin 25) indicates to the host that valid data read from the disk is on the bus. The falling edge of the Drive I/O Write signal (pin 23) indicates that data on the bus to be written on disk is valid.

The Drive 16-bit I/O signal (pin 32) indicates whether the read or write transfer comprises 8 or 16 bits. The signal is active to indicate 16-bit transfers.

Normally, AT Attachment transfers are accomplished through programmed I/O, the standard mode of operation using the standard ATA hard disk BIOS. However, the AT Attachment standard optionally supports Direct Memory Access transfers. Two signals control handshaking during DMA data moves. The drive signals that it is ready to read data and transfer it in DMA mode by asserting the DMA Request signal (pin 21). The computer host acknowledges that it is ready to accept that data with the DMA Acknowledge signal (pin 29). If the host cannot accept all the data at once, it removes the DMA Acknowledge signal until it is ready to receive more.

In DMA write operations, the host PC uses DMA Acknowledge to indicate that it has data available and the active drive uses DMA Request for handshaking to control the flow of data. The Drive I/O Read and Write signals indicate in which direction the data should flow (as a disk read or write).

An AT Attachment disk drive can interrupt the host computer to gain immediate attention by activating the Drive Interrupt signal (pin 31). On programmed I/O transfers, the drive generates an interrupt at the beginning of each block of data (typically a sector) to be transferred. On DMA transfers, the interrupt is used only to indicate that the command has been completed. (The interrupt used is determined by the host's circuitry.)

A drive can signal to the host computer that it is not ready to process a read or write request using the I/O Channel Ready signal (pin 27). Normally, this signal is activated; the drive switches it off when it cannot immediately respond to a request to transfer data.

The Drive Reset signal (pin 1) causes the drive to return to its normal power-on state, ignoring transfers in progress and losing the contents of its registers (returning them to their default values). Normally, the drive is activated briefly (for at least 25 microseconds) when the host computer is turned on so that it will initialize itself. Activating this signal thereafter will cancel the command in progress and reinitialize the drive.

The Passed Diagnostics signal (pin 34) is used by the slave drive to indicate to its host that it is running its diagnostics. The "Passed" in the name does not mean that the diagnostics are completed successfully but that the results are ready to be passed along to the host system. Actual results (and the command to actually execute diagnostics) is given through the AT Attachment registers.

The Spindle Sync/Cable Select signal (pin 28) can be used at the drive manufacturer's option to make the drives spin synchronously (as is required by some drive-array technologies) or to set drive identification as master or slave by the cable rather than using a jumper or switch on the drive. When used as a spindle-synchronizing signal, the master drive generates a periodic pulse (typically once each revolution of the disk, although the actual timing is left to the drive manufacturer), and the slave uses this signal to lock its spin to the master. When this connection is used as a cable-select signal, supplying a ground on pin 28 causes a drive to function as the master (drive 0); leaving the connection open causes the connected drive to act as the slave (drive 1).

A single signal, termed Drive Active/Drive 1 Present located on pin 39, indicates that one of the drives is active (for example, to illuminate the drive activity indicator on the system front panel). The same pin is used by the host signal to determine whether one or two AT Attachment drives are installed when the power is switched on. The drive assigned as the slave is given a 400-millisecond period during system startup to put a signal on this pin to indicate its availability; after waiting 450 milliseconds to give the slave drive time to signal, the master drive puts its signal on the pin to indicate its presence to the host computer. It switches its signal off and converts the function of the signal to drive activity when the drive accepts its first command from the host computer or after waiting 31 seconds, whichever comes first.

As comprehensive as the AT Attachment standard is, it doesn't define everything. Most important, it governs only the connection between the PC and drive. Everything upstream—that is, inside the computer—is left to the designer of the host PC. AT Attachment does not indicate the logical location of its control registers. The decoding logic that determines those values is part of the host adapter circuitry of the PC. The system BIOS (or add-in BIOS) provides the needed information for establishing the link.

The system BIOS is thus critical to getting AT Attachment drives to operate properly. Some older BIOSs may not be able to properly control AT Attachment drives. In particular, AMI BIOSs dated before April 9, 1990, were not completely compatible. To use an AT Attachment drive in a system with one of these older BIOSs, you must replace the BIOS.

Logical Interface

The AT Attachment interface logically links to the rest of your PC through a series of registers. The standard does not constrain the port addresses used by these registers. Their location is set by the BIOS writer and chipset designer of your PC. The registers are generally inside the motherboard chipset, and the BIOS must be written to match. Add-in host adapters include their own registers and matching add-on BIOS.

Applications and operating systems that use the BIOS never need know the location of these ports. Software drivers for operating systems that bypass the BIOS must be written with the proper register addresses.

Register Addresses

Most chipset makers use the same range of addresses for the I/O ports used in communicating with their AT Attachment interfaces. Consequently, a single set of register addresses has become a de facto standard in nearly all PCs. Table 9.13 lists these register addresses.

TABLE 9.13   AT Attachment Primary Port Host System Registers

Register	Read Function	Write Function
01F0h	Read Data	Write Data (16 Bits)
01F1h	Error register	Set Features Data
01F2h	Status of sector count	Write sector count
01F3h	Starting sector	Write sector
01F4h	Cylinder low location	Write cylinder low location
01F5h	Cylinder high location	Write cylinder high location
01F6h	Head/device selection	Write device/head selection
01F7h	Device Status	Device command
03F6h	Alternate Status	Device Control
03F7h	Drive Address	

Secondary Host Adapters

Most modern host adapters include a secondary port—another connector to plug in a cable for two more ATA devices. In most systems, the primary port conforms to one of the advanced specifications (for example, EIDE) and the secondary port offers more modest basic ATA speed enhanced only by ATAPI support for a CD drive. The design of the ATA interface requires a separate set of input/output ports for communicating with this second connection.

The logical location of the ports used by both the primary and secondary AT Attachment host adapters is not fixed and can be set at any of several ranges of values that the hardware manufacturer chooses. The chosen I/O port addresses only need to be reflected in the BIOS routines for Interrupt 13(Hex) service and the software drivers used to control the board. Nevertheless, most manufacturers use the same ports and interrupts for their primary and secondary AT Attachment ports. Table 9.14 lists the usual address ranges and interrupt assignments.

TABLE 9.14   Typical AT Attachment Port and Interrupt Assignments

Interface number	Primary (CS0)	Secondary (CS1)	IRQ number
1	01F0h-01F7h	03F6h-03F7h	14
2	0170h-0177h	0376h-0377h	15 or 10
3	01E8h-01Efh	03EEh-03Efh	12 or 11
4	0168h-016Fh	036Eh-036Fh	10 or 9

Within each range, the function of each of the eight I/O ports follows the assignments given in Table 9.13 (the previous table).

SCSI

Pronounced "scuzzy" by much of the computer industry (and much less often "sexy" by its most fervent advocates), SCSI is a system-level interface that provides what is essentially a complete expansion bus into which to plug peripherals. SCSI isn't simply a connection that links a device or two to your PC. Rather, it functions like a sub-bus. SCSI devices can exchange data between themselves without the intervention of the host computer's microprocessor. In fact, they can act across the SCSI bus even while other transfers are shifting across the host computer's normal expansion bus.

Originally simply a means to add hard disk drives to minicomputers, SCSI has evolved into a complete interconnection system that can link hard disk drives, CD ROM players, scanners, and even arrays of hard disks to any kind of computer.

Background

In its latest dress, SCSI is a wide-reaching system with both hardware and software aspects. It is not a single standard but a group that is linked together by a common set of commands. When most people speak of SCSI, they actually mean the hardware connection system that's technically termed the *SCSI parallel interface*. Although this interface is only one physical manifestation of SCSI, it is the most common aspect now found in PCs. There is much more to SCSI than the connector on the back end of hard disks, however.

Today, the SCSI system is a three-tier hierarchy. The top level is the command structure that gives your PC control of all the SCSI hardware. This is the realm of the software driver inside your PC. The middle level comprises the protocol, the software structure used to move the commands through the SCSI system to the various SCSI devices. This is the code generated by your PC's software driver that travels across the SCSI hardware system and gets interpreted by each SCSI device. The bottom tier is the hardware itself, the ports, cables, and connectors that link the SCSI devices together. This level is your primary concern because this is the one level that requires your hands-on participation. To make the SCSI system work, you have to plug together all the SCSI hardware properly. Once you've installed the SCSI drivers, all the software work is in the hands of the programmers. You have no options to tinker or change it.

Each of the primary types of devices that you might connect to a SCSI port has its own command standard. Under the SCSI-3 rubric, these commands have been grouped into five types: *block commands* to control devices such as hard disk drives, *stream commands* for regulating such products as tape drives, *graphics commands* for printers, *medium changer commands* for such things as CD ROM juke boxes, and *controller commands* for disk arrays.

The SCSI system ties together these four command sets with an overall primary SCSI command set, governed by its own standard. This primary command set is the one feature shared by all SCSI devices and software. It is what makes them SCSI.

The primary command set sends out a common set of instructions to all SCSI hardware. The protocol layer interprets and converts these instructions into the form that works with each of four hardware systems currently incorporated into the SCSI family. Each hardware system has its own corresponding protocol layer. Typically, your SCSI host adapter implements the protocol layer and produces the requisite signals for sending through the various SCSI connections.

History

The original SCSI standard evolved from another interface called SASI, the Shugart Associates Standard Interface. This interface was developed in 1981 by hard disk pioneer

Shugart Associates working with NCR Corporation. Together, they developed SCSI as an 8-bit parallel connection between host computers and disk drives. Later that year, the X3T9 committee of the American National Standards Institute used the SASI specification as the foundation for its work on a parallel interface standard. That standard, now known as SCSI-1, was formally approved in 1986.

Even before the ANSI acceptance of SCSI, manufacturers were wary of the shortcomings in the original specification. In 1985, device manufacturers approached the group working on the standard with proposals to increase the mandatory requirements of the SCSI standard. Because the standard was already near completion and the industry was impatient, ANSI adopted SCSI while at the same time formed a new group to develop a set of commands for SCSI with broader application, eventually published—although not as an official standard—as the *common command set*.

Because the common command set was not a mandatory part of SCSI, each device manufacturer made its own interpretation of it. As a result, individual SCSI devices often required their own driver software and many combinations of SCSI devices simply wouldn't work together at all.

In 1991, a revision of SCSI was introduced to help fix some of the problems in mating SCSI devices, as well as to increase the speed of SCSI transfers. Referred to as SCSI-2, the new standard integrated a complete software-control system called the common command set with several optional hardware enhancements. These included the broadening of the 8-bit SCSI data bus to wide SCSI, which can use 16 or 32 data lines. These would double the effective peak transfer rate of the interface to 10 or 20MB/sec. In addition, the top speed of SCSI transfers was doubled with the addition of fast SCSI. With an 8-bit bus width, fast SCSI pushed transfer rates up to 10MB/sec; wide and fast SCSI could peak at 20 to 40MB/sec. Wide SCSI also expands the number of possible devices connected to a single host adapter channel to 15.

Almost immediately after the SCSI-2 standard was approved, the industry began work on its successor, SCSI-3, to refine the standard further. Although not formally approved at the time this was written, SCSI-3 has been out in draft for long enough that most manufacturers have incorporated its requirements into their designs. For the purposes of this discussion, SCSI-3 is considered the current standard.

Rather than a single standard, SCSI-3 has become an umbrella that covers a multitude of individual hardware and protocol standards. Notably, it divorces software from hardware so that the common command set and the various cabling systems go their separate directions. At that, SCSI itself becomes a command protocol and the various interconnection standards control how you wire your peripherals together.

At the hardware level, SCSI-3 carries over the traditional SCSI design with its own refinements and adds three other options for linking SCSI devices. The traditional SCSI wiring system becomes the *SCSI parallel interface* (SPI). The other three interconnection systems give you high-speed serial choices. *Serial storage architecture* currently delivers two channels of 20MB/sec transfer rate for full duplex operation. (A device can transmit and receive simultaneously at that data rate.) *P1394* gives a 100MB/sec serial system that plugs together like a set of stereo components. *Fibre channel arbitrated loop* provides a 100MB/sec system that uses simple plug-in connections for disk drives and a bridge to optical fiber with even higher speeds. These hardware standards give SCSI-3 enough headroom to take peripheral connections into the next generation—and the next incarnation of SCSI.

Standards

SCSI has a bad, and often undeserved, reputation for being confusing to set up. Many people considered prayers as necessary as hardware know-how in setting up a SCSI system. Be that as it may, the real confusion in SCSI comes in the nomenclature. Although all SCSI devices speak a common language, most people use their own definitions of the words that describe different SCSI versions. Not only has the official standard gone through three distinct incarnations, but also manufacturers have concocted their own labels for some of the variations available under the SCSI-3 umbrella. Many of the more common usages are misleading if not outright wrong.

This section attempts to clear up some of the confusion and fit the pieces of the jigsaw puzzle together.

SCSI-1

The original version of SCSI now is termed SCSI-1 to distinguish it from its heirs. As the progenitor, SCSI-1 inspired the work that has led to today's SCSI standard. SCSI-1 embraces only little more than the parallel wiring interface that serves as the basis for the current SPI design.

SCSI-1 devices need not understand the common command set. As a consequence, early SCSI devices exhibited a variety of incompatibilities with one another. The only way of being certain that a given SCSI-1 device would work with another—including simple connections between host adapter and hard disk drive—was to buy a pair specifically matched by a peripheral manufacturer. Although many manufacturers later adapted the common command set to their SCSI-1 devices, you have no assurance that a given SCSI-1 device will work with more modern SCSI implementations.

SCSI-2

The big demarcation between what is now called SCSI-1 and SCSI-2 is the command set. The move to SCSI-2 broadened the SCSI command set and made many previously optional features mandatory. The aim of this change was to eliminate inter-compatibility problems—that is, to assure you would have no (or at least less) difficulty in getting SCSI devices to work with one another. At the same time, SCSI-2 added *optional* higher speed transfer modes. Because these higher speed modes are optional, a given product can conform with the SCSI-2 standard and *not be any faster* than a SCSI-1 drive. It could even perform more slowly. In other words, a label that claims SCSI-2 is not a guarantee of superior performance.

In common parlance, this distinction is often blurred. When most PC people claim a hard disk drive is SCSI-2, they usually mean that it can transfer data faster than a drive following the SCSI-1 standard. Most of the time, such references to SCSI-2 really mean the product implements Fast SCSI, discussed later. Similarly, some folks use the moniker SCSI-3 to mean Wide SCSI, a feature of SCSI-3 that was actually introduced in SCSI-2.

At the hardware level, SCSI-2 starts with the same parallel interface first used with SCSI-1. In addition, it adds new hardware options: Fast SCSI that alters some timing parameters for higher throughput, Wide SCSI for greater bus width for increased performance and more devices per SCSI port, and several new connector options.

SCSI-2 eliminated some of the little-used options that the initial SCSI standard allowed. These included the single initiator option, the non-arbitrating systems option, the non-extended sense data option, and the reservation queuing option. The command set aimed at read-only devices was changed to a CD ROM command. And SCSI-2 eliminated the one of the shielded connectors endorsed by the original standard.

SCSI-2 also made some of the original SCSI options into mandatory requirements. Under SCSI-2, devices must provide for parity checking the data bus. All devices must support SCSI messaging. Any SCSI device may provide termination power, but all initiators must provide termination power. In addition, SCSI-2 shaved some timing specifications to allow for higher speed.

SCSI-2 also added several new performance-improving options. The combination of revised timing and synchronous data transfers allows for transfers of 10MB/sec. An option for wide buses increases the data path and doubles or quadruples the peak transfer rate. *Tagged command queuing* improves host performance by allowing your PC (or other SCSI host) to send several commands through the SCSI system at the same time or send one command the previous one completes. Your PC doesn't have to wait for the SCSI system to be ready before it sends more commands, which means less waiting—at least if your operating system can carry on while a command is pending. (DOS and Windows 95 cannot.)

SCSI-2 also improves the connectability of traditional SCSI parallel wiring, adding new high-density connector alternatives and improved bus termination.

SCSI-2 also significantly broadens the command set. From being exclusively a hard disk interface, SCSI-2 embraces communications as well as other storage devices. It incorporates specific command sets for read-only and erasable optical devices in addition to CD

ROM. Other commands control devices that can change their medium, such as optical juke boxes. SCSI-2 also includes commands for printers (carried over from the original SCSI), scanners, and communications equipment.

SCSI-3

SCSI-3 provides mechanisms for using the common command set across several hardware-connection schemes. In addition to parallel SCSI, essentially what we know as SCSI-2 today, the new standard will support serial SCSI based on the P1394 standard (see Chapter 20, "Peripheral Ports"), a fiber optical connection, and several others. Moreover, parallel SCSI is enhanced into 16-bit SCSI, which increases the device total that can be connected to a single SCSI bus to 16. SCSI-3 also takes care of some of the details, officially standardizing the P-connector used in most wide SCSI-2 implementations.

The speed of SCSI-3 depends on its hardware implementation. The cabling methods and speed of SCSI-2 are still allowed, but new transmission systems allow transfer rates in excess of 100MB/sec. SCSI-3 incorporates four wiring standards, SPI, P1394, SSA, and FC-AL:

SPI is the *SCSI-3 parallel interface*, the traditional SCSI wiring system with some new embellishments. When most people and manufacturers talk about SCSI-3, they really mean SPI. Although SCSI-3 embraces the same hardware configurations as SCSI-2 and is backward compatible, it tightens the requirements for signal and cabling over SCSI-2. Ultra SCSI and Ultra 2 SCSI are SPI implementations with increased bus speeds, as discussed later in this chapter in the section "SCSI Parallel Interface."

P1394 is an IEEE standard for a 100 megabits per second (and faster) serial interface that's known in the Macintosh world as *Firewire*. It is discussed in detail in Chapter 20.

SSA stands for *system storage architecture*, a high-speed interface design created primarily by IBM. It is discussed in Appendix N, "Less Popular Disk Interfaces."

FC-AL stands for *fibre channel arbitrated loop*, an offshoot of the development of a fiber optical interconnection system that doesn't actually use fiber optics. It is discussed in Appendix N.

Organization

The American National Standards Institute, ANSI, maintains the official SCSI standards. SCSI standards in their final, published form are available only from ANSI.

The SCSI T10 Committee actively develops the various SCSI standards. It provides recommendations to ANSI, which, on its approval, sanctions the specifications as industry standards. The committee acts as a forum for introducing and discussing proposals for the standard. It maintains a Web site at http://www.t10.org/.

The SCSI Trade Association promotes the use of SCSI and devices that adhere to that standard. The association maintains a Web site at `http://www.t10.org/`.

SCSI Parallel Interface

The basic SCSI hardware interface is a parallel connection on a multi-conductor cable called the *SCSI parallel interface*, or SPI. This standard is an outgrowth of the original SCSI interface. In original form, the SCSI interface comprised an 8-bit bus with a ninth parity bit for error detection and a maximum clock speed of 5MHz. Since then, three versions of the SPI system have been developed, the most recent of which (SPI-3) pushes the width of the bus to 16 bits (not counting parity) and clock speed to 80MHz.

More than a means of linking storage devices as was the original SCSI system, SPI was designed to be an expansion bus that could link any of a variety of device types to your PC through a single-port connection. The first SCSI design linked up to seven SCSI devices to one SCSI port through a simple daisy chain. The expanded bus afforded by SPI increased the number of devices per port to 15 (or 16 if you count the host adapter). All the devices function independently, under the control of the host system through the host adapter that provides the SCSI port.

SCSI parallel interface allows for both asynchronous and synchronous transfers. *Asynchronous transfers* allow data to be sent at irregular intervals using start and stop bits to mark the beginning and ends of data bytes. *Synchronous transfers* use system timing to define data bytes. Because synchronous transfers require less overhead—fewer bits transferred and less processing of the data—it can be faster.

Wiring for the SCSI parallel interface takes the form of a cable-based bus for internal devices. External connections are topographically identical—a bus—but use a daisy-chain connection system. This relatively simple wiring scheme gets complicated by the sanctioned variations in bus width and speed and by the need for terminating the connections to maintain signal integrity.

Performance

Most people quote one or two numbers for SCSI speed and base all their judgments on those figures. Speed across a SCSI parallel interface connection is not a simple thing, however. It suffers many variations and practical limitations in addition to options in the standard. In other words, just because a device is SCSI does not mean you'll see 10MB/sec—or 20 or 40 or whatever—when it comes to plugging everything together.

The speed limit of current SPI connections gets set by two primary factors, bus speed and bus width. In asynchronous connections, the length of the connection and transfer overhead mix in to reduce the actual throughput beneath the limit set by the clock speed.

To get the real issue out of the way first, Table 9.15 lists the nomenclature and speed limits (more correctly, peak transfer rates) of today's common parallel SCSI connection systems.

TABLE 9.15   Comparison of SCSI Parallel Interface Performance Specifications

Interface Name	Bus width	Bus Speed	Peak transfer rate
Plain SCSI (SCSI-2)	8 bits	5MHz	5Mbytes/sec
Fast SCSI	8 bits	10MHz	10Mbytes/sec
Wide SCSI	16 bits	5MHz	10Mbytes/sec
Fast Wide SCSI	16 bits	10MHz	20Mbytes/sec
Ultra SCSI	8 bits	20MHz	20Mbytes/sec
Ultra Wide SCSI	16 bits	20MHz	40Mbytes/sec
Ultra2 SCSI	8 bits	40MHz	40Mbytes/sec
Ultra2 Wide SCSI	16 bits	40MHz.	80Mbytes/sec
Ultra160/m SCSI	8 bits	40MHz	80Mbytes/sec
Ultra160/m Wide SCSI	16 bits	40MHz	160Mbytes/sec

Clock Speed

Strictly speaking, in asynchronous form the SCSI parallel interface has no clock as does a PC expansion bus. No single oscillator shepherds every byte down the bus. However, the various signals on the bus have rigidly defined durations that, when put in practice, set a limit on the peak transfer rate of the overall system.

In synchronous SCSI, which is unhindered by the need for interlocked handshaking (and runs as close to an open-ended oscillator as anything in SCSI, the cycle time of the bus arises from the combination of the assertion period and negation period. The assertion period is the time allowed for SCSI devices to ready their signals and place them on the bus. The negation period is the time allowed for removing the signals.

Under the SCSI-1 specification, 90 nanoseconds was allocated to each of these actions. A full transfer cycle across the SCSI bus consequently required 180 nanoseconds. Assuming a perfect signaling system and no overhead, that timing allows for a peak transfer rate of about 5.5MB/sec. The 5.0MB/sec figure often quoted for SCSI-1 is both an approximation and the maximum practical speed of many commercial products.

SCSI-2 shaved the cycle times and specifically defined a cycle time of 100 nanoseconds. This rate allows for a peak transfer rate of 10MB/sec. This figure is often quoted as *Fast SCSI*, although the term actually applies to any speed in excess of 5.0MB/sec. Note that proclaiming a device to be Fast SCSI automatically implies an allegiance to at least the SCSI-2 standard. The reduced cycle times required for this rate are not possible under SCSI-1.

Shorter timing cycles and faster speeds are permitted under the SPI standards. Officially, each of these modes is termed "Fast" followed by the clock speed. When used without a numerical designation, Fast SCSI refers to the 10MHz speed.

Fast-20 doubles that speed to 20MHz and a cycle time of 50 nanoseconds. Throughout the industry, this speed is commonly known as *Ultra SCSI*, usurping what was once a proprietary term for a somewhat different combination of technologies.

Fast-40 SCSI again doubles the speed—to 40MHz—by halving the cycle time to 25 nanoseconds. This speed level is now commonly called *Ultra2 SCSI*.

Fast-80 SCSI doubles throughput but retains the same cycle time and clock speed. To achieve higher throughput, it relies on double-clocking, shifting data on both the rising and falling sides of the timing signals. In its wide, 16-bit form, Fast-80 SCSI has been termed SCSI 160m.

As a practical matter, modern SCSI drives can use single-ended signaling at speeds up to and including Ultra SCSI—providing you follow the cable length constraints listed later in this chapter in the section "Maximum Cable Length." The speed of Ultra2 and Fast-80 SCSI requires differential signaling.

Handshaking

SCSI devices can use asynchronous or synchronous transfer protocols when communicating. Asynchronous SCSI transmissions are slower because they require more overhead—a handshake signal for every byte transferred. Synchronous SCSI transfers require less overhead. You can mix both asynchronous and synchronous devices in a single SCSI system.

Asynchronous SCSI transfers operate as a handshaking system. First, a device issues a request (signaling REQ) and waits for an acknowledgment (ACK) to be sure its request was received before doing anything else. In every step and every byte of the transfer, this two-step process must take place. Actual transfers require four steps: First, one device sends the REQ and it is answered by ACK. The first device turns off its REQ and waits for the other device to switch off its ACK before the first device can go on to the next byte.

Each of these handshakes must travel down the SCSI cable, so the signal must go back and forth through the cable twice for each transfer. Although electrical signals are fast, they travel at a finite and measurable speed, about one third the speed of light in a vacuum. In typical SCSI cables, it takes a signal about 5.25 nanoseconds to move one meter. This travel time is termed the propagation delay, and it is the primary constraint on the speed of asynchronous SCSI transfers in long cables. The longer the cable, the longer the delay.

Although the original SCSI standard puts a speed limit of 1.25MB/second on asynchronous transfers, that rate applies only to the longest permitted cables, 25 meters. Shorter cables can achieve higher rates using asynchronous transfers.

The overhead involved in transferring each byte across the parallel SCSI bus using asynchronous signaling is about 160 nanoseconds. Adding in the propagation delay sets the minimum cycle time and maximum transfer rate of the connection. Table 9.16 shows the relationship between the timing, cable legnth, and speed in simple parallel SCSI.

TABLE 9.16 SCSI Maximum Asynchronous Transfer Rate Versus Cable Length

Cable length (meters)	Propagation delay (ns.)	Overhead (nanoseconds)	Cycle time (nanoseconds)	Transfer rate (MB/sec)
0.3	6.3	160	166	6.0
1	21	160	181	5.5
3	63	160	223	4.5
5	105	160	265	3.8
10	210	160	370	2.7
15	315	160	475	2.1
25	525	160	685	1.5

Synchronous SCSI requires an acknowledgment for each request sent, but it allows the acknowledgment to be delayed. Consequently, a device can send packets one after another without enduring the propagation delays required in interlocked handshaking. Synchronous SCSI operates at a speed determined by its cycle time without regard to propagation delay. In other words, the speed of synchronous SCSI is independent of cable length.

Bus Width

Because the SCSI parallel interface is exactly that, it transfers data more than one bit at a time. Initially, designers conceived SCSI as a byte-wide interface, but the SCSI-2 revision brought options for 16-bit and 32-bit bus widths. The 16-bit connection is termed *Wide SCSI.*

These wider buses directly translate into greater bus throughput. The overhead for each transfer is the same, regardless of bus width. Consequently, 16-bit SCSI achieves twice the transfer rate as 8-bit SCSI. Although SCSI proposals once provided the potential for

32-bit connections, which would quadruple the 8-bit transfer rate, the latest incarnation of SPI only blesses 8- and 16-bit bus widths.

Wide SCSI brings an additional benefit. The SCSI parallel interface uses a hardware scheme for selecting a device to send or receive data. The number of devices that can share a single SCSI connection depends on the individual addressability of the devices. The cabling that adds extra bus connections also brings additional lines for addressing devices.

External Factors

As a practical matter, the most onerous limits on the performance of SCSI devices are unrelated to the hardware connections of the interface. That's exactly as it should be; in the best implementations, the interface is invisible with no overall effect on peripheral performance.

The obvious limit on device performance is the rate at which a given device reads its medium. Although a cache can improve the apparent performance of a system, on extended or random transfers, caches fail and throughput falls to the speed imposed by the mechanism.

The speeds of the various SCSI systems, all the way to Fast-80, all represent the *peak* transfer rate. It is the maximum speed potential of the system that may be achieved when a drive unloads a burst of data from an on-board cache. Non-cached transfers slow to the limit set by the mechanical performance of the drive. Moreover, because the SCSI bus is a shared resource, the demands of other devices on the bus can cut the throughput of an individual device.

Capacity and Addressing

SCSI devices store data in the form of blocks. Each block is assigned an address, and a host indicates which block to read or write by its address. The size of each block and the number of available addresses constrain the capacity of any given device.

The original SCSI command structure provided 21 bits for identifying block addresses, sufficient for 2,097,152 blocks. With hard disk drives that used blocks of standard 512-byte sectors, this addressing scheme allow for drives storing up to 1GB.

The SCSI-2 refinement allows for a full three bytes (24 bits) for encoding block addresses by taking advantage of three bits reserved under the earlier implementation. SCSI host adapters designed to that standard can access up to 16,777,216 blocks, which with sector-size blocks limits capacity to 8GB, or 8,589,934,592 bytes. Larger drives could be accommodated by defining blocks as multiple sectors.

Increasing block size is a band-aid solution, one that only covers up an underlying problem. Consequently, the current SCSI block commands now include a second form of read, write, and related commands that allocate four bytes (32-bits) for block addresses. Using the new commands, the system can address up to 4,294,967,296 blocks, enough to handle devices storing two terabytes (2,199,023,255,552 bytes) of data.

Early SCSI host adapters suffered another limit resulting from the translation of DOS cylinder-head-sector addresses into SCSI's logical block address format by commercial SCSI host adapters. One of the most common translation algorithms mapped 1MB of disk capacity to each logical cylinder. The capacity of the drive determined the number of cylinders reported to your PC. Each of these cylinders appeared to your PC as if it had 63 sectors and 32 heads.

This simple translation scheme suffers one severe constraint. The DOS Interrupt 13(Hex) routines recognize only 1,024 cylinders, constricting drive addressing to 1,024MB. Even when drives had larger capacities, only the first gigabyte could be addressed.

Note that the translation algorithm and this restriction are functions of the design choices in creating a specific SCSI host adapter. Once host adapter makers recognized the problem (about the time 1GB disk drives were arriving on the marketplace in force), they altered their algorithms to handle greater capacities. Nevertheless, should you plug a large SCSI drive into an older host adapter, you will not be able to use its entire capacity. By 1994, most makers had moved to more advanced translations schemes. For example, the Adaptec 1542B suffers a 1GB addressing limit, but the 1542C does not.

Note, too, that because the translation algorithm is a design choice in the host adapter, different host adapters sometimes use their own algorithms that may be incompatible with other SCSI host adapters. As a result, when you move a disk from an older to newer host adapter, your files may appear scrambled (if the drive works at all). Your data is, in fact, intact as long as you don't write to the drive, and you can recover all your files by reinstalling the drive on the old host adapter. To move to the new host adapter, back up your files from the drive using the old host adapter, reinstall (and reformat) the drive with the new host adapter, and restore your files from the backup.

You face another constraint with middle-aged host adapters. An older host adapter may not be able to handle 32-bit block addresses and could constrain your use of disks with larger capacities. In general, if you use a host adapter that supports the fastest transfer mode supported by your drive, you should encounter no addressing limits. All UltraSCSI host adapters, for example, should have no problems with large drives. If, however, you try to use a large UltraSCSI drive with an old ordinary SCSI host adapter (which technically should work because SCSI devices negotiate the speed to use), you may not be able to reach the full capacity of the drive—nor would you take advantage of its full speed potential.

Wiring

Because SCSI is a bus, its wiring is essentially simple. The pins of the connectors on one device are directly linked to the pins of the same position (and function). You can run a straight cable (no twists or crossovers) from the host adapter to one SCSI device and then on to the next. Unfortunately, reality interferes with this idealized connection system. All of the variations of the parallel interface need to be taken into account. As a result, the mechanics of the actual cabling vary with bus speed and width whether your SCSI connections are strictly inside your PC, external to it, or both.

SCSI also saddles you with two other worries, device identification and termination. The proper operation of a SCSI system requires that you get both of these setup chores right.

SCSI Identification

Because SCSI is a bus, all devices are simultaneously connected and receive all transmissions (commands and data). Commands are routed to individual SCSI devices by identifying them by their SCSI addresses. Standard SCSI systems use eight dedicated lines in the SCSI cable for identifying devices. Each device uses one line, allowing eight unambiguous addresses, which translate into SCSI identification, or SCSI ID, numbers. In 8-bit SCSI systems, these are usually designated in standard Arabic numerals as SCSI ID numbers 0 through 7. Wide SCSI systems expand the identification possibilities to 0 through 15. In either case, one number (usually the highest) is reserved for the SCSI host adapter. The other addresses, 0 through 6 or 0 through 14, can be assigned to any device connected anywhere in the SCSI chain. Each address is assigned a priority to the device using it with the host adapter as 7 or 15 having the top priority and 0 having the lowest priority.

In the latest SCSI systems that operate under the plug-and-play aegis, you don't have to worry about these numbers. The *SCAM* system—which stands for SCSI Configured AutoMagically—does exactly what its name implies, querying each SCSI device and assigning non-conflicting ID numbers to each one it finds. For SCAM to work, of course, your host adapter, operating system, and SCSI devices must comply with the standard. Note, by the way, the magical part of the name was applied in the initial standard, although some less inspired engineers are apt to interpret the name to be SCSI Configured Automatically.

If you have an older host adapter and a mess of old SCSI devices, you'll be left to configuring them without prestidigitation. And that's where the complication of SCSI begins. Except for the arbitrary address of 7 assigned to the host adapter (or 15 in Wide SCSI systems), you assign the addresses that each SCSI device uses. The most basic rule is simple: SCSI ID numbers must be unique, so never assign to two or more devices in the same SCSI chain the same ID number.

In the formal SCSI scheme of things, you can assign any number to any device, as long as you configure your software properly. The SCSI specification does not reserve any particular number for any device. As a practical matter, you cannot be so cavalier about the ID numbers that you use for different devices. One concern is matching your software. A SCSI driver may require that you indicate the SCSI address that you assign to your CD ROM player. The software for the CD ROM player may demand that you assign a particular address to the player in order for it to work.

If there is any one guide to follow, it is the model set by Adaptec, the largest maker of SCSI host adapters. To provide some consistency for its host adapters that emulate Western Digital WD1002 controllers so that they can boot your PC, Adaptec chose rather pragmatically that you *must* assign your boot hard disk drive (if it is a SCSI drive) ID number zero. Oddly, this is the device that the SCSI arbitration system assigns the *least* priority. Nearly all manufacturers of SCSI host adapters and PCs now follow this convention.

Early Adaptec host adapters had built in BIOSs that enabled the boot drive and one additional drive to link to your PC without an additional software driver. For your second drive to be recognized when using this kind of controller, the second hard disk must have ID number 1.

The latest Adaptec host adapters include an advanced BIOS capable of recognizing up to seven hard disk drives, giving you the freedom to assign them any ID, *providing you give the boot device ID 0*. The BIOS recognizes disk drives (and dispenses drive letters) according to the order of the ID you assign. The lower numbers get the first drive letters.

Some Adaptec host adapters put one more restriction on your freedom in assigning device IDs. Removable media devices—which include CD players, CD recorders, and tape drives—should not be assigned ID numbers 0 or 1. The BIOSs of these adapters may not properly operate with removable media devices with these lower ID numbers and may not properly handle media changes. Consequently, you should assign any removable media devices connected to your host adapter an ID number above 1 but not in conflict with your host adapter. Table 9.17 summarizes the best choices for device ID assignments in SCSI systems.

TABLE 9.17 Typical SCSI ID Number Assignments

Wide SCSI ID (16-bit)	Narrow SCSI ID (8-bit)	Priority	Usual assignment
0	0	Lowest	Boot hard disk drive
1	1	Low	Second hard disk drive
2-14	2-6	Ascending	Removable media devices
15	7	Highest	SCSI host adapter

Internal SCSI devices such as hard disks typically have several jumpers or switches on each device that set its SCSI ID. The location of these selectors varies but is usually easy to find. Look for a set of jumpers with some form of the legend "ID" silk-screened on the circuit board. Older drives often offer a row of 7 jumper pairs numbered 0 through 6 with one jumper spanning a single pair. With these, setting the ID is easy. Move the jumper to the ID number you want. Other drive manufacturers use a binary code to set the ID, so you'll face a set of three header pin pairs that require from zero to three jumpers depending on the ID you want.

Newer drives typically use a binary code assigning ID number. Four pairs of pins allow the choice of any ID from 0 to 15. Figure 9.8 gives an example of this binary coding scheme.

FIGURE 9.8
SCSI ID binary code shown as jumper positions.

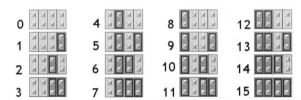

Drives vary in the location and labeling of these identification pins, so you should check with the instructions supplied with a given drive or the drive maker's Web site for guidance in setting the ID number you want.

External SCSI devices commonly use two forms of selector switches for choosing the SCSI ID number assigned to the device, pushbutton and rotary switches. Figure 9.9 illustrates both of these selectors.

FIGURE 9.9
The pushbutton (left) and rotary selector switches for setting a SCSI ID.

Pushbutton selectors allow you to ratchet up and down the series of identification numbers by pressing two push-tabs on the selector. Some switches cycle around and around without stopping; others limit their movement at zero and seven. You only need to push the appropriate button until you see the SCSI ID you want in the small adjacent window.

Rotary switches select the SCSI ID numbers like an old-fashioned television channel selector, the miniature equivalent of the rotating knob. Most of these rotary switches require a small screwdriver to adjust, preventing them from getting inadvertently changed by bumping the back of the SCSI device.

Note that nothing in the design of the SCSI parallel interface precludes two PCs sharing one chain of SCSI devices *except* for SCSI identification numbers. Because each device in a single chain must have a unique ID, two host adapters assigned SCSI ID 7 cannot co-exist. If you can alter the ID number assigned to the SCSI host adapter in either PC, however, you can connect both in a single SCSI chain. Either PC will be able to access the various device. In theory, the two PCs could transfer files between one another as well, but most SCSI software makes no provision for such installations.

Cable Connections

Once you've manually configured your SCSI devices with the proper ID numbers (or left matters to the Fates under SCAM), you have to connect them all together. The SCSI system uses a straightforward daisy-chain wiring system; each device connects to the next one down the line.

The exact mechanics of the wiring system depends on whether you have internal or external SCSI devices or a mixture of both.

Internal Devices

An internal SCSI system is like a flexible expansion bus. Instead of connectors to a printed circuit board, the bus takes the form of a ribbon cable and the expansion connectors are plugs on the cable. One end of the cable plugs into your SCSI host adapter. Each drive attaches to one of the plugs in the cable.

All plugs on the cable have identical signals, so you can use any convenient connector for any SCSI device. The devices and host adapter use SCSI ID numbers to sort out which commands and data go where.

For best operation, always plug a device into the last connector at the end of the cable. When this device is terminated (see "Terminations" later in this chapter), it prevents signal reflections from the end of the wire that might interfere with the operation of the SCSI system.

Modern SCSI devices may use 50-, 68-, or 80-pin connectors. The last two (and one form of the first) all are molded in a vague "D" shape that acts as a key so you cannot plug in a drive improperly. Older 50-pin connectors sometimes are not keyed and can pose orientation problems.

As with nearly all ribbon cable systems, a red (or sometimes blue) stripe on one edge of the cable used by SCSI devices marks the polarity of the cable. The stripe corresponds to pin one of the SCSI connector. Most internal 50-pin SCSI connectors and receptacles are also keyed with a tab and corresponding notch in the middle of one long edge of the connector and receptacle. When you look into the holes of the cable-mounted female SCSI connector with the keying tab on top, pin one (and the red stripe) appear on the left, as shown in Figure 9.10.

FIGURE 9.10

The keying of an internal SCSI cable connector.

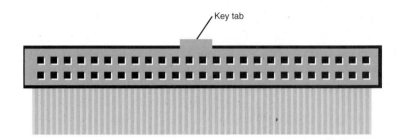

Key tab

The SCSI cable in systems with 50-pin and 68-pin connectors links both control and data signals. However, it does not provide power to the individual internal SCSI devices. Each SCSI device will also require you to plug in its own power connector. The 80-pin SCA system includes power in its connections.

Drives that use the 80-pin system are designed for hot-swapping. You can plug them in at any time, even when your computer is running. The other connection systems require that you switch off your computer before you plug in a drive.

External Devices

External SCSI cabling is somewhat different from that of internal devices. Using the external SCSI cabling system, you run a cable from the host adapter to the first device in the external SCSI chain. For the next device, you plug another cable into the first device and then plug the other end of the cable into a second device. Just continue in the same manner adding another cable for each additional device.

Most external SCSI devices have two SCSI connectors to facilitate their daisy-chain connection. It doesn't matter which of the two connectors on the SCSI device you use to attach each cable. Functionally, both connectors are the same; each is equally adept at handling incoming and outgoing signals.

The empty jack on the last device gets a terminator (unless the device has other provisions for termination). The complete wiring system is a daisy chain as shown in Figure 9.11.

Wider bus SCSI systems may require *two* cables to link each device in the chain. The cables run in parallel following the same daisy-chain path as a single cable SCSI system.

FIGURE 9.11
*External wiring of the
SCSI parallel interface.*

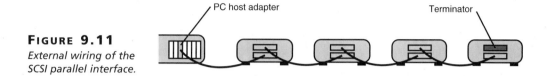

As long as the SCSI system is properly terminated, cable length is not supposed to matter, providing the each of the cables is between 18 inches (one-half meter) and six feet (two meters) long. High-frequency electrical signals such as those used by SCSI sometimes act differently from what the rules predict, so the length and placement of the cables may affect SCSI operation. Rearranging the cables in a recalcitrant system can sometimes bring the entire SCSI chain to life.

After you finish connecting your SCSI cables, be sure to snap in place the retaining clips or wires on each SCSI connector to be sure that each connector is held securely in place. This mechanical locking is particularly important with SCSI connections because the wiring works like old-fashioned Christmas lights; if one goes out, they all go out. Not only will whatever SCSI device that has a loose connector be out of touch, all other devices after the loose connector in the chain also will lose communication. Moreover, because the chain will no longer be terminated properly, even the devices earlier in the chain may not work reliably. Locking the wire on each SCSI connector will help ensure that none of the connectors accidentally gets loosened.

Mixed Devices

When your SCSI system has a mixture of internal and external devices, the wiring is exactly as you would expect—a mixture of both of the preceding schemes. Most SCSI host adapters have connectors that allow you to link both internal and external devices at the same time. The individual rules for internal and external wiring apply to the respective parts of the system. The only change is in terminating the system, as discussed in the next section.

Terminations

Eventually, all SCSI daisy chains must come to an end. You will have one last device to which you have no more peripherals to connect. To prevent spurious signals bouncing back and forth across the SCSI cable chain, the SCSI standard requires that you properly terminate the entire SCSI system. The SCAM system can automatically activate the proper terminations in a SCSI system. For manual settings, the SCSI-2 standard allows for two methods of terminating SCSI buses.

Alternative 1 is the old-fashioned (original SCSI) method of passive terminations using only resistors. Electrically, the terminator is the equivalent of a voltage source of three volts in series with a 132-ohm resistor. This value is achieved by connecting a single-ended signal through a 220-ohm resistor to the TERMPWR line and through a 330-ohm resistor to ground. Figure 9.12 shows this kinds of a passive SCSI termination. All signals on the SCSI bus (except those labeled ground, TERMPWR, or reserved by the standard) require this kind of termination at each end of the bus. Alternative 1 terminations work well when four or fewer devices are connected to the SCSI bus.

FIGURE 9.12

Passive SCSI termination.

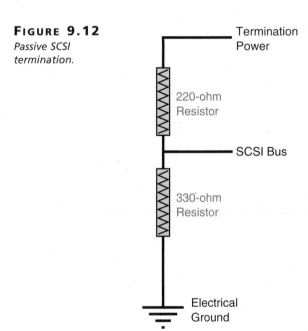

Termination Power

220-ohm Resistor

SCSI Bus

330-ohm Resistor

Electrical Ground

Note that if you attempt to measure the resistance of a SCSI termination, you will find a much lower resistance than that shown, on the order of 75 to 90 ohms. Although each SCSI bus connection is isolated and runs to one of the lines of the bus individually, the other end of each of the two termination resistors of all SCSI lines goes to either the termination power or ground. When you measure across any resistor in a SCSI terminator, you're actually measuring a complex circuit that includes a series/parallel combination of all the resistors in the termination system.

Alternative 2 uses active termination. The terminator uses a voltage regulator to source a 2.85 VDC level in series with a 110-ohm resistor. This active termination reduces the susceptibility of the bus to noise, particularly when cables are long or many devices are connected to the bus. The active voltage regulator assures that no matter the number of loads on the bus, the termination voltage will remain constant. Figure 9.13 shows the connections of an active SCSI termination.

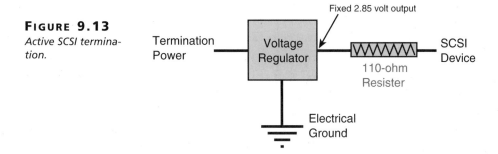

FIGURE 9.13
Active SCSI termination.

If you attempt to measure an active termination, you will always read a value above 110 ohms because the 110-ohm resistor will be in series with the circuit you measure, however you measure it. Because the voltage regulator is an active component, you will measure different resistances across it depending on the polarity of the voltage from your meter. You can thus easily distinguish an active termination from a passive termination; the former has a higher resistance, one that varies with the polarity of the leads of the multimeter you use for your measurements.

Active termination offers several advantages that increase the reliability of SCSI transfers. By providing a more stable termination, it helps reduce noise on the SCSI cable. It also helps maintain signal integrity by clamping the overshoot of signal pulses. It reduces the electrical requirements, cutting the current drawn through the termination power line. An active termination generally provides a more accurate termination resistance. Consequently, the SCSI-2 standard recommends active terminations for both ends of all SCSI buses. In addition, the active termination scheme allows device makers to design systems in which a drive's termination is switched on or off as a single logic gate instead of requiring mechanical switches.

Differential signals use a different termination method. All signals are terminated at each end of the cable with a network having two 330-ohm resistors and a 150-ohm resistor arranged to provide the equivalent of a 122-ohm impedance. The TERMPWR line connects to the negative signal line through a 330-ohm resistor, the negative signal line is connected to the positive through the 150-ohm resistor, and the positive signal line is connected to the ground through the second 330-ohm resistor.

SCSI initiators supply the termination power to their TERMPWR connections through diodes to prevent termination power from other devices from flowing back into the device. Although targets devices do not need to supply terminator power, any SCSI device is permitted to supply terminator power.

A third form of termination called *forced perfect termination* is rarely used. FPT uses diodes to regulate the power on the SCSI bus.

In classic SCSI implementations, the three most popular physical means of providing a SCSI termination are internally with resistor packs, externally with dummy termination plugs, and using switches. SCSI-2 systems with active terminations usually use switches.

Resistor packs are components attached directly to circuit boards. Unlike the other interfaces, SCSI devices typically use three (instead of one) resistor packs for their terminations. Most PC-based SCSI host adapters and hard disks come with termination resistors already installed on them.

You easily can identify terminating resistors as three identical components about an inch long and one-quarter to three-eighths inch high and hardly an eighth inch thick. Most commonly, these resistor packs are red, brownish yellow, or black and shiny, and they are located adjacent to the SCSI connector on the SCSI device or host adapter. When necessary, you remove these terminations simply by pulling them out of their sockets on the circuit board. Figure 9.14 shows two of the most common styles of terminating resistor packs, those in DIP and SIP cases.

FIGURE 9.14

Passive terminators, SIP shown on the left, DIP on the right.

External SCSI terminators are plugs that look like short extensions to the SCSI jacks on the back of SCSI devices. One end of the terminator plugs into one of the jacks on your SCSI device, and the other end of the dummy plug yields another jack that can be attached to another SCSI cable. Some external terminators, however, lack the second jack on the back. Generally, the absence of a second connector is no problem because the dummy plug should be attached only to the last device in the SCSI chain.

Switches, the third variety of termination, may be found on both external and internal drives. Sometimes a single switch handles the entire termination, but occasionally a SCSI drive will have three banks of DIP switches that all must be flipped to the same position to select whether the termination is active. These switches are sometimes found on the SCSI device or on the case of an external unit.

A few external SCSI devices rely on the terminators on the drives inside their cases for their terminations. For these, you must take apart the device to adjust the terminators.

According to the SCSI specification, the first and last device in a SCSI chain must be terminated. The first device is almost always the SCSI host adapter in your PC. If you install a single internal hard disk to the host adapter, it is the other end of the chain and requires termination. Similarly, a single external hard disk also requires termination.

With multiple devices connected to a single host adapter, the termination issue becomes complex. Generally, the host adapter will be one end of the SCSI chain except when you have both internal and external devices connected to it. Then, and only then, should you remove the terminations from your host adapter. In that case, the device nearest the end of the internal SCSI cable should be terminated as should the external device at the end of the daisy chain of cables—the only external device that likely has a connector without a cable plugged into it. Remove or switch off the terminators on all other devices.

Maximum Cable Length

SCSI host adapter maker Adaptec provides the rules of thumb in Table 9.18 as recommendations for the maximum cable length under various SCSI standards, speeds, and number of connected devices.

TABLE 9.18   Maximum Recommended SCSI Cable Lengths

SCSI Standard	Bus clock	Devices	Maximum cable length	
			Meters	Feet
SCSI	5MHz	<7	6	16
Fast SCSI	10MHz	<7	3	9
Fast/Wide SCSI	10MHz	<15	3	9
UltraSCSI	20MHz	>4	1.5	4.5
UltraSCSI	20MHz	<4	3	9
Ultra2 SCSI	40MHz	>2	12	36

Source: Adaptec Corporation

The general rule underlying these recommendations is to divide 30 by the bus clock to derive the maximum recommended cable length in meters. The rule does not apply to Ultra2 SCSI because of the special low voltage differential signals used under that standard.

Cables

In the current SCSI scheme of things, only two different cable types are used. These are designated the A cable and the P cable.

The *A cable* has 50 conductors and serves for all eight-bit SPI systems, both single-ended and differential. Similarly, the 68-conductor *P cable* serves wide signaling systems.

The purpose assigned each conductor in the cable varies with the type of signaling used and the connector system. The allowed variety is wide. In fact, the cable is a minor concern compared to connector considerations.

Connectors

More than any other standard PC wiring system, SCSI suffers a plague of connectors. Not only do internal and external devices use different connector styles, but also both come in wide variety. Beside separate internal and external connector styles, the system also suffers from generational differences.

The SPI-3 specifications acknowledges eight connector systems—four nonshielded alternatives for internal devices and four shielded systems for external devices. In the past, PC makers have used other designs to suit their particular requirements.

For the most part, a SCSI connector is like a shoe. If it fits, use it. All too often, however, your SCSI device comes equipped with a connector that looks weirdly different from that on the cable you're trying to snap onto it. You can prevent problems by checking the connector type used by the SCSI cables in your PC and matching any device you buy to your cabling. SCSI devices—hard disk drives in particular—often have several connector options. When buying a new drive, choose the one that fits.

Adapters are also available for matching unlike connectors. Within the limitations noted in the next section, an adapter is often sufficient to get any SCSI device to link up with any host adapter. If you have a hot soldering iron and want to make your own adapter, you'll find the pin-outs of all the SCSI connector options in Appendix ZZ, "Connectorama."

To buy or make an adapter or to select the right connector on a new drive, you need to know what you're talking about. What follows is a brief outline of all the popular SCSI connector types.

50-Pin Internal Connectors

The initial incarnation of the SCSI interface was the basic 50-contact pin connector used on the first SCSI drives. Officially, this system is termed the *nonshielded connector alternative 2*.

Basically a glorified header, this connector featured two parallel rows of pins in a rectangular array, the centers of the pins separated at increments of 0.1 inch both horizontally and vertically. Figure 9.15 shows the male connector of this type as you would find it on the rear of a SCSI device.

FIGURE 9.15

The 50-pin non-shielded connector alternative 2, narrow-bus SCSI drive connector.

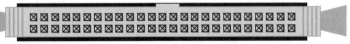

At one time, nearly all SCSI devices that use the eight-bit implementation of the standard used this connector. However, both SPI-2 and SPI-3 offer another 50-pin nonshielded design that's more compact and more consistent with current circuit design practices.

Termed the *nonshielded connector alternative 1*, this design also uses two parallel rows of pins. As with the older connector, the rows are spaced on 0.1-inch centers, but the individual pins in each row are spaced at only half that distance, 0.05 inch. The female receptacle is molded with a vague "D" shape. The male connector has a matching extended D-shaped perimeter that protects the pins. Drives use the female connector as a jack. Figure 9.16 shows this connector.

FIGURE 9.16

The 50-pin non-shielded connector alternative 1.

Although both nonshielded connector alternatives 1 and 2 have 50 pins, the functions assigned each pin differ between the two alternatives. In fact, there are four variations: single-ended alternative 1, single-ended alternative 2, differential alternative 1, and differential alternative 2. You cannot tell the four options apart by merely looking at the connector. You must check the specifications of the drive to determine the signal type it uses.

50-Pin External Connectors

The most common form of external SCSI connectors has 50 pins arranged in two rows of 25 and looks like an enlarged Centronics printer connector. This connector is termed the *shielded connector alternative 2* under SPI-2 and SPI-3. It is still the most common 50-pin connector used by external SCSI devices and is shown in Figure 9.17.

FIGURE 9.17

The 50-place ribbon connector, shielded connector alternative 2.

The shielded connector alternative 1 also offers 50 pins to external devices. It uses the same layout and signal system as the alternative 1 nonshielded connector except the mating portions of the connector are metal shields. Figure 9.18 shows this connector.

As with the nonshielded 50-pin connectors, shielded connector alternatives 1 and 2 differ in the functions assigned each pin. The pin-outs of the connector alternatives are the same as for the nonshielded versions. Because of the physical similarity and identical pin-out, you can plug a raw drive into an external shielded alternative 1 connector (providing you don't mix the single-ended and differential signaling systems). The nonshielded and shielded versions of alternative 2 also share the same signal assignments to their pins, but the connectors are physically incompatible.

FIGURE 9.18

The 50-place external shielded connector alternative 1.

Some older external SCSI devices and host adapter used classic D-shell connectors with proprietary signal assignments. Although they are sometimes classed as 50-pin connectors because they offer essentially the same signals as the standard 50-pin SCSI system, the D-shell configuration actually only allows odd numbers of pins. They never attracted a following because they were simply ungainly, about four inches long. These resemble the alternative 1 connectors, but the pins are round rather than square, more widely spaced, and staggered. Figure 9.19 shows this large connector.

FIGURE 9.19

The non-standardized "50-pin" D-shell connector.

More popular was a design that trimmed the length of the D-shell connector in half by similarly trimming the pin count. These shorter, 25-pin D-shell connectors saved space and were popularized by Apple Computer for its Macintosh equipment. The connectors are identical to those used by most computer makers for their parallel port connections. Despite the similarity, the signals on the SCSI and parallel ports are entirely different and should *never* be connected together.

To reduce the number of pins required, this style of connector eliminates many of the ground return signals used in single-ended SCSI. These connectors do not have enough connections for differential signals. Figure 9.20 shows this connector.

68-Pin Connectors

Wide SCSI requires more connections than are possible with a 50-pin connector. To accommodate all of the required signals, the SPI standards specify a set of 68-pin connectors. This connector system offers both nonshielded and shielded alternatives for internal and external devices.

Both the nonshielded and shielded versions use essentially the same design and the same signal assignments. The chief difference is the roughly D-shaped metal shield surrounding the contacts of both male and female connectors, the shield also protecting the bare pins of the male connector, much as in a classic D-shell connector.

FIGURE 9.20

The female 25-pin D-shell connector used by some SCSI products.

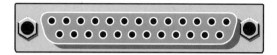

Both connectors are termed "alternative 3." That is, the internal set makes up *nonshielded connector alternative 3* and the external set *nonshielded connector alternative 3*. Many sources refer to either the shielded or nonshielded connector simply as a "SCSI-3" connector. Do not be misled by this label, which is best seen as an abbreviation for "SCSI alternative 3 connector." All SCSI-3 systems *do not* use this connector system. In fact, the SCSI-3 standard allows any of the eight connector alternatives—as well as the connectors for the various other physical interconnection systems besides SPI.

The pins of the alternative 3 connectors are arranged in two rows of 34 male contacts. The pins within each row are located on 0.05-inch centers, and the two rows are spaced on 0.10-inch centers. Figure 9.21 shows the shielded version of this connector.

FIGURE 9.21

The 68-place shielded connector alternative 3.

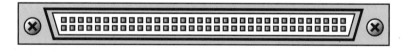

The SPI specifications allow for a second style of shielded 68-pin connector that looks like a miniaturized version of the classic 50-place external SCSI ribbon connector. Termed the *shielded connector alternative 4*, it uses the same pin-outs as alternative 3. Instead of pins, it has two rows of ribbon contacts spaced at 0.0315-inch intervals. Figure 9.22 shows this connector.

FIGURE 9.22

Shielded connector alternative 4.

80-Pin SCA

Hot-swapping drives requires that both control signals and drive power be connected quickly and easily. To accommodate the needed power signals, drive makers developed the 80-pin SCSI connector system, which is often called SCA (which stands for *Single Connector Attachment*). Under SPI rubric, this is the *nonshielded connector alternative 4*. Figure 9.23 shows this connector.

FIGURE 9.23

The 80-pin SCA connector.

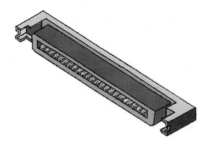

The SCA connector is designed chiefly for internal use—sliding drives into racks. There is not external equivalent to the SCA connector.

All the pins on the connector on the SCA device are the same length. On the host end, however, several of the pins are extended so that they make contact first when the drive gets plugged in. These longer pins (numbers 1, 36–43, 45, 46, and 78–80) ground the drive, supply power to it, and set its SCSI ID number. The added length assures that the drive powers up properly and is properly identified before it presents signals to the bus.

Mixing SCSI Standards

SCSI comes in so many flavors that you're likely to have devices that follow two or more standards that you'll want to hook together in a single chain. With modern host adapters that allow you to configure the transfer characteristics assigned to each SCSI ID, you can freely mix standards with a reasonable chance that you can get everything to work together. Better still, you can tune all devices to operate at their maximum transfer rate with but a few exceptions.

In most cases, however, you can't just string together a mixed collection of SCSI peripherals with complete impunity. You still have to consider issues of bus width, signal type (single-ended or differential), and clock speed to make optimal connections. Some things just won't fit—and others you may not want to fit.

Bus Width

The problem with bus width appears fundamental. Some devices use 50-pin connectors, some 68-pin, and some 80. For the most part, however, the issue is purely mechanical. If you can make the connector fit, use it.

If you have any wide devices at all whether internal or external, you'll need a 68-connector cable from your host adapter. You need all 68 pins to carry the necessary wide signals. Your problem then becomes ones of simply linking 50-pin devices to the 68-pin connection. The answer is simple: What you need is adapters.

With an *internal* chain of mixed devices, you'll need an adapter for each *narrow* SCSI device you want to plug into the wide chain.

To mix wide and narrow SCSI devices together in an *external* SCSI daisy chain, you need to follow one rule: Wide goes first. Connect the wide devices together and closest to the host adapter. After the last wide device, use an adapter to go from 68-pin to 50-pin connections. Then, finish the bus with your narrow devices.

Hot-swap drives that use the 80-pin SCA system require their own adapters. They combine the control and data signals from the P-cable system with the power required to run the drive.

Signaling System

The original SCSI specifications allowed for two types of SCSI buses: single-ended and differential. These quite different signaling systems are inherently incompatible. Although adapters help mate them together, dangers remain. For example, connecting a single-ended device such as a CD drive to a differential host adapter or a differential drive to a single-ended host adapter may physically damage both the host adapter and the drive. Because the SCSI connector system does not distinguish between signal types, you must be sure of the signal types used by all the devices in your SCSI system before making the first connection.

Single-Ended SCSI

Single-ended SCSI uses an unbalanced or single-ended electrical signal—a single wire for each signal, with all signals in the bus using a single common ground return. Differential SCSI uses balanced or differential signals. Each signal on the SCSI bus has its own return line that is isolated from the reference ground. Differential SCSI signals use twisted-pair wiring. Most SCSI implementations have been single-ended because they require half the pins, cheaper wire, and simpler electronics than do differential SCSI implementations.

As with all single-ended electrical systems, single-ended SCSI is more prone to picking up noise and interference than differential SCSI. As a result, the specifications for SCSI systems that use single-ended signals limit cable lengths to no more than 6 meters (just under 20 feet). Differential SCSI allows for bus lengths up to 25 meters (about 82 feet). You must have at least one-third meter (about 12 inches) of cable between SCSI devices, so the shortest possible SCSI cable is that length. External SCSI cables should be shielded.

Differential SCSI

The fastest and most reliable signaling system used by parallel SCSI uses differential signals. Differential signaling is more reliable at long distances and higher speeds. Fast SCSI systems generally use differential signals. Although single-ended signals are not precluded for Fast SCSI operation by the standard, no current implementations exist.

Differential signals represent information as the potential *difference* between two conductors. That is, the voltage difference you measure between the two wires encodes the information that's conveyed. In differential signaling systems, the signals in the two wires are exact opposites of one another. When added together, they cancel out. When subtracted—finding the difference—they combine to an absolute value twice the sum of the absolute value of each one. Noise and interference, which typically add equally to each signal, cancel out when the signals get subtracted.

Clock Speed

Although the different top speeds of SCSI devices might appear to be a problem and limit all the devices, no matter how fast, to the speed constraints of the slowest, the issue never arises. The SCSI host adapter only communicates with a single device at a time, and those communications monopolize the SCSI bus while they are taking place. In today's SCSI systems, transfers do not go directly between devices but instead must travel through the host adapter. For example, to back up a hard disk, the disk first sends a block of data to the host adapter, which temporarily stores the data in system memory. When the disk finishes sending its block, the host adapter moves the data from memory to the tape drive. Consequently, the two SCSI devices—hard disk and tape drive—communicate with the host adapter independently of one another and may operate at different speeds.

A modern host adapter can adjust its speed to suit whatever devices with which it communicates. In general, it will set itself to transfer data to each device at the top speed at which that device can operate.

The one big exception to the "any speed" rule is Ultra2 SCSI. Put simply, you cannot attach an ordinary SCSI device to an Ultra2 SCSI port and expect Ultra2 SCSI peripherals to operate at top speed. The issue is not really speed, however. All Ultra2 SCSI devices use LVD (Low Voltage Differential) signaling. Most ordinary SCSI devices use (SE) single-ended signaling. When you plug an SE device into the Ultra2 bus, the bus reverts to SE operation; otherwise, damage would result. The SCSI host adapter would send the negative-going differential voltages into a direct short-circuit, signal pins grounded in the single-ended device. Although reverting to single-ended operation minimizes the chance for damage, it also limits the speed potential to ordinary UltraSCSI because the highest speeds of Ultra2 SCSI require the added integrity of differential signaling.

Operating System Support

Most SCSI host adapter circuitry, including that built into motherboards, includes a feature called WD1002 emulation or simply "a BIOS." Both mean the same thing: ROM or flash memory in a host adapter includes code telling your system how to use the SCSI subsystem to boot up your PC. This code is sufficient for your PC and its operating system to recognize two hard disks, the boot drive and one other. At that point, built-in support for the SCSI system in many PCs runs out of gas, although some server systems designed particularly for SCSI operating have BIOS code that allows them to boot from a SCSI CD drive as well. Without further help, neither your PC nor its operating system will be able to use other SCSI devices, notwithstanding that your PC lists a whole array of SCSI devices when it boots up. Worse, the firmware code that gets your two hard disks going operates in real mode using 16-bit code. Its performance lags far behind what you'd expect from a 32-bit protected-mode system.

The SCSI system requires several software drivers to operate properly. In particular, your operating system needs to load a driver to match the needs of SCSI to its own operation, another to control the host adapter hardware, and one for each of the SCSI devices you connect. The drivers install like any others as part of the hardware installation process through your operating system.

If you don't already have an operating system installed on your PC and you have a SCSI CD drive, you may have to load the drivers before you can set up the operating system from its CD. Microsoft includes the necessary SCSI drivers on its startup disks for the full-fledged versions of Windows. Note that Windows has no idea what equipment you have in your PC until it gets running, so it attempts to load a whole range of drivers as it sets itself up; the ones that load properly and run are the ones it uses.

Operation and Arbitration

All devices connected to a single SCSI bus function independently, under the control of the host system through the SCSI adapter. Rather than just use signals on dedicated conductors on the bus that can be understood by devices as dumb as a light bulb, SCSI presupposes a high degree of intelligence in the devices it connects and provides its own command set—essentially, its own computer language—for controlling the devices.

Boot Up

Most software drivers search for their target devices when they are booted into your system. Consequently, all your external SCSI devices should be running when you switch on your PC. Turn on your SCSI devices before you switch on your PC or use a power director (outlet box) that ensures that your entire computer system—PC and SCSI peripherals—switches on simultaneously.

Arbitration

Not only is SCSI more like an expansion bus of a computer than a traditional hard disk interface, but it also resembles today's more advanced Micro Channel and NuBus designs. Like the latest computer buses, SCSI provides an arbitration scheme. Arbitration enables the devices connected to the bus to determine which of them can send data across the bus at a given time. Instead of being controlled by the host computer and suffering delays while its microprocessor does other things, the arbitration of the SCSI bus is distributed among all the devices on the bus.

Arbitration on the SCSI bus is handled by hardware. Each of the up to seven SCSI devices is assigned a unique identifying number, usually by setting jumpers or DIP switches on the drive in a manner similar to the Drive Select jumpers on an ST506 device.

When a device called the initiator wants to access the SCSI bus, it waits until the bus is free and then identifies itself by sending a signal down one of the SCSI data lines. At the same time, it transmits a signal down another SCSI data line corresponding to the other SCSI device, called the target, that it wants to interact with. The eight data lines in the SCSI connection allow the unique identification of seven SCSI devices and one host.

Note that SCSI devices can initiate arbitration on their own, independent of the host. Two SCSI devices also can transfer information between one another without host intervention. A SCSI hard disk, for example, may back itself up to a SCSI tape drive without requiring the attention of (and robbing performance from) its host computer. Better than background operation, this form of backup represents true parallel processing in the computer system.

In addition, SCSI provides for reselecting. That is, a device that temporarily does not need bus access can release the bus, carry out another operation, and then resume control. You can command a disk drive to format and it can carry out that operation without tying up the bus, for example. The net result is, again, true parallel processing.

Because SCSI is a high-level interface, it also isolates the computer from the inner workings of the peripherals connected to it. The SCSI standard allows hard disks to monitor their own bad tracks independently from the computer host. The disk drive reassigns bad tracks and reports back to its computer host as if it were a perfect disk. In addition, hard disk drives can be designed to automatically detect sectors that are going bad and reassign the data they contain elsewhere, all without the host computer or the user ever being aware of any problems.

Floppy Disk Interface

The floppy disk connection stands as the one stalwart in disk interfaces. Circuitry, signals, connectors, and cabling for floppy disk drives has changed minimally even after more than a decade and a half. With little effort, you could plug a 160KB floppy disk drive left over from the very first PC into a modern Pentium III Xeon computer.

Part of the reason for this immutability is that the function of the floppy disk hasn't changed over the years. The floppy disk remains a boot device, a data exchange system, and a backup system. At one time, it was your only choice for each of these functions. The world has, of course, changed in the intervening years, and the floppy disk is at best the fallback choice for each of these functions. Your needs and the rest of your PC hardware have long passed by floppy technology. In the next few years, the floppy disk and its interface may be left behind.

Moreover, the floppy disk interface has not been entirely immutable. Its speed has notched up twice, its connectors have changed, and the range of devices linking to it has broadened. For example, the floppy disk interface connection scheme is also used by a number of inexpensive tape backup systems.

Note that the interface used by floppy disk drives is undergoing transition. New, high-capacity drives may use the ATA or SCSI interfaces. External floppy disk drives used by some sub-notebook PCs are shifting to the USB interfaces. Some external drives use a parallel port. Eventually, one or several of these interfaces may entirely supplant the conventional floppy disk interface, but for now, nearly every new PC has a floppy interface buried somewhere inside.

Background

In its heart and in operation, the floppy disk interface is much like a glorified serial port that's had a few new command lines added to it to handle the particular functions associated with the floppy disk drive. Only a few signals are required to control the two floppy disk drives normally attached by a single cable to the controller.

Two Drive Select signals are used to individually select either the first or second drive, A or B. (In four-drive systems, the signals for A in the second cable control drive C, and those of B control D.) If the signal assigned to a particular drive is not present, all the other input and output circuits of the drive are deactivated, except for those that control the drive motor. In this way, two drives can share the bulk of the wires in the controller cable without interference. However, this control scheme also means that only one drive in a pair can be active at a time. You can write to drive B at the same time as you read from drive A. That's why you must transfer the data held on a disk (or file) from one drive into memory before you can copy it to another drive.

One wire is used for each drive to switch its spindle motor on and off. These are called, individually, Drive Select A and Drive Select B. Although it is possible to make both motors spin simultaneously, rules laid down by IBM admonish against activating these two lines to make both floppy disk drive motors run at the same time. (This saves power in the severely constrained PC system and is a moot issue in the single-drive XT system.) The two drives in your PC may run simultaneously for brief periods due to a delay built into most drives that keeps their motors running for a few seconds after the Motor Enable signal stops.

Two signals in the floppy disk interface control the head position of each of the attached drives. One, Step Pulse, merely tells the stepper motor on the drive with its Drive Select active to move one step—that's exactly one track—toward or away from the center of the disk. The Direction signal controls which way the pulses move the head. If this signal is active, the head moves toward the center.

To determine which of the two sides of a double-sided disk to read, one signal, called Write Select, is used. When this signal is active, it tells the disk drive to use the upper head. When no signal is present, the disk drive automatically uses the default (lower) head.

Writing to disk requires two signals on the interface. Write Data contains the information that's actually to be written magnetically onto the disk. It consists of nothing but a series of pulses corresponding exactly to the flux transitions that are to be made on the disk. The read/write head merely echoes these signals magnetically. As a fail-safe that precludes the possibility of accidentally writing over valuable data, a second signal called Write Enable is used. No write current is sent to the read/write head unless this signal is active.

Four signals are passed back from the floppy disk drive to the controller through the interface. Two of these help the controller determine where the head is located. Track 0 indicates to the controller when the head is above the outermost track on the disk so that the controller knows from where to start counting head-moving pulses. Index helps the drive determine the location of each bit on a disk track. One pulse is generated on the Index line for each revolution of the disk. The controller can time the distance between ensuing data pulses based on the reference provided by the Index signal.

In addition, the Write Protect signal is derived from the sensor that detects the existence or absence of a write-protect tab on a diskette. If a tab is present, this signal is active. The

Read Data signal comprises a series of electrical pulses that exactly match the train of flux transition on the floppy disk.

Controllers

The basic purpose of the floppy disk controller is to convert the requests from the BIOS or direct hardware commands that are couched in terms of track and sector numbers into the pulses that move the head to the proper location on the disk. For the most efficient operation, the controller must also remember where the head is located, index the head as necessary, and report errors when they occur.

In its translation function, the floppy disk controller must make sense from the stream of unformatted pulses delivered from the drive. It first must find the beginning of each track from the Index pulse and then mark out each sector from the information embedded in the data stream. When it identifies a requested sector, it must then read the information it contains and convert that information from serial to parallel form so that it can be sent through the PC bus. In writing, the controller must first identify the proper sector to write to—which is a read operation—and then switch on the write current to put data into that sector before the next sector on the disk begins.

Most of the hard work of the controller is handled by a single integrated circuit, the 765 controller chip. The 765 works much like a microprocessor, carrying out certain operations in response to commands that it receives through registers connected to your computer's I/O ports. This programmability makes the 765 and the floppy disk controllers made from it extremely versatile, able to adapt to changes in media and storage format as the PC industry has evolved. None of the essential floppy disk drive parameters are cast in stone or the silicon on the controller. The number of heads, tracks, and sectors on a disk are set by loading numbers into the registers of the 765. The values that the controller will use are normally loaded into the controller when you boot up your computer. You ordinarily don't have to worry about them after that. With the right on-board support circuitry and BIOS code, the same controller can often handle floppy disks ranging from ancient 8-inch monsters to the latest extra-density (2.88MB) 3.5-inch pocket-liners. Because older designs could not foresee the potential of future floppy disk formats, however, not all controllers are compatible with all floppy disk formats. To get full use of more recent floppy configurations, you'll need a version of DOS or other operating system designed to accommodate them (see Chapter 25, "Power").

Special software can reprogram your controller to make it read, write, and format floppy disks that differ from the PC standard. The most common today is the Distribution Media Format used by Microsoft to stuff extra information on floppy disks used for distributing software.

In its original implementation, the floppy disk controller required its own, full-size expansion board. Engineers soon moved the necessary circuitry to the motherboard. Eventually, it became a basic part of every chipset. Nearly all modern PCs take advantage of this technology and provide a connector for a floppy disk drive system on their motherboards.

Cabling

The original PC floppy system is the standard for nearly all floppy disk systems. It was designed so that you can install floppy disk drives with a minimum of thought—which gives you an idea of what manufacturers think of their assembly line workers. Once you understand a few simple rules, you can do as good a job as—or better than—they can.

Drive Select Jumpers

The cabling used in a floppy disk subsystem apparently presumes that a drive attached to it already knows whether it is supposed to be drive A or B in your system. However, for compatibility reasons, all floppy disk drives are created equal with a common design for all drive letters. For a given floppy disk drive to assume the identity of A or B, drive manufacturers equipped their products with DIP switches or jumpers to select the appropriate appellation. With these drive select jumpers, most floppy disk drives allow you to select one of four potential identities.

For reasons related to their function—they essentially switch some of the connections delivered by the cable—drive select jumpers can usually be found on a drive near the edge connector onto which you attach the cable. Usually, you'll be faced with an array of jumpers or switches, probably either, each labeled with a not-too-meaningful combination of two or three letters and numbers. The drive select jumpers can be identified (when they are labeled) by the two-character prefix DS. From there, different disk drive manufacturers go in two directions. Some start numbering the drive select settings with one and count up to four; others start with one and venture only as far as three.

Drive Select Settings

In the PC way of doing things, the drive or the floppy disk cable determines which of two drives is A and which is B.

To configure a floppy disk drive for installation in a standard PC system, you should invariably set it as the second drive, paying no attention to whether it will be A or B. With drives with which the drive select jumpers are numbered starting with zero all floppy disk drives should be set as one. With drives with which the number of the drive select jumpers begins with one, all drives should be set as two.

Drive Cabling

The special twist that sorts out the drive identities is exactly that; a group of five conductors in the floppy disk cable are twisted in the run to one of its connectors. This twist reverses the drive select and motor control signals in the cable as well as rearranges some of the ground wires in the cable (which effectively makes no change).

Because all drives are set up as the second drive, this reversal makes the drive attached to the cable after the twist the first drive, drive A. In other words, drive A is attached to the connector at the end of the cable, the one where the wire twist takes place. Drive B is attached to the connector in the middle of the length of the cable. The third connector, at the end of the cable with no twist, goes to the floppy disk controller or host adapter. Figure 9.24 illustrates the floppy disk cable and the proper connections.

FIGURE 9.24

Classic floppy drive cable showing proper connections.

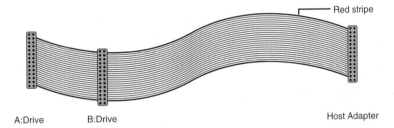

Red stripe

A:Drive   B:Drive   Host Adapter

Single Drive and Straight-Through Cables

With hard disk drives, you can use a straight-through cable (that is, one without the twist near the last connectors) to operate a single disk drive by moving the drive select jumper of the connected hard disk to the first drive position. This tactic will not work with floppy disk drives. The twisted part of the cable moves not only the drive select conductor but also the motor control conductor. You cannot, therefore, use a straight-through cable with a single floppy disk drive in your computer system.

If you make your own floppy disk cable to handle a single drive, you'll have to abide by the IBM drive select numbering scheme. You have to make a twist in the conductors.

Connectors

Physical aspects of the floppy disk interface have changed subtly over the years. The original PC floppy-disk controller used an edge connector to attach to the floppy-disk cable. Since about 1984, controllers generally have used pin connectors, although edge connector products appear into the 1990s. Similarly, the connectors on floppy disks migrated from edge connectors to pin connectors. Nearly all old 5.25-inch drives use edge connectors; nearly all modern 3.5-inch drives use pin connectors. Figure 9.25 contrasts the two connector styles.

No matter the style of connector that's used by host adapter or disk drive, the same signals appear at the same pins. Not only does this arrangement make wiring consistent, but also it allows cables to include both connector styles without wiring more complicated with the require twist between drives A and B. Table 9.19 gives the signal assignments for standard PC floppy disk interface connections at both the host adapter end and either floppy disk drive connector.

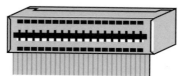

TABLE 9.19　Floppy Disk Cable Connector Pin Assignments

Drive A: connector	Drive B: connector	Host internal	Host (XT) external	Function
34-pin	**34-pin**	**34-pin**	**37-pin**	
1 1	1	20	Ground	
2 2	2	1	Unused	
3 3	3	21	Ground	
4 4	4	2	Unused	
5 5	5	22	Ground	
6 6	6	3	Unused	
7 7	7	23	Ground	
8 8	8	6	Index	
9 9	9	24	Ground	
16	10	10	NC	Motor Enable A
15	11	11	25	Ground
14	12	12	NC	Drive Select B
13	13	13	26	Ground
12	14	14	NC	Drive Select A
11	15	15	27	Ground
10	16	16	NC	Motor Enable B
17	17	17	28	Ground
18	18	18	11	Direction (Stepper Motor)
19	19	19	29	Ground
20	20	20	12	Step Pulse
21	21	21	30	Ground

Drive A: connector	Drive B: connector	Host internal	Host (XT) external	Function
34-pin	**34-pin**	**34-pin**	**37-pin**	
22	22	22	18	Write Data
23	23	23	31	Ground
24	24	24	14	Write Enable
25	25	25	32	Ground
26	26	26	15	Track 0
27	27	27	33	Ground
28	28	28	16	Write Protect
29	29	29	34	Ground
30	30	30	17	Read Data
31	31	31	35	Ground
32	32	32	13	Select Head 1
33	33	33	36	Ground
34	34	34	4	Unused
NC	NC	NC	5	Unused
NC	NC	NC	7	Motor Enable C
NC	NC	NC	8	Drive Select D
NC	NC	NC	9	Drive Select C
NC	NC	NC	10	Motor Enable D
NC	NC	NC	37	Ground

In addition to the edge or pin connector on the card, some floppy disk controllers provide a second, 37-pin connector on the card retaining bracket. All the signals necessary for running a third and a fourth floppy disk are available there. Most newer floppy disk controllers only provide for two drives, although a few four-drive controllers are available from third-party manufacturers.

Terminations

The floppy disk system developed for the first PCs required you pay attention to terminations. The last drive on the cable (which usually was the A drive) required a termination. The other drive was forbidden from being terminated.

For practical reasons, termination is no longer a concern. The problems of termination have proven minimal, so manufacturers simply include a termination on all drives and design floppy disk controllers to work adequately whether they have one or two terminations on a given cable.

Power Connections

All drives require power to run their motors and their control electronics, and most drives regardless of size or interface use the same kind of power connection. The primary are devices incorporated into PC Cards, portable PC AT Attachment drives, and SSA drives, which integrate their power leads into their signal interface connectors. Nearly all other drives use a standard device power plug—a nylon connector that accommodates four separate wires, one of which is redundant or a miniature power plug with three connections. This book discusses these mass storage power connectors and power requirements in Chapter 25, in the sections "Power Supplies" and "Power Protection."

Hard Disks

In most PCs, the hard disk is the principal mass storage system. It holds all of your programs and data files and must deliver them to your system at an instant's notice. Hard disks differ in technology, interface, speed, and capacity—all of which are interrelated.

Important issues in selecting a new drive as a replacement or upgrade for your PC include the following:

Issue	Advice
Interface	Determines whether you can connect a given drive to your PC. Be sure the interface used by the drive matches the host adapter in your PC—PC makers prefer ATA (or UDMA) drives; workstations and servers lean toward SCSI.
Data rate	An interface sub-issue. Modern interfaces let you plug-in drives matching any revision-level of the interface, but you'll only get top performance only if both the drive and PC match the same standard level. A UDMA/66 drive is wasted on a PC that supports only UDMA/33, just as an Ultra 2 SCSI drive is wasted in a plain Ultra SCSI system.
Connector	Part of the interface but a separate issue, particularly with SCSI drives. Although you can adapt an SCA drive to a 68-pin cable and system (and vice versa), you'll need a $40-50 adapter.
Capacity	Buy the biggest drive you can afford. An extra gigabyte or two will stave off your outgrowing the drive for a few weeks or months.
Speed	Although not as much an issue as it once was, all else equal you should prefer the faster drive. The easiest (though not necessarily best) modern performance measure is rotation rate. A 7200 RPM drive is superior; a 10,000 RPM drive will make the other kids on the block envy yours.
Package	A new or upgrade drive must fit where you want it. Although the issue is particularly critical in the tight confines of notebook PCs, small desktop systems may limit your drive choices as well.
BIOS	Not in the drive but in your PC—your BIOS must allow you to use the full capacity of your hard disk drive. Older BIOSs may constrain you from addressing all the bytes on the drive.

A PC without a hard disk demonstrates solid-state senility; all that's left of long-term memory are the brief flashbacks that can be loaded (with great effort and glacial speed) by floppy disks, tape, or typing. What's left is a curiosity to be nursed along until death overtakes it—probably your own—because a PC without a hard disk will make you wish you were dead.

The hard disk is the premiere mass storage device for today's PCs. No other peripheral can approach the usefulness of the hard disk's combination of speed, capacity, and straightforward user installation. Your PC's hard disk stores your files and extends the RAM capacity of your PC with virtual memory. It deals in megabytes, hundreds or thousands of them. In one second, the disk must be able to remember or disgorge the information equivalent of the entire contents of a physics textbook or novel. And it must be equally capable of casting aside its memories and replacing them with revised versions to keep your system up to date. That's a big challenge, particularly for a device that may be no larger than a deck of playing cards and uses less power than a nightlight.

Perhaps the most amazing thing about hard disks is their ability to keep up with the needs of contemporary programs. The first PCs didn't even have hard disks. The first drives were about half the size of a shoebox and held 10MB, a fraction of what you need for a single Windows program. Today's hard disk takes up about a tenth the space and holds 100 times the data—or more. In fact, the standard unit of measurement for disk capacity has shifted a thousand-fold, from megabytes to gigabytes. Yet all the while, the cost of hard disks has been plummeting, not just the cost per megabyte but the basic price of the standard equipment drive.

Depending on your needs and demands, hard disks can be expensive or cheap. Like tires, power tools, and companions, they come in various sizes and speed ratings. You can scrounge through ads and find decade-old hard disk drives that will still plug into your PC at prices that will make Scrooge smile—and you weep while you wait and wait for its ancient technology to catch up with the demands of a modern microprocessor.

In truth, today's hard disk drives have little in common with their forebears of as few as five years ago. Modern hard disks take up less space, respond faster, have several times the capacity, last several times as long, and have nowhere near the failure potential of older drives. A modern drive won't even plug into your PC the same way early hard disks did. New and constantly evolving interfaces promise to keep pushing up speeds while making installation easier.

Although the standards of speed and quality among hard disks have never been higher, sorting among your options has never been tougher. As the range of available products grows wider, the differences between the competition at each level have narrowed. Finding the one right hard disk now more than ever requires understanding what's inside a drive, what the different mechanisms and technology are, and what best mates with a modern machine.

Background

Because of their ability to give nearly random access to data, magnetic disk drives have been part of computers since long before there were PCs. The first drives suffered from the demands of data processing, however, and quickly wore out. Their heads ground against their disks, leaving dust were data had been. For fast access, some lined dozens of heads along the radius of the disk, each sweeping its own dedicated range of disk and data. Such designs had fast access speeds, dependent only on the speed of the spin of the disk (which is still an issue, even today), and minimal maintenance worries because they had a minimum of moving parts. But the size of the heads and the cost of arraying a raft of them meant such drives were inevitably expensive. Although not a major problem with mainframe computers priced in the millions, pricing a PC with such a drive would put computer within the budgets solely of those with personal Space Shuttles in their garages.

The breakthrough came at IBM's Hursley Labs near Winchester in England. Researchers there put a single head to work scanning across the disk to get at every square inch (England had not yet gone metric) of its surface. Their breakthrough, however, totally eliminated the wear of head against disk and was destined to set the standard for computer storage for more than three decades. By floating—actually flying—the read/write head on a cushion of air, the head never touched the disk and never had a chance to wear it down. Moreover, the essentially friction-free design allow the head to move rapidly between positions above the disk.

This original design had two sections, a "fixed" drive that kept its disk permanently inside the drive and a removable section that could be dismounted for file exchange or archiving. Each held 30MB on a platter about 14 inches across. During development, designers called the drive a 30/30 to reflect its two storage sections. In that Remington used the same designation for its most famous repeating rifle—the gun that won the West—this kind of drive became known as a *Winchester disk drive*.

The name "Winchester" first referred to the specific drive model. Eventually, it was generalized to any hard disk. In the computer industry, however, the term was reserved for drives that used that same head design as the original Winchester. New disk drives—including *all* of those now in PCs—do not use the Winchester head design.

Besides Winchester, you may also hear other outdated terms for what we today call a "hard disk." Many folks at IBM still refer to them as "fixed disks." When computer people really want to confound you, they will sometimes use another IBM term from the dark ages of computing, *DASD*, which stands for Direct Access Storage Device. No matter the name, however, today all hard disks are essentially the same in principle, technology, and operation.

Technologies

The hard disk is actually a combination device, a chimera that's part electronic and part mechanical. Electrically, the hard disk performs the noble function of turning evanescent pulses of electronic digital data into more permanent magnetic fields. As with other magnetic recording devices—from cassette recorders to floppy disks—the hard disk accomplishes its end using an electromagnet, its read/write head, to align the polarities of magnetic particles on the hard disks themselves. Other electronics in the hard disk system control the mechanical half of the drive and help it properly arrange the magnetic storage and locate the information that is stored on the disk.

Mechanism

The mechanism of the typical hard disk is actually rather simple, comprising fewer moving parts than such exotic devices as the electric razors and pencil sharpener. The basic elements of the system include a stack of one or more platters—the actual hard disks themselves. Each of these platters serves as a substrate upon which is laid a magnetic medium in which data can be recorded. Together, the platters rotate as a unit on a shaft, called the spindle. Typically, the shaft connects directly to a spindle motor that spins the entire assembly.

Rotation

Hard disks almost invariably spin at a single, constant rate measured in revolutions per minute, or RPM. This speed does not change while the disk is in operation, although some disks may stop to conserve power. This constant spin is technically termed *constant angular velocity recording*. This technology sets the speed of the disk's spin at a constant rate so that in any given period over any given track, the drive's read/write head hangs over the same length arc (measured in degrees) of the disk. The actual length of the arc, measured linearly (in inches or centimeters), varies depending on the radial position of the head. Although the tiny arc made by each recorded bit has the same length when measured angularly (that is, in degrees), when the head is farther from the center of the disk, the bit-arcs are longer when measured linearly (that is, in inches or millimeters). Despite or because of the greater length of each bit toward the outer edge of the disk, each spin stores the same number of bits and the same amount of information. Each spin at the outer edge of the disk stores exactly the same number of bits as those at the inner edge.

Constant angular velocity equipment is easy to build because the disk spins at a constant number of RPM. Old vinyl phonograph records are the best example of constant angular velocity recording; the black platters spun at an invariant 33, 45, or 78 RPM. Nearly all hard disks and all ISO standard magneto-optical drives use constant angular velocity recording.

A more efficient technology, called *constant linear velocity recording*, alters the spin speed of the disk depending on how near the center tracks the read/write head lies so that in any given period the same length of track passes below the head. When the head is near the outer edge of the disk, where the circumference is greater, the slower spin allows more bits and data to be packed into each spin. Using this technology, a given-size disk can hold more information.

Figure 10.1 illustrates the on-disk difference between the two methods of recording. The sector length varies in constant angular velocity but remains constant using constant linear velocity. The number of sectors is the same for each track in constant angular velocity recording but varies with constant linear velocity.

FIGURE 10.1
Comparison of constant angular and line velocity recording methods.

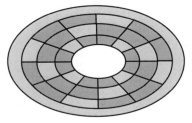 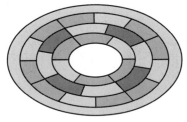

Constant Angular Velocity   Constant Linear Velocity

Constant linear velocity recording is ill-suited to hard disks. For the disk platter to be properly read or written, it must be spinning at the proper rate. Hard disk heads regularly bounce from the outer tracks to the inner tracks as your software requests them to read or write data. Slowing or speeding up the platter to the proper speed would require a lengthy wait, perhaps seconds because of inertia, which would shoot the average access time of the drive through the roof. For this reason, constant linear velocity recording is used for high-capacity media that don't depend so much on quick random access. The most familiar is the Compact Disc, which sacrifices instant access for sufficient space to store your favorite symphony.

Modern hard disks compromise between constant angular velocity and constant linear velocity recording. Although they maintain a constant rotation rate, they alter the timing of individual bits depending on how far from the center of the disk they are written. By shortening the duration of the bits (measured in microseconds) over longer tracks, the drive can maintain a constant linear length (again, measured in inches or whatever) for each bit. This compromise technique underlies *multiple zone recording* technology, which we will more fully discuss later.

Speed

The first disk drives (back in the era of the original IBM Winchester) used synchronous motors. That is, the motor was designed to lock its rotation rate to the frequency of the

AC power line supplying the disk drive. As a result, most motors of early hard disk drives spun the disk at the same rate as the power line frequency, 3,600 resolutions per minute, which equals the 60 cycles per second of commercial power in the United States.

Synchronous motors are typically big, heavy, and expensive. They also run on normal line voltage—117 volts AC—which is not desirable to have floating around inside computer equipment where a couple of errant volts can cause a system crash. As hard disks were miniaturized, disk makers adopted a new technology—the servo-controlled DC motor— that eliminated these problems. A servo-controlled motor uses feedback to maintain a constant and accurate rotation rate. That is, a sensor in the disk drive constantly monitors how fast the drive spins and adjusts the spin rate should the disk vary from its design specifications.

Because servo motor technology does not depend on the power line frequency, manufacturers are free to use any rotation rate they want for drives that use it. Early hard disks with servo motors stuck with the standard 3,600 RPM spin to match their signal interfaces designed around that rotation rate. Once interface standards shifted from the device level to the system level, however, matching rotation speed to data rate became irrelevant. With system-level interfaces, the raw data is already separated, deserialized, and buffered on the drive itself. The data speeds inside the drive are entirely independent from those outside. With this design, engineers have a strong incentive for increasing the spin rate of the disk platter: The faster the drive rotates, the shorter the time that passes between the scan of any two points on the surface of the disk. A faster spinning platter makes a faster responding drive and one that can transfer information more quickly. With the design freedom afforded by modern disk interfaces, disk designers can choose any spin speed without worrying about signal compatibility. As a result, the highest performing hard disks have spins substantially higher than the old standard; some rotate as quickly as 10,000 or 12,000 RPM.

Note that disk rotation speed cannot be increased indefinitely. Centrifugal force tends to tear apart anything that spins at high rates, and hard disks are no exception. Disk designers must balance achieving better performance with the self-destructive tendencies of rapidly spinning mechanisms. Moreover, overhead in PC disk systems tends to overwhelm the speed increases won by quickening disk spin. Raising speed results in diminishing returns. According to some developers, the optimum rotation rate (the best tradeoff between cost and performance) for hard disks is between 4,500 and 5,400 RPM, although newer drives are pushing the optimum price point to 7,200 RPM.

Latency

Despite the quick and constant rotation rate of a hard disk, it cannot deliver information instantly on request. There's always a slight delay that's called latency. This term describes how long after a command to read to or write from a hard disk the disk rotates to the proper angular position to locate the specific data needed. For example, if a program requests a byte from a hard disk and that byte has just passed under the read/write head, the disk must spin one full turn before that byte can be read from the disk and sent to the program. If read and write requests occur at essentially random times in regard to the spin of the disk (as they do), on the average the disk has to make half a spin before the read/write head is properly positioned to read or write the required data. Normal latency at 3,600 RPM means that the quickest you can expect your hard disk—on the average—to find the information you want is 8.33 milliseconds. For a computer that operates with nanosecond timing, that's a long wait, indeed.

The newer hard disks with higher spin speeds cut latency. The relationship between rotation and latency is linear, so each percentage increase in spin pushes down latency by the same factor. A modern drive with a 5,400 RPM spin achieves a latency of 5.6 milliseconds.

Standby Mode

During operation, the platters in a hard disk are constantly spinning because starting and stopping even the small mass of a two-inch drive causes an unacceptable delay in retrieving or archiving your data. This constant spin assures that your data will be accessible within the milliseconds of the latency period.

In some applications, particularly notebook computers, the constantly spinning hard disk takes a toll. Keeping the disk rotating means constant consumption of power by the spindle motor, which means shorter battery life. Consequently, some hard disks aimed at portable computers are designed to be able to cease spinning when they are not needed. Typically, the support electronics in the host computer determine when the disk should stop spinning. In most machines that means if you don't access the hard disk for a while, the computer assumes you've fallen asleep, died, or had your body occupied by aliens and you won't be needing to use the disk for a while. When you do send a command to read or write the disk, you then will have to wait while it spins back up to speed—possibly as long as several seconds. Subsequent accesses then occur at high hard disk speeds until the drive thinks you've died again and shuts itself down.

The powering down of the drive increases the latency from milliseconds to seconds. It can be a big penalty. Consequently, most notebook computers allow you to adjust the standby delay. The longer the delay, the more apt your drive will be spinning when you want to access it—and the quicker your PC's battery will discharge. If you work within one application, a short delay can keep your PC running longer on battery power. If you shift between applications when using Windows or save your work often, you might as well specify a long delay because you disk will be spinning most of the time, anyway. Note, too, that programs with autosaving defeat the purpose of your hard disk's standby mode, particularly when you set the autosave delay to a short period. For optimum battery life, you'll want to switch off autosaving—if you have sufficient faith in your PC.

Data Transfer Rate

The speed of the spin of a hard disk also influences how quickly data can be continuously read from a drive. At a given storage density (which disk designers try to make as high as possible to pack as much information in as small a package as possible), the quicker a disk spins, the faster information can be read from it. As spin rates increase, more bits on the surface of the disk pass beneath the read/write head in a given period. This increase directly translates into a faster flow of data—more bits per second.

The speed at which information is moved from the disk to its control electronics (or its PC host) is termed the data transfer rate of the drive. Data transfer rate is measured in megabits per second, megahertz (typically these two take the same numeric value), or megabytes per second (one eighth the megabit per second rate). Higher is better.

The data transfer rates quoted for most hard disks are computed values rather than the speeds you should expect in using a hard disk drive in the real world. A number of factors drive down the actual rate at which information can be transferred from a disk drive.

The measure of the actual amount of useful information that moves between a disk drive and your PC is called the *throughput*. It is always lower—substantially lower—than the disk's data transfer rate. The actual throughput achieved by a drive system varies with where the measurement is made because each step along the way imposes overhead. The throughput between your drive and controller is higher than between drive and memory. And the actual throughput to your programs—which must be managed by your operating system—is slower still. Throughput to your operating system on the order of a few hundred kilobytes per second is not unusual for hard disk drives that have quoted transfer rates in excess of 10 or 20 megabytes per second.

Platters

The disk spinning inside the hard disk drive is central to the drive—in more ways than one. The diameter of this platter determines how physically large a drive mechanism must be. In fact, most hard disk drives are measured by the size of their platters. When the PC first burst upon the world, hard disk makers were making valiant attempts at hard disk platter miniaturization, moving from those eight inches in diameter (so-called 8-inch disks) to 5.25-inch platters. Today, the trend is to ever-smaller platters. Most large-capacity drives bound for desktop computer systems now use 3.5-inch platters. Those meant for PCs in which weight and size must be minimized (which means, of course, notebook and smaller PCs) have platters measuring 2.5, 1.8, or 1.3 inches (currently the smallest) in diameter. (See Chapter 26, "Cases," for form-factor details.)

To increase storage capacity in conventional magnetic hard disk storage systems, both sides of a platter are used for storing information, each surface with its own read/write head. (One head is on the bottom where it must fly below the platter.) In addition, manufacturers often put several platters on a single spindle, making a taller package with the same diameter as a single platter. The number of platters inside a hard disk also influences the speed at which data stored on the hard disk can be found. The more platters a given disk drive uses, the greater the probability that one of the heads associated with one of those platters will be above the byte that's being searched for. Consequently, the time to find information is reduced.

Adding platters has drawbacks besides increasing the height of a drive. More platters means greater mass so their greater inertia requires longer to spin up to speed. This is not a problem for desktop machines; power-on memory checks typically take longer than even the most laggardly hard disk requires to spin up. But an additional wait is annoying in laptop and notebook computers that slow down and stop their hard disks to save battery energy. Additionally, because each surface of each platter in a hard disk has its own head, the head actuator mechanism inevitably gets larger and more complex as the number of platters increases. Inertia again takes its toll, slowing down the movement of the heads and increasing the access time of the drive. Of course, drive makers can compensate for the increased head actuator mass with more powerful actuators, but that adds to the size and cost of the drive.

Substrates

The platters of a conventional magnetic hard disk are precisely machined to an extremely fine tolerance measured in microinches. They have to be; remember, the read/write head flies just a few microinches above each platter. If the disk juts up, the result is akin to a DC-10 encountering Pike's Peak, a crash that's good for neither airplane nor hard disk. Consequently, disk makers try to ensure that platters are as flat and smooth as possible.

The most common substrate material is aluminum, which has several virtues. It's easy to machine to a relatively smooth surface. It's generally inert, so it won't react with the material covering it. It's non-magnetic, so it won't affect the recording process. It's been used for a long while (since the first disk drives) and is consequently a familiar material. And above all, it's cheap.

A newer alternative is commonly called the glass platter, although the actual material used can range from ordinary window glass to advanced ceramic compounds akin to Space Shuttle skin. Glass platters excel at exactly the same qualities as do aluminum platters. On the positive side, they hold the advantage of being able to be made smoother and allowing read/write heads to fly lower. But because glass is newer, it's less familiar to work with. Consequently, glass-plattered drives are moving slowly into the product mainstream.

Areal Density

The smoothness of the substrate affects how tightly information can be packed on the surface of a platter. The term used to describe this characteristic is *areal density*, that is, the amount of data that can be packed onto a given area of the platter surface. The most common unit for measuring areal density is megabits per square inch. The higher the areal density, the more information can be stored on a single platter. Smaller hard disks require greater areal densities to achieve the same capacities as larger units. Current products achieve values on the order of 500 to 1,000 megabits per square inch.

A number of factors influence the areal density that can be achieved by a given hard disk drive. The key factor is the size of the magnetic domain that encodes each bit of data, which is controlled in turn by several factors. These include the height at which the read/write head flies and the particle (grain) size of the medium.

Manufacturers make read/write heads smaller to generate smaller fields and fly them as closely to the platter as possible without risking the head running into the jagged peaks of surface roughness. The smoothness of the medium limits the lowest possible flying height; a head can fly closer to a smoother surface.

The size of magnetic domains on a disk is also limited by the size of the magnetic particles themselves. A domain cannot be smaller than the particle that stores it. At one time, ball mills ground a magnetic oxide medium until the particle size was small enough for the desired application. Platters were coated with a slurry of the resulting magnetic material. Modern magnetic materials minimize grain size by electroplating the platters.

Oxide Media

The first magnetic medium used in hard disks was made from the same materials used in conventional audio recording tapes, ferric or ferrous oxide compounds—essentially fine grains of rather exotic rust. As with recording tape, the oxide particles are milled in a mixture of other compounds, including a glue-like binder and often a lubricant. The binder also serves to isolate individual oxide particles from one another. This mud-like mixture is then coated onto the platters.

The technology of oxide coatings is old and well developed. The process has been evolving for more than 50 years and now rates as a well-understood, familiar—and obsolete—technology. New hard disk designs have abandoned oxide media and with several good reasons. Oxide particles are not the best storers of magnetic information. Oxides tend to have lower coercivities and their grains tend to be large when compared to other, newer media technologies. Both of these factors tend to limit the areal density available with oxide media and have rendered oxide coatings obsolete. The slight surface roughness of the oxide medium compounds that of the platter surface, requiring the hard disk read/write head to fly farther away from it than other media, which reduces maximum storage density. In addition, oxide coatings are generally soft and are more prone to getting damaged when the head skids to a stop, when the disk ceases its spin, or when a shock to the drive causes the head to skitter across the platter surface, potentially strafing your data as effectively as an attack by the Red Baron.

Thin-Film Media

In all current hard disk drives, drive makers have replaced oxide coatings with thin-film magnetic media. As the name implies, a thin-film disk has a microscopically skinny layer of a pure metal, or mixture of metals, mechanically bound to its surface. These thin films can be applied either by plating the platter much the way chrome is applied to automobile bumpers or by sputtering, a form of vapor plating in which metal is ejected off a hot electrode in a vacuum and electrically attracted to the disk platter.

Thin-film media hold several special advantages over oxide technology. The very thinness of thin-film media allows higher areal densities because the magnetic field has less thickness in which to spread out. Because the thin-film surface is smoother, it allows heads to fly closer. Thin-film media also has higher coercivities, which allows smaller areas to produce the strong magnetic pulses needed for error-free reading of the data on the disk.

One reason that thin film can be so thin and support high areal densities is that, as with chrome-plated automobile bumpers and faucets, plated and sputtered media require no binders to hold their magnetic layers in place. Moreover, as with chrome plating, the thin films on hard disk platters are genuinely hard, many times tougher than oxide coatings. That makes them less susceptible to most forms of head crashing; the head merely bounces off the thin-film platter just as it would your car's bumpers.

Contamination

Besides shock, head crashes can also result from contaminants such as dust or air pollution particles on the media surface that can strike the head and upset its flight. The head touching the disk surface may result in a nick to the media, which not only destroys the storage ability of the media in the area struck by the head but also can loosen particles of media that can, in turn, cause further contamination and crashing.

Fortunately, the almost universal use of thin-film media and more robust drive mechanisms has made head crashes things of the past. Although you should still be careful with your hard disk (no sense tempting fate or your service contract), in normal use you need not worry about crashes. Most of today's hard disk drives are designed for the rigors of portable computers—that means, the computer moving during operation, say when the airline hits a pocket of turbulence—so a nudge now and again won't destroy the disk.

To be on the safe side, and to help guard against contamination of the platter surface with dust, hair, and other floating gunk, most hard disks keep all their vulnerable parts in a protective chamber. In fact, this need to avoid contamination is why nearly all PC hard disks use non-removable media, sealed out of harm's way.

The disk chamber is not completely air tight. Usually, a small vent is designed into the system to allow the air pressure inside the disk drive to adjust to changes in environmental air pressure. Although this air exchange is minimal, a filter in this vent system traps particles before they can enter the drive. Microscopic pollutants, such as corrosive molecules in the air, can seep through the filter, however, potentially damaging the disk surface. Although the influx of such pollutants is small—the hard disk vent does not foster airflow, only pressure equalization—it is best not to operate a hard disk in a polluted environment. You wouldn't want to be there to use it, anyhow.

Read/Write Heads

Besides the platters, the only other moving part in most hard disk drives is the head system. In nearly all drives, one read/write head is associated with each side of each platter and flies just above or below its surface. Each of these read/write heads is flexibly connected to a more rigid arm, which supports the flying assembly. Usually, several of these arms are linked together to form a single moving (usually pivoting) unit.

Physical Design

The head is loosely connected to the actuator so that it can minutely rise or fall. When the hard disk drive is turned off or in sleep mode so that its platters are not spinning, the head rests lightly against them by a slight spring force. The physical design of the head makes it into an airfoil much like an airplane wing. As the platters spin, they drag the air in contact with them along for the ride. The moving air creates a slight breeze which, like the air whisking past the airplane wing, generates lift on the hard disk head's airfoil. The head rises, flying a few millionths of an inch above the spinning surface of the platter.

Altitude Effects

The height at which the read/write head of a hard disk flies is one factor in determining the ultimate storage capacity of the drive. Magnetic fields spread out with distance, so the farther the head is from the disk, the larger the apparent size of the field is generated by a flux transition on the disk. Moving the head closer shrinks the apparent size of the flux transitions, allowing them to be packed closer together on the disk surface and increasing the capacity of the disk. The typical first-generation hard disk head flew about 10 to 12 microinches—millionths of an inch—above the surface of the platter. Modern disk drive heads fly closer, on the order of five microinches. These lower heights are possible thanks to smoother platters and smooth thin-film media.

Contact Heads

Magnetic fields spread out with distance, so the closer the read/write head flies to the platter surface, the more focused its fields and the smaller the area it can write to and read from. Lowering the flying height of a hard disk head therefore increases its potential storage capacity.

The limiting case is flying at zero altitude. Flying at such a low height is fraught with danger. Just as trees, barns, and other obstacles loom in the way of low-flying aircraft, surface imperfections of hard disks can have similar deleterious consequences on a low-flying head. When the head has no ground clearance, it runs into a further problem—friction. The head constantly rubbing against the disk surface will soon wear something out. It doesn't matter whether the platter or the head succumbs, the result is the same—a dysfunctional disk.

Nevertheless, the optimum flying height for a hard disk head is zero. Drive makers have found a way around the problem of friction—constant lubrication for the head in the form of a viscous liquid. In effect, the head swims instead of flies, and the liquid prevents both from wearing out. In coming years, expect to see these contact disks as an alternative to flying head designs.

Electrical Design

Flying is a means to an end, not the ultimate purpose of the read/write head. The real job of the head is to create or detect the magnetic pulses on the disk platter that correspond to the data you store there. Modern hard disks use one of two basic designs to accomplish this design purpose, inductive and magneto-resistive.

Inductive Heads

An *inductive read/write head* is nothing more than a miniature electromagnet akin those of childhood experimentation. Wrap a long length of wire around a nail, connect the two ends of the wire to the positive and negative terminals of a battery, and the nail becomes an electromagnet. The electricity flowing through the wire *induces* a magnetic field in the nail. In the inductive read/write head, the wire is called the *coil* and the part that acts as the nail is the *core*. The principle is the same. The disk drive electronics sends a current through the read/write head coil, which induces a magnetic field in the core. The magnetic field alters the orientation of the magnetic particles on the nearby platter. The read process simply reverses the relationship. The magnetic fields of the particles on the platter slightly magnetize the core which, in turn, induces a small voltage in the coil. The disk drive electronics detect the small voltage fluctuations in the coil and interprets them as data.

The physical design of the core allows focusing the head's read and write abilities into a small area. Instead of a long, thin nail, the core is folded so that its two poles (ends) are not quite touching, separated by a thin gap. This design concentrates the magnetic field into the tiny gap. The first practical read/write heads, those in vintage tape recorders, had nothing more than air in the gap. Basic disk drive read/write heads fill the gap with a non-magnetic metal. Such designs are termed *metal-in-gap* heads. Modern read/write heads replace the coil of wire with a thin layer of copper deposited in coil form as a film. Called *thin-film heads*, their technology allows finer, lower-mass coils that are easier and less expensive to fabricate.

Magneto-Resistive Heads

The latest trend in head design is *magneto-resistive read/write* heads. These heads work on an entirely different physical principle from inductive heads. They measure the change in electrical resistance that a magnetic field causes in some materials. The disk drive electronics sends a small, constant current through the magneto-resistive material (usually an alloy of iron and nickel) and measures the change voltage across the head; as the resistance of the head goes up, the voltage goes down. The change is minuscule but easily detectable by modern precision electronics.

The magneto-resistive action is one-way. It can be used only to detect changes in magnetic fields. It cannot create the fields. In other words, the magneto-resistive principle works only for read operations. Consequently, disk drives with magneto-resistive heads actually have combination heads, a magneto-resistive read head combined with an inductive write head. Dividing the functions of a read/write head into separate elements allows each to be tailored to best operation. The magneto-resistive design allows higher frequency operation, which equates to greater storage densities and operating speeds.

Write Pre-Compensation

Constant angular velocity recording has another drawback. The shorter sectors closer to the spindle require data to be packed into them more tightly, squeezing the magnetic flux reversals in the recording medium ever closer together. The ability of many magnetic media to hold flux transitions falls off as the transitions are packed more tightly; pinched together, they produce a feebler field and induce a lower current in the read/write head.

One way of dealing with this problem is to write on the disk with a stronger magnetic field as the sectors get closer to the spindle. By increasing the current in the read/write head when it writes nearer the center of the disk, the on-disk flux transitions can be made stronger. They can then induce stronger currents in the read/write head when that area of the disk is read.

This process is called write pre-compensation because the increased writing current compensates for the fall-off in disk responses nearer its center at a place logically before the information is stored on the disk. Drives with system-level interfaces automatically make the necessary compensation. Your PC must instruct older device-level interfaced drives when to add the necessary write pre-compensation. Some drives, particularly older models, require that you indicate the write pre-compensation cylinder when you set up your system. Modern drives do not. When you don't need write pre-compensation, you should specify either cylinder 0 or 65535, depending on your PC's BIOS, to indicate not to apply write pre-compensation.

Head Actuators

Each read/write head scans the hard disk for information. Were the head nothing more than that, fixed in position as is the head of a tape recorder, it would only be able to read a narrow section of the disk. The head and the entire assembly to which it is attached must be able to move in order to take advantage of all the recordable area on the hard disk. The mechanism that moves the head assembly is called the head actuator. Usually, the head assembly is pivoted and is swung across the disk by a special head actuator solenoid or motor.

Modern head actuator designs also help increase hard disk capacity. This increase is achieved by precision. One of the most important limits on the density of data storage in a disk system is the ability of the mechanism to exactly and repeatedly locate a specific location on the disk surface that stores a bit of information. The more precise the mechanism, the tighter it can pack data. The better actuators (along with the dimensional stability of the rigid platters themselves) are used in the hard disk for a more stable, more precise storage environment that can reliably pack information at a greater density.

The head actuator is part of an electro-mechanical system that also includes the electronics that control the movement of the head. Two distinct types of electronic systems are commonly used in hard disk designs, open-loop actuators and closed-loop actuators. Open-loop systems are essentially obsolete in modern hard disk drives, notable only for the role they played in disk development.

Specific types of hard disk mechanisms are associated with these open-loop and closed-loop design techniques. Most open-loop systems used band-stepper technology. Today's closed-loop hard disks almost universally use servo-voice coil actuators.

Whether the "loop" is open or closed merely indicates if direct feedback about the head position is used in controlling the actuator. An open-loop system gets no direct feedback; it moves the head and hopes that it gets to the right place. Closed-loop systems give the drive feedback about the location of the read/write head over the platters. Consequently, closed-loop drives can have higher storage densities because the head can be more precisely placed when it knows its exact location above the disk platters.

Band-Stepper Actuators

The first PC-size hard disks used the same head-moving mechanism as floppy disks. Called a *band-stepper actuator*, it used a stepping motor to generate the force to move the head. A stepping motor is a special direct current motor that turns in discrete increments in response to electrical pulses from the control electronics instead of spinning. The electronics of the band-stepper system send out a given number of pulses and assume the stepper motor rotates that number of steps. The band of the band-stepper is simply a thin strip of metal that couples the rotating shaft of the motor to the linear travel of the head. Each pulse from the control electronics thus moves the head across one track of the hard disk.

The band-stepper design is no longer used because it had severe shortcomings. The speed at which this form of actuator can operate is limited by the rate at which pulses can reliably be sent to the motor, so band-stepper drives were inevitably slow. Although electrically simple and low cost, the band-stepped design limits the maximum number of tracks on a disk to a few hundred because its open-loop design cannot accurately target finely spaced tracks. Today's gigabyte drives would not be possible with band-stepper actuators.

Servo-Voice Coil Actuators

The closed-loop system gets a constant stream of information regarding the head position from the disk, so it always knows exactly where the head is. The system determines the location of the head by constantly reading from a special, dedicated side of one platter—the servo surface—which stores a special magnetic pattern that allows the drive mechanism to identify each storage location on the disk. Some more recent magnetic hard disks put the servo information on the same recording surface as the stored data. This combined data-and-servo system is called embedded servo technology.

The most common of the closed-loop actuator systems uses a voice coil mechanism that operate like the voice coil in a loudspeaker and are therefore called servo-voice coil actuators. In this design, a magnetic field is generated in coil of wire (a solenoid) by the controlling electronics, and this field pulls the head mechanism against the force of a spring. By varying the current in the coil, the head mechanism is drawn farther from its anchoring spring and the head moves across the disk. The voice coil mechanism connects directly to a pivoting arm, which also supports the read/write head above the platter. The varying force of the voice coil swings the head radially in an arc across the platter surface.

Because of its closed-loop nature, the servo-voice coil system doesn't have to count out each step to the disk location it needs to travel to. It can quickly move to approximately the correct place and in milliseconds fine-tune its location based on the servo information. This speed, and the tight track spacing afforded by closed-loop positioning, has made servo-voice coil hard disks the current choice of all major hard disk manufacturers.

Dual-Actuator Drives

Even the servo-voice coil mechanism has to obey the laws of physics. It cannot move the head instantly from one track to another, so there is always a slight delay when the head has to search out a particular byte. One of the principal goals in improving hard disk performance is minimizing this delay. Drive makers have squeezed about all they can get out of traditional mechanisms by reducing the mass (and thus inertia) of the head assembly. Dramatic speed improvements require a radical change.

One such departure from traditional design first developed by Conner Peripherals was the dual-actuator hard disk. Instead of a single head per platter, the Conner design used two, each attached to its own independent actuator. Either head could scan across the entire surface of the platter. With properly designed electronics, this mechanism could cut latency in half on isolated disk operations and eliminate the delays imposed by head movement on back-to-back read or write requests. In addition, by installing the two head actuators at diametrically opposed positions across the disk, the design could halve latency. The drive electronics could determine which head was nearest the desired data and use it for the read or write operation. Because one of the heads has to be within half a revolution of the desired data, the rotational latency is one half the time it takes the platter to make a complete spin.

Clever as it was, this design failed to catch on because another technology delivered the same benefits and more. As noted in Chapter 8, "Mass Storage Technology," a disk array gains the benefit of dual or even multiple actuators but puts them in separate drives controlled by special electronics so that they act as one. Arrays cut both access time and latency thanks to their multiple actuators and improved reliability.

Landing Zone

Hard disks are most vulnerable to head crash damage when they are turned off. As soon as you flick the off switch on your computer, the platters of its hard disk must stop spinning, and the airflow that keeps the heads flying stops. Generally, the airflow decreases gradually, and the head slowly progresses downward, eventually landing like an airplane on the disk media.

In truth, however, any head landing is more of a controlled crash and holds the potential for disk damage. Consequently, most hard disks—even those with thin-film media—have a dedicated *landing zone* reserved in their media in which no data can be recorded. This landing zone is usually at the inner edge of the actual data storage area.

Park-and-Lock

Usually, a software command is necessary to bring the head to the landing zone and hold it there while the disk spins down. This process is called *head parking*. The first hard disks had no special provisions for parking their heads and required a specific software command to move their heads to the landing zone. All modern hard disks are designed so that whenever their power is switched off, the head automatically retracts to the landing zone before the disk spins down. Such drives are said to have automatic head parking. In addition, the most modern drives latch their heads in the landing zone after power is removed. The latch prevents an impact or other shock to the system from jarring the head out of the landing zone and, in the process, bouncing it across the vulnerable medium. This feature is generally termed *automatic park-and-lock*. All portable and most desktop drives now incorporate it.

Thermal Compensation

All materials expand and contract as temperatures change, and the metals used in constructing hard disk drives are no exception. As a drive operates, it generates heat from the motors that spin its platters, the actuator that moves the heads, and the electronics that control its operation. This heat causes the various components of the drive to slightly expand, changing its dimensions slightly but measurably. Because of the miniaturization of modern hard disks that packs thousands of tracks in an inch, even this slight thermal expansion can alter the geometry of the drive sufficiently that heads and tracks can move from their expected positions.

To compensate for such changes, most hard disk drives periodically perform a *thermal calibration*, or T-cal. The disk moves its heads to read special calibration tracks to re-establish a proper reference for head positioning. Drive manufacturers developed their own algorithms for determining when their drives would perform thermal calibration, for example, at fixed intervals or upon the occurrence of seek errors. In general, the thermal compensation takes priority over normal read operations and sometimes imposes a delay when you request data. The delay can amount to several dozen milliseconds because the drive's heads must move to the calibration tracks before fulfilling any data requests.

To avoid the delays imposed by thermal calibration, many high-performance drives have the ability to delay the calibration until the completion of a read operation to avoid the interrupt of the delivery of prolonged sequential data streams such as those that might occur in playing back a video clip. Most drives calibrate all heads simultaneously, which results in the drive being unavailable for reading or writing data for the milliseconds required by the re-calibration. A few drives can now re-calibrate heads individually, allowing the other heads to retrieve data at the same time.

Geometry

A combination of the hard disk mechanism, its controller, and the software operating it all dictates the manner in which data is arranged on the platter. Unlike floppy disks, which are often interchanged, hard disks need not fit any particular standard because their media are never at large; they are always sealed inside the drive mechanism. Because platters cannot be removed from drives (providing you don't take matters into your own hands with a can opener and crowbar), they have no need for interchangeability. The physical layout of the data on disk is thus left to the imagination of the disk's designer.

The disk designer is not given free reign, however, because of one overriding necessity—compatibility with your operating system and hardware standards. Certain disk parameters must arbitrarily be set at values that true compatibility requires. Of course, where there's a roadblock, there's an engineer with a pocket calculator figuring out exactly how much effort sidestepping it will take. Today's advanced drive electronics allow the designers the widest possible latitude is selecting hard disk parameters; whatever doesn't match the PC standard, the electronics fake so your PC doesn't know about the rules violations. Consequently, what your PC sees follows the PC standard to the letter, but what goes on inside the drive is the engineer's business.

To understand this parameter monkey business, you first need to know a bit of hard disk geography—where the drive puts your bytes. The storage arrangement is called the drive's geometry, and it determines the setup parameters of the drive used in its installation.

Tracks

No matter the type of magnetic media or style of head actuator used by a disk, the read/write head must stop its lateral motion across the disk whenever it reads or writes data. While it is stationary, the platter spins underneath it. Each time the platter completes one spin, the head traces a full circle across its surface. This circle is called a *track*.

A disk drive stores the data bits of a given track sequentially, as if it were a strip of tape spliced end-to-end. With every spin, the same data passes the head as long as the drive holds in the same place. The electronics of the drive select which portion of the track to read (or write) to find a random block of data.

Cylinders

Each head traces out a separate track across its associated platter. The head actuator locks all the heads together so that all are at the same position from the center of the disk along a given radius. Because the combination of all the tracks traced out at a given head actuator position forms the skeleton of a solid cylinder, such a vertical stack of tracks is often termed exactly that: a *cylinder*.

The number of cylinders in a drive is the same as the number of tracks on a platter in that drive. Both numbers are permanently determined when the manufacturer makes the drive. In most drives, the number of cylinders is set by a magnetic pattern called a *servo pattern*. Older hard disks dedicated one surface of a platter to this servo information. Most modern disks put the servo information on the same surface as the stored data. The servo information gets read along with the data, and the drive electronics sort everything out—using the servo information to find its place and sending the data to your applications. This kind of hard disk is called an *embedded servo drive*.

The more cylinders in the drive, the more data the drive can store. The maximum number of cylinders is limited by physical factors inherent in the technology used by the drive. Using more tracks on each platter squeezes the tracks closer together and forces them to be smaller. The minimum width of a track is set by the size of the head but is limited by other factors—such as how closely the head flies to the disk surface—that also limit the amount of information that the drive can fit into each track. Once, hard disk drives had as few as 312 cylinders. Modern drives have thousands.

Sectors

Most hard disk systems further divide each track into short arcs termed sectors, and the sector is the basic storage unit of the drive. Some operating systems use the sector as their basic storage unit as does, for example, the NTFS system used by Windows NT and

Windows 2000. Under the VFAT system of Windows 95 and Windows 98, however, the operating system gathers together several sectors to make its basic unit of storage for disk files, the cluster.

Sectors can be soft, marked magnetically with bit-patterns embedded in the data on the track, or hard, set by the drive mechanism itself. Soft sectors are demarcated using a low-level format program, and their number can vary almost arbitrarily, depending on the formatting software and the interface used for connecting the disk. Disks with device-level interfaces are essentially soft-sectored. For all practical purposes, disks with system-level interfaces are hard-sectored because their sector size is set by the servo information encoded on the drive platters, which cannot be changed once the drive leaves the factory. Magneto-optical cartridges are hard-sectored by an embedded optical format pre-recorded on the medium.

In the PC hard disk industry, the size of a sector is, by convention, almost universally 512 bytes. The number of sectors per track depends on the design of the disk. The sector count on any given track of older hard disks is the same as every other track because of their use of constant angular velocity recording. Device-level interfaces required certain specific numbers of tracks per sector because of the rate at which bits had to be read from the disk. ST506 disks that used MFM recording usually had 17 sectors per track. With RLL recording, ST506 disks typically had 25 or 26 sectors per track. ESDI disks generally operated with 34 sectors per track. The oldest AT Attachment (IDE) hard disks also put the same number of sectors on each track, but the system-level interface allowed designers to choose any value they wanted.

Most modern hard disk drives use a technique called *multiple zone recording*, which puts variable numbers of sectors on each track. MZR allows the drive maker to use the storage capacity of the magnetic medium more efficiently.

A disk with a fixed number of sectors per track stores data at lower densities in its outer tracks than it does in its inner tracks. Only the innermost tracks pack data at the highest density allowed by the medium. All the other tracks must be recorded at a lower density, an inevitable result of the constant angular velocity recording used by hard disks and the fixed frequency of the data signals.

Multiple zone recording allows the drive to maintain a nearly constant data density across the disk by dividing it into zones. The drive alters the frequency of the data signals to match each zone. Using higher frequencies in the zones near the outer tracks of a disk increases their data density to about that of the inner tracks. This, in turn, can substantially increase overall disk capacity without compromising reliability or altering the constant spin needed for quick access.

Sometimes, MZR technology is described as Zoned Constant Angular Velocity (ZCAV) recording, a term which confirms that the spin rate remains the same (constant angular velocity) but the platter is divided into areas with different recording densities (zones). Seagate Technologies uses a proprietary form of MZR called Zone-Bit Recording— different name, same effect.

The MZR drive must somehow mask its actual physical characteristics so that it looks to your PC as if it has a standard geometry, such as tracks of 17 sectors, each sector storing 512 data bytes. Many operating systems can't deal with disks that magically change from 17 sectors per track one minute to 23 sectors and then to 31. This masking process is simplified by using a system-level interface that already uses sector translation.

Physical Format

The geometry of a disk drive describes only the numbers of the various drive parameters— cylinders, heads, and sectors. The drive *format* describes the arrangement and alignment of these parameters.

Disk geometry fixes the tracks as concentric circles with the sectors as small arcs within each track. The format defines the location of the sectors in regard to one another—that is, the order in which they are read. Sectors need not be read one after another in a given track. Moreover, their starting edges need not exactly align on the disk.

Sector Identification

Neither tracks nor sectors are engraved on the surface of individual platters. They are instead defined magnetically by coded bit-patterns recorded on the disk. Before data can be written on such a disk, the sectors have to be marked to serve as markers so that the information can later be found and retrieved. The process by which sectors are defined on the hard disk is called low-level formatting because it occurs at a control level below the reaches of normal Windows commands.

Three methods have found general application in defining tracks: simply by the count of the stepper motor in the oldest band-stepper drives, by the permanently recorded track servo data on the dedicated servo surface of old servo-voice coil drives, and by embedded servo data in modern drives.

In classic hard disk drives, special bit-patterns on the disk serve as sector identification markings. The patterns indicate the start of the sector and encode an ID number that gives the sector number within the track. The sector ID precedes each sector; error-correction data typically follows each sector. In normal operation, the disk servo system seeks a particular track, and then the drive begins to read sector IDs until it finds the sector that your PC has requested.

The sector ID can consume a significant portion of the available space on each disk track, about 10 percent. Consequently, manufacturers have sought means to eliminate it. For example, the *No-ID Format* developed by IBM eliminates sector IDs by putting a format map in RAM. The map tells the drive where on each track each sector is located and which sectors have been marked bad. The map, for example, tells the drive how many sectors are on a track in a zoned recording system and where each begins in reference to the track servo information embedded on the disk. This format also improves access speed because the drive can immediately locate a given sector without detours in chasing replacements for defective sectors.

Sector Interleave

Back in the days when microprocessors lagged hard disk performance, system engineers worried about adequately slowing drive performance to achieve an optimum match with the host PC. Sector interleaving was the primary method of achieving the happiest marriage. Interleave is no longer an issue with most modern hard disks.

The sector interleave of a hard disk refers to the relationship of the logical arrangement of sectors in a track to their actual physical arrangement. For example, sectors might be numbered 1 through 17 with data stored sequentially in them. But on the disk, consecutively numbered sectors need not be laid next to each other. The actual order is not important to the disk controller because it reads the sector identification (essentially the number assigned the sector) rather than check the sector position on the disk when it needs to find a particular sector. This mapping between the logical and physical sector locations is determined by the low-level format of the hard disk.

Sector interleaving works by forcing the disk drive to skip a given numbers of sectors when your operating system tells it to read consecutive sectors. For example, Windows may instruct the drive to read sectors one and two. The hard disk system reads sector one, and then the arrangement of sectors causes it to skip the next six sectors before reading the sector bearing the number two identification. The time that elapses while the six unread sectors pass by gives the host computer a chance to catch up with the disk.

The ratio of the length of a sector to the distance between the start of two logically consecutive sectors is termed the interleave factor. Because the length used for measuring interleave is one sector, often only the right-hand factor in the ratio is used to describe the interleave. Thus, a disk in which no sectors are skipped would be said to have an interleave factor of 1:1, or simply one. If five sectors are skipped between each one that's used, the interleave factor would be 1:6, or six.

Although interleaving would appear to invariably slow the transfer rate of a disk system, the optimum interleave actually helps improve performance. Higher or lower interleave values impair performance—and setting the interleave too low has the most dramatic and deleterious effect. Consider, for example, what happens when a PC is not ready for the next sector being read from the disk; the disk must complete an entire spin before the sector can be read again, typically a delay of about 17 milliseconds (at 3,600 RPM). If skipping one sector is sufficient to give the PC time to catch up, the added delay is only one millisecond (assuming 17 sectors per track). In this case, the proper interleave makes the disk system 17 times faster than not interleaving, a compelling argument for achieving the optimum interleave.

Note that erring on the high side yields less of a penalty than using too low of an interleave. Skipping an extra sector delays the next sector read by only one millisecond, compared to the 17 milliseconds imposed by erring on the low side.

Interleave is not an issue with hard disks that have track buffers because these drives read an entire track at a time, sending out the sector information from within the track only as your PC requests it. Because nearly all modern disk drives use track buffering, interleave is no longer a factor in installing a new drive.

If you have to tangle with an old drive and old PC, however, interleave may rear its ugly head when you low-level format the drive. Because the optimum interleave varies with the ability of your PC to accept data, better formatting programs let you test a given drive in a given PC to determine the optimum interleave. Because of the tremendous penalty for setting interleave factors too low, PC makers were often overly conservative in specifying interleave factors for their products. Although a 1:1 interleave might appear best, it rarely is. If the old drive lacks track buffering, the best interleave in usually two if its PC host uses a 286 or faster microprocessor.

Cylinder Skewing

After the disk drive head finishes reading one track, it must be repositioned slightly to read the next. As with any mechanical movement, repositioning the head requires a slight time. Although brief, this repositioning period is long enough that should the head try moving from the end of one track to the beginning of another, it gets there too late. Consequently, you have to wait while the whole track passes below the head until it is ready to read the beginning of the second track.

This problem is easily solved by the simple expedient of not aligning the starting points of all tracks along the same radial line. By offsetting the beginning of each track slightly from the end of the preceding track, the travel time of the head can be compensated for. Because the beginning of the first sector of each track and cylinder do not line up but are somewhat skewed, this technique is called track skewing or cylinder skewing.

Addressing

Hard disks are random access devices but operate at the sector level rather than with individual bytes. The drive locates and identifies any given sector by the cylinder position to which it moves the head actuator, the number corresponding to one of the heads in the stack, and by the sector number on the track. These three values—the cylinder, the head, and the sector—give an immutable *physical address* to each and every sector on the disk.

The drive doesn't know what's stored in any given sector and it doesn't care. It just moves its heads to the appropriate position and carries out a read or write command there.

Typically, a command to a hard disk drive works its way through several levels in your PC. When your application software requests data from the disk, it sends a command to your operating system. The application identifies what it wants by the name of the file or, in later requests, as a *file handle*. A file handle is a number the operating system assigns to the filename when it is opened. The handle is an expedient that's more convenient for the operating system to work with, a couple of bytes instead of 255 or so alphanumeric characters. The operating system translates the name or handle into terms the disk drive understands and sends the request to the drive.

CHS Addressing

Early hard disks required that the operating system identify each sector by its exact physical address. The operating system would send out a command specifying which cylinder, head, and sector the disk was to retrieve or write. Because of the three values the operating system would send out to identify data sectors, this form of addressing is usually called cylinder-head-sector addressing, or more commonly *CHS addressing*.

This physical addressing gives all the work of running the disk drive to the operating system. The drive itself is a simple automaton, moving its actuating arms only on explicit command. The operating system keeps track of which sectors store each block of a file. If a sector on the disk goes bad, the operating system has the responsibility of not issuing a command to use it.

The technology behind CHS addressing has no inherent problems. It is still used internally by hard disk drives no matter their size. But implementations of CHS addressing at the PC level have severe shortcomings.

All the shortcomings of CHS addressing date back to the first PC hard disk drives. When drivers were incorporated into PCs, hardware and software manufacturers (basically IBM and Microsoft at the time) allocated space to store the individual cylinder, head, and sector values. The values they chose were generous, at least considering that the hard disk drive they were designed for had 312 cylinders, 4 heads, and 17 sectors for a full 10MB of storage. Both early PC hardware and software allowed for 1,024 cylinders, 255 heads, and 63 sectors—that's 10 bits to store cylinders, 8 to store heads, and 6 to store sectors. The head and sector counts start with one instead of zero, trimming each value from its potential maximum by one. In theory, those values are good enough for storing 8,422,686,720 bytes.

Unfortunately, the values were ill-chosen in regard to the physical configuration of disk drives. Few drive makers have configured products with even 16 heads. The maximum cylinder count of 1,024, however, was quickly exceeded by hard disk makers. Using strict physical CHS addressing, the cylinders beyond 1,024 on larger drives were inaccessible to PCs.

Although theoretically the 1,024 cylinder maximum imposes only an 8GB limit on capacity, the odd requirements of geometries allowed for physical CHS addressing effectively limits practical hard disks to less than 80 to 120MB. For obvious reasons, no current hard disk drives use direct physical CHS addressing.

Sector Translation

The primary strategy used by hard disk makers to sidestep the 1,024 cylinder limit imposed by direct physical CHS addressing by PCs is *sector translation*. The electronics of the hard disk translate the CHS values sent out by your PC's operating system into different values that the hard disk can use for its physical addressing of sectors. Although your PC still sends out CHS values—and thus remains compatible with conventional PC hardware and software—these addresses do not directly correspond to sectors on the disk. The drive electronics re-maps the CHS values it receives to the actual CHS values it uses.

Sector translation allows a disk drive to appear that it has a different arrangement of cylinders, heads, and sectors than it actually does. In other words, its *logical geometry*, the CHS values your PC thinks the drive has, is different from its physical geometry. For example, although a drive might have 2,048 cylinders and 3 heads, the drive electronics are designed to respond as if the drive was actually built with only 1,024 cylinders and 6 heads. Because the drive appears to have only 1,024 sectors, your PC can address all of its storage.

Sector translation also allows drive makers to use zoned recording to squeeze more sectors into the longer tracks near the outer edge of hard disk platters. Although PCs expect all tracks to have the same sector count, the sector translation of a drive can mask the differing sector counts in the various zones of the disk. As a result, sector translation lets a drive maker increase the capacity of a hard disk at a given areal density.

Because the translation occurs in the drive hardware itself, neither you nor your system has to worry what the actual physical cylinder and head arrangement might be. Sector translation works most effectively on embedded interface drives—AT Attachment and SCSI—which give the disk designer full control over all aspects of the disk controller hardware.

With some disk drives, manufacturers have taken sector translation one step further. The drive can adjust the translation so that its logical geometry matches the drive parameters set in your PC. For example, some older Seagate AT Attachment drives checked your system to see what drive geometry it expected, and then the drive changed like a chameleon to match that configuration.

In theory, sector translation allows drives as large as 8GB to work with standard PC hardware and software that use the default Interrupt 13 disk access routines. A mismatch between the CHS addressing limits of Interrupt 13 and the AT Attachment interface constrains accessible disk capacities to 528MB. (See the section "Capacity Limits," later in this chapter.)

Automatic sector translation has one drawback, however. After you format a drive that uses automatic sector translation, the logical configuration of your data is set and cannot be changed without reformatting the drive. Although the drive can still automatically adapt to match your PC if you should change the drive parameters in its CMOS memory, your data cannot.

A problem arises if the CMOS configuration memory of your PC becomes corrupted. For example, if you replace the battery in your PC and have to reconfigure your system, you have to remember the old drive parameters you set to recover the data you stored. If you want to transfer a drive and its data between different systems, you have to be sure to use the same setup parameters in each system.

Unfortunately, an automatic sector translation drive offers no help in what parameters to use other than telling you its capacity. Consequently, as a future reference, you should label your hard disk with the parameters (or drive type) you set when you format it.

Logical Block Addressing

Once a hard disk has enough on-board intelligence to translate CHS addressing, there is no longer a need to follow the CHS convention when sending addresses to a disk drive. The drive can map any value to the physical CHS addresses of individual sectors.

The most popular method of addressing data on disk drives is now *logical block addressing*. Under the LBA scheme, each sector on the disk is numbered. The sector numbers run sequentially from the first usable sector to the last. To access a given sector, your PC sends out the sector number. The drive then translates that number into the physical CHS value of that sector to access the requested data.

Logical block addressing has greater flexibility than CHS addressing, hinted at by the name. LBA can be used for addressing devices other than disk drives. Any device that segments its data into blocks, which can be virtually any size, can use LBA. Tape drives that use the SCSI or AT Attachment interfaces use LBA.

PCs expect hard disks to have a sector size of 512 bytes. Consequently, most LBA schemes for hard disk drives use a block size of 512 bytes. This block size constrains individual hard disk capacity to 8GB using the ATA and SCSI interfaces. (See the section "Capacity Limits.")

The SCSI interface always uses LBA. Most PC-based SCSI host adapters translate CHS addresses generated by PCs into LBA values so that they are compatible with Interrupt

13. The AT Attachment interface makes LBA optional. To use LBA, you must have an LBA-compatible drive (nearly all ATA drives with more than 0.5GB capacity allow the use of LBA) and driver software for your operating system that knows how to use LBA. Windows 95 has built-in LBA addressing support in its driver library.

Sector Remapping

Eliminating the constraints of direct physical CHS addressing brings another benefit, the ability of a disk drive to automatically alter its address map. This ability, called *sector remapping*, allows a hard disk to avoid storing data on sectors or tracks that have doubtful, dangerous, or damaged magnetic media that would otherwise put your data at risk. Using sector remapping, the drive can substitute a different physical sector for the bad one while maintaining the same logical sector or block address. Modern hard disks remap sectors by performing *automatic reallocation*. Upon encountering a bad sector, they automatically locate a new sector to store the data, move the data to that sector, and update their tables to substitute the new sector address. The process is invisible to you, handled at the hardware level by the drive.

Disk Parameters

Taken together, the number of platters (or heads), the number of cylinders, and the point at which write pre-compensation begins make up the set of disk parameters. With drives that use device-level interfaces and older ATA drives, these three numbers are required by the disk drive controller to properly operate a disk drive.

Modern hard disk interfaces can identify themselves to your PC. Use your PC's setup function to configure your AT Attachment (IDE or UDMA) drive as "AUTO," and your BIOS will query the drive, determine its parameters, and automatically load them. The identification functions even identify the make and model of your hard disk so your PC can display it as it boots up.

Very early computers hardwired disk parameters into their firmware, which made changing drives troublesome. The setup system through which you had to type in the specific parameters used by your PC's hard drive was seen as an improvement. It allowed you to match most hard disk drives to your system—provided you knew all the numbers your PC needed.

When the BIOS of your PC does not know how to automatically access the formatting information encoded in your hard disks, you have to revert to this old system and manually enter the parameters when you set up your PC. With a modern hard disk using the AT Attachment interface and automatic translation mode, you don't have to worry about exactly matching these parameters. As long as you set your system with any parameters that yield the proper drive capacity, the disk itself makes the right parameter match.

Modern SCSI host adapters use their own BIOSs and operate independently from your PC's setup parameters. (Some AT Attachment host adapters have their own BIOSs and therefore do not require parameter setting, either.) With most PCs when you connect a SCSI drive alone, you should usually set up your system as if it has no hard disks. The SCSI host adapter takes care of the details, reading the drive parameters from the drive itself and relaying the setup information to your PC. Most add-in SCSI systems prefer to stay invisible to your PC's built-in disk system. If all you have is a SCSI drive, you tell your PC (through its setup system) that you have *no* hard disk drives.

File System

To store a file on disk, the FAT file system breaks it down into a group of clusters, perhaps hundreds of them. Each cluster can be drawn from anywhere on the disk. Sequential pieces of a file do not necessarily have to be stored in clusters that are physically adjacent.

The earliest—and now obsolete—versions of the FAT file system followed a simple rule in picking which clusters are assigned to each file. The first available cluster, the one nearest the beginning of the disk, is always the next one used. Therefore, on a new disk, clusters are picked one after another, and all the clusters in a file are contiguous.

When a file is erased, its clusters are freed for reuse. These newly freed clusters, being closer to the beginning of the disk, are the first ones chosen when the next file is written to disk. In effect, a FAT-based file system first fills in the holes left by the erased file. As a result, the clusters of new files may be scattered all over the disk.

The earliest versions of the FAT file system use this strange strategy because they were written at a time when capacity was more important than speed. The goal was to pack files on the disk as stingily as possible. For more than a decade, however, the FAT system has used a different strategy. Instead of immediately trying to use the first available cluster closest to the beginning of the disk, the file system attempts to write on never-before-used clusters before filling in any erased clusters. This helps assure that the clusters of a file are closer to one another, a technique that improves the speed of reading a file from the disk.

File Allocation Table

To keep track of which cluster belongs in which file, the Windows 95 and Windows 98 file systems use a File Allocation Table, or FAT, essentially a map of the clusters on the disk. When you read to a file, a FAT-based file system automatically and invisibly checks the FAT to find all the clusters of the file; when you write to the disk, it checks the FAT for available clusters. No matter how scattered over your disk the individual clusters of a file may be, you—and your software—only see a single file.

FAT-based file systems simply number all the clusters in a manner similar to the way a disk drive numbers logical blocks. The operating system keeps track of which cluster number and in what order clusters have been assigned to a given file. The operating system stores most of the cluster data in the file allocation table.

The FAT file system works by chaining together clusters. The directory entry of a file or subdirectory contains several bytes of data in addition to the file's name. Along with the date the file was last changed and the file's attributes is the number of the first cluster used to store the file or subdirectory.

When the operating system reads a file, it first checks the directory entry to find the first cluster number. In addition to reading the data from the cluster from the disk, the operating system also checks the file allocation table for the entry with the number corresponding to the first cluster number. This FAT entry indicates the number of the *next* cluster in the file. After reading that cluster, the operating system checks the entry corresponding to that cluster number to find the next cluster. If the file has no additional clusters, the cluster entry has a value of 0FF(Hex). The operating system assigns unused clusters—those available for adding to files to store data—the value of zero.

When the standard FAT-based PC operating system erases a file, it merely changes the first character of the file name in the directory entry to 0E5(Hex) and changes all the FAT entries of the file to zero. Because the rest of the directory information remains intact (at least until the file system runs out of space for directory information and overwrites the entries of erased files), it can be recovered to help reconstruct accidentally erased files. Unerase and undelete utilities check the directory for entries with the first character of 0E5(Hex) and display what it finds as candidates for recovery. From the remaining directory data, the unerasing program can locate the first cluster of the file. Finding the remaining clusters from the FAT is a matter of making educated guesses.

The FAT of a disk is so important that Windows guards against losing its data by putting two complete (and identical) copies of the FAT end-to-end on the disk.

Clusters

As clever as using clusters to allocate file data may be, the technique has its drawback. It can be wasteful. Disk space is divvied up in units of a cluster. No matter how small a file (or a subdirectory, which is simply a special kind of file) may be, it occupies at a minimum one cluster of disk space. Larger files take up entire clusters, but any fractional cluster of space that's left over requires another cluster. On average, each file on the disk wastes half a cluster of space. The more files, the more waste. The larger the clusters, the more waste. Unless you work exclusively with massive files, increasing cluster size to increase disk capacity is a technique to avoid whenever possible.

DOS versions through 3.3 used FATs with 12-bit entries for cluster numbers, allowing a total of 4,096 uniquely named clusters. With 8,192 byte clusters, the maximum possible disk (or partition size) was 33,554,432—the infamous old DOS 32MB limit. DOS 4.0 and later allow 16-bit FAT entries, which allow a total of 65,536 uniquely named clusters. With cluster size kept at a space-saving 2,048 bytes, the maximum possible disk size is 134,217,728 (or 128MB). Larger disks or partitions—up to 512MB—are accommodated by increasing cluster size, stepwise, through 4,096 to 8,192 bytes. DOS 5.0 can handle even larger disks by dividing them into multiple partitions, each kept within the limits imposed by the combination of cluster and FAT entry size.

DOS 5 and 6 are also designed to use the smallest cluster size possible for a given disk capacity. Consequently, disks with capacities up to 134,217,728 bytes could be addressed as a single unit with 2,048-byte clusters. With 8,192-byte clusters, the maximum size of a single unit or disk partition is 536,870,912 bytes. Both DOS 5 and 6 handle larger disks but require partitioning them into these half-gigabyte chunks. Table 10.1 lists the allocation unit sizes used by 16-bit FAT for various disk capacities.

TABLE 10.1   Drive Capacity Versus Cluster Size in 16-Bit FAT Systems

Drive Capacity	Cluster Size
0 to 15MB	8KB
16 to 127MB	2KB
128MB to 255MB	4KB
256MB to 511MB	8KB
512 MB to 1,023MB	16KB
1,024MB to 2,047MB	32KB

Microsoft's 16-bit FAT structure imposes another problem, a maximum supported disk size of 2GB. In the fall of 1996 Microsoft quietly revised its FAT system to accommodate 32-bit entries. The new system, called FAT32, reserves 4 of its 32 bits for future purposes, so each cluster is actually identified with a 28-bit value. Using FAT32, Windows 95 accommodates drives up to 2,048GB and on smaller disks stores files more efficiently with smaller clusters (see Table 10.2).

TABLE 10.2   Drive Capacity Versus Cluster Size in 32-Bit FAT Systems

Drive Capacity	Cluster Size
0 up to 6GB	4KB
6GB up to 16GB	8KB
16GB up to 32GB	16KB
32GB up to 2,048GB	32KB

Microsoft eased FAT32 onto the market. It first became available in Windows 95 version 950b, which was offered only to PC manufacturers for pre-loading on their products. It is now a standard part of Windows 98 and NT 4.0.

Microsoft elected not to provide FAT32 as a consumer update for Windows 95 because it could not be installed as an easy revision. FAT32 required updates to all the Windows 95 disk-based utilities such as FDISK, SCANDISK, and DEFRAG as well as the disk driver (VFAT.VXD). You must re-partition your hard disk and start from scratch. Moreover, your old third-party utilities (think Norton) won't work under FAT32, so you must contact the publisher of your utilities for updates. The better strategy is to move to Windows 98, which natively supports FAT32.

If you don't want to change over to Windows 98, you can trim the cluster waste without the hassle of upgrading to FAT32. All you need is DriveSpace 3, which is included on Microsoft's Plus! Utilities disk. DriveSpace allocates files in sectors of 512 bytes instead of clusters, eliminating the cluster overhead entirely. Moreover, if you're worried about the reliability of disk-compression, you can install DriveSpace 3 *without* compression by selecting No Compression (Fastest) from the Advanced settings menu and then installing DriveSpace. If you have a lot of small files on your system, you can save dozens of megabytes of disk space.

Compression

The DriveSpace file system used by Windows works with individual sectors instead of clusters when storing compressed data in the compressed volume file. The file system takes uncompressed data one cluster at a time and maps it in compressed form into sectors in the compressed volume file. To locate which sector belongs to each file, it used a special FAT called the MDFAT (Microsoft DoubleSpace FAT, DoubleSpace being the DriveSpace predecessor), which encodes the first sector used for storing a given cluster, the number of sectors required for coding the cluster, and the number of the cluster in the uncompressed volume that's stored in those sectors. When the operating system needs the data from a file, the file system first searches for the clusters in the main disk FAT and then looks up the corresponding starting and length values from the MDFAT. With that information, the operating system locates the data, uncompresses it, and passes it along to your applications.

To speed up operations when writing compressed data to disk, the operating system uses a second kind of FAT in the compressed volume file. Called the BitFAT, this structure reports which sectors reserved in the compressed volume file hold active data and which are empty. The BitFAT uses only one bit for each sector as a flag to indicate whether a sector is occupied.

New Technology File System

Windows NT and Windows 2000 give you two choices for file systems, the same old FAT-based system used since time began and the newer Windows NT File System, usually termed NTFS.

The centerpiece of the NTFS is the *Master File Table*, which stores all of the data describing each directory and file on a given disk. The basic data about each file is contained in a file record in the Master File Table. These file records may be two, four, or eight sectors long (that is, 1KB, 2KB, or 4KB). The first 16 records are reserved for system use to hold data of special *metadata* files, the first of which stored the attributes of the Master File Table itself.

To NTFS, a file is a collection of *attributes*, each of which describes some aspect of the file. One of the attributes is the name of the file; another is the data contained in the file. Others may include who worked on the file and when it was last modified. The Master File Table tracks these attributes. To identify attributes, the file system assigns each file a unique ID number, a 48-bit value (allowing nearly 300 trillion entries).

Instead of the clusters used by the FAT system, NTFS uses the sector as its basic unit of storage. Sectors on a disk or partition are identified by Relative Sector Numbers, each of which is 32 bits long—sufficient to encode 4,294,967,296 sectors or a total disk space of 2,048GB. Sectors are numbered sequentially, starting with the first one in the partition. Files are allocated in multiples of single sectors; directories, however, are made from one or more blocks of four sectors.

Each file or directory on the disk is identified by its File NODE, which stores descriptive data about the file or directory. This information includes file attributes, creation date, modification dates, access dates, sizes, and a pointer that indicates in which sector the data in the file is stored. Each File NODE is one sector (512 bytes) long. Up to 254 bytes of the File NODE of a disk file store an extended file name, which can include uppercase and lowercase characters, some punctuation (for example, periods), and spaces.

An NTFS disk organized its storage from a root directory. In an NTFS system, however, the root directory does not have a fixed location or size. Instead, the root directory is identified by reference to the disk Super Block, which is a special sector that is always kept as the 16th sector from the beginning of the HPFS partition. The 12th and 13th bytes— that is, at an offset of 0C(Hex) from the start of the block—of the Super Block points to the location of the root directory File NODE. Free space on the disk is identified by a bitmapped table.

As with other FNODEs, a pointer in the root directory FNODE stores the location of the first block of four sectors assigned to the root directory. The root directory is identical to the other directories in the HPFS hierarchy, and like them, it can expand or shrink as the number of files it contains changes. If the root directory needs to expand beyond its initial four sectors, it splits into a tree-like structure. The File NODE of the root directory then points to the base File NODE of the tree, and each pointer in the tree points to one directory entry and possibly a pointer to another directory node that may in turn point to entries whose names are sorted before the pointer entry. This structure provides a quick path for finding a particular entry, along with a simple method of scanning all entries.

NTFS can accommodate any length file (that will fit in the partition, of course) by assigning multiple sectors to it. These sectors need not be contiguous. NTFS, however, pre-allocates sectors to a file at the time it is opened, so a file may be assigned sectors that do not contain active data. The File NODE of the file maintains an accurate total of the sectors that are actually used for storing information. This pre-allocation scheme helps prevent files from becoming fragmented. Normally, the block of sectors assigned to a file will be contiguous, and the file will not become fragmented until all the contiguous sectors have been used up.

Two types of sectors are used to track the sectors assigned a given file. For files that have few fragments, the File NODE maintains a list of all the relative sector numbers of the first sector in a block of sectors used by the file as well as the total number of sectors in the file before those of each block. To capture all the data in a file, the operating system finds the relative sector number of the first block of sectors used by the file and the total number of sectors in the block. It then checks the next relative sector number and keeps counting with a running total of sectors in the file.

If a file has many fragments, it uses a tree-style table of pointers to indicate the location of each block of sectors. The entry in the file's File NODE table then stores pointers to the sectors, which themselves store pointers to the data. Each of these sectors identifies itself as to whether it points to data or more pointers with a special flag.

Besides its huge capacity, NTFS has significant advantages when dealing with large hierarchies of directories, directories containing large number of files, and large files. Although both the NTFS and FAT use tree-structured directory systems, the directories in the NTFS are not arranged like a tree. Each directory gets stored in a tree-like structure that, coupled with the pre-sorting of entries automatically performed by the NTFS, allows faster searches of large directories. NTFS also arranges directories on the disk to reduce the time required to access them; instead of starting at the edge of the disk, they fan out from the center.

The Master File Table attempts to store all the attributes of a file in the record it associates with that file. When the attributes of a file grow too large to be held in the MFT record, the NTFS just spreads the attribute data across as many additional disk clusters records to create as many *non-resident attributes* as are needed to hold the file. The Master

File Table keeps track of all the records containing the attributes associated with a given file by the file's ID number.

This system allows any file to grow as large as the complete storage space available while preserving a small allocation unit size. No matter how large a disk or partition, NTFS never allocates space in increments larger than 4KB.

Capacity Limits

Over the years, the capacities of hard disks in PCs have been constrained by a number of limits, as small as 10MB as noted in Table 10.3. Today, only two primary limits remain, and these should gradually fade from importance. From the box, Windows NT 4.0 suffers a 2GB constraint on boot volumes. Early Windows 95 and NT systems using the old 16-bit FAT system suffer a similar limit on all partitions. Although later Windows 95 did not suffer such a constraint nor do systems running Windows 98 or Windows 2000, the BIOS of some PCs may limit access to hard disks larger than 8GB.

TABLE 10.3   Chief Historic Hard Disk Capacity Constraints

Limit	Maximum Bytes	Primary Cause
10MB	10,485,760	Hardware design
16MB	16,777,216	12-bit FAT
32MB	33,554,432	Number of FAT entries (16KB)
128MB	134,217,728	2KB cluster size
528MB	528,482,304	Mismatch between ATA and BIOS
2GB	2,147,483,648	16-bit FAT
8GB	8,589,934,592	24-bit LBA addresses

The 16-bit FAT structure was the culprit that imposed the 2GB limit on early Windows 95 partitions. The maximum cluster size supported by the operating system was 64 sectors or 32,768 bytes. That cluster size and the maximum of 65,536 FAT entries resulted in a maximum addressable partition size of 2,147,483,648 bytes, or 2GB. Moving to a 32-bit FAT with the latter Windows 95 version breaks through this limit.

Logical Block Addressing suffers from its own disk addressing limit. The chief constraint of LBA is the address size. Both the early standard SCSI and AT Attachment (IDE or EIDE) interfaces allocated 24 bits to block addresses. This scheme permitted a maximum of 16,777,216 blocks. Because PCs work with disk sectors of 512 bytes, this allowed for a maximum addressable physical disk size of 8,589,934,592 bytes, or 8GB, using current forms of logical block addressing.

Of course, larger disks are now in everyday use, and the standards have been amended to accommodate them. During the transition to the new standards, PC makers got around the old limits by instructing their systems to wield larger blocks of data. By doubling sector size to 1KB, they doubled the addressable capacity. Quadrupling sector size quadrupled addressable capacity, and so on.

The 8GB limit may be enforced by factors in the BIOSs of earlier PCs. If your PC refuses to allow you to create a partition larger than 8GB, your first step should be to seek a BIOS upgrade for your PC.

Another solution is to use special drive installation software such as On-Track Computer System's Disk Manager and Storage Dimension's SpeedStor, which install driver software to enable your system to handle larger drives.

Performance Issues

When shopping for hard disks, many people become preoccupied with disk performance. They believe that some drives find and transfer information faster than others. They're right. But the differences between state-of-the-art hard disk drives are much smaller than they used to be, and in a properly setup system, the remaining differences can be almost completely equalized.

The performance of a hard disk is directly related to design choices in making the mechanism. The head actuator has the greatest effect on the speed at which data can be retrieved from the disk, the number of platters exerting a smaller effect. Because the head actuator designs used by hard disk makers have converged, as have the number of platters per drive because of the height restrictions of modern form factors, the performance of various products has also converged.

Clearly, however, all hard disks don't deliver the same performance. The differences are particularly obvious when you compare a drive that's a few years old with a current product. Understanding the issues involved in hard disk performance will help you better appreciate the strides made by the industry in the last few years and show you what improvements may still lie ahead.

Average Access Time

You've already encountered the term latency, which indicates the average delay in finding a given bit of data imposed because of the spin of the disk. Another factor also influences how long elapses between the moment the disk drive receives a request to reveal what's stored at a given place on the disk and when the drive is actually ready to read or write at that place—the speed at which the read/write head can move radially from one cylinder to another. This speed is expressed in a number of ways, often as a seek time. Track-to-track seek time indicates the period required to move the head from one track to the next.

More important, however, is the average access time (sometimes rendered as average seek time), which specifies how long it takes the read/write head to move on the average to any cylinder (or radial position). Lower average access times, expressed in milliseconds, are better.

The type of head actuator technology, the mass of the actuator assembly, the physical power of the actuator itself, and the width of the data area on the disk all influence average access time. Smaller drives have some inherent advantages in minimizing average access time. Their smaller, lighter head and actuators have less inertia and can accelerate and settle down faster. More closely spaced tracks mean the head need travel a shorter distance in skipping between them when seeking data.

Real-world access times vary by more than a factor of 10. The first PC-size hard disks had access times hardly better than floppy disks, sometimes as long as 150 milliseconds. The newest drives are usually below 10 milliseconds; some are closer to 6 milliseconds.

How low an average access time you need depends mostly on your impatience. Quicker is always better and typically more costly. You can feel the difference between a slow and fast drive when you use your PC, particularly when you don't have sufficient memory to hold all the applications you run simultaneously. Once access time is below about 10 microseconds, however, you may be hard-pressed to pay the price of improvement.

Disk makers have explored all sorts of exotic technologies to reduce access time. Some primeval hard disks had a dozen or more fixed heads scanning huge disks. Because the heads didn't move, the access time was close to zero—more correctly, half the latency of the drive. About a decade ago, drive makers experimented with dual-actuator drives; two heads mean less than half the waiting because with an intelligent controller, the drive could overlap read and write requests. None of these technologies made it into the PC mainstream because an even better idea—one much simpler and cheaper—has taken the forefront, the disk array (a technology now more commonly termed RAID for Redundant Array of Inexpensive Drives). Instead of multiple actuators, RAID relies on multiple *drives* to cut access time. At the same time, RAID can increase transfer rate and reliability.

Advanced disk controllers, particularly those used in disk arrays, are able to minimize the delays cause by head seeks using a technique called elevator seeking. When confronted with several read or write requests for different disk tracks, the controller organizes the requests in the way that moves the head the least between seeks. Like an elevator, it courses through the seek requests from the lower numbered tracks to the higher numbered tracks and then goes back on the next requests, first taking care of the higher numbered tracks and working its way back to the lower numbered tracks. The data gathered for each individual request is stored in the controller and doled out at the proper time.

Elevator seeking improves performance in drive systems that receive multiple requests for data near simultaneously. DOS and its offspring Windows 95 and 98 are single-threaded operating systems (no matter what Microsoft says) and cannot take full advantage of this access-acceleration technique. DOS requires that each seek request be fulfilled before it sends the next to the disk. In systems based on Windows NT and Windows 2000 as well as most network operating systems, however, multiple seek requests can and do occur simultaneously. Elevator seeking can substantially cut the disk access time in such systems.

Data Transfer Rate

Once a byte or record is found on the disk, it must be transferred to the host computer. Another disk system specification, the data transfer rate, reflects how fast bytes are batted back and forth, affecting how quickly information can shuttle between microprocessor and hard disk. The transfer rate of a disk is controlled by a number of design factors completely separate from those of the average access time.

Through the years, the factor constraining the transfer rate of particular computer systems has shifted from the host microprocessor, to the disk interface, to the bus, and the disk drive. With the microprocessors in the earliest PCs (those made before 1984), for example, even the slowest disks dished out data faster than the system could possibly consume it. The next generation systems were faster than the early disk interfaces. Once drive makers conquered that problem, they faced constraints enforced by the ISA expansion bus. When PCI broke that barrier, the drive mechanism itself began to set the limit. As a result, the speed at which disks spin has become one of the more important measures in disk performance.

The transfer rate of a hard disk is expressed in megahertz (MHz) or megabytes per second (or MB/sec, which is one eighth the megahertz rate). The very first hard disks (those that followed the now-ancient ST506 standard) suffered a peak transfer rate of 0.625 MB/sec. Today's best drives do a bit better—the Ultra 2 Wide SCSI interface can pass along information at 80MB/sec—if the drive's heads can read data fast enough. UltraDMA or ATA-4 Mode 2 hard disks peak at 33 MB/sec; UDMA/66 or ATA-5 Mode 4 disks reach up to 66 MB/sec.

Today's disk and bus interfaces are rarely the bottlenecks constricting disk transfer rates. Although hard disk interface speed far exceeds the maximum potential of the ISA expansion bus, about 8 MB/sec, they are well within the 132 MB/sec capabilities of the basic PCI bus. Physical factors in the construction of the drive nearly always constrain the transfer rate to values below the potential of the bus or interface. The primary constraint results from the combination of the speed of a disk's spin and its track density—that is, the number of 512-byte sectors in each track. The faster the platter spins and the denser the data on each track, the more information that passes under the read/write head in a given period. With device-level interfaces, this raw stream of data is what is passed through the interface; the product of spin speed and the capacity of each track yields the raw data rate.

Note that the interface used by a hard disk does not accurately portray the sustained transfer rate. The drive can only maintain that speed while its on-board buffer is discharged. It is then constrained by how quickly it can physically read data from the disk. As a result, rotation rate gives a good (but still approximate) indication of drive transfer performance.

Disk Caching

The ultimate means of isolating your PC from the mechanical vagaries of hard disk seeking is disk caching. Caching eliminates the delays involved in seeking when a read request (or write request in a system that supports write caching) involves data already stored in the cache; the information is retrieved at RAM speed. Similarly, the cache pushes the transfer rate of data stored in the cache up to the ceiling imposed by the slowest interface between the cache and host microprocessor. With an on-disk cache, the drive interface will likely be the primary constraint; with a hardware cache in the disk controller or host adapter, the bus interface is the limit; with a software cache, microprocessor and memory access speed are the only constraints.

AV Drives

Multimedia and non-linear editing are popular applications for large capacity drives that have their own particular needs. They demand almost sequential access to the storage system to store and retrieve long sections of real-time audio and video data. For such applications, drive makers developed *AV drives* that are optimized for audio and video applications.

More important than capacity is speed. Unlike normal hard disks that must provide instant access to completely random data, AV drives are designed for high-speed sequential access. Audio and video files tend to be long and linear, read sequentially for long periods. Access time is not as important for such applications as is a high sustained data transfer rate. For example, most video production today requires data rates of 27MB/sec but use compression ratios averaging about 10 to 1 to produce a data stream of about 2.7MB/sec that needs to be stored and retrieved. To achieve the highest possible performance, they add extensive buffering and may sacrifice or delay some data integrity features.

To handle AV data as fast as possible, AV drives generally have very high rotational rates, some up to 10,000 RPM, and newer drives will undoubtedly climb higher. In addition, most include large embedded buffers so that they can maintain high data throughputs even when incrementing between tracks and encountering errors. AV drives also attempt to maintain data contiguity, keeping sequential sectors in the data stream together so that head movement can be minimized.

To achieve the high transfer rates required by video applications, AV drives need to use every speed-up trick they can find. These run a wide range, and most involve trading off absolute data security to eliminate interruptions in the high-speed flow of information. The hard disk industry rationale for this design is that video data, unlike spreadsheets or databases, tolerates errors well, so a short sequence of bad data won't hurt anything. After all, a single sector isn't even a third of a line of uncompressed video. The video subsystem can correct for such one-time errors in part of a line, masking them entirely.

One way to prevent interruptions in the flow of data is to alter error handling. Engineers usually require that most hard disk drives attempt to reread the disk when they encounter an error. Most manufacturers use elaborate algorithms to govern these rereads, often minutely changing the head position or performing an entire thermal calibration. If these are not successful, the drive may invoke its error-correction code to reconstruct the data. AV drives alter these priorities. Because error correction is entirely electronic and imposes no mechanical delays, AV drives use it first to attempt error recovery. Only after error correction fails may the drive try to reread the data, often for a limited number of retries.

Advanced hard disks log the errors that they encounter so that they may be used later for diagnostics. The logging operation itself takes time and slows disk performance. AV drives delay error logging until it does not interrupt the data stream.

One feature that slows down conventional drives is sector remapping, which AV drives avoid to eliminate its performance penalties. The remapping process imposes delays on the flow of data because the read/write head of the drive must jump from one place to another to write or retrieve the data from the remapped sector at the time of the data access. AV drives often avoid auto-relocation to prevent interruption of the flow of high-speed data.

The possibility of uncorrected errors occurring in the reading and writing of your data makes AV drives unsuitable for critical data applications. When used for their design purpose, however, AV drives deliver excellent performance with reasonable levels of risk.

Installation

Installing a hard disk drive involves several issues. You must physically fit the drive into your PC—or find some other place to put it. You must make the various electrical connections to it, not only the control and data signals that travel through the interface but also power and, usually, a drive activity indicator. You'll find these physical issues discussed in Chapter 25.

Once you have your drive in place and spinning, you're still not finished. Despite all the wiring you've done, all the skinned knuckles, and all the curses that have driven both friends and family to some place where the air is cleaner, your PC may not know, understand, or believe that you've actually done any work. It may simply refuse to recognize your handiwork until you tell it what you've done. In other words, you have to reconfigure your PC so that it can operate your drive.

There's more. Depending on the kindness of your drive supplier (or lack of same), you may be stuck with the several steps of the logical preparation of the drive. Although few hard disks today require low-level formatting, you may still need to partition and format your drive before you can use it. In spite of all the seeming complications that computer and mass storage industries have shoved in your way, the installation process can be straightforward, manageable, and even easy, if you take it one step at a time.

As with any hardware you install in your PC, the process of adding or replacing a hard disk varies with the vintage of the system and the software that you use. Before Windows 95 and the advent of Plug and Play, the process involved was entirely manual. The new innovations simplify some steps but leave many of the configuration steps unchanged.

The process of matching a drive to your PC has several steps. First, you must identify the kind of drive you have so that your system knows how to use it. You may then need to add a low-level format. Next, you decide on how to divide up the capacity of the drive, assigning it to one or more partitions. Finally, you format each partition individually. The various steps of the process take different forms depending on the operating system that you use.

Of course, before you need to worry about any of these steps, you must prepare any drive you want to install to match your PC. The preparatory steps depend on the interface that it uses and are explained in Chapter 8, "Mass Storage Technology." Here's a quick summary to get you started: The majority of new drives will be either EIDE or SCSI. You must configure the EIDE drive as master or slave, depending how you want it to work in your PC. You must assign an unused device ID and properly set the termination of any SCSI drive that you install. Once your drive is configured, you can plug it into the appropriate cable.

Drive Recognition

Once your hard disk is physically installed and properly connected to your PC, you must ensure that your system recognizes the drive. Nothing is quite so frustrating as plugging in a new hard disk, switching on your PC, and not finding a new drive letter. Before a hard disk will be recognized by most PC operating systems as a new drive letter, your PC needs to know that you've installed the drive and the drive itself must have electronic markings on it that the operating system can identify. Sometimes, your PC will automatically recognize when you've installed a new drive. With some interfaces and older PCs, however, you must let your system know that you've added a hard disk by identifying its parameters using your system's setup procedure. Your PC adds the necessary electronic markings to the drive when you partition it. Until you've partitioned a new drive, your operating system will not recognize it (unless, of course, the supplier of the drive has been kind enough to partition it for you). Older hard disks may require low-level formatting before you can partition them.

The process of preparing your drive so that your PC will recognize it consequently requires as many as three steps: using BIOS setup to identify drive parameters, low-level formatting, and partitioning. Most new drives will require only the last of these steps.

BIOS Setup

Ordinarily, the BIOS setup of a modern hard disk only requires that you check to be sure your system properly configured itself automatically. When it boots up, your PC's BIOS will search for the hard disk drives that are installed in your system, query them as to make, model, and setup parameters, and then add the appropriate values to its drive tables.

If you are installing a new disk in an old PC or an old disk in a new PC, however, the automatic setup may not work; your drive may lack the ability to identify itself or the BIOS may be unable to query the drive. In such situations, your PC will need to know how many cylinders, heads, and sectors to use—and perhaps more esoteric information such as write pre-compensation and landing zone identification—before it can take control and test the drive.

A few old, small drives let you choose the drive settings by drive type, a numeric value from 1 to 15 (or 45 or so). Of course, you need to know the type number your PC maker assigned to the make and model of the hard disk that you have. These values differed among PC makers, so setup could be a challenge. During the transition to modern automatic drive typing, most PCs allowed you to enter custom configuration values for your hard disk. With these systems, you would typically select drive type 47 (or another value that your BIOS may reserve for this function), and then you enter the parameters used by your drive.

Note that both the drive type number and the user-configurable parameters get stored in CMOS memory. If your old PC's CMOS loses power because its battery runs down or gets disconnected and your PC cannot automatically identify your drive, your system won't be able to boot up. Your PC simply won't be able to locate the drive. You will have to reenter the parameters through the normal BIOS setup procedures. If when you boot up your PC fails to recognize a hard disk that has otherwise been working well, the first thing to check is the drive type in your BIOS setup.

Low-Level Formatting

A new hard disk is like a newborn babe: Although some abilities are built in, its mind and memory are essentially blank. It has to learn about the world before it can do what it was designed for. For example, many drives must construct the individual sectors that they use for storage from the undifferentiated lengths of individual tracks.

Much like floppy disk drives, the organization of a hard disk drive is called its format. Hard disks differ from floppies in that two levels of organization wear the same title—the low-level format and the operating system format. Both are necessary to use a given disk, and each has its own role and requires it own procedure to set up.

Nearly all hard disk drives are sold with their low-level formats already in place so you ordinarily don't have to go through the low-level process with a new drive. Some older drives, in fact, warn that you should not low-level format them at all. When something goes really awry with your system and you want to obliterate all traces of your operating system and disk partitions, low-level formatting may be recommended.

Modern drives know how to low-level format themselves. You just have to tell them to start the process. Most new PC BIOSs allow you to start the process through your PC's setup procedure. Usually, you'll find a "disk utilities" or "disk maintenance" option that will give you access to the low-level formatting procedure. SCSI host adapters typically include similar access through *their* setup procedure.

With some old disks and systems, you may encounter the need to deal with *bad tracks*. In the manufacture of hard disk platters, defects occasionally occur in the magnetic medium. These defects will not properly record data. Sectors in which these defects occur are called *bad sectors*; the tracks containing the sectors are, as you may have guessed, the bad tracks.

Modern hard disks incorporate automatic defect management. They find bad spots in their media and automatically remap them. Because the drive takes care of defect management, your PC never knows that there are bad spots on the hard disk. Your PC sees a perfect disk. Although Logical Block Addressing makes automatic defect management particularly easy, any drive with sector translation can use the technology. Only drives that use direct physical addressing cannot use this technology.

Older drives that lack automatic defect management require some help from your PC. Your computer can deal with bad sectors by locking them out of normal use. During the low-level formatting process, the sectors that do not work properly are recorded and your system is prevented from using them. The only ill effect of reserving these bad sectors is that the available capacity of your hard disk may diminish by a small amount.

Some low-level formatting programs require that you enter bad sector data before you begin the formatting process. Although this seems redundant—the format program checks for them anyhow—it's not. Factory checks for bad sectors are more rigorous than the format routine. This close scrutiny helps minimize future failure. Tedious as it is, you should enter the bad sector data when the low-level format program calls for it. The list of bad sectors is usually on a sheet of paper accompanying the disk drive or on a label affixed to the drive itself.

The only time that a bad sector is an evil thing is when it occurs on the first track of the disk. The first track (Track 0) is used to hold partition and booting data. This information must be located on the first track of the disk. If it cannot be written there, the disk won't work. Should you get a hard disk with a bad Track 0, return it to the dealer from whom you bought it. If you reformat a disk after a head crash and discover Track 0 is bad during the format process, you need a new disk.

Partitioning

Once the low-level format is in place on a hard disk, you must partition it. Partitioning is a function of the operating system. It sets up the logical structure of the hard disk to a form that is compatible with the operating system.

Under Windows 95 and Windows 98, you must partition your hard disk in MS DOS mode or from the MS DOS prompt by running a utility called FDISK. If you don't, you'll get an error message when you boot up your system. You'll find FDISK in the COMMAND folder in your WINDOWS folder of your C: drive.

In general, partitioning is a way that you divide your physical hard disk into the equivalent of several logical disk drives. Each behaves as if it were a separate hard disk. The purpose of partitioning is threefold: It helps organize your disk; it allows you to take advantage of larger disks than the logical structure of your operating system may be able to handle; and it allows you to keep several separate operating systems and file systems on one physical disk drive.

Your PC keeps track of disk partitions using a master partition table located in the first physical sector of a hard disk. It is offset from the start of the disk—that is, sector 00(Hex), cylinder 00(Hex), head 00(Hex)—by 364 bytes. In other words, the master partition table is at offset 01BE(Hex) from the beginning of your hard disk. The master partition table consists of 64 bytes, which is subdivided into four 16-byte entries to accommodate the four possible partitions. Each one is identified as to its type using an ID number.

Extended DOS partitions each have their own partition tables to store the values needed to define their logical volumes (known as extended volumes). Each of these extended volumes starts with its own extended partition table that uses a format identical to the master partition table. If a disk has more than one extended volume, the extended partition table of the first points to the next volume, so the partition tables form a chain.

The first byte in the master partition table is a boot flag; it indicates whether the partition is bootable. A bootable partition has a value of 80(Hex) here (and has the necessary code to boot the system in its first sector). Non-bootable partitions are marked with the value 00(Hex). Of DOS partitions, only the primary partition is bootable.

The partition table defines the size of a partition by its starting and ending sectors. The three bytes starting at offset 01(Hex) encode the starting head, sector, and cylinder numbers. The three bytes starting at 05(Hex) encode the ending head, sector, and cylinder numbers. In both cases, the head number is a full byte value; the sector number is coded as the lower six bits of the second byte; and the cylinder number takes the upper two bits of this byte and all eight bits of the next byte. Together, these values define the maximum disk geometry that this partitioning scheme can accommodate: 256 heads (8 bits); 64 sectors (6 bits); and 1,024 cylinders (10 bits).

The byte trapped between the starting and ending sector data at offset 04(Hex) is the System Indicator Byte, which defines the file system used inside the partition.

A double word (four bytes) at offset 08(Hex) stores the starting sector number relative to the first sector on the disk. Another double word at 0C(Hex) stores the length of the partition in sectors.

Left to itself, your operating system will automatically assign drive letters to your disks and partitions. When your PC boots up, your PC normally scans through the partition table to find the boot partition. As the boot process unfolds, Windows assigns logical drive letters to each volume that it sets up. First, it searches through all of the physical hard disks in your system that contain primary partitions and assigns them identifying letters in sequence starting with C: for the boot drive. After all primary partitions have been identified, it continues to assign drive letters to volumes in extended partitions, dealing with all the volumes of one physical hard disk before going on to the next.

You can override these automatic choices using various utilities.

FDISK as used by Windows 95 and Windows 98 is a primitive and unyielding program that forces you to make menu choices and requires that you make the choices in the correct order. Figure 10.2 shows the initial screen from the latest incarnation of FDISK, that included with Windows 98.

FIGURE 10.2

Initial screen of the FDISK disk partitioning program.

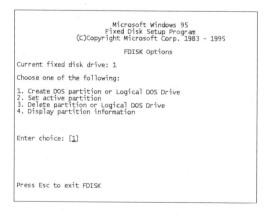

```
                        Microsoft Windows 95
                        Fixed Disk Setup Program
                  (C)Copyright Microsoft Corp. 1983 - 1995

                          FDISK Options

Current fixed disk drive: 1

Choose one of the following:

1. Create DOS partition or Logical DOS Drive
2. Set active partition
3. Delete partition or Logical DOS Drive
4. Display partition information


Enter choice: [1]




Press Esc to exit FDISK
```

In general operation, FDISK will prompt you in the correct order for the necessary functions, selecting first to create a new partition, recommending the maximum size for the partition, and setting the partition active. The only time to select less than the maximum FDISK permits for partition size is should you want to divide your drive into separate partitions, each with its own drive letter, for ease of access or to minimize cluster size. If you do not use the entire disk for your first partition, you can create more partitions and then assign a logical drive letter to each.

FDISK does not allow you to alter the size of partitions once you've made them. You must first delete the partitions on your disk and then start from the beginning should you want to change the configuration or size of the partitions on your disk. If you change the partitions on your hard disk, you will lose their previous contents. Back up first.

Some SCSI hard disks present a problem to Windows 95 or Windows 98. They need to be configured for Interrupt 13 access before Windows can properly partition them. To adjust this setting through Windows, select Device Manager from the System icon in the Control Panel folder, which you can open from the Settings selection from the Start button. Or right-click your mouse on the My Computer icon, select Properties from the menu that pops up, and then select the Device Manager option.

Select the disk drive you want to partition. Device Manager will display an entry for hard disks. Click the plus sign to the left of Disk Drive entry to list the drives installed in your PC. You will see a display like that shown in Figure 10.3.

FIGURE 10.3

Properties screen for the selected disk drive.

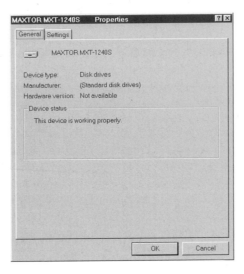

Most SCSI host adapters will automatically set the Interrupt 13 option and not allow you to change it. In such cases, Windows will check the selection and gray it out, as shown in Figure 10.4.

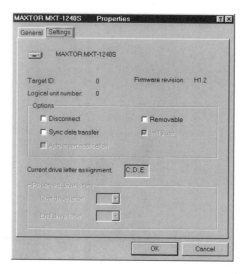

If when you open the Setting tab you see that the Interrupt 13 option is not selected, put
your mouse on the box to the right of Int13 Unit and click to put a check mark in the
box. Click Okay and then reboot your system from the Shut Down selection from the
Start button. You can then partition your SCSI hard disk. Although these steps are not
necessary for most hard disks, Microsoft recommends that you go through the preliminary steps to assure your SCSI hard disk is marked as an Int13 Unit.

Formatting

The final step in preparing a disk for use is formatting it with the operating system you
intend to use. With Windows 95 or Windows 98, that means selecting Format from the
file menu when you've highlighted the icon for the drive or running the FORMAT program from the MS-DOS prompt. The "fast format" option of the current FORMAT program does not overwrite the data areas of a hard disk (which means it won't rejuvenate
them). It simply refreshes the file allocation table. (That's why you can unformat disks; by
storing a copy of the FAT elsewhere on the disk, the unformatting program can reconstruct the FAT to find all the files hidden by the formatting operation.)

Reliability

You trust your valuable data to your hard disk. You naturally expect to be able to find what
you want when you want it. You don't want to see such ominous messages as "General
Disk Failure" when you're preparing next year's budget (or explaining what went awry
with last year's). You want your drive to be as reliable as, say, a brick.

Unfortunately, judging the reliability of the average hard disk these days by just looking at it is about as worthwhile as looking at a brick. Little of the electronics is visible and even less of the mechanism. For all intents, purposes, and assessments, the hard disk is a sealed black box that won't reveal its secrets without the aid of a can opener. And should you use such means to investigate a disk in the store, your salesperson will be happy to present you with a bill for your subject drive after he recovers from his myocardial infarction.

MTBF

Your alternative is taking the salesperson's word, and at best he'll quote whatever lies the drive maker tells him. Most of these lies are numeric, the most commonly quoted being the Mean Time Between Failures, or MTBF.

The MTBF of a hard disk should give you a general indication of its reliability, but today the figures are almost ridiculous. Where drives were once rated at about 25,000 hours, most are now rated in the range 100,000 to 160,000 hours; that's 11 to 18 years. Some manufacturers now list their MTBF figures as 300,000 or more hours—34 years. Your PC (or you, for that matter) should last as long. A long MTBF is an assurance of a long-lasting drive. But you'll also want to consider how the manufacturer backs up its MTBF claim. A 500,000-hour MTBF is meaningless if the manufacturer gives you only a 90-day warranty.

S.M.A.R.T. Technology

Most disk drive failures need not be surprises. The typical disk fails like a sinking ship, slowly slipping into the abyss. If the captain can give the warning to abandon ship soon enough—and if life jackets are available—everyone on board could be saved. If you know your disk is slowing dying, you can back up your files and be prepared for the ultimate disaster.

The trick is for the disk to warn you about an impending failure *before* your data get lost—and that's precisely the goal of Self-Monitoring, Analysis and Reporting Technology, or S.M.A.R.T., a feature of most modern hard disk drives. As the name implies, S.M.A.R.T. puts the disk drive to work monitoring its own health. It analyzes the operation of the drive and reports to your PC when the drive begins to act as though it is in its death throes. S.M.A.R.T. does not extend the life of a disk drive nor does it automatically protect you from failures. It is only an early warning system—and a limited one at that. S.M.A.R.T. does not warn before any and all failures, only some of them, and fortunately the majority of them. Just as a lifeboat cannot guarantee your survival, S.M.A.R.T. gives you an extra chance, reducing the odds that you'll lose vital information.

Disks fail in a variety of ways. Some failures are unpredictable and usually catastrophic. Others involve the gradual degradation of the operation of one or more parameters of the drive. The drive can monitor these parameters and when it detects one becoming marginal or close to failure, it can issue a warning.

The various S.M.A.R.T. standards govern how predicted failures get reported to your PC and the response to the warning but do not cover the conditions inside the drive that result in warnings. Each drive maker choose which parameters to monitor and how to interpret the changes that occur within the drive. In general, there are several parameters that may indicate a hard disk drive is failing. Some of these factors include

- **The height at which the read/write head flies.** A decrease in flying height may lead to a head crash.

- **The data throughput of the drive.** Throughput decreases as errors cause the drive to retry read or write operations, which indicate impending unreliability.

- **The time required for the drive to spin up to speed.** A longer spin-up time can indicate bearing or lubricant degradation or even an electronic degradation that may lead to failure.

- **Sectors that get automatically relocated.** Most drives automatically and invisibly move data to safe sectors. Many sectors requiring relocation in a short time indicates a failing drive.

- **The number of errors encountered in seeking data.** Read errors indicate an impending failure in the medium, head, or electronics of the drive.

- **The speed at which the drive can access data.** If the drive encounters errors and must make multiple tries to read data, its seek time will increase.

- **The number of retries required to read data.** An increase in the count of the number of errors encountered presages drive failure.

- **The number of times the drive must recalibrate itself.** Drives periodically calibrate themselves to optimize their operation. A drive that must retry its calibration repeatedly is suffering degradation that may lead to failure.

History

S.M.A.R.T. represents the combination of two independently developed error prediction systems. In the early 1990s, IBM developed a technology call Predictive Failure Analysis (PFA) for hard disk drives that monitored several disk attributes such as the flying height of the read/write head to anticipate failures. Later Compaq, in conjunction with drive makers Conner, Quantum, and Seagate, developed its own failure prediction system, which it called IntelliSafe. On May 12, 1995, Compaq put its technology in the public domain through the Small Form Factor Committee at its specification SFF-8035. The five largest American disk drive makers at the time then joined together to develop S.M.A.R.T. by combining IntelliSafe, PFA, and original ideas.

Standards

S.M.A.R.T. is not a single standard. The two major disk drive interfaces, ATA and SCSI, use different signaling systems, which have their own requirements for reporting through the connection system. Consequently, S.M.A.R.T. works differently under the two standards, although a given drive mechanism will monitor the same conditions no matter its interface. Only the means of reporting varies.

The Small Form Factor Committee SFF-8035 still governs S.M.A.R.T. in the ATA environment. In the SCSI environment, the equivalent standard is ANSI-SCSI Informational Exception Control (IEC) document X3T10/94-190.

Warranty

Rather than take the manufacturer's word, you may want to see how the manufacturer backs up what it says. That is, check the warranty. Hard disk drives may be warranted by the vendor or the manufacturer. You'll probably depend more on the vendor's warranty, so that should be your first concern.

The easy-to-quantify issue is the length of the warranty. A hard disk warranty should extend for at least 90 days. You'll find that better products—and better vendors—offer hard disk warranties measured in years.

How that warranty is honored is important. Because you have no control over what happens to a drive that you return for repair, you should prefer a warranty that gives you a replacement drive (at least if the product dies in its first few weeks of life) rather than risk getting your old drive back as a time bomb, waiting to go off the second the warranty expires.

Manufacturers' warranties are trickier to get a handle on. In general, the warranty period starts when the product is sold to your vendor, not to you, so it may expire sooner than you think. Worse, a manufacturer may choose not to recognize its warranty if you don't buy from an authorized dealer. So it's important to clarify whether you get a manufacturer's warranty when you buy your drive.

At least the drive manufacturer has the facilities for properly handling repairs and a reputation to uphold, so you shouldn't worry about having your drive repaired rather than replaced by the manufacturer.

Support

Of course, the warranty does you no good if the drive works in the abstract but not inside your PC. Depending on the manufacturer of the hard disk, you may have one or two avenues of support for the drive you buy to help overcome such problems. In most cases, the preferred first choice for support is the vendor who sold you the drive. You'll want to check out what the drive vendor offers.

Before you buy, ask the salesman about his company's support policy. Check to see whether the vendor even has a support number. Because you'll probably install your drive in the evening, you'll want to be sure that the number is staffed at any conceivable hour you might call (around the clock). Check whether the support line is toll-free and that there are enough people to answer your questions immediately. You don't want to have to wait—perhaps forever—for someone to call you back.

Some vendors depend solely on the drive manufacturer's support staff. Drive makers run a wide range in the support they offer end users. Some won't even talk to you. They deal only with vendors, not with the real users of their products. Others prefer that you start with your dealer but will help in a pinch. Some have consumer support lines, and a few are even toll-free.

Floppy Disks

The floppy disk is the premiere data exchange medium for PCs and the most popular backup system. Except for a few notebook computers, all PCs come with at least one floppy disk drive as standard equipment. Although floppy disk drives come in a variety of sizes and capacities (disks measure from 2.5 to 8 inches in diameter and store from 160KB up to 120MB each), all work in essentially the same way.

The floppy is ubiquitous but not unique. This chapter discusses several varieties, including:

Standard	Capacity	In short
8-inch	1 MB	The original floppy disk used in small computers before such things as personal computers were developed. Now extinct.
5.25-inch	1.2 MB	The first floppy disks to be used in PCs and once the dominant standard. Some people still use them. And some people like their sushi grilled. (Why bother?)
3.5-inch	1.44 MB or 2.88 MB	Today's standard floppy disk used in both desktop and notebook PCs. The high-capacity version (2.88MB) has caught on about as well as disposable sports cars.
LS-120	120 MB	An open-standard improved floppy disk system can also read and write ordinary 3.5-inch floppies.
Zip	100 MB or 200 MB	A proprietary floppy disk system with 100MB or 200 MB capacity that's widely used for exchanging large files.
HiFD	200 MB	A proprietary floppy disk system that wants to become a standard that puts 200 MB on a 3.5-inch disk.

Since the first PC booted up, the floppy disk has been a blessing and a curse, subject of the same old saw usually reserved for kids, spouses, and governments—"You can't live with them, and you can't live without them."

You can't live without floppy disks because they provide the one universal means of information interchange, data storage, and file archiving used by PCs. They're convenient—you can stuff half a dozen floppy disks into a shirt pocket—and easy to use. Slide a disk into a slot, and you've got another megabyte or so online. Push a button, pop out the disk, and you're ready for another megabyte. No other medium is so simple and universal. Tape cartridges come in dozens of formats; cartridge disks require software drivers and their own maintenance software; CDs add that complication and make recording an expensive proposition with a recording CD drive costing as much as some PCs alone.

Despite the appeal of floppies, most people have a hard time living with floppy disks because of their frustration factor. Floppy disks have traditionally been slow and small. No matter how much a floppy disk holds, it will be a few kilobytes shy of what you need. Moreover, floppy disks are plagued by problems. Subtle magnetic differences between disks often have no apparent effect until months after you've trusted your important data to a disk that can no longer be read. A profusion of standards means you need to carefully match disks to drives, drives to controllers, and the whole kaboodle to DOS. You never seem to have the right drive to match the disk that came in the box of software—or enough space for all the drives you need to match the proliferating floppy disk standards. Indeed, floppies are like taxes—something that everyone lives with and no one likes.

Background

The floppy disk itself is only part of a system. Just as a nail is worthless in the abstract (without the hammer to drive it in place and the arm to swing the hammer), so is a floppy disk, unless you have all the other parts of the system. These include the floppy disks themselves, called the media, the floppy disk drive mechanism, the floppy disk drive controller, and the disk operating system software. All four elements are essential for the proper (and useful) operation of the system.

The floppy disk provides a recording medium that has several positive qualities. The flat disk surface allows an approximation of random access. As with hard disks, data are arranged in tracks and sectors. The disk rotates the sectors under a read/write head, which travels radially across the disk to marks off tracks. More importantly, the floppy disk is a removable medium. You can shuffle dozens of floppies in and out of drives to extend your storage capacity. The floppy disk in the drive provides online storage. Offline, you can keep as many floppy disks as you want.

The term "floppy disk" is one of those amazingly descriptive terms that abound in this age of genericisms. Inside its protective shell, the floppy disk medium is both floppy, (flexible) and a wide, flat disk. The disks are stamped out from wide rolls of the magnetic medium like cutting cookies from dough.

The wide rolls look like hyperpituitary audio or video tape, and that's no coincidence. Its composition is the same as for recording tape—a polyester substrate on which a magnetic oxide is bound. Unlike tape, however, all floppy disks are coated with magnetic material on both sides. The substrate is thicker than tape, too, about three mils, compared to one mil or less for recording tape. After all, if floppies were thinner, they'd be too floppy.

To protect it, the floppy resides in a shell. The first floppies had a truly floppy protective shell, one made out of thicker but still flexible Mylar. Today, the floppy fits into a hard case and overall is not very floppy. The disk inside, the one made from the media, remains floppy so the name remains the same—uniquely accurate in a world of computers inhabited by spinning fixed disks and recordable read-only memory.

That said, the floppy disk has taken on more forms than a schizophrenic changeling. Over the years, the floppy has adapted to various sizes, storage densities, format, and recording technologies. The traditionally magnetic-only medium has taken an optical boost to squeeze in ever more data into as little rust as possible. From an initial 160KB, floppy disk capacity has grown almost a thousand-fold, to 120MB, all while the available area for storing data was cut in half. Although some folks scoff and say that floppy disk technology hasn't kept up with processing power and hard disk capacity, all have grown at about the same rate, now with about a thousand-fold improvement from their beginnings. And all bear as little resemblance to their progenitors as we do the slime from which we arose.

History

The concept of the floppy disk arose long before the PC was conceived. When the floppy was first conceived, personal computers didn't exist and no one appeared to have any need for the medium as a data exchange. IBM is usually credited with the creation of the floppy, but one that neither looked nor operated like today's floppies. The most obvious difference between the first floppy and current disks was that it was bigger, an 8-inch disk in a slightly larger Mylar envelop (like that of the more modern 5.25-inch floppy disks). Rather than a read/write medium, it was more an early CD ROM, a read-only disk for distributing information. In particular, IBM used it to store diagnostic programs and microcode for its large computer system, instead of tape (too cumbersome and many applications didn't require such a large capacity) or memory chip (too expensive). These first floppies held about 100KB of data and program code using single-density recording on a single side of the medium. By 1973, the 8-inch floppy had been adapted to a convenient read-write medium suitable for both the original application and for storage for data-entry systems such as IBM's DisplayWriter word processing system.

The 8-inch floppy disk had a number of features going for them that made them desirable as a computer data storage medium. They were compact (at least compared to the ream of paper that could hold the same amount of information), convenient, and standardized. Above all, they were inexpensive to produce and reliable enough to depend on. From the computer hobbyists' standpoint, their random access ability made them a godsend for good performance, at least when compared to the only affordable alternative, the cassette tape.

In 1976, Shugart Associates introduced the 5.25-inch floppy disk, a timely creation that exactly complemented the first commercial PCs, introduced at about the same time. (Both Apple Computer and Microsoft Corporation were founded in 1976; although fledgling Microsoft offered a BASIC interpreter as its first product, its operating system for floppy disks did not arrive until 1981.) Because these were smaller than the older 8-inch variety, these 5.25-inch floppies were called diskettes by some. The name later spread to even smaller sizes of floppy disk.

In 1980, Sony Corporation introduced the 3.5-inch floppy disk of the same mechanical construction that we know today. The initial reception was lukewarm to say the least. The 5.25-inch disk was the unassailable storage standard. The little disks, however, gained a foothold in the small computer marketplace when Apple adopted them for their initial Macintosh in 1984. In the PC industry, however, the 3.5-inch floppy remained off limits until about 1986 when the first notebook computers needed a more compact storage system. Its place was assured when first IBM and then the rest of the computer industry moved to the new diskette size.

Computer makers experimented with all sort of floppy formats, including disks as small as 2.5 inches introduced by Zenith Data Systems for an early sub-notebook PC. None of these alternate formats have survived, although in 1996, Iomega Corporation was exploring a 2-inch new-technology floppy with about 20MB capacity.

As data needs increased, media and drive manufacturers made several attempts at creating larger capacity floppies. Extra-high density 3.5-inch floppies, which doubled traditional floppy capacity to 2.88MB, remain available but little used. In 1988, the floptical drive bumped single-disk capacity to 20MB but never won more than a small market niche.

In 1996, the PC market saw the introduction of two floppy systems with capacities over 100MB. Iomega Corporation, one of the vendors of floptical systems, developed a proprietary system called the Zip drive with a capacity targeted at exactly the 100MB level. Shortly thereafter, an industry consortium promoted the LS-120 or *SuperDisk* system with not only slightly greater capacity (about 120MB, hence the name), but also backward compatibility with 1.44MB floppy disks. In 1998, other manufacturers unveiled two large-capacity floppy disk systems. Caleb Technology demonstrated a 144MB system, and Fuji and Sony showed a 200MB system, both of which were backward compatible with conventional 1.44MB media. In addition, Iomega pushed the capacity of the Zip system to 250MB.

Media

The traditional floppy disk medium itself is the thin, flexible disk inside the protective shell. This disk is actually a three-layer sandwich, the meat of which is a polyester substrate that measures about 3.15 mils (thousandth of an inch) or 80 micrometers thick. The bread is the magnetic recording medium itself, a coating less than one-thousandth of an inch thick on each side of the substrate.

Nearly all floppy disks use this same substrate. An exception is the advanced-technology LS-120 system, which uses a slightly thinner substrate (2.5 mils) that's cut from a different plastic, polyethylene terathalate (PET). This substrate is more flexible than the traditional polyester to let the LS-120 medium bend better around the head for more reliable contact.

The floppy disk medium starts out as vast rolls of the substrate that are coated in a continuous process at high speed. The stamping machine cuts individual disks from the resulting roll or *web* of medium like a cookie cutter. After some further mechanical preparation (for example, a metal hub is attached to the cookies of 3.5-inch disks), another machine slides the disks into their protective shells.

Sides and Coatings

No matter the substrate, a mixture of magnetic oxide and binder coat both sides of the substrate. Even so-called "single-sided" disks are coated on both sides.

Even though all traditional floppy disks have an oxide coating on both sides, media makers sometimes offer *single-sided disks*. Instead of omitting the coating on one side (which might make the disk vulnerable to warping from temperature or humidity changes), the manufacturer simply skips testing one side, certifying only one side will accept the data without error. By convention, the bottom surface of the disk is used in single-sided floppy disk drives.

The actual testing of the floppy disk is one of the most costly parts of the manufacturing process. Testing two sides takes more time and inevitably results in more rejected disks. Two sides simply provide more space in which problems can occur. Both single-sided and double-sided floppy disks may be made from exactly the same batch of magnetic medium.

In years gone by, some particularly frugal floppy disk users trimmed the price they paid for floppy disks by substituting their own testing (during the floppy disk format process) for that ordinarily performed by the manufacturer. They bought single-sided disks and attempted to format them double-sided. Every disk they successfully formatted on both sides was a bonus. What they really accomplished was shifting the cost of testing the medium from the manufacturer to themselves; their bargain was paid for by their own time. The economics of today's floppy disks make such bargains dubious. When double-sided disks cost 25 cents, single-sided disks must be cheap indeed (if they are even available) to make the procedure pay off.

Magnetic Properties

The thickness of the magnetic coating on the floppy disk substrate varies with the disk type and storage density. In the most common disk types, it measures from 0.035 mil to 0.1 mil (that is, 0.9 to 2.5 micrometers). In general, the higher the storage density of the disk, the thinner the magnetic coating. The individual particles are also finer grained. Table 11.1 lists the coating thicknesses for common floppy disk types.

Although all common floppy disk coatings use ferric oxide magnetic media, engineers have tailored the magnetic particles in the mix to the storage density at which the disks are used. The higher storage density media generally have higher coercivities, as shown in Table 11.1.

TABLE 11.1   Floppy Disk Media Characteristics

Disk Type	Coating Thickness	Coercivity
5.25-inch double density	2.5 micrometers	290 oersteds
5.25-inch high density	1.3 micrometers	660 oersteds
3.5-inch double density	1.9 micrometers	650 oersteds
3.5-inch high density	0.9 micrometers	720 oersteds

Despite the names used by various floppy disk types, all floppy disk drives use MFM (Modified Frequency Modulation) recording that produces double-density recording. In other words, both normal and high-density disks are double density, even though many manufacturers reserve the "double-density" term for lower capacity 5.25-inch floppy disks. Some computers used floppies termed *quad-density* with capacities in between those of normal and high-density floppies (720K on a 5.25-inch disk), but this format never found general acceptance.

Extra-high density disks (that is, 2.88MB floppies) use a novel technology called *perpendicular recording*. In conventional floppy disks, the grains of magnetic medium are aligned flat against the substrate, and the write process aligns them along a radius of the disk. The particles of medium used in perpendicular recording are arranged vertically so that one end of each particle points toward the substrate. A special read/write head in the disk drive changes the vertical orientation of the magnetic field of the media particles. In addition, extra-high density disks use a high coercivity barium-ferrite recording medium.

You will see no visual difference between the media of different coercivities and thus storage densities. The coating looks about the same in any case. Despite the visual similarity of the disk types, however, the two 5.25-inch media types have widely different coercivities; those of 3.5-inch disks differ, too, but only to a minor extent. When you format a floppy disk, the capacity you select tells your floppy disk drive to adjust to match the coercivity of the magnetic medium used by the disk. The disk drive can't adjust by itself. From the medium alone, a disk drive cannot tell the characteristics of the disk you've given it.

Although the shell designs of more recent floppy disks such as those of the 3.5-inch size incorporate a physical means of encoding the usable storage density, 5.25-inch floppies make no such distinction. Consequently, you can slide a double-density 5.25-inch disk into a high-density drive and force it to be formatted as a high-density disk. Although sometimes you'll get a large number of errors, many double-density floppy disks format just fine at high density. Only with the passing of time does the difference in coercivities take its toll. As these wrongly formatted disks age, they develop read errors much more quickly than properly formatted disks. Wrongly formatted floppies may become unreliable in a matter of a few months.

Disk

PCs have used two primary types of floppy disk. Before today's 3.5-inch floppy was accepted as the standard, the 5.25-inch disk reigned supreme. New PCs now are almost exclusively equipped with 3.5-inch disk drives. The larger disks survive mainly in archives of old files and programs that still occasionally need to be read.

Although the two disk sizes use nearly identical technologies, their mechanical construction and logical formatting are entirely different. They, of course, require their own drives, although combination drives—essentially two floppy disk drives that fit into a single drive bay with a single combined front panel—were popular for several years to accommodate people retaining an attachment to the old disks.

Microsoft has supported nine different floppy disk formats. As each was introduced, Microsoft adapted its DOS operating system to match. Although older versions of DOS cannot handle disks made for later versions, newer versions are all backward compatible with old disk formats. The latest version of DOS, which is actually part of the Windows 95/98 operating systems, recognizes all nine floppy disk types. Table 11.2 lists the formats of conventional PC floppy disks as well as their DOS requirements.

TABLE 11.2   Conventional Floppy Disk Formats

Diameter (Inches)	Density or Format	Sectors per Track	Tracks per Side	Sides	Capacity in Bytes	DOS Version Required
5.25	Double	8	40	1	163,840	1.0
5.25	Double	9	40	1	184,320	2.0
5.25	Double	8	40	2	327,680	1.1
5.25	Double	9	40	2	368,640	2.0
5.25	High	15	80	2	1,228,800	3.0
3.5	Double	9	80	2	737,280	3.2
3.5	High	18	80	2	1,474,560	3.3
3.5	Extra	18	160	2	2,949,120	5.0
3.5	DMF	21	80	2	1,720,320	3.3

To squeeze more storage onto each high-density floppy and cut the number of disks that they have to use to distribute applications, many software publishers sometimes use Microsoft's *Distribution Media Format* (DMF) on their floppy disks. This variation in the high-density design allows them to fit 1,720,320 bytes on a standard high-density 3.5-inch floppy disk in place of the more normal 1,474,560 bytes (nominal 1.44MB). The DMF format differs from the standard DOS format in that it uses 21 sectors per track instead of the normal 18. DMF squeezes more sectors on each track by reducing the inter-record gap (the space between sectors) down to nine bytes.

The differences go deeper, however. Each track uses a 2:1 interleave factor so that sectors do not appear in order. This interleaving results in slower reading because the disk has to spin around twice for each track to be read. The DMF format also skews the sectors on adjacent tracks by three sectors so that sector one on track four sits next to sector one on track two.

The small inter-record gap makes DMF disks difficult to write on with normal floppy disk drives. In fact, Microsoft calls DMF a read-only format. In any case, you cannot write to DMF disks using ordinary software. However, several special utilities are available for copying and even creating DMF disks. Note that Microsoft enforces a limit of 16 entries in the root directory of a DMF disk by only allocating a single cluster to serve as the root, so DMF formatted disks usually use a subdirectory structure for their contents.

By itself, DOS cannot read a DMF floppy. Consequently, DMF floppies are used only when a program requires multiple floppy disks for its installation. The first disk of the installation package—usually called the *setup disk*—loads software that reprograms your floppy disk controller to read the DMF disks.

IBM developed its own extra-capacity format for the distribution of OS/2 diskettes called XDF. Although XDF uses many of the same capacity-enhancing principles as DMF, the actual format on the disk is different and incompatible with DMF. As with DMF floppies, installation programs that use disks in XDF format reprogram your floppy controller to properly read the disks.

3.5-Inch Floppies

In developing the 3.5-inch floppy disk, Sony Corporation took a proven storage mechanism and endowed it with several improvements to make it more convenient and rugged. The obvious change was, of course, size. As new magnetic media became available, Sony put them to work in its various storage products such as audio and video tape. Using a magnetic material more advanced than conventional floppy disks allowed maintaining the same disk capacity as existing 5.25-inch disks while shrinking the area used for data storage by three quarters (that is, quadrupling the areal density). Initial single-sided 3.5-inch floppies—which were used by Macintosh computers but never PCs—stored 360KB per disk, the same as a double-sided 5.25-inch disk at the time. The first notebook PCs to accommodate the 3.5-inch disk size used double-density, double-sided disks with a capacity of 720KB. When the makers of desktop machines finally adopted the 3.5-inch size as standard, they used only high-density disks with a capacity of 1.44MB.

Shell

The chief improvements brought by Sony's 3.5-inch disk design were mechanical. Magnetically and logically, the disks work the same as the first 8-inch floppies. Drives, too, are basically the same, only miniaturized to suit the medium and modern PCs.

Most notable of the Sony innovations to the 3.5-inch disk was its tough, high-impact plastic shell. Originally only available in a rich blue color you dream the ocean to be, the shell protects the magnetic medium inside from whatever terrors lurk in your world, be they teething infants, churning chair casters, or simple carelessness. The tough shell allows you to put a label on the disk and then write whatever identification you want on it, even with a ballpoint pen. The thinner shells of earlier disks could not protect the media within from pen points, so writing on a label already affixed to an early floppy could crease the medium and make it unreadable. Figure 11.1 shows the shell of a 3.5-inch floppy disk and its notable external features.

FIGURE 11.1

Layout of 3.5-inch floppy disk.

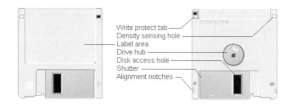

The shell of a 3.5-inch floppy disk measures 3.7 inches (94 millimeters) front-to-back and just over 3.5 inches (90 millimeters) wide. Each disk is a little more than one-eighth inch (3.3 millimeters) thick. A single disk weighs just over three quarters of an ounce, about 22 grams. Despite its 3.5-inch name, the media disk inside the shell actually measures about 3.4 inches (nominally 86 millimeters) across.

Unlike the bigger disks, which leave a large head-access swath of the disk vulnerable to dirt, dust, and fingerprints, the 3.5-inch design covers the vulnerable head-access area with a spring-loaded sliding metal shield or *shutter*. It opens automatically only when you insert a disk into a drive and slides closed when you pop the disk from the drive. The shutter is an effective dust shield that prevents contaminants from collecting on the medium surface whenever the disk is out of its drive. This protection means that 3.5-inch disks include all the protection they need and don't need an additional sleeve or shuck that older floppy disks required.

Liners

As protective as the hard shell of 3.5-inch floppies may be, the medium needs protection from it as well. A thin sheet of unwoven cloth akin to a loose-woven paper towel cushions each side of the medium from the shell. The interlocked threads of the liner serve as a slipsheet and dust collector. Light contact with the strands of the liner let the medium slide with little friction. At the same time, the material sweeps dust and particles from the surface of the medium so that it doesn't scrape against the read/write head of the drive.

Hub

One area of older floppies that sustained the most damage was the hub hole. Every time you slide a disk into a drive, drive hubs clamp onto the disk to hold and spin it. The hub entered the drive hole and forced the entire disk into the proper position for proper reading and writing. At times, the hub clamping down damaged the edges of the hole. After a disk suffered enough damage, it could become unreliable or unusable. The only protection to the hub hole offered by older floppy disks was an optional reinforcing ring some manufacturers elected to add to the perimeter of the hub hole.

The 3.5-inch floppy eliminates such problems by using a sturdy metal hub with a square center spindle hole that mates with the mechanism of the disk drive. The stamped steel hub resists damage. The single rectangular cut-out in the hub allows the drive mechanism to unambiguously identify the radial alignment of the disk. The cut-out serves as a mechanical reference for the position of data on the disk. The hub itself is glued to the disk media.

Insertion Key

A 3.5-inch floppy disk has four edges and two sides, giving you eight possible ways to try to slide it into your disk drive, only one of which is correct. Although the over-square design of the floppy shell prevents you from sliding a disk in sideways, you can still shove one in backward or upside down. To assure that you don't damage your disk drive by improperly inserting a disk, the shell of 3.5-inch floppies is keyed by a notch in one corner. A tab in the drive blocks this corner so if the notch is not present, you cannot slide the disk all the way into the drive. The last few millimeters of sliding in the disk open the shutter and load the heads against the disk, so the notch prevents the heads from ramming against floppy's shell instead of the access area.

Molded into the plastic of the shell is a small arrow that serves as a visual reminder to you. It points to the edge of the disk that you should slide into your disk drive, just in case the shutter is not enough guidance.

Write Protection

The fundamental design of the floppy disk is to serve as a read/write medium so that you can store information on it and read it back. Sometimes, however, you might want to protect the data on a floppy disk from change. For example, you might back up your archives to floppy disk. Software vendors prefer protection against writing to the distribution disks holding their programs so that you don't accidentally erase the code and become a support problem for them.

The 3.5-inch floppy design incorporates a *write-protect tab* that allows you to make any floppy disk a read-only medium. The design uses a hole and a plastic slider. When the slider blocks the hole, you can read, write, and format the disk. When the slider is moved back to reveal the hole, an interlock on the drive prevents you from writing to the disk. You can move the slider back and forth to write-protect a disk and then make it writable again as often as you want.

Software vendors often remove the slider entirely. Without the slider, the write-protected hole cannot be covered and the disk is permanently write-protected. You can, however, circumvent even this "permanent" form of write-protection by blocking off the write-protect hole. The easiest way is to cover both sides of the hole with opaque tape to make a distribution disk writable. This method is not without its dangers, however. If the tape does not stick tightly to the disk, it can jam the drive mechanism, likely preventing you from popping or pulling the disk out of the drive.

Density Key

So that your disk drive can determine the type of magnetic medium on your disk so that its electronics can be adjusted to match the disk's coercivity, 3.5-inch floppy disks incorporate a *density key*. This key is actually the presence or absence of a hole in one corner of the disk shell. Double-density disks lack a hole. High-density disks have a hole. An extra high-density notch marks disks with 2.88MB capacity. Higher density disks also have a visual indication of their capacity—for example, the stylized "HD" silk-screened near the shutter of high-density disks.

The connections between many floppy disk drives and the host PC often do not properly relay the density key information to the PC and its operating system. When the density key information is not available, you can format a double-density disk as high density. In years gone by, some enterprising manufacturers also offered hole punches designed to add a density-key hole to double-density disks so you could format them as high density. Although the difference in coercivities between double- and high-density media is modest, there are other differences in the formulation of the media that make double-density disks unreliable at high-density capacities. Moreover, the hole punches often left residue in the form of small particles of plastic to contaminate the disks. (At the factory, the density key is molded rather than punched.) These contaminants can shorten the life of the medium or damage your disk drive. The low cost of today's high-density disks render such overly frugal after-engineering an even more dubious value.

Format

Four formats are commonly used for 3.5-inch floppy disks, three of which are supported on PCs. (PCs do not support single-sided 3.5-inch floppy disk formats.) Your disk drives and operating system automatically adjust to the format of the disks you attempt to read, providing your drive is capable of reading the format. All higher capacity drives can read formats of lower capacity. Table 11.3 summarizes the essential characteristics of these four formats for 3.5-inch floppy disks.

TABLE 11.3   3.5-Inch Floppy Disk Characteristics

Capacity	Units	360KB	720KB	1.44MB	2.88MB
Sides	Number	1	2	2	2
Tracks	Number	80	80	80	80
Sectors per track	Number	9	9	18	36
Sector size	Bits	512	512	512	512
Rotation rate	RPM	300	300	300	300
Data transfer rate	Kbps	500	500	500	1,000

Capacity	Units	360KB	720KB	1.44MB	2.88MB
Bit density (max)	BPI	8,717	8,717	17,434	34,868
Track density	TPI	135	135	135	135
Coercivity	Oersteds	650	650	720	1,200

The capacity of a floppy disk is set when the disk is formatted. Using options of the DOS FORMAT command or the Format option from the Windows menu associated with your floppy disk drive, you can select the capacity of new floppy disks (or reformat floppies to change their capacity). Preformatted disks relieve you of the chore of formatting floppies yourself, although you can always format over the factory format to change the capacity of a disk.

To format a floppy through Windows, click the icon of your floppy disk drive and then choose the Format option. You'll see a screen like the one shown in Figure 11.2.

FIGURE 11.2

The Windows 95 Format options screen.

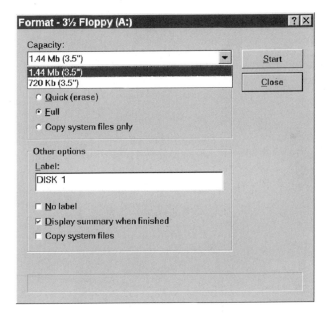

Depending on the capacity of the disk you insert in your drive and the wiring of your PC, Windows may give you the option of formatting at double, high, or extra density. Clicking the down arrow at the Capacity option (or typing Alt+P) will reveal the capacities the operating system will allow you to use.

Double density is the starting format for 3.5-inch floppy disks. It uses 80 tracks with 9 sectors per track. The tracks are spaced at 135 to the inch (about 5.3 to the millimeter).

The small diameter disk only allows a swath about 0.6 inch (15 millimeters) wide around the disk for reading and writing. The high-density format merely doubles the number of sectors per track, packing the data in twice as tightly.

Because 3.5-inch floppy disks spin at a fixed speed of 300 RPM, doubling the density of the data on each track also boosts the speed at which the information is read from the disk. The basic reading speed of 250 kilobits per second for double density is doubled to 500Kbps with high-density disks.

Extra-high density disks again double the sector count on each track, to 36 sectors per track, without changing the number of tracks or their spacing. Again, this increase in storage density also increases the read and writing speed, to 1000Kbps.

Note that the capacities of *all* floppy disks are given with the format in place. The formatting data steals away some of the usable storage area of the disk. Floppy disk makers occasionally list the unformatted capacities of their products. The unformatted capacity of a double-density (720KB formatted) disk is 1MB; that of a high-density (1.44MB formatted) disk is 2MB; that of an extra-high density (2.88MB formatted) disk is 4MB.

100MB and Larger Technologies

With the typical program stretching out for dozens of megabytes and hard disk capacities measured in gigabytes, the lowly floppy disk is woefully outclassed. Backing up an entire hard disk might take a crate of floppies and several evenings to complete. A single program might include more disks than a chiropractor's nightmare.

The gap between need and reality is so great that a simple improvement in floppy capacity won't suffice. Computer and media companies consequently tried more radical solutions to the problem, re-engineering the floppy disk concept. (The more radical—and possibly right-thinking—simply look to CD-Recordable to assume the role formerly held by floppy disks.) The result was not one but two mutually incompatible new generation floppy disk-based storage systems, each with a capacity of 100MB or more.

Iomega Zip Disk

First on the market was the Zip disk, developed by Iomega Corporation. Although initially a proprietary system, Iomega has licensed Zip to other companies. Both drives and media are now available from multiple sources, although the format is totally under the control of Iomega.

100MB

As you might expect, Zip can be seen as an outgrowth of floptical technology, but Iomega put the capacity and speed of Zip more in the range of small hard disks. The Zip medium uses an optically read servo track to allow repeatable head positioning in fine increments, fine enough to allow for a scant 100MB per disk cartridge. Each cartridge holds exactly 100,431,872 bytes, which is a true 95.8MB. The same Zip drives work with nominal 25MB cartridges, which hold 25,107,968 actual bytes.

Because of the laser/mechanical formatting of the disks, low-capacity Zip disks cannot be reformatted to higher capacity. In fact, the servo tracks cannot be erased by any means that would not destroy the cartridge.

The shell of the Zip disk makes it a true cartridge. To achieve speeds in the hard disk range, the medium must spin at a high rate, and the friction from rubbing against a liner is an anathema to speed. The thicker cartridge gives the Zip disk spinning room and enables it to rotate at 2,968 RPM. In addition, the Zip drive has hard disk-like access speeds, with the first generation of drives having a 26 millisecond average access time. The disk requires about three seconds to spin up to speed or spin down, which becomes a factor only when exchanging cartridges.

The actual Zip media disk inside a cartridge measures true 3.5 inches across. Consequently, the cartridge must be larger than conventional 3.5-inch floppies and MO cartridges (magneto-optical cartridges, discussed on the CD-ROM), measuring 3.7 inches (94 millimeters) square and a quarter inch (6.35 millimeters) thick. These dimensions alone make the Zip disk incompatible with traditional floppy disks.

Zip drives read only Zip disks. Products using any of three interfaces—IDE, parallel port, and SCSI—are available. Current generation drives operate only as slaves or with identifications that do not allow booting PCs. The interface used by the drive dramatically affects performance. The SCSI drives can transfer information about three times faster than parallel-interfaced models. In any case, the actual throughput of the drive system is throttled by the rate at which the media is read, 1.4MB per second.

Instead of using a mechanical write-protect mechanism on the cartridge shell, Zip disks are write-protected electronically. The Iomega system provides three protection modes with optional password access limits as part of its ZipTools software. The three modes include conventional write protection that prevents the inadvertent alteration of data on the disk; read/write protection, which requires a password to access data on the disk; and unprotect until eject, which lets you work with the data on the disk but protects the disk when you remove it from the drive. The same software that adds write protection is required to remove it. Passwords, however, are not recoverable—even by Iomega.

250MB

By increasing the density of storage on slightly modified media, in 1998 Iomega was able to boost the capacity of the Zip system by a factor of two and a half without major modifications to the drive mechanism. As a result, Iomega was able to offer an improved system with 250MB capacity at the same initial price as the original Zip drive.

Thanks to the increased lineal density of data on the 250MB Zip tracks, the data through-put of the new system is more than two times greater than the old, although access time remains comparable. Actual throughput may be limited by the drive interface. High-capacity Zip drives use the same interfaces as the old, and performance through parallel ports is compromised.

Although both drive and disks of the high-capacity system look outwardly identical to their forebears, they have been altered inside. The drive electronics have been adapted to accommodate the higher read and write rates required by the new media. The storage medium, too, has been improved for higher density storage. Disks with 250MB capacity are rejected outright by older drives as incompatible.

On the other hand, high-capacity Zip drives are fully backward compatible with old media. New 250MB drives can read and write 100MB disks. Old drives, however, can nei-ther read nor write 250MB media.

LS-120

Now promoted as *SuperDisk*, the LS-120 format was jointly developed by Compaq Computer Corporation, the storage products division of 3M Company (now Imation Corporation), Matsushita-Kotobuki Electronics Industries, Ltd., and O. R. Technology, the parent company of Optics Research, Inc., to be the next generation of floppy disk drive. The first LS-120 drives were marketed in March 1996. These drives, made by MKE, were installed in Compaq PCs and used media manufactured by 3M. The drives use optical technology developed by ORT.

Outwardly, a SuperDisk resembles an ordinary 3.5-inch floppy diskette. The only obvious difference is the shape of the shield over the head slot. Instead of rectangular, the SuperDisk wears a roughly triangular shield. Figure 11.3 shows an LS-120 diskette.

FIGURE 11.3
An LS-120 diskette.

Format

Each LS-120 diskette can store up to 125,829,120 bytes or 120MB, accounting for the designation of the drive. Not all of that capacity is usable. As with conventional floppy disks, part of the total capacity must be devoted to the FAT and directory data.

The SuperDisk drive combines two technologies to increase its capacity, an opto-mechan-ical laser servo system and zoned recording.

The major increase comes from increasing the track density to 2,490 per inch, achieved using the laser servo system. The small diameter of the disk only allows 1,736 tracks per side at this density. Even so, it requires a special medium, a two-layer metal particle compound.

For compatibility with PC hardware and software, the track layout of the LS-120 medium is mapped to a logical format (the way the drive appears to your PC) having 960 tracks per side. This mapping results in the drive—which has two heads, one for each disk side—appearing to your system as if it has eight heads.

The LS-120 system uses zoned recording with 55 different zones across the radius of each disk. The number of sectors per track varies from 51 on the innermost tracks to 92 at the outer edge. Table 11.4 lists the physical and logical formats of an LS-120 diskette.

TABLE 11.4   LS-120 Disk Format

Format Type	Cylinders	Heads	Sectors
Physical	1,736	2	51 to 92 (zoned recording)
Logical	960	8	32

The LS-120 disks spin at a constant 720 revolutions per minute. As a result of the constant spin and varying sector count, an LS-120 drive reads data from the disk at a rate that changes with the track position of the read/write head. Near the center of the disk, the transfer rate is lowest, about 400 KB/sec. At the outer edge, the transfer rate reaches 665 KB/sec. Initial LS-120 drives had an average access time of about 70 milliseconds. Table 11.5 lists the specifications of the LS-120 disk and its format.

TABLE 11.5   LS-120 Specifications

Feature	Specifications
Media diameter	3.5 inches
Recording medium	Metal particle
Capacity (formatted)	120MB
Bytes per sector	512
Sectors per track	51–92 (ZBR)
Track data capacity	26,112–47,616KB
Tracks per surface	1,736
Track density	2,490 tracks per inch

continues

TABLE 11.5 Continued

Feature	Specifications
Areal density	33,660 flux changes/inch
Recording surfaces (sides)	2
Track pitch	10.2 µm
Peak transfer rate	3.20 to 5.33 MB/sec
Throughput	313–571
Estimated life	5 million passes

Technology

The stepper motor-based open-loop mechanisms used by conventional floppy disk drives cannot correctly position a read/write head with sufficient precision to reliably locate the fine tracks used by the LS-120 system. To achieve the necessary track density, the LS-120 system used an embedded-servo system. Servo data is etched into the disk during factory preparation. The LS-120 drive then uses a laser to detect and read the etched servo information from the disk and align the read/write head properly on each track. In fact, the "LS" designation is an abbreviation for "laser servo."

The read/write head has two gaps, one used for the fine tracks used in high-density recording and one used for working with conventional double-density and high-density floppy disk media. The laser servo design does not increase the capacity of conventional floppy disk media.

Compatibility

Unlike Zip disk drives, LS-120 drives are backward compatible with standard 1.44MB floppy disks. The drives can both read and write standard floppies, and the 1.44MB floppies written on a LS-120 drive are readable by conventional floppy disk drives. Because of the higher spin speed of the LS-120 drive, however, it can achieve a higher transfer rate with a 1.44MB floppy—approximately 2.5 times higher—than a conventional floppy disk drive.

The LS-120 media are designed to appear as write-protected to conventional 1.44MB floppy disk drives by virtue of a cut-out that corresponds to the write-protect hole in a conventional floppy. Consequently, there is no risk of damage to data by inadvertently sliding a LS-120 disk into a conventional floppy disk drive.

The LS-120 media is beyond the control capabilities of the chip on the controllers for conventional floppy disk drives. The initial LS-120 drives instead used an IDE interface.

Caleb UDH

In 1998, a relatively unknown company, Caleb Technology, released its own proprietary high-capacity floppy disk system. The first product was a drive, the Caleb UDH144. An outgrowth of the conventional 1.44MB 3.5-inch floppy disk drive, the Caleb unit maintains backward compatibility with older media and can both read and write conventional 3.5-inch floppy disks formatted to either 720KB or 1.44MB capacity.

As with the LS-120 system, the Caleb drive squeezes more into the confines of a small floppy by increasing the track density. With 2,705 tracks per inch, it beats even the LS-120 system for density. In addition, it more than triples the data density on each track, to 58,600 flux changes per inch (58.6 FCI), leading to its capacity advantage over the less dense LS-120 system.

The Caleb UHD144 drive uses the familiar IDE/ATAPI connection system so that it is easy to add to most PCs. With proper BIOS support in its computer host, the Caleb drive is fully bootable and can entirely eliminate the need for a conventional floppy disk drive.

Table 11.6 compares the basic specifications of the Caleb system to that of a conventional 3.5-inch floppy disk.

TABLE 11.6 Comparison of Caleb and Conventional Floppy Disks

	Caleb UDH	*Conventional Floppy*
Capacity (MB)	144	1.44
Seek time (ms)	<30	79
Data transfer rate (MB/min)	57	7.5
Spin speed (RPM)	1,000	600
Track density (TPI)	2,705	135
Data density (FCI)	58,600	17,000
Areal density (MB/in^2)	158	2.3

HiFD

Introduced in 1998 with spotty distribution, the HiFD floppy disk system represents the combined efforts of Fuji and Sony. Using the former's media technology and the latter's drive-making expertise, the two companies created another high-performance, high-capacity floppy disk system, one capable of packing 200MB per disk. HiFD, a 200MB high-performance system, also features backward compatibility with older floppies.

As with the SuperDisk, the HiFD system is backward compatible with standard floppy disks, understandable because Sony created the current 3.5-inch floppy physical format. HiFD drives can both read and write conventional floppies.

When they shift into HiFD gear, the drives are able to move data at a 3.6 MB/sec peak rate, about 60 times faster than the conventional 3.5-inch floppy drive. Because of the high linear density of the HiFD disk and the 3,600 RPM rotational speed of the HiFD drive, HiFD is fast enough to play back full motion video. In addition, the dual discrete gap head, (flying head type) similar to those used in hard disk drives, and a high-speed head actuator with VCM (voice coil motor) provide the quick access speed.

To achieve its high storage density, the HiFD system used Fuji's ATOMM technology to double-coat the Mylar substrate of the floppy medium. Where the magnetic coatings on conventional floppy disks are from 2 to 5 microns thick, the ATOMM (a rather strained acronym—Advanced super Thin-layer high-Output Metal Media) coating is about 0.5 micron. The thinner, pure metal medium allows for recording shorter wavelengths, which directly translates into higher data density. Key to the density is creating a smooth surface on which to evaporate the magnetic metal medium. ATOMM uses an extra plating layer of titanium to provide the required smooth substrate.

Thanks to the high-density medium, the HiFD system is able to spread 2,822 tracks along an inch of the radius of a 3.5-inch disk (111 tracks per millimeter). The linear density of storage within each track is almost 30 times greater, from 79 to 87 kilobits per inch. Table 11.7 summarizes the physical format of the HiFD system.

TABLE 11.7 HiFD Specifications

Feature	Specification
Capacity	200MB (formatted)
Size	94 mm × 90 mm × 3.3 mm
Track pitch	9 micrometers
Track density	2,822 TPI (111 tracks/mm)
Linear recording density	87–79 kb/in (3.43-3.11 kb/mm)
Encoding/decoding method	PRML (16-17 code)
Transfer rate	3.6 MB/s (max.)

Drives

As computer equipment goes, floppy disk drives are simple devices. The essential components are a spindle motor, which spins the disk, and a stepper motor that drives a metal
band in and out to position the read/write heads, an assembly that is collectively called the
head actuator. A manual mechanism is provided for lowering a hub clamp to center and
lock the disk in place and to press the heads against the surface of the disk. In all except
the single-sided drives of the original PC, two heads pinch together around the disk to
read and write from either side of the medium. The tracks on either side of the disk are
interleaved so that one head is slightly offset above the other.

In more than two decades of development, about the only refinement made to the conventional floppy disk mechanism has been miniaturization. Not only have disks shrunk,
but the size of the drives for a given disk format have been reduced as well. Some floppy
disk drives are less than half an inch tall. No matter their size, however, all conventional
floppy disk drives work in essentially the same way.

Mechanical Design

To carry out their design purpose, all floppy disk drive mechanisms must be able to carry
out a few basic tasks. They have to spin the disks at a uniform speed. They must also
move their read/write heads with sufficient precision to locate each and every data track
on a given disk. And the open-loop head-positioner design requires a known starting
place, an index, which the drive must be able to locate reliably.

Speed Control

All of the electronics packed onto the one or more circuit boards attached to the drive
unit merely control those simple disk drive operations. A servo system keeps the disk spinning at the correct speed. Usually, an optical sensor looks at a stroboscopic pattern of
black dots on a white disk on the spindle assembly. The electronics count the dots that
pass the sensor in a given period to determine the speed at which it turns, adjusting it as
necessary. Some drives use similar sensors based on magnetism rather than optics, but
they work in essentially the same way—counting the number of passing magnetic pulses
in a given period to determine the speed of the drive.

Head Control

Other electronics control the radial position of the head assembly to the disk. The stepper
motor that moves the head reacts to voltage pulses by moving one or more discrete steps
of a few degrees (hence the descriptive name of this type of motor). Signals from the
floppy disk controller card in the host computer tell the disk drive which track of the disk
to move its head to. The electronics on the drive then send the appropriate number of
pulses to the stepper motor to move the head to the designated track.

The basic floppy disk mechanism receives no feedback on where the head is on the disk. It merely assumes it gets to the right place because of the number of steps the actuator makes. Because the drive does its best to remember the position of the head, hard reality can leave the head other than in its expect place. For instance, you can reach in and manually jostle the head mechanism. Or you might switch off your computer with the head halfway across the disk. Once the power is off, all the circuitry forgets, and the location of the head becomes an unknown.

Note that the stepper motors in most double-density floppy disk drives sold today are capable of tracing out all 40 tracks used by the PC floppy disk format. Some earlier computers did not require all 40 tracks. Consequently, some drives made for these computers—usually those drives closed out at prices that seem too good to be true—may not have a full 40-track range. Caveat emptor!

Head Indexing

So that the head can be put in the right place with assurance, the drive resorts to a process called indexing. That is, it moves the head as far as it will go toward the edge of the disk. Once the head reaches this index position, it can travel no farther, no matter how hard the actuator tries to move it. The drive electronics make sure that the actuator moves the head a sufficient number of steps (a number greater than the width of the disk) to assure that the head will stop at the index position. After the head has reached the index position, the control electronics can move it a given number of actuator steps and know exactly where on the radius of the disk the head is located.

Extra-High Density Considerations

To cope with the extra-high density recording medium, extra-high density floppy disk drives required a radical innovation—an extra head for each surface. The extra-high density medium is so difficult to work with that it requires a separate erase head. The extra head is fixed to the same actuator as the read/write head and moves with it track-to-track. When writing data, the erase head prepares the area for the read/write head by aligning the disk flux transitions in the same direction. The read/write heads then can change their orientation to record data.

Control Electronics

Although operating a floppy disk drive seems simple, it's actually a complex operation with many levels of control. When you press the Save button while running an application program, your button press does not connect directly to the drive. Instead, the keystroke is detected by your computer's hardware and recognized by its BIOS. The BIOS, in turn, sends the appropriate electronic code to your application program. The program then probably makes one or more requests to DOS to write something to disk. DOS sends instructions to the BIOS, and the BIOS sends codes to ports on the disk control hardware. Finally, this hardware tells the drive where to move its head and what to do once the head gets where it's going.

The penultimate piece of hardware in this chain is the floppy disk controller. It has two purposes in operating your system's floppy disks. One is to translate the logical commands from your computer system, which are usually generated by the BIOS, into the exact electrical signals that control the disk drive. The other function is to translate the stream of pulses generated by the floppy disk head into data in the form that your computer can deal with.

Operation

The best way to understand the operation of the floppy disk controller is to examine the signals that control the floppy disk drive and those that the drive sends to its computer host.

Two of these signals, Drive Select A and Drive Select B, are used to individually select either the first or second drive, A or B. (In four-drive systems, the signals for A in the second cable control drive C, and those of B control D.) If the signal assigned to a particular drive is not present, all the other input and output circuits of the drive are deactivated, except for those that control the drive motor. In this way, two drives can share the bulk of the wires in the controller cable without interference. However, this control scheme also means that only one drive in a pair can be active at a time. You can't write to drive B at the same time you read from drive A. That's why you must transfer the data held on a disk (or file) from one drive into memory before you can copy it to another drive.

One wire is used for each drive to switch its spindle motor on and off. These are called, individually, Drive Select A and Drive Select B. Although it is possible to make both motors spin simultaneously, rules laid down by IBM for the vary first PCs admonish against activating these two lines to make both floppy disk drive motors run at the same time. (The intention was to save power in the severely constrained PC system, an issue that disappeared with the next PC model and is no longer of any consequence. Not only is power more than adequate, but also all modern PCs have but a single drive.) Two signals control the head position. One, Step Pulse, merely tells the stepper motor on the drive to move one step (that's exactly one track) toward or away from the center of the disk. The Direction signal controls which way the pulses move the head. If this signal is active, the head moves toward the center.

To determine which of the two sides of a double-sided disk to read, one signal, called Write Select, is used. When this signal is active, it tells the disk drive to use the upper head. When no signal is present, the disk drive automatically uses the default (lower) head.

Writing to disk requires two signals. Write Data comprises the information that's actually to be written magnetically onto the disk. It consists of a series of pulses corresponding exactly to the flux transitions that are to be made on the disk. The read/write head merely echoes these signals magnetically. As a failsafe to preclude the possibility of accidentally writing over valuable data, a second signal called Write Enable is used. No write current is sent to the read/write head unless this signal is active.

The data rate of the data signal varies with the disk drive type. A normal density floppy accepts and sends data at a rate of 250 kilobits per second. A high-density drive operates at 500 kilobits per second. An extra-high density drive operates at one megabit per second.

The controller receives four signals back from the floppy disk drive. Two of these help the controller determine where the head is located. Track 0 indicates to the controller when the head is above the outermost track on the disk so the controller knows from where to start counting head-moving pulses. Index helps the drive determine the location of each bit on a disk track. One pulse is generated on the Index line for each revolution of the disk. The controller can time the distance between ensuing data pulses based on the reference provided by the Index signal.

The Write Protect signal is derived from the sensor that detects the existence or absence of a write-protect tab on a diskette. If a tab is present, this signal is active.

The Read Data signal comprises a series of electrical pulses that exactly match the train of flux transition on the floppy disk. The data rates correspond to those used for writing to the disk.

In its control function, the floppy disk controller must convert the requests from the BIOS or direct hardware commands that are couched in terms of track and sector numbers into the pulses that move the head to the proper location on the disk. For the most efficient operation, the controller must also remember where the head is located, index the head as necessary, and report errors when they occur.

In its translation function, the floppy disk controller must make sense from the stream of unformatted pulses delivered from the drive. It first must find the beginning of each track from the Index pulse and then mark out each sector from the information embedded in the data stream. Once it identifies a requested sector, it must then read the information it contains and convert it from serial to parallel form so that it can be sent through the PC bus. In writing, the controller must first identify the proper sector to write to (which is a read operation) and then switch on the write current to put data into that sector before the next sector on the disk begins.

Hardware

Most of the hard work of the controller is handled by a single integrated circuit, the 765 controller chip. (In contemporary PCs, the function of the 765 is often integrated inside chipsets.) The 765 works much like a microprocessor. It carries out certain operations in response to commands that it receives through registers connected to your computer's I/O ports.

This programmability makes the 765 and the PC-style floppy disk controller extremely versatile. None of the essential floppy disk drive parameters are cast in stone or the silicon on the controller. The number of heads, tracks, and sectors on a disk are set by loading numbers into the registers of the 765. Usually, the normal PC operating values are loaded into the controller when you boot up your computer. You ordinarily don't have to worry about them after that.

Integration

PC makers have used three distinct styles of floppy disk controller—standalone, combined, and integrated. The original design used by IBM in the first PC was a standalone floppy disk controller, an expansion board that did nothing else but operate floppy disk drives—up to four of them. The floppy disk controller of the PC AT and most PCs of its generation were combined with the hard disk controller. Most new PCs have their floppy disk controllers built into their motherboard circuitry. All three of these designs are still in use.

In any case, the circuitry is the same. The speed of the floppy disk interface is so low that bus interfaces and other connection issues are moot. The difference in circuit location only reflects the overall system manufacturer's design choice. The last, most integrated form yields the least expensive overall PC. In fact, floppy disk circuitry is often built into motherboard chipsets to facilitate complete integration. Aftermarket motherboards sometimes omit the floppy circuitry, allowing the manufacturer to shave a few pennies from the cost of the board and forcing you to get an AT-style controller that combines both hard and floppy disk sections. For specialized applications, dedicated floppy disk controllers remain on the market. One manufacturer even combines a PC Card slot adapter with floppy disk controller and drive.

Setup

Conventional floppy disk drives require only a simple, step-by-step installation procedure. Drives are physically installed in whatever bays are available and whichever one fits, as discussed in Chapter 25, "Cases." A single cable carries all control and data signals to two drives, wired as shown in Chapter 9, "Storage Interfaces." Most new technology drives include their own installation instructions, which usually amount to little more than screw the drive in, load the driver, and call technical support.

Once you've physically installed and connected a conventional floppy disk drive, you have one further step to perform: You must configure your system to accept it. Your PC needs to know the type of drive you've installed so that it can properly program the controller. Normally, all you need to do is make the appropriate selection from your PC's setup menu.

Whether a given format of drive will work with your PC is another issue, fortunately one that has become easier with the demise of more demanding old systems. To help you get a new drive running, we'll first take a quick look at support issues and then run through the normal floppy disk setup procedure, including a glance at the issue of disk compression.

Drive Support

Because all conventional floppy disk drives use the same controller electronics, whether a given size and format of floppy will work with your PC is a BIOS issue. The BIOS determines the parameters your PC can support. Nearly all PCs made in the last decade support all conventional floppy disk formats. Installing a higher-capacity drive in an older system requires at least a BIOS upgrade.

New technology drives require their own levels of system support. Extra-high density floppies require both hardware and software support specifically designed for them—that includes drive, controller, and BIOS. The Zip disk and LS-120 systems require only the matching interface. Iomega supplies drivers to support Zip disks with most popular operating systems. Support for the LS-120 system is built into all Windows versions since Windows 95.

Setup

Floppy disk drives are typically your third concern in setting up your PC—right after the time and date. Most system setup programs put queries about floppy disks at the top of the list, probably because the associated parameter values are first in CMOS memory.

In general, you only need to select the appropriate capacity for your disk drive from the four or five available selections: 360KB, 1.2MB, 720KB, 1.44MB, and 2.88MB. All you need to do is make the right match to your drives. If you accidentally make the wrong selection, you'll know as soon as your system runs through its Power-On Self Test and the drive makes an ugly sound as if it's trying to push its motor and electronics out the drive slot. Despite the noise, the floppy may pass the POST evaluation even if you've configured the wrong type. It won't, however, work properly when you try to read and write disks. If you run setup again and set the correct drive type, you shouldn't hear the ugly noise again.

Note that if you only install one disk drive, DOS will recognize it as both Drive A: and Drive B:, prompting you to change disks to keep the two drives straight. This two-drive emulation allows you to make disk copies even with one disk drive. Windows 95 is more concrete and recognizes a single drive as exactly that.

Compression

Disk compression works with floppy disks just as it does with hard disk drives. Floppy disks impose an additional complexity in that they are removable, and your PC has no way of knowing whether the floppy you slide into one of its drives is compressed. To take care of this problem, Microsoft operating systems require that you *mount* a compressed floppy disk drive after you boot your system or change floppy disks.

The current versions of DriveSpace used by DOS and Windows have built-in *auto-mounting* capabilities. When you boot your PC or slide a floppy into a drive, the floppy disk drive software used by the operating system spins the disk, reads from its boot sector to determine whether the floppy is compressed, and mounts the disk if it is compressed. With early versions of Windows, the auto-mount feature required about 4KB of real-mode memory. Consequently, Microsoft allowed you to switch off the feature and save previous kilobytes of real-mode memory by clearing the Automatically Mount option in the DriveSpace Advanced menu. Under Windows 95/98, auto-mounting does not impinge on real-mode memory, but it can nevertheless be switched off. To do so, clear the appropriate box, as shown in Figure 11.4, in the Settings page of the Advanced menu choice that appears when you run DriveSpace.

FIGURE 11.4

Switching off auto-mounting in Windows.

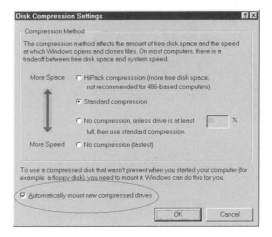

If you switch auto-mounting off and slide a compressed floppy into your drive, the floppy will appear to have nearly all of its space used up even though only a single small file will appear in directory display. Typically, the file will be named READTHIS.TXT and its contents will include instruction to mount the floppy. The rest of the floppy's capacity is devoted to serving as a repository for compressed data even if you have stored no files on the compressed floppy.

To see the compressed files or to allow your programs to use them, you must used DriveSpace to mount the floppy manually. Run the DriveSpace program, and select the appropriate disk drive and the Advanced option. Choose the Mount option from the menu that drops down, as shown in Figure 11.5.

FIGURE 11.5

Manually mounting a floppy disk drive using DriveSpace.

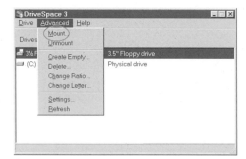

As with hard disk drives, under the compression systems used by Microsoft the operating system creates a Compressed Volume File that stores the data you compress onto floppy. The CVF appears as a file on your physical floppy disk drive using the name DRV-SPACE.000 as a default. This file has the hidden, system, and read-only attributes, so it is normally invisible when you use the DIR command.

The operating system assigns a drive letter to the CVF so that you can work with it as if it were a physical drive. By default, Microsoft operating systems reassign and hide the drive letter of the physical floppy disk drive when it uses a CVF on the drive.

Compact Disks

From a simple stereo component, the Compact Disc has blossomed into today's premiere digital exchange medium. A single disc can slip up to 680MB of information into your PC. When you need more storage, the CD's designated successor, the DVD, takes over, packing up to 18GB on the same size silver disc. Both CDs and DVDs can store just about anything digital using a variety of audio, video, and data formats. Pre-recorded discs are fast and cheap to make. Special disc drives even let you craft your own CDs and DVDs.

Issues in judging CD and DVD drives in new PCs or consider drives as upgrades or replacements:

Issue	Advice
Format	DVD does everything that CD does (at least in playing back), so a DVD drive is the better, forward-looking choice
Speed	Faster is better. Look for at least a 24x CD drive or a 2x to 5x DVD drive. Multiply DVD speeds by 6 to get the approximate equivalent CD speed.
Interface	ATAPI drives are cheaper but SCSI CD drives do better digital audio extraction (handy for making MP3 files)
Video decoder	Required for watching DVD movies; irrelevant for CDs. Hardware decoders faster than software and produce better images—but hardware costs more.
Writability	CD-R drives let you make your own CDs but CD-RW do that and more, so CD-RW is the better choice. Writable DVD remains unproven.
Changers	So far, CD-only. Let you keep several discs almost on-line but clumsy software can be a headache—physically changing discs is often faster and less troublesome

Star Wars writ small—that's a succinct and surprisingly accurate description of modern optical storage systems. Precision flashes of light blast pits into a high-tech medium, leaving it permanently scarred. Every time you load a CD or DVD into your drive, the battle starts anew, although most of the time the robots throttle back the lasers to preserve the information pitted on the disc.

Certainly, there are more practical ways of looking at CDs and DVDs. Today, one or the other is as necessary in a new PC as a hard disk drive or even microprocessor. After all, without a way to read CDs, you couldn't load the latest software onto your PC, and without the software, it would be as useless as a system without a brain. The CD and DVD provide a convenient distribution medium. A CD holds more megabytes than even most bloated programs need. A DVD boosts that capacity fivefold—for now—and puts the latest widescreen movies with full surround sound inside your PC's drive.

Modern innovations to optical technology enable some drives to create as well as read discs, turning the optical medium into a backup and archiving system *par excellence*. The latest twist endows disc drives with the ability to reuse discs so you can update your archives. Although they are not nearly so fast as today's hard disk drives, a rewriteable optical drive is probably more versatile and more secure. The discs you write are apt to outlive the PC you make them on; they are likely even to outlive *you*.

Although the CD and DVD are often treated as two different systems, they share a common heritage and technology. The DVD is really only the second generation of optical disc storage for PCs. The major technical differences are a result of improvements in technology over the nearly two-decade history of the CD medium. No revolutionary changes separate the two. In fact, the biggest changes only reflect new formats created to take advantage of the larger capacity the technical refinements permit.

History

The history of the CD and DVD begins at about the same time as that of the PC and for years ran parallel but unconnected to computer technology. Developed by the joint efforts of Philips and Sony Corporation in the early 1980s, when the digital age was taking over the stereo industry, the Compact Disc was first and foremost a high-fidelity delivery medium. Initially released in the United States in 1983 (in Japan, the CD got a one-year head start, officially released in 1982 according to Sony), within five years it had replaced the vinyl phonograph record as the premiere stereophonic medium because of its wide range, lack of noise, invulnerability to damage, and long projected life.

Engineers set many of the practical aspects of the CD around the requirements of music recording. For example, they selected the 70 or so minutes of music capacity as one of the core specifications in designing the system because a primary design goal was to fit the entirety of Beethoven's Ninth Symphony, without interruption, on a single disc. As the

CD rose to prominence as the primary distribution medium for pre-recorded music, computer engineers eyed the shiny medium with a covetous gleam in their eyes. They saw the digital storage provided by the disc as repository for more megabytes than anyone had reason to use. After all, data is data (okay, data are data) no matter whether the bytes encode a symphony or an operating system. (Remember, these were the days when the pot at the end of the rainbow held a 20 or 30MB hard disk.) When someone got the idea that a plastic puck that cost a buck to make and retailed for $16.99 could be filled with last year's statistics and marketed for $249, the rush was on. The Compact Disc became the CD ROM (which stands for Compact Disc, Read-Only Memory), and megabytes came to the masses.

Soon, sound became only one of the applications of the Compact Disc medium. The original name had to be extended to distinguish musical CDs from all the others. To computer people, the CD of the stereo system became the CD-DA, *Compact Disc, Digital Audio*.

Engineers tinkered with the storage format of the CD to stuff the discs with other kinds of data. Philips optimized the medium for interactive applications—multimedia presentations and games—to create CD-I, which stands for *Compact Disc Interactive*. Some even thought that compression—a lot of it—could fit video on the discs. *Compact Disc-Video* succeeded in squeezing video on the little discs, but not very much and not very well. Viewable video had to wait another string of developments and the new generation of optical storage.

DVD was the needed innovation. The initials stand for Digital Versatile Disc, although the system was first termed the Digital Video Disc before the adoption of the current technical standards.

The roots of DVD go back to two competing proposals, both of which had the primary intent of storing video on a disc the same size as a CD. The original developers of the Compact Disc, Philips and Sony, backed a format they called MMCD for *Multimedia Compact Disc* (they owned the CD name so they took advantage of it). The other camp, led by Matsushita, Time Warner, and Toshiba, developed their own, incompatible format they called *SD*.

For a while, the industry appeared poised for a repeat of the Beta-VHS debacle that put two mutually incompatible videotape cassette formats on the market for nearly a decade. In September 1995, the industry appeared to come to its senses, hammering out a single standard agreeable to both camps. To distinguish it from the earlier efforts and reflect the expanded range of possibilities afforded by the new medium, the format was re-christened with *versatile* replacing the *video* of the earlier proposals. Credit for developing the initial standard is generally given an industry consortium that included Hitachi, JVC, Matsushita, Mitsubishi, Philips, Sony, Thompson, Time Warner, and Toshiba.

Where the CD started as a single-purpose device and later grew to accommodate applications its developer never could have foreseen, DVD started from the beginning as a multi-purpose technology. Computer data storage was part of the format from its inception. In fact, IBM spearheaded the unification efforts. In the long run, DVD is meant to replace just about every consumer media storage and playback system. The developers of the DVD believe that it will quickly replace videocassettes, audio CDs, and all the various CD-based computer storage systems—and probably serve several more purposes no one has yet guessed. Although anyone can make such speculations, in the case of the DVD developers they carry weight. After all, the developers make the same VCRs, CD players, and other devices they expect their new wonder-child to replace.

As with CDs, each application format for the DVD will have its own sub-designation. These include DVD-Video for video applications such as the distribution of motion pictures; DVD-Audio, as a high-quality audio disc with capabilities far beyond today's 16-bit discs; and DVD-ROM for the distribution of computer software and other data.

When it came to developing a recordable format for DVD, various members of the consortium that developed the original DVD standard went their own ways. As a result, at least four recordable formats are now being marketed—DVD-R, DVD-RAM, DVD-RW, and DVD+RW.

Despite these differences and the wide variety of formats now used in PC optical storage systems, the underlying technology for all remains the same—a spinning disc is the target for *Star Wars* refugee laser.

Technology

Cheap and easy duplication make PC optical disc storage an ideal distribution medium. Its versatility (the same basic technology stores data, sound, and video) came about because all engineers eagerly search for big, cheap storage. Both the Compact Disc and Digital Versatile Disc have both of those virtues by design.

One of the great virtues of any kind of optical storage is data density; little discs mean a lot of megabytes. By using light beams provided by lasers, optical storage earns several advantages. Lenses can focus a beam of light—particularly the coherent beam of a laser—to a tiny spot smaller than the most diminutive magnetic domain writeable on a hard disk drive. Unlike the restricted magnetic fields of hard disks that have to be used within a range of a few millionths of an inch, light travels distance with ease. Leaping along some 5.9 trillion miles in a year, some beams have been traveling since almost the beginning of the universe 10 to 15 billion years ago. A small gap between the source and storage medium is consequently no problem. The equipment that generates the beam of light that writes or reads optical storage need not be anywhere near the medium itself, which gives equipment designers more freedom than they possibly deserve.

The basic idea behind optical disc storage is that you can encode binary data as a pattern of black and white splotches just as on and off electrical signals can. You can make your mark in a variety of ways. The old reliable method is plain, ordinary ink on paper. The bar codes found universally on supermarket products do exactly that.

Reading the patterns of light and dark takes only a *photo-detector*, an electrical component that reacts to different brightness levels by changing its resistance. Light simply allows electricity to flow through the photo-detector more easily. Aim the photo-detector at the bar code, and it can judge the difference in reflected light between the bars and background as you move it along (or move the product along in front of it). The lasers that read in the check-out quicken the scan. The photo-detector watches the reflections of the red laser beam and patiently waits until a recognizable pattern—the bar code as the laser scans across it—emerges from the noise.

You could store the data of a computer file in one gigantic bar code and bring back paper tape as a storage medium—one long strip of bars that stretches past the horizon. Even if you were willing to risk your important data to a medium that turns yellow and flakes apart under the unblinking eye of the sun like a beach bum with a bad complexion, you'd still have all the joy of dealing with a sequential storage medium. That means renew your subscriptions to your favorite magazines because you'll have a lot of waiting to do.

The disc, with its random access abilities, is better suited as a storage system. Its two-dimensional storage makes randomly accessing a particular block of data a matter of milliseconds rather than miles. The choice of a fast-spinning disc was obvious even to the audio-oriented engineers who put the first Compact Disc systems together. They had a successful pattern to follow: the old black vinyl phonograph record. The ability to drop a needle on any track of a record had become ingrained in the hearts and minds of music lovers for more than 100 years. Any new music storage system needed equally fast and easy access to any selection. The same fast and easy access suits computer storage equally well.

Optical storage brings another benefit. The optical patterns that encode data in both the CD and DVD systems can be formed mechanically. Both systems use physical pits that show up as small black holes against a shiny silver background as the dark and bright spots to optically code data. The pits are mechanical features that can be duplicated mechanically. The process is inexpensive and fast. Machines can flawlessly mold multiple copies in a few seconds, and with multiple master molds, a factory can crank out a million copies in a few days. In other words, optical technology allows duplicating megabytes, even gigabytes, *en masse*. Magnetic media, on the other hand, can duplicate data only byte-by-byte.

Medium

The heart of both the Compact Disc and Digital Versatile Disc systems is the disc medium itself. Its design, based on a pattern of dots that can be read optically but mass-produced mechanically, makes optical storage the fastest and least expensive medium for duplicating hundreds of megabytes of data.

The flat disc shape also offers a distinct advantage. Machines can mold copies of discs by stamping them between dies instead of filling a three-dimensional mold with a casting liquid. This stamping process has a long history. It has been used for over a century in duplicating recording music—first with shellac and clay to copy Emil Beliner's first phonograph records and then with vinyl for old-fashioned record albums. Duplicating CDs and DVDs requires extra precision and a few extra steps, but it remains essentially the same stamping process.

The disc duplicating process begins with a disc master. A mastering machine equipped with a high-powered laser blasts the pits in a blank disc—the recording master—to make an original mechanical recording. Then, the master is made into a mold called a stamper. A negative copy is electroplated onto the master and then separated from it, leaving the master unscathed. One master can make many duplicate molds, each which is then mounted in a stamping machine. The machine heats the mold and injects a glob of plastic into it. After giving the plastic a chance to cool, the stamping machine ejects the disc and takes another gulp of plastic.

In making a CD or DVD, another machine takes the newly stamped disc and aluminizes it so that it has a shiny, mirror-like finish. To protect the shine, the disc is laminated with a clear plastic cover that guards the mechanical pattern from chemical and physical abuse (oxidation and scratches). Finally, another machine silk-screens a label on the disc. It is packaged, shrink-wrapped, and sent off to a warehouse or store.

The DVD process differs in that a disc can have multiple layers. In the current process, a separate master is made for each layer. The layers are stamped out separately, each only half as thick as a complete disc. The two complete layers are then fastened together with a special transparent glue.

In theory, a disc could be any size, and setting a standard is essentially an exercise in pragmatism. Size is related to playing time. The bigger the disc, the more data it holds, all else being equal. If you want to store a lot of data, a big disc has its allure. On the other hand, a platter the size of a wading pool would win favor with no one but plastics manufacturers. You can also increase the capacity of a disk by shrinking the size of every stored bit of digital code, but the practical capabilities of technology limit how small you can make a bit. In trying to craft a standard, engineers have to balance the convenience of small size, the maximum practical storage density, and a target for the amount of information they need to store.

In the late 1970s when Philips and Sony were developing the CD, the maximum practical storage density of the then-current technology was about 150MB per square inch. The arbitrary design goal of about 70 minutes per disc side (enough room for Beethoven's Ninth) dictated about 650MB at the data rate selected (which itself was a tradeoff between data requirements and sound quality). The result was that the design engineers found a 120 millimeter (that's about 4.6 inches) platter to be their ideal compromise. A nice, round 100 millimeters was just too small for Beethoven.

For portable applications, the engineers came up with a smaller form factor for discs, 80 millimeters (about 3.1 inches). Once plated and given its protective plastic coating, either size of CD is about 1.2 millimeters (about 0.05 inch) thick.

For DVDs, the same sizes have been retained. This expedient allows the same equipment used to make CDs with only minor modification to stamp out DVDs.

The DVD medium differs from conventional CDs in that discs can use both sides for recording data and multiple layers on each side. As noted earlier, current technology fabricates each DVD in two pieces, each 0.6 millimeter thick, which are later cemented together. Cemented back-to-back, the disc gains two sides. Cemented so the face of one butts the back of the other, the disc gains two layers. The latter configuration allows you to play both recorded surfaces without flipping the disc over.

Under the DVD standards, eight possible types of disc are currently defined, depending on the size, number of sides, and number of layers. Table 12.1 summarizes the various DVD types and their storage capacities.

TABLE 12.1 DVD Types and Capacities

Name	Diameter	Capacity	Sides	Layers
DVD-1	8cm	1.36GB	1	1
DVD-2	8cm	2.48GB	1	2
DVD-3	8cm	2.72GB	2	1
DVD-4	8cm	4.95GB	2	2
DVD-5	12cm	4.38GB	1	1
DVD-9	12cm	7.95GB	1	2
DVD-10	12cm	8.75GB	2	1
DVD-18	12cm	15.9GB	2	2

Initial releases conform to DVD-5 standard. This format was tailored to the needs of the motion picture and videocassette industry. It allows a standard Hollywood-style movie to fit on a single disc. Unlike videocassettes, however, the movie will have digital quality images and sound, and not just stereo sound but full eight-channel surround. In that the cost of duplicating DVDs is a fraction of that of videocassettes, the software industry will be urging you into the new medium as fast as it can. In that you should easily be able to see and hear the difference, you shouldn't need too much encouragement.

The DVD format allows your disc drive to read the two layers in either of two ways, determined when the disc is recorded. PTP (parallel tracking path) tracks are read in *parallel*. Your drive reads both layers at nearly the same time in parallel. In practice, the two tracks may contain the same material in different formats—one might hold a standard aspect ratio image and the other a widescreen image—allowing you to switch between them instantly. OTP (opposite tracking path) tracks are read sequentially. The drive reads one layer to its end and then reverses and reads the second layer in the *opposite* direction. To minimize changeover time when the read head reverses direction, the drive starts reading the bottom layer from the inside out and then switches to reading the inside layer from the outside in. Discs that use OTP tracks are sometimes described as *reverse-spiral dual-layer* (RSDL) discs. Some disc producers prefer them because they offer a longer (nearly) continuous playing time.

The first DVDs were mostly two-sided, single-layer DVD-10 discs, usually a motion picture in full-frame format on one side and widescreen on the other. One reason was that drives capable of reading two-layer discs required more development and that all DVD drives can handle two-sided discs, providing you physically flip the disc to access the other side.

A modern DVD drive distinguishes the separate layers of a multiple-layer disc by selective focus. To read the bottom layer, it simply focuses on its pits. To read the upper layer, it focuses through the semi-transparent lower layer to the upper layer. The separation between the two layers, about 20 to 70 microns, is sufficient for each layer to have a distinct enough focus for them to be distinguished. When the laser beam in your DVD player is out of focus, it scans such a wide area that the out-of-focus pattern simply doesn't register.

Four-layer DVDs, which have two layers of data on each of their two sides, require a not-quite-perfected manufacturing process that writes two layers simultaneously on each of the two halves that are cemented to make the completed disc.

Materials

The recording material used by read-only, recordable, and rewritable optical disc systems are quite different because each system operates on different physical principles. Read-only media depend on fast, mechanical reproduction of discs. Recordable media require a one-use material with a long life. Rewriteable media require a medium that can be cycled between states so that it can be erased and reused.

Read-Only

Every Compact Disc is a three-layer sandwich. The bulk of the disc is a transparent poly-carbonate plastic substrate called the *carrier*. It is made from the material injected into the stamping press; the machine smashes flat a warm glob of raw plastic and embosses the spiral pattern of pits, encoding the digital data into one of its surfaces. The aluminum coating that makes the disc reflective (except for the data pits) is vapor plated on the polycarbonate substrate to a thickness of about one-tenth micron. To protect the aluminum from oxidation (which would darken it and make the pattern of pits difficult or impossible to read), it is protected with a final layer of lacquer about 200 microns thick.

The laser in a disc drive reads from *reflective* side of the disc. That is, the laser reads through the thick carrier to the aluminized layer. The label of the disc gets silk-screened onto the thin protective lacquer coating. Note that the coating is about one thousand times thinner than the carrier on the reflective side. As a result, a compact disc is more vulnerable to damage on the label side. Although a scratch here may not interfere with the reading of the disc, it may allow air to come into contact with the aluminized layer and oxidize it, ruining the discs.

The construction of multilayer DVDs is similar except the polycarbonate carrier is only half as thick. Double-sided and double-layer discs cement two half-thickness discs together. DVD-5 discs (single-sided, single-layer) cement a dummy half-thickness disc to the back of the one active layer. In any case, in the center of the disk the protective plastic layer is replaced with a transparent plastic cement, which seals the aluminized layer on the lower half of the disc and binds the upper half to it.

Compared to vinyl phonograph records or magnetic discs, CDs and DVDs offer a storage medium that is long-lived and immune to most abuse. The protective clear plastic layer resists physical tortures. (In fact, Compact Discs and one-sided DVDs are more vulnerable to scratches on their label side than the side that is scanned with the playback laser.) The data pits are sealed within layers of the disc itself and are never touched by anything other than a light beam; they never wear out and acquire errors only when you abuse the discs purposely or carelessly (for example, by scratching them against one another when not storing them in their plastic jewel boxes). Although error correction prevents errors from showing up in the data, a bad scratch can prevent a disc from being read at all. Although the smaller features used by the DVD system for storing data are more vulnerable (one scratch can wipe out more stored data), the DVD system has a more robust error-correction system that more than compensates.

Recordable

Discs used in CD recorders differ in two ways from those used by conventional CD players—besides being blank when they leave the factory. CD-R discs require a recordable surface, something that the laser in the CD recorder can alter to write data. This surface takes the form of an extra layer of dye on the CD-R disc. Recordable CDs also have a formatting spiral permanently stamped into each disc.

As with other CDs, a recordable disc has a protective bottom layer or carrier of clear polycarbonate plastic that gives the disc its strength. A thin reflective layer is plated on the polycarbonate to deflect the CD beam back so that it can be detected by the drive. Between this reflective layer and the normal protective top lacquer layer of the disc, a CD-R disc has a special dye layer. The dye is photoreactive and changes its reflectivity in response to the high-power mode of the CD recorder's laser. Figure 12.1 shows a cross-section of a typical CD-R disc.

FIGURE 12.1

Cross-section of recordable CD media using cynanine dye (not to scale).

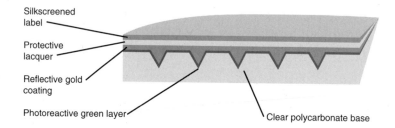

Silkscreened label

Protective lacquer

Reflective gold coating

Photoreactive green layer

Clear polycarbonate base

The CD-R medium records information by burning the dye layer in the disc. By increasing the power of the laser in the drive to 4 to 11 milliwatts, its beam heats the dye layer to about 250 degrees (Celsius). At this temperature, the dye layer melts and the carrier expands to take its place, creating a non-reflective pit within the disc.

Three compounds are commonly used for photo-reactive dyes used by CD-R discs. These are most readily distinguished by their color, either green, gold, or blue.

> **Green.** The dye used in green CD-R discs is based on a cynanine compound. The Taiyo Yuden company developed this photoreactive dye, which was used for the first CD-R discs, including those used during the development of the CD-R standards. Even now, green CD-R discs are believed to be more forgiving laser power variations during the read and write processes. The green cynanine dye is believed to be permanent enough to give green CD-R discs a useful life of about 75 years. In addition to Taiyo Yuden, several companies, including Kodak, Ricoh, TDK, and Verbatim, make or have made green CD-R discs.

> **Gold.** Gold CD-R discs used a phthalocyanine dye developed by Mitsui Toatsu Chemicals. The chief advantage of gold over green discs is longer life because the dye is less sensitive to bleaching by ambient light. If it were on a dress or shirt, it would be more colorfast. Gold CD-R discs are believed to have a useful life of about 100 years. Some people believe that gold discs are also better for high-speed (2x or 4x) recording than are green discs. Mitsui Toatsu and Kodak manufacture most gold CD-R discs.

Blue. The most recent of the CD shades is blue, a color that results from using cynanine with an alloyed silver substrate. The material is proprietary and patented by Verbatim. According to some reports, it is more resistant to ultraviolet radiation than either green or gold dyes and makes reliable discs with low block error rates.

Some manufacturers use multiple layers of dyes on their discs, sometimes even using two different dyes. The multiple-layer CD-R discs are often described as green-green, gold-gold, or green-gold depending on the colors of the various layers.

Additionally, the reflective layers of recordable CDs also vary in color. They may be silver or gold, which subtly alters the appearance of the dye.

There should be no functional difference between the different CD-R colors; all appear the same hue to the monochromatic laser of a CD drive that glows at a wavelength of 780 nanometers. But although all of the CD-R materials reliably yield approximately the same degree of detectable optical change, as a practical matter they may act differently. Some early CD ROM readers may have varying sensitivities to the materials used in CD-R discs and will reliably read one color but not another. There is no general rule about which color is better or more suited to any particular hardware. Moreover, the dyes behave differently when illuminated by the 680 nanometer lasers of the DVD system and may be unreadable in first-generation DVD drives. The best strategy is to find what works for you and stick with it.

No matter the dye used, recordable CD media are not as durable as commercially stamped CDs. They require a greater degree of care. They are photosensitive, so you should not expose them to direct sunlight or other strong light sources. The risk of damage increases with exposure. The label side of recordable CDs is often protected only by a thin lacquer coating. This coating is susceptible to damage from solvents such as acetone (fingernail polish remover) and alcohol. Many felt-tip markers use such solvents for their inks, so you should never use them for marking on recordable CDs. The primary culprits are so-called permanent markers, which you can usually identify by the strong aroma of their solvents. Most fine-point pen-style markers use aqueous inks, which are generally safe on CD surfaces. Do not use ballpoint, fountain pen, pencil, or other sharp-tipped markers on recordable CDs because they may scratch through the lacquer surface and damage the data medium.

The safest means of labeling a recordable CD is using a label specifically made for the recordable CD medium. Using other labels is not recommended because they may contain solvents that will attack the lacquer surface of the CD. Larger labels may also unbalance the disc and make reading it difficult for some CD players. In any case, once you put a label on a recordable CD, do not attempt to remove it. Peeling off the label likely will tear off the protective lacquer and damage the data medium.

Eraseable/Rewriteable

The CD-RW system is based on *phase-change* media. That is, the reflective layer in the disc is made from a material that changes in reflectivity depending on whether it is in an amorphous or crystalline state. The most common medium is an alloy of antimony, indium, silver, and tellurium, which has an overall silver color.

In its crystalline state, the medium has a reflectivity of about 15 to 25 percent. In its amorphous state, the reflectivity falls a few percent—enough to be reliably detected by the laser-based disc-reading system.

A blank disc has all of its reflective medium in its crystalline state. To record data, the drive increases laser power to between 8 and 15 milliwatts and heats the medium to above its 500- to 700-degree (Celsius) melting point. The operation is straightforward and equivalent to the CD-R writing process except for laser power.

Erasing the disc complicates things. To completely erase a disc and restore it to its original crystalline state, the disc must be annealed. The reflective layer is heated to about 200 degree Celsius and held at that temperature while the material recrystallizes. The process requires about 37 minutes for a complete disc. On-the-fly erasing of a disc is possible by selectively annealing small areas of the disc with the laser at moderate power. The annealed areas may be rewritten with higher laser power.

Physical Format

The medium provides space to store information, but a complete storage system requires something more. It needs a standardized method of organizing that information. That organization may take several levels—a physical level and one or more logical levels. The physical level or format determines how densely information fits onto the medium and how it is accessed. The logical level determines how it is addressed and used.

The physical format of the Compact Disc and Digital Versatile Disc share a characteristic with hard disks that's the same with most disc-based media: The information is arranged *around* the disc in long arcs. But where hard disks and floppy disks make those arcs into concentric tracks, the CD and DVD turn the arc into a long spiral. As a result, CDs don't have tracks like hard disks. They have one continuous track. DVDs have multiple tracks but only one on each layer.

The difference is that hard disks are meant to be a random access medium. CDs and DVDs are designed for sequential access. The CD was optimized for storing music, which usually is a continuous and uninterrupted stream of data. The DVD was primarily optimized for video, which also requires a continuous and uninterrupted stream. In scanning a single spiral track, the reading mechanism never has to pause to jog to a new position. As long as it follows the track, it's where it needs to be.

CDs and DVDs also differ from hard and floppy disks in that they do not spin at a constant rate. Drives adjust the speed of the spin so that they read the same number of data pits of the same size in any given period. Technically speaking, hard and floppy disks spin with *constant angular velocity*. In any given period (say a millisecond), the disk always • rotates by the same size angle. In contrast, CDs and DVDs are a constant *linear velocity medium*. In any given period, they spin the same linear length of track past the reading mechanism. As a result, near the center of a CD or DVD where the diameter is small, the disc must spin faster to present the same length of track to the reading mechanism.

The actual linear velocity used by the original Compact Disc system was 1.2 meters per second. As a result, the spin varied from about 400 revolutions per minute (RPM) at the inner diameter to about 200RPM at the outside edge. Higher speed drives, discussed later, spin at multiples of this rate. Under the basic Digital Versatile Disc standard, a single-layer disc spins at a constant linear velocity of 3.49 meters per second. As a result, discs' spin rates must vary from 600 RPM at the outer edge to about 1,200RPM at the inner edge of the recordable area. Multilayer discs spin somewhat faster, 3.68 meters per second. Although DVD drives in computers may spin at faster rates, the DVD players you connect to your video system are locked to this speed.

With each spin of a disc, the track advances outward from the center of the disc, a distance called the *track pitch*. In the case of CDs, the track pitch is 1.6 micrometers. The individual pits on the track that encode data bits are at least 0.83 micrometers long. The raw data rate at the basic speed of the CD system is 4.3218 megabits per second. In original trim as an audio playback device, the actual data throughput was 150 kilobytes per second (1.2 Mbits/sec) after demodulating, decoding, error correction, and formatting the raw signal.

DVD storage is considerably denser. Most significantly, all measurements can be smaller because the DVD system uses a shorter wavelength laser, 650 to 680 nanometers compared to 780 nanometers used by CDs. Standard DVD track pitch measures 0.74 microns. On a single layer disc, each data pit is about 0.40 micron long. On double-layer discs, pits measure 0.44 micron. The basic data rate for DVD is 26.16 megabits per second. Subtract out the overhead, and the net rate is about 11.08 megabits per second. Table 12.2 summarizes the physical format of CDs and DVDs.

TABLE 12.2	CD and DVD Physical Formats		
	CD	*Single-Layer DVD*	*Double-Layer DVD*
Disc diameter	120 or 80 mm	120 or 80 mm	120 or 80 mm
Track pitch	1.6 nm	0.74 nm	0.74 nm
Standard read velocity	1.2 m/sec	3.49 m/sec	3.68 m/sec

continues

TABLE 12.2   Continued

	CD	Single-Layer DVD	Double-Layer DVD
Minimum pit length	0.83 micron	0.4 micron	0.44 micron
Laser wavelength	780 nm	680 nm	680 nm
Basic read rate	4.3218 Mbits/sec	26.16 Mbits/sec	26.16 Mbits/sec

Both CD-R and CD-RW blank discs (as well as their DVD equivalents) have a physical format already laid down on them. Each has one continuous spiral track at the standard pitch (1.6 microns for CDs). In addition, this track *wobbles* with a period of 22.05 kilohertz and an excursion of 0.3 microns. That is, the smooth spiral actually has a superimposed S-shape. The CD drive detects this wobble and uses it to control the rotation rate of the disc. The wobble is frequency modulated by a one kilohertz signal that provides an absolute timebase for the drive.

Drives

The hundreds or thousands of megabytes on your CDs and DVDs would do you no good without a means for reading them. That means is the optical disc drive. A CD drive or CD ROM reader gives you access only to CDs, be they audio or data discs. All DVD drives can read both CDs and DVDs, although early drives often cannot read discs written with CD-R and CD-RW drives.

With the price difference between CD and DVD drives disappearing, there's less reason than ever to consider a CD drive. A DVD drive will do everything the CD does (but likely better). Performance and compatibility are no longer issues. Consequently, in any new PC, a DVD drive is the preferred option.

All optical disc drives in PCs can play back audio CDs. The multimedia standards require that drives on multimedia PCs have both a front panel headphone jack and volume control. All drives also have an audio connector on their rear panels for linking to your sound board. This connector provides analog audio—that is, the sound from a disc that has already been decoded from its original digital format. Drives also have standard mass storage interface jacks (typically AT Attachment or SCSI) to send digital data to your PC.

In theory, you can recover digital audio through this connection. Drives differ in their ability to deliver usable audio in digital form, however, a feature called *digital audio extraction*. For example, if you wanted to capture a track from an audio CD to convert into an MP3 file, you would need a drive that supports digital audio extraction. Most SCSI-based drives handle DAE better than AT Attachment drives, although ATA drives have improved substantially in this ability over the last few years. If you plan to work with audio in digital form from your CDs, you'll want to look for DAE support.

Technology

Dedicated home DVD players have video jacks, but the DVD drives in PCs do not. The circuitry required to decompress video data is just too complex to build into the current generation of drives. For video playback in your PC, the DVD reader must plug into a *MPEG decoder* that typically slides into an expansion slot and directly links to your PC's video system.

Nearly all optical disc drives for desktop PCs are fit into a standard half-height, 5.25-inch drive bay. The discs themselves are too big to squeeze into drives that would fit a 3.5-inch bay. Notebook drives are usually thin, often no taller than a floppy disk drive. Modern optical disc drives use *tray loading*, which means you simply put a disc into the tray that slides out of the drive. In other words, modern drives do not require you put a disc into a *caddy*, a protective cartridge.

Early in the history of CD drives, three forms of caddies were in use, but now the few drives still using caddies have settled on one. The most common was initially used by Denon, Hitachi, some Matsushita, Sony, Toshiba, and newer NEC drives. It is the survivor. Its design resembles a 3.5-inch floppy disc with a single metal shutter that slides back to let the drive optics see the disc. You open the caddy by squeezing tabs at the end opposite the shutter to drop in a disc.

The other two caddy designs have essentially disappeared from the market. The Philips-style caddy was transparent smoked plastic and opened by pressing two tabs; the CD slid inside between large white plastic pincers. The other style was that used by the old NEC CDR-77/88 drive.

Some people buy a caddy for each disc they have because of this convenience and the extra protection the carrier affords the disc—no scratches and no fingerprints, guaranteed! This can be a particular advantage if your system gets heavy use by younger folk or uncaring office personnel. A caddy can extend the life of your investment in optical media.

Caddies make it easier to operate an optical drive with its disc slot or tray oriented vertically. Although most tray-loading drives have no difficulty reading discs when the drive is oriented vertically, loading the disc can be a problem. Drives typically have retractable clips in their trays to keep the disc from sliding from the tray as it loads. Adjusting and learning to use these clips is more an art than a science.

Speed

When Philips and Sony originally propounded the Compact Disc system, memory was expensive and PCs were only for hobbyists. Players had to read audio data from each disc at the same rate as it was to be played. Higher speeds were irrelevant. Once PCs adopted the CD, however, audio speed became a horrendous hold-up. Audio CD speed was slower than that of a modern floppy disk, and floppy disks were too slow.

Data, unlike music, need not abide by the constraints of real-time playback. It wasn't long before computer engineers took advantage of a simple expedient to speed up the CD drives connected to PCs. They made the discs spin faster—and faster—and faster. From humble beginnings of only twice as fast as ordinary audio CDs, they have revved up to as high as 50 times faster.

Drive makers describe the speed of their product using the "x" factor. The base speed of an audio CD drive is 1x. A 2x drive spins twice as fast. A 12x drive spins 12 times faster and so on.

After about 12x, the rotation rates for CDs become awesome. When reading from the inside of the disk, a 12x rate amounts to about 4,800 RPM. At the outer edge, the disc spins at half that rate. Higher speed factors (for example 20x, 36x, or 50x) are comparably faster. Not only is spinning the disc at these rates a challenge, but also altering the spin speed from the inner to outer reaches of the disc is tricky and time-consuming. The need to change speeds can really slow down random access.

In data applications, a constant data rate is unnecessary. With that gem of wisdom in mind, drive makers developed CD players with a constant spin rate, which, with a logic peculiar to the computer market, are known as *variable speed drives*. Although spin rate is constant, the data rate the drives deliver is not. It is twice as high at the outer edge of the disc as it is at the inner edge. The x-factor of the drive varies with the data rate.

As any cynic would expect, drive manufacturers invariably quote the *fastest* speed that variable speed drives could possibly deliver. In practical use, drives almost never achieve this rate. Discs are written to be read from the center of the disc outward—that is, from the point at which they deliver their lowest reading speed. They reach their highest speed only at the outer edge of the disc. In that most discs are not completely filled with data, drives never read far enough across the disc to reach their top speed. More reputable computer makers are beginning to describe variable speed drives by listing both their slowest and fastest speed, such as 12/24x.

On the other hand, variable speed drives have an advantage in random access. Because they spin your discs at a constant rate, you don't have to wait for the drive to alter its speed to match the rate required at a particular place on the disc.

Note, too, that high-speed drives impose an access penalty. Drives with faster speed ratings require more time to spin your discs up to the proper speed. That means you have to wait longer after you slide a disc into the drive before you can read it. The problem is particularly severe with portable computers, which stop their discs from spinning after a minute or so to conserve power. Each time the drive powers down, you have to wait for it to spin the disc back up to speed before you can read from it.

The x-factor for DVD drives is not the same as for CD drives. As with the CD, the DVD speed ratings are pegged to the base data rate of the original video-only DVD system. The linear velocity of the DVD system is about 2.98 times faster than the linear velocity of the CD. But drive electronics don't care about linear speed. They lock onto the data rate. The data format of the CD has larger features than that of DVDs. The minimum pit length, for example, is 0.83 microns for CDs and only 0.4 for DVDs. For a given data rate, the CD must spin about twice as fast as a DVD to produce the same data rate, the 26.16 Mbits/sec basic read rate of DVDs. Add the increased linear velocity to the change required by feature size and read rate, and the result is that a 1x DVD drive best reads data at about six times the base CD rate. Consequently, every DVD "x" is worth about six "xs" from a CD drive. Table 12.3 gives a comparison of some common CD and DVD speeds (assuming a constant data rate).

TABLE 12.3   Comparison of CD and DVD Drive Speed Factors

CD Factor	DVD Factor	Raw Data Rate
1x	0.17x	4.32 Mbits/sec
2x	0.33x	8.64 Mbits/sec
4x	0.67x	17.3 Mbits/sec
6x	1x	26.2 Mbits/sec
12x	2x	52.4 Mbits/sec
18x	3x	78.6 Mbits/sec
20x	3.3x	86.4 Mbits/sec
24x	4x	105 Mbits/sec
30x	5x	131 Mbits/sec
36x	6x	157 Mbits/sec
40x	6.7x	173 Mbits/sec

Because the coding system used by DVDs is more efficient than that used by CDs, a DVD drive extracts more information at a given raw data rate. The user data rate from a 1x DVD drive *reading a DVD* is about nine times that from a 1x CD drive *reading a CD*.

In general, a faster drive is a better drive—providing you can put up with the extended spin-up times of really quick disc drives. Some software makes particular speed demands from CD drives. The minimum speed requirement usually is in the range of 4x to 6x. All CD drives in new PCs deliver at least 12x, so you should encounter no problem with software speed compatibility. Similarly, the base DVD rate is fast enough for most applications, although you may prefer the quicker load times afforded by a 4x or faster DVD drive.

When you play audio from CDs or movies from DVDs, high drive speeds and x-factors make no difference. A faster drive will not produce a higher-quality signal from these iso-synchronous sources. Only when you read computer data from disc do the x-factors matter. For example, play a CD so you can listen to it, and your drive will operate at 1x. When you attempt to extract digital data from the same audio CD to create an MP3 file, however, the drive may shift to a higher speed—if your PC can process the data fast enough. Extraction need not occur in real-time.

Access Time

Compared to magnetic hard disks, all optical disc readers are laggardly beasts. Mass is the reason. The read head of an optical drive is substantially more massive than the flyweight mechanisms used in hard disks. Instead of a delicate read/write head, the CD or DVD drive has a large optical assembly that typically moves on a track. The assembly has more mass to move, which translates into a longer wait for the head to settle into place. Optical drives consequently have hefty access times; where the typical hard disk drive now has an average access time of 9 milliseconds or less, a quick optical drive is about one-tenth the speed (with an average access time about 90 to 100 milliseconds).

As noted earlier, the constant linear velocity system used by some drives also slows the access speed. Because the spin rate of the disc platter varies depending on how far the read/write head is located from the center of the disc, as the head moves from track to track, the spin rate of the disc changes. With music, which is normally played sequentially, that's no problem. The speed difference between tracks is tiny, and the drive can quickly adjust for it. Make the optical drive into a random-access mechanism, and suddenly speed changes become a big issue. The drive might have to move its head from the innermost to outermost track, requiring a drastic speed change. The inertia of the disc spin guarantees a wait while the disc spins up or down.

Changers

As disc collections grow, the old idea from the stereo system—the disc or record changer—becomes increasingly compelling. You can load up several discs and have them at ready access. No more shuffling through stacks of discs and jewel cases. You can keep your favorite discs just a keystroke away. CD changers are now readily available. DVD changers are not.

The first CD ROM changers were, in fact, derived from those used in stereo systems. Pioneer adapted its six-CD cartridge to computer use to create the first changer—only natural in that Pioneer has patented that changer design. More recently, other manufacturers have developed changers that don't need cartridges. As with single disc CD drives, the choice between cartridge and free-disc system is one of preference. Either style of drive works.

Similarly, CD changers operate at the same speeds as single-CD units, although the fastest changers lag well behind the fastest single-disc drives. Today, 8x changers are commonplace. Unfortunately, software has not tracked the developments in CD changers. Both applications and operating systems have problems with the multi-disc drives.

Most driver software for CD changers assign separate drive letters to each disc (or disc position) in the changer. A four-disc changer would thus get four drive letters. To access the disc in a particular changer slot, you only need to use the appropriate drive letter.

Life isn't so simple, however. Most CD-based applications don't expect being loaded into a changer and react badly. Although some applications will run no matter where you load them, some will force an icon to pop on your screen and ask in which slot to find the disc. Some are worse: They will refuse to run except in a favored slot with the favored drive letter. Worse, the error message you get won't help you find the problem. It may tell you that the program can't find its drive even if you've installed the program for that exact drive. The only solution is to find the slot the program favors and always use that slot for that particular program.

Windows outsmarts itself by testing and sensing all the drives that are connected to it. As a result, when Windows boots up it will chunk through each slot in your CD changer and wait for it to come up to speed. In that spinning up and down each disc may take 20 seconds, cycling through the whole changer can add minutes to the already long boot-up interval. In addition, some changer drivers do not interface well with Windows and may not properly inform Windows when you change discs. Change discs without closing a program, and the system may hang until you slide the program's disc back into the right slot and close it properly. Moreover, many programs remember what drive letter you installed them as. If you try to use a CD-dependent application in a slot other than the one from which it was installed, the application may not run.

Certainly, better drivers and applications that are more aware will come onto the market. But you should beware that, as with any new technology, CD changers are not perfect.

Controls

Nearly all optical disc drives have an eject button on the front panel. Pressing this button causes the drive to spin down the disc inside the drive (if there is one) and then side out the tray or pop out the caddy should one be used. Pressing the button again slides the tray back in. Usually pressing on the open tray will also trigger the drive to slide all the way in.

The MPC (Multimedia PC) specifications established by the Multimedia PC Marketing Council (http://www.spa.org/mpc) require a volume control on the front panel of any CD drive you have in your multimedia PC. This control is useful if you decide to use your drive for playing back music while you work. You can plug headphones into the jack on the front of the drive (also required by the MPC standards) and use the volume control to adjust the loudness of the playback independent of the CD control software you run on your PC. The front panel volume control usually does not control the output on the audio connector on the rear of the drive.

Some CD and DVD drives have extended control panels, usually with the standard motion controls as found on dedicated disc players: stop, play, fast forward, rewind, track forward, and track back. Although these controls are not required, they can be handy when you use the DVD player in your PC for playing video through an external monitor.

With the exception of the volume control, all of the front panel control functions (including eject) can be operated through suitable software.

Compatibility

DVD drives are required to be able to play back audio CDs made under the Red Book standard. (See the following section, "Standards.") Although as a digital system that can read CD ROM data, DVD could be compatible with any CD, this is not always the case. Most DVD systems cannot handle interactive Green Book CDs. The dye used in many CD-R media is invisible to DVD wavelengths, so early DVD drives may be unable to read the CD-R discs you make. Drive makers have adopted a number of strategies to enable their newer DVD drives to properly read CD-Rs. Of course different CD-R media use different dyes, so you might find your DVD drive works with some CD-Rs and not with others. CD-RW media complicate matters because the medium is not as reflective as that used by pre-recorded CDs and DVDs. Manufacturers have developed a "MultiRead" label to assure you that the drive will read CD ROM, CD-R, and CD-RW media. DVD drives are not required to be able to read CD-Video disc (White Book), but most can; it takes no great technical feat because the DVD drive can read the CD medium and the MPEG-2 circuitry in the DVD drive also handles the MPEG-1 of CD-Video. DVD players can read data from Enhanced CDs made under the Blue Book standard, including music CDs.

Standards

Because both the Compact Disc and Digital Versatile Disc were conceived as distribution media for software—in this case, "software" meaning audio for the CD, video for the DVD—standardization has been of the utmost importance. Without hard and fast standards, you could not be sure that the disc you buy will play back in your drive. Consequently, every format of disc has an official standard that guides both drive and disc makers so their products can be compatible.

The Sony-Philips standards are published in books that are commonly referred to by the colors of their covers. This small rainbow covers all currently recognized CD standards and was recently (1999) enlarged to embrace the new Super Audio CD. The DVD standards, promulgated by the DVD Forum and published by Toshiba, wear more prosaic identifying names based on a simple letter designation. The five standards recognized at the time of this writing include those for audio, video, read-only data, write-once data, and read/write data. Table 12.4 summarizes these standards.

TABLE 12.4   CD and DVD Standards

Book	Name	Application	Standard
Book A	DVD-ROM	Data distribution	
Book B	DVD-Video	Consumer video playback	
Book C	DVD-Audio	Consumer audio playback	
Book D	DVD-WO (DVD-R)	Write-one data storage	
Book E	DVD-E (DVD-RW)	Rewriteable data storage	
Red Book	CD-DA	Consumer audio playback	ISO 10149
Scarlet Book	SA-CD	Super Audio CD	Pending
Orange Book	CD-R, CD-RW	Writeable and rewriteable data storage	
Yellow Book	CD ROM	Data distribution	ISO 10149:1989 (E)
Green Book	CD-I	Interactive CDs	
Blue Book	CD-Extra, CD-Plus	Stamped multi-session CDs	
White Book	CD-V	Consumer video playback	

The primary DVD standard is maintained by Toshiba Corporation. It is freely available but hardly free. Anyone can obtain a copy from the DVD Forum at http://www.dvdforum.org after paying a $5,000 fee and signing a non-disclosure agreement.

Each of the most widely used of the CD and DVD standards is separately discussed in the following sections. Less popular formats (CD-I, CD-Video) as well as proprietary formats (including PhotoCD) are covered on the CD-ROM.

Note that the original format for CDs was audio. The data format, CD ROM, was separately developed around the audio parameters. In DVD, the original format was DVD-ROM with the first application, DVD-Video, being a subset of the DVD-ROM format.

CD-DA

CD-DA, which stands for Compact Disc, Digital Audio, is standardized in the Red Book. It was the original Compact Disc application, storing audio information in digital form. The name Red Book refers to the international standard (ISO 10149), which was published as a book with a red cover and specifies the digitization and sampling rate details, including the data-transfer rate and the exact type of pulse code modulation used.

Under the standard, a CD-DA disc holds up to 74 minutes of stereo music with a range equivalent to today's FM radio station. The high end goes just beyond 15KHz (depending on the filtering in the playback device); the low end, nearly to DC. The system stores audio data with a resolution of 16 bits, so each analog audio level is quantified as one of 65,536 levels. With linear encoding, that's sufficient for a dynamic range of 96 decibels, that is, 20log(162). To accommodate an upper frequency limit of 15KHz with adequate roll-off for practical anti-aliasing filters, the system uses a sampling rate of 44.1KHz.

Under the Red Book standard, this digital data is restructured into 24-byte blocks, arranged as six samples of each of a pair of stereophonic channels (each of which has a depth of 16 bits). These 24 bytes are encoded along with control and subchannel information into the 588 optical bits of a small frame, each of which stores about 136 microseconds of music. Ninety-eight of these small frames are grouped together in a large frame, and 75 large frames make one second of recorded sound.

In CD-DA systems, the large frame lacks the sync field, header, and error-correction code used in CD ROM storage, discussed later. Instead, the error-correction and control information is encoded in the small frames. The necessary information to identify each large frame is spread through all 98 bits of subchannel Q in a given large frame. One bit of the subchannel Q data is drawn from each small frame.

From the subchannel Q data, a sector is identified by its ordinary playing time location (in minutes, seconds, and frame from the beginning of the disc). The 98 bits of the subchannel Q signal spread across the large frame is structured into nine separate parts: a two-bit synchronization field; a four-bit address field to identify the format of the subchannel Q data; a four-bit control field with more data about the format; an eight-bit track number; an eight-bit index number; a 24-bit address counting up from the beginning of the track (counting down from the beginning of the track in the pre-gap area); eight reserved bits; a 24-bit absolute address from the start of the disc; and 16 bits of error-correction code. At least 9 of 10 consecutive large frames must have their subchannel Q signals in this format.

In the remaining large sectors, two more subchannel Q formats are optional. If used, they must occur in at least one out of 100 consecutive large frames. One is a disc catalog number that remains unchanged for the duration of the disc; the other is a special recording code that is specific and unchanging to each track.

Super Audio CD

The Scarlet Book covers the Super Audio CD, the DVD/CD hybrid developed jointly by Philips and Sony to compete with DVD-Audio. Using two-layer technology, it couples a conventional CD-A layer for compatibility with old equipment with a DVD-like layer for higher-quality audio using Sony's proprietary Direct Stream Digital (DSD) encoding technology (described later). The format specifications were released in March 1999.

The DSD encoding system provides frequency response to 100KHz and a dynamic range in excess of 120dB. Although few people can hear anything beyond 20KHz, the highest quality analog master tapes recorded at a speed of 30 inches per second often have information out to 50KHz. The high frequency range of DSD will finally put to rest complaints that digital doesn't sound as good as analog.

The DSD system uses one-bit sampling at a 2.8224MHz rate, the same as used in high-quality PCM encoding system that use 64x over-sampling. Instead of converting the resulting code to PCM (Pulse Code Modulation), the DSD system records the one-bit sample values. *Delta sigma modulation* determines the one-bit value for each sample; that is, the sample represents the sum (sigma) of the changes (delta) of the signal. The system maintains a running total of the bits representing the strength of the analog waveform. At each sampling interval, it compares the present value with the previous value. If the new value is higher than the previous value, the system adds a logical 1 to the code stream. If the current value is lower than the previous value, the system adds a logical 0 to the code stream. If a value does not change, it is nevertheless evaluated and will produce an alternating pattern of 1s and 0s that correct one another.

The overall result is that a rising (positive) waveform will be a dense string of 1s and a full falling (negative) waveform will be a dense string of 0s. Consequently, this form of modulation is often termed *Pulse Density Modulation*, or PDM. As with all digital signals, the PDM output is resistant to noise and distortion—and alteration to the signal smaller than an entire pulse will be ignored in processing and excluded from the reconstructed signal. Unlike coded digital signals, however, PDM (and a similar digital modulation system, *Pulse Width Modulation*) signals are closely allied to their analog equivalent. The pulses in the signal mimic the analog signal in strength and frequency. In fact, a simple low-pass filter can convert the digital signals into analog form.

In the case of Sony's DSD, the simple analog conversion isn't very good. Digital artifacts make the simple conversion noisy. The Sony system uses high-order filtering to move the noise out of the audio band.

The CD-compatible layer of a Super Audio CD is created during mastering through a process Sony calls *Super Bit Mapping Direct* downstream conversion. It is essentially the same process used in mastering ordinary audio CDs from 64x over-sampled masters.

Although the standard Super Audio CD format uses two audio channels of DSD signals, the specification allows for up to six such channels for future applications. In addition, storage space outside the audio signal area is reserved for text, graphics, or videos—for example, to accompany the audio presentation.

The Super Audio CD also includes provisions for watermarking (invisibly indicating the origin of the media) discs through coding embedded in the wobble of the track. This feature can be used for tracking the origins of a particular disc (for example, for controlling disc piracy) or in copy protection schemes.

According to Sony, a Super Audio CD will play in any drive, CD, DVD, or SA CD. In a CD drive, it will deliver better than CD quality thanks to the super bitmapping downstream conversion. Current DVD drives will also play the discs with CD quality. The true beauty of the disc will come out only on special SA CD players or a future generation of DVD drives that have the proper playback algorithms.

CD ROM

Yellow Book, first introduced in 1984, describes the data format standards for CD ROM discs (Compact Disc, Read-Only Memory) and includes CD-XA, which adds compressed audio information to other CD ROM data. Yellow Book divided CD ROM operation into two modes. Mode 1 is meant for ordinary computer data. Mode 2 handles compressed audio and video data. Because Yellow Book discs can contain audio, video, and data in their two modes, they are often termed *mixed mode* discs. Yellow Book is the standard that first enabled multimedia CDs. It is now an internationally recognized standard as ISO 10149:1989 (E).

As the full name implies, CD Read-Only Memory is fundamentally an adaptation of the Compact Disc to store digital information; rock-and-roll comes to computer storage. Contrary to the implications of the name, however, you can write to CD ROM discs with your PC, providing you buy the right (which means expensive) equipment. For most applications, however, the CD ROM is true to its designation; it delivers data from elsewhere into your PC. Once a CD ROM disc is pressed, the data it holds cannot be altered. Its pits are present for eternity.

In the beginning, CD ROM was an entity into itself, a storage medium that mimicked other mass storage devices. It used its own storage format. The kind of data that the CD ROM lent itself to was unlike that of other storage systems, however. The CD ROM supplied an excellent means for distributing sounds and images for multimedia systems; consequently, engineers adapted its storage format to better suit a mixture of data types. The original CD ROM format was extended to cover these additional kinds of data with its Extended Architecture. The result was the Yellow Book standard.

Logical Format

As with other disc media, the CD divides its capacity into short segments called sectors. In the CD ROM realm, however, these sectors are also called large frames and are the basic unit of addressing. Because of the long spiral track, the number of sectors or large frames per track is meaningless; it's simply the total number of sectors on the drive. The number varies but can reach about 315,000 (for example, for 74 minutes of music).

Large frames define the physical format of a Compact Disc and are defined by the CD ROM media standards to contain 2,352 bytes. (Other configurations can put 2,048, 2,052,

2,056, 2,324, 2,332, 2,340, or 2,352 bytes in a large frame.) The CD ROM media standards allow for several data formats within each large frame, dependent on the application for which the CD ROM is meant. In simple data storage applications, data mode one, 2,048 bytes in a 2,352-byte large frame actually store data. The remaining 304 bytes are divided among a synchronization field (12 bytes), sector address tag field (4 bytes), and an auxiliary field (288 bytes). In data mode two, which was designed for less critical applications not requiring heavy-duty error correction, some of the bytes in the auxiliary field may also be used for data storage, providing 2,336 bytes of useful storage in each large frame. Other storage systems allocate storage bytes differently but in the same large frame structure.

The four bytes of a sector address tag field identify each large frame unambiguously. The identification method hints at the musical origins of the CD ROM system; each large frame bears an identification by minute, second, and frame, which corresponds to the playing time of a musical disc. One byte each is provided for storing the minute count, second count, and frame count in binary-coded decimal form. BCD storage allows up to 100 values per byte, more than enough to encode 75 frames per second, 60 seconds per minute, and the 74 minute maximum playing time of a Compact Disc (as audio storage). The fourth byte is a flag that indicates the data storage mode of frame.

In data mode one, the auxiliary field is used for error detection and correction. The first four bytes of the field stores a primary error-detection code and are followed by eight bytes of zeros. The last 276 hold a layered error-correction code. This layered code is sufficient for detecting and repairing multiple-bit errors in the data field.

Extended architecture rearranges the byte assignment of these data modes to suit multi-session applications. In XA Mode 2 Form 1, the 12 bytes of sync and 4 of header are followed by an 8-byte subheader that helps identify the contents of the data bytes, 2,048 of which follow. The frame ends with an auxiliary field storing 4 bytes of error detection and 276 bytes of error-correction code. In XA Mode 2 Form 2, the auxiliary field shrinks to 4 bytes; the leftover bytes extending the data contents to 2,324 bytes.

Data Coding

The bytes of the large frame do not directly correspond to the bit-pattern of pits that are blasted into the surface of the CD ROM. Much as hard disks use different forms of modulation to optimize both the capacity and integrity of their storage, the Compact Disc uses a special data-to-optical translation code. Circuitry inside the Compact Disc system converts the data stream of a large frame into a bit-pattern made from 98 small frames.

Each small frame stores 24 bytes of data (thus 98 of them equal a 2,352-byte large frame) but consists of 588 optical bits. Besides the main data channel, each small frame includes an invisible data byte called the subchannel and its own error-correction code. Each byte of this information is translated into 14 bits of optical code. To these 14 bits, the signal processing circuitry adds 3 merging bits, the values of which are chosen to minimize the low-frequency content of the signal and optimize the performance of the phase-lock loop circuit used in recovering data from the disc.

The optical bits of a small frame are functionally divided into four sections. The first 27 bits comprise a synchronization pattern. They are followed by the byte of subchannel data, which is translated into 17 bits (14-bit data code plus 3 merging bits). Next comes the 24 data bytes (translated in 408 bits), followed by 8 bytes of error-correction code (translated into 136 bits).

The subchannel byte actually encodes eight separate subchannels, designated with letters from P through W. Each bit has its own function. For example, the P subchannel is a flag used to control audio muting. The Q subchannel is used to identify large frames in audio recording.

As with a hard disk, this deep structure is hidden from your normal application software. The only concern of your applications is to determine how the 2,048 (or so) bytes of active storage in each large frame are divided up and used. The CD ROM drive translates the block requests made by the SCSI (or other interface) into the correct values in the synchronization field to find data.

Sessions

A session is a single recorded segment on a CD that may comprise multiple tracks. The session is normally recorded all at once in a single session, hence the name. Under the Orange Book standard, a session can contain data, audio, or images.

On the disc, each session begins with a lead-in, which provides space for a table of contents for the session. The lead-in length is fixed at 4,500 sectors, equivalent to one minute of audio or 9MB of data. When you start writing a session, the lead-in is left blank and is filled in only when you close the session.

At the end of the last session on the disc is a lead-out, which contains no data but only signals to the CD player that it has reached the end of the active data area. The first lead-out on a disc measures 6,750 sectors long, the equivalent of 1.5 minutes of audio or 13MB of data. Any subsequent lead-outs on a single disc last for 2,250 sectors, half a minute or about 4MB of data.

Addressing

The basic addressing scheme of the Compact Disc is the track, but CD tracks are not the same as hard disk tracks. Instead of indicating a head position or cylinder, the track on a CD is a logical structure akin to the individual tracks or cuts on a phonograph record.

A single Compact Disc is organized with up to 99 tracks. Although a single CD can accommodate a mix of audio, video, and digital data, each track must be purely one of the three. Consequently, a disc mixing audio, video, and data would need to have at least three tracks.

The tracks on a disc are contiguous and sequentially numbered, although the first track containing information may have a value greater than one. Each track consists of at least 300 large frames (that's four seconds of audio playing time). Part of each track is a transition area called pre-gap and post-gap areas (for data discs) or pause areas (for audio discs).

Each disc has a lead-in area and a lead-out area corresponding to the lead-in and lead-out of phonograph records. The lead-in area is designated track zero, and the lead-out area is track 0AA(Hex). Neither is reported as part of the capacity of the disc, although the subchannel of the lead-in contains the table of contents of the disc. The table of contents lists every track and its address (given in the format of minutes, seconds, and frames).

Tracks are subdivided into up to 99 indices by values encoded in the subchannel byte of 9 out of 10 small frames. An index is a point of reference that's internal to the track. The number and location of each index is not stored in the table of contents. The pre-gap area is assigned an index value of zero.

Capacity

The nominal maximum capacity of a CD amounts to 74 minutes of music recording time or about 650MB when used for storing data. These capacities are only approximate, however. A number of factors control the total capacity of a given disc. For example, mass-produced audio CDs sometimes contain more than 74 minutes of sound because disc makers can cram more onto each disc by squeezing the track on the glass master disc into a tighter, longer spiral. This technique can extend the playing time of a disc to 80 minutes or more.

The special CDs that you can write on with your PC cannot benefit from this tighter-track strategy because their spiral is put in place when the discs are manufactured. The standard formats yield four capacity levels on two different sizes of disc, as discussed in the section "CD-Recordable." In any case, these numbers represent the maximum storage capacity of a recordable CD. Nearly anything you do when making a CD cuts into that capacity.

Although 650MB seemed generous at one time—even as recently as a few years ago—the needs of modern PCs are quickly overwhelming the CD. These demands have added impetus to develop the much higher capacity DVD.

Format

The Yellow Book describes how to put information on a CD ROM disc. It does not, however, define how to organize that data into files. In the DOS world, two file standards have been popular. The first was called High Sierra format. Later, this format was upgraded to the current standard, the ISO 9660 specification.

The only practical difference between these two standards is that the driver software supplied with some CD ROM players, particularly older ones, meant for use with High Sierra formatted discs may not recognize ISO 9660 discs. You're likely to get an error message that says something like "Disc not High Sierra." The problem is that the old version of the Microsoft CD ROM extensions—the driver that adapts your CD ROM player to work with DOS—cannot recognize ISO 9660 discs.

To meld CD ROM technology with DOS, Microsoft Corporation created a standard bit of operating code to add onto DOS to make the players work. These are called the DOS CD ROM extensions, and several versions have been written. The CD ROM extensions before Version 2.0 exhibit the incompatibility problem between High Sierra and ISO 9660. The solution is to buy a software upgrade to the CD ROM extensions that came with your CD ROM player from the vendor who sold you the equipment. A better solution is to avoid the problem and ensure any CD ROM player you purchase comes with version 2.0 or later of the Microsoft CD ROM extensions.

ISO 9660 embraces all forms of data you're likely to use with your PC. Compatible discs can hold files for data as well as audio and video information.

For Windows 95, Microsoft created another set of extensions to ISO 9660. Called the *Joliet CD ROM Recording Specification*, these extensions add support for longer filenames—but to 128 characters instead of the 255-character maximum of Windows 95—as well as nesting directories beyond eight levels, allowing directory names to use extensions, and broadening the character set. To maintain compatibility with ISO 9660, the extra Joliet data must fit in a 240-character limit, foreclosing on the possibility of encoding all Windows 95 directory data.

CD-Recordable

Orange Book is the official tome that describes the needs and standards for Compact Disc-Recordable (CD-R) systems. It turns the otherwise read-only medium into a write-once medium so you can make your own CDs. Introduced in 1992, the Orange Book standard introduced multi-session technology. A multi-session disc can contain blocks of data written at different times (sessions). Each session has its own lead-in track and table of contents.

Developed jointly by Philips and Sony (sound familiar?), the Orange Book defines both the physical structure of recordable CDs and how various parts of the data area on the disc must be used. These include the program area, which holds the actual data the disc is meant to store, a program memory area that records the track information for the whole disc and all the sessions it contains, the lead-in and lead-out areas, and a power calibration area that's used to calibrate the power of the record laser.

The nature of the CD ROM medium and operation of CD recorders make the creation and writing of a CD ROM a more complex operation than simply copying files to a hard disk drive. Because CD ROMs are essentially sequentially recorded media, the CD recorder wants to receive data and write it to disc as a continuous stream. In most CD recorders, the stream of data cannot be interrupted once it starts. An interruption in the data flow can result in an error in recording. Moreover, to obtain the highest capacity possible from a given CD, you want to limit the number of sessions into which you divide the disc. As noted earlier, each session steals at least 13MB from disc capacity for the overhead of the session's lead-in and lead-out.

If your system cannot supply information to your CD recorder fast enough, the result is a *buffer underrun error*. When you see such an error message on your screen, it means your CD recorder has exhausted the software buffer and run out of data to write to the disc. The later section, "Underrun," tells how to avoid underrun errors when writing discs.

Depending on the manufacturer of your CD recorder and the software accompanying it, you may have a choice of more than one mode for copying data to CD. In general, you have two choices, building a CD image on your hard disk and copying that image intact to your CD. Some manufacturers call this process "writing on the fly." From a hardware standpoint, this is the easiest for your system and CD recorder to cope with because the disc image is already in the form of a single huge file with all of the directory structures needed for the final CD in their proper places. Your system needs only ready your hard disk and send a steady stream of data to the CD recorder.

The alternative method is to create the CD structure in its final form on the CD itself. Some manufacturers call this "writing a virtual image." In making a CD by this method, your CD recorder's software must follow a script or database to find which files it should include on the disc and locate the files on your hard disk. The program must allocate the space on your CD, dividing it into sectors and tracks, while at the same time reading the hard disk and transferring the data to the CD.

Capacity Issues

With a read-only medium, you normally don't have to concern yourself with the issue of storage capacity. That's for the disc maker to worry about; the publisher has to be sure everything fits. With about 650MB of room on the typical CD and many products requiring only a few megabytes for code, the big problem for publishers is finding enough stuff to put on the disc so that you think you're getting your money's worth.

The advent of recordable CDs changes things entirely. With CDs offering convenient long-term storage for important files such as graphic archives, you'll be sorely tempted to fill your CDs to the brim. You'll need to plan ahead to make all your files fit.

CD ROMs have substantial overhead that cuts into their available capacity. If you don't plan for this overhead, you may be surprised when your files don't fit.

Raw Capacity

CD ROM capacities are measured in minutes, seconds, and sectors based on the audio format from which engineers derived the medium. Recordable CDs come in four capacities: 18 and 21 minute discs are 80 millimeters in diameter; 63 and 74 minute discs are 120 millimeters in diameter.

Two kinds of file overhead (discussed in the following sections) affect the number of bytes available on a given recordable CD that are actually used for storage. One is familiar from other mass storage devices, resulting from the need to allocate data in fixed-size blocks. The other results from the format structure required by the CD standards.

Logical Block Padding

As with most hard and floppy discs, CD ROMs allocate their storage in increments called *logical blocks*. Although logical block sizes of 512, 1,024, and 2,048 bytes are possible with today's CD drives, only the 2,048-byte logical block format is in wide use. If a file is smaller than a logical block, it is padded out to fill a logical block. If a file is larger than one logical block, it fills all its logical blocks except the last, which is then padded out to be completely filled. As a result of this allocation method, all files except those that are an exact multiple of the logical block size require more disc space than their actual size. In addition, all directories on a CD require at least one logical block of storage.

That said, CD ROMs are typically more frugal with their storage than today's large hard disks. The standard DOS and Windows 95 disc formats require allocation units called clusters of 16KB for discs with capacities between 1 and 2GB, so they waste substantially more space on allocation unit padding than do CDs.

Format Overhead

In addition to the block-based overhead shared with most mass storage devices, CD ROMs have their own format overhead that is unique to the CD system. These are remnants of the audio origins of the CD medium.

Because audio CDs require lead-in and lead-out tracks, the Yellow Book standard for CD ROM makes a similar allowance. The specifications require that data on a CD ROM begin after a two second pause, followed by a lead-in track 6,500 sectors long. Consequently, the first two seconds of storage space and the lead-in area on a CD are not usable for data. These two seconds comprise a total of 150 sectors each holding 2,048 bytes, which trims the capacity of the disc by 307,200 bytes. The 6,500 sector lead-in consumes another 13,312,000 bytes. The lead-out gap at the end of a storage session and pregap that allows for a subsequent session consume another 4,650 sectors or 9,523,200 bytes.

The ISO 9660 file structure also eats away at the total disc capacity. The standard reserved the first 16 sectors of the data area—that's 32,768 bytes—for system use. Various elements of the disc format also swallow up space. The root file, primary volume descriptor, and volume descriptor set terminator each require a minimum of one sector. The path tables require at least two sectors. The required elements consequently take another 5 sectors or 10,120 bytes of space. Discs with complex file structures may exceed these minimums and lose further storage space.

The more sessions you divide a given CD into, the less space will be available for your data. Each session on a multi-session CD requires its own lead-in. Consequently, each session requires at least 13MB of space in addition to the file structure overhead.

Operation

Creating a CD is a complete process. The drive doesn't just copy down data blocks as your PC pushes them out. Every disc, even every session, requires its own control areas to be written to the disc. Your CD-R drive doesn't know enough to handle these processes automatically because the disc data structure depends on your data and your intentions. Your CD-R drive cannot fathom either of these. The job falls to the software you use to create your CD-R discs.

Your CD creation software organizes the data for your disc. As it sends the information to your CD-R drive, it also adds the control information required for making the proper disc format. After you've completed writing to your disc, the software fixates the disc so that it can be played. The last job is left to you—labeling the disc so you can identify the one you need from a stack more chaotic than the pot of an all-night poker game.

Speed

As with ordinary CD ROMs, the speed of CD-R drives is the transfer rate of the drive measured in multiples of the basic audio CD speed, 150 KB/sec. The very first CD recorders operated at 1x speed, and each new generation has doubled that speed. The fastest drives currently operate at 4x, although technical innovation can increase that just as it has improved basic CD speed.

Most CD recorders have two speed ratings, one for writing and one for reading. The writing speed is invariably the same or less than the reading speed. Advertisements usually describe drives using two numbers, the writing speed (lower number) first. The most common speed combinations are: 1x1, single-speed read and write; 1x2, single-speed write and double-speed read; 2x2, double-speed writing and reading; 2x4, double-speed writing and quadruple-speed reading; and 4x4, quadruple-speed in both writing and reading.

How fast a CD recorder writes is only one factor in determining how long making one or more CDs will take. Other variables include your system, writing mode (whether you try to put files together for a CD session on the fly or try to write a disc image as one interrupted file), and the number of drives.

Your system and writing mode go hand-in-hand. As noted later, a CD recorder requires a constant, uninterrupted stream of data to make a disc. The speed at which your PC can maintain that data flow can constrain the maximum writing speed of a CD-R drive. Factors that determine the rate of data flow include the speed of the source of the data (your hard disk), the fragmentation of the data, and the interfaces between the source disc and your CD recorder.

Most CD recorders have built-in buffers to bridge across temporary slow-downs in the data supply, such as may be involved in your hard disk's read/write head repeatedly moving from track to track to gather together a highly fragmented file or when an older, non-A/V drive performs a thermal calibration. Even with this bridge action, however, such hard disk slow-downs reduce the net flow of data to the CD recorder. If you try to create a CD by gathering together hundreds of short hard disk files on the fly, your hard disk may not be able to keep up with the data needs of a 4x CD recorder. In fact, if the files are many and small, the hard disk may not even be able to maintain 1x speed, forcing you to resort to making an image file before writing to disc.

On the other hand, one manufacturer (Mitsumi) reports that higher writing speeds produce more reliable CDs. At the 1x writing speed, the laser remains focused on a given disc area longer, possibly overheating it. In other words, you may want to avoid 1x speed unless the performance of your system and its software requires it. Although early software, drives, and PCs often could not keep up with speeds in excess of 1x, most current products do not have difficulties at higher speeds.

When you have to produce a large number of CDs quickly, one of the best strategies is to use multiple drives. Five drives writing simultaneously cuts the net creation time of an individual CD by 80 percent. Because the drives write exactly the same data, your PC needs to prepare only a single data-stream so underrun worries are no greater than when using a single drive. For moderate volume applications, stacks of CD writers can make a lot of sense—and CDs. For large volume applications (generally more than a few hundred), pressing CDs is the most cost-effective means of duplication, albeit one that requires waiting a few days for mastering and pressing.

Disc Writing Modes

Depending on your CD-R drive and your CD creation software, you may have your choice of the mode you use for writing to your CD. The mode determines what you can write to your discs and when. Typically, you don't have to worry about the writing mode because your software takes care of the details automatically. However, some drives and software may be limited to the modes under which they can operate.

The basic CD writing modes are four: track-at-once, multi-session, disc-at-once, and incremental writing. Each has its own requirements, limitations, and applications.

Track-at-Once

The most basic writing method for CDs is the creation of a single track. A track can be in any format that your CD-R drive can write, for example, a CD ROM compatible disc or a CD-DA disc for your stereo system. The track-at-once process writes an entire track in a single operation. A track must be larger than 300 blocks and smaller than the total capacity of the disc minus its overhead.

Writing track-at-once requires only that you designate what files you want to put on a CD. Your CD creation software takes over and handles the entire writing process.

Originally, the big limitation of track-at-once writing was that you could write only one track on a disc in a single session. Consequently, unless you had a lot to write to your disc already prepared beforehand, this process was wasteful of disc space. Some modern CD systems can add one track at a time to a disc within a single session, even allowing you to remove the disc from the drive and try it in another in the middle of the process.

Each track has overhead totaling 150 blocks of overhead for lead-in, lead-out, pre-gap, and linking. CD standards allow 99 tracks per disc; consequently if your tracks are small, you may waste substantial capacity. Writing the maximum number of blocks of minimal size (300 blocks plus 150 blocks of overhead each) will only about half-fill the smallest, 18 minute CD (44,550 blocks on a 81,000 block disc).

Track Multi-Session

Sometimes called *track incremental* mode, *track multi-session* mode is the most common means of allowing you to take advantage of the full capacity of CDs. Track multi-session writing allows you to add to CDs as you have the need for it by dividing the capacity of the disc into multiple sessions, up to about 50 of them. Each session has many of the characteristics of a complete CD, including its own lead-in and lead-out areas as well as table of contents.

In fact, the need for these special formatting areas for each session is what limits the number of sessions on the disc. The lead-in and lead-out areas together require about 13.5MB of disc space. Consequently, CDs with a total capacity of 680MB can hold no more than about 50 sessions.

When the CD standards were first created, engineers didn't even consider the possibility that individual consumers would ever be able to write their own discs. Consequently, they assumed that all discs would be factory mastered in a single session. They designed early CD drives to recognize only one session on a disc. Many older CD ROM drives (particularly those with 1x and 2x speed ratings) were single-session models and cannot handle multi-session discs written in track multi-session mode. Single-session drives generally read only the first session on a disc and ignore the rest.

Another problem that may arise with multi-session discs is the mixing of formats. Many CD players are incapable of handling discs on which CD ROM Mode 1 or 2 sessions are mixed with XA sessions. The dangerous aspect of this problem is that some CD mastering software (and CD drives) allow you to freely mix formats in different sessions. You may create a disc that works when you read it on your CD drive that cannot function in other CD drives. The moral is not to mix formats on a disc. (Don't confuse format with data type. You can freely mix audio, video, and pure data as long as they are written in the same format, providing the one you choose is compatible with all three data types.)

Most modern CD-R machines allow you to write more than one track in a given session. The advantage of this technique is the elimination of most of the 13.5MB session overhead. Instead of lead-in and lead-out tracks, each pair of tracks is separated by 150 blocks (two seconds) of pre-gap—overhead of only about 300KB. The entire session must, of course, be framed by its own lead-in, table of contents, and lead-out areas.

In multi-session discs, the drive writes to the lead-in area after it finishes with the data on the disc. The lead-in contains the table of contents for the session as well as an indication of the remaining writeable area on the disc. The lead-in of the last session on the disc indicates that no more sessions are present, closing the disc.

Disc-at-Once

Old-fashioned vinyl phonograph records were cut as a single, continuous process. From the moment the cutting stylus plunked down on the master disc until it finished the disc spinning around in the capture track, the mastering process had to be free of interruptions. After all, any gap in the spiral track of the phonograph record would stall your record player. To cut a master record, the engineers prepared a master tape that was complete in every detail of everything that was to go on the final disc, including blank tape for the gaps between cuts on the final disc.

The CD equivalent to making such a master disc is the disc-at-once process. As with cutting a master record, the disc-at-once process must be completely free from interruption from the beginning of the lead-in area to the completion of the lead-out area. The table of contents, all tracks, and the Q channel must all be prepared before the writing process begins. The entire disc will be written in one swoop in the order that the formatting data appear on the disc. (For example, the lead-in will be written before the data.) Typically, to make a CD using disc-at-once writing, you'll prepare an exact image of the CD and store it on a hard disk. The hard disk must be A/V rated so that it does not interrupt the data stream for thermal calibration or other housekeeping and thus cause buffer underrun. (See the section "Underrun" later in this chapter.)

In effect, disc-at-once is a combination of track-at-once and multi-session writing that simply extends across the entire CD (or as much of it as will ever be used).

Disc-at-once is the recording method that must be used when you prepare a disc to serve as master for making mass-produced CDs. Because the laser never turns off, a disc recorded using the disc-at-once mode contains no link blocks.

Packet Writing

If you could make a CD-R work like a conventional hard disk, it would be capable of *incremental writing*. That is, you could add data to your disc whenever you needed to simply by saving a file. In CD terminology, this is called *packet writing*. With appropriate software drivers, you can drag and drop files to your CD recorder as if it were a hard disk drive.

In this context, a packet is a block of data smaller than a track. Your drive accepts the packet and writes it to the disc, identifying it with four blocks of lead-in information, two of lead-out, and a link block. Each packet thus suffers seven blocks or about 15KB of overhead in addition to that required for directory information.

The ISO 9660 file system comes up short in packet writing. It requires that all the file information be written in the table of contents when you create a session. Multi-session discs sidestep this problem by creating a new file system every time you write a new session—with all the overhead of a complete file system; whoops, there goes another 13.5MB. Packet writing thus requires drives and software that follow the UDF (Universal Data Format) system, discussed in the section "DVD-ROM" later in this chapter.

Underrun

No matter the mode, the CD writing process is continuous start to finish. The laser switches on at the beginning of a session and remains in continuous operation until that session is finished. The CD format requires the interleaving of data between blocks during the writing process to help ensure data integrity. To properly interleave the data, the drive needs an overview of it. To gain this overview, the drive has a data buffer from which it draws the data to write.

For the laser in a CD-R drive to operate continuously, it must have a continuous supply of data to keep its buffer filled with enough information to properly perform the interleaving. If at any time it runs out of data to write, the writing process is interrupted. Unlike hard disks, the CD drive can't pick up where it left off on the next spin of the disc. The error resulting from the interruption of the data flow is termed *buffer underrun*.

CD players see the interrupted session as an error (which it is) that may render the disc unplayable. In other words, buffer underrun ruins a disc. Better CD-R drives allow you to close the interrupted session and recover the remaining space on the disc for other sessions.

You can prevent this error by increasing the size of the buffer if your software allows it. Or you can better prepare your files for transfer to CD. In particular, build a CD image on a hard disk that can be copied on the fly to the CD.

The best strategy is to give over your PC to the CD writing process, unloading any TSR programs, background processes, or additional tasks in a multitasking system. Screen savers, pop-up reminders, and incoming communications (your modem answering the phone for data or a fax) can interrupt your CD session and cause you to waste your time, a session, or an entire disc.

Your system needs to be able to find the files it needs to copy to your CD ROM as efficiently as possible. Copying multiple short files can be a challenge, particularly if your hard disk is older and slower or fragmented. CD recorder makers recommend discs with access times faster than about 19 milliseconds. An AV-style hard disk is preferable because such drives are designed for the smooth, continuous transfer of data and don't interrupt the flow with housekeeping functions such a thermal calibration. You'll also want to be sure that your files are not fragmented before transferring them to CD. Run your defrag utility before writing to your CD.

Testing

To prevent your wasting discs with inadvertent data underruns, most CD-R mastering software makes a trial run or test of the recording session before actually committing your data to disc. The test involves performing exactly the same steps as the actual write operation—including operating the laser in the drive in its write mode—but keeps the power of the laser at read level. The CD-R drive runs through the entire write operation but the lower power of the laser prevents it from affecting (and potentially ruining) a disc.

If the recording software discovers a problem during recording that would cause an underrun or other problem, it will advise you how to sidestep the problem, typically by stepping down to a lower writing speed on your CD-R drive or, as a last resort, defragmenting your hard disk.

The only problem with pre-write testing is that the trial run takes as long as writing everything to your disc, essentially doubling the write time of every disc you make. Most CD mastering programs allow you to switch off this pre-write testing. Although you do this at your own peril (and the expense of ruined CDs), if you're making a batch of discs it is a viable time-saving option. In general, if you can write the first disc successfully, you can run through dozens of additional copies without worry.

Fixation

Before a CD that you write can be read by a CD ROM drive or the audio CD player in your stereo system, it must have an overall table of contents that follows the ISO 9660 standard. The process of finishing the disc for reading is termed *fixation*. In the process of fixation, the disc is *finalized* when your CD-R drive writes an overall *absolute lead-in area* and *absolute lead-out area* for the entire disc.

Multi-session drives also can create discs that are *fixated for appending*. The individual sessions each have their own table of contents that reflects the sessions actually written on the disc, but the disc lacks the overall lead-in and lead-out areas. When you've added the last session to the disc, the *finalization* process writes an indication on the disc that no further sessions are present and then writes the overall disc lead-in and lead-out areas, completing a table of contents compatible with the ISO 9660 standard. Most CD mastering programs refer to this finalization process as *closing* the disc.

Software that performs packet writing—for example, Sony's CDRFS (Compact Disc Recordable File System)—may require a process termed *freezing* the disc before you can use packet-written discs in ordinary CD players. The freezing process writes lead-in and lead-out areas on the disc. After a disc has been frozen, you can still write additional sessions onto it providing, of course, additional capacity is available. The freeze process only subtracts from the available capacity, draining away the 13MB of overhead required by any single session.

Labeling

The last step in preparing a CD-R disc for use is labeling it so that you can later identify its contents without having to shove it into your CD drive first. You have your choice of several options—each with its own requirements and limitations—for labeling your CDs.

The easiest way to label a CD is just scribble on its back surface, the one that has the manufacturer's logo and other information already printed on it. You can directly write anywhere on this side of the disc. However, to prevent damage to the disc, damage that won't be immediately apparent but may gradually cause the disc to deteriorate, you should only use a permanent marker that uses water-soluble ink. Markers with the traditional "Magic Marker" smell have volatile solvents that can leech through the protective coating on your CDs and affect the data storage layers. Never use ballpoint pen, pencil, or any sharp instrument to label discs. Nor should you use the traditional alternative to sharp objects, crayons, because they leave residue that may flake off into the drive mechanism when the disc plays. Moreover, discs get hot inside the drive, which can melt the crayon wax, allowing it to gum up the works.

Labels will give your discs a more professional look because you can take advantage of the full facilities of your computer printer to render high-quality text and multi-color artwork.

Again, the chemicals in the adhesives of some labels can have long-term deleterious effects on the CD medium. Choose only labels specifically designed for CDs.

Some people have reported problems with labels in high-speed (8x and 10x) CD players. They believe that the labels shift the balance of the disc in the drive, causing it to shake as it spins. Drive manufacturers do not believe that such small differences in balance affect drive performance. However, because of the high speed at which discs spin in some players, surface irregularities such as wrinkled or folded labels may create turbulence and unsteadiness in the rapidly spinning discs. Ensure that your labels lie flat against the disc surface and do not overhang the edge of the disc. Don't try pulling a label from a disc, even one that's only partially stuck, because you may rip part of the surface of the disc along with the adhesive.

Several manufacturers offer special printers designed specifically for low-volume CD writing. Models based on thermal-wax technology create on-disc labels that look like they have been silk-screened. This technology will work with almost any recordable CD. Other CD-R labeling machines use ink-jet technology. These require specially prepared discs that have a specially prepared labeling area to which ink-jet ink can adhere.

Typically, you'll label a disc after you've finished writing the last session to it. Some drive makers recommend that you label your discs *before* you start writing, however. The label may change some performance characteristics (optical or mechanical) of the drive. For example, some CD-R drives have Optimal Power Control circuits that ensure the writing laser is operating at peak efficiency, changing its intensity to match the reflectivity of the disc. If you label the disc before you write to it, the electronics of the drive can often compensate for the changes the label makes. As a result, your discs will be more reliable.

CD-Rewriteable

CD-RW stands for CD-Rewriteable, meaning that these drives can create new CDs that you can erase and use again. In fact, you can treat a rewriteable CD as if it were a big floppy disc drive or slow hard disk drive. All CD-RW drives also function as CD-R drives and they are standardized under the Orange Book just as are CD-R drives.

The difference between CD-R and CD-RW is in the media. Put a blank CD-R disc in a CD-RW drive, and you make a permanent record that you cannot change. With a CD-RW disc, you can rewrite and reuse disc space, thanks to its phase-change medium.

CD-RW drives are actually the third incarnation of phase-change technology. The first drives, under the Phase Change Recordable banner, or PCR, were made by Toray Industries. They used a medium slightly larger than CDs, 130 millimeters in diameter as opposed to the CD's 120 mm, and were consequently physically incompatible with CD drives. Both sides of the disc had a recordable surface, allowing for a total capacity of 1.5GB per disc. Panasonic's PD discs reduced the size of the disc to the same as CDs and modified the storage format. The actual writing format uses sectors of 512 bytes versus the 2,048-byte or larger sectors used by CD, so PD disc are also logically incompatible with CDs. You cannot duplicate a CD on the PD medium. Moreover, the logical format of the PD system limits its capacity to 650MB per disc as opposed to the 680MB total of CDs. Further, the phase-change material used by the Panasonic PD drives is not compatible with the optical heads and electronics of CD drives. Although the electronics of the Panasonic drives were adapted to handle either phase-change or conventional CD media, PD discs work only in PD drives.

Because of the lower reflectivity of CD-RW media, phase-change discs often are unreadable in early (pre-1998) CD ROM and CD-R drives. Newer drives have compensatory circuitry built in called *automatic gain control.*

In operation, a CD-RW drive can function more like a conventional hard disk than a CD-R. The drive can update the disc table of contents at any time so you can add files and tracks without additional session overhead. Under Windows, you typically drag and drop files to your CD-RW drive just like you would with any other disk. Note, however, that the format used during CD-RW operation is usually different from that of conventional CDs. To read a CD-RW disc in a CD ROM or CD-R drive, the disc must be closed, an operation that effectively reorganizes its format. In the typical implementation, the reorganization process requires blank space on the disc, so you cannot fill a CD-RW disc with data and expect to later use it in another drive.

DVD-ROM

To your PC, the storage on a DVD looks much like that of any disk system. Information is organized into 2KB blocks that correspond to the clusters on disk systems. The file structure takes the form of Micro UDF/ISO Bridge format. In effect, it bridges two storage formats. *Universal Data Format* was designed by the Optical Storage Technology Association, a group of companies involved in optical data storage, to make data stored on optical discs independent of any operating system (hence, "universal"). The goal was to allow you to write an optical disc on your computer and read it on any other computer in the world, regardless of operating system or microprocessor or even whether it was powered by electricity or steam. UDF defines the data structures (partitions, files, sectors), error correction, character sets, and the read/write method of the DVD system. ISO 9660 defines the tree-oriented directory structure (the same as on computer CDs) compatible with Windows and other popular operating systems. The overall structure of the disc fits the UDF format with the ISO 9660 structure on top, the intent being to eventually eliminate ISO 9660 support.

As this is written, the UDF specification has incremented up to version 2.0, the level that OSTA recommends DVD-ROM publishers follow. DVD-Video discs and players are locked to the UDF version 1.02 specifications. You can download both versions of the specification in their entirety from `www.osta.org`.

The Micro UDF/ISO Bridge format imposes some limits on DVDs. One oft-quoted limit is a maximum file size of 1GB. This constraint applied only to DVD-Video discs. Although it seems incompatible with two hours of continuous video playback, the DVD system was design to agglomerate multiple small files (including video, audio, and control information), process them together, and output a single continuous video stream.

On the disc itself, the block is chopped and scattered to help in error recovery. The tiny size of the pits on the disc means that a splotch or scratch will likely span a considerable storage area. Spreading the data out scatters potential read errors into small pieces in different storage units so that they can be more readily detected and corrected.

Each 2KB block is translated into a 2,064-byte physical sector for storage on the disc. The sector gets further subdivided into 12 rows of 172 bytes each. The central 10 rows store only data. The first starts with a 12-byte sector header to identify the storage unit. Four bytes provide the actual ID information with two additional bytes used for error correction dedicated to the ID data. The remaining six bytes in the header are reserved. The following 160 bytes in the first row contain data. The last row of each sector ends with four bytes of error detection and correction information for the data area of the sector.

Sixteen sectors are then interleaved together to form a larger storage unit, the block. Ten bytes of error-correction code are added to each row in the block, and the resulting overall block gains another 16 rows of error-correction code. The result is a block of 37,856 bytes with about 15 percent of its contents devoted to error-correction information. These blocks are then written sequentially to the disc.

The DVD-ROM format allows for both constant linear velocity and constant angular velocity recording. The former favors capacity in sequential access applications (audio and video). The later improves random access speed for data applications but reduces the capacity of each layer. Although it is an inherent part of the DVD-ROM specification, the chief application of CAV recording in DVD has been the various rewriteable formats.

The required support to read UDF-based DVD-ROM discs is built into Windows 98 and will be part of Windows 2000. Earlier Windows versions will require add-in drivers, which are usually included with DVD drives. In addition to decoder software, playback of DVD-Video requires DirectShow 5.2 or newer, which is included with Windows 98. More recent versions can be downloaded from Microsoft's Web site at `www.microsoft.com`. Again, DVD drives usually include the necessary decoder (as software or as a separate hardware MPEG-decoder board) as well as DirectShow.

DVD-Video

The DVD-Video system devotes one track to video information that may use either MPEG1 or MPEG2 encoding. All commercial discs use MPEG2 because it simply looks (and works) better. A dedicated DVD player can render into video for either your television or monitor. With current technologies, a DVD-ROM player in a PC works best with a separate hardware-based MPEG2 decoder. Only the fastest PC processor can decode MPEG2 in real time, and even these don't work as well as dedicated hardware decoders. Moreover, because your PC must devote nearly all of its power to decoding the video, there's little left for doing other work at the same time.

DVD-Video would not be possible without compression (nor would any other digital video system be practical). DVD-Video data originates with a bit rate of 124 Mbits/sec, and it must be compressed down to the maximum rate permitted under the DVD standard, 9.6 Mbits/sec. The average bit rate is about 3.5 Mbits/sec. Despite the heavy-duty compression, DVD still delivers about twice the resolution of VHS videocassettes. A typical DVD-Video system produces horizontal resolution of about 500 lines compared to less than 240 lines for a VHS tape.

DVD-Video goes far beyond today's VHS and CD-Video systems. It allows both conventional-style images with the 4:3 aspect ratio as well as those with the 16:9 ratio favored by high-definition television systems. DVD players are required to have built-in filters to translate 16:9 images into the full-width of a 4:3 aspect ratio screen, in other words, built-in letterbox format translation. The DVD players will also allow you zoom in to fill the screen height with a 16:9 image and pan to either side of the picture. The MPEG-2 encoding delivers about four times the spatial resolution as MPEG-1 used by some CD systems and allows a high-quality display with 480 lines of 720 pixels each to fit into a 4 MB/sec data stream. As with any video compression technique, the exact data rate depends on the complexity of the image. Typically, a high-quality image requires *less* data than a low-quality one plagued by noise. The onscreen resolution produced by a DVD system is in the range of 480–500 horizontal lines. Unlike other video systems—VCRs and LaserDisc systems—DVD stores video images in component format, separate red, green, and blue images. Other consumer formats use composite video.

DVD-Video also introduces the concept of *subpictures*, which are additional images of limited color depth that can be multiplexed with the main audio and video data. The DVD standards allows for up to 32 subpictures, which typically will be menus for control systems, subtitles for foreign language films, or production credits. Each subpicture can measure as large as 720 by 480 pixels in four colors.

Note that DVD video is not High Definition Television. About the only thing in common between the two is the 16:9 aspect ratio supported by both. DVD video is more closely aligned with standard NTSC video, offering quality similar to that in the television studio.

An HDTV image has about five times the number of pixels as the DVD video format. Its compressed format requires about twice the data rate (about 19.4 Mbits/sec). Certainly, the DVD-18 medium has enough capacity to store HDTV, but it will require a new storage and playback format to cope with the HDTV data rate.

DVD mimics HDTV by offering a wide aspect ratio format. The DVD standard allows for both the old television and video aspect ratio of 4:3 and the HDTV aspect ratio of 16:9. The wide aspect ratio images have the same number of pixels as 4:3 images. The image is compressed anamorphically to fit. On playback, the ostensibly square pixels get stretched horizontally to the wider aspect ratio. The standard allows the display of wide aspect ratio images in three different ways, which you can select when playing back a disc:

Letterbox mode fills the width of the screen with the full width of the image, leaving black bands 60 lines high at the top and bottom of the screen.

Pan and scan mode fills the full narrow screen with a window into the wide image. The window is dynamic. The disc stores cues determined by the director of the film or producer of the DVD that guide the window to follow the action in the image.

Widescreen mode provides a full-width image on a 19:6 aspect ratio screen.

The audio accompanying DVD video can take any of many forms. The most common (used on nearly all releases of theatrical movies) is Dolby Digital. Although the Dolby Digital system can accommodate up to 5.1 channels of PCM audio, the standard embraces less as well—including simple monophonic and stereophonic recordings. In other words, a label proclaiming "Dolby Digital" on a movie box does not guarantee anything in the way of true multi-channel sound.

The required audio support depends on the standard followed by the recorded video. Discs containing NTSC video (the standard in North America and Japan) are required to use Dolby Digital. Discs containing PAL video (Europe and most of the rest of the world) must use MPEG 2 audio. Other audio formats may optionally accompany either video standard.

The DVD-Video standard accommodates eight tracks of audio, each track being a single data stream that may comprise one or more audio channels. Each of these channels may use any of five encoding systems. In addition to Dolby Digital (with up to 5.1 channels per track), all DVD drives must also be able to decode PCM audio, up to 8 channels per track (potentially 64 channels per disc, but real data rates ordain the channel count be lower), and MPEG audio (up to 7.1 channels per track). Optional decoding systems—which may or may not be included within the circuitry of a given DVD drive but can be attached as an accessory—include *Digital Theater Sound* (DTS) and *Sony Dynamic Digital Sound* (SDDS). Chapter 18, "Audio," discusses these systems in more detail.

Video DVDs are burdened with several layers of copy protection that are entwined both with hardware and operating system software. Copy-protection occurs at three levels—analog, serial copy protection, and digital encoding:

Analog copy protection alters the video output so that the signal appears corrupted to VCRs when you attempt to record it. The current *Analog Protection System*, or APS, adds a rapid modulation to the colorburst signal (called a *colorstripe*) and pulses in the vertical blanking signal (termed *AGC* because it is meant to confuse the Automatic Gain Control of VCRs). Computer video boards with conventional analog video outputs (composite or S-video) must incorporate APS. DVD-Video discs themselves control whether the APS system is used on playback by signaling to the disc player to switch APS on or off.

Serial copy protection encodes in the signal whether it can be copied. The *copy generation management system* adds information to line 21 of the NTSC video signal to tell equipment whether copying is permitted. Although DVD-Video encodes line 21 differently, the information is regenerated into the analog video output of DVD players and computer video boards.

Digital encoding encrypts the digital form of media files, requiring the video player know the key necessary for decrypting the code. The DIVX licensing system works through digital encoding.

In addition, DVDs are marked with a regional code, a number that specifies the part of the world in which playback of the DVD's content is permitted. The DVD player checks to see whether a region code on the software matches that encoded into its hardware. If the two don't match, the disc won't play. DVD media boxes are marked with the region code as a number on a globe icon, the number corresponding to one of six regions as listed in Table 12.5.

TABLE 12.5   DVD Regional Codes

Code Number	Region
1	Canada, United States (including US territories)
2	Egypt, Europe, Japan, Middle East, South Africa
3	East and Southeast Asia
4	Central and South America, Caribbean, Australia, New Zealand, Pacific Islands
5	Africa, former Soviet Union, Indian subcontinent, Mongolia, North Korea
6	China

DVD-Audio

Ever since the introduction of the CD-DA format, audio purists have insisted that it was not good enough. They could hear a definite digital sound (whatever that might be) that interfered with their enjoyment of music. They were quick to point out that tradeoffs made in the design of the CD-DA format slighted sound quality. The relatively low sampling rate required to pack enough information on a disc required high-order low-pass filtering to keep digital artifacts out of the audio, and even then, the upper cut-off frequency must be too low to accommodate everything that old analog tape recorders could capture.

The huge capacity of the DVD system eliminates the need for the tradeoffs of the CD-DA system and unleashes the potential for superb audio quality—good enough to satisfy listeners with 24-karat ears. The audio-only implementation of DVD—termed *DVD-Audio*—isn't just for purists, however. The system can use the multi-gigabyte storage of the medium for super-quality audio, additional channels, or both.

Where CDs are built around a 44.1KHz sampling rate, DVD supports both this rate (and the whole Red Book standard) as well as 48KHz, the same as professional audio systems, and a super-high quality 96KHz sampling rate. In addition to today's 16-bit digital audio, DVD will also support 24-bit audio as well as several compressed multi-channel formats to accompany video. The multi-channel audio standards vary with the video standard used, with Dolby AC-3 (eight-channel audio) for NTSC video.

The options allowed the producer for linear PCM are wide. The system supports up to six channels with bit depths of 16, 20, or 24. Recording may use either of two bit-rate families—the 44.1KHz of Red Book audio supplemented by 88.2 and 176.4KHz multiples or a 48KHz base rate supplemented by 96 and 192KHz multiples. The highest sampling rate and bit-depth (192KHz at 24 bits) allows response to nearly 96KHz with a dynamic range approaching 144dB. The maximum data rate of the system, 9.6 Mb/sec, constrains the system to two channels of these highest-quality signals and the storage capacity of the DVD system limits playing time (at this quality level) to about 67 minutes.

To extend playing time, the DVD-Audio standard allows for data compression of various sorts, including MPEG. Most intriguing is *MLP*, which stands for Meridian Lossless Packing. As the name implies, this system works like file compression and reduces data redundancies in the digital audio but allows the original signal to be perfectly reconstructed during decoding. Compression extends playing time enough to allow up to about 135 minutes of 6-channel 24-bit audio sampled at the 96KHz rate.

To make six-channel audio compatible with two-channel stereo sound systems, DVD-Audio incorporates a special *System-Managed Audio Resource Technique*, or SMART (entirely different from S.M.A.R.T. hard disk failure-prediction technology). This system allows the producer of an audio DVD to determine the optimum mixdown that combines the channels together for each selection on each disc. The mixdown information is stored as a table of coefficients—the level assigned to each channel in the mix—and each selection on the disc can have a particular table assigned to it. Each disc can accommodate up to 16 tables.

DVD-Audio discs also accommodate other kinds of data in addition to digital audio. The standard allows for including up to 16 still images in each track and for synchronizing a display of lyrics with the music. In addition, the DVD-Audio system provides for computer-style navigation through a screen-oriented menu system (or a simplified control system for audio players without computer displays).

Writeable DVD Formats

The next step after the DVD is the equivalent of CD-RW, a rewritable DVD. Although such drives are available, they are problematic. Currently, rewriteable DVD drives use any of three mutually incompatible recording formats, and there's no telling which if any of them will be the eventual standard. The drives are also quite expensive. Unless you're a gadgetophile or tinkerer, you'll probably want to avoid these products until things settle down. The following sections provide a quick run-down.

DVD-R

A write-once medium equivalent to CD-R, DVD-R uses the same dye-polymer technology on preformatted discs. At present, DVD-R drives can store only 3.9GB of data, although a capacity of 4.7GB is expected in drives by year end. DVD-R is not expected to be a major consumer medium but will find application in a sort of pre-press application—producing sample discs before DVDs are commercially stamped. This system does not appear targeted at home use. The first drives cost nearly $20,000, and the second generation still cost about $5,000. Officially, the DVD-R format is the ECMA-279 standard.

DVD-RW

Based on the DVD-R format, DVD-RW can store only 3.9GB of data per disc, although a capacity of 4.7GB was promised by the end of 1999. DVD-RW drives are in the same price range as DVD-R drives, making its chief market the preparation of DVD-ROM discs rather than as a consumer product. A DVD-RW disc can be rewritten approximately 1,000 times, allowing producers to work out the details of their creations.

DVD-RAM

The DVD Forum's chief entry as a consumer-level writeable DVD format, DVD-RAM promises to extend CD-RW technology to multiple gigabytes. In its initial incarnation, DVD-RAM discs could pack only 2.6GB, but manufacturers are working on extending that capacity to 4.7GB per disc. As with CD-RW, DVD-RAM uses phase-change media and a wobble groove pressed into the black discs to establish system timing when writing data. With an initial price in the $500–800 range, DVD-RAM was designed to compete with cartridge discs such as Iomega's Jaz drives. Its estimated life is more than 100,000 write cycles. (Reading is unlimited.) Hitachi is developing a version of DVD-RAM that uses a disc eight centimeters in diameter for camcorders.

DVD+RW

Jointly developed by Philips and Sony, DVD+RW is also based on CD-RW technology and is actually a more straightforward outgrowth of that format. It uses phase-change media and a preformatted wobble track for setting timing during the write process. The data format on the disc is the same as DVD-ROM as are its basic operating modes. For random access applications, the system uses zoned constant angular velocity recording, which limits disc capacity to about 2.8GB per side. A second generation of drives is projected to be compatible with the DVD-R and DVD-RW systems and store up to 4.7GB per disc. Sony claims DVD+RW drives will have full reading and writing backward compatibility with all major optical storage formats, including CD ROM, CD-R, CD-RW, CD audio and video, DVD-ROM, and DVD-Video discs. Although not supported by the DVD Forum, the DVD+RW format is standardized at ECMA-247.

Tape

Tape is for backup—your insurance that a disaster doesn't erase every last vestige of your valuable data. You also can use some of the standardized tape systems as exchange media—the floppy disk for the age of megabytes. Tape systems come in a number of formats with different capacities, speeds, and levels of convenience. The best, however, is the one that's easiest to use.

Best Backup Choices

Medium	Also known as	Advantages and disadvantages
Quarter-inch Cartridges	QIC, DC600	The first, the oldest, and ageing technology. Moderate capacity, moderate speed, moderate media cost, moderate drive cost
Mini-cartridges	Travan, Ditto	Moderate cartridge costs, moderate capacity, lowest initial price
DDS	DAT	Low cartridge cost, moderate capacity, moderate speed, compact, moderate purchase price
DLT	Digital Linear Tape	High cartridge cost, high speed, high capacity, high purchase price
LTO	Linear Tape Open	High cartridge cost, high speed, high capacity, high purchase price
CD-R	CD-Read only	Cheap medium but only one use, moderate speed, low capacity, low purchase price
CD-RW	CD Read/write	Moderate medium cost, moderate speed, low capacity, low purchase price
Duplicate disk		Lowest price all around but not a true backup system, limited protection

Faith is trusting your most valuable possessions—purportedly to protect them—to a sealed black box filled with fragile machinery you don't understand honed to split-hair tolerances and vulnerable to a multitude of ills—electroshock, impact, even old age. One misstep and your treasures can be destroyed.

Such groundless, even misguided, trust has no place in business and definitely no role in the rigorous world of personal computers, but that's exactly what you show every time you save a file to your hard disk drive. You send data to a complex, sealed black box with the hope of someday retrieving it. Technology has given us this faith, but just in case the faith is misused, technology has also bequeathed us the backup system.

A backup system will help you sleep at night—not with narcotic action (tape is definitely not habit-forming) but with peace of mind. You won't have to worry about your PC exploding from overload, the office burning down from spilled midnight oil, or thieves stealing your PC and all your business records with it. With a suitable backup system, you can quickly make a copy of your most valuable data on a movable medium that you can take to preserve somewhere safe. When disaster strikes—as it inevitably does—you always have your backup copy ready to replace the original.

The concept is simple but far from perfect. A backup system requires a combination of contradictory features. It must be permanent but reusable, secure but portable, reliable but cheap, easy-to-use but a piece of PC equipment. Three principal types storage equipment best fit the bill, recordable and rewritable compact discs (discussed in the previous chapter), cartridge disks (discussed on the CD-ROM) and tape, the subject of this chapter.

Background

Tape was the first magnetic mass storage system used in computers, harking back to the days of room-size Univacs and vacuum tubes. It first proved itself as a convenient alternative to punched cards and punched paper tape—the primary storage system used by mainframe computers. Later, information transfer became an important use for tape. Databases could be moved between systems as easily as carting around one or more spools of tape. After magnetic disks assumed the lead in primary storage, tape systems were adapted to backing them up.

Tape joined in personal computing already enjoying many of the benefits of its evolution in the mainframe environment. Never considered as primary storage—except in the nightmares of the first PC's original designers who thoughtfully included a cassette port on the machine for its millions of users to ignore—tape started life in the PC workplace in the same role it serves today, as a basic backup medium. Since the first systems, tape has grown in stride with the disks that it serves to back up. From initial systems able to store only about 30MB per tape, modern systems pack gigabytes into a compact, convenient cartridge.

With half a century of development behind it, tape has the potential to play a major role in your PC, not just protecting your data but also as an archival and exchange medium. Tape is unmatched as a low-cost medium for reliably holding data for the long term. Today's tape cartridges are the best way to secure gigabytes of data in a single convenient package, the best way of keeping multiple copies of your most important files so you won't risk losing your information assets even if the worst disaster befalls your PC, home, or office.

Over the long history of the PC, every few years tapes get eyed as a distribution exchange medium, too—a way for software publishers to get their products to you. When programs grew beyond the capacity of a reasonable number of floppy disks, some publishers toyed with tape systems to distribute their products. The idea never caught on, and the compact disc summarily squelched such thoughts—at least for now. But with some programs now claiming nearly a dozen CDs and DVD-ROM yet nascent, the time may come when some engineer decides that the 40GB capacity of a DDS-5 cartridge, no bigger than an audio cassette, makes a wonderful distribution and exchange medium. After all, pigs have grown wings, at least in *some* alternate realities.

Medium

As a physical entity, tape is both straightforward and esoteric. It is straightforward in design, providing the perfect sequential storage medium—a long, thin ribbon that can hold orderly sequences of information. The esoteric part involves the materials used in its construction.

Tape

The tape used by any system consists of two essential layers—the backing and the coating. The backing provides the support strength needed to hold the tape together while it is flung back and forth across the transport. Progress in the quality of the backing material mirrors developments in the plastics industry. The first tape was based on paper. Shortly after the introduction of commercial tape recorders at the beginning of the 1950s, cellulose acetate (the same plastic used in safety film in photography for three decades previously) was adopted. The state-of-the-art plastic is polyester, of double-knit leisure-suit fame. In tape, polyester has a timeless style of its own—flexible and long-wearing with a bit of stretch. It needs all those qualities to withstand the twists and turns of today's torturous mechanisms, fast shuttle speeds, and abrupt changes of direction. The typical tape backing measures from one-quarter mil (thousandth of an inch) to one mil thick, about 10 to 40 microns.

The width of the backing varies with its intended application. Wider tapes offer more area for storing data but are most costly and, after a point, become difficult to package. The narrowest tape in common use, cassette tape, measures 0.150 inches (3.8 millimeters) wide. The widest in general use for computing measures 0.5 inches (12.7 millimeters). Equipment design and storage format determine the width of tape to be used.

Coatings have also evolved over the decades, as they have for all magnetic media. Where once most tapes were coated with doped magnetic oxides, modern coatings include particles of pure metal in special binders and even vapor-plated metal films. Tape coatings are governed by the same principles as other magnetic media; the form is different but the composition remains the same. As with all magnetic storage systems, modern tape media have higher coercivities and support higher storage densities.

Cartridges

Taken by itself, tape is pretty hard to get a handle on. Pick up any reasonable length of tape, and you'll have an instant snarl on your hands. The only place that tape is used by itself is in endless loops (one ends splice to the other) in special bins used by audio and video duplicating machines. In all other applications, the tape is packaged on reels or in cartridges.

Reels came first. A spool onto which a length of tape gets wound, the reel is the simplest possible tape carrier. In this form, tape is called *open reel*. Normal tape transport requires two reels, one to supply the tape and one to take up the tape after it passes past the read/write heads. The principal problem with reel-based systems is manual tape handling. To use a tape reel, you must slide it onto a hub, pull out a leader, thread it past the read/write heads, and wrap it around the hub of the take-up reel. In addition, the tape must be physically turned over to use its second side (if it has one) or rewound when you're done with it. Although the path taken by recording tape is less tortuous than that of movie film, many people are challenged to thread it properly. Automatic threading systems are complex and, when badly implemented, unreliable. Although open-reel tape remains in use, most PC applications avoid it.

Putting tape in a cartridge adds a permanent package that both provides protection to the delicate medium and makes it more convenient to load. The most basic cartridge design, that used by the LTO Ultrium standard, a system for computers more powerful than PC and computer networks, simply packages a reel of tape in a plastic shell and relies on an automatic threading mechanism in the drive itself.

All current PC-size tape systems, including quarter-inch cartridges, and also four-millimeter and eight-millimeter helical tape systems, use cassette-style cartridges that include both the supply and take-up reels in a single cartridge. The origin of this design is traceable back to the original audio cassette.

Developed—and patented—by the Dutch Philips conglomerate, the audio cassette was just one of many attempts to sidestep the need for threading open-reel tapes. The idea did not originate with Philips, however. An earlier attempt by RCA, which used a similar but larger cassette package, failed ignobly in the marketplace. The *Compact Cassette*, as it was labeled by Philips, was successful because it was more convenient and did not aspire so high. It was not designed as a high-fidelity medium but grew into that market as technology improved its modest quality. The RCA cartridge was about the size of a thin book, but the Compact Cassette fit into a shirt pocket and was quite at home when it was on the go in portable equipment. Size and convenience led to its adoption as the auto-sound medium of choice, pushing aside both eight-track cartridges, becoming the general high-fidelity medium of choice, earning the majority of the pre-recorded music market before the introduction of the compact disc.

The basic cassette mechanism simply takes the two spools of the open-reel tape transport and puts them inside a plastic shell. The shell protects the tape because the tape is always attached to both spools, eliminating the need for threading across the read/write heads and through a drive mechanism. The sides of the cassette shell serve as the sides of the tape reel—holding the tape in place so that the center of the spool doesn't pop out. This function is augmented by a pair of Teflon slip sheets, one on either side of the tape inside the shell, that help to eliminate the friction of the tape against the shell. A clear plastic window in either side of the shell enables you to look at how much tape is on either spool—how much is left to record on or play back.

The reels inside the cassette themselves are merely hubs that the tape can wrap around. A small clip that forms part of the perimeter of the hub holds the end of the tape to the hub. At various points around the inside of the shell, guides are provided to ensure that the tape travels in the correct path.

The cassette also incorporates protection against accidental erasure of valuable music or information. On the rear edge of the cassette—away from where the head inserts—are a pair of plastic tabs protecting hole-like depressions in the shell. A finger from the cassette transport attempts to push its way into this hole. If it succeeds, it registers that the cassette is write-protected. Breaking off one of these tabs therefore protects the cassette from accidental erasure. To restore recordability, the hole needs only to be covered up. Cellophane or masking tape, or even a Band-Aid or file folder label, works for that purpose. Two such tabs exist—one to protect each side of the tape. The tab in the upper-left corner protects the top side of the cassette. (Turn the cassette over, and the other side becomes the top—but the tab that allows recording on this side still appears in the upper-left corner.)

More recent audio cassettes may have additional notches on the rear edge to indicate to the automatic sensing cassette desk the type of tape inside the cassette shell. Audio tape comes in four varieties that require different settings on the cassette recording for optimal operation.

More recent tape cartridges have altered some of the physical aspects of the cassette design but retain the underlying technologies. For example, the shell of the audio cassette is thickened at the open edge to allow the record/playback head and the drive puck to be inserted against the tape and the tape is unprotected in the head-access area. All other data tape cartridges have a nearly uniform thickness and provide some kind of door to protect the tape from damage. Although other data tape cartridges do not use the same tab-and-hole mechanism for write protection, all incorporate write protection of some kind. Most make it reversible using a sliding tab or rotating indicator. And, of course, other data cartridges use tapes of different widths than audio-style cassettes. The exact design of a cartridge depends on the goals, knowledge, and prejudices of its designers.

The development of cartridges, no matter their physical embodiment, has had a vital effect on tape backup. All claims of the convenience of tape backup are based on this ease of loading the cartridges. But people still decry the inconvenience of tape backup; they just shift the blame to the software.

Technologies

Tape systems are often described by how they work, that is, the way they record data onto the tape. For example, although the term "streaming tape" that's appended to many tape drives may conjure up images of a cassette gone awry and spewing its guts inside the dashboard of your card (and thence to the wind as you fling it out the window), it actually describes a specific recording mode that requires an uninterrupted flow of data. At least four of these terms—start-stop, streaming, parallel, and serpentine—crop up in the specifications of common tape systems for PCs.

Start-Stop Tape

The fundamental difference between tape drives is how they move the tape. Early drives operated in *start-stop mode*; they handled data one block (ranging from 128 bytes to a few kilobytes) at a time and wrote each block to the tape as it was received. Between blocks of data, the drive stopped moving the tape and awaited the next block. The drive had to prepare the tape for each block, identifying the block so that the data could be properly recovered. Watch an old movie that shows mainframe computers with jittering tape drives, and you'll see the physical embodiment of start-stop tape.

The earliest PC tape systems operated in start-stop mode. They had to. The computers and their disks were so slow that they could not move data to the drive as fast as the drive could write it to tape. Modern PCs, disks, and tape drives are all faster, and they use large memory buffers to assure that the tape-bound data forms an uninterrupted stream. Tape drives usually shift to start-stop mode only when an intervening circumstance—for example, an important task steals so much microprocessor time that not enough is available to prepare data for the tape—temporarily halts the data flow. The drive then will often rewind to find its place before accepting the next block of data and starting the tape in motion again.

Streaming Tape

When your PC tape drive gets the data diet it needs, bytes flow to the drive in an unbroken stream and the tape runs continuously. Engineers called this mode of operation *streaming tape*.

Drives using streaming-tape technology can accept data and write it to tape at a rate limited only by the speed the medium moves and the density at which bits are packed—the linear density of the data on the tape. Because the tape does not have to stop between blocks, the drive wastes no time. The streaming design also lowers the cost of tape drives because the drives do not have to accelerate the tape quickly or brake the motion of the tape spools, allowing a lighter weight mechanism to be used. Nearly all PC tape drives are now capable of streaming data to tape.

Parallel Recording

Just as disk drives divide their platters into parallel tracks, the tape drive divides the tape into multiple tracks across the width of the tape. The number of tracks varies with the drive and the standard it follows.

The first tape machines used with computer systems recorded nine separate data tracks across the width of the tape. The first of these machines used *parallel recording* in which they spread each byte across their tracks, one bit per track with one track for parity. A tape was good for only one pass across the read/write head, after which the tape needed to be rewound for storage. Newer tape systems elaborate on this design by laying 18 or 36 tracks across a tape, corresponding to a digital word or double word, written in parallel.

Parallel recording provides a high transfer rate for a given tape speed because multiple bits get written at a time but makes data retrieval time-consuming; finding a given byte might require fast forwarding across an entire tape. In addition, the read/write heads and electronics are necessarily complicated. The head requires a separate pole and gap for each track. To prepare the signals for each head gap, the tape drive requires a separate amplifier. These complications increase the cost of tape drives that use parallel recording.

Serpentine Recording

Most PC tape systems use multitrack drives but do not write tracks in parallel. Instead, they convert the incoming data into serial form and write that to the tape. Serial recording across multiple tracks results in a recording method called serpentine recording.

Serpentine cartridge drives write data bits sequentially across the tape in one direction on one track at a time, continuing for the length of the tape. When the drive reaches the end of the tape, it reverses the direction the tape travels and cogs its read/write head down one step to the next track. At the end of that pass, the drive repeats the process until it runs out of data or fills all the tracks. Figure 13.1 shows the layout of tracks across a tape using four tracks of serpentine recording.

FIGURE 13.1

Layout of four tracks using serpentine recording.

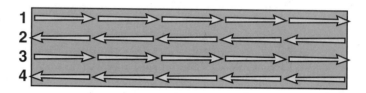

A serpentine tape system can access data relatively quickly by jogging its head between tracks because it needs to scan only a fraction of the data on the tape for what you want. Additionally, it requires only a single channel of electronics and a single pole in the read/write head, lowering overall drive costs. Modern serpentine systems may use more than 50 tracks across a tape.

Helical Recording

The basic principle of all the preceding tape systems is that the tape moves past a stationary head. The speed the tape moves and the density of data on the tape together determine how fast information can be read or written, just as the data density and rotation rate of disks control data rate. Back in the '50s, however, data rate was already an issue when engineers tried to put television pictures on ordinary recording tape. They had the equivalent of millions of bytes to move every second, and most ordinary tape systems topped out in the thousands. The inspired idea that made video recording possible was to make the head move as well as the tape to increase the relative speed of the two.

Obviously, the head could not move parallel to the tape. The first videotape machines made the head move nearly perpendicular to the tape movement. Through decades of development, however, rotating a head at a slight angle to the tape so that the head traces out a section of a helix against the tape has proven to be the most practical system. The resulting process is called *helical-scan recording*. Today, two helical-scan systems are popular, eight millimeter and DAT (Digital Audio Tape).

In a helical-scan recording system, the rotating heads are mounted on a drum. The tape wraps around the drum outside its protective cartridge. Two arms pull the tape out of the cartridge and wrap it about halfway around the drum. (Some systems, such as unlamented Betamax, wrap tape nearly all the way around the drum.) So that the heads travel at an angle across the tape, the drum is canted at a slight angle, about five degrees for eight-millimeter drives and about six degrees for DAT. The result is that a helical tape has multiple parallel tracks that run diagonally across the tape instead of parallel to its edges. These tracks tend to be quite fine; some helical systems put nearly 2,000 of them in an inch.

In most helical systems, the diagonal tracks are accompanied by one or more tracks parallel to the tape edge used for storing servo control information. In video systems, one or more parallel audio tracks may also run the length of the tape. Figure 13.2 shows how the data and control tracks are arranged on a helical tape.

FIGURE 13.2
Helical-scan recording track layout.

— Data tracks

— Control tracks

Helical-scan recording can take advantage of the entire tape surface. Conventional stationary-head recording systems must leave blank areas—guard bands—between the tracks containing data. Helical systems can and do overlap tracks. Although current eight-millimeter systems use guard bands, DAT writes the edges of tracks over one another.

This overlapping works because the rotating head drum actually has two (or more) heads on it, and each head writes data at a different angular relationship (called the azimuth) to the tracks on the tape. In reading data, the head responds strongly to the data written at the same azimuth as the head and weakly at the other azimuth. In DAT machines, one head is skewed 20 degrees forward from perpendicular to its track; the other head is skewed backward an equal amount.

Formats

Each of these various recording methods, along with physical concerns such as tape width and cartridge design, allows for a nearly infinite range of tape recording systems. When you try to make sense of backup systems, it often seems as though all of the possibilities have been tried in commercial products.

The number of formats used by PC tape systems is indeed diverse. Search for the one perfect backup system, and you'll be confronted by more "standards" than in any other area of personal computing. One tape industry organization alone publishes hundreds of tape standards, and a wide variety of competing systems and standards thrive outside of those definitions. Worse, many of the standards don't guarantee intercompatibility among products that abide them. All too often, you can buy a tape drive that conforms to an industry standard but will not read tape written by another manufacturer's drive that follow the same standard.

In other words, tape standards and the resulting formats often serve as points of departure rather than bastions of rigid conformity. If nothing else, however, they can help guide us on a quick tour of your various options in the world of tape.

The chief division among tape systems is between linear recording and helical recording systems.

Linear Recording Tape Systems

The most straightforward tape systems use simple linear recording. That is, they simply move the tape past a stationary head as did the very first audio tape recorders. Linear recording is the old reliable in tape technology. The process and methods have been perfected (as much as that is possible) over more than five decades of use.

The oldest of the tape systems, progenitor of all, is *open-reel tape*. These are the big spools of black tape that chug through science fiction movies throughout the 1950s and 1960s. Its half-inch width lined with nine parallel tracks, this format was the first standard among computers—mainframes and minicomputers alike—and probably the last universal tape standard that allowed free interchange of data and media between different computer systems.

All other linear tape systems are just open-reel tape with the reels enclosed. The chief differences are in the size of the cartridges. All of the various linear systems share a common technology, so all benefit from the improvements in technology; through the years, the capacity of a given length of tape has multiplied so that cassette-size cartridges now hold more megabytes than the biggest open reel of days gone by.

The first tape medium used by PCs was the audio cassette. As with other hobby-style computers of the early 1980s, PCs could write programs and data to audio cassette tapes by using tones from what was essentially a modem. The speed was slow—on the order of 1,000 bytes per second—but then again, so was everything else. The "quick" floppy disk elbowed it into ignominy—you know how slow floppies are, so it's almost frightening to imagine something much, much slower.

Before finally disappearing from the scene, cassettes reared up twice again in purely digital formats as D/CAS and DCC. Both were proprietary systems (D/CAS from Teac, DCC from Philips), and both failed to win wide market acceptance in the late 1980s and early 1990s.

Oddly enough, only the oldest linear tape cartridge format caught on among PCs, the quarter-inch cartridge. Engineers miniaturized the same underlying technology to make the mini-cartridge, and when the mini-cartridge proved too small, they un-miniaturized it into the Travan and QIC-EX format. All of these linear formats are still popular among PCs along with a newcomer that's winning acceptance in larger systems, Digital Linear Tape.

Quarter-Inch Data Cartridges

A few years after Philips introduced the cassette to take dictation, 3M Company first offered a quarter-inch tape cartridge as a data recording medium. First put on the market in 1972, these initial quarter-inch cartridges were designed for telecommunications and data acquisition applications calling for the storage of serial data, such as programming private business telephone exchanges and recording events. No one imagined that the quarter-inch cartridge would evolve into the premiere personal computer backup medium; no PCs existed at the time.

The initial concept behind the quarter-inch tape cartridge appears to be the same as that of the cassette: Put the two spools of tape from the open-reel system into an easy-to-handle plastic box. In function, operation, and construction, the cassette and cartridge are entirely different because the needs of dictation and data storage are entirely different. Compared to the cassette, the tape cartridge requires greater precision and smoother operation. To achieve that end, a new mechanical design was invented by Robert von Behren of the 3M Company, who patented it in 1971—the quarter-inch cartridge mechanism.

Instead of using the capstan drive system like cassettes, the quarter-inch cartridge operates with a belt drive system. A thin, isoelastic belt stretches throughout the cartridge mechanism, looping around (and making contact with) both the supply and take-up spools on their outer perimeters. The belt also passes around a rubber drive wheel, which contacts a capstan in the tape drive.

The capstan moves the belt but is cut away with a recess that prevents it from touching the tape. The friction of the belt against the outside of the tape reels drives the tape. This system is gentler to the tape because the driving pressure is spread evenly over a large area of the tape instead of pinching the tape tightly between two rollers. In addition, it provides for smoother tape travel and packing of the tape on the spools. The tape is wound and the guide and other parts of the mechanism arranged so that the fragile magnetic surface of the tape touches nothing but the read/write head (see Figure 13.3).

For sturdiness, the cartridge is built around an aluminum baseplate. The rest of the cartridge is transparent plastic, allowing the condition of the tape and the mechanism to be readily viewed.

The essence of the design is that the cartridge itself acts as the tape drive. It contains the tape guides, the tape, and the tape-moving mechanism. Although that means that the data cartridge is somewhat more expensive to make, drives are less expensive because they essentially need only a motor and a head. The design also ensures the best possible consistency of tape alignment and minimizes the need for adjustments to the drive.

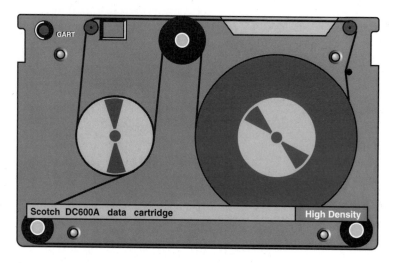

This basic design underlies the quarter-inch data cartridge and the mini-cartridge—both of which have declined in importance—and currently popular tape formats, including Travan and QIC-EX.

Early Systems

The initial cartridge, called the DC300A by 3M Company, held 300 feet of tape in a package almost the size of a paperback book—a full 6 by 4 by 5/8 inches. The cartridge mechanism was designed to operate at a speed of 30 inches per second, using phase encoding (single-density recording) to put a density of 1,600 bits per inch serially (one track at a time) on the tape—a data rate of 48 kilobits per second. Two or four tracks were used one at a time. Drives for this format were made by 3M Company, Kennedy, Qantax, DEI, and, briefly, IBM.

In 1979, DEI quadrupled the speed and capacity of the quarter-inch cartridge by introducing a drive that recorded four tracks in parallel, still at 30 inches per second and 1,600 bits per inch. The new mechanism achieved a 192 kilobits-per-second data rate using standard DC300A tapes. Even though these cartridges only held 1.8MB unformatted—1MB formatted, the same as an eight-inch floppy disk—using this recording method, the data rate was high enough to interest the computer industry.

A year later, another four-track drive for the DC300A cartridge was introduced. The capacity of the system was increased to about 15MB by shifting to modified frequency modulation (MFM) recording and pushing the data density to 6,400 bits per inch. Although the 192 kilobits-per-second transfer rate and 30 inches-per-second speed were maintained, data was transferred serially, one track at a time. As late as 1988, this groundbreaking drive was still in production, although it was no longer used in mass market PC products, being superseded in those applications by higher capacity systems.

Since then, tape lengths have again been increased, to as much as 900 feet, although the most popular length is the 600 feet contained in the cartridges that were initially designated DC600. Current implementations of cartridge technology—no matter the length of tape they contain—use cartridges the same size and shape as the 3M originals. However, capacities have blossomed into the gigabyte range thanks to multi-track heads, high-density recording media, and error correction. Existing standards put up to 13GB in a single cartridge. The ultimate capacity of the format is believed to be about 100GB per cartridge.

The DC600 cartridge is now a thing of the past—but in name only. New designations have been added to take into account other media and tape length differences that affect storage capacities. The generic name for a full-size quarter-inch tape cartridge is officially the *Data Cartridge*, and commercial products are designated by model numbers reflecting their capacities or, occasionally, the industry standards they abide by. Tapes for earlier cartridge standards follow a regular naming rule. The model number starts with DC (for Data Cartridge); a "6" is carried over from the earlier "600" designation (the length of the tape in the cartridge); and three digits (or so) indicate the tape capacity.

In a quest to shrink the size (or form factor) of tape drives down to something more suitable for desktop PCs, tape and drive manufacturers developed a miniaturized version of the standard data cartridge, which they called the *mini-cartridge*. Inside its smaller shell, the drive mini-cartridge retains the same mechanism as its larger forebear. Table 13.1 lists the capacities and other characteristics of these basic data cartridges and mini-cartridges.

TABLE 13.1   Capacities and Characteristics of Tape Cartridges

Cartridge Type	Cartridge Size	Nominal Capacity	Tape Length (Feet)	Tracks on Tape	Recording Density (Flux Transitions per Inch)	Compatible Systems
DC 100A	1/8-inch	67MB	140	2	3,200	HP-85
DC 300A	Data	2.9MB	300	4	3,200	QIC-11
DC 300XL/P	Data	45MB	450	9	3,200-10,000	QIC-11/24
DC 600A	Data	60MB	600	9	10,000	QIC-24
DC 600HW	Data	60MB	600	11	10,000	Sentinal
DC 1000	1/8-inch	20MB	185	12	12,500	Irwin 10/20
DC 2000	Mini	40MB	205	20	10,000	QIC-40/100
DC 2080	Mini	80MB	205	32	15,000	QIC-80

continues

TABLE 13.1 Continued

Cartridge Type	Cartridge Size	Nominal Capacity	Tape Length (Feet)	Tracks on Tape	Recording Density (Flux Transitions per Inch)	Compatible Systems
DC 2120	Mini	120MB	307.5	32	15,000	QIC-80/128
DC 2155	Mini	155MB	307.5	29	18,000	MT-01N
DC 2255	Mini	255MB	295	40	22,125	QIC-3010-MC
DC 2300	Mini	560MB	215	40	38,750	Excel 1G
DC 2500	Mini	500MB	295	40	44,250	QIC-3020-MC
DC 2555	Mini	555MB	295	40	50,800	QIC-3030-MC
DC 2750	Mini	750MB	295	40	38,750	EXB-2501
DC 6037	Data	37MB	155	18	12,500	QIC-120/150
DC 6150	Data	150MB	620	18	12,000	QIC-120/150
DC 615A	Data	15MB	150	9	10,000	QIC-24
DC 6250	Data	250MB	1020	18	12,500	QIC-120/150
DC 6350	Data	320MB	620	26	20,000	QIC-525
DC 6525	Data	525MB	1020	26	20,000	QIC-525
Magnus 1.0	Data	1GB	760	30	45,000	QIC-1000
Magnus 1.2	Data	1.2GB	950	30	45,000	QIC-1000
Magnus 1.35	Data	1.35GB	760	30	38,750	QIC-1350
Magnus 1.6	Data	1.6GB	950	30	38,750	QIC-1350
Magnus 2.0	Data	2GB	950	42	50,800	QIC-2GB
Magnus 2.1	Data	2.1GB	950	30	50,800	QIC-2100

Only the media was the same in early products based on quarter-inch cartridges. Each drive manufacturer went in its own direction, varying not only the number of tracks and density of data on the tape, but also how the tape drive connected with its computer host.

Every tape system was proprietary, a situation that doesn't give a computer supervisor a feeling of security when a lifetime of data is packed onto cartridges. Proprietary standards mean that whatever is stored on tape is at risk to the whims of the manufacturer. A discontinued product line could render tape unreadable in the future as drives break down. Moreover, the diversity of tape systems meant that each manufacturer essentially had to start from scratch in developing each model.

To try to lessen the chaos in the tape cartridge marketplace, a number of tape drive manufacturers—including DEI, Archive, Cipher Data, and Tandberg—met together at the National Computer Conference in Houston in 1982. They decided to form a committee to develop standards so that a uniform class of products could be introduced. The organization took the name Working Group for Quarter-Inch Cartridge Drive Compatibility, a name often shortened into QIC committee. In November 1987, the organization was officially incorporated as Quarter-Inch Cartridge Standards, Inc.

The QIC committee consisted primarily of drive manufacturers who did not sell directly to the PC market and initially concerned itself with physical standardization. Data formats were left for system integrators to develop—and, in general, each one designed his own. With time, the committee has developed into a trade association, and it recognizes the need for format standardization, too. Today, it promulgates standards at all levels of the application of tape. Table 13.2 summarizes the data cartridge standards adopted by QIC to date.

TABLE 13.2   QIC Data Cartridge (DC6000-style) Standards

Standard	Native Capacity	Tracks	Bits per Inch	Tape Speed (Inches per Second)	Tape Coercivity (Oersteds)	Original Adoption Date
QIC-24-DC	60MB	9	8,000	90	550	22–Apr–83
QIC-120-DC	125MB	15	10,000	90	550	30–Oct–85
QIC-150-DC	150/250MB	18	10,000	90	550	12–Feb–87
QIC-525-DC	320/525MB	26	16,000	90/120	550	24–May–89
QIC-1000-DC	1.2GB	30	36,000	53.3/80	550	24–Oct–90
QIC-1350-DC	1.6GB	30	51,667	90/120	900	24–May–89
QIC-2GB-DC	2.5GB	42	40,640	70.9	900	4–Jun–92
QIC-2100-DC	2.6GB	30	67,773	91.5/120	900	20–Jun–91

continues

TABLE 13.2   Continued

Standard	Native Capacity	Tracks	Bits per Inch	Tape Speed (Inches per Second)	Tape Coercivity (Oersteds)	Original Adoption Date
QIC-4GB-DC	4GB	45	50,800		900	4-Mar-93
QIC-5GB-DC	5GB	44	96,000	90	900	3-Dec-92
QIC-5010-DC	13GB	144	67,773	30/60/120	900	27-Feb-92
QIC-5210-DC	25GB	144	76,200			31-Aug-95
QIC-6000C	6GB	96	50,800			6-Feb-91

Source: *Quarter-Inch Cartridge Standards, Inc.,* www.qic.org, *1999*

The first standard developed by the committee to reach the marketplace in a commercial product was QIC-24, a nine-track version of a DC300 tape drive. The standard was formally approved in April 1983, and the first commercial units shipped later that year. QIC-24 (now QIC-24-DC, the suffix indicating Data Cartridge, QIC's designation for larger tape cartridges) achieved its 60MB of storage per tape at a density of 8,000 bits per inch. Using one-track-at-a-time serpentine recording at 90 inches per second, the system sent 720 kilobits of data per second through its QIC-02 interface.

Since then, the story of data cartridges is a continuing increase in capacity won through increasing the density of storage. New standards push up the number of bits per inch storage along the length of the tape and the number of tracks lined with data across the tape.

Some of the transitional standards have been left behind, such as QIC-120-DC, which put 125MB on cartridges using 15 tracks of data written at 10,000 bits per inch. But an improvement on that standard coming just two years later in 1987 remains in use. QIC-150-DC used a slight change in geometry along with longer tapes to double cartridge capacity. Using the same data density as its predecessor standard, QIC-150-DC put 18 tracks across the tape. With shorter tapes (DC6150), the QIC-150-DC drives slide 150MB into a cartridge; longer DC6250 tapes hold up to 250MB using the same. As of early 1999, both Tandberg and Wangtek offer drives compatible with QIC-150-DC.

The next capacity push came in May 1989, with the adoption of QIC-525-DC (formerly designated QIC-320). By increasing both linear and densities by 60 percent (to 16,000 bits per inch and 26 tracks), drives abiding this standard packed up to 525MB on DC6525 tapes (320MB on D6320 tapes). In addition, an optional tape speed increase to 120 inches per second allowed the raw transfer rate to climb to 1.92 megabits per second from tape to controller. The standard also allows for a slower, 90 inches-per-second speed and read compatibility with QIC-120-DC and QIC-150-DC tapes. QIC-525-DC drives also remained available in 1999.

In October 1990, QIC adopted the last standard to use its traditional tape medium—that is, 550 Oersted magnetic tape using group-coded recording—QIC-1000-DC. Packing 30 tracks across the tape and recording with a bit density of 36,000 per inch, the new format fit up to 1.2GB per tape cartridge. Although the new standard lowered maximum tape speed to 80 inches per second (53.3 inches per second could also be used), the higher density yielded a faster raw transfer rate, about 2.8 megabits per second. QIC-1000-DC drives could read tapes made under all previous QIC data cartridge standards except for QIC-24-DC. Drives conforming to QIC-1000-DC remained available through 1999.

At the same time QIC-525-DC was adopted, however, QIC also pushed data cartridges into the future with new technologies. The QIC-1350-DC standard introduced a new data coding method—1,7 Run Length Limited—and new, higher-coercivity (900 Oersted) media. The new tape and coding let manufacturers push data density up to 51,667 bits per inch. Using 30 tracks across the tape, QIC-1350-DC can fit 1.6GB on a cartridge. At its 120 inches-per-second top tape speed (90 inches per second also allowed), the system can achieve a raw transfer rate of about 6.2 megabits per second. QIC-1350-DC drives could also read QIC-525-DC and QIC-1000-DC tapes.

Using longer tapes and a somewhat higher data density (67,773 bits per inch), the QIC-2100-DC standard, adopted in June 1991, stretched single cartridge capacity to 2.6GB. QIC-2100-DC drives also read tapes made under the QIC-1350-DC standard.

To bring a bit more sense to the confusing nomenclature, QIC started using tape capacity as part of the drive designation in 1992 and added three new standards to push quarter-inch cartridges into competition with new helical formats blazing the trail into multi-giga-byte territory. QIC-2GB-DC sliced 900 Oersted tape into 42 tracks at a data density of 40,640 bits per inch, cramming 2.5GB onto a single cartridge. QIC-5GB-DC pushed the bit density to 96,000 per inch and added two tracks (to 44) to fit up to 5GB per cartridge. QIC-5010-DC put up to 13MB on a tape by lining up 144 thin tracks across the quarter-inch tape with data at a bit density of 67,773 per inch. Of these, QIC-5GB-DC reaches the highest raw transfer rate (about 8.6 megabits per second at 90 inches per second) and the greatest compatibility. DC-5GB-DC drives can read any earlier QIC data cartridge physical format. Tandberg offers drives using the QIC-2GB-DC, QIC-4GB-DC, QIC-5010-DC, and QIC-5210-DC formats.

Mini-Cartridges

If standard quarter-inch cartridges have a drawback, it's their size. Squeezing a drive to handle a 6x4 cartridge into a standard 5.25-inch drive bay is a challenge; fitting one in a modern 3.5-inch bay is an impossibility. Seeking a more compact medium, quarter-inch cartridge makers cut their products down to size, reducing tape capacity while preserving the proven drive mechanism. The result was the mini-cartridge. The smaller size was adopted by the QIC committee, which now promulgates a standard for it. Table 13.3 summarizes QIC's mini-cartridge standards.

TABLE 13.3   QIC Mini-Cartridge (DC2000-style) Standards

Standard	Native Capacity	Tracks	Bits per inch	Tape Speed (Inches per Second)	Tape Coercivity (Oersteds)	Original Adoption Date
QIC-40-MC	60 MB	20	10,000	25/50	550	4-Jun-86
QIC-80-MC	125MB	28	14,700	25/50	550	3-Feb-88
QIC-100-MC	40MB	24	10,000	60	550	19-Mar-85
QIC-128-MC	128MB	32	16,000	90	550	23-May-89
QIC-3010-MC	255MB	40	22,125	22.6	900	10-Jun-93
QIC-3020-MC	500MB	40	44,250	22.6	900	21-Jun-91
QIC-3030-MC	580MB	40	40,600	60	900	18-Apr-91
QIC-3040-MC	840MB	42/52	40,600	70.9	900	9-Dec-93
QIC-3080-MC	1.6GB	60	60,000	30-80	900	30-Jan-94
QIC-3210-MC	1.8/2.3GB	56/72	76,200		1800	16-Mar-95
QIC-3090-MC	2GB	48	93,333	56.5	1800	30-Jan-94
QIC-3110-MC	2GB	48	70,000		1800	30-Jan-94
QIC-3070-MC	4GB	144	67,773	N/A	900	27-Feb-92
QIC-3095-MC	4GB	72	50,800		900	13-Dec-95
QIC-3220-MC	10GB	106	79,800		1650	27-Aug-97
QIC-3230-MC	15.5GB	180	76,200		1800	15-Jun-95

Source: Quarter-Inch Cartridge Standards, Inc., `www.qic.org`, *1999*

Because 3M Company introduced the first mini-cartridge with the designation DC2000, many people in the computer industry persist in calling all mini-cartridges "DC2000-style" cartridges. Mini-cartridges actually come in a variety of designations. As with the current model numbers of DC600-size cartridges, the model designations of most mini-cartridges encode the cartridge capacity as their last digits. For example, a DC2080 cartridge is designed for 80MB capacity; a DC2120 for 120MB.

The mini-cartridge package measures just under 3.25x2.5 by 0.625 inches. As originally developed, it held 205 feet of tape with the same nominal quarter-inch width used by larger cartridges, hence the initial "2" in the designation.

One big advantage of the smaller cartridges is that drives for them easily fit into standard 3.5-inch bays. On the other hand, cartridge capacities are necessarily lower than full-size cartridges if just because less room for tape is available inside. From humble beginnings

(40MB total capacity), the storage reserves of mini-cartridges have grown to 15.5GB under current QIC standards. The QIC committee envisions the small cartridges eventually holding up to 30GB.

The number of mini-cartridge tape drive manufacturers is surprisingly small. At one time or another, about nine companies were in the industry: Alloy, Braemar, Cipher, Colorado Memory Systems, Conner, Irwin, Mountain, 3M Company, and Wangtek. Industry consolidation has dramatically reduced the ranks of cartridge drive makers. For example, Maynard acquired Irwin; Archive acquired Maynard; Conner acquired Archive; and Seagate acquired Conner. Hewlett-Packard acquired Colorado Memory Systems. Other makers simply dropped out of the market. Major drive makers now include Aiwa, Hewlett-Packard, Seagate, and Tandberg. In 1998, 3M company spun off its media operations to form Imation.

The first major mini-cartridge standard to win wide acceptance was QIC-40-MC, adopted in June 1986. With a cartridge capacity of 40MB, the standard aimed at inexpensive backup and took advantage of a spare channel of most floppy disk drive controllers. Although both the capacity and speed, which was limited by that of the interface, are laughable compared to modern needs and products, QIC-40-MC readily handled early backup needs.

QIC-40-MC arrayed 20 tracks in parallel across the width of the tape, with each track divided into 68 segments of 29 sectors of 1,024 bytes each. This format packed data at a density of 10,000 bits per inch. The drives used the same modified frequency modulation (MFM) recording as floppy disks. (After all, the signals came from the same controller.) The data rate of the controller set the speed of the tape—25 inches per second with a 250 kilobits-per-second controller (one that could use only 5.25-inch floppy disks) or 50 inches per second with a 500 kilobits-per-second controller.

The QIC standards refined this basic format to double capacity to the QIC-80-MC format. Through use of longer tapes that used the same magnetic coating, QIC-80-MC allowed up 120MB per cartridge.

The QIC-80-MC data format remains popular and serves as the foundation of the Iomega Ditto tape backup system. Ditto, however, has kept pace with increasing hard disk capacities by opting for larger cartridges that hold more tape—enough for one gigabyte of uncompressed data storage. The Seagate Tape*Stor system also uses the QIC-80-MC format.

To increase the capacity of mini-cartridges to keep pace with fast-growing hard disks, QIC switched to new, higher coercivity media for all its later mini-cartridge standards. Starting in 1991, all QIC mini-cartridge standards are based on tape with 900 Oersted or higher coercivities. This break with the past is reflected in a new nomenclature, which no longer corresponds to capacity.

QIC adopted the first of these new standards in April 1991 and brought the same high-speed technology used by larger data cartridges to the mini-cartridge format. Originally designated QIC-470 and QIC-555M but later renamed QIC-3030-MC, the new standard pushed up data density to 40,600 bits per inch thanks to the improved tape coating. To increase the data rate to 2.5 megabits per second, the standard upped the tape speed to 60 inches per second and shifted to a SCSI connection. To maximize capacity, the QIC-3030-MC standard specified 40 tracks across the quarter-inch tape width, yielding 580MB on a standard 900 Oersted QIC-143 cartridge. The new design was unlike anything else in the mini-cartridge arena, so QIC-3030-MC drives were not backward compatible with any previous standard.

A few months later, in June 1991, QIC adopted another standard in the same capacity range, QIC-3020-MC (previously designated as QIC-385 and QIC-500M), that allowed drives to read QIC-40-MC and QIC-80-MC cartridges. As with those predecessors, QIC designed this new format to use floppy disk or AT Attachment (IDE) interfaces. To accommodate these interfaces, QIC lowered the tape speed to 22.6 inches per second while maintaining a high data density (44,250 bits per inch). As with QIC-3030-MC, QIC-3020-MC put 40 tracks across the tape, allowing the two standards to share the same physical mechanism with only a firmware change needed to alter the speed and data density. The resulting format packed 500MB on a standard QIC-143 mini-cartridge.

The QIC-3020-MC data format remains popular. Aiwa, HP, and Iomega use the format for drives offering capacities from 3.2GB to 10GB.

To counter the threat from helical media, in February 1992 QIC introduced a refined version of QIC-3030-MC that could pack up to 4GB of uncompressed data on a single mini-cartridge. Achieving that capacity required slicing the tracks thinly—144 of them across the tape—and increasing linear density up to 67,773 bits per inch. Drives complying with the resulting standard, designated QIC-3070-MC, also can read QIC-3030-MC tapes.

In June 1993, QIC adopted a lower capacity version of QIC-3020-MC as QIC-3010-MC. By halving the data density, the new standard halved the capacity of the tape with all other vital parameters unchanged. The resulting standard is less demanding on equipment and results in less dense storage, which should be more reliable. Because of its heritage, QIC-3010-MC drives can read QIC-40-MC and QIC-80-MC tapes. Moreover, QIC-3030-MC drives can read QIC-3010-MC tapes, but lower capacity drives cannot read the tapes made on higher capacity mechanisms.

Competing directly with Digital Audio Tape (discussed later) in the low-gigabyte backup range are two standards adopted by QIC in January 1994. QIC-3080-MC puts up to 1.6GB on a now-standard 900 Oersted mini-cartridge by laying 60 tracks across the tape with a linear data density of 60,000 bits per inch with a tape speed of 30 to 80 inches per second. QIC-3090-MC increases per-cartridge storage with higher data densities made possible by 1,300 Oersted tape. A single QIC-3090-MC holds up to 2GB spread across 48 tracks at a linear density of 93.333 bits per inch. In the QIC-3090-MC system, the tape travels at 56.5 inches per second.

The QIC-3095-MC format is the most popular for high-end mini-cartridge drives. Aiwa, HP, Seagate, and Tandberg offer systems with capacities from 8 to 20GB.

QIC-3070-MC, adopted February 1992, specifies laying 144 tracks across a 900 Oersted quarter-inch tape at a linear density of 67,773 bits per inch, a total of about 4GB per tape. The drives use special cartridges (QIC-138) but can read tapes made under the QIC-3030-MC standard as well as its own.

The availability of even higher coercivity media led QIC to adopt several new cartridge standards in 1994 and 1995, all in the multiple gigabyte range (see Table 13.3 earlier).

QIC Wide

Today, the standard hard disks in many new PCs have grown to twice that capacity without resorting to data compression. To help the familiar cartridges cope with larger drives, Sony Corporation added 68 percent more capacity by squeezing in wider tape to make *QIC-Wide* cartridges; the new "quarter-inch" cartridges hold tape measuring eight millimeters (0.315 inch) across. Other cartridge manufacturers have since adopted the format, and cartridges are available from many suppliers.

The capacity of a single QIC-Wide cartridge starts at 200MB uncompressed and runs up to 4GB using advanced tape coatings, drives, and data compression. Surprisingly, the wider tape doesn't fatten prices. Other than alter the size of the cartridge slot and the distance the head must rise and fall to accommodate the greater number of tracks across the tape, QIC-Wide does not alter the underlying technology. Table 13.4 lists the characteristic of commercial mini-cartridges from one manufacturer (Sony).

TABLE 13.4   Commercial QIC-Wide Mini-Cartridge Specifications

Standard	Native Capacity	Tracks	Bits per inch	Tape Speed (Inches per Second)	Tape Coercivity (Oersteds)	Data Transfer Rate
QW5122F	208MB	36	14,700	34	550	62.5KB/sec
QW3000XL	1.0GB	52	40,600	70	900	300KB/sec
QW3010XLF	425MB	50	22,125	22.6	900	125KB/sec
QW3020XLF	849MB	50	22,125	22.6	900	250KB/sec
QW3080XLF	2.0GB	77	60,000	78	900	225KB/sec
QW3095XLF	2.0GB	77	67,733	78	900	225KB/sec
QW3210XLF	2.3GB	72	76,300	47.2	1800	300KB/

In 1995, Conner, Iomega, HP, 3M Company, and Sony joined together to create a new tape system that could push mini-cartridges to yet higher capacities. They called their creation Travan, a coined word. The underlying concept was less creative than the name, however. They achieved higher capacities by adding more tape, made possible by making the cartridge bigger.

The increase in cartridge size appears in three dimensions. The cartridges are wider, deeper, and taller. The added height allows the use of wider tape, the same eight-millimeter (0.315-inch) tape used by the QIC-Wide format, the format pioneered by Sony. The wider tape permits an increase in track count by about 30 percent (from 28 to 36 in the initial Travan format).

In addition, Travan adds an extra half inch to the width and depth of cartridges. The Travan cartridge measures 0.5 by 3.6 by 2.8 inches (HWD), smaller in the front (3.2 inches) than the rear where the tape spools reside. Internally, the Travan cartridge uses the same 3M mechanism as other quarter-inch cartridges and must be formatted before use.

Although the increase seems modest, it allows the tape capacity to more than double, from 307 feet in a DC2120 cartridge to 750 feet in the Travan. The extra size gives Travan a distinctive shape, basically rectangular with two corners curved in to make sliding in a cartridge easier. Figure 13.4 shows a Travan cartridge.

FIGURE 13.4
A Travan tape cartridge.

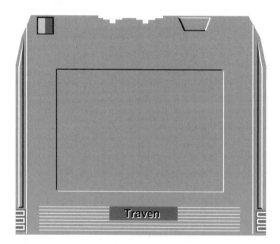

The combination of more tracks and greater tape length was sufficient to boost single cartridge capacity to 400MB (uncompressed) in the initial Travan implementation. Nothing about the Travan design impairs making further improvements, so whatever developments add to the capacity of standard mini-cartridges can be directly reflected in increased Travan capacities. In fact, since its introduction, Travan has been improved three times, each change about doubling single-cartridge capacities.

The first change, creating TR-2, boosted the coercivity of the medium and allowed for a 50 percent increase in data density, both in a greater number of tracks and a higher linear density on each track. The next change doubled linear density again without altering the track count to create TR-3. Another increase in linear density and matching increase in track count boosted the TR-4 Travan implementation to 4GB per cartridge. Table 13.5 summarizes the characteristics of the various Travan implementations.

TABLE 13.5   Travan tape cartridge specifications

Model	TR-1	TR-2	TR-3	TR-4
Capacity, uncompressed	400MB	800MB	1.6GB	4GB
Capacity, compressed	800MB	1.6GB	3.2GB	8GB
Minimum transfer rate	62.5KB/sec	62.5KB/sec	125KB/sec	567KB/sec
Maximum transfer rate	125KB/sec	125KB/sec	250KB/sec	567KB/sec
Media length	750 ft.	750 ft.	750 ft.	740 ft.
Media width	.315 in.	.315 in.	.315 in.	.315 in.
Media coercivity	550 Oe	900 Oe	900 Oe	900 Oe
Tracks	36	50	50	72
Data Density	14,700 ftpi	22,125 ftpi	44,250 ftpi	50,800 ftpi
Interface	Floppy	Floppy	Floppy	SCSI/E-IDE
Read/write compatibility	QIC-80	QIC-3010	3020/3010	3080/3095
Read-only compatibility	QIC-40	QIC-80	QIC-80	QIC-3020

Perhaps the most notable part of the Travan design is its compatibility. A Travan drive accepts standard DC2000 cartridges and QIC-Wide cartridges as well as its own native media; that's two different cartridge sizes and tape widths in one drive. Compatibility extends to both reading and writing all three cartridge styles. The various Travan implementations also feature backward compatibility. The more recent standards can read tapes made under the earlier Travan standards.

QIC-EX

As long as the cartridge in a QIC drive sticks out, as does Travan, you might as well let it all hang out. That dated cliché underlies the philosophy of QIC-EX. By allowing a cartridge to stick out of the drive nearly three inches, QIC-EX accommodates up to 1,000 feet of tape in the QIC format. That's more than double the capacity of ordinary mini-cartridges. Increase the tape width to QIC-Wide's eight millimeters, and you can fit gigabytes onto a standard tape cartridge. Figure 13.5 shows the dimensions of a QIC-EX cartridge.

FIGURE 13.5

Dimensions of a QIC-EX tape cartridge.

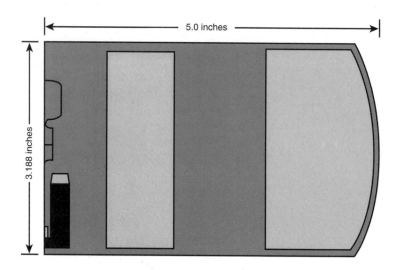

Unlike Travan, which requires a wider drive with a wider throat to accommodate the wider cartridges, the QIC-EX design is the same width as standard mini-cartridges. QIC-EX tape consequently fit into most mini-cartridge drives to give an instant capacity increase.

Data Compression

Another way to increase the capacity of tape cartridges is with data compression. You can nominally double the capacity of any tape backup using data compression software. In fact, QIC standards cover two compression algorithms. QIC-122 is based on the same algorithm used by Stac Electronics commercial Stacker software. QIC-130 is a compression standard developed by Hewlett-Packard that uses an algorithm called DCLZ, which stands for Data Compression according to Lempel and Ziv. Both QIC compression methods rely on the same underlying compression principle: They reduce repetitive data to a short token that refers to a longer block of data kept in a dictionary. They work by checking the incoming data stream for sequences recorded in the dictionary, replacing each one it finds with the corresponding token. Either algorithm provides a data-dependent apparent increase in cartridge capacity averaging around a factor of two.

With the exception of the three earlier data cartridge standards (QIC-24-DC, QIC-120-DC, and QIC-150-DC), QIC standards allow manufacturers to optionally choose either variety of compression for their products. Mini-cartridge manufacturers have the same choice, except under the QIC-100-MC and QIC-128-MC standards (for which no compression standard has been adopted) and QIC-3010-MC and QIC-3020-MC (for which QIC has adopted only the QIC-122 compression standard).

Cartridge Compatibility

Compatibility remains a thorny issue with quarter-inch tape cartridges. Tapes of the same physical size fit into drives regardless of format, but to operate properly, they must be matched to the mechanism because of differing coercivities. With the few exceptions noted earlier, tapes made under one standard are unreadable by drives following another standard. The exceptions, however, enable you to install a new drive without the need to update and replace all your backup tapes.

Compatibility concerns run deeper, however. Even if two drives follow a given QIC standard, they may not produce tapes that are interchangeable between them. Some QIC standards define only the physical format of data on the tape—that is, the number of tracks and bits per inch. Individual managers are left to decide how that storage should managed, for example, by dividing it into blocks or sectors. Some QIC standards do define a logical format for tape-based data, but they fall short of actually specifying the exact arrangement of the tape file structure. That's left to the individual software developer who makes the backup program to run the tape system. As a result, although tapes are interchangeable between different drives and can be read without regard to the equipment used, your backup software might not be able to make sense of the results. Because there's no compatibility of file structure, you can read every byte on a tape in any system, but all you might end up with is a big pile of data; files can run into one another and even intermingle.

Some QIC standards are designed to permit interchangeability. In fact, two QIC standards (QIC-140 and QIC-141) specify read-only mini-cartridges and data cartridges designed for distributing software. The use of cartridge tape has not, however, won wide acceptance for program distribution. The cost of mass producing CD-ROMs is much lower, although tape can be competitive with recordable Compact Discs when distribution requires only a few copies.

Digital Linear Tape

Strictly speaking, all of the preceding tape formats from open reel through QIC cartridges are digital linear tape formats. They move tape at a high speed across a stationary read/write head, which scans digital signals. One system, however, calls itself *Digital Linear Tape* with capital letters—a cartridge-based system using half-inch tape that runs at speeds in excess of 100 inches per second (about 3 meters per second). Rather than simply descriptive, the name—or more particularly, its initials, *DLT*—is meant to emphasize its relationship with the popular DAT (Digital Audio Tape, discussed later in the chapter) helical format. Both are high-capacity systems designed for backing up today's huge hard disks and multi-gigabyte drive arrays.

DLT distinguishes itself with more than a different middle initial. According to its developer, both DLT media and head mechanisms have five times the working life of their

DAT equivalents. Moreover, the capacities of the latest DLT systems put the helical formats to shame. Currently, single cartridge capacity is 20GB (40GB with compression) and even greater capacities are in the offing. As with eight-millimeter helical systems, DLT also lends itself to automation, and DLT jukeboxes could potentially give terabytes of data hands-free automatic access. The developer of DLT technology estimates that a single cartridge ultimately will be able to store 200GB and transfer data at more than 20 MB/sec when the technology is fully refined.

The huge capacities of DLT cartridges hint at the origins of the technology. Originally, it was meant as a mini-computer backup system. First offered commercially by mini-computer maker Digital Equipment Corporation in the early 1980s, the system was actually developed by Quantum Corporation. Although drives are available from a variety of sources under different proprietary names, all currently are manufactured by Quantum.

Tape speed makes DLT stand out from other linear storage tape systems. The current Quantum DLT4000 operates with a tape speed of 150 inches per second when reading or writing. Other linear systems approach this speed only when in a fast transport such as rewinding. This high speed gives the DLT system a tape-to-head that's actually in excess of the common helical tape systems, which directly translates into higher data transfer rates, a sustained transfer rate of 10.0 MB/sec when using data compression, 5.0 MB/sec without.

One of the advantages of the DLT system is obvious: With one less thing moving (the head), there's less to go wrong. Indeed, DLT systems are inherently simpler than helical systems. As a practical matter, however, the drives are nearly as complex. To isolate the tape movement across the heads from the vagaries of the hub and cartridge, the DLT drive pulls a length of tape from the cartridge and threads it across the head.

The durability of the DLT media and mechanism arise indirectly from the application of linear tape technology. Tapes last longer because they undergo less stress and flexing than in helical systems. The DLT system does not require the tape wrap more than halfway around a spinning head-wheel. Nor need the tape sharply bend as it starts and ends its wrap around the head, as shown in Figure 13.6. In addition, the force of contact between tape and head in the linear scan system is substantially less than that of a helical system.

As a result of its less tortuous tape path, DLT tapes are rated for 500,000 passes compared to the 2,000 passes of helical systems. Because in average use the tape will shuttle past the heads dozens of times (up to 64 to cover all the tracks), DLT tapes are rated for 10,000 cartridge uses. In addition, DLT heads are rated for 10,000 hours of operation versus 2,000 hours for eight-millimeter systems because the lower tape tension of the DLT system results in less wear.

FIGURE 13.6

Comparison of helical and linear scan tape paths.

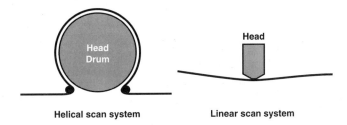

Helical scan system   Linear scan system

One distinct disadvantage of the DLT system is the time it takes to load a tape, which may approach 90 seconds. As soon as you slide a cartridge into a drive, it takes a few seconds to pull the tape out and thread it across the head. The next step is the penalty. Because of the narrow tracks spread across the tape, the drive has to align itself and its electronics to match the tape. It does this by reading two calibration tracks on the tape and fine-tuning its head positioning and amplifier gain to match the tape. (If the drive cannot properly calibrate itself, it warns that you should clean its heads.) Once the drive is calibrated, it backs up to the beginning of the tape and reads the directory, which the drive stores in memory to help find files on the tape fast. Although this lengthy wait may leave you strumming the tabletop with your fingertips, it's not a significant penalty for automated backup using cartridge jukeboxes, the primary application intended for the technology.

Current DLT systems spread from 128 or 206 tracks across the half-inch width of the tape. Earlier drives with 128 tracks read or write two tracks at a time, so scanning a complete tape takes 64 passes. The newest drive, the DLT 7000, has four channel electronics to read or write four tracks at a time, requiring 53 passes to cover a complete tape.

To minimize scanning time, DLT drives use serpentine recording. In addition, the tape directory data includes track location. When a DLT drive seeks a file, it checks the directory (stored in memory as well as on the tape), increments its head to the proper track, and then can find the file as fast as it can scan across the tape, taking no longer than one pass across the length of the tape. The rated access times of current drives vary from 45 to 68 seconds with a maximum time from the beginning of the tape to any file of 90 seconds. Table 13.6 summarizes some of the specifications of current DLT models.

TABLE 13.6   Digital Linear Tape Drive Models Specifications Compared

	DLT 7000	DLT 4000	DLT 2000	Units
Native capacity	35	20	10	Gigabytes
Native transfer rate	5	1.5	1.25	MB/sec
Tracks	208	128	128	Units
Track density	416	256	256	Tracks per inch
Recording density	86,000	86,000	62,500	Bits per inch
Access time	60	68	45	Seconds

DLT tape cartridges measure 4.2 inches square and are one-half inch thick. Various DLT drives use different types of tape with from 1,100 feet of 0.5 mil tape to 1,823 feet of 0.3 mil tape inside a single cartridge. The various DLT drive models are backward compatible with the media used by previous models. For example, a DLT 7000 drive can read and write all DLT tape formats with cartridge capacities from 2.6 to 35GB.

Linear Tape Open

When the industry slotted DLT as a proprietary format, Hewlett-Packard, IBM, and Seagate jointly developed an alternative planned to be an open format for a linear tape medium that the entire tape industry could support. To promote its non-proprietary nature, the group announced its new idea to the world on April 7, 1998, and called it *Linear Tape Open*, or LTO.

LTO is a single on-tape format that accommodates two different styles of cartridge, Accelis and Ultrium. The two cartridges are physically very different from one another and each requires its own matching drive. The primary design goal of Accelis is fast access; of Ultrium, huge capacity. Both formats share a common head and track layout, the same number of channels, and the same servo control technology. Drives for the two cartridge styles similarly share circuitry (including LSI chips) and use similar code structures.

Initial LTO drives will write four or eight parallel data channels much like venerable nine-track tape and IBM's 3480 cartridge system that's discussed on the CD-ROM. The LTO format divides the width of the tape into multiple *bands*, each of which has its own servo channels. Current drives spread two or four bands across the tape, depending on cartridge format.

The read/write heads of the drive make multiple passes back and forth across the tape within each band so that a single band contains from 96 to 128 tracks of data in addition to the servo information. The number of tracks in the format remains constant for each cartridge type no matter whether a drive has four or eight channels. The LTO drive's heads physically step up or down to access tracks within each band and to move between bands.

To aid in tracking each band and locating data on the tape, the top and bottom of each band include a servo track. These servo tracks include timing data as well as longitudinal information, which tells the drive exactly where on the length the head is reading or writing.

LTO pushes beyond other linear tape technologies into high-density territory, packing 100 megabits per square inch of medium. The initial drives that follow the LTO format use RLL data coding with built-in error correction and an improved compression algorithm that nominally doubles storage over the native capacity of each cartridge. Future LTO formats will use partial-response maximum likelihood (PRML) technology instead of RLL.

LTO embeds the error-correction information in the data channels instead of using a separate track. The error-correction code extends two dimensionally, both across time and across tracks. The LTO group claims the ECC is powerful enough to allow the reliable reading of data even should an entire track along with 1 percent of the remaining data get lost. Drives also use *dynamic rewrite* technology that automatically writes another copy of a data block that is bad in some tracks.

Each LTO cartridge contains a 32-kilobit RAM chip that electronically stores data location information for the cartridge. The drive uses non-contact technology (essentially radio waves) to read the chip without the tape needing to move. The drive can locate active data or blank areas to write upon without scanning the entire tape.

For speed, Accelis uses a two-spool cartridge so that the tape can shuttle quickly back and forth. In addition, Accelis loads with the tape in the middle position (rather than at one end of the tape, as with other two-spool formats) so that the most distant data is only half a tape length away. An Accelis cartridge is a bit longer but narrower than a QIC-EX cartridge and measures 5.4 inches (137 millimeters) long, 2.3 inches (59 millimeters) wide, and 0.6 inches (16 millimeters) thick. The Accelis package is not quite rectangular with one shorter side (the front) slightly angled. Figure 13.7 shows an Accelis cartridge.

FIGURE 13.7

An Accelis LTO cartridge.

Each Accelis cartridge holds 216 meters of tape measuring eight millimeters across. The two bands written across the tape each hold 128 tracks for a total of 256 tracks across the width of the tape.

The Accelis initial design provided access to any point on a tape within 10 seconds. Each cartridge holds 25GB of data without compression with two eight-channel data bands spread across the width of the tape. Initial systems offered transfer rates from 10 to 20 MB/sec. Eventually, the standard envisages cartridges holding 200GB (uncompressed) and transferring data from 80 to 160 MB/sec.

Ultrium is a single-spool design like IBM's own 3480/3490 tape cartridge system (from which it was apparently derived). The second spool—the *take-up reel*—is inside the drive. When you slide an Ultrium tape into its drive, a coupler grabs a pin that's attached to the end of the tape and then pulls the tape from the cartridge and around the take-up reel. The reel then pulls the tape across the heads.

To gain capacity, Ultrium uses wider tape than Accelis—half an inch wide—with more tracks spread across its width—384 tracks in four 96-channel bands. Each Ultrium cartridge is nearly square, 4.1 inches (105 millimeters) wide, 4.0 inches (102 millimeters) deep, and 0.8 inches (21.5 millimeters) thick. Figure 13.8 shows an Ultrium cartridge.

FIGURE 13.8
An Ultrium cartridge.

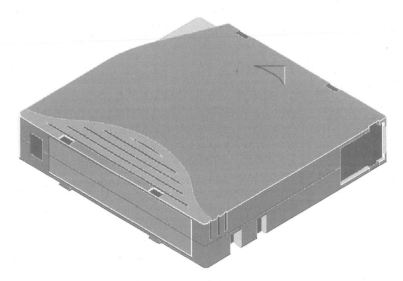

The initial Ultrium design could pack 100GB without compression in a single cartridge holding 600 meters of tape with cartridges of 30GB (180 meters) and 50GB (300 meters) also available. The format eventually should permit single-cartridge capacities of about 800GB with transfer rates of 80 to 160 MB/sec.

The LTO group maintains an informational Web site at www.lto-technology.com.

Helical-Scan Systems

Although helical-scan recording was originally designed for video signals, it is also an excellent match for digital data. The high tape-to-head speed can translate to high data transfer rates. Although the narrow data tracks potentially increase the noise content of the recorded signal, digital technology handily avoids the noise. As with all digital signals, the electronics of the helical-scan tape system simply ignore most of the noise, and error-correction takes care of anything that can't be ignored.

Helical-scan systems are the children of the digital age. They trade the mechanical precision required in the linear scan systems for servo-controlled designs. Servo mechanisms in the helical-scan recorder control both the tape speed and head speed to assure that the read/write head exactly tracks the position of the tracks on the tape. Although servo electronics can be built with other technologies, digital electronics and miniaturization make the required circuitry trivial, a single control chip. Moreover, servo control automatically compensates for inaccuracies in the operation and even construction of the tape transport system. This design allows manufacturers to use less expensive fabrication processes and helps the mechanism age gracefully, adjusting itself for the wear and tear of old age.

Three different helical-scan systems are currently used in tape systems for digital data, eight-millimeter tape, four-millimeter tape (which is formally called the Digital Data Standard, or DDS), and a proprietary system sold by Pereos (discussed on the CD-ROM).

Eight Millimeter

Probably the most familiar incarnation of eight-millimeter tape is in miniaturized camcorders. Sony pioneered the medium as a compact, high-quality video recording system. The same tapes were later adapted to data recording by Exabyte Corporation and first released on the PC market in 1987.

Video recorders have in the past been used as the basis of tape backup systems. However, these relied on converting digital computer signals into an analog format that could be recorded on tape as if it were a video signal. Alpha Microsystems used this approach in a product the company calls Videotrax, which used a single expansion card in the host computer to convert hard disk or other system data into NTSC (National Television Standards Committee) video signals. The resulting signals were then stored on a conventional videocassette recorder. The eight-millimeter helical system created by Exabyte, on the other hand, records digital data in a digital format without conversion. In fact, the Exabyte system shares only the cassette with the eight-millimeter video recording system. The signals and equipment are entirely different.

The eight-millimeter cassette resembles an audio cassette because it has two hubs within its plastic shell, but the tape is much wider (eight millimeters, of course, is 0.315 inch compared to 0.150 inch for cassette tape) and a hinged door on the cassette protects the tape from physical damage. The cassette itself measures 3.75 inches by 2.5 inches and about half an inch thick.

In the original Exabyte eight-millimeter digital recording system, the head drum rotated at 1,800 revolutions per minute and the tape traveled past it at 10.89 millimeters per second to achieve a track density of 819 per inch and a flux density of 54 kilobits per inch—enough to squeeze 2.5GB on a single cartridge. Improvements extended the capacity to 5GB without compression and up to 10GB with compression. The tape can be rapidly shuttled forward and backward to find any given location (and block of data) within about 15 seconds.

Eight-millimeter drives tend to be quite expensive. Complete systems cost thousands of dollars. A raw drive alone can cost more than $1,000. Its primary market is backing up file servers, machines that can benefit from its huge capacity.

Advanced Intelligent Tape

One of the biggest problems with tape is the need to scan through the entire ribbon to find out what's there. Although a number of companies have developed data formats with a directory structure, these add time to the backup and restoration process and usually require formatting the tape before its use—all of which make tape inconvenient. Sony developed an alternative technology. By incorporating non-volatile RAM memory into the shell of an eight-millimeter tape, a tape drive can quickly retrieve directory information without the need to scan the tape. It doesn't have to read the tape at all to find out what's there.

This memory is what makes Sony's *Advanced Intelligent Tape* so smart. Each cartridge has 16KB for storing table-of-contents and file location information. Each cartridge can store 25MB of uncompressed data. With data compression, the AIT system can achieve transfer rates of 6 MB/sec and a capacity of 50MB per cartridge.

Despite being based on eight-millimeter technology, AIT is not backward compatible with the older medium. AIT drives reject conventional eight-millimeter tapes as unsupported media and hardware write protection prevents older drives from altering AIT tapes.

Digital Data Storage

Developed originally as a means to record music, the *Digital Data Storage* first saw commercial application as *Digital Audio Tape*, or DAT, a name sometimes applied to the system even when it is used for storing computer data. The technology was first released as a computer storage medium in 1989. Using a tape that's nominally four millimeters wide (actually 3.81 millimeters or 0.150 inch, the same as cassette tape), the system is sometimes called four-millimeter tape. The thin tape fits into tiny cartridges to store huge amounts of data.

The first DAT system could pack 1.3GB into a cassette measuring only 0.4x2.9x2.1 inches (HWD). The result was, at the time, the most dense storage of any current computer tape medium, 114 megabits per square inch on special 1450 Oersted metal particle tape (the same material as used by eight-millimeter digital tape systems). A cassette held either 60 or 90 meters of this tape. The shorter tapes stored 1.3GB; the longer tapes, 2.0GB.

Under the aegis of Hewlett-Packard and Sony Corporation, in 1990 this format was formalized as DDS, sometimes listed as DDS-1 (to distinguish it from its successors). The same format underlies DDS-DC, which adds *data compression* to the drive to increase capacity. Although at first DDS was listed in some literature (and in an earlier edition of this book) as an abbreviation for Digital Data Standard, the DDS organization that coordinates the specification renders it officially as *Digital Data Storage*.

In 1993, the same companies updated the standard to DDS-2, doubling both the data transfer speed and capacity of the system as well as introducing new 120-meter cassettes using a tape coated with a metal powder medium.

In 1995, the standard got upped again to DDS-3, which can pack up to 12GB on each cartridge or 24GB of compressed data. In addition, the DDS-3 standard allows for transfers at double the DDS-2 rate with speed potential of up to 1.5 megabits per second (discounting the effects of compression). DDS-3 uses the same tape media as its predecessor format but increases the data density to 122 kilobits per inch. The key to this higher density is a new technology termed *partial-response maximum likelihood* (PRML).

Announced in 1998 with products expected in late 1999, DDS-4 further enhances the four-millimeter format to provide 20GB of storage on a single tape. Part of the capacity increase results from longer tapes, to 155 meters per cartridge. In addition, DDS-4 reduces track width by 25 percent. Because of its higher data density, DDS-4 also gains a bit of speed. The standard allows for transfer rates from 1 to 3 megabits per second.

DDS-5, planned for the year 2001, aims for a native capacity of 40GB per cartridge, achieved through the use of longer (yet again) tapes, higher density recording using a PRML read channel (see Chapter 9, "Storage Interfaces"), and increased channel efficiency. Designers anticipate transfer rates of up to 6 megabits per second for DDS-5 drives.

Table 13.7 summarizes the various DDS implementations.

Table 13.7   Summary of DDS specifications

Format	*DDS*	*DDS-DC*	*DDS-2*	*DDS-3*	*DDS-4*	*DDS-5*
Year introduced	1989	1991	1993	1995	1999	2001
Cartridge capacity	1.3GB	2.0GB	4.0GB	12GB	20GB	40GB
Transfer rate	183 Kbit/sec	183 Kbit/sec	360 to 750 Kbit/sec	720 kbit/sec to 1.5 Mbit/sec	1 to 3 Mbit/sec	1 to 6 Mbit/sec
Tape length	60 m	90 m	120 m	125m	155 m	NA

In a DDS drive, the tape barely creeps along, requiring about three seconds to move an inch—a tape speed of eight millimeters per second. The head drum, however, spins rapidly at 2,000 revolutions per minute, putting down 1,869 tracks across a linear inch of tape with flux transitions packed 61 kilobits per inch.

DAT technology has two important strengths: access speed and capacity. In the audio realm, the DAT medium was designed for rapid access to information—finding a musical selection. Consequently, when translated into the computer realm, DAT could locate a file in about 15 seconds. Although access speed is of little importance for backups, quick times make for easy file restorations.

The estimated life for the tape in a DDS cartridge is 2,000 passes over a given section of tape. In that a normal backup or restoration session can push a tape through up to six passes over some sections, the practical life of a cartridge amounts to about 100 insertions or sessions. If you enforce a weekly backup schedule using a given cartridge for backup once each week, you should replace cartridges after about two years of regular use.

The first DAT systems shared tapes with audio DAT recorders. Since that time, however, the later DDS standards have required improved magnetic media with higher coercivities. As a result, to get the highest reliability you must use a tape made to the standard that matches your drive. Although you may be able to read older tapes in a later DDS drive, successful writing (where coercivity comes into play) is less probable. Similarly, DDS tape will not work in your DAT recorder. The DDS Manufacturers Group, the organization that coordinates DDS activities, has also developed a technology called *Media Recognition System* that is able to detect audio DAT tapes. The DDS organization has developed distinctive logos for each level of the DDS hierarchy so that you can readily distinguish tapes and drives. Figure 13.9 shows the logos for DDS-2 through DDS-4.

FIGURE 13.9

The official DDS-2, DDS-3, and DDS-4 logos.

DDS-2   DDS-3   DDS-4

Hewlett-Packard and Sony hold intellectual property rights to DDS technology, and all drives using DDS must be licensed by them. The DDS Manufacturers Group maintains a Web site at www.dds-tape.com.

Choosing a Backup System

Tape has several advantages, but it is not the only backup system that you can use. What you want depends on the kind of protection you need and how much you want to pay.

With the price of PCs now averaging in the vicinity of $1,000 and good-performing systems available for half that if you turn over the right rocks, a $2,000 backup system doesn't make much sense. In fact, only the various styles of mini-cartridge and DDS drives make sense for an individual PC. Eight-millimeter, AIT, DLT, and both LTO's Accelis and Ultrium formats make sense only for larger computer systems and networks where drives that cost several thousand dollars make good business sense.

The entry level for a tape system is about $200, which buys a mini-cartridge system capable of storing 2 to 8GB. A basic DDS system with similar capacity but faster access and lower media costs will cost three or more times as much. Some of the alternatives to a tape backup system provide better value, although they offer different forms of protection. Among your choices are a second PC or disk drive, a cartridge disk drive, a CD-Recordable or CD-RW drive, and a true tape backup system.

Another PC

When you upgrade from one PC to another or if you have both a notebook and desktop PC, you can use one as the backup for the other. This strategy has a singular advantage: You have a complete backup system. If something happens to one PC, you can continue your work on the other.

In that you probably already have a second PC if you've recently upgraded to a new machine, this strategy seems natural. To make it work effectively, however, you must duplicate your files from one system to the other. The best way is with a small (two nodes are sufficient) local area network. All the software you need comes with any modern operating system, and the additional hardware is minimal: a pair of network interface cards and a hub or cross-over cable. Chapter 23, "Networking," gives you step-by-step instructions for getting a small network going.

If you have both a notebook and desktop PC, a network is still the best way to move files back and forth, but there are others. You can link your two systems together with a *LapLink* cable (parallel or serial, usually supplied with *LapLink* software from Traveling Software) or a special USB cable that allows two masters to interconnect.

The two PC strategy has its limitations. It is a one-shot backup system. You don't have a continuing series of backups to rely on if you need to go back to a particular version of an ever-changing file. Moreover, making a backup to another PC is still bothersome, and you're apt to get behind and not have the backup copies you want when you need them.

Fortunately, you can make an automatic backup system using some of the old utilities built into Windows and the operating system's own System Agent function.

Duplicate Disk

A duplicate hard disk has the same weaknesses as a second PC and lacks the biggest advantage of that strategy. Moreover, if you keep both hard disks in one PC, both are vulnerable to the same physical dangers. As with a second PC, you can maintain a single backup copy with a second hard disk. Better still, a RAID 0 system will automatically make a backup for you that guards against hardware failure. On the other hand, because the RAID system automatically and nearly instantly duplicates the data on one disk to the other, this strategy will not give you a copy of a file that you can step back to if you inadvertently change the original for the worse.

A duplicate disk excels when you need to restore a backed-up file. You can probably restore a whole directory faster than you can locate the right tape to make a restoration from. Of course, your selection of backups to restore from will be small unless you arrange a chronological hierarchy of backups on your second hard disk.

You can guard against some of the eggs-in-one-basket dangers by making your second drive *removable*. By installing your drive in a *portable rack* (described in Chapter 26, "Cases"), you can pull it out of your PC at the end of the day and lock it up—or take it home with you. You can even use several different drives as sort of a backup system. Although drives remain more costly than data cartridges, the gap is narrowing. A $200 UDMA hard disk can give you 10GB of backup protection.

Cartridge Disk

A cartridge disk is a seeming panacea, one that combines all the advantage of tape backups with the speed and flexibility of a second hard disk drive. You can keep multiple disk copies of your important files, lock the cartridge disks safely away, and develop a true backup system so that you can go back to earlier versions of changing files. At the same time, cartridge disks deliver performance comparable to a conventional hard disk drive.

The drawback of cartridge disk systems are capacity and cost. Today's largest disk cartridges hold 2GB, about a quarter the storage on current basic Travan systems. Moreover, the disk cartridges are more expensive both per cartridge and per gigabyte of storage.

CD-Recordable and CD-RW

Optical storage in the form of a CD-R or CD-RW drive offers an intriguing backup alternative. Recordable CDs are now inexpensive enough to make a valuable archiving system. Although you cannot change the content of a CD-R once you've written it, this immutability suits backup applications in which you need to access files in their original form or early versions of changing files.

A CD-RW drive goes further and can function as true backup system that lets you regularly rotate discs in weekly and monthly cycles. In fact, CD-RW systems offer many of the same advantages of cartridge magnetic disk systems. CD-RW drives are neither as fast nor as convenient as cartridge magnetic disks for everyday use as a primary storage system. CD-RW media are, however, less costly per gigabyte of storage.

The chief drawback of current optical media is the limited capacity of each disc, about 650MB based on CD standards. You'll need several discs to make a complete system backup. The hidden ace of optical storage is, of course, the DVD-RW system. Such drives can back up about 5GB per disc, but at the time this is being written, the wide availability of affordable drives is more dream than reality.

Tape Systems

Each of the many tape formats currently available has its own strengths as the backbone of a backup system. Price alone makes two formats the best choices for backing up individual PCs. The low cost of drives compatible with Travan and QIC-EX cartridges makes them the best choice if your budget is tight. In early 1999, $200 buys 8GB of backup. DDS drives are more expensive (from $500 to $700 for a low-end product as this is written) but promise lower costs per gigabyte thanks to inexpensive cartridges. DDS drives also offer faster access to your backup files.

Operation

When buying a tape drive or its media, you confront other issues besides the tape format. Among these are the way the drive installs in (or out) of your PC and the media that you slide into the drive.

The first thing you must consider is that tape—or any backup system—is not something that's fun to work with. Rather than something you enjoy doing, it's something you have to do. Far from a miracle or wonder drug, tape backup is more like castor oil for your computer: It's unpalatable and has little perceived value in the abstract, no matter what you have to pay for it. You put up with it because you've been told it's good for you in some way that you hope to never test. No matter how much sugar is mixed in with it, you still wish it (and the need for it) would go away. It won't, so you might as well swallow hard and take advantage of the protection tape offers you and your PC. The best you can hope for is getting it over with quickly.

Portable Drives

Internal and external units are generally much the same; the only effective difference is that you need a free drive bay to install an internal system. External systems tend to be costlier because they require a case and a connecting cable. However, they offer the advantage that they are portable. You can shuttle a single backup drive between several PCs (providing that you equip each with the necessary host adapter).

Better still are portable drives that link to PCs through standard bidirectional parallel ports (EPP or ECP, see Chapter 21, "Legacy Ports"). Because nearly every PC has a parallel port built in, you can shuttle one of these machines around without the worry of adding host adapters. Using conventional parallel ports, such drives can attain the speeds of other units that use floppy disk interfaces. Linked with Enhanced Parallel Ports, they can rival backup systems with SCSI connections. If you have a number of PCs to regularly back up, a single external tape drive can do the job for all. You can even use it as a data transport system to move files or entire environments between PCs.

Many new drives use the USB interface. As in other applications, USB fits in between parallel and SCSI in speed. Before you opt for USB, however, insure both your PC and its operating system have USB support, as noted in Chapter 20, "Peripheral Ports." Windows NT through version 4.0 does not support USB, and Windows 95 may require an update.

Internal, single-system drives are the choice when you don't want clutter or you want to save the cost the drive manufacturer charges for packaging and powering an external unit. As with other peripherals you install internally, you must have a free bay for an internal tape drive, and the bay requires front panel access. Nearly all internal tape drives require the power as used by disk drives—positive 5 volts DC for their logic, 12 volts for their drive motors—and they link to your PC's power supply with a standard drive power connector.

Network Backups

Backing up an individual PC can be a bore. Backing up a dozen makes skipping work to have a root canal sound like a desirable alternative. Making multiple backups can be a manageable task and is usually the best way to make the most of a backup system.

Networking and backups go hand-in-hand. The very existence of the network implies important work is being done, or is supposed to be done—work that would be tragic to lose. The value of the data makes the cost of a reasonable backup system trivial in comparison. In addition, the network permits backups to be centralized so that one backup system and one operator can take care of all the data. One drive serves all PCs just as with a portable backup unit, but you're not burdened with the bother of plugging it in and unplugging it to move between PCs.

Working over a network poses no inherent problem for tape backup hardware. As with making individual backups, the chief concerns are capacity and speed. You need enough capacity to accommodate all your files on a reasonable number of tapes—which may mean a single tape if you don't want to station someone near the tape drive to change tapes and you cannot afford a tape jukebox. The backup system should be fast enough that it finishes one backup before the next one is scheduled. The high-capacity backup systems designed for networks have no problems in this regard, but smaller tape cartridge systems that interface through floppy disk ports may make backing up a large drive a continuous process.

The more important issue in backing up networks is software. Your software will determine how and how well you make backups of your network. There are two basic strategies for network backups, backing up server files and backing up individual PC files. The server strategy implies that you have a server-based network typical of most businesses that consolidates your important data files on the server. Backing up the server is much like backing up an individual PC, but there are more data and more directories. Backing up individual PCs in the peer-to-peer networks that are more common in homes and workgroups requires backup software that's capable of addressing multiple disk drives spread across the network. Not all backup systems can automate peer backups, so checking the capabilities of network backup software becomes a critical concern.

Backup Software

The tape drive is only part of a true backup system. Just as important is the software that runs the system. The software determines what you can do with a tape drive and how you do it.

Almost universally, today's backup software gives you (or should give you) menu control and some means of automating your regular backup procedure—for example, a batch mode or command-driven option. If you make only occasional backups, you probably do not want to spend the time learning an elaborate command structure, so these menu-controlled systems are often best. However, if you want to automate the backup process and make untended backups, you'll want either software that can be run in command mode or a program that has provisions to automatically swing into action while you count sheep, worrying whether it will actually work and whether you've left your PC switched on.

In general, the following two backup techniques have evolved—image and file-by-file backups—with manufacturers each developing their own format standards for their own tapes.

Image Backups

The image backup is a bit-for-bit copy of the original disk. Bytes are merely read from the disk and copied on tape without a glance to their content or structure. Because little processing overhead is involved, these image backups can be fast.

With early backup systems, a major problem with image backups was that they typically required restoring to exactly the same drive as was backed up because they read the bad tracks with the good and unused disk areas with those that are used. Obviously, this technique was not very versatile when you wanted to exchange data between systems—or if your hard disk crashed and had to be replaced.

Backup software writers solved this problem by adding intelligence to the restoration program so that it could build the needed structure when moving files back to disk from tape. Although modern PC backup software often lacks an image mode, the backup systems for larger computer systems may still include this mode. Having such an image backup can be invaluable because it allows the restoration of the full operating environment of a large, multi-user computer system.

File-by-File Backups

The alternative to image backups is file-by-file backups. These record the structure of the data as it is backed up. File-by-file backups are more efficient because they back up only the data you need to back up, even allowing you to select individual files. Most PC backup systems use this method exclusively.

Recording file structure seems a natural part of the backup process. In fact, image backup appeared chiefly for performance reasons. Processing overhead slows the file-by-file backup process, and early PCs were not fast enough to handle this overhead while keeping tape streaming. Most modern PCs can keep up with the fastest tape systems.

File-by-file backups impose another penalty. Most systems record a directory of the files and backup sessions on each tape, usually reserving a portion of the tape for the directory. Maintaining this directory adds time to the backup process. Before it begins making a backup, most backup software compiles the directory, stealing several minutes even before the tape starts unreeling. Some software checks and updates the directory at the end of each backup session as well, adding more minutes to the backup.

File-by-file backup systems afford several methods of selecting files to be written to tape. A *full backup* captures all or nearly all of the files on your disk. Most backup software automatically excludes system files from backups but may allow you the option of streaming even these to tape. *Incremental backups* only capture the files that you have created or modified since your last full backup session. Usually only a few files on your PC change each day, so an incremental backup can be incredibly fast. The only problem is that incremental backups complicate file restoration. To restore your complete disk, you must first restore the full backup and then each incremental backup in order. *Selective backups* allow you to specify which files to copy to tape. Most backup software lets you choose files from a tree-structured menu display or by typing in a file name or some identifying characteristic. Selective backups eliminate all the chaff and so make backing up quick. On the other hand, they shift the burden of managing your files and backups to you.

To help you organize selective backups, most backup software lets you choose files by identifying characteristics. The most popular of these, which should be expected as normal file selection options, include archive bits, which indicate whether a file has been previously backed up; date and time stamps, which enable you to back up files changed after a given date and time; and subdirectory searches, which include all the files in the daughter directories of the one being backed up. Some software also enables you to specifically exclude files from a backup session, either by name or tagging.

Most tape systems enable you to give a name to every backup session that can later be read to identify a tape if, for example, you neglect to put a physical label on it. Many backup systems also enable you to embed a password so that the secrecy of your data will not be compromised if a tape is lost or stolen.

Error handling is an important aspect of backup software. Some backup programs quit when they encounter an error—such as a disk error when reading a file to be backed up or finding a tape error—and you're forced to start the entire process all over again. When you're several hours into a backup session or have spent considerable time selecting files, that's not a happy situation. Unfortunately, there's no way you can tell how accommodating a particular program is in error handling except in checking reviews.

Verification

There's nothing worse than a false sense of security, thinking you're protected when you're not. Having a backup that cannot be restored or a backup containing one or more errors (which in itself may prevent restoration) can give you that false security.

Some tape systems perform *read-after-write verification* or data checking. That is, after they write bits to tape, they read them back to be sure that everything was properly written to tape. For this system to work, the tape drive requires separate write and read heads or a dual-gap head that has separate gaps for writing to and reading from tape. Although read-after-write verification makes hardware more complex and expensive (and is consequently only included in more expensive systems), it requires no additional time in making a backup.

To assure that your backups can accomplish their goal of making restorable tapes even with inexpensive tape drives that lack read-after-write verification, most backup software includes a *verification option*. That is, after you've completed your backup, the tape drive rewinds and makes a file-by-file comparison of everything on the tape. This verification doubles the time required for making a backup.

Tape Requirements

With any removable media system, the cost of the medium can quickly eclipse the price of the hardware. Consequently, you will be tempted to limit the number of tapes in which you invest.

For most backup scenarios, you will want sufficient media capacity to hold a minimum of three complete backups. For greater peace of mind or more elaborate backup rituals—such as keeping a separate backup for each day of the week—your media needs increase. Most people actively use between 6 and 10 tapes in their regular backup routine.

You also should figure in the cost of periodically replacing any media that can wear out. All tape media and all disks except for cartridge hard disks eventually wear out.

The exact amount of life to expect from a particular medium depends on your own personal paranoia. One major media manufacturer pegged cartridge tape life at 5,000 to 6,000 passes across the read/write head, clearly more than you'll want to endure over the life of your PC, or your own life, for that matter. On the other hand, cautious mainframe managers may routinely replace open-reel tapes after they've been used as few as 50 times. A good compromise is to replace your backup tapes at least annually. Too many other things can go wrong with backups to risk the small expense of assuring yourself of good tape quality.

Media Matching

As with other removable media drives, cartridges (or whatever) serve as the raw material that a tape drive works upon. Although most tape media are entirely different from tape cartridges used in audio and video products, some data tape cartridges are physically similar to their other worldly counterparts—in particular eight-millimeter and DAT cassettes. Considering the premium prices charged for data-certified media, substituting audio or video cassettes can be tempting, indeed. Even within the realm of computer products, it is sometimes tempting to substitute a cheaper mini-cartridge for those officially sanctioned for a tape drive.

Tape vendors note that data tapes are engineered with different characteristics such as coercivity and retentivity than are tapes made for audio/visual applications. They warn that mismatches between the needs of a machine and the characteristics of the media may result in poor performance—even unusable backups. Although in the case of eight-millimeter analog video and digital data tapes, the argument is compelling, it is less so for DAT and DDS cartridges. Eight-millimeter systems are designed primarily for network and larger computer backup, and risking their data to save a few dollars on a cartridge is false economy indeed. On the other hand, both DAT and DDS use digital technology, and DDS is eminently suited for backing up the gigabyte-level drives in modern PCs. There appears little penalty in substituting DAT for DDS cartridges. The only factor weighing against the strategy is that the price difference between the two different media is disappearing. Moreover, DDS is catching on faster than DAT ever did, so DDS tapes may actually be more readily obtainable. In other words, in a pinch you can use DAT tapes in your DDS drive, but there's little point in doing so.

Backup Strategy

The best backup system is the one that you are most likely to use—and use routinely. No matter how good or expensive it is, a backup system is worthless if you never bother to put it to work. The easiest and most convenient backup system to operate is the one least likely to be ignored—and the one most likely to help when disaster strikes.

No matter what backup hardware you choose, you still need a backup *system*. That system requires more than just hardware, even more than software. To make it work, you must adhere to a strict backup routine after you make one overall backup of all the files on your hard disk.

If you plan to oversee all your backups as they happen, the fastest backup system is always the more endurable. If your time is valuable and you don't mind leaving your PC running overnight (and you have the faith that it will, indeed, continue to run overnight), taking advantage of automatic backup programs makes the time spent backing up meaningless. If you don't have to wait, it doesn't matter how long it takes.

Even a slow backup system is better than none, and even an occasional backup beats not having any. All it takes is one disk crash, however, for you to learn how important it is to take the time—no matter how long—to keep your backups current.

To cut the time required for backing up, most backup software publishers recommend making a full backup when you set up your backup system and then at predetermined, widely spaced intervals afterward (typically weekly or bi-weekly). Daily (or as often as you feel necessary), you fill in the gap with incremental backups. This strategy ensures that all of your files are on tape so you can make a complete recovery from even a huge disaster. It saves both tape and time.

With some backup systems, the full-and-incremental strategy won't save as much time as you think. The tape drive may have to scan from the beginning of your tape to the end of the data to find where to begin adding your incremental files. Scanning the tape and writing to the tape may take exactly the same amount of time, so making a full backup actually takes no longer. Moreover, having several full backups helps assure you that you'll have at least one that will be completely restorable.

The best backup system is the one that enforces the routine you are most likely to follow—the one that ensures that you have protection when the worst does happen. A backup system that does not get used (or used often) is not a backup system at all.

Input Devices

Input devices are the means by which you move information into your PC—the primary means by which you interact with your personal computer. The various available devices span an entire range of technologies, from the tactile to the vocal. Although they work in different ways, all accomplish the same task: They enable you to communicate with your computer.

Important Issues in Keyboard Design

Feature	In Short
Touch	The force required to activate keys can be light (soft) or heavy (hard) with or without a snap-over feel (tactile feedback). The best combination is what feels right to you.
Layout	The arrangement of keys for desktop keyboards is nearly universal but notebook designs vary enough to be maddening in moving between machines. Most people prefer the familiar, although you can learn to live with anything, including the Dvorak arrangement.
Ergonomics	Plain flat keyboards can cause or encourage repetitive stress injury; angled ergonomic designs may soothe hands that tire from long bouts of continuous keystroking.
Interface	The PS/2 (six-pin) interface has become almost universal among removable keyboards, but the PC industry wants you to move to USB. Be sure to match the interface when replacing your keyboard.
Cable	Short coiled cables may make lightweight keyboards snap from your hands. Long cables give more freedom in operation. You can totally liberate yourself with a wireless keyboard.

The Most Popular PC Pointing Devices

Pointing device	In Short
Mouse	The first and still the most popular pointing device but requires desktop real estate and moving your hand from the keyboard (good for ergonomics but bad for typing efficiency). Prolonged use can tire your whole arm.
Trackball	Takes up less space and requires less movement to navigate through screens and programs, and it generally causes less fatigue during prolonged use. Designs are diverse, so you must choose one that fits your hand and style.
TouchPad	Perhaps the most popular notebook computer pointing device. Good designs work well but beware of poor implementations that cause inadvertent mouse movement and key activation.
Trackpoint	Designed for typing efficiency—your fingers need never leave the home row when moving the mouse—but some people find it clumsy and unnatural.
Joystick	Not really a pointing device but a game controller. Modern controllers can be as elaborate as a starship bridge—which is perfect if that's the onscreen world you intend to control.

You don't buy a PC as a big, full box that you can shake your data out of as if it were a giant digital saltcellar. The lure of the PC is that you can fill it with what you want—your programs, your data, your hopes, your dreams, your arcade games. The problem you face is getting all that stuff *into* your PC. Certainly you can download programs, files, and other delights from the Internet or copy disks you buy in the store or coerce from your friends. But if you want to make your personal computer really personal, you need a way to fill it with your personal thoughts, sketches, and ideas.

The one needed element is the input device, a channel through which you can pass data and commands to your PC. Absent a silico-cerebral mind link that makes sense only to science fiction writers, that connection inevitably involves some kind of mechanical device. Commands, data, and ideas have to be reduced to physical form to exit your mind and enter your PC. The input device converts the mechanical into the electronic form that your PC can understand.

The basic electro-mechanical interface is the switch. A computer can detect the state of a switch by sensing the electrical flow through it. (The switch is on if electricity flows; off if it does not.) Thus with a single switch, you could communicate with your PC exactly one bit at a time—a daunting task if you want to create a multi-megabyte database.

You can speed the communications by employing several switches, a whole bank of them. In fact, early computers were programmed exactly in that way—as are computers today. However, instead of using old-fashioned toggle switches, today's computers use pushbuttons. Instead of sending a single on/off state to the computer, each button sends a series of them, pulses, to your computer. The pulses make up a digital code, and each button sends a different one to indicate a letter of the alphabet or other symbol. This entire bank of switches is called a *keyboard*, and despite the best efforts of designers and executives, it remains the primary input device used by today's PCs.

Keyboards have shortcomings. The primary one is that they are relatively inefficient at relaying spatial information to your computer; they send symbols, not places. A number of applications, however, depend on knowing where rather than what—moving a cursor, for example. The computer knows what you want to move (the cursor); it just needs the spatial information about where to put it. A whole menagerie of input devices has arisen to improve on the keyboard's ability to point to a place—mice, trackballs, joysticks, pens, and digitizing tablets.

As computers moved into the graphic realm with the aid of pointing devices, they also developed the need to acquire huge blocks of graphic data from external sources. That is, when all else fails to convey what you want to say, you paint your PC a picture. But you need a means of converting a physical (optical) image into electronic form. The scanner and digital camera fill this need.

Keyboards

The primary input device for most computer systems is the keyboard, and until voice recognition systems are perfected to the point that they can recognize continuous speech, the dominance of the keyboard is not likely to change. Even then, the keyboard will probably remain unapproachable for speed and accuracy for years to come. The keyboard also is more suited to data entry in open offices, airplanes, and anywhere your privacy is not ensured and your sanity not beyond reproach.

When you buy a new PC, the keyboard is the least of your worries. After all, the manufacturer takes care of it for you. Nearly every desktop PC comes completely equipped with a keyboard (otherwise, the PC wouldn't be much good for anything). Notebook PCs have their keyboards completely built in. Moreover, keyboards are pretty much all the same these days—or at least they all look the same. Over the last decade, the key layout has become almost completely standardized, the one true keyboard design that might have been ordained by God. With a desktop machine, you get 101 keys on a surfboard-shaped panel that monopolizes your desktop or overflows your lap. With a notebook PC, you're stuck with whatever the computer maker thought best for you and the market value of its executive stock options.

The default keyboard that comes with your PC is more variable than you might think, however. Underneath all those keys, you might find one or another exotic technology that would seem best left to the realm of engineers. But the technology used by your keyboard determines not only how it works, but also how long it works and how much you will enjoy working with it. It may even influence whether keyboarding is a time of pleasure or pain. The underlying differences are enough to make you consider casting aside the (usually) cheap, default keyboard the maker of your desktop PC packed in the box and getting something more suitable to your fingers and your work. When you consider a notebook PC, a difference in keyboards may be enough to make you favor one machine over another, particularly when the rest of the two systems are well matched.

Technologies

The keyboard concept—a letter for every pushbutton—is almost ancient, dating back to the days of the first typewriter. The design seems fixed in stone. Actually, it's the product of something even more immovable, human inertia. The basic layout and function of the keyboard has changed little since the last half of the 19th century, and the mold for the PC refinement was first cast in 1987. No matter what PC you buy today, you're almost certain to get a keyboard that follows the now industry-standard design. That's good because you can confront any PC and start working in seconds. But that's also bad when those seconds stretch to hours of uninterrupted typing.

All keyboards have the same function: detecting the keys pressed down by your fingers and relaying that information to your computer. Even though two keyboards may look identical, they may differ considerably in the manner in which they detect the motion of your fingers. The technology used for this process—how the keyboard works electrically—can affect the sturdiness and longevity of the keyboard. Although all operate in effect as switches by altering the flow of electricity in some way, the way those changes are detected evolved into an elaborate mechanism. The way that technology is put into action affects how pleasant your typing experience is.

Nearly every technology for detecting the change in flow of electricity has been adapted to keyboards at one time or another. The engineer's goal has been to find a sensing mechanism that combines accuracy—detecting only the desired keystroke and ignoring errant electrical signals—with long life (you don't want a keyboard that works for six words), along with the right "feel," the personal touch. In past years, keyboard designers found promise in complex and exotic technologies such as Hall-effect switches, special semiconductors that react to magnetic field changes. The lure was the wonder of magnetism; nothing need touch to make the detection. A lack of contact promised a freedom from wear, a keyboard with endless life.

In the long run, however, the quest for the immortal keyboard proved misguided. Keyboards rated for tens of millions of keypresses met premature ends with a splash from a cup of coffee. In the end, manufacturers opted for the simplest and least expensive, hard contact technology, as close to a plain switch as you can get without a wallplate. The chief alternative, capacitive technology, led the pack at the start. It was more reliable, longer lived, more complicated, and (for a long while) more popular. It was also more expensive; in today's dollars, the keyboard of the first PC cost more than an entire current computer system. Something had to give.

Contact

The direct approach in keyboards is using switches to alter the flow of electricity. The switches in the keyboard do exactly what all switches are supposed to do: open and close an electrical circuit to stop or start the flow of electricity. Using switches requires simpler (although not trivial) circuitry to detect each keystroke, although most switch-based PC keyboards still incorporate a microprocessor to assign scan codes and serialize the data for transmission to the system unit.

Design simplicity and corresponding low cost have made switch-based keyboards today's top choice for PCs. These keyboards either use novel technology to solve the major problem of switches—a short life—or just ignore it. Cost has become the dominant factor in the design and manufacture of keyboards. In the trade-off between price and life, the switch-based design is the winner.

Three switch-based keyboard designs have been used in PCs: mechanical switches, rubber domes, and membrane switches.

Mechanical switches use the traditional switch mechanism, precious metal contacts forced together. In the *discrete switch* design, the switch under each keyboard station is an independent unit that can be individually replaced. Alternately, the entire keyboard can be fabricated as one assembly. Although the former might lend itself to easier repair, the minimum labor charge for computer repair often is higher than the cost of a replacement keyboard.

The contact in a mechanical switch keyboard can do double duty, chaperoning the electrical flow and positioning the keycaps. Keyboard contacts can operate as springs to push the keycap back up after it has been pressed. Although this design is compelling because it minimizes the parts needed to make a keyboard, it is not suited to PC-quality keyboards. The return force is difficult to control and the contact material is apt to suffer from fatigue and break. Consequently, most mechanical switch keyboards incorporate springs to push the keycaps back into place as well as other parts to give the keyboard the right feel and sound.

Although several manufacturers have built keyboards with mechanical switches, the design has fallen from favor. Probably less than 2 percent of all keyboards use discrete switches.

Rubber dome keyboards combine the contact and positioning mechanisms into a single piece. A puckered sheet of elastomer—a stretchy, rubber-like synthetic—is molded to put a dimple or dome under each keycap, the dome bulging upward. Pressing on the key pushes the dome down. Inside the dome is a tab of carbon or other conductive material that serves as one of the keyboard contacts. When the dome goes down, the tab presses against another contact and completes the circuit. Release the key, and the elastomer dome pops back to its original position, pushing the keycap back with it.

The rubber dome design initially won favor on notebook computers where its resistance to environmental stress (a euphemism for "spilled coffee") was a major strength. The design also is inexpensive to manufacture. The switches for the entire keyboard can be molded as one piece about as easily as making a waffle. The design was readily adapted to desktop keyboards and provides the foundation for many inexpensive, lightweight models.

Properly designed, a rubber dome keyboard has an excellent feel; the give of the individual domes can be tailored to enable you to sense exactly when the switch makes contact. A poor design, however, makes each keypress feel rubbery and uncertain. Moreover, some elastomers have a tendency to become stiff with age with the result that some keys can become recalcitrant.

Membrane keyboards are similar to rubber domes except they use thin plastic sheets—the membrane—printed with conductive traces rather than elastomer sheets. Most designs uses a three-sheet sandwich—top and bottom sheets with printed contacts and a central insulating sheet with holes at each key position that holds the contacts apart. The top sheet is dimpled, and pressing down on the dimple pushes the top contact down to meet the bottom contact. The dimple snaps from one position to another, giving a distinct tactile feedback that indicates when you've pressed a key.

The membrane design often is used for keypads to control calculators and printers because of its low cost and trouble-free life. The materials making contact can be sealed inside the plastic, impervious to harsh environments.

By itself, the membrane design makes a poor computer keyboard because its contacts require only slight travel to actuate. However, an auxiliary key mechanism can tailor the feel (and key travel) of a membrane keyboard and make typing on it indistinguishable from working with a keyboard based on another technology.

Non-Contact

The biggest problem with all contact keyboards is the contacts themselves. Although switches work well for room lights, they are fickle when it comes to the minuscule voltages and currents used by computer systems. At a microscopic (and microtemporal) level, making a contact is an entire series of events: Tiny currents start and stop flowing until finally good contact is made and the juice really gets going. The brief pulses that precede making final contact aren't apparent when you throw a light switch, but a computer can detect each little pulse as a separate keystroke. Keyboards have special circuits called *debouncers* that make your keypresses unambiguous. However as contacts age, they oxidize. Oxidation puts a less-conductive layer of oxide on the contacts and makes your keypresses even less reliable—to the point they cannot be unambiguously detected.

Early in the history of the PC, manufacturers scorned contact keyboards because they knew traditional contact materials were fated to short lives, not the tens of millions of keystrokes they expect from keyboards. Modern keyboards use ceramics and exotic metals that, resistant to oxidation, can achieve the required life.

The most popular of non-contact designs was the *capacitive* keyboard. Capacitance is essentially a stored charge of static electricity. Capacitors store electricity as opposite static charges in one or more pairs of conductive plates separated by a non-conductive material. The opposite charges create an attractive field between one another, and the insulating gap prevents the charges from coming together and canceling out one another. The closer the two charged plates are, the stronger the field and the more energy can be stored. Moving the plates in relation to one another changes their capacity for storing charge, which in turn can generate a flow of electricity to fill up the increased capacity or drain off the excess charge as the capacity decreases. These minute electrical flows are detected by the circuitry of a capacitive keyboard. The small, somewhat gradual changes of capacity are amplified and altered so that they resemble the quick flick of a switch.

The first PC keyboards and some of the more robust designs of the past all used capacitive technology. The best of these designs could work reliably for 100 million keystrokes compared to 10 to 15 million for most contact designs. Although that extended life may be commendable, most people never typed even 10 million keystrokes during the lifetime of their PCs. They usually move on to another computer well before the keyboard wears out. The added cost of the capacitive design consequently yields no additional useful life and the design has fallen from favor. The last capacitive keyboard from a major manufacturer rolled out of the Key Tronic Corporation factory in early 1999.

Touch

Today, the principal dividing line between keyboards is not technology but touch—what typing actually feels like. A keyboard must be responsive to the touch of your fingers; when you press down, the keys actually have to go down. More than that, however, you must feel like you are typing. You need tactile feedback, sensing through your fingers when you have activated a key.

The most primitive form of tactile feedback is the hard stop; the key bottoms out and stops moving at the point of actuation. No matter how much harder you press, the key is unyielding, and that is the problem. To assure yourself that you are actuating the key, you end up pressing harder than necessary. The extra force tires you out more quickly.

One alternative is to make the key actuate before the end of key travel. Because the key is still moving when you realize that it registered your keystroke, you can release your finger pressure before the key bottoms out. You don't have to expend as much effort, and your fingers don't get as tired.

The linear travel or linear touch keyboard requires that you simply press harder to push a key down. In other words, the relationship between the displacement of the key and the pressure you must apply is linear throughout the travel of the key. The chief shortcoming of the linear touch keyboard is that your fingers have no sure way of knowing when they have pressed down far enough. Audible feedback, a click indicating that the key has been actuated, can help, as does the appearance onscreen of the character you typed. Both slow you down, however, because you are calling more of your mind into play to register a simple keystroke. If your fingers could sense the actuation of the key themselves, your fingers could know when to stop reflexively.

Better keyboards provide this kind of tactile feedback by requiring you to increase pressure on the keyboard keys until they actuate and then dramatically lowering the force you need to press down farther until you reach the limit of travel. Your fingers detect the change in effort as an over-center feel. Keyboards that provide this positive over-center feel are generally considered to be the best for quick touch-typing.

A spring mechanism carefully tailored to abruptly yield upon actuation of each key was the classic means of achieving a tactile feel and could be adapted to provide an audible "click" with every keypress. The spring mechanism also returns the key to the top of its travel at the end of each keystroke. The very first PC keyboards were elaborate constructions that used a separate spring assembly for each key. Modern keyboards use a single overall spring assembly or, more likely, an elastic rubber dome that pops between positions. Dome-based keyboards give satisfying tactile feedback, but individual keys may sporadically require increased force for a stroke or two, subverting their smooth operation. Nevertheless, the low cost and good reliability makes dome technology popular among keyboard makers.

Soft-touch keyboards use a compressible foam to work as the spring mechanism as well as to cushion the end of each keystroke. Soft-touch keyboards give a more linear feel but are preferred by some people for exactly the same reason others dislike them—their lack of snap and quiet operation.

Another influence on the feel of a keyboard is the force required to actuate a key. Some keyboards require you to press harder than others. In general, however, most keyboards require between 1.9 and 2.4 ounces to actuate a key. Stiff keyboards can require as much as three ounces.

On March 22, 1999, Key Tronic Corporation introduced the first varied key-feel keyboard, one that required differing amounts of pressure to activate its keys. Called *ErgoForce* by its developer, its varied key pressures are tailored to the fingers expected to activate them. For example, the "a" key that is usually operated by the left little finger requires only 1.25 ounces (35 grams) of force to activate, but the spacebar requires 2.3 ounces (80 grams). The location of each key determines one of five levels of effort to activate—35, 45, 55, 65, or 80 grams. According to the manufacturer, the tailored effort makes typing easier and improves the level of typing comfort for people using a keyboard for long periods.

Keyboards also differ in how far you must press down on a key to actuate it. Full-travel keyboards require your fingers to move down between 0.14 and 0.18 of an inch to actuate a key. Studies show that the full-travel design helps typists achieve high speeds and lower error rates. In laptop and notebook computers where every fraction of an inch counts, however, keyboards sometimes are designed with less than full travel. A short-travel keyboard actuates with less than about 0.10 inch of key travel. Whether you can live with—or even prefer—a short-travel keyboard is a personal issue.

Legends

Each key on a keyboard bears a legend identifying the letter, symbol, or function it activates. These legends are usually applied using one of three technologies.

Double-shot keycaps have the legend molded in. Making each keycap is a two-step process. Black plastic is molded into the inner shape of the keycap that attaches to the switch mechanism. The legend protrudes from the top of this inner cap. Then, light plastic is molded over and around the inner cap with the legend showing through the top.

Using the double-shot technique, each keycap for each key is a separate and different part that must be individually installed in the correct position on the keyboard as the final step in the production process. Assembly is complex and stock-keeping parts and completed keyboards can be costly. Although once popular, this technology has fallen from favor.

Pad printed keycaps have their legends stamped into place. A machine inks on the legends on all the keys on a fully manufactured keyboard at one swoop. Then, a transparent protective layer is applied over the ink and is baked to a permanent finish. Notebook computers and keyboards with light legends over dark caps often have their keys pad printed. In the case of notebooks, the assembled keyboard gets baked before the keyboard is installed on the PC.

Laser-marked keycaps have their legends burned into place with a laser. The process is akin to a laser printer that operates on keycaps rather than plastic. The complete keyboard is put into a big machine with a laser and mirrors, and the laser burns the legends into all the keycaps in one operation. The advantage of the process is that the legends only need to be applied at the last moment, right before the keyboard is shipped out with a new PC, and the language and layout of the keyboard need not be set until then. The process is fast, the legends are long-lived, and stock-keeping is simplified. Most new keyboards are now laser marked.

Layouts

On a full-size keyboard, the spacing between the keycaps for individual character keys is 0.75 inch (19 millimeters), center-to-center. The keycaps themselves are about 0.5 inch (12.5 millimeters) across at the top, dished to help you place your fingers. The shape of this curve is somewhat arbitrary. Most American designs put a concave cylindrical curve (it's curved only around the longitudinal axis) on the top of the keys; some European designs use a concave spherical curve.

QWERTY

The one unvarying aspect of keyboards also seems the oddest—the un-alphabetical arrangement of the alphabet keys. Anyone new to typing will be amazed and perplexed at the seemingly nonsensical arrangement of letters on the keys of the typical computer keyboard. Even the name given to this esoteric layout has the ring of some kind of black magic or odd cabala—QWERTY. Simply a list of the first six characters of the top row of the nominal arrangement, the absurd name harks back to the keyboard of the first practical typewriter.

There is no doubt that the standard arrangement is not the only possible ordering of the alphabet; in fact, there are 26! (or 26 factorial, exactly 403,291,461,126,605,635,584,000,000) different possible arrangements of letters alone, not to mention the further complications of using rows of different lengths and non-alphabetic keys. QWERTY is not the only possible layout, and it's probably not the best. Nor is it the worst. But it is the standard that millions of people have spent years mastering.

A legend surrounds the QWERTY key arrangement. The typewriter was invented in 1867 by Christopher Sholes, and his very first keyboard had its letter keys arranged alphabetically. Within a year of his invention, however, Sholes discovered what he viewed as a superior arrangement, QWERTY.

According to the common myth, Sholes created QWERTY because typists pounded on keys faster than the simple mechanisms of the first typewriters could handle their strokes. The keys jammed. The odd QWERTY arrangement slowed down the typists and prevented the jams.

Sholes left no record of how he came upon the QWERTY arrangement, but it certainly was not to slow down speedy typists. High typing rates imply modern-day touch-typing, 10 fingers flying across the keyboard. This style of typing did not arise until about 10 years after Sholes had settled on the QWERTY arrangement. Typewriter development was indeed slow; the Shift key wasn't added to the basic design to permit lowercase characters until 1878!

Other hypotheses about the QWERTY placement also lead to dead ends. For example, breaking a strict alphabetic order to separate the keys and prevent the type bars (the levers that swing up to strike letters on paper) from jamming doesn't make sense because the arrangement of the type bars has no direct relationship to the arrangement of keys.

Dvorak-Dealey

The most familiar challenger to QWERTY, one that crawls in a distant second in popularity and use, is the Dvorak-Dealey letter arrangement, named for its developers, August Dvorak and William L. Dealey. The name is often shortened to Dvorak. Figure 14.1 shows the Dvorak layout applied to a typical keyboard.

The Dvorak-Dealey design incorporates several ideas that should lead to faster typing. A basic goal is to foster the alteration of hands in typing. After you strike one letter with a key under a finger of your left hand, the next key you'll want to press likely is under a right-hand finger. This hand alteration is a faster typing strategy. To make hand alteration more likely, the Dvorak-Dealey arrangement places all vowels in the home row under the left hand's fingertips and the consonants used most often in the right hand's home row.

Note that the Dvorak-Dealey arrangement was developed for speed and does nothing to make the keyboard more alphabetic or easier to learn to use.

FIGURE 14.1

Dvorak-Dealey key layout.

The first publication of the Dvorak-Dealey keyboard was in the 1936 book *Typewriting Behavior*, authored by the developers of the new letter arrangement. To back up the philosophic and theoretical advantages attributed to the Dvorak-Dealey arrangement, tests were conducted in the 1930s on mechanical typewriters, amounting to typing races between the QWERTY and Dvorak-Dealey key arrangements. Dvorak and Dealey ran the tests, and—not surprisingly—they came out the winner by factors as large as 30 percent.

Dvorak believed in both his keyboard and his test results and wrote papers promoting his ideas. Alas, the more he wrote, the greater his claims became. Articles such as "There Is a Better Typewriter Keyboard" in the December 1943 issue of *National Business Education Quarterly* has been called by some experts "full of factual errors." Tests run by the United States Navy and the General Accounting Office reported much more modest results for Dvorak.

Notwithstanding the exaggerated claims, the Dvorak layout does offer some potential advantages in typing speed, at least after you become skilled in its use. The penalty for its increased typing throughput is increased difficulty in typing when confronted with a QWERTY keyboard.

The design of the PC makes converting to Dvorak relatively easy. Whereas typewriters have to be redesigned for the new key arrangement, you can just plug a new keyboard into your PC. Commercial Dvorak keyboards often are available by special order.

In fact, if you don't mind your keytop legend bearing no likeness to the characters that actually appear on your screen (and in your files), you can simply reprogram your PC to think that it has a Dvorak keyboard by intercepting the signals sent by the keyboard to your computer and converting them on the fly.

Windows makes specific provisions for the Dvorak key arrangement. The standard keyboard driver allows you to select the Dvorak option. From Windows Control Panel, select the Keyboard icon. Next, select the Language tab, on which you'll find a Properties button. Clicking this button will reveal a screen like that shown in Figure 14.2, which allows you to choose the keyboard language. The Dvorak layout is available as an option in the United States layout, as shown in the figure.

FIGURE 14.2

Selecting the Dvorak layout in Windows.

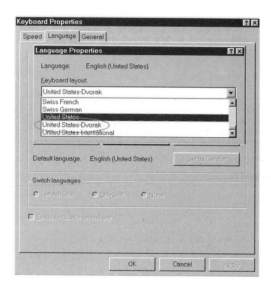

Control and Function Keys

The classic key layouts fail when it comes to computer keyboards. The array of keys they offer simply doesn't match the needs of a computer control system. Certainly the alphabet hasn't changed—at least over the 125-year history of the QWERTY arrangement. But computers have needs not addressed by the letters of the alphabet or basic numerals. They require navigation keys and buttons to control system functions. Even that's not enough to provide an easy-to-use control system for applications and operating systems. In addition (as well as subtraction and other math operations), a dedicated numeric keypad can help immensely when your work involves entering a lot of numbers.

Each additional key adds another option in laying out the keyboard. Another word for it is potential chaos. Although computer manufacturers have exploited some of the opportunities to craft their own, peculiar keyboards—particularly in notebook computers—the basic design has gravitated toward a single standard.

A common design for all keyboards seems an obvious idea, but it didn't arise spontaneously. After a short, wrenching evolution between 1981 and 1987 involving three major design changes, the layout has remained subject to tinkering. The last significant change came when Microsoft added three keys tied specifically to functions in the Windows operating system. Although most keyboard makers stick to this arrangement, they sometimes alter the size and shape of some keys—just enough to frustrate you during your first attempts to use an unfamiliar computer.

IBM set the basic configuration after the six-year gestation. Its first design attempt came with the original PC in 1981 and had 83 keys. In 1984, the company revised the layout to an 84-key arrangement more closely matched to the company's esteemed Selectric business typewriters. After complaints from computer neophytes that the function keys, arranged in two rows to the left of the main keypad, didn't correspond to the help legends that sometimes appeared in a row at the bottom of the screen, IBM created a third design. An attempt to answer every complaint about keyboards in a single design, IBM opted for the straightforward solution. To add extra features, it added keys, making a total of 101. Termed the Advanced Keyboard by IBM, it is also commonly called the Enhanced Keyboard. Figure 14.3 illustrates the United States layout of the Advanced Keyboard.

FIGURE 14.3
IBM Advanced Keyboard layout.

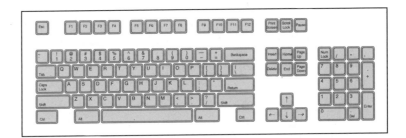

The key additions were several. A new, dedicated cursor control pad was provided separate from the combined numeric and cursor pad, and several other control keys were duplicated in another small pad. Two new function keys (F11 and F12) were added, and the whole dozen were moved to a top row, above and slightly separated from the alphanumeric area. Duplicate Ctrl and Alt keys were provided at either side of the spacebar, and the Caps Lock was moved to the former location of the Ctrl key.

A few functions of Windows don't fall readily under the caps of 101-key keyboards. To better match the operation of Windows, many keyboard makers now add three additional keys—two Windows keys and a pop-up menu key—in the otherwise vacant area around the spacebar, which has also shrunk to provide more room. The two Windows keys, identified by the zooming window logo on their caps, serve as attention keys to pop you into the Windows Task Manager. One is located on the left of the spacebar between the Ctrl and Alt keys. The other fits on the right, just right of the Alt key. The third key serves to select the item at which the mouse cursor points. It is located to the right of the right Windows key.

Most makers of Windows keyboards also modify other keys for easier typing. In particular, they enlarge the Enter key to the size used by the lamented 84-key design. To provide the extra key area, the backslash shrinks and moves upward, sandwiched between a shortened Backspace key and the plus/equals key. Figure 14.4 illustrates the most common form of the 104-key Windows keyboard.

FIGURE 14.4

Layout of the 104-key Windows keyboard.

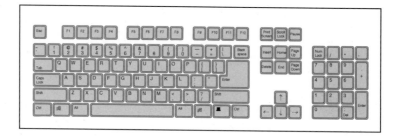

Ergonomic Designs

No one likes to type, except possibly masochists and men from Mars. For most people, typing is a pain. In fact, extended typing without taking a break can cause pain and worse, occupational ailments such as carpal tunnel syndrome (see Appendix C, "Health and Safety"). The best way to avoid such problems is to avoid typing, yet another good reason to quit early each day. When you can't avoid pounding on the keyboard all day long, the next best choice is to find a keyboard that minimizes the pain.

Human factors specialists who deal in the science of how people relate to the workplace and machines, called *ergonomics*, point out that the keyboard was not designed with human beings in mind. The original layout of keys in four (or five or six) rows was a mix of the arbitrary and the needs of the original lever-operated typewriter mechanism. As good as straight rows are for pounding on paper, they are an anathema for most human hands. Normal typing forces you to splay your hands apart, bend them at the wrists, and keep them in that position all the while you type away. The bend stresses the ligaments in your wrist as well as squeezes the nerves that lead into your hand through the carpal tunnel (essentially a hole in the bones of your wrist). Over time, the stress adds up and may eventually impair the functioning of your hands.

Computer keyboards do not suffer the same constraints as the keyboards of mechanical typewriters. Designers can put the key switches in any positions they choose. Some of the more imaginative designs result in *ergonomic keyboards*. These split the alphanumeric keypad in two and angle the two halves in respect to one another. The result in an odd-looking keyboard—at least to the eyes of those long used to the mechanical typewriter design—that's supposed to make typing less painful.

The theory underlying the ergonomic design is that the typing position of your hands on the split keypad lets you keep your wrists straight. Your hands follow more of the natural position they would assume when hanging down at your sides (hence the name of Microsoft's *Natural Keyboard*). Because there is less stress, prolonged typing should be less painful on a split-pad keyboard.

With old-fashioned keyboards and especially those of mechanical typewriters, you must bend your wrist in another direction, vertically, for normal typing. When your arm lies flat on your desk, you must angle your hands upward to reach the keys of a keyboard lying atop your desk. When you use the little feet at the back of your keyboard to angle your keyboard further, you must bend your wrists even more.

As with the horizontal bending of your wrists, these vertical bends can also cause stress and, possibly, carpal tunnel syndrome or other occupational ailments. Consequently, many keyboards have extended wrist rests that force you to minimize the bending of your wrists.

Unlike changes to the layout of keycaps, these ergonomic designs require a brief (if any) training period in which to accustom yourself. They might seem odd at first, but you can quickly start using them effectively. The choice of regular or ergonomic designs is simply a matter of your own preference or a doctor's recommendation.

Convenience Functions

No matter its layout, a keyboard beckons you with the same warm welcome as a swamp stewing with alligators. Despite the improvements made through the years with softer keys and even revised arrangements, typing remains a chore about as much fun as plucking chickens and just as likely to result in repetitive strain injury. Little wonder each new keyboard alternative, no matter how wild-eyed or specious, gets more media attention than would the Loch Ness monster arriving in Washington in a UFO piloted by Elvis.

Although engineers can't change the need for typing, they have found myriad ways to make the chore a little less onerous. Along the way, they have also made the keyboard more flexible and more forgiving toward people who lack full dexterity. These convenience functions can make typing a bit more bearable—or even possible.

Typematic

With most computer keyboards, when you press down and hold a key, after a short delay the keyboard begins to send a continuous sequence of the character you've pressed, ending only when you release the key. The key-repeating feature is usually called *typematic*, a combination of *typ[e]ing* and auto*matic*. Your keyboard generates the continuous stream of typematic characters, but you can command the keyboard to change the speed at which it shoots out individual characters and the delay before typematic kicks in. The typematic rate is measured in characters per second. The usual default for this setting is about 15 characters per second.

Engineers can add the typematic function almost anywhere in the chain from your fingertips to your application. Some keyboards have built-in typematic functions. Many BIOSs make the keyboard typematic feature adjustable at the hardware level. For example. the advanced setup section of the AMI BIOS provides individual settings for typematic values. The parameter Typematic Rate Delay adjusts how long you can lean on a key before the automatic character repetition begins. The default is usually around half a second (500 milliseconds).

Because the hardware-level typematic feature of a keyboard operates independently from your system and its software, it can let you overwhelm your system with more characters than it can handle. For example, on some PCs you can hold a key down for several seconds and start your PC angrily beeping at you. The same thing can occur unintentionally. If you push your keyboard into something on your desk that presses on a key, your PC may respond with angry chatter that sounds like a mouse using Morse code. The solution to the problem is, of course, to let go of the key.

RepeatKeys

Under current consumer versions of Windows, Microsoft repackages the familiar typematic function as its RepeatKeys accessibility option. The RepeatKeys function allows you to adjust the typematic rate or disable it entirely at the operating system level, giving you provisions for controlling the typematic feature of your keyboard through a simple menu interface.

The Speed tab of the Keyboard Properties windows gives you control of both the typematic rate delay and typematic rate, although it calls these features the character repeat delay and the repeat rate, respectively. To access these settings, select the keyboard icon in Control Panel and then click on the Speed tab. You'll see a screen like that shown in Figure 14.5.

Adjust the delay and repeat rate by moving the sliders with your mouse. If you click on the white box labeled "Click here and hold down a key to test repeat rate," you can monitor your settings. (This feature is welcome because Windows does not deign to tell you the exact period of the delay or true character per second rate of the typematic action.) You can also toggle the feature on and off with the designated emergency hot key, pressing and holding the right shift key down for at least eight seconds.

BounceKeys, FilterKeys, and SlowKeys

Under Windows, *FilterKeys* is essentially the opposite of typematic. Instead of multiplying a lone keypress, it suppresses bursts of short-duration keypresses, either repeated presses of a single key or a fast sequence of different keys. When filtering through repeated presses of the same key, Microsoft uses the term *BounceKeys* for this function. When the system filters through bursts of different keys, Microsoft calls it *SlowKeys*.

FIGURE 14.5

Adjusting the keyboard typematic feature through Windows.

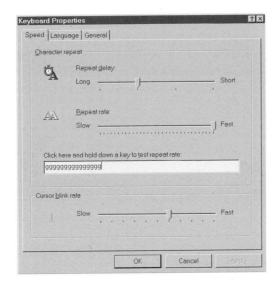

For example, should you accidentally brush across the tops of several in-between keycaps as you move your finger from one key to another, SlowKeys squelches the inadvertent keypresses. In other words, the SlowKeys function makes Windows disregard a brief touch of any key or sequence of keys. It works by delaying the onset of the typematic function by requiring you press a key for a longer period before the machine-gun onslaught of typematic characters begins.

Similarly, BounceKeys bridges together rapid-fire presses of a single key to yield the equivalent of one keystroke.

So that Windows can distinguish between your accidental and intentional keypresses, when the FilterKeys function is active you must firmly press each key you want to register until its associated character appears on the screen. Although this need will slow down the work of a proficient and fully able typist, it speeds up the work of the less able by eliminating many mistakes.

You can adjust the sensitivity of both BounceKeys and SlowKeys—adjusting how long you must press each key before it registers—through the Accessibility Options icon in Control Panel. Once you open the icon, you'll see an Accessibility Properties dialog, like that shown in Figure 14.6.

The Keyboard tab of Accessibility Properties lets you turn on and off FilterKeys (as well as other keyboard options). You adjust the individual BounceKeys and SlowKeys values by pressing the Settings button under FilterKeys. When you do, you'll see a new screen like that shown in Figure 14.7.

FIGURE 14.6

The Keyboard tab of Accessibility Properties under Windows.

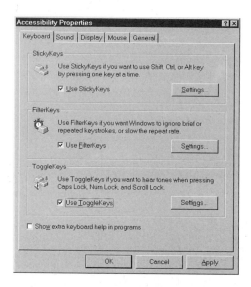

FIGURE 14.7

Adjusting FilterKeys settings under Windows.

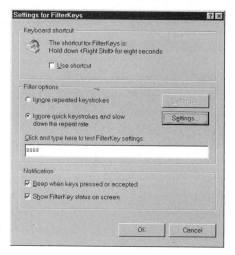

By checking the Use Shortcut box, you can activate and disable your FilterKeys selections without opening the Accessibility Properties folder. To simply turn it on or off, activate the designated hot key by pressing and holding down the right shift key for at least eight seconds.

BounceKeys and SlowKeys have individual settings for their associated delays, which you can adjust by clicking on the Settings box adjacent to the description of the function. (When you disable a function, Windows will not allow you to change its settings, graying out the Settings button.)

StickyKeys

In normal operation, a keyboard's keys have momentary action. They register a keypress and release, waiting for the next keypress. Only the "locking" keys—Caps Lock, Num Lock, and Scroll Lock—have a toggle action by which one press activates their function, which remains in effect until a second press deactivates it. The momentary mode of operation is perfect for normal typing except when your software calls upon you to press several keys simultaneously and your fingers won't reach or because of a physical limitation you simply can't press more than one key at a time. The *StickyKeys* feature of Windows latches the modifier keys that turn alphanumeric characters into function and control keys. These modifier keys include Alt, Ctrl, and Shift. When StickyKeys is activated, the modifier keys latch much like Caps Lock does. The latching operation allows you to press keys in sequence and have your software think you pressed them simultaneously.

The latch operation of StickyKeys has two modes, automatic and manual release. Automatic release is the normal operating mode of StickyKeys. You can select manual release in addition to automatic release when configuring StickyKeys.

Automatic release makes the modifier key stick only for the length of a command. When you press a modifier key once, it latches only until you press another key that is not a modifier (that is, a normal alphanumeric or symbol key). For example, to signal the Alt+F combination to your software when StickyKeys is in operation, you press Alt and then F, and the Alt key automatically releases after the command.

Manual release keeps the modifier key latched until you tell it to unlatch. Pressing the modifier key twice in a row activates it and keeps it active until you overtly specify its release by striking the key a third time. For example, press Ctrl twice, and every letter key you strike thereafter becomes a control code. You must then press Ctrl again to use the alphanumeric keys normally.

You initially configure StickyKeys as an Accessibility Option from Windows' Control Panel. Later, you can use the same system to control the operation of StickyKeys or you can activate and deactivate it using a hot key.

To configure StickyKeys, select the Accessibilities Options from Control Panel. Then, click on the Settings button adjacent to the StickyKeys selection. You should see a new dialog like that shown in Figure 14.8.

As with other Accessibilities Options, the settings of the StickyKeys menu are straightforward. Clicking the shortcut box gives you hot key control of StickyKeys, allowing you to turn the function on and off at will. The first option box lets you switch on the manual toggle release function of StickyKeys.

FIGURE 14.8

The StickyKeys configuration screen.

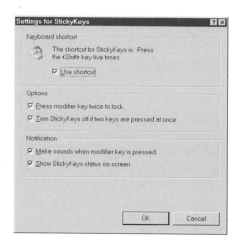

ToggleKeys

Every modern keyboard has visual indicators for the status of the latching keys Caps Lock, Num Lock, and Scroll Lock. But if you're a touch typist, you don't look at the keyboard—or at least you shouldn't. Moreover, if your vision or mobility is impaired, you might not be able to look down at the keyboard to observe the status lights.

To help you monitor the state of the latching keys without glancing at the keyboard LEDs, Microsoft added the *ToggleKeys* feature to Windows. ToggleKeys gives you an audible indication each time you activate or deactivate one of the latching keys. Activate a latching key, and ToggleKeys gives a low beep through the system speakers. Deactivate the key, and ToggleKeys responds with a low beep.

You can activate ToggleKeys as an Accessibility option from the Windows 95 Control Panel. It's the last option listed in the Keyboard tab.

You can also switch ToggleKeys on and off on the fly when you enable its shortcut key, holding down Num Lock for five seconds. Selecting the Settings button in the ToggleKeys section of the Keyboard tab opens a dialog with a check box for selecting the use of the shortcut keys, as shown in Figure 14.9.

Electrical Function

In the macroscopic world in which we live, switches operate positively without hesitation or doubt. Switch on a light, and it comes on like, well, a light. In the realm of microelectronics, however, switches are not so certain in their first steps toward changing state. As a switch makes contact, it hesitates, letting tiny currents flow and then halting them—then letting more flow. These initial jitters are called switch bounce, and it results from a number of causes. The contact materials of most switches are far from perfect. They may become coated with oxidation or other impurities, and they often don't mesh together perfectly. The contacts touch, bounce, and cut through the crud and finally mate firmly together. In the process, many tiny pulses of electricity can slip through. These pulses aren't enough to affect a light bulb but can be more than sufficient to confuse a semiconductor circuit.

FIGURE 14.9

Activating the ToggleKeys shortcut key under Windows.

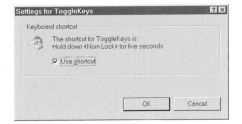

For use in computer circuits, switches require special electronics to remove the jitters, to debounce their contacts. Such debouncing circuits monitor the switch contacts and change the hesitating initial stabs at changing state into a sharp, certain switch. Unfortunately, each switch contact requires its own debouncer. This is not much of a concern with a single switch but can be a nightmare for the designer who must debounce the 101 switches in a typical keyboard.

Instead of individual debouncing, computer keyboards use a different process for eliminating the hesitation from keyboard switches. The keyboard electronics do not detect when each switch changes but check periodically to see whether a switch has changed. When the electronics note a change in the state of a switch corresponding to the press of a key, they generate an indication of the switch switching that is sent along to your PC.

This process has its own shortcomings. The go-and-look method of detection adds a brief wait to signaling each keypress. Moreover, each and every key must be individually checked. But the high speed of today's computer circuits makes this system entirely workable. The process is reduced to a routine; the keyboard electronics scan each key at rates approaching a million times every second, looking for a change in the state of any key. In general, a microprocessor (an 8048-series device in the most popular keyboards) scans the keyboard for current changes every few microseconds, and the minute current flow caused by a keystroke can be detected. Because a slight chance exists that random noise—the stuff that must be debounced away—could cause a current pulse similar to that generated by a keystroke, keyboards may require that the increased current flow be detected during two or more consecutive scans of the keyboard.

In today's PCs, the keyboard can use either of two technologies to relay the effects of your keypresses to your computer. In the traditional design, used in systems since the first PCs, the keyboard sends data to your PC in the form of scan codes. The personal computer industry is making an effort to shift keyboard communications from scan codes to formatted data sent through the USB port.

Keyboard Port

In the traditional (legacy) keyboard design, the keyboard connects to your PC and sends its codes called a *scan code* through a specialized serial port. A microprocessor in the keyboard assigns a code of pulses to your every keypress, and a second processor called a *keyboard controller* converts the scan code pulses into bus-compatible data using a hexadecimal code.

When it receives a scan code, the keyboard controller chip issues an interrupt to notify your PC's microprocessor that you've pressed a key and it had better do something about it. To service the interrupt, your computer sorts through the scan codes and figures out which keys are pressed and in which combination. The program code for doing this is part of your system's BIOS. The computer remembers the condition of the locking shift keys by changing special memory locations, called *status bytes*, to reflect each change made in their condition.

Each press of a key generates two different scan codes—one when the key is pushed down and another when it pops back up. The two-code technique allows your computer system unit to tell when a key is pressed and held down—for example, when you hold down the Alt key while pressing a function key.

Rather than a single standard for scan codes, there are three. These comprise three operating modes and correspond to the three generations of keyboard development. Mode 1 is the system used by the original 83-key keyboard of the first PCs. Mode 2 is the system used by the 84-key keyboard of the PC AT. Mode 3 is the system introduced with the 101-key keyboard design that's now ubiquitous among PCs. In general, more modern keyboards can emulate older models by shifting their operating modes based on commands sent to the keyboard by your PC.

In any given operating mode, each key generates a unique scan code. Even if the same legend appears on two keys, such as the duplicate number keys in the alphanumeric and numeric-and-cursor keypads, the individual keys generate different codes. The code for a given key is determined by its position and is not affected when the Caps Lock or other Shift key is in effect. In Mode 1, all scan codes are single bytes and the make and break codes of individual keys are different. In Modes 2 and 3, scan codes may be one or more bytes. In general, the make code is a single byte and the break code is two bytes, the byte F0(Hex) followed by the make code. You'll find a list of legacy port keyboard scan codes in Appendix D, "Data Coding."

Although scan codes were originally fixed to key positions rather than characters, when manufacturers alter the arrangements of their auxiliary keys, they maintain the same scan codes for the character as in the basic design. Otherwise, every key layout would generate different scan codes and confuse both your PC and you as you type. Foreign languages have their own scan code mappings. Each different keyboard design for a specific language puts different characters on punctuation keys and so the scan codes elicited by these characters will vary in languages other than English.

Modern 101-key and 104-key keyboards have two Enter keys, one on the alphanumeric keypad, the scan code for which is listed with the rest of the keys in this pad, and a second one in the numeric/cursor keypad. This second Enter key—as well as each of the duplicate number and math function keys on the numeric/cursor keypad—has its own scan code. As a result, your PC can distinguish *which* Enter (or number key or whatever) you press, just as it can distinguish between left and right shift keys. Although for most operations the two keys work identically, in some cases they do not. For example, hot keys sequences often make use of one or the other of the shift keys but not both.

All PC keyboards have dedicated *function keys* that have no predefined role. What they do often changes with each application that you run, although some programmers strive for a bit of consistency (such as making F1 elicit help and F10 exit). The function keys may be arrayed in two vertical rows of 5 on an 83-key or 84-key keyboard or as a single horizontal row of 12 on 101-key and 104-key keyboards. In either arrangement, the scan codes of these keys are the same, although the scan codes of F11 and F12 won't be available from keyboards with only 10 function keys.

Each key of the dedicated cursor keypad that's interposed between the alphanumeric and numeric/cursor keypads on 101-key and 104-key keyboards also generates scan code distinct from the keys with duplicate functions located elsewhere.

Normally, you do not have to deal with scan codes (which is why they got stuck in an appendix in this edition). The computer makes the translation to numbers and letters automatically and invisibly. The converted information is used in generating the information that appears on your monitor screen, and it is also made available to the applications you run and even the programs you write. Sometimes, however, when you write your own programs, it is useful to detect every key change. You may, for example, want to cause something to happen when a certain key combination is pressed. Your program need only to read the keyboard input port and compare what it finds there to a scan code chart.

Your computer receives these scan codes at a special I/O port that operates much like a serial port without explicitly following the RS-232 standard. Instead of an array of data and handshaking signals, the keyboard uses only two. By activating or deactivating these two signals in combinations, the system manages communications both from the keyboard and, in all but the initial PC keyboard design, from the host system. Although the very first PCs used a one-way flow of data from the keyboard to your PC, current keyboards use a bidirectional interface with its own command protocol.

Protocol

Keyboards use different serial codes for bytes depending on operating mode. In Mode 1, the standard protocol uses nine bits per byte. The first bit is a start bit, which must be a logical 1. The eight data bits follow in sequence, ordered from least significant to most. In Modes 2 and 3, keyboards use an 11-bit protocol. Each byte begins not with a start bit but with a logical zero. Next, the eight data bits follow in sequence, least to most significant. Next comes a parity bit. All keyboard use odd parity, so this bit is set to a logical one or zero so that an odd number of logical ones appear in the combination of eight data and one parity bits. The protocol ends with a stop bit, which is always a logical one. Table 14.1 lists the details of this protocol.

TABLE 14.1 Standard Keyboard Serial Byte Protocol

Bit Number	Function	Mode 1	Modes 2 and 3
1	Start bit	1	0
2	Data bit 0	Least significant bit	Least significant bit
3	Data bit 1		
4	Data bit 2		
5	Data bit 3		
6	Data bit 4		
7	Data bit 5		
8	Data bit 6		
9	Data bit 7	Most significant bit	Most significant bit
10	Parity	Not used	Depends on data
11	Stop bit	Not used	1

The signaling and handshaking system is quite elaborate. The keyboard uses the clock line to send out signals that synchronize the bits on the data line with the receiver in your PC. In addition, the PC uses the clock line to throttle the flow of data from the keyboard. The clock line uses *tri-state logic*, which allows both ends of the connection to alter the signal. Normally, the keyboard supplies a voltage to the clock line and interrupts it to provide the synchronizing signal. Your PC can also pull down the voltage—essentially shorting it out without harm to the keyboard—as a means to signal its data needs. The data line also uses tri-state logic.

The keyboard monitors the status of both the data and clock lines to determine when it can send information to your PC. Only when both the clock and data lines are high, not pulled low by your PC, will the keyboard send character data to your PC. When the clock line is low, the keyboard holds any characters it wants to send in its buffer. If the clock line is high but the data line is held low by your PC, the keyboard waits to receive a command sent from your PC. The keyboard monitors the clock line throughout the transmission of each byte, and if your PC pulls the line low before your keyboard sends off the parity bit, the keyboard stops its transmission and holds the character in its buffer, waiting until the clock line going high signals that it can retry its transmission.

To send a command byte to the keyboard, your PC first checks to see whether any data is coming its way. To immediately stop the data flow, it pulls the clock line low. Then, by letting the clock line go high again and pulling the data line low, it signals the keyboard that it will send data. The keyboard then counts the bits on the data line. If it receives the correct number, it sends an acknowledgment byte, FA(Hex), back to the PC. If the bit count is wrong, it asks for a retransmission with the FE(Hex) command.

Software Commands

Your PC has a modest repertory of commands that it can issue to the keyboard to adjust its internal operation. It can alter the operating mode of the keyboard (and hence which scan codes it sends out) with the command F0(Hex) followed by the mode number. It can also alter the typematic rate using command F3(Hex) or alter the status of the locking key indicators with command ED(Hex). Table 14.2 summarizes the commands that your PC can send your modern keyboard. Very old keyboards, such as the 83-key models accompanying the first PCs, cannot receive these instructions because of their unidirectional interface. When in Mode 1, keyboards only respond to the Reset command FF(Hex), but they then can switch to another mode to act upon other instructions.

TABLE 14.2   Commands Sent to the Keyboard from the Host PC

Byte Value	Command Definition
ED	Change keyboard indicators (bitmapped) Bit 0, Scroll Lock Bit 1, Num Lock Bit 2, Caps Lock
EE	Echo

continues

TABLE 14.2   Continued

Byte Value	Command Definition
EF	Invalid command
F0	Set keyboard mode to byte following (1, 2, or 3) 00 = Keyboard sends out current setting 01 = Switch to Mode 1 02 = Switch to Mode 2 03 = Switch to Mode 3
F1	Invalid command
F2	Send keyboard ID
F3	Set repeat delay and rate to bit-coded value Format 0ddbbaaa Delay = (dd+1) * 250 msec Rate = (8 + aaa) * 2 ^bb * 4 msec
F4	Clear buffer
F5	Restore default settings and wait for enable
F6	Restore default settings
F7	Set all keys typematic
F8	Set all keys make/break
F9	Set all keys make
FA	Set all keys typematic/make/break
FB	Set key type typematic
FC	Set key type make/break
FD	Set key type make
FE	Error; requests retransmission
FF	Reset keyboard

In addition to its scan codes, the keyboard has a modest range of commands and status information it can relay back to your PC. For example, it can tell your PC that it has too many characters in its in-board buffer, whether it has properly received a command from the PC, and the status of its internal self test. Table 14.3 lists these commands and status signals.

TABLE 14.3 Commands Sent from the Keyboard to the Host PC

Byte Value	Command Definition
00	Buffer overflow (Modes 2 and 3)
AA	Self-test passed
F0	Byte that follows is break code
FA	Acknowledge last command
FD	Self test failed
FC	Self test failed
FE	Last command in error; re-send
FF	Buffer overflow (Mode 1)
E0	Byte that follows is scan/release code Mode 2

To start communications, the keyboard starts by sending a series of the self-test passed character—AA(Hex)—to your PC using the wrong parity to indicate that it has not been initialized. When your PC has gone through the boot process sufficiently to be ready to accept data, it sends an error acknowledgment to the keyboard—FE(Hex). The keyboard responds by correcting the parity and sending the self-test passed character, providing of course it passed its internal self test. At this point, the keyboard and PC are ready for normal operation.

Host Interface

The keyboard interface inside your PC is a complete subsystem with its own dedicated microprocessor. The original design used an Intel 8042 microprocessor for handling keyboard communications, but in modern PCs, circuitry equivalent to such a microprocessor is typically built into the chipset. This microprocessor monitors the data and clock lines linking it to the PC, deciphers the serial code, and repackages it in parallel form for passing on to your PC.

Your PC receives data from the keyboard interface and sends data to it through a pair of I/O ports. When it has a byte ready for processing by your PC, it generates a hardware interrupt.

In modern PCs, the location of keyboard ports and the interrupt generated by the controller may vary with the hardware design and BIOS of your PC. If you are curious, you can check the ports used from the Windows Control Panel by selecting the Keyboard icon and then the Resources tab. You'll see a display like that shown in Figure 14.10.

FIGURE 14.10

Windows 95 display of the resources used by the keyboard subsystem.

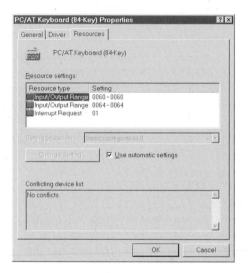

After your PC acknowledges the hardware interrupt, the keyboard controller passes a scan code sent from the keyboard to your system, and the keyboard BIOS routine determines the character to be sent to your operating system. The standard BIOS interrupt processing routine generates a second interrupt that permits a subroutine to process the scan code before it gets processed into a character. Under Windows, these BIOS routines are replaced by keyboard drivers that perform the same functions. By default, current consumer versions of Windows install two keyboard drives—a real-mode driver (KEY-BOARD.DRV) and a protected-mode driver (VKD.VXD). You can see the drivers installed in your system or change the drivers using the Driver tab of the Keyboard Properties dialog in Windows, as shown in Figure 14.11.

Compatibility

The scan codes produced by all PC-compatible keyboards are the same, but not all keyboards are the same. When IBM developed its Personal Computer AT, the inner function of the keyboard was reconsidered, and IBM elected to make the keyboard programmable. Old keyboards—those shipped with the 8088-based PC and XT models—were one-way devices, sending scan codes to their host computers in a constant monologue. Today's keyboards accept commands from the computer and even have their own language.

Although you will never have to deal with the keyboard language (it's for programmers and hardware designers), it does make the pre- and post-AT keyboard designs incompatible. An AT keyboard does not work with PC and XT system units, nor does an XT keyboard work with today's computers.

FIGURE 14.11

Windows display of installed keyboard drivers.

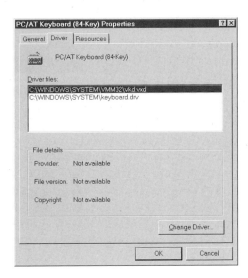

IBM eliminated worries about keyboard compatibility in its own product line by changing its keyboard connectors in 1987 (but too late—for three years the company manufactured AT computers with the same keyboard connector as used by XT systems). Other keyboard makers compensated by putting switches on their products to select their compatibility. A few keyboards automatically detect the type of circuitry in your computer and adjust themselves accordingly.

Some keyboards, however, are not adjustable. Because XT-style systems and keyboards have been left far behind, many keyboard makers now feel safe in ignoring backward compatibility with them. Unless you have an ancient system that pre-dates the 1984 AT keyboard design change, you should not have to worry about the compatibility of your keyboard.

Windows generally can identify your keyboard when it scans your hardware and set itself up accordingly. If you have reason to believe that its choice was incorrect or if you want to manually install a keyboard into Windows for any reason, Windows gives you that option. You access the keyboard selection in the General tab of the Keyboard Properties menu. To open the Keyboard Properties menu, select the Keyboard icon in Control Panel.

If the keyboard Windows displays is not the one that you want, click on the Change button. Windows will respond with a list of keyboards it inherently knows how to manage, as shown in Figure 14.12.

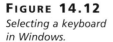

FIGURE 14.12

Selecting a keyboard in Windows.

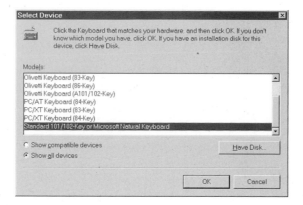

As with installing any hardware into your PC, Windows lets you install keyboards without built-in Windows support using drivers supplied by the keyboard maker. If the keyboard you want to use is not listed as one of those directly supported, click on Have Disk and slide the floppy disk or CD supplied by your keyboard vendor in the appropriate drive slot when Windows instructs you to. You specify a disk location and complete the installation process as you would with any other hardware device.

Connections

The scan-code system and serial signaling simplify the connection scheme used by PC keyboards. Scan codes are sent from the keyboard to the computer serially so that only one wire conductor is needed to convey the keyboard data information. A second conductor is required to serve as a return path for the data signal; as a ground, it serves as a common return for all other circuits in the keyboard cable. To synchronize the logic in the keyboard with that in the computer, a separate wire is used for a keyboard clock signal. A fourth and final wire is used to supply the keyboard with the five-volt direct current power that it needs to operate. These four conductors are all that is necessary to link keyboard to computer.

The physical embodiment of those signals is the keyboard connector. Nearly all keyboard and PC makers use exactly the same connectors, one of two styles originally introduced by IBM.

The most popular keyboard connector is the one that IBM chose for its original series of personal computers. This system is based on a standard five-pin DIN connector that's used by a number of other applications, such as MIDI cables.

The five pins form a semicircle spread across one half of the connector. A stamped groove in the shield around the pins keys the connector for proper insertion. The pins of the connector are shorter than the shield, so you can slide the connector into a jack and rotate it until the groove engages in the jack. The connector will then slide into the jack without your worrying about bending pins. Figure 14.13 shows this connector and the layout of its pins and signals.

FIGURE 14.13

Pin layout and signal assignments of PC keyboard connector.

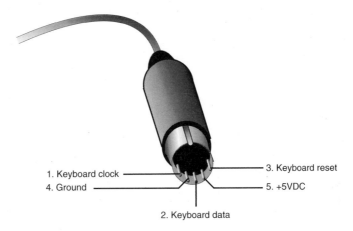

1. Keyboard clock
4. Ground
2. Keyboard data
3. Keyboard reset
5. +5VDC

You'll face one surprise should you attempt to fashion the wiring of a keyboard connector on your own. The layout of the pins in the connector is not exactly straightforward. The pins are not laid out in order but follow an irregular sequence, as shown in the figure.

Pin one of the connector is assigned to the keyboard clock signal used to synchronize the keyboard and PC; two, the keyboard data signal; four, the ground; five, the five-volt electrical supply. One of the connections provided by the keyboard plug—pin three—is assigned to carry a signal to reset the keyboard, but it is normally not used and need not be connected in normal keyboard cabling. Table 14.4 summarizes the pin-out of a standard five-pin PC keyboard connector.

TABLE 14.4   Five-Pin DIN Keyboard Connector Pin-Out

Pin	Description	Direction
1	+Keyboard clock	In
2	+Keyboard data	In
3	Reserved	Out
4	Ground	N/A
5	+5 V	Out

Early keyboards use pin three for the PC to send a reset signal to the keyboard. In modern keyboards, the reset signal is not required because the keyboard protocol includes a software reset command. The PC/XT style 83-key keyboard used an explicit reset signal on pin three as did some IBM-manufactured 84-key keyboards. Other manufacturers of 84-key keyboards usually did not use an external reset signal. Consequently, sometimes incompatibilities would appear if you plugged an IBM keyboard into a non-IBM system. Since the acceptance of the 101-key and 104-key designs, this problem no longer occurs.

Many manufacturers use an alternate standard for their keyboards, one using miniature six-pin DIN connectors. This design is usually called *PS/2-style* because IBM introduced it with its PS/2 computers in 1987. The six pins are arrayed in a circle around a rectangular plastic tab that, along with three guides in the shield, keys the connector against improper insertion. As with the five-pin connector, the pin numbers follow an irregular pattern. Figure 14.14 shows the six-pin miniature DIN keyboard connector and its signal layout.

FIGURE 14.14

The six-pin miniature DIN keyboard connector.

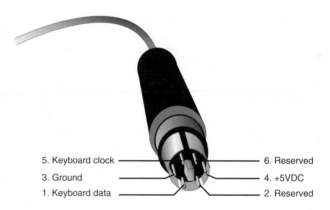

5. Keyboard clock ——————— 6. Reserved

3. Ground ——————— 4. +5VDC

1. Keyboard data ——————— 2. Reserved

The wiring of the six-pin miniature DIN connector is similar to that of the older five-pin design; the signals are the same, only rearranged. Again, only four pins are significant to keyboard use: Pin one is assigned keyboard data; pin three, ground; pin four, five volts; pin five, keyboard clock. Pins two and six are reserved, and the shield is attached as a chassis ground. Table 14.5 lists the signal assignments on the PS/2-style keyboard connector.

TABLE 14.5   Six-Pin Miniature DIN Keyboard Connector Pin-Out

Pin	Description	Direction
1	Data	In
2	Reserved	N/A

Pin	Description	Direction
3	Ground	N/A
4	+5 V	Out
5	Clock	In
6	Reserved	N/A
Shield	Ground	N/A

Because the five-pin and six-pin keyboard connectors use the same signals with only a slight rearrangement, a simple adapter will convert one style of connector to another. These keyboard adapters are readily available on the PC parts market. If you're so inclined, you can make your own using the interconnection guide in Table 14.6.

TABLE 14.6   Keyboard Connector Adapter Wiring Scheme

PC Connector Five-Pin DIN	PS/2 Connector Six-Pin Mini-DIN	Signal Function
1	5	Clock
2	1	Data
3	2	Reserved
4	3	Ground
5	4	+5 volts
NC	6	Reserved

Besides redesigning the PC end of the keyboard connection for its PS/2 machines, IBM also altered its keyboard to accept different keyboard cables by making the cable itself detachable from the keyboard. This detachable design makes the cable easy to service (by replacing it) and a single keyboard adaptable to between five-pin and six-pin cabling standards. The keyboard-to-cable connection uses a modular (AMP) jack on the rear of the keyboard with a matching plug on the cable, as shown in Figure 14.15.

As shown in the figure, this modular connector has the following signal assignments: A, reserved; B, keyboard data; C, ground; D, keyboard clock; E, five volts; F, reserved. The gold contacts of the connector are labeled in reverse alphabetical order from left to right. Table 14.7 summarizes these signal assignments.

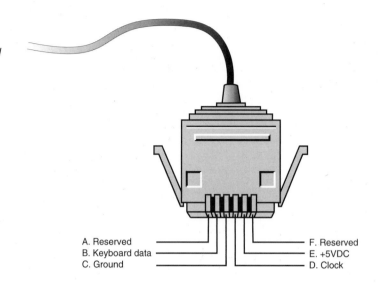

FIGURE 14.15

The modular key-board connector and signal assignments.

A. Reserved
B. Keyboard data
C. Ground
F. Reserved
E. +5VDC
D. Clock

TABLE 14.7   Modular Keyboard Connector Pin-Out

Pin	Description	Direction
A	Reserved	N/A
B	Data	Out
C	Ground	N/A
D	Clock	Out
E	+5 V	In
F	Reserved	N/A
Shield	Ground	N/A

USB Port

As PCs shift to the use of the *Universal Serial Bus*, keyboard connections will move to this high-speed interface. USB-based keyboards were displayed as early as February 1996, but the early introduction proved premature. Even in 1999, PC makers prefer the conventional keyboard interface because it is cheap and reliable despite admonitions from Intel and Microsoft to move to USB. As the interface matures, however, USB keyboards are destined to become more popular.

Because USB is designed and designated a universal interface, one that will link devices other than keyboards, it is treated in a separate chapter devoted to modern PC interfaces, Chapter 20, "Peripheral Ports."

The inner workings of USB keyboards are immaterial to your PC. It just looks for data packets received through the USB port. Any packets containing keyboard data get routed by the USB driver to the keyboard driver of the operating system. Then, the operating system pulls the data from the packets to see what you've typed. If your PC wants to send a command to the keyboard, it notifies the keyboard driver, which generates the code of the command and passes it along to the USB driver, which routes it out the port and to your keyboard as another packet on the USB circuit.

The flaw in this design is that it doesn't work until the operating system and its USB drivers load. Before then, the keyboard driver has no route through which to get keystroke codes. That's all right because if the operating system hasn't loaded, the keyboard driver won't have loaded, either. With neither USB nor keyboard driver running, your PC faces a problem if it needed to read the keyboard while booting up—for example, to step through the setup menu.

Your PC's BIOS makes up for this flaw. It patches together the old and new keyboard systems.

Pointing Devices

To many people, the keyboard is the most formidable and forbidding aspect of a PC. The keys might as well be teeth ready to chomp down on their fingers as soon as they try to type. Typing just isn't something that comes naturally to most people. Learning to type takes months or years of practice—practice that's about as welcome as a piano lesson on a sunny afternoon when the rest of the neighborhood kids are playing outside.

Moreover, keyboards don't do well at indicating things on the screen.

Mice

One idea aimed at making the computer more accessible is the mouse. The idea was developed by Douglas C. Engelbart during his tenure at the Stanford Research Institute between 1957 and 1977 and first found fame as the pointing device coupled with a graphical/menu-driven onscreen user interface developed at the Palo Alto Research Center of Xerox Corporation. The underlying concept is to allow a computer user to indicate what function he wants his computer to carry out by selecting from a list of commands presented as a menu. The user points at the menu selection by physically moving the pointing device, which causes a corresponding onscreen movement of the cursor. One or more buttons atop the device enables the user to indicate that he wants to select a menu item.

The device is small enough to fit under the palm of a hand with the button under a fingertip. The cord connecting the device to its computer host trailing like a tail and the need to make the device scurry around the desktop to carry out its function quickly earned it the name mouse. The whole process of moving the mouse and its onscreen representation is termed dragging the mouse.

Apple Computer, understanding the need to make computers more accessible by making them easier to use, incorporated the best of the Palo Alto ideas into its Macintosh, including the mouse. IBM, more performance than ease-of-entry oriented, only made the mouse a built-in feature of its personal computers with the introduction of the Micro Channel PS/2 line, each machine of which incorporates a special mouse port in its motherboard circuitry.

Mice can be distinguished by four chief differences: the technology they use; the number of buttons they have; the manner in which they connect with their computer hosts; and the protocol or language they use to encode the information they send to your PC.

Technology

As a mechanical transducer, a mouse somehow has to be able to detect its motion across your work surface. Although engineers have a wide range of position-sensing technologies to choose from—they could even use the satellite-based Global Positioning System to determine the absolute location of the mouse and deduce changes—only two techniques have actually been used in practice. These include mechanical sensing and optical sensing. Nearly all mice today use mechanical sensing.

Mechanical Mice

The first mouse was a mechanical design based on a small ball that protruded through its bottom and rotated as the mouse was pushed along a surface. Switches inside the mouse detected the movement and relayed the direction of the ball's rotation to the host computer.

Although the ball is free to rotate in any direction, only four directions are detected, corresponding to two axes of a two-dimensional coordinate system. The movement in each of the four directions is quantified (in hundredths of an inch) and sent to the host as a discrete signal for each discrete increment of movement.

The mechanical mouse works on just about any surface. In general, the rotating ball has a coarse texture and is made from a rubbery compound that gets a grip even on smooth surfaces. In fact, you can even turn a mechanical mouse upside down and spin the ball with your finger (although you'll then have difficulty fingering the pushbuttons!).

On the other hand, the mechanical mouse requires that you move it across a surface of some kind, and all too many desks do not have enough free space to give the mouse a good run. (Of course, if all else fails, you can run a mechanical mouse across your pants leg or skirt, but you're likely to get some odd looks.) In addition, mechanical parts can break. A mechanical mouse tends to pick up dirt and lint that can impede its proper operation. Regularly clean your mechanical mouse even if you think your desktop is spotless.

Inside the mechanical mouse, the ball rolls against two perpendicular sensors. These sensors generate electrical pulses as they rotate, and the mouse sends the pulses to your PC. By counting the number of pulses in each direction, your computer can calculate the movement of the mouse.

The sensors can use various technologies. For example, the wheel may be optically encoded with an alternating pattern of black and white (or clear and opaque) and a photodetector senses the changes. Or the sensor may use electromagnetic technology, sensing as a pattern of magnetic material passes a detector.

Optical Mice

The only widely used alternative technology to the mechanical mouse once was the purely optical mouse. Instead of a rotating ball, the optical mouse used a light beam to detect movement across a specially patterned mouse pad. No moving parts mean that the optical mouse has less to get dirty or break.

The typical optical mouse uses two pairs of LEDs and photodetectors on its bottom, one pair oriented at right angles to the other. Its matching mouse pad is coated with an overlapped pattern of blue and yellow grids. Each pair of LEDs and photodetectors detects motion in either direction across one axis of the grid. A felt-like covering on the bottom of the mouse makes it easy to slide across the plastic-coated mouse pad.

The big disadvantage of the optical mouse is that it requires that you use its special mouse pad and put the pad somewhere. The pad itself could get dirty, be damaged, or simply get lost. On humid days, the plastic coating of the pad might stick to your bare forearm and lift off in sheets. For these and other reasons, purely optical technology has fallen from favor in mouse design.

Buttons

In purest form, the mouse has exactly one pushbutton. Movement of the mouse determines the position of the onscreen cursor, but a selection is made only when that button is pressed, preventing any menu selections that the mouse is inadvertently dragged across from being chosen.

One button is the least confusing arrangement and the minimum necessary to carry out mouse functions. Operating the computer is reduced to nothing more than pressing the button. Carefully tailored menu selections allow the single button to suffice in controlling all computer functions. The Apple Macintosh uses this kind of mouse with one button.

Two buttons allow more flexibility, however. For example, one button can be given a "Do" function and a second, an "Undo" function. In a drawing program, one button might "lower" the pen analog that traces lines across the screen and the other button might "lift" the pen.

Of course, three buttons would be even better. The programmer would have still more flexibility. Maybe four buttons would—but as the number of mouse buttons rises, the mouse becomes increasingly like a keyboard. It becomes a more formidable device with a more rigorous learning curve. A profusion of mouse buttons is counterproductive.

Three buttons is the practical limit because three positions are available for index, middle, and ring fingers while the thumb and pinkie grab the sides of the mouse. Most applications use two or fewer buttons, and the most popular mice are the two-button variety. There's nothing wrong with three-button mice—they can do everything two-button mice can and more—but most applications don't require the extra button. A good mouse driver will let you program the function of the extra button (and the other buttons as well) so you can make it do what you want.

Interfaces

To communicate its codes to your computer, the mouse must be connected in some way. Mice connect with PCs through any of three ways: a serial port, a built-in dedicated mouse port, or a special adapter that plugs into an expansion slot. Mice that use these methods are called (respectively) serial mice, proprietary mice, and bus mice.

Serial Mice

Most mice adapt to a port that is generally available—the standard serial port. Called serial mice, they simply plug in and deliver their movement codes to the serial port. Driver software for operating the mouse can give the mouse priority by generating an interrupt whenever a new mouse movement code appears at the port. The driver then passes along the mouse code to the software in control.

In general, mice make no onerous demands on the serial port. They operate at a low communication rate, 1,200 bits per second, and adapt to any available port. However, because every mouse movement generates a serial-port interrupt, if your system has more than two serial ports, you have to be careful which port you assign your mouse. Because serial ports 1 and 4 (that is, the ports that DOS calls COM1 and COM4) share interrupt four and serial ports 2 and 3 (COM2 and COM3) share interrupt three, a mouse can conflict with another device connected to the other port sharing its interrupt. It's always best to plug your mouse into the port that does not have to share its interrupt (for example, COM1 if your PC has three serial ports) to avoid surprises—the kind that can crash your PC.

Bus Mice

Another way to avoid serial port conflicts is to avoid serial ports. Sometimes, this strategy is forced upon you; your PC has only two ports and you have a modem and plotter connected and you want to plug in a mouse. The alternative is attaching the mouse to a dedicated mouse adapter that plugs into your computer's expansion bus. These so-called bus mice work identically to serial mice except that they use their own dedicated ports.

In most cases, these special mouse ports conform to the RS-232 standard and act just like serial ports except that they cannot be directly accessed by DOS because the operating system doesn't know to what I/O addresses the ports are assigned. Otherwise, a bus mouse is just like any other mouse. It can use optical or mechanical technology and have any number of buttons.

If you have a spare serial port, you probably will want a serial mouse because you pay extra for the bus mouse's adapter card. If you are short on serial ports, however, you likely will want a bus mouse.

Proprietary Mice

Some PCs, such as the IBM PS/2 series and some Compaq computers, have built-in mouse ports. These make mouse matters elementary. You simply plug the mouse into the mouse port without worrying about interrupt conflicts or tying up a serial port. At heart, these proprietary mouse ports are just bus mouse connections built into your PC. (Some compatible machines just slide a bus adapter into an expansion slot. IBM builds the circuitry onto the motherboard.)

From a performance standpoint, the style of mouse you choose makes little difference. All three kinds of mouse interfaces use the equivalent of a serial connection. The principal factors in choosing one over the other are the resources of your PC.

Obviously, you need a serial port if you want to attach a serial mouse that plugs into such a port. If you have a spare serial port, a serial mouse is the least expensive way of adding a pointing device to your PC.

Most people, however, have designs on all their serial ports and consequently do not want to tie them up with a mouse cable. The bus mouse provides an out. The bus mouse host adapter does not steal a COM port from DOS nor does it share one of the serial port interrupts, the sharing of which often causes problems with modem communications. The only problems associated with using a bus mouse are finding a spare slot into which to slide the host adapter and the extra cash to pay for the additional hardware. A bus mouse and a serial mouse work effectively the same way. Which you choose makes no difference to your software.

If your system has a built-in mouse port, you may be stuck needing a proprietary mouse. Although your source of supply may be more limited (and the mice consequently more costly), a proprietary mouse is the easiest of all to install.

USB Mice

As with all PC peripherals, mice are migrating (albeit slowly) to the USB connection. As with other USB devices, USB-based mice pass the data they generate—position and key-press information—in the form of serial packets that chain through the USB and mouse drivers for processing and execution.

The USB connection does nothing to alter the operation of the mouse. Its chief effect, at least for now, is to increase the cost of the mouse. In the long run, it should help eliminate interrupt conflicts and simplify PC manufacture.

Drivers

Mice convert the motions they detect into a digital code that can be processed or analyzed by your PC. The only loose end is what code the mouse uses. A standard mouse code would help software writers craft their products to better take advantage of mice. A standard mouse code would be so useful, in fact, that the industry has come up with four distinct standards, called mouse protocols. These standards were developed by four of the major forces in the mouse industry, and each bears its originator's name. These include Microsoft, Mouse Systems Corporation (for a period known as MSC Corporation), Logitech, and IBM Corporation. The first three were designed for individual mouse products created by the respective companies. The IBM protocol was introduced with the PS/2 series of computers, which came equipped with a built-in jack that accepted a mouse.

In truth, you don't need to know the details of any of these protocols. You only need to know that they exist and that they are different. Match the protocol used by your mouse to your applications.

Today, the Microsoft mouse protocol is the most prevalent, but some mouse manufacturers enhance their mice in their own ways, perhaps making additional features programmable. To take advantage of these features, you use the proper proprietary protocol. You select this protocol when you install your mouse. In normal circumstances, Windows will find and recognize your mouse and install the proper driver software for it.

You can also install a new mouse manually. Windows gives you at least two ways of accomplishing the installation. You can choose the Add New Hardware icon in Control Panel and then choose to install a mouse. Or you can select the Mouse icon in Control Panel, select the General tab, and then click on the Change button. In either case, you'll have an opportunity to select from one of the mice for which Microsoft has built-in drivers or supply your own drivers from disk.

To select a built-in driver, click on the Show All Devices radio button. Then, select a manufacturer and product, as shown in Figure 14.16.

FIGURE 14.16

Selecting a mouse for which Windows has a built-in driver.

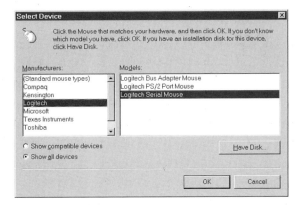

If you're in doubt, remember that most mice sold today can emulate the Microsoft mouse protocol. Those that have this emulation built in to their hardware can be directly substituted for a Microsoft mouse. Others require the use of drivers to make the match.

If you want to check which drivers are installed for your particular mouse, you must use the Windows Device Manager. Select the System icon from Control Panel and then click on the Device Manager tab. You should find a mouse icon in the list. Clicking on the plus sign by the icon will display the mice you have installed. Highlight a particular mouse and then click on the Properties button. To see the drivers in use, click on the Driver tab of the Mouse Properties dialog, as shown in Figure 14.17.

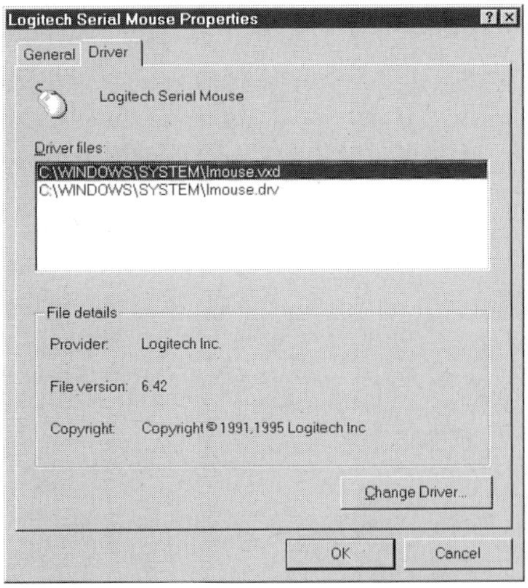

FIGURE 14.17

The Driver tab on the Mouse Properties screen.

You're likely to see two driver entries. One is a real-mode driver (with the .DRV extension), and the other is a protected-mode driver (with the .VXD extension). You can change the driver from this screen, for example, to make an upgrade, by clicking on the Change Driver button.

Resolution

Mice are sometimes rated by their resolution—the number of Counts Per Inch, or CPI, that they can detect. When a mouse is moved, it sends out a signal indicating each increment of motion it makes as a single count. The number of these increments in an inch of movement equals the mouse's CPI rating.

The higher the CPI, the finer the detail in the movement the mouse can detect. Unless the mouse driver compensates, higher resolution has an odd effect. More resolution translates into faster movement of the mouse pointer onscreen because the screen pointer is controlled by the number of counts received from the mouse, not the actual distance the mouse is moved. Consequently, a higher resolution mouse is a faster mouse, not a more precise mouse.

The true limit on how precisely you can position your mouse cursor is your own hand. If you want to be more accurate with your mouse, you can compensate for your human limitations by opting for less resolution from your mouse. Because you have to move your mouse physically farther for each onscreen change, a lower mouse resolution helps you put the cursor where you want it.

Customization

Windows requires a pointing device of some kind, and a mouse is its preferred device. Along with this requirement comes a degree of flexibility. Windows allows you to tailor the operation of your mouse to match your working style.

The Mouse Properties menu, which you can activate by clicking on the Mouse icon in Windows Control Panel, allows you to adjust the operation of your mouse buttons, the pointers that appear onscreen, and the speed of cursor movement.

The Buttons tab, as shown in Figure 14.18, gives you the choice of right- or left-handed mouse operation. The two radio buttons let you swap the functions of the right and left mouse buttons. Right-handed operation is the default. In addition, this tab lets you alter the speed at which your double-clicking will be properly recognized. Moving the slider adjusts the double-click speed. Adjust it until you achieve consistent operation when you double-click in the test area.

FIGURE 14.18

*The Windows Mouse
Properties Buttons
tab.*

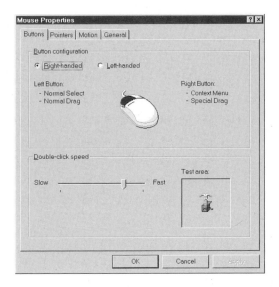

The Pointers tab allows you to select the onscreen cursors (which Microsoft calls *pointers*) that correspond to your mouse position. During the operation of Windows, the shape of the pointer changes to reflect the operating mode of the mouse. You can change each of these pointers to suit your personal taste through the Mouse Properties dialog box, as shown in Figure 14.19. Before you have any alternate pointers to change to, however, you'll have to choose the additional mouse pointers option when you install Windows or obtain additional pointers elsewhere. The various display schemes included with the Microsoft Plus! Utilities package include several sets of additional pointers. You can also find alternate pointers on the Internet.

The final bit of customization, the Motion tab, allows you to change the speed at which the mouse pointers are updated on the screen. Selecting a faster speed makes the pointer respond more quickly to the movement of your mouse. However, in some cases—such as when using a notebook PC's low-contrast LCD screen—very fast operation may make the pointer hard to spot. A slower pointer speed can give your eye more time to spot the elusive pointer.

The Motion tab also lets you select *pointer trails*, lingering after-images of the pointer that follow its movement. These trails help make the motion of your mouse more apparent, especially on LCD screens. If you have trouble finding your mouse pointer when you work with your notebook PC, turn on the pointer trails and set a relatively long persistence, as shown in Figure 14.20.

FIGURE 14.19

Choosing alternate pointers through the Mouse Properties screen.

FIGURE 14.20

Long persistence pointer trails set under Windows.

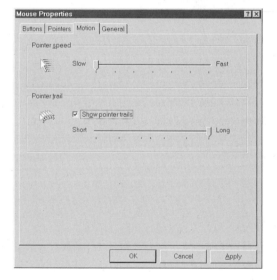

Working Without a Mouse

A mouse (or mouse-like pointing device) is now required for modern graphics-oriented operating systems such as Windows 98 and Windows NT. All current computer specifications require a mouse or other pointing device as basic equipment. Nevertheless, you can operate a PC without a mouse. For example, the Windows family of operating systems includes keyboard-only commands that duplicate all mouse functions. These functions are hardly intuitive, but they do allow you to navigate through the operating system.

Many applications are not so forgiving. Their functions may require a mouse. Without a pointing device, you may be forced to stare helplessly at a screen that's out of your reach and control.

Windows incorporates a feature called MouseKeys that lets you get more mouse-like functions from your keyboard. After you activate MouseKeys, the combined numeric-cursor keypad supplements the control of the mouse cursor. Pressing a number key (except 0 and 5) moves the cursor in the associated direction. To move in larger increments, hold the Ctrl key while pressing a number. Holding Shift gives greater precision by reducing the movement for each keypress to a single pixel in the specified direction.

Other keys take on the functions of mouse buttons. To single-click, press 5; to double-click, press the plus sign (+) on the numeric keypad. The slash (/) and minus sign (–) take on the functions of the left and right mouse buttons, and the asterisk (*) between them activates both button functions at once.

To drag an object using MouseKeys, first position the mouse cursor on the object. Then, press Ins. The object will move with the mouse cursor as you move it. To drop the object, press Del. Table 14.8 summarizes the functions of these keys when MouseKeys is active.

TABLE 14.8 Key Definitions Under MouseKeys

Key	Function (Numeric Keypad Only)
1	Move mouse cursor left and down
2	Move mouse cursor down
3	Move mouse cursor right and down
4	Move mouse cursor left
5	Single-click left mouse button
6	Move mouse cursor right
7	Move mouse cursor left and up
8	Move mouse cursor up
9	Move mouse cursor right and up
Ctrl	Magnify mouse movement
Shift	Precision mouse movement
+	Double-click left mouse button
Ins	Start to drag an object
Del	Drop an object being dragged

continues

TABLE 14.8 Continued

/	Left mouse button
-	Right mouse button
*	Both mouse buttons

MouseKeys is an accessibility option. You can turn it on and off several ways—through a menu, with hot keys, or using the Num Lock button—once you've set it up. To make the initial configuration of MouseKeys, you must use Windows Control Panel. Select the Accessibility Options icon in Control Panel and then click on the Mouse tab. You'll see a menu like that shown in Figure 14.21.

FIGURE 14.21

The MouseKeys control dialog under Windows.

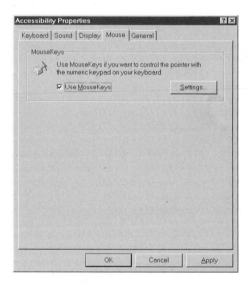

To enable the operation of the MouseKeys functions, you must click on the Use MouseKeys box. Once you've activated MouseKeys, you can adjust its configuration, for example, to alter the speed of MouseKeys or to give yourself a shortcut for turning MouseKeys on and off.

Clicking on Settings will open a new dialog like that shown in Figure 14.22.

The various settings for MouseKeys are straightforward. Click the Use Shortcut box to allow activating and disabling MouseKeys using hot keys. Adjust the sliders to vary the speed of cursor movement under MouseKeys. Click the appropriate radio button to allow you to share the MouseKeys function with normal cursor movement or numeric entry on your keypad.

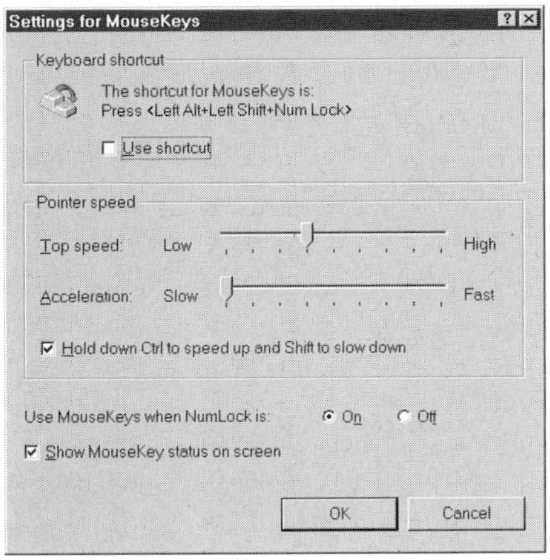

FIGURE 14.22

MouseKeys configuration options under Windows.

Trackballs

Just like the namesake in the Rodentia, the computer mouse needs room to roam and ends up almost anywhere. A mouse does not stay put because moving around is in its nature—and that's how you use it.

The problem is that many folks do not have room for a roaming rodent. Their desks are just too cluttered or they are traveling with a laptop and neglected to carry a desk along with them into the coach-class cabin. More insidious issues also involve mice. Pushing a plastic rodent requires clumsy, wasteful, and tiring whole-arm movements. Mice are inefficient and exhausting.

The leading mouse alternative, the trackball, eliminates these problems. Essentially a mouse turned upside down, the trackball is much like it sounds—an often big ball that, when rotated, causes the screen pointer (mouse cursor) to track its movements. The trackball spins in place and requires no more desk space than its base, a few square inches. Portable trackballs are designed to clip onto laptop and notebook computers, extending the width of the machine by no more than a couple of inches.

Switches

As with mice, trackballs also require switches so that you can indicate when the cursor is pointing to what you want. Most trackballs have two or three pushbuttons that duplicate the selection functions of mouse buttons. Although some trackballs boast four buttons, the foursome typically functions as two duplicate pairs—mirror images—so that one trackball can serve either a right or left hand.

No standard exists for switch placement on trackballs because no consensus exists on how you are supposed to operate a trackball. Some are designed so that you spin the ball with your fingers. Others prefer that your thumb do the job. Which is better depends on who you believe and how you prefer to work.

A company that makes trackballs which operate with the fingers maintains that your fingers are more agile than your thumb so they are more precise at spinning the ball. A competing company that makes a trackball designed for thumb control says that the thumb has more muscle control than the fingers. Some makers wisely don't take sides and make trackballs that can be used equally adeptly by the posed or opposed digit.

Ball Size

Another trackball design choice is the size of the ball itself and how it is retained inside the mechanism. Various products range in dimensions from the size of a shooter marble to those equaling cue balls. Bigger once was thought to be better, but the trackballs built into laptop and notebook computers are making smaller sizes popular. (In fact, the most compelling reason that big trackballs are big is that a ready supply of balls is available on the pool table.)

Because no definitive study has shown the superiority of any particular size for a trackball, the best advice is to select one that feels best to you—or the one that comes already attached to your PC.

As with the balls in mechanical mice, trackballs naturally attract dirt. Although the trackball doesn't pick up dirt from rolling around, dust does fall upon the ball and the oils from your fingers collect there, too. A readily removable ball can be quickly and easily cleaned. This sort of serviceability is absent from many trackball designs—something to consider if you plan to use your trackball for a long time.

Handedness

Most mice are symmetrical. Although two- and three-button mice define different functions for their left- and right-side buttons, most enable you to flip the functions of the buttons to suit right- or left-hand operation if what button falls under a given finger is important to you.

Trackballs, however, are sometimes asymmetrical. In itself, that can be good. An asymmetrical trackball can better fit the hand that it is designed for, right or left. But this handedness among trackballs poses a problem when you make your purchase; you have to determine whether you want a right- or left-handed trackball. Which you need does not necessarily correspond to the way you write. Some left-handed people prefer right-handed trackballs (and some righties like lefties). Consequently, a right-handed trackball isn't always the best choice for a right-handed person. Before you buy a one-handed trackball, make sure that you know which hand you will favor in using it. If you switch hands when you tire from using one hand for spinning your trackball all day long, you may not want a product with definite handedness at all.

Interfaces

To communicate with your programs, trackballs must send positioning information back to your PC exactly as mice must. Because mice came first and have established workable protocols, trackball makers simply adopted the various mouse standards as their own. Consequently, most trackballs mimic the Microsoft mouse and use exactly the same protocol. Other trackballs are designed to plug directly into IBM's PS/2s as mouse substitutes, so they use IBM's mouse protocol.

As with mice, the protocol used by a trackball must match that supported by your PC and its software. Other than that issue of compatibility, you don't need to worry about trackball protocols.

Resolution

As with mice, trackballs are sometimes rated in resolution, the number of counts per inch of movement (CPI). As with mouse resolution, these numbers don't necessarily indicate precision. A higher number of counts per inch actually can make a trackball less precise to use. A trackball with a high number of counts per inch moves your onscreen pointer a greater distance for every degree of spin you give the ball. As a result, the high CPI trackball makes the onscreen cursor move faster but with less control. A low number of counts per inch means that you must spin the ball farther to move the cursor, giving you greater precision in your control.

Most trackball manufacturers now give you several choices for the effective resolution of their products so that you can tailor its actions and reactions to match the way you work. In addition, most trackball makers offer ballistic operation in which the translation of ball movement to onscreen cursor change varies with the speed of the ball's spin. This yields fast positioning without loss of precision. The only problem is getting used to such non-linear control in which the speed at which you spin the trackball has as much (sometimes more) effect as how far you spin it.

Unlike most other peripherals, no one trackball is objectively better than the rest. Operating any of them is an acquired talent like brain surgery, piano-playing, or hair-combing. Any judgment must be subjective, and which is better suited for a particular user depends most on personal preference and familiarity.

Non-Ball Trackballs

In the endless quest for the ultimate pointing device for laptop and notebook computers, designers have developed a number of intriguing ideas that either have not caught on or have not yet had time to catch on. Two of the most promising are the Isopoint device and the pointing stick.

Invented by Craig Culver, the Isopoint device acts like a trackball that uses a rolling bar instead of a ball. Designed to be located just below the spacebar of your keyboard, the

Isopoint is perfectly placed for you to operate with one of your thumbs. To move your onscreen cursor vertically, you roll the Isopoint bar as if it were a one-dimensional trackball. To move left or right, you push the spring-loaded roller, and the force you apply determines the speed the cursor races along. To click as you would a mouse, press down on the roller. Auxiliary switches on either side of the roller can be added to replicate the function of the extra buttons on two- and three-button mice.

The technology behind the Isobar isn't revolutionary; it just uses switches and encoders as does a mouse or trackball. The genius is the shape and location. Easy to grope and find, it fits right under your thumb without taking up too much room. Unlike the trackballs added to laptop computers, you don't have to take your fingers from the home row to use the Isopoint device. The disadvantage of the product is, as with any other revolutionary idea, it's different.

The pointing stick (called Trackball II in IBM notebooks) was developed by Ted Selker and Joseph D. Rutledge of IBM's Thomas J. Watson Research Center and was first used in IBM notebook computers. In principle, the pointing stick is a miniature joystick that's stuck between the "G" and "H" keys of a conventional keyboard. The pointing stick protrudes just two millimeters above the normal typing surface. Its position enables you to maneuver it with either index finger while the rest of your fingers remain in the home row. Because in normal touch-typing your fingers should never cross the G-H boundary, it does not interfere with normal typing. The selection function of mouse buttons is given over to bar keys at the lower edge of the keyboard, adjacent to the spacebar.

Unlike joysticks, the pointing stick itself does not move. Instead, it reacts to pressure. IBM believes the key to the success of the pointing stick is the algorithm it uses to determine the speed to move your onscreen cursor. In general, the more force you apply to the pointing stick, the faster the cursor moves—up to a maximum speed that corresponds to your ability to follow the cursor motion (as determined by human-factor experiments in the Watson lab).

TouchPads

In their developmental years, notebook computers used a variety of pointing devices. Several tried integrated trackballs. The designer's whims determined placement— sometimes at the corner of the screen, sometimes below the keypad. In any case, the balls were small (they had to be to fit in a portable system), and the perfectly located trackball was rare, indeed.

Hewlett-Packard developed a pop-out mouse tethered to the right side of the system. The system detected mouse movement through the thin, flat tether so you could hold the mouse in the air and its movements would nevertheless register. The downside was the need for space on the right, either air or desktop, a requirement not easily met in crowded aircraft.

The notebook industry needed a better alternative for a pointing device and found it in the TouchPad. (The name is a trademark of Synaptics Corporation.) Almost by default, the TouchPad became the most popular pointing device for notebook systems. It wasn't that the TouchPad necessarily was so good. All the alternatives were worse. Figure 14.23 shows a TouchPad.

FIGURE 14.23

A TouchPad on a notebook PC.

The TouchPad detects the location of your finger on the pad by detecting the electrical capacitance of your finger. Your finger attracts a minute static electrical charge, which causes a small current flow in the circuitry of the TouchPad. The electronics associated with the TouchPad detects this minute current from two adjacent edges of the pad, so it can precisely locate your finger in two dimensions. By following changes in the current, it can determine the motion of your finger across the pad.

Mechanically, the foundation of the TouchPad is a printed circuit board. The top of the board holds a pattern of conductive sensor lines etched into place. The bottom of the board holds the electronics that make the pad work. A layer of Mylar covers the top of the board to protect it and give your finger a smooth surface to trace across. Current designs are capable of resolving 1000 points/inch (40 points/mm).

A TouchPad is inherently an absolute position detector. The electronics of the pad converts this absolute location information it determines into mouse-like relative motion that can be sent to your PC in standard mouse protocol.

The TouchPad can be completely sealed from any kind of contamination, so it is an excellent choice as a pointing device for a machine that has to operate in a hostile environment. On the other hand, useful TouchPads must be large enough to conveniently register your finger movements. That means they steal space from the top of your notebook PC. Most notebook PC makers take advantage of this space requirement to give you a hand-rest below the keyboard—and to give the manufacturer more room for the components inside the computer.

PC makers can choose from several sizes of TouchPad for their products. Typically, the active pad surface measures 62 by 46.5 millimeters, although larger (90.6 by 72.1 millimeters) and smaller versions (55.9 by 32.9 millimeters or less) are also readily available.

Most manufacturers locate the TouchPad just below the spacebar on their keyboards. This location allows you to use your thumbs to move the mouse so you don't have to take your hands from the home row when typing, an important consideration if you touch-type on your PC. Notebook PCs differ in the height and sensitivity of their TouchPads. Although the differences are subtle, they affect usability. If the TouchPad height is wrong for your typing system, you're likely to inadvertently move the mouse, even activate it. You'll want to try out the keyboard and the TouchPad of any portable PC that has one before you commit to buying it.

TrackPoint

Invented by IBM, which has trademarked the name and patented the technology, the TrackPoint system puts a small rubber nub between the lower corners of the G and H keys of your keyboard. Figure 14.24 shows the placement of the TrackPoint.

The nub—which typically is removable in case you wear it smooth—mechanically connects to a pair of solid-state pressure sensors mounted at right angles to one another. When you press against one side of the TrackPoint device, it senses the pressure you apply even though the nub itself does not move. The TrackPoint electronics and software driver convert this pressure data into an indication of relative motion. The harder you press, the greater the signal the pressure sensor generates, and the faster it tells your PC to move the mouse pointer. The paired sensors give you two axes of control corresponding to moving the mouse along its X and Y axes.

The TrackPoint system has several advantages. Its location allows you to move the mouse without removing your fingers from the home row while you're typing. It is entirely solid-state and sealed so it, like a TouchPad, is environmentally rugged. It has no moving parts to wear out—except for the pointing nub, which you can readily replace. The disadvantage is that many people find it unnatural to use until they have acquired experience using it.

FIGURE 14.24
A TrackPoint device in its native environment.

Joysticks and Paddles

Mice don't fall readily to hand for games and some other applications. Running a mouse across a pad is a relatively leisurely activity, at least in the PC scheme of things. Games require fast action, reactions rather than the measured responses you're apt to apply to your mouse. Moreover, games are based more on absolute positions rather than the relative locations that mice specify best. Consequently, games demand a different kind of pointing device, one that handles instant reactions and accompanying abuse, one that evaluates each response independently rather than based on previous movements. The input device that fulfills these requirements and has become the input choice for most games—at least until the advent of 3D technology and virtual reality—is the *joystick*.

A combination of tiller and throttle, the joystick is a two-dimensional absolute position sensor. That means it distinguishes a specific location on a plane—left and right as does the tiller of a boat, forward and reverse as does the throttle. The positions it indicates are absolute, anchored to a specific reference on the screen, in contrast to the mouse, which indicates relative positions based on previous movements. In other words, a joystick indicates a place, but the mouse indicates motion.

A *paddle* is the poor relation of the joystick, one stripped of half of its assets. Where the joystick points in two dimensions, the paddle has only one. Instead of specifying a location on a plane, the paddle indicates a position on a line. As with the joystick, however, the position a paddle indicates is absolute, referenced to a fixed position on your screen.

Technology

The joystick indicates locations as resistance values, one value for the x-coordinate of the location, a second value for the y-coordinate. When you move the joystick, you shift the arms of a pair of variable resistors arranged perpendicular to each other, changing the resistance value. Over its complete range, the resistance value changes from 0 to 100,000 ohms.

Your PC senses the resistance of the joystick position as a voltage. This voltage changes linearly as you move the joystick. Consequently, game port inputs are analog signals. The game port converts each of the analog signals it senses into a single digital pulse, the duration of which is directly proportional to the resistance values in the joystick sensor. By timing the length of this pulse, your PC can determine the position of the joystick.

Each joystick or paddle also has a button. Pressing a joystick or paddle button simply closes a circuit; it acts as a switch.

Interface

In the PC scheme of things, a joystick connects to your PC through a special adapter called a *game port*. Although sometimes called a joystick port, the same connection also hosts paddles. The game port provides connections for one or two joysticks using one 15-pin D-shell connector like that shown in Figure 14.25.

FIGURE 14.25
The 15-pin female D-shell connector used by game ports.

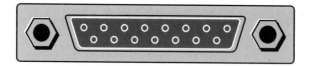

Alternately, you can connect four paddles to one game port. The game port has one input for each joystick to sense whether this switch is open or closed. Table 14.9 lists the functions of the 15 pins of the standard game port when used for joysticks or paddles.

TABLE 14.9 Game Port Joystick and Paddle Pin Definitions

Pin	Name	*Joystick Function*	*Paddle Function*
1	+5 VDC	Joystick A coordinate common	Paddle A coordinate high
2	Button 4	Joystick A pushbutton high	Paddle A pushbutton high
3	Position 0	Joystick A x-coordinate wiper	Paddle A coordinate wiper
4	Ground	Joystick A pushbutton return	Paddle A pushbutton return
5	Ground	Not used	Paddle B pushbutton return
6	Position 1	Joystick A y-coordinate wiper	Paddle B coordinate wiper
7	Button 5	Not used	Paddle B pushbutton high
8	+5 VDC	Not used	Paddle B coordinate high
9	+5 VDC	Joystick B coordinate common	Paddle C coordinate high
10	Button 6	Joystick B pushbutton high	Paddle C pushbutton high
11	Position 2	Joystick B x-coordinate wiper	Paddle C coordinate wiper
12	Ground	Joystick B pushbutton return	Paddle C/D pushbutton return
13	Position 3	Joystick B y-coordinate wiper	Paddle D coordinate wiper
14	Button 7	Not used	Paddle D pushbutton high
15	+5 VDC	Not used	Paddle D coordinate high

For a game port, determining what you've done with your joystick is all a matter of timing. Your PC checks the joystick position and switches condition interactively by sending an OUT instruction to the joystick port at 0201(Hex). This instruction starts the timing pulses. The first four bits of the output of the 0201(Hex) port go high at the start of the timing pulse and remain high for the period corresponding to the resistance value of the associated joystick position. The upper four bits of this port indicate the status of the associated switches.

If you're detail oriented, you'll want to known that the minimum length of this pulse is 24.2 microseconds. Each ohm of resistance stretches the pulse by 0.011 microsecond, so at maximum resistance, the length of the pulse is 1124.2 microseconds.

Graphic Devices

Graphic devices are special peripherals that let you transfer the images that you see into digital form that your PC can process and publish. Strictly speaking, they are input devices, but they differ fundamentally in that other input devices are meant to control your PC, but graphic input devices only supply visual information for your PC to process. The two chief graphic input devices used in modern PC systems are the scanner and digital camera.

The most important issues in choosing a scanner

Feature	In short
Optical resolution	The quality of the scanning element in a scanner determines the sharpest details it can capture. Entry level scanners start at 300 dpi; good scanners offer 1200 dpi. Serious graphic and photographic work (slide scanners) require even higher resolutions.
Interpolated resolution	Scanner software can simulate higher resolutions by mathematically adding dots between those actually scanned. Save interpolation until after scanning because interpolated images take more room but hold no additional information. Don't be misled by high interpolated resolution—you can interpolate 9600 dpi from a newspaper photograph.
Color bits	The more bits of color, the more realistic the image and the more range the scanner has to cope with marginal images. Entry level starts at 30 bits; 36-bits marks the mainstream. Some top-quality scanners now promise 48-bit color.
Design	Flatbed scanners do 3D and anything you can lay on their glass—great for graphics—but drum (page) scanners quickly run through piles of text. Now-rare hand scanners let you capture library text into your notebook PC.
Interface	Parallel is cheap and slow; SCSI is fastest and costliest; and USB fits in-between. After your first few scans speed will become important so you'll want to spend the extra cash for SCSI.

The most important issues in choosing a digital camera

Feature	In short
Resolution	Set image sharpness but more importantly determines how large an image you can print before it begins to look like you've printed it too large. Megapixel (roughly 1280 by 1024) is good enough for Internet publishing and snapshots but look for two megapixels for quality work.
Color depth	More bits to the color give you more range to work with (like film latitude). Early, inexpensive cameras started with 24-bit color but better cameras give you 36-bits of range.
Zoom	Optical zoom gets you closer and gives versatility in image composition. Good cameras start with 3x zoom. Digital zoom interpolates the image—it makes it bigger without adding information or quality.
Interface	You want a fast interface to download images from your camera to your PC. Early cameras used serial ports—which means slow. Better designs use USB or, faster still, FireWire. Make sure your PC has a port to match.
Storage format	Tiny SmartMedia or small CompactFlash give your camera megabytes of storage for dozens of images—more is always better. Some cameras use floppy disks that make moving images to your PC easy but offer small capacity.

You and your PC live in different worlds. You live in a visual world in which sight is your foremost sense, a world of colors and shapes and (you hope) beauty. Your PC resides in the digital domain where all is data—numbers, characters, or reduced to the fundamentals, electrical pulses. Bringing those two worlds together takes more than a spaceship with a towrope as might suffice for Venus and Mars. You need a translator, one conversant in both images and electricity. You need a graphic input device. Specifically, you need a scanner or a digital camera.

The scanner can convert anything you have on paper—or, for that matter, anything reasonably flat—into computer-compatible electronic form. Dot-by-dot, a scanner can reproduce photos, line drawings, even collages in detail sharper than your laser printer can duplicate. Better yet, equip your PC with optical character recognition software and the images your scanner captures of typed or printed text can be converted into ASCII files for your word processor, database, or publishing system. Just as the PC opened a new world information management to you, a scanner opens a new world of images and data to your PC.

The digital camera captures what you see in the real world. It grabs a view of not only three-dimensional objects but also entire scenes in their full splendor. As the name implies, the digital camera is the computer equivalent of that old Kodak, one that produces files instead of film. It captures images in a flash—or without one in bright daylight—and requires no processing other than what you do with your photo editing software. It probably tops the list of most wanted PC peripherals because it's not only a useful tool but also a neat toy that turns anyone into an artist and can add a good dose of fun to an otherwise drab day at the PC.

Scanners

The essence of any scanner is elementary. The scanner detects differences in the brightness of reflections off an image or object using an array of light sensors. In most cases, the scanner has a linear array of these sensors, typically charge-coupled devices, or CCDs, squeezed together hundreds per inch in a narrow strip that stretches across the full width of the largest image that can be scanned. The width of each scanning element determines the finest resolution the scanner can detect within a single line. The narrower each scanning element and the closer they are all packed together, the higher the resolution and the finer the detail that can be captured.

This line-up of sensors registers a single, thin line of the image at a time. Circuitry inside the scanner reads each sensing element one-by-one in order and creates a string of serial data representing the brightness of each point in each individual scan line. Once the scanner has collected and arranged the data from each dot on the line, it advances the sensing element to read the next line.

Types

How the view of the scanning sensor moves to that next line is the fundamental design difference between scanners. Somehow, the long line of sensing elements must shift their attention with extreme precision over the entire surface of the image to be captured. Nearly all scanners require a mechanical sweep of the sensors across the image, although a few low-resolution scanners use video technology. To make a sweep in a mechanical scanner, two primary strategies have emerged. One requires the image sensor to move across a fixed original; the other moves the original in front of a fixed scanner. With a video scanner, nothing moves except an electron beam.

Drum Scanners

Not a tool for checking out percussive musical instruments, the *drum scanner* specializes in capturing images from paper. It works like a printing press in reverse. You feed a piece of paper that bears the image you want to capture into the scanner, and the paper wraps around a rotating drum that spins the image past a sensor string that's fixed in place inside the machine.

The first scanners, invented long before the PC, used the drum design. Drum scanning technology was the core of early facsimile machines and, even earlier, made wire-photo images possible and allowed newspapers to move photographs through the same wires used for telegraphing the text of stories.

The spinning drum of the scanner allows its image sensor to trace down the page being scanned one line at a time. As each line gets captured, the electronics of the scanner advance the paper the height of a single scan line. This movement determines the height of each line and the vertical resolution of the scanner. The image sensor itself determines the horizontal resolution.

The drum design lends itself to document processing. The mechanism puts the paper being scanned in motion, so adding a page feeder is a relatively simple addition. Because of their orientation to scanning printed pages, drum scanners are sometimes termed *page scanners*.

Drum scanners are moderate in price and compact in size because their mechanisms are relatively simple. However, that mechanism imposes a stiff penalty; only thin, flexible images can be scanned. In general, that means normal paper. Books (at least while intact) and solid objects are off limits. Only certain sizes of paper may be accepted. Although this may be no disadvantage in a character-recognition and document processing applications, it may be frustrating when you want to pull an image off a large sheet without resorting to scissors or a photocopier first.

Flatbed Scanners

The *flatbed scanner* takes the opposite tack and moves the sensor instead of the paper or image. This form of scanner earns its name from the flat glass surface upon which you must place the item to be scanned, face down. The scanning sensors are mounted on a bar that moves under the glass, automatically sweeping across the image. The glass surface allows the sensors to see up to the image.

Flatbed scanners have precision mechanisms that step the sensors or image a small increment at a time, each increment representing a single scan line. The movement of the mechanism, which is carefully controlled by the electronics of the scanner, determines the height of each line (and thus the resolution of the scanner in that direction).

Flatbed scanners are like copying machines in that anything that you can lay flat on their glass faces can be scanned—books, magazines, sections of poster, even posteriors and other part of your anatomy if you get imaginative, bored, or drunk. Of course, the scanned image can be no larger than the scanner bed.

In the past, the chief drawback of the flatbed scanner has been price. Manufacturers have refined flatbed technology to the point that their prices overlap other technology and some products rank among the least expensive scanners available. Although the bargain machines skimp on image quality, they deliver results eminently suitable to casual applications.

Hand Scanners

Hand scanners make you the motive force that propels the sensor over the image. You hold the T-shape hand scanner in the palm of your hand and drag it across the image you want to scan. A string of sensors peers through a plastic window in the bottom of the hand scanner to register the image.

Hand scanners must cope with the vagaries of the sweep of your all-too-human hand. If you move your hand at a speed other than that at which the scanner expects, lines will be scanned as too wide or too narrow, resulting in image distortion. At best, the aspect ratio may be off; at worse, the scanned image will look as wavy as the Atlantic under the influence of an errant typhoon. To avoid such disasters, the hand scanner uses a feedback mechanism that tracks the position of the image. Most have a roller that presses down against the image you're scanning to sense how fast you drag the scanner along. The rate at which the roller spins gives the scanner's electronics the feedback it needs about scanning speed. From this information, the software that controls the hand scanner can give each scanned dot its proper place.

Because they omit the most expensive parts of most scanners—the precision mechanism for moving the paper or sensor—hand scanners should have an edge in price. In reality, the advantage is negligible. Some low-end flatbed scanners are actually less expensive than typical hand scanners. But handheld technology does retain a singular advantage. Hand scanners are compact and easy to carry. You could plug one into your notebook PC and carry the complete system to the neighborhood library to scan from books in its collection. Hand scanners can also be quick because you can make quick sweeps of small images instead of waiting for the lumbering mechanism of another scanner type to cover a whole sheet. Hand scanners may also adapt to some non-flat surfaces and three-dimensional objects. For example, most will easily cope with the pages of an open atlas or gothic novel—although few can do a good job on a globe or watermelon.

On the downside, the small size of the hand scanner means a single pass of the scanner will cover an image no more than about four inches wide. Although that's enough for a column of text and most scanners offer a means of pasting together parallel scans of larger drawings and photos, the narrow strips of scan make dealing with large images inconvenient. On the other hand (and in the other direction), because a hand scanner is not limited by a scanning mechanism, it can allow you to make absurdly long scans, typically limited only by the scanning software you use.

Note that hand scanning is like typing—a learned skill. To use a hand scanner effectively, you'll have to practice until you learn to move the scanner smoothly and at the proper speed, which means very slowly at high resolutions.

Video Scanners

A *video scanner* is the electronic equivalent of a photographic copy stand. The video scanner uses a conventional video camera to capture an image. Most video scanners permanently mount the camera on a stand and give you a stage on which you put the item to be scanned. The stage may have a backlight to allow you to scan photographic slides or negatives, or it may be a large bed for sheets of paper or even three-dimensional objects.

Video scanners avoid all the problems and inaccuracies imposed by mechanical scans. They have the potential for the greatest precision. Typically, however, video scanners yield the lowest quality. Like a video camera, video scanners require a CCD element for every pixel they scan, and affordable two-dimensional CCD arrays have only a few hundred thousand pixels. Because video scanners use the same CCD arrays as video cameras, they have the same resolution as video cameras, not measured in dots per inch but in pixels across the entire image. They are suited to snapshots and catalog illustrations but not to rendering high-quality scans.

Slide Scanners

The *slide scanner* is not a special technology but rather a special implementation of flatbed or video scanner technology. A flatbed-style slide scanner is optimized for the higher-resolution needs of scanning small photographic transparencies or negatives but relies on a modified flatbed scanner mechanism. It needs only more precision in its control because of the smaller side of the scanned area. A video slide scanner is subject to the same limitations as any video scanner—chiefly low resolution—but gives you an inexpensive means of capturing limited-resolution snapshot-quality images from slides and negatives.

Features

Beside their basic mechanism, scanners are distinguished by their features. Among these are whether the scanner can produce color images, how fast it can make a scan, the dynamic range it can handle, its resolution, and whether it can recognize text characters and translate them into characters rather image data. In addition, some scanners allow you to install optional accessories such as transparency adapters and sheet feeders to take care of your more special scanning needs.

Color Versus Monochrome

The base-level distinction between scanners is like that of television sets, color or monochrome. And as with televisions, the distinction is basically between the least that will get you a picture and what you'll really be happy with. Color scanners can do anything a grayscale scanner can do but with full spectral fidelity. Moreover, most can stoop to making quick scans in monochrome. You can even convert captured color images to grayscale at any later date when your needs require it. Although you can make a color scan using a monochrome scanner, the challenge and results are about on par with teaching your cat to bark.

True to their name, monochrome scanners perceive the world in one color or, rather, without distinguishing between colors. Better termed *grayscale scanners*, they are able to see only levels of brightness without separating light by its hue. They are innately simpler than color scanners, they are often faster, and invariably they are lower in cost. In fact, the least expensive minimum among scanners is a grayscale handheld unit.

Monochrome isn't only for cheapskates. For many applications, monochrome is sufficient. For example, if all you want to do is capture text with optical character recognition technology, you don't need more. Grayscale scanning works for desktop publishing, too, when your intent is to get it out in black-and-white. You don't have to pay for color that you can't use.

Color can be an issue even with monochrome scanners. Most scanners provide their own sources of illumination for scanning images. (This eliminates one variable from the scanning process and makes for more uniform and repeatable scans.) Although the color of illumination might seem immaterial for a monochrome scanner, that's not necessarily true. Illumination color becomes important when you want to scan from color originals.

For example, some hand scanners use red light-emitting diodes (LEDs) for illumination. LEDs have long, trouble-free lives. But when colored objects are illuminated in their red light, the brightness reflected from the image does not correspond to the brightness the human eye would perceive in white light. Green illumination gives a better approximation of the human eye's perception of tones. Colored images captured by a scanner that uses red illumination may seem tonally incorrect. Flesh tones, in particular, scan too lightly. Caucasian skin tones may come out too white; brown or black skin tones may appear almost Caucasian. For line drawing and text recognition applications, however, red can sometimes be better. Red pencil or ink marks on an image won't reproduce, so you can sketch or comment in red and not have it show in your scans.

Scanning Speed

Early color scanners give monochrome models a hefty edge in performance. The earliest color scanners were *three-pass* machines. That is, they required three passes to make a complete image, one pass for each of the primary colors. These ancient scanners used three separate light sources of different colors and took a full scan in each color. Nearly all modern scanners use *one-pass* designs. They have a single light source and rely on filtering in their photodetectors to sort out the colors. One-pass color scanners can operate just as quickly as monochrome models, although transferring a large color image measuring dozens of megabytes still takes longer than moving a monochrome image one-third its size.

The speed at which the scanning CCD moves across the image area is only one factor in the total time required to make a scan. Most scans require at least two separate passes. First, you command the scanner to make a *pre-scan*, a relatively quick, low-resolution pass across the image that helps you establish its brightness range and also lets you target a specific area for scanning. Then, you make the actual scan at the resolution you want.

In addition, the interface used by a scanner influences the speed of scans. The high-resolution bit images produced by the scanner represent a huge amount of data—megabytes—and a slow interface constricts its flow. Of the commonly used interfaces, a parallel connection is slowest and SCSI fastest. The difference may be a factor of two or three or more. USB-based scanners fall between the other two.

If the scan you want to make is large, you also have to wait for image processing, both in the scanning software and in the host application. Very large scans can add minutes or more to the total scan time if you exceed the memory capabilities of your PC. Although Windows can take advantage of virtual memory to let you capture images of nearly any size, this technology uses your disk drive for extra storage space, which adds the seek, writing, and reading times to the total time of your scan. If you plan to regularly make large scans, you'll speed things up more by adding memory to your PC—in the dozens of megabytes—than looking for a faster scanner.

Dynamic Range

The compass of color a scanner can discern or the number of brightness levels from black to white a grayscale scanner can distinguish is termed the scanner's *dynamic range*. The most common means of expressing dynamic range is bit depth, the number of bits needed to digitally encode the total color capacity. The most common scanners can distinguish 256 (8-bit), 1,024 (10-bit), or 4,096 (12-bit) brightness levels in each primary color. Just to make the scanner seem more capable, scanner manufacturers total up the number of colors within the scanner repertory, so you'll see 24-bit, 30-bit, and 36-bit color scanners.

The actual dynamic range and the bit depth of a scanner are not necessarily the same. A high-quality scanner will be able to resolve the number of brightness levels its bit depth implies. The bit depth actually specifies the range of the analog-to-digital converters that convert the level detected by the scanner's CCD sensors into digital signals. Taking advantage of that bit depth requires that the scanned image be properly focused on the CCD sensor under optimal illumination. If the focus of the scanner's optics is off, pixels will blur into one another and lower image contrast and the dynamic range of the scanner. Similarly, if the illumination provided for the image during the scan is uneven, the variations will wipe out some of the available brightness levels of the dynamic range. Consequently, two scanners with the same number of bits quoted for their dynamic range may, in fact, have different actual dynamic ranges.

Most PCs can, of course, display from 256 to 16.7 million different hues—that is, 8-bit to 24-bit color. When that is more than you or your software wants to manage, their palettes can easily be scaled back, either through hardware controls or through software, to an even smaller bit depth. With even a minimal 24-bit scanner capable of giving your software more than enough color, the extra bits of higher cost scanners might seem superfluous.

Those extra bits are very useful, however, when the scanner pre-processes image data before passing it along to your PC. A scanner with 36-bit dynamic range can capture all the shades and hues of an image and let you process them down into 24-bit color for your PC to use. You get to choose how to handle the conversion, compressing the dynamic range or cutting off colors you don't want to use. The extra bits assure that your scanner can capture all the detail in the darkest shadows and brightest highlights. When you use a transparency adapter, greater dynamic range helps you compensate for thinner or denser originals, potentially yielding workable scans from transparencies you can barely see through.

Many scanners have automatic modes through which they determine the proper brightness and contrast ratios to take best advantage of the translation of the scanner's dynamic range into the 24-bit color (or other level of color) used by your PC. The most common means of making this optimization is to pre-scan the image. The scanner then checks the brightest and darkest points of the scanned area. Using these values to establish the actual range of brightness and color in the image, the scanner can adjust its transformation to yield the image with the greatest tonal range to your applications.

Just as color scanners have different spectral ranges, grayscale scanners differ in the number of shades they can detect. At the bottom are the plain black and white machines that recognize no intermediary tones. From there, the grayscale range increases as powers of two. A few years ago, a scanner with a range of 16 grays was top of the line. Today, most grayscale scanners have a range of 256 levels, which matches 8-bit encoding (one byte per pixel) and matches most monitor display capabilities.

Most grayscale scanners can also be set to recognize fewer gray tones, usually the selection is between 2 (black and white) 16, 64, and 256 grays. The more grays you select, the larger the resulting image file will be but the more realistic the image will appear. A limited gray range is useful for text recognition and for capturing line drawings, but you'll want a wide range of grays to capture photographs.

Resolution

Scanners differ in the resolution at which they can capture images. All scanners have a maximum mechanical limit on their resolution. It's equal to the smallest step that their sensor can be advanced. Typically, a minimal scanner will start with about 300 dots per inch and go up from there in regular steps like 600, 1,200, and then 2,400 dots per inch. Special-purpose slide scanner achieve resolutions as high as 10,000 dots per inch. Because it represents the limit of the quality the scanner hardware is able to resolve, this measurement is often termed the *hardware resolution* of the scanner or the *optical resolution* of the scanner.

Beyond the mechanical resolution of a given scanner, the control software accompanying the scanner often pushes the claimed resolution even higher, to 4,800 or even 9,600 dots per inch even for an inexpensive scanner. To achieve the higher resolution figures, the control software interpolates dots. That is, the software computes additional dots in between those that are actually scanned.

This artificial enhancement results in a higher resolution value quoted for some scanners as *interpolated resolution*. Although interpolating higher resolution adds no more information to a scan—which means it cannot add to the detail that you've scanned—it can make the scan look more pleasing. The greater number of dots reduces the jaggedness or stairstepping in the scan and makes lines look smoother.

The new dots created by interpolation add to the size of the resulting scanned file, possibly making a large file cumbersome indeed. In that interpolation adds no new information, it need not be done at the time of scanning. You can store a file made at the mechanical resolution limit of your scanner and then later increase its apparent resolution through interpolation without wasting disk space storing imaginary dots.

As with colors and shades of gray, a scanner can easily be programmed to produce resolution lower than its maximum. Lower resolution is useful to minimize file size, to match your output device, or simply to make the scanned image fit on a single screen for convenient viewing. Although early scanners and their control software shifted their resolution in distinct increments—75, 150, and 300 dpi, for example—modern scanner-plus-software combinations make resolution continuously variable within wide limits.

The actual hardware resolution of a scanner is fixed across the width of the image by the number of elements in the CCD sensor that determines the brightness of each pixel. The hardware resolution along the length of the scan is determined by the number of steps the CCD sensor takes as it traverses the image area. The size of these steps is also usually fixed. Scanning software determines lower as well as higher resolution values by interpolating from the hardware scan. Consequently, even when set for 50 dpi, a scanner would sense at its hardware resolution level, deriving the lower resolution figure through software from its higher capabilities.

Transparency Adapters

As with people, scanners are not blessed with the ability to see in the dark. To make a proper scan—that is, one that doesn't resemble a solar eclipse in a coal mine—the scanner needs a light source. All scanners have their own, built-in and usually calibrated light sources. In drum and flatbed scanners, the light source is inside the mechanism, typically one or three cold cathode tubes that glow brightly. Handheld scanners often use LEDs (light emitting diodes) as their illumination source. In any case, in normal operation the light *reflects* from the material being scanned, and the CCD sensors in the scanner measure the brightness of the reflected light.

Some source materials fail to reveal their full splendor under reflected light. The most important of these are transparencies such as photographic slides or presentation foils. These are designed to have light shine through them, that is, transmitted light.

To properly scan these media, the scanner must put the media between its light source and its sensor. Slide scanners have the source for transmitted light built in. Most other desktop scanners have an optional secondary source for transmitted light called a *transparency adapter*. The secondary light source tracks the CCD sensor as it scans across the image but from the opposite side of the original.

Most commonly, the transparency adapter takes the form of a thicker cover over the glass stage on which you lay your originals to be scanned. A few scanners have add-on arms that scan over the top of the transparencies you lay on the stage. The latter style works well but does not hold original transparencies as flat against the stage as do the former styles.

Optical Character Recognition

Scanners don't care what you point them at. They will capture anything with adequate contrast, drawings, or text. However, text captured by a scanner will be in bit-image form, which makes it useless to word processors, which use ASCII code. You can translate text in graphic form into ASCII codes in two ways—by typing everything into your word processor or by using optical character recognition. Add character recognition software to your scanner, and you can quickly convert almost anything you can read on your screen into word processor, database, or spreadsheet files. Once the realm of mainframe computers and special hardware costing tens of thousands of dollars, OCR is now within the reach of most PCs and budgets.

Early OCR software used a technique called *matrix-matching*. The computer would compare small parts of each bit image it scanned to bit-patterns it had stored in a library to find what character was the most similar to the bit-pattern scanned. For example, a letter "A" would be recognized as a pointed tower 40 bits high with a 20-bit wide crossbar.

Matrix-matching suffers a severe handicap; it must be tuned to the particular typeface and type size you scan. For example, an Italic "A" has a completely different pattern signature from a Roman "A," even within the same size and type family. Consequently, a matrix-matching OCR system must have an enormous library of bit-patterns (requiring a time-consuming search for each match), or the system must be limited to matching a few typestyles and fonts. Even then, you will probably have to tell the character recognition system what typeface you want to read so it can select the correct pattern library. Worse, most matrix-matching systems depend on regular spacing between characters to determine the size and shape of the character matrix, so these systems work only with mono-spaced printing such as that generated by a typewriter.

Most of today's OCR systems use *feature-matching*. Feature-matching systems don't just look and compare but also analyze each bit-pattern that's scanned. When it sees the letter "A," it derives the essential features of the character from the pattern of bits—an up slope, a peak, and a down slope with a horizontal bar across. In that every letter "A" has the same characteristic features—if they didn't your eyes couldn't recognize each one as an "A," either—the feature-matching system doesn't need an elaborate library of bit-patterns to match nearly any font and type size. In fact, feature-matching recognition software doesn't need to know the size or font of the characters it is to recognize beforehand. Even typeset text with variable character spacing is no problem. Feature-matching software can thus race through a scan very quickly while making few errors.

Sheet Feeders

The typical OCR application involves transferring the information content of multiple pages into electronic form. You must, of course, scan each page separately to derive its information content. With long documents, the chore is time-consuming and usually not the most productive way to spend your working hours.

A sheet feeder automatically runs each sheet of a multiple-page document through a scanner. Although a sheet feeder is easiest to implement with a drum scanner because the scanner has to put the paper in motion anyway, some flatbed scanners have built-in or optional sheet feeders as well.

Sheet feeders are useful primarily for OCR applications. Graphic scanning usually involves individual setup of each page or image. Actually loading a page into the scanner is a trivial part of the graphic scan. Adding a sheet feeder to a scanner used primarily for graphics is consequently not cost-effective.

Sheet feeders require loose sheets. They cannot riffle through the pages of a book or other bound document. When a job requires high productivity and the information is more valuable than the printed original, some people cut apart books and similar materials for scanning using a sheet feeder. In any case, you'll probably find a staple-puller to be a worthy accessory to your sheet feeder.

Electrical Interfacing

At least six different interface designs are or have been used by scanners—SCSI (the Small Computer System Interface), GPIB (General Purpose Interface Bus), standard serial, parallel, USB, and proprietary. Almost all current products rely on parallel, SCSI, or USB connections.

Parallel models plugs into legacy printer ports. Most have special cables or connectors that allow you to link your printer to the same port used by the scanner. With modern port-driver software, parallel-interfaced scanners are the easiest to get running; they come to life almost as soon as you plug them in (and install the drivers). The parallel interface is also inexpensive.

The downside of the parallel connection is performance. It is the slowest of the scanner links and may double the scan time of a typical page.

The SCSI interface, on the other hand, is fast—the fastest scanner connection in use. The penalty is, of course, the need to tangle with a SCSI connection. This need not be a problem. When the SCSI-based scanner is the only device plugged into a SCSI port, getting the scanner to work is about as easy as with a parallel port. Adding a scanner to a long SCSI chain is as fraught with problems are linking any additional SCSI device.

The other problem with SCSI-based scanners is that they require a SCSI port. Most SCSI-based scanners come with their own SCSI host adapters and cables. (This is one reason the SCSI interface adds to the cost of a scanner.) Installing the adapter in an expansion slot complicates the installation process. Worse, if you want to use a SCSI scanner with a notebook computer, you'll need to purchase a PC Card SCSI adapter.

USB scanners fit in the middle. Although they require a free USB port, nearly all new PCs (including notebooks) have at least one. Scanners fit readily into USB's plug-and-play system but suffer from the same teething difficulties as other USB products. Although USB scanning is quicker than parallel, it is not as fast as SCSI scanning.

Application Interfacing

As with other input devices, scanners have their own control and signaling systems that must link to your software to be used effectively (or at all). Early scanners used their own proprietary application interfaces to relay commands and data. Consequently, each scanner required its own software or drivers. Oftentimes, you could only use the scanner manufacturer's own software to grab images.

Thanks to a concerted effort by the scanner industry, that situation has changed. Now you can expect any scanner to work with just about any graphics program. Moreover, scanning is consistent across applications. The same screens that control your scanner in Photoshop appear in Corel PhotoPaint.

Central to this standardization is Twain. First released in early 1992, Twain is a scanner software interface standard developed by a consortium scanner and software makers called (in its final form) the Working Group for Twain. The primary companies involved in forming the working group included Aldus Corporation, Caere Corporation, Eastman Kodak Company, Hewlett-Packard, and Logitech.

The Twain name requires some explanation. Twain is not an acronym, so only its initial letter needs to be capitalized. Rendering Twain in all capital letters is a typographic error. That said, the promoters of the standard usually write it in all capital letters as if it were an acronym.

Officially, the Twain developers have explained that the name is a reference to the purpose of the interface. Not an acronym, it derives from making the twain (an archaic word for "two") meet, the two of the twain being applications and scanners. However, a few wags insist that Twain stands for "Technology Without An Interesting Name."

When the Twain interface was being developed, it wore a number of different names. The most common of these were *Direct-Connect* and *CLASP*, the latter of which stands for the Connecting Link for Applications and Source Peripherals. The developers of Twain considered these and others as the formal names of the interface. After searching through lists of trademarks in use, however, they found so many conflicts they felt that lawsuits would be a distinct possibility were any of the developmental names to be used. Instead, they chose the name Twain to, in the words of one of the developers, "describe this interface which brings together two entities, applications and input devices."

Twain links programs and scanner hardware, giving software writers a standard set of function calls by which to control the features of any scanner. One set of Twain drivers will handle any compatible scanning device. Because the Twain connection has two ends—your scanner and your software—to take advantage of it requires both be Twain compatible.

Twain defines its hardware interface as its source. The source is hardware or firmware in a scanner that controls the information that flows from the scanner into Twain. The scanner maker designs the source to match its particular hardware and interface. Your software links to the Twain source through a source manager, which is essentially a set of program calls.

Twain takes the form of a software driver. The original driver was written in 16-bit code and takes the name TWAIN.DLL. The working group has also created a fully 32-bit version of the driver called TWAIN32.DLL. Both the 16- and 32-bit versions work with Windows 95 and NT as well as more recent Windows versions.

Operation

Despite the advances made in PCs and software, making a scan still is not a matter of simply pushing a button. Getting the best quality of graphic images and the most useful data file requires several steps. Before you begin, you have to consider exactly what you want from your image, what format you want (black-and-white, grayscale, or color), the resolution, and the file format in which you want to save it. Then, you must make a preliminary scan to help define the image area and dynamic range. After making adjustments, you can finally make your scan. Before you save the image, however, you may want to tweak it with your graphic software to crop off unwanted areas, sharpen or soften the details, and fine-tune its tonal range.

Pre-Scanning

The first step in making a graphic scan is the preliminary scan or *pre-scan*. You make a quick scan of the image, usually at low resolution, that allows you to delimit the physical area to be scanned and make a first stab at optimizing the dynamic range of the scan. With most scanning software, the pre-scan covers the full width of the imaging area because there's no speed penalty for taking in the whole width; the CCD sensor automatically covers everything. On the other hand, you can limit the length of the pre-scan to minimize sensor movement and speed up the pre-scan. One-pass scanners will likely make their pre-scans in full color; three-pass engines usually restrict themselves to monochrome images so they need to make only one pass.

Defining the Imaging Area

When the pre-scan completes, your imaging software should give you the opportunity to define the imaging area, typically by putting a frame around it. As you move to higher resolutions, it becomes increasingly important to tightly define the imaging area to limit the amount of data force-fed to your application. By eliminating extraneous areas from your image at this point, you can cut both storage space requirements and image processing time.

Dynamic Range Adjustments

In addition, your scanner control software should give you an opportunity to adjust image brightness, contrast, and color. This stage is critical for obtaining the best possible image, the one most suited to later manipulation.

If you're making black-and-white scans, at this point you can set the threshold at which the scanner judges each pixel either black or white. If you're scanning line art, you'll want to set the threshold so as to minimize noise in the image. If you're scanning a grayscale or color image, the threshold setting can have a major effect on the image and its quality. If you cannot make a precise adjustment at this point because of the small size of the image displayed after the pre-scan, you may be better off making a grayscale scan and converting it to black and white with your image processing software where you should have more control.

In making grayscale scans, you'll want to set the brightness and contrast of the image to maximize image quality. These controls determine how the scanning software processes the dynamic range of the scanner into the 256 shades of gray used by most graphics software for monochrome images. You may also be able to switch the polarity of the image, turning a negative into a positive image.

All of the dynamic range controls interact. The basic controls are brightness and contrast. For the best scans, you'll need to adjust contrast so that the brightest area of the scan matches the brightest white that your software accepts and the darkest area is the maximum black. The brightness control shifts the range of grays up and down, contrast adjusts the width of the range. Most software gives you more advanced control such as histogram and gamma control. The histogram will show you the most prevalent tones in the image. It may allow you to cut off excess whites or blacks to limit the dynamic range that is imaged. You may also be able to shift the midpoint of the rendering to bias the image toward brightness or darkness. The gamma control also lets you adjust the mapping of tones. Generally speaking, a low gamma compresses high and low tones and extends the rendering of middle tones, whereas a high gamma extends the ranges of brights and darks while compressing the mid-tones. High gamma images appear to have more contrast, although strictly speaking gamma and contrast are not the same thing.

In making color scans, you also need to optimize the dynamic range of the scanner. In most cases, you use the same controls as for adjusting a grayscale image. In addition, you may have the opportunity to adjust some aspects of the color of the scan, including making color shifts and adjusting saturation.

Defining Scan Area

Because of the prodigious amount of data created in a full-page, full-color scan, most scanner software allows you to limit the area of a scan to something that produces a more reasonable number of bytes. This expedient saves not only storage but also time because fewer bytes need to move through the interface.

Typically, you define the area to be scanned by outlining or drawing a box around your selection on the pre-scanned image. In most cases, you'll want to be generous in the amount of area you select because you can always crop off the excess at the edges. If you fail to scan enough area, however, the only cure is to make another scan.

Setting Resolution

Before you make your scan, you should also set or double-check the resolution setting of the scanner. Although you may find it tempting to scan at the highest resolution to get the most detail in the resulting image, such a strategy wastes both time and disk space. Higher resolutions result in more data to manipulate. You'll waste time in manipulating a large image if you're just going to shrink it down to size later.

Some people recommend that you do not scan at any resolution higher than the maximum hardware resolution of the scanner. Higher resolutions, being interpolated, add no new information. You can manipulate your image at hardware resolution and, when you're done, scale it larger without losing quality. Your image processing software likely can interpolate as well or better than the scanner hardware.

If you're scanning photographs, one third of the resolution of your printer often is sufficient. Most printers use super-pixels for halftoning. That is, the printer uses a block of four, nine, or more dots to represent each image pixel. Most color printers use even larger super-pixels to render wide palettes. The big exceptions are continuous tone printers such as dye-sublimation machines in which you can control the hue of each pixel. When scanning for them, you should set the scanner resolution to the same as the printer resolution for optimum quality.

If you're scanning images to later be made into color separations, a good starting point is setting resolution at twice the line frequency of the printing screen. For example, if your scanned image will be reproduced in a glossy magazine printed using a 133 lines-per-inch screen, scan at a resolution of 266 dots per inch.

When you plan to scan only for presentation on your computer monitor, set the resolution so that the image size in pixels matches your display resolution. The required resolution may be surprisingly low. For example, if you want to make a full-page image fit on a VGA screen, you'll want to set the resolution to yield an image 480 pixels high—just over 40 dots per inch for a page 11 inches long.

Digital Cameras

Push the button and digital electronics will do the rest. Forget the yellow or green boxes and snub your nose at the one-hour photo place. The digital camera doesn't need film—that's the whole point of it—and it doesn't need a film company. No need for the photofinisher any more, either. Better than Polaroid, you don't have to wait to see what develops or suffer the agonizing wait as colors fill in through the fog. Instantly, you know what went wrong (and with photography, something *always* goes wrong—the challenge is finding the least-wrong image) and whether you need to snap again. You can review a half a dozen shots at a time *in the camera*, choose the ones you want, and take some more without wasting an inch of film. When you're done, download everything into your PC where you can digitally edit and enhance your images until everything is perfect. And finally, you can put to work that photo-quality printer that came with your PC or move clips into your digital documents or even post them on your Web site.

The digital camera is the facilitating device for *digital photography*, often called *non-silver photography* because of its lack of reliance on conventional photographic film. Film depends on the photosensitivity of silver salts. Several silver compounds change color when struck by photons of light, and the chemical development process allows the work of one photon to be magnified to affect thousands or millions of atoms of silver. In digital photography, photons are detected electrically by an *image sensor* that's so sensitive there's no need for the chemical amplification of the film developer.

Imaging Sensors

The image sensor is the heart of the digital camera. It captures the image, registering it in a form that can later be used. Film captures the image chemically; the energy in photons of light changes the atomic bonds in molecules that result in a change in the reflectance of those molecules. The image sensor captures the image electrically. It detects photons and translates their energy into a minute electrical current that circuits can sense, amplify, digitize, and store.

Many people call image sensors *CCDs*, the name of the technology used by most digital camera image sensing devices. Although CCDs are used in most cameras, some companies have adopted a similar technology that's usually termed CMOS. Yes, it's the same name as the memory used for system configuration data in your PC because the image sensors and the memory use the same semiconductor technology—Complimentary Metal-Oxide Semiconductor technology.

CMOS promises to be less expensive than CCD although with some sacrifice in quality. The most notable product using a CMOS sensor is the Barbie Digital Camera sold by Mattel. Camera makers note, however, that improvements in technology have made

CMOS quality competitive with CCD—and have made CCD pricing competitive with CMOS.

For purposes of this story, we'll use CCD to refer to sensors generally and distinguish CMOS only where there may be important technological differences.

Although the term "CCD" usually is used in the singular, the actual image sensor requires an array of CCDs. The mere presence of light is not as important as its pattern, which makes up the actual image. A single CCD (or CMOS sensor) element registers only a single point. Consequently, what's normally called a CCD is actually an array of individual CCD elements. In video cameras, the CCD elements get arranged as a matrix. (The CCDs used in scanners typically are arranged as a thin straight line.) Camera circuitry samples each element in turn to scan an image frame.

Size

Image sensors come in various sizes. Typically they measure one-quarter, one-third, or one-half inch (diagonally). All else equal, the larger the CCD, the greater the number of elements that can be packed into the array. The number of elements determines the resolution of the image signal produced by the CCD. This number is related to, but is not the same as, the number of pixels in an image.

Size of the sensor affects other elements of the camera design. For example, the coverage of the lens usually is tailored to match the sensor size. (That's one reason why camera makers cannot simply put CCDs inside ordinary 35mm cameras; today's practical sensors are substantially smaller than 35mm film and would only register a fraction of the image from the lens.)

Resolution

The maximum possible resolution is set by the number of pixels that the CCD can sense. The keyword in digital photography currently is *megapixel*—that is, a million pixels. Photographers see the million pixel mark as distinguishing good cameras from bad. A camera with more than a million pixels produces an image almost as good as a 35mm point-and-shoot camera. Fewer pixels result in marginal image quality—or worse.

The number of total pixels is directly related to the resolution of a CCD. If you know the number of CCD elements in a sensor (video cameras are sometimes described by this figure), you can determine its highest possible resolution using these formulae:

Horizontal resolution = 4 * sqr(number of pixels/12)

Vertical resolution = 3 * sqr(number of pixels/12)

To determine the number of pixels in the image, divide the number of CCD elements by three. Divide this figure by twelve, and then determine the square root of the result. Horizontal resolution is four times this figure; vertical resolution, three times the figure.

In general, digital camera resolution levels parallel those of computer display systems. The minimal modern digital camera boasts VGA resolution, 640 by 480 pixels. Megapixel cameras start at 1,280 by 1,024 pixels.

Sensitivity

Image sensors vary in their sensitivity to light. The best can detect a single photon. Those in digital cameras require dozens of photons to make a detected signal. The inherent sensitivity of the image sensor is not, however, directly relevant to practical photography. Other aspects of the design of the camera overwhelm concerns about the native sensitivity of image sensors. The most important of these is the lens.

Lenses

A camera is just a box that prevents light from getting on film or its modern-day equivalent. Almost any light-tight box will do, including a full-size room. Camera, after all, means room. The most important add-on for the camera is the lens. The lens determines the quality of the image that's formed inside the camera. The lens and its quality determine what kind of image your camera can collect and to a great degree set the ultimate quality of picture you can hope to take.

You can take photographs without a lens; that's the principle behind pinhole photography. But nearly all cameras have lenses for one very good reason: A lens collects a lot of light. It lets a lot more light into the camera box. That gives the camera more light to work with and makes exposures quicker. The lens also affects the view, what the camera sees. It alters the aesthetics of the image you make.

Aperture

Literally speaking, an aperture is nothing more than a hole, and that's what it means for cameras. The aperture is the hole in the lens through which light can get to the film—or the CCD sensor (in the case of a digital camera). You can't poke your finger through the hole, however, because it is inside the lens. Only light goes through it.

In photography, digital or otherwise, the aperture is more important than a mere hole. It's a variable hole, one you can make larger or smaller to let more or less light reach the film or sensor. A larger aperture lets more light in; smaller lets in less.

Varying the size of the aperture helps a camera of any kind cope with light conditions. When light is too bright, it can overwhelm the CCD; too dim, and the CCD might not be able to find enough photons to make an image. With film, too much light results in overexposure; too little, underexposure. To prevent these problems, most cameras use wider apertures in dim light.

Autoexposure

The oldest cameras required that the photographer determine the proper aperture to properly expose film. Although some photographers guessed at the proper aperture to use—for example, relying on the little drawings that used to come with the film showing bright sunny days and clouds—most photographers relied on light meters to measure the brightness of the scene they were photographing.

Along with all the other paraphernalia, the photographer had to tote along a separate light meter. It didn't take engineers long to figure out that they could incorporate the light meter to the camera itself. As camera mechanisms became more sophisticated and technology advanced, the camera designers removed the human variable from reading the light meter, allowing the camera to read its own meter and adjust the aperture accordingly. The result was the *autoexposure* camera.

All but a brave few cameras (mostly those designed for professionals who know more than any dumb meter, at least in their own minds) now incorporate autoexposure. All digital cameras automatically set their apertures.

The mechanism for setting the aperture is termed the *iris* of the camera, and it corresponds to the iris of the human eye. By sliding thin plates called *iris blades*—in manual mode typically by rotating a ring around the lens termed, appropriately enough, the aperture ring—you can adjust the size of the hole between the blades and thus the aperture.

Although the irises of most lenses approximate it, the aperture need not be round. Square works as well as circular with little effect on the image. Critical photographers can, however, notice a difference in photographs because bright spots that are out of focus in the image made by a lens take on the shape of the lens aperture. The effect is often subtle, but to some photographers, it can have a dramatic effect on subjective image quality.

The size of the aperture is measured as an *f-stop*. Most commonly, the f-stop is a number in the geometric series 1.4, 2.0, 2.8, 4.0, 5.6, 8.0, 11.0, 16.0, 22, 32. The series is designed so that the next higher stop cuts the light transmitted through the lens to half the value of the previous stop. An f-stop setting of 8.0 allows half as much light into the camera as a setting of 5.6. (The sequence is simpler than it looks. Each f-stop differs from its predecessor by the square root of two, the results rounded.) Table 15.1 lists the ISO standard (nominal) f-stops, the actual (computed) f-stop, and relative light values.

TABLE 15.1 F-stops

Nominal Stop (ISO)	Actual Stop and Half-Stop	Light Value (Relative f/1.0)
1	1.00	1.00
	1.19	1.41
1.4	1.41	2.00
	1.68	2.83

Nominal Stop (ISO)	Actual Stop and Half-Stop	Light Value (Relative f/1.0)
2	2.00	4.00
	2.38	5.66
2.8	2.83	8.00
	3.36	11.31
4	4.00	16.00
	4.76	22.63
5.6	5.66	32.00
	6.73	45.25
8	8.00	64.00
	9.51	90.51
11	11.31	128.00
	13.45	181.02
16	16.00	256.00
	19.03	362.04
22	22.63	512.00
	26.91	724.08
32	32.00	1,024.00
	38.05	1,448.15
45	45.25	2,048.00
	53.82	2,896.31
64	64.00	4,096.00

Although the sequence of numbers is now an arbitrary sequence, the value of the f-stop is scientifically defined. It is the focal length of the lens divided by the apparent aperture of the lens. (It's not the actual size of the hole in the iris but the size of the hole visible through the lens; the glass in the lens can magnify the aperture or even make it appear smaller.) For example, a lens with a 50 millimeter focal length set at f-stop 4 would have a visible aperture of 12.5 millimeters. This relationship leads to the common way of writing f-stop settings. A setting of four is usually written as f/4. In other words, it is the f(ocal length) divided by four.

Lenses are usually described by the widest aperture at which they can be set, for example, f/1.4 or f/2.8. Sometimes, the widest aperture setting falls between the numbers of the standard f-stop sequence, for example, f/2.3, but the value represents the same concept.

Many zoom lenses are marked with two f-stops, for example, f/2.8-4.3. The two values do not represent the total range of stops available from the lens. Rather, they represent the range of minimum f-stop values. The formula for determining the f-stop of a lens requires the size of the aperture to vary with the focal length of the lens at a constant f-stop setting. A longer lens requires a wider aperture for the same f-stop setting.

Zoom lenses are able to vary their focal lengths to change the size of the image they make in your camera. Nearly all zoom lenses automatically change the aperture as you zoom to maintain a constant f-stop setting. The physical diameter of the lens limits its maximum aperture; the hole in the iris can't be bigger than the lens itself. When the focal length is set shorter, however, the largest possible aperture represents a wider (lower value) f-stop, which is desirable because it allows more light into the lens so that you can take photographs in dimmer light. Consequently, lens makers let you take advantage of the wider f-stop settings at shorter focal lengths, and the minimum f-stop value varies with the focal length setting of the lens. The highest f-stop number represents the widest setting at the longest focal length setting of the lens. The lower value represents the widest f-stop setting possible at the most favorable focal length setting.

When using a lens, the aperture or f-stop setting can have a dramatic effect on the final image beyond setting exposure. The f-stop determines the *depth of field* (more correctly, the depth of *focus*) in the image.

Focal Length

Technically speaking, the focal length of a lens is the distance from its nodal point to the plane of focus of its image of an object an infinite distance from the lens—that is, where the image appears sharpest. Although this highly technical concept appears to have no practical value in judging cameras or lenses, focal length has an important ramification. It determines the field of view a lens provides or, the corollary, the size of the image. As a practical matter, a lens with a short focal length provides a wide field of view and makes things look smaller and farther away. A long lens provides a narrow field of view and large images that look closer. The choice of focal length also affects other aspects of the "look" of the image, issues of aesthetics better addressed in art texts than a hardware book.

Wider, smaller, larger, and closer are all relative concepts. With lenses, such terms relate to a "normal" lens. For some reason not readily apparent, the photographic world has decided a normal lens has a field of view of 46 degrees. That is, the angle between the camera and the left side of what it sees is 46 degrees from a line draw to the rightmost side of the image. On a 35 millimeter camera, that means a 50 millimeter lens is "normal."

Not everyone agrees. Some people believe a normal lens should have a focal length the same size as the image format. A diagonal line across a frame of 35 millimeter film measures 43 millimeters, so that should be the "normal" focal length. Others have compared paintings to actual views and discovered that many artists seem to focus on a view approximating that taken with about a 90 millimeter lens in the 35 millimeter format. The focal length required for this normal field of view for a quarter-inch CCD is about 7 millimeters; for a third-inch CCD, 6.9 millimeters; for a half-inch CCD, 9.3 millimeters. Table 15.2 compares the field of view for lens focal lengths in various imaging formats.

TABLE 15.2   Image Sensor Sizes

Format	6×4.5	35mm	1 in CCD	3/4 in CCD	1/2 in CCD	1/3 in CCD	1/4 in CCD
Units	Centimeters	Millimeters	Millimeters	Millimeters	Millimeters	Millimeters	Millimeters
Diagonal	7.50	43.27	25.40	19.05	12.70	8.47	6.35
115.00	2.39	13.78	8.09	6.07	4.05	2.70	2.02
110.00	2.63	15.15	8.89	6.67	4.45	2.96	2.22
105.00	2.88	16.60	9.75	7.31	4.87	3.25	2.44
100.00	3.15	18.15	10.66	7.99	5.33	3.55	2.66
95.00	3.44	19.82	11.64	8.73	5.82	3.88	2.91
90.00	3.75	21.63	12.70	9.52	6.35	4.23	3.17
85.00	4.09	23.61	13.86	10.39	6.93	4.62	3.46
80.00	4.47	25.78	15.14	11.35	7.57	5.05	3.78
75.00	4.89	28.19	16.55	12.41	8.28	5.52	4.14
70.00	5.36	30.90	18.14	13.60	9.07	6.05	4.53
65.00	5.89	33.96	19.93	14.95	9.97	6.64	4.98
60.00	6.50	37.47	22.00	16.50	11.00	7.33	5.50
55.00	7.20	41.56	24.40	18.30	12.20	8.13	6.10
50.00	8.04	46.39	27.24	20.43	13.62	9.08	6.81
45.00	9.05	52.23	30.66	23.00	15.33	10.22	7.67
40.00	10.30	59.44	34.89	26.17	17.45	11.63	8.72
35.00	11.89	68.61	40.28	30.21	20.14	13.43	10.07
30.00	14.00	80.74	47.40	35.55	23.70	15.80	11.85
25.00	16.92	97.58	57.29	42.96	28.64	19.10	14.32
20.00	21.27	122.69	72.03	54.02	36.01	24.01	18.01

continues

TABLE 15.2 Continued

Format	6×4.5	35mm	1 in CCD	3/4 in CCD	1/2 in CCD	1/3 in CCD	1/4 in CCD
Units	Centimeters	Millimeters	Millimeters	Millimeters	Millimeters	Millimeters	Millimeters
15.00	28.48	164.32	96.47	72.35	48.23	32.16	24.12
10.00	42.86	247.27	145.16	108.87	72.58	48.39	36.29
8.00	53.63	309.37	181.62	136.21	90.81	60.54	45.40
6.00	71.55	412.79	242.33	181.75	121.16	80.78	60.58
5.00	85.89	495.48	290.88	218.16	145.44	96.96	72.72
4.00	107.39	619.50	363.68	272.76	181.84	121.23	90.92
3.00	143.21	826.14	484.99	363.74	242.50	161.66	121.25
2.00	214.84	1,239.37	727.58	545.69	363.79	242.53	181.90
1.00	429.71	2,478.93	1,455.27	1,091.45	727.64	485.09	363.82

Zoom

Technically speaking, a zoom lens is one that allows you to change its focal length within a given range. For most people, however, the results of the zooming process are more important. Zooming lets you change the size of the image in your viewfinder, on your film, and in your files. You zoom in to make things bigger, as if you had stepped closer to whatever you're photographing. Zooming out makes things smaller so you can fit more of your subject into the frame. Zooming has other effects, too, changing the depth of field and compressing distance, concepts that we'll discuss later.

All zooming is in the lens with chemical photography. Digital photography adds another way to zoom—the electronic or digital zoom. Although both produce the same effect, they achieve it in different ways that have important results for what you see in the final image. The two forms of zoom are complementary. They can be used together, and often are, to increase zoom range.

Optical Zooming

The classic zoom is optical with all the zoom effect created by the lens. The optical principle is actually simple. A zoom lens adds another lens that acts as a magnifier, increasing the size of the image by apparently increasing the focal length of the original lens. The magnifying effect changes with the distance of the magnifier from the original lens, so by sliding the magnifier, you can continuously change the focal length of the original lens.

In practice, zoom lenses are not so simple. They are among the most complex optical devices in common use. They have multiple lens elements to correct for image problems and distortions added by the zoom process, for example, maintaining that constant f-stop setting as the focal length of the lens changes.

Maintaining the quality of the image produced by a lens throughout its zoom range has always been a challenge for optical designers. Thanks to modern computers, they have become adept at creating superb zoom lenses. The designs are complex, however, and that means that they can be costly to produce. That's the chief disadvantage of the optical zoom.

The quality—meaning the sharpness, contrast, and color saturation—of the image produced by a modern zoom lens does not change as you zoom through the entire range of the lens. Keep that in mind. It's the chief advantage of the optical zoom.

Digital Zooming

Optical zooming works on the image before it is actually formed on the CCD inside a digital camera. Digital zooming, in contrast, manipulates the image after it is registered by the CCD. In effect, digital zooming is nothing more than interpolating the image to a different size. The process is exactly the same as you can do with image editing software inside your PC. It's called digital zooming only because it takes place within the digital camera with the results showing in the camera's viewfinder.

As with any interpolation, quality can suffer. The interpolation process cannot create image data that's not there to start with. Because the zooming process typically fills the entire frame with an image taken from a fractional part of the frame and discards the rest, the zoomed image inevitably is of lower quality than the full-frame image.

The exception to this is when you work at less than the full resolution of the camera, for example, taking only a VGA image (640 by 480 pixels) from a high-resolution (say SXGA with 1,280 by 960 pixels) camera. In that case, the zoom selects pixels from the original full-frame image instead of interpolating them, so there's no quality loss in zooming; the quality is already compromised by the selection of lower resolution.

Digital zooming has another downside. It's wasteful. It creates a larger file and more data without adding information. Because digital zooming is nothing more than interpolation, you can achieve the same effect with your image editing software. Increasing the file size in the camera simply doesn't make sense. It gives you more data to store in your camera, transfer down to your PC, and hold in files, without adding any information. From that point of view, there's little reason for using digital zooming *except if you want to see an enlarged image in your camera*. In all other cases, you'll be better off to do the zooming with your PC's software.

Zoom Range

The zooming range of lenses is measured in its own x-factor. The "x" represents the longest focal length of the zoom lens divided by its shortest focal length. For example, a 50 to 150mm zoom lens is described as a 3x zoom. At that, the x-factor describes the power of the zoom to increase the linear dimensions of the images it produces. With a 3x zoom, for example, the greatest magnification of its image will be three times taller and three times wider than at its least magnification.

A larger zoom range is better than a small one and, of course, typically more costly. Be alert that sometimes camera makers publish the total zoom capabilities of their cameras as a single figure that's a product of both optical (useful) and digital (doubtful) zoom capabilities. For example, a camera advertised with 6x zoom capabilities will have 3x optical zoom and a 2x digital zoom. For most practical purposes, you can consider such a camera to have merely 3x capabilities.

Supplemental Lenses

Just as modern lenses are made from multiple elements, you can add additional elements to a lens to change its fundamental characteristics. For example, put a positive (convex) element in front of a camera lens, and you will change its focus; it will focus nearer. Additional elements that you can attach to the basic lens of your camera are called *supplemental lenses*. Some digital camera makers call them *conversion lenses*.

Four types of supplemental lenses are sometimes available:

- **Telephoto converters** make distant images closer and larger without affecting the camera's ability to focus at faraway objects.

- **Close-up converters** allow your camera to fill its frame with the image of a nearby object. You can photograph things closer to your camera, but when using the converter, you can no longer focus on faraway objects.

- **Wide-angle converters** allow your camera to take in more panoramic views. This converter will add drama to landscape photos but can be even more useful indoors when you can't otherwise get far enough from large subjects (for example, groups of people) to fit them entirely in the frame.

- **Fisheye converters** take wide-angle to the extreme, giving you a 180 degree view by bending the straight lines of the image to fit the frame.

Which of these four types of converters is available to you depends on what your camera maker offers or whether aftermarket products fit the camera you choose. If you want to experiment with additional telephoto reach or wide-angle panoramas, check to see which options you can buy before you purchase a new digital camera.

Shutters

The role of the shutter in a camera is to *limit* the amount of light getting in. Certainly, too much light will overexpose film and overwhelm CCDs, but constraining the quantity of light isn't the only function of the shutter. After all, reducing the aperture will similarly prevent overexposure. The shutter controls exposure by its duration, the period during which light is allowed into the camera. Images often change over time; people blink, horses gallop, racecars race, grass grows, and paint peels. By limiting the time during which light is gathered, the shutter can capture a small slice of the image during which movement is minimal, even invisible. A fast shutter can simply stop motion—more correctly, the blurring effects of motion on captured images.

Shutter Speeds

Over the years, shutter speeds have been standardized in a sequence in which each speed is one-half the next fastest, effectively cutting the light passes through by one half. Consequently, each step in shutter speed alters the amount of light reaching film or image sensor by the same amount as the change in one standard f-stop. Table 15.3 lists the standard shutter speeds.

TABLE 15.3   Shutter speed sequence

Indication on camera	*Actual exposure period*
1	1 second
2	0.5 second
4	0.25 second
8	0.125 second
15	0.073 second
30	0.033 second
60	0.0167 second
125	0.008 second
250	0.004 second
500	0.002 second
1000	0.001 second
2000	0.0005 second
4000	0.00025 second

Shutter speed settings are typically displayed on conventional cameras without the "1/" indication. Consequently, the notch for a shutter speed of 1/125th second will be identified as simply 125.

Cameras differ in the speeds they make available to you. Only more expensive, professional-grade cameras offer the highest speeds, 1/2000th second and greater.

Choosing a shutter speed is not arbitrary. You (or the program of an automatic camera) must consider several issues. The two most important are proper exposure and the minimization of the effect of camera shake.

With 35 millimeter cameras, the oft-stated rule for the slowest shutter speed that yields sharp images when the camera is handheld is one over the focal length of the lens (or shorter). For example, with a standard 50 millimeter lens, the slowest speed recommended for handheld exposures is 1/60th second. Some people are able to make sharp exposures at speeds a notch or two slower than the general rule. But when you need to make an exposure longer than these recommendations, you should mount your camera on a tripod to prevent shake. A tripod is not a cure-all, however. Even a tripod won't prevent the image blurring because of subject movement.

Exposure Sensing

The most important job for any camera is controlling light. The camera stops all light from getting to its film or image sensor except for the tiny bit that leaks through the lens. Even this thin stream of light must be carefully controlled. Too little light, and the image won't register. Too much and your film gets overexposed or your image sensor gets overwhelmed (or injured).

Cameras control the light that forms the image in two ways: using a shutter to limit the time light flows to film or sensor and using the aperture to control the flow of light during that period. The challenge facing cameras and their operators is knowing how much light to let through. At that point, you or your camera can adjust the shutter and aperture to allow a fraction of the light of the original scene flow into your camera.

The problem becomes one of measuring the brightness of the scene you want to photograph. A special device called a light meter does exactly that. From the name of the device, the process of determining the brightness of a scene is called light metering or exposure metering.

The brightest thing that most people have to photograph is a sunny day. Although some days are sunnier than others and some locations are brighter than others (a cloudless day skiing is probably the brightest of all), this level of illumination sets the upper limit for the brightness of anything you're likely to want to photograph.

How bright the world is depends on where you look. A clear day in Aspen is brighter than a night in Carlsbad Caverns, and you would expect your camera to adjust for the difference. But the camera faces a problem when it comes to real-world photographic situations. A given scene is likely to contain a range of brightnesses, and the brightness level a meter measures will depend on where it looks.

Brightness is a property not of each scene but of each part of a scene. As long as the world isn't a uniform gray, some parts of a scene will be brighter than others. This inevitable difference in brightness is good; without it, we wouldn't see anything. But it poses a difficult question for exposure metering: Where should you measure brightness?

Answering that question is tough because it has no one correct answer. Certainly, there are obvious choices: measure everything, measure the brightest spot, average the brightest and darkest areas, measure only the center, and so on. Although almost any strategy results in an image, often acceptable, none will always produce the best possible image. Finding a way of evaluating image brightness in the greatest number of situations has challenged camera designers since they first glued selenium cells on the fronts of their products.

The advent of the digital camera alters only the mechanics of the situation. Cameras for chemical photography rely on add-on electronic brightness-measuring devices called photocells. The size, cost, and placement of photocells has inevitably limited the camera designer's choices in metering. Digital cameras (and video cameras, for that matter) produce a measurable electronic brightness signal for every pixel. The camera designer must only choose how to combine those signals to control the aperture and shutter.

The issue is not only which pixels to sample but what importance to assign to the signal from each one—that is, the weight to assign to each of potentially a million or more signals. The guiding factor is as much aesthetic as engineering, however. Through the years, a number of schemes have been tried, increasing in complexity as technology has allowed. The primary choices are three (in order of introduction): full-screen, spot, and matrix, together lumped together as metering patterns.

The most advanced form of pattern metering doesn't just integrate a brightness level over the entire scene or a 10 degree spot. Instead, it uses computer-based intelligence to deduce what you're trying to photograph—not quite a canned aesthetic sense but no more than a step away. Instead of a single metering sensor, camera makers spread several of them in a matrix across the image. Each one sends a separate signal to a small computer in the camera, which then looks for a pattern in the relative brightnesses striking the various sensors.

Camera makers have discovered that certain patterns of brightness—for example, bright around the edges but dark in the center—are trademarks of common photographic situations. The example would indicate a backlighted subject, perhaps a portrait of some-one with the sun behind. Once the camera identifies the photographic situation, it adjust the waiting of the various sensor elements in its metering matrix. For example, instead of simply adjusting for the overall brightness of the image, the camera would, based on its judgment of the image composition, meter to the center of the image where the actual subject lay, ignoring the bright backlighting.

Exposure Control

Metering only creates information. The next issue is what to do with the information that the metering system develops. The choices are two: Either let the camera deal with it or leave it for you to deal with. In other words, choose either automatic or manual exposure control.

Manual

Manual exposure is the old-fashioned way. You read the meter (which may be inside the camera and displayed in the viewfinder of a modern digital camera) and then adjust both the shutter speed and lens aperture to match its recommendations. Old match-needle metering required you simply to adjust the camera so that the needle of its light meter moved to the center of its display; newer cameras may ask you to make adjustments until a red LED turns green or some such nonsense.

For the most part, manual exposure systems existed because camera makers had not yet learned how to make them automatic. Manual exposure still gives you the utmost in con-trol, however. It allows you to control the depth of field of your photographs, the amount of blurring from image movement, and similar aesthetic pictorial features. If you have the least pretense toward making artistic photographs, you'll want a camera that allows you to step backward to manual exposure control.

Automatic

Automatic exposure is not a single miracle, it's several. Autoexposure systems may operate in any of three distinct modes and may even allow you to choose which to use:

- **Aperture priority** asks you to set the lens aperture and automatically adjusts the shutter speed for proper exposure.
- **Shutter priority** asks you to set the shutter speed, and the camera automatically adjusts the aperture for proper exposure.
- **Programmed** asks only that you point the camera in the general direction of what you want to photograph, and the camera adjusts both shutter speed and lens aper-ture according to a stored program.

The programs used by programmed exposure systems vary at the discretion of the camera manufacturer. Some favor shorter exposures to lessen the chance of blurring with long lenses. Some favor smaller apertures to yield more depth of field to simplify the job of autofocus systems. More expensive cameras allow you to select from different programs to match the photographic situation you face. Some cameras even let you tailor your own programs or select from more exotic programs stored on removable memory cards.

In any case, most cameras set off flashing lights, beeps, or sirens to warn when you try to photograph a scene out of the range of the automatic exposure system's capabilities to assure a proper exposure. (A few snotty cameras may even prevent you from taking a photo that they think they cannot properly expose.) Usually, adjusting the parameter that's left to manual control (the aperture or shutter that has priority) will resolve these difficulties unless the scene is just too dark.

The compromise between automatic and manual exposure is to handle things automatically but give you a veto. That is, the camera will find its own way but allow you to take over when things get too challenging.

To allow you to override the automatic exposure system and fine-tune the exposure of your images, most cameras provide *exposure compensation controls*. These are also called backlight switches or something similar in recognition of the situation most often requiring compensation: When the source of light is behind the actual subject, making the background substantially brighter than the foreground. The exposure compensation control simply tells the camera to overexpose the overall image to bring the actual subject into the proper exposure range. This overexposure is also useful for other special situations such as snowy ski scenes or bright sandy beaches. Although advanced matrix-metering systems supposedly cope with this sort of lighting, a camera with exposure compensation gives you a degree of control without sacrificing general automatic operation.

Exposure Range

The variety of lighting situations with which a digital camera can cope, from dark to bright, is the exposure range of the camera. This value represents the combination of its sensitivity and the adjustments available for dealing with excess light using its shutter and aperture controls as well as electron image adjustments (such as AGC, automatic gain control).

Camera makers commonly express exposure range in EV, the exposure value, a figure that represents all the combinations of shutters speeds and apertures that present the same amount of light to the film or image sensor. A one unit change in EV is equivalent to double the amount of light (or changing shutter speed or aperture by one full notch). To express the ability of a digital camera to cope with real-world scenes, the EV must be expressed as an equivalent ISO speed rating.

A value of EV 14 is equivalent to the classic "bright sunny day" at ISO 100. A digital camera with an exposure range of EV 5 to EV 16 can handle well-lit interiors to sunny skiing scenes.

Because the maximum aperture of modern zoom lenses changes with the focal length setting, the exposure range will similarly change. Consequently, some camera manufacturers will list the exposure range of their products both in wide (W) and telephoto (T) zoom settings.

Cameras face exposure range problems not only between scenes but also within scenes. Not all scenes are evenly lit. Some have spots that are very bright or dim. The difference between the brightest and dimmest part of a scene is its contrast ratio. Dealing with large contrast ratios is the most difficult challenge faced by any imaging technology.

Flash

No matter how sensitive a film or CCD is, none can find an image in absolute darkness. When it's truly dark, there are no photons available to register on film or CCD. To allow you to take photographs even when insufficient light is available, most point-and-shoot cameras (including the less inexpensive digital models) incorporate their own photon source—a flash. As the name implies, a flash unit makes a flash of bright light. Although once based on contained explosions sealed inside small light bulbs, today's flash units rely on the excitation of xenon gas to produce a brief but bright light pulse. The brevity of the flash allows the near-instant illumination to stop motion (the object illuminated can't move far during the brief pulse during which it is illuminated) much as a mechanical stroboscope apparently stops motion. Repeating flashes can thus operate as stroboscopes, too, and consequently some photographers call their xenon-based flash units strobes. Another common term is speedlight, probably created by anxious marketers wanting consumers to disregard the lengthy period required by their products to recharge between flashes.

When judging flash units or the flash incorporated into a camera, several issues are important. These include the guide number, exposure control, red-eye reduction, and possibility of external connections.

The guide number of a flash unit allows you to determine the aperture setting of your camera for proper exposure using the flash. Guide numbers depend on film speed, so you'll see them listed as something like "Guide number 50 with ASA 100 film." The guide numbers for the built-in flashes of digital cameras are calibrated to the sensitivity of the CCD, so they don't have to include an ASA number, although some manufacturers note the ASA equivalent.

Most of the time, you don't have to bother. All digital camera flashes are automatic. They are designed to provide just the right amount of light to properly illuminate your subject when taking a picture. The guide number is useful in that it allows you to determine the maximum distance at which your flash will be effective. But you'll usually see this distance listed in the specifications of your camera, so you don't even have to bother with the math.

Simple physics limits the range of any flash. Beams of light inevitably spread, no matter how hard engineers work to keep them concentrated. Even lasers spread out, and regular light doesn't fare nearly so well. As the light beam spreads, the same number of photons must spread over a larger area, leaving fewer of them in a given space, and fewer photons means dimmer light.

The worst case for this diminution of light intensity is the point source; light leaks off in every direction. In such situations, light follows the inverse square law. Its intensity diminishes as to the square of the distance. Move twice as far away from the light source, and its intensity is cut to a quarter. The reason is that as you travel linearly away from the light source, you've moving in one dimension. But the light gets spread out in two dimensions, high and wide, which translates to height times width.

The designers of flashes use reflectors and sometimes even lenses to control the spread of light. They don't want to minimize it because then you might get a thin but powerful pencil-like beam of light that would brightly illuminate a tiny dot on the subject you're photographing. Instead, designers tailor the spread of light to be approximately equal to the area the camera lens sees.

From the spread of light, you can deduce how much it diminishes with distance using simple trigonometry. Better still is to let the camera maker do the work and look at the value given for the maximum distance at which the flash is usable. This distance takes in not only the spread of the light beam but also its initial intensity and the minimum intensity needed to make a picture. It is the maximum working distance you can use with the flash and camera.

Focusing

All lenses must be focused to present a sharp image. At the point of focus, the light rays emanating from any point on the subject are brought back together again as a single point in the resulting image—or as close as possible to a single point. Rays of light (photons) leave the subject in many directions. A few of them strike the lens. The wider the lens aperture, the more of them the lens can collect. Then, the job of the curved surface of the lens is to nudge the photons in a new direction. The curve of the lens varies the nudging for the different angles at which the photons left the subject. The problem is that once the lens nudges the photons, they keep traveling straight. The photons from any given point will converge on a point at a distance from the lens. At greater or lesser distances than the point at which they all meet, they may be close together but are still spread apart in the shape of the aperture. When you focus a lens, you move the lens closer or farther from the film or image sensor to make the distance proper.

That's all well and good. You'd think that you'd be able to set the focus once and forget it. Light, alas, isn't so cooperative. The photons from the subject spread more the farther your lens is from the subject; the angle at which they strike the lens and the amount of corresponding nudge they get from the lens both change with the result the distance of the lens to the properly focused image changes.

You and your camera must compensate for these changes to make sharp pictures. *Conventional focusing*, the traditional way, is to move the lens closer or farther from the film or sensor. A more modern technique is *internal focusing*, which alters elements within the lens to change the alteration of angles between the elements—with exactly the same effect as moving the lens in relation to the film or sensor. Either technique works. The lens designer chooses which to use based on his own criteria.

From a more practical standpoint, the *means* by which the focus gets changed is more important. Three different types of focusing systems are possible: fixed focus, manual focus, and autofocus.

Fixed Focus

Fixed focus is not focusing at all. The lens itself and its distance to the film or sensor is physically fixed. As a result, a fixed focus lens creates a sharp image at only one distance to its subject. Everything else (and often just plain everything) is out of focus. Although this situation would seem highly undesirable and even unacceptable in a camera, fixed focus often works and is popular in inexpensive cameras.

Fixed focus works best when its shortcomings are hidden by other shortcomings in the camera system. If a lens never produces a truly sharp image, you'll never be able to tell when it is out of focus. Consequently, the limitations of inexpensive lenses cover up the lack of true focus.

The fixed focus system takes advantage of another optical property. Wider angle lenses make focusing less critical; consequently, most fixed focus lenses are a bit wider than "normal." In the realm of 35 millimeter photography (to which most lens-length comparisons are made), instead of a normal 50mm focal length, a fixed focus lens will be around 35mm.

A smaller aperture makes focusing less critical; consequently, fixed focus lens are rarely fast. A smaller aperture gives a lens greater depth of field because it cuts off the more divergent beams of photons that would have to be focused. A fixed focus lens takes advantage of this greater depth of field by eliminating the ability to focus. The fixed focus lens is actually focused at a moderate distance and depends on the depth of field of its small aperture to make greater and lesser distances *appear* to be in focus.

As long as you don't more than moderately magnify the image made by a fixed focus lens—for example, limiting the enlargement of a negative to 4 by 6 inches—you won't notice the slight out-of-focus nature of most of the images. Inexpensive digital cameras have low enough resolution that the out-of-focus properties of the image are lost in the other deficiencies of the system. These cameras cannot resolve enough detail to make any loss of focus apparent.

In short, fixed focus lenses depend on the concept of good enough. The images they make are good enough for the way they are normally displayed. If you don't want more than snapshot quality, they are good enough.

Autofocus

Short of cutting off vital parts of the anatomy (like heads or the tops thereof) the most common complaint during the golden days of chemical photography was that an image was blurred or out of focus. True blurring arises from moving the camera during exposure, a defect that is cured by image stabilization, as noted later.

A good autofocus system is more accurate than most people at adjusting the focus of a camera. Autofocus systems are generally faster at focusing than are mere human beings. And autofocus systems are more reliable. They do not forget to focus the camera before that once-in-a-lifetime shot.

On the other hand, people are more creative than autofocus systems. If you want to take more than mere snapshots, you'll probably want an autofocus system that you can defeat so you can manually adjust your camera's focus to suit your own artistic tastes.

Autofocus systems are either passive or active. *Passive autofocus* systems look at a scene and attempt to figure out what the correct focus is. *Active autofocus* systems work like radar or sonar. They send out a signal, usually infrared, watch for its reflections, and judge from the time elapsed between transmission and reception how far the signal traveled.

Both sorts of autofocus achieve their intended purpose, at least most of the time. Active systems can be fooled more easily, however. For example, Polaroid cameras use a very effective sonar-based autofocus system that's among the most accurate systems in use. But if your subject is behind a window, the sound waves from the sonar system bounce off the glass rather than the subject, so the camera focuses on the window and leaves the subject a blur. Moreover, active autofocus systems have a finite range. The sound or light they send out is effective only for a limited distance. For normal length lenses, that distance is the equivalent of infinity focus, so this shortcoming poses no problem. With long telephoto lenses, however, the active autofocus system may run out of range before the lens.

Passive autofocus systems work like the human visual system by trying to make lines sharp. To do so, the passive autofocus system requires something to focus on, a subject with a definite outline in high contrast. Without adequate image contrast, the autofocus system won't work. It is particularly susceptible to darkness because low light levels usually reduce contrast (less light means less overall range in brightness, which means less contrast). Passive systems don't work at all in the dark. Active systems have no problem with darkness.

Most autofocus systems for cameras don't bring objects into absolute focus. Rather, they have a stepped focus system that adjusts the lens to accommodate a range of distances for the subject. Cameras may have as few as three focus ranges or *steps*. More is better, but infinity is unnecessary.

White Balance

The *white balance* control of a camera allows you to adjust it for the varying *color temperature* of the scene that you wish to photograph. (You'll find a full discussion of color temperature in Chapter 18, "Displays.") Although color temperature is a complex concept, the effect of white balance is easy to judge. Most digital cameras have automatic white balance systems that adjust to the available light. Some digital cameras also let you make manually settings for sunny, cloudy, incandescent, fluorescent, and flash lighting conditions.

Image Storage

The film used in chemical photography provides two discrete functions. Not only does it sense and capture the original image, but it is also a storage system for the image. Once you capture something on film, it's there forever—or at least until the dyes fade or the film itself chemically deteriorates. Both forms of degradation have been reduced using modern materials so that the images you capture on film are likely to last longer—substantially longer—than you are.

The images that a CCD detects are not nearly so permanent. Unless you take some corrective action, they disappear nearly instantly. The corrective action your camera takes is to transfer the data gather by the CCD into solid-state memory. This expedient assures that the image won't disappear, at least as long as the memory works.

You probably don't want to keep all your images inside your camera.

Modern digital cameras combine their storage and transfer functions. Most use small *flash memory* cards to hold your images. These cards are removable so that you can quickly transfer the images, for example, sliding them into a reader connected to your PC. Today's digital cameras use one of two incompatible formats for their flash memory cards, either CompactFlash or SmartMedia. A third storage format developed by Sony, *MemoryStick*, will soon join the fray in products from Casio Computer, Fujitsu, Olympus Optical, Sanyo Electric, and Sharp. In addition, one brand of digital camera relies on floppy disks to store and transfer images. Earlier digital cameras and many lesser expensive models have built-in memory. That is, the flash memory chips are part of the camera's circuitry itself and cannot be removed. As long as the camera has sufficient capacity for your purposes, this built-in memory is not a problem. After all, you can just download the images from inside the camera into your PC and free up all the memory for reuse.

Because all of these media are removable, they also serve as a way to move images from your camera to your PC, either directly or through adapters. Physically moving a memory card or floppy disk is many times quicker than pushing files through a serial port; once you plug the card or disk into your PC, you can move the images at bus speed or disk speed instead of serial port speed. Although some of the latest digital cameras have high-speed USB or FireWire (sometimes called i.Link on cameras) ports for image transfer, moving files in bulk form on a card or disk still remains a convenient alternative.

At least one brand and series of products—Sony's Mavica—relies on conventional floppy disks as its primary image storage medium. Considering that the company credits itself with creating the 3.5-inch floppy disk format, the choice is understandable.

Floppy disk storage has several strong points for digital camera storage:

- **Familiarity** Floppy disks are like the Big Mac—familiar, the same the world over, and perhaps none too good for you. Among PCs, the floppy disk has long been the least common denominator. The medium and mechanisms have been around so long, manufacturers must have gotten them right. Anyone more hip than Rip van Winkle knows all he needs to know about floppy disks, including where to shove them.

- **Cost** If nothing else, floppy disks are cheap. They aren't just close to free. Without much effort, they can be free. Computer and office supplies dealers often make boxes of floppies loss leaders, not only low-priced but even free after a mail-in rebate. If you can't score a deal like that, you can always recycle old floppies such as those sent holding software trials or given you by friends. If you do have to stoop to paying for floppies, they should not cost more than a quarter each; that's about $.15 per megabyte. Compare that to the alternative, solid-state cards that run $10 per megabyte, and there is no comparison.

- **Compatibility** Floppy disks are one of the few universals in modern technology. Every PC has a drive slot, so you don't need extra adapters to move images from your camera to your PC. You don't have to tangle with cable nor wait while megabytes crawl through a slow serial connection.

But flash memory cards and sticks beat floppy disks for digital camera storage in several areas:

- **Capacity** Floppy disks have proven themselves inadequate to the task of regular PC storage because they no longer store enough to make them a worthwhile medium. Program and data files have just grown too much over the years. As camera resolutions increase, the ability of floppies to store a reasonable number of images becomes doubtful. As it stands, the floppy is successful in the Mavica chiefly because Sony has limited camera resolution to the VGA level. Today's XGA and better cameras come with card memory more than double the capacity of a floppy disk.

- **Reliability** A floppy disk has many moving parts—spinning disks, jogging heads—and anything moving is prone to stop moving. The mechanical aspects of the floppy drive inside a camera are the most failure prone, especially when you consider you will expect your camera to work under all sorts of adverse conditions, from gentle rain to raging blizzards. (What good is your camera if it fails you when you see Elvis in a parka?) Moreover, the floppy medium itself is far from trouble-free. Disks are vulnerable to all sorts of environmental dangers.

- **Power consumption** Spinning the motors that drive the floppy disk is the most energy-hungry part of digital cameras that use them. The battery life of such cameras will be demonstrably shorter than those using only solid-state storage. Moreover, spinning up the floppy adds its own bit of extra waiting in making an exposure.

As far as capacity is concerned, Sony's new HiFD disks, which store 200MB each, could give the medium a big edge in mobile image storage. But all the other drawbacks remain. The universal compatibility disappears. And no camera using the new format has yet been marketed.

Compression

Most digital cameras give you the option of storing your images at two or more quality levels, which trade good looks for more compact storage. Although some early digital cameras distinguished their quality levels by their actual resolution, more modern cameras operate at one or two basic resolutions and trade off higher compression for greater storage capacity. When decoded, the more highly compressed images yield lower quality—they typically look fuzzier—but nevertheless display at the basic resolution level of the camera.

The compression method of choice is JPEG, which stands for the Joint Photographic Experts Group, a committee that hammered out standards for the algorithms. JPEG is lossy compression, which means that some information gets sacrificed in the effort to shrink file size. The lost information can never be regained, so once an image is compressed, its original quality can never be restored.

At moderate levels of compression, the losses made by JPEG compression show up as a loss of image sharpness. However, if you examine a reconstructed JPEG image at high magnification, you can see patterns that arise from the compression algorithm. As you increase the JPEG compression ratio, these artifacts become obvious: The image loses definition and finally falls apart so that your eye can no longer make sense from it.

Nearly all graphic editors support the JPEG file format, so the use of JPEG compression is a positive feature of any digital camera. Be wary of any camera that uses a proprietary compression scheme that requires its own software to display or edit images.

The storage or operating modes of most modern digital cameras correspond to the degree of JPEG compression used. The best quality mode—often called exactly that—uses the least compression, typically file size reduction by about a factor of four. The next increment down may compress by a factor of 12. Economy or low-quality mode may compress by a factor of 36 or more. Alternately, the economy mode may ratchet resolution down by one giant notch.

In economy mode, some cameras may have a low-resolution mode in which images are stored at a resolution level lower than the native resolution of the image sensor. In most cases, this will be VGA resolution, 640 by 480. Each image at VGA resolution requires only one-quarter the storage of the 1,280 by 960 images typical of modern digital cameras (using the same degree of compression).

If your camera gives you a choice between high compression or low resolution for its economy mode, try them both. Each produces its own distinctive quality that becomes increasingly apparent as you magnify the image. Use the one most pleasing to you.

Viewfinders

The viewfinder is named after its function: It helps you find the view that you want to photograph. On still cameras, a viewfinder can be as simple as a frame that works like a gun sight or as complex an optical system as the Hubble Space Telescope. Today's digital cameras give you a direct preview of exactly (or nearly so) the image the camera will capture, devoid of peculiarities of old-fashioned film-based camera's viewfinders. (Under those black drapes, view camera photographers saw the world upside-down when framing pictures; those with waist-level viewfinders saw the world rightside-up but with left and right reversed.) In contrast, the viewfinder of a digital camera is direct and easy-to-use—but not without its own issues and concerns.

In photography, several terms have developed specialized meanings. A plain viewfinder does nothing but give you a view. It can be as simple as two frames that you line up to locate the image that the camera will picture. Digital cameras add *video viewfinders* or *LCD panels* to help you compose images.

Optical viewfinders use a combination of lenses that work like a telescope, giving you a view at a glance so you don't have to line up frames. The lenses are small and separate from the lens in the camera used to take the actual picture. Most inexpensive (under $1,000) digital cameras have optical viewfinders.

Strictly speaking, a *rangefinder* doesn't give you a view. It only tells you the distance to an object. A coupled rangefinder is connected to the focus of the camera lens so that as you adjust it to the proper range, it automatically sets the focus distance on the lens through a mechanical linkage. Rangefinders are unnecessary (at least camera makers think so) on modern autofocus cameras; the camera is faster and more accurate than you are, so why bother with an expensive rangefinder?

Modern *reflex cameras* use the camera lens as part of the viewfinder so you see the image seen by the lens. A mirror reflects the lens image up into the viewfinder, the reflection being the camera's reflex. As used in the photographic industry, a reflex viewfinder is any viewfinder that gains its image through the taking lens of the camera so that, as they say in desktop publishing, what you see is what you get. A reflex viewfinder does not have to offer a direct sight path through the taking lens but nevertheless shows what the taking lens sees. For example, the LCD panel on your camera is a reflex viewfinder in this sense.

A reflex viewfinder allows you to see the effects of zooms. Moreover, the reflex viewfinder gives you a detailed color image without the need for expensive color LCD displays or their associated circuitry. But because you don't see how the camera's electronics are affecting the image, you can only guess at effects such as fade-outs.

Optical reflex viewfinders do not depend on the camera's electronics. Instead, the viewfinder splits the lens image between the camera sensor and the viewfinder. You see the image produced by the lens as it is going into the camera. The SLR cameras of chemical photography—SLR stands for single-lens reflex cameras—allow you to peer through the taking lens of the camera by dropping a mirror in the pathway of the image. The mirror bounces the image through a prism or complex mirror system and into your eye. You see what the camera lens sees. When you take a picture, the mirror lifts up and out of the path of the lens so the image heads directly for the film.

LCD Panel Viewers

The LCD panels on digital cameras serve two purposes. They allow you to review the images that you've captured. In addition, they can let you preview the image before you capture it, acting as a supplemental viewfinder.

Conventional *video viewfinders* give you a small monitor to watch that's built into an ocular like a traditional movie camera viewfinder. The tiny screen—a small picture tube on older video cameras but usually an LCD panel in modern units—shows the image in stark monochrome along with warning lights and indicators. The miniature monitor lets you view all the effects the camera generates, even monitor tapes you've made.

Big-screen or *view-screen viewfinders* give you a larger LCD display meant to be watched like a television set instead of a pirate's telescope. It gives the best possible view of the image before and after recording. Using big-screen viewfinders can seem unnatural to anyone used to the peep-show method of previewing images in other camera formats.

Even though you may plan to use your digital camera solely to take still photographs, you need to be concerned about the moving image in the viewfinder and its frame rate. As with all video systems (and the viewfinder is actually just a dedicated video system), the frame rate determines how natural movements look on the screen. But your concern is not natural movement but fast updates. You need the screen to continuously adjust the image to reflect what the camera lens sees. If the screen does not update fast enough, the jerkiness of the image may make framing the scene more difficult. You might even lose that critical moment you want to photograph between screen updates.

As with video systems, 30 frames per second is sufficient for the appearance of continuous motion. You can probably make do with half that rate. Slower display systems are apt to be bothersome at best, possibly frustrating.

In framing a shot, the only image display you'll want is a full-screen view of what your camera sees. But when you review the photos that you've taken, you'll find that additional viewing modes are helpful. You'll want a digital camera that supports several viewing modes. Some of these include single image mode, multiple image mode, and slide show mode:

Single Image What you see is what you get is the basic function of the viewfinder in review mode. In single image mode, that's all you see—a one-shot view. Most cameras will let you set through all of the images that you've exposed so that you can look at them one at a time. Although you can't compare shots (except in your mind), you will see the greatest possible level of detail. Single image mode is the basic viewing mode for digital cameras in review mode and usually the only preview view.

Slide Show Long before we had home videos to bore our friends and neighbors through wintry evenings, God gave us the slide show. You'd drag out a rolled-up screen that never properly unrolled, plug in the projector, and flash side after slide, one at a time, on the screen. The slide show mode of a digital camera's electronic viewfinder operates similarly, a one-after-another display of the images in its memory. This mode allows you to briefly view all the photos you've captured before deciding to chuck them all and start over.

The slide show lets you assess the mass of your work in full detail. At that, it can be quite useful in making a quick evaluation of your technical prowess. As with the presentation of single images, it does not allow you to make quick comparisons.

Multiple Image In multiple image mode—sometimes called thumbnail mode—your camera breaks its viewfinder into a matrix of individual images, typically an array of four or nine. Although each image is a fraction of its individual size (one quarter or one ninth), this mode allows you to make side-by-side comparisons. You can pick out an image to keep or trash in one quick glance. This mode is particularly useful when you urgently need more memory and want to eliminate wasted shots to gain memory space.

Zoom The small screen and low pixel count in digital camera LCD displays can make checking image details difficult. Consequently, many cameras incorporate a electronic zoom mode in their viewfinder systems. Typically, this mode will let the

LCD panel display one pixel for each pixel in the captured image, which magnifies the image by a factor of two to four. Although you cannot see the entire image at one time, you can usually pan across its width and height to check each pixel. If you're critical about the images you take, you'll want zoom mode. For ordinary snapshots, however, you may find it unnecessary and may not miss the feature in a camera that lacks it.

If you plan only to use your LCD panel to review images, you don't much care about where it is on your camera. You can just tilt the camera to the viewing angle you prefer. If, however, you want to use the panel as a viewfinder, the mounting of the LCD is decidedly important. It must be located so you can view it conveniently while pointing the camera lens at your subject. Not all digital cameras have LCD panels that let you do this conveniently.

A common location for the LCD panel is on the back of the camera. That's fine for reviews, but previews force you to hold the camera a foot or so in front of your face to compose images. It's not exactly the natural way to take a photograph.

Adjustable panels allow you to swivel the LCD to whatever position is most comfortable for you to view it. In particular, you can tilt it upward so that it functions as a waist-level viewfinder, which many professional photographers prefer, particularly for portrait photography.

Connections

The chief reason to shift to digital photography is to have images ready for use in computer applications. With the images already in digital form, you need bother with no intermediary steps such as photo processing. The only challenge is getting the image from the camera into your computer.

This need creates several concerns in buying a digital camera—platform compatibility, interface, video output, and connectors. Failure to match any of these to your hardware will make your images more difficult to use, if not unusable.

Platform Compatibility

When digital camera makers talk about platforms, they mean the combination of your PC and its operating system. The need for compatibility with your particular platform arises not from the camera hardware itself—a digital camera is a stand-alone imaging device—but from the software you need to run to transfer the images from the camera to your PC.

As with any other software, the primary requirement is matching your operating system. Most digital cameras will come with software that works with all popular operating systems, typically separate programs for the Windows family (including Windows 95, Windows 98, and Windows NT) and the Macintosh. The software may require a specific version of the operating system, such as NT version 4.0 or later or Mac OS 7.1 or later.

The image transfer software will also make its own demands for disk space and memory. The disk requirements do not include any consideration of archive space, so if you're planning to store your digital images, you'd better reserve a few gigabytes. Better still, invest in a CD-R drive so that you can make permanent copies of your images on the long-lasting CD medium.

Interface

Downloading images from camera to PC also requires some kind of connection. Among current digital cameras, four interfaces are popular—standard serial, USB serial, FireWire (also known as IEEE 1394 and i.Link), and PC Card.

The standard serial connection accommodates the widest range of PC but is also the slowest connection in general use. A so-called "high-speed" serial interface in the PC realm operates at a speed of 115,200 bits per second, a rate that may demand 10 minutes to download the contents of a modest-size camera memory. The Mac world fares a bit better; the standard serial interface on the Mac can accept information about 8 times faster, 921 kilobits per second.

Some newest digital cameras take advantage of the Universal Serial Bus port design. This interface, which is standardized across computer platforms, operates at about 12 megabits per second—fast enough to empty a memory card in a few seconds. USB is the preferred connection system for state-of-the-art digital cameras. Of course, your PC or Mac will need a USB port to plug into, and older computer models may lack one. You can always add a USB port as an expansion card.

Making USB function effectively also requires software support, however. Although USB support is built into Windows 98, Windows 95 includes only add-on USB support and even that is only part of release 2 of the operating system. For your Mac, you'll want OS 8.0 or newer.

Although the IEEE 1394 interface has not lived up to its expectations as a general-purpose connection system, the digital imaging world has embraced it fondly under the names FireWire and i.Link. It is the connection of choice for digital video systems and a growing number of digital cameras. It's even faster than USB (by almost an order of magnitude) and eventually should be nearly as convenient (although support is not built into any operating system as yet).

The last interface available with many digital cameras takes advantage of the removability of their card-based flash memory. Although many early digital cameras had "built-in" memory—a way of saying "non-removable" with a more positive spin—you should demand removable storage on any new camera so you can also use it as a file interchange medium.

Video Output

Another way to get images from a digital camera to your PC is as video. Many digital cameras have video outputs that allow you to use them as video cameras with any standard video accessories such as monitors and VCR. If your PC has a video input or a video capture system, you can also transfer images in the form of video signals. Digital still cameras with video outputs usually provide motion picture video images at their outputs. Note, however, that the quality of image available through a video output is always lower (usually substantially so) than you get with other connection systems. The actual quality depends on the video interface provided by the camera.

NTSC

The most common video signal from digital cameras and the one with lowest quality is the standard *NTSC signal*, described more fully in Chapter 16, "The Display System." Better camcorders and video accessories use *S-video* connections. Although not as high in quality as transferring images digitally, S-video currently offers the best means of transferring analog video images in real-time. S-video connections are consequently desirable on any digital camera.

Connectors

At its best, the digital camera is a completely self-contained image-capturing system, no strings—and no wires—attached. You need nothing, least of all cables and connections, to make it work.

That's an ideal world, perhaps. But you still have to get the images out of the camera. And if you want to keep battery expenses in check during your studio work, you'll want to plug into the power line. All of these link-ups require making a connection with your camera.

The earliest digital cameras used simple serial ports, which made for mighty slow transfers. Because standard serial connectors are large and most digital cameras small, many manufacturers opted for non-standard connectors for these ports, which makes replacement cables expensive and difficult to find. Newer digital cameras are migrating to the USB system, which overcomes these problems.

Power

Digital cameras are electronic devices and consequently need a steady supply of electricity. With today's technologies, their needs border on the prodigious and often sneak to the far side of the border. That power has to come from somewhere, and the places of choice are two—from self-contained batteries or from utility-supplied electricity through an external transformer, the ubiquitous power brick.

Batteries

Unlike camcorders, the batteries for most digital cameras are standard sizes. Most digital cameras use standard AA or AAA batteries, typically about four (the number needed to get enough voltage for conventional logic circuits). Most manufacturers generously include batteries with their products.

Unlike camcorders, most digital cameras use standard-size batteries as rechargeables—again those ordinary AA and AAA sizes. Although nickel-based rechargeables (nicads and NiMH batteries) do not produce as much voltage as ordinary alkaline cells (a nominal 1.2 volts for nickel-based batteries versus 1.5 for alkalines), the nickel cells have higher current capacities and work well meeting the extreme demands of digital cameras. Most digital cameras are, in fact, designed to accommodate a range of voltages, typically from 4.8 volts (four nickel cells) to 6.0 volts (four alkalines).

Some cameras include rechargeable batteries. Most allow the use of rechargeable batteries, although they lack the provisions for actually charging the batteries. The economics of the rechargeable choice are personal to you. In the long run, rechargeables are more economical and make more sense environmentally. But they are not as convenient as slipping in a set of batteries when you need them, and the initial price can be forbidding.

Note that digital cameras are noted for their prodigious appetite for batteries when you switch on their LCD viewfinders. With some cameras, you may be lucky to make 12 exposures and download them on a single set of batteries. These needs make another good argument for rechargeables.

AC Power

Nearly all digital cameras make provisions for plugging in an AC adapter. Many, however, make the AC adapter an option—often an expensive option. Personally, I think that's almost criminal considering the power needs of some cameras. I would recommend boycotting manufacturers that don't include an AC adapter with their products, which would cut your camera choices to about zero. So you're stuck buying the AC adapter. Just be sure to figure its cost into the total price you end up paying for your camera.

Physical Issues

Although the end product of photography—the image—is the most important consideration in choosing a camera, you can't ignore the physical entity of the camera itself. You have to hold the camera in your hands to use it—or to screw it on a tripod to use it (whether you can is another issue to consider). Indeed, the physical reality of the camera is something you'll grow to love or loathe regardless of the quality of the images it captures.

What follows is essentially a verbal checklist of physical issues you should consider in making your choice of digital cameras.

Dimensions

Those advertising pictures that show your favorite camera candidate suspended in air and surrounded with an angelic halo mislead more than inform. Without context, you have no idea how big the blasted camera really is and whether it will fit into your hands or require an auxiliary crane to carry about. Some supposedly compact digital cameras are bigger than you might think. It's best to check the spec sheet before you make up your mind. Better still, wrap your hands around the model you favor and be sure it's a good fit for your grip before a surprise of bulk turns your joy of ownership into an eternal gripe.

Weight

There's less air in a digital camera, so the compact models tend to be heavier than their conventional equivalents. Don't be surprised if the little thing weighs more than you expect or threatens to slice through your neck thanks to the thin, coarse strap the manufacturer supplies that the swinging camera turns into a hacksaw.

Controls

Although digital cameras typically have fewer controls than, say, the space shuttle, they are often just as perplexing. A camera may have only a switch and a couple buttons, but those few do-dads may command dozens of functions using a menu system designed by someone with less command of the English language than an engineer. You may never understand all the functions—or want to.

You should at least be able to reach them. That's the first rule. Make sure the controls on the camera are compatible with your hands. Make sure you can reach all the buttons and switches without a flashlight and magnifying glass. Make sure you can push the buttons without a specially designed, $10 option, pointed stick. And make sure you can understand what the labels mean and whether they have any relevance to what the controls really do.

Although the advice sound repetitive, it's still and always true: There's no other way to be sure other than actually trying out each camera before you buy.

Tripod Mount

Trivial as it may seem, a hole for screwing a digital camera into a tripod is a useful feature. Certainly many, if not most, digital cameras will be used for snapshots. Most people put cameras on tripods only for getting the sharpest in quality from their exposures, and the limited resolution of digital cameras inherently constrains sharpness. But there is another reason for a tripod mount: Digital cameras are inherently excellent *video* cameras. Even low-end digital cameras have resolution abilities well beyond most camcorders. Even digital camcorders fall short of better digital cameras. A good digital camcorder boasts 300,000 to 500,000 pixels in its CCD. With a digital camera, you can get 1,200,000 to 1,500,000 pixels for about half the price.

Of course, the digital camera lacks any provision for recording. But you can stream video to a PC with an MPEG encoder to capture video as well as any digital camcorder. You'll need a high-speed interface such as IEEE 1394 (also known as FireWire or I.link) to move the data from camera to PC.

With a tripod adapter, your digital camera then becomes a television camera that boasts specs as good as studio models. Choose a video-style tripod with fluid panning, and you'll be in the video production business.

The shortcoming of a digital camera for this purpose is the zoom of the lens. You'll be lucky to get 3x zoom in a digital camera. A digital camcorder might, once you allow for all the digital and optical zoom options, boast 100x zooming.

Lens Capping

As with all cameras, the lenses of digital cameras are vulnerable to a number of woes. Dust and fingerprints on the lens surface can impair image quality temporarily—until you get time to clean them off. Scratches permanently impair image quality. Even faint, light scratches, called cleaning marks by used equipment dealers, reduce contrast and sharpness subtly.

The cure for lens damage is replacement—of the whole camera if the lens is not removable. A better idea is prevention, protecting the lens from damage and, incidentally, from dust and fingerprints.

The first line of defense is the lens cap, a cover that puts a barrier between the lens and physical trauma. Working against ordinary lens caps is the inconvenience of snapping them on and off. With point-and-shoot cameras, manufacturers have created a number of self-capping designs that automatically slide a cover over the lens when you turn the camera off or put it away, sliding the cover away and revealing the lens automatically when you put it into action.

Digital camera makers haven't yet learned this lesson. Although many digital cameras are patterned after the point-and-shoot model, few are self-capping. Camera makers don't even include conventional lens caps with many of their products. You're left to find a lens cap yourself—if you can find one that fits—or venture into hard reality unprotected.

Professional photographers often put a clear glass filter on their camera lenses as a semi-permanent lens cap that they don't have to take on and off. Others use UV (ultraviolet) or skylight (faint pink) filters for the same purpose. You can do the same with your digital camera if you can find filters that fit your camera.

The Display System

Your PC's display system allows you to see exactly what your PC is doing as it works. Because it gives you instant visual feedback, the display system makes your PC interactive. The display system also affects the speed of your PC and your pleasure (or pain) in using your machine. PCs use a number of different technologies in creating their displays, and the choice determines what you see, how sharply you see it, and how quickly the image appears. This chapter presents an overview of PC display technology; the next two cover the devices that put this technology to work.

Basic display system features

Feature	In Short
Teletype text mode	Displays pre-formed characters (and primitive graphics built from characters) in strict serial order only. Your PC boots in teletype text mode, and HTML text is displayed much in a teletype-like mode.
Character-mapped mode	Allows positioning text and graphic characters anywhere on the screen.
Bit-mapped graphics mode	Allows your PC to control every pixel on the screen individually. Windows and all of its applications run in bit-mapped mode.
2D acceleration	Allows the graphic subsystem to draw ordinary images (such as presentation graphics) independently from your PC's microprocessor, which speeds up screen updates.
3D acceleration	Allows the graphic subsystem to add depth effects to your graphics using hardware separate from your microprocessor, giving fast, realistic displays. Nearly all PC graphics systems now used 3D acceleration.
Video overlay	Allows your graphics system to combine video images from a separate source (which may be inside your PC) with the graphics it draws so you can see video in an onscreen window (without imposing the burden of video regeneration on your PC microprocessor).
MPEG decoding	Allows your PC to regenerate video images from compressed files; hardware decoding works independently from your microprocessor to speed up (and improve the quality) of resulting video images.

Seeing is believing. If you couldn't see the results of your calculations or language manipulations, the personal computer would be worthless as a tool. You need some way of viewing the output of the computer system to know what it has done and why you're not wasting your time feeding it data.

Although every PC worth using today paints an image of Windows across a display screen akin a television set, nothing about computers or even information technology demands an image anything like what you get. Nowhere is it written that you must see what your computer does. After all, the computers in your car work invisibly, nursing your car along without revealing a single thought (unless to complain with a "Check engine" light). Rather than paint you a picture, your PC could talk to you; speech synthesis, in fact, gives computers a voice that can open a new world to the visually impaired.

Out of all the potential technologies for giving you feedback about what your computer is doing, the one almost universal choice is the one you see on your screen. It's entirely visual. More specifically, it is a color bitmapped graphic image on a video display system. That description is intentionally specific. Each word is important because it represents a pragmatic choice among many technologies. What you see is bitmapped rather than character-based, graphic rather than text-based; color rather than monochrome; video rather printed on paper or stroked across a vector screen.

The chosen few technologies do not have a monopoly, however. The challengers make appearances more often than you might suspect. You'll find the future still holds a lot of the past. Log onto the Internet, for example, and your PC will work hard to convert character-based signals more suited to an ancient teletype machine into a bitmapped form that will fit on your screen.

In practice, the total entity made from these technologies is your PC's *display system*. At the hardware level, it comprises two distinct parts. The *display* is the screen you see, either as a separate monitor or as a panel that's a permanent part of your PC. The display adapter, which may be a separate expansion board or built into your system's motherboard, converts the logical signals in your PC to the form digestible by the display. Each of these hardware devices is important enough to earn its own chapter—the two following this one.

In this chapter, we'll take a look at the technologies behind the screens, how your PC conceives its visual output, how it organizes visual information, how it stores that information, and how it sends it along to the rest of the display system.

Background

PC displays were not always this good—and they are not always as good as they can be. The roots of the high-resolution screen with vivid, moving 3D graphics are humble, indeed. They reach back to the uncertain first days of computers—a time before monitors, even before monitor technology was developed. Even today, when stripped of its software, a PC display system is a homely thing, designed for nothing more than pasting white text on a black screen—or, as was the case with the first PCs, green on black. On its own, your PC thinks in text alone and even that in not a very aesthetic way. The words it generates have the same old clunky monospaced characters as an old-fashioned typewriter.

Fortunately, PC display systems are amenable to dressing up, loading software that gives them spectacular graphic abilities. The key to that is the graphic environment, part of today's modern operating systems. The software—actually, layer upon layer of it—tells your PC how to paint pictures and do a job good enough that Rembrandt would be amazed (if just the PC alone wouldn't do it for a 17th century artist).

Teletype Output

The starting point for PC display systems must be the computer. When engineers ushered Harvard Mark I in 1943, there was no such thing as a computer monitor. Television itself was little more than a bluish dream in the minds of broadcasters, barely off to a flickery black-and-white start (the first commercial licenses went into effect in July 1941) and then put on hold for the years of World War II. The first computers were mechanical devices that had no ports or even electrical signals for linking up to embryonic TVs. Consequently, these first data processing machines shared the same output technology that was used by their predecessor, the mechanical adding machine—printed paper. The telegraph industry had long before figured out how to actuate the keys of a typewriter to electrical control, creating the first electrical printer called the *teletype*.

Developed to convey words and numbers across continents, the teletype took electrical codes and converted them to keystrokes that printed characters on paper. The classic teletype merely relayed keystrokes made on one keyboard to the distant printer, sort of like a stretched, transcontinental typewriter. The computer added a novel twist: A machine created the keystrokes from scratch instead of merely registering the finger presses of a human. These early computers fed characters to the teletype printer the same way as if they had begun at some different keyboard—one character at a time in a long series.

Teletypes had a long association with early computers. Even today, the data that's sent by a computer to its output device as a string of printable characters is still termed *teletype output*. The character string, if converted to the correct code, would run a mechanical teletype happily through reams of coarse paper.

Video Terminals

Although the teletype has reached a status somewhere between endangered species and museum piece, the teletype output method of data transmission and display still does service to today's high-tech toys. Instead of hammering away at paper, however, these machines send their character strings at the electronic equivalent of the teletype, the computer terminal. These terminals are often called *Video Data Terminals* (sometimes Video Display Terminals), or VDTs, because they rely on video displays to make their presentations to you. They are terminal because they reside at the end of the communications line, in front of your eyes.

A terminal at its most rudimentary is the classic *dumb terminal*. This device is mentally challenged not only by its lack of processing abilities but also in the way it displays what you see. It puts each character on its screen exactly as it is received through the umbilical cable linking it to its computer host. It's teletype printing on a phosphor coated screen instead of paper. The refinements are few; instead of rattling off the edge of the paper, a too-long electronic line more likely will "wrap" or scroll down to the line below. The terminal never runs out of paper; it seemingly has a fresh supply of blank screen below that rolls upward as necessary to receive each additional line. Alas, the output it generates is even more tenuous than the flimsiest tissue and disappears at the top of the screen, perchance never to be seen again.

The brains in a *smart terminal*, on the other hand, allow it to recognize special commands for formatting its display and may even be able to do some computer-like functions on its own. In fact, today's highly regarded *Network Computer* is little more than a smart terminal with a more powerful processor and a new name meant to erase old, bad memories. Despite its brain power, the smartest of terminals (and even NCs) are often relegated to working as ordinary dumb terminals and simply relaying characters and commands to their screens.

A few other characteristics that distinguish the operation of a mechanical teletype are carried over into the display of teletype output on video terminals. The paper on which the teletype prints upon moves but in one direction. Neither the paper nor the output of the teletype ever goes backwards. Like a stock ticker, the teletype merely churns out an unending string of text. The teletype cannot type over something it did before, and it cannot jump ahead without patiently rolling its paper forward as if it has printed so many blank lines.

In the electronic form of the computer terminal, the teletype method of text-handling means that when one character changes on the screen, a whole new screen full of text must be generated and sent to the terminal. The system cannot back up to change the one character, so it must rush headlong forward, reworking the whole display along the way.

Mammoth primeval computers and rattling teletypes might seem to share little in common with the quiet and well-behaved PC sitting on your desk. The simplest of programs, however, still retain this most primitive way of communicating with your video screen. They generate characters and send them one by one to the video display, only instead of traveling across the globe, the text merely shuffles from one place in memory to another inside the machine. These programs in effect operate as if the video system of your computer was the screen of a terminal that mimics an age-old teletype.

BIOS Support

This method of display is understandably often called a *teletype display*, and it is the basic display mode even in modern PCs. Teletype display technology is a vestige of PC ancestry that's used both by rudimentary programs and sophisticated email systems.

On its own, a teletype display is the only kind of image a PC can generate. It is the highest level of support provided by the system BIOS in most PCs and is thus required to make a PC a PC.

The basic PC BIOS gives several layers of teletype output. In the most primitive, a program must load one character at a time into a microprocessor register, issue a *video interrupt*—specifically, Interrupt 010(Hex)—and wait while the microprocessor checks where to put the character (a several step process in itself), pushes the character into the appropriate place in memory, and finally returns to the program to process the next character. The most advanced teletype mode lets a program put an entire line of text on the screen through a similar, equally cumbersome process.

In basic teletype mode, characters are written on the screen from left to right, from screen top to bottom, merely scrolling after each line is full or ended with a carriage return. More advanced display technologies are able to write anywhere on the monitor screen using formatting instructions much as smart terminals do. For example, commands in the PC BIOS let your programs locate each character anywhere on the screen.

HTML

The great advance made in communications by the Internet has at its heart teletype technology. Your PC displays basic Web text in teletype style—one character at a time as if it came as part of a string from a teletype. The chief difference between what came across the teletype wire and through your Internet connection is the code. Teletypes used Baudot; the Web uses *Hypertext Markup Language*, HTML, layered upon the ordinary ASCII code that specifies individual letters.

HTML uses the processing power of the PC to improve on basic teletype technology. Certainly, it's quieter. Unlike a teletype machine, your screen does not chatter like the teeth of a freezing epileptic. More importantly, the HTML character stream includes formatting codes that allow it to specify type size and faces, even colors. Although your PC still pops each character on your screen in the order it appears in the HTML string, it can make changes in the appearance of each character based on the in-stream codes.

The codes act as switches. When one appears in the data stream, it switches on a text feature—for example, turning the text red. All later text gets displayed in red until another HTML code turns it off or sets another color.

Some HTML codes affect the formatting of characters displayed on your PC's screen, for example, indenting lines. This formatting is relative rather than absolute. Its effects vary depending on the size and shape of your Web display. For example, a simple tab might take up half a column in a narrow window on your display or a few character widths in a wide one. In this way, HTML operates like a teletype; the characters in the HTML stream come out without regard to the size or shape of the display medium.

More recent revisions to HTML allow the Web to go beyond minimally formatted text. Tables allow you to create more structure in your text displays. In addition, you can embed streams of images with your text characters. Even these elements, however, are handled like the letters and numbers relayed to an old teletype display. In other words, old ideas don't die. They just go online.

Character Technologies

The most notable aspect of teletype technology is that it is *character oriented*. The smallest unit of information it deals with is a text character. At the times when your PC steps back to this technology of yesteryear—for example, the first few moments of booting up, before it spins its disks to load the basic code of your operating system, or when you read your email—your computer lets you see its world only in terms of letters and numbers.

Somehow, your PC must organize the characters it wants to display. Teletype machines handle this matter mechanically. They simply stamp each character on a piece of paper. The typing automatically organizes the text and an inky image preserves it. Your PC isn't so lucky. It has to organize the text in electronic form, it has to be able to move the character representations around inside its circuitry, and it has to keep the characters you see glowing on a screen that would rather remain permanently black.

Your system has two alternative ways of dealing with the characters it wants to put on your screen. It can store and manipulate them in the form of individual characters. Or it can break the characters down into tiny pieces called a *bitmap*, in which each piece represents one of the bright dots appearing on your computer display. Your PC uses both of these technologies every day. Although Windows treats your entire display screen as one giant bitmap, applications running under Windows often send information to the operating system to display in character form.

Character Mapping

When your PC deals with characters as a fixed unit, one code per indivisible character, it uses a technology termed *character mapping*. The name refers to the character map, a special range of addresses that's sometimes called screen memory or display memory. The memory of the character map is reserved for storing the characters that will appear on the screen. Simple programs such as your PC's bootup BIOS routines write text on the screen by pushing bytes into the proper places in that memory. Just as a street on a roadmap corresponds to the location of a real street, each byte of display memory corresponds to a character position on the screen.

The most common operating mode of the character-mapped display systems used by PCs divide the screen into a matrix (essentially a set of pigeon holes with each hole corresponding to one position on the screen) that measures 80 characters wide and 25 high. To display a character on the screen, a program loads the corresponding code into the memory location associated with its matrix cell. To put the image on the screen, the display system reads the entire matrix, translates it into a serial data stream that scans across the monitor screen, and moves the data to the video output. In other words, it creates the exact bit-pattern that will appear on the screen on-the-fly, computing each nanosecond of the video signal in real-time. From there, the signal is the monitor's problem.

For your programs, writing characters to the screen is simply a matter of writing directly to screen memory. Consequently, this display technique is often called direct writing. It is the fastest way to put information on a PC screen. Character mapping is also more versatile than teletype technology. Programs can push characters into any screen location in any order that they please—top, bottom, left, or right, even lobbing one letter atop another, overwriting the transitory existence of each.

Once an advanced operating system like Windows loads, however, your PC steps away from character mapping. The operating system imposes itself between your programs and the BIOS. The operating system captures the characters your text-oriented programs attempt to fling directly at the screen. The operating system then recomputes the map, making it larger or smaller and, in the latter case, moving it to a designated area of the screen.

This versatility makes character mapping fast. When PCs had hardly enough power to figure out they were switched on, character-mapped applications gave the fastest possible displays. Screen updates sped by quickly because the system used direct access to the screen and did not go through the multiple steps required by the teletype routines of the BIOS. Moreover, only the character (or characters) needing to be changed had to be pushed into place. Once a character was pushed into the display memory matrix, it stayed there until changed by the program that put it there—or any other software that reached into that area of memory.

Direct Writing

This quick way of putting characters on the screen is often termed *direct writing* because programs simply move the code assigned to a character directly to the memory location corresponding to that character's screen position—a one-step process that requires only one microprocessor instruction.

Direct writing makes a specific demand from programs using it: They need to know the exact location of each screen memory address. For all applications to work on all PCs, the addresses used by each system must be the same—or there needs to be some means of determining what addresses are used. The designers of the first PC reserved two *character buffers*, blocks of addresses (one for color text, one for monochrome) in High DOS Memory for holding characters for screen memory. Although these locations never became an official standard, software writers found direct writing to these locations to be the only way to get acceptable speed from their software. The industry's reliance on these addresses made them into unofficial standards with which no manufacturer bothers to tamper. It also complicated the lives of the programmers writing new operating systems; capturing direct writes to memory is more complex than intercepting BIOS calls.

In basic text modes, your PC uses one set of screen memory addresses when it is operating in color and the other set when in monochrome. To determine which mode your system is currently using, the PC BIOS provides a special flag—called the *video mode flag*, although originally termed the video equipment flag—located at absolute memory location 0463(Hex).

When the video mode flag is set to 0D4(Hex), your system is running in color and the chain of addresses starting at 0B8000(Hex) is used for text screen memory. In monochrome, the flag is set to 0B4(Hex) to indicate the use of addresses starting at 0B0000(Hex). For compatibility reasons, all newer PC video systems are also capable of operating through these same addresses even though they may store additional video information elsewhere. These address ranges are off limits to programs and for storing the BIOS code of expansion boards.

Character Boxes

In text modes, the display memory addresses hold codes that have nothing to do with the shapes appearing on the monitor screen except as a point of reference. The actual patterns of each character that appears on the screen are stored in a special ROM chip called the *character ROM* that's part of the video circuitry of the computer. The code value that defines the character is used by the video circuitry to look up the character pattern that matches it. The bit-pattern from the character ROM is scanned and sent to the screen to produce the final image.

Modern display adapters allow you to download your own fonts (typefaces) into on-board RAM that's reserved from the same block that would serve as the character map. These downloaded fonts can be used as if they were located in ROM with the same ease of manipulation as ROM-based fonts. Downloaded fonts appear just the same whether pushed on the screen through the teletype or direct-access technique.

Each onscreen character is made from an array of dots, much like the text output of a teletype or dot-matrix printer. PC and display adapter manufacturers use several video standards to build individual characters out of different size dot arrays. The framework in which the dots of an individual character are laid out, called the *character box*, is a matrix like a crossword puzzle. The character box is measured by the number of dots or cells comprising its width and its height. For example, Figure 16.1 shows a series of characters formed in character boxes measuring 15 by 9 cells.

The text modes used by various early display standards all had their own, distinctive character boxes. The standard Video Graphics Array (VGA) text screen uses a 9-by-16 character box. Each character takes up a space on the screen measuring 9 dots wide and 16 dots high. Other operating modes and display systems use character boxes of different sizes. Earlier standards include Monochrome Display Adapter, which used a character box measuring 9 by 14; Color Graphics Adapter, which used 8 by 8; and the Enhanced Graphics Adapter, 8 by 14.

FIGURE 16.1

Characters each formed in a 9-by-15 cell box.

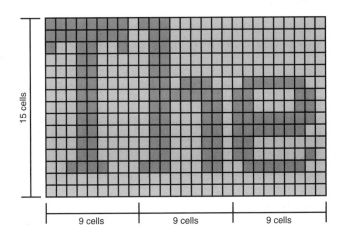

The last vestige of character mode display technology that remains under Windows 95 and 98 is its DOS box. (In Windows NT, the equivalent is *command mode*.) You can select the height and width of the character box used in the DOS box to adjust the size of the windows in which your character-based applications run in text mode. From the box, Windows 95 comes with a selection of character box sizes you can select from. The Microsoft Plus! utility adds several more.

You can change the size of the character box in windowed DOS mode from the tool bar on your DOS window or from the properties screen for your application. Make your selection from the left-most entry on the tool bar. Click on the down arrow, and Windows will show you the character box sizes available to you with a display like that in Figure 16.2.

FIGURE 16.2

Selecting a character box for a windowed DOS box.

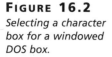

The size of the character box does not exactly describe how large each character is or how many dots are used in forming it. To improve readability, individual characters do not necessarily take up the entire area that a character box affords. For instance, text characters on most monochrome displays keep one row of dots above and one below those used by each character to provide visible separation between two adjacent lines of text on the screen.

Video Attributes

The character-mapped displays of most PC video systems do not store each letter adjacent to the next. Instead, each onscreen character position corresponds to every other byte in screen memory; the intervening bytes are used as *attribute bytes*. Even numbered bytes store character information; odd bytes, attributes.

The attribute byte determines the highlighting or color of displayed character that's stored in the preceding memory byte. The codes used in monochrome and color displays are different. Monochrome characters are allowed the following attributes: normal, highlighted (brighter onscreen characters), underlined, and reserve-video characters (dark on light instead of the normal light on dark). The different attributes can be combined, although in the normal scheme of things, highlighted reverse-video characters make the character background brighter instead of highlighting the character shape itself. These monochrome display attributes are listed in Table 16.1.

TABLE 16.1 Monochrome Display Attributes

Byte Value	Attribute
00	Non-display
01	Underline
07	Normal
09	Intensified underline

Background

Byte Value	Attribute
0F	Intensified
71	Reverse video underline
77	Reverse video
79	Reverse video intensified underline
7F	Reverse video intensified
81	Blinking underline
87	Blinking normal
89	Blinking intensified underline
8F	Blinking intensified
F1	Blinking reverse video underline
F7	Blinking reverse video
F9	Blinking intensified reverse video underline
FF	Blinking intensified reverse video

Color systems store two individual character hues in the attribute byte. The first half of the byte (the most significant bits of the digital code of the byte) code the color of the character itself. The latter half of the attribute (the least significant bits) code the background color. Because four bits are available for storing each of these colors, this system can encode 16 foreground and 16 background colors for each character (with black and white considered two of these colors). In normal operation, however, one bit of the background color code indicates a special character attribute—blinking. This attribute allows any color combination to blink but also cuts the number of hues available for backgrounds in half (to eight colors—all intensified color choices eliminated). When you or your software needs to be able to display a full 16 background colors, a status bit allows the character flashing feature to be defeated. Color display attributes are shown in Table 16.2.

TABLE 16.2   Color Display Attributes

Nibble Value	Foreground Color	Background Color	Flashing
0	Black	Black	No
1	Blue	Blue	No
2	Green	Green	No

continues

TABLE 16.2 Continued

Nibble Value	Foreground Color	Background Color	Flashing
3	Red	Red	No
4	Cyan	Cyan	No
5	Magenta	Magenta	No
6	Brown	Brown	No
7	Light gray	Light gray	No
8	Dark gray	Black	Yes
9	Bright blue	Blue	Yes
A	Bright green	Green	Yes
B	Pink	Red	Yes
C	Bright cyan	Cyan	Yes
D	Bright magenta	Magenta	Yes
E	Yellow	Brown	Yes
F	White	Light gray	Yes

Because each character on the screen requires two bytes of storage, a full 80-character column by 25-character row of text (a total of 2,000 characters) requires 4,000 bytes of storage. In the basic PC monochrome video system, 16KB are allotted to store character information. The basic (and basically obsolete) color system reserved 64KB for this purpose.

Video Pages

The additional memory does not go to waste, however. It can be used to store more than one screen of text at a time, with each separate screen called a video page. Either basic video system is designed to quickly switch between these video pages so that onscreen images can be changed almost instantly. Switching quickly allows a limited degree of animation. The technique is so useful that even today's most advanced 3D graphics boards use it, although with pictures instead of text.

Two-Dimensional Graphics

Graphics are such a central part of the displays of all modern computers that it's hard to imagine PCs without the ability to paint picture-perfect images on their screens. Yet the first PCs relegated graphics to the after-thought department. Simply adding color required a revolutionary new display system.

The only graphics available on the first PCs were block graphics, akin in more than name to the first toys of toddlers, mere playthings that you wouldn't want to use for serious work. The first real PC graphic display system made television look good, which in any other context would be an insurmountable challenge to the imagination. The foundation of the new display systems—called bitmapped graphics—proved powerful enough that in a few years, PC display quality not only equaled televisions but also PCs were used in *making* television images. The modern PC graphic system has taken a further step beyond and attempts to build a real (or real-looking) three-dimensional reality.

The development of PC graphics is best described as accumulation rather than evolution. Each new system builds upon the older designs, retaining full backward compatibility. Even the latest 3D graphic systems retains the ability to work with the first rudimentary block graphics. Just as you share genes with some of the lowest forms of life, such as bacteria, planaria, and politicians, your sleek new PC comes complete with state-of-the-art 1981 graphic technology.

Block Graphics

You don't need a lot of computer power and an advanced operating system to put graphics on your screen, which is good because in the early years PCs didn't have a lot of power or decent operating systems. In fact, even teletypes that are able only to smash numbers and letters on paper can print primitive graphic images. By properly selecting characters, standing far from printouts, and squinting, you could imagine you saw pictures in some printouts (a triangle of text might vaguely resemble a Christmas tree, for example). Some people still go to elaborate length to create such text-based images to pack into their email. But such text-based images could hardly be confused with photographs unless your vision was quite bad, your standards quite low, or your camera very peculiar.

When PCs operate like teletypes, their graphic output faces the same limitations as printouts; characters can only approximate real-world images. To improve matters, the designers of the original PC took advantage of the extra potential of storing characters as byte values. Because one byte can encode 256 different characters, and the alphabet and other symbols total far short of that number, the first PC's designers assigned special characters to some of the higher-numbered bytes in its character set. Beyond dingbats and foreign language symbols, a few of the extra characters were reserved for drawing graphic images from discrete shapes and patterned blocks that partly or entirely fill in the character matrix.

When your PC is operating in text mode, such as in the DOS box, you can still create rough graphic images by strategically locating these character blocks on the screen so that they form larger shapes. Other extra characters comprise a number of single and double lines as well as corners and intersections of them to draw borders around text areas. The characters are building blocks of the graphics images, and consequently, this form of graphics is termed block graphics. Figure 16.3 shows the block graphic characters in the standard PC character set.

FIGURE 16.3
Standard PC block graphic characters.

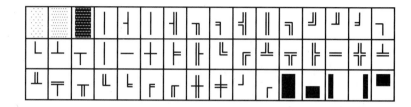

To a PC display system, block graphics are considered text and are handled exactly like ordinary text characters. All of the text attributes are available to every character of block graphics, including all of the available text colors, highlighting, and inverse video characteristics. The characters are also pushed onto the screen in text mode, which gives them high speed potential, but they are available only in text mode or Windows's DOS box. Because they use the high-order ASCII characters—foreign territory for most seven-bit email systems—you cannot ordinarily use them for images in ordinary email.

Bitmapped Graphics

Windows marked the transition of the primary operating mode of PC display systems. From character-based displays, Windows ushered in the age of the bitmapped display. *Bitmapped graphics* improve the poor quality of block graphics by making the blocks smaller. The smaller the blocks making an image, the finer grain and the more detail it can show. Physical aspects of the display system impose a distinct and unbreakable limit on how small each block can be—the size of the individual dots that make up the image on the video screen. The sharpest and highest quality image that could be shown by any display system would individually control every dot on the screen.

These dots are often called *pixels*, a contraction of the descriptive term picture element. Like atomic elements, pixels are the smallest building blocks from which known reality can be readily constructed.

The terms dot and pixel are often used as synonyms, but their strict definitions are somewhat different. When a system operates at its limits, putting as many dots on the screen as it is physically capable of handling, the number of dots and the number of pixels are the same. Often, however, systems operate with somewhat less sharpness than they are capable with the result that one pixel may be made from several onscreen dots.

The most straightforward way of handling the information to be displayed on such a screen is to assign some part of memory to each pixel, just as two bytes are given over to each character of a character-mapped display. In the PC scheme of things, because the data controlling each pixel is stored as one or more memory bits, this kind of display system is often called bitmapped graphics. Alternately, because each pixel or point on the video screen can be separately addressed through memory, this method of controlling the video display is often called *all points addressable* graphics or an APA display.

In the bitmapped graphics system, display memory stores an exact electronic representation of the onscreen image. It's actually a time slice of what you see; the software running on your PC is constantly sending new data into display memory to update the screen image. The memory temporarily stores or buffers the changes' frame until they are read out as a complete image frame dozens of times per second. Because of this function, graphic display memory is often called the frame buffer.

As with character-mapped memory, programmers have their choice of methods to write bitmapped graphics to your monitor screen. The PC BIOS provides basic support that allows any bit on the screen to be altered by programs. Using the BIOS to alter individual pixels is, however, a slow and painstaking process. Most applications write directly to the frame buffer to achieve satisfactory performance.

Bitmapped graphics hold the potential for being much sharper than block graphics. More pixels mean more detail. The number of dots on a screen and the ultimate number of pixels are many times the number of characters that are displayed on that same screen, from 64 to 126 times greater. However, bitmapped graphics imposes its own, interrelated penalties—memory usage and speed.

The amount of memory required by a graphic display system depends on two factors: the sharpness of the display image and the number of colors (or gray levels) that are to be displayed. Each increase in sharpness and number of colors means that your PC is putting more detail (more information) on its screen and storing more information in its display buffer. As a result, it must move around more information (more bytes) and that means more work. And the harder your PC works, the longer it takes to complete its job.

Vector Graphics

Bitmapped graphics is sometimes termed *raster graphics* because the technology organizes the screen into a series of lines called a raster that's continually scanned dozens of times a second. Although raster graphics are the basis of all PC displays—as well as today's television and video systems—it's not the only way to put a computer image on a monitor. A completely different technique does not regularly scan the screen at all. Instead, it precisely controls the circuitry operating the horizontal and vertical deflection yokes. It doesn't trace scan lines but instead draws figures the same way you would as a series of strokes of a paintbrush. To keep the screen lit, it constantly retraces the figures.

Because the signals controlling the monitor drive the electron beam in the CRT as a series of vectors, this image-making technique is usually termed *vector graphics*. Alternately, this kind of display system is sometimes called a *stroker* because of the kinship to drawing brushstrokes. Although not used on PCs, the term pops up occasionally in the descriptions of expensive computerized workstations.

Resolution

The number that quantifies the possible sharpness of a video image is called resolution. It indicates how many individual pixels an image contains that your display system will spread across the width and height of the screen. Because your PC generates the image as an electrical signal completely independent from your computer monitor (it would make the same image even if your monitor wasn't connected to the computer at all), physical properties of the monitor (such as its physical dimensions) play no part in resolution measurements. In other words, the number of pixels in an image does not vary with the size of the screen that it is displayed upon. Resolution is expressed without reference to units of linear measurement; resolution is described in pixels or dots rather than dots per inch. For example, a standard VGA display has a resolution of 640 pixels horizontally by 480 pixels vertically in its native graphics mode. (A peculiarity of the VGA system makes its text and graphics resolutions different. VGA text has a resolution of 720 by 400 pixels.)

Dots per inch is a measure of actual onscreen sharpness, and it depends both on resolution and the size of the resulting image. At the same resolution, a larger screen has less sharpness than a smaller screen—all else being equal. For example, a VGA image that measures 15 inches diagonally will have 640 pixels across one of its 12-inch long horizontal lines. On a perfect monitor, its sharpness would be 53 dots per inch. On a perfect 10-inch screen, the sharpness would measure 80 dots per inch.

The higher the resolution of an image, the more pixels it will contain. The more pixels, the more memory needed to store them.

Graphic Attributes

How much memory required for a given resolution depends on a second factor in addition to the number of pixels—the number of bits assigned to each pixel. At a minimum, each pixel requires a single bit of storage. That bit can be used to code either of two conditions—whether the pixel is illuminated on the screen or invisibly dark. In the simplest bit-image graphic system, one bit of memory would then be used to map the condition of each pixel in the video display.

What's lacking from this primitive mapping system is contrast and color. All bits are treated the same and their associated pixels look about the same, either on or off. The result is a single-hued picture with no variation or shading, essentially the same sort of an image as a line drawing. Although that may be sufficient for some purposes—for instance, the display of a chart or graph that mimics the monochrome look of ink-on-paper—color and contrast can add impact.

The way to add color to bitmapped images is much the same as adding color to character-based displays, adding attribute information. Additional memory is devoted to storing the attribute of each bit. The bitmapped system works somewhat differently from the character-based mode, however. All of the memory devoted to a bit is used to describe it. Not a byte needs to be devoted to identifying a character or pattern for each picture element because each one is essentially a featureless dot.

Color Planes

A single bit per pixel results in what graphics folk call a two-color system because it puts everything in black and white; each pixel is either on or off. Putting more color in the image requires encoding more information—more bits and more memory. Adding a second bit per pixel doubles the number of possible displayable colors. (Shades—degrees of darkness or light—are considered different colors in the terminology of computer graphics.) Every additional bit assigned to each pixel likewise doubles the number of possible colors. Hence with n bits, $2n$ colors are possible.

In computer graphics, the number of bits that are assigned to coding color information is sometimes described as the number of color planes. This term relates to the organization of display memory. The memory map of the graphic image can be visualized much like a Mercator projection of the world with latitude and longitude lines corresponding to the different positions of the bits corresponding to pixels in the image. Additional bits per each pixel add a third dimension, much like layers of maps stacked atop one another, a series of flat planes containing the color information.

Because the more colors used in an image, the better the apparent image quality and the more lifelike its appearance, the temptation is to increase the bit-depth of each pixel as high as possible. But the more colors or color planes, the more storage needed for encoding each pixel. Moreover, much to the dismay of purveyors of video memory, the human eye is limited in its ability to resolve individual colors: Most people can distinguish only a few million distinct colors. Color monitors are even more limited in the number of colors that they can display. Most monitors top out at about 262,144 colors, corresponding to the capabilities of an 18-bit display system. Once these limits are reached and enough memory is assigned each pixel, further improvements do not improve appearances.

The practical limit on color is a bit-depth of 24 bits, which allows a system to store and theoretically display any of 16,777,216 hues. Display systems with this bit-depth are termed 24-bit color or true color systems because they can store sufficient information to encode more colors than anyone could possibly see; they hold a truly accurate representation of any color.

Although some of the capabilities of true color display systems are superfluous because they exceed human abilities to distinguish colors, true color is a convenient system for designers because it assigns one byte of storage for each of the three additive primary colors (red, green, and blue) to each pixel. This three-byte-per-pixel memory requirement imposes severe processing overhead on high resolution systems. It can also strain storage systems.

Some newer display systems have a 32-bit color mode. Instead of allocating the additional byte of storage to color information, however, most of these 32-bit systems put the extra bits to work as an alpha channel. The bits in the alpha channel hold control rather than color information. In effect, the alpha channel provides a storage place for special effects information. The bits in the alpha channel normally are not tallied in counting color planes.

The math for finding the amount of memory required to display a color graphics screen is straightforward. Simply multiply the number of pixels on the screen—that is, the resolution—by the bit-depth of each pixel, and then divide by eight to translate bits into bytes. For example, a so-called XGA screen with 1024 by 768 pixels comprises exactly 786,432 pixels. If you want True Color (one byte of storage per color or a total of 24 bits per pixel), you need 18,874,368 bits to store the image data; that's 2,359,296 bytes. A display adapter with only 2MB won't handle that combination of colors and resolution, but (rounding up to the next generally available increment) a board with 4MB will do nicely.

Table 16.3 summarizes the memory required for common resolutions at various bit depths.

TABLE 16.3   Display Memory Required for Given Resolution and Color Depth

Resolution	Mono	16 Colors	256 Colors	High Color	True Color
Bits per pixel	1	4	8	16	24
Bytes/pixel	0.125	.5	1	2	3
640¥480	38,400	153,600	307,200	614,400	921,600
800¥600	60,000	240,000	480,000	960,000	1,440,000
1,024¥768	98,304	393,216	786,432	1,572,864	2,359,296
1,152¥864	124,416	497,664	995,328	1,990,636	2,985,984
1,280¥1,024	163,840	655,360	1,310,720	2,621,440	3,932,160
1,600¥1,200	240,000	960,000	1,920,000	3,840,000	5,760,000
1,920¥1,340	321,600	1,286,400	2,572,800	5,145,600	7,718,400
2,048¥1,536	393,216	1,572,864	3,145,728	6,291,456	9,437,184

The values shown in this table refer only to two-dimensional display systems. The three-dimensional systems that are becoming popular gorge themselves on memory. Most have two frame buffers to take advantage of the double-buffering and use additional memory in rendering the image, for example, to serve as a z-buffer. Because 3D rendering is computationally intensive, most systems limit the working resolution of their 3D images, reducing their memory requirements in 3D mode.

Color planes are related to memory banks but are not exactly the same thing. For instance, to map more memory into the limited address space reserved for video using the old VGA memory apertures, some video adapters use bank-switching techniques to move video memory bytes in and out of the address range of the host microprocessor. In some video modes, these banks correspond exactly to the color planes used by the video adapter. In other modes, several planes of video information may be stored in each bank by using bits in each byte of screen memory to indicate individual colors.

Color Coding

The best and the worst display systems assign the same number of bits to each of the three primary colors—a bit or an entire byte. For intermediary color depths, however, the base-two digital nature of the PC and the three-fold nature of color vision come into direct collision. For example, if you want to assign a single byte to store the colors of each pixel, how can you evenly allocate eight bits among three colors? With two bytes per pixel, how do you divide 16 by 3 evenly?

You don't. But you don't have to. You don't even have to code colors as a mix of red, green, and blue.

Because the human eye is most sensitive to green and its shadings (probably something to do with primitive humans living in an environment lush with chlorophyll-green plants), some color coding systems split their bit assignments evenly and assign the odd bit to green. For example, when the first PC engineers designed a 16-bit VGA color system, they assigned five bits to red and blue and gave six to green.

Color Spaces

In mixing colors to produce a full spectrum, the number of hues any system can produce is limited by the range of its medium. Because most systems of colors involve three signals such as the three primary colors of light, mapping them requires three dimensions, which in turn defines a volume or space. The range of colors that a specific system can handle consequently is called the *color space*. In the RGB system used by PC monitors, the range of red, green, and blue signals defines the three dimensions of the color space, but the RGB system is only one possible color space.

Some image systems encode colors by an entirely different manner. One of the most common (used by the Kodak PhotoCD system) is to encode colors by brightness (technically called luminance and abbreviated as Y) and two color (or chromaticity) values (abbreviated C1 and C2) that essentially correspond to coordinates on a map of colors. The mathematical relationship between these three signals is defined by the PhotoCD standard (see Chapter 12, "Compact Disks"), optimized for the requirements of the PhotoCD system.

In more general form, the signals used are termed Y, Cr, and Cb. In effect, Y is the luminance or overall image brightness, derived by totaling together all three of the RGB signals. Cr represents the difference between the red and luminance signal. Cb represents the difference between the blue and the luminance signal. Subtract Cr from Y and you get the red signal. Subtract Cb from Y and you get blue. Subtract both the resulting red and blue signals from Y and you get green.

A related system used by composite video signals transforms the YCrCb signals into intensity, hue, and saturation. In the intensity/hue/saturation color space, intensity describes one axis of the color space. Saturation is defined as the distance from the intensity axis, and hue is the direction from the axis. Together, these three measures—two distances and an angle—define the three dimensions of the space. In effect, hue is represented as an angle in the phase relationship between two signals.

In conventional video signals as used by televisions, VCRs, and other video equipment, the intensity information is called the luminance signal, and it takes the form of a standard black-and-white television signal. The saturation information is represented as the corresponding amplitude of an added signal called the *color burst*. The phase relationship between the luminance signal and the color burst defines the hue. In this way, the three dimensions of the video color space are cleverly encoded in two signals.

Print-oriented workers prefer to think and store colors in a color space defined by the ink colors used in printing—cyan, magenta, and yellow—which are often abbreviated CMY (or sometimes, CMYK—the K stands for black, which is used in four-color process printing to add depth to the colors).

These different color spaces and coding methods are useful to particular output devices—CMYK colors for storing images that eventually will be printed and published; luminance and chrominance coding for images that will eventually be used in broadcast-style (as opposed to computer) video systems. To be displayed by normal computer monitors, they must be translated from their native format to the RGB signals used by PC monitors.

Color Mapping

Another method of encoding colors in memory that requires translation has found greater use in PCs, particularly when a manufacturer wants to scrimp on video memory. A technique called *color mapping* stores only code numbers for colors, allowing each code number to stand for almost any color. One code number gets stored in video memory for each onscreen pixel. The display system matches the stored numeric code values to a color lookup table, or CLUT, that tells which color corresponds to each number and then that color is sent along to the monitor. Because of the nature of colors in the real world, color mapping can lead to substantial economies in display memory.

When the values stored in screen memory directly indicate what color appears on the screen—each possible color getting an assigned code whether or not it is used—the colors are said to be *direct mapped*.

Direct mapping allows any pixel to be any color, but most images are made from far fewer colors. After all, there are only 307,200 pixels on the VGA screen, so you can't possibly display all 16 million colors allowed by a 24-bit VGA system at the same time. If you're judicious about your color pruning and the colors you display, you can make amazingly realistic images using a few bytes of storage by limiting the number of colors you put on the screen (which limits the storage you need). The problem is, of course, the optimum color selection for one image isn't the same as another. A polar bear in a snowstorm is predominantly white; a black bear in a cave on a starless night would be predominantly black; and a still frame from a blockbuster action movie would likely be mostly red.

The colors assigned to storage can be made to adapt to the image using the color lookup table. In effect, the CLUT serves as a spectral map. A limited amount of storage makes up the guideposts or pointers that indicate which particular color in a wide overall selection called a palette belongs to a particular pixel. The number of guideposts determine how many different colors can be on the screen at the same time. The number of colors in the palette is constrained by the size of the pointer. Each pixel on the screen needs only enough storage to indicate which pointer to use. For example, a VGA system using a single byte of storage for each pixel could access a color lookup table with 256 pointers—that is, 2^8—allowing 256 different colors on the screen at a time. Each pointer has 18 bits of storage, allowing access to a palette of 262,144 different hues—almost enough to make each pixel a different color.

Color lookup tables conserve both memory and speed. The march of technology makes these issues increasingly irrelevant, however. As memory and microprocessor power becomes cheaper and screen resolution higher, CLUTs have become rarer. Although VGA uses them, the high-resolution display systems on most PC do not. Even so, you still run into this technology in another place where conserving memory becomes important—storing graphic images. The GIF files used for many Web images often use color mapping and lookup tables to reduce the number of bytes required for storing an image.

Graphic Commands

The secret weapon of achieving high speed in any graphics system is the high-level graphic command. By combining all the tiny steps of complex screen operations into a single routine, some of the most intricate onscreen images can be encoded as a few commands. Not only do high-level graphic commands make programs more compact, but also they allow your PC's microprocessor to offload the work of building images in the frame buffer.

Your microprocessor uses the high-level graphic commands to send instructions to a graphic subsystem. In today's PCs, that means a graphic accelerator chip or a 3D accelerator. The accelerator executes the commands to move pixels around in the frame buffer.

The range of these graphic commands is large. Each accelerator chip has its own repertory of them. The most common among them are the following.

Bit Block Transfers

Bit block transfers are instructions that tell the graphic chip to move data from one place to another in display memory. Instead of moving each byte of screen data through memory, the microprocessor only needs to tell the graphic chip what block to move (the source of the data) and where to put it (the destination). The graphic chip then carries out the entire data transfer operation on its own.

Often shortened to BitBlt, bit block transfers are most commonly used for scrolling the image up the screen. You can easily see the effect the command makes in video performance. When you scroll a bit image up the screen using a graphic chip, the top part of the image often snaps into its new position, leaving a black band at the bottom of the screen that slowly fills with the remainder of the image. The initial quick move of the top of the image is made entirely in display memory using BitBlts. The rest of the image must be brought into display memory through the I/O bus or local bus, resulting in delays.

Drawing Commands

Drawing commands tell the graphic chip how to construct part of an image on the screen— drawing a line, rectangle, or arc or filling a closed figure with a solid color or pattern. Often called graphic primitives, these commands break the image into its constituent parts that can be coded digitally to build a shape on the screen.

Before your PC's microprocessor puts a line on the screen, it first has to compute where each bit of the line will appear. It must compute the coordinates of each pixel to appear on the screen and then transfer the change into display memory across the bus. With a graphic chip, the microprocessor only needs to indicate the starting and ending points of a line to the chip. The graphic chip then computes the pixels and puts the appropriate values in display memory.

Sprites

Sprites are small images that move around the screen as a unit, much like an onscreen mouse pointer. General purpose microprocessors have no provisions for handling sprites, so they must compute each bit of the sprite image anew every time the sprite moves across the screen. Many graphic chips have built-in abilities to handle sprites. They store the bit-pattern of the sprite in memory and only need instructions indicating where to locate the sprite on the screen. Instead of redrawing the sprite, the graphic chip need only change the coordinates assigned to its onscreen image, essentially only remapping its location.

Windowing

Windowing is one of the most common features of today's graphic operating systems. Each task is given an area of the screen dedicated to its own operations and images. Keeping straight all the windows used by every task is a challenge for a general-purpose microprocessor. Graphic and 3D accelerator chips, however, are usually designed to manage windows using simple commands. Once an onscreen window is defined, it can be manipulated as a single block rather than as individual bytes. The windowing operations can be strictly software manipulations, or the graphic chip may include special hardware provisions for streamlining the control of the windows.

In a conventional windowing system, software controls the display of each window. The layout of the screen is calculated, and the proper values for each pixel are plugged into the appropriate locations in the memory map. The image is generated by reading each memory location in sequence and using the information it contains to control the intensity of the electron beam in the display as it sweeps down the screen. Every memory location is scanned sequentially in a rigid order.

Hardware windowing works by slicing up the frame buffer. Although each dot on the screen has one or more bits of memory assigned to it, the map no longer needs to be an exact coordinate-for-coordinate representation of the screen. The video chip no longer scans each memory location in exact sequential order as the video beam traces down the screen. Instead, the memory scanned to control the beam is indicated by pointers, which guide the scan between different memory areas. Each memory area pointed to represents an onscreen window.

Each window can be individually manipulated. The memory used by a window can even be mapped into the address range of the system microprocessor while the rest of the screen is handled separately. As a consequence, most of the calculating normally required to change a window is eliminated. Screen updates speed up substantially.

Panning

Hardware panning takes advantage of the some of the memory in the video system that's not needed as a frame buffer. For example, your video board may have 2MB of memory but use only 1.5MB to store a full 1,024-by-768 pixel image with 16-bit color. The extra half megabyte of memory can hold an image that's bigger than that displayed on the monitor screen; the monitor image essentially becomes a window into display memory. Instead of stretching out for 1,024 by 768 pixels, for example, the extra display memory might allow the filling of an 1,152-by-864 pixel map. To pan the onscreen image one way or another on the screen, the display circuits only need to change the address of the area routed through the output of the board. Changing addresses is much faster than moving blocks of bytes with BitBlt instructions, so hardware panning takes place very quickly—as long as the video board's memory holds the entirety of the image to be displayed. This technique is most useful when you have an older monitor that's not quite up to today's high scan rates; you put as much image on your screen as your monitor can tolerate while organizing your work across a larger desktop.

Depending on the hardware and drivers you've installed in your PC, Windows allows you to adjust the size of your desktop and onscreen display independently through the Settings tab of Display Properties.

Three-Dimensional Graphics

All of the latest display adapters claim to have the capacity to display three-dimension images. In other words, they claim to be *3D boards*. In terms of a display adapter, 3D means more and less than it seems. 3D does not mean what it did in the 1950s when your parents or grandparents put on blue-and-red glasses with cardboard frames to watch *The Creature from the Black Lagoon* jump out of the movie screen. In computer terms, that kind of 3D is a *stereoscopic display*, and you'll find more about on the CD-ROM.

In computer terms, 3D means adding simulated depth to the flat images on a monitor screen. But a 3D graphics adapter does more than add the appearance of a third dimension. It also gives 3D motion to your images to add excitement to games and attention-grabbing effects to your presentations.

Indeed, the motion part of the 3D board's job is its toughest assignment. It must not only make 3D images, but also it has to make them fast enough (at least 15 frames per second) that you think they are moving rather than just flashing at you.

Generating those images takes more processing power than was available in a PC a few years ago. They have to move megabytes, even hundreds of them, every second. They have to cope with mathematical functions you probably never knew existed in high school—and frightened you into an arts degree once in college. Yet they now encapsulate all the power they need in today's graphic accelerators. Better still, most of the math is gone. When developers write programs, they only need call the advanced functions built into programming interfaces such as Microsoft's DirectX.

No matter what you use your 3D board for, it needs to handle a few basic functions to generate its illusion of 3D reality. These functions can take place in hardware or software; that is, your graphic accelerator can take care of the heavy-duty computing itself or rely on your PC's microprocessor to do the hard work and merely pass along conventional two-dimensional functions to your 3D board. Obviously, a 3D board is supposed to do all the 3D work itself, but DirectX will take over if your board doesn't have the hardware functions it needs.

Tessellation

Computers face a problem in creating and manipulating three-dimensional objects. Computers work only with numbers, so the objects must be mathematically described for the computer to have any idea of how to deal with them. Finding a set of equations to describe a complex object is a daunting task, so daunting that programmers don't dare face it. Instead, they break complex objects into easily describable pieces and use the computer to manipulate those pieces. What they do is make their images the same way a mosaic artist makes a picture from small tiles.

The process of breaking the image into tile-like pieces is termed *tessellation*. The term comes from the name given to one of the mosaic artist's tiles, *tessera*. (The plural form is *tesserae*.)

In 3D graphics, the computer manipulates each tessera individually. When its transformation is complete, the computer recombines all the tesserae to create the original object. To eliminate the seams between the individual tesserae and other artifacts of the manipulation, the graphics system *filters* the resulting image combination.

In practical 3D display systems, the tesserae are polygons, usually triangles. The performance of 3D processors is often expressed in the number of polygons (or triangles) that can be rendered in a second. The number has to be prodigious. A complex object may require 20,000 or more polygons. Rotate it with 15 updates per second, and your graphic chip has to render 300,000 polygons per second.

The polygons-per-second description of a product really doesn't reveal a lot. The rendering time for any polygon depends on its shading, texture, and other attributes. Chip makers rate their products with their theoretical capabilities, and you can guess whether they would use best-case (monochrome, smooth surface triangles) or worst-case (True Color, polygons with complex textures, filtering, and anti-aliasing) conditions.

Texture Mapping

At this level, the individual tesserae of the image would have the appearance of an armor plate or a stealth fighter. Each one would be a single, solid, unrelieved color. Outside of jousts and midnight bombings, reality rarely looks so armor-plated. Real objects have shading and texture that makes them look, well, realistic.

To add realism to the 3D objects your computer generates, the graphic system adds texture. Through a process called *texture mapping*, a two-dimensional texture is applied to the surface of each tessera making up the image. In effect, the texture is glued to each surface of the image.

In the texture-mapping process, the computer starts out with an image of the texture. The complete texture is broken into small constituent parts similar to the pixels in a video image. Each of these pieces is termed a *texel*. The computer manipulates the texture by rotating and scaling it and applying perspective techniques to make it correspond to the manipulations performed on the tessera to which it is applied. The computer then maps the texels to pixels.

Because of the manipulations of the tesserae and texture, one pixel does not always correspond to one texel. Typically, the position of a given pixel appears between texels. Simply applying the color of the closest texel to the pixel results in an unrealistic image. The image may get blocky as multiple pixels take on the same color, or it may shimmer with slight movements as pixel values shift dramatically between texel values. To prevent these effects, the graphic system may apply *bilinear filtering* during the texture-mapping process. The pixel color value takes on a value intermediate between the colors of the four adjacent texels. The result is a more realistic appearance of the texture color, particularly as the image is moved or rotated.

Most 3D systems store their textures in several different levels of detail for situations requiring different 3D depths and resolutions. Typically, each level is designed for half the resolution of the preceding one, so a collection would include textures at resolutions of 100 percent, 50 percent, 25 percent, and 12.5 percent. Each texture level is prefiltered and tuned to the best appearance at its resolution level. Taken together, the stored collection of a single texture at various levels of detail is termed a *mip map*.

Objects can appear at any depth in the image, but the mip map stores only discrete levels of detail. At some depths, the texture applied to a polygon will require a level of detail between those in the mip map. The 3D processor interpolates an intermediate texture using a technique termed *tri-linear filtering*. The processor first performs bi-level interpolation (bi-level filtering), then applies a further linear interpolation between the detail levels on either side of the polygon's depth.

Texture mapping is one of the most complex of the operations required in three-dimensional graphic systems. Making the necessary calculations for mapping and filtering may take up half or more of the processing time for the image. Consequently, texture mapping benefits greatly from hardware acceleration.

Depth Effects

What separates ordinary graphic displays from 3D displays is the appearance of depth to the image. In a 3D image, some objects appear closer than others. The difference in depth is, of course, an illusion because the face of the picture tube or LCD remains flat. The 3D display system must fool the eye into believing it perceives depth.

The problem is not new to 3D display systems. Ever since the first cave artists scratched walls with charcoal and ochre, they have attempted to add depth to their paintings and drawings. Over the years, they discovered (and often rediscovered) the techniques of perspective and other means that take advantage on the depth cues the human eye uses to put distant objects in their places.

Recession

One of the primary depth cues to the human eye is image size. The smaller an object of a known size appears to be, the farther away it seems. Three-dimensional graphic systems use a technique termed *perspective divide* to simulate this effect. To make distant objects smaller, the graphic system scales distances in the x- and y-coordinates of the image by a factor that is proportional to the z-coordinate. In simplest form, distances in the x-y coordinate system are divided by the z value; the larger the z, the smaller objects become.

The effect is the same as one-point perspective in the art world. Parallel lines, such as railroad tracks, converge at a single point in the distance; as z approaches infinity, the values of x and y approach zero and the coordinates collapse into a point.

Atmospheric Perspective

Artists have long used the technique of *atmospheric perspective* to add depth to paintings. Because of the effects of looking through a long reach of atmosphere, which isn't perfectly clear because of the haze of dust and water vapor suspended in it, distant objects appear paler and bluer than nearer objects. Artists capitalize on this visual effect and mix white and a trace of blue with the color of objects that are supposed to appear in the distance in their paintings.

The corresponding technique in three-dimensional computer graphics is termed *fogging*. To make an object appear more distant, the graphic system adds a fixed color called the *fog color* to the hue of the object. The amount of fog color added increases with the apparent distance of the object. Because the fogging technique corresponds to the appearance of natural haze, the technique is sometimes called by that name, *haze*. This technique is also called *depth cueing*.

Lighting Effects

Photographers and artists quickly learn that lighting is the key to making their two-dimensional images appear to represent three dimensions. The pattern and depth of bright areas and shadows allow the human eye to determine depth and the relative locations of objects. When an object sits between another object and the light source, the first object is brightly lit, and the second object is in shadow. The technique of rendering images using the effects of light and shadow is called *chiaroscuro*, from the Italian for "clear-dark." *Chiaroscuro* rendering is one of the great challenges facing the 3D graphic system.

Ray Tracing

The most powerful and compelling way to render the lighting of a three-dimensional scene uses the technique of *ray tracing*. The computer follows or traces the path of every light ray that impinges on the scene. The process is complex. The computer determines which object each ray strikes based on the direction of the origin of the ray. After the ray strikes the object, the computer determines how much of the ray illuminates the object and is reflected. Based on the angle of the object surface to the light beam, the computer determines a new path for the reduced beam and plots it to the next object, continuing until the beam is so diminished that it has no further effect. Once all the rays have been traced, the computer sums up the amount of light that has struck each surface. Those surfaces with the most rays are the brightest; those with few rays are in shadow.

Of course, to make the math tractable, the computer deals with only a reduced set of rays; the more, the better the rendering. The math is so complex that PCs cannot perform ray tracing on reasonably sized images in real-time. The technique works extremely well for static images (if you're patient) but requires each frame of an animate be individually rendered, taking perhaps a minute per frame. The ray-tracing technique consequently is not suitable to generating compelling 3D animations in real-time.

Shading

PC graphic systems use a simplified means of creating the *chiaroscuro* effect called shading. In the simplest form, the computer determines the angle of a surface to the light source and, using the reflectivity of the surface, computes how bright the surface should be rendered. *Gouraud shading*, also known as *smooth shading*, takes an additional step. It interpolates lighting values across the face of a surface to give gradual color transitions from a bright edge to a dim edge.

Z-Buffering

One way to eliminate the display of hidden surfaces is to track the depth of picture elements. The depth—or the distance away from you the element is supposed to appear—is assigned a value. This value corresponds to the position of the element on the z-axis of the three-dimensional coordinate system. In the *z-buffering* technique, this depth value gets stored in a special *z-buffer*. As the graphic chip updates the image, it compares the z value of each pixel to that stored in the z-buffer. When the z value in the buffer is less than that of the newly rendered pixel, the old value is nearer and would obscure the new value, so the new value is discarded. If the new value is lower and would thus appear in front of the old value, the old value gets discarded, replaced by the new value.

Transparency

Not all objects in the real world are opaque. If they were, seeing through the windshield of your car would be a much greater challenge. Making an object appear transparent on your computer screen is a similar challenge for your display system. It must track not only multiple levels of objects but also the effects of one on the others.

To account for the effects of a transparent object sitting in front of another object, many 3D imaging systems store a transparency attribute for colors in addition to the normal red, green, and blue values. The storage for this additional attribute data is termed the *alpha channel*. Commonly, the alpha channel is an extra 8 bits added to the 24 bits used to store True Color pixel data, resulting in a 32-bit storage system or 4 bytes per pixel. Most systems assign higher values to greater opacity, so 255 would be totally opaque and 0 totally transparent.

When calculating the appearance of a given pixel, the graphic processor uses the alpha channel values to determine its resulting color through a process termed *alpha blending*. The processor adds a fraction of the color of the transparent object set by the alpha channel value to the color of the background object. Mixing the colors together gives the appearance that the background color is seen through a layer of the transparent object.

By itself, of course, alpha blending only changes the color of pixels. You need more to give the true illusion of transparency. The viewer's eye also takes cues from the shape of the transparent object (defined by the color change made by the alpha blending) as well as the difference between the background color seen with and without the transparent mask. The programmer must take all of these factors into account to produce a compelling three-dimensional image.

Double Buffering

To create smooth animation, 3D display adapters use the technique of *double buffering*. As the name implies, this technology puts two frame buffers in control of the graphics chip.

The *front buffer* corresponds to the traditional display buffer, connected to the rasterization circuitry that reads it sequentially and sends the video data to the screen. While the front buffer is scanned, the graphics chip draws in the *back buffer*, where the rendering operation is hidden and access is not limited by the timing of the rasterization process. Once the graphics chip completes its drawing, the two buffers are switched; the back buffer becomes the front buffer and the image drawn in it gets sent to the display. The graphic chip can then begin drawing in the new back buffer.

By cycling between the two buffers, double buffering allows a fast but limited form of animation. It also achieves the same end as double-ported video RAM without using expensive, specialized memory chips. At the same time, it eliminates the appearance of the drawing process on the screen.

Signals

Most discussion of PC graphics ends with the frame buffer, where the image gets temporarily stored. After all, once you've got all the pixels arranged the way you want them in memory, shipping them off through a cable to your display should be a simple matter. It isn't. The image must be transformed from its comparatively static position in screen memory to a signal that can traverse a reasonable interface; after all, the cable for a parallel interface capable of moving data for nearly a million pixels would likely be thicker than the average PC. Consequently, the frame buffer image must be serialized for transmission.

This need became evident when television was invented. The system developed by Philo T. Farnsworth (one of several folks credited with inventing television) relied on scanning images that naturally produced a serial data stream. Although television has improved somewhat since the 1920s when Farnsworth was developing it (technically, at least), the transmission system remains essentially the same for today's analog video signals as well as the connections between PCs and their displays.

The in-your-face full-screen image gets sliced thin and converted into a single serial signal. In effect, the technology converts two physical dimensions into one physical and one time dimension. Such serialization process fits the needs of the transmission system and the display hardware, including both early image acquisition and display devices, in particular, the television picture tube.

Technically termed a *cathode ray tube*, or CRT, the device earns its name because it shoots an electron beam from a cathode (an electron emitter) to light the phosphors of the screen. The single data stream of the television signal corresponds to the single electron beam inside the tube, and changes in the beam directly reflect changes in the data. The single data streams also suited the television transmission system; one data stream requires only one channel, which simplifies the design of transmitters and receivers.

Modern technology no longer requires (or desires) the image serialization developed for television. For example, the LCD monitors in notebook computers don't require scanning or serialized signals. Digital television systems move images in compressed form that bears little resemblance to the original image (at least until it is decoded). Nevertheless, for convenience and compatibility the serial format survives in the connection between your desktop PC and its external monitor.

Scanning

The dimensional transformation required by the television system is accomplished by the technique of scanning. The first television cameras traced an electron beam across the projection of an image on a special material that changed its electrical characteristics in response to the bright and dark areas of a scene. By focusing the electron beam, the camera could detect the brightness of a tiny spot in the scene. By dividing the scene into dots the size of its sensing spot and rapidly examining each one, the camera could gather all the data in the image.

Although there's no naturally required order to such an examination, the inventors of television looked to what we humans have been doing for centuries—reading. We read text one line at a time, progressing from left to right across each line. The various inventors of television (and there are many competing claims to the honor) followed the same pattern, breaking the image into lines and scanning the dots of each line from left to right. This process is called *scanning*.

To make a scan in a classic television camera, the electron beam is swept across the image by a combination of magnetic fields. One field moves the beam horizontally, and another vertically. Circuitry in the camera supplies a steadily increasing voltage to two sets of deflection coils to control the sweep of the beam. These coils are electromagnets, and the increasing voltage causes the field strength of the coils to increase and deflect the beam farther. At the end of the sweep of a line, the field that controls the horizontal sweep of the electron beam is abruptly switched off, returning the beam to the starting side of the screen. Likewise, when the beam reaches the bottom of the screen, the field in control of the vertical sweep switches off. The result is that the electron beam follows a tightly packed zigzag path from the top of the screen to the bottom.

The primary difference between the two sweeps is that several hundred horizontal sweeps take place for each vertical one. The rate at which the horizontal sweeps take place is called the *horizontal frequency* or the line rate of the display system. The rate at which the vertical sweeps take place is called the *vertical frequency* or frame rate of the system because one complete image frame is created every time the beam sweeps fully down the screen.

The television receiver scans the inside of the CRT in exactly the same fashion. In fact, its electron beam is precisely synchronized to that of the camera. The one-line-at-a time, left-to-right scan nicely accomplishes the required dimensional conversion.

The video circuits of your PC have to carry out a similar conversion. The only difference is that the image is laid out in a logical two-dimensional array in memory instead of a physical two-dimensional array on a camera tube (or, more likely today, CCD or charge-coupled device). The process in the video circuits of the computer is elegant in its simplicity. Addresses in the memory map are just read off in sequential order, one row at a time. A special electronic circuit called the *video controller* scans the memory addresses, reads the data value at each address, and sends the data out in one serial data stream.

Synchronizing Signals

The biggest complication to scanning memory to produce a video signal is getting the timing right. Because of the dimensional conversion, timing determines the location of each dot on the screen. If the timing is off, the location of each dot will be off, and the image won't look anything like it is supposed to.

To assure that an image stored in your PC's frame buffer is properly reconstructed, the horizontal and vertical frequencies of the scan of the frame buffer memory must exactly match that of your monitor. To ensure these frequencies do match, your PC and all video systems packages samples of these critical frequencies along with the data.

These frequency samples are called *synchronizing signals*. They take the form of sharp pulses that the circuitry inside your monitor converts to the proper scanning signals. The video controller in your PC generates these pulses as it makes its memory scan, sending out one (the horizontal synchronizing signal) before each line in the image and one (the vertical synchronizing signal) before the beginning of each image frame. The monitor uses the pulses to trigger its sweep of each line and to reset to the top of the image to start the scan of the next frame.

The video controller doesn't scan at just any frequency. It uses standard frequencies that vary with the geometry of the image—its height and width along with the frame rate. The monitor is tuned to expect these frequencies, using the synchronizing signals only to achieve a precise match.

Broadcast television and single-wire video systems combine both synchronizing signals with the data signal. In the production studio and the connection between your PC and monitor, however, the one-wire limit can be lifted. These systems often give synchronizing signals their own, dedicated connections. There are, in fact, four common ways of combining or not combining video data and synchronizing signals:

- **Composite video** is the all-together-now approach that puts all video data and the two required synchronizing signals into one package for single-wire or single-channel transmission systems.

- **Composite sync** combines the horizontal and vertical synchronizing signals together and puts them on one wire. Another, separate wire carries the image data.

- **Separate sync** gives a separate wire and connection to the image data and the horizontal and vertical synchronizing signals.

- **Sync-on-green** combines the vertical and horizontal synchronizing signals together and then combines that with the data for the green data channel.

In any of these four systems, the relative timing of the synchronizing and data signals is the same. The chief difference is in the wiring. A composite video system requires only one wire. The other systems use three wires for data (one for each primary color). Sync-on-green thus requires only three connections; composite sync requires four (three colors, one sync); and separate sync requires five (three colors, two sync). The standard video system in most PCs uses composite sync; the signal monitor cable has four separate connections for image data and synchronizing signals.

Retrace

The data corresponding to the dots on the screen don't fill a video signal wall-to-wall. The physics of the first television systems saw to that. To make the image you see, the electron beam in the CRT of a classic television set traces a nearly horizontal line across the face of the screen and then, in an instant, flies back to the side of the screen from which it started, lower by the width of the line it already traced out. This quick zipping back is termed *horizontal retrace*, and although quick, it cannot take place instantly because of the inertia inherent in electrical circuits. Consequently, the smooth flow of bytes must be interrupted briefly at the end of each displayed line (else the video information would vanish in the retrace). The video controller must take each retrace into account as it serializes the image.

In addition, another variety of retrace must occur when the electron beam reaches the bottom of the screen when it's finished painting a screen-filling image: *vertical retrace*. The beam must travel as quickly as possible back up to its starting place, and the video controller must halt the flow of data while it does so.

Blanking

During retrace, if the electron beam from the gun in the tube were on, it would paint a bright line diagonally across the screen as the beam returns to its proper position. To prevent the appearance of this distracting line, the beam is forcibly switched off not only during retrace but also during a short interval on either side to give the beam time to stabilize. The interval in which the beam is forced off and cannot be turned on by any degree of programming is called *blanking* because the electron beam can draw nothing but a blank on the screen.

The classic television signal cleverly combines synchronization, retrace, and blanking together. The horizontal synchronizing signal is a strong pulse of the opposite polarity of the image data that lasts for the retrace period. The negative nature of the signal effectively switches off the electron beam, and the frequency of the signal effectively synchronizes the image.

Front and Back Porches

Most computer monitors don't fill their entire screens with data. They center (or try to) the image within darkened borders to minimize the image distortions that sneak in near the edges of the screen. To produce these darkened, protected areas, the electron beam is held at the level that produces a black image for a short while before and after the data of each image line is displayed. The short interval before the data of a line begins is termed the *front porch* of the signal. The interval after the end of the data but before the synchronizing signal is called the *back porch*. If you examined the signal, you'd see that it dips down for blanking and pops up to an intermediate height (called *black level* by broadcasters) to create the porches between blanking and data. Use your imagination and the black-level signals look like shelves—or porches.

Television and composite video systems put the color burst that helps decode the color in the signal on the back porch.

Although LCD screens don't need to worry about retrace (or even scanning across the screen), to be compatible with the video signals already used by PCs, they must make allowances for the timing of the non-data parts of the signal, including retrace and blanking.

Vertical Interval

The period during which the screen is blanked during the vertical retrace is called, appropriately, the *vertical interval*. Its physical manifestation is the wide black horizontal bar that's visible between image frames when your television screen or computer monitor picture rolls and requires adjustment of the vertical hold control. The big black bar corresponds to the time during which the signal carries no video information.

The vertical interval is a carry-over from the early days of television when vacuum tube electronics needed time to "recover" between fields and frames. It allowed voltages inside the circuitry of the TV set to retreat to the proper levels to begin the next field. Modern electronics—say, for example, those of televisions made in the last 30 years—don't really require the long duration of the vertical interval. Consequently, broadcasters have found the time devoted to it useful for stuffing in extra information. Television stations add a *Vertical Interval Test Signal*, or VITS, to monitor operation of their transmitters and associated equipment. The text for the closed captioning system is also encoded during the vertical interval, as are all sorts of other miscellaneous data.

You can even see some of it should you have an older television on which you can twist the "vertical hold" control. Gently adjust it so you can see the big, black bar of the vertical interval, and you'll notice it's not so black any more. The broken horizontal lines within the vertical interval are caused by the data encoded there.

Although computers don't stuff data into the vertical intervals of their monitor signals, proprietary hardware can grab the data put into broadcast signals and deliver it to your PC.

Video Integration

Video has become an intrinsic part both of what PCs do and what you expect from your PC. PCs are now regularly used to produce videos, including those for presentation on television, even on networks. At the other end of the channel, PCs display video images—from television using a TV adapter board or from a DVD drive. Video images inevitably confront the PC display system, and dealing with them can be a challenge.

You can convert the output of your PC into a conventional video image suitable for your VCR or video monitor using any of a number of adapters. VGA-to-video is particularly easy and inexpensive because the VGA system has its roots in American commercial television standards. Mixing video with computer images on your PC display is more difficult because modern high-resolution PC graphics systems share little in common with ordinary video images. Converting video images to match the signals inside your PC video system takes more processing power than usually is available. Consequently, some manufacturers cheat with a technique called *video overlay*.

Going the other way, when you want to work with a video image on your PC—either as still graphics or as full-motion video—you must somehow get the signals into your PC. This technology is termed *video capture*.

Standards

When it comes to images, the standard most widely used stares you in the face, literally, for several hours a day. The unblinking eye of the television set defines the most widely used image communication system in the world. Considering when the basic television standards were created, their longevity has been amazing, particularly compared to the short tenure of PC standards; the basic television signal was defined half a century ago. Only recently has it come under threat by digital and high-definition technologies.

Ordinary PC displays and video boards don't work with the same image formats and signals as do televisions and VCRs. Television came first, of course, and until recently had no need for discussions of such things as bitmaps. Transmission rather than storage was the issue with television—moving its signals in real-time. For the first few years of television, in fact, the only way to store its images was to photograph them.

The primary concern with television signals was getting them from one point to another at the lowest possible cost in equipment, signal processing, and bandwidth. The quality of the display on your PC's monitor leaves ordinary television far behind. You'd have no reason to take a step backward to television quality were it not for the collision course steered both by computer and television dream engineers. Eventually, they foresee, your computer and television combined into one box—probably including your stereo, game, home control, and mind control systems as well.

This grand union is what multimedia has been about all along. Multimedia combines TV and PC to make something that we hope won't sink us in alphabet soup. Your PC will eventually make and control the images you view on your television screen. Those images—at least for now—use their own standards that are unlike anything in computer-dom.

First, a bit of definition. *Video* means "I see" in Latin. The word "television" is a hodge-podge derived from the Greek for "distant" and Latin for "sight." Television is what is broadcast or transmitted over a distance. Video is up close and personal.

When we talk of "video" among PCs, however, we mean an electrical signal that encodes an image in raster form, hence the term "video board." When people involved with television speak of video, they mean a particular form of this signal, one with well-defined characteristics we'll list shortly. A distant-sight television signal takes this video signal and modulates a carrier wave (corresponding to the television channel) with it. Video signals range in frequency from zero to a half dozen megahertz. Television signals start out at 60MHz and extend upward to nearly 10 times that. Television sets tune in television signals, receiving them on their antenna inputs. Monitors display video signals.

Although one standard currently dominates video signals in the United States and Japan, other standards are used elsewhere in the world. In addition, a secondary standard termed S-video appears in high-quality video applications.

NTSC

The most common form of video in North America and Japan wears the designation NTSC, which stands for *National Television Standards Committee*, an industry organization formed in the early 1950s to create a single signal standard for color television. At the time, CBS had been broadcasting for over a year with an electro-mechanical color system that essentially spun a color wheel in front of the camera and a matching wheel in front of the monitor. RCA, owner of rival NBC, proposed an all-electronic alternative. The RCA system had the advantage that it was backward compatible with black-and-white television sets, but the CBS system was not. The NTSC was formed chiefly to put an impartial stamp of approval on the RCA system.

The RCA system was the prototype for all color television today. Each pixel gets scanned in each of the three primary colors. Although studio equipment may pass along the three colors separately like the RGB signals in PCs, for broadcast they are combined together with synchronizing signals to create NTSC video.

The magic is in the combining process. For three independent variables—the three colors—they needed to have three separate signals but not necessarily the three original signals. By transforming the signals mathematically, they found a clever way to package them as one.

First came a transformation of color space. For compatibility with monochrome, they combined all three signals together. This produced a signal they called *luminance*, which encoded all the brightness information in the television image. The luminance signal was essentially a monochrome signal and produced an entirely compatible image on black-and-white television sets. The name of the luminance signal is often abbreviated as Y.

The other two signals they used encoded difference information—the difference between luminance and the red signal and the difference between luminance and the blue signal—which allowed the reconstruction of the original red and blue signals. Subtract red and blue from the luminance signal, and the remainder was green. This method of encoding colors assured monochrome compatibility. In the NTSC system, the difference signals are called I and Q.

The next step the NTSC used was to combine the two difference signals into a single signal that could carry all the color information, one called *chrominance* (abbreviated as C). Engineers used quadrature modulation to combine the two signals into one. The result was that colors are encoded into the chrominance signal as a phase angle.

Together, the luminance and chrominance signals provided a guide to a map of colors, a polar chart. The chrominance encodes the angle between the color and the x-axis of the chart, and the luminance indicates the distance from the origin to the color.

To fit the chrominance signal in where only luminance should fit, engineers resorted to putting chrominance on a subcarrier. That is, they modulated a carrier wave with the chrominance signal and then added it to the luminance signal. Although the subcarrier had much less bandwidth than the main luminance channel, the process was effective because the human eye is less sensitive to color differences than brightness differences.

The NTSC chose a frequency of 3.58MHz as the color subcarrier frequency. The chrominance is thus an amplitude modulated signal centered at 3.58MHz. To avoid interference with the luminance signal, the NTSC process eliminates the carrier and lower sideband of the chrominance signal after the modulation process.

The NTSC process has two drawbacks. The luminance signal must be cut off before it reaches 3.58MHz to avoid interfering with the subcarrier. This frequency cap limits the highest possible frequencies in the luminance signal, which means that the sharpness of the image is reduced from what it would be using the full bandwidth (4.5MHz for the video signal) of the channel. Chrominance carries even less detail.

The basic frame rate of a video signal is about 29.97 per second. Each frame is made from two interlaced fields, so the field rate is 59.94Hz. Each frame is made from 525 lines, of which about 480 are visible and the rest are devoted to vertical retrace. Ideally, a studio image would have about 640 pixels across a line. Black-and-white television images may be that sharp. However, the 3.58MHz bandwidth imposed by the NTSC color process constrains the luminance signal bandwidth to 400 to 450 pixels horizontally. Although that might sound paltry, a good home VCR may be able to store images with about half that resolution.

S-Video

The constraints of NTSC color are required because of the need for backward compatibility. The color signal had to fit into exactly the same bandwidth as a black-and-white signal. In effect, NTSC gives up a bit of black-and-white resolution to fit in the color information.

Video signals that never make it to the airwaves need not suffer the indignities required by the NTSC broadcast standard. Studio signals have always transcended broadcast standards; studio RGB signals have full bandwidth, high-resolution (640-pixel) images in each of their three colors. To raise home viewing quality, VCR designers came up with a way to get more quality in color signals by avoiding the NTSC process.

The part of the NTSC process that most limits visual quality is squeezing the color signal onto its subcarrier. By leaving the video in two parts, separate luminance and color signals, the bandwidth limitation can be sidestepped. This form of video is termed *S-video*, short for separate video. High-end VCRs, camcorders, and monitors use often use S-video signals.

Other than not modulating chrominance onto a subcarrier, the color encoding method used by S-video is identical to that of NTSC. The three RGB color signals are combined into luminance and chrominance using exactly the same formulae. Although you cannot substitute one signal for the other, the innards of S-video monitors need not be radically different from those of NTSC displays. The level of quality is often quite visibly different. S-video components may have twice the horizontal resolution as composite video.

Note that once a signal is encoded as NTSC, information is irretrievably lost. There's no point to decoding an off-the-air television signal to S-video. The only time S-video helps is when you have a source of the signals that has never been NTSC encoded.

International Standards

The United States pioneered color television, and the rest of the world learned from its mistakes. The NTSC system is used only in North America and Japan. The rest of the world does things a bit differently. Most of the world uses a color system called PAL. France and most of the nations that were the USSR, such as Russia and Ukraine, use a system called SECAM.

PAL

With the benefit of hindsight, the engineers who developed the PAL standard added a twist to the signals they used for color television. By reversing the phase of one of the chrominance signals (R-Y) after every scan line, they were able to make the color in images more stable. Any phase distortion that arises during the broadcast of such a signal can be reduced by the use of a simple delay line in a television receiver. The change of phase gave the system its name; PAL stands for *Phase Alternating Line*.

By itself, the change of phase doesn't yield higher resolution. When PAL was developed, however, the engineers chose different parameters that do yield a better image. Most nations that use PAL have a power-line frequency of 50Hz instead of the 60Hz common in North America. Consequently, they chose 50Hz as the field rate (yielding a frame rate of 25Hz). This change allowed time to put more lines on the screen, 625 in PAL. To improve horizontal resolution, most PAL systems use a subcarrier frequency of 4.43MHz, allowing both luminance and chrominance a wider bandwidth.

SECAM

In 1959, France developed a system called *Sequence Couleur a Memoire* (in English, sequential color with memory), commonly known by its abbreviation, SECAM. Instead of one quadrature modulated color subcarrier, SECAM uses two FM subcarriers, one for each chrominance signal. The luminance portion of its signal is the same as PAL with the same frame rate and line count. Table 16.4 summarizes the characteristics of the major television standards used in the world today.

TABLE 16.4   International television standards

Name	Field rate	Frame rate	Lines per frame	Sub-carrier type	Sub-carrier freq.	Audio carrier offset	Channel width
Units	Hz	Hz	None	None	MHz	MHz	MHz
NTSC	59.94	29.97	525	AM	3.58	4.5	6
PAL	50	25	625	AM	4.43	6	8
PAL-M	59.94	29.97	525	AM	4.43	6	8
PAL-N	50	25	625	AM	3.58	4.5	6
SECAM	50	25	625	FM	4.43	6	8

The signals of all three color systems are mutually incompatible. The different number of pixels alone is sufficient to guarantee that images meant for the European systems won't work with NTSC. Even videotapes must be translated to move their images between any two of the standards, a process that uses a device appropriately called a *standards converter*.

As long as you stick to one standard, you shouldn't encounter problems. However, many video accessories for PCs are available to meet NTSC, PAL, and SECAM specifications. Be sure to match the standard you buy to what you want to watch—and what's compatible with the video system you intend to use.

Video Overlay

One of the heaviest burdens on the video system is the processing required to combine picture information from several sources—for example, when you want to put a video display on screen with several other windows. Although combining this image data is no problem for a graphic accelerator, it can be time-consuming—so time-consuming as to make real-time video displays impossible with all but the latest chips. To give adequate performance with earlier generation accelerators, hardware designers used another strategy to combine video with other PC graphic information. Instead of processing the data streams as software, they used hardware to add together the different image signals.

The one design problem these engineers faced was how to tell the hardware where to locate the video image. After all, they couldn't overwrite the entire screen (if they did, there would be no reason to combine images), nor could they write on the screen at random because they would risk obscuring important information.

To supply the needed location information, these design engineers turned to an old television technology called *chroma keying*. This process works by substituting one image for a key part of another image. Typically, the key would be identified by its color or chroma, and the color of choice was a sky blue. This color is preferred because it's optically the opposite of average Caucasian flesh tones so is least apt to make parts of people disappear on the screen.

In PCs, this process is called *overlay technology*. In its most common form, it used a supplemental video board that intercepted the signals sent toward your monitor by your primary video board. The software controlling the overlay board would use standard Windows instructions to put a blank window on the screen where the video was to appear. The overlay board would then key the video into the window. In this way, your graphic software and even your PC's microprocessor never need to deal with processing the video. In fact, the video never even makes it as far as the expansion bus. It is isolated on the overlay board. You get full motion video on your screen with virtually no impact on the performance of your PC.

Video Capture

Gathering up video images so that they can be used by your programs—*video capture*—requires hardware that combines aspects of a more traditional video board and a digital video camera. Traditional video images are analog signals and require an *analog-to-digital converter*, or A-to-D converter, to put them in a form usable by your PC.

The A-to-D converter works by sampling the voltage level of the video at each pixel position of the video image and assigning a digital value to it. In most systems, the signal is first decoded into your computer's standard RGB format to determine the strengths of individual colors before sampling. Typically, the image gets stored in a buffer and is sampled from the buffer rather than from the real-time video signal. The buffer helps bridge between the different timings and formats of the video signal and its target digital form.

Most PC video capture systems do not convert a full-motion, full-resolution video stream into digital form. True real-time sampling is beyond the capabilities of PCs if just because of the data rates involved. Converting a full NTSC video image into 24-bit RGB data in real-time would require a data rate of at least 36 megabits per second, beyond the capabilities of even the most advanced disk interface. Instead, video capture systems trim the resolution or frame rate of the video signal to fit within the data-handling capabilities of your PC. You can consequently get a small image with a reasonable frame rate or a full-size still-frame image. The latter technology underlies the *video frame grabber* that lets you capture individual video frames as still images.

Practical video frame grabbers are often small, external boxes that plug into a parallel port on your PC. You supply a video signal to the frame grabber while watching the image on an external video monitor, not your PC's display system. When you see the frame you want to grab, you trigger the frame grabber to capture it. The frame grabber stores the image in its buffer and spools it into your PC at a rate the parallel port will accept.

Many overlay boards allow you to capture the video signals they display. Moreover, they save on the need for an external video monitor by displaying the video image as an overlay on your PC's monitor screen. Because of their bus connection, they can glean moving images, although at a reduced resolution and frame rate.

Professional-level video-capture systems approximate full-screen, full-motion video using image compression. High-powered hardware reduces the data required for the video signal to a rate compatible with the PC's abilities. Note that this compression must be performed in special hardware circuitry because it requires extensive processing power. Moreover, it must be compressed before it gets handed down to your PC because the uncompressed video will quickly overload your expansion bus.

Image Compression

Computer video puts a golden gleam in the eyes of the makers of memory and mass storage systems. They know that nothing has powered the growth of their industries as much as the move to putting real video into PCs. Nothing eats memory and storage faster than full-motion, full-color video. The math is enough to make the manufacturers drool. Full-color video, which requires 3 bytes per pixel, at 640×480 resolution equals nearly 1MB of digital data per frame. At the 30 frames per second used in the United States and most of the Western Hemisphere (or even the 25 frames per second standard in Europe and elsewhere), a video producer could easily use up 1GB of hard disk space in storing less than one minute of uncompressed digital video information.

Of course, memory and mass storage are only a matter of money. The real problem blossoms when you go online and try to move video through an ordinary modem connection. The problem is severe when packaging video clips on CD and even worse when you try to make a multimedia link through a modem. Ordinary video is simply too bulky for ordinary use on your PC.

The secret that makes images and videos readily transportable and lets you put video on ordinary CDs as well as the latest, high-capacity DVDs is *image compression*. As with data compression, image compression reduces the size of files by eliminating redundant or otherwise unnecessary information. Image compression goes further, however. It throws away some information in a quest for smaller files; in other words, most image compression is lossy. The most popular image compression systems prove themselves acceptable in two ways: They throw away only information that psychovisual studies indicate is the least apparent, and they allow you to tailor the amount of discarded data to yield the compromise between size and quality that looks best to your eye.

Video compression takes the next step and analyzes the changing aspects of a series of images to find the best way of reducing their data needs. Video compression systems usually mix together several technologies to achieve compression ratios of hundreds to one (compared to the nominal two-to-one average compression ratio of non-lossy systems). Although both still-image compression and video compression share a number of characteristics and technologies, each presents its own problems and compression opportunities.

Note that some file types—such as the GIF files included in nearly every Web page—are compressed but, strictly speaking, don't use image compression. Instead, they compress the image as data (data compression). The difference is that image compression analyzes the image from a visual perspective, but data compression doesn't care how the image looks—or whether the data is even an image. GIF files may also palletize an image with color lookup tables, but such processing is not usually regarded as true image compression.

Normal still-image compression programs work two dimensionally, analyzing areas and reducing the data required for storing them. The most popular is called JPEG, initials that stand for the Joint Photographic Experts Group, which developed the standard. Video compression works three dimensionally; in addition to working over areas, it works in time. It takes advantage of how little actually changes from frame to frame in a video image. Only the changes get stored or transmitted; the static parts of the image can be ignored. For example, when someone moves against a backdrop, only the pixels in the moving character need to be relayed to the data stream. The most popular form is called MPEG, for the Motion Picture Experts Group, an organization similar to JPEG (part of the same overall body) but separate from it.

Filters and Codecs

Compressing still and video image data streams is so different that developers use distinct terminologies when speaking of the conversion process. Moreover, they even handle the conversion software differently.

The program routines that compress still images are usually termed *filters*. Most graphic applications have several filters built in to handle a variety of different compression systems and file formats.

Video compression requires either a software- or hardware-based processor that is termed a *codec*, short for compressor/decompressor. The most efficient software codecs are proprietary designs that rely on patented technology. Each has its own advantages (such as speed of processing, high compression ratio, or good image quality) that make it best suited for a given type of application. Consequently, many codecs remain in common use. Most multimedia applications include the appropriate codec in their playback software or work with those assumed to be installed in your operating system.

Although MPEG is widely used—it forms the basis for both video CDs and DVDs—it is extremely processor-intensive. Best results require dedicated image-conversion hardware, although Intel claims the Pentium Processor with MMX Technology can decipher MPEG-1 images in real-time. Several lesser compression systems that require only software codecs are often used by multimedia systems. Windows 95 includes support for four of these alternate multimedia codecs, including Cinepak, Intel Indeo, Microsoft run-length encoding, and Microsoft Video 1.

You can view the video codecs installed in your Windows 95 system by opening the Multimedia icon in Control Panel, choosing the Advanced tab, and double-clicking on Video Compression Codecs. You'll see a display like that in Figure 16.4.

FIGURE 16.4

Windows display of video codecs.

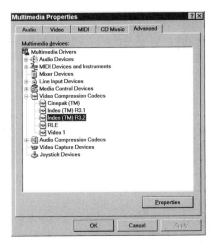

Windows 95 handles codec installation as part of its *hardware* installation wizard. Codecs install as drivers. As you step through the wizard menus, simply specify that you want to install specific hardware and then choose Sound, Video, and Game controllers from the list on the first screen. The wizard will give you the installation menu, as shown in Figure 16.5.

Select the hardware that will use the codec. Then, slide the disk containing the codec in a drive and click on Have Disk, and Windows 95 should find the codec and install it in your system.

JPEG

Today's top choice for still-image compression is JPEG. Just as a celebrity is someone who is well-known for being well-known, JPEG is popular because of its popularity. It's nearly universal, exactly what it was designed to be. One reason is that JPEG has something for everyone; it can deliver high compression ratios, completely lossless image quality, and layered transmission that lets you quickly send rough images that progressively fill in with detail. Of course, JPEG is no panacea, and gaining one advantage means losing another. Specifically, when you opt for high compression, you lose image quality. This point is, however, that JPEG gives you the choice. When it does compress, it minimizes the apparent loss in image quality.

FIGURE 16.5

The Windows codec installation wizard.

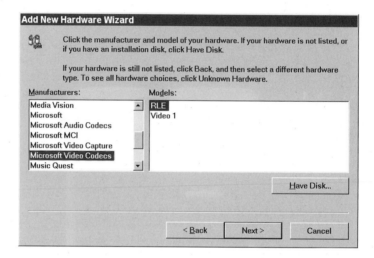

The standard gains these advantages by being a non-standard, the kind of thing you'd expect to be crafted by a committee. In the case of JPEG, however, the variability translates into the versatility that's the standard's strongest point. JPEG allows many options in the image processing used for compression, maintaining order by giving a standard system for documenting the steps taken so that they can be reversed to reconstitute the image. All the compression details are listed in the header of the image file or at the beginning of a transmitted data stream.

JPEG is at its best compressing color images because it relies on psychovisual perception effects to discard image data that you might not be able to perceive. It also works on grayscale images but yields lower compression ratios at a given quality level. It does not work well on monochrome (two-tone or black-and-white) images and requires that color-mapped images be converted to a conventional, continuous-tone color format before processing—which, of course, loses the compression effect of the color mapping.

JPEG processing involves several steps, some of which are optional. Several of these steps may reduce the amount of detail in the image, and thus its quality. The JPEG standard allows you to select the amount of information that's thrown away in these steps so you can control how well an image reconstructed from the compressed data will resemble the original. One option is lossless, which throws away no information other than that which would be redundant. This typically compresses an image file to 50 percent of its original size. Even invoking lossy compression, you can reconstruct an image visually indistinguishable from the original with a reduction to 33 percent of the original. The loss becomes apparent somewhere around reductions to 5 to 10 percent of the original data size. You can brute-force the image data down to 1 percent of the original size, although the results will resemble more a new work of computer art than whatever masterpiece you started with.

Baseline Compression

The starting point for the JPEG compression process is a *baseline* compression algorithm that's defined by the standard. All JPEG systems must be able to handle this baseline algorithm, and most go no further. Even the baseline algorithm allows for several optional processing steps.

The first step in the baseline JPEG transformation is the optional translation of the color space in which the image is stored. Most PC display systems use RGB data for storing and displaying images, but a luminance/chrominance color space allows the JPEG system to better compress the image. Moving to a luminance/chrominance color space allows the next optional step to reduce the image data by about one third without any apparent loss in detail.

If the image is stored in a luminance/chrominance color space, the compression system can reduce the resolution of the chrominance information without reducing the perceived resolution of the image. Human eyes cannot see color differences as sharply as it can detect changes in brightness. Preserving the high resolution of the luminance information makes the overall image appear sharp even when the actual resolution of the color information is reduced.

The resolution is reduced by averaging together adjacent pixels, a process termed *downsampling*. The average can be taken either horizontally or vertically—the pixels may be either side-by-side or one above the other—or the pixels can be averaged in both directions. In typical JPEG processing, two pixels are averaged horizontally without vertical averaging (termed *2h1v sampling*) or two pixels are averaged both horizontally and vertically (termed *2h2v sampling*). Because 2h1v sampling reduces the size of two of the three image components by half, it yields a one-third reduction in the size of the image data. By reducing the two components to one-quarter their unprocessed size, 2h2v sampling results in an overall reduction of the image data by one half.

Another data conversion step is key to the sliding compressibility scale of JPEG. Using a mathematical function called a *discrete cosine transformation*, or DCT, image pixels are converted into a frequency map. The transformation results in a series of numbers that represent the pixels in increasing detail. JPEG slices the image into blocks of 64 made from squares of pixels measuring 8 to a side. After the discrete cosine transformation, the image becomes 64 values, the first of which contains the lowest frequency of the block—corresponding to an overall average of the block data. Each value supplies higher frequency data until the last, which yields the data necessary to run the DCT algorithm backwards and completely reconstruct the image. The DCT process does *not* compress the image. Nor does it affect the quality of the reconstructed image, within the limits of the precision of the calculations. Strictly speaking, however, the DCT process is not completely lossless because of the inevitable round-off errors in its calculation. Truly lossless JPEG compression consequently does not use the DCT.

The bulk of the compression in the JPEG process comes from applying *quantization coefficients* to the values derived by the DCT. JPEG applies a separate coefficient to each of the 64 DCT values. Different combinations of coefficients affect the relationship between compression ratio and quality. Getting the best compromise is a black art only slightly less arcane than curing warts, making yourself invisible, or putting a curse on your neighbors. The values used may vary with each image, so the JPEG data stream or file of any image contains a complete table of all 64 values used in that particular image. Most software that produce images with JPEG compression simply use the values given as examples by the JPEG committee. Although the exact amount varies with the coefficients used, this step results in the greatest amount of compression in the JPEG system and the greatest amount of information loss.

The values resulting after the application of the quantization coefficients are finally compressed as ordinary digital data. The JPEG standard allows two chief options, Huffman coding (which essentially replaces a string with a single value and a multiplier) or arithmetic coding. Although the latter results in files that may be 5 to 10 percent smaller, the algorithm is patented and requires licensing. Most JPEG systems use only Huffman coding.

To enable a JPEG decoder to properly reconstruct the image, the encoder adds a header to the image data that defines the various steps taken in processing the image, including the table of quantization coefficients. Standard JPEG image disk files have yet another header added to further identify the image. Microsoft has defined and published a specific file format for JPEG images and the associated header.

Hierarchical Mode

Programmers sometimes find having different resolutions of an image available to be useful. For example, they might want to be able to display the image as a small thumbnail or as a completely detailed high-resolution image. Having the image encoded at different resolutions in the same file minimizes the processing time when an application needs a specific resolution level (providing, of course, the resolution the application wants is one at which the image has been encoded).

For such applications, JPEG includes a *hierarchical mode*. The hierarchy is a set of the image encoded at each discrete resolution level. A single JPEG file might include an 80 by 60 pixel thumbnail, a 320 by 240 pixel low-resolution image, a 640 by 480 VGA image, and a 2,048 by 1,536 high resolution version. A program need only decode one of them and need not bother with the time-consuming processing of the high-resolution image if its application does not require all the detail.

Progressive Mode

In some applications—chiefly those that involve sending image data through low-speed communications channels—getting a rough draft of a image can be useful. For example, while surfing the Internet, you may visit a site and want a quick glimpse of what's there without waiting a few aeons while a full page of graphic images loads through a modem already gasping for life. The image draft lets you quickly decide to linger or jump further afield, partly anaesthetizing the pain of laggardly telecommunications. Better Web browsers take advantage of the *progressive mode* of the JPEG standard to make quick drafts of images, steadily building the quality as you allow more time for the additional image data to slide into your system.

Progressive mode is a special case of hierarchical mode in which the images at various resolution levels are arranged progressively from the lowest in detail to the most detailed. In progressive mode, the DCT coefficients of an image get sent incrementally as successive scans of the image. With each scan, a new level of detail gets layered onto the image. The first consists of a few single-color blocks. With each later scan, the number of blocks increases as their size decreases and more color is piled on. Because the initial scan contains little detail, it transfers quickly, and each later level takes progressively longer.

Although more convenient in data transfer applications, the designers of JPEG decided not to make progressive mode universal. Each scan of the image must be separately and fully decoded, and each consumes a dollop of microprocessor time. A normal, non-progressive JPEG image gets reconstructed in a single decode. For a given level of detail in the final image, progressive mode is slower.

Lossless Mode

Although JPEG is primarily a lossy compression system, the versatile standard also incorporates a *lossless mode* for special applications. Lossless mode operates differently from setting the highest quality level. In making the discrete cosine transforms in its normal operation, JPEG must round off values, and the tiny fractions lost in rounding cannot be recovered when the image is reconstructed. To store images with no loss in quality, JPEG's lossless mode avoids the use of the discrete cosine transforms (as well as downsampling the chrominance channels).

In lossless mode, JPEG uses a simple compression algorithm that encodes each pixel as the difference between its value and that of the previous pixel. The resulting data stream further compressed with the same Huffman or arithmetic coding used in lossy JPEG.

Lossless mode is often used in conjunction with hierarchical or progressive mode. It allows the final layer of a progressive reconstruction of the image to be a perfect replica. A reconstructed lossless JPEG image will develop fewer artifacts if it is later compressed again.

Motion JPEG

If you want to create a video, you need to string together a series of individual images. Encode each one using the JPEG algorithm, and you have a compressed movie. Such a design underlies the technology of *Motion JPEG*.

This approach has both advantages and disadvantages. Because each frame in a motion JPEG video is complete in itself—essentially just a still image—you can pull any image out of the sequence and use it as a still photo. You can grab one frame at random, decode it, and get an image on your screen. In other words, motion JPEG gives you complete random access. In addition, you can control the size of the images used in the sequence, so you can determine the resolution of the final display and, by adjusting the algorithm, the quality of the display. Motion JPEG also specifies a means of adding an accompanying audio channel to the image.

The price you pay for all of this versatility is that motion JPEG isn't very good at encoding. It compresses in only two dimensions (the height and width of the image) and essentially ignores the third (time). With most video images, the greatest saving you can gain through compression comes in the time dimension. That's a fundamental problem. What motion JPEG does worst is what benefits video compression the most.

MPEG

The videos that you're most likely to display on your PC use MPEG compression. MPEG stands for the *Moving Picture Experts Group*. As with JPEG, MPEG is a committee working under the joint direction of the International Standards Organization (ISO) and the International Electro-Technical Commission (IEC). The formal name of the group is ISO/IEC JTC1 SC29 WG11. The stuff after the organization simply further delineates the organization: JTC stands for Joint Technical Committee, Subcommittee 29, Workgroup 11. It began its life in 1988 under the leadership of Leonardo Chairiglione and Hiroshi Yasuda.

Despite the similarity of names, the JPEG and MPEG groups are separate and share few members. Some of the technologies used by the two compression systems are similar, but they are meant for different kinds of data. The most prominent point of divergence is that

MPEG achieves most of its data reduction by compressing in the time dimension, encoding only differences between frames in video data.

Standards

MPEG includes multiple standards for encoding not only video but also the accompanying audio. Over the years, it has progressed through several levels with increasing sophistication and quality.

The first MPEG standard, now usually called MPEG-1 but formally titled "Coding of Moving Pictures and Associated Audio for Digital Storage Media at up to About 1.5 Mbits/s" became an international standard in October 1992. It has four parts. The actual compression of video or video signals is covered under International Standard 11172-2. Related parts describe compressing audio signals, synchronizing audio and video, and testing for compliance with the standard.

The reason MPEG-1 is used by CD-i (interactive Compact Discs) is that it achieves a data rate that is within the range of CD drives. To get down that low with the technology existing at the time the standard was developed, the system sacrifices resolution. At best, an MPEG-1 image on CD-i has about one-quarter the pixels of a standard TV picture. MPEG also requires hefty processing power to reconstruct the moving image stream, which is why CD-i players can display it directly to your TV or monitor, but only the most powerful PCs can process the information fast enough to get it to your display without dropping more frames than an art museum in an earthquake. If you're used to the stuff that pours out of a good VCR, this early MPEG looks marginal, indeed.

MPEG-2 was meant to rectify the shortcomings of MPEG-1, at least regarding image quality. The most apparent difference appears on the screen. The most common form of MPEG-2 extends resolution to true TV quality, 720 pixels horizontally and 480 vertically, while allowing for both standard and wide-screen formats (4:3 and 16:9 aspect ratios). Although MPEG-2 benefits from advances in compression technology, this higher quality also demands more data. The TV-quality image format requires a bandwidth of about 4Mbps. Beyond that, the MPEG-2 standard supports resolutions into ionspheric levels. All MPEG-2 chips are also required to step back and process MPEG-1 formats.

In addition to high-quality video, MPEG-2 allows for 5.1 audio channels—that is, left and right main channels (front), left and right rear channels (surround), and a special effects channel for gut-thumping rumbles limited to no higher than 100Hz. (The ".1" in the channel description refers to the 100Hz limit.) MPEG-1 only allows for a single stereo pair.

What was initially MPEG-3 has been incorporated into MPEG-2. The concept behind MPEG-3 was to make a separate system for High Definition TV for images with resolutions up to 1,920 by 1,080 pixels with a 30Hz frame rate. Fine-tuning the high levels of

MPEG-2 worked well enough for HDTV images that there was insufficient need to support a separate standard.

MPEG-4 is slated to go the opposite direction, aimed at very low data rate applications that transfer information in the range of 4,800 to 64,000 bits per second. Such low rates are suited to moving images through conventional modems for videophones or small screen video conferencing. The image itself would have low resolution (about 176 by 144 pixels) and a low frame rate, on the order of 10Hz.

Processing

MPEG-1 processing starts out with steps similar to JPEG to capitalize on the same principles. Images are first converted to luminance/chrominance (YUV) color space, allowing a reduction of resolution in the chrominance channels without an apparent visual effect. The MPEG-1 system allows for encoding images as large as 4,095 by 4,095 pixels at 60 frames per second. Among PCs, the format most widely used is termed *Constrained Parameters Bitstream* (CPB).

To make the data generated by the MPEG-1 system manageable, in 60Hz frame-rate NTSC-based video systems, the starting resolution of CPB is limited to 352 by 240 pixels. The 50Hz PAL and SECAM systems alter the number of lines in a frame to 288. After conversion, the resolution of the chrominance channels is reduced to 176 by 120 pixels.

At this point, MPEG-1 goes its own direction and begins its time compression. The image frame is sliced into blocks. In the luminance channel, these blocks measure 16 pixels by 16 pixels. In the chrominance channels, they measure 8 pixels by 8 pixels. The different sizes cover exactly the same area of the image because of the lower resolution of the chrominance channels. Taken together, the three blocks (one luminance, two chrominance) describing a common image area are termed a *macroblock*. The MPEG encoder examines the macroblocks of two frames to find which are the same, which are close matches, and which are wildly different. Depending on the type of frame, it can compare the preceding frame or the following frame for correspondences. It determines the level of difference between the macroblocks of the two frames. If the blocks are too different, the encoder keeps the new data; otherwise, it works with the difference information. With this data, it computes a discrete cosine transform for each macroblock, which the system further manipulates, reducing both the data and detail of the image. The encoder then applies conventional data compression (Huffman coding) to the results of these operations to create the final data set.

Frames in MPEG-1 compression are divided into three types:

- I-frames are intra frames. These are frames encoded without reference to other frames. They are basically still images that serve as a starting point from which differences made by images changes are referenced.

- P-frames are predicted frames. A predicted frame represents the difference between the current image and the one generated by the frame before it. The P-frame includes difference data (vector and difference DCT coefficients) as well as blocks of new data for image areas that don't match those of the previous frame.

- B-frames are bidirectional frames. Blocks in these frames encode changes either from the frame before or from the next frame. The encoder checks to see which direction works best to code the image—forward, back, and then averaging between. If the changes can't be encoded, then the encoder uses new data. The averaging helps the B-frame reduce noise in low bit-rate systems. The penalty is added complexity in the processing (and thus hardware).

Note that although only I-frames are complete in themselves, any kind of frame can contain original information in the form of I-frame macroblocks.

To allow for random access to individual frames, MPEG-1 requires an I-frame at least every 0.4 second. That works out to every 12 frames in the 30 frame-per-second NTSC world (which means the US and Japan). MPEG does not require any particular sequence of frame types. The code stream indicates which types of frame are used when. In a typical encoding, the pattern of frames would run like this:

I B B P B B P B B P B B I B B P B B P B B P B B I ...

Clever as MPEG technology is, it cannot predict the future. Calculating some of the B-frames requires knowledge of the frame that comes after it in the sequence. As a result, frames need not be sent or stored in strict sequence. Moreover, the MPEG decoder needs to decode frames and keep several of them in memory to properly decode subsequent frames. Add in all the mathematical calculations required to reconstruct each frame, and the heavy processing needs of the MPEG system become quickly obvious. The use of B-frames also imposes a slight delay in the output signal because the system has to read several frames ahead of what it actually displays.

In MPEG-2, the equivalent of CPB is called *low level*, and the most popular application will probably be *main level*, which delivers decoded output at about the level of today's studio television systems. Table 16.5 lists the characteristics of the various MPEG-2 levels.

TABLE 16.5   Characteristics of MPEG-2 Levels

Level	Maximum Image Size	Frames Rate	Pixels Rate	Maximum Bit Rate
Low	352×240	30 per sec	3.05 MB/sec	4 Mbits/sec
Main	720×480	30 per sec	10.40 MB/sec	15 Mbits/sec
High 1440	1,440×1,152	30 per sec	47.00 MB/sec	60 Mbits/sec
High	1,920×1,080	30 per sec	62.70 MB/sec	80 Mbits/sec

Low level under MPEG-2 is essentially the same as CPB video under MPEG-1. The most common form is main level, which is used by DVD systems. The two high levels are aimed specifically at professional video recording.

Interfacing

As with all other hardware, linking video and display circuitry to your PC has two aspects, hardware and software. The hardware side governs both the electrical and logical connections, which are discussed in the next chapter. The software side determines how information and instructions wend their way from your PC to the video system.

The software side is the more complex because interactions occur at several levels. Each video board maker designs its product to recognize a given set of instructions, typically to carry out functions in 2D drawing and 3D rendering. These *board-level commands* are specific to each accelerator and video board. To enable your operating system to communicate with the board, a video driver translates the operating system functions into these board-level commands. At the other side of the system, your application software sends graphic commands to the operating system using the application program interface (API) of the operating system.

Drivers

If there is any weakness in improving display performance with graphic accelerators and graphic processors, it is the need for these special high-level commands. Unless a program includes the requisite instructions, the graphic chips will never swing into action. Any investment in this extra-cost hardware would be wasted.

Consequently, programs must be specially written to take advantage of your system's graphic hardware. In itself, that need might not seem troublesome—until you consider that more than a dozen graphic chips are in use and each has its own individual command set. To recognize and use all the available chips, a program would have to pack itself with instructions for each of the chips with which it might potentially be used. With the proliferation of different chips, the necessary code would grow inside programs like a digital cancer, swelling programs with tumors of code that will eventually doom performance.

Software drivers help programmers sidestep the need for overloading their programs with graphic code. The program itself is written to the most common subset of high-level graphic commands available from most graphic chips. The programmer uses his own, proprietary command for each of those functions. He then creates a separate program called a software driver that translates his commands into those used by a specific graphic chip or board build from a specific chip. When the microprocessor in the PC encounters one of the program's graphic instructions, the software driver tells the microprocessor the proper instruction to send to the graphic chip, which then carries out the operation.

Although this design makes your life easier, it fosters nightmares for most programmers—if they can even get enough sleep to have a nightmare. This strategy requires the programmer of even the simplest graphic program to be familiar with all available graphic hardware. He needs to be both a software and hardware wizard in a world where expertise in one or the other field is rare enough already.

At one time, programmers avoided the problem by leaving the writing of software drivers to the makers of display adapters, which simply shifted the requirement of double expertise from the software company to the hardware company. You were left to install the hardware maker's drivers for each of your applications—if the hardware maker chose to write a driver for the applications you favored.

The real solution to the problem was the development of the graphic operating environment, which eventually evolved into the modern operating system. This latter approach adds yet another layer of software with the environment/operating system bridging between your applications and hardware driver. Every layer of software takes a performance toll, so the flowering of this technology came only when PCs and graphic accelerators were fast enough to hide all the behind-the-scenes work. The hefty demands of graphics is what sets the minimum requirement for most advanced operating systems at the 486 microprocessor level.

Most operating systems include drivers for the most common video devices available at the time of the release of the operating system. Hardware makers often tailor their products to the existing drivers. Often, these built-in drivers match not a particular video board but rather a given chipset. These are often termed *generic drivers* because most video boards using the target chipset will operate with them. If a chipset maker develops a new product after the release of the operating system, it may develop its own generic drivers for that chipset.

If a video board developed after the release of the operating system (or version of an operating system) does not work optimally with a generic driver, the board maker will usually develop its own device driver to match the board. Often, a board maker will develop its own drivers to take advantage of an exclusive feature of its product. In general, the board maker's drivers will outperform the generic drivers included with the operating system or developed by the chip maker. (Sometimes, the chip maker's drivers won't work at all with a given board.) The general rule is that the more specific the driver, the faster it will be.

In a quest to gain or keep a perceived performance lead, some video board manufacturers rush out improved drivers as fast as they can. And they rush out even newer drivers to fix the bugs in the ones rushed out earlier. At times, it can seem like the board maker is offering drivers *du jour*. Because of the tentative nature of some display drivers, the best strategy when you encounter a problem with a video board is to first be sure you have the latest drivers. Most board makers let you download their latest drivers from their Web sites or, occasionally, a bulletin board system.

With modern operating systems, you install video drivers as part of the hardware installation process. If you choose hardware that's specifically supported by the operating system, the operating system will install its own drivers. By clicking on the Have Disk option, you can install drivers supplied by the maker of your video board by sliding the disk distributed with the board when you are prompted to do so.

Most video board makers will outline the exact process required to update their drivers when they release new versions. Sometimes to properly install updated drivers, you must uninstall a product and then reinstall it with the new drivers. Otherwise, your operating system might think you have two video boards—one using the old drivers and one using the new. The easiest way to remove a video board is through Device Manager. Highlight your video board and then click the Remove button.

Application Program Interfaces

The graphic operating system works by giving programmers a set of software routines called *hooks* that each programmer can use to elicit certain images on the video display. The operating system translates the hook commands into its own common language, which is translated by the driver software into a form understood by the graphic accelerator. Application writers need only concern themselves with the operating environment hooks.

The entire set of program hooks is called the *application program interface*, or API. Some hardware makers omit the redundant word *program*, so these hooks are sometimes called simply the application interface, or AI. Whatever the name, these command compendia make the intermediate translation step that allows software and hardware to come together. The application program interface is the official means of controlling the display system (or linking with display software) that's documented by the maker of the device. The connection can work through any of a variety of links—from direct control of hardware registers to a top layer of software that interacts with specific drivers.

For the programmer, the application program interface is an instruction manual that tells him how to work with the various features built into a display system. You, as a PC user, never need to deal with the application program interface. Your only concern is that you have the right driver for your hardware. The hardware maker writes (or contracts with someone to write) a driver that bridges between the operating system and the hardware.

In that one company develops, publishes, and controls nearly all the operating system software used by PCs, you'd think that programmers would have only one API to worry about. The operating system has become a mere foundation for wildly divergent applications, each of which has its own distinctive needs. One API to fit all possible applications would be unwieldy at best. No one, however, wants suffer the old malaise of requiring a different driver for each application. The solution to this problem is the compromise, a multiplicity of interfaces optimized for particular kinds of software applications (for example, games or interactive video).

Windows GDI

The API used for graphics by early versions of Windows was called the Windows *Graphic Device Interface*, or GDI. It handles all the display functions programs normally need. It allows programs to draw images on the screen as well as create boxes, menus, and windows with simple commands.

The GDI is the default graphic system used by Windows, which isn't necessarily bad. The latest versions use full 32-bit technology—one characteristic that distinguishes the generation between Windows 3.1 and Windows 95. The design of the GDI is optimized for two-dimensional application graphics, providing font, drawing, and interface primitives to your programs. Current versions of the GDI also include a device-independent bitmap (DIB) engine that enables programmers to put bit-images on any display hardware that has a Windows driver.

DirectX

The next step and next generation in linking graphic software through the Windows system is Microsoft's *DirectX*. The name reflects the design goal—to make the link between your software and display hardware more direct for improved performance, particularly on complex graphic tasks such as fast-moving videos and 3D displays. The improved speed and hardware links provided by DirectX are aimed specifically at making the PC—and the Windows environment in particular—a viable platform for the most demanding of all PC graphic applications: games.

The various DirectX application program interfaces tightly mesh with what Microsoft calls a *hardware abstraction layer* (termed HAL, but no relation to the *2001: A Space Odyssey* computer). The HAL provides the interface with a common feature set that's independent of the exact hardware you've installed. If the particular device you install does not have a feature required by the application program interface, DirectX interposes a *hardware emulation layer* (HEL). Operating in parallel with the HAL, the HEL uses software routines to create whatever high-level functions the target hardware does not support. For example, if a given 3D accelerator supports bi-linear filtering but not tri-linear filtering, commands for bi-linear filtering would be routed through HAL and tackled by the accelerator chip; commands for tri-linear filtering would be handled through software, putting the computation burden on your PC's microprocessor.

Which path the program calls from your applications take depends on the DirectX drivers you install. A generalized driver, such as those supplied by Microsoft, take few hardware features for granted and emulate most operations through HEL. DirectX drivers supplied by an expansion board maker should be expected to route more functions through HAL to better exploit hardware power. Other than measuring performance, you have no way of knowing which route your graphic commands take. The path through HEL is usually slower.

DirectX does not supplant other APIs. Rather, it works in conjunction with them. For example, when adding OpenGL to Windows 95, drafting and engineering programs link into OpenGL, which then ties to your hardware through DirectX.

The current DirectX family of interfaces has five major sections, two of which are aimed at onscreen graphics. DirectDraw handles the functions of the GDI and accelerates two-dimensional graphics. Direct3D provides a repertory of 3D graphic commands using both 3D accelerator hardware and ordinary graphic accelerators. DirectInput provides a link between applications and specialized input devices such as joysticks, pedals, and exotic virtual-reality equipment. DirectPlay links your PC with applications running through a modem or network. DirectSound works with audio devices.

Because DirectX is not a standard part of Windows 95, most manufacturers of hardware that use it include the necessary DirectX drivers with their products. Newer versions of Windows will include built-in DirectX support.

Display Adapters

The hardware that changes your pulsing digital PC's thoughts into the signals that can be displayed by a monitor is called the display adapter. Over the years, the display adapter has itself adapted to the demands of PC users, gaining color and graphics abilities as well as increasing its resolution and range of hues. A number of standards—and standard setters—have evolved, each improving the quality of what you see on your monitor screen. Although display adapters themselves may disappear from PCs, they will leave a legacy in the standards they set.

Basic display adapter (graphics board) features

Feature	In short
Accelerator	The actual chip that does the work of generating the onscreen image. The type of chips (2D or 3D as well as brand and model) ultimately controls the performance of the video system.
Memory	Used by the accelerator to create and store the onscreen image. More is better, allowing more colors and higher resolutions. Most modern PC start with 4MB of display memory.
Bandwidth	The electronic limit on the displayable video signals. Higher bandwidths allow the video system to display sharper images and update them more often.
Resolution	The measurement of the sharpness of the image a graphics board can produce. All PCs start with 640 by 480 pixels (VGA) and may go as high as 1600 by 1200 pixels.
Bus interface	How the video system links to the rest of your PC's circuitry. Faster bus interfaces allow for faster screen updates. The lowest common denominator is PCI. AGP is better (and usually standard) but 2x and 4x AGP improve performance.
Video interface	How a graphics board links to your display. Most PCs now use analog output through a VGA connector but digital interfaces are becoming popular for flat panel displays.

Making light of electronic signals requires no extraordinary skill or complex circuitry. All it takes is a light bulb and a press of a finger on a willing wall switch. Beyond that, however, things get more difficult. Imagine mastering more than a million light bulbs, each with a dimmer rather than a switch, and perfectly adjusting each one half a hundred times a second.

Of course, that's exactly the kind of chore you bought your computer for. Not just any computer will do, though. It needs special circuitry to take control of that light show. Not only must it be able to switch on and off the lights, dimming them when appropriate, but also it has to remember how each is supposed to be set. And it has to imagine, visualize, and draw the patterns that the lights will reveal. In a modern PC, all of these functions are adeptly handled by the display adapter, circuitry that adapts computer signals to those that control your monitor. In most machines, the display adapter is a special expansion board that serves primarily to make graphic images, hence the display adapter is often called a graphics board. Because the graphic board sends out signals in a form that resemble (but are not identical to) those of your home video system, they are often termed *video boards*. Notebook PCs lack video boards—they typically lack any conventional expansion boards at all—but all of them also include display adapter circuitry on their motherboards.

No matter its name, the function of display adapter circuitry is the same—control. The adapter controls every pixel that appears on your computer display. But there is one more essential element. Just any control won't do. Give a room full of monkeys control of a million light dimmers (you'll need a mighty large room or a special breed of small, social simians) and the resulting patterns might be interesting—and might make sense at about the same time your apes have completed duplicating the works of Shakespeare. The display adapter circuitry also organizes the image, helping you make sense from the chaos of digital pulses in your PC. It translates the sense of your computer's thoughts into an image that makes sense to you.

Key to the display adapter's ability to organize and communicate is standardization—the rules that let your computer and its video circuitry know the correct way to control the image on your monitor. Computer makers build their display circuits to conform to certain industry standards, and programmers write their magnum opuses to match. The standards control the quality of the images that you see—most importantly color, resolution, and refresh. Working within these standards, video board makers do their best to eke the most speed from their circuits. Their efforts relentlessly push at the standards. Something's got to give, and not surprisingly, it has been the standards. Your demands for more speed and quality have pushed the PC industry through the reigns of several hardware standards and into a new realm where traditional hardware standards no longer matter.

Ground zero in a modern PC display is called VGA, named after IBM's pioneering Video Graphics Array that was introduced in 1987. This little bit of history remains the default mode of nearly every PC video system. Switch on your PC, and it begins life as a VGA system. Only after your operating system loads its video drivers does it switch to the resolution you set. The first screen you see, usually the Windows splash screen announcing your investment in making Bill Gates's fortune, pops on your screen courtesy of VGA. When you can't get anything to work and your Windows-based PC snarls into service in safe mode, VGA is what you see. Much as you might want to, you can't get away from VGA.

But VGA is still just for starters. Except for the lowliest of notebook systems, every PC today strives higher. The best display systems put more than six times as much detail on your screen in more colors than you can name (or even distinguish). Choose wisely and you can get a PC display that's better than you see in the movies. And that's the way it should be because PCs are making those movies, too.

Background

Since the introduction of the PC, display adapters and display standards have evolved hand-in-hand. Programmers have followed close behind, often prodding to push things ahead even faster. Over the years, several standards have emerged, unleashing their momentum as great waves, splashing across the industry, ebbing away, and leaving puddles of advocates slowly evaporating in the heat of the latest innovations. Thanks to the acceptance of Windows, hardware standards have declined in importance. Compatibility between your programs and display system is now controlled by software drivers.

In the beginning, the only way to assure your programs could work with your display system was to ensure your PC followed an accepted hardware standard. Display adapter makers followed *de facto* industry standards for everything from memory locations to port addresses to the fonts of the character generator. Standards, however, held back progress. Manufacturers pushed beyond them to achieve better onscreen images.

Electrical compatibility issues cannot so easily be wallpapered over, however. A display adapter must electrically connect with both your PC and your display. The evolution of hardware standards for these connections has made it possible to plug just about any display into your PC and get a picture. Getting the best images—the sharpest, most colorful, and quickest—still requires careful matching of standards, however.

History

Although beauty lies in the beholder's eye, the first PC's screen was something only a zealot (or a secretary under duress) could love—ghostly green text that lingered on as the screen scrolled, crude block graphics, the kinds of stuff you thought you outgrew when you graduated from crayons to pencils. The most positive thing you could say for the original display system—the *Monochrome Display Adapter*, or MDA, which IBM introduced with its first PC in 1981—was that you never had any trouble making up your mind about what you wanted. Nor did you have to worry about compatibility—or such trivialities as art, color, aesthetics, or creativity. Only later in 1982 did IBM add color in its *Color Graphics Adapter*, or CGA, system, creating an entirely different display system, incompatible with MDA hardware but (mostly) compatible with PC software. This ancient transition has set the pattern for every change in PC display systems. Backward compatibility is an expected part of any new standard. Change your display system, and you expect your old software will continue to run.

The result of this expectation often has challenged hardware designers in crafting new products. It also results in a little bit of MDA and CGA in even the latest display systems in the newest PCs. Should you dig up a PC program written in 1981 from a fossil stratum filled with mastodons, saber-toothed cats, and Irish elk, your newest PC won't harbor a bit of doubt about how to handle images designed to display on the ancient hardware.

IBM's next stab at PC video was the *Enhanced Graphics Adapter*, or EGA, introduced in 1984. EGA combined both monochrome and color together in one board, though only one at a time (you had to set switches on the board to make it act as one or the other), and mixed in higher-resolution graphics. It worked with monitors made for either the MDA or CGA standards as well as with its own, incompatible higher-resolution standard. In retrospect, it was sort of like mating a Ford Model T with a steamboat and tying an outboard motor behind. It proved to be a technological dead end. Although current display systems still can handle software crafted for EGA, its hardware design holds only historic interest.

The *Video Graphic Array*, or VGA, introduced by IBM in 1987, represented a thorough rethinking of display technology—thorough and forward-thinking enough that it forms the basis of all modern display adapters. Strip your PC down to its minimal configuration without fancy operating systems, without driver software, without acceleration, and you'll see VGA. The least of laptop computers may, in fact, go no further. But VGA provided a solid foundation on which all of today's graphic technology was built. It remains the one enduring standard in PC display systems.

Not that no one has tried to set other hardware standards. IBM created two other hardware systems that expanded on VGA. Its *8514/A* display system, known only as the model number of the initial IBM video board, was introduced along with VGA as a higher-resolution alternative in 1987. It won little favor because its hardware used a flickery interlaced monitor (see Chapter 18, "Displays") and because, in a fit of corporate hubris, IBM initially refused to disclose the details of its operation. When the company improved on the 8514/A to create its *Extended Graphics Array*, or XGA, in 1990, few others adopted it. Unlike 8514/A, however, IBM revealed all about XGA in hopes of making it an open standard.

Two aspects of XGA survive. As with 8514/A, XGA was an accelerated video system. As such, it paved the way for today's graphic accelerators and 3D accelerators. The commands that controlled it serve as the core of instructions for most accelerated display hardware. The XGA name also is occasionally used as a description of video systems with 1,024-by-768 pixel resolution. This usage is usually incorrect in that the defining characteristic of XGA (at least when it was introduced) was its software interface of graphic commands.

The lack of any pace-setting standard beyond the basic VGA resolution level did not stop the makers of video boards from exploring higher resolution levels. As they created new products, they were careful to duplicate VGA while adding their own extensions at resolution levels and operating frequencies of their own choosing. These extended VGA boards quickly became known as Super VGA, although only the VGA part had any semblance to a standard. Nearly all were incompatible with one another at higher resolutions, requiring special drivers for DOS and any applications you wanted to push beyond VGA. Most of these early products operated at 800-by-600 pixel resolution; many reached to 1,024 by 768. What level you could actually use was another matter. You had to match your monitor as well as your software to your video board.

Resolution wasn't so much a problem as was the timing of signals. Without a standard for guidance, video board makers set the timing of their video signals—the relationship between the sync pulses and the beginning of the picture—at whatever value they thought appropriate. Timing differences translate to differences in the position of the video image on the monitor screen. Although multi-scanning monitors, which were just coming on to the market in force, could accommodate a variety of resolution levels, they couldn't by themselves sort out the timing differences. Because of the differences, the image made by one video board might appear squarely in the center of a monitor, but that from another might lose its right edge behind the screen bezel. Worse, when shifting resolutions the position of the image might change dramatically. As a result every time you shifted resolution levels, you'd have to tweak the image size and positioning controls on your monitor—if your monitor gave you image size and positioning controls.

Few people liked this system. Most people complained and blamed the makers of monitors. After all, it was the monitors that needed adjustment. The video industry needed a timing standard, and the driving force behind that standard was, quite naturally, at the time the leading maker of multi-scanning monitors, NEC Technologies. While standing in his kitchen amid dishes packed for moving from California to Chicago in 1987, Jim Schwabe of NEC got the idea for a new organization of video companies to hammer out a set of timing standards. He even thought of a name for the group, the *Video Electronics Standards Association*, or VESA.

Within the first three years of its existence, VESA came to embrace literally every maker of display adapters, most monitor manufacturers, and even large computer companies like

IBM and Compaq. VESA quickly grew into the display industry forum. All current hardware standards beyond VGA widely recognized by the PC industry have been developed by VESA.

VESA sorted out the timing problem by publishing a set of Discrete Monitor Timing standards that not only define the synchronizing rates at various resolution levels but also specify the relative timing of the sync and image signals to assure standardized image placement. To tackle the job of matching software and high-resolution video modes, the organization developed the *VESA BIOS Extensions*, or VBE, through which programs can determine the capabilities of video boards and how to access high-resolution modes. In addition, the organization shepherded the first local bus standard onto the market and developed internal interfaces for multimedia circuitry inside PCs. It continues to develop new standards for the timing and connection of video systems.

With VESA resolving most of the hardware problems, standardization issues for the most innovative of today's display technologies—2D and 3D graphics acceleration—have shifted upstream. Your software must be able to link with the instruction sets controlling the accelerators. This task is now handled by your PC's operating system, which for most people means Windows. In effect, Windows pushes the PC video standard back to where it was originally envisioned: as a software interface.

Video Board Types

The design of the PC requires that every video board actually be two boards in one. All video boards need VGA compatibility to assure that they will work properly as your PC wakes up. At boot time, the video board must work in its most primitive mode—one compatible with all PC software written since time began. All PCs boot in VGA mode and remain in that mode until your operating system loads the proper software drivers to move your display system into its high-resolution operating mode. If something goes wrong and your system cannot load its drivers, VGA mode remains to help you sort things out. For example, the safe mode of Windows operates in VGA mode without requiring special drivers to load.

In operating mode, conventional hardware compatibility standards do not matter. The drivers bridge across any oddities and mysteries. Compatibility means only that you have a driver that matches both your video board and operating system. Meet that one requirement, and anything goes.

This design has won video board makers complete freedom in crafting high-resolution, high-performance products. It underlies the use of both 2D and 3D graphic accelerators. It also means that conventional video standards are essentially irrelevant. For their high-resolution modes, board makers can choose whatever system resources (I/O ports and memory addresses) and whatever set of commands that they want to use.

Display adapters inside PCs made in the last decade can be classed as one of the following four types:

VGA boards, the most basic video boards that match the VGA standard using a dumb frame buffer and nothing more.

Super VGA (SVGA) boards that follow the VESA standards for higher resolutions but use dumb frame buffers and offer no acceleration.

Graphic accelerator boards that work with 2D drawing commands and deliver high resolutions.

3D accelerator boards that work with 3D commands.

Modern PCs rely on 3D accelerators almost exclusively. Each of the four board types in this list is backward compatible with the types preceding it. A 3D accelerator board can also handle 2D drawing as well as basic Super VGA and VGA displays—and probably better because the 3D product has the benefit of newer technology. The price difference between 2D and 3D accelerator chips is negligible, so 3D technology is the obvious choice.

Dumb frame buffers are essentially obsolete, but they cannot be ignored. You'll find them in older PCs, and you'll find their technologies lurking inside even the latest designs. They're worth taking a look at, providing you don't look too long.

The term "Super VGA" survives mostly as an indicator of video resolution. In this nomenclature, a Super VGA or SVGA video system (usually found in a notebook computer) produces 800-by-600 pixel resolution.

Circuits

The display system in PCs usually takes the form of a video (or graphic) board. Some PCs integrate the functions of the video board with their motherboards, but the circuitry and even the logical host connection are exactly the same as they would be with a separate video board.

No matter its placement, the video circuitry performs the same functions. In its frame buffer (or in main memory in systems using Unified Memory Architecture), it creates the image your PC will display. It then rasterizes the memory-mapped image and converts the digital signals into the analog format compatible with your monitor.

The modern video board usually has five chief circuits that carry out these functions, although some boards lack some of these elements. A *graphic accelerator* chip builds the image, taking commands from your software and pushing the appropriate pixel values into the frame buffer. By definition, VGA and Super VGA boards lack an accelerator chip and require your microprocessor to construct the image. *Memory* forms the frame buffer that stores the image created on the board. A *video controller* reads the image in the frame buffer and converts it to raster form. A *RAMDAC* then takes the digital values in the raster and converts them into analog signals of the proper level. And a *video BIOS* holds extension code that implements VGA and Super VGA functions and allows the board to work without your operating system installing special drivers.

Accelerator Chips

Of all the chips on a video board, the most important is the graphic accelerator. The chip choice here determines the commands the board understands—for example, whether the board can carry out 3D functions in its hardware or depends on your PC to process 3D effects. The speed at which the accelerator chip operates determines how quickly your system can build image frames. This performance directly translates into how quickly your system responds when you give a command that changes the screen (for example, dropping down a menu) or how many frames get dropped when you play back a video clip. The accelerator also limits the amount and kind of memory in the frame buffer as well as the resolution levels of the images that your PC can display, although other video board circuits can also impose limits. In short, the graphic accelerator is the most important chip in the entire video system.

That said, the accelerator is optional, both physically and logically. Old video boards lack accelerators, hence they are not "accelerated." That means your PC's microprocessor must execute all drawing instructions. In addition, even boards with accelerators may not accelerate all video operations. The board may lack commands to carry out some video tasks or the board's driver may not take advantage of all the features of the board's accelerator. In such circumstances, the drawing functions will be emulated by a Hardware Emulation Layer by your operating system—which means that your microprocessor gets stuck with the accelerator's drawing work.

Note that the MMX instructions of newer Intel microprocessors overlap the functions of graphic accelerators. Streaming SIMD extensions add performance to most graphic operations, complementing MMX. In UMA (Unified Memory Architecture) PCs, these technologies can take the place of a dedicated graphics accelerator. In PCs with frame buffers, these features work in conjunction with the graphic accelerator. They speed up your PC's ability to calculate what images look like, for example, decompressing stored images or calculating wireframes for your drafting program. The graphic accelerator actually paints the final image that will appear on your screen based on the data determined by your PC's microprocessor.

Background

The graphic accelerator is an outgrowth of an older chip technology, the *graphic coprocessor*. An early attempt to speed up the display system, the graphic coprocessor was introduced as a supplemental microprocessor optimized for carrying out video-oriented commands.

The graphic coprocessor added speed in three ways. By carrying out drawing and image manipulation operations without the need for intervention by the microprocessor, the coprocessor freed up the microprocessor for other jobs. Because the graphic coprocessor was optimized for video processing, it could carry out most image-oriented operations faster than could the microprocessor even if the microprocessor were able to devote its full time to image processing. The graphic coprocessor also broke through the bus bottleneck that was (at the time of the development of graphic coprocessor technology) choking video performance. When the microprocessor carried out drawing functions, it had to transfer every bit bound for the monitor through the expansion bus—at the time, the slow ISA bus. The coprocessor was directly connected to the frame buffer and could move bytes to and from the buffer without regard to bus speed. The microprocessor only needed to send high-level drawing commands across the old expansion bus. The graphic coprocessor would carry out the command through its direct attachment to the frame buffer.

The workstation market triggered the graphic coprocessor. Microprocessor makers altered their general purpose designs into products that were particularly adept at manipulating video images. Because the workstation market was multi-faceted with each different hardware platform running different software, the graphic coprocessor had to be as flexible as possible—programmable just like their microprocessor forebears.

These coprocessors joined the PC revolution in applications that demanded high-performance graphics. But the mass acceptance of Windows made nearly every PC graphics-intensive. The coprocessor was left behind as chip makers targeted the specific features needed by Windows and trimmed off the excess—programmability. The result was the fixed-function graphic coprocessor, exactly the same technology better known now as the graphic accelerator.

Graphic coprocessors never died. Rather, they went into the witness protection program. The latest generation of the chips once called coprocessors are now termed *Digital Signal Processors* (DSP) and are still exploited in specialized, high-performance video applications.

The most recent evolution of graphic acceleration technology has produced the *3D accelerator*. Rather than some dramatic breakthrough, the 3D accelerator is a fixed-function graphic coprocessor that includes the ability to carry out the more common 3D functions in its hardware circuitry. Just as an ordinary graphic accelerator speeds up drawing and windowing, the 3D accelerator gives a boost to 3D rendering.

As with the microprocessors, graphic and 3D accelerators come in wide varieties with different levels of performance and features. Each maker of graphic accelerators typically has a full line of products ranging from basic chips with moderate performance designed for low-cost video boards to high-powered 3D products aimed at awing you with benchmark numbers far beyond the claims of their competitors and, often, reality.

The first significant fixed-function graphic accelerators were made by S3 Corporation. The company prefers to think of its name as S-cubed, but it is generally pronounced S-three (the name is derived from Solid State Systems). The company's 86C911 chip set the pace for the first generation of accelerators. Stripped to its essentials, the chip was a hardware implementation of the features most relevant to Windows applications, drawn from the instruction set of the IBM Extended Graphics Array (XGA) coprocessor. Designed to match the ISA bus, the S3 86C911 used 16-bit architecture all around—internally and linking it to its 1MB maximum of VRAM. Although it could handle resolutions up to 1,280 to 1,024, its color abilities were limited by its RAMDAC connection.

Other manufacturers followed with their own 16-bit chips; most jumped directly into the second generation with 32-bit chips. The race quickly evolved into one of wider and wider internal bus width, up to 128 bits. Most chips now use 64-bit or wider technology, both for internal processing and for accessing the frame buffer.

Features

Bits aren't everything. The performance and output quality of a graphic accelerator depend on a number of design variables. Among the most important of these are the width of the registers it uses for processing video data, the amount and technology of the memory it uses, the ability of the chip to support different levels of resolution and color, the speed rating of the chip, the bandwidth of its connection to your PC and display, and the depth and extent of its command set, as well as how well those commands get exploited by your software. A final difference that's declining importance with the acceptance of graphic operating systems is the accelerator's handling of standard VGA signals.

Register Width

Graphic accelerators work like microprocessors dedicated to their singular purpose, and internally they are built much the same. The same design choice that determines microprocessor power also affects the performance of graphic accelerator chips. The internal register width of a graphic accelerator determines how many bits the chip works with at a time. As with microprocessors, the wider the registers, the more data that can be manipulated in a single operation.

The basic data type for modern graphic operations is 32 bits; that's the requirement of 24-bit True Color with an alpha channel. Most graphic and 3D accelerators at least double that and can move pixels two (or four) at a time in blocks.

Because the graphic or 3D accelerator makes the video circuitry of your PC a separate, isolated system, concerns about data and bus widths elsewhere in your PC are immaterial.

The wide registers in graphic accelerators work equally well no matter whether you run 16-bit software (DOS, Windows 95, and Windows 98) or 32-bit software (Windows NT and Windows 2000), no matter what microprocessor you have or what bus you plug your video board into.

Memory Technology

Graphics accelerators can be designed to use standard dynamic memory (DRAM), dual-ported video memory (VRAM), or either type. VRAM memory delivers better performance because it can handle its two basic operations (writing and reading, corresponding to image updates and writing to the screen) simultaneously. VRAM is, however, more expensive than DRAM. Although memory prices are always falling, many manufacturers skimp here to deliver products at lower prices.

The prodigious amounts of memory required by large frame buffers, double-buffering, Z-buffering, and other 3D operations make memory speed an important issue in the design of video boards. Manufacturers are adapting all major high-speed memory technologies to their products. In the next few years, the industry is likely to move to RAMBus memory because of its wide bandwidth. Some boards using RAMBus are already available and demonstrate excellent speed in operations normally constrained by memory speed. The Accelerated Graphic Port is optimized for operation with RAMBus memory or Intel's promised nDRAM, which is derived from RAMBus technology.

Resolution Support

The design of a graphic accelerator also sets the maximum amount of memory that can be used in the frame buffer, which in turn sets upper limits on the color and resolution support of a graphic accelerator. Other video board circuit choices may further constrain these capabilities. In general, however, the more memory, the higher the resolution and the greater the depth of color the accelerator can manage.

Every graphic accelerator supports three basic resolutions: standard VGA 640-by-480 pixel graphics, Super VGA 800 by 600 pixels, and 1,024 by 768 pixels. Beyond the basic trio, designers often push higher, depending on other constraints. Besides the standard increments upward (1,280 by 1,024 and 1,600 by 1,200 pixels), some makers throw in intermediate values so that you can coax monitors to their maximum sharpness for the amount of memory you have available for the frame buffer.

Color Support

Many of today's graphics accelerators are all-in-one video solutions, so they contain RAMDACs as well as video controller circuitry. These built-in RAMDACs obey the same rules as standalone chips, as discussed later. Foremost in importance is the color depth the chips can produce. Some graphic accelerators rely on standard VGA-style DAC and are limited to 18-bit VGA-style color (6 bits of each primary color) and can only discriminate between 262,144 colors. Most newer graphic accelerators with built-in DACs have full 24-bit (or 32-bit) color support, enabling them to display the 16.7 million hues of True Color. Most 3D accelerators depend on external RAMDACs so their color capabilities are determined by board design rather than the chip.

Speed Rating

The higher the resolution a graphic accelerator produces, the more pixels it must put on the screen. At a given frame rate, more pixels means each one must be produced faster; it gets a smaller share of each frame. Consequently, higher-resolution accelerator chips must be able to operate at higher speeds. For 1,024 by 768 resolution with a 75Hz frame rate, 80MHz is sufficient; for 1,280 by 1,024, 100MHz is sufficient (110MHz is better); for 1,600 by 1,200 resolution, 150MHz is needed, although 135MHz is sufficient should screen updating be limited to lower frame rates. As the demand for higher refresh rates increases, so do the speed requirements of graphic accelerators. Some chips now run as fast as 180 or 200MHz and are able to display their highest resolutions at their highest frame rates—if you can afford a monitor that can accept the signals.

Bus Bandwidth

Although graphic and 3D accelerators minimize the need for your system to ship data wholesale across an expansion bus, some types of images can only be built by moving bits through the bus. Bitmapped and video images in particular require heavy bus interaction.

Early graphic accelerators were limited by design to 16-bit interfaces because they were engineered before local bus technology appeared on the scene. They only needed to match to ISA, and 16-bits sufficed. The advent of local buses forced the new generation of chips onto the scene to take advantage of the higher possible bus throughput. Most current-generation graphic accelerators have full 32-bit interfaces to match with the leading local buses.

As the Accelerated Graphic Port moves into PCs, you can expect chips with 64-bit interfaces to dominate. After all, a 64-bit bus offers no advantage if the accelerator chip can't accommodate its data.

Besides needing a link to the system bus, graphic accelerators also couple with their own frame buffers. The width of this connection need not match that of the bus interface. For better performance, many graphic accelerators use wider connections to their video memory. Most modern chips have a 64-bit or 128-bit memory connection.

Operating System Support

The same graphic or 3D accelerator chip may deliver wildly different performance when installed in different video boards, even boards with substantially similar circuitry. One of the chief reasons for performance differences among different brands of video board is not in the hardware but the software support. Drivers can radically alter the performance of a given accelerator chip. After all, the chip only processes instructions. If the instructions are optimized, the performance of the chip will be optimum. To be useful at all, a video board must have drivers to match the operating system you want to use, as noted in the Drivers section in Chapter 16, "The Display System."

VGA Support

In the minute or two your system is booting before the operating system and its video drivers load, your video board must operate in a standard, BIOS-mediated mode. By default, nearly all video boards start off operating as if they were standard VGA boards. Consequently, every video board must have VGA support of some kind built into its hardware. Most graphic accelerator makers have integrated all the needed VGA functions into their chips. A few rely on external chips for VGA text and images.

Functionally, your software won't notice a difference between the location of the VGA support circuitry or how it performs. Once your operating system loads its video drivers, all that VGA stuff is long forgotten. The only time VGA mode comes into play is when you operate your PC without its video drivers, for example, in MS DOS mode or when booting from a DOS disk (but not in a DOS box). As long as your video board has basic VGA support, you can get going. Issue of performance are essentially immaterial to the normal operation of your system.

Video Controllers

The primary job of the video controller in desktop PCs, that use picture tubes, is to serialize the data in display memory. The conversion often is as convoluted as a video game maze. The resemblance between the memory map and the onscreen image is only metaphoric. The rows and columns into which the memory of the chips of the frame buffer are organized have no relationship to the rows and columns of pixels on your monitor screen. The bytes of video information are scattered between a handful of memory chips or modules, sliced into several logical pages, and liberally dosed with added-in features such as cursors and sprites. Somehow, all the scattered bytes of data must get organized and find their way to the monitor. In addition, the monitor itself must be brought under the control of the computer, synchronized in two dimensions.

The video controller generates the actual scanning signals. Using the regular oscillations of a crystal, the controller generates a *dot clock*, a frequency corresponding to the rate at which it will scan the data for the pixels to appear on the screen. The controller divides down this basic operating frequency to produce the horizontal synchronizing frequency and, from that, the vertical synchronizing frequency. From these frequencies, the controller can create a monitor signal that lacks only data image data. In real-time, the controller scans through the memory addresses assigned to each pixel on the screen in the exact order in which each pixel will appear on the screen. The time at which each address gets read exactly matches the time and position the pixel data appears in the final video output signal.

In modern analog PC video systems, the controller doesn't read memory directly. Rather, the digital data scanned by the controller from memory gets routed first through the RAMDAC, which converts the data from digital to analog form. The video controller then adds the analog data to the scanning signals to create the video signal that gets passed along to your monitor.

The video controller may draw pixel data from places other than the frame buffer. The circuits used by PCs generate the cursor that appears on the screen in text modes. Or it may add in the bit-values associated with a sprite. By re-routing its scan, it can make hardware windows.

In addition, the hardware video controller circuitry in PCs stores values for different operating modes and provides a means for your programs to readily select among these modes. PC controllers also allow the mixing together of pixel values using various logical operations in the hardware, for example, letting the pixels of one object reverse the color of the area of the image that it sits upon.

CRT Controller

In the language of PC engineering, the part of the video circuitry that performs the actual scanning operation is called the *CRT controller* because the signals it generates actually control the sweep of the electron beam in the CRT or picture tube of your monitor. In the first PCs, the CRT controller was a separate integrated circuit, the 6845 made by Motorola. This chip originally was not designed for computers but as a generalized scan-maker for any sort of electronic device that might plug into a television set or monitor. The engineers that designed the first PCs chose it because it was a readily available, off-the-shelf product that made the development of video boards relatively easy and cheap. Long ago, most video board manufacturers switched to custom-designed and manufactured CRT controllers, often a part of other PC video circuitry. Even the most advanced of these chips emulate the 6845 in their basic operating modes. When software calls upon the video system to operate in one of the original PC's modes to display text or low-resolution graphics, all CRT controllers react the same way to basic hardware instructions.

Software takes command of the 6845 through the chip's registers. Programs send instructions by loading the appropriate digital values in the registers. They access the registers through the input/output ports of your PC.

The registers that control the 6845 video controller chip or its equivalent in a video chipset are not directly available to your system. That is, these registers are not directly mapped to your PC's ports. Instead, they require a two-step access process that uses two ports, one that selects the register to access and one that acts as the portal to the register. A program first sends the value of the 6845 register it wants to control to the CRT *index register* on the video board. The index register acts like the channel selector on an old-fashioned television, tuning in the right 6845 register for access. Then, your program sends the data or instruction to the selected 6845 register through the CRT *control register*.

The location of these two registers varies, depending on whether your PC is operating in monochrome or color mode. The index register is located at 03B4(Hex) during monochrome operation or 03D4(Hex) during color. The control register is at 03B5(Hex) during monochrome or 03D5(Hex) during color.

You don't normally deal with the registers of the CRT controller. BIOS routines take care of all the changes you or your applications normally need to make to the CRT controller's settings. Programs need only call the appropriate BIOS routine or operating system function (which may, in turn, reach into the BIOS) to command the CRT controller.

In the first application of the 6845 controller in PCs used in early (and now obsolete) video boards, the circuitry of the video board enabled your software to command 18 of the registers of the controller chip. These 18 registers and their functions are listed in Table 17.1.

TABLE 17.1   6845 Controller Registers in Early PC Display Systems

Register Number	Description	Programming Unit	Access
00H	Horizontal total	Character	Write Only
01H	Horizontal displayed	Character	Write Only
02H	Horizontal sync position	Character	Write Only
03H	Horizontal sync width	Character	Write Only
04H	Vertical total	Row	Write Only
05H	Vertical total adjust	Scan line	Write Only
06H	Vertical displayed	Row	Write Only
07H	Vertical sync position	Row	Write Only
08H	Interlace mode	None	Write Only
09H	Maximum scan line address	Scan line	Write Only
0AH	Cursor start	Scan line	Write Only
0BH	Cursor end	Scan line	Write Only
0CH	Start address (high)	None	Write Only
0DH	Start address (low)	None	Write Only

continues

TABLE 17.1   Continued

0EH	Cursor (high)	None	Read/Write
0FH	Cursor (low)	None	Read/Write
10H	Light pen (high)	None	Read Only
11H	Light pen (low)	None	Read Only

In the VGA system, the function of the 6845 chip was taken over by the CRT controller circuits inside a dedicated video chip designed particularly for making PC displays. The VGA system altered some of the register assignments of the initial video board designs to eliminate unused features (for example, light pen support) and add versatility by giving control of a wider range of parameters. Using the same two-step register-to-port mapping system, the VGA design gives access to 24 registers on the CRT controller. Table 17.2 lists the address assignments of these registers.

TABLE 17.2   CRT Controller Registers in VGA Display Systems

Register Number	Description	Programming Unit	Access
00H	Horizontal total	Character	Read/write
01H	Horizontal display end	Character	Read/write
02H	Start horizontal blanking	Character	Read/write
03H	End horizontal blanking	Character	Read/write
04H	Start horizontal retrace	Row	Read/write
05H	End horizontal retrace	Scan line	Read/write
06H	Vertical total	Row	Read/write
07H	Overflow	Row	Read/write
08H	Present row scan	None	Read/write
09H	Maximum scan line	Scan line	Read/write
0AH	Cursor start	Scan line	Read/write
0BH	Cursor end	Scan line	Read/write
0CH	Start address high	None	Read/write
0DH	Start address low	None	Read/write
0EH	Cursor location high	None	Read/write
0FH	Cursor location low	None	Read/write
10H	Vertical retrace start	None	Read/write

Circuits

Register Number	Description	Programming Unit	Access
11H	Vertical retrace end	None	Read/write
12H	Vertical display enable end		Read/write
13H	Offset		Read/write
14H	Underline location		Read/write
15H	Start vertical blanking		Read/write
16H	End vertical blanking		Read/write
17H	CRTC mode control		Read/write
18H	Line compare		Read/write

Some registers in the VGA controller chip take on different functions. For most operations, these differences are masked by the BIOS, providing your software accesses the controller through BIOS routines. The differences become readily apparent when software takes direct hardware control. The inconsistent register assignments occur only on functions not normally used by application software. For example, the horizontal and vertical scanning signals usually get changed only by switching modes through function calls that use the BIOS to find the proper registers.

VGA Controller

By itself, however, the 6845 does not make a complete video control system. After all, there's more to making an image than just scanning memory. A video board in a PC has to track a wide variety of settings in maintaining its video display. For example, it needs to remember whether it is operating in color or monochrome mode, the number of colors to use, whether it is mapping colors from a palette, which colors or palette to use, and so on. All video boards consequently add to the circuitry of the basic controller. In the first PCs, engineers added only a handful of discrete circuits to the 6845 to make the complete controller.

By the time they designed the VGA system, the extra controller circuitry had become so complex that it required a dedicated ASIC (application-specific integrated circuit) termed, appropriately, the *VGA chip*. The same controller circuitry—and more—is often built into 2D and 3D graphic accelerator chips.

All the functions of the VGA chip are controlled through a wide set of registers. For backward compatibility with old software, the VGA chip provides both the CRT index and CRT control registers at their familiar port addresses. Other VGA functions use a variety of addresses that are consistent among all PCs. The VGA ports are within the range 0C0(Hex) to 0DF(Hex) and cannot be used for other devices. Table 17.3 lists the registers of the VGA chip and the ports normally used for accessing these registers.

TABLE 17.3   Standard VGA Register Assignments

Register Name	Class	Read or Write	Mono Port	Color Port	Index
Miscellaneous output	General	Write	03C2	03C2	N/A
Miscellaneous output	General	Read	03CC	03CC	N/A
Input status 0	General	Read only	03C2	03C2	N/A
Input status 1	General	Read only	03BA	03DA	N/A
Feature control	General	Write	03BA	03DA	N/A
Feature control	General	Read	03CA	03CA	N/A
Video subsystem enable	General	Read/write	03C3	03C3	N/A
Address	Attribute	Read/write	03C0	03C0	N/A
Palette (x16)	Attribute	Write	03C0	03C0	00-0F
Palette (x16)	Attribute	Read	03C1	03C1	00-0F
Attribute mode control	Attribute	Write	03C0	03C0	10
Attribute mode control	Attribute	Read	03C1	03C1	10
Overscan color	Attribute	Write	03C0	03C0	11
Overscan color	Attribute	Read	03C1	03C1	11
Color plane enable	Attribute	Write	03C0	03C0	12
Color plane enable	Attribute	Read	03C1	03C1	12
Horizontal PEL panning	Attribute	Write	03C0	03C0	13
Horizontal PEL panning	Attribute	Read	03C1	03C1	13
Color select	Attribute	Write	03C0	03C0	14
Color select	Attribute	Read	03C1	03C1	14
Index register	6845 chip	Read/write	03B4	03D4	N/A
CRT control register	6845 chip	Read/write	03B5	03D5	N/A
Address	Sequencer	Read/write	03C4	03C4	N/A
Reset	Sequencer	Read/write	03C5	03C5	00
Clocking mode	Sequencer	Read/write	03C5	03C5	01
Map mask	Sequencer	Read/write	03C5	03C5	02
Character map select	Sequencer	Read/write	03C5	03C5	03
Memory mode	Sequencer	Read/write	03C5	03C5	04
Address	Graphic	Read/write	03CE	03CE	N/A

Circuits

Register Name	Class	Read or Write	Mono Port	Color Port	Index
Set/reset	Graphic	Read/write	03CF	03CF	00
Enable set/reset	Graphic	Read/write	03CF	03CF	01
Color compare	Graphic	Read/write	03CF	03CF	02
Data rotate	Graphic	Read/write	03CF	03CF	03
Read map select	Graphic	Read/write	03CF	03CF	04
Graphics mode	Graphic	Read/write	03CF	03CF	05
Miscellaneous	Graphic	Read/write	03CF	03CF	06
Color don't care	Graphic	Read/write	03CF	03CF	07
Bit mask	Graphic	Read/write	03CF	03CF	08
PEL address	DAC	Read/write	03C8	03C8	N/A
PEL address	DAC	Write only	03C7	03C7	N/A
DAC state	DAC	Read only	03C7	03C7	N/A
PEL data	DAC	Read/write	03C9	03C9	N/A
PEL mask	DAC	Read/write	03C6	03C6	N/A

To achieve complete backward compatibility with older display systems, the VGA system also uses the same mode-dependent ports as the first PC video boards. In monochrome mode, the controller uses 03B0(Hex) through 03BB(Hex); in color mode, 03D0(Hex) through 03DB(Hex). These ranges include access to the CRT controller.

Hardware Cursor

When designing the first PC, IBM's engineers decided to use the CRT controller to generate a hardware cursor in text mode rather than rely on each software application to make its own cursor. Because of this design choice, the PC hardware sets the flash rate of the text-mode cursor, and it cannot be changed. Software (such as No-Squint Laptop Cursor) can only simulate different flashing rates by superimposing a different rate on the inviolable hardware rate. The size of the cursor is, however, programmable through the registers that access the CRT controller. In graphics modes—which means everything except MS DOS mode under Windows—the operating system generates the cursor and controls its flash rate.

The size of the cursor is varied by altering two registers. You load the cursor start register (bits 0 to 4) with the binary value of the row in the character matrix that you want to be the top line of the cursor, and you load the cursor end register (bits 0 to 4) with the last line of the cursor. By altering these values, you can make the cursor a block that fills an entire character position, a single scan line, or anything in between. Normally, the cursor is a two-scan-line underline. You can turn the cursor completely off by altering bit 5 of the cursor start register.

To send values to the cursor start register, you use the two-step process outlined earlier to access the 6845 registers. First, you load the CRT controller address register with the value of 0A(Hex), and then you set the value of the start line in that register. You reach the cursor end register by setting the CRT controller address register to 0B(Hex). The difference between the two register settings determines the height (size) of the cursor.

RAMDACs

Modern computer monitors use analog signals so that the signals supplied them do not limit the range of color that they can display. The data stored in your PC's frame buffer is digital because, well, everything in your PC is digital. Moreover, no convenient form of analog memory is available. As a result of this divergence of signal types, digital in and analog out, your video board must convert the digital data into the analog form compatible with your monitor. The chip that performs this magic is termed a *digital-to-analog converter*. Sometimes, it may be referred as a *RAMDAC*—the RAM for Random Access Memory—because its digital data originates in memory.

RAMDACs are classified by the number of digital bits in the digital code they translate. The number of bits translates into the number of signal levels that can appear in its output signal. For example, an 8-bit RAMDAC converts the levels encoded in 8-bit digital patterns into 256 analog levels. In a monochrome system, each one of those levels represents a shade of gray.

In color systems, each primary color or channel requires a separate DAC, a total of three. Video RAMDACs usually put all three converter channels into a single package, although some older video boards may use separate DAC chips for each color channel. Total up the number of bits across all three channels of each RAMDAC, and you'll get the number of bit-planes of color that a system can display, its palette. Most of the RAMDACs in today's video systems have three 8-bit channels, allowing them to generate the 16.7 million hues of True Color.

RAMDACs are also speed-rated. The RAMDAC chip must be fast enough to process each pixel that is to be displayed on the screen. The higher the resolution of the image you want to display, the higher the speed required from your RAMDAC. The required speed corresponds directly to the *dot-clock* (the number of pixels on the screen times the refresh rate). To accommodate high-resolution displays, some RAMDACs are rated as high as 200MHz, although 135MHz chips are currently more common. A 135MHz RAMDAC easily can handle a 1,280-by-960 pixel display with an 85Hz refresh rate.

When memory prices were high a few years ago, two specialized RAMDACs tantalized the PC industry with a promise of better, more realistic quality without increasing the memory needs of standard VGA adapters—the Color-Edge Graphic system developed by Edsun Laboratories (now part of Analog Devices) and HiColor RAMDACs from Sierra Semiconductor. Both were innovative attempts to more efficiently encode color or color transition data to make images that appear more realistic without substantially increasing the memory needs of a video board. Low memory prices have made direct-referenced color—standard 8-, 16-, and 24-bit color coding—the universal technology.

Memory

On a video board, memory mostly means frame buffer. Every video board includes a good dose of some kind of RAM for holding the bitmap of the image that appears on the screen. In addition, 3D accelerators need memory for their special operations. Double-buffering, as the name implies, doubles the memory needs by putting two separate frame buffers to work. Z-buffering and working memory for the calculations of the 3D accelerator also increase the memory needs of the video board.

The requirements of the graphic or 3D accelerator determines the type of memory required. The manufacturer of the video board sets the amount actually included on the board. Some manufacturers provide sockets to allow you to later upgrade to increase the resolution or color depth capabilities of your video system. As memory prices have fallen to the point that sockets are an appreciable fraction of the cost of adding memory, manufacturers have resorted to providing separate board models with differing memory dosages, all soldered down and not upgradable. These boards make it imperative that you decide on the resolution and color depth you require before you make a purchase. You have to balance your budget, the capabilities and limitation of your monitor, and the height and breadth of your aspirations.

In general, your choice of graphic chip will determine the memory technology used on a given video board. When you're buying a board, you'll want the highest performance memory possible.

Frame Buffer Address

So the microprocessor in your PC can directly manipulate the pixels on your screen, it must have direct access to the frame buffer. In other words, the addresses assigned to the memory in the frame buffer must be within the address range of your microprocessor. In addition, the microprocessor must know what these addresses are. The addresses must be standardized, or some means of informing the microprocessor of the identity of these addresses must be standardized.

Early video systems, up to and including VGA, located their frame buffers at standard addresses. Current systems still use (or emulate using) these addresses. In addition, they may have their own frame buffers for high-resolution displays.

The old video standards use three address ranges that are all in High DOS memory. This location was required because all three standards evolved during a time when microprocessors limited to operating in real mode was prevalent, even the only chips available. Although only limited ranges of addresses were available in High DOS memory, the low resolutions and color depths of the earliest of these systems allowed the frame buffers to fit into its confines adequately.

By the time of VGA, however, display memory requirements had already exceeded the space available in High DOS. To fit the necessary pixels into the small space real mode allowed, the VGA system resorted to the old trick of paging memory, switching blocks of addresses in and out of the real-mode address range. The default VGA standard and many VESA Super VGA systems remain confined by this technology.

Video systems not needing or wanting to look back to the days of real-mode-only microprocessors take advantage of the widest address range possible with protected-mode addressing. Many of these systems use linear memory apertures for their frame buffers.

Monochrome Modes

In the original monochrome text mode, the character buffer was located at base address 0B0000(Hex). The system reserved a 32KB range of addresses for video storage, with the last available address at 0B7FFF(Hex). Each character position on the screen uses two bytes of memory. The first byte stores the character value; the second byte, the character attribute. The entire character buffer, holding 2,000 characters arrayed as 80 columns by 25 rows, stretches for a bit less than 4KB. The address range allows for up to eight pages of displayable text. The active page was selected through BIOS functions.

Modern display adapters likely do not put any memory in this address range. To achieve compatibility with old software, they trap address requests to this range and remap them to the physical addresses used by their own character buffers. This remapping is invisible to you and your software, so when you shift your video system into monochrome text mode, it can address the old ranges just as if you'd taken your PC back in a time machine to 1981.

A graphic display system developed by Hercules Computer Technology, Inc., also used the memory range assigned to monochrome text. Before VGA, this system, which was based on the design of the *Hercules Graphics Card*, or HGC, was the reigning monochrome graphics standard. It used a frame buffer comprising 64KB of RAM functionally arranged in two contiguous 32KB banks with base addresses of 0B0000(Hex) and 0B8000(Hex). Each of these banks stored a single page of monochrome graphics. Because the upper page overlapped the range assigned to other purposes (the low-resolution color frame buffer), Hercules boards always booted up with only the half of their memory in the monochrome address range active. A configuration register located at I/O port 03BF(Hex) activated the second bank. Poking zero into the second bit (bit 1) of the register at this port disabled the second bank of memory. Poking a one enabled the second bank.

In its graphics mode, the Hercules board generated a 720-by-348 bitmapped image with two brightness levels: black and white. Eight contiguous onscreen pixels are controlled by each byte of the frame buffer, 90 bytes to each 720-pixel line. The most significant bit of each byte corresponds to the leftmost onscreen pixel stored in the byte. The Hercules system interleaved screen lines in the frame buffer so that contiguous lines in memory display four lines apart on the screen.

Low-Resolution Color Modes

The first graphics modes available to the PC operated at low resolutions, limited by the memory available in the address range assigned to the first graphic frame buffer. This range stated absolute memory location 0B8000(Hex) and ran to 0BFFFF(Hex), a range of only 32KB. Although modern display systems do not use this range for active memory, in color modes they remap addresses to this range to their own frame buffers to achieve backward compatibility with old software.

The storage arrangement in low-resolution color modes separated odd- and even-numbered scan lines. For example, in the "high-resolution" (640-by-200) mode of this system, which allowed only one bit per pixel, it stored even-numbered scan lines, starting with zero, one after the other. The odd-numbered scan lines were stored in sequence starting at an address 2000(Hex) higher. When multiple bits are assigned to an individual pixel, they are stored as sequential bits in a given byte of storage, four pixels per byte in the early "medium-resolution" (320-by-200 pixel) mode.

Color text modes work like monochrome text modes, interleaving a byte of character with a byte of character attribute for each onscreen character position. However, color text mode has two differences—the character attributes control the color of the character. In addition, the character buffer is located at the same base address as the low-resolution color frame buffer with a base address of 0B8000(Hex).

VGA Modes

Even in the early 1980s, a frame buffer of 32KB proved inadequate. To allow for more space in the frame buffer, IBM developed a paged frame buffer for its EGA system. This same memory arrangement is used today for the VGA system upon which all current video boards are based.

In moving to paged memory, IBM also moved the frame buffer to its current location at a base address of 0A0000(Hex), the very bottom of High DOS memory. The full expanse of the system's display memory is usually split four ways into 64KB banks, although a two-way 128KB-bank split is also possible. The latter mode extends across the ranges used by the old monochrome and low-resolution color frame buffers.

A register called the map mask register, which is part of the VGA chip, controls which banks the system microprocessor addresses through a 64KB range of high memory addresses. The VGA specification puts the map mask register at I/O port 03C5(Hex). Several registers actually share this port address to economize on port usage. The VGA sequencer register at port address 03C4(Hex) controls the function of the port used by the map mask register. When the sequencer register is set to the value 02(Hex), port 03C5(Hex) gives access to the map mask register.

The map mask register has four control bits. In the VGA's original 16-color mode, each bit nominally controls a bit plane and switches the intensity on or off red, green, and blue signals (listed from most significant bit to least). Unlike most bank switching systems, the VGA system allows multiple banks to be switched on simultaneously. This scheme allows an onscreen hue that's mixed from more than one color to be loaded in a single cycle. For example, if your system could only activate the VGA banks individually, writing a bright white dot would take four separate operations—writing a bit of one color, switching banks, and then writing another color, and so on. By activating all four banks simultaneously, writing the white bit takes only one switch and write operation.

Addressing within each bank is linear in the original 16-color VGA graphic mode. That is, the memory arrangement puts onscreen pixels and lines into memory in the same order that they appear on the screen. The bit data in a byte from most significant to least significant bit corresponds to an onscreen sequence of eight pixels in a line from left to right.

In 256-color mode, each byte of memory defines the color of a single pixel. The bank-control logic of the VGA system divides the 256KB of memory for onscreen pixels into four 64KB blocks. These banks essentially duplicate one another but provide a convenient way of scanning color plane data into the RAMDAC. Because there are eight color signals per pixel, and the VGA system is designed to scan four color planes at a time, the 256-color pages are scanned twice to make the transfer.

In text modes, the VGA memory banks act as if they are at the old mode locations and are similarly interleaved: odd bytes of display memory in the first bank; even bytes in the second bank. In normal text-mode operation, this corresponds to putting the character values in the first bank and attribute data in the second bank. The various pages of character memory start at each 2KB paragraph address boundary. For example, when operating in color text mode, the first page will be based at 0B8000(Hex), the second page at 0B8800(Hex), and so on.

The mechanics of the address remapping used by the VGA system are relatively straight-forward. A register in the VGA control circuitry acts as the switch. The memory map register controls the base address of the VGA's video memory and the page size of each bank.

Accessing the memory map register is a two-step process. First, the graphic address register at the microprocessor I/O port must be set with a value of 06(Hex) to enable writing to the memory map register through the VGA's miscellaneous register at the microprocessor port address 03C2(Hex), an address shared with a number of other functions. Bits 2 and 3 in the memory map register control bank address and size.

Setting bit 3 of the memory map register to zero locates the base address of the frame buffer at 0A0000(Hex). Bit 2 then controls bank size. Set to zero, it specifies two 128KB banks; set to one, it indicates four 64KB banks.

When bit 3 of the memory map register is set to one, bank size is set at 32KB and bit 2 controls the base address used by the two permitted banks. With bit 2 set to zero, the buffer base address is 0B0000(Hex); when set to one, the buffer base address is 0B8000(Hex).

Other Apertures

The VGA paged memory system allows larger frame buffers with the simple expedient of adding pages. The price of this simplicity is complication. To directly access the various pages, programmers have to keep track of many pages, 32 of them for a board with a 2MB frame buffer. In addition, memory access and scanning get slowed down by the need to shift pages multiple times per frame.

With the shift to protected mode, the use of larger address ranges for the frame buffer became feasible. The first widely available display system to take advantage of the vast space afforded by protected-mode memory was the XGA system.

In its initial incarnation, XGA allowed for three different frame buffer locations termed *memory apertures*. The basic aperture was the old page VGA frame buffer in High DOS memory. In addition, XGA opened two protected-mode apertures.

A 1MB aperture allowed XGA memory to be controlled through a 1MB window, which can be located on any 1MB boundary within the first 16MB of protected-mode memory. To accommodate larger frame buffers up to 4MB, this aperture was also paged. This compromise enlarged-but-paged design permitted a large frame without robbing too much memory from the limited range of the 286 and 386SX microprocessors. You'll find more about memory apertures and problems resulting from their placement in Chapter 4, "Memory."

XGA also permitted a large *linear aperture* in protected-mode memory beyond the lower 16MB. The design permits complete freedom in the placement of this buffer, although normally, it will be located at addresses high enough to not interfere with physical RAM. Modern 3D accelerators may use linear apertures as large as 64MB. The address range used by these boards is assigned dynamically by the PCI system. The plug-and-play configuration process automatically finds a range that does not conflict with other system devices or resources.

BIOS

The built-in BIOS of the traditional PC includes a section of code for handling video, but its support is limited to the early dumb frame buffer boards used in the first PCs, the MDA and CGA boards noted among the obsolete standards. All video boards since (and including) the also obsolete EGA included their own add-in BIOSs containing code for the added functions brought by the board. During boot-up, your PC loads the vectors to this add-in BIOS code so that your programs can call the routines to display images on the screen. If just for compatibility with the boot-up VGA standard, all video boards, including the latest 3D accelerators, include their own BIOS code.

Depending on the video board, this BIOS code may be contained in 8-bit or 16-bit memory, even in 32-bit computers. The narrow bus and the slow access times for the EPROM memory chips make this BIOS code some of the slowest to execute on most PCs. To get this code up to speed, most PCs shadow the video BIOS code. After your operating system loads its video drivers, shadowing and the BIOS itself become irrelevant. The driver software bridges your applications (through the operating system) to the hardware. The BIOS simply gets ignored.

If you weren't forced to sometimes run DOS applications and diagnose system problems before your operating system boots up, you could ignore the BIOS, too, a relic of a bygone era. But even when you're running the most exotic 3D graphics, the BIOS remains on your video board waiting, just waiting, until you need it again—sort of Puff the Magic BIOS.

PC Video BIOS

Because the original PC was designed to be able to operate even without an operating system—it had its own, built-in programming language—its original BIOS was written to include the ability to take care of all normal display function, albeit at a rather rudimentary level. By issuing software interrupt 10(Hex) with one register (AH) of the microprocessor loaded with the proper value, the BIOS would locate the ports used by the display adapter and instruct it to carry out the appropriate function. The range of these functions was modest. The basic functions of the video BIOS interrupt are listed in Table 17.4.

TABLE 17.4 PC BIOS Interrupt 10(Hex) Functions

AH Value	Function
00H	Set video mode
01H	Set cursor type
02H	Set cursor position
03H	Read cursor position
04H	Read light pen position
05H	Select active display page
06H	Scroll active page up
07H	Scroll active page down
08H	Read character and attribute at cursor position
09H	Write character and attribute at cursor position
0AH	Write character only at cursor position
0BH	Set color palette
0CH	Write dot
0DH	Read dot
0EH	Write teletype (one character)
0FH	Current video state

The original intention of the design of the original PC was that all video operations were to be handled by the BIOS. To draw graphics on the screen, programs were supposed to repeatedly call function 0C(Hex) of the video BIOS. This design was supposed to ensure the hardware independence of PC software so that the frame buffer could be moved anywhere in memory. The price of this versatility was performance. Using the BIOS required that dozens of microprocessor instructions write each pixel, and in the days when PCs ran at less than 1/100th their current rate, you might raise a forest of bristle-cone pines waiting for an image to paint on the screen. This laggardly performance led programmers to write directly to the frame buffer and basically ignore the BIOS.

VGA BIOS

When PCs gain new, higher-resolution modes, larger frame buffers, and more colors, their video BIOSs got updated to match. The EGA system was first to add extensively to the BIOS, but the lasting improvements came later, with VGA.

Because it required operating modes not conceived at the time the original PC BIOS was written, the VGA display system required its own BIOS extensions, a total of nine new functions. The first computers to use VGA incorporated the display circuitry on their motherboards and put the necessary code into the system BIOS. ROM chips on add-in VGA boards extended the BIOS in the PCs into which the boards were installed. Table 17.5 lists the functions added by the revised VGA BIOS.

TABLE 17.5   VGA BIOS Extensions

AH Value	Function
10H	Set palette registers
11H	Character generator
12H	Alternate select
13H	Write string
14H	Load LCD character font
15H	Return physical display parameters
16H	Reserved
17H	Reserved
18H	Reserved
19H	Reserved
1AH	Read/write display combination code
1BH	Return functionality or state information
1CH	Save/restore video state

By the time VGA was developed, direct writing was the standard means of writing to the video board. The VGA BIOS extensions don't make any attempt at handling all-points-addressable graphics. Most of the new codes, in fact, are concerned with identifying the hardware of the display system.

Super VGA

Display systems that went beyond VGA had one inherent problem—the lack of a standard to follow. VESA sought to establish a standard but due to the diversity of products and functions chose not to mandate a strict hardware standard. Instead, it left the design details of the inner workings of higher-resolution display adapters to the engineers working for board makers. VESA chose a system approach, defining what went in and what came out, essentially making the high-resolution video board a magical black box.

Circuits

On the output side, VESA developed standards and guidelines for monitor timings. At the other end, it created an extension to the standard VGA BIOS. These *VESA BIOS Extensions* aimed exclusively at eliminating compatibility worries. They did nothing for the regular handling of video signals. Programmers did, after all, prefer writing to frame buffers.

Compared to the standard video support built into the basic PC BIOS, that provided by the VESA extension is modest. The additional code holds no new text or individual bit-handling routines. Instead, the extension simply provides information that your video drivers and applications need to be able to use the higher resolutions of a Super VGA display adapter. The VESA BIOS Extensions simply told them where to find the frame buffer and how to operate the various features of the video board. Rather than a secret recipe, the VESA BIOS Extension is the key that unlocks the secret. The video driver software uses the key to put display bits into the proper pixel positions.

One of the most important functions of the VESA BIOS Extension is to report which modes a particular display adapter understands and displays from among the range supported by the VESA standard. These cover all the major resolution levels and color depths currently used by display adapters.

Windows has, of course, made the VESA BIOS a less critical issue. Normal second-to-second operation of most video boards runs through the drivers installed particularly for each board. The driver gives the fastest possible access to the full range of features of the board.

Nevertheless, the VESA BIOS survives today, to the extent of being recently revised to its third incarnation, published on September 16, 1998. The new version, VBE 3.0, operates as dual-mode code, able to be called in real mode through the standard interrupt 10(Hex) method or in protected mode as program calls. Through the VESA BIOS, your PC can control a video board with generic drivers, or the board's drivers can access hardware code to control special features.

The basic VESA BIOS interface takes advantage of the standard IBM video function calls that are activated with software interrupt 010(Hex). The VESA BIOS Extension adds one additional function call, 04F(Hex), which is otherwise unused. By loading different parameters when making this function call, software can elicit a number of functions from the VESA BIOS Extension. Table 17.6 lists the basic VESA BIOS Extension function calls.

TABLE 17.6 Basic VBE Function Calls

Function Number	Associated Operations
00H	Return VBE controller information
01H	Return VBE mode information

continues

TABLE 17.6 Continued

Function Number	Associated Operations
02H	Set VBE mode
03H	Return current VBE mode
04H	Save/restore state
05H	Display window control
06H	Set/get logical scan line length
07H	Set/get display start
08H	Set/get DAC palette format
09H	Set/get palette data
0AH	Return VBE protected-mode interface

Version 2.0 extended the VESA BIOS to include multimedia facilities, including control of audio and MIDI control systems. Each of these uses its own function call to send the appropriate information to inquiring software.

Mode Numbers

VESA developed its very first mode to extend ordinary VGA systems to 800-by-600 pixel resolution. By the time the association had begun its work, individual manufacturers had already developed their own modes. VESA chose to number its own mode 06A(Hex) and used it as a phantom mode; when this VESA mode was elicited, the display adapter actually switched to one of its own, native modes that supported the 800-by-600 pixel resolution level.

Originally, IBM provided eight bits for tracking video modes. To prevent confusion between proprietary video modes and VESA standards, VESA extended the range to 15 bit values. All modes agreed upon after the original 800-by-600 pixel standard were given 15-bit mode numbers, and the original 06A(Hex) mode was given an alternate number, 101(Hex). Table 17.7 lists the VESA video modes.

TABLE 17.7 Commonly Used Video Mode Numbers

Mode Number	Text or Graphic	Originator	Graphic Resolution			Text Resolution	
			Horizontal	Vertical	Colors	Columns	Rows
0	Text	IBM	-	-	-	40	25
1	Text	IBM	-	-	-	40	25

Circuits

Mode Number	Text or Graphic	Originator	Graphic Resolution			Text Resolution	
			Horizontal	Vertical	Colors	Columns	Rows
2	Text	IBM	-	-	-	80	25
3	Text	IBM	-	-	-	80	25
4	Graphic	IBM	320	200	4	-	-
5	Graphic	IBM	320	200	4	-	-
6	Graphic	IBM	640	200	2	-	-
7	Text	IBM	-	-	-	80	25
8	Graphic	IBM	160	200	16	-	-
9	Graphic	IBM	320	200	16	-	-
A	Graphic	IBM	640	200	4	-	-
B	Graphic	Proprietary	704	519	16	-	-
D	Graphic	IBM	320	200	16	-	-
E	Graphic	IBM	640	200	16	-	-
F	Graphic	IBM	640	350	2	-	-
10	Graphic	IBM	640	350	16	-	-
11	Graphic	IBM	640	480	2	-	-
12	Graphic	IBM	640	480	16	-	-
13	Graphic	IBM	320	200	256	-	-
22	Text	Ahead	-	-	16	132	44
23	Text	Ahead	-	-	16	132	25
24	Text	Ahead	-	-	16	132	28
25	Graphic	Ahead	640	480	16	-	-
26	Graphic	Ahead	640	480	16	-	-
2F	Text	Ahead	-	-	16	160	50
32	Text	Ahead	-	-	16	80	34
33	Text	Ahead	-	-	16	80	34
34	Text	Ahead	-	-	16	80	66
42	Text	Ahead	-	-	4	80	34

continues

TABLE 17.7 Continued

Mode Number	Text or Graphic	Originator	Graphic Resolution			Text Resolution	
			Horizontal	Vertical	Colors	Columns	Rows
43	Text	Ahead	–	–	4	80	45
50	Graphic	Proprietary	640	480	16	–	–
50	Text	Ahead	–	–	2	132	25
50	Text	MXIC	–	–	16	132	25
50	Text	MXIC	–	–	16	132	30
51	Text	Ahead	–	–	4	132	28
52	Text	Ahead	–	–	2	132	44
53	Graphic	Proprietary	800	560	16	–	–
55	Graphic	MXIC	800	600	16	–	–
56	Graphic	MXIC	1,024	768	16	–	–
57	Graphic	MXIC	640	350	256	–	–
58	Graphic	Proprietary	800	600	16	–	–
58	Graphic	MXIC	640	400	256	–	–
59	Graphic	Proprietary	720	512	16	–	–
59	Graphic	MXIC	640	480	256	–	–
5A	Graphic	MXIC	800	600	256	–	–
5B	Graphic	MXIC	1,024	768	256	–	–
60	Graphic	Ahead	640	400	256	–	–
61	Graphic	Ahead	640	480	256	–	–
62	Graphic	Ahead	800	600	256	–	–
63	Graphic	Ahead	1,024	768	256	–	–
6A	Graphic	VESA	800	600	16	–	–
70	Graphic	Proprietary	800	600	16	–	–
70	Graphic	Ahead	720	396	16	–	–
71	Graphic	Proprietary	800	600	16	–	–
71	Graphic	Ahead	800	600	16	–	–
73	Graphic	Proprietary	640	480	16	–	–

Mode Number	Text or Graphic	Originator	Graphic Resolution			Text Resolution	
			Horizontal	Vertical	Colors	Columns	Rows
74	Graphic	Ahead	1,024	768	16	-	-
75	Graphic	Ahead	1,024	768	4	-	-
76	Graphic	Ahead	1,024	768	2	-	-
77	Graphic	Proprietary	752	410	16	-	-
79	Graphic	Proprietary	800	600	16	-	-
100	Graphic	VESA	640	400	256	-	-
101	Graphic	VESA	640	480	256	-	-
102	Graphic	VESA	800	600	16	-	-
103	Graphic	VESA	800	600	256	-	-
104	Graphic	VESA	1,024	768	16	-	-
105	Graphic	VESA	1,024	768	256	-	-
106	Graphic	VESA	1,280	1,024	16	-	-
107	Graphic	VESA	1,280	1,024	256	-	-
108	Text	VESA	-	-	-	80	60
109	Text	VESA	-	-	-	132	25
10A	Text	VESA	-	-	-	132	43
10B	Text	VESA	-	-	-	132	50
10C	Text	VESA	-	-	-	132	60
10D	Graphic	VESA	320	200	32K	-	-
10E	Graphic	VESA	320	200	64K	-	-
10F	Graphic	VESA	320	200	16M	-	-
110	Graphic	VESA	640	480	32K	-	-
111	Graphic	VESA	640	480	64K	-	-
112	Graphic	VESA	640	480	16M	-	-
113	Graphic	VESA	800	600	32K	-	-
114	Graphic	VESA	800	600	64K	-	-
115	Graphic	VESA	800	600	16M	-	-
116	Graphic	VESA	1,024	768	32K	-	-

continues

TABLE 17.7 Continued

Mode Number	Text or Graphic	Originator	Graphic Resolution			Text Resolution	
			Horizontal	Vertical	Colors	Columns	Rows
117	Graphic	VESA	1,024	768	64K	-	-
118	Graphic	VESA	1,024	768	16M	-	-
119	Graphic	VESA	1,280	1024	32K	-	-
11A	Graphic	VESA	1,280	1024	64K	-	-
11B	Graphic	VESA	1,280	1024	16M	-	-
11C	Graphic	VESA	1,600	1200	32K	-	-
11D	Graphic	VESA	1,600	1200	64K	-	-
11E	Graphic	VESA	1,600	1200	16M	-	-
81FF	Special VESA memory preservation mode						

For software using the VESA BIOS Extensions, finding the available modes is only a start. Your software uses the information reported back by the VESA BIOS extension to determine whether it can operate at the resolution and color level you want. Once the software is certain it can operate in the proper mode, it must then find out how. By sending another function code to the VESA BIOS Extension, your software can determine the location and control system for the memory banks used by the frame buffer for a given video mode. In fact, the latest VBE, version 2.0, encourages but does not require support of these mode numbers. According to the VBE 2.0 specifications, future resolutions and color depths will be defined by VESA display manufacturers.

Internal Interfaces

The video system in your PC must somehow link up with the rest of its circuitry. In most display systems, the connection is intimate. It gives your PC's microprocessor the power to directly intervene and inject data such as an image bitmap right into the frame buffer. That means that the frame buffer must be within the addressing range of the microprocessor.

Only in UMA systems is the frame buffer actually part of the main memory system, accessible through the memory bus. In all other PCs, the frame buffer links to the rest of the system through a bus. In old systems, this link was the standard expansion bus or its equivalent. In modern PCs, the video link is directly through the PCI bus or its AGP offshoot.

In modern multimedia PCs, the display adapter may not be the only board processing video. Video capture, editing, and compression systems may require dedicated hardware that works in conjunction with your display adapter. To work properly, the auxiliary system and your graphics adapter need an *inter-card connection*, a dedicated high-speed connection, one separate from the expansion bus.

Bus Interfaces

In the basic PC design, the frame buffer is not part of the memory system used by your PC's microprocessor for running programs. Although the frame buffer may be directly addressed by the microprocessor, either fully or through a window, it connects through the expansion bus circuitry rather than the memory bus. This design is a carry-over from the primitive days of the first PC. The designers of the PC consigned the frame buffer and the rest of the display system to a separate expansion board that necessarily connected through the expansion bus. Not only was there not enough room on the first PC motherboards to incorporate all the video components, but also this design added flexibility. You could upgrade the video capabilities of your PC by merely exchanging graphics boards.

For the sake of design and operational consistency, most PCs use the bus interface to link to their video circuitry even when the video system is part of the motherboard. Upgrading the video on these systems requires switching off the motherboard video circuitry, usually with a hardware jumper or as a configuration setting.

There's nothing inherently wrong with using the bus connection for video operations; it works, doesn't it? As a practical matter, however, the bus-based design imposes a singular limitation: The bus constrains video performance. A low-bandwidth bus means poor video speed. One of the major thrusts in PC design over the last decade has been to accelerate video performance by increasing the bandwidth of this bus connection.

ISA

The first decade of PCs used whatever bus they had for linking to their graphics adapters. It all started with the 8-bit bus of the original PC. With the advent of the AT and its 16-bit ISA expansion bus, the advantage of using a wider bus connection became obvious. Display adapter boards with 16-bit interfaces proved themselves substantially faster than boards with 8-bit connectors. With twice the bus width, 16-bit adapters could acquire display data quicker, delivering almost the expected doubling of performance.

Around 1987, some PC manufacturers, including industry leaders Compaq and IBM, rethought the reason for plugging video into expansion slots. The increased scale of integration left room on the motherboard that might be used by display circuitry, and that's where cost-conscious manufacturers put it. At first, they used the same circuitry as the I/O bus to assure compatibility. Although the video circuitry was physically relocated to the motherboard, it remained electrically and logically connected through the same old bus control circuitry. This design expedient assured that any video operation would properly find the frame buffer and video controller exactly where it was expected.

Local Bus

By the early 1990s, microprocessors began to generate video data faster than the standard expansion buses could carry it. This shortfall became obvious as the 386 family of microprocessors became popular. The power of the 386 made multitasking and graphic operating environments popular. Shifting to graphics increased the amount of data that had to be moved in and through the video system, from a few kilobytes to hundreds of thousands per frame, millions per second for anything approaching real-time action. The old expansion bus connection choked under the load. Video speed became the chief performance constraint on PCs.

The industry response was to develop the local bus, as discussed in Chapter 7, "The Expansion Bus." Local bus brought an order of magnitude improvement in throughput—first VL Bus, then PCI.

Although PCI gave a near-quantum boost to bus performance, the demand for greater graphics speed soon outran the capabilities of even that bus. Intel's response was to enhance PCI to provide a single slot with accelerated performance, the Accelerated Graphic Port, or AGP.

Accelerated Graphic Port

The Accelerated Graphic Port is not a display standard in that it does not specify color, resolution, or other aspects of the look of your monitor screen. Rather, it is a connection standard that describes a new, high-speed bus connection between the video system in your PC and its microprocessor and memory. In effect, it is a specialized expansion bus, one that recalls local bus designs. You might even consider it the second generation of local bus for video systems.

The AGP design originated in Intel labs and was officially released as a standard (version 1.0) on July 31, 1996. As you might expect from a new bus design from Intel, it is based on the PCI design and follows basic PCI protocol and signaling. Because it's high speed—potentially four times that of today's PCI—it uses its own, incompatible connector design and imposes tight restrictions on design layouts. Intel specifically matched the design to the Pentium Pro microprocessor, noting that the faster cache and floating-point processor designs in the Pentium Pro give it superior performance in systems designed for 3D graphics. A lesser processor would make the AGP into the equivalent of an hourglass shaped like a cylinder instead of having its distinctive wasp-waist; turn it upside down, and all the sand would instantly glob to the bottom, just as the data would wing through the AGP with bandwidth to spare.

On May 4, 1998, Intel revised the AGP design to version 2.0. The improvements were twofold. By adding a transfer mode, Intel created a new quadruple-speed mode for AGP. In addition, the new specification allows for lower-voltage operation. In addition to the 3.3-volt design of AGP 1.0, the revision allows for 1.5-volt operation as well.

Note that Windows NT 4.0 does not include full support for AGP. Utilizing all the features of the slot requires DirectX support, and the first incarnation of Windows NT with built-in support is Windows 2000. Windows NT 4.0 will run with AGP video boards, but that operating system only extends support to two-dimensional graphics modes.

More than just another link, however, the AGP incorporates dedicated pipelined access to main memory. Coupled with its wide bandwidth, its design allows an accelerator chip on an AGP expansion board to use main memory for video functions such as z-buffering, texture mapping, and alpha blending.

Although based on revision 2.1 of the PCI specifications, the AGP design goes beyond them with three innovations: pipelined memory that eliminates wait states, separate address and data lines on the bus to cut the necessary number of cycles per transfer, and a timing specification allowing operation at 133MHz across a 32-bit bus, allowing for throughput on the order of 500 MB/sec. The actual clock speed of the AGP bus is 66MHz, matching the PCI 2.1 specs. To achieve the higher data rates, the AGP system relies on more exotic technologies, discussed in the sections "2x Transfer Mode" and "4x Transfer Mode," later in this chapter.

The AGP shares the same physical address space for memory with the PCI system and microprocessor. It uses a 32-bit address bus that can handle up to a 4GB address range. Matching its 32-bit data bus, AGP transfers always move data in 8-byte blocks, double the granularity of standard PCI transfers (which slices data into 4-byte blocks). To accommodate smaller data types, the AGP interface can also use PCI transfer modes.

Despite its PCI foundation, AGP has its own set of commands and transfer protocol. The AGP interface hardware supports both the AGP transfers and traditional PCI transfers as separate modes.

Unlike PCI, where address and data cycles are intimately linked, the AGP modes disconnects them. This allows other data to intervene in between. This design allows the system to keep the pipeline filled. Each access request across the AGP is sent to a queue while it awaits the transfer of its associated data. The AGP devices track the access requests and data in their hardware. Access requests in the queue are prioritized into high- and low-priority sub-queues. PCI transfers have their own queue.

The AGP design allows for a maximum of 256 transactions in the pipeline at once, although hardware capabilities will further constrain the pipeline. When the plug-and-play system sets up the AGP board, the AGP hardware reports the maximum depth that the pipeline can support in its host computer.

On the other hand, the AGP transfer modes allow access only to memory. It does not link to input/output ports or configuration memory. In addition, to help the AGP achieve its high speed, its design cuts it free from cache snooping, so changes made through AGP are not necessarily reflected in the memory cache.

Architecture

AGP clearly shows the new role of video in the future of the PC. Through AGP, video is given its own dedicated interface and connection. It does not share a bus with expansion boards or even memory. It has a direct reach to the high holy sanctum of the PC, the microprocessor and chipset.

In effect, the AGP is a fourth bus in a modern PC, added to the expected compatibility bus (ISA), high-speed expansion bus (PCI), and memory bus. The signals for AGP arise in the same system control logic that links to the PCI bridge and main memory in the PC. As shown in Figure 17.1, the AGP design gives the graphics chip of a PC the same direct connection with the chipset as honors the microprocessor, PCI bridge, and memory system.

FIGURE 17.1

Block diagram show-ing the role of AGP in modern system archi-tecture.

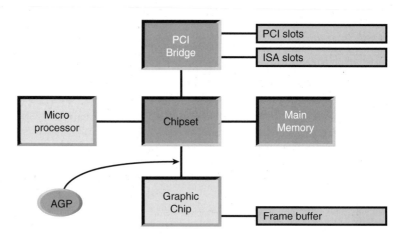

AGP operates solely between two devices. By design, one of these must be the system memory controller, which is normally part of the PC's chipset. To the AGP system, the chipset is the target device and AGP transfers are controlled by the graphics board at the other end of the connection, which is the master. In PCI transfer modes, the host chipset operates as a PCI sequencer, which is capable of service as both master and target. The video board only need operate as a PCI target, although it may have master functions as well.

Operation

Intel envisioned that the AGP would be used in two different ways. Its DMA model pic-tured AGP as a fast channel for moving large blocks of data between a dedicated frame buffer and main system memory. Your PC's graphic chip would work conventionally, working in the memory on the expansion board, carrying out most operations directly in the frame buffer. The system would use DMA transfers across the AGP to move bit image data from system memory to the frame buffer. The execute model sees the AGP as a means of connecting the graphic accelerator to main memory. The accelerator chip on the video board can use main memory for the execution of high-level functions such as anti-aliasing and 3D rendering. The graphic chip would use the AGP to draw data from system memory and hold intermediate results, loading the final data of the image into the local frame buffer.

In either case, transfers are mediated in the same way. First, either end of the connection negotiates to use the interface.

When operating in its native AGP mode, the graphics controller starts each transaction by making an access request to the system board chipset. The chipset then schedules its action on the request, working around other tasks that involve the bus. The chipset can accumulate several graphics requests and begin to process them while waiting for the actual data transfer to take place. In effect, the processing steps involved in the transfer requests are pipelined much like instructions in an advanced microprocessor.

The transfer requests in the pipeline are split into two queues, one with high priority and one with low priority, for each read and write request. The AGP system puts the responsibility for tracking the status of all the transfers on the graphics controller requesting them, and the controller determines the number of requests waiting in each queue. The chipset processes the request—for example, transferring data from system memory to the frame buffer—as free time in the system allows it. It can process requests from the various queues as system resources allow, so it may interleave the processing of read and write requests.

When operating in its PCI mode, the graphics controller acts like any PCI device. Although the basic design of the AGP system gives separate control to the PCI transactions across the bus, the PCI transfers are not pipelined like the native AGP transactions.

The signals used for AGP transfers are built on a foundation of the PCI bus. The AGP standard augments the PCI standard with special control signals Intel terms sideband signals. They alter the timing of the PCI bus to allow higher data throughput. The PCI data and bus control lines still channel information during AGP transfers, but a new signal termed PIPE# defines the AGP transfer much as the FRAME# signal defines PCI transfers. The complete signal assignments of the AGP are listed on the CD-ROM.

When the PIPE# signal is active, the system operates in the AGP 2X transfer mode and moves data across the bus twice during each cycle. Request queuing, pipelining, parallel execution, and the double-time transfer cycle all contribute to the higher throughput of the AGP interface.

AGP-defined protocols (such as pipelining) are overlaid on the PCI bus at a time and in a manner that a PCI bus agent (non-AGP) would view the bus as idle. Both pipelined access requests (read or write) and resultant data transfers are handled in this manner. The AGP interface uses both PCI bus transactions without change, as well as AGP pipelined transactions as defined herein. Both of these classes of transactions are interleaved on the same physical connection. The access request portion of an AGP transaction (bus command, address, and length) is signaled differently than is a PCI address phase. The information is still transferred on the AD and C/BE# signals of the bus as is the case with PCI 6 but is identified or framed with a new control signal, PIPE#, in a similar way to which PCI address phases are identified with FRAME#.

2X Transfer Mode

For high-performance systems in which the 266 MB/sec potential of basic AGP is inadequate, the original AGP specification allowed for higher-speed transfers in its *2x transfer mode*. Using the proven technique called *double-clocking*, 2x mode pushes the maximum potential throughput of the AGP system to 533 MB/sec.

Double-clocking makes the clock signal do double duty, keying transfers to both its leading and trailing edges. That is, the transition marking the beginning of the clock signal triggers one transfer across the bus, and the transition ending the clock pulse triggers another. In most logic systems and basic AGP mode, only the leading edge of the clock signals valid data, allowing the transfer.

To improve the reliability of 2x transfer mode, it uses three *strobe* signals rather than the clock itself. The clock signal originates in your PC as part of its array of PCI signals. In contrast, the device sending data generates the strobe signals. When your PC sends data to the AGP board, the PC creates the strobes. When the AGP board sends data to your PC, the AGP board creates the strobes. Because the sending device generates both the data and strobe signals, the timing relationship between the two can be more precisely controlled.

The strobe signals appear only within the interconnection between the AGP transmitting and receiving circuits and the hardware connection between them. In AGP terminology, this is the *inner loop*. The rest of the AGP system is the *outer loop*.

The specification defines individual strobe signals for the low and high 16 bits of the AGP bus as well as the sideband. The AGP circuitry issues the strobe signals at the same frequency as the AGP clock, but the specification more rigidly defines the timing of the strobes. The high and low phases of the strobe signal are equal, so leading and trailing edges of the signals are evenly spaced and transfers keyed to the edges occur uniformly.

4X Transfer Mode

In enhancing the performance of AGP, the Intel engineers faced a major problem. The original design already strained at the high-frequency limit of the connector system. Increasing the speed of AGP would require a redesign with expensive new technologies. To avoid most of these issues, the Intel engineers kept their changes inside the inner loop, designing a more elaborate strobe system.

To create 4x transfer mode, Intel's engineers doubled the frequency of the strobe signals and double-clocked the data keyed to them. This change again doubles the potential throughput of the system, yielding a maximum rate of 1,066 MB/sec.

With the increase in strobe frequency comes a need for a tighter definition of the timing of the signals. Intel created the necessary precision by adding three more strobe signals. Each one is paired with one of the 2x transfer mode signals but is the opposite polarity, turning each strobe into a differential pair. When one of the strobes in a pair transitions from high to low, the other moves from low to high. At one instant during the paired transitions, at approximately midway between them, the voltage values of the two signals are equal; on a timing chart, the values cross. The 4x transfer mode keys each transfer to one of these crossings. Because these crossings occur twice in each strobe cycle and the strobe frequency is twice the basic AGP clock frequency, transfers occur at four times the basic AGP rate.

Intel took another step to help AGP achieve the speed required by 4x transfer mode. It lowered the voltage of the signals, which helps deal with the capacitance inherent in any bus system. All AGP boards that operate in AGP 4x transfer mode must use 1.5-volt signaling.

Expansion Cards

The AGP design assumes that the 3D accelerator chip and frame buffer will have a home on an expansion board rather than the motherboard, although nothing about the interface design precludes putting all the circuitry on the motherboard. In a typical PC, an expansion slot supporting the AGP connection fits on the motherboard like a PCI slot, with the same spacing and dimensional requirements. Although a given PC or motherboard may omit a PCI slot in favor of an AGP connection, AGP is electrically separate from the PCI slots and does not reduce the number of slots that may be connected to a single bridge.

The AGP circuit board design is built around a conventional PCI card, at least for use in full-size computers—those matching (or approximating) the ATX design. For these systems, the original AGP standard provided for the two sizes of card. A full-size AGP board measures 4.2 inches (107 millimeters) tall and 12.28 inches (312 millimeters) long. Short cards measure only 6.875 inches (175 millimeters) long. Figure 17.2 illustrates these principal dimensions.

FIGURE 17.2

Dimensions of an ATX-size AGP video board.

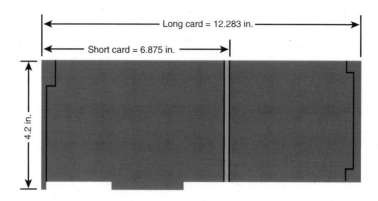

For low-profile computers that match the NLX standards, the revised AGP 2.0 standard provides a special, low-slung card form factor that allows the AGP-based graphics adapter to plug into the motherboard rather than the riser that accommodates other expansion boards. Figure 17.3 shows the dimensions of the NLX-style AGP board.

FIGURE 17.3

Dimensions of an NLX-style AGP video board.

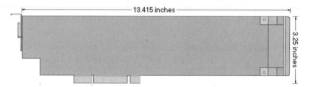

The slot spacing for AGP expansion boards in ATX computers is the same as for PCI and ISA boards, 0.8 inch. AGP boards in such systems use the same retaining bracket design as ordinary PCI boards. The NLX design, however, requires a special bracket, as shown in Figure 17.4.

FIGURE 17.4

The NLX-style AGP retaining bracket.

Connector

Although the AGP slot in a PC uses an edge connector, it is an entirely different connector from those used in PCI slots. This physical difference assures against inserting an expansion board in an inappropriate slot. Other aspects of AGP further constrained the design of the connector. The chosen design interleaves contacts at two depths inside the connector with the mating fingers on the edge connector arranged in a flip-flop pattern, as shown in Figure 17.5.

FIGURE 17.5
Layout of the high-density contacts on an AGP edge connector.

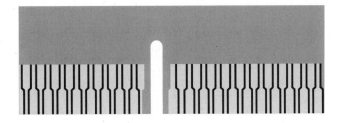

The interleaved contact fingers on the AGP card make hot-plugging AGP boards impossible. That is, you should not slide an AGP board into its slot when the power is on to your PC. When you slide a board into a slot, the contact fingers closest to the edge of the board are apt to wipe across the connector contacts for the deeper contacts. Even a quick wipe can send weird, even damaging signals through the card and your PC. Intel recommends that you slide AGP boards into their slots as straight as you can without rocking them back and forth to seat them in the connector. Even when the power is off, the side-to-side wiping action can damage the miniaturized contacts in the AGP connector.

UMA

Unified Memory Architecture is an alternate way to design a PC for lower-cost construction. It actually can have a beneficial effect on video performance. Because the frame buffer is integrated into the main memory of the PC, bitmaps don't have to cross any I/O bus at all. Of course, the memory used by the frame buffer cannot also be used by programs, but today's memory prices makes this loss of storage almost inconsequential.

To provide a common standard to which designers could create the electrical and logical interface between the video system using UMA and the core logic of a PC, VESA developed its own standard called *VESA Unified Memory Architecture*. First published in March 1996, VUMA allows for adding external devices to your PC that can share direct access to its main memory system to use it as a frame buffer. Although UMA has become popular in low-cost PCs, even with this standard, add-on devices that use the technology have not become popular.

Inter-Card Interfaces

Your graphics adapter generates all the signals that your monitor displays. Normal PC monitors have no provisions for mixing together video signals from several different sources and displaying them together.

Sometimes, however, you do want to mix video sources together. For example, if you have a TV adapter in your PC, you may want to display the television signal along with

Windows, perhaps as a window alongside your other applications. Somehow, your PC must be able to join together the two signals sources *before* the final signals get sent to your monitor.

Mixing the signals digitally is an onerous chore, one that may be within the capabilities of today's microprocessors but that would leave little power left over for other chores. Overlay technology, discussed in the previous chapter, eliminates nearly all of the processor overhead. But it leaves a nagging problem—bringing the two signals (video and PC graphics) together within your PC.

The modern trend is to take care of everything—video and graphics—on one board or on a graphics board with a daughterboard devoted to video. A proprietary connector on the graphics board passes the signals back and forth.

When you want to mix products from different manufacturers, for instance, the MPEG decoder that accompanied a new DVD drive and the graphics adapter that came with your PC, you face the video connection challenge. Over the years, several inter-card connection schemes have been developed and standardized.

Loop-Through

The one universal design is the *loop-through* board. This simple expedient intercepts the signal from your graphic adapter at its external connection—the one that would otherwise go directly to your monitor—and interposes another board. A short *loop-through cable* plugs into the output on the back of your graphics board and then stretches over to an input on the video board. The signals mix on the video board, and you plug your monitor into an output on that board.

As a practical matter, you unplug your monitor from your graphics adapter and plug it into the video board. Then, you connect your graphics adapter and video board with a short cable on the back of your PC. The short cable sticks out in a semicircle—almost a loop—on the back of your PC.

As clumsy as this connection system is, it is effective for overlay boards. Some recent MPEG decoders still rely on loop-through technology.

VGA Auxiliary Video Connector

Internal connections are neater and to some degree more reliable. After all, you're less likely to unplug them accidentally.

The prototype for all internal inter-card video connection schemes was the VGA Auxiliary Video Connector introduced by IBM in 1987. More often termed the *VGA Feature Connector*, it permitted add-on accessories to share signals and control the VGA circuitry on a graphics board (or motherboard) to the extent of switching off VGA entirely. This original design used an edge connector, as shown in Figure 17.6. You'll find a pin-out of its signals in Appendix TK.

FIGURE 17.6
The VGA Auxiliary Video connector.

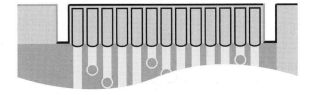

VESA Feature Connector

Despite its wide adoption when VGA boards were popular, the VGA feature connector was essentially a proprietary design. VESA used it as the basis for its own *VESA Feature Connector*, which became an industry standard. The chief difference is that the VESA design uses a pin connector, as shown in Figure 17.7, instead of an edge connector.

FIGURE 17.7
The VESA feature connector. Pin Z1 is at the right rear.

VESA Advanced Feature Connector

Both the VGA and VESA feature connectors are limited to the signals used by the VGA system itself and were not useful beyond a 640-by-480 pixel resolution in 256 colors. To satisfy the need for a high-performance channel for linking graphics and video systems, VESA designed a new, high-performance connection called the *VESA Advanced Feature Connector*.

This March 1994 design had 150 MB/sec throughput through a 16-bit or 32-bit data channel operating at a maximum clock speed of 37.5MHz with support for resolutions up to 1,024 by 768. In its fullest 32-bit implementation, the VAFC used an 80-pin high-density connector with 0.1-by-0.05 inch pin spacing. Its pin-out is given in Appendix TK.

VESA Media Channel

To move uncompressed video through computer systems and multimedia equipment derived from PC technology in real-time, in September 1994, VESA published another high-speed bus interface called the *VESA Media Channel*. It was designed to link multimedia devices within a PC or other equipment independent of the PCI bus.

VM Channel is a 32-bit bus operating at speeds as high as 33MHz that supports full arbitration between up to 15 interconnected devices. Exchanges across the VM Channel are broadcast rather than exchanged. That is, when a source sends out video data, the bus carries the data to all the devices connected to the bus. Each device determines whether it should accept and use the data.

To achieve its high data rate, the VM Channel operates essentially isosynchronously, but a not-ready signal inhibits the transmission of data from the source device so that unused or superfluous information does not waste bus bandwidth. When a device takes control of the VM Channel and then receives a not-ready indication, control passes from that device to the next one that needs to transfer data across the channel.

The standard VM Channel connector is an edge connector with the contact fingers spaced with the centers 0.05 inches apart. You'll find the connector on the top of both ISA and PCI video boards. Figure 17.8 illustrates this connector. The signals on the pin are listed in Appendix TK.

FIGURE 17.8
VESA Media Channel card edge connector.

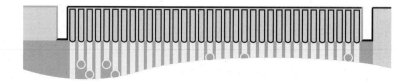

VESA Video Interface Port

The current VESA-approved link between video devices is the VESA *Video Interface Port*, first introduced in June 1997. Initially, it was meant to provide a higher-performance alternative to the Feature Connector to allow high-speed transfers of video data between expansion boards independent of the expansion bus. In October 1998, the standard was revised to the now-current version 2.0 to better accommodate MPEG decoders and the signals of HDTV systems.

Operation

In operation, your PC's graphics board works like any other hardware device, controlled through Windows by a device driver installed specifically for that particular model (and revision) of graphics adapter. There is a difference, however. Your graphics adapter is a boot device. It must operate as your PC boots up so you can monitor the progress of the process. You may also need to see what your PC is doing so that you can configure it. Consequently, the graphics adapter must be able to operate independently from any operating system.

The BIOS provides the functions needed during the boot process. It also provides default functionality. That is, if you do not install a driver, it provides the least common denominator for the operation of your video system.

To provide a common basis for this default operation, all graphics adapters start their operation in VGA mode. That is, they emulate the basic VGA system of years gone by. In safe mode, for example, Windows steps back to VGA mode.

VGA also provides a solid model for understanding the basic operation of your PC's graphics adapter. VGA operation is still shared by *all* graphics adapters in your PC, and they all build upon basic VGA functions.

Boot-Up

IBM introduced VGA to the world in 1987 as perhaps the only enduring part of its Micro Channel PS/2s. The VGA name is derived from the name IBM gave to a VLSI chip. This chip, the *Video Graphics Array*, integrated all the functions of the video controllers used in previous IBM designs so that it was entirely backward compatible with older software. The Video Graphics Array used gate array technology (which means a lot of logic circuits are dedicated to their function instead of being programmable like a microprocessor). Because it generated video signals, the Video Gate Array name was a natural. These features, which are taken for granted today, all originated with VGA.

Because of its designed-in backward compatibility, the VGA system carries a lot of baggage, most of it odd-shaped and tattered. Ordinary VGA systems operate at any of four resolutions, depending on the video mode your software requests. Its signals switch between three image heights and two refresh (vertical synchronizing) rates as it changes resolution.

Text Modes

The default operating mode of the VGA system, the one that you see when your PC first starts and displays characters to tell you what it is, is a character-mapped carry-over from the very first PC display system. This allows your PC to boot up with text messages on your screen so you can read diagnostic messages and enjoy the copyright messages of the various BIOS add-ins you've installed. This text is arrayed in 80 columns across your screen, 25 rows high.

Although VGA allows both color and monochrome operation, nearly all PCs start in color mode. The chief distinguishing characteristic of this mode is that the VGA system locates its character buffer at base address 0B8000(Hex) and allows you or your software to choose any of 16 foreground colors and 8 background colors for each text character. You can also make individual characters blink. (Some software exchanges the ability to make individual characters blink with an extra eight background colors.) In monochrome text mode, you can select character attributes instead of colors. The available attributes include character intensity (bright or dim), underlining, reverse video, and blinking.

The distinction between color and monochrome text modes is important because software that writes directly to video memory may not be able to find the screen if your system is in the wrong mode. Monochrome memory is at a different address—0B0000(Hex)—and text sent the wrong place won't appear on your screen. In the early 1990s, this problem sometime reared up when you plugged a monochrome monitor into your PC and VGA shifted to monochrome mode while your PC still wrote to the color mode memory locations. Nothing but a cursor appeared on your screen. The problem disappeared along with monochrome monitors.

The basic VGA system includes three fonts, its native 9-by-16 characters and two for backward compatibility with lower resolution standards, an 8-by-8 font and a 9-by-14 font. In addition, it allows the downloading of up to eight more fonts, each with 256 characters. By sacrificing eight of the possible character foreground colors, the VGA system allows the use up to 512 different characters on the screen at a time. The necessary 512-character fonts (up to four may be used) are simply downloaded in the positions used by two of the smaller fonts.

The cursor on the VGA system follows the model discussed earlier, its blink rate fixed by hardware but its size adjustable through the 6845 control registers.

Graphics Modes

The native graphics modes of the VGA system operate with a resolution of 640 pixels horizontally and 480 pixels vertically. This resolution is the highest supported by standard VGA systems and the mode used in Windows safe mode. Because most monitor screens have an aspect ratio of 4:3, each pixel occupies a perfectly square area on the screen. Other display standards (indeed, other VGA display modes) produce elongated pixels that complicate the math needed to draw shapes on the screen.

Because VGA was created at a time when memory was expensive, it uses color mapping. That is, to broaden its apparent range of colors and to generate more life-like images, the VGA standard takes advantage of a color lookup table to maps hues. Each of the 256 entries in the color lookup table encodes one of 262,144 hues.

The maximum number of hues in basic VGA results from the color generation system of the VGA electronics. The original VGA system produces analog signals to drive its monitors, and these analog signals are derived from three six-bit digital-to-analog converters. In early VGA circuitry, all three DAC channels were integrated into a single chip. Each six-bit DAC channel encodes 64 intensities of a primary color (red, blue, or green). Combined together, 64 plus 64 plus 64 (that is, 64 times 3, or 2^{18}) distinct combinations of color levels are possible, the 262,144 hue potential. Although most graphics boards offer more colors at the 640-by-480 pixel resolution level, these are not VGA modes and are not supported by the standard VGA drivers.

The actual color lookup table in the original VGA circuitry was part of its RAMDAC chip, which provided 256 registers, each capable of storing the necessary 18-bit color code.

Monochrome Detection and Operation

Two pins in the VGA connector allow the detection of display type. Monochrome monitors assign pin 12 the function of video ground and provide no pin or connection on pin 11. Color displays are wired in the opposite manner: The connector from the monitor has no pin 12 and uses pin 11 as a video ground. This digital ground function is also duplicated on pin 10 so monitors lacking either sensing pin will still properly receive all image signals.

As a default, the VGA circuitry sends out only the signal assigned to the color green when it detects a monochrome monitor. Of course, the color repertory of the VGA system is compromised by this operation, but the VGA compensates by translating the colors into up to 64 shades of gray, a result of the green signal being capable of handling 26 discrete intensities, limited by the 6-bit green channel of the DAC.

Normal Operation

Windows remains in VGA mode while it is loading its drivers and initializing itself. Just before it starts loading programs, it switches over to the video mode you've chosen through the Display Properties menu.

The driver software tells Windows about the capabilities of your graphics board, which constrains your choices as to resolution and color depth and, in conjunction with information provided by your monitor, refresh rate. The color depth and resolution settings interact, limited by the amount of memory available to your display system, as discussed in the section "Color Planes" in Chapter 16.

CHAPTER

18

Displays

A display is the keyhole you peer through to spy on what your PC is doing. You can't do your work without a display, and you can't work well without a good one. The final quality of what you see—the detail, sharpness, and color—depends on the display you use. No longer a function only of TV-like monitors, today's computer displays increasingly rely on new technologies to achieve flat screens and high resolutions.

Technology	Your choices are two: the traditional CRT and the flat panel. The former is bulky and cheap; the latter, expensive, thin, and electrically frugal.
Screen size	Bigger lets you see more detail at higher resolutions. Most people consider 17-inch displays necessary for resolutions higher than 1024×768 (which is standard for 15-inch flat panel displays).
Resolution	Most monitor makers usually mean addressability when describing resolution. In other words, the number of pixels a monitor can display, at least in theory.
Dot, slot, or pixel pitch	The distance between the physical elements of the display, usually the smallest detail the monitor can display. The smaller the display, the finer the pitch required for a given resolution to be displayed.
Sharpness	The quality of the image that you can actually see.
Refresh rate	How often the onscreen image gets repainted. Low rates may appear to flicker. High resolution may force you to use lower refresh rates. Most people consider 70 Hz adequate; 75 Hz, better.
Connectors	The jacks on the back of the monitor. Standard VGA jacks work okay to about 1280×1024 resolution. Separate BNC jacks better handle analog signals at high resolutions. Flat panel displays work better with digital interfaces.

You cannot see data. The information your computer processes is nothing but ideas, and ideas are intangible no matter whether they're in your mind or your computer's. Although you can visualize your own ideas, you cannot peer directly into the pulsing digital thought patterns of your computer. You probably have no right to think that you could; if you can't read another person's thoughts, you should hardly expect to read the distinctly non-human circuit surges of your PC.

Although most people—at least those not trained in stage magic—cannot read thoughts per se, they can get a good idea of what's going on in another person's mind by carefully observing his external appearances. Eye movements, facial expressions, gestures, and sometimes even speech can give you a general idea about what that other person is thinking, although you will never be privy to his true thoughts. So it is with computers. You'll never be able to see electrons tripping through logical gates, but you can get a general idea of what's going on behind the screens by looking into the countenance of your computer—its display. What the display shows you is a manifestation of the results of the computer's thinking.

The display is your computer's line of communication to you, much as the keyboard enables you to communicate with it. Like even the best of friends, the display doesn't tell you everything, but it does give you a clear picture, one from which you can draw your own conclusions about what the computer is doing.

Because the display has no direct connection to the computer's thoughts, the same thoughts—the same programs—can generate entirely different onscreen images while working exactly the same way inside your computer. Just as you can't tell a book's contents from its cover, you cannot judge the quality of a computer from its display.

What you can see is important, however, because it influences how well you can work with your computer. A poor display can lead to eyestrain and headaches, making your computer literally a pain to work with. A top-quality display means clearly defined characters, sharp graphics, and a system that's a pleasure to work with.

Background

Although the terms are often used interchangeably, a display and a monitor are distinctly different. A *display* is the image-producing device itself, the screen that you see. The *monitor* is a complete box that adds support circuitry to the display. This circuitry converts the signals sent by the computer (or some other device, such as a videocassette recorder) into the proper form for the display to use. Although most monitors operate under principles like those of the television set, displays can be made from a variety of technology, including liquid crystals and the photon glow of some noble gases.

Because of their similar technological foundations, monitors to a great extent resemble the humble old television set. Just as a monitor is a display enhanced with extra circuitry, the television is a monitor with even more signal conversion electronics. The television incorporates into its design a tuner or demodulator that converts signals broadcast by television stations or a cable television company into about the same form as those signals used by monitors. Beyond the tuner, the television and monitor work in much the same way. Indeed, some old-fashioned computer monitors work as televisions as long as they are supplied the proper signals.

New monitors have developed far beyond their television roots, however. They have greater sharpness and purity of color. To achieve these ends, they operate at higher frequencies than television stations can broadcast.

Computer displays and monitors use a variety of technologies to create visible images. A basic bifurcation once divided the displays of desktop computers and those of laptop machines. Most desktop computers use systems based on the same cathode ray tube (CRT) technology as that used in the typical television set. Laptop and notebook computers chiefly use liquid crystal displays (LCDs). Today, the LCD is making inroads on the desktop as demand and developments in manufacturing technology push down their almost astronomic prices. There's little doubt that flat-screen technologies will eventually replace the classic CRT in *all* applications (including television, whatever television will be in the future). But don't expect the immediate demise of the CRT.

Earlier predictions of a rapid move to LCDs (including in the last edition of this book) had to be revised not because of changes in technology but because of economics. The 1997 collapse of the Asian economy led to the postponement of the construction of LCD fabrication plants. Without the anticipated added capacity, demand began to outrun supply in early 1999 and, from that perspective, price *increases* were expected by the end of that year. This situation will likely delay the ascent and dominance of LCDs by several years. In the meantime, LCD prices may temporarily reverse their downward trend as manufacturers try to squeeze extra profits out of their production shortfalls.

Meanwhile, CRTs continue to get better—brighter and less expensive. CRTs still hold the edge in critical applications: They can reproduce more colors and can make better color matches with print media in critical applications. Moreover, today's CRTs are sharper than LCDs. Affordable LCDs top out at 1,024-by-768 pixel resolution. CRTs in the same price range regularly reach 1,600 by 1,200 pixels. CRTs also offer wider viewing angles and brighter images.

In fact, the glaringly apparent difference between thin and fat displays hides far greater internal dissimilarities. About the only characteristic the two technologies share is that they make images. CRTs and LCDs differ not only in how they form images but also in how they are viewed and how they are best connected to your PC. Consequently, we'll look at the two types of displays separately, starting historically with CRTs.

Cathode Ray Technology

The oldest electronic image-generating system still in use is the *cathode ray tube*. The name is purely descriptive. The device is based on a special form of vacuum tube—a glass bottle that is partially evacuated and filled with an inert gas at very low pressure. The tube of the CRT is hardly a tube, but is more flask shaped with a thin neck that broadens like a funnel into a wide, nearly flat face. Although CRTs appear to be made like simple bottles—in fact, people in the monitor business sometimes refer to CRTs as "bottles"—its construction is surprisingly complex and involves a variety of glasses of many thicknesses. The face of the typical CRT, for example, often is about an inch thick.

The "cathode" in the CRT name is a scientific term for a negatively charged electrode. In a CRT, a specially designed cathode shoots a beam or ray of electrons toward a positively charged electrode, the anode. (Electrons, having a negative charge, are naturally attracted to positive potentials.) Because it works like a howitzer for electrons, the cathode of a CRT is often called an *electron gun*.

The electrons race on their ways at a substantial fraction of the speed of light, driven by the high voltage potential difference between the cathode and anode, sometimes as much as 25,000 volts.

At the end of their flight to the anode, the electrons crash into a layer of a coating made from phosphor compounds that has the wondrous property of converting the kinetic energy of the electrons into visible light.

Physical Characteristics

The CRT is a physical entity that you can hold in your hand, drop on the floor, and watch shatter. Little of its design is by chance; nearly every design choice in making the CRT has an effect on the image that you see.

Four elements of the CRT exert the greatest influence on the kind and quality of an image made by a monitor. The phosphors chosen for the tube affect the color and persistence of the display. The electron guns actually paint the image, and how well they work is a major factor in determining image sharpness. In color CRTs, the shadow mask or aperture grille limits the ultimate resolution of the screen. The face of the screen and the glare reflected from it affect both image contrast and how happy you will be in working with a monitor.

Phosphors

At the end of the electrons' short flight from the gun in the neck of a CRT to the inside of its wide, flat face lies a layer of a phosphor-based compound with a wonderful property: It glows when struck by an electron beam. The image you see in a CRT is the glow of the electrically stimulated phosphor compounds, simply termed phosphors in the industry. Not all the phosphorous compounds used in CRTs are the same. Different compounds and mixtures glow various colors and for various lengths of time after being struck by the electron beam.

The type of phosphor determines the color of the image on the screen. Several varieties of amber, green, and whitish phosphors are commonly used in monochrome displays. Color CRT displays use three different phosphors painted in fine patterns across the inner surface of the tube. The patterns are made from dots or stripes of the three additive primary colors—red, green, and blue—arrayed next to one another. A group of three dots is called a *color triad* or *color triplet*.

One triad of dots makes up a picture element, often abbreviated as *pixel* (although some manufacturers prefer to shorten picture element to *pel*).

The makers of color monitors individually can choose each of the three colors used in forming the color triads on the screen. Most monitor makers have adopted the same phosphor family, which is called P22 (or B22, which is the same thing with a different nomenclature), so the basic color capabilities of most multihued monitors are the same.

The color monitor screen can be illuminated in any of its three primary colors by individually hitting the phosphor dots associated with that color with the electron beam. Other colors can be made by illuminating combinations of the primary colors. By varying the intensity of each primary color, the tube can display a nearly infinite spectrum.

Monochrome displays have their CRTs evenly coated with a single, homogenous phosphor so that wherever the electron beam strikes, the tube glows in the same color. The color of the phosphors determines the overall color that the screen glows.

Three colors remain popular for monochrome computer displays—amber, green, and white. Which is best is a matter of both preference and prejudice. Various studies support the superiority of each of these colors:

> **Green**. Green screens got a head start as PC displays because they were IBM's choice for most of its terminals and the first PC display—as well as classic radar displays and oscilloscopes. It is a good selection for use where ambient light levels are low; part of its heritage is from the days of oscilloscope and radar screens (most of which remain stubbornly green). Over the last few years, however, green has fallen from favor as the screen of choice.

Amber. In the 1980s, amber-colored screens rose in popularity because they are, according to some studies, easier on the eyes and more readable when the surrounding environmental light level is bright. Yellow against black yields one of the best perceived contrast combinations, making the displays somewhat easier on your eyes. Amber also got a push as a de facto European monitor standard.

White. Once, white screens were something to be avoided, if only from their association with black-and-white televisions. A chief reason was that most early monochrome displays used a composite interface and gave low onscreen quality.

White now dominates VGA monochrome displays—at least the few still available. Green and amber remain in use only in specialized applications.

If you look closely, you might see fine specs of colors, such as a bright yellow dappled into so-called "white" phosphors. Manufacturers mix together several different phosphors to fine-tune the color of the monochrome display—to make it a cool, blue television "white" or a warm, yellowish paper "white."

You'll find no good dividing line between ordinary white and *paper-white* displays. In theory, paper-white means the color of the typical bond paper you type on, a slightly warmer white than the blue-tinged glow of most "white" monitors. But "paper-whiteness" varies with who is giving the name.

Background Color

Often ignored, yet just as important to screen readability as the phosphor colors, is the background color of the display tube. Monochrome screen backgrounds run the full range from light gray to nearly black. Darker screens give more contrast between the foreground text and the tube background, making the display more readable, particularly in high ambient light conditions.

The background area on a color screen—that is, the space between the phosphor dots—is called the *matrix*, and it is not illuminated by the electron beam. The color of the matrix determines the color screen's background color (usually termed *matrix color*)—what it looks like when the power is off—pale gray, dark green-gray, or nearly black. Darker and black matrices give an impression of higher contrast to the displayed images. Lighter gray matrices make for purer whites. The distinctions are subtle, however, and unless you put two tubes side-by-side, you're unlikely to detect the difference.

Color Temperature

If your work involves critical color matching, the color temperature of your monitor can be an important issue. White light is not white, of course, but a mixture of all colors. Alas, all whites are not the same. Some are richer in blue, some in yellow. The different colors of white are described in their color temperature, the number of Kelvins (degrees Celsius above absolute zero) that a perfect luminescent body would need to be to emit that color.

Like the incandescence of a hot iron horseshoe in the blacksmith's forge, as its temperature gets higher the hue of a glowing object shifts from red to orange to yellow and on to blue-white. Color temperature simply assigns an absolute temperature rating to these colors, as shown in Figure 18.1.

FIGURE 18.1

The color temperatures associated with various conditions.

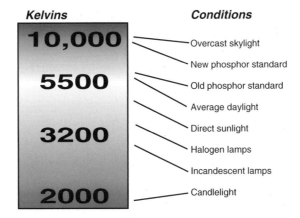

Kelvins — Conditions

10,000 — Overcast skylight
— New phosphor standard
5500 — Old phosphor standard
— Average daylight
— Direct sunlight
3200 — Halogen lamps
— Incandescent lamps
2000 — Candlelight

For example, ordinary light bulbs range from 2,700 to 3,400 Kelvins. Most fluorescent lights have non-continuous color spectra rich in certain hues (notably green), and lack others, making assigning a true color temperature impossible. Other fluorescent lamps are designed to approximate daylight with color temperatures of about 5,000 Kelvins.

The problem with color matching arises because pigments and paper only reflect light, so their actual color depends on the temperature of the light illuminating them. Your monitor screen emits light, so its color is independent of illumination; it has its own color temperature that may be (and is likely) different from that lighting the rest of your work. Monitors are designed to glow with the approximate color temperature of daylight rather than incandescent or fluorescent light.

Alas, not everyone has the same definition of daylight. Noonday sun, for instance, ranges from 5,500 to 6,000 Kelvins. Overcast days may achieve a color temperature of 10,000 Kelvins because the scattered blue glow of the sky (higher color temperature) dominates the yellowish radiation from the sun. The colors and blend of the phosphors used to make the picture tube screen and the relative strengths of the electron beams illuminating those phosphors determine the color temperature of a monitor. Some engineers believe the perfect day is a soggy, overcast afternoon suited only to ducks and Englishmen and opt to run their monitors with a color temperatures as high as 10,000 Kelvins. Others, however, live in a Kodachrome world where the color temperature is the same 5,300 Kelvins as a spring day with tulips in the park.

Persistence

CRT phosphors also differ in persistence, which describes how long the phosphor glows after being struck by the electron beam. Most monitors use medium persistence phosphors.

Persistence becomes obvious when it is long. Images take on a ghostly appearance, lingering for a few seconds and slowly fading away. Although the effect may be bothersome, particularly in a darkened room, it's meant to offset the effect of another headache-producer, flicker.

Exactly what it sounds like, flicker is the quick flashing of the screen image caused by the image decaying before it gets rescanned by the electron beam. The persistence of vision (a quality of the human visual system) makes rapidly flashing light sources appear continuously lit. Fluorescent lights, for example, seem to glow uninterruptedly even though they switch on and off 120 times a second (twice the nominal frequency of utility-supplied electricity).

The lingering glow of long-persistence phosphors bridges over the periods between passes of electron beams when they stretch out too long for human eyes to blend them together. Long-persistence phosphors are thus often used in display systems that are scanned more slowly than usual, such as interlaced monitors (described later). The IBM Monochrome display, perhaps the most notorious user of long-persistence green phosphors, is scanned 50 times a second instead of the more normal (and eye-pleasing) 60 or more.

Long-persistence phosphors need not be green, however. Long-persistence color systems also are available for use in applications where flicker is bothersome. Most often, long-persistence color phosphors are used in interlaced systems that are scanned more slowly than non-interlaced displays.

Long-persistence phosphors also frustrate light pens, which depend on detecting the exact instant a dot of phosphor lights up. Because of the lingering glow, most light pens perceive several dots to be lit simultaneously. The pen cannot zero in on a particular dot position on the screen.

Electron Guns

To generate the beams that light the phosphors on the screen, a CRT uses one or more electron guns. An electron gun is an electron emitter (a cathode) in an assembly that draws the electrons into a sharp, high-speed beam. To move the beam across the breadth of the tube face (so that the beam doesn't light only a tiny dot in the center of the screen), a group of powerful electromagnets arranged around the tube called the yoke bend the electron beam in the course of its flight. The magnetic field set up by the yoke is carefully controlled and causes the beam to sweep each individual display line down the face of the tube.

Monochrome CRTs have a single electron gun that continuously sweeps across the screen. Most color tubes have three guns, although some color televisions and monitors boast "one-gun" tubes, which more correctly might be called "three guns in one." The gun count depends on the definition of a gun. Like all color CRTs, the one-gun tubes have three distinct electron-emitting cathodes that can be individually controlled. The three cathodes are fabricated into a single assembly that allows them to be controlled as if they were generating only a single beam.

In a three-gun tube, the trio of guns is arranged in a triangle. So-called "one-gun" tubes arrange their cathodes in a straight line, often earning the epithet *inline guns*. In theory, inline guns should be easier to set up, but as a practical matter, excellent performance can be derived from either arrangement.

The three guns in a color CRT emit their electrons simultaneously, and the three resulting beams are steered together by force of a group of electromagnets around the neck of the tube called the yoke. Monitors provide individual adjustments, both mechanical and electrical, for each of the three beams to ensure that each beam falls exactly on the same triplet of color dots on the screen as the others. Because these controls help the three beams converge on the same triad, they are called *convergence controls*. The process of adjusting them is usually termed color *alignment*.

Convergence

The three electron beams inside any color monitor must converge on exactly the right point on the screen to illuminate a single triad of phosphor dots. If a monitor is not adjusted properly—or if it is not designed or made properly—the three beams cannot converge properly to one point. Poor convergence results in images with rainbow-like shadows and a loss of sharpness and detail. Individual text characters no longer appear sharply defined but become two- or three-color blurs. Monochrome monitors are inherently free from such convergence problems because they have but one electron beam. Figure 18.2 simulates the effect of poor convergence.

FIGURE 18.2
Excellent (left) and poor convergence on a monitor screen.

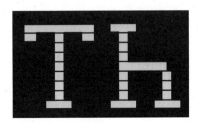 

Convergence problems are a symptom rather than a cause of monitor deficiencies. Convergence problems arise not only from the design of the display, but also from the construction and setup of each individual monitor. Convergence (and convergence problems) can vary widely from one display to the next and may be aggravated by damage during shipping.

The result of convergence problems is most noticeable at the screen periphery because that's where the electron beams are the most difficult to control. When bad, convergence problems can be the primary limit on the sharpness of a given display, having a greater negative effect than wide dot-pitch or low bandwidth (discussed later).

Many monitor makers claim that their convergence is a given fraction of a millimeter at a particular place on the screen. If a figure is given for more than one screen location, the center of the screen invariably has a lower figure—tighter, better convergence—than a corner of the screen.

The number given is how far one color may spread from another at that location. Lower numbers are better. Typical monitors may claim convergence of about 0.5 (one-half) millimeter at one of the corners of the screen. That figure often rises 50 percent higher than the dot-pitch of the tube, making the convergence the limit on sharpness for that particular monitor.

Misconvergence problems often can be corrected by adjusting the monitor, usually using the monitor's internal convergence controls. A few, high-resolution (and high-cost) monitors even have external convergence adjustments. But adjusting monitor convergence is a job for the specialist—and that means getting a monitor converged can be expensive, as is any computer service call.

Many monitor makers now claim that their products are converged for life. Although this strategy should eliminate the need to adjust them, it also makes it mandatory to test your display before you buy it. You don't want a display that's been badly converged for life.

Purity

The ability of a monitor to show you an evenly lit screen that does not vary in color across its width is termed *purity*. A monitor with good purity will be able to display a pure white screen without a hint of color appearing. A monitor with poor purity will be tinged with one color or another in large patches. Figure 18.3 illustrates the screens with good and poor purity.

FIGURE 18.3
Comparison of good and bad monitor purity.

Excellent purity   Poor purity

Poor purity often results from the shadow mask or aperture grille of a cathode ray tube becoming magnetized. Degaussing the screen usually cures the problem. Most larger monitors have built-in automatic *degaussers*.

You can degauss your monitor with a degaussing loop designed for color televisions, or even a bulk tape eraser. Energize the degausing coil or tape eraser in close proximity to the screen, and then gradually remove the coil to a distance of three or more feet away before switching it off. The gradually declining alternating magnetic field will overpower the static field on the mask, and the gradual removal of the alternating field will prevent the strong field from establishing itself on the mask.

Shadow Masks

Just pointing the electron beams at the right dots is not enough because part of the beam can spill over and hit the other dots in the triplet. The result of this spillover is a loss of color purity; bright hues become muddied. To prevent this effect and make images as sharp and colorful as possible, most color CRTs used in computer displays and televisions alike have a *shadow mask*—a metal sheet with fine perforations in it—located inside the display tube and a small distance behind the phosphor coating of the screen.

The shadow mask and the phosphor dot coating on the CRT screen are critically arranged so that the electron beam can only hit phosphor dots of one color. The other two colors of dots are in the "shadow" of the mask and cannot be seen by the electron beam.

The spacing of the holes in the shadow mask to a great degree determines the quality of the displayed image. For the geometry of the system to work, the phosphor dots on the CRT screen must be spaced at the same distance as the holes in the mask. Because the hole spacing determines the dot spacing, it is often termed the *dot-pitch* of the CRT.

The dot-pitch of a CRT is simply a measurement of the distance between dots of the same color. It is an absolute measurement, independent of the size of the tube or the size of the displayed image.

The shadow mask affects the brightness of a monitor's image in two ways. The size of the holes in the mask limits the size of the electron beam getting through to the phosphors. Off-axis from the guns—that is, toward the corners of the screen—the round holes appear oval to the gun and less of the beam can get through. As a result, the corners of a shadow mask screen are often dimmer than the center, although the brightness difference may not be distinguishable.

The mask also limits how high the electron beam intensity can be in a given CRT. A stronger beam—which makes a brighter image—holds more energy. When the beam strikes the mask, part of that energy is absorbed by the mask and becomes heat, which raises the temperature of the mask. In turn, this temperature rise makes the mask expand unpredictably, distorting it minutely and blurring the image. To minimize this heat-induced blur, monitor makers are moving to making shadow masks from materials that have a low coefficient of thermal expansion. That is, they change size as little as possible with temperature. The alloy Invar is favored for shadow masks because of its capability to maintain a nearly constant size as it warms.

Aperture Grilles

With all the problems associated with shadow masks, you might expect someone to come up with a better idea. Sony Corporation did exactly that, inventing the Trinitron picture tube.

The Trinitron uses an *aperture grille*—slots between a vertical array of wires—instead of a mask. The phosphors are painted on the inner face of the tube as interleaved stripes of the three additive primary colors. The grille blocks the electron beam from the wrong stripes just as a shadow mask blocks it from the wrong dots. The distance between two sequential stripes of the same color is governed by the spacing between the slots between the wires—the slot-pitch of the tube. Figure 18.4 illustrates slot-pitch and dot-pitch. Because the electron beam fans out as it travels away from the electron gun and stripes are farther from the gun than is the mask, the stripes are spaced a bit farther apart than the slot-pitch. Their spacing is termed screen-pitch. For example, a 0.25 millimeter slot-pitch Trinitron might have a screen-pitch of 0.26 millimeter.

FIGURE 18.4
Measuring dot-pitch and slot-pitch.

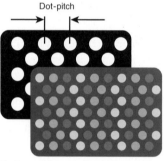

Dot-pitch

Shadow mask

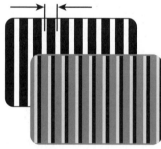

Slot-pitch

Aperture grille

The wires of the aperture grille are quite thick, about two thirds the width of the slot-pitch. For example, in a Trinitron with a 0.25 slot-pitch, the grille wires measure about 0.18 millimeters in diameter because each electron beam is supposed to illuminate only one third of the screen. The wires shadow the other two thirds from the beam to maintain the purity of the color.

The aperture grille wires are held taut, but they can vibrate. Consequently, Trinitron monitors have one or two thin tensioning wires running horizontally across the screen.

Although quite fine, these wires cast a shadow on the screen that is most apparent on light-colored screen backgrounds. Some people find the tensioning wire shadows objectionable, so you should look closely at a Trinitron before buying.

Trinitrons hold a theoretical brightness advantage over shadow-mask tubes. Because the slots allow more electrons to pass through to the screen than do the tiny holes of a shadow mask, a Trinitron can (in theory) create a brighter image. This added brightness is not borne out in practice. However, Trinitrons do excel in keeping their screens uniformly bright. The aperture grille wires of a Trinitron block the beam only in one dimension and so don't impinge as much on the electron beam at the screen edges.

Thanks to basic patents, Sony had exclusive rights to the Trinitron design. However, those patents began expiring in 1991, and other manufactures were quick to begin working with the technology. Other patents, however, cover manufacturing and other aspects of building successful Trinitrons. Consequently, the expected flood of Trinitron clones never appeared. In fact, the only new alternative to the Trinitron was introduced by Mitsubishi in 1993. Called Diamondtron by its manufacturer, the new design is based on aperture grille technology but uses a refined electron gun. Whereas the Trinitron combines three guns into a single focusing mechanism, the Diamondtron gives each gun its own control. According to Mitsubishi, this refinement allows more precise beam control and a more accurate and higher-resolution image.

Required Dot-Pitch

No matter whether a monitor uses a shadow mask with a dot-pitch or an aperture grille with a slot-pitch, the spacing of image triads on the screen is an important constituent in monitor quality. A monitor simply cannot put dots any closer together than the holes in mask or grille allow. It's easy to compute the pitch necessary for a resolution level in a computer system. Just divide the screen size by the number of dots required to be displayed.

For example, a typical small display measures 14 inches diagonally. A horizontal line stretching across the full width of such a screen would measure 11.2 inches, or about 285 millimeters. To properly display an SVGA image (800 pixels by 600 pixels), it would require a dot-pitch of 0.36 millimeter or smaller (that is, 285/800 millimeter or less). Often, a monitor's image is somewhat smaller than full-screen width and such displays require even finer dot-pitch. The larger the display, the coarser the dot-pitch can be for a given level of resolution.

Line Width

Another factor limits the sharpness of monitor images: the width of the lines drawn on the screen. Ideally, any vertical or horizontal line on the screen will appear exactly one pixel wide, but in practical monitors, the width of a line may not be so compliant. If lines are narrower than one pixel wide, thin black lines will separate adjacent white lines and wide white areas will be thinly striped in black. If the line width exceeds the size of a pixel, the display's ability to render fine detail will be lost.

The ideal line width for a monitor varies with the size of the screen and the resolution displayed on the screen. As resolution increases, lines must be narrower. As screen size goes up (with the resolution constant), line width must increase commensurately. You can calculate the required line width the same way as for the previous dot-pitch example. The line width should equal the maximum dot-pitch you calculate. In other words, for the 14-inch screen at SVGA resolution, you'd want a line width of 0.36 millimeters.

Several factors influence the width of lines on the screen. The monitor must be able to focus its electron beam into a line of ideal width. However, width also varies with the brightness of the beam; brighter beams naturally tend to expand out of focus. Consequently, when you increase the brightness of your monitor, the sharpness of the image may decline. For this reason, test laboratories usually make monitor measurements at a standardized brightness level.

Screen Curvature

Most CRTs have a distinctive shape. At one end, a narrow neck contains the electron gun or guns. Around the neck fits the deflection yoke, an external assembly that generates the magnetic fields that bend the electron beams to sweep across the inner surface of the wide face of the tube. The tube emerges from the yoke as a funnel-like flaring, which enlarges to the rectangular face of the screen itself. This face often (but becoming much less common) is a spherically curving surface.

The spherical curve of the face makes sense for a couple of reasons. It makes the distance traveled by the electron beam more consistent at various points on the screen, edge to center to edge. A truly flat screen would require the beam to travel farther at the edges than at the center and would require the beam to strike the face of the screen obliquely, resulting in image distortion. Although this distortion can be compensated for electrically, the curving screen helps things along.

In addition, the CRT is partly evacuated, so normal atmospheric pressure is constantly trying to crush the tube. The spherical surface helps distribute this potentially destructive force more evenly, making the tube stronger.

Screen curvature has a negative side effect. Straight lines on the screen appear straight only from one observation point. Move your head closer, farther away, or to one side, and the supposedly straight lines of your graphics images will bow this way and that.

Technology has made the reasons underlying spherical curved screens less than compelling. The geometry of inline guns simplifies tube construction and alignment sufficiently that cylindrically curved screens are feasible. They have fewer curvilinear problems because they warp only one axis of the image. Trinitrons characteristically have faces with cylindrical curves. Most shadow-mask tubes have spherical faces.

In the last few years, the technical obstacles to making genuinely flat screens have been surmounted. A number of manufacturers now offer flat-screen monochrome displays, which are relatively simple because compensation for the odd geometry is required by only one electron beam.

The first color flat screen was Zenith's *flat tension-mask* system. The tension mask solves the construction problems inherent in a flat-screen color system by essentially stretching the shadow mask. Although so-called "flat-square" tubes are neither flat nor square, several CRT manufacturers now offer truly flat screens based on a variety of technologies.

Besides the easier geometry offered by true flat-screen CRTs, they bring another benefit. The curved screen on conventional tubes reflects light from nearly the entire area in front of the tube. No matter where you point the display, it's sure to pick up some glare. True flat-screen tubes reflect glare over a very narrow angle. If you point a flat-screen display slightly downward, most of the room glare will reflect down onto your keyboard and away from your eyes.

Resolution Versus Addressability

The resolution of a video system refers to the fineness of detail that it can display. It is a direct consequence of the number of individual dots that make up the screen image, and thus is a function of both the screen size and the dot-pitch.

Because the size and number of dots limit the image quality, the apparent sharpness of screen images can be described by the number of dots that can be displayed horizontally and vertically across the screen. For example, the resolution required by the Video Graphics Array system in its standard graphics mode is 640 dots horizontally by 480 vertically. Modern display systems may produce images with as many as 1,600 by 1,200 dots in their highest resolution mode.

Sometimes, however, the resolution available on the screen and that made by a computer's display adapter are not the same. For example, a video mode designed for the resolution capabilities of a color television set hardly taps the quality available from a computer monitor. On the other hard, the computer-generated graphics may be designed for a display system that's sharper than the one being used. You might, for instance, try to use a television in lieu of a more expensive monitor. The sharpness you actually see would then be less than what the resolution of the video system would have you believe.

Actual resolution is a physical quality of the video display system—the monitor—that's actually being used. It sets the ultimate upper limit on the display quality. In color systems, the chief limit on resolution is purely physical—the convergence of the system and the dot-pitch of the tube. In monochrome systems, which have no quality-limiting shadow masks, the resolution is limited by the bandwidth of the monitor, by the highest frequency signal with which it can deal. (Finer details pack more information into the signals sent from computer system to monitor. The more information in a given time, the higher the frequency of the signal.)

A few manufacturers persist in using the misleading term addressability to describe the quality of their monitors. Addressability is essentially a bandwidth measurement for color monitors. It indicates how many different dots on the screen the monitor can point its electron guns at. It ignores, however, the physical limit imposed by the shadow mask. In other words, addressability describes the highest quality signals the monitor can handle, but the full quality of those signals are not necessarily visible to you onscreen.

Anti-Glare Treatment

Most mirrors are made from glass, and glass tries to mimic the mirror whenever it can. Because of the difference between the index of refraction of air and that of glass, glass is naturally reflective. If you make mirrors, that's great. If you make monitors—or worse yet, use them—the reflectivity of glass can be a big headache. A reflection of a room light or window from the glass face of the CRT can easily be brighter than the glow of phosphors inside. As a result, the text or graphics on the display tends to "wash out" or be obscured by the brightness.

The greater the curvature of a monitor screen, the more apt it is to have a problem with reflections because more of the environment gets reflected by the screen. A spherical monitor face acts like one of those huge convex mirrors strategically hung to give a panoramic view of shoplifters or cars sneaking around an obscured hairpin turn. The flatter the face of the monitor, the less of a worry reflections are. With an absolutely flat face, a slight turn of the monitor's face can eliminate all glare and reflections.

You can't change the curve of your monitor's face. However, help is available. Anti-glare treatments can reduce or eliminate reflections from the face of most CRTs. Several glare-reduction technologies are available, and each varies somewhat in its effectiveness.

Mesh

The lowest tech and least expensive anti-glare treatment is simply a fabric mesh, usually nylon. The mesh can either be placed directly atop the face of the screen or in a removable frame that fits about half an inch in front of the screen. Each hole in the mesh acts like a short tube, allowing you to see straight in at the tube but cutting off light from the sides of the tube. Your straight-on vision gets through unimpeded, but glare that angles in doesn't make it to the screen.

As simple as this technique is, it works amazingly well. The least expensive after-market anti-glare system uses mesh suspiciously similar to pantyhose stretched across a frame.

Unfortunately, this mesh has an unwanted side effect. Besides blocking the glare, it also blocks some of the light from the screen and makes the image appear darker. You may have to turn the brightness control up to compensate, which may make the image bloom and lose sharpness.

Mechanical

Glare can be reduced by mechanical means—not a machine that automatically intercepts glare before it reaches the screen, but mechanical preparation of the screen surface. By lightly grinding the glass on the front of the CRT, the face of the screen can be made to scatter rather than reflect light. Each rough spot on the screen that results from the mechanical grinding process reflects light randomly, sending it every which direction. A smooth screen reflects a patch of light all together, like a mirror, reflecting any bright light source into your eyes. Because the light scattered by the ground glass is dispersed, less of it reaches your eyes and the glare is not as bright. However, because the coarse screen surface disperses the light coming from inside the tube as well as that reflected from the tube face, it also lessens the sharpness of the image. The mechanical treatment makes text appear slightly fuzzier and out-of-focus, which to some manufacturers is a worse problem than glare.

Coating

Glare can be reduced by applying coatings to the face of the CRT. Two different kinds of coatings can be used. One forms a rough film on the face of the CRT. This rough surface acts in the same way as a ground-glass screen would, scattering light.

The screen also can be coated with a special compound such as magnesium fluoride. By precisely controlling the thickness of this coating, the reflectivity of the surface of the screen can be reduced. The fluoride coating is made to be a quarter of the wavelength of light (usually of light at the middle of the spectrum). Light going through the fluoride and reflecting from the screen thus emerges from the coating out of phase with the light striking the fluoride surface, visually canceling out the glare. Camera lenses are coated to achieve exactly the same purpose—the elimination of reflections. A proper coating can minimize glare without affecting image sharpness or brightness.

Polarization

Light can be polarized; that is, its photons can be restricted to a single plane of oscillation. A polarizing filter allows light of only one polarization to pass. Two polarizing filters in a row can be arranged to allow light of only one plane of polarization to pass (by making the planes of polarization of the filters parallel), or the two filters can stop light entirely when their planes of polarization are perpendicular.

The first filter lets only one kind of light pass; the second filter lets only another kind of light pass. Because none of the second kind of light reaches the second filter, no light gets by.

When light is reflected from a surface, its polarization is shifted by 90 degrees. This physical principle makes polarizing filters excellent reducers of glare.

A sheet of polarizing material is merely placed a short space in front of a display screen. Light from a potential source of glare goes through the screen and is polarized. When it strikes the display and is reflected, its polarization is shifted 90 degrees. When it again reaches the filter, it is out of phase with the filter and cannot get through. Light from the display, however, only needs to go through the filter once. Although this glow is polarized, there is no second screen to impede its flow to your eyes.

Every anti-glare treatment has its disadvantage. Mesh makes an otherwise sharp screen look fuzzy because smooth characters are broken up by the cell structure of the mesh. Mechanical treatments are expensive and tend to make the screen appear to be slightly "fuzzy" or out of focus. The same is true of coatings that rely on the dispersion principle. Optical coatings, Polaroid filters, and even mesh suffer from their own reflections. The anti-glare material itself may add its own bit of glare. In addition, all anti-glare treatments—polarizing filters in particular—tend to make displays dimmer. The polarizing filter actually reduces the brightness of a display to one-quarter its untreated value.

Even with their shortcomings, however, anti-glare treatments are amazingly effective. They can ease eyestrain and eliminate the headaches that come with extended computer use.

Deflection Angle

Another difference between CRTs is their *deflection angle*, which measures the maximum degree the tube allows its electron beam to bend. This corresponds to the angle at which the tube flares out. A tube with a narrow deflection angle will be long with a small screen. A wide deflection angle permits large screens with shorter tubes. Ideally, the best tube would be the shortest, but as the deflection angle increases, it becomes more difficult to control the electron beam and make a perfect image. Consequently, lower deflection angles usually produce better images. Improved technology has allowed deflection angles to increase while maintaining image quality. This allows monitors to be shorter and take up less desk space.

A monitor can deflect the electron beam inside its CRT both left and right of the center line path the beam would take without deflection. By custom, the deflection angle listed for a given CRT is the total deflection from maximum left to maximum right. Until the late 1990s, nearly all computer monitors used CRTs with deflection angles of 90 degrees. Television sets, which can get by with less image quality, typically use 110-degree tubes. In 1999, computer monitors with 100-degree tubes began to enter the market.

Image Characteristics

The electronics of a monitor control the size, shape, and other aspects of the quality of the image it displays. Each of these aspects of the image is defined and characterized in a number of ways. The most rudimentary is screen size. Although the chief limit on image size is physical—the bigger your monitor screen, the larger the images it can make—the electronics in the monitor control how large the image is on the screen. Because of the underscanning common among computer monitors, the actual image size is almost always smaller than the screen. The aspect ratio of the image describes its shape independent of its size. Most monitors give you a variety of controls to alter the size and shape of the image, so you are the final arbiter of what things look like on your monitor screen.

Screen Size

The most significant measurement of a CRT-based monitor is the size of its screen. Although seemingly straightforward, screen size has been at best an ambiguous measurement, and at worst downright misleading.

The confusion all started with television, where confusion often begins. The very first television sets had round CRTs, and their size was easy to measure—simply the diameter of the tube. When rectangular tubes became prevalent in the 1950s, the measurement shifted to the diagonal of the face of the tube. The diagonal was, of course, the closest equivalent to the diameter of an equivalent round tube. It was also the largest dimension that a television manufacturer could reasonably quote.

Unlike television images, which usually cover the entire face of the CRT, computer monitors limit their images. The image is most difficult to control at the edges of the screen; monitor makers maintain higher quality by restricting the size of the image. They mask off the far edges of the CRT with the bezel of the monitor case.

That bezel means that no image can fill the entire screen—at least no image that you can entirely see. The tube size becomes irrelevant to a realistic appraisal of the image. Some monitor makers persisted in using it to describe their products. Fortunately, most of the industry recognized this measuring system as optimistic exaggeration and began using a more realistic diagonal measurement of the actual maximum displayable image area.

VESA adopted the diagonal of the maximum image area as the measurement standard in its *Video Image Area Definition* standard, version 1.1, which it published on October 26, 1995. This standard requires that screen image area be given as horizontal and vertical measurements of the actual active image area when the monitor is set up by the manufacturer using the manufacturer's test signals. The dimensions must be given in millimeters with an assumed maximum variance of error of plus and minus two percent. Wider tolerances are allowed but must be explicitly stated by the manufacturer. In no case can the expressed image dimensions exceed the area visible through the monitor bezel.

Because the aspect ratio of PC monitor displays is 4:3, computation of the horizontal and vertical screen dimensions from the diagonal is easy. The diagonal represents the hypotenuse of a 3-4-5 right triangle, and that ratio applies to all screen sizes. Table 18.1 lists the dimensions for the most common nominal screen sizes.

TABLE 18.1   Nominal CRT Screen Dimensions

Diagonal	Horizontal	Vertical	Horizontal	Vertical
	Millimeters		Inches	
14 inches	284	213	11.2	8.4
15 inches	305	229	12	9
16 inches	325	244	12.8	9.6
17 inches	345	259	13.6	10.2
20 inches	406	305	16	12
21 inches	427	320	16.8	12.6

Portrait displays, which are designed to give you a view more like the printed sheets that roll out of your laser printer and into envelopes, merely take an ordinary CRT and turn it on its side. The market is not large enough to justify development of custom CRTs for portrait applications. Moreover, the 4:3 aspect ratio works fine because the "active" image on a sheet of letterhead—the space actually occupied by printing once you slice off the top, bottom, left, and right margins—is about 8 by 10 inches, a nearly perfect fit on a standard picture tube. When measuring the images on these portrait displays, horizontal becomes vertical and all measurements rotate 90 degrees.

Overscan and Underscan

Two monitors with the same size screens may have entirely different onscreen image sizes. Composite monitors are often afflicted by *overscan*; they attempt to generate images larger than their screen size, and the edges and corners of the active display area may be cut off. (The overscan is often designed so that as the components inside the monitor age and become weaker, the picture shrinks down to normal size, likely over a period of years.) *Underscan* is the opposite condition: The image is smaller than nominal screen size. For a given screen size, an overscanned image will appear larger at the expense of clipping off the corners and edges of the image as well as increasing distortion at the periphery of the image. Underscanning wastes some of the active area of the monitor screen. Figure 18.5 illustrates the effects of underscanning and overscanning on the same size screen.

Underscan is perfectly normal on computer displays and does not necessarily indicate any underlying problems unless it is severe—for example, when it leaves a two-inch black band encircling the image. Underscanning helps keep quality high because image geometry is easier to control nearer the center of the screen than it is at the edges. Pulling in the reigns on the image can ensure that straight lines actually are displayed straight. Moreover, if you extend the active image to the very edge of the bezel, if you change your viewing position so that you are not facing the screen straight on, the edge of the image may get hidden behind the bezel. The glass in the face of the screen is thicker than you might think, on the order of an inch (25 millimeters), enough that the third dimension will interfere with your most careful alignment.

FIGURE 18.5
Underscan and over-scan.

On the other hand, although overscan gives you a larger image and is the common display mode for video systems, it is not a good idea for PC monitor images. Vital parts of the image may be lost behind the bezel. You may lose the first character or two from each line of type of one edge of a drafting display to overscan. With video, however, people prefer to see as big an image as possible and usually pay little attention to what goes on at the periphery. Broadcasters, in fact, restrict the important part of the images that they deal with to a *safe area* that will be completely viewable even on televisions with substantial overscan.

Aspect Ratio

The relationship between the width and height of a monitor screen is termed its aspect ratio. Today, the shape of the screen of nearly every monitor is standardized, as is that of the underlying CRT that makes the image. The screen is 1.33 times wider than it is high, resulting in the same 4:3 aspect ratio used in television and motion pictures before the widescreen phenomenon took over. Modern engineers now prefer to put the vertical number first to produce aspect ratios that are less than one. Expressed in this way, video has a 3:4 aspect ratio, a value of 0.75.

The choice of aspect ratio is arbitrary and a matter of aesthetics. According to classical Greek aesthetics, the *Golden Ratio*, with a value of about 0.618, is the most beautiful. The exact value of the Golden Ratio is irrational: (SQRT(5)–1)/2. Its beauty is mathematical as well as aesthetic, the solution to the neat little equation $x+1 = 1/x$. (Hardly coincidentally, expressed as a ratio of horizontal to vertical, the Golden Ratio becomes 1.618, the solution to $x–1 = 1/x$.)

Various display systems feature their own aspect ratios. The modern tendency is toward wider aspect ratios. For example, High Definition Television (HDTV) stretches its aspect ratio from the 3:4 of normal video and television to 9:15. The normal negatives you make with your 35mm camera have a 4:6 aspect ratio. The reason video is so nearly square carries over from the early days of television, when cathode ray tubes had circular faces. The squarer the image, the more of the circular screen that was put to use. Figure 18.6 compares the aspect ratios of three common display systems.

FIGURE 18.6
Aspect ratios of display systems.

The image on your monitor screen need not have the same aspect ratio of the tube, however. The electronics of monitors separate the circuitry that generates the horizontal and vertical scanning signals and results in their independent control. As a result, the relationship between the two can be adjusted, and that adjustment results in an alteration of the aspect ratio of the actual displayed image. For example, by increasing the amplification of the horizontal signal, the width of the image is stretched, raising the aspect ratio.

Normally, you should expect that the relative gains of the horizontal and vertical signals will be adjusted so that your display shows the correct aspect ratio on its screen. A problem develops when a display tries to accommodate signals based on different standards. This mismatch proved particularly troublesome with VGA displays because the VGA standard allowed images made with three distinct line counts—350, 400, and 480—to provide compatibility with old standards and software. All else being equal, an image made from 350 lines is less than three-quarters the height of a 480-line image. To compensate, VGA uses the polarity of the horizontal and vertical synchronizing signals to indicate the number of lines in the image so that a monitor can compensate. Because Windows runs VGA displays at only the 640-by-480 pixel resolution level, this compensation is of no practical importance.

Image Sizing

Monitor makers developed *autosizing* technology to compensate for different video standards. Autosizing works by examining the video signal and automatically adjusting the monitor to compensate for different line widths and screen heights. True autosizing works regardless of the signal going to the monitor, and scales the image to match the number of display lines.

The match is not always perfect. Monitors may get close to a perfect display, but the image may be offset to one side of the screen or otherwise amiss. Analog display signals are sensitive to the precise timing of the signals, and deviations from the timing the monitor expects results in the display errors. Usually, you'll have to touch up the automatic setting made by your monitor.

Autosizing is often keyed to display modes. That is, instead of trying to maintain a constant size regardless of the input signal, the monitor classifies inputs into limited ranges. When coupled with memory inside the monitor, this expedient allows you to manually adjust images at several resolutions to perfection. When you switch between resolutions, the monitor retrieves your touched-up settings from memory and adjusts itself accordingly.

Although autosizing is helpful in setting up your display, Windows has diminished the importance of the ability to quickly switch between modes. Windows sticks with one resolution setting and stays there all the while you work unless you manually alter the resolution through the Display Properties menu.

Image Distortion

Between the electron guns and the phosphors in a cathode ray tube, the electron beam passes through an electronic lens and deflection system that focuses and steers the beam to assure that its path across the screen is the proper size and in the proper place. The electronics of the monitor control the lens and deflection system, adjusting it throughout the sweep of the electron beam across the screen. In addition to their other chores, the electronics must compensate for the difference in the path of the electron beam at different screen positions. Modern monitors do a magnificent job of controlling beam placement.

When the control system is not properly adjusted, however, the image may exhibit any of a number of defects. Because these defects distort the image from its desired form, they are collectively called *image distortion*.

The two most common forms of image distortion are barrel distortion and pincushion distortion. *Barrel distortion* causes vertical or horizontal lines in the image to bow outward so that the center of the lines lies closer to the nearest parallel edge of the screen. *Pincushion distortion* causes the vertical or horizontal lines in the image to bow inward so that the center of the lines is closer to the center of the screen. Figure 18.7 shows these two kinds of image distortion.

Barrel and pincushion distortion arise from the same cause, improper image compensation, and are essentially opposites of one another. Overcompensate for pincushion distortion and you get barrel distortion. Collectively, the two are sometimes simply called *pincushioning* no matter which way the lines bow.

FIGURE 18.7

Barrel and pincushion distortion.

No distortion   Barrel   Pincushion

Pincushioning is always worse closer the edges of the image. All monitors have adjustments to compensate for pincushioning, although these adjustments are not always available to you. They may be hidden inside the monitor. Other monitors may include pincushioning adjustments in their control menus. Technicians usually use test patterns that display a regular grid on the screen to adjust monitors to minimize pincushioning. You can usually use a full-screen image to adjust the pincushioning controls so that the edges of the desktop background color are parallel with the bezel of your monitor.

Less common is *trapezoidal distortion*, which leaves lines at the outer edge of the screen straight but not parallel to the bezel. In other words, instead of your desktop being a rectangle, it is a trapezoid with one side shorter than its opposite side. As with pincushioning, all monitors have controls for trapezoidal distortion, but not all make them available to you as the user of the monitor. If your monitor does have an external control for trapezoidal distortion, you adjust it as you do for pincushioning.

Image Controls

A few (far from a majority) monitors make coping with underscan, overscan, and odd aspect ratios simply a matter of twisting controls. These displays feature horizontal and vertical size (or gain) controls that enable you to adjust the size and shape of the image to suit your own tastes. With these controls—providing they have adequate range—you can make the active image touch the top, bottom, and sides of the screen bezel, or you can shrink the bright area of your display to a tiny (but geometrically perfect) patch in the center of your screen.

Size and position controls give you command of how much screen the image on your monitor fills. With full-range controls, you can expand the image to fill the screen from corner to corner or reduce it to a smaller size that minimizes the inevitable geometric distortion that occurs near the edges of the tube. A full complement of controls includes one each of the following: horizontal position (sometimes termed phase), vertical position, horizontal size (sometimes called width), and vertical size (or height).

A wide control range is better than a narrow one. Some monitors skimp on one or more controls and limit you in how large you can make the onscreen image. Worse, sometimes a monitor maker doesn't include a control at all. For example, some monitors have no horizontal size controls. As a result, you cannot adjust both the size and aspect ratio of the image.

The optimum position for these controls is on the front panel, where you can both adjust them and view the image at the same time. Controls on the rear panel require you to have gorilla-like arms to reach around the monitor to make adjustments while checking their effect.

Image controls come in two types: analog and digital.

Analog controls are the familiar old knobs like those you find on vintage television sets. Twist one way and the image gets bigger; twist the other and it shrinks. Analog controls have one virtue: Just by looking at the knob you know where they are set, whether at one or the other extreme of their travel. The control itself is a simple memory system; it stays put until you move it again. Analog controls, however, become dirty and wear out with age, and they usually enable you to set but one value per knob—one value that must cover all the monitor's operating modes.

Digital controls give you pushbutton control over image parameters. Press one button, and the image gets larger or moves to the left. Another compensates in the opposite direction. Usually, digital controls are linked with microprocessor, memory, and mode-sensing circuitry so that you can preset different image heights and widths for every video standard your monitor can display.

Digital controls don't get noisy with age and are more reliable and repeatable, but you never know when you are approaching the limit of their travel. Most have two-speed operation: Hold them in momentarily and they make minute changes; keep holding down the button and they shift gears to make gross changes. Of course, if you don't anticipate the shift, you'll overshoot the setting you want and spend a few extra moments zeroing in on the exact setting.

Size and position controls are irrelevant to LCD and similar alternate display technologies. LCD panels are connected more directly to display memory so that memory locations correspond nearly exactly to every screen position. There's no need to move the image around or change its shape because it's forever fixed where it belongs.

Most CRT-based displays also carry over several controls from their television progenitors. Nearly every computer monitor has a brightness control, which adjusts the level of the scanning electron beam; this in turn makes the onscreen image glow brighter or dimmer. The contrast control adjusts the linearity of the relationship between the incoming signal and the onscreen image brightness. In other words, it controls the brightness relationship that results from different signal levels—how much brighter high intensity is. In a few displays, the brightness and contrast function are combined into a single "picture" control. Although a godsend to those who might get confused by having to twiddle two knobs, the combined control also limits your flexibility in adjusting the image to your liking.

Other controls ubiquitous to televisions usually are absent from better computer monitors because they are irrelevant. Vertical hold, color (saturation), and hue controls only have relevance to composite video signals, so they are likely only to be found on composite-interfaced displays. The vertical hold control tunes the monitor to best decipher the vertical synchronizing signal from the ambiguous composite video signal. The separate sync signals used by other display standards automatically remove any ambiguity. Color and hue only adjust the relationship of the color subcarrier to the rest of the composite video signal, and have no relevance at all to non-composite systems.

Flat Panel Display Technology

Throughout the age of television, predictions of the future have almost universally included big, flat TV screens. Almost as soon as the first CRTs cast their blue spells in living rooms across the world, everyone knew they were only temporary technology. Something better would soon come along. Of course, at the same time pundits predicted an autogyro in every garage. That was about 60 years ago, and few folks have sprung for an autogyro in that time. (Few even remember what an autogyro is.) Although engineers never really pursued the dream of universal personal aircraft, they have attacked the flat-screen challenge with verve and a variety of approaches. They haven't quite achieved the sixty-year-old dream, but they are getting close.

Although the old dream offered encouragement, the real impetus for flat-screen technology arose from more mundane concerns. Conventional CRTs are simply impractical for portable computers, as anyone who once toted a 40-pound first-generation movable computer knows. The glass in the tube itself weighs more than most of today's notebook machines, and running a CRT steals more power than portables budget for all their circuitry and peripherals. From necessity sprung technology—actually several of them—that have made flat screns not only practical but inevitable. Although conventional CRT displays still hold an edge on the desktop (you get more screen for your money), their advantage is fading. Within the next decade—or less—conventional displays are apt to be as obsolete as, well, the autogyro.

LCD

The winner in the display technology competition was the Liquid Crystal Display, the infamous LCD. Unlike LED and gas-plasma displays, which glow on their own, emitting photons of visible light, LCDs don't waste energy by shining. Instead, they merely block light otherwise available. To make patterns visible, they either selectively block reflected light (reflective LCDs) or the light generated by a secondary source either behind the LCD panel (backlit LCDs) or adjacent to it (edgelit LCDs). The backlight source is typically an electroluminescent (EL) panel, although some laptops use Cold-Cathode

Fluorescent (CCF) for brighter, whiter displays with the penalty of higher cost, greater thickness, and increased complexity.

Nematic Technology

A number of different terms describe the technologies used in the LCD panels themselves, terms such as supertwist, double supertwist, and triple supertwist. In effect, the twist of the crystals controls the contrast of the screen, so triple supertwist screens are contrastier than ordinary supertwist.

The history of laptop and notebook computer displays has been lead by innovations in LCD technology. Invented by RCA in the 1960s (General Electric still receives royalties on RCA's basic patents), LCDs came into their own with laptop computers because of their low power requirements, light weight, and ruggedness.

An LCD display is actually a sandwich made from two plastic sheets with a very special liquid made from rod-shaped or nematic molecules. One important property of the nematic molecules of liquid crystals is that they can be aligned by grooves in the plastic to bend the polarity of light that passes through them. More importantly, the amount of bend the molecules of the liquid crystal gives to the light can be altered by sending an electrical current through them.

Ordinary light has no particular orientation, so liquid crystals don't visibly alter it. But polarized light aligns all the oscillations of its photons in a single direction. A polarizing filter creates polarized light by allowing light of a particular polarity (or axis of oscillation) to pass through. Polarization is key to the function of LCDs.

To make an LCD, light is first passed through one polarizing filter to polarize it. A second polarizing filter, set to pass light at right angles to the polarity of the first, is put on the other side of the liquid crystal. Normally, this second polarizing filter stops all light from passing. However, the liquid crystal bends the polarity of light emerging from the first filter so that it lines up with the second filter. Pass a current through the liquid crystal and the amount of bending changes, which in turn alters the amount of light passing through the second polarizer.

To make an LCD display, you need only to selectively apply current to small areas of the liquid crystal. The areas to which you apply current are dark; those that you don't are light. A light behind the LCD makes the changes more visible.

Over the past few years, engineers have made several changes to this basic LCD design to improve its contrast and color. The basic LCD design outlined here is technically termed twisted nematic technology, or TN. The liquid molecules of the TN display in their resting state always bend light by 90 degrees, exactly counteracting the relationship between the two polarizing panels that make up the display.

By increasing the bending of light by the nematic molecules, the contrast between light and dark can be increased. An LCD design that bends light by 180 to 270 degrees is termed a supertwist nematic, or simply supertwist display. One side effect of the added twist is that the appearance of color artifacts results in the yellowish green and bright blue hues of many familiar LCD displays.

This tinge of color can be canceled simply by mounting two supertwist liquid crystals back-to-back so that one bends the light in the opposite direction of the other. This design is logically termed a double supertwist nematic (or simply double supertwist) display. This LCD design is currently popular among laptop PCs with black-and-white VGA-quality displays. It does have a drawback, however. Because two layers of LCD are between you and the light source, double supertwist panels appear darker or require brighter backlights for adequate visibility.

Triple supertwist nematic displays instead compensate for color shifts in the supertwist design by layering both sides of the liquid crystal with thin polymer films. Because the films absorb less light than the twin panels of double supertwist screens, less backlight—and less backlight power—is required for the same screen brightness.

Cholesteric Technology

In 1996, the Liquid Crystal Institute of Kent State University developed another liquid crystal technology into a workable display system and began its commercial manufacture. Termed cholesteric LCDs, this design uses crystals that switch between transmissive and reflective states instead of twisting. These changes are more directly visible and require no polarizers to operate. In that polarizing panels reduce the brightness of nematic displays by as much as 75 percent, cholesteric LCDs can be brighter. Early screens are able to achieve high contrast ratios without backlights.

Cholesteric screens have a second advantage. They are bi-stable. That is, maintaining a given pixel in either the transmissive or reflective phase requires no energy input. Once switched on, a pixel stays on until switched off. The screen requires power only to change pixels. In fact, a cholesteric screen will retain its last image even after it is switched off. Power usage in notebook PC applications is likely to be as low as 10 percent that of nematic panels.

The fabrication technologies used to make the cholesteric displays also allow for finer detail. Kent State has already demonstrated grayscale panels with resolutions as high as 200 pixels per inch. Although initial production was limited to grayscale displays, color cholesteric panels are currently under development.

Passive Matrix

Nematic LCDs also come in two styles, based on how the current that aligns their nematic molecules is applied. Most LCD panels have a grid of horizontal and vertical conductors, and each pixel is located at the intersection of these conductors. The pixel is darkened simply by sending current through the conductors to the liquid crystal. This kind of display is called a passive matrix.

Active Matrix

The alternate design, the active matrix, is more commonly referred to as Thin Film Transistor (TFT) technology. This style of LCD puts a transistor at every pixel. The transistor acts as a relay. A small current is sent to it through the horizontal and vertical grid, and in response the transistor switches on a much higher current to activate the LCD pixel.

The advantage of the active matrix design is that a smaller current needs to traverse the grid so the pixel can be switched on and off faster. Although passive LCD screens may update only about half a dozen times per second, TFT designs can operate at ordinary monitor speeds—10 times faster. That increased speed equates to faster response; for example, your mouse won't disappear as you move it across the screen.

The disadvantage of the TFT design is that it requires the fabrication of one transistor for each screen pixel. Putting those transistors there requires combining the LCD and semiconductor manufacturing processes. That's sort of like getting bricklayers and carpenters to work together.

Double-Scanned Displays

To achieve the quality of active matrix displays without paying the price, engineers have upped the scan on passive panels. Double-scanned passive panels work exactly like the name says: They scan their screens twice in the period that a normal screen is scanned only once. Rather than go over each pixel two times, a double-scanned display divides the screen into two halves and scans the two halves at the same time. The idea is something like interlacing CRT screens, lowering the required scanning frequency, but the arrangement and effect are different. Double-scanned displays split the screen in the middle into upper and lower halves. The split means that each pixel gets twice as long for updates as would be the case if the whole screen were scanned at the same frequency. As a result, double-scanning displays can eke out extra brightness, contrast, and speed. They do not, however, reach the quality level set by active matrix screens.

Sometimes manufacturers use the abbreviation *DSTN* to indicate double-scanned displays. It is an acronym for Double-scanned Super-Twist Nematic. *HPA*, which stands for High Performance Addressing, is an improved double-scanned technology. Note that both DSTN and HPA display systems use passive matrix technology.

Response Time

The LCD panel equivalent of persistence is *response time*. Charging and discharging individual pixels requires a finite period, and the response time measures this period. The time to charge and the time to discharge a given pixel can, and often are, different and are typically individually specified. For example, the off time of some active screens may be twice that of the on time.

The ambient temperature can have dramatic effects on the response time of an LCD panel. At freezing, the response time of a panel may be three times longer (slower) than at room temperature.

At room temperature, an active matrix display pixel has a response time on the order of 10–50 milliseconds.

Color Issues

The displayable range of colors of today's LCD panels is more limited than that of CRT displays. Although the color shortfall recommends against using a desktop LCD panel in color-critical applications such as prepublishing, the range is more than broad enough to present realistic full-color images. In fact, unless you need to do Pantone matching, you're unlikely to notice the lack of color range.

A related problem with LCD panels has been control of color temperature. Early LCD panels have had almost random color temperatures; they were set at whatever the commonly available backlights would permit. Modern displays have advanced to the point that many now offer selectable color temperatures, typically a daylight value (in the range of 5000 Kelvins), a "bluish" hot temperature (in the 9000-Kelvin range), and an adjustable user-defined temperature.

Field Emission Displays

The chief challenger to the Liquid Crystal Display is the *Field Emission Display*, or FED. Several manufacturers are actively developing FED technology. The technology was first described by Charles A. Spindt and other researchers in 1989, and the first FED-based monochrome screen was demonstrated in 1991. Color followed a few years later. Commercial FED panels were offered in early 1996, although with smaller dimensions than are required for PC displays. Although FED displays were expected in notebook PCs in 1997, the technology proved slow in coming. Pixtech demonstrated a working 15-inch color screen in 1998, but it has yet to see production. In fact in early 1999, Pixtech promised a color screen with 320-by-200 resolution and Futuba offered a VGA-resolution screen, albeit small and green. Manufacturers remain at work developing small (2.5-inch) panels for hand-held televisions and large panels (40 inches) for wall-hung displays.

In a radical bit of retro design, the FED uses the same basic illumination principle as the cathode ray tube. A flux of electrons strikes phosphor dots and causes them to glow. As with the CRT, the electrons must flow through a vacuum, so the FED panel is essentially a flattened vacuum tube. Instead of a single electron gun for each color, however, the

FED uses multiple, microscopic cones as electron emitters. Several hundred of these cathode emitters serve each image pixel. Each group of emitters has its own drive transistor, much like an active matrix LCD panel. Each emitter is cone shaped, a configuration that favors electron emission.

At the other side of the panel, each pixel has a conventional trio of phosphor dots, one for each primary color. Each dot has associated with it a separate transparent anode that attracts the electron flux. To separate the three colors of the pixel, the drive electronics activate each of the three anodes in sequence so the total display time of the pixel is split in thirds, one third for each color. The whole assembly fits between two glass panels, which form the bottle of the vacuum tube. Figure 18.8 illustrates the construction used by one FED manufacturer.

FIGURE 18.8

Cross-section of a Field Emission Display.

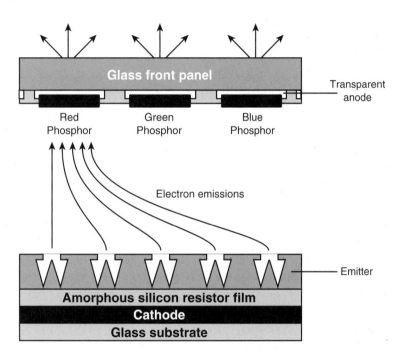

The short travel of the electron flux in the FED dramatically reduces the voltage required for the operation of the device. The anode in a FED may be only about 200 microns from the nearest cathode. Instead of a potential of thousands of volts between the anode and cathode, the FED operates at about 350 volts. The FED is essentially a current device, relying on a high current in the form of a dense flux of electrons to provide sufficient illumination. This high current presents one of the major technological obstacles to designing successful FEDs. Conventional phosphors deteriorate rapidly with the onslaught of electrons, quickly and readily burning in.

A FED behaves more like a CRT than an LCD. Its electron currents respond quickly to changes in their drive voltages. The response time of a FED display is typically a few microseconds, compared to the millisecond responses of LCD panels. FEDs also have wider viewing angles than LCD panels. The image on a FED screen is viewable over an angle of about 160 degrees, much the same as a CRT. In addition, FED technology promises to be more energy efficient than LCDs, capable of delivering about the same screen brightness while using half the power.

Currently, two camps appear to be evolving. Low voltage FEDs, such as those made by Futuba and Pixtech, require about 500 volts to operate. High voltage FEDs, in development by Candescent and Sony, require about 5,000 volts. The developers of the high-voltage technology believe it promises brighter screens and longer life, although the voltage requirements make it a worse match for notebook PCs. It will more likely find application in traditional CRT-style applications: desktop computer monitors and television sets.

Suspended Particle Devices

One of several technologies informally termed "light valves," *suspended particle devices*, or SPDs, throttle the transmission of light by varying their transparency under electrical control. Rather than generate light itself, the SPD modulates a separate light source, much like an LCD does. The similarities to LCDs run deeper. SPDs can be manufactured in the same facilities that make LCDs, with few changes to the process.

As the descriptive name implies, an SPD uses particles suspended in a liquid or, alternately, a film in which droplets of liquid containing suspended particles are embedded. This medium is sandwiched between transparent plates of glass or plastic with a conductive coating. The particles are key to the operation of the display. In their normal, relaxed state, they align randomly, diffusing and blocking the passage of light. A voltage applied across the two plates forces the particles to align, making them transparent. The effect is quick, and by varying the application of voltage, the degree of transparency can be controlled.

The developers of SPD technology note that it holds several advantage over LCDs. The SPD should allow higher contrast, greater brightness, and wider viewing angles because it does not require polarizers (each of which cuts light transmission by half). This design also makes SPDs less complex—which means they should be easier and less expensive to fabricate.

Manufacturers are exploring the possibility of using SPDs for notebook PC displays, but no current SPD product offers the color and resolution levels of today's LCDs. So far, the technology has shown its best promise in making *smart windows*. These have nothing to do with the operating system. Rather, they are traditional glass windows that can change from transparent to opaque as suits your needs.

Electroluminescent Displays

The backlights used by many LCD displays use electroluminescent technology. Some manufacturers are working to develop flat-panel displays that do away with the LCD and instead use an EL panel segmented into individual pixels. Monochrome screens have already been developed, but color screens are problematic. Although green and blue EL elements have operating lives long enough for commercial applications—in excess of 5,000 hours—current red EL elements operate only about half as long. The longer wavelength of red light requires higher currents, which shortens the life of the materials. Manufacturers believe, however, that the technology will be successful in the next few years. Its primary application is expected to be wall-hung displays.

Gas-Plasma

One alternative is the gas-plasma screen, which uses a high voltage to ionize a gas and cause it to emit light. Most gas-plasma screens have the characteristic orange-red glow of neon because that's the gas they use inside. Gas-plasma displays are relatively easy to make in the moderately large sizes perfect for laptop computer screens, and they yield sharpness unrivaled by competing technologies. However, gas-plasma screens also need a great deal of power—several times the requirements of LCD technology—at high voltages, which must be synthesized from low-voltage battery power. Consequently, gas-plasma displays are used primarily in AC-power portables. When used in laptops, the battery life of a gas-plasma-equipped machine is quite brief, on the order of an hour.

LED

In lieu of the tube, laptop designers have tried just about every available alternative display technology. These include the panels packed with light-emitting diodes—the power-on indicators of the 1980s—that glow at you as red as the devil's eyes. But LEDs consume extraordinary amounts of power. Consider that a normal, full-size LED can draw 10 to 100 milliwatts at full brilliance and that you need 100,000 or so individual elements in a display screen; you get an idea of the magnitude of the problem. Certainly, the individual display elements of an LED screen would be smaller than a power-on indicator and consume less power, but the small LED displays created in the early days of portable PCs consumed many times the power required by today's technologies. LEDs also suffer in that they tend to wash out in bright light and are relatively expensive to fabricate in large arrays.

Practical Considerations

Today, the choice for flat-panel displays involves exactly one technology, the LCD. Even so, a number of variables makes one display system more appealing than another. When buying a notebook PC, the display is one of the factors guiding your decision. Whether a given system is right for you often depends on the size and resolution of the display. In selecting a flat-panel display for a desktop PC, you must confront another issue: the interface used by the display system.

Resolution

Onscreen resolution is an important issue with flat-panel displays; it determines how sharp text characters and graphics will appear. Commercial LCD products available as standalone displays for desktop PCs and built into notebook computers typically achieve one of three resolution levels.

VGA is today's minimum. You'll find its 640-by-480 pixel resolution only in the least expensive of modern notebook systems. It's adequate for note-taking and other single-minded applications but falters when you want to work in multiple windows or work on large spreadsheets.

SVGA usually refers to the 800-by-600 pixel resolution level. This is today's workhorse resolution, found both in moderately priced notebook computers and smaller desktop flat-panel displays (12 to 14 inches). The popularity of this resolution reflects it being a good compromise between price and usability.

XGA usually refers to the 1,024-by-768 pixel resolution level. This is temporarily the top of the line for notebook PCs and for reasonably affordable desktop displays.

Beyond XGA, the terminology is less uniform. However, the display industry now uses several additional acronyms for resolution levels up to 2,048 by 1,536 pixels. Table 18.2 lists these common resolution names.

TABLE 18.2   Resolution Levels and Associated Tags

Name	Horizontal Pixels	Vertical Pixels	Aspect Ratio
VGA	640	480	.75
SVGA	800	600	.75
XGA	1,024	768	.75
SXGA	1,280	1,024	.75
UXGA	1,600	1,200	.75
HDTV	1,920	1,080	.56
QXGA	2,048	1,536	.75

LCDs have an inherent resolution that's a physical property of the panel. Pixels are a physical feature of the screen. An XGA screen, for example, has exactly 1,024 active picture elements arranged across its width. This fact makes the measure of *pixel-pitch* (analogous to dot-pitch) less relevant than with CRT displays. All displays of a given size and resolution will have the same pixel-pitch.

As a result of this arrangement, LCD panels have a preferred operating resolution, one that matches the physical resolution. Although some analog LCD systems can simulate lower resolutions (and to some degree higher resolutions), they achieve optimum performance with the correct match.

Size

Unlike CRT-based monitors, the entire area of an LCD display is usable. Because the image is a perfect fit into the pixels of the LCD display, there are no issues of underscan and overscan. The size of the screen is the size of the image.

The VESA Video Image Area Definition standard applies to LCDs just as it does to CRTs. Most LCD panel makers, however, specify the dimensions of their products with the same diagonal that served manufacturers so well for color televisions. Common sizes range from 10.4 inches to 15 inches, with even larger sizes available for specialized desktop applications.

Because most LCD panels are used on notebook PCs, their size is ultimately constrained by the dimensions of the computer itself. For notebook machines that approximate the size of a stack of true notepads, the maximum screen size is about 12.1 inches. Some manufacturers (notably NEC) have developed notebook PCs with larger screens, but the computers themselves are necessarily larger in length and width. Larger LCD panels are slated to replace CRTs as the basis for desktop and, in a new application, wall-hung displays. Some manufacturers are experimenting with screens as large as 42 inches across for such applications.

In desktop applications LCD displays are, inch for inch, more generous than CRT monitors. That is, the workable image (and visual impression) presented by the LCD appears about the size of a CRT display one step larger. The image on a 15-inch LCD looks comparable to that on a 17-inch CRT. Figure 18.9 compares the screen size of a 15-inch LCD and a 17-inch CRT.

Interface

Flat panels differ substantially from CRTs. Most flat-panel display systems have a fixed number of pixels. That is, a flat panel claiming 1,024-by-768 resolution has an array of active (illuminating) elements measuring exactly 1,024-by-768 pixels. CRTs have no fixed pixel positions; they will display the number of pixels embedded in a scan line. Although CRTs cope well with analog interfaces, flat panels do not.

To see anything on a flat panel using an analog interface such as the standard VGA connector, the resolution in the video signal must match that of the display. Even then, however, the match is likely not to be perfect. Transitions between pixels in the analog signal may not line up with the actual elements of the flat-panel screen. As a result, the onscreen image may display odd artifacts such as one or more vertical lines or a shimmer to the image. To cope with such problems, most flat-panel displays with analog inputs have a phase control that you adjust when you set up the monitor.

FIGURE 18.9

Image size on CRT and LCD monitors compared.

That said, the autosizing of today's analog desktop LCD monitors easily outclasses that of conventional CRT displays. Although you'll be faced with the same image size and position controls on an analog-interfaced LCD as with a conventional CRT, the automatic settings do an excellent job of properly sizing and locating the image on the display.

Flat-panel display systems work best with digital interfaces that target each pixel specifically. Notebook computers, with their directly connected displays, work well because they supply their flat-panel displays with digital data. Desktop flat-panel displays work best with digital interfaces such as the Digital Video Interface, or DVI, which is described later. With a digital connection, you need not make any adjustments to get a proper display. If anything, a tweak of the contrast control will yield the best possible image.

Electronics

The image you see onscreen is only part of the story of a complete display system. The video signals from your PC must be amplified and processed by the electronics inside the monitor to achieve the right strength and timing relationships to put the proper image in view.

The basic electronic components inside a monitor are its video amplifiers. As the name implies, these circuits simply increase the strength (amplify) of the approximately one-volt signals they receive from your PC to the thousands of volts needed to drive the electron beam from cathode to phosphor. Monochrome monitors have a single video amplifier; color monitors, three (one for each primary color).

In an analog color monitor, these three amplifiers must be exactly matched and absolutely linear. That is, the input and output of each amplifier must be precisely proportional, and it must be the same as the other two amplifiers. The relationship between these amplifiers is called color tracking. If it varies, the color of the image on the screen won't be what your software had in mind.

The effects of such poor color tracking are all bad. You lose precision in your color control. This is especially important for desktop publishing and presentation applications. With poor color tracking, the screen can no longer hope to be an exact preview of what eventually appears on paper or film. You may even lose a good fraction of the colors displayable by your video system.

What happens is that differences between the amplifiers cause one of the three primary colors to be emphasized at times and de-emphasized at others, casting a subtle shade on the onscreen image. This shading effect is most pronounced in gray displays; the dominant colors tinge the gray.

Although you don't have to worry about color tracking in a monochrome display, the quality of the amplifier nevertheless determines the range of grays that can be displayed. Aberrations in the amplifier cause the monitor to lose some of its grayscale range.

The relationship between the input and output signals of video amplifiers is usually not linear. That is, a small change in the input signal may make a greater than corresponding change in the output. In other words, the monitor may exaggerate the color or grayscale range of the input signal; contrast increases. The relationship between input and output is referred to as the gamma of the amplifier. A gamma of one would result in an exact correspondence of the input and output signals. However, monitors with unity gammas tend to have washed out, pastel images. Most people prefer higher gammas, in the range 1.5 to 1.8, because of their contrastier images.

Synchronizing Frequency Range

At one time, engineers locked computer monitors to one standard, much as video monitors lock to standard NTSC or PAL video signals. To access higher resolutions, however, monitor makers abandoned such *fixed-frequency* monitors and opted for *multiscanning monitors* that could lock on a wide range of signals. Almost all new computer monitors use multiscanning technology.

Coping with today's variety of signal standards makes mandatory a monitor's ability to synchronize with the widest possible range of synchronizing frequencies. You have two frequencies to worry about. The *vertical synchronizing frequency*, sometimes called the refresh rate or frame rate, determines how often the complete screen is updated. The *horizontal synchronizing frequency* (or horizontal scan rate) indicates the rate at which the individual scan lines that make up the image are drawn. These frequency ranges are important to you because they determine with which video standards the monitor can work.

The starting point for the scan rate of a modern monitor is the 31.5KHz used by the VGA system. All current monitors require compatibility with this scan rate to make legible displays when your PC boots up. (Under the DVI standard, discussed later, new digitally interfaced monitors can emulate this mode, although DVI itself will make scan rate issues irrelevant.) A higher maximum scan rate is always better.

The lowest frame rate normally required is the 59Hz used by some early VESA modes, although today you'll only run into such low refresh rates with old display adapters. You'll want a new monitor that supports the highest possible frame rate, as high as 85Hz under some VESA standards.

Scan rate, refresh rate, and resolution interact. Table 18.3 lists the scanning frequencies of most common computer display systems.

TABLE 18.3   Scanning Frequencies Specified by Monitor Standards

Standard	Resolution	Vert. Sync (Frame Rate)	Horiz. Sync (Line Rate)
MDA	720×350	50Hz	18.3KHz
CGA	640×200	60Hz	15.75KHz
EGA	640×350	60Hz	21.5KHz
MCGA (Graphics)	640×480	60Hz	31.5KHz
MCGA (Text)	720×400	70Hz	31.5KHz
VGA (Graphics)	640×480	60Hz	31.5KHz
VGA (Text)	720×400	70Hz	31.5KHz
Macintosh	640×480	67Hz	35.0KHz
XGA-2	640×480	75.0Hz	39.38KHz
VESA	640×480	75Hz	37.5KHz
Apple Portrait	640×870	76.5Hz	70.19KHz
VESA guideline	800×600	56Hz	35.5KHz
VESA guideline	800×600	60Hz	37.9KHz
VESA standard	800×600	72Hz	48.1KHz

Electronics

Standard	Resolution	Vert. Sync (Frame Rate)	Horiz. Sync (Line Rate)
VESA standard	800×600	75Hz	46.875KHz
RasterOps &	1,024×768	75.1Hz	60.24KHz
Supermac	1,024×768	75.1Hz	60.24KHz
VESA guideline	1,024×768	60Hz	48.3KHz
VESA standard	1,024×768	70.1Hz	56.5KHz
VESA standard	1,024×768	75Hz	60KHz
8514/A	1,024×768	44Hz*	35.5KHz
XGA	1,024×768	44Hz*	35.5KHz
XGA-2	1,024×768	75.8Hz	61.1KHz
Apple 2-page	1,152×870	75Hz	68.68KHz
VESA standard	1,280×1,024	75Hz	80KHz

Note that the legacy 8514/A and XGA systems have very low frame rates, 44Hz, because they are interlaced systems. To properly display these signals, a monitor must have sufficient range to synchronize with the field rate of these standards, which is twice the frame rate.

Interlacing

Most computer display systems use *progressive scanning*. That is, the system starts by displaying the first (top) line in the video image and then displays each subsequent line, one after the other down the screen. Televisions and video systems use *interlaced scanning*. Instead of scanning lines sequentially from top to bottom, each frame of the image is broken into two fields. One field consists of the odd-numbered lines of the image, the other, the even-numbered lines. The electron beam sweeps across and down, illuminating every other line, and then starts from the top again and finishes with the ones it missed on the first pass.

This technique achieves an apparent doubling of the frame rate. Instead of sweeping down the screen 30 times a second (the case of a normal television picture), the top-to-bottom sweep occurs 60 times a second. Whereas a 30 frame-per-second rate would noticeably flicker, the ersatz 60 frame-per-second rate does not—at least not to most people under most circumstances. Some folks' eyes are not fooled, however, so interlaced images have earned a reputation of being flickery. Figure 18.10 compares progressive and interlaced scanning.

FIGURE 18.10
Progressive versus interlaced scanning.

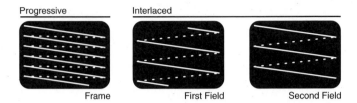

Interlacing is used on computer display signals to keep the necessary bandwidth down. A lower frame rate lowers the required bandwidth of the transmission channel. Although interlaced scanning should have been forgotten along with the 8514/A and original XGA display systems, it occasionally pops up in computer displays—typically low-priced monitors that claim high resolutions. Be wary of any monitor that specifies its maximum resolution as interlaced.

Bandwidth

Perhaps the most common specification usually listed for any sort of monitor is bandwidth, which is usually rated in megahertz. Common monitor bandwidths stretch across a wide range; figures from 12 to 200MHz are sometimes encountered.

In theory, the higher the bandwidth, the higher the resolution and sharper the image displayed. In the case of color displays, the dot-pitch of the display tube is the biggest limit on performance. In a monochrome system, however, bandwidth is a determinant of overall sharpness. The PC display standards do not demand extremely wide bandwidths. Extremely large bandwidths are often superfluous.

The bandwidth necessary in a monitor is easy to compute. A system ordinarily requires a bandwidth wide enough to address each individual screen dot, plus an extra margin to allow for retrace times. (Retrace times are those periods in which the electron beam moves but does not display, for instance, at the end of each frame when the beam must move from the bottom of the screen at the end of the last line of one frame back up to the top of the screen for the first line of the next frame.)

A typical color display operating under the VGA standard shows 288,000 pixels (a 729-by-400 pixel image in text mode) 70 times per second, a total of 20.16 million pixels per second. An 800-by-600 pixel Super VGA display at 75Hz must produce 36 million pixels per second.

Synchronizing signals require their own slice of monitor bandwidth. Allowing a wide margin of about 25 percent for retrace times, it can thus be seen that for most PC applications, a bandwidth of 16MHz is acceptable for TTL monitors, and 10MHz of bandwidth is sufficient for sharp composite video displays—figures well within the claims of most commercial products. For VGA, 25MHz is the necessary minimum.

Multiplying the dot-clock by 25 percent yields an acceptable estimate of the bandwidth required in a monitor. For the standards IBM promulgated, the company listed actual bandwidth requirements. Table 18.4 summarizes these requirements and calculates estimates for various PC display standards.

TABLE 18.4   Dot-Clocks and Recommended Bandwidths for Video Standards

Video Standard	Dot-Clock	Recommended Bandwidth
MDA	12.6MHz	16.3MHz
CGA	7.68MHz	14.3MHz
EGA	13.4MHz	16.3MHz
PGC	18.4MHz	25MHz
VGA (350- or 480-line mode)	18.4MHz	25MHz
VGA (400-line mode)	20.2MHz	28MHz
8514/A	34.6MHz	44.9MHz
VESA 800×600, 75Hz	36MHz	45MHz
VESA 1,024×768, 75Hz	60MHz	75MHz
VESA 1,280×1,024, 75Hz	100MHz	125MHz

Although these estimates are calculated using the dot-clock of the display, the relationship between dot-clock and bandwidth is not as straightforward as the calculations imply. Because in real-world applications the worst-case display puts an illuminated pixel next to a dark one, the actual bandwidth required by a display system should be one-half the dot-clock plus system overhead. A pair of on/off pixels exactly corresponds to the up and down halves of a single cycle. The higher bandwidth you calculate from the dot-clock allows extra bandwidth that gives greater image sharpness; sharply defining the edges of a pixel requires square waves, which contain high-frequency components. Consequently, the multiplication of the dot-clock by display overhead offers a good practical approximation of the required bandwidth, even though the calculations are on shaky theoretical ground.

Energy Star

Compared to some of the things that you might connect to your PC, a monitor consumes a modest amount of electricity. A laser printer can draw as much as a kilowatt when its fuser is operating. A typical PC requires 100 to 200 watts. A typical monitor requires only about 30 watts. Unlike the laser fuser, however, your monitor may stay on all day long, and an office may have hundreds of them, each continually downing its energy dosage.

Those watts add up, not just in their power consumption but also their heat production that adds to the load on the office air conditioning.

To help cut the power used by computer equipment, the Environmental Protection Agency started the Energy Star program, which seeks to conserve power while computers and their peripherals are in their idle states. For monitors, Energy Star means that the monitor powers down to one of two lower-power conditions or shuts off entirely when its host computer has not been used for a while.

Energy Star compliant monitors have four operating modes: on, standby, suspend, and off. During normal operation, when the monitor displays an active image generated by your PC, it is on. In standby mode, the monitor cuts off the electron beam in its CRT and powers down some of its electronics. It keeps the filament or heat of the CRT hot (the part that has to warm up to make the tube work) so that the monitor can instantly switch back to its on state. In suspend mode, the filament and most of the electronics of the monitor switch off. Only a small portion of the electronics of the monitor remain operational to sense the incoming signals, ready to switch the monitor back on when the need arises. This conserves most of the power that would be used by the monitor but requires the CRT to heat up before the monitor can resume normal operation. In other words, the monitor trades rapid availability for a reduction in power use. In off mode, the monitor uses no power but requires you to manually switch it on.

To enable your PC to control the operating mode of your monitor without additional electrical connections, VESA developed its Display Power Management Standard. This system uses the two synchronizing signals your video board supplies to your monitor to control its operating mode. To signal the monitor to switch to standby operation, your video card switches off only its horizontal sync signal. To signal the monitor to switch to suspend mode, your video board cuts both the video signal and the vertical sync but leaves the horizontal sync on. In off mode, all signals are cut off. Table 18.5 summarizes these modes.

TABLE 18.5   VESA Display Power Management Summary

Monitor State	Video	Vertical Sync	Horizontal Sync	DPMS	Recovery Time	Power Savings
On	On	On	On	Mandatory	None	None
Standby	On	On	Off	Optional	Short	Minimal
Suspend	Off	Off	On	Mandatory	Longer	Substantial
Off	Off	Off	Off	Mandatory	Warm-up	Maximum

Advanced operating systems monitor your system use and send out the standby and suspend signals when you leave your system idle for a predetermined time. Your video driver software controls the DPMS signals. Note that screensaver software defeats the purpose of DPMS by keeping your system active even when it is not in use. You can trim your power usage by relying on DPMS rather than a screensaver to shut down your monitor.

Many monitors made before the DPMS standard was created often incorporate their own power-saving mode that's initiated by a loss of the video signal for a predetermined time. In other words, they sense when your screen is blank and start waiting. If you don't do something for, say, five minutes, they switch the monitor to standby or suspend, regardless of the state of the synchronizing signals. The DPMS system is designed so that these monitors, too, will power down (although only after the conclusion of both the DPMS and their own internal timing cycles).

To enable the DPMS system under Windows, you must tell the operating system that your monitor is Energy Star compliant. If your monitor is in the Windows database, Windows will know automatically whether the monitor is compliant. You can also check the Energy Star compliance in the Change Display Settings screen. You must also activate the DPMS screen blanker from the Screen Saver tab of your Display Properties screen.

Identification

The prevalence of multiscanning monitors with wildly different capabilities makes getting the most from your investment a challenge. You must be able to identify not only the display abilities of the monitor, but also those of your video board, and then make the best possible match between them. If you're wrong, you won't get everything that you've paid for. Worse, you might not see anything intelligible on your screen. Worse still, you face a tiny chance of actually harming your monitor or video board.

Hardwired Coding

The problem is neither new nor one that arose with multiscanning systems. When the VGA system was new, IBM developed a rudimentary system for letting its PCs determine the type of monitor that was connected—limited, of course, to the monitors IBM made. The system had limited capabilities. It could identify whether the monitor was monochrome or color and whether it met merely the VGA standard or advanced into higher resolution territory. At the time, IBM only offered four monitors, and that modest range defined the extent of the selection.

The IBM scheme was to use three of the connections between the monitor and the video board to carry signals identifying the monitor. These first signals were crude—a simple binary code that put the signal wire either at ground potential or with no connection. Table 18.6 lists this coding system.

TABLE 18.6   Monitor Identification Coding used by IBM

Display type	Size	IBM model	ID 0	ID 1	ID 2
Monochrome	12 inch	8503	NC	Ground	NC
Color	12 inch	8513	Ground	NC	NC
Color	14 inch	8512	Ground	NC	NC
Hi-resolution	15 inch	8514	Ground	NC	Ground

Display Data Channel

This rudimentary standard was not up to the task of identifying the wide range of monitor capabilities that became available in the years after the introduction of VGA. Yet adding true plug-and-play capabilities to your PC requires automatically identifying the type of monitor connected to your PC so that the display adapter (and the rest of the system) can be properly configured. To meet this challenge, VESA developed the *Display Data Channel (DDC)*, an elaborate monitor identification system based on the same connections as the early IBM system but with greatly enhanced signals and capabilities.

Through the DDC, the monitor sends an *Extended Display Identification*, or EDID, to your PC. In advanced form, the DDC moves data both ways between your monitor and your PC using either the I^2C or ACCESS.bus serial interfaces . The DDC2B standard uses I^2C bus signaling on two of the wires of the monitor connection to transfer data both ways between the monitor and its attached video board. DDC2AB uses a full ACCESS.bus connection and protocol, which allow you to connect other computer peripherals (for example, your keyboard) to your monitor rather than the system unit.

All levels of the DDC system gain information about your monitor in the same way. The monitor sends out the EDID as a string of serial bits on the monitor data line, pin 12. Depending on the level of DDC supported by the monitor, the EDID data stream is synchronized either to the vertical sync signal generated by the video board present on pin 14 of 15-pin video connectors or to a separate serial data clock (SCL) that's on pin 15 in DDC2 systems. One bit of data moves with each clock cycle. When the system uses vertical sync as the clock, the data rate will be in the range 60 to 85Hz. With DDC compliant monitors, your video board can temporarily increase the vertical sync frequency to up to 25KHz to speed the transmission of this data. Using the SCL signal when both video board and monitor support it, data rates as high as 100KHz are possible.

The serial data takes the form of nine-bit sequences, one per byte. The first eight bits encode the data, most significant bit first. The last bit can be either a zero or one at the choice of the monitor manufacturer. The only restriction is that the ninth bit must have the same value for every byte.

The DDC system sends data from the monitor to your display adapter in 128-byte blocks. The first of these is the EDID block. It is optionally followed by an Extended EDID block or additional proprietary manufacturer data blocks. Table 18.7 lists the structure of the basic EDID.

TABLE 18.7   Basic EDID Structure

Start Byte	Length	Description
0	8 bytes	Header
8	10 bytes	Vendor/product identification ·
18	2 bytes	EDID version/revision
20	15 bytes	Basic display parameters/features
35	19 bytes	Established/standard timings
54	72 bytes	Timing descriptions × 4 (18 bytes each)
126	1 byte	Extension flag
127	1 byte	Checksum

The header is always the same data pattern and serves to identify the EDID information stream. The vendor identification is based on EISA manufacturer identifications. The product identification is assigned by the manufacturer. It includes the month and year of manufacture of the monitor.

The basic display parameters that EDID relays to your system include the maximum size of your monitor's display, expressed as the largest width and height of the image area. Your applications or operating system can use this information to automatically set the proper scaling for fonts displayed on the screen. The timing data includes a bit representing the ability to support each of the various VESA standards so that your system can determine the possible modes and frequencies your monitor can use.

In addition to basic DDC support, VESA provides for two higher levels of standardization. The DDC2B system uses the Philips I2C signaling system to transfer data bidirectionally across the interface. The DDCAB system includes full ACCESS.bus support that supplies a low-speed serial interconnection bus suitable for linking such peripherals as keyboards and pointing devices through the monitor.

Because standard expansion buses do not provide suitable connections for routing ACCESS.bus signals, VESA has defined an auxiliary connector for the purpose, a five-pin *Berg* connector. Table 18.8 lists the signal assignments of this connector.

TABLE 18.8   Access Bus Connector Signal Assignments

Pin	Function
1	Ground
2	Mechanical key
3	Serial data (SDA)
4	+5V ACCESS.bus supply voltage
5	Data clock (SCL)

Monitors that are compliant with DDC use the same connectors as ordinary VGA displays. All the active video and synchronizing signals are located on the same pins of the connector, regardless of the DDC level the monitor uses or even if it doesn't use DDC at all. The only difference is the definition of the monitor identification signals. DDC1 video boards sacrifice the Monitor ID bit 1 pin, number 12, as a channel to receive identification data from your monitor. DDC2 systems make this signal bidirectional and take over pin 15 for carrying the clock signal. In any case, pin 9 may be used to supply five volts for running accessory devices. Table 18.9 lists the signal assignments of the VGA 15-pin connector under DDC.

TABLE 18.9   VESA Display Data Channel Signal Assignments

Pin	DDC1 Host	DDC2 Host	DDC1, DDC2 Display
1	Red video	Red video	Red video
2	Green video	Green video	Green video
3	Blue video	Blue video	Blue video
4	Monitor ID bit 2	Monitor ID bit 2	Optional
5	Return	Return	Return
6	Red video return	Red video return	Red video return
7	Green video return	Green video return	Green video return
8	Blue video return	Blue video return	Blue video return
9	+5V (optional)	+5V (optional)	+5V load (optional)
10	Sync return	Sync return	Sync return
11	Monitor ID bit 0	Monitor ID bit 0	Optional
12	Data from display	Bidirectional data	Bidirectional data

Electronics

Pin	DDC1 Host	DDC2 Host	DDC1, DDC2 Display
13	Horizontal sync	Horizontal sync	Horizontal sync
14	Vertical sync	Vertical sync	Vertical sync
15	Monitor ID bit 3	Data clock (SCL)	Data clock (SCL)

Manual Configuration

If your monitor or video board does not support any level of the DDC specification, you will be left to configure your system on your own. In general, you won't need to perform any special configuration to a multiscanning monitor to match it to your video board if the signals from the video board are within the range of the monitor. That's the whole point of the multiscanning display: It adjusts itself to accommodate any video signal.

That said, you may not get the most from your monitor. You might slight on its refresh rate and quickly tire your eyes with a flickering display. Worse, you might exceed its capabilities and end up with a scrambled or blank screen.

Windows includes its own configuration process that attempts to optimize the signals of your compliant video adapter with your monitor type. Windows already knows what video board you have; you have to tell it when you install your video drivers. Without a DDC connection, however, Windows is cut off from your monitor, so you must manually indicate the brand and model of monitor you're using.

You make these settings by clicking on the Change Display Type button in the Settings tab of your Display Properties dialog. Click on the button, and you see a screen like that shown in Figure 18.11.

FIGURE 18.11

The Change Display Type screen in Windows.

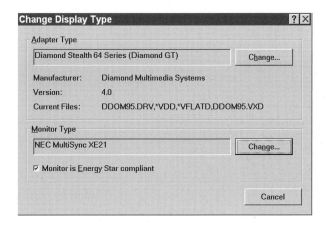

Interfacing and Connectors

The video connection carries the image between your video board and monitor.

Monitors can be grouped by the display standard they support, mostly based on the display adapter card they are designed to plug into. One basic guide that helps you narrow down the compatibility of a display just by inspecting its rear panel is the input connector used by the monitor. After all, if you cannot plug a monitor in to your computer, odds are it is not much good to you.

You likely encounter one of three styles of connector on the back of your PC. These include legacy connectors, used by display systems too ancient to worry about; analog systems used by the majority of today's display systems; and new digital interfaces that are beginning to appear on the market and mark the look (and connection) of things to come.

Legacy Connectors

The first video connector used by PCs was the nine-pin D-shell connector, as shown in Figure 18.12. It is now used only by legacy video systems and serves mostly as a warning that you may encounter trouble in trying to match your video system to a monitor. Appendix L covers the various obsolete video systems that lurk behind this connector.

FIGURE 18.12
A nine-pin D-shell jack used by legacy video systems.

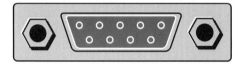

Analog Connection Systems

Three styles of connectors are shared by different PC video standards. By name, these three connectors are the RCA-style pin jack, the nine-pin D-shell, and the 15-pin "high-density" D-shell. In addition, some high-resolution monitors use three or more BNC connectors for their input signals.

Pin Jacks

The bull's eye jack used on stereo and video equipment is used by most manufacturers for the composite video connections in PC display systems, although a wealth of monitors and television sets made by innumerable manufacturers also use this connector. This connector does give you many choices for alternate displays—that is, if you don't mind marginal quality.

Composite monitors (those dealing with the composite video and NTSC color only) rank among the most widely available and least expensive in both color and monochrome. Even better quality television sets have such jacks, as shown in Figure 18.13, available.

FIGURE 18.13

A pin jack used by composite video I signals.

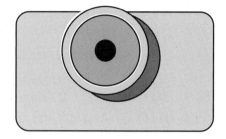

Although you can use any composite video display with a CGA or compatible color card, the signal itself limits the possible image quality to okay for monochrome, acceptable for 40-column color, and unintelligible for 80-column color. Nevertheless, a composite video display—already a multipurpose device—becomes even more versatile with a computer input.

Daisy-Chaining

A side benefit of pin plug and composite video displays is that most have both input and output jacks. These paired jacks enable you to daisy-chain multiple monitors to a single video output. For example, you can attach six composite video monitors to the output of your computer for presentations in a classroom or boardroom.

In many cases, the jacks just loop through the display (that is, they connect together). The display merely bridges the input video signal and alters it in no other manner. You can connect a nearly unlimited number of monitors to these loop-through connections with no image degradation. Some monitors, however, buffer their outputs with a built-in video amplifier. Depending on the quality of the amplifier, daisy-chaining several of these monitors can result in noticeable image degradation.

One way to tell the difference is by plugging the output of the display into the output of your computer. Most amplifiers don't work backwards, so if the display has a buffering amplifier, nothing appears onscreen. If you do get an image comparable to the one you get when plugging into the input jack, the signal just loops through the display.

Analog Voltage Level

The specifications of composite monitors sometimes include a number describing the voltage level of the input signal. This voltage level can be important when selecting a composite display because all such monitors are essentially analog devices.

In analog monitors, the voltage level corresponds to the brightness the electron beam displays onscreen. A nominal one-volt peak-to-peak input signal is the standard in both the video and computer industries and should be expected from any composite monitor. The VGA system requires a slightly different level—0.7 volts.

Termination

For proper performance, a composite video signal line must be terminated by an impedance of 75 ohms. This termination ensures that the signal is at the proper level and that
aberrations do not creep in because of an improperly matched line. Most composite input
monitors (particularly those with separate inputs and outputs) feature a termination switch
that connects a 75 ohm resistor across the video line when turned on. Only one termination resistor should be switched on in any daisy chain, and it should always be the last
monitor in the chain.

If you watch a monitor when you switch on the termination resistor, you'll notice that the
screen gets dimmer. That's because the resistor absorbs about half the video signal.
Because composite video signals are analog, they are sensitive to voltage level. The termination cuts the voltage in half and consequently dims the screen by the same amount.
Note that the dim image is the proper one. Although bright might seem better, it's not. It
may overload the circuits of the monitor or otherwise cause erratic operation.

Composite monitors with a single video input jack and no video output usually have a termination resistor permanently installed. Although you might try to connect two or more
such monitors to a single CGA composite output (with a wye cable or adapter), doing so
is unwise. With each additional monitor, the image gets dimmer (the signal must be split
among the various monitors) and the CGA adapter is required to send out increasing current. The latter could cause the CGA to fail.

VGA Connectors

The most common connector on PC monitors is the *15-pin high-density D-shell* connector.
Originally put in use by IBM for its first VGA monitors, it has become adopted as an
industry standard for all but the highest performance computer displays.

Because the signals generated by the VGA are so different from those of previous IBM
display systems, IBM finally elected to use a different, incompatible connector so the
wrong monitor wouldn't be plugged in with disastrous results. Although only nine connections are actually needed by the VGA system (11 if you give each of the three video
signals its own ground return as IBM specifies), the new connector is equipped with 15
pins. It's roughly the same size and shape as a 9-pin D-shell connector, but before IBM's
adoption of it, this so-called high-density 15-pin connector was not generally available.
Figure 18.14 shows this connector.

In addition, to allow for four video signals (three primary colors and separate sync) and
their ground returns, the VGA connector provides a number of additional functions. In
the original VGA design, it enabled the coding of both monitor type and the line count of
the video signal leaving the display adapter. The modern adaptation of the connector to
the VESA DDC standard redefines several pins for carrying data signals, as noted earlier.
Table 18.10 lists the signal assignments of the VGA connector.

FIGURE 18.14

A 15-pin mini D-shell connector used by VGA and similar video systems.

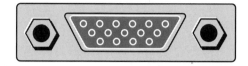

TABLE 18.10   VGA and Super VGA Connector Pin-Out

Pin	Function
1	Red video
2	Green video
3	Blue video
4	Reserved
5	Ground
6	Red return (ground)
7	Green return (ground)
8	Blue return (ground)
9	Composite sync
10	Sync return (ground)
11	VESA Display Data Channel
12	Reserved
13	Horizontal sync
14	Vertical sync
15	VESA Display Data Channel

IBM's 8514 and 8515 displays, as well as 8514/A and XGA display adapters, also use the same connector even though they at times use different signals. Again, however, IBM has incorporated coding in the signals to ensure that problems do not arise. The 8514/A and XGA adapters can sense the type of display connected to them and do not send out conflicting signals. The 8514 and 8515 monitors operate happily with VGA signals, so problems do not occur if they are plugged in to an ordinary VGA output.

The advantage of the 15-pin connector is convenience. One cable does everything. On the downside, the connector is not arranged for proper high-speed operation, and its deficiencies can limit high-frequency performance, which in video terms equates to sharpness when operating at high resolutions and refresh rates. Consequently, the highest resolution systems often forego the 15-pin connector for separate BNC connectors for each video channel.

BNC Connectors

True high-resolution systems use a separate coaxial cable for every signal they receive. Typically, they use BNC connectors to attach these to the monitor. They have one very good reason: Connectors differ in their frequency-handling capabilities, and capacitance in the standard 15-pin high-density D-shell connector can limit bandwidth, particularly as signal frequencies climb into the range above 30MHz. BNC connectors are designed for frequencies into the gigahertz range, so they impose few limits on ordinary video signals.

Monitors can use three, four, or five BNC connectors for their inputs. Figure 18.15 shows an array of five BNC connectors on the rear of a monitor.

FIGURE 18.15

A monitor with five BNC connectors for input.

A three-connector system integrates both horizontal and vertical synchronizing signals with the green signal. The resulting mix is called sync-on-green. Others use three connectors for red, green, and blue signals, and a fourth for horizontal and vertical sync combined together. This scheme is called composite sync. Five connector systems use three color signals: one for horizontal sync and one for vertical sync. These are called separate sync systems.

Enhanced Video Connector

VESA approached the problem of insufficient bandwidth with its *Enhanced Video Connector*. In addition to providing a high bandwidth digital and *analog* signal path, EVC added monitor identification facilities and sufficient additional signals to permit linking complete multimedia systems with a single plug. The final EVC standard allowed for four wide-bandwidth video signals along with 30 other data connections in a connector not much larger than today's VGA.

Unlike other connector standards, the EVC was not designed to accommodate any new kinds of signals. Instead, it is a carrier for existing interconnection standards. It allows grouping together nearly all of the next generation of high-speed computer connections in a single cable. The point is that you can put your PC on the floor, run an EVC connection to your monitor, and connect all your desktop accessories—keyboard, mouse, printer—to your monitor. The snarl of cables leading to the distant PC disappears thanks to the magic of the EVC.

In addition to RGB video with composite sync, the EVC standard includes provisions for composite and S-video signals as well as international video standards (PAL and SECAM) in systems that support DDC for monitor identification and negotiation. Connections are also provided for analog audio signals (both inputs and outputs). To connect additional peripherals, EVC also accommodates both Universal Serial Bus and IEEE 1394 ("FireWire") high-speed serial interface signals. Other connections provide DC power for charging notebook computers.

The centerpiece of the EVC design is the Molex *MicroCross* connection system, which uses four pins for video connections separated by a cross-shaped shield. The design links coaxial cables and allows for bandwidths of 500MHz. The additional data signals are carried through 30 additional contacts arranged in a 3-by-10 matrix. Figure 18.16 shows the contact arrangement on an EVC connector.

FIGURE 18.16
The VESA Enhanced Video Connector.

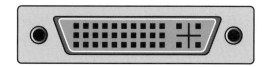

Although the EVC design is not a true coaxial connector, it provides a good impedance match (within 5 percent of a nominal 75 ohms) and shielding that is 98 percent effective. The signal bandwidth of the connection is approximately 2GHz.

All EVC connectors do not have to include all the signals specified by the standard. System designers are free to choose whatever signals they would like to include. That said, VESA recommends that manufacturers adopt one of three levels of support or signal sets for EVC for their products. These include Basic, Multimedia, and Full.

The Basic signal set is the minimum level of support required for devices using EVC. It includes only the video signal lines and DDC. At the Basic level, EVC operates as a standard video connector, much like today's VGA connector but with greatly improved bandwidth. The DDC connection allows the monitor and its host to negotiate the use of higher-resolution signals. VESA recommends that the Basic signal set be included in any subset of the EVC signals that a system designer chooses to support.

The Multimedia signal set adds audio support to the Basic signal set, allowing a single cable to carry video and audio to a suitable monitor. VESA foresees that the Multimedia signal set will usually be supplemented with USB signaling.

Full support includes all signal options in one connector.

Acceptance of EVA was neither instant nor overwhelming. However, with digital display connection systems—in particular, DVI—adopting the EVC style of connector, EVC will likely grow in importance as a high-performance analog connection system—perhaps the swan song of analog connection technology.

Digital Connection Systems

Flat-panel displays made the need for a high-performance digital display interface obvious. Analog-interface flat panels work but are only an interim solution.

Among the other problems with the standard analog links so popular on today's monitors, one stands in the way of getting truly high-resolution images on your monitor—limited bandwidth. The now dominant VGA connector has a maximum bandwidth of about 150MHz, so it already constrains the quality of some display systems. Conventional high-frequency video connectors (primarily BNC) require a separate cable for each video signal and allow no provisions for auxiliary functions such as monitor identification.

Achieving a single standard has been problematic for the industry, however. In the last few years, various groups have developed at least three specifications, all promoted as "standards." Despite the infighting among the promoters of each, the three are not in competition but represent the evolution of what will likely be the dominant standard for the future, the *Digital Video Interface*, or DVI.

Plug and Display

VESA called initial attempts at a digital video connection system *Plug and Display*, a clever turn on the plug-and-play system. Introduced in June 1997, the design basically grafted digital signals onto the EVA connector and used a complex coding system to keep connections straight.

Key to making Plug and Display work is *PanelLink* technology, developed by Silicon Image, Inc. A high-speed all-digital serial connection combines electrical and logical innovations to achieve a bandwidth above 150 MB/sec with high reliability.

The technology underlying PanelLink is called *transition minimized differential signaling*, or TMDS. It works at two levels. It begins with a form of group coding. The serial stream of display data first gets translated into a new bit pattern using 10 bits to encode each byte using only the bit-patterns that minimize the number of transitions between logical high and low. Each of the three primary color signals is separately coded.

The resulting stream of bits is sent through a balanced two-wire transmission system. In addition, the bit-patterns chosen for the original code are also chosen to balance the period the signal is high and low so that the voltage of the differential signal is zero. These techniques minimize crosstalk and interference, making the signal more reliable and easier to control.

VESA added the Plug and Display signals to its Enhanced Video Connector, using the shape of the shield around the plug and jack to code the signal type, acting as a physical key so that you could not mismatch your display and graphics adapter. Figure 18.17 illustrates this coding system.

FIGURE 18.17

*Plug and Display con-
nector coding.*

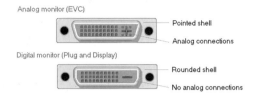

Analog monitor (EVC)

Pointed shell

Analog connections

Digital monitor (Plug and Display)

Rounded shell

No analog connections

From 1997 through early 1999, the Plug and Display connector was popular among digital desktop LCD panels. Among computer manufacturers, the primary supporter of the standard was IBM. The closely related DVI connection will likely replace Plug and Display, leaving it a historic note.

Digital Flat Panel Port

The Plug and Display connection system did not win universal acceptance. Some makers of computers, monitors, and graphics adapters thought the connector too complex and too large. In particular, they found mounting a Plug and Display connector and a conventional VGA connector (for backward compatibility) on a single card retaining bracket impractical. To develop an alternative, a group of 14 companies—all VESA members—formed the Digital Flat Panel Group.

The fruit of their efforts was another digital display connection standard, one electrically similar to Plug and Display but physically incompatible because of the choice of a different, smaller connector. The current (and final) version of the underlying specification, the *Digital Flat Panel port* standard, was published May 4, 1998. Table 18.11 lists the signal assignments of connectors that follow this standard.

TABLE 18.11 Digital Flat Panel Display Connector Signal Assignments

Pin	Mnemonic	Function
1	TX1+	Channel 1 TMDS positive differential output
2	TX1-	Channel 1 TMDS negative differential output
3	SHLD1	Shield for channel 1
4	SHLDC	Shield for clock
5	TXC+	Reference clock positive differential output
6	TXC-	Reference clock negative differential output
7	GND	Logic ground
8	+5V	Logic +5 VDC supply

continues

TABLE 18.11   continued

Pin	Mnemonic	Function
9	Reserved 9	Reserved
10	Reserved 10	Reserved
11	TX2+	Channel 2 positive differential output
12	TX2-	Channel 2 negative differential output
13	SHLD2	Shield for channel 2
14	SHLD0	Shield for Channel 0
15	TX0+	Channel 0 positive differential output
16	TX0-	Channel 0 negative differential output
17	Reserved 17	Reserved
18	HPD	Hot plug detection
19	DDC_DAT	DDC2B data
20	DDC_CLK	DDC2B clock

As with Plug and Display, the DFP system uses TMDS signaling. Unlike Plug and Display, the DFP port hardware incorporates no analog signals even as options. This expedient allows the use of a compact 20-pin miniature ribbon connector like that shown in Figure 18.18.

FIGURE 18.18

The Digital Flat Panel port display connector.

With good industry support thanks to its adoption by DFP group member Compaq Computer Corporation, the DFP port connector found favor on many commercial products. However, before its use became widespread, it was overtaken by yet another new design, one that will likely dominate the flat-panel display industry: the Digital Video Interface.

Digital Video Interface

For the makers of displays and graphic adapters, the coexistence of two standards and two connectors for the same purpose and products was not a good thing. Board makers, for example, were forced either to take sides and reduce their potential market or to develop two different products to match the competing standards. Although many people saw the weakness of having dueling standards, it took the influence of Intel to change things.

In late 1998, Intel rounded up the usual suspects to work on yet another digital display standard. The result was the Digital Display Working Group, initially comprising representatives from both the Plug and Display and DFPP camps—Intel, Compaq, Fujitsu, Hewlett-Packard, IBM, NEC, and Silicon Image.

The working group took the best of the two earlier standards and developed the *Digital Video Interface* as kind of the greatest hits of monitor connectors. The standard was adopted and published by VESA as DVI version 1.0 on April 2, 1999. Number Nine Visual Technology demonstrated the first product to use the interface, the SR9 graphics adapter, on May 19, 1999.

DVI shares the connector design and some of the non-video data signals with Plug and Display, but it breaks off the integral USB port from the connector. Although the DVI standard does not preclude USB in displays, to do so they must use a separate connection for the USB signals.

Although DVI uses the same TMDS signals as Plug and Display and DFPP, it doubles the effective bandwidth of these signals with the simple expedient of using two of them. Both are locked to the single clock channel provided by the interface, so they are automatically synchronized to each other. Each color signal has two signals, which are interleaved so data is spread between the two channels of a given color, creating what is essentially a parallel connection. Display systems may use either the one channel system or two channels, but the DVI specification draws a hard line between the two. Signals requiring a bandwidth of less than 165MHz must use the single-channel system. Systems requiring larger bandwidths must use two channels.

The three signal paths of DVI are not names with colors, although they correspond to red, green, and blue data. Each signal path actually carries three interleaved channels of data. The signal path used by blue data, for example, also carries a horizontal synchronizing signal and a vertical synchronizing signal. The two channels in the remaining pair of signal paths are currently reserved and have no assigned function.

Analog video is an optional part of DVI. Rather than shape, the DVI connector uses the cross-pin in the connector as a key for the presence of analog signals. The same connector can be used for all analog or all digital systems.

Analog signals, when present, are located in the four quadrants around the keying cross in the connector. Table 18.12 shows the signal assignments for the DVI connector.

TABLE 18.12   Signal Assignments for the DVI Connector

Pin	Function	Pin	Function	Pin	Function
1	TMDS Data2 -	9	TMDS Data1-	17	TMDS Data0-
2	TMDS Data2 +	10	TMDS Data1 +	18	TMDS Data0 +
3	TMDS Data2/4 Shield	11	TMDS Data1/3 Shield	19	TMDS Data0/5 Shield
4	TMDS Data4 -	12	TMDS Data3 -	20	TMDS Data5 -
5	TMDS Data4 +	13	TMDA Data3 +	21	TMDS Data5 +
6	DDC Clock	14	+5 V Power	22	TMDS Clock Shield
7	DDC Data	15	Ground	23	TMDS Clock +
8	Analog Video Sync	16	Hot Plug Detect	24	TMDS Clock -
C1	Analog Red	C2	Analog Green	C3	Analog Blue
C4	Analog Horizontal Sync	C5	Analog Ground		

Audio

The noise-making spectrum of PCs ranges from the beeps and squeaks of the tiny internal speaker to an aural rush equal in quality to today's best stereo CDs. PCs can generate, manipulate, record, and play back sounds of all sorts and even control other noise-makers such as music synthesizers. Today's high-quality sound capability distinguishes multimedia PCs from ordinary, visual-bound systems.

The most important audio features of a modern PC

Feature	Benefit
Basic sound system	Allows your PC to beep
Sound board	Gives your PC the ability to capture and reproduce sounds and music. May be integrated into your motherboard
Microphone	Captures live sound. May be used to record music, make voice annotations, or turn your PC into a speakerphone
Loudspeakers	Give your PC a voice so you can hear—or feel—the sounds and effects generated by your programs
CD Drive	Lets your PC play pre-recorded discs (and, of course, stores data files. A CD-R drive lets you records CDs for your stereo system
Synthesizer	Sound board feature that allows your PC to create new musical sounds
MIDI	Allows you to control external electronic musical instruments with your PC
MP3	Standard file format for compressed music that lets you turn your PC into a jukebox

Of the five senses, most people only experience personal computers with four: touch, smell, sound, and sight. Not that computers are tasteless—although a growing body of software doesn't even aspire that high—but most people don't normally drag their tongues across the cases of their computers. Touch is inherent in typing and pushing around a mouse or digitizer cursor. Smell is more limited still—what you appreciate in opening the box holding your new PC or what warns you when the fan in the power supply stops, internal temperatures rise, and roasting resistors and near inflammatory components begin to melt.

Most interactions with PCs involve sight: what you see on the monitor screen and, if you're not a touch typist, a peek down at the keyboard. High-resolution graphics make sight perhaps the most important part of any PC—or at least the most expensive.

To really experience your PC, however, you need an added sensual dimension—sound. In fact, sound distinguishes the ordinary PC from today's true multimedia machine. Most PCs are mainly limited to visual interaction. A multimedia PC extends the computer's capabilities of interacting with the world to include sound. It can generate sounds on its own, acting like a music synthesizer or noise generator, and it can control external devices that do the same thing through a MIDI interface. It can record or sample sounds on any standard computer medium (the hard disk being today's preferred choice) with sonic accuracy every bit as good (even better) than commercial stereo CDs. All the sounds it makes and stores can be edited and manipulated: Tones can be stretched, voices shifted, noises combined, music mixed. It can play back all the sounds it makes and records with the same fidelity, pushing the limits of even the best stereo systems.

The advent of multimedia made higher-quality external (or monitor-mounted) speakers mandatory in most home PCs. Unfortunately, the native endowment of most business PCs is naught but a squeaker of a loudspeaker that makes soprano Mickey Mouse sound like the Mormon Tabernacle Choir in comparison. The tiny little speaker is an artifact of the first PCs, the designers of which simply thought sound unnecessary. After all, the noise that calculating machines made was to be avoided. All they thought important were warning signals, so that's all the PC got. Images fared little better: Text screen little hinted at today's graphic potential of the PC.

Fortunately, any audible omissions made by the maker of your PC can be corrected by adding external speakers and, if necessary, a sound board. A basic requirement of a multimedia PC and included in most home systems, the sound board gives your PC the capability to synthesize and capture a variety of sounds, play them back, and control external devices.

Background

Sound is a physical phenomenon, best understood as the rapid change in air pressure. When a physical object moves, it forces air to move also. After all, air and the object cannot take up the same place at the same time. Air is pushed away from the place the object moves to and rushes into the empty place where the object was. Of course, the moving air has to come from somewhere. Ideally, the air pushed out of the way would retreat to the vacuum left behind when the object moved. Unfortunately, the air, much like any physical entity, cannot instantly transport itself from one place to another. The speed at which the air moves depends on its density; the higher the pressure, the greater the force pushing the air around. Indeed, moving the object creates an area of high pressure in front of it— where the air wants to get out of the way—and low pressure behind. Air is dumb—or, in today's politically correct language, knowledge challenged. The high pressure doesn't know that an exactly matching area of low pressure exists behind the object, so the high pressure pushes out in all directions. As it does, it spreads out and the pressure decreases.

Simply moving an object creates a puff of air. Sound arises when the object moves rapidly, vibrating. As it moves one way, it creates the high pressure puff that travels off. It moves back, and a corresponding low pressure pulse pops up and follows the high pressure. As the object vibrates, a train of these high- and low-pressure fronts moves steadily away from it.

The basic principles of sound should be obvious from this rudimentary picture. Sound requires a medium for transmission. The speed of sound depends not on the moving object but on the density of the air (or other medium). The higher the density, the faster the sound moves. The intensity of the sound pressure declines with distance as more air interacts with the compression-decompression cycles. Unconstrained, this decline would follow the infamous inverse-square law because as the sound travels in one dimension, it must spread over two. By confining or directing the air channel, however, you can alter the rate of this decay.

Human beings have a mechanism called the ear that detects pressure changes or sound waves. The ear is essentially a mechanical device, a transducer, that's tuned to react to the pressure changes that make up what we call sound.

To fit its digital signals into this world of pressure waves is a challenge for the PC in several ways. The PC needs a convenient form for manipulating sound. Fortunately, sound has an analog in the electronic world called *analog audio*, which uses electrical signals to represent the strengths of the pressure waves. PCs turn these electrical signals into *digital audio* that's compatible with microprocessors, other digital circuits, and sound systems. Of course, the PC is not limited to sounds supplied by others; it can create the digital signals itself, a process termed *synthesis*. To turn those digital signals into something that approaches sound—back to audio again—your PC uses its own audio circuitry or a *sound board* that includes both a digital-to-analog converter and an amplifier. (The sound board also likely contains a synthesizer of some kind.) Finally, your PC plugs into *loudspeakers* that convert the audio into pressure waves once again.

Analog Audio

As a human sensation, sound is an analog phenomenon. It has two primary characteristics—loudness (or amplitude) and frequency—that vary over a wide range with a infinite range of variations between its limits. Sounds can be loud or soft or any gradation in between. Frequencies can be low or high or anything in between.

Frequency

Sound frequencies are measured in *Hertz*, just like the frequencies of computer clocks or radio signals. The range of frequencies that a human being can hear depends on his age and sex. Younger and female ears generally have wider ranges than older and male ears. Most sources list the range of human hearing as 20 Hertz to 15,000 Hertz (or as high as 20,000 Hertz if your ears are particularly good).

Lower frequencies correspond to bass notes in music and the thumps of explosions in theatrical special effects. High frequencies correspond to the "treble" in music, the bright, even harsh sounds that comprise overtones in music—the brightness of strings, the tinkle of jingle bells—as well as hissy sounds like sibilants in speech, the rush of waterfalls, and overall background noise.

Low frequencies have long wavelengths, in the range of 10 feet (3 meters) for middle bass notes. The long wavelengths allow low frequencies to easily bend around objects and, from a single speaker, permeate a room. Moreover, human hearing is not directionally sensitive at low frequencies. You cannot easily localize a low-frequency source. Acoustical designers exploit this characteristic of low frequencies when they design low-frequency loudspeakers. For example, because you cannot distinguish the locations of individual low-frequency sources, a single speaker called a *subwoofer* is sufficient for very low frequencies even in stereo and multichannel sound systems.

High frequencies have short wavelengths, measured in inches or fractions of an inch (or centimeters). They can easily be blocked or reflected by even small objects. Human hearing is acutely sensitive to the location of higher-frequency sources.

Amplitude

Amplitude describes the strength or power of the sound. The amplitude of sound traveling through the air is usually expressed as its *sound pressure level*, or SPL. The threshold of human hearing is about 0.0002 microbar—which means a pressure change of 1/5,000,000,000th (one five billionth) of normal atmospheric pressure. In other word, the ear is a sensitive detector of pressure changes. Were it any more sensitive, you might hear the clink of Brownian motion as dust particles ricochet through the air.

In audio systems, electrical signals take the place of sound pressure waves. These signals retain the characteristic frequencies of the original sounds, but their amplitude refers to variations in electrical strength. Usually, the *voltage* in an audio system represents the amplitude of pressure of the original sound waves.

Decibels

A term that you'll usually see engineers use in measuring amplitude loudness is the *decibel*. Although the primary unit is actually the *Bel*, named after Alexander Graham Bell, the inventor of the hydrofoil (and, yes, the telephone), engineers find units of one-tenth that quantity to be more manageable.

The decibel represents not a measuring unit but a relationship between two measurements. The Bel is the ratio between two powers expressed as a logarithm. For example, a loud sound source may have an acoustic power of one watt, but a somewhat softer source may only generate one milliwatt of power, a ratio of 1,000:1. The logarithm of 1,000 is 3, so the relationship is 3 Bels or 30 decibels; one watt is 30 decibels louder than one milliwatt.

In addition to reducing power relationships to manageable numbers, decibels also approximately coincide with the way we hear sounds. Human hearing is also logarithmic. That means that something twice as loud to the human ear does not involve twice the power. For most people, for one sound to appear twice as loud as another it must have 10 times the power. Expressed as dB, this change is an increase in level of 3 dB because the logarithm of 10 is 0.3, so the relationship is 0.3 Bels or 3 decibels.

Engineers also use the decibel to compare voltages and sound pressures. The relationship and math are different, however, because in a circuit in which everything else is held constant, the voltage will be proportional to the square root of the power. Consequently, a doubling of voltage represents a 6 dB change.

Most commonly, you'll see dB used to describe signal-to-noise ratios and frequency response tolerances. The unit is apt in these circumstances because it is used to reflect relationships between units. Sometimes, however, people express loudness or signal levels as a given number of dB. This usage is incorrect and meaningless because it lacks a reference value. When the reference unit is understood or specified, however, dB measurements are useful.

Any unit may be used as a reference for measurements expressed in dB. Several of these have common abbreviations, as listed in Table 19.1.

TABLE 19.1 References Units in dB Measurements

Abbreviation	Reference Unit
0 dBj	1 millivolt
0 dBv	1 volt
0 dBm	1 milliwatt
0 dBk	1 kilowatt

In sound systems, the dBm system is most common. The electronic industry adopted (in May 1939) a power level of one milliwatt in a 600 ohm circuit as the standard reference for 0 dBm.

You'll also encounter references to *volume units*, or VU, as measured by the classic VU meter. A true VU meter is strictly defined and the zero it indicates reflects a level 4 dB above 0 dBm. The meters on tape and cassette recorders have VU designations but are not strictly speaking VU meters. They are usually referenced to a specific recording level on the tape. Similarly, meters on radio transmitters are often calibrated in VU, but zero corresponds not to the input line level but the output modulation level; 0 VU usually means 100 percent modulation.

Impedance

Nearly all practical electrical circuits waste some of the electricity flowing through them, the exception being exotic superconducting designs made from exotic materials that operate at very low temperatures. This electrical waste becomes heat. It makes both toasters and microprocessors hot.

Engineers call the characteristic of a direct current circuit that causes this waste *resistance* because it describes how a material resists the flow of electricity. Resistance is measured in a unit called the *ohm* after German physicist G. S. Ohm. Neat electrical trivia: The opposite of resistance is conductivity, for which the measuring unit is the mho.

The alternating current used by audio circuits complicates matters. Some electrical devices conduct some frequencies better than others. This frequency-sensitive opposition to the flow of alternating current is called *reactance*. The sum of the resistance and reactance of a circuit at a given frequency is called its *impedance*.

Impedance is an important measure in audio circuits. It governs how well the two ends of a connection in an electrical circuit match. When the impedance of a source does not match the impedance of the target device, electrical power gets wasted. In theory, matching impedances is the best policy; a circuit achieves optimum power transfer with matched impedances.

Power is a primary concern when mating amplifiers and loudspeakers, so impedance matching is the primary tactic when connecting speakers. Moreover, if a speaker has too low of an impedance, it may draw currents in excess of the capabilities of the output circuits of the amplifier, potentially overloading and perhaps damaging the amplifier. Impedance matching is also important in high-frequency network signals because the energy that is not transferred becomes noise in the network that may interfere with its proper operation.

In low-level audio circuits, power transfer is not a critical issue. More important is the signal voltage because low-level circuits are generally treated as voltage amplifiers. The critical issue is that the voltage levels expected by the circuits you connect together are the same. Most low-level circuits use *bridging* connections in which a high impedance input gets connected to a low impedance output. Bridging connections waste power, but that's generally not a concern with voltage amplifiers.

These unmatched impedances work to your benefit in two particular instances with PCs and their sound systems. Many sound boards provide only speaker outputs. You can usually connect these directly to the AUX input of a stereo amplifier without overpowering the circuits because of the impedance mismatch. For example, a 1 watt amplifier with an 8 ohm output impedance produces only about 125 millivolts, just about right for AUX inputs rated for 100 to 150 millivolt signals. Similarly, most headphones have high internal impedances (for example, 600 ohms), so they can plug into speaker outputs without submitting their transducers and your ears to the full power of the amplifier. Plug 600 ohm headphones into an 8 ohm amplifier output, and only 1/75th of the power gets through.

Distortion

No one is perfect, and neither are audio amplifiers. All analog audio amplifiers add subtle defects called *distortion* to the sound. In effect, distortion adds unwanted signals—the defects—to the desired audio. The most common way to express distortion is the ratio between the unwanted and wanted signals expressed as a percentage. In modern low-level circuits, the level of added distortion is vanishingly small, hundredths of a percent or less, and is often lost in the noise polluting the signal. Only if your hearing is particularly acute might you be able to detect the additions.

In power amplifiers, the circuits that produce the high-level signals used to operate non-powered loudspeakers, the addition of distortion can rise to levels that are not only noticeable but also objectionable, from one-tenth to several percent. Power amplifier distortion also tends to increase as the level increases—as you turn the volume up.

Better amplifiers produce less distortion. This basic fact has direct repercussion when it comes to getting the best sound quality from a PC. The sound boards typically found in PCs produce a lot of distortion. You can often get appreciably better audio quality by plugging your stereo system (which is designed for low distortion even at high power levels) into the low-level outputs of your sound board so that the audio signal avoids the sound board's own power amplifier. In fact, better quality sound boards often lack power amplifiers in the recognition that any included circuitry is apt to be of lower sound quality due to the restrictions of installing them on a circuit board with limited power supply capacity.

Digital Audio

Computers, of course, use digital signals, as do many modern stereo components such as Compact Disc players and Digital Audio Tape systems. Once a sound signal is translated from analog into digital form, it becomes just another form of data that your PC can store or compute upon. Digital technology adds new terms to the audio vocabulary and raises new concerns.

Digital recording of sound turns music into numbers. That is, a sound board examines audio waveforms thousands of times every second and assigns a numerical value to the strength of the sound every time it looks; it then records the numbers. To reproduce the music or noise, the sound board works backward. It takes the recorded numbers and regenerates the corresponding signal strength at intervals exactly corresponding to those at which it examined the original signal. The result is a near-exact duplication of the original audio.

The digital recording process involves several arbitrary variables. The two most important are the rate at which the original audio signal is examined—called the sampling rate—and the numeric code assigned to each value sampled. The code is digital and is defined as a given number of bits, the bit-depth or resolution of the system. The quality of sound reproduction is determined primarily by the values chosen for these variables.

Sampling Rate

The sampling rate limits the frequency response of a digital recording system. The highest frequency that can be recorded and reproduced digitally is half the sampling frequency.

This top frequency is often called the Nyquist frequency. Higher frequencies become ambiguous and can be confused with lower-frequency values producing distortion. To prevent problems, frequencies higher than half the sampling frequency must be eliminated—filtered out—before they are digitally sampled. Because no audio filter is perfect, most digital audio systems have cut-off frequencies somewhat lower than the Nyquist frequency. The Compact Disc digital audio system is designed to record sounds with frequencies up to about 15KHz, and it uses a sampling rate of 44.1KHz. Table 19.2 lists the sampling rates in common use in a variety of applications.

TABLE 19.2 Common Digital Sampling Rates

Rate (Hz)	Application
5,563.6	Apple Macintosh, lowest quality
7,418.3	Apple Macintosh, low quality
8,000	Telephone standard
8,012.8	NeXT workstations
11,025	PC, low quality (1/4th CD rate)
11,127.3	Apple Macintosh, medium quality
16,000	G.722 compression standard
18,900	CD-ROM/XA long-play standard
22,050	PC, medium quality (1/2 CD rate)
22,254.5	Basic Apple Macintosh rate
32,000	Digital radio, NICAM, long-play DAT, HDTV
37,800	CD-ROM/XA higher-quality standard
44,056	Professional video systems
44,100	Basic CD standard
48,000	DVD, Audio Codec '97, professional audio recording
96,000	DVD at highest audio quality

The odd numbers used by some of the standards are often less arbitrary than they look. For example, the 22,254.5454Hz rate used by Apple Macintosh system matches the horizontal line rate of the video display of the original 128K Macintosh computer system. For Mac people, that's a convenient number. The 44,056 rate used by some professional video systems is designed to better match the sampling rate to the video frame rate.

Resolution

The number of bits in a digital code, or *bit-depth*, determines the number of discrete values it can record. For example, an 8-bit digital code can represent 256 distinct objects, be they numbers or sound levels. A recording system that uses an 8-bit code can thus record 256 distinct values or steps in sound levels. Unfortunately, music and sounds vary smoothly rather than in discrete steps. The difference between the digital steps and the smooth audio value is distortion. This distortion also adds to the noise in the sound recording system. Minimizing distortion and noise means using more steps. High-quality sound systems—that is, CD-quality sound—require a minimum of a 16-bit code.

Bandwidth

Sampling rate and resolution determine the amount of data produced during the digitization process, which in turn determines the amount that must be recorded. In addition, full stereo recording doubles the data needed because two separate information channels are required. The 44.1KHz sampling frequency and 16-bit digital code of stereo CD audio result in the need to process and record about 150,000 bits of data every second, about 9MG per minute.

For full CD compatibility, most newer sound boards have the capability to digitize at the CD level. Intel's Audio Codec '97 specification requires a bit more, a 48KB sampling rate, and undoubtedly stereophiles will embrace the extraordinarily high optional 96KB sampling rate allowed by the DVD standard. For most PC operations, however, less can be better; less quality means less data to save in files and ship across the Internet. The relatively low quality of loudspeakers attached to PCs, the ambient background noise in offices, and the noise the PC and its fan and disks make themselves make the nuances of top-quality sound inaudible anyway.

To save disk space and processing time, PC sound software and most sound boards give you the option of using less resource-intensive values for sampling rate and bit-depth. Moreover, many older sound boards were not powerful enough for full CD quality. Consequently, you will find sound boards that support intermediary sampling frequencies and bit densities. Many older sound boards also limit themselves to monophonic operation. The original Multimedia PC(MPC) specification only required 8-bit digitization support. Most sound boards support 22 and 11KHz sampling; some offer other intermediate values such as 8, 16, or 32KHz. You can trim your data needs in half simply by making system sounds monophonic instead of stereo.

If you are making original recordings of sounds and music, you will want to use as high a rate as is consistent with your PC's resources. Often, the application will dictate your format. For example, if you want to use your CD-R drive to master audio CDs, you'll need to use the standard CD format, stereo 16-bit quantization at a 44.1KHz sampling rate. On the other hand, the best tradeoff between quality and bandwidth for Internet-bound audio is 11KHz sampling with 8-bit quantization.

Note that the format of the data sets a limit on quality without determining the actual quality of what you will hear. In other words, you can do better than the quality level you set through choice of bit-depth and sampling rate. The shortcomings of practical hardware, particularly inexpensive sound boards and loudspeakers, destine that the quality of the sound that actually makes it into the air will be less realistic than the format may allow.

Transmission

Moving digital audio around is the same as sending any digital signal. You can move files through any convenient port.

You can usually move CD-quality audio through a 10Base-T network with no problem. For example, you can put WAV files on a server and play them back smoothly on any PC connected to the network—that is, unless you put your PC to work on other jobs that are extremely resource intensive or your network bears heavy traffic.

USB provides a quick and easy connection and is coming into use for digital recording and editing. The bandwidth of USB is, however, constrained. After allowing for handshaking and other transmission overhead, you can expect to route about six simultaneous CD-quality digital audio signals through a USB connection.

The Web provides a big challenge for audio. Real-time audio playback across the Web is inevitably a big compromise, one that relies on heavy compression that restricts bandwidth, which in turn limits frequency response and guarantees a high noise level.

If you don't need real-time audio playback—if you're collecting music rather than listening to it—you can move any kind of digital audio through any channel. Ordinary telephone connections make the time involved prodigious, especially if you want to move raw CD-quality audio for an album collection. Consequently, most music now moves across the Web in compressed form, although using more aurally friendly algorithms such as MP3 (described later) and newer, related systems.

Compression

The Internet is not the only place where the size of digital audio files becomes oppressive. At about 10MB per minute, audio files quickly grow huge. Archiving more than a few sound bites quickly becomes expensive in terms of disk space.

To squeeze more sound into a given amount of storage, digital audio can be compressed like any other data. Actually, audio lends itself to compression. The more efficient algorithms take into account the special character of digital sound. The best rely on psychoacoustic principles, how people actually hear sound. They discard inaudible infor-mation, not wasting space on what you cannot hear.

The algorithms for compressing and decompressing digital audio are sometimes called *codecs*, short for compressors/decompressors. Several have become popular for different applications. Windows includes support for the CCITT G.711 A-law and u-lw, DSP Group TrueSpeech, IMA ADPCM, GSM 6.10, Microsoft ADPCM, and Microsoft PCM converter codecs. You can view the audio codecs installed in your Windows 95 system by opening the Multimedia icon in Control Panel, choosing the Advanced tab, and double-clicking on Audio Compression Codecs. You'll see a display like that in Figure 19.1.

FIGURE 19.1

A display of the installed audio codecs under Windows 95.

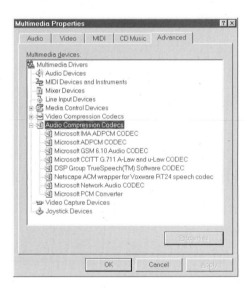

Other than to view this list, you normally won't have to deal with the various codecs. Windows automatically uses the appropriate codec when necessary to play back an audio file. When recording, your software will prompt you to select the codec to use if a selection is available.

The Internet has brought other compression systems to the forefront. Although nothing inherent in the Web requires them, because they reduce the size of audio files (and hence their transmission time), they have made audio distribution through the Web practical. More than that, high-quality compressed audio and the Web are revolutionizing how music gets distributed.

TrueSpeech

Ground zero for online sound and Windows compression is the TrueSpeech system, which is both an international standard and a standard part of Windows. TrueSpeech, developed by the DSP Group, was adopted as G.723 by the International Telecommunications Union(ITU) as the audio standard for video conferencing over ordinary telephone connections. Microsoft also incorporated TrueSpeech as a real-time audio playback technology that could be bundled with the Windows 95 operating system.

Originally created when 14,400 bps modems were the norm, TrueSpeech was optimized for that data rate, compressing the 64 kbits/sec rate used for ordinary telephony to below the modem rate. The basic TrueSpeech compression algorithm is lossy, so it sacrifices quality in favor of data rate. Moreover, the TrueSpeed system uses only one compression ratio, optimized for the 14,400 bps rate. As a consequence, switching to a higher speed connection will not improve its quality. At its target rate, however, is works well and delivers better quality than the popular RealAudio system (discussed later). Further, TrueSpeech incorporates no mechanism to assure real-time reconstruction of transmissions, so if a connection is slow, the audio will be interrupted.

MPEG

Although usually regarded as a video standard, the MPEG standards discussed in Chapter 16, "The Display System," also describe the audio that accompanies its moving images. The applications of MPEG audio are widespread; its compression system is used by Digital Compact Cassettes, digital broadcasting experiments, and the DVD.

MPEG audio is not one but a family of audio coding schemes based on human perception of sound. The basic design has three *layers*, which translate directly into sound quality. The layers, numbered 1 through 3, form a hierarchy of increasing complexity that yield better quality at the same bit rate. Each layer is built upon the previous one and incorporates the ability to decode signals coded under the lower layers. Table 19.3 summarizes the MPEG audio layers.

TABLE 19.3   MPEG Layers and Bit Rates Compared

Layer	Allowed Range	Target or Optimum	Sample Application
1	32 to 448 kbits/sec	192 kbits/sec	Digital Compact Cassette
2	32 to 384 kbits/sec	128 kbits/sec	MUSICAM (Broadcasting)
3	32 to 320 kbits/sec	64 kbits/sec	DVD, Internet sound

As the layer number increases, the encoding becomes more complex. The result is a greater amount of compression. Because greater compression requires more processing, there is apt to be more latency (signal delay) as the layer number increases.

The layer number does not affect perceived sound quality. All layers permit sampling frequencies of 32, 44.1, or 48 kbits/sec. No matter the layer, the output quality is dependent on the bit rate allowed; the higher the bit rate, the higher the quality. The different standards allow higher quality to be maintained at lower bit rates. At their target bit rates, all three layers deliver sound quality approaching that of CDs.

Unlike other standards, MPEG does not define compression algorithms. Instead, the layers provide standards for the data output rather than how that output is achieved. This descriptive approach allows developers to improve the quality of the algorithms as the technology and their discoveries permit. Header information describes the level and methodology of the compression used in the data that follows.

MPEG is asymmetrical in that it is designed with a complex encoder and a relatively simple decoder. Ordinarily, you will decode files. Only the producer or distributor of MPEG software needs an encoder. The encoding process does not need to (and often does not) take place in real-time. All layers use a polyphase filter bank with 32 subbands. Layer 3 also adds a MDCT (Modified Discrete Cosine Transform) that helps increase its frequency resolution.

MP3

The dominant sound of the Internet is MP3, shorthand for MPEG, Level 3, as discussed earlier. (It does not stand for MPEG 3; there is no such standard, at least not yet.) Although MP3 seems to threaten to replace the Compact Disc as today's reigning music distribution standard with dedicated players ready to stand in for WalkPeople, it's really little more than a standard—but one around which an industry is gathered. MP3 takes advantage of the high compression afforded under the MPEG audio standard and uses it as the basis for a file system, which serves as a basis for today's MP3 hardware.

The advantage of MP3 is simply compression. It squeezes audio files into about 1/12 of the space raw digital audio data would require. As a result, music that would nominally require a 50MB file under the WAV format only takes about 4MB. Smaller files mean less transmission time so that entire albums can reasonably be sent across the Internet. It also allows a substantial length of music (an hour or more) to be encoded into solid-state memory and carried about in a no-moving-parts player.

Better still, by squeezing the size of the MP3 file, the data rate required for playing back a file in real-time can be similarly reduced. Instead of requiring the approximately 1.2 mbits/sec to move two CD-quality audio channels, MP3 files need only 64 kbits/sec for near-CD-quality playback. Although that's not slow enough for real-time playback through a 56K modem (remember, MP3 files are already compressed so modem-based compression cannot appreciably speed up transfer rates), real-time playback is possible with an ISDN terminal adapter (with a good 128K connection and fast server), cable "modems," and ADSL connections. With light network traffic and a 56K modem, you can expect to download an MP3 files from the Web in two to four times its actual playing time.

Because MP3 is part of the MPEG-1 standard, it accommodates only stereo. MPEG-2 is designed for surround sound using up to eight channels. In the works is a new level of compression, often referred to as MP4, which will extend MP3-like compression to surround sound systems.

The tradeoff to gain the compactness of MP3 files is data processing. Decoding the audio data from an MP3 file requires a lot of microprocessor power. Typically, you'll need at least a 100MHz Pentium microprocessor to decode an MP3 file in real-time, for example, to listen to a musical selection. Encoding into the MP3 format requires even greater power. Expect to consume nearly the entire resources of a 300MHz Pentium II microprocessor in encoding files in real-time to the MP3 format.

You can recognize MP3 files by the extension MP3. Note that some encoding programs that generate MP3 files allow you to choose the "level" of processing—typically Level 1, 2, or 3. These selections correspond to the levels under the MPEG standard and represent higher degrees of compression (smaller files and lower data rates) as the numbers ascend, but only Level 3 creates true MP3 files. Nearly all MP3 decoders will handle whatever level you choose, so go for the lower numbers if you want the highest quality and don't mind giving up more disk space.

AAC

AT&T developed Advanced Audio Compression as a refinement to MP3. As you would expect, more work resulted in better compression—smaller files and higher quality. At the same time, AT&T added a locking scheme to AAC.

VQF

Similar to MP3, VQF is a somewhat more advanced audio compression developed primarily by Yamaha that yields files about one third smaller than their MP3 equivalent yet maintains higher apparent audio quality. The penalty is that both encoding and decoding under VQF is more processor intensive; it takes about 20 percent longer than with MP3. Packing data more densely is simply more work. VQF was developed by Toshiba, which rigidly maintains control over its use.

SDMI

To develop a single secure format capable of handling audio downloads and playback, the Recording Industry Association of America (RIAA) organized the Secure Digital Music Initiative (SDMI) in December 1998. The organization, which quickly grew to accommodate 110 members, most of which are equipment makers and recording companies, plans to create a standard for portable digital music players capable of subverting piracy. Similar to the Liquid Audio system, the standard will allow you to download cuts from the Internet (which may require paying a fee), play the files on a portable device similar to the Diamond Multimedia RIO MP3 player, or cut your own CD from them with your CD-R drive. A watermark in the file encodes your rights to the music—whether you are allowed to copy, make a disk, or just listen to it. The SDMI group solicited proposals for the standard in March 1999, hoping to have a standard in place soon enough to allow compatible devices to be marketed for the 1999 Christmas season.

Looped Sound

When you want to include sound as a background for an image that your audience may linger over for a long but predetermined time, for example, to add background sounds to a Web page, you can minimize the storage and transmission requirements for the audio by using *looped sound*. As the name implies, the sound forms an endless loop, the end spliced back to the beginning. The loop can be as short as a heartbeat or as long as several musical bars. The loop simply repeats as long as the viewer lingers over the Web page. The loop only requires as much audio data as it takes to code a single pass, no matter how long it plays.

No rule says that the splice between the end and beginning of the loop must be inconspicuous, but if you want to avoid the nature of the loop becoming apparent and distracting, it should be. When looping music, you should place the splice so that the rhythm is continuous and regular. With random sounds, you should match levels and timbre at the splice. Most PC sound editors will allow you to finely adjust the splice. Most Internet sound systems support looped sounds.

Synthesis

Making a sound electronically is easy. After all, any AC signal with a frequency in the range of human hearing makes a noise when connected to a loudspeaker. Even before the age of electronics, Hermann Helmholtz discovered that any musical tone is made from vibrations in the air that correspond to a periodic (but complex) waveform. Making an electronic signal sound like something recognizable is not so simple, however. You need exactly the right waveform.

The basic frequency-generating circuit, the oscillator, produces a very pure tone, so pure that it sounds completely unrealistic—electronic. Natural sounds are not a single frequency but collections of many, related and unrelated, at different strengths.

A tone from a musical instrument, for example, comprises a single characteristic frequency (corresponding to the note played) called the fundamental and a collection of other frequencies, each a multiple of the fundamental, called overtones by scientists or partials by musicians. The relationship of the loudness of the overtones to one another gives the sound of the instrument its distinctive identity, its timbre, and makes a note played on a violin sound different from the same note played on a flute. Timbre is a product of the many resonances of the musical instrument, which tend to reinforce some overtones and diminish others.

Noises differ from musical tones because they comprise many, unrelated frequencies. White noise, for example, is a random collection of all frequencies.

The one happy result of all sounds being combinations of frequencies (a principle discovered in relation to periodic waves by Jean Baptiste Joseph Fourier in the late 18th century) is that creating any sound requires only putting together frequencies in the right combination. So synthesizing sounds should be easy; all you need to know is the right combination. At that, synthesis becomes a little daunting. Trial-and-error experimentation at finding the right combinations is tedious at best because the number of frequencies and the possible strengths of each frequency are both infinite, so you end up dealing with numbers that strain most pocket calculators—like infinity times infinity. Add in the fact that natural sounds vary from one instant to the next, meaning that each instant represents a different frequency combination, giving you yet another infinity to deal with, and sound synthesis suddenly seems to slip to the far side of impossible.

In truth, the numbers are much more manageable than the dire situation outlined in the preceding paragraph. For example, musical sounds involve only a few frequencies—the fundamental and overtones within the range of human hearing (both in frequency range and strength). But synthesizing sounds from scratch remains a challenge. Reality cannot yet be synthesized. Even the best synthesis systems only approach the sound of real-world musical instruments and not-so-musical noises. The best—or most real—sound quality produced by a sound board is thus not synthesized but recorded. The best synthesizers sound like synthesizers even when they attempt to emulate an acoustical instrument such as a piano. You don't have to be particularly musically attuned to distinguish a real instrument from a synthesized one. But that's not necessarily a quality judgment. Some synthesizers sound better than others. Although one may not be more realistic sounding than another, it may be more pleasing. In fact, high-end synthesizers are treasured for their unique musical characteristics much as Steinway or Bosendorfer pianos are. Just don't expect a synthesizer to exactly replicate the sound of your Steinway.

Electronic designers have come up with several strategies that synthesize sound with varying degrees of success. Many techniques have been used to make synthesizers, including subtractive synthesis, additive synthesis, frequency modulation, and wave table synthesis.

Subtractive Synthesis

The first true music synthesizers (as opposed to electronic instruments, which seek to replicate rather than synthesize sounds) used analog technology. The first of these machines were created in the late 1950s and were based on the principle of subtractive synthesis. These early synthesizers generated tones with special oscillators called waveform generators that made tones already rich in harmonics. Instead of the pure tones of sine waves, they generated square waves, sawtooth waves, and odd intermediary shapes. In itself, each of these oscillators generated a complex wave rich in harmonics that had its own distinctive sound. These initial waveforms were then mixed together and shaped using filters that emphasized some ranges of frequencies and attenuated others. Sometimes, one tone was used to modulate another to create waveforms so strange they sounded like they originated in foreign universes.

Analog synthesis was born in an age of experimentation when the farthest reaches of new music was being explored. Analog synthesizers made no attempt to sound like conventional instruments; after all, conventional instruments could already do that and the outposts of the avant garde had traipsed far beyond the fringes of conventional music. The goal of analog synthesis was to create new sounds—sounds not found in nature, sounds never before heard, sounds like the digestive system of some giant dyspeptic dinosaur. Analog synthesizers sounded unmistakably electronic.

As the depths of new music were being plumbed, digital technology appeared as an alternative to analog designs. The first digital synthesizers sought merely to duplicate the function of the analog units using an alternate technology that gave greater control. In fact, digital synthesis gave so much control over sounds that it became possible not just to create new sounds, but also to create (or at least approximate) any sound. The goal of synthesis also shifted to mimicking conventional instruments—that is, expensive, handcrafted instruments—with cheap, sound-nearly-alike digital substitutes. With one mass-produced electronic box—the digital synthesizer—a musician could put an entire orchestra at his fingertips.

Additive Synthesis

Recreating the sounds of actual instruments required entirely different technologies than had been used in new-sound synthesizers. The opposite of a subtractive synthesizer is an additive synthesizer. Instead of starting with complex waves and filtering away the unwanted parts, the additive synthesizer builds sounds in the most logical way—by adding together all the frequencies that make up a musical sound. Although this chore was difficult if not impossible with analog circuitry, the precision of digital electronics made true additive synthesis a reality. The digital additive synthesizer mathematically created the pattern that mixing tones would create. The resulting digital signal would then be converted into an analog signal (using a digital-to-analog converter) that would drive a loudspeaker or recording system.

The additive synthesizer faced one large problem in trying to create life-like sounds: The mix of frequencies for each note of an instrument is different. In fact, the mix of frequencies changes from the initial attack when a note begins (for instance, when a string is struck by a piano hammer) to its final decay. To produce sounds approaching reality, the synthesizer required a complete description of every note it would create at various times in its generation. As a result, a true additive-type digital synthesizer is a complex—and expensive—device.

Practical sound synthesis for PC peripherals is based on much more modest technologies than purely additive synthesis. Two primary alternatives have become commercially popular in the synthesizers incorporated into PC sound boards. These are FM synthesis and wave table synthesis.

FM Synthesis

While working at Stanford Artificial Intelligence Laboratories in 1973, John M. Chowning made an interesting discovery. Two pure sine wave tones could be combined together to make interesting sounds using frequency modulation. Although the principle corresponded to no natural phenomenon, it could be used to create sounds with close-to-natural attacks and decays.

The resulting FM synthesis works by starting with one frequency or tone called a carrier and altering it with a second frequency called a modulator. When the modulator is a low frequency of a few Hertz, the carrier frequency rises and falls much like a siren. When the carrier and modulator are close in frequency, however, the result is a complex wave. Varying the strength of the modulator changes the mix of frequencies in the resulting waveform, altering its timbre. (Changing the strength of the carrier merely makes the sound louder or softer.) By changing the relationship between the carrier and modulator, the timbre changes in a natural-sounding way.

A basic FM synthesis system needs only two oscillators producing sine waves to work. However, a synthesizer with a wider combination of carriers and modulators can create an even more complex variety of waveforms and sounds. Each of the sine waves produced by an FM synthesizer is called an operator. Popular synthesizers have four to six operators.

The greatest strength of FM synthesis is that it is inexpensive to implement; all it takes is a chip. On the other hand, FM synthesis cannot quite duplicate real-world sounds. The sounds created through FM synthesis are recognizable—both as what they are supposed to represent and as synthesized sounds.

Wave Table Synthesis

An alternate technique used for creating sounds is wave table synthesis. Also known as sampling, wave table synthesis starts not with pure tones but with representative waveforms for particular sounds. The representations are in the form of the sound's exact waveform, and all the waveforms that a product can produce are stored in an electronic table, hence the name of the technology. The waveforms for a given instrument or sound are only templates that the synthesizer manipulates to produce music or what is supposed to pass as music. For example, the wave table may include a brief burst of the tone of a flute playing one particular note. The synthesizer can then alter the frequency of that note to play an entire scale and alter its duration to generate the proper rhythm.

Although wave table synthesis produces more life-like sounds than FM synthesis, it is not entirely realistic because it does not replicate the complete transformation of musical sounds from attack to decay nor the subtle variation of timbre with the pitch produced by a synthesized instrument. Some wave table synthesizers have specific patterns for the attack, sustain, and decay of notes but mathematically derive the transitions between them. These come closer to reality but still fall short of perfection. In general, wave table synthesized notes all have the same frequency mix and consequently have a subtle but unreal sameness to them.

On the other hand, wave table synthesis is the PC hardware-maker's delight. Because all the waveforms are stored digitally just like all other sounds, they can be reconstituted without any special hardware such as synthesizer chips. All that's needed is an audio digital-to-analog, which has to be incorporated in any multimedia PC anyway. A programmer can create the necessary waveforms for any sound he can imagine using software alone. The only trouble is that putting together the necessary waveforms digitally takes a lot of processor power, so much that older, slower PCs can't handle the chore in real-time. When the process need not be done in real-time, however, your PC can transform synthesizer instructions (typically in the form of a MIDI file) into synthesized music without additional expensive synthesis hardware. MIDI Renderer uses this technique to endow MIDI files with top-quality synthesized sound.

Wave table synthesizer boards sidestep the demand for processor power by incorporating their own processing abilities. To keep their performance as high as possible, many of these products put the reference waveforms they need into ROM memory, saving any delays that might be needed for disk access. The downside of this fast storage is that the waveform reference hogs storage space. Many hardware-based waveform synthesizers have hundreds of thousands of bytes of wave table ROM; some have multiple megabytes of reference waveforms.

Advanced Techniques

Scientifically inclined musicians and musically inclined scientists are never satisfied with the sound of synthesized instrument—and never will be until they can make an all-electronic violin sound better than a Stradivarius in good hands. As modern electronics puts more processing power in their hands, they are developing ever more elaborate techniques to generate the most realistic sounds possible.

The latest trend is modeling actual instruments. They make mathematical models of musical instruments that reflect how the physical attributes of the instrument affect the sounds it makes. Instead of deconstructing the waveform the instrument makes, they seek to construct the waveform in the same manner as the instrument itself. For example, they might start with a basic tone generated by scraping a string with a bow (an elaborate model in itself) and then temper it with the resonances of the instrument's body.

Another aspect of advanced synthesis designs is increased control. Current synthesizers distill a musician's (or program's) control of an instrument to a few parameters: the press and release of a key and "touch," the speed at which the key is struck. Although this description is reasonably complete for a keyboard instrument, it ignores the modulations possible with bowed instruments or those through which the musician blows. The newest synthesizers often include a more elaborate control system focused on an additional sensor such as an instrument-like tube the musician blows through. The musician can then use his breath pressure to continuously signal the synthesizer how to modulate the music.

Although these experimental synthesizers are currently aimed at live performance, nothing prevents the acquisition of their control information for automated playback or editing. MIDI does not currently accommodate the increased data needs of such synthesizers, but new standards will undoubtedly accompany any new technology synthesizers into the market mainstream.

Internet Sound Systems

Go online and you'll be confronted with a strange menagerie of acronyms describing sound systems promising everything from real-time delivery of rock concerts, background music from remote radio stations a zillion miles away, and murky audio effects percolating in the background as you browse past pages of uninteresting Web sites. All of this stuff is packaged as digital audio of some kind, else it could never traverse the extent of the Internet. Rather than straight digital audio, however, it is processed and compressed into something that fits into an amazingly small bandwidth. Then, to get it to you, it must latch on to its own protocol. It's amazing that anything gets through at all, and in truth, some days (and connections) are less amazing than others.

The biggest hardware obstacle to better Internet sound is bandwidth. Moving audio digitally consumes a huge amount of bandwidth, and today's typical communications hardware (discussed in Chapter 22, "Telecommunications") is simply not up to the chore. A conventional telephone conversation with a frequency response of 300 to 3,000 Hertz—hardly hi-fi—gets digitized by the telephone system into a signal requiring a bandwidth of 64,000 bits per second. That low-fidelity data is a true challenge to cram through a modem that has but a 28,800 or even 33,400 bits-per-second data rate. As a result, all Internet sound systems start with data compression of some kind to avoid the hardware-imposed bandwidth limits.

The Internet poses another problem for audio systems: The Web environment itself is rather inhospitable to audio signals. From its inception, the Net was developed as an asynchronous packet-switched network. Its primary protocol, TCP, was not designed for the delivery of time-critical isosynchronous data such as live audio. When downloading a file (or a Web page, which is essentially a file as well), it doesn't matter whether a packet gets delayed, but a late packet in an audio stream is less than worthless; it's an interruption that can ruin whatever you're listening to. Some Internet sound systems abandon TCP for audio transfer and use the UDP protocol instead, which can complicate matters with systems and firewalls designed expressly for TCP. Other Internet sound systems rely on TCP, citing that it assures top audio quality in transferred files.

Several streaming audio players are available for download from the Web. The three most popular are Internet Wave from Vocaltec (`http://www.vocaltec.com`), RealAudio from Progressive Networks (`http://www.realaudio.com`) and Shockwave from Macromedia (`http://www.macromedia.com`). To play sounds from all the sites on the Web, you need all three.

Internet Wave uses ordinary TCP to distribute audio, which means it goes everywhere normal Web pages do and all audio packets are guaranteed to be delivered. Current versions work at any of four recommended source sampling rates, 5,500, 8,000, 11,025, or 16,000Hz so quality ranges from telephone level to radio broadcast quality in mono. Internet Wave audio uses two files on the server, a media file with the extension .VMF and a stub file, .VMD. Along with players, a beta version of the encoder is available for free download from the Vocaltec site.

RealAudio is distributed free as a low-fidelity player; it delivers AM radio quality sound both online and offline (from files you've previously downloaded). You must buy server support and the production version of the full-featured hi-fi RealAudio player. Both are monophonic only. The latest RealAudio server can automatically negotiate the correct bandwidth (lo-fi or hi-fi) to send you. RealAudio uses UDP for file transfer so it gains some speed at the penalty of possibly losing packets (and quality). RealAudio files have the extension .RA.

Shockwave is aimed primarily at delivering audio to accompany multimedia presentations made for playing back through Macromedia's Director program but can also direct streaming audio through the Internet. A number of sites use Shockwave to delivery streaming audio using TCP. The Shockwave format allows for a variety of quality levels including full CD-quality stereo. Shockwave audio files wear the extension .SWA.

Multichannel Sound

When sound recording first became possible, people were so thrilled to hear anything at all that small issues like sound quality were unimportant to them. A tiny voice against a scratchy background sounded as real as a loving coo whispered in their ears. As new technologies such as electronic recording processes brought more life-like qualities to reproduced sound, people discovered that recordings had a missing dimension. In real life, they could hear depth, but the single horn on top of the old Victrola compressed the sound down to a single point.

Trying to recover the depth of sound recording has occupied the minds of engineers and researchers almost since the advent of electronic recording in the 1920s. Their aim has been to reproduce the entire listening experience so that you don't just hear the music but feel like you are immersed in it, sitting in a concert hall rather than your living room.

Stereo

The most natural improvement was stereophonic recording. The idea was simple, even intuitive. Scientists knew that people were able to localize sound because they had two ears. At the time, they didn't know exactly what allowed your hearing to determine locations, but they found that reproducing music through two speaker systems with separately recorded signals created a miraculous effect: Instead of hearing sound from one speaker or the other, the ears of the listeners were fooled into hearing sounds coming from the entire space *between* the speakers.

Binaural

Closely related to stereo is *binaural* recording. As with stereo, binaural uses two recording channels, but binaural requires a special recording method for creating those signals that uses tiny microphones placed inside the ears of a dummy head. Playback, too, differs from ordinary stereo. In its purest form, binaural systems require headphones instead of loudspeakers. In effect, the binaural system records the sounds that reach the dummy's ears directly into your ears.

The difference between stereo and binaural is astounding. Unlike simple stereo systems, binaural creates a convincing illusion of three-dimensional space. Listen to a conventional stereo recording on headphones, and all the sounds appear to emanate from inside your head. The only spread is between your ears. With a binaural recording, the sound appears to come from all around, outside your head, surrounding you. You are convincingly transported to the place and position of the dummy head used in making the original recording.

Without headphones, the binaural illusion disappears. To most people, a binaural recording played through loudspeakers sound like a conventional stereophonic recording.

The development of binaural recording paralleled conventional stereo. Although initially more a laboratory curiosity, in the 1960s and early 1970s record companies released a few commercial binaural disks and radio stations transmitted a few binaural broadcasts of classical music and, rarely, rock concerts. Unfortunately, the artificial head recording technique was incompatible with the multi-track studio tapes used for the vast majority of popular and rock discs, so the technology never transcended its status as a laboratory curiosity.

Quadraphonic

An abortive attempt at creating a three-dimensional sound stage appeared in the form of quadraphonic recording in the early 1970s. The idea was simple: To create listening space around and behind the listener, two recording channels and speakers dedicated to them were added behind the listener. Essentially, it was stereo squared.

The problem with quad was not the concept but the available technology for broadcasting and recording discs. At the time quad was invariably a compromise. Because of the limitations of analog technology, engineers were invariably forced to squeeze in four channels where only two were meant to fit. The most common method involved a sacrifice in channel separation. To achieve compatibility with conventional stereo, the engineers combined the front and back information for each of the two stereo channels. They then piggybacked difference information—the back channel minus the front channel—on top of the front-plus-back signal using a form of phase modulation (quadrature modulation, which, despite the similarity of names, is not related to the quadraphonic concept). These systems provided a front-to-back channel separation of about six decibels—much less than the 20 to 30 dB of separation for the front channels but sufficient (or so the engineers said) for providing the illusion of depth.

Only tape systems could provide four full bandwidth and completely separate audio channels. At the time, however, the only legitimate tape systems with quality suitable for music recording used cumbersome open-reel tape. The audio cassette was still in its infancy.

Although the Compact Disc would have permitted true quadraphonic recording with four equal channels (although with a halving of playing time), it came too late. By the time of the introduction of the CD, consumer-level quad was long a dead issue. It had never made it into Disco let alone the 1980s. Worse, quad bore the stigma of unfulfilled promises along with skepticism about its origins. Many people suspected the stereo industry introduced and promoted quad solely to sell more stereo equipment at a time when hardware sales were flagging. Because of its bad name, the advent of technology capable of handling quad was not sufficient to resurrect it and modern systems carefully avoid any association with it. Note that no new technology professing to be "surround sound" uses four speakers.

3D Sound

The notion that two channels of sound is all that you need for two ears is hard to shake. Somehow with just two ears, most people are able to perceive sound in three dimensions; you can tell not only whether a sound source is left or right of you but also whether it is above, below, or anywhere else. Two ears shouldn't be sufficient for 3D, but (obviously) they are. Binaural recording-and-playback shouldn't work.

As early as the first studies of stereo sound, scientists have puzzled over this anomaly. They discovered that two ears alone aren't enough. The ears had to be coupled to a powerful computer—the human brain. The brain exploited subtle differences in the signals received in each ear, differences cause by the odd shape of the human ear (in some people odder than others), and extracted enough information not only for depth but also for height and everything else.

Once they figured out how people could deduce depth from the signals from two ears, engineers went to work reversing the process. They figured if they altered the signal before it was played back, they could add cues that would fool listeners into thinking they heard sound in three dimensions when played through two speakers.

Surround Sound

Although surround sound is a relatively new innovation for home listening, it actually predates two-channel stereo by decades. The first commercial presentation of surround sound came with Walt Disney's animated feature film *Fantasia*, released in 1941 with a six-channel soundtrack. Although not known then as "surround," similar multichannel formats became popular in cinematic productions during the 1950s as movie producers attempted to fight the defection of their audience to the small screens of television sets. They stretched their already-giant movie screens with Cinerama and Cinemascope and filled the auditoriums with six or more sound channels. Although these systems were formally classed as "stereo," industry insiders began to refer to the speakers in the sides and rear of the auditoriums as "surrounds," and soon the technology became *surround sound*.

Although "surround sound" does not inherently imply any specific number of channels, the most popular format made four the basic standard. In 1976, Dolby Laboratories introduced Dolby optical stereo sound, a system that used noise reduction to coax high-quality sound from optical sound tracks. Until then, most movies with surround sound used magnetic soundtracks, a technology that adds to the cost and complication of printing films. Optical soundtracks are printed in the same operation as the images. Fitting four channels into the optical soundtrack required matrixing, the same technique that put quadraphonic sound on vinyl phonograph discs.

The difference between this four-channel form of surround sound and quad is the arrangement of channels. Quad uses four equal speakers in the corners of the listening space—a square. Surround uses a diamond arrangement with two primary speakers—one left, one right—a center speaker and a rear speaker. Not only is this arrangement effective in producing an illusion of an all-encompassing sound field, but it is also more amenable to the matrixing technique that combines four channels into two. Videocassettes labeled "Dolby Surround" use this technology.

Dolby Pro Logic adds signal steering to the basic surround sound arrangement. That is, it is able to emphasize (or exaggerate) the surround sound effect by selectively altering the balance between channels in response to coding in the original two-channel signal. Both Dolby Surround and Dolby Pro Logic are analog technologies, although the latter uses digital logic to control the balance between channels.

In discussing surround sound, the arrangement of speakers is often abbreviated in what looks like a fraction—two numbers separated by a slash. The first number represents the speakers in front of the listener; the latter number, the speakers behind the listener. Table 19.4 lists the common surround sound configurations.

TABLE 19.4   Surround Sound Channel Configurations

Designation	Common Name	Speakers Used							
		Front Left	Front Center	Front Right	Mid Left	Mid Right	Rear Left	Rear Center	Rear Right
1/0	Mono	o	o	X	o	o	o	o	o
2/0	Stereo	X	o	X	o	o	o	o	o
3/0	Center-channel stereo	X	X	X	o	o	o	o	o
2/1	Three-channel surround	X	o	X	o	o	o	X	o
2/2	Quadraphonic	X	o	X	o	o	X	o	X
3/2	Standard surround	X	X	X	o	o	X	o	X
5/2	Enhanced surround	X	X	X	X	X	X	o	X

Further complicating the designations is a decimal component sometimes listed in the count of channels, for example, 5.1 or 7.1. The decimal indicates an additional sound source that doesn't quite reach to being a full-range channel because of limited bandwidth. Sometimes, this extra channel is termed the *low-frequency effects* (LFE) channel. Its frequency range is limited to that of non-directional low frequencies (below 100 to 150Hz) as would be used to power a subwoofer. Nearly all theater-style surround sound systems use an LFE channel to accentuate explosions and other impacts so that their low-frequency components might be felt as readily as they are heard.

AC-3

More commonly known as Dolby Digital (Dolby Labs holds patents on the perceptual encoding system it uses), AC-3 is a 5.1 channel sound system. In other words, it uses five full-bandwidth (20Hz to 20KHz) channels along with one reduced-bandwidth (20Hz to 120Hz) channel dedicated to low-frequency effects. Speakers for a full-fledged AC-3 system are arrayed in the 3/2 configuration with three in front—left, center, and right—and two in the rear (left and right). The subwoofer can be put in any convenient location. AC-3 also allows for other configurations, including plain mono and stereo.

AC-3 is the standard sound format of movies distributed on DVD, having been approved for that purpose in December 1995. In the DVD system, all six channels of AC-3 are discrete, separately recorded and isolated from the others. The full-bandwidth channels are encoded with a sampling rate of 48KHz and a depth of 16 bits.

In operation, AC-3 compresses the raw audio data encompassing all the channels down to a bit rate that can range from 64 kbits/sec to 448 kbits/sec. Typically in stereo, the bit rate will be 192 kbits/sec. In full 5.1 channel configuration, the bit rate runs about 384 kbits/sec.

AC-3 is the standard for sound on NTSC-based DVD-Video discs. In addition, it has also been adopted as the sound system for the American digital television transmission standard (ATSC). As such, the full text of the AC-3 standard is available from the ATSC Web site at www.atsc.org.

DTS

Digital Theater Systems, or DTS, began as a proprietary system for providing top-quality digital surround sound to motion picture theaters. Using the same encoding and compression system as it applied to professional applications, DTS created an alternative audio format for digital source material. The DTS system is an option for both audio and video DVDs. Nearly all DVD players lack the facility for decoding DTS signals, although you can usually connect an auxiliary processor to handle them.

As with most of the sound formats for DVD, the DTS system began as an enhancement for theatrical films. The professional DTS system syncs a CD-based digital playback system with movie projectors using a time code encoded along with conventional sound tracks on the film itself. The time code allows the digital audio source to be exactly locked to the film even after editing or repairing (cutting and splicing) the film.

In DVD form, the DTS sound stream encodes up to 5.1 channels sampled at 48KHz with a depth of up to 20 bits. It allows all standard channel combinations from mono to 3/2 surround with an LFE channel. The chief advantage of DTS is that it uses a lower compression ratio (about 4 to 1) than does Dolby Digital. As a result, it holds the potential of delivering higher-quality audio. As a result, the bit stream may have a data rate from 64 to 1,536 kbits/sec.

SDDS

By acquiring Columbia Pictures, Sony became a major player in the motion picture business. The company is not only active in software but also developed its own high-quality digital surround system called Sony Dynamic Digital Sound, or SDDS. Based on the same compression system used by the zombie Minidisc system, SDDS can encode up to eight channels in a 1,280 kbits/sec stream. Typically, it samples 5.1 or 7.1 channels at 48KHz and a depth of 16 bits. SDDS is an optional DVD format.

Capturing Sounds

If you're not content using the sound given you by others and you don't want to go to the trouble of synthesizing your own, you may look longingly at all the noise already available to you that just isn't in PC-compatible form. You might have a stack of old vinyl albums that you want to transfer to CD, you might want to move a cut from a CD into an MP3 file for more compact listening on your notebook PC while you travel, or you might want to steal a sound from a television program or movie to spice up your PC's otherwise drab responses. (My system has Homer Simpson crying "Doh!" every time I hit the wrong key.) Equipped with a modern sound board and suitable software, your PC can readily capture any audio source you have for whatever purpose you want.

As with most computing matters, however, you have several choices in capturing sounds. You can directly transfer the digital data from CD, you can digitize analog data from conventional audio sources, or you can make original recordings. Each technique has its own methodology and produces different results.

CD Ripping

Audio Compact Discs already contain digital audio information, so you might think that capturing the data would be easy. After all, your PC already can tap its built-in CD drive to get the data it needs to set up programs. Matters are not quite so simple, however. As noted in Chapter 12, "Compact Discs," the Red Book format for audio CDs is substantially different from the Yellow Book standard used by digital data CDs. The differences extend to formatting and error correction. Simply put, your ears tolerate audio errors much better than digital systems tolerate errors in code. Although a data error may be inaudible to you when you listen to a CD playing back, the data stream may include errors that will send digital circuits into conniptions. If your PC cannot detect the audio errors, they will be faithfully encoded as digital data in the proper format but with the wrong value. Transient audio errors become a permanent part of the data—and the digitally encoded audio that you listen to.

The ability for a CD to deliver audio in digital form to your PC is called *digital audio extraction*. The process requires special software that has come to be known as the *CD ripper*. Similarly, the extraction process is often called *CD ripping*.

CD drives differ widely in their ability to yield pure audio data. Most early drives cannot faithfully extract audio data. They are unable to properly frame that audio data into digital form, resulting in jitter. The aural result is distortion in the digital audio, most often in the form of loud clicks that repeat throughout a transfer, sort of like someone has thoroughly rubbed 80 grit sandpaper over your favorite vinyl album.

Note that the quality of digital audio extraction is primarily dependent on the CD drive that you use. First-generation ATAPI-based CD drives often are poor at digital audio extraction. Early SCSI drives fare much better. Modern ATAPI drives usually yield good-quality transfers.

CD ripping is fast. With a fast microprocessor, your PC will likely rip through CDs at the fastest speed at which your CD drive is capable. In other words, you may be able to rip CD files in from 1/6 to 1/32 of the time it would take the cut to play back.

Analog Capture

The alternative to ripping digital audio is to capture audio in analog form and convert it to digital. All sound boards have analog-to-digital converter circuits that carry out this process, which is nothing more than ordinary audio sampling. You only need supply the analog source to your sound board and specify the parameters of the sample—bit rate and bit-depth.

Internal CD

If your source material is a CD, you can use the internal CD drive of your PC for analog capture even if it is not capable of digital audio extraction. Use the mixer software supplied with your sound board to specify the CD drive as the source and mute or switch off other sources. Your sound board will then sample only the audio from your CD.

The quality you get from analog capture will be lower than with direct extraction. Your samples will pick up all noise and distortion present in the analog circuitry of your sound board, which can be substantial. For example, although the noise floor of CD audio is about 96 dB below peak level, going through the analog audio circuitry of both the CD drive and sound board may increase the noise to only 60 to 70 dB below peak audio. This level of noise is often not objectionable and can actually sound superior to audio extracted from a marginal CD drive that is rife with clicks and pops. In fact, this noise level is comparable with optimum FM radio reception. If you are a purist, you can remove most of the residual noise with the digital noise reduction functions available in some audio editing programs.

Another disadvantage of analog capture of CD audio is speed. Analog capture is a real-time process. Sampling a cut from a CD will require precisely the playback time of the cut. In addition, you may need to edit what you've captured, trimming the silence from the beginning and end of the cut.

External Components

You can also capture sounds from external components using the auxiliary input that's available on most (but not all) sound boards. The auxiliary input functions exactly like the input to a cassette recorder. The audio signals you plug in there are routed through the mixer function of the sound board to its analog-to-digital converter to be sampled. Once digitized, you can use the audio data exactly like that ripped from CD.

You can plug an external audio CD player directly into the auxiliary input of your sound board. Better still, you can connect the recorder outputs of your receiver to the auxiliary input of your sound board and use your PC as if it were a cassette recorder, using the receiver to select the external audio source you want to record.

The mixer software supplied with most sound boards also has a MIDI input that allows you to translate MIDI files—both those you make and those you obtain elsewhere—into digital audio files that you can play back like any other music file. You can make recordings by selecting the MIDI source and using any sound recording software. Note, however, that most sound boards use their own MIDI circuitry to synthesize the sounds so the capabilities and idiosyncrasies of your sound board will determine the musical voices in the MIDI recordings that you make.

Microphone Inputs

The worst way to capture audio from a CD is to shove a microphone in front of a speaker. Not only does the quality suffer the indignity of conversion from digital to analog format, but it also suffers the substantial shortcomings of both the speaker and the microphone. You might just as well listen to a friend play the CD over the telephone.

Microphones are the only way to capture live sounds, be it your own speech or the band infesting your garage that no amount of Warfarin will deter. Most sound boards have microphone inputs that allow you to plug in directly and start recording simply by selecting the microphone (or mic) source in your sound board's mixer program.

That said, you should be aware that most sound board microphone inputs are designed primarily for speech. Although they are able to accept a wide frequency range, they have a high noise level because their circuits are immersed inside the noisy electronics of your computer. You can obtain better quality recordings by using an external microphone preamplifier such as that in a mixing console (or "board").

Note that most sound board microphone inputs are stereophonic and use stereophonic miniature jacks having three connections—tip, ring, and sleeve. A single monophonic microphone with a standard miniature plug (tip and sleeve) usually won't work with these inputs. Adapters are readily available to let you use a single microphone with a stereo input or to combine the signals from two microphones into a single plug to match your sound board. Modern microphones designed for PC applications are usually equipped with stereo plugs to match the inputs of sound boards.

Legal Issues

Commercial recordings—in general, that means all the CDs that you've bought—are protected by copyright laws. You should not post what you've captured or sampled on the Internet. You should not use material in a production (for example, a slide show, training video, or simply as background sound) without the permission of the copyright holder.

You should never sell a copy of anything that you've sampled from a copyrighted source such as a CD.

You can back up a CD that you have bought to an MP3 file for your personal use, for example, to make an MP3 file that you can listen to on a portable player (such as Diamond Multimedia's Rio MP3 player). Current copyright law allows you to make a single backup of copyrighted software that you have bought. It's no different from making a copy of a disk on a cassette to play in your car. (Although some folks question the legality of making such copies, as long as you make only one copy for personal use only, you won't have to worry about the copyright police pounding on your door.) On the other hand, it is both illegal and immoral to copy tracks from discs that you have borrowed from a friend or library.

Hardware

The job of the audio circuitry in your PC is to set the air in motion, making sounds that you can hear to alert you, to entertain you, to amaze you. PCs have had sound circuitry from the very beginning. But in the beginning of PCs, as in the beginning of life on earth, things were primitive, about the audio equivalent of amoebic blobs bobbing along en masse in black swamps. From humble beginnings, however, PC sound systems have evolved to parity with the stuff in all but the best and most esoteric stereo systems.

From the standpoint of a computer, sound is foreign stuff. Indeed, it's something that happens to stuff—air—while the computer deals with the non-stuff of logical thoughts. Video images are much more akin to computer electronics; at least the photons that you see are electromagnetic. Sound is purely mechanical, and that makes the computer's job of dealing with it tough. To make sound audible, it somehow has to do something mechanical. It needs a transducer, a device that transmits energy from one system to another—from the electrical PC to the kinetic world of sound.

Basic Sound System

Although the audio abilities of some PCs rival the best stereo systems, the least common denominator among them is low indeed. The basic sound system that you're assured of finding in all PCs is exactly the same primitive design that IBM bolted into its original PC.

To be charitable, the basic PC sound system wasn't designed for high fidelity. In fact, it was conceived as a beeper. Its goal was to generate pure if harsh tones to alert you to events occurring in your PC, such as the beep code of the BIOS. After all, in 1981 computers didn't sing opera.

This basic sound system has three components, a tone generator, an amplifier, and a loudspeaker—all three of which must be called rudimentary because there's nothing lower on the scale. When all worked together, you could make your PC beep as easily as typing Ctrl+I. The frequency and amplitude of the tone was predetermined by IBM's engineers. You were lucky to get any noise at all, let alone a choice.

Clever programmers quickly discovered that they could easily alter the tone, even play short ditties with their data. As programmers got clever, they found they could modulate the primitive sound system and indeed make the PC sing. Considering the standard equipment, you can make your PC sound surprisingly good just by adding the right driver to Windows.

Tone Generator

The fundamental tone generation circuit is the oscillator, the same as the clock that generates the operating frequency of your PC's microprocessor. The only difference is that the tone generator operates at lower frequencies, those within the range of human hearing (once they are translated into sounds).

The first PCs used one of the channels of the 8253 or 8254-2 timer/counter integrated circuit chips as the required oscillator. Modern PCs integrate the same functions into their chipsets.

No matter the implementation, the circuits work the same. The timer develops a train of pulses by turning a voltage on and off. The timing of these cycles determines the frequency of the tone the circuit produces.

The PC timer/counter chip starts with a crystal-controlled fixed frequency of 1.19MHz and divides it down into the audio range. A register in the timer chip stores a 16-bit divisor by which value the timer reduces the oscillator frequency. Loading the highest possible value into the divisor register (65,535) generates the lowest possible tone the basic PC sound system can produce, about 18Hz, low enough to strain the limits of normal hearing were the PC's speaker able to reproduce it. Divisor values above about 64 produce tones beyond the upper range of human hearing.

To use the timer to generate tones in a PC, you must first set up the timer/oscillator chip by writing the value 0B6(Hex) to the timer's control port at I/O port address 043(Hex). The frequency divisor for the PC tone generator then gets loaded into the I/O port at 042(Hex). This 8-bit port expects to receive two data bytes in sequence, the least significant byte first.

Because of the circuit design of the PC, these tones are produced as square waves, which means they are not pure tones but are rich in overtones or harmonics. Musically, they sound harsh—exactly what the doctor (or engineer) orders for warning tones.

The basic PC sound system was designed to produce tones of the frequency set by the divisor for short periods. These sounding periods are defined by gating the output of the oscillator on and off.

To turn the speaker on, you activate bit 0 of the register at I/O port 061(Hex). Resetting this bit to zero switches the speaker off. (You must exercise care when tinkering with these bits; other bits in this register control the keyboard.)

In this basic operating mode, the dynamics of the signal are limited. The output of the timer/oscillator chip is set at a constant level—the standard digital signal level—so the sound level produced by the speaker does not vary. All the sounds produced by the PC's motherboard have the same level. Some tones generated by the PC timer sound louder than others primarily because they are more obnoxious. They are made from the exact right combination of frequencies to nag at the aesthetic parts of your brain. That's about all they were designed to do. Listen long enough and you'll agree that the PC's designers succeeded beyond their wildest dreams at creating obnoxious sound.

Using a technique called pulse-width modulation, programmers discovered they could use even this primitive control system to add dynamics to the sounds they generated. Pulse-width modulation uses the duty cycle of a high-frequency signal coupled with a low-pass filter to encode the loudness of an analog signal equivalent. The loudness of a sound corresponds to the length of a signal pulse of a high-frequency carrier wave. A soft sound gets a brief pulse, and loud sounds are full-strength square waves. The low-pass filter eliminates the high carrier frequency from the signal and leaves a variable strength audio signal (the modulation).

Amplifier

The output of the tone-generator chip is too weak for sounding a speaker at a listenable level. The chip simply cannot supply enough current. The standard way to boost signal strength is with an amplifier. The basic PC sound system uses a simple operational amplifier. Modern systems incorporate this circuitry into the basic motherboard chipset. In any case, even with the boost, the signal amounts to only about 100 to 200 milliwatts, not enough to shake a theater.

The standard PC design also adds a low-pass filter and a current-limiting resistor between the driver and the loudspeaker. The low-pass filter eliminates frequencies higher than normal hearing range (and some in the upper ranges that you probably can readily hear). PCs often use higher frequencies to make audible sounds, and the low-pass filter prevents these artifacts from leaking into the speaker. In other words, it smoothes things out.

A resistor (typically about 33 ohms) in series with the loudspeaker prevents the internal loudspeaker of a PC from drawing too much current and overloading the driver circuit. A resistor also lowers the loudness of the speaker because it absorbs some power as part of the current-limiting process. Although some circuit-tinkerers bypass this resistor to make their PCs louder, doing so risks damage to the driver circuit.

Loudspeaker

The actual noisemaker in the PC's basic sound system is a small, two- to three-inch dynamic loudspeaker. To most PC designers, the internal loudspeaker is an obligatory headache. They have to put one somewhere inside the PC no matter how inconvenient. Usually, the speaker gets added almost as an afterthought. After all, all you have to do is hear it. You don't have to hear it well.

Because PC designers make no effort at optimizing the quality of the sound of the basic speaker, it is usually unbaffled. Its small size and acoustic prevent it generating any appreciable sound at low frequencies. Its physical mounting and design limit is high-frequency range. Outside of replacing the loudspeaker with something better, you cannot do anything to break through these limits.

In most PCs, the speaker connects to the motherboard using a simple, short two-wire twisted-pair cable. The motherboard usually, but not always, includes a four-pin loudspeaker connector. In many PCs, one of the pins is removed for keying the polarity of the speaker connection. One matching hole in the speaker cable connection often is blocked. Only two pins of the four pins of the motherboard connector are active, the two at the ends of the connector. The center one or two pins aren't connected to anything. Figure 19.2 shows this connection.

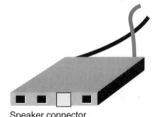

Motherboard connector   Speaker connector

In most PCs, the loudspeaker is electrically floating. That is, neither of its terminals is connected to the chassis or any other PC wiring except for the short to which it is soldered. When the speaker is electrically floating, the polarity of its connection is irrelevant so the keying of the connection is essentially meaningless. In other words, if the speaker connector on your PC is not keyed—if all four pins are present in the motherboard connector and none of the holes in the speaker connector is plugged—don't worry. The speaker will operate properly no matter how you plug it in.

Drivers

Other than beeping to indicate errors, the basic sound system in a PC has a life of leisure. If left to its own devices, it would sit around mute all the while you run your PC. Applications can, however, take direct hardware control and use the basic sound system for audible effects. For example, text-to-speech converters can use the basic sound system with pulse-width modulation techniques to simulate human speech.

Under all versions of Windows, only the native tone-generating abilities of the basic sound system get used, again just to beep warnings. Microsoft and some others have developed speaker drivers that allow the built-in basic sound system to play more elaborate noises such as the Windows sound when starting the operating system. These drivers let you play WAV files only. They do not synthesize sounds, so they cannot play MIDI files nor do they work with most games.

The prototype of these drivers is called the *Windows Speaker Driver* and was developed by Microsoft strictly for Windows 3.1. The speaker driver has not been updated for more recent versions of Windows. In fact, the history of the speaker driver is even more checkered; it was included with the beta test versions of Windows 3.1 but not the release version. During the development of Windows 3.1, Microsoft found that this driver sometimes misbehaved with some programs. To avoid support headaches, Microsoft elected not to include the driver in the basic Windows 3.1 package. The driver is included in the Microsoft Driver Library, and Microsoft does license it to developers to include with their products. It remains available from a number of sources, as are other, similar drivers.

These drivers will work under Windows 95, although Microsoft offers no explicit support of such operation. If you're used to simple beeps, these drivers sound amazingly convincing. They are not, however, a substitute for a real sound system based on a sound board.

Sound Boards

Clearly, the basic sound system in PCs is inadequate for the needs of modern multimedia. Getting something better requires additional circuitry. Traditionally, all of the required electronics get packaged on a single expansion card termed a *sound board*. Higher-quality audio has become such a necessity in modern PCs that most new notebook machines include all of the circuitry of a sound board on their motherboards. Many new desktop PCs and replacement motherboards also make all of the functions of a sound board an integral part of their designs. The physical location of the circuits is irrelevant to their normal operation. Electrically and logically, they are equivalent.

To cope with the needs of multimedia software and the demands of human hearing and expectation, the sound board needs to carry out several audio-related functions using specific hardware features. Foremost is the conversion of digital sound data into the analog form that speakers can shake into something that you can hear using a digital-to-analog converter. In addition, most sound boards sample or record sounds for later playback with a built-in analog-to-digital converter. They also create sounds of their own using a built-in synthesizer. Sound boards also include mixer circuits to combine audio from all the sources available to your PC—typically a microphone, the output of the sound board's digital-to-analog converter (which itself combines the synthesizer, WAV files read from disk, and other digital sources), the analog audio output of your PC's CD player, and an auxiliary input from whatever audio source tickles your imagination. Finally, the sound board includes an amplifier that takes this aural goulash and raises it to ear-pleasing volume.

Sound boards may include additional functions, one of which is required by the various multimedia PC specifications—a MIDI interface. This additional connection lets you link your PC to electronic musical instruments, for example, allowing your PC to serve as a sequencer or, going the other way, connecting a keyboard to control the sound board's synthesizer. Some makers of sound boards want their products to act as single-slot multimedia upgrades, so they include CD drive interfaces on their sound boards.

Sound boards can be distinguished in several ways. The most important of these divisions are the three Cs of sound boards—compatibility, connections, and quality. Compatibility determines the software with which a given sound board will work. The connections the board supports determines what you can plug in, usually MIDI and CD devices. Quality influences how satisfied you will be with the results, essentially whether you will be delighted or dismayed by your foray into multimedia.

Compatibility

Compatibility often is the most important because if your software can't coax a whimper from your sound board, you won't hear anything no matter what you plug in or how well the circuitry on the board might be able to do its job. Compatibility issues arise at two levels, hardware and software. More practically, you can regard these levels as DOS and Windows compatibility (or games and Windows, if DOS is foreign to your nomenclature).

For the most part, compatibility refers to the synthesizer abilities of a sound board. For your games to make the proper noises, it must be able to tell the sound board exactly what to do, when and whether to belch and boom. Your software needs to know which ports access the functions of the sound board. To work with games at the DOS level (and below), many of these features must be set in hardware, although you will still have to install driver software. At the Windows compatibility level, driver software determines compatibility. The DOS level of compatibility is more rigorous. It is also the level you require if you want to be able to run the full range of PC games.

Most games and other software require compliance with two basic de facto industry standards, Ad Lib and SoundBlaster. Beyond this, some games may also require features of particular sound boards.

Ad Lib

The basic level of hardware compatibility required for DOS games is with Ad Lib, the maker of one of the first sound boards to gain popularity in the sound-board business. Because it had the widest user base early when noisy games were becoming popular, many game programmers wrote their products to take advantage of the specific hardware features of the Ad Lib board. Even the newest hardware standards for sound board, Audio Codec '97, requires basic Ad Lib compatibility.

SoundBlaster

Another company, Creative Labs, entered the sound board business and built upon the Ad Lib base. Its SoundBlaster product quickly gained industry acceptance as a superset of the Ad Lib standard; it did everything the Ad Lib board did and more. The SoundBlaster found a huge market and raised the standard for sound synthesis among game products. Because programmers directly manipulated the hardware registers of the SoundBlaster to make the sounds they wanted, to run most games and produce the proper sounds you need a sound board that is hardware compatible with the SoundBlaster. Several iterations of SoundBlaster hardware were produced; the minimal level of compatibility to expect today is with version SoundBlaster 1.5.

The SoundBlaster relies on a particular integrated circuit to produce its array of synthesized sounds, the Yamaha YM3812. This chip has a single output channel, so it can produce only monophonic sound even when it is installed on a sound board that's otherwise called stereo. Some sound boards use two of these chips to produce stereo. The YM3812 has a fix repertory of 11 voices, 6 of which are instrumental and 5 for rhythm.

A newer FM synthesis chip has become popular on better sound boards, the Yamaha YMF262 or OPL3. Not only does the OPL3 have more voices—20—but it also uses more sophisticated synthesis algorithms for synthesis. It also can produce a full stereo output. Because it is backward compatible with its forebear, sound boards using it can gain both better synthesis and SoundBlaster compatibility.

The degree of SoundBlaster compatibility is critical when you're investigating portable PCs because the hardware needs of the SoundBlaster are incompatible with the PC Card standard. The PC Card bus in current form (version 2.1) does not include all of the signals needed by the SoundBlaster interface. Although PC Card-based sound boards can approximate true SoundBlaster compatibility, they cannot, for example, play Doom. To avoid the problem, many notebook computer manufacturers add SoundBlaster circuitry to the motherboards so you don't need to use PC Card.

The SoundBlaster interface works by sending data through two control ports, an address/status port located at 0388(Hex) and a write-only data port at 0389(Hex). These ports serve to access the SoundBlaster's 244 internal registers. The SoundBlaster also assigns four ports to speakers with addresses that vary with the base address you assign the board. By default, the data ports for the left speaker are at 0220(Hex) and 0221(Hex); for the right speaker, 0222(Hex) and 0223(Hex). You can make music by sending data directly to these ports. Most hardware-level programming, however, takes the form of sending function calls through the SoundBlaster's driver software, which uses a software interrupt for access to its functions.

To activate a SoundBlaster function, you load the appropriate values required by a given function call into specific registers of your PC's microprocessor and then issue the designated software interrupt. The function to be called is designated in the BX register of the microprocessor; the BH half of the register indicates one of five major functions handled by an individual driver (control, FM synthesis, voice from disk, voice from memory, or MIDI), and the BL register indicates exactly what to do. Table 19.5 summarizes these functions.

TABLE 19.5 SoundBlaster Function Calls

Function Name	Register Settings			Additional Comments
	BH	BL	CX	
Get SBSIM version number	0	0	Not used	On exit, AH=major version number; AL=minor version number.
Query drivers	0	1	Not used	On exit, AX bit values show drivers in use; bit 0=FM; bit 1=voice from disk; bit 2=voice from memory; bit 3=control; bit 4=MIDI.
Load file into extended memory	0	16	Not used	AX indicates file type (0=VOC file); CX, SBSIM handle to use; DS:DX points to file name.
Free extended memory	0	19	Not used	AX indicates SBSIM handle of file to be cleared.
Start FM sound source	1	0	0	SBSIM file handle in AX.
Play FM sound	1	1	0	
Stop FM sound	1	2	0	
Pause FM sound	1	3	0	

Hardware

Function Name	Register Settings			Additional Comments
	BH	*BL*	*CX*	
Resume FM sound	1	4	0	
Read FM sound source	1	5	0	On exit, AX=0 indicates sound is stopped; AX=FFFF indicates sound is playing.
Start voice from disk	2	0	0	SBSIM file handle in AX.
Play voice from disk	2	1	0	
Stop voice from disk	2	2	0	
Pause voice from disk	2	3	0	
Resume voice from disk	2	4	0	
Read voice from disk	2	5	0	On exit, AX=0 indicates sound is stopped; AX=FFFF indicates sound is playing.
Start voice from memory	3	0	0	AX points to file in conventional memory; DX:AX points to file in extended memory.
Play voice from memory	3	1	0	
Stop voice from memory	3	2	0	
Pause voice from memory	3	3	0	
Resume voice from memory	3	4	0	
Read voice from memory status	3	5	0	On exit, AX=0 indicates sound is stopped; AX=FFFF indicates sound is playing.
Show volume level	4	0	Not used	On entry, AX shows source; on exit, AH=left channel volume, AL=right channel volume.
Set volume level	4	1	Not used	On entry, AX indicates source to change; DH=left volume, DL=right volume.
Get gain setting	4	2	Not used	On entry, AX=1; on exit, AH=left channel gain, AL=right channel gain.
Set gain	4	3	Not used	On entry, AX=1; DH=left channel gain, DL=right channel gain.

continues

TABLE 19.5   Continued

Function Name	Register Settings			Additional Comments
	BH	BL	CX	
Show tone settings	4	4	Not used	On entry, AX=0 for treble, AX=1 for bass; on exit, AH=left channel setting, AL=right channel.
Set tone	4	5	Not used	On entry, AX=0 for treble, AX=1 for bass; DH=left channel setting, DL=right channel.
Start MIDI source	5	0	0	SBSIM file handle in AX.
Play MIDI source	5	1	0	
Stop MIDI source	5	2	0	
Pause MIDI source	5	3	0	
Resume MIDI source	5	4	0	
Read MIDI status	5	5	0	On exit, AX=0 indicates sound is stopped; AX=FFFF indicates sound is playing.

When the SoundBlaster interface driver loads, it chooses the first available interrupt within the range 080(Hex) to 0BF(Hex) inclusive. Programs needing to use its function calls can find the interrupt by looking for the signature "SBSIM" offset 103(Hex) bytes from the start of the interrupt vector segment address.

Windows

To produce sounds under Windows, a sound board requires a Windows-compatible software driver. With the right driver, a sound board can play the standard Windows sounds as well as any WAV files you like even if it does not have hardware compatibility with the Ad Lib or SoundBlaster standards. Because WAV files are digitally recorded audio data, they do not require synthesis. All Windows sounds, from the log-in noise to the standard riff when you make an error, are WAV files.

Newer drivers for sound boards should be compatible with DirectSound, the audio portion of the DirectX set of application interfaces.

Audio Codec '97

In developing its own two-chip audio system for PCs, Intel Corporation published the specifications of the system as if it were a standard by which all audio systems could be measured. The result, termed *Audio Codec '97*, represents a reasonable target for the designers of audio systems and may well become the standard that Intel planned. The two chips comprise a controller that handles all digital operations and an analog chip that turns the computer signals into audio. The two are connected by a five-wire serial connection termed the *AC link*.

The heart of the design is two digital-to-analog converters capable of operating at a 48KHz sampling rate to generate a pair of stereo audio channels. The specification requires that the controller be able to simultaneously process four signals, two inputs and two outputs. Each channel must be able to translate the signals to or from at least six sampling rates to the 48KHz basic rate of the system. These include 8.0, 11.025, 16.0, 22.05, 32.0, 44.1KHz. To maintain true hi-fi quality, the specification requires a single-to-noise ratio of 90 dB.

The DACs are fed by a mixer that accepts inputs from all the digital sources in the PC, including the synthesizer section of the Intel codec chipset. For inputs, the system includes a pair of analog-to-digital converters that also operate at 48KHz as well as an optional third, matching channel dedicated as a microphone input.

Control

The DirectX interface also provides a means through which application software can control multimedia equipment. In addition, the various Multimedia PC specifications also require that sound boards incorporate two very specific control functions for external devices, a CD interface and a MIDI interface. It also must incorporate an analog mixer to control audio levels.

CD Interface

Augmenting its synthesis and sampling functions, an MPC-compliant sound board must also be able to control a CD ROM drive. Besides controlling the drive, the sound board must also have a direct connection to the CD ROM drive for audio information, delivered in analog rather than digital form.

The CD interface circuitry on the sound board usually takes one of three forms—an ATAPI-compatible AT Attachment (IDE) connector, a SCSI port, or a proprietary port. Although common among early sound boards, particularly those sold in kits as complete multimedia upgrades, the acceptance of the low-cost AT Attachment interface for CD ROM drives has greatly diminished proprietary offerings.

The intent of the CD ROM interface is to assure that you can connect a CD drive to your PC because you need the drive if you want even a pretense of multimedia capabilities. If your PC has a suitable interface or even a CD drive already attached, the sound board port is superfluous. In fact, the interface on a sound board is better ignored. Standalone ATA and SCSI host adapters usually deliver better performance than the circuitry built into sound boards; for example, you may have a PCI-based disk interface that will have substantially wider bandwidth than the ISA-based interface on the sound board. Although the sound board interface will usually have sufficient performance for mid-range CD drives, it may be hard-pressed to keep up with a 12x or 16x drive and definitely will be out of its league with a hard disk. In other words, don't even think of connecting a hard disk drive to the SCSI port on a sound board. If the board gives you the option, switch off the interface circuitry or simply don't install the driver for it. That way, you can put the system resources otherwise used by the port to better use.

MIDI

The MPC specification also requires that a compliant sound board include a Musical Instrument Device Interface, or MIDI, port. Most people don't put this port to work. Its primary application is in making music with your PC rather than playing back what someone else has already written. You don't even have to have a MIDI port to play back the music files that encode MIDI instructions. Your playback software will usually route the MIDI instructions to the synthesizer circuitry on your sound board, generate the music there, and play it through the mixer and amplifier on the sound board. The MIDI instructions never need to cross the MIDI port.

That said, if you want to use your PC as a sequencer to record, edit, and play back your own musical compositions or if you want to use an external piano-style (as opposed to typewriter) keyboard to operate your sound board's synthesizer, your MIDI port will be your lifeline. Appendix X, "MIDI," discusses the MIDI interface in detail.

The MIDI standard describes the signals and protocols that travel through the connections between MIDI devices. It does not govern how the MIDI port links to your PC. Although in theory your PC could use any ports and addresses for controlling its MIDI circuitry, a standard evolved early in the history of MIDI in PCs. Roland Corporation developed a very popular MIDI adapter, its model MPU-401. To get the best performance from their programs, the writers of music software took direct hardware control of the MPU-401. The resources used by the MPU-401 quickly became the standard in the industry. The MIDI circuitry of most sound boards mimic the MPU-401, and most MIDI software requires MPU-401 compatibility.

Mixers

In addition to commanding external devices, sound boards also provide important control functions for music making and audio playback. The mixer circuitry in the sound board serves as a volume control for each of the various sources that it handles.

An audio *mixer* combines several signals into one, for example, making the distinct signals of two instruments into a duet in one signal. Most audio mixers allow you to individually set the volume levels of each of the signals that they combine.

Mixers work by summing their input signals. *Analog mixers* work by adding together their input voltages. For example, an analog mixer would combine a 0.3-volt signal with a 0.4-volt signal to produce a 0.7-volt signal. *Digital mixers* combine digital audio signals by adding them together mathematically using their digital values. The results are the same as in analog mixing; only the type of audio signal differs.

In your PC, however, the difference is significant. The sound board performs analog mixing in real-time in its on-board circuitry. Most PCs use their microprocessors to do digital mixing, and they usually don't make the mix in real-time. For example, your PC may mix together the sounds from two files and let you later play back the combination.

All sound boards incorporate mixer circuitry that lets you combine all the analog signals the board works with. The resulting audio mixture goes to your speakers and the analog-to-digital converter on the board so that you can record it into a file.

To control the relative volume levels of the various mixer inputs, most sound board makers provide mixer software that gives you an onscreen slider to adjust each input interactively.

Quality

In sound boards, quality wears more than one face. Every board has designed-in abilities and, likewise, limits that control what the board might possibly do. Lurking beneath, however, is the quality that a given board can actually produce. Dreams and reality being as they are, most sound boards aspire higher than they perform. This difference is hardly unexpected and would not be an issue were not the difference so great. A sound board may have specifications that put it beyond Compact Disc quality and yet perform on par with an ancient AM radio crackling away in a thunderstorm.

In general, most sound boards list their abilities in the range of digital signals they manage. That is, a given sound board may support a range of sampling frequencies and bit-depths. Nearly any modern sound board worth considering for your PC will list capabilities at least as good as the 44.1KHz sampling and 16-bit resolution of the CD medium. Newer boards should accommodate the 48KHz sampling of professional audio and the DVD system.

In terms of digital quality, the CD rates should be good for a flat frequency response from DC to 15KHz with a signal-to-noise ratio of about 96 decibels. Commercial sound boards miss both of those marks.

The shortfalls arise not in the digital circuitry; after all, *any* changes in a digital signal, including those that would degrade sound quality, are errors, and no modern PC should let errors arise in the data it handles. Rather, the analog circuitry on the sound board teases, tortures, and truncates the signals that travel through it. Both frequency response and dynamic range suffer.

Most of the time, the manhandling of the audio signals makes little difference. When sounds play through typical PC loudspeakers, you probably won't hear the deficiencies. Most inexpensive PC speakers (which means most PC speakers) are so bad that they mask the signal shortfalls. Listen through headphones or through a good stereo system, however, and the problems become readily apparent.

Many sound boards shortchange you on frequency response. Certainly, the sampling rate of a digital system automatically imposes a limit on the high frequencies that the system can handle. At the other end of the sound spectrum, there should be no such limitation. A digital system should easily be capable of encoding, storing, and reproducing not only the lowest frequencies that you can hear but also sounds lower than you can hear and even levels of direct current. Less expensive sound boards do not dip so low, however. In fact, many boards cannot process low-frequency sounds within the range a human hears, often missing the fundamental frequencies of bass notes and the stomach-wrenching rumbles of computer game special effects. These limits arise in the analog circuitry on the board from the coupling of AC signals through the various amplifier stages.

Most common analog systems require coupling capacitors between amplifier stages (and in the output) to block both supply voltages and direct current errors from interfering with the amplified audio signal. The size of the capacitor (its rating in *microfarads*, a unit of measure of electrostatic capacity) determines the low-frequency limit of the overall system. Larger capacitors are more expensive and harder to place on compact circuit boards, so manufacturers of budget products are apt to skimp on capacitor size. Better audio circuits use larger capacitors that pass lower frequencies or direct-coupled designs that totally eliminate their need (and push response down to DC).

The size of any capacitor in the amplifier output is particularly critical because as the power level increases, the required capacity to pass a given frequency increases. Consequently, the first place the low-frequency limit of a sound board suffers usually is in its power amplifier, the part that provides a high-level signal suitable for unpowered speakers. It is not unusual for low-priced sound boards to cut off sounds below 150Hz, which means few bass frequencies get through. Because the low frequencies are not present at the speaker jacks of such sound boards, plugging in better amplified speakers or even your stereo system will do nothing to ameliorate the low-frequency deficiencies. Line-level outputs, as opposed to speaker outputs, are more likely to preserve low frequencies, and they should be preferred for quality connections.

The other signal problem with inexpensive sound boards is noise. The noise level in any digital system is constrained by the bit-depth, and the typical 16-bit system pushed the noise floor down below that of many stereo components. Listen critically to the sounds from many sound boards and CD ROM drives, however, and you'll hear squeaks and peeps akin the conversations of Martians as well as more mundane sounds such as swooshes and hiss. Most of these sounds are simply extraneous signals intercepted by the sound board, mixed with the sounds you want to hear, and amplified to offend your ears. Not only do these arcane sounds interfere with your listening enjoyment, but they may also make their imprint on the sounds you digitize and store, forever preserving the marginal quality of your poor choice of sound board for posterity. Most sound boards keep the level of these noises below that which you can hear through inexpensive speakers, but listen to soft music from your CD drive, and you may find your peace shattered by Martian madness.

Better sound boards incorporate shielding to minimize the pick-up of extraneous noises. For example, the circuit traces on the boards will be shielded by *ground planes*, extra layers of circuit traces at ground potential covering the inner traces of multilayer printed circuit boards. Only the best sound boards can digitize analog signals without raising the overall noise level well above the 92 to 96 dB promised by good CD drives.

If you plan on using a sound board for transferring analog audio to digital form, for example, to back up your old vinyl phonograph records to CD, you will want a sound board that guarantees low noise and low-frequency response extending down to 20Hz.

USB Speakers

An intriguing new technology combines digital audio and the USB interface to make *USB speakers*. Instead of using a high-power analog interface, USB speakers accept audio in digital form straight from the USB port. The necessary analog-to-digital conversion circuitry is built into the speakers. In theory, USB speakers can eliminate the need for a sound board.

The concept eliminates the need for almost any analog circuitry inside your PC and cuts the interference from the digital signals in there. The result is that the low-level noises that you can hear through your speakers when your hard disk rattles into action (as well as any strange sounds that appear when your PC engages in heavy-duty processing) disappear. In addition, the speaker maker can tailor the D-to-A converter and amplifier to exactly match the speaker. It also eliminates a confusing jack from the back of your PC and integrates all of your PC's wiring into the USB system.

USB speakers have shortcomings, too. Digital audio eats a big chunk from the available USB bandwidth; as a practical matter, once you account for overhead the speaker connection swallows up about one third of the USB channel's bandwidth. Moreover, the speaker connection is only one function of a sound board. USB speakers do nothing to assume the other sound board functions. For example, they provide no microphone input. Although you could, in theory, link your microphone to your PC with a USB connection, too, USB mikes are as rare as unicorns or OS/2 on home PCs.

The USB speaker does nothing for other sound board connection functions. Although the USB port might serve the game port and disk interface functions, it won't handle MIDI without an add-on converter. And it won't allow playback from conventional CD drives that link to your sound board with an analog wire for the normal playback of music CDs.

In other words, USB speakers currently leave too many loose ends. Despite the predictions of some optimistic writers, USB speakers won't totally eliminate sound boards for quite a while.

Transducers

The bridge between the electronic world of audio (both analog and digital) and the mechanical world of sound is the acoustic transducer. The microphone converts sound into audio, and the loudspeaker converts audio into sound.

Microphones

All sound boards have microphone inputs to enable you to capture your voice in the digital medium. You can use digital transcriptions of your voice to annotate reports, spreadsheets, and other files or incorporate them into multimedia presentations. With a suitable sound board, you can even connect high-quality microphones to your PC and make digital recordings of music, edit them, and write them to CDs to play in your stereo system.

The job of the microphone is simple: to translate changes in air pressure into voltage changes. The accuracy of the microphone's translation determine the quality of the sound that can be recorded. No microphone is perfect. Each subtly distorts the translation, not making the results unidentifiable but minutely *coloring* the captured sound. One side of the microphone designer's art is to make these colorations as pleasing as possible. Another side of the art is to attempt to make the microphone work more like the human ear and tuning in only to what you want to hear, rejecting unwanted sounds.

Technologies

Engineers can use any of several technologies to build microphones. The microphones that you're most likely to connect to a sound board to capture your voice are dynamic. A dynamic microphone acts like a small electrical generator or dynamo, using a moving magnetic field to induce a current in a coil of wire. To detect changes in air pressure, a dynamic microphone puts a *diaphragm* into the path of sound waves. The diaphragm is typically made from lightweight plastic and formed into a domed shape or something even more elaborate to stiffen it. The diaphragm connects to a lightweight coil of wire called a *voice coil* that's wrapped around a small, usually cylindrical, permanent magnet. The voice coil is suspended so that it can move across the magnet as the diaphragm vibrates. The moving coil in the permanent magnetic field generates a small voltage, which provides the signal to the microphone input of your sound board.

Most microphones used for recording music today use a different operating principle. Called *condenser microphones* (or sometimes, capacitor microphones), they modify an existing voltage instead of generating a new one. In a classic condenser microphone, the diaphragm acts as one plate of an electrical capacitor (which in the days of vacuum tubes was often called a condenser, hence the name of the microphone). As the diaphragm vibrates, the diaphragm capacitance changes, which in turn modifies the original voltage.

Directionality

Microphones are often described by the *directionality*, how they responds to sounds coming from different directions. An *omnidirectional microphone* does not discriminate between sounds, no matter what direction they come from. It hears everything the same in a full circle around the microphone. A *unidirectional microphone* has one preferred direction in which it hears best. It partially rejects from other directions. Most unidirectional microphones are most sensitive to sounds directly in front of them. Sounds in the preferred direction are called *on-axis sounds*. Those that are not favored are called *off-axis sounds*. The most popular unidirectional microphone is called the *cardioid microphones* because of the heart-like shape of its pattern of sensitivity, *kardia* being Greek for heart. Hypercardioid microphones focus their coverage more narrowly while maintaining the basic cardioid shape. *Bidirectional microphones* are, as the name implies, sensitive to sounds coming from two directions, generally the front and rear of the microphone that resembles the numeral "8." Consequently, bidirectional microphones are sometimes called figure-eight microphones. This design is chiefly used in some special stereophonic recording techniques. Figure 19.3 illustrates the major types of microphone directional patterns.

FIGURE 19.3
Microphone directional patterns.

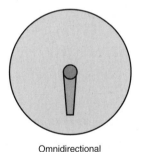 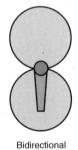 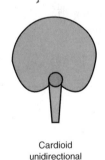

Omnidirectional   Bidirectional   Cardioid
                                                        unidirectional

The inexpensive microphones that accompany cassette tape recorders and some sound boards are typically omnidirectional dynamic microphones. If you want to minimize external noises or office commotion when annotating documents, a better unidirectional microphone will often make a vast improvement in sound quality.

Electrical Characteristics

The signals produced by microphones are measured in several ways. The two most important characteristics are impedance and signal level.

Microphones are known as low impedance (from 50 to 600 ohms) and high impedance (50,000 and more ohms). Some microphones have switches that allow you to change their impedance. Plugging a microphone of one impedance into a circuit meant for another results in low power transfer—faint signals. Nearly all professional microphones and most other microphones now operate at low impedance as do most microphone inputs. If your microphone has an impedance switch, you'll usually want it set to the low (150 ohm) position.

The signal levels produced by microphones are measured in millivolts or dB (decibels) at a given sound pressure level. This value is nominal. Loud sounds produce higher voltages. Most microphones produce signals described as –60 to –40 dBv and will work with most microphone inputs. If you shout into any microphone, particularly one with a higher output (closer to –40 dB), its output level may be too high for some circuits to process properly, particularly those in consumer equipment—say your PC's sound board. The high level may cause distortion. Adding an *attenuator* (or switching the microphone with output level switches to a lower level) will eliminate the distortion.

Microphone signals can be balanced or unbalanced. Balanced signals require two wire and a ground; unbalanced, one wire and a ground. Balanced signals are more immune to noise. Unbalanced signals require less sophisticated electronic input circuitry. Most sound boards use unbalanced signals. Most professional microphones produce balanced signals.

You can often convert a balanced signal into an unbalanced one (so you can connect a professional microphone to your sound board) by tying together one of the two signal wires of the balanced circuit with the ground. The ground and the other signal wire then act as an unbalanced circuit.

Connectors

Both inexpensive microphones and sound boards use the same kind of connector known as a miniature phone plug. Better quality, professional microphones with balanced signals typically use XLR connectors (named after the model designation of one of the original designs) with three pins for their two signals and ground. In these connectors, pin one is always ground. In balanced circuits, pin two carries the positive signal; pin three, the negative. When used in unbalanced circuits, pins one and three are usually connected together.

Phone plugs have two or three connections. The end of the plug is called the *tip*, and the shaft of the connector is called the *sleeve*. Some connectors have a third contact in the form of a thin ring between the tip and the sleeve. This is called the *ring*. Figure 19.4 illustrates a typical phone plug.

FIGURE 19.4
Components of a typical phone plug.

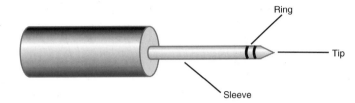

In unbalanced audio circuits, the tip is always connected to the hot or positive signal wire, and the sleeve is connected to the shield or ground. With balanced signals, positive still connects to the tip, negative connects to the ring, and the shield or ground goes to the sleeve. In stereo connections, the left channel goes to the tip, the right channel to the ring, and the common ground or shield goes to the sleeve.

Loudspeakers

From the standpoint of a PC, moving air is a challenge as great as bringing together distant worlds, the electronic and the mechanical. To make audible sounds, the PC must somehow do mechanical work. It needs a transducer, a device that transmits energy from one system to another—from the electrical PC to the kinetic world of sound. The device of choice is the dynamic *loudspeaker*, invented in 1921 by Kellogg Rice.

The dynamic loudspeaker reverses the dynamic microphone design. An electrical current activates a *voice-coil* (a solenoid or coil of wire that gives the speaker its voice) that acts as an electromagnet, which is wrapped around a permanent magnet. The changing current in the voice-coil changes its magnetic field, which changes its attraction and repulsion of the permanent magnet, which makes the voice-coil move in proportion to the current change. A diaphragm called the *speaker cone* is connected to the voice-coil and moves with the voice-coil to create the pressure waves of sound. The entire assembly of voice-coil, cone, and supporting frame is called a speaker *driver*.

The art of loudspeaker design only begins with the driver. The range of human hearing far exceeds the ability of any driver to reproduce sound uniformly. Accurately reproducing the full range of frequencies that you can hear requires either massive electronic compensation (called *equalization* by audio engineers) or using multiple speaker drivers, with each driver restricted to a limited frequency range.

Commercial speaker systems split the full audible frequency range into two or three ranges to produce *two-way* and *three-way* speaker systems. Modern systems may use more than one driver in each range so a three-way system may actually have five drivers.

Woofers operate at the lowest frequencies that mostly involve bass notes, usually at frequencies of 150 Hertz and lower. *Tweeters* handle the high frequencies associated with the treble control, frequencies that start somewhere in the range 2,000 to 5,000 Hertz and wander off to the limits of human hearing. *Midrange* speaker drivers take care of the range in between. A *cross-over* divides the full range of sound into the individual ranges required by the specialized speaker drivers.

The term subwoofer is also used to describe a special, auxiliary baffled speaker system meant to enhance the sound of ordinary speakers by extending their low-frequency range. Because the human ear cannot localize low-frequency sounds, you can place this sub-woofer anywhere in a listening room without much effect on stereophonic imaging. The other, smaller speakers are often termed satellite speakers.

Baffles and Enclosures

The low-frequency range is particularly difficult for speaker systems to reproduce. The physics of sound requires that more air move at lower frequencies to achieve the same pressure changes or loudness, so larger speakers do a better job generating low-frequency sounds. But the packaging of the speaker also influences its low-frequency reproduction. At low frequencies, the pressure waves created by a loudspeaker can travel a substantial distance in the time it takes the speaker cone to move in and out. In fact, when frequencies are low enough the air has time to travel from the high-pressure area in front of the speaker to the low-pressure area behind an outward-moving speaker cone. The moving air cancels out the air pressure changes and the sound. At low frequencies—typically those below about 150Hz—a loudspeaker in free air has little sound output. The small size and free-air mounting of the loudspeakers inside PCs severely constrain their ability to reproduce low frequencies.

To extend the low-frequency range of loudspeakers, designers may install the driver in a cabinet that blocks the air flow from the front to the back of the speaker. The cabinet of a speaker system is often termed a baffle or enclosure. Strictly speaking, the two terms are not equivalent. A *baffle* controls flow of sound, but an *enclosure* is a cabinet that encircles the rear of the speaker.

Not just any cabinet will do. The design of the cabinet influences the ultimate range of the system as well as its ability to deliver uniform frequency response. As with any enclosed volume, the speaker enclosure has a particular resonance. By tuning the resonance of the enclosure, speaker system designers can extend the frequency range of their products. Larger enclosures have lower resonances, which helps accentuate the lowest frequencies speaker drivers can produce.

Most speaker enclosures use one of two designs. *Acoustic suspension* speaker systems seal the low-frequency driver in a cabinet, using the confined air to act as a spring (which in effect "suspends" the speaker cone in its resting position). A *ducted* speaker or *tuned-port* speaker or *bass reflex* speaker puts a vent or hole in the cabinet. The vent both lowers the resonance of the enclosure and, when properly designed, allows the sound escaping from the vent to reinforce that produced by the speaker driver. Ducted speakers are consequently more efficient, producing louder sounds for a given power, and can be smaller for a given frequency range.

Although tuning a speaker cabinet can extend its frequency range downward, it can't work magic. The laws of physics stand in the way of allowing a speaker of a size that would fit on your desk or bookshelf or inside a monitor from reproducing bass notes at levels you can hear. For most business applications, reproducing low frequencies isn't necessary and may even be bothersome to co-workers in adjacent cubicles when you start blasting foreign agents and aliens.

Subwoofers and Satellites

A *subwoofer* extends the low-frequency abilities of your PC's sound system for systems that need or require it. The distinguishing characteristic of the subwoofer is that it is designed to supplement other speaker systems and reproduce only the lowest audible frequencies, typically those from 20 to 100 Hertz. Because these low frequencies are essentially non-directional (your ear cannot tell where they are coming from), a single subwoofer suffices in stereo and multichannel sound systems.

The classic speaker system puts all the drivers for various frequency ranges in a single cabinet to produce a *full-range speaker system*. One major trend in speaker design is to abandon the full-range layout and split the cabinetry. Designers put the midrange speakers and tweeters into small cabinets called *satellite speakers* and rely on one or two subwoofers to produce the low frequencies. Practical considerations underlie this design. The small size of the satellites allows you to place them where convenient for the best stereo imaging, and you can hide the non-directional woofers out of sight. Figure 19.5 shows a satellite-subwoofer combination.

Flat-panel speakers ordinarily must take on huge dimensions to reproduce low frequencies. Some of the most exalted flat-panel designs stretch floor to ceiling. Using a subwoofer, flat panels can be more modest in size. One manufacturer, Sonigistix, has adopted flat-panel speakers as computer satellites, noting the unique directional characteristics of the design allows better imaging for a single listener, focusing the sound on the listener and minimizing room reflections. Figure 19.6 shows flat-panel speakers complementing a flat-panel display system.

Passive and Active Systems

The speakers you add to your PC typically come in one of two types, active or passive. The difference is that *active speakers* have built-in amplifiers, but *passive speakers* do not.

Most speaker systems designed for stereo systems are passive. They rely on your receiver or amplifier to provide them with the power they need to make sound. Most computer speakers are active with integral amplifiers designed to boost the weak output of the typical sound board to the level required for filling a room with sound.

FIGURE 19.5
Satellite speakers combined with a sub-woofer.

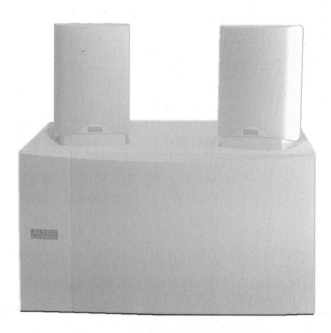

FIGURE 19.6
Monsoon flat-panel speakers with a flat-panel display.

The amplifiers in active speakers are like any other audio amplifiers with output power measured in watts (and in theory matched to the speakers) and quality measured in terms of frequency response and distortion. The big difference is that most active speakers, originally designed for portable stereos, operate from battery power. If you plan to plug active speakers into your desktop PC, ensure that you get a battery eliminator power supply so you can plug them into a wall outlet. Otherwise if you're serious about multimedia, you'll be single-handedly supporting the entire battery industry.

Most sound boards produce sufficient power to operate small passive speaker systems. Their outputs are almost uniformly about four watts because all use similar circuitry to generate the power. This level is enough even for many large stereo-style passive speaker systems. Active speakers still work with these higher-powered sound boards and in many cases deliver better (if just louder!) sound through their own amplifiers.

Installation

Sound boards are heavy feeders when it comes to system resources. A single sound board may require multiple interrupts, a wide range of input/output ports, and a dedicated address range in High DOS memory. Because of these extensive resource demands, the need for numerous drivers, and often-poor documentation, sound boards are the most frustrating expansion products to add to a PC. In fact, a sound board may be the perfect gift to surreptitiously gain revenge letting you bury the hatchet with an estranged friend without the friend knowing you've sliced solidly into his back.

Some of the connections and concerns in installing a sound board have already been discussed in other contexts. The CD drive audio connection was discussed in Chapter 12. The digital control interface for CD drives present on some sound boards were discussed in Chapter 9, "Storage Interfaces." Those, however, are the simple connections for the sound board. The actual audio issues are more complex.

System Resources

Most of the difficulties in installing a sound board arise from the multiple functions expected from it. Because of the need for hardware compatibility with both the Ad Lib and SoundBlaster standards, any sound board must duplicate all the registers and other hardware features of those products for their synthesizers to work with older games. MIDI software often requires a specific port assignment. Controlling the analog-to-digital conversion and analog mixer circuits requires additional controls. Specific enhancements as well as CD ROM interfaces must also be addressed.

Depending on the vintage of the sound board you want to install, most current sound boards use electronic settings compatible with the plug-and-play standard. Older boards may force you to tangle with a bank of DIP switches or a row or two of jumpers to select the resources used by the board. A number of boards are transitionary; they use electronic settings but do not fully support Plug and Play. Your owners' manual should document what form these settings take, and if manual configuration is required, it should list the factory defaults (always a good starting place) and how to make changes.

Even when you must configure your sound board manually, you don't have full freedom of choice. Should you want to run DOS-based games, many of the resource assignments are pre-ordained. For example, you must use DMA channel 1. DOS games require SoundBlaster compatibility, and the SoundBlaster's DMA usage is set to channel 1. If you don't want to play games, however, another channel choice may be more appropriate. Higher DMA channel numbers are all 16-bit transfers, and lower DMA channels (1, 2, and 3) are only 8 bits wide. Achieving the highest degree of SoundBlaster compatibility also dictates setting the base I/O port assignment for your sound board to 220(Hex), the default assignment of the SoundBlaster. In addition, the default SoundBlaster interrupt assignment is 5. You can use alternate settings for the interrupt and I/O port settings because the SoundBlaster allows for alternate values. However, you'll have to alter the options used with your sound board driver software to match your manual configuration. Under Windows 95, you may have to alter the resource settings assigned the sound board through Device Manager.

Most electronically configured sound boards automatically adjust themselves to the settings you make through Device Manager. Others do not. You may have to run the software setup program supplied by the sound board maker and then adjust Device Manager to reflect your new settings. Moreover, sometimes the resources automatically assigned by Windows 95 during hardware installation to boards that do not fully support the plug-and-play standard can cause conflicts. If your sound board does not work after installation, you should try alternate resource settings first.

A further installation difficulty is that Windows may not automatically exclude from management the memory range used by your sound board. Should your sound board not work at its alternate resource settings, check the memory addresses it uses and ensure they are excluded from management.

Old drivers can also cause problems with sound boards. When installing a new sound board driver, you'll also want to remove any old sound board drivers that you've previously installed. The procedure is specific to your operating system. For example, under the Windows 3.1 family, you would select Remove from the Drivers menu, highlight the old driver name, and click on OK. You may need to eliminate references to old sound board drivers from your CONFIG.SYS file even when running under Windows 95. When upgrading from Windows 3.1 to Windows 95, some sound board makers require that you manual delete the old Windows 3.1 drivers by erasing them from your disk to prevent later problems. The general rule is to install *only* the latest drivers and remove all old sound board drivers.

Audio Connections

Most sound boards have integral audio amplifiers designed for power external speakers. Because of constraints imposed by your PC, however, these amplifiers are rudimentary. Typically, they produce little output power—usually between 100 milliwatts and one watt.

Worse, many cut off low frequencies below 100 Hertz, the very frequencies that have the most impact in the sound effects often played through sound boards. Although you can connect an auxiliary amplifier and speaker system to your sound board to overcome the power shortage, you usually cannot overcome the low frequency cut-off.

Speaker Wiring

Commercial computer speakers make wiring easy. Most sound boards use stereophonic miniature phone jacks for their outputs, and speaker systems designed for computers have matching plugs. The wires from both speaker systems in a stereo pair may join at this plug; the two speakers share a single plug. Often, however, each speaker has its own wire and plug. These systems require that you chain the speakers. Again, you face two design variations.

In one variation, the speakers are not quite identical. One of them, usually the left speaker, has a jack near where the wire leads into the speaker. In this case, you plug the left speaker into your sound board and plug the right speaker into a jack on the left speaker. If you accidentally plug the right speaker into the sound board, you won't hurt anything but you won't have a place to plug in the left speaker.

The other variation uses speakers that both have jacks on the back. You can plug either speaker into your sound board and plug the other speaker into the first. Although the wires carry both signals through both speakers, the right speaker only taps the right signal, and the left speaker taps only the left signal.

You're not limited to commercially designated computer speakers. You can plug high-efficiency stereo speakers or power speakers designed for portable personal stereo systems directly into your sound board. Or you can plug your sound board into the auxiliary jack (or CD jack) of a receiver or preamplifier and route the sound through an ordinary stereo system. Commercial adapter cables are readily available to convert the single stereo miniature phone plug into two pin (or phono) plugs for your stereo.

If you choose to connect your own speaker to a sound board, be they commercial speaker systems or drivers you have lying around from that old autosound installation that went awry, be certain you match levels and impedances. Most sound boards are rated to deliver full power into loads with a four ohm impedance. Higher impedance causes no worry because a higher impedance load typically reduces the drain on an amplifier (making it less prone to overloading and failure). Although a lower impedance can be dangerous, nearly all speakers have a four ohm or greater impedance. The only time you may encounter a lower impedance is if you try to connect two speakers in parallel to one channel of your sound board. Don't try it.

Adding subwoofers complicates matters. Passive subwoofers usually incorporate their own cross-overs that intercept low frequencies and prevent them from being passed on to the rest of your speakers. Consequently, the subwoofer must be connected between your ordinary speakers and amplifier. When you connect a single subwoofer and satellites, all signals first go to the subwoofer, and the satellites plug into the subwoofer. Systems with two subwoofers pair one subwoofer with one satellite, so the wire from each channel leads to the associated subwoofer, thence its satellite. Active subwoofers, when not part of a speaker package, typically bridge your amplifier outputs, wired in parallel to your existing speakers.

A surround sound amplifier makes subwoofer wiring easy: Most surround systems provide dedicated subwoofer outputs.

Amplifier Wiring

If you want the best sound quality, you may be tempted to plug your sound board into your stereo system. For such purposes, you can consider your stereo an active speaker system. Just connect an unused input of your receiver or preamp to the output of your sound board. (The auxiliary output is best, but the speaker output will likely work, too.) If your PC and stereo are not both properly grounded, however, you may inadvertently cause damage. With improper grounding, there can be odd voltage differences between the chassis of your PC and stereo system—enough of a difference that you can draw sparks when plugging in the audio cable. This can have detrimental effects on both computer and stereo circuitry. In other words, make sure that you properly ground both PC and stereo.

Most sound board outputs are high level, meant for direct connection with loudspeakers. Using high-power buffer circuits, they can drive low-impedance loads presented by loudspeakers, typically 4 to 16 ohms. Although these connections are designed for loudspeakers, they match the high-level audio inputs of most preamplifiers and receivers well enough that you can usually connect them directly with a patch cord.

Do not worry about blasting a full watt into the input of your receiver. The input circuits of your receiver or preamplifier are sensitive to the voltage level rather than the power in the signal. Because amplifier inputs typically have a high input impedance—at least 2,000 ohms and possibly as high as 100,000 ohms—little of the current in the sound board output can flow through the amplifier input circuit. The voltage levels match well enough that the signals are compatible, although you may have to adjust the volume control on high-powered sound boards to prevent overloading your receiver's inputs with too much voltage.

A sound board with a one watt output into a four ohm load produces a two volt output. A 100-milliwatt sound board produces a 0.62 volt output, again assuming a four ohm impedance. Most high-level receiver and preamplifier auxiliary inputs operate with a voltage level of 0.1 to 1 volt. Do not, however, plug the speaker output signals of your sound

Installation

board into microphone inputs. The voltage levels in the sound board signal will likely overload most microphone inputs.

If you choose to make a direct connection to a receiver or other external amplifier, turn down the volume or loudness control on both your sound board and receiver to a minimal level before you begin. Play some sound through your sound board and slowly increase the volume control on your receiver to the position you use for your normal listening level. Finally, increase the level of your sound board until it reaches a pleasing listening level through your receiver.

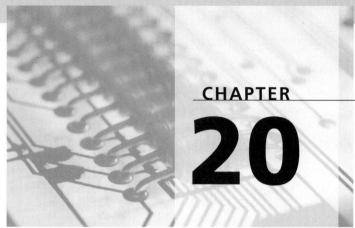

CHAPTER

20

Peripheral Ports

Ports provide the link between your PC and external peripherals. Although many current PCs include traditional ports adapted from other applications— the legacy serial and parallel designs—the ports of choice in the future follow standards designed specifically for PCs. All of these use serial communications and take advantage of modern electronics for automatic configuration with a minimum of hassle. Your choices include USB for versatility, FireWire for speed, and IrDA for wireless connectability.

Preferred peripheral ports for today's PCs

Port	Chief advantage	Top speed	Devices per port	Chief applications
IrDA	Wireless flexibility	4 Mbits/sec	126	Keyboards, PDAs, printers
USB	Connect anything	12 Mbits/sec	127	Keyboards, mice, scanners, printers
Firewire	Speed	800 Mbits/sec	16	Digital video

In a politically correct world, the old saw, "No man is an island," no longer works. Made PC, it would read, "No person is an island." But the real truth is that no PC is an island. Hermits thrive in caves, alone and happy for their isolation. Your PC, however, does not.

No PC has everything you need built into it. The PC gains its power from what you connect to it—its peripherals. Somehow, your PC must be able to send data to its peripheral. It needs to connect, and it makes its connections through its ports.

Right now, the PC is about to undergo a revolution in port technology. The ports that have traditionally connected peripherals to PCs, the RS-232C serial port and the parallel port, have their pink slips in hand. New PCs are slated to go without them. In the eyes and minds of the promoters of PC technology (which means Intel and Microsoft), these old friends among connections are *legacy ports*. To prepare you for the brave new interconnected world, we've left them to their own chapter, Chapter 21, "Legacy Ports."

Today's port choices differ from the legacy designs. Instead of being imported from other applications to personal computing, they were crafted in the modern world. That means more than just speed. The new interfaces have enough built-in intelligence that, their designers believe, you don't need any. Plug in a connector, and the interface circuitry does the rest. Moreover, engineers have painstakingly designed the system with plugs and jacks that prevent you plugging in anything improperly, no matter how hard you try.

Today's PCs include two or three of these modern interfaces. Those that you're likely to encounter include

> *Universal Serial Bus*, or USB, is today's general-purpose choice. It combines moderate performance with a goof-proof connection system. As its name implies, USB acts as a true bus that can link up to 127 devices to your PC without worries about matching connectors and cables (although it remains a wire-based design). Speed takes a quantum leap over legacy ports with a peak data rate of 12 megabits per second as well as a low-speed mode that operates at 1.5 megabits per second. To make the "universal" in the name a reality, the design goal of the new standard aims low: USB was designed to be a low-cost interface, cheap enough for every PC.

> *FireWire*, perhaps better known among PC users by its technical name of IEEE 1394, races far ahead of USB, starting almost 10 times faster and racing to rates normally reserved for UHF television stations. Pushing serial technology further still, FireWire has a starting data rate of 100 megabits per second with rates as high as 3.2 gigabits per second envisioned. More expensive to implement than USB, it fits with the new SCSI-3 scheme of things and offers a reliable means of linking high-speed peripherals such as hard disks and real-time video systems to PCs.

> *IrDA*, an acronym for its sanctioning organization, the Infrared Developers Association, is a wireless connection system with modest performance. Although based on legacy serial technology, it adds such modern concepts as automatic device identification and improved performance.

In addition, some PC peripherals use a connection system termed *ACCESS.bus.* This interface is an inexpensive but low-speed serial connection to link multiple undemanding devices with your PC. Rather than speed, its advantage over legacy serial port designs is versatility. It can connect more devices to your PC than all the legacy ports you or your system could stand. Moreover, it is a simple standard, one without a confusion of cables and connectors.

Table 20.1 compares these port alternatives as well as their legacy predecessors.

TABLE 20.1   A Comparison of Serial Interfaces

Standard	Data Rate	Medium	Devices per Port
RS-232C	115,200 bps	Twisted-pair	1
ACCESS.bus	100 kbps	4-wire shielded cable	125
IrDA	4 mbps	Optical	126
USB	12 mbps	Special 4-wire cable	127
USB-2.0	120 to 240 mbps	Special 4-wire cable	127
IEEE 1394	100 mbps to 800 mbps (3,200 mbps proposed)	Special 6-wire cable	16

All of these connection systems use *serial* technology. That is, they treat data one dimensionally, as a long stream or series of bits. From this common ground, each goes its own direction. At heart, however, all involve the same repackaging of data to make it fit a channel with a single stream of data (see "Legacy Serial Ports" in Chapter 21 for a fuller explanation of serial technology.)

Background

No matter the name and standard, all serial ports are the same, at least functionally. Each takes the 8, 16, or 32 parallel bits your computer exchanges across its data bus and turns them sideways—from a broadside of digital blips into a pulse chain that can walk the plank, single file. This form of communication earns its name "serial" because the individual bits of information are transferred in a long series.

The change marks a significant difference in coding. The bits of parallel data are coded by their position. That is, the designation of the bus line they travel confers value. The most significant bit travels down the line designated for the most significant signal. With a serial port, the significance is awarded by timing. The position of a bit in a pulse string gives it its value. The later in the string, the more important the bit.

In a perfect world, a single circuit—nothing more than two wires, a signal line and a ground—would be all that was necessary to move this serial signal from the one place to another without further ado. Of course, a perfect world would also have fairies and other benevolent spirits to help usher the data along and protect it from all the evil imps and energies lurking about, trying to debase and disgrace the singular purity of serial transfer.

The world is, alas, not perfect, and the world of computers even less so. Many misfortunes can befall the vulnerable serial data bit as it crawls through its connection. One of the bits of a full byte of data may go astray, leaving a piece of data with a smaller value on arrival as it had at departure—a problem akin to shipping alcohol by a courier service operated by dipsomaniacs. With the vacancy in the data stream, all the other bits will slip up a place and assume new values. Or the opposite case: In the spirit of electronic camaraderie, an otherwise well-meaning signal might adopt a stray bit as a child takes on a kitten, only to later discover the miracle of pregnancy and a progeny of errors that ripple through the communications stream, pushing all the bits backward. In either case, the prognosis is not good. With this elementary form of serial communications, one mistaken bit either way, and every byte that follows will be in error.

Establishing reliable serial communications means overcoming these bit-error problems and many others as well. Thanks to some digital ingenuity, however, serial communications work and work well—well enough that you and your PC can depend on them.

Clocking

In computers, a serial signal is one in which the bits of data of the digital code are arranged in a series. They travel through their medium or connection one after another as a train of pulses. Put another way, the pattern that makes up the digital code stretches across the dimension of time rather than across the width of a data bus. Instead of the bits of the digital code getting their significance from their physical position in the lines of the data bus, they get their meaning from their position in time. Instead of traveling through eight distinct connections, a byte of data, for example, makes up a sequence of eight pulses in a serial communications system. Plot signal to time, and the serial connection turns things sideways from the way they would be inside your PC.

Do you detect a pattern here? Time, time, time. Serial ports make data communications a matter of timing. Defining and keeping time become critical issues in serial data exchanges.

Engineers split the universe of serial communications into two distinct forms, synchronous and asynchronous. The difference between them relates to how they deal with time.

Synchronous communications require the sending and receiving system—for our purposes, the PC and printer—to synchronize their actions. They share a common time base, a serial *clock*. This clock signal is passed between the two systems either as a separate signal or by using the pulses of data in the data stream to define it. The serial transmitter and receiver can unambiguously identify each bit in the data stream by its relationship to the shared clock. Because each uses exactly the same clock, they can make the match based on timing alone.

In *asynchronous communications*, the transmitter and receiver use separate clocks. Although the two clocks are supposed to be running at the same speed, they don't necessarily tell the same time. They are like your wrist watch and the clock on the town square. One or the other may be a few minutes faster even though both operate at essentially the same speed: A day has 24 hours for both.

An asynchronous communications system also relies on the timing of pulses to define the digital code. But they cannot look to their clocks as infallible guidance. A small error in timing can shift a bit a few positions, say from the least significant place to the most significant, which can drastically affect the meaning of the digital message.

If you've ever had a clock that kept bad time—for example, the CMOS clock inside your PC—you probably noticed that time errors are cumulative. They add up. If your clock is a minute off today, it will be two minutes off tomorrow. The longer time elapses, the bigger the difference in two clocks will be apparent. The corollary is also true: If you make a comparison over a short enough period, you won't notice a shift between two clocks even if they are running at quite different speeds.

Asynchronous communications banks on this fine slicing of time. By keeping intervals short, they can make two unsynchronized clocks act as if they were synchronized. The otherwise unsynchronized signals can identify the time relationships in the bits of a serial code.

Isochronous communications involve time-critical data. Your PC uses information that is transferred isochronously in real-time. That is, the data are meant for immediate display, typically in a continuous stream. The most common examples are video image data that must be displayed at the proper rate for smooth full-motion video and digital audio data that produces sound. Isochronous transmissions may be made using any signaling scheme, be it synchronous or asynchronous. They usually differ from ordinary data transfers in that the system tolerates data errors. It compromises accuracy for the proper timing of information. Although error correction in a conventional data transfer may require the retransmission of packets containing errors, an isochronous transmission lets the errors pass through uncorrected. The underlying philosophy is that a bad pixel in an image is less objectionable that image frames that jerk because the flow of the data stream stops for the retransmission of bad packets.

Frames

The basic element of digital information in a serial communication system is the data *frame*. Think of the phrase as a time frame, the frame bracketing the information as a frame surrounds a window. The bits of the digital code are assigned their value in accordance with their position in the frame. In a synchronous serial communications system, the frame contains the bits of a digital code word. In asynchronous serial communications, the frame also contains a word of data, but it has a greater significance. It is also the time interval in which the clocks of the sending and receiving systems are assumed to be synchronized.

When an asynchronous receiver detects the start of a frame, it resets its clock and then uses its clock to define the significance of each bit in the digital code within the frame. At the start of the next frame, it resets its clock and starts timing the bits again.

The only problem with this system is that an asynchronous receiver needs to know when a frame begins and ends. Synchronous receivers can always look to the clock to know, but the asynchronous system has no such luxury. The trick to making asynchronous communications work is unambiguously defining the frame. Today's asynchronous systems use *start bits* to mark the beginning of a frame and *stop bits* to mark its end. In the middle are a group of *data bits*.

The start bit helps the asynchronous receiver find data in a sea of noise. In some systems, the start bit is given a special identity. In most asynchronous systems, it is twice the length of the other bits inside the frame. In others, the appearance of the bit itself is sufficient. After all, without data, you would expect no pulses. When any pulse pops up, you might expect it to be a start bit.

Each frame ends with one or more stop bits. They assure the receiver that the data in the frame is complete. Most asynchronous communication systems allow for one, one and a half, or two stop bits. Most systems use one because that length makes each frame shorter (which, in turn, means that it takes a shorter time to transmit).

The number of data bits in a frame varies widely. In most asynchronous systems, there will be from five to eight bits of data in each frame. If you plan to use a serial port to connect a modern serial device to your PC, your choices will usually be to use either seven bits or eight bits, the latter being the most popular.

In addition, the data bits in the frame may be augmented by error-correction information called a parity bit, which fits between the last bit of data and the stop bit. In modern serial systems, any of five varieties of parity bits are used: odd, even, space, mark, and none.

The value of the parity bit is keyed to the data bits. The serial transmitter counts the number of digital ones in the data bits and determines whether this total is odd or even.

In the odd parity scheme, the transmitter will turn on the parity bit (making it a digital one) only if the total number of digital ones in the data bits is odd. In even parity systems, the parity bit is set as one only if the data bits contain an even number of digital ones. That is, in odd parity systems, the parity bit gets set to insure the total number of active (usually high) bits is odd. In even parity, the parity bit gets set so the total number of active bits is even. In mark parity, the parity bit is always a mark, a digital one. In space parity, the parity bit is always a space, a digital zero. With no parity, no parity bit is included in the digital frames, and the stop bits immediately follow the data bits.

By convention, the bits of serial data in each frame are sent least significant bit first. Subsequent fits follow in order of increasing significance. Figure 20.1 illustrates the contents of a single data frame that uses eight data bits and a single stop bit.

FIGURE 20.1

A serial data frame with eight data bits and one stop bit.

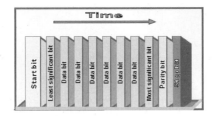

Packets

A frame corresponds to a single character. Taken alone, that's not a whole lot of information. A single character rarely suffices for anything except answering multiple-choice tests. To make something meaningful, you combine a sequence of characters together to form words and sentences.

The serial communications equivalent of a sentence is a *packet*. A packet is a standardized group of characters and frame that makes up the smallest unit that conveys information through the communications system.

Background

As the name implies, a packet is a container for a message, like a diplomatic packet or envelope. The packet holds the data. In addition, in most packetized systems, the packet also includes an address and, often, a description of its contents. Packets may also include extra data to assure the integrity of their contents—for example, an error-detection or error-correction scheme of some sort. Figure 20.2 shows the constituents of a typical data packet.

FIGURE 20.2

Constituents of a typical data packet.

The exact constituents of a packet depend on the communication protocol. In general, however, all packets have much the same construction. They begin with a symbol or character string that allows systems listening in to the communication channel to recognize the bit-pattern that follows as a packet.

Each packet bears an address that tells where it is bound. Devices listening in on the communication channel check the address. If it does not match their own or does not indicate that the packet is being broadcast to all devices—in other words, the packet wears an address equivalent to "occupant"—the device ignores the rest of the packet. Communications equipment is courteous enough not to listen in on messages meant for someone else.

Most packets include some kind of identifying information that tells the recipient what to do with the data. For example, a packet may bear a marker to distinguish commands from ordinary data.

The bulk of the packet is made from the data being transmitted. Packets vary in size and hence the amount of data that they may contain. Although there are no hard and fast limits, most packets range from 256 to 2,048 bytes.

Error Handling

Because no communication channel is error free, most packets include error-detection or error-correction information. The principle behind error-detection is simple: Include duplicate or redundant information that you can compare to the original. Because communication errors are random, they are unlikely to affect both of two copies of the transmitted data. Compare two copies sent along and if they do not match, you can be sure one of them changed during transmission and became corrupted.

Many communications systems don't rely on complex error-correction algorithms as are used in storage and high-quality memory systems. Communication systems have a luxury storage systems do not: They can get a second chance. If an error occurs in transmission, the system can try again—and again—until an error-free copy gets through.

As a function of communication protocol, packets are part of the software standard used by the communication system. Even so, they are essential to making the hardware—the entire communication system—work properly and reliably.

History

Nearly every serial communication system now uses packets of some kind. In retrospect, the idea of using packets seems natural, the logical way of organizing data. In fact, however, the concept of using packets as a method of reliably routing data through communication systems rates as an invention with a clear-cut history. The first inkling of the concept of packet-based communications dates back as early as 1960 when Paul Baran working at Rand Corporation conceived the idea of a redundant, packet-switched network. At the time, nothing came of the idea because the chief telecommunications supplier in the United States, AT&T, regarded a communication system or network based on packets as unbuildable. AT&T preferred switching signals throughout its vast network, a technology with which the company had become familiar after nearly a century of development.

In 1965, Donald Watts Davies, working at the British National Physics Laboratory, independently conceived the idea of packetized communications and it was he who coined the name "packet." Baran called them data blocks and his version of packet switching was "distributed adaptive message block switching." The direct ancestor of today's Internet, ARPAnet (see the next chapter), development of which began in 1966, is usually considered the first successful packetized communication system.

Universal Serial Bus

In 1995, three drawbacks of legacy serial ports nagged at PC developers. They were slow, fraught with interconnection difficulties, and constraining, allowing only one device for every port connector on the back of a PC. Determined to design a better interface, Compaq, Digital, IBM, Intel, Microsoft, NEC, and Northern Telecom pooled their efforts and laid the groundwork for the *Universal Serial Bus*—better known as USB. Later that year, they started the Universal Serial Bus Implementers Forum and in 1996 unveiled the new interface to the world.

Aimed at replacing both legacy serial and parallel port designs, the USB design corrected for all three of the shortcomings. To improve performance, it boasted a 12 mbits/sec data rate (with an alternative low-speed signaling rate of 1.5 mbits/sec). To eliminate wiring hassles and worries about connector gender, cross-over cables, and device types, they developed a strict wiring system with exactly one type of cable to serve all interconnection needs. And to allow one jack on the back of a PC to handle as many peripherals as necessary, they designed the system to accommodate up to 127 devices per port. In addition, they built in plug-and-play support so that every connection could be self-configuring. You could even hot-plug new devices and use them immediately without reloading your operating system.

The USB design also includes an optional power distribution function that allows a single connection to supply the electricity a peripheral needs along with the data connection. This feature makes possible lower-cost peripherals that need no power supply of their own.

It was a connection system to dream of. And for years, that's about all you could do. Although the first USB products were quick in coming—Key Tronic unveiled a USB keyboard in January 1997—the system was slow in taking off. By the beginning of 1999, the USB Implementers Forum was boasting that 100 USB devices were available, a tiny fraction of the number linking through legacy ports. In May 1999, one developer described the USB situation as simply a "mess."

Worse, even though the USB standard had not won wide acceptance, its successor was already in the works. In February 1999, work on the successor interface, USB 2.0, began.

Yet the port remains the industry's best hope at straightening out the confusion of connecting peripherals. By then, USB was an integral part of the Device Bay standard (see Chapter 26, "Cases") and was a recommended part of every new PC under the joint Intel/Microsoft PC 99 specifications. Despite the rocky beginnings, USB provides (or will provide) the basic mechanism for connecting most, if not all, peripherals to your PC. Everything from your keyboard to cash register drawer can connect simply and quickly with a USB plug, at least once the standard matures.

Background

Designed for those who would rather compute than worry about hardware, the premise underlying USB is the substitution of software intelligence for cabling confusion. USB handles all the issues involved in linking multiple devices with different capabilities and data rates with a layer cake of software. Along the way, it introduces its own, new technology and terminology.

USB divides serial hardware into two classes, hubs and functions. A USB *hub* provides jacks into which you can plug functions. A USB *function* is a device that actually does something. USB's designers imagined that a function may be anything that you can connect to your computer, including keyboards, mice, modems, printers, plotters, scanners, or whatever.

Rather than a simple point-to-point port, the USB acts as an actual bus that allows you to connect multiple peripherals to one jack on your PC with all of the linked devices sharing exactly the same signals. Information passes across the bus in the form of packets, and all functions receive all packets. Your PC accesses individual functions by adding a specific address to the packets, and only the function with the correct address acts on the packets addressed to it.

The physical manifestation of USB is a port, a jack on the back of your PC or in a hub. Although your PC's USB port can handle up to 127 devices, each physical USB port connects to a single device. To connect multiple devices, you need multiple jacks. Typically, a new PC comes equipped with two USB ports. When you need more, you add a *hub*, which offers multiple jacks to let you plug in several devices. You can plug one hub into another to provide several additional jacks and ports to connect more devices.

The USB design envisions a hierarchical system with hubs connected to hubs connected to hubs. In that each hub allows multiple connections, the reach of the USB system branches out like a tree—or a tree's roots. Figure 20.3 gives a conceptual view of the USB wiring system.

FIGURE 20.3

USB hierarchical inter-connection scheme.

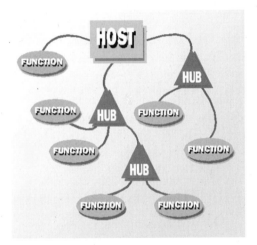

Your PC acts as the base hub for a USB system and is termed the *host*. The circuitry in your PC that controls this integral hub and the rest of the USB system is called the *bus controller*. Each USB system has one and only one bus controller.

The USB system doesn't care which device you plug into which hub or how many levels down the hub hierarchy you put a particular device. All the system requires is that you properly plug everything together following its simple rule—each device must plug into a hub—and the USB software sorts everything out. This software, making up the *USB protocol*, is the most complex part of the design. In comparison, the actual hardware is simple—but the hardware won't work without the protocol.

The wiring hardware imposes no limit on the number of devices and functions that you can connect in a USB system. You can plug hubs into hubs into hubs fanning out into as many ports as you like. You do face limits, however. The protocol limits the number of functions on one bus to 127 because of addressing limits. Seven bits are allowed for encoding function addresses, and one of the potential 128 is reserved.

Practical systems are unlikely to tap the full interconnection potential of USB. Although there's no theoretical reason that you cannot connect the full 127 devices, as a practical matter no one ever has successfully accomplished that feat (at least so far). The record number of devices connected to a single USB port is 101, made in a demonstration at Intel's Developer's Forum on September 14, 1998, in Palm Springs, CA.

In addition, the wiring limits the distance at which you can place functions from hubs. The maximum length of a USB cable is five meters. Because hubs can regenerate signals, however, your USB system can stretch out for greater distances by making multiple hops through hubs.

As part of the plug-and-play process, the USB controller goes on a device hunt when you start up your PC. It interrogates each device to find out what it is. It then builds a map that locates each device by hub and port number. These become part of the packet address. When the USB driver sends data out the port, it routes it to the proper device by this hub-and-port address.

Wiring with USB is, by design, trouble-free. Because all devices receive all signals, you face no issues of routing. Because each port has a single jack that accepts one and only one connector—and a connector of a specific matching type—you don't have to worry about adapters, cross-over cables or the other minutiae required to make old-style serial connections work.

On the other hand, USB requires specific software support. Any device with a USB connector will have the necessary firmware to handle USB built in. But your PC will also require software to make the USB system work. Your PC's operating system must know how to send the appropriate signals to its USB ports. In addition, each function must have a matching software driver. The function driver creates the commands or packages the data for its associated device. An overall USB driver acts as the delivery service, providing the channel—called in USB terminology a *pipe*—for routing the data to the various functions. Consequently, each USB you add to your PC requires software installation along with plugging in the hardware.

Connectors

The USB system involves four different styles of connectors, two chassis-mounted jacks and two plugs at the ends of cables. Each jack and plug comes in two varieties, A and B.

Hubs have *A jacks*. These are the primary outward manifestation of the USB port—the wide, thin USB slots you'll find on the back of your PC. The matching *A plug* attaches to the cable that leads to the USB device. In the purest form of USB, this cable is permanently affixed to the device and you need worry about no other plugs or jacks.

This configuration may someday become popular when manufacturers discover they can save the cost of a connector by integrating the cable. Unfortunately, too many manufacturers have discovered by putting a jack on their USB devices they save the cost of the cable by not including it with the device.

Universal Serial Bus

To accommodate devices with removable cables (and manufacturers that don't want to add the expense of a few feet of wire to their USB devices), the USB standard allows for a second, different style of plug and jack meant only to be used for inputs to USB devices. If a USB device (other than a hub) requires a connector so that, as a convenience, you can remove the cable, it uses a USB *B jack*, a small, nearly square hole into which you slide the mating *B plug*.

The motivation behind this multiplicity of connectors is to prevent rather than cause confusion. All USB cables will have an A plug at one end and a B plug at the other. One end must attach to a hub and the other to a device. You cannot inadvertently plug things together incorrectly.

Because all A jacks are outputs and all B jacks are inputs, only one form of detachable USB cable exists—one with an A plug at one end and a B plug at the other. No cross-over cables or adapters are needed for any USB wiring scheme.

Cable

The physical USB wiring uses a special four-wire cable. Two conductors in the cable transfer the data as a differential digital signal. That is, the voltage on the two conductors is of equal magnitude and opposite polarity so that when subtracted from one another (finding the difference) the result cancels out any noise that ordinarily would add equally to the signal on each line. In addition, the USB cable includes a power signal, nominally five volts DC, and a ground return. The power signal allows you to supply power for external serial devices through the USB cable.

The two data wires are twisted together as a pair. The power cables may or may not be.

To achieve its high data rate, the USB specification requires that certain physical characteristics of the cable be carefully controlled. Even so, the maximum length permitted any USB cable is five meters.

One limit on cable length is the inevitable voltage drop suffered by the power signal. All wires offer some resistance to electrical flow, and the resistance is proportional to the wire gauge. Hence, lower wire gauges (thicker wires) have lower resistance. Longer cables require lower wire gauges. At maximum length, the USB specification requires 20 gauge wire, which is one step (two gauge numbers) thinner than ordinary lamp cord.

The individual wires in the USB cable are color-coded. The data signals form a green-white pair, the +Data signal on green. The positive five-volt signal rides on the red wire. The ground wire is black. Table 20.2 outlines this color code.

TABLE 20.2   USB Cable Color Code

Signal	Color
+Data	Green
–Data	White
VCC	Red
Ground	Black

Normally, you cannot connect one PC to another using USB. The standard calls for only one USB controller in the entire interconnection system. Physically, the cabling system prevents you from making such a connection. Some people have reported seeing cables with A plugs on each end, a design not only prohibited by the USB specification but also guaranteed to back the port circuitry of your PC.

The exception to this rule is the LapLink *purple cable* developed and sold by Traveling Software. In addition to having A plugs on each end, it has a lump in the middle, akin a snake that's gorged itself on a cow. The bulge hides a secret; it contains active circuitry that buffers the connection and translates the communications to allow one of the two connected PCs to appear like an ordinary USB device rather than a host. Getting such a connection to work requires additional software which, hardly coincidentally, Traveling Software sells.

Software Support

Most new PCs have one or more USB ports built in. To use the port, hardware is not enough, however. It also requires software support, which usually takes the form of one or more drivers for your operating system. Windows 98 and Windows 2000 have built-in support for USB. The original release of Windows 95 did not. Versions 4.00950B or later of Windows 95 do include support that will allow the use of USB. Windows NT 4.0 and earlier NT versions have no intrinsic USB support, and no add-on drivers are available to add it. To use USB with NT, you must upgrade to Windows 2000.

Note that the later versions of Windows 95 that are capable of using USB also require Microsoft's USB Supplement to make the interface functional. (Earlier versions of Windows 95 do not support USB even with the supplement.) Even the supplement has suffered teething pains. Early versions—specifically 4.03.1212—don't work at all and may not even initialize the USB ports in some PCs. You need version 4.03.1214 or newer to make USB work.

If you've already installed USB Supplement 4.03.1212, you cannot simply replace it with version 4.03.1214. The old version makes changes to your system's Registry that the new version cannot deal with. You must delete three entries from your Registry before installing the new supplement version. The entries you must delete include the following:

```
hkey_local_machine\enum\root\usb

hkey_local_machine\enum\usb

hkey_local_machine\enum\system\currentcontrolset\services\class\usb
```

Data Coding

To help ensure the integrity of the high-speed data signal, the USB system uses a combination of NRZI data encoding and bit stuffing. NRZI coding (Inverse No Return to Zero) uses a change in signal during a given period to indicate a logical zero and no change in a period to indicate a logical one. Figure 20.4 illustrates the NRZI translation scheme. Note that a zero in the code stream triggers each transition in the resulting NRZI code. A continuous stream of logical zeros results in an on-off pattern of voltages on the signal wires, essentially a square wave.

FIGURE 20.4
NRZI coding scheme used by USB.

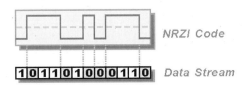

The NRZI signal is useful because it is self-clocking. That is, it allows the receiving system to regenerate the clock directly from the signal. For example, the square wave of a stream of zeros acts as the clock signal. The receiver adjusts its timing to fit this interval. It keeps timing even when a logical one in the signal results in no transition. When a new transition occurs, the timer resets itself, making whatever small adjustment might be necessary to compensate for timing differences at the sending and receiving end.

Ordinarily, a continuous stream of logical ones would result in a constant voltage, an extended stream without transitions. If the length of such a series of logical ones were long enough, the sending and receiving clocks in the system might wander and lose their synchronicity. *Bit stuffing* helps keep the connection in sync.

The bit stuffing technique used by the USB system injects a zero after every continuous stream of six logical ones. Consequently, a transition is guaranteed to occur at least every seven clock cycles. When the receiver detects a lack of transitions for six cycles and then receives the transition of the seven, it can reset its timer. It also discards the stuffed bit and counts the transition (or lack of it) occurring at the next clock cycle to be the next data bit.

Protocol

As with all more recent interface introductions, the USB design uses a packet-based protocol.

All message exchanges require the exchange of three packets. The exchange begins with the host sending out a *token packet*. The token packet bears the address of the device meant to participate in the exchange as well as control information that describes the nature of the exchange. A *data packet* holds the actual information that is to be exchanged. Depending on the type of transfer, either the host or the device will send out the data packet. Despite the name, the data packet may contain no information. The exchange ends with a *handshake packet*, which acknowledges the receipt of the data or other successful completion of the exchange. A fourth type of packet, called special, handles additional functions.

All packets must start with two components, a sync field and a packet identification. Each of these components is one byte long.

The *sync field* is a series of bits that produce a dense string of pulse transitions using the NRZI encoding scheme required by the USB standard. These pulses serve as a consistent burst of clock pulses that allow all the devices connected to the USB bus to reset their timing and synchronize themselves to the host. As encoded, the sync field appears as three on/off pulses followed by a marker two pulses wide. The raw data before encoding takes the value 00000001(Binary), although the data is meaningless because it is never decoded.

The *packet identifier* byte includes four bits to define the nature of the packet itself and another four bits as check bits that confirm the accuracy of the first four. Rather than a simple repetition, the check bits take the form of a one's complement of the actual identification bits (every zero is translated into a one). The four bits provides a code that allows the definition of 16 different kinds of packets.

USB uses the 16 values in a two-step hierarchy. The two more significant bits specify one of the four types of packets. The two lesser significant bits subdivide the packet category. Table 20.3 lists the PIDs of the four basic USB packet types.

TABLE 20.3   USB Packet Identifications

Bit-Pattern	Packet Type
XX00XX11	Special packet
XX01XX10	Token packet
XX10XX01	Handshake packet
XX11XX00	Data packet

Token Packets

Only the USB host sends out token packets. Each token packet takes up four bytes, which are divided into five functional parts. Figure 20.5 graphically shows the layout of a token packet.

FIGURE 20.5

Functional parts of a USB token packet.

The two bytes take the standard form of all USB packets. The first byte is a sync field that marks the beginning of the token's bit stream. The second byte is the *packet identification*.

The PID byte defines four types of token packet. These include an out packet that carries data from the host to a device; an in packet that carries data from the device to the host; a setup packet that targets a specific endpoint; and a start of frame packet that helps synchronize the system. Table 20.4 matches the PID code with the token packet type.

TABLE 20.4 Token Packet Types

Packet Identification Byte	Token Packet Type
00011110	Out
01011010	Start of Frame (SOF)
10010110	In
11010010	Setup

For in, out, and setup token packets, the seven bits following the PID encode the *address field*, which identifies the device that the host wants to command or send data. Four additional bits supply a *endpoint* number. An endpoint is an individually addressable section of a USB function. Endpoints give hardware designers the flexibility to divide a single device into logically separate units. For example, a keyboard with an built-in trackball might have one overall address to act as a single USB function. Assigning individual endpoints to the keyboard section and the trackball section allows device designers to individually address each part of the overall keyboard.

Start of frame packets differ from other USB packets in that they are broadcast. All devices receive and decode but do not acknowledge them. The 11 bits that would otherwise make up the address and endpoint fields indicate a frame number. The host sends out one start of frame packet each millisecond, as the name suggests, defining the beginning of the USB's one-millisecond frame. The host assigns frame numbers incrementally, starting with zero and adding one for each subsequent frame. When it reaches the maximum

11-bit value (3,072 in decimal), it starts over from zero. Figure 20.6 graphically illustrates a start of frame packet.

FIGURE 20.6

Constituents of a USB start of frame form of token packet.

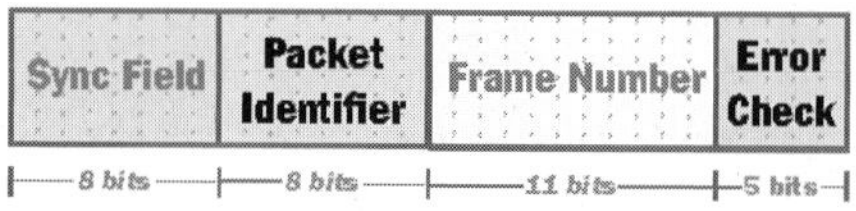

Sync Field	Packet Identifier	Frame Number	Error Check
8 bits	8 bits	11 bits	5 bits

All token packets end with five bits of cyclic redundancy check information. The CRC data provides an integrity check of the address field and endpoint. It does not cover the PID, which has its own, built-in error correction.

Data Packets

The actual information transferred through the USB system takes the form of data packets.

As with all USB packets, a data packet begins with a one-byte sync field followed by the packet identification. The actual data follows as a sequence of zero to 1,023 bytes. A two-byte cyclic redundancy check verifies the accuracy of only the data field. The PID field relies on its own redundancy check mechanism. Figure 20.7 graphically illustrates a USB data packet.

FIGURE 20.7

Constituents of a USB data packet.

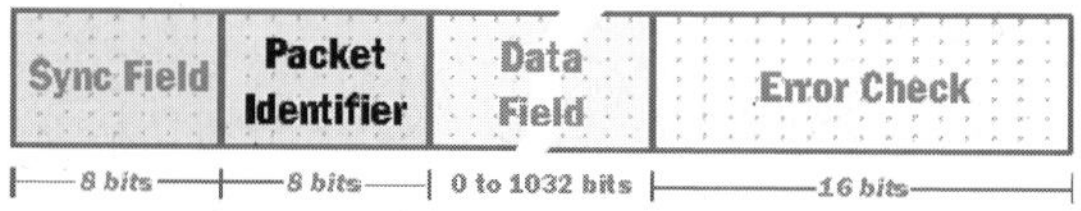

Sync Field	Packet Identifier	Data Field	Error Check
8 bits	8 bits	0 to 1032 bits	16 bits

The PID field ostensibly defines two types of data packets, Data 0 and Data 1. Table 20.5 lists the coding applied to these packets. Functionally, however, the two data types (and hence the PIDs) form an additional error-checking system between the data transmitter and receiver. The transmitter toggles between Data 0 and Data 1 to indicate that it has received a valid acknowledgment of the receipt of the preceding data packet. In other words, it confirms the confirmation.

TABLE 20.5   USB Data Packet Types

Packet Identification	Data Packet Type
00110011	Data 0
10110010	Data 1

For example, the transmitter sends out a data packet of the type Data 0. After the receiver successfully decodes the packet, it sends an acknowledgment signal back to the transmitter in the form of a handshake packet. If the transmitter successfully receives and decodes the acknowledgment, the next data packet it sends will be Data 1. From this change in data packet type, the receiver knows that its acknowledgment was properly received.

Handshake Packets

Handshake packets are two bytes long, comprising a sync field and a packet identification. Figure 20.8 graphically illustrates a USB handshake packet.

FIGURE 20.8

Constituents of a USB handshake packet.

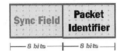

USB 2.0

On February 23, 1999, a new group led by Compaq, Hewlett-Packard, Intel, Lucent, Microsoft, NEC, and Philips announced it had begun development of a revised USB standard, version 2.0.

The key change is an increase in performance, upping speed from 12 mbits/sec to 120 to 240 mbits/sec. The new system will incorporate all the protocols of the old and is expected to be fully backward compatible. Devices will negotiate the highest common speed and use it for their transfers. Connectors and cabling will likely remain unchanged.

Because new chipsets supporting the higher speed likely would be no more expensive than current chips, the increased performance of USB 2.0 will come essentially free. The developers expect most PC makers to move to the new standard as it becomes available, probably in the year 2000.

At the time of the announcement of the new version, its developers hoped to have a preliminary specification prepared and posted at the USB Web site by the end of 1999.

Standard

The USB standard is maintained by the USB Implementers Forum, which can be reached at the following address:

> USB Implementers Forum
> 5440 SW Westgate Dr.
> Suite 217
> Portland, OR 97221
> Phone: 503-296-9892
> Fax: 503-297-1090

You can download a complete copy of the current version of the specifications from the USB Web site at www.usb.org.

IEEE 1394

Also known as FireWire and I.link and DV, IEEE 1394 is a serial interface that's aimed at high-throughput devices such as hard disk and tape drives as well as consumer-level multimedia devices such as digital camcorders, digital VCRs, and digital televisions. Originally, it was conceived as a general-purpose interface suitable for replacing legacy serial ports but with blazing speed. In other words, it appeared destined for the same applications as USB. With the passage of time, however, the interface has been repositioned to complement USB. Where USB takes the low road, IEEE 1394 takes the high—that is, the high-speed route.

For the most part, IEEE 1394 is a hardware interface. It specifies speeds, timing, and a connection system. The software side is based on SCSI. In fact, IEEE 1394 is one of the several hardware interfaces included in the SCSI-3 standards.

One IEEE 1394 port holds the potential of linking all the high-speed devices your PC normally needs, linking up to 16 peripherals. Easier to plug together than ordinary stereo components, IEEE 1394 eliminates the wiring confusion that scares technophobes from trying and using computer technology. If you can manage plugging your PC into a wall outlet, you can connect up the most elaborate multimedia system. In short, IEEE 1394 is key to pushing computing technology into home and everyday entertainment.

Although as FireWire the interface has found some acceptance among users of the Apple Macintosh computer, acceptance of the IEEE 1394 connection among PC people—users or designers—has been slow in coming. At a networking conference in early 1999, the general consensus was that IEEE 1394 makes a splendid connection for digital video but offers no unique benefit for mass storage devices. On the other hand, the promoters of Device Bay (see Chapter 26) have adopted IEEE 1394 for high-speed transfers. Although current Microsoft operating systems offer no integral support for IEEE 1394, both Service Pack 1 for Windows 98 and the initial release of Windows 2000 will support the OpenHCI implementation of IEEE 1394. On the other hand, Intel, which had once promised IEEE 1394 support in its chipsets, has quietly backpedaled and announced its latest chipsets will not include integral IEEE 1394 support.

Background

Development of the new standard began more than a decade ago when the IEEE (Institute of Electrical and Electronic Engineers) assigned a study group the task of clearing the murk of thickening morass of serial standards in September 1986. Hardly four months later (in January 1987), the group had already outlined the basic concepts underlying IEEE 1394, some of which still survive in today's standard—including low cost, a simplified wiring scheme, and arbitrated signals supporting multiple devices. Getting the devil out of such details as operating speed and the technologies needed to achieve it took years as needs, visions, and visionaries changed. Consensus on the major elements of the standard—including the connector and the bus management—came only in 1993, and the standard reached final form in late 1994. Achieving its worthy goals required four break-through new technologies, including a novel encoding system that made high speed safe for serial data, a self-configuration system that moved the headaches of setup from users to the port circuitry, a time-based arbitration system that guarantees all of the many devices linked to a single port all have fair and guaranteed access, and a means of deliver-ing time-critical data such as video without affecting the transfer of serial data.

IEEE 1394 truly offers something for everyone—today's relatively skilled PC user, tomor-row's casual home user, and even machine makers.

The key to the power of IEEE 1394 is speed. The initial design of IEEE 1394 sets up a 100 mbits/sec data transfer protocol. In addition, the initial standard defined two higher-speed data rates for future upgrades, 200 and 400 mbits/sec. Revisions have pushed that rate to 800 mbit/sec, and new proposals promise to extend the port's capabilities to 3200 mbits/sec. For manufacturers, the cost of IEEE 1394 may prove most alluring. IEEE 1394 has the potential of reducing the cost of external connections to PCs both in terms of money spent and panel usage. Both of these savings originate in the design of the IEEE 1394 connector. IEEE 1394 envisions a single six-wire plastic connector replacing most if not all of the standard port connectors on a PC. As with today's SCSI, one IEEE 1394 port on a PC allows you to connect multiple devices, up to 16 in current form.

The connector itself will cost manufacturers a few cents, but the connectors alone for a RS-232 port can cost several dollars (and that can be a significant portion of the price of a peripheral or even PC). Moreover, a standard serial connector—that 25-pin D-shell con-nector—by itself is much too large for today's miniaturized systems. For example, the old-fashioned serial connector is too large to fit on a PC Card.

As less skilled people start tinkering with PCs and try linking them into multimedia sys-tems, the simplified setup and wiring of IEEE 1394 should earn their praises. Today's high-performance interface choice, SCSI, is about as friendly as a hungry bear awakened from hibernation. Although backed by strong technology, SCSI is a confusion of connec-tors, cables, terminators, and ID numbers. Wise folks find the best strategy is to stay out of the way. Where cabling a SCSI system means following rules more obscure than those of a fantasy adventure game, IEEE 1394 has exactly one wiring requirement: All IEEE 1394 devices in a system must connect together without loops. There are no terminations to worry about, no different cable types such as straight-through and cross-over, no cable length concerns, no identification numbers, and no connector genders to change. You simply plug one end of an IEEE 1394 cable into a jack on the back of the two devices you want to link. Most IEEE 1394s will have two or three jacks, so you can wire together elaborate webs. As long as no more than one circuit runs between any two IEEE 1394 devices, the system will work. It's even easier than a stereo system because there are no worries about input and output jacks.

Down deeper, however, IEEE 1394 is more complex. Instead of simply converting the PC's parallel data into a serial format, IEEE 1394 is a complex communication system with its own transfer protocol requiring new application-specific integrated circuits. Although those initially will be expensive—an estimated $15 per IEEE 1394 device— throughout the history of PCs, the cost of standard silicon circuits has plummeted while the cost of connectors continued to climb. Moreover, the current cost isn't entirely out of line with today's serial technology, where a 16550AFN UART alone can cost $5 to $10. Just as the electrically more complex AT interface replaced older interfaces for hard disks, IEEE 1394 stands to step in place of the serial port.

Performance

For today's PC users, speed is the probably the most important aspect of IEEE 1394. Serial connections exchange simplicity for the constraints of moving one bit at a time through a narrow data channel. For example, the legacy serial port on your PC tops out at 115,200 bits per second. Although the top rate is set by the timebase design of the original IBM PC of 1981, electrical issues such as interference and wire capacitance constrain RS232 transmissions to substantially slow data rates on longer connections.

In contrast, IEEE 1394 *started* with a raw data rate of 100 megabits per second and pushed upward from there. The Device Bay implementation of the connection standard requires a minimum speed of 800 mbits/sec. Current work aims at extending the standard up to 3,200 mbits/sec.

Although IEEE 1394 imposes substantial software overhead because of its packet-based nature and the need for addressing and arbitration, it still offers enough bandwidth to carry three simultaneous video signals or 167 CD-quality audio signals at its base 100 mbits/sec rate. In current form, it allows hard disks to match the 10 MB/sec transfer rate of Fast SCSI-2 connections.

Timing

Reliability is a problem with any high-speed circuit, and the designers of IEEE 1394 faced a formidable challenge. More than does any comedian, IEEE 1394 depends on precise timing. The meaning of each bit in a transmission depends on when the bit gets regis-tered. At the high data rates of IEEE 1394, signal jitter becomes a major problem. Each bit must be defined to fit precisely into a frame 10 billionths of a second long; the slight-est timing error can cause an error. In designing IEEE 1394, engineers tried elaborate coding schemes to eliminate jitter problems. In the end, they created an entirely new sig-naling system.

To minimize noise, data connections in IEEE 1394 use differential signals. Legacy serial ports use single-ended signals. One wire carries the data, and the ground connection serves as the return path. Differential signaling uses two wires that carry the same signal but of different polarities. Receiving equipment subtracts the signal on one wire from that on the other to find the data as the difference between the two signals. The benefit of this scheme is that any noise gets picked up by the wires equally. When the receiving equipment subtracts the signals on the two wires, the noise gets eliminated; the equal noise signals subtracted from each other equal zero.

IEEE 1394 goes further, using *two* differential wire pairs. One pair carries the actual data; the second pair, called the strobe lines, complements the state of the data pair so that one and only one of the pairs changes polarity every clock cycle. For example, if the data line carries two sequential bits of the same value, the strobe line reverses polarity to mark the transition between them. If a sequence of two bits changes the polarity of the data lines (a one followed by a zero or zero followed by a one), the strobe line does not change polarity. Summing the data and strobe lines together exactly reconstructs the clock signal of the sending system, allowing the sending and receiving devices to precisely lock up.

Setup

Similar to the SCSI parallel interface, IEEE 1394 allows you to connect multiple devices together and uses an addressing system so the signals sent through a common channel are recognized only by the proper target device. The linked devices can independently communicate among themselves without the intervention of your PC.

To communicate, however, devices must be able to identify one another. Providing proper ID has been one of the recurring problems with SCSI, requiring you to set switches on every SCSI device and then indicate your choices when configuring software. IEEE 1394 eliminates such concerns with its own automated configuration process.

Whenever a new device gets plugged into an IEEE 1394 system (or when the whole system gets turned on), it starts its automatic configuration process. By signaling through the various connections, each device determines how it fits into the system, either as a root node, a branch, or a leaf. Each IEEE 1394 system has only one root, which is the foundation around which the rest of the system organizes itself. The node also sends out a special clock signal. IEEE 1394 devices with only one connection are leaves; those that link to multiple devices are branches. Once the connection hierarchy is set up, the IEEE 1394 devices determine their own ID numbers from their locations in the hierarchy and send identifying information (ID and device type) to their host.

Arbitration

IEEE 1394 also relies on timing for its arbitration system. As with a SCSI, USB, or network connection, IEEE 1394 transfers data in packets, a block of data preceded by header that specifies where the data goes and its priority. In the basic cable-based IEEE 1394 system, each device sharing a connection gets a chance to send one packet in an arbitration period that's called a fairness interval. The various devices take turns until all have had a chance to use the bus. After each packet gets sent, a brief time called the *subaction gap* elapses, after which another device can send its packet. If no device starts to transmit when the subaction gap ends, all devices wait a bit longer, stretching the time to an arbitration reset gap. After that time elapses, a new fairness interval begins, and all devices get to send one more packet. The cycle continues.

To handle devices that need a constant stream of data for real-time display, such as video or audio signals, IEEE 1394 uses a special isochronous mode. Every 125 microseconds, one device in the IEEE 1394 that needs isochronous data sends out a special timing packet that signals isochronous devices can transmit. Each takes a turn in order of its priority, leaving a brief isochronous gap delay between their packets. When the isochronous gap delay stretches out to the subaction gap length, the devices using ordinary asynchronous transfers take over until the end of the 125-microsecond cycle when the next isochronous period begins.

The scheme guarantees that video and audio gear can move its data in real-time with a minimum of buffer memory. (Audio devices require only a byte of buffer; video may need as many as six bytes!) The 125-microsecond period matches the sampling rate used by digital telephone systems to help IEEE 1394 mesh with ISDN (Integrated Service Digital Network) telephone systems. (As IEEE 1394 was being developed, engineers were optimistic about ISDN and wary of ADSL.)

For manufacturers, the cost of IEEE 1394 may prove most alluring. IEEE 1394 has the potential of reducing the cost of external connections to PCs both in terms of money spent and panel usage. Both of these savings originate in the design of the IEEE 1394 connector. IEEE 1394 envisions a single six-wire plastic connector replacing most if not all of the standard port connectors on a PC. As with today's SCSI, one IEEE 1394 port on a PC allows you to connect multiple devices, up to 16 in current form.

The connector itself will cost manufacturers a few cents, but the connectors alone for a RS-232 port can cost several dollars (and that can be a significant portion of the price of a peripheral or even PC). Moreover, a standard serial connector—that 25-pin D-shell connector—by itself is much too large for today's miniaturized systems. It can't fit a PCMCIA card by any stretch of the imagination.

Down deeper, however, IEEE 1394 is more complex. Instead of simply needing an UART, IEEE 1394 is a complex communication system with its own transfer protocol requiring new application-specific integrated circuits. Although those initially will be expensive—an estimated $15 per IEEE 1394 device—throughout the history of PCs, the cost of standard silicon circuits has plummeted while the cost of connectors continued to climb. Moreover, the current cost isn't entirely out of line with today's serial technology, where a 16550AFN UART alone can cost $5 to $10. Just as the electrically more complex AT interface replaced older interfaces for hard disks, IEEE 1394 stands to step in place of the serial port.

Similar to the SCSI parallel interface, IEEE 1394 allows you to connect multiple devices together and uses an addressing system so the signals sent through a common channel are recognized only by the proper target device. The linked devices can independently communicate among themselves without the intervention of your PC.

Architecture

IEEE 1394 is a true architecture that is built from several layers, each of which defines one aspect of the serial connection. These layers include a bus-management layer, a transaction layer, a link layer, and a physical layer.

Bus-Management Layer

The bus-management layer of the IEEE 1394 standard defines the basic control functions as well as the control and status registers required by connected devices to operate their ports. This layer handles channel assignments, arbitration, mastering, and errors.

Transaction Layer

The protocol that governs transactions across the IEEE 1394 connection is called the transaction layer. That is, this layer mediates the read and write operations. To match modern PCs, the transaction layer is optimized to work with 32-bit double words, although the standard also allows block operations of variable length. This operation of this layer was derived from the IEEE 1212 parallel data-transfer standard.

Link Layer

The logical controls on the data across the IEEE 1394 wire is the link layer, making the transfer for the transaction layer. Communications are half-duplex transfers, but the link layer provides a confirmation of the reception of data. Double-word transfers are favored, but the link layer also permits exchanges in variable-length blocks.

Physical Layer

The actual physical connections made by IEEE 1394 are governed by the physical layer. This part of the standard includes both a protocol and the medium itself. The physical protocol sublayer controls access to the connection with full arbitration. The physical medium sublayer comprises the cable and connectors.

The IEEE 1394 wiring standard allows for up to 32 hops of 4.5 meters (about 15 feet) each. As with current communications ports, the standard allows you to connect and disconnect peripherals without switching off power to them. You can daisy-chain IEEE 1394 devices or branch the cable between them. When you make changes, the network of connected devices will automatically reconfigure itself to reflect the alterations.

Cabling

In initial form, the physical part of IEEE 1394 will be copper wires. The standard cable is a complex weaving of six conductors. Data will travel down two shielded twisted-pairs of AWG 28 gauge wire with a nominal impedance of 110 ohms. In addition, two AWG 22 gauge wires carry power at 8 to 40 volts with sufficient current to power a number of peripherals. Another shield will cover the entire collection of conductors. A small, six-pin connector will link PCs and peripherals to this cable. Figure 20.9 shows this connector.

FIGURE 20.9
*An IEEE 1394
connector.*

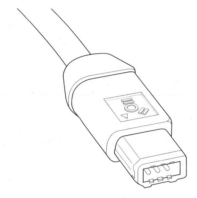

The IEEE 1394 wiring scheme depends on each of the devices that are connected together to relay signals to the others. Pulling the plug to one device could potentially knock down the entire connection system. To avoid such difficulties and dependencies, IEEE 1394 uses its power connections to keep in operation the interface circuitry in otherwise inactive devices. These power lines could also supply enough current to run entire devices. No device may draw more than 3 watts from the IEEE 1394 bus, although a single device may supply up to 40 watts. The IEEE 1394 circuitry itself in each interface requires only about 2 milliwatts.

IrDA

The one thing you don't want with a portable PC is a cable to tether you down, yet most of the time you have to plug into one thing or another. Even a simple and routine chore such as downloading files from your notebook machine into your desktop PC gets tangled in cable trouble. Not only do you have to plug in both ends, reaching behind your desktop machine only a little more elegantly than fishing into a catch basin for a fallen quarter—and, more likely than not, unplugging something else that you'll inevitably need later only to discover the dangling cord—but also you've got to tote that writhing cable along with you wherever you go. There has to be a better way.

There is. You can link your PC to other systems and components with a light beam. On the rear panel of many notebook PCs, you'll find a clear LED or a dark red window through which your system can send and receive invisible infrared light beams. Although originally introduced to allow you to link portable PCs to desktop machines, the same technology can tie in peripherals such as modems and printers, all without the hassle of plugging and unplugging cables.

History

On June 28, 1993, a group of about 120 representatives from 50 computer-related companies got together to take the first step in cutting the cord. Creating what has come to be known as the *Infrared Developers Association*, or IrDA, they aimed at more than making your PC more convenient to carry. They also saw a new versatility and, hardly incidentally, a way to trim their own costs.

The idea behind the get-together was to create a standard for using infrared light to link your PC to peripherals and other systems. The technology had already been long established, not only in television remote controls but also in a number of notebook PCs already in the market. Rather than build a new technology, the goal of the group was to find common ground, a standard so that the products of all manufacturers could communicate with the computer equivalent of sign language.

Hardly a year later on June 30, 1994, the group approved its first standard. The original specification, now known as IrDA version 1.0, essentially gave the standard RS-232C port an optical counterpart, one with the same data structure and, alas, speed limit. In August 1995, IrDA took the next step and approved high-speed extensions that pushed the wireless data rate to four megabits per second.

Overview

More than a gimmicky cordless keyboard, IrDA holds an advantage that makes computer manufacturers—particularly those developing low-cost machines—eye it with interest. It can cut several dollars from the cost of a complex system by eliminating some expensive hardware, a connector or two and a cable. Compared to the other wireless technology, radio, infrared requires less space because it needs only a tiny LED instead of a larger and costlier antenna. Moreover, infrared transmissions are not regulated by the FCC as are radio transmissions. Nor do they cause interference to radios, televisions, pacemakers, and airliners. The range of infrared is more limited than radio and restricted to line-of-sight over a narrow angle. However, these weaknesses can become strengths for those who are security conscious.

The original design formulated by IrDA was for a replacement for serial cables. The link was envisioned as a half-duplex system. Although communications would go in both directions, only one end of the conversation sends out data at any given time.

To make the technology easy and inexpensive to implement with existing components, it was based on the standard RS-232C port and its constituent components, such as UARTs. The original IrDA standard called for asynchronous communication using the same data frame as RS-232C and the most popular UART data rates from 2,400 to 115,200 bits per second.

To keep power needs low and prevent interference among multiple installations in a single room, IrDA kept the range of the system low. The expected separation between devices using IrDA signals to communicate was about one meter (three feet). Some links are reliable to two meters.

Similarly, the IrDA system concentrates the infrared beam used to carry data because diffusing the beam would require more power for a given range and be prone to causing greater interference among competing units. The laser diodes used in the IrDA system consequently focus their beams into a cone with a spread of about 30 degrees.

After the initial serial-port replacement design was in place, IrDA worked to make its interface suitable for replacing parallel ports as well. That goal lead to the creation of the IrDA high-speed standards for transmissions at data rates of 0.576, 1.152, and 4.0 megabits per second. The two higher speeds use a packet-based synchronous system that requires a special hardware-based communication controller. This controller monitors and controls the flow of information between the host computer's bus and communications buffers.

A watershed of differences separate low-speed and high-speed IrDA systems. Although IrDA designed the high-speed standard to be backward compatible with old equipment, making the higher speeds work requires special hardware. In other words, although high-speed IrDA devices can successfully communicate with lower-speed units, such communications are constrained to the speeds of the lower-speed units. Low-speed units cannot operate at high speeds without upgrading their hardware.

IrDA defines not only the hardware but also the data format used by its system. The group has published six standards to cover these aspects of IrDA communications. The hardware itself forms the *physical layer*. In addition, IrDA defines a *link access protocol* termed IrLAP and a *link management protocol* called IrLMP that describe the data formats used to negotiate and maintain communications. All IrDA ports must follow these standards. In addition, IrDA has defined an optional *transport protocol* and optional *plug-and-play* extensions to allow the smooth integration of the system into modern PCs. The group's IrCOMM standard describes a standard way for infrared ports to emulate conventional PC serial and parallel ports.

Physical Layer

The physical layer of the IrDA system encompasses the actual hardware and transmission method. Compared to other serial technologies, the hardware you need for an IrDA port would appear to be immaterial. After all, it *is* wireless. However, your PC still needs a port capable of sending and receiving invisible light beams.

A growing number of notebook computers have built-in IrDA facilities. In fact, IrDA is one of the more important features to look for in a new notebook computers.

Desktop machines are another matter. The IrDA wave hasn't yet struck them. Fortunately, you can add an IrDA port as easily as plugging in any serial cable. For example, the Adaptec AirPort plugs into a serial port and gives you an optical eye to send and receive IrDA signals.

The AirPort is only the first generation of IrDA accessories for desktops. By its nature, it is limited to standard serial port speeds. After all, it can't run faster than the signals coming to it. IrDA ports that take advantage of the newer, higher speeds will require direct connection to your PC's expansion bus (or a more advanced serial port such as the Universal Serial Bus, discussed earlier).

In any case, the optical signals themselves form what the IrDA calls the physical layer of the system. IrDA precisely defines the nature of these signals.

Infrared Light

Infrared light is invisible electromagnetic radiation that has a wavelength longer than that of visible light. Where you can see light that ranges in wavelength from 400 Angstroms (deep violet) to 700 Angstroms (dark red), infrared stretches from 700 Angstroms to 1,000 or more. IrDA specifies that the infrared signal used by PCs for communication have a wavelength between 850 and 900 Angstroms.

Data Rates

All IrDA ports must be able to operate at one basic speed, 9,600 bits per second. All other speeds are optional.

The IrDA specification allows for all the usual speed increments used by conventional serial ports from 2,400 bps to 115,200 bps. All of these speeds use the default modulation scheme, Return-to-Zero Invert (RZI). High-speed IrDA version 1.1 adds three additional speeds, 576 kbps, 1.152 mbps, and 4.0 mbps.

No matter the speed range implemented by a system or used for communications, IrDA devices first establish communications at the mandatory 9,600 bps speed using the link access protocol. Once the two devices establish a common speed for communicating, they switch to it and use it for the balance of their transmissions.

Pulse Width

The infrared cell of an IrDA transmitter sends out its data in pulses. Unlike the electronic logic signals inside your PC, which are assumed to remain relatively constant throughout a clock interval, the IrDA pulses last only a fraction of the basic clock period or bit cell. The relatively wide spacing between pulses makes each pulse easier for the optical receiver to distinguish.

At speeds up to and including 115,200 bits per second, each infrared pulse must be at least 1.41 microseconds long. Each IrDA data pulse nominally lasts just 3/16th of the length of a bit cell, although pulse widths a bit more than 10 percent greater remain acceptable. For example, each bit cell of a 9,600 bps signal would occupy 104.2 microseconds (that is, one second divided by 9,600). A typical IrDA pulse at that data rate would last 3/16th that period or 19.53 microseconds.

At higher speeds, the pulse minima are substantially shorter, ranging from 295.2 nanosecond at 576 kbps to only 115 nanoseconds at 4.0 mbps. At these higher speeds, the nominal pulse width is one quarter of the character cell. For example, at 4.0 mbits/sec, each pulse is only 125 nanoseconds long. Again, pulses about 10 percent longer remain permissible. Table 20.6 summarizes the speeds and pulse lengths.

TABLE 20.6 IrDA Speeds and Modulation

Signaling Rate	Modulation	Pulse Duration
2.4 kbits/sec	RZI	78.13 µs
9.6 kbits/sec	RZI	19.53 µs
19.2 kbits/sec	RZI	9.77 µs
38.4 kbits/sec	RZI	4.88 µs
57.6 kbits/sec	RZI	3.26 µs
115.2 kbits/sec	RZI	1.63 µs
0.576 mbits/sec	RZI	434.0 ns
1.152 mbits/sec	RZI	217.0 ns
4.0 mbits/sec	4PPM, single pulse	125 ns
4.0 mbits/sec	4PPM, double pulse	250.0 ns

Modulation

Depending on the speed at which a link operates, it may use one of two forms of modulation. At speeds lower than 4.0 mbits/sec, the system employs *Return-to-Zero Invert* (RZI) modulation. Actually, RZI is just a fancy way of describing a simple process. Each pulse represents a logical zero in the data stream. A logical one gets no infrared pulse. Figure 20.10 shows the relation between the original digital code, the equivalent electrical logic signal, and the corresponding IrDA pulses.

FIGURE 20.10
Relationship between original code and the IrDA pulses.

IrDA Pulses

Logic Level

`0 1 0 0 1 1 1 0` *Original Code*

At the 4.0 mbits/sec data rate, the IrDA system shifts to *pulse position modulation*. Because the IrDA system involves four discrete pulse positions, it is abbreviated 4PPM.

Pulse position modulation uses the temporal position of a pulse within a clock period to indicate a discrete value. In the case of IrDA's 4PPM, the length of one clock period is termed the *symbol duration* and is divided into four equal segments termed *chips*. A pulse can occur in one and only one of these chip segments, and which chip the pulse appears in—its position inside the symbol duration or clock period—encodes its value. For example, the four chips may be numbered 0, 1, 2, and 3. If the pulse appears in chip 2, it carries a value 2 (in binary, that's 10). Figure 20.11 shows the pulse position for the four valid code values under IrDA at 4.0 mbps/sec.

FIGURE 20.11
Pulse positions for the four valid code values of 4PPM under IrDA.

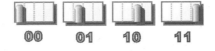

00   01   10   11

The IrDA system uses group coding under 4PPM. Each discrete pulse in one of the four possible positions indicates one of four two-bit patterns. Each pulse in the IrDA 4PPM system thus encodes two bits of data and four clock periods suffice for the transfer of a full byte of data. Table 20.7 lists the correspondence between pulse position and bit-patterns for IrDA's 4PPM.

TABLE 20.7 Data to Symbol Translation for IrDA 4PPM Code

Data Bit Pair	4PPM Symbol
00	1000
01	0100
10	0010
11	0001

IrDA requires data to be transmitted only in 8-bit format. In terms of conventional serial port parameters, a data frame for IrDA comprises a start bit, 8 data bits, no parity bits, and a stop bit for a total of 10 bits per character. Note, however, that zero insertion may increase the length of a transmission, although any inserted zeroes are removed automatically by the receiver and do not enter the data stream. No matter the form of modulation used by the IrDA system, all byte values are transmitted the least significant bit first.

Bit Stuffing

Note that with RZI modulation, a long sequence of logical ones will suppress pulses for the entire duration of the sequence. For example, a sequence of the byte value 0FF(Hex) will include no infrared pulses. If this suppression extends for a long enough period during synchronous communication, the clocks in the transmitter and receiver may become unsynchronized. To prevent the loss of sync, moderate-speed IrDA systems use a technique called *bit stuffing*.

Moderate-speed IrDA systems operate synchronously using long data frames that are self-clocking. To avoid long periods without pulses, these systems rely on *bit stuffing*. After a predetermined number of logical ones appear in the data stream, the system automatically inserts a logical zero. The zero adds a pulse that allows the transmitter and receiver to synchronize their clocks. When it detects an extended period without pulses, the receiver automatically removes the extraneous stuffed pulse from the data stream.

Moderate-speed systems stuff a zero at the conclusion of each string of five logical ones. The system calculates its CRC error-correction data before the data gets stuffed. The receiver strips off the stuffed bits before performing its CRC.

Bit stuffing is only required during synchronous transmissions. Because low-speed IrDA systems operate asynchronously, there is no need for bit stuffing. Nor is bit stuffing necessary at IrDA's highest speed because 4PPM modulation guarantees a pulse within each clock period.

Format

The IrDA system doesn't deal with data at the bit or byte level but instead arranges the data transmitted through it in the form of packets, which the IrDA specification also terms *frames*. A single frame can stretch from 5 to 2,050 bytes (and sometimes more) in length. As with other packetized systems, an IrDA frame includes address information, data, and error correction, the last of which is applied at the frame level. The format of the frame is rigidly defined by the IrDA Link Access Protocol standard, discussed later.

Aborted Frames

Whenever a receiver detects a string of seven or more consecutive logical ones—that is, an absence of optical pulses—it immediately terminates the frame in progress and disregards the data it received (which is classed as invalid because of the lack of error-correction data). The receiver then awaits the next valid frame, signified by a start-of-frame flag, address field, and control field. Any frame that ends in this summary manner is termed an *aborted frame*.

A transmitter may intentionally abort a frame or a frame may be aborted because of an interruption in the infrared signal. Anything that blocks the light path will stop infrared pulses from reaching the receiver and, if long enough, abort the frame being transmitted.

Interference Suppression

High-speed systems automatically mute lower-speed systems that are operating in the same environment to prevent interference. To stop the lower-speed link from transmitting, the high-speed system sends out a special *Serial Infrared Interaction Pulse* at intervals no longer than half a second. The SIP is a pulse 1.6 microseconds long follow by 7.1 microseconds of darkness, parameters exactly equal to a packet start pulse. When the low-speed system sees what it thinks is a start pulse, it automatically starts looking for data at the lower rates, suppressing its own transmission for half a second. Before it has a chance to start sending its own data (if any), another SIP quiets the low-speed system for the next half second.

Link Access Protocol

To give the data transmitted through the optical link a common format, the Infrared Data Association created its own protocols. Its Link Access Protocol describes the composition of the data packets transmitted through the system. IrLAP is broadly based on the asynchronous data communications standards used in RS232C ports (no surprise here) that is, in turn, adapted from the more general HDLC, High-level Data Link Control. Note that although the overall operation of the IrDA link is the same at all speeds, IrDA defines different protocols for its low and high speeds.

Primary and Secondary Stations

The foundation of IrLAP is distinguishing primary and secondary stations. A *primary station* is the device that takes command and controls the link transfers. Even when a given link involves more than two devices, all transmissions must either go to or come from the primary station. That is, all secondary devices send data only to the primary station. The primary station, however, can target a single secondary station or broadcast its data to all secondary stations.

In any IrDA connection, there can be only one primary station. The role of primary station does not automatically fall on a given device. For example, your PC is not automatically the primary station in the sessions in which it becomes involved. At the beginning of any IrDA link, the stations negotiate for the roles they will play. After one device becomes the primary station, it retains that role until the link is ended.

An IrDA link begins when a device seeks to connect with another. The first device may directly request a link to a known device or it may sniff out and discover a device to which to make a connection. For example, a notebook PC could continuously search for a desktop mate, and when it finally comes into range with one, it begins to negotiate a link.

To begin the link, the first device sends out a connection request at the universal 9,600 bps speed. This request includes the address of the initiating device, the speed at which it wants to pursue the link, and other parameters. The responding device assumes the role of the secondary station and sends back identifying information, including its own address and its speed capabilities. The two devices then change to a mutually compatible speed and the initiating device, as the primary station, takes command of the link. Data transfer begins.

Frame Types

Three types of frames are used by IrLAP, following the model of HDLC. *Information frames* transfer the actual data in a connection. *Unnumbered frames* perform setup and management tasks. For example, an unnumbered frame can establish a connection, remove a connection, or search out or discover devices with which to make a connection. *Supervisory frames* help control the flow of data between stations. For example, a supervisory frame may be used to acknowledge the receipt of a given frame or to warn that a given station is busy.

Each frame is bracketed by two or more start fields at its beginning and one or more stop fields at its conclusion. If a frame is not bracketed by the proper flags, it will be ignored.

Next comes the address field, which identifies the source and destination of the packet. The control field identifies the type of packet, whether it contains data or control information. The data field is optional because some packets used to control the link need no data. The data field can be any length up to and including 2,045 bytes but must be a multiple of eight bits. The frame ends with a frame check sequence used to detect errors and one or more stop flags. Figure 20.12 shows the layout of a typical IrDA frame.

FIGURE 20.12
Constituents of a high-speed IrDA data frame (packet).

The start flag is simply a specific bit-pattern that indicates the beginning of a field. It serves to get the attention of the receiver. The exact pattern used for the start flag depends on the speed of the data. At speeds of 115,200 bps and below, the start flag is the

byte value 0C0(Hex). A frame may include more than one start flag. The stations participating in a link negotiate the number to use. Table 20.8 summarizes the components in an
IrDA synchronous data frame at low data rates.

TABLE 20.8 IrDA Low-Speed (2,400 to 115,200 bps) Frame Components

Mnemonic	Definition	Length	Value
STA	Start flag	8 bits	0C0(Hex)
ADDR	Address field	8 bits	Varies
DATA	Control field	8 bits	Varies
DATA	Information field	2,045 bytes	Varies
FCS	Error-correction field	16 bits	CRC
STO	Stop flag	8 bits	0C1(Hex)

At higher speeds, both start and end flags are given the value 07E(Hex). Each frame must
have at least two start flags. A transmitter can insert additional start flags, which are
ignored by the receiver. If a transmitter outputs two IrDA frames back to back, the data in
the two frames will be separated by at least one stop flag and two start flags. If the transmitter sends two frames that are not back-to-back, the stop flag of the first frame and the
first start flag of the second frame must be separated by at least seven pulse-free clock
cycles. Table 20.9 summarizes the components in an IrDA synchronous data frame.

TABLE 20.9 IrDA Synchronous Data Frame Components at 576 kbps and Higher

Mnemonic	Definition	Length	Value
STA	Start flag	8 bits	07E(Hex)
ADDR	Address field	8 bits	Varies
DATA	Control field	8 bits	Varies
DATA	Information field	<2,046 bytes	Varies
FCS	Frame check sequence	16 bits	CRC error detection
STO	Stop flag	8 bits	07E(Hex)

Addressing

The address field identifies the secondary station participating in the communications
link. When the primary station transmits a packet, the address identifies the secondary
station to which the packet is destined. When a secondary station transmits a packet, the
address identifies the secondary station. The first bit identifies the direction of the

transmission, 1 from the primary station, 0 from the secondary station. The remaining seven bits are the actual address. Two of the 128 possible addresses are reserved. The address 0000000(Binary) identifies the primary station. The address 1111111(Binary) identifies a packet as global, which means that it is transmitted to all secondary nodes participating in the link. The addressing scheme constrains the number of IrDA devices in a given system to 127—the primary station and 126 secondary stations.

Error Detection

The error-correction field is two bytes long. Its value is computed from the bits in the entire frame except for the start and end flags. In other words, the error correction covers not only the information field but also the address and control fields.

IrDA error correction is based on the cyclical redundancy check adopted by the ITU. It is similar but not identical to the error detection used in the XMODEM file transfer protocol.

The value of the cyclical redundancy check is computed using the following algorithm:

$$CRC(x) = x^{16} + x^{12} + x^5 + 1$$

Link Management Protocol

Before an IrDA system can exchange data, it must establish a link. The IrDA created a standard procedure for creating and managing links called the Link Management Protocol. This standard covers all aspects of establishing and ending communication between IrDA devices, including such aspects as link initialization, discovering the addresses of available devices, negotiating the speed and format of the link, disconnection, shutdown, and the resolution of device conflicts. Many aspects of IrLMP were derived from the more general HDLC protocols. Because of the broadcast nature of the infrared signal, however, the IrDA group developed its own system for detecting the presence of devices and resolving conflicts among them.

One of the biggest problems faced by IrLMP is the dynamic nature of wireless connections. You can bring new devices into the range of a master at any time or similarly remove them, changing the very nature of the connection. The master must be able to determine the devices with which it can communicate and keep alert for changes. It must be able to search out not only those devices within its range (and operating in a compatible mode) but also new devices that you suddenly introduce. Moreover, it must be able to determine when each device involved in a communication session ceases to participate—either by being turned off or by being moved out of range. Where traditional hardwired serial connections had the luxury of status signals that allow the easy monitoring of the status of the connection and the devices linked through it, infrared devices have nothing but pulses of light linking them.

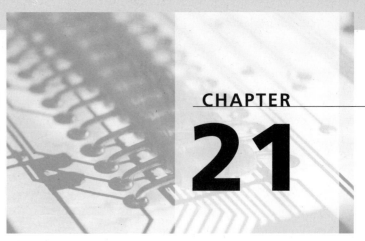

Legacy Ports

The traditional way of connecting peripherals to your PC has been using serial or parallel ports. Although the two largest corporations controlling what goes into PCs—Intel and Microsoft—have ordained that traditional ports will go the way of all things, they persist like other quaint notions, say freedom of expression. Most PCs still have these legacy ports and hundreds of millions of peripherals require them to link to your PC. Although Intel and Microsoft can turn their backs on traditional port technology, neither you nor this book can. Consequently, this chapter covers the ins and outs of the traditional PC serial and parallel ports.

A quick comparison of legacy ports

Feature	Serial port	Parallel Port
Speed	115 Kbits/sec	800 Kbits/sec (as EPP)
Cable length	Over 100 feet, but speed limited	10 feet maximum
Cable conductors used	3 to 9	25
Devices per port	1	Usually 1 but up to 127 under ECP
Origins	Telephone company	Printer company
Chief applications	Mice, modems, digital cameras	Printers, portable disk and tape drives

You've heard the arguments. The metric system is good for you. It simplifies measurements and conversions. It's easier to use. Even the names of the units make more sense. And more than 20 years since the government of the United States declared the country would switch over to the almost universal metric system, milk still comes in quart bottles (more likely, cartons—we have made progress), two-by-fours are still measured in inches (and they still measure 1-5/8 by 3-1/2 inches), and you count your weight in pounds and height in inches. The moral here is not that metric is bad but that change takes time. Only when the *Star Trek* generation takes control of the dairies, construction trades, and what's left of your mind will you switch to measuring in meters, liters, and grams.

So it is with PC ports. Everyone knows that USB and FireWire are better. They're faster. They're easier. They have fewer calories. The PC industry is bent on a serious brainwashing campaign to convince you how wonderful the new interfaces are. But look at the reality beyond the claims, cajoling, and lies, and the future is plain. You're still going to connect your printer with a parallel port as long as you find a parallel port on your printer.

For almost two decades, the serial port has been the least common denominator of computer communications, an escape route for your long distance messages but one burdened by its own ball and chain. From the perspective of modern interconnection systems, however, the legacy serial port hobbles your PC with data rates out of the dark ages. The classic serial port was a carry-over from a previous generation of technology, the age of the black Bakelite telephone. Its low speed was a sad match for the quick pulse of the PC. It was like having a medieval scribe ink out your PC's owners' manual in glorious Gothic script—a trial of your patience that took little advantage of current technology. (Then again, some PC documentation arrives so late you just *might* suspect some scribe to be scrawling it out with quill and oxgall ink.) Although PCs generate millions of characters per second, legacy serial ports dole out a few hundred or thousand in the same time.

The least common denominator is the RS-232C port, standard equipment on nearly every PC since 1984. Throughout the first decade and a half of personal computing, serial port meant only RS-232C. But the standard is even older than the first PCs, having been a telephone system standard long before. And like most of the carry-overs from early technology, RS-232C brought its own baggage—a speed limit more severe than a stern first grade teacher who believes that rulers are for discipline rather than measurement. USB truly is faster. And once you see all the connector permutations bequeathed the world by RS-232C, you'll appreciate the straightforward simplicity of USB. But you'll still need a serial port to link to that old modem, your Windows CE handheld computer, or an older digital camera.

When it comes to connecting peripherals to your PC, the parallel port appears to have come as the answer to your prayers. Here was a foolproof connection. You could plug in a cable and expect everything to work. No switches to worry about, no mode commands, no breaking out the break-out box to sort through signals with names that sound suspiciously similar to demons from Middle Earth.

The alternate name, *printer port*, hints at the weakness of the parallel design. The connection was originally engineered only for one-way links with printers.

The simplicity of the parallel connection evaporated when it proved too intriguing for engineers. Seeking it was inherently faster than the only other standard PC port at the time, the RS-232 serial port. By tinkering with the parallel port design, the engineers first broke the intimate link between the port and your printer and opened it as a general-purpose high-speed connection. Not satisfied with a single standard, they developed several. In the process, the port lost its trouble-free installation.

Today, the legacy parallel port is not a singular thing. Through the years, a variety of parallel port standards have developed. Today, you face questions about three standard connectors and four operational standards, not to mention a number of proprietary detours that have appeared along the way. Despite their innate differences—and often great performance differences—all are termed *parallel ports*. You may face combinations of any of the three connectors with any of the four operational standards in a given connection. With just a look, you won't be able to tell the difference between them or what standard the connection uses. In fact, you might become aware of the differences only when you start to scratch your head and wonder why your friends can unload files from their notebook computers 10 times faster than you can.

Legacy Serial Ports

The classic serial port in your PC wears a number of different names. IBM, in the spirit of bureaucracy, sanctions an excess of syllables, naming the connection an "asynchronous data communications port." Time-pressed PC users clip that to "async port" or "comm" port. Officialdom bequeaths its own term. The variety of serial links accepted by the PC industry operates under a standard called RS-232C (one that was hammered out by an industry trade group, the Electronics Industry Association, or EIA), so many folks call the common serial port by its numerical specification, an RS-232 port.

So far, we've discussed time in the abstract. But serial communications must occur at very real data rates, and those rates must be the same at both ends of the serial connection, if just within a frame when transmissions are asynchronous. The speed at which devices exchange serial data is called the *bit rate*, and it is measured in the number of data bits that would be exchanged in a second if bits were sent continually. You've probably encountered these bit rates when using a modem. The PC industry uses bit rates in the following sequence: 150; 300; 600; 1,200; 2,400; 4,800; 9,600; 19,200; 38,400; 57,600; and 115,200.

This sequence results from both industry standards and the design of the original IBM PC. The PC developed its serial port bit rate by using an oscillator that operates at 1.8432MHz and associated circuitry that reduces that frequency by a factor of 1,600 to a basic operating speed of 115,200 bits per second. For this base bit rate, a device called a *programmable divider* mathematically creates the lower bit rates used by serial ports. It develops the lower frequencies by dividing the starting rate by an integer. By using a divisor of three, for example, the PC develops a bit rate of 38,400 (that is, 115,200/3). Not all available divisors are used. For example, designers never set their circuits to divide by five.

You may have noticed that some modems use speeds not included in this sequence. For example, today's popular V.34 modems operate at a base speed of 28,800 bits per second. The modem generates this data rate internally. In general, you connect your PC to the modem so that it communicates at a higher bit rate, and the modem repackages the data to fit the data rate it uses by compressing the data or telling your PC to halt the flow of information until it is ready to send more bits.

The accepted standard in asynchronous communications allows for a number of variables in the digital code used within each data frame. When you configure any serial device and an RS-232 port, you'll encounter all of these variables: speed, number of data bits, parity choices, and number of stop bits. The most important rule about choosing which values to use is that the transmitter and receiver—your PC and the serial device— must use exactly the same settings. Think of a serial communications as an exchange of coded messages by two spies. If the recipient doesn't use the same secret decoder ring as the sender, he can't hope to make sense out of the message. If your serial peripheral isn't configured to understand the same settings your PC sends out in its serial signals, you can't possibly hope to print anything sensible.

Normally, you'll configure the bit rate of the serial port on a peripheral using DIP switches or the serial peripheral's menu system. How to make the settings will vary with the serial device you are installing, so you should check its instruction manual to be sure.

Windows takes direct control of the port and provides its own menu system for setting it up. Usually, the driver associated with your peripheral will handle these details. For example, when you configure a modem, Windows automatically takes care of the port details. If you want to change setting directly, you'll have to dig in through the Control Panel. Choose Device Manager after double-clicking on the System icon. Find the port you want to configure—expanding the list under the Ports (COM & LPT) icon if necessary—highlight it, and then click on the Properties button. The various tabs give you intimate control.

Electrical Operation

Serial signals have a definite disadvantage compared to parallel: Bits move one at a time. At a given clock rate, fewer bits will travel through a serial link than a parallel one. The disadvantage is on the order of 12 to 1. When a parallel port moves a byte in a single cycle, a serial port take around a dozen—eight for the data bits, one for parity, one for stop, and two for start. That 9,600 bits-per-second serial connection actually moves text at about 800 characters per second.

Compensating for this definite handicap, serial connections claim versatility. Their signals can go the distance. They can travel not just the mile or so you can shoot out the signal from your standard serial port, but the thousands of miles you can make by modem—tied, of course, to that old serial port.

The tradeoff is signal integrity for speed. As they travel down wires, digital pulses tend to blur. The electrical characteristics of wires tend to round off the sharp edges of pulses and extend their length. The farther a signal travels, the less defined it becomes until digital equipment has difficulty telling where the one pulse ends and the next begins. The more closely spaced the pulses are (and, hence, the higher the bit rate), the worse the problem becomes. By lowering the bit rate and extending the pulses and the time between them, the farther the signal can go before the pulses blend together. (Modems avoid part of this problem by converting digital signals to analog signals for the long haul. PC networks achieve length and speed by using special cables and signaling technologies.)

The question of how far a serial signal can reach depends on both the equipment and wire that you use. You can probably extend a 9,600 bps connection to a hundred feet or more. At a quarter mile, you'll probably be down to 1,200 or 300 bps (slower than even cheap printers can type).

Longer wires are cheaper with serial connections, too, a point not lost on system designers. Where a parallel cable requires 18 to 25 separate wires to carry its signals, a serial link does with three: one to carry signals from your PC to the serial peripheral, one to carry signals from the serial peripheral to PC, and a common or ground signal that provides a return path for both.

The electrical signal on a serial cable is a rapidly switching voltage. Digital in nature, it has one of two states. In the communications industry, these states are termed space and mark like the polarity signals. *Space* is the absence of a bit, and *mark* is the presence of a bit. On the serial line, a space is a positive voltage, a mark is a negative voltage. In other words, when you're not sending data down a serial line, it has an overall positive voltage on it. Data will appear as a serial of negative-going pulses. The original design of the serial port specification called for the voltage to shift from a positive 12 volts to negative 12 volts. Because 12 volts is an uncommon potential in many PCs, the serial voltage often varies from positive 5 to negative 5 volts.

Connectors

The physical manifestation of a serial port is the connector that glowers on the rear panel of your PC. It is where you plug your serial peripheral into your computer. And it can be the root of all evil—or so it will seem after a number of long evenings during which you valiantly try to make your serial device work with your PC, only to have text disappear like phantoms at sunrise. Again, the principle problem with serial ports is the number of options that it allows designers. Serial ports can use either of two styles of connectors, each of which has two options in signal assignment. Worse, some manufacturers venture bravely in their own directions with the all-important flow control signals. Sorting out all of these options is the most frustrating part of serial port configuration.

25-Pin

The basic serial port connector is called a 25-pin D-shell. It earns its name from having 25 connections arranged in two rows that are surrounded by a metal guide that takes the form of a rough letter D. The male variety of this connector—the one that actually has pins inside it—is normally used on PCs. Most, but hardly all, serial peripherals use the female connector (the one with holes instead of pins) for their serial ports. Although both serial and parallel ports use the same style 25-pin D-shell connectors, you can distinguish serial ports from parallel ports because on most PCs the latter use female connectors. Figure 21.1 shows the typical male serial port DB-25 connector that you'll find on the back of your PC.

FIGURE 21.1

The male DB25 connector used by serial ports on PCs.

Although the serial connector allows for 25 discrete signals, only a few of them are ever actually used. Serial systems may involve as few as three connections. At most, PC serial ports use 10 different signals. Table 21.1 lists the names of these signals, their mnemonics, and the pins to which they are assigned in the standard 25-pin serial connector.

TABLE 21.1   25-Pin Serial Connector Signal Assignments

Pin	Function	Mnemonic
1	Chassis ground	None
2	Transmit data	TXD
3	Receive data	RXD
4	Request to send	RTS
5	Clear to send	CTS
6	Data set ready	RTS
Pin	*Function*	*Mnemonic*
7	Signal ground	GND
8	Carrier detect	CD
20	Data terminal ready	DTR
22	Ring indicator	RI

Note that in the standard serial cable, signal ground (which is the return line for the data signals on pins 2 and 3) is separated from the chassis ground on pin 1. The chassis ground pin is connected directly to the metal chassis or case of the equipment much like the extra prong of a three-wire AC power cable and provides the same protective function. It assures that the case of the two devices linked by the serial cable are at the same potential, which means you won't get a shock if you touch both at the same time. As wonderful as this connection sounds, it is often omitted from serial cables. On the other hand, the signal ground is a necessary signal that the serial link cannot work without. You should never connect the chassis ground to the signal ground.

9-Pin

If nothing else, using a 25-pin D-shell connector for a serial port is a waste of at least 15 pins. Most serial connections use fewer than the complete 10; some as few as 4 with hardware handshaking, 3 with software flow control. For the sake of standardization, the PC industry sacrificed the cost of the other unused pins for years until a larger—or smaller, depending on your point of view—problem arose: space. A serial port connector was too big to fit on the retaining brackets of expansion boards along with a parallel connector. In that all the pins in the parallel connector had assigned functions, the serial connector met its destiny and got miniaturized.

The problem arose when IBM attempted to put both sorts of ports on one board inside its Personal Computer AT when it was introduced in 1984. To cope with the small space available on the card retaining bracket, IBM eliminated all the unnecessary pins but kept the essential design of the connector the same. The result was an implementation of the standard serial port that used a 9-pin D-shell connector. To trim the 10 connections to 9, IBM omitted the little-used chassis ground connection.

As with the 25-pin variety of serial connector, the 9-pin serial jack on the back of PCs uses a male connector. This choice distinguishes it from the female 9-pin D-shell jacks used by early video adapters. (The MDA, CGA, and EGA systems all used this style of connector.) Figure 21.2 shows the 9-pin male connector that's used on some PCs for serial ports.

FIGURE 21.2

The male DB-9 plug used by AT-class serial devices.

Besides eliminating some pins, IBM also rearranged the signal assignments used in the miniaturized connector. Table 21.2 lists the signal assignments for the 9-pin serial connector introduced with the IBM PC-AT and now the most popular form of the legacy serial port.

TABLE 21.2   IBM 9-Pin Serial Connector

Pin	Function	Mnemonic
1	Carrier detect	CD
2	Receive data	RXD
3	Transmit data	TXD
4	Data terminal ready	DTR
5	Signal ground	GND
6	Data set ready	DSR
7	Request to send	RTS
8	Clear to send	CTS
9	Ring indicator	RI

Other than the rearrangement of signals, the 9-pin and 25-pin serial connectors are essentially the same. All the signals behave identically no matter the size of the connector on which it appears.

Motherboard Headers

When a serial port is incorporated into motherboard circuitry, the motherboard maker may provide either a D-shell connector on the rear edge of the board or a header from which you must run a cable to an external connector. The pin assignments on these motherboard headers usually conform to that of a standard D-shell connector, allowing you to use a plain ribbon cable to make the connection.

Intel, however, opts for a different pin assignment on many of its motherboards. Table 21.3 lists the pin assignments of most Intel motherboards.

TABLE 21.3   Intel Motherboard Serial Port Header Pin Assignments

Motherboard Header Pin	Corresponding 9-Pin D-Shell Pin	Function
1	1	Carrier detect
2	6	Data set ready
3	2	Receive data
4	7	Request to send
5	3	Transmit data
6	8	Clear to send
7	4	Data terminal ready
8	9	Ring indicator
9	5	Signal ground
10	No connection	No connection

Signals

Serial communications is an exchange of signals across the serial interface. These signals involve not just data but also the flow-control signals that help keep the data flowing as fast as possible—but not too fast.

First, we'll look at the signals and their flow in the kind of communication system for which the serial port was designed, linking a PC to a modem. Then, we'll examine how attaching a serial peripheral to a serial port complicates matters and what you can do to make the connection work.

Definitions

The names of the signals on the various lines of the serial connector sound odd in today's PC-oriented lingo because the terminology originated in the communications industry. The names are more relevant to the realm of modems and vintage teletype equipment.

Serial terminology assumes that each end of a connection has a different type of equipment attached to it. One end has a *data terminal* connected to it. In the old days when the serial port was developed, a terminal was exactly that—a keyboard and a screen that translated typing into serial signals. Today, a terminal is usually a PC. For reasons known but to those who revel in rolling their tongues across excess syllables, the term Data Terminal Equipment is often substituted. To make matters even more complex, many discussions talk about *DTE* devices—which means exactly the same thing as "data terminals."

The other end of the connection had a *data set*, which corresponds to a modem. Often, engineers substitute the more formal name Data Communication Equipment or talk about *DCE* devices.

The distinction between data terminals and data sets (or DTE and DCE devices) is important. Serial communications were originally designed to take place between one DTE and one DCE, and the signals used by the system are defined in those terms. Moreover, the types of RS-232 serial devices you wish to connect determine the kind of cable you *must* use. First, however, let's look at the signals, and then we'll consider what kind of cable you need to carry them:

Transmit Data—The serial data leaving the RS-232 port travels is called the *transmit data* line, which is usually abbreviated TXD. The signal on it comprises the long sequence of pulses generated by the UART in the serial port. The data terminal sends out this signal, and the data set listens to it.

Receive Data—The stream of bits going the other direction—that is, coming in from a distant serial port—goes through the receive data line (usually abbreviated RXD) to reach the input of the serial port's UART. The data terminal listens on this line for the data signal coming from the data set.

Data Terminal Ready—When the data terminal is able to participate in communications, that is, it is turned on and in the proper operating mode, it signals its readiness to the data set by applying a positive voltage to the *data terminal ready* line, which is abbreviated as DTR.

Data Set Ready—When the data set is able to receive data, that is, it is turned on and in the proper operating mode, it signals its readiness by applying a positive voltage to the *data set ready* line, which is abbreviated as DSR. Because serial communications must be two-way, the data terminal will not send out a data signal unless it sees the DSR signal coming from the data set.

Request To Send—When the data terminal is on and capable of receiving transmissions, it puts a positive voltage on its *request to send* line, usually abbreviated RTS. This signal tells the data set that it can send data to the data terminal. The absence of a RTS signal across the serial connection will prevent the data set from sending out serial data. This allows the data terminal to control the flow of the data set to it.

Clear To Send—The data set, too, needs to control the signal flow from the data terminal. The signal it uses is called *clear to send*, which is abbreviated CTS. The presence of the CTS in effect tells the data terminal that the coast is clear and the data terminal can blast data down the line. The absence of a CTS signal across the serial connection will prevent the data terminal from sending out serial data.

Carrier Detect—The serial interface standard shows its roots in the communication industry with the *carrier detect* signal, which is usually abbreviated CD. This signal gives a modem, the typical data set, a means of signaling to the data terminal that it has made a connection with a distant modem. The signal says that the modem or data set has detected the carrier wave of another modem on the telephone line. In effect, the carrier detect signal gets sent to the data terminal to tell it that communications are possible. In some systems, the data terminal must see the carrier detect signal before it will engage in data exchange. Other systems simply ignore this signal.

Ring Indicator—Sometimes, a data terminal has to get ready to communicate even before the flow of information begins. For example, you might want to switch your communications program into answer mode so that it can deal with an incoming call. The designers of the serial port provided such an early warning in the form of sending the *ring indicator* signal, which is usually abbreviated RI. When a modem serving as a data set detects ringing voltage—the low-frequency, high-voltage signal that makes telephone bells ring—on the telephone line to which it is connected, it activates the RI signal, which alerts the data terminal to what's going on. Although useful in setting up modem communications, you can regard the ring indicator signal as optional because its absence usually will not prevent the flow of serial data.

Signal Ground—All of the signals used in a serial port need a return path. The signal ground provides this return path. The single ground signal is the common return for all other signals on the serial interface. Its absence will prevent serial communications entirely.

Flow Control

This hierarchy of signals hints that serial communications can be a complex process. The primary complicating factor is handshaking or flow control. The designers of the serial interface recognized that some devices might not be able to accommodate information as fast as others could deliver it, so they built handshaking into the serial communications hardware using several special control signals to compensate.

The flow-control signals become extremely important when you want to use a serial connection to a slow device such as a plotter. Simply put, plotters aren't as quick as PCs. As you sit around playing FreeCell for the fourteenth hand while waiting for the blueprint of your dream house to roll out, that news comes as little surprise. Plotters are mechanical devices that work at mechanical speed. PCs are electronic roadrunners. A modern PC can draw a blueprint in its memory much quicker than your plotter can ink it on paper.

The temptation for your PC is to force-feed serial devices, shooting data out like rice puffs from a cannon. After the first few gulps, however, force-fed serial devices will choke. With a serial connection, the device might let the next salvo whiz right by. Your plotter may omit something important—such as bedroom walls and bathroom plumbing—and leave large gaps in your plan (but, perhaps, making your future life somewhat more interesting). Flow control helps throttle down the onslaught of data to prevent such omissions.

The concept underlying flow control is the same as for parallel and other ports: Your peripheral signals when it cannot accept more characters to stop the flow from your PC. When the peripheral is ready for more, it signals its availability back to your PC. Where the traditional parallel port uses a simple hardware scheme for this handshaking, flow control for the serial port is a more complex issue. As with every other aspect of serial technology, flow control is a theme overwhelmed by variations.

The chief division in serial flow control is between hardware and software. *Hardware flow control* involves the use of special control lines that can be (but don't have to be) part of a serial connection. Your PC or peripheral signals whether it is ready to accept more data by sending a signal down the appropriate wire. *Software flow control* involves the exchange of characters between PC and serial peripheral. One character tells the PC your peripheral is ready and another warns that it can't deal with more data. Both hardware and software flow control take more than one form. As a default, PC serial ports use hardware flow control (or hardware handshaking). Most serial peripherals do, too.

Hardware Flow Control

Several of the signals in the serial interface are specifically designed to help handle flow control. Rather than a simple on-and-off operation, however, they work together in an elaborate ritual.

The profusion of signals seems overkill for keeping a simple connection such as that with a plotter under control, and it is. The basic handshaking protocol for a serial interface is built around the needs of modem communications. Establishing a modem connection and maintaining the flow of data through it is one of more complex flow-control problems for a serial port. Even a relatively simple modem exchange involves about a dozen steps with a complex interplay of signals. The basic steps of the dance would go something like this:

1. The telephone rings when a remote modem wants to make a connection. The data set sends the ring indicator signal to the data terminal to warn of the incoming call.

2. The data terminal switches on or flips into the proper mode to engage in communications. It indicates its readiness by sending the data terminal ready signal to the data set.

3. Simultaneously, it activates its request to send line.

4. When the data set knows the data terminal is ready, it answers the phone and listens for the carrier of the other modem. If it hears the carrier, it sends out the carrier detect signal.

5. The data set negotiates a connection. When it is capable of sending data down the phone line, it activates the data set ready signal.

6. Simultaneously, it activates its clear to send line.

7. The data set relays bytes from the phone line to the data terminal through the receive data line.

8. The data terminal sends bytes to the data set (and thence the distant modem) through the transmit data line.

9. Because the phone line is typically slower than the data-terminal-to-data-set link, the data set quickly fills its internal buffer. It tells the data terminal to stop sending bytes by deactivating the clear to send line. When its buffer empties, it reactivates clear to send.

10. If the data terminal cannot handle incoming data, it deactivates its request to send line. When it can again accept data, it reactivates the request to send line.

11. The call ends. The carrier disappears, and the data set discontinues the carrier detect signal, clear to send signal, and data set ready signal.

12. Upon losing the carrier detect signal, the data terminal returns to its quiescent state, dropping its request to send and data terminal ready signals.

Underlying the serial dance are two rules. First, the data terminal must see the data set ready signal as well as the clear to send signal before it will disgorge data. Second, the data set must see the data terminal ready and request to send signals before it will send out serial data. Interrupting either of the first pair of signals will usually stop the data terminal from pumping out data. Interrupting either of the second pair of signals will stop the data set from replying with its own data.

The carrier detect signal may or may not enter into the relationship. Some data terminals require seeing the carrier detect signal before they will transmit data. Others just don't give a byte one way or the other.

Software Flow Control

The alternative means of handshaking, software flow control, requires your serial peripheral and PC to exchange characters or tokens to indicate whether they should transfer data. The serial peripheral normally sends out one character to indicate it can accept data and a different character to indicate that it is busy and cannot accommodate more. Two pairs of characters are often used, XON/XOFF and ETX/ACK.

In the XON/XOFF scheme, the XOFF character sent from your serial peripheral tells your PC that its buffer is full and to hold off sending data. This character is also sometimes called DC1 and has an ASCII value of 19 or 013(Hex). It is sometimes called Ctrl+S. (With some communications programs, you can hold down the Ctrl key and type S to tell the remote system to stop sending characters to your PC.) Once your serial peripheral is ready to receive data again, it sends out XON, also known as DC3, to your PC. This character has an ASCII value of 17 or 011(Hex). It is sometimes called Ctrl+Q. When you hold down Ctrl and type Q into your communications program, it cancels the effect of a Ctrl+S.

ETX/ACK works similarly. ETX, which is an abbreviation for end text, tells your PC to hold off on sending more text. This character has an ASCII value of 3 (decimal or hexadecimal) and is sometimes called Ctrl+C. ACK, short for acknowledge, tells your PC to resume sending data. It has an ASCII value of 6 (decimal or hexadecimal) and is sometimes called Ctrl+F.

There's no issue as to whether hardware or software flow control is better. Both work and that's all that's necessary. The important issue is what kind of flow control your serial peripheral and software use. You must assure that your PC, your software, and your serial peripheral use the same kind of flow control.

Your software will either tell you what it prefers or give you the option of choosing when you load the driver for your peripheral. On your serial peripheral, you select serial port flow control when you set it up. Typically, this will involve making a menu selection or adjusting a DIP switch.

Cables

The design of the standard RS-232 serial interface anticipates that you will connect a data terminal to a data set. When you do, all the connections at one end of the cable that links them are carried through to the other end, pin-for-pin, connection for connection. The definitions of the signals at each end of the cable are the same, and the function and direction of travel (whether from data terminal to data set or the other way around) of each is well defined. Each signal goes straight through from one end to the other. Even the connectors are the same at either end. Consequently, a serial cable should be relatively easy to fabricate.

In the real world, nothing is so easy. Serial cables are usually much less complicated or much more complicated than this simple design. Unfortunately, if you plan to use a serial connection for a printer or plotter, you have to suffer through the more complex design.

Straight-Through Cables

Serial cables are often simpler than pin-for-pin connections from one end to the other because no serial link uses all 25 connector pins. Even with the complex handshaking schemes used by modems, only nine signals need to travel from the data terminal to the data set, PC to modem. (For signaling purposes, the two grounds are redundant; most serial cables do not connect the chassis ground.) Consequently, you need only make these 10 connections to make virtually any data terminal to data set link work. Assuming you have a 25-pin D-shell connector at either end of your serial cable, the essential pins that must be connected are 2 through 8, 20, and 22 on a 25-pin D-shell connector. This is usually called a 9-wire serial cable because the connection to pin 7 uses the shield of the cable rather than a wire inside. With 9-pin connectors at either end of your serial cable, all 9 connections are essential.

Not all systems use all the handshaking signals, so you can often get away with fewer connections in a serial cable. The minimal case is a system that uses software handshaking only. In that case, you need only three connections: transmit data, receive data, and the signal ground. In other words, you need only connect pins 2, 3, and 7 on a 25-pin connector or pins 2, 3, and 5 on a 9-pin serial connector—providing, of course, you have the same size connector at each end of the cable.

Although cables with an intermediary number of connections are often available, they are not sufficiently less expensive than the nine-wire cable to justify the risk and lack of versatility. So you should limit your choices to a nine-wire cable for systems that use hardware handshaking or three-wire cables for those that you're certain use only software flow
control.

Manufacturers use a wide range of cable types for serial connections. For the relatively low data rates and reasonable lengths of serial connections, you can get away with just about everything, including twisted-pair telephone wire. To ensure against interference, you should use shielded cable, which wraps a wire braid or aluminum-coated plastic film about inner conductors to prevent signals leaking out or in. The shield of the cable should be connected to the signal ground. (Ideally, the signal ground should have its own wire, and the shield should be connected to the chassis ground, but most folks just don't bother.)

Adapter Cables

If you need a cable with a 25-pin connector at one end and a 9-pin connector at the other, you cannot use a straight-through design even when you want to link a data terminal to a data set. The different signal layouts of the two styles of connector are incompatible. After all, you can't possibly link pin 22 on a 25-pin connector to a non-existent pin 22on a 9-pin connector.

This problem is not uncommon. Even though the nine-pin connector has become a de facto standard on PCs, most other equipment, including serial plotters, printers, and modems, have stuck with the 25-pin standard. To get from one connector type to other, you need an adapter. The adapter can take the form of a small assembly with a connector on each end of an adapter cable, typically from six inches to six feet long.

Although commercial adapters are readily available, you can readily make your own. You'll find the wiring in the Appendix, "Connectorama," on the CD-ROM.

Cross-Over Cables

As long as you want to connect a computer serial port that functions to a modem, you should have no problem with serial communications. You will be connecting a data terminal to a data set, exactly what engineers designed the serial systems for. Simply sling a cable with enough conductors to handle all the vital signals between the computer and modem and *voila*! Serial communications without a hitch. Try it, and you're likely to wonder why so many people complain about the capricious nature of serial connections.

When you want to connect a plotter or printer to a PC through a serial port, however, you will immediately encounter a problem. The architects of the RS-232 serial system decided that both PCs and the devices are data terminals, or DTE devices. The designations actually made sense, at least at that time. You were just as likely to connect a serial printer (such as a teletype) to a modem as you were a computer terminal. There was no concern about connecting a printer to a PC because PCs didn't even exist back then.

When you connect a plotter or printer and your PC—or any two DTE devices—together with an ordinary serial cable, you will not have a communication system at all. Neither machine will know that the other one is even there. Each one will listen on the serial port signal line that the other is listening to, and each one will talk on the line that the other talks on. One device won't hear a bit the other is saying.

The obvious solution to the problem is to switch some wires around. Move the transmit data wire from the PC to where the receive data wire goes on the plotter or printer. Route the PC's receive data wire to the transmit data wire of the plotter or printer. A simple *cross-over cable* does exactly that, switching the transmit and receive signals at one end of the connection. A *cross-over adapter* shrinks the cross-over cable down into a single connector.

Many of the devices that you plug into a PC are classed as DTE or data terminals just like the PC. All of these will require a cross-over cable. Table 21.4 lists many of the devices you might connect to your PC and whether they function as data terminals (DTE) or data sets (DCE).

TABLE 21.4   Common Serial Device Types

Peripheral	Device Type	Cable Needed to Connect to PC
PC	DTE	Cross-over
Modem	DCE	Straight-through
Mouse	DCE	Straight-through
Trackball	DCE	Straight-through
Digitizer	DCE	Straight-through
Scanner	DCE	Straight-through
Serial printer	DTE	Cross-over
Serial plotter	DTE	Cross-over

Some serial ports on PCs (and some serial devices, too) offer a neat solution to this problem. They allow you to select whether they function as a DTE or DCE with jumpers or DIP switches. To connect one of these to a plotter or printer using an ordinary straight-through cable, configure the PC's serial port as DCE.

This simple three-wire cross-over cable works if you plan to use only software flow control. With devices that require hardware handshaking, however, the three-wire connection won't work. You need to carry the hardware handshaking signals through the cable. And then the fun begins.

Your problems begin with carrier detect. The carrier detect signal originates on a data set, and many data terminals need to receive it before they will send out data. When you connect two data terminals together, neither generates a signal anything like carrier detect, so there's nothing to connect to make the data terminals start talking. You have to fabricate the carrier detect signal somehow.

Because data terminals send out their data terminal ready signals whenever they are ready to receive data, you can steal the voltage from that connection. Most cross-over cables link their carrier-detect signals to the data terminal ready signal from the other end of the cable.

Both data terminals will send out their data terminal ready signals when they are ready. They expect to see a ready signal from a data set on the data set ready connection. Consequently, most cross-over cables also link data terminal ready on one end to data set ready (as well as carrier detect) at the other end. Making this link allows the two data terminals at either end of the cable to judge when the other is ready.

The actual flow-control signals are request to send and clear to send. The typical cross-over cable thus links the request to send signal from one end to the clear to send connection at the other end. This link will enable flow control—providing, of course, the two data terminal devices follow the signaling standard we outlined earlier. Table 21.5 summarizes these connections.

TABLE 21.5   Basic Cross-Over Cable for Hardware Handshaking (25-Pin Connectors)

PC End	Function	Device End
2	Transmit data	3
3	Receive data	2
4	Request to send	5
5	Clear to send	4
6	Data set ready	20
7	Signal ground	7

TABLE 21.5   Continued

PC End	Function	Device End
8	Carrier detect	20
20	Data terminal ready	6
20	Data terminal ready	8

Unfortunately, this cable may not work when you link many serial devices to the typical PC. A different design that combines the request to send and clear to send signals and links them to carrier detect at the opposite end of the cable often works better than the preceding by-the-book design. The wiring connections for this variety of cross-over cable are listed in Table 21.6.

TABLE 21.6 Wiring for a Generic Cross-Over Serial Cable (25-Pin Connectors)

PC End	Function	Device End
2	Transmit data	3
3	Receive data	2
4	Request to send	8
5	Clear to send	8
6	Data set ready	20
7	Signal ground	7
8	Carrier detect	5
8	Carrier detect	4
20	Data terminal ready	22
20	Data terminal ready	6
22	Ring indicator	20

A number of printers vary from the signal layout ascribed to RS-232 connections. You'll find some helpful adapter designs in Appendix TK, "Connectorama."

One way to avoid the hassle of finding the right combination of hardware handshaking connections would appear to be letting software do it—avoiding hardware handshaking and instead using the XON/XOFF software flow control available with most serial devices. Although a good idea, even this expedient can also cause hours of headscratching when nothing works as it should—or nothing works at all.

When trying to use software handshaking, nothing happening is a common occurrence. Without the proper software driver, your PC or PS/2 has no idea that you want to use software handshaking. It just sits around waiting for a DSR and a CTS to come rolling in toward it from the connected serial device.

You can sometimes circumvent this problem by connecting the data terminal ready to data set ready and request to send to clear to send within the connectors at each end of the cable. This wiring scheme satisfies the handshaking needs of a device with its own signals. But beware: This kind of subterfuge will make systems that use hardware handshaking print, too, but you'll probably lose large blocks of text when the lack of real handshaking lets your PC continue to churn out data even after your printer shouts "Stop!"

Finally, note that some people call cross-over cables *null modem cables*. This is not correct. A null modem is a single connector used in testing serial ports. It connects the transmit data line to the receive data line of a serial port as well as crossing the handshaking connections within the connector as described earlier. Correctly speaking, a null modem cable is equipped with this kind of wiring at both ends. It will force both serial ports constantly on and prevent any hardware flow control from functioning at all. Although such a cable can be useful, it is not the same as a cross-over cable. Substituting one for the other will lead to some unpleasant surprises—text dropping from sight from within documents as mysteriously and irrecoverably as D.B. Cooper.

UARTs

A serial port has two jobs to perform. It must re-package parallel data into serial form, and it must send power down a long wire with another circuit at the end, which is called driving the line.

Turning parallel data into serial is such a common electrical function that engineers created special integrated circuits that do exactly that. Called *Universal Asynchronous Receiver/Transmitter* chips, or UARTs, these chips gulp down a byte or more of data and stream it out a bit at a time. In addition, they add all the other accouterments of the serial signal—the start, parity, and stop bits. Because every serial practical connection is bidirectional, the UART works both ways, sending and receiving, as its name implies.

Because the UART does all the work of serializing your PC's data signals, its operation is one of the limits on the performance of serial data exchanges. PCs have used three different generations of UARTs, each of which imposes its own constraints.

The choice of chip is particularly critical when you connect your serial port to modem to it. When you communicate online with a modem, you're apt to receive long strings of characters through the connection. Your PC must take each character from a register in the UART and move it into memory. When your PC runs a multitasking system, it may be diverted for several milliseconds before it turn its attention to the UART and gathers up the character. Older UARTs must wait for the PC to take away one character before they can accept another from the communications line. If the PC is not fast enough, the characters pile up. The UART doesn't know what to do with them, and some of the characters simply get lost. The latest UARTs incorporate small buffers or memory areas that allow the UART to temporarily store characters until the PC has time to take them away. These newer UARTs are more immune to character loss and are preferred by modem users for high-speed communications.

When you connect a printer to a serial port, you don't have such worries. The printer connection is more a monologue than a dialogue; your PC chatters out characters and gets very little backtalk from your printer. Typically, it will get only a single XOFF or XON character to tell the PC to stop or start the data flow. Because there's no risk of a pile-up of in-bound characters, there's no need for a buffer in the UART.

If you have both a modem and a serial printer attached to your PC, your strategy should be obvious: The modem gets the port with the faster UART. Your printer can work with whatever UART is left over.

In the past, PC makers used any of three discrete UART chips in their products—chips designated 8250, 16450, and 16550A. Modern PCs include the function of one or two UARTs in their chipsets, so discrete UARTS chips (but not their functions) are unnecessary. These integral UARTs usually are functionally equivalent to the 16550A discrete chip.

In theory you should not need to worry about the type of UART in your newer PC. However some inexpensive expansion products such as I/O boards and modems may use the older UART designs. Consequently you should be aware of the differences between the various UART chips.

8250

The first UART used in PCs was installed in the original IBM PC's Asynchronous Communications Adapter card in 1981. Even after a decade and a half, it is still popular on inexpensive port adapter expansion boards because it is cheap. It has a one-byte internal buffer that's exactly what you need for printing or plotting applications: It can hold the XOFF character until your PC gets around to reading it. It is inadequate for reliable two-way communications at high modem speeds.

16450

In 1984, designers first put an improved version of the 8250, the 16450 UART, in PCs. Although the 16450 has a higher-speed internal design, it still retains the one-byte buffer incorporated into its predecessor. Serial ports built using it may still drop characters under some circumstances at high data rates. Although functionally identical, the 16450 and 8250 are physically different (they have different pin-outs), and you cannot substitute one in a socket meant for the other.

16550A

The real UART breakthrough came with the introduction of the 16550 to PCs in 1987. The first versions of this chip proved buggy, so it was quickly revised to produce the

16550A. It is commonly listed as 16550AF and 16550AFN, with the last initials indicating the package and temperature rating of the chip. The chief innovation incorporated into the 16550 was a 16-byte *first-in, first-out buffer* (or FIFO). The buffer is essential to high-speed modems operating in multitasking systems, making this the chip of choice for communications.

To maintain backward compatibility with the 16450, the 16550 ignores its internal buffer until it is specifically switched on. Most communications programs activate the buffer automatically. Physically, the 16550 and 16450 will fit and operate in the same sockets, so you can easily upgrade the older chip to the newer one.

Register Function

The register at the base address assigned to each serial port is used for data communications. Bytes are moved to and from the UART using the microprocessor's OUT and IN instructions. The next six addresses are used by other serial port registers, in order: the interrupt enable register, the interrupt identification register, the line control register, the modem control register, the line status register, and the modem status register. Another register, called the divisor latch, shares the base address used by the transmit and receive registers and the next higher register used by the interrupt enable register. It is accessed by toggling a setting in the line control register.

This latch stores the divisor that determines the operating speed of the serial port. Whatever value is loaded into the latch is multiplied by 16. The resulting product is used to divide down the clock signal supplied to the UART chip to determine the bit rate. Because of the factor of 16 multiplication, the highest speed the serial port can operate at is limited to 1/16 the supplied clock (which is 1.8432MHz). Setting the latch value to its minimum, one, results in a bit rate of 115,200.

Registers not only store the values used by the UART chip but also are used to report back to your system how the serial conversation is progressing. For example, the line status register indicates whether a character that has been loaded to be transmitted has actually been sent. It also indicates when a new character has been received.

Although you can change the values stored in these registers manually using Debug or your own programs, for the most part you'll never tangle with these registers. They do, however, provide flexibility to the programmer.

Instead of being set with DIP switches or jumpers, the direct addressability of these registers allows all the vital operating parameters to be set through software. For instance, by loading the proper values into the line control register, you alter the word length, parity, and number of stop bits used in each serial word.

Buffer Control

Operating system support for the buffer in the 16550 appeared only with Windows 3.1. Even then, it was limited in support to Windows applications only. DOS applications require internal FIFO support even when they run inside Windows 3.1. Windows for Workgroups (version 3.11) extended buffer support to DOS applications running within the operating environment. The standard communications drivers in Windows 95 and 98 operating systems will automatically take advantage of the 16550 buffer when the chip is present.

Under Windows, you can control the FIFO buffer through the Device Manager section of the System folder found in Control Panel. Once you open Control Panel, click on the System icon. Click the Device Manager tab and then the entry for Ports, which will expand to list the ports available in your system. Click on the COM port you want to control, and then click the Properties button below the list, as shown in Figure 21.3.

FIGURE 21.3

Windows Device Manager screen.

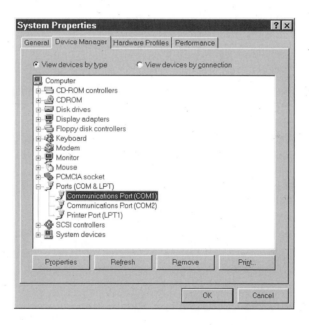

From the Communications properties screen, click on the Port Settings tab. In addition to the default parameters set up for your chosen port, you'll see a button labeled Advanced. Clicking on it will give you control of the FIFO buffer, as shown in Figure 21.4.

FIGURE 21.4

*Disabling or enabling
your UART FIFO
buffer under
Windows.*

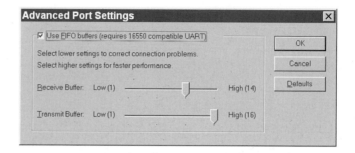

Windows defaults to setting the FIFO buffer on if you have a 16550 UART or the equivalent in your PC. That's the minimum you should expect in a new PC and the minimum Windows expects, too. To switch the buffer off, click on the checked box labeled Use FIFO buffers.

Identifying UARTs

One way of identifying the type of UART installed in your PC is to look at the designation stenciled on the chip itself. Amid a sea of prefixes, suffixes, data codes, batch numbers, and other arcana important only the chip makers, you'll find the model number of the chip.

First, of course, you must find the chip. Fortunately, UARTs are relatively easy to find. All three basic types of UARTs use exactly the same package, a 40-pin DIP (Dual Inline Package) black plastic shell that's a bit more than 2 inches long and 0.8 inch wide. Figure 21.5 shows this chip package. These large chips tend to dominate multifunction or port adapter boards on which you'll typically find them. Some older PCs have their chips on their motherboards.

FIGURE 21.5
The 40-pin DIP package used by UARTs.

Unfortunately, the classic embodiment of the UART chip is disappearing from modern PCs. Large ASICs (Application-Specific Integrated Circuits) often incorporate the circuitry and functions of the UART (or, more typically, two of them). Most PCs consequently have no UARTs for you to find, even though they have two built-in serial ports.

The better way to identify your UARTs is by checking their function. That way, you don't have to open up your PC to find out what you've got. Better still, you can be sure that the chip will act the way it's supposed to. Snooper programs will check out your UART quickly and painlessly. Better still, you can determine the kind of UARTs in your PC (as well as a wealth of other information) using Microsoft Diagnostics, the program MSD.EXE, which is included with the latest versions of Windows. After you run MSD, you'll see a screen like that shown in Figure 21.6.

FIGURE 21.6

The opening screen of the Microsoft Diagnostics program.

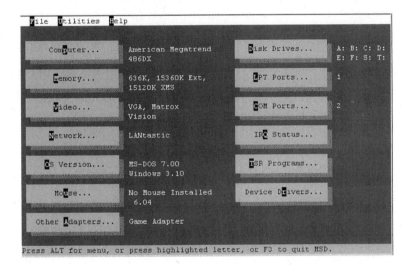

From the main menu, choose the COM ports option by pressing C on your keyboard. The program will respond by showing you the details of the serial ports that you have installed in your system with a screen like that shown in Figure 21.7.

FIGURE 21.7

The Microsoft Diagnostics display of communications port parameters.

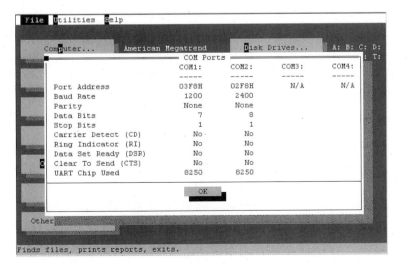

The last line of the display lists the UART chip used by each of your PC's serial ports. Use the more recent chip for your external modem if you have the choice; the 8250 chips (as shown in the sample screen) are suitable for plotters, printers, mice, and other slow-moving critters.

Enhanced Serial Ports

Serious modem users may install an Enhanced Serial Port in their PCs, which act like a 16550 but incorporate higher-speed circuitry and a much larger buffer. Because you have to install such an option yourself, you should know whether you have one. Most Enhanced Serial Ports are identified as 16550 UARTs by snooping programs. They were introduced primarily to take advantage of higher modem speeds. Parallel modems and new serial port designs such as USB provide a means of achieving the same end using recognized industry standards, so you may want to avoid enhanced serial ports.

Logical Interface

Your PC controls the serial port UART through a set of seven registers built into the chip. Although your programs could send data and commands to the UART (and, through it, to your serial device) by using the hardware address of the registers on the chip, this strategy has disadvantages. It requires the designers of systems to allocate once and forever the system resources used by the serial port. The designers of the original IBM PC were loathe to make such a permanent commitment. Instead, they devised a more flexible system that allows your software to access ports by name. In addition, they worked out a way that port names would be assigned properly and automatically even if you didn't install ports in some predetermined order.

Port Names

The names they assigned were COM1 and COM2. In 1987, the designers of DOS expanded the possible port repertory to include COM3 and COM4. Under Windows 3.1, up to nine serial ports could be installed in a PC using DOS conventions, although no true standard for the higher port values exists. Windows 95 and later versions have enhanced its support of serial ports to extend to 128 potential values. The implementation of these ports is handled by the device driver controlling them.

Before Windows 95, operating systems followed the DOS conventions for naming ports. The names that get assigned to a serial port depend on the input/output port addresses used by the registers on the UART. PCs reserve a block of eight I/O ports for the seven UART registers. These eight addresses are sequential, so they can be fully identified by the first, the *base address* of the serial port.

Because of their long use, the first two base addresses used by the serial ports are invariant, 3F8(Hex) and 2F8(Hex). Although the next two sometimes vary, the most widely used values for the next two base addresses are 3E8(Hex) and 2E8(Hex). When a PC boots up, DOS reads all base address values for serial ports and then assigns port names to them in order. Under this scheme, serial port names are always sequential. In theory, you could skip a number from the ordered list of base addresses and still get a sequence of serial port names starting with COM1. In a four-port system, the values would be assigned as listed in Table 21.7.

TABLE 21.7   Default Settings for DOS and Windows Serial Ports

Port Name	Base Address	Interrupt
COM1	03F8(Hex)	4
COM2	02F8(Hex)	3
COM3	03E8(Hex)	4
COM4	02E8(Hex)	3

Current Windows versions search the nominal base addresses for serial ports and assign its serial port driver to those that are active. Devices out of the normal range—including the serial ports built into internal modems—require their own drivers to match their hardware. Windows doesn't worry whether port names get assigned in order, so you can easily have a system with only COM1 and COM3.

Interrupts

Serial ports normally operate as interrupt-driven devices. That is, when they must perform an action immediately, they send a special signal called an interrupt to your PC's microprocessor. When the microprocessor receives an interrupt signal, it stops the work it is doing, saves its place, and executes a special software routine called the *interrupt handler*.

A serial port generates a hardware interrupt by sending a signal down an *interrupt request line*, or IRQ. Unless interrupts are shared, each serial port needs its own interrupt. Unfortunately, the number of available interrupts is typically too small for four serial ports to get their own IRQs. In many computers, only interrupts 3 and 4 are typically used by serial ports. When you have more than two serial ports installed in such a system, some ports must share interrupts. Conflicts can arise in systems that only let you use these two interrupts when two serial devices on different ports trigger the same interrupt at the same time. The result can be characters lost in serial port communications, mice that refuse to move, and even system crashes.

Windows can help resolve serial port interrupt conflict problems. Normally, the operating system automatically identifies your serial ports. You can change the automatic settings using the Resources tab in the Communications Port Properties dialog box, as shown in Figure 21.8. You access this folder exactly as you do when you change FIFO buffers settings as described earlier.

FIGURE 21.8

The Resources tab on the Communications Port Properties folder.

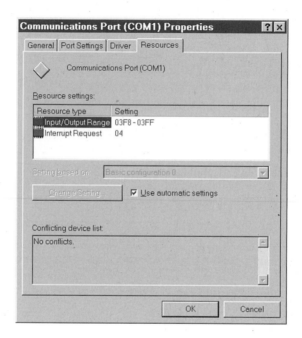

Parallel Ports

The defining characteristic of the parallel port design is implicit in its name. The port is parallel because it conducts its signals through eight separate wires—one for each bit of a byte of data—that are enclosed together in a single cable. The signal wires literally run in parallel from your PC to their destination—or at least they did. Better cables twist the physical wires together but keep their signals straight (and parallel).

In theory, having eight wires means you can move data eight times as fast through a parallel connection than through a single wire. All else being equal, simple math would make this statement true. Although a number of practical concerns make such extrapolations impossible, throughout its life, the parallel port has been known for its speed. It beat its original competitor, the RS-232 port, hands down, outrunning the serial port's 115.2 kbits/sec maximum by factors from two to five even in early PCs. The latest incarnations of parallel technology put the data rate through the parallel connection to over 100 times faster than the basic serial port rate.

In simple installations, for example, when used for its original purpose of linking a printer to your PC, the parallel port is a model of installation elegance. Just plug your printer in, and the odds are that it will work flawlessly—or that whatever flaws appear won't have anything to do with the interconnection.

Despite such rave reviews, parallel ports are not trouble-free. All parallel ports are not created equal. A number of different designs have appeared during the brief history of the PC. Although new PCs usually incorporate the latest, most versatile, and highest speed of these, some manufacturers skimp. Even when you buy a brand new computer, you may end up with a simple printer port that steps back to the first generation of PC design.

A suitable place to begin this saga is to sort out this confusion of parallel port designs by tracing its origins. As it turns out, the history of the parallel port is a long one, older than even the PC, although the name and our story begins with its introduction.

History

Necessity isn't just the mother of invention. It also spawned the parallel port. As with most great inventions, the parallel port arose with a problem that needed to be solved. When IBM developed its first PC, its engineers looked for a simplified way to link to a printer, something without the hassles and manufacturing costs of a serial port. The simple parallel connection, already used in a similar form by some printers, was an elegant solution. Consequently, IBM's slightly modified version became standard equipment on the first PCs. Because of its intended purpose, it quickly gained the "printer port" epithet. Not only were printers easy to attach to a parallel port, but also they were the only thing that you could connect to these first ports at the time.

In truth, the contribution of PC makers to the first parallel port was minimal. They added a new connector that better fit the space available on the PC. The actual port design was already being used on computer printers at the time. Originally created by printer maker Centronics Data Computer Corporation and used by printers throughout the 1960s and 1970s, the connection was electrically simple, even elegant. It took little circuitry to add to a printer or PC even in the days when designers had to use discrete components instead of custom-designed circuits. A few old-timers still cling to history and call the parallel port a *Centronics* port.

The PC parallel port is not identical to the exact Centronics design, however. In adapting it to the PC, IBM substituted a smaller connector. The large jack used by the Centronics design had 36 pins and was too large to put where IBM wanted it—sharing a card-retaining bracket with a video connector on the PC's first Monochrome Display Adapter. In addition, IBM added two new signals to give the PC more control over the printer and adjusted the timing of the signals traveling through the interface. All that said, most Centronics-style printers worked just fine with the original PC.

At the time, the PC parallel port had few higher aspirations. It did its job and did it well, moving data one direction—from PC to printer—at rates from 50 to 150 kilobytes per second. It, or subtle variations of it, became ubiquitous if not universal. Any printer worth connecting to a PC used a parallel port (or so it seemed).

In 1987, however, IBM's engineers pushed the parallel port in a new direction. The motivation for the change came from an odd direction. The company decided to adopt the 3.5-inch floppy disk drives for its new line of PS/2 computers at a time when all the world's PC data was mired on 5.25-inch diskettes. The new computers made no provision for building in the bigger drives. Instead, IBM believed that the entire world would instantly switch over to the new disk format. People would need to transfer their data once and only once to the new disk format. To make the transfer possible, the company released its *Data Migration Facility*, a fancy name for a cable and a couple disks. You used the cable to connect your old PC to your new PS/2 and software on the disks to move files through the parallel port from the old machine and disks to the new.

Implicit in this design is the ability of the PS/2 parallel port to receive data as well as send it out, as to a printer. The engineers tinkered with the port design and made it work both ways, creating a *bidirectional parallel port*. Because the design's intimate connection with the PS/2, it is sometimes termed the *PS/2 parallel port*.

The Data Migration Facility proved to be an inspirational idea despite its singular shortcoming of working in only one direction. As notebook computers became popular, they also needed a convenient means to move files between machines. The makers of file transfer programs such as Brooklyn Bridge and LapLink knew a good connection when they saw it. By tinkering with parallel port signals, they discovered that they could make any parallel port operate in both directions and move data to and from PCs.

The key to making bidirectional transfers on the old-fashioned one-way ports was to redefine signals. They redirected four of the signals in the parallel connector that originally had been designed to convey status information back from the printer to your PC. These signals already went in the correct direction. All that the software mavens did was to take direct control of the port and monitor the signals under their new definitions. Of course, four signals can't make a byte. They were limited to shifting four bits through the port in the backward direction. Because four bits make a nibble, the new parallel port operating mode soon earned the name *nibble mode*.

Four-bits at a time had greater implications than just a new name. Half as many bits also means half the speed. Nibble mode operates at about half the normal parallel port rate—still faster than single-line serial ports but not full parallel speed.

If both sides of a parallel connection had bidirectional ports, however, data transfers ran at full speed both ways. Unfortunately, as manufacturers began adapting higher-performance peripherals to use the parallel port, what once was fast performance became agonizingly slow. Although the bidirectional parallel port more than met the modest data transfer needs of printers and floppy disk drives, it lagged behind other means of connecting hard disks and networks to PCs.

Engineers at network adapter maker Xircom Incorporated decided to do something about parallel performance and banded together with notebook computer maker Zenith Data Systems to find a better way. Along the way, they added Intel Corporation and formed a triumvirate called Enhanced Parallel Port Partnership. They explored two ways of increasing the data throughput of a parallel port. They streamlined the logical interface so that your PC would need less overhead to move each byte through the port. In addition, they tightly defined the timing of the signals passing through the port, minimizing wasted time and helping assure against timing errors. They called the result of their efforts the *Enhanced Parallel Port*.

On August 10, 1991, the organization released its first description of what they thought the next generation of parallel port should be and do. They continued to work on a specification until March 1992, when they submitted release 1.7 to the Institute of Electrical and Electronic Engineers (IEEE) to be considered as an industry standard.

Although the EPP version of the parallel port can increase its performance by nearly tenfold, that wasn't enough to please everybody. The speed potential made some engineers see the old parallel port as an alternative to more complex expansion buses like the SCSI system. With this idea in mind, Hewlett-Packard joined with Microsoft to make the parallel port into a universal expansion standard called the *Extended Capabilities Port* (or ECP). In November 1992, the two companies released the first version of the ECP specification aimed at computers that use the ISA expansion bus. This first implementation adds two new transfer modes to the EPP design—a fast two-way communication mode between a PC and its peripherals and another two-way mode with performance further enhanced by simple integral data compression—and defines a complete software control system.

The heart of the ECP innovation is a protocol for exchanging data across a high-speed parallel connection. The devices at the two ends of each ECP transfer negotiate the speed and mode of data movement. Your PC can query any ECP device to determine its capabilities. For example, your PC can determine what language your printer speaks and set up the proper printer driver accordingly. In addition, ECP devices tell your PC the speed at which they can accept transmissions and the format of the data they understand. To assure the quality of all transmissions, the ECP specification includes error detection and device handshaking. It also allows the use of data compression to further speed transfers.

On March 30, 1994, the IEEE Standards Board approved its parallel port standard, *IEEE-1284-1994*. The standard included all of the basic modes and parallel port designs, including both ECP and EPP. It was submitted to the American National Standards Institute and approved as a standard on September 2, 1994.

The IEEE 1284 standard marks a watershed in parallel port design and nomenclature. The standard defines (or redefines) all aspects of the parallel connection, from the software interface in your PC to the control electronics in your printer. It divides the world of parallel ports in two: *IEEE 1284 compatible devices*, which are those that will work with the new interface, which in turn includes just about every parallel port and device ever made; and *IEEE 1284 compliant devices*, those which understand and use the new standard. This distinction is essentially between pre- and post-standardization ports. You can consider IEEE 1284 *compatible* ports to be "old technology" and IEEE 1284 *compliant* ports to be "new technology."

Before IEEE 1284, parallel ports could be divided into four types: standard parallel ports, bidirectional parallel ports (also known as PS/2 parallel ports), Enhanced Parallel Ports, and Extended Capabilities Ports. The IEEE specification redefines the differences in ports, classifying them by the transfer mode they use. Although the terms are not exactly the same, you can consider a standard parallel port one that is able to use only nibble-mode transfers. A PS/2 or bidirectional parallel port from the old days is one that can also make use of byte-mode transfers. EPP and ECP ports are those that use EPP and ECP modes, as described by the IEEE 1284 specification.

EPP and ECP remain standards separate from IEEE 1284, although they have been revised to depend on it. Both EPP and ECP rely on their respective modes as defined in the IEEE specification for their physical connections and electrical signaling. In other words, IEEE 1284 describes the physical and electrical characteristics of a variety of parallel ports. The other standards describe how the ports operate and link to your applications.

Connectors

The best place to begin any discussion of the function and operation of the parallel port is the connector. After all, the connector is what puts the port to work. It is the physical manifestation of the parallel port, the one part of the interface and standard you can actually touch or hold in your hand. It is the only part of the interface that most people will ever have to deal with. Once you know the ins and outs of parallel connectors, you'll be able to plug in the vast majority of PC printers and the myriad other things that now suck signals from what was once the printer's port.

Unfortunately, as with the variety of operating modes, the parallel port connector itself is not a single thing. Parallel port connectors come in enough different and incompatible designs to make matters interesting, enough subtle wiring variations to make troubleshooting frustrating, and enough need for explanation that this book can find its way into a fifth edition. Although the long-range prognosis for those suffering from connector confusion is good—eventually parallel ports will gravitate to a single connector design—in the short-term matters are destined only to get more confusing.

Before the IEEE 1284 standard was introduced, equipment designers used either of two connectors for parallel ports. On the back of your PC, you would find a female 25-pin D-shell connector, IBM's choice to fit a parallel port within the confines allowed on the MDA video adapter. On your printer, you would find a female 36-pin ribbon connector patterned after the original Centronics design. In its effort to bring standardization to parallel ports, the IEEE used these two designs as a foundation, formalizing them into the standard and giving them official names, the 1284-A and 1284-B connectors. The standard also introduced a new, miniaturized connector, 1284-C, similar to the old Centronics ribbon connector but about half the size.

The A Connector

The familiar parallel port on the back of your PC was IBM's pragmatic innovation. At the time of the design of the original PC, many computers used a 37-pin D-shell connector for their printer ports that mated with Centronics-style printers. This connector was simply too long (about four inches) for where IBM wanted to put it. Slicing off 12 pins would make a D-shell connector fit, and it still could provide sufficient pins for all the essential functions required in a parallel port as long as some of the ground return signals were doubled (and tripled) up. Moreover, the 25-pin D-shell was likely in stock on the shelves wherever IBM prototyped the PC because the mating connector had long been used in serial ports. IBM chose the opposite gender (a female receptacle on the PC) to distinguish it from a serial connection.

To retain compatibility with the original IBM design, other computer makers also adopted this connector. By the time the IEEE got around to standardizing the parallel port, the 25-pin D-shell was the standard. The IEEE adopted it as its 1284-A connector. Figure 21.9 shows a conceptual view of the A connector.

FIGURE 21.9

The IEEE 1284 A connector, a female 25-pin D-shell jack.

The individual contacts appear as socket holes, spaced at intervals of one-tenth inch, center to center. On the printer jack as it appears in the illustration, pin 1 is on the upper right, and contacts are consecutively numbered right to left. Pin 14 appears at the far right on the lower row, and again the contacts are sequentially numbered right to left. (Because you would wire this connector from the rear, the contact number would appear there in the more familiar left to right sequence.) The socket holes are encased in plastic to hold them in place, and the plastic filler itself is completely surrounded by a metal shell that extends back to the body of the connector. The entire connector measures about two inches wide and half an inch tall when aligned as shown in the illustration.

The studs at either side of the connector are 4-40 jack screws, which are essentially extension screws. They fit into the holes in the connector and attach it to a chassis. Instead of slotted heads, they provide another screw socket to which you can securely attach screws from the mating connector.

As a receptacle or jack for mounting on a panel such as the back of your PC, this connector is available under a number of different part numbers, depending on the manufacturer. Some of these include AMP 747846-4, Molex 82009, and 3M Company 8325-60XX and 89925-X00X. Mating plugs are available as AMP 747948-1, Molex 71527, and 3M 8225-X0XX.

Of the 25 contacts on this parallel port connector, 17 are assigned individual signals for data transfer and control. The remaining eight serve as ground returns. Table 21.8 lists the functions assigned to each of these signals as implemented in the original IBM PC parallel port and most compatible computers until the IEEE 1284 standard was adopted. In its compatibility mode, the IEEE standard uses essentially these same signal assignments.

TABLE 21.8   The Original PC Parallel Port Pin-Out

Pin	Function
1	Strobe
2	Data bit 0
3	Data bit 1
4	Data bit 2
5	Data bit 3
6	Data bit 4

Pin	Function
7	Data bit 5
8	Data bit 6
9	Data bit 7
10	Acknowledge
11	Busy
12	Paper end (out of paper)
13	Select
14	Auto feed
15	Error
16	Initialize printer
17	Select input
18	Strobe ground
19	Data 1 and 2 ground
20	Data 3 and 4 ground
21	Data 5 and 6 ground
22	Data 7 and 8 ground
23	Busy and fault ground
24	Paper out, select, and acknowledge ground
25	Auto feed, select input, and initialize printer ground

Under the IEEE 1284 specification, the definition of each signal on each pin is dependent on the operating mode of the port. Only the definition changes; the physical wiring inside your PC and inside cables does not change. If it did, shifting modes would be far from trivial. The altered definitions change the protocol, the signal handshaking that mediates each transfer.

A single physical connector on the back of your PC can operate in any of these five modes, and the signal definitions and their operation will change accordingly. Table 21.9 lists these five modes and their signal assignments.

TABLE 21.9   IEEE 1284-A Connector Signal Assignments in All Modes

Pin	Compatibility Mode	Nibble Mode	Byte Mode	EPP Mode	ECP Mode
1	nStrobe	HostClk	HostClk	nWrite	HostClk
2	Data 1	Data 1	Data 1	AD1	Data 1
3	Data 2	Data 2	Data 2	AD2	Data 2
4	Data 3	Data 3	Data 3	AD3	Data 3
5	Data 4	Data 4	Data 4	AD4	Data 4
6	Data 5	Data 5	Data 5	AD5	Data 5
7	Data 6	Data 6	Data 6	AD6	Data 6
8	Data 7	Data 7	Data 7	AD7	Data 7
9	Data 8	Data 8	Data 8	AD8	Data 8
10	nAck	PtrClk	PtrClk	Intr	PeriphClk
11	Busy	PtrBusy	PtrBusy	nWait	PeriphAck
12	PError	AckDataReq	AckDataReq	User defined 1	nAckReverse
13	Select	Xflag	Xflag	User defined 3	Xflag
14	nAutoFd	HostBusy	HostBusy	nDStrb	HostAck
15	nFault	nDataAvail	nDataAvail	User defined 2	nPeriphRequest
16	nInit	nInit	nInt	nInt	nReverseRequest
17	nSelectIn	1284 Active	1284 Active	nAStrb	1284 Active
18	Pin 1 (nStrobe) ground return				
19	Pins 2 and 3 (data 1 and 2) ground return				
20	Pins 4 and 5 (data 3 and 4) ground return				
21	Pins 6 and 7 (data 5 and 6) ground return				
22	Pins 8 and 9 (data 7 and 8) ground return				

Pin	Compatibility Mode	Nibble Mode	Byte Mode	EPP Mode	ECP Mode
23	Pins 11 and 15 ground return				
24	Pins 10, 12, and 13 ground return				
25	Pins 14, 16, and 17 ground return				

Along with standardized signal assignments, IEEE 1284 also gives us a standard nomenclature for describing the signals. In Table 21.9 and all following that refer to the standard, signal names prefaced with a lowercase "n" indicate that the signal goes negative when active; that is, the absence of a voltage means the signal is present.

Mode changes are negotiated between your PC and the printer or other peripheral connected to the parallel port. Consequently, both ends of the connection switch modes together so the signal assignments remain consistent at both ends of the connection. For example, if you connect an older printer that only understands compatibility mode, your PC cannot negotiate any other operating mode with the printer. It will not activate its EPP or ECP mode, so your printer will never get signals it cannot understand. This negotiation of the mode assures backward compatibility among parallel devices.

The B Connector

The parallel input on the back of your printer is the direct heir of the original Centronics design, one that has been in service for more than two decades. Figure 21.10 offers a conceptual view of this connector.

FIGURE 21.10
The IEEE 1284-B connector, a 36-pin ribbon jack.

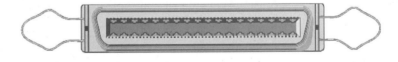

At one time this connector was called an "Amphenol" connector after the name the manufacturer of the original connector used on the first ports, an Amphenol 57-40360. Amphenol used the trade name "Blue Ribbon" for its series of connectors that included this one, hence the ribbon connector name.

Currently, this style of connector is available from several makers, each of which uses its own part number. In addition to the Amphenol part, some of these include AMP

555119-1, Molex 71522, and 3M Company 3367-300X and 3448-62. The mating cable plug is available as AMP 554950-1 or Molex 71522.

The individual contacts in the 36-pin receptacle take the form of fingers or ribbons of metal. In two 18-contact rows, they line the inside of a rectangular opening that accepts a matching projection on the cable connector. The overall connector from edge to edge measures about 2.75 inches long and about 0.66 inches wide. The individual contacts are spaced at 0.085 inch center to center. On the printer jack as it appears in the illustration, pin 1 is on the upper right, and contacts are consecutively numbered right to left. Pin 19 appears at the far right on the bottom row, and again the contacts are sequentially numbered right to left. (In wiring this connector, you would work from the rear, and the numbering of the contacts would rise in the more familiar left to right.)

The assignment of signals to the individual pins of this connector has gone through three stages. The first standard was set by Centronics for its printers. In 1981, IBM altered this design somewhat by redefining several of the connections. Finally, in 1994, the IEEE published its standard assignments, which, like those of the A connector, vary with operating mode.

The Centronics design serves as the foundation for all others. It, with variations, was used by printers through those made in the early years of the PC. Table 21.10 shows its signal assignments. This basic arrangement of signals has been carried through, with modification, to the IEEE 1284 standard. As far as modern printers go, however, this original Centronics design can be considered obsolete. Those printers not following the IEEE standard invariably use the original PC layout.

TABLE 21.10 Centronics Parallel Port Signal Assignments

Pin	Function
1	Strobe
2	Data bit 0
3	Data bit 1
4	Data bit 2
5	Data bit 3
6	Data bit 4
7	Data bit 5
8	Data bit 6
9	Data bit 7
10	Acknowledge

Pin	Function
11	Busy
12	Paper end (out of paper)
13	Select
14	Signal ground
15	External oscillator
16	Signal ground
17	Chassis ground
18	+5 VDC
19	Strobe ground
20	Data 0 ground
21	Data 1 ground
22	Data 2 ground
23	Data 3 ground
24	Data 4 ground
25	Data 5 ground
26	Data 6 ground
27	Data 7 ground
28	Acknowledge ground
29	Busy ground
30	Input prime ground
31	Input prime
32	Fault
33	Light detect
34	Line count
35	Line count return (isolated from ground)
36	Reserved

The Centronics layout includes some unique signals not found on later designs. The line count (pins 34 and 35) connections provide an isolated contact closure each time the printer advances its paper by one line. The light detect signal (pin 33) provides a indication whether the lamp inside the printer for detecting the presence of paper is functioning. The external oscillator signal (pin 15) provides a clock signal to external devices, one generally in the range of 100KHz to 200KHz. The input prime signal (pin 31) serves the same function as the later initialize signal. It resets the printer, flushing its internal buffer.

The original PC design eliminated the signals (but essentially only renames input prime) and added two new signals, auto feed and select input, discussed later. This layout remains current as IEEE 1284 compatibility mode on the 1284-B connector. Its signal assignments are listed in Table 21.11.

TABLE 21.11 IBM Parallel Printer Port Signal Assignments

Pin	Function
1	Strobe
2	Data bit 0
3	Data bit 1
4	Data bit 2
5	Data bit 3
6	Data bit 4
7	Data bit 5
8	Data bit 6
9	Data bit 7
10	Acknowledge
11	Busy
12	Paper end (out of paper)
13	Select
14	Auto feed
15	No connection
16	Ground
17	No connection
18	No connection
19	Strobe ground
20	Data 0 ground
21	Data 1 ground
22	Data 2 ground

Pin	Function
23	Data 3 ground
24	Data 4 ground
25	Data 5 ground
26	Data 6 ground
27	Data 7 ground
28	Paper end, select, and acknowledge ground
29	Busy and fault ground
30	Auto feed, select in, and initialize ground
31	Initialize printer
32	Error
33	No connection
34	No connection
35	No connection
36	Select input

As with the A connector, the IEEE 1284 signal definitions on the B connector change with the operating mode of the parallel port. The signal assignments for each of the five IEEE operating modes are listed in Table 21.12.

TABLE 21.12 IEEE 1284-B Connector Signal Assignments in All Modes

Pin	Compatibility Mode	Nibble Mode	Byte Mode	EPP Mode	ECP Mode
1	nStrobe	HostClk	HostClk	nWrite	HostClk
2	Data 1	Data 1	Data 1	AD1	Data 1
3	Data 2	Data 2	Data 2	AD2	Data 2
4	Data 3	Data 3	Data 3	AD3	Data 3
5	Data 4	Data 4	Data 4	AD4	Data 4
6	Data 5	Data 5	Data 5	AD5	Data 5
7	Data 6	Data 6	Data 6	AD6	Data 6
8	Data 7	Data 7	Data 7	AD7	Data 7

continues

TABLE 21.12   Continued

Pin	Compatibility Mode	Nibble Mode	Byte Mode	EPP Mode	ECP Mode
9	Data 8	Data 8	Data 8	AD8	Data 8
10	nAck	PtrClk	PtrClk	Intr	PeriphClk
11	Busy	PtrBusy	PtrBusy	nWait	PeriphAck
12	PError	AckDataReq	AckDataReq	User defined 1	nAckReverse
13	Select	Xflag	Xflag	User defined 3	Xflag
14	nAutoFd	HostBusy	HostBusy	nDStrb	HostAck
15	Not defined				
16	Logic ground				
17	Chassis ground				
18	Peripheral logic high				
19	Ground return for pin 1 (nStrobe)				
20	Ground return for pin 2 (data 1)				
21	Ground return for pin 3 (data 2)				
22	Ground return for pin 4 (data 3)				
23	Ground return for pin 5 (data 4)				
24	Ground return for pin 6 (data 5)				
25	Ground return for pin 7 (data 6)				
26	Ground return for pin 8 (data 7)				
27	Ground return for pin 9 (data 8)				
28	Ground return for pins 10, 12, and 13 (nAck, PError, and Select)				

Pin	Compatibility Mode	Nibble Mode	Byte Mode	EPP Mode	ECP Mode
29	Ground return for pins 11 and 32 (Busy and nFault)				
30	Ground return for pins 14, 31, and 36 (nAutoFd, nSelectIn, and nInit)				
31	nInit	nInit	nInit	nInit	nReverse Request
32	nFault	nDataAvail	nDataAvail	User defined 2	nPeriph Request
33	Not defined				
34	Not defined				
35	Not defined				
36	nSelectIn	1284 Active	1284 Active	nAStrb	1284 Active

Again, the port modes and the associated signal assignments are not fixed in hardware but change dynamically as your PC uses the connection. Although your PC acts as host and decides which mode to use, it can only negotiate those that your printer or other parallel device understands. Your printer (or whatever) determines which of these five modes could be used while your PC and its applications pick which of the available modes to use for transferring data.

The C Connector

Given a chance to start over with a clean slate and no installed base, engineers would hardly come up with the confusion of two different connectors with an assortment of different, sometimes-compatible operate modes. The IEEE saw the creation of the 1284 standard as such an opportunity, one which they were happy to exploit. To eliminate the confusion of two connectors and the intrinsic need for adapters to move between them, they took the logical step: They created a third connector, IEEE 1284-C.

All devices compliant with IEEE 1284 Level 2 must use this connector. That requirement is the IEEE's way of saying, "Let's get rid of all these old, confusing parallel ports with their strange timings and limited speed and get on with something new for the next generation." Once the entire world moves to IEEE 1284 Level 2, you'll have no need of compatibility, cable adapters, and other such nonsense. In the meantime, as manufacturers gradually adopt the C connector for their products, you'll still need adapters but in even greater variety.

All that said, the C connector has much to recommend it. It easily solves the original IBM problem of no space. Although it retains all the signals of the B connector, the C connector is miniaturized, about half the size of the B connector. As a PC-mounted receptacle, it measures about 1.75 inches long by .375 inch wide. It is shown in a conceptual view in Figure 21.11.

FIGURE 21.11
Conceptual view of the 1284-C parallel port connector.

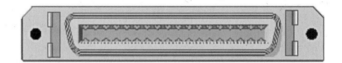

The actual contact area of the C connector is much like that of the B connector with contact fingers arranged inside a rectangular opening that accepts a matching projection on the mating plug. The spacing between the individual contacts is reduced, however, to 0.05 inches, center to center. This measurement corresponds to those commonly used, on modern printed circuit boards.

The C connector provides a positive latch using clips that are part of the shell of the plug. The clips engage latches on either side of the contact area, as shown in the figure. Squeezing the side of the plug spreads the clips and releases the latch.

The female receptacle (as shown) is available from a number of manufacturers. Some of these include AMP 2-175925-5, Harting 60-11-036-512, Molex 52311-3611, and 3M 10236-52A2VC. Part numbers of the mating plug include AMP 2-175677-5, Harting 60-13-036-5200, Molex 52316-3611, and 3M 10136-6000EC.

Every signal on the C connector gets its own pin and all pins are defined. As with the other connectors, the signal assignments depend on the mode in which the IEEE 1284 port is operating. Table 21.13 lists the signal assignments for the 1284-C connector in each of the five available modes.

TABLE 21.13   IEEE 1284-C Connector Signal Assignments in All Modes

Pin	Compatibility Mode	Nibble Mode	Byte Mode	EPP Mode	ECP Mode
1	Busy	PtrBusy	PtrBusy	nWait	PeriphAck
2	Select	Xflag	Xflag	User defined 3	Xflag

Pin	Compatibility Mode	Nibble Mode	Byte Mode	EPP Mode	ECP Mode
3	nAck	PtrClk	PtrClk	Intr	PeriphClk
4	nFault	nDataAvail	nDataAvail	User defined 2	nPeriphRequest
5	PError	AckDataReq	AckDataReq	User defined 1	nAckReverse
6	Data 1	Data 1	Data 1	AD1	Data 1
7	Data 2	Data 2	Data 2	AD2	Data 2
8	Data 3	Data 3	Data 3	AD3	Data 3
9	Data 4	Data 4	Data 4	AD4	Data 4
10	Data 5	Data 5	Data 5	AD5	Data 5
11	Data 6	Data 6	Data 6	AD6	Data 6
12	Data 7	Data 7	Data 7	AD7	Data 7
13	Data 8	Data 8	Data 8	AD8	Data 8
14	nInit	nInit	nInit	nInit	nReverseRequest
15	nStrobe	HostClk	HostClk	nWrite	HostClk
16	nSelectIn	1284 Active	1284 Active	nAStrb	1284 Active
17	nAutoFd	HostBusy	HostBusy	nDStrb	HostAck
18	Host logic high				
19	Ground return for pin 1 (Busy)				
20	Ground return for pin 2 (Select)				
21	Ground return for pin 3 (nAck)				
22	Ground return for pin 4 (nFault)				
23	Ground return for pin 5 (PError)				
24	Ground return for pin 6 (data 1)				

continues

TABLE 21.13 Continued

Pin	Compatibility Mode	Nibble Mode	Byte Mode	EPP Mode	ECP Mode
25	Ground return for pin 7 (data 2)				
26	Ground return for pin 8 (data 3)				
27	Ground return for pin 9 (data 4)				
28	Ground return for pin 10 (data 5)				
29	Ground return for pin 11 (data 6)				
30	Ground return for pin 12 (data 7)				
31	Ground return for pin 13 (data 8)				
32	Ground return for pin 14 (nInit)				
33	Ground return for pin 15 (nStrobe)				
34	Ground return for pin 16 (nSelectIn)				
35	Ground return for pin 17 (nAutoFd)				
36	Peripheral logic high				

Adapters

The standard printer cable for PCs is an adapter cable. It rearranges the signals of the A connector to the scheme of the B connector. Ever since the introduction of the first PC, you needed this sort of cable just to make your printer work. Over the years, they have become plentiful and cheap. If you want to build your own adapter cables, you'll find the correct wiring in Appendix TK.

To cut costs, many makers of adapter cables group all the grounds together as a single common line so that you need only 18 instead of 25 conductors in the connecting cable. Cheap adapters *that do not meet the IEEE 1284 standard* use this approach.

A modern printer cable should contain a full 25 connections with the ground signals divided up among separate pins. A true *IEEE 1284 printer cable* is equipped with an A connector on one end and a B connector on the other with the full complement of connections in between.

As new peripherals with the 1284-C connector become available, you'll need to plug them into your PC. To attach your existing PC to a printer or other device using the C connector, you'll need an adapter cable to convert the A connector layout to the C connector design. On the other hand, if your next PC or parallel adapter uses the C connector and you plan to stick with your old printer, you'll need another variety of adapter, one that translates the C connector layout to that of the B connector.

Cable

The nature of the signals in the parallel port are their own worst enemy. They interact with themselves and the other wires in the cable to the detriment of all. The sharp transitions of the digital signals blur. The farther the signal travels in the cable, the greater the degradation that overcomes it. For this reason, the maximum recommended length of a printer cable was 10 feet. Not that longer cables will inevitably fail—practical experience often proves otherwise—but some cables in some circumstances become unreliable when stretched for longer distances.

The lack of a true signaling standard before IEEE 1284 made matters worse. Manufacturers had no guidelines for delays or transition times, so these values varied among PC, printer, and peripheral manufacturers. Although the signals might be close enough matches to work through a short cable, adding more wire could push them beyond the edge. A printer might then misread the signals from a PC, printing the wrong character or nothing at all.

Traditional printer cables are notoriously variable. As noted in the discussion of adapters, manufacturers scrimp where they can to produce low-cost adapter cables. After all, cables are commodities and the market is highly competitive. When you pay under $10 for a printer cable that comes without a brand name, you can never be sure of its electrical quality.

For this reason, extension cables are never recommended for locating your printer more than 10 feet from your PC. Longer distances require alternate strategies—opting for another connection (serial or network) or getting a printer extension system that alters the signals and provides a controlled cable environment.

What length you can get away with depends on the cable, your printer, and your PC. Computers and printers vary in their sensitivity to parallel port anomalies such as noise, crosstalk, and digital blurring. Some combinations of PCs and printers will work with lengthy parallel connections, up to 50 feet long. Others match-ups may balk when you stretch the connection more than the recommended 10 feet.

The high-speed modes of modern parallel ports make them even more finicky. When your parallel port operates in EPP or ECP modes, cable quality becomes critical even for short runs. Signaling speed across one of these interfaces can be in the megahertz range. The frequencies far exceed the reliable limits of even short runs of the dubious low-cost printer cables. Consequently, the IEEE 1284 specification precisely details a special cable for high-speed operation. Figure 21.12 offers a conceptual view of the construction of this special parallel data cable.

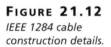

FIGURE 21.12
IEEE 1284 cable construction details.

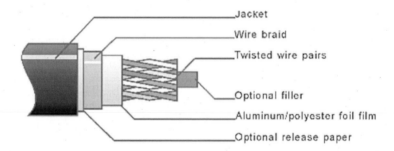

Jacket
Wire braid
Twisted wire pairs
Optional filler
Aluminum/polyester foil film
Optional release paper

Unlike standard parallel wiring, the data lines in IEEE 1284 cables must be double shielded to prevent interference from affecting the signals. Each signal wire must be twisted with its ground return. Even though the various standard connectors do not provide separate pins for each of these grounds, the ground wires must be present and run the full length of the cable.

The difference between old-fashioned "printer" cables and those that conform to the IEEE 1284 standard is substantial. Although you can plug in a printer with either a printer or IEEE 1284 compliant cable, devices that exploit the high-speed potentials of the EPP or ECP designs may not operate properly with a non-compliant cable. Often even when a printer fails to operate properly, the cable may be at fault. Substituting a truly IEEE 1284 compliant cable will bring reluctant connections to life.

Electrical Operation

In each of its five modes, the IEEE 1284 parallel port operates as if it were some kind of completely different electronic creation. When in compatibility mode, the IEEE 1284 port closely parallels the operation of the plain vanilla printer port of bygone days. It allows data to travel in one direction only, from PC to printer. Nibble mode gives your printer (or more likely, another peripheral) a voice and allows it to talk back to your PC. In nibble mode, data can move in either of two directions, although asymmetrically.

Information flows faster to your printer than it does on the return trip. Byte mode makes the journey fully symmetrical.

With the shift to EPP mode, the parallel port becomes a true expansion bus. A new way of linking to your PC's bus gives it increased bidirectional speed. Many systems can run their parallel ports 10 times faster in EPP mode than in compatibility, nibble, or byte mode. ECP mode takes the final step, giving control in addition to speed. ECP can do just about anything any other expansion interface (including SCSI) can do.

Because of these significant differences, the best way to get to know the parallel port is by considering each separately as if it were an interface unto itself. Our examination will follow from simple to complex, which also mirrors the history of the parallel port.

Note that IEEE 1284 deals only with the signals traveling through the connections of the parallel interface. It establishes the relationship between signals and their timing. It concerns itself neither with the data that is actually transferred, command protocols encoded in the data, nor with the control system that produces the signals. In other words, IEEE 1284 provides an environment under which other standards such as EPP and ECP operate. That is, ECP and EPP modes are not the ECP and EPP standards, although those modes are meant to be used by the parallel ports operating under respective standards.

Compatibility Mode

The least common denominator among parallel ports is the classic design that IBM introduced with the first PC. It was conceived strictly as a interface for the one-way transfer of information. Your PC sends data to your printer and expects nothing in return. After all, a printer neither stores information nor creates it on its own.

In conception, this port is like a conveyor that unloads ore from a bulk freighter or rolls coal out of a mine. The raw material travels in one direction. The conveyor mindlessly pushes out stuff and more stuff, perhaps creating a dangerously precarious pile, until its operator wakes up and switches it off before the pile gets much higher than his waist.

If your printer had unlimited speed or an unlimited internal buffer, such a one-way design would work. But like the coal yard, your printer has a limited capacity and may not be able to cart off data as fast as the interface shoves it out. The printer needs some way of sending a signal to your PC to warn about a potential data overflow. In electronic terms, the interface needs feedback of some kind; it needs to get information from the printer that your PC can use to control the data flow.

To provide the necessary feedback for controlling the data flow, the original Centronics port design and IBM's adaptation of it both included several control signals. These were designed to allow your PC to monitor how things are going with your printer—whether data is piling up, whether it has sufficient paper or ribbon, whether the printer is even turned on. Your PC can use this information to moderate the outflowing gush of data or to post a message warning you that something is wrong with your printer. In addition, the original parallel port included control signals sent from your PC to the printer to tell it *when* the PC wants to transfer data and to tell the printer to reset itself. The IEEE 1284 standard carries all of these functions into compatibility mode.

Strictly speaking, then, even this basic parallel port is not truly a one-way connection, although its feedback provisions were designed strictly for monitoring rather than data flow. For the first half of its life, the parallel port kept to this design. Until the adoption of IEEE 1284, this was the design you could expect for the port on your printer and, almost as likely, those on your PC.

Each signal flowing through the parallel port in compatibility mode has its own function. These signals include eight data lines, a strobe line, a busy line, an acknowledge line, select, paper empty, fault, initialize printer, select input, and auto feed XT.

Data Lines

The eight *data lines* of the parallel interface convey data in all operating modes. In compatibility mode, they carry data from the host to the peripheral on connector pins 2 through 9. The higher numbered pins are more significant to the digital code. To send data to the peripheral, the host puts a pattern of digital voltages on the data lines.

Strobe Line

The presence of signals on the data lines does not, in itself, move information from host to peripheral. As your PC gets its act together, it may change the pattern of data bits. No hardware can assure that all eight will always pop to the correct values simultaneously. Moreover, without further instruction your printer has no way of knowing whether the data lines represent a single character or multiple repetitions of the same character.

To assure reliable communications, the system requires a means of telling the peripheral that the pattern on the data lines represents valid information to be transferred. The *strobe line* does exactly that. Your PC pulses the strobe line to tell your printer that the bit-pattern on the data lines is a single valid character that the printer should read and accept. The strobe line gives its pulse only after the signals on the data lines have settled down. Most parallel ports delay the strobe signal by about half a microsecond to assure that the data signals have settled. The strobe itself lasts for at least half a microsecond so that your printer can recognize it. (The strobe signal can last up to 500 microseconds.) The signals on the data lines must maintain a constant value during this period and slightly afterward so that your printer has a chance to read them.

The strobe signal is negative going. That is, a positive voltage (+5VDC) stays on the strobe line until your printer want to send the actual strobe signal. Your PC then drops the positive voltage to near zero for the duration of the strobe pulse. The IEEE 1284 specification calls this signal *nStrobe*.

Busy Line

Sending data to your printer is thus a continuous cycle of setting up the data lines, sending the strobe signal, and putting new values on the data lines. The parallel port design typically requires about two microseconds for each turn of this cycle, allowing a perfect parallel port to dump out nearly half a million characters a second into your hapless printer. (As we will see, the actual maximum throughput of a parallel port is much lower than this.)

For some printers, coping with that data rate is about as daunting as trying to catch machine gun fire with your bare hands. Before your printer can accept a second character, its circuitry must do something with the one it has just received. Typically, it will need to move the character into the printer's internal buffer. Although the character moves at electronic speeds, it does not travel instantaneously. Your printer needs to be able to tell your PC to wait for the processing of the current character before sending the next.

The parallel port's *busy line* gives your printer the needed breathing room. Your printer switches on the busy signal as soon as it detects the strobe signal and keeps the signal active until it is ready to accept the next character. The busy signal can last for a fraction of a second (even as short as a microsecond) or your printer could hold it on indefinitely while it waits for you to correct some error. No matter how long the busy signal is on, it keeps your PC from sending out more data through the parallel port. It functions as the basic flow-control system.

Acknowledge Line

The final part of the flow-control system of the parallel port is the *acknowledge line*. It tells your PC that everything has gone well with the printing of a character or its transfer to the internal buffer. In effect, it is the opposite of the busy signal, telling your PC that the printer is ready rather than unready. Where the busy line says "Whoa!" the acknowledge line says "Giddyup!" The acknowledge signal is the opposite in another way; it is negative going and busy is positive going. The IEEE 1284 specification calls this signal *nAck*.

When your printer sends out the acknowledge signal, it completes the cycle of sending a character. Typically, the acknowledge signal on a conventional parallel port lasts about 8 microseconds, stretching a single character cycle across the port to 10 microseconds.

(IEEE 1284 specifies the length of nAck to be between 0.5 and 10 microseconds.) If you assume the typical length of this signal for a conventional parallel port, the maximum speed of the port works out to about 100,000 characters per second.

Select

In addition to transferring data to the printer, the basic parallel port allows your printer to send signals back to your PC so your computer can monitor the operation of the printer. The original IBM design of the parallel interface includes three such signals that tell your PC when your printer is ready, willing, and able to do its job. In effect, these signals give your PC the ability to remote sense the condition of your printer.

The most essential of these signals is *select*. The presence of this signal on the parallel interface tells your PC that your printer is online. That is, your printer is switched on and is in its online mode, ready to receive data from your PC. In effect, it is a remote indicator for the online light on your printer's control panel. If this signal is not present, your PC assumes that nothing is connected to your parallel port and doesn't bother with the rest of its signal repertory.

Because the rest state of a parallel port line is an absence of voltage (which would be the case if nothing were connected to the port to supply the voltage), the select signal takes the form of a positive signal (nominally +5VDC) that *in compatibility mode* under the IEEE 1284 specification stays active the entire period your printer is online.

Paper Empty

To print anything, your printer needs paper, and the most common problem that prevents your printer from doing its job is running out of paper. The *paper empty* signal warns your PC when your printer runs out. The IEEE 1284 specification calls this signal *PError* for "paper error," although it serves exactly the same function.

Paper empty is an information signal. It is not required for flow control because the busy signal more than suffices for that purpose. Most printers will assert their busy signals for the duration of the period they are without paper. Paper empty tells your PC about the specific reason that your printer has stopped data flow. This signal allows your operating system or application to flash a message on your monitor to warn you to load more paper.

Fault

The third printer-to-PC status signal is *fault*, a catch-all for warning of any other problems that your printer may develop—out of ink, paper jams, overheating, conflagrations, and other disasters. In operation, fault is actually a steady-state positive signal. It dips low (or off) to indicate a problem. At the same time, your printer may issue its other signals to halt the data flow, including busy and select. It never hurts to be extra sure. Because this signal is negative going, the IEEE specification calls it *nFault*.

Initialize Printer

In addition to the three signals your printer uses to warn of its condition, the basic parallel port provides three control signals that your PC can use to command your printer without adding anything to the data stream. Each of these three provides its own hard-wired connection for a specific purpose. These include one to initialize the printer, another to switch it to online condition if the printer allows a remote-control status change, and a final signal to tell the printer to feed the paper up one line.

The *initialize printer* signal helps your computer and printer keep in sync. Your printer can send a raft of different commands to your printer to change its mode of operation, change font, alter printing pitch, and so on. Each of your applications that share your printer might send out its own favored set of commands. And many applications are like sloppy in-laws who come for a visit and fail to clean up after themselves. The programs may leave your printer in some strange condition, such as set to print underscored bold-face characters in agate size type with a script typeface. The next program you run might assume some other condition and blithely print out paychecks in illegible characters.

Initialize printer tells your printer to step back to ground zero. Just as your PC boots up fresh and predictably, so does the printer. When your PC sends your printer the initialize printer command, it tells the printer to boot up, that is, reset itself and load its default operating parameters with its start-up configuration of fonts, pitches, typefaces, and the like. The command has the same effect as you switching off the printer and turning it back on and simply substitutes for adding a remote-control arm on your PC to duplicate your actions.

During normal operation, your PC puts a constant voltage on the initialize printer line. Removing the voltage tells your printer to reset. The IEEE 1284 specification calls this negative-going signal *nInit*.

Select Input

The signal that allows your PC to switch your printer online and offline is called *select input*. The IEEE 1284 specification calls it *nSelectIn*. It is active, forcing your printer online, when it is low or off. Switching it high deselects your printer.

Not all printers obey this command. Some have no provisions for switching themselves online and offline. Others have setup functions (such as a DIP switch) that allow you to defeat the action of this signal.

Auto Feed XT

At the time IBM imposed its print system design on the rest of the world, different printers interpreted the lowly carriage return in one of two ways. Some printers took it literally. Carriage return mean to move the printhead carriage back to its starting position on the left side of the platen. Other printers thought more like typewriters. Moving the printhead full left also indicated the start of a new line, so they obediently advanced the paper one line when they got a carriage return command. IBM, being a premiere typewriter maker at the time, opted for this second definition.

To give printer developers flexibility, however, the IBM parallel port design included the *Auto Feed XT* signal to give your PC command of the printer's handling of carriage returns. Under the IEEE 1284 specification, this signal is called *nAutoFd*. By holding this signal low or off, your PC commands your printer to act in the IBM and typewriter manner, adding a line feed to every carriage return. Making this signal high tells your printer to interpret carriage returns literally and only move the printhead. Despite the availability of this signal, most early PC printers ignored it and did whatever their setup configuration told them to do with carriage returns.

Nibble Mode

Early parallel ports used unidirectional circuitry for their data lines. No one foresaw the need for your PC to acquire data from your printer, so there was no need to add the expense or complication of bidirectional buffers to the simple parallel port. This tradition of single-direction design and operation continues to this day in the least expensive (which, of course, also means "cheapest") parallel ports.

Every parallel port does, however, have five signals that are meant to travel from the printer to your PC. These include (as designated by the IEEE 1284 specification) nAck, Busy, PError, Select, and nFault. If you could suspend the normal operation of these signals temporarily, you could use four of them to carry data back from the printer to your PC. Of course, the information would flow at half speed, four bits at a time.

This means of moving data is the basis of *nibble mode*, so called because the PC community calls half a byte (or those four bits) a nibble. Using nibble mode, any parallel port can operate bidirectionally—full speed forward but half speed in reverse.

Nibble mode requires that your PC take explicit command and control the operation of your parallel port. The port itself merely monitors all of its data and monitoring signals and relays the data to your PC. Your PC determines whether to regard your printer's status signals as backward-moving data. Of course, this system also requires that the device at the other end of the parallel port—your printer or whatever—know that it has switched into nibble mode and understand what signals to put where and when. The IEEE 1284 specification defines a protocol for switching into nibble mode and how PC and peripherals handle the nibble-mode signals.

The process is complex, involving several steps. First, your PC must identify whether the peripheral connected to it recognizes the IEEE standard. If not, all bets are off for using the standard. Products created before IEEE 1284 was adopted relied on the software driver controlling the parallel port to be matched to your parallel port peripheral. Because the two were already matched, they knew everything they needed to know about each other without negotiation. The pair could work without understanding the negotiation process or even the IEEE 1284 specification. Using the specification, however, allows your PC and peripherals to do the matching without your intervention.

Once your PC and peripheral decide they can use nibble mode, your PC signals to the peripheral to switch to the mode. Before the IEEE 1284 standard, the protocol was proprietary to the parallel port peripheral. The standard gives all devices a common means of controlling the switchover.

After both your PC and parallel port peripheral have switched to nibble mode, the signals on the interface get new definitions. In addition, nibble mode itself operates in two modes or phases, and the signals on the various parallel port lines behave differently in each mode. These modes include reverse idle phase and reverse data transfer phase.

In *reverse idle phase*, the PtrClk signal (nAck in compatibility mode) operates as an attention signal from the parallel port peripheral. Activating this signal tells the parallel port to issue an interrupt inside your PC, signaling that the peripheral has data available to be transferred. Your PC acknowledges the need for data and requests its transfer by switching the HostBusy signal (nAutoFd in compatibility mode) low or off. This switches the system to *reverse data transfer phase*. Your PC switches the HostBusy signal high again after the completion of the transfer of a full data byte. When the peripheral has mode data ready and your PC switches HostBusy back low again, another transfer begins. If it switches low without the peripheral having data available to send, the transition re-engages reverse idle phase.

During reverse data transfer phase, information is coded across two transfers as listed in Table 21.14. In effect, each transfer cycle involves to epicycles that move one nibble. First, your peripheral transfers the four bits of lesser significance and then the bits of more significance.

TABLE 21.14 Data Bit Definitions in Nibble Mode

Signal	First Epicycle Contents	Second Epicycle Contents
nFault	Least significant bit	Data bit 5
Xflag	Data bit 2	Data bit 6
AckDataReq	Data bit 3	Data bit 7
PtrBusy	Data bit 4	Most significant bit

Because moving a byte from peripheral to PC requires two nibble transfers, each of which requires the same time as one byte transfer from PC to peripheral, reverse transfers in nibble mode operate at half speed at best. The only advantage of nibble mode is its universal compatibility. Even before the IEEE 1284 specification, it allowed any parallel port to operate bidirectionally. Because of this speed penalty alone, if you have a peripheral and parallel port that lets you choose the operating mode for bidirectional transfers, nibble mode is your *least* attractive choice.

Byte Mode

Unlike nibble mode, byte mode requires special hardware. The basic design for byte mode circuitry was laid down when IBM developed its PS/2 line of computers and developed the Data Migration Facility. By incorporating bidirectional buffers in all eight of the data lines of the parallel port, IBM enabled them to both send and receive information on each end of the connection. Other than that change, the new design involved no other modifications to signals, connector pin assignments, or the overall operation of the port. Before the advent of the IEEE standard, these ports were known as PS/2 parallel ports or bidirectional parallel ports.

IEEE 1284 does more than put an official industry imprimatur on the IBM design, however. The standard redefines the bidirectional signals and adds a universal protocol of negotiating bidirectional transfers.

As with nibble mode, a peripheral in byte mode uses the PtrClk signal to trigger an interrupt in the host PC to advise that the peripheral has data available for transfer. When the PC services the interrupt, it checks the port nDataAvail signal, a negative-going signal that indicates a byte is available for transfer when it goes low. The PC can then pulse off the HostBusy signal to trigger the transfer using the HostClk (nStrobe) signal to read the data. The PC raises the HostBusy signal again to indicate the successful transfer of the data byte. The cycle can then repeat for as many bytes as need to be sent.

Because byte mode is fully symmetrical, transfers occur at the same speed in either direction. The speed limit is set to the performance of the port hardware, the speed at which the host PC handles the port overhead, and by the length of timing cycles set in the IEEE 1284 specification. Potentially, the design could require as little as four microseconds for each byte transferred, but real-world systems peak at about the same rate as conventional parallel ports, 100,000 bytes per second.

Enhanced Parallel Port Mode

When it was introduced, the chief innovation of the Enhanced Parallel Port was its improved performance, thanks to a design that hastened the speed at which your PC could pack data into the port. The EPP design altered port hardware so that instead of using byte-wide registers to send data through the port, your PC could dump a full 32-bit word of data directly from its bus into the port. The port would then handle all the conversion necessary to repackage the data into four byte-wide transfers. The reduction in PC overhead and more efficient hardware design enabled a performance improvement by a factor of 10 in practical systems. This speed increase required more stringent specifications for printer cables. The IEEE 1284 specification does not get into the nitty-gritty of linking the parallel port circuitry to your PC, so it does not guarantee that a port in EPP mode will deliver all of this speed boost. Moreover, the IEEE 1284 cable specs are not as demanding as the earlier EPP specs.

EPP mode of the IEEE 1284 specification uses only six signals in addition to the eight data lines for controlling data transfers. Three more connections in the interface are reserved for use by individual manufacturers and are not defined under the standard.

A given cycle across the EPP mode interface performs one of four operations: writing an address, reading an address, writing data, or reading data. The address corresponds to a register on the peripheral. The data operations are targeted on that address. Multiple data bytes may follow a single address signal as a form of burst mode.

nWrite

Data can travel both ways through an EPP connection. The *nWrite* signal tells whether the contents of the data lines are being sent from your PC to a peripheral or from a peripheral to your PC. When the nWrite signal is set low, it indicates data is bound for the peripheral. When set high, it indicates data sent from the peripheral.

nDStrobe

As with other parallel port transfers, your system needs a signal to indicate when the bits on the data lines are valid and accurate. EPP mode uses a negative-going signal called *nDStrobe* for this function in making data operations. Although this signal serves the same function as the strobe signal on a standard parallel port, it has been moved to a different pin, that used by the nAutoFd signal in compatibility mode.

nAStrobe

To identify a valid address on the interface bus, the EPP system uses the nAStrobe signal. This signal uses the same connection as does nSelectIn during compatibility mode.

nWait

To acknowledge that a peripheral has properly received a transfer, it deactivates the negative-going *nWait* signal (making it a positive voltage on the bus). By holding the signal positive, the peripheral signals the host PC to wait. Making the signal negative indicates that the peripheral is ready for another transfer.

Intr

To signal the host PC that a peripheral connected to the EPP interface requires immediate service, it sends out the *Intr* signal. The transition between low and high states of this signal indicates a request for an interrupt (that is, the signal is edge-triggered). EPP mode does not allocate a signal to acknowledge that the interrupt request was received.

nInit

The escape hatch for EPP mode is the *nInit* signal. When this signal is activated by making it low, it forces the system out of EPP mode and back to compatibility mode.

Extended Capabilities Port Mode

When operating in ECP mode, the IEEE 1284 port uses seven signals to control the flow of data through the standard eight data lines. ECP mode defines two data transfer signaling protocols—one for forward transfers (from PC to peripheral) and one for reverse transfers (peripheral to PC)—and the transitions between them. Transfers are moderated by closed-loop handshaking that guarantees that all bytes get where they are meant to go, even should the connection be temporarily disrupted.

Because all parallel ports start in compatibility mode, your PC and its peripherals must first negotiate with one another to arrange to shift into ECP mode. Your PC and its software initiate the negotiation (as well as manage all aspects of the data transfers). Following a successful negotiation to enter ECP mode, the connection enters its forward idle phase.

HostClk

To transfer information or commands across the interface, your PC starts from the forward idle phase and puts the appropriate signals on the data line. To signal to your printer or other peripheral that the values on the data lines are valid and should be transferred, your PC activates its *HostClk* signal, setting it to a logical high.

PeriphAck

The actual transfer does not take place until your printer or other peripheral acknowledges the HostClk signal by sending back the *PeriphAck* signal, setting it to a logical high. In response, your PC switches the HostClk signal low. Your printer or peripheral then knows it should read the signals on the data lines. Once it finishes reading the data signals, the peripheral switches the PeriphAck signal low. This completes the data transfer. Both HostClk and PeriphAck are back to their forward idle phase norms, ready for another transfer.

nPeriphRequest

When a peripheral needs to transfer information back to the host PC or to another peripheral, it makes a request by driving the *nPeriphRequest* signal low. The request is a suggestion rather than a command because only the host PC can initiate or reverse the flow of data. The nPeriphRequest typically causes an interrupt in the host PC to make this request known.

nReverseRequest

To allow a peripheral to send data back to the host or to another device connected to the interface, the host PC activates the *nReverseRequest* signal by driving it low, essentially switching off the voltage that otherwise appears there. This signals to the peripheral that the host PC will allow the transfer.

nAckReverse

To acknowledge that it has received the nReverseRequest signal and that it is ready for a reverse-direction transfer, the peripheral asserts its *nAckReverse* signal, driving it low. The peripheral can then send information and commands through the eight data lines and the PeriphAck signal.

PeriphClk

To begin a reverse transfer from peripheral to PC, the peripheral first loads the appropriate bits onto the data lines. It then signals to the host PC that it has data ready to transfer by driving the *PeriphClk* signal low.

HostAck

Your PC responds to the PeriphClk signal by switching the *HostAck* signal from its idle logical low to a logical high. The peripheral responds by driving PeriphClk high. When the host accepts the data, it responds by driving the HostAck signal low. This completes the transfer and returns the interface to the reverse idle phase.

Data Lines

Although the parallel interface uses the same eight data lines to transfer information as do other IEEE 1284 port modes, it supplements them with an additional signal to indicate whether the data lines contain data or a command. The signal used to make this nine-bit information system changes with the direction of information transfer. When ECP mode transfers data from PC host to a peripheral (that is, during a forward transfer), it uses the HostAck signal to specify command or data. When a peripheral originates the data being transferred (a reverse transfer), it uses the PeriphAck signal to specify command or data.

Logical Interface

All parallel ports, no matter the speed, technology, or operating mode, must somehow interface with your PC, its operating system, and your applications. After all, you can't expect to print if you can't find your printer, so you shouldn't expect your programs to do it, either. Where you might need a map to find your printer, particularly when your office makes the aftermath of a rock concert seem organized, your programs need something more in line with their logical nature that serves the same function. You look for a particular address on a street. Software looks for function calls, interrupt routines, or specific hardware parameters.

That list represents the steps that get you closer to the actual interface. A function call is a high-level software construct, part of your operating system or a driver used by the operating system or your applications. The function call may in turn ask for an interrupt, which is a program routine that either originates in the firmware of your PC or is added by driver software. Both the function call and interrupt work reach your interface by dipping down to the hardware level and looking for specific features. Most important of these are the input/output ports used by your parallel interface.

Input/Output Ports

The design of the first PC linked the circuitry of the parallel port to the PC's microprocessor through a set of *input/output ports* in your PC. These I/O ports are not ports that access the outside world but rather are special way a microprocessor has to connect to circuitry. An I/O port works like a memory address; the microprocessor signals the address value to the PC's support circuitry and then it sends data to that address. The only difference between addressing memory and I/O ports is that data for the former goes to the RAM in your PC. In the latter case, the addressing is in a separate range that links to other circuitry. In general, the I/O port addresses link to registers, a special kind of memory that serves as a portal for passing logical values between circuits.

The traditional design for a parallel port used three of these I/O ports. The EPP and ECP designs use more. In any case, however, the I/O ports take the form of a sequential block. The entire range of I/O ports used in a parallel connection usually gets identified by the address of first of these I/O ports (which is to say the one with the lowest number or address). This number is termed the *base address* of the parallel port. Every parallel port in a given PC must have a unique base address. Two parallel ports inside a single PC cannot share the same base address, nor can they share any of their other I/O ports. If you accidentally assign two parallel ports the same base address when configuring your PC's hardware, neither will likely work.

The original PC design made provisions for up to three parallel ports in a single system, and this limit has been carried through to all IBM-compatible PCs. Each of these has its own base address. For the original PC, IBM chose three values for these base addresses, and these remain the values used by most hardware makers. These basic base addresses are 03BC(Hex), 0378(Hex), and 0278(Hex).

Manufacturers rarely use the first of these, 03BC(Hex). IBM originally assigned this base address to the parallel port that was part of the long-obsolete IBM Monochrome Display Adapter, or MDA, card. IBM kept using this name in its PS/2 line of computers, assigning it to the one built-in parallel port in those machines. There was no chance of conflict with the MDA card because the MDA cannot be installed inside PS/2s. Other computer makers sometimes use this base address for built-in parallel ports. More often, however, they use the base address of 0378(Hex) for such built-in ports. Some allow you to assign either address—or even 0278(Hex)—using their setup program, jumpers, or DIP switches.

Device Names

These base address values are normally hidden from your view and your concern. Most programs and operating systems refer to parallel ports with port names. These names take the familiar line printer form: LPT1, LPT2, and LPT3. In addition, the port with the name LPT1 can also use the alias PRN.

The correspondence between the base address of a parallel port and its device name varies with the number of ports in your PC. There is no direct one-to-one relationship between them. Your system assigns the device names when it boots up. One routine in your PC's BIOS code searches for parallel ports at each of the three defined base addresses in a fixed order. It always looks first for 03BC(Hex), then 0378(Hex), and then 0278 (Hex). The collection of I/O ports at the first base address that's found gets assigned the name LPT1; the second, LPT2; the third, LPT3. The BIOS stores the base address values in a special memory area called the *BIOS data area* at particular absolute addresses. Because I/O port addresses are 16 bits long, each base address is allocated two bytes of storage. The base address of the parallel port assigned the LPT1 is stored at absolute memory location 0000:0408; LPT2, at 0000:040A; LPT3, 0000:040C. This somewhat arcane system assures you that you will always have a device called LPT1 (and PRN) in your PC if you have a parallel interface at all, no matter what set of I/O ports it uses.

Interrupts

The design of the original PC provided two interrupts for use by parallel ports. Hardware interrupt 07(Hex) was reserved for the first parallel port, and hardware interrupt 05(Hex) was reserved for the second.

DOS, Windows, and most applications do not normally use hardware interrupts to control printers. When interrupts run short in your PC and you need to find one for a specific feature, you can often steal one of the interrupts used by a printer port.

The key word in the discussion of parallel port interrupts is *printer*. If you use your parallel port for some other purpose, you may not be able to steal its interrupt. Drivers for

EPP and ECP ports may use interrupts, and modems that use parallel ports usually make use of interrupts. If you need an interrupt and you're not sure whether your parallel port needs it, try reassigning it where you need it. Then, try to print something while you use the feature that borrowed the interrupt. If there's a problem, you'll know it before you risk your data to it.

Port Drivers

The PC printer port was designed to be controlled by a software driver. Under DOS, you might not notice these drivers because they are part of your PC's ROM BIOS. The printer interrupt handler is actually a printer driver.

In reality, only a rare program uses this BIOS-based driver. It's simply too slow. Because the hardware resources used by the parallel port are well known and readily accessed, most programmers prefer to directly control the parallel port hardware to send data to your printer. Many applications incorporate their own print routines or use printer drivers designed to take this kind of direct control.

More advanced operating systems similarly take direct hardware control of the parallel port through software drivers that take over the functions of the BIOS routines. Under Windows 95 or 98, you can check or change the parallel port driver of your system through the Printer Port properties folder. To access this folder, run Device Manager. From the Start button, select Settings and then Control Panel. Click on the System icon in Control Panel. Select the Device Manager tab. Click on the line for Ports (COM and LPT) and then highlight the LPT (Printer) port for which you want to check the driver. Finally, click the Properties button. You'll see a screen like that shown in Figure 21.13.

Under the heading Driver files, you'll see your parallel port drivers listed. You can change the driver used by this port by clicking on the Change Driver button under Windows 95 or Update Driver under Windows 98. If you have Windows 95, you'll see a window like that shown in Figure 21.14.

Windows 98 gives you a wizard to update your printer port, but after you step through it you'll face a Models list screen like that in Figure 21.14. You'll have a quicker time if you tell the Windows wizard *not* to search for hardware but instead to display all of the drivers so you can select the one you want.

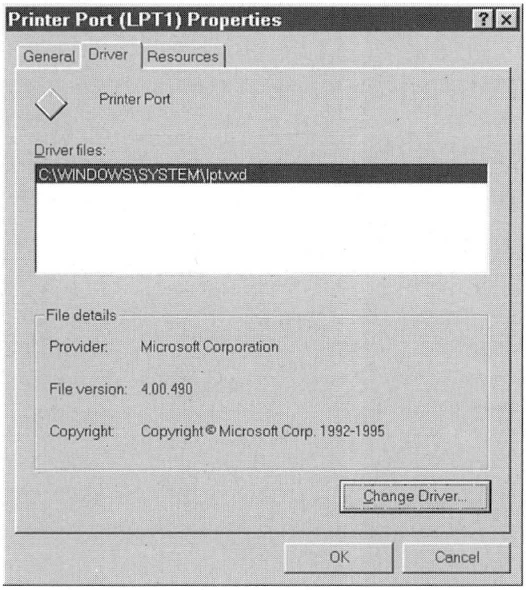

FIGURE 21.13

The Windows parallel port properties dialog.

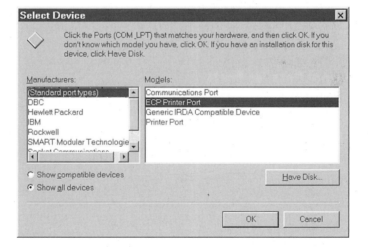

FIGURE 21.14

Updating your parallel port driver under Windows.

By default, the Models list will include only those drivers that are compatible with the port that the Windows Plug and Play system has detected in your PC. The list will change with the manufacturer you highlight. You can view all the available drivers from a given manufacturer (or the standard drivers) by selecting Show all devices. If the driver you want is not within the current repertory of your Windows system, you can install a driver from a floppy or CD ROM disk (or one that you've copied to your hard disk) by clicking the Have Disk button, which prompts you for the disk and path name leading to the driver.

To install a new driver, highlight it and click the OK button. Windows takes care of the rest.

Control

Even in its immense wisdom, a microprocessor can't fathom how to operate a parallel port by itself. It needs someone to tell it how to move the signals around. Moreover, the minutiae of constantly taking care of the details of controlling a port would be a waste of the microprocessor's valuable time. Consequently, system designers created help systems for your PC's big brain. Driver software tells the microprocessor how to control the port. And port hardware handles all the details of port operation.

As parallel ports have evolved, so have these aspects of their control. The software that controls the traditional parallel port that's built into the firmware of your PC has given way to a complex system of drivers. The port hardware, too, has changed to both simplify operation and to speed it up.

These changes don't follow the neat system of modes laid down by IEEE 1284. Instead, they have undergone a period of evolution in reaching their current condition.

Traditional Parallel Ports

In the original PC, each of its parallel ports linked to the PC's microprocessor through three separate I/O ports, each controlling its own register. The address of the first of these registers serves as the base address of the parallel port. The other two addresses are the next higher in sequence. For example, when the first parallel port in a PC had a base address of 0378(Hex), the other two I/O ports assigned it had addresses of 0379(Hex) and 037A(Hex).

The register at the base address of the parallel port serves a data latch called the *printer data register*, which temporarily holds the values passed along to it by your PC's microprocessor. Each of the eight bits of this port is tied to one of the data lines leading out of the parallel port connector. The correspondence is exact. For example, the most significant bit of the register connects to the most significant bit on the port connector. When your PC's microprocessor writes a value to the base register of the port, the register latches those values until your microprocessor sends newer values to the port.

Your PC uses the next register on the parallel port, corresponding to the next I/O port, to monitor what the printer is doing. Termed the *printer status register*, the various bits that your microprocessor can read at this I/O port carry messages from the printer back to your PC. The five most significant bits of this register directly correspond to five signals appearing in the parallel cable: bit 7 indicates the condition of the busy signal; bit 6, acknowledge; bit 5, paper empty; bit 4, select; and bit 3, error. The remaining three bits of this register (bits 2, 1, and 0—the least significant bits) served no function in the original PC parallel port.

To send commands to your printer, your PC uses the third I/O port, offset two ports from the base address of the parallel port. The register there, called the *printer control register*, relays commands through its five least significant bits. Of these, four directly control corresponding parallel port lines. Bit 0 commands the strobe line; bit 1, the auto feed XT line; bit 2, the initialize line; and bit 3, the select line.

To enable your printer to send interrupts to command the microprocessor's attention, your PC uses bit 4 of the printer control register. Setting this bit high causes the acknowledge signal from the printer to trigger a printer interrupt. During normal operation your printer, after it receives and processes a character, changes the acknowledge signal from a logical high to a low. Set bit 4, and your system detects the change in the acknowledge line through the printer status register and executes the hardware interrupt assigned to the port. In the normal course of things, this interrupt simply instructs the microprocessor to send another character to the printer.

All of the values sent to the printer data register and the printer control register are put in place by your PC's microprocessor, and the chip must read and react to all the values packed into the printer status register. The printer gets its instructions for what to do from firmware that is part of your system's ROM BIOS. The routines coded for interrupt vector 017(Hex) carry out most of these functions. In the normal course of things, your applications call interrupt 017(Hex) after loading appropriate values into your microprocessors registers, and the microprocessor relays the values to your printer. These operations are very microprocessor intensive. They can occupy a substantial fraction of the power of a microprocessor (particularly that of older, slower chips) during print operations.

Enhanced Parallel Ports

Intel set the pattern for Enhanced Parallel Ports by integrating the design into the 386SL chipset (which comprised a microprocessor and a support chip, the 386SL itself and the 82360SL I/O subsystem chip, which together required only memory to make a complete PC). The EPP was conceived as a superset of the standard and PS/2 parallel ports. As with those designs, compatible transfers require the use of the three parallel port registers at consecutive I/O port addresses. However, it adds five new registers to the basic three. Although designers are free to locate these registers wherever they want because they are accessed using drivers, in the typical implementation, these registers occupy the next five I/O port addresses in sequence.

EPP Address Register

The first new register (offset three from the base I/O port address) is called the *EPP address register*. It provides a direct channel through which your PC can specify addresses of devices linked through the EPP connection. By loading an address value in this register, your PC could select among multiple devices attached to a single parallel port, at least once parallel devices using EPP addressing become available.

EPP Data Registers

The upper four ports of the EPP system interface (starting at offset four from the base port) link to the *EPP data registers*, which provide a 32-bit channel for sending data to the EPP data buffer. The EPP port circuitry takes the data from the buffer, breaks it into four separate bytes, and then sends the bytes through the EPP data lines in sequence. Substituting four I/O ports for the one used by standard parallel ports moves the conversion into the port hardware, relieving your system from the responsibility of formatting the data. In addition, your PC can write to the four EPP data registers simultaneously using a single 32-bit double-word in a single clock cycle in computers that have 32-bit data buses. In lesser machines, the EPP specification also allows for byte-wide and word-wide (16-bit) write operations through to the EPP data registers.

Unlike standard parallel ports that require your PC's microprocessor to shepherd data through the port, the Enhanced Parallel Port works automatically. It needs no other signals from your microprocessor after it loads the data in order to carry out a data transfer. The EPP circuitry itself generates the data strobe signal on the bus almost as soon as your microprocessor writes to the EPP data registers. When your microprocessor reads data from the EPP data registers, the port circuitry automatically triggers the data strobe signal to tell whatever device that's sending data to the EPP connection that your PC is ready to receive more data. The EPP port can consequently push data through to the data lines with a minimum of transfer overhead. This streamlined design is one of the major factors that enables the EPP to operate so much faster than standard ports.

Fast Parallel Port Control Register

To switch from standard parallel port to bidirectional to EPP operation requires only plugging values into one of the registers. Although the manufacturers can use any design they want, needing only to alter their drivers to match, most follow the pattern set in the SL chips. Intel added a software-controllable *fast parallel port control register* as part of the chipset. This corresponds to the unused bits of the standard parallel port printer control register.

Setting the most significant bit (bit 7) of the fast parallel port control register high engages EPP operation. Setting this bit low (the default) forces the port into standard mode. Another bit controls bidirectional operation. Setting bit 6 of the fast parallel port control register high engages bidirectional operation. When low, bit 6 keeps the port unidirectional.

In most PCs, a EPP doesn't automatically spring to life. Simply plugging your printer into EPP hardware won't guarantee fast transfers. Enabling the EPP requires a software driver, which provides the link between your software and the EPP hardware.

Extended Capabilities Ports

As with other variations on the basic parallel port design, your PC controls an Extended Capabilities Port through a set of registers. To maintain backward compatibility with products requiring access to a standard parallel port, the ECP design starts with the same trio of basic registers. However, it redefines the parallel port data in each of the ports' different operating modes.

The ECP design supplements the basic trio of parallel port registers with an additional set of registers offset at port addresses 0400(Hex) higher than the base registers. One of these, the *extended control register*, controls the operating mode of the ECP port. Your microprocessor sets the operating mode by writing to this port, which is located offset by 0402(Hex) from the base register of the port. The ECP port uses additional registers to monitor and control other aspects of the data transfer. Table 21.15 lists the registers used by the ECP, their mnemonics, and the modes in which they function.

TABLE 21.15   Extended Capabilities Port Register Definitions

Name	Address	Mode	Function
Data	Base	PC, PS/2	Data register
ecpAFifo	Base	ECP	ECP FIFO (address) buffer
DSR	Base+1	All	Status register
DCR	Base+2	All	Control register
cFifo	Base+400	EPP	Enhanced Parallel Port FIFO (data) buffer
ecpDFifo	Base+400	ECP	ECP FIFO (data) buffer
tFifo	Base+400	Test	Test FIFO
cnfgA	Base+400	Configuration	Configuration register A
cnfgB	Base+401	Configuration	Configuration register B
ecr	Base+402	All	Extended control register

As with other improved parallel port designs, the ECP behaves exactly like a standard parallel port in its default mode. Your programs can write bytes to its data register (located at the port's base address just as with a standard parallel port) to send the bits through the data lines of the parallel connection. Switch to EPP or ECP mode, and your programs can write at high speed to a register as wide as 32 bits. The ECP design allows for transfers 8, 16, or 32 bits wide at the option of the hardware designer.

To allow multiple devices to share a single parallel connection, the ECP design incorporates its own addressing scheme that allows your PC to separately identify and send data to up to 128 devices. When your PC wants to route a packet or data stream through the parallel connection to a particular peripheral, it sends out a channel address command through the parallel port. The command includes a device address. When an ECP parallel device receives the command, it compares the address to its own assigned address. If the two do not match, the device ignores the data traveling through the parallel connection until your PC sends the next channel address command through the port. When your PC fails to indicate a channel address, the data gets broadcast to all devices linked to the parallel connection.

Performance Issues

As with any interface, you want your parallel connection to operate at the highest possible speed. The speed of a parallel connection can be difficult to pin down. Several variables affect it. For example, the parallel cable itself sets the upper limit on the frequencies of the signals that the port can use, which in turn limits the maximum data rate. At practical cable lengths, which means those less then the recommended 10-foot maximum, cable effects on parallel port throughput are minimal. Other factors that come into play include the switching speed of the port circuitry itself, the speed at which your PC can write to various control and data registers, the number of steps required by the BIOS or software driver to write a character, the ability of the device at the other end of the connection to accept and process the data sent to it, and the delays necessary in the timing of the various parallel port signals that are necessary to ensure the integrity of the transfer.

Timing

The timing of parallel port signals is actually artificially slow to accommodate the widest variety of parallel devices. Because the timing was never standardized before the IEEE 1284 specification, manufacturers had to rely on loose timing—meaning a wider tolerance of errors achieved through a slower signaling rate—to assure any PC could communicate with any printer or other parallel peripheral.

When system timing of an older standard parallel port is set at the minima that produces the widest compatibility, the transmission of a single character requires about 10 microseconds. That speed yields a peak transfer rate of 100,000 bytes per second.

Operated at the tightest timing allowed by the IEEE 1284 specification, a conventional parallel port can complete a single character transfer cycle in 4 microseconds, yielding a peak throughput of 250,000 bytes per second.

Add in all the overhead at both ends of the connection, and those rates can take a bad tumble. With a fast PC and fast peripheral, you can realistically expect 80 to 90 KB/sec through the fastest conventional parallel port.

The EPP specification allows for a cycle time of one-half microsecond in its initial implementations. That translates to a peak transfer rate of 2 MB/sec. In actual operation with normal processing overhead, EPP (and ECP) ports come close to half that rate, around 800 KB/sec.

Such figures do not represent the top limit for the EPP design, however. In future versions of the EPP standard, timing constraints may be tightening to require data on the interface to become valid within 100 nanoseconds. Such future designs allow for a peak transfer rate approaching 8 MB/sec. Such a rate actually exceeds the speed of practical transfers across the ISA bus. Taking full advantage of an EPP connection will require a local bus link.

Data Compression

One effective way of increasing the speed of information through any interface is to minimize the number of bytes you have to move. By compressing the digital code—that is, reducing it to a more bit-efficient format—you can reduce the number of bytes needed to convey text, graphics, and files. Already popular in squeezing more space from disks (for example, with DriveSpace and Stacker), tapes in backup systems, and modem connections, data compression is also part of the Extended Capabilities Port standard.

As an option, the ECP system allows you to compress the data you send through the parallel interface to further increase the speed of transfers. The port circuitry itself handles the compression and decompression, invisible to your PC and its software as well as to the peripheral at the other end of the connection. The effect on your transfers is the same as increasing the speed of the signals across the parallel cable but without all the electrical problems.

The ECP design uses a simple form of compression called *Run Length Encoding*, or RLE. As with any code, RLE can take many different forms but the basic principle is the same. Long repetitions of the same digital pattern get reduced to a single occurrence of the pattern and a number indicating how many times the pattern is repeated. The specific RLE algorithm used by the ECP system works at the byte level. When the same byte is repeated in a sequence of data, the system translates it into two bytes: one indicating the original code and a multiplier. Of course, if bytes do not repeat this basic form, RLE is counterproductive. Using two bytes to code one accomplishes increases the number of bytes required for a given amount of data. To minimize the impact of this expansion, the RLE algorithm used by the ECP system splits the difference. Half the possible byte values are kept untouched and are used by the code to represent the same single byte values as in the incoming data stream. The other byte values serve as multipliers. If the same byte as that used by a multiplier appears in the incoming data stream, it must be represented by two bytes (the byte value followed by a multiplier of one). This system allows two bytes to encode repeated character streams up to 128 bytes long.

At its best, this system can achieve a compression ratio of 64 to 1 on long repetitions of a single byte value. At worst, the system expands data by a ratio of 1 to 2. With real-world data, the system achieves an overall compression ratio approaching 2 to 1, effectively doubling the speed of the parallel interface, whatever its underlying bit-per-second transfer rate.

RLE data compression can be particularly effective when you transfer graphic images from your PC to your printer. Graphic images often contain long sequences of repeated bytes representing areas of uniform color. RLE encoding offers little benefit to textual exchanges because text rarely contains long repetitions of the same byte or character. Of course, sending ordinary text to a printer usually doesn't strain the capabilities of even a standard parallel port, so the compression speed boost is unnecessary.

Bus Mastering

System overhead is the bane of performance in any data transfer system. The more time your PC's microprocessor spends preparing and moving data through the interface, the less of its time is available for other operations. The problem is most apparent during background printing in PCs using older, slower microprocessors. Most applications give you the option of printing in the background so you can go on to some other task while your PC slowly spools out data to your printer. All too often, the PC slows down so much during background printing that it's virtually useless for other work. This problem occurs in PCs as powerful as 486-based machines.

The slowdown has several sources. Your microprocessor may have to rasterize a full-page image itself (as it often does when printing from Windows) or it may spend its time micro-managing the movement of bytes from memory to the registers of the parallel interface. Although system designers can't do anything to improve the speed of the former case, short of using a more powerful microprocessor, they have developed several schemes to minimize system overhead. One dramatic improvement comes with sidestepping the printer BIOS routines and taking direct control of the interface circuitry. Another is to take a job from the microprocessor and give it to some other circuit. This last expedient underlies the technology of *bus mastering*.

Bus mastering can improve overall system (and printing) performance two ways. The circuit managing the transfers can be more efficient than your microprocessor at the chore. It may be able to move bytes faster. And by removing responsibility from your microprocessor, it prevents data transfers from bogging down the rest of your PC. Your microprocessor has more of its time for doing whatever a microprocessor does.

In systems that allow the bus mastering of parallel port, the transfers are typically managed by your system's DMA (Direct Memory Access) controller. Your microprocessor sets up the transfer—specifying where the bytes are coming from, where they are to go, and how many to move—and lets the DMA controller take over the details. The DMA controller then takes control of the bus, becoming its master and moving the bytes across it.

Bus-mastered parallel transfers have not won wide favor. The technology does not work well on the ISA expansion bus, and IBM introduced it late in the life of the Micro Channel system. Moreover, the high processing speed of modern 486 and better microprocessors coupled with comparatively low throughput of the standard parallel interface makes the bus mastering an unnecessary complication. Although not currently applied to PCI or VL Bus systems (both of which support bus mastering), the technology could give a boost to EPP and ECP performance because of the higher throughput and simplified means of transfer bytes to those interfaces.

Plug and Play

The Plug and Play system developed by computer manufacturers with the intention of making your life simpler—or at least dealing with the setup of your PC easier—extends to input/output ports and printers. Plug and Play technology allows your PC to detect and identify the various hardware devices that you connect to your computer. For example, a printer that understands and uses the Plug and Play system can identify itself to your PC and tell your PC which software driver is best to use.

The basic mechanism required for the Plug and Play system to work for printers is built into the IEEE 1284 specification. The actual identification and matching of drivers gets handled by your PC's operating system.

Benefits

Equipment made in accord with the Plug and Play specification tells your PC the system resources it needs, and your PC can then automatically assign those resources to the equipment. Unlike when you set up hardware yourself, your PC can infallibly (or nearly so) keep track of the resource demands and usages of each device you connect. Plug and Play technology lets your PC not only resolve conflicts between devices that need the same or similar hardware resources, but also the system prevents conflicts from occurring in the first place.

When connecting a printer, you only need to concern yourself, if at all, with two aspects of Plug and Play—how it configures your ports and how it deals with your printer itself. Although you shouldn't even have to worry about these details most of the time, understanding the magic can help you better understand your PC and subvert the system when it creates instead of eliminates a problem.

Printers that conform to the requirements of the Plug and Play system enable several automatic features. A printer can then specify its *device class*, and the Plug and Play operating system will install features and drivers that work with that device class. The system allows your printer to identify itself with a familiar name instead of some obscure model number and use that name throughout the configuration process. That way, you can understand what's going on instead of worrying about some weird thing in your computer with a name that looks eerily like the markings on the side of a UFO. And the Plug and Play printer can tell you what other peripherals that it works with.

Requirements

For the Plug and Play system to work at all, you need to run an operating system that has Plug and Play capabilities. Windows 95 was the first operating system to fully support the technology.

Ideally, your PC and all the peripherals connected to it will comply with the Plug and Play specifications. If you buy a new PC in these enlightened times, you should expect that level of compliance. If you have an older system (or a new system into which you've installed old peripherals), however, you probably won't have full Plug and Play compliance. That's okay because in most cases a Plug and Play operating system can make do with what you have. For example, Windows can identify your printer as long as it follows the Plug and Play standard—even if you have cluttered your PC with old expansion boards that don't mesh with the standard.

To automatically identify your printer, the Plug and Play system needs only to be able to signal to your printer and have it send back identification data. Your parallel port is key to this operation, but the demands made from it for Plug and Play operation are minimal. The port may use any of the standard IEEE connector designs. It must also support, at minimum, nibble-mode bidirectional transfers. Nearly every parallel port ever made fits these requirements. Plug and Play prefers a port that follows the ECP design, and for the sake of maximum printer performance, so should you.

Of course, a printer must have built-in support of the Plug and Play standard if it is to take advantage of the technology. The primary need is simple. Your printer must be able to send to your PC Plug and Play identification information so your PC will know what kind of printer you've connected. So that your system can be certain about the kind of printer you have, it requires three forms of identification called *key values*. Three additional key values optimize the operation of the Plug and Play system.

Operation

The IEEE 1284 specification provides a mechanism through which your PC's operating system can query a device connected to a parallel port. When your PC sends out the correct command, the printer responds first by sending back two bytes indicating how much identification data it has stored. This value is the length of the identification data in bytes, including the two length-indicating bytes. The first byte of these is the more significant.

After your PC gets the length information, it can query your printer for the actual data with another command. Your Plug and Play printer responds by sending back the key value information stored inside its configuration memory (which may be ROM, Flash RAM, or EEPROM).

The three required identifications for Plug and Play to work are the manufacturer, command set, and model of your printer. Each of these is stored as a string of case-sensitive characters prefaced by the type of identification. The IEEE 1284 specification abbreviates these identifications as MFG, CMD, and MDL. For example, your printer might respond with these three required values like this:

```
MFG: Acme Printers; CMD: PCL; MDL: Roadrunner 713
```

The manufacturer and model identifications are unique to each manufacturer. These values should never change and typically will be stored in ROM inside your printer. Ideally, the command set identification tells your computer what printer driver to use, Hewlett-Packard's Printer Control Language (PCL) in the sample line. Although it is often a fixed value in a given printer, if your printer allows you to plug in additional emulations or fonts, the value of the command set identifier should change to match. Note that Windows ignores the command set key value. Instead, when it automatically sets up your printer driver, it relies on manufacturer and model information to determine which driver to use.

Windows generates its own internal Plug and Play identification for working with key value data. It generates its ID value by combining together the manufacturer and model values and appending a four-digit checksum. If the manufacturer and model designations total more than 20 characters, Windows cuts them off at 20 characters but only *after* it calculates the checksum. The result is a string 24 or fewer characters long. Finally, Windows adds the preface LPTENUM\ (indicating the parallel port enumerator) so that it knows the path through which to find the printer. The result is the printer's Plug and Play ID that Windows uses internally when matching device drivers to your printer. For example, the internal Windows ID for a Hewlett-Packard LaserJet 4L printer would be the following character string:

```
LPTENUM\Hewlett-PackardLaserC029
```

Printer manufacturers can add, at their option, other identification information to the Plug and Play key values. The IEEE 1284 specification envisions comment and active command set entries. Microsoft defines its own trio of options: class (abbreviated CLS), description (or DES), and compatible ID (or CID). These values are not case sensitive.

The class key value describes the general type of device. Microsoft limits the choices to eight: FDC, HDC, Media, Modem, Net, Ports, or Printer.

The description key value is a string of up to 128 characters that is meant to identify the Plug and Play device in a form that human beings understand. Windows uses the description when referring to the device onscreen when it cannot find a data (INF) file corresponding to the device. Normally, Windows would retrieve the onscreen identification for the device from the file. The description key value keeps things understandable even if you plug in something Windows has never encountered before.

The compatible ID key value tells Windows if your printer or other device will work exactly like some other product for which Windows might have a driver. For example, it allows the maker of a printer cloned from an Epson MX-80 to indicate it will happily use the Epson printer driver.

Once Windows has identified your printer, its command set, and compatibilities, it uses these values to search for the data it needs to find the drivers required by your printer and properly configure them. Of course, you always have the option to override the automatic choices when you think you know better than Mother Microsoft.

Telecommunications

The greatest power and strength in using a computer comes not from sitting at a solitary keyboard but by connecting with other machines and networks. You can exchange files, programs, images, and information across telephone lines. But because most of today's local telephone lines are analog and computers are stolidly digital, you need a modem to match them. Modem speeds and variety (including fax modems) are greater than ever before.

Your telecommunication connection choices

Connection	Maximum speed	Advantages	Disadvantages
V.90 Modem	56 Kbit/sec	Slow	Cheap; universally available
ISDN	128 Kbit/sec	Standardized	Spotty availability; can be expensive; not very fast
DSL (G.Lite)	1.544 Mbit/sec	Fast	Spotty availability; Pricing varies with location; Must be near central office
Leased line (T1)	1.544 Mbit/sec	Fast	Expensive (both in installation and monthly charges)
Cable Modem	10 Mbit/sec	Very fast; usually inexpensive	Spotty availability
Direct Satellite	400 Kbits/sec	Available almost anywhere	Moderate speed; works best with buffering

Your PC achieves its peak power when it reaches out and touches the universe of other computers. Using the telecommunications power of your PC, you can link up with the World Wide Web, download the latest driver software, play games internationally, find the most obscure facts, or simply fax your lunch order to the corner deli. The PC can do all this and more with a single connection to the outside world. The prime target is, of course, the Internet.

For years, that connection was the same one you used to reach for making dates, ordering pizza, or raving to the town council. By adding a modem to your PC, you could adapt it to the telephone line and use your PC for exactly the same things. The old phone line was a strange world to your PC, full of primitive and dangerous signals. It was the world of analog, and it required special equipment—like that modem—to make a connection.

Just as computer technology has invaded everything else in the world, it wormed its way into the international telephone system as well. The new generation of telecommunications extends your PC with the signals it knows best, digital. A number of these new digital services promise your PC faster and more reliable distant communications. Everyone wants to get in the act—and money—of linking your PC digitally. Not just your telephone company but also the cable company and even satellite operators want you to plug into (and pay for) their services.

Without a doubt, digital services are the best way to connect to the Internet and the rest of the world. But digital services aren't always available. As the 20th century ends, *most people* still do not have access to high-speed digital communications. The issue is simple. Although you can invest a thousand dollars and have a state-of-the-art PC tomorrow, telephone and cable companies have to spend hundreds of millions of dollars to accommodate digital communications with your PC. Forward-thinking communications companies have already made much of that investment and offer high-speed access in selected markets across the United States; by selected we mean, of course, the cable or telephone company has selected the areas in which people are wealthy or foolish enough to pay a steep tab for leading-edge technology. Over the next few years, however, high-speed digital communications will trickle down to the rest of the world.

Consequently, modem-based analog communications remains the best (and often, only) choice for most people. We'll take a look at it first and then see why digital will be the better choice—when you can get your hands and bytes on it.

Analog Services

A modem is standard equipment in every new PC and with good reason. You need a modem to go online and link with the World Wide Web. Consider a PC without a modem, and you might as well buy a vacuum cleaner.

Today's modem is a world apart from those of only a few years ago, and the difference is speed. A modem that doesn't run at least 14,400 bits-per-second is simply too slow to use on the Internet and a drag for any other kind of telecommunications. Modern modems start there and reach from 28,800 bps to 33,600 bps and even 56,000 bps. In fact, the next modem you buy may even exceed those speeds and—despite the name—probably won't even be a modem.

With all of these changes in modem technology, one question remains: Why do you need this extra piece of hardware to make your PC telecommunicate? After all, both your PC and telephone talk with the same stuff, electricity, and move messages back and forth with ordinary electrical signals. Were not the giant corporations specializing in computers and telephones not such avowed rivals, you might suspect that they were in cahoots to foist such a contrived accessory on the computer marketplace.

Step back and look at what a modem does, however, and you will gain new respect for the device. In many ways, the modern modem is a miracle worker. A true time machine, a modem bridges between today's digital computer technology and the analog telephone interface that was devised more than a century ago. Although digital telephone and telecommunications services are inching their way into homes and offices, most telephone connections still rely on analog signals for at least part of their journey. Even these digital services require something like a modem to make a connection. Although most people call such digital linking devices modems, too, strictly speaking they are *terminal adapters*. Nevertheless, no matter whether you have old-fashioned analog or modern fast and expensive digital telephone service, you need a box between your PC and the phone line. And most folks will call it a modem.

Beyond converting digital and analog signals, the best of today's modems can squeeze more than a dozen data bits through a cable where only one should fit. A fax modem can even cram a full-page image through a thin 22-gauge telephone wire in about 15 seconds.

The classic modem is a necessary bridge between digital and analog signals. The modern modem usually does much more than connect. Most are boxes chock full of convenience features that can make using them fast, simple, and automatic. The best of today's modems not only make and monitor the connection but even improve it. They dial the phone for you, remembering the number you want, and they will try again and again. A modem will listen in until it's sure of good contact and only then let you transmit across the telephone line. Some even have built-in circuits to detect and correct the inevitable errors that creep into your electrical conversations.

Background

A true modem is a necessary evil in today's world of telecommunications because we still suffer from a telephone system that labors under standards devised even before electronics were invented, at a time when solid-state digital circuitry lay undreamed, almost a hundred years off. The first words out of Dr. Bell's speaking telegraph were analog electrical signals, the same juice that flows through the receiver of your own telephone. Although strictly speaking, digital communications are older than the invention of the telephone—the conventional telegraph predates the telephone by nearly 30 years (Samuel F.B. Morse wondered what God had wrought in 1844)—current digital technology is a comparatively recent phenomenon.

The telephone system was designed only to handle analog signals because that's all that speaking into a microphone creates. Over the years, the telephone system has evolved into an elaborate international network capable of handling millions of these analog signals simultaneously and switching them from one telephone set to another anywhere in the world. In the last couple of decades, telephone companies have shifted nearly all of their circuits to digital. Most central office circuitry is digital. Nearly every long distance call is sent between cities and countries digitally. In fact, the only analog part of most telephone connections is the *local loop*, the wires that reach out from the telephone exchange to your home or office (and likewise extend from a distant exchange to the telephone of whomever you're calling).

The chief reason any analog circuitry remains in the telephone system is that there are hundreds of millions of plain old telephone sets (which the technologically astute call simply POTS) dangling on the ends of telephone wires across the country. Even the wires between you and your telephone exchange are probably capable of adroitly dealing with digital signals. If you're willing to pay a premium—both for new equipment and for extra monthly charges—you can go all digital with ISDN or DSL (discussed later). As long as you stick with your POTS, however, you'll still need a modem for communications.

Even with digital service, you still need a box or modem-like expansion board between the digital circuitry of your PC and the digital phone line. The terminal adapter helps match the signal standards between the different types of hardware. More importantly, at least from the perspective of your telecommunications service provider (once quaintly known as the "telephone company"), the terminal adapter protects the telephone network from strange and spurious signals originating in your PC. It assures that the digital phone network gets exactly the kinds of signals it requires.

Modulation

The technology that allows modems to send digital signals through the analog telephone system is called *modulation*. In fact, the very name "modem" is derived from this term and the reciprocal circuit (the demodulator) that's used in reception. Modem is a foreshortening of the words modulator/demodulator.

Modulation, and hence modems, are necessary because analog telephone connections do not allow digital, direct current signals to pass. The modulation process creates analog signals that contain all the digital information of the computer original but which can be transmitted through the voice-only channels of the telephone system.

More generally, modulation is the process of adapting a signal to suit a communications medium by using the otherwise incompatible signal to modify another signal that's compatible with the medium. In the case of a modem, modulation uses the digital data signal to modify an analog signal so that the combination of the two can travel through the analog telephone system.

The modulation process begins with a constant signal called the *carrier*, which carries or bears the load of the digital (modulating) information. In most modulation systems, the carrier is a steady-state signal of constant amplitude (strength) and frequency and coherent phase, the electrical equivalent of a pure tone. Because it is unchanging, the carrier itself is devoid of content and information. It's the equivalent of one, unchanging digital bit. The carrier is simply a package, like a milk carton. Although you need both the carrier and milk carton to move its contents from one place to another, the package doesn't affect the contents and is essentially irrelevant to the product. You throw it away once you've got the product where you want it.

The signal that's electrically mixed with the carrier to modify some aspect of it is given the same name as the process, *modulation*. The carrier wave and modulation are not simply mixed together. If they were, the modulation would be simply filtered away by the incompatible communications medium. Instead, the modulation alters the carrier wave in some way so that the carrier wave retains its essential characteristics and remains compatible with its medium.

A modem modulates an analog signal that can travel through the telephone system with the digital direct current signals produced by your PC. The modem also demodulates incoming signals, stripping off the analog component and passing the digital information to your PC. The resulting modulated carrier wave remains an analog signal that—usually—easily whisks through the telephone system.

The modulation process has two requirements. The first is the continued compatibility with the communications medium so that the signal is still useful. Second, you must somehow be able to separate the modulation from the carrier so that you can recover the original signal.

Demodulation is the signal recovery process, the complement of modulation. During demodulation, the carrier is stripped away and the encoded information is returned to its original form. Although logically just the complement of modulation, demodulation usually involves entirely different circuits and operating principles, which adds to the complexity of the modem.

The modulation/demodulation process brings several benefits, more than enough to justify the complication of combining signals. Because electronic circuits can be tuned to accept the frequency of one carrier wave and reject others, multiple modulated signals can be sent through a single communications medium. This principle underlies all radio communication and broadcasting. In addition, modulation allows digital, direct-current-based information to be transmitted through a medium, such as the telephone system, that otherwise could not carry direct current signals.

Just as AM and FM radio stations use different modulation methods to achieve the same end, modem designers can select from several modulation technologies to encode digital data in a form compatible with analog transmission systems. The different forms of modulation are distinguished by the characteristics of the carrier wave that are changed in response to changes in data to encode information. The three primary characteristics of a carrier wave that designers might elect to vary for modulation are its amplitude, its frequency, and its phase. Modern modems take advantage of all of these kinds of modulation.

Carrier Wave Modulation

The easiest way to understand the technique of modulation is to look at its simplest form, *carrier wave* modulation, which is often abbreviated as CW, particularly by radio broadcasters.

We've previously noted that a digital signal, when stripped to its essential quality, is nothing more than a series of bits of the information that can be coded in any of a variety of forms. We use 0s and 1s to express digital values on paper. In digital circuits, the same bits take the form of the high or low direct current voltages, the same ones that are incompatible with the telephone system. However, we can just as easily convert digital bits into the presence or absence of a signal that can travel through the telephone system (or be broadcast as a radio wave). The compatible signal is, of course, the carrier wave. By switching the carrier wave off and on, we can encode digital 0s and 1s with it.

The resulting CW signal looks like interrupted bursts of round sine waves, as shown in Figure 22.1.

FIGURE 22.1
Carrier wave modulation.

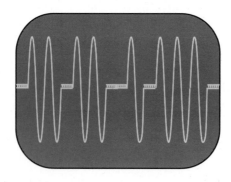

The figure shows the most straightforward way to visualize the conversion between digital and analog, assigning one full wave of the carrier to represent a digital one and the absence of a wave a zero. In most practical simple carrier waves systems, however, each bit occupies the space of several waves. The system codes the digital information not as pulses per se but as time. A bit lasts a given period regardless of the number of cycles occurring within that period, making the frequency of the carrier wave irrelevant to the information content.

Although CW modulation has its shortcomings, particularly in wire-based communications, its retains a practical application in radio transmission. It is used in the simplest radio transmission methods, typically for sending messages in Morse code.

One of the biggest drawbacks of carrier wave modulation is ambiguity. Any interruption in the signal may be misinterpreted as a digital zero. In telephone systems, the problem is particularly pernicious. Equipment has no way of discerning whether a long gap between bursts of carrier is actually significant data or a break in or end of the message.

Frequency Shift Keying

A more reliable way of signaling digital information is to use separate and distinct frequencies for each digital state. For example, a digital 1 would cause the carrier wave to change to a higher frequency much as it causes a higher voltage. A digital 0 would shift the signal to a lower frequency. Two different frequencies and the shifts between them could then encode binary data for transmission across an analog system. This form of modulation is called *frequency shift keying*, or FSK, because information is encoded in (think of it being "keyed to") the shifting of frequency.

The "keying" part of the name is actually left over from the days of the telegraph when this form of modulation was used for transmitting Morse code. The frequency shift came with the banging of the telegraph key.

In practical FSK systems, the two shifting frequencies are the modulation that is applied to a separate (and usually much higher) carrier wave. When no modulation is present, only the carrier wave at its fundamental frequency appears. With modulation, the overall signal jumps between two different frequencies. Figure 22.2 shows what an FSK modulation looks like electrically.

Frequency shift keying is used in the most rudimentary of popular modems, the once-ubiquitous 300 bits-per-second modem that operated under the Bell 103 standard. This standard, which is used by most modems when operating at a 300 bits-per-second data rate, incorporates two separate FSK systems each with its own carrier frequencies, one at 1,200 and another at 2,200 Hertz. Space modulation (logical zeros) shifts the carrier down by 150 Hertz, and mark modulation pushes the carrier frequency up by an equal amount. Because the FSK modulation technique is relatively simple and the two frequencies so distinct even through bad connections, the 300 bps speed of the Bell 103 standard is the most reliable, if slowest, common modem standard.

FIGURE 22.2
Frequency shift keying.

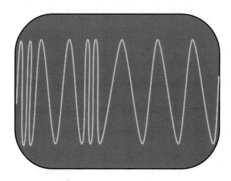

Amplitude Modulation

Carrier wave modulation is actually a special case of *amplitude modulation*. Amplitude is the strength of the signal or the loudness of a tone carried through a transmission medium, such as the telephone wire. Varying the strength of the carrier in response to modulation to transmit information is called amplitude modulation. Instead of simply being switched on and off as with carrier wave modulation, in amplitude modulation the carrier tone gets louder or softer in response to the modulating signal. Figure 22.3 shows what an amplitude modulated signal looks like electrically.

FIGURE 22.3
Amplitude modulation, signal strength (vertical) versus time (horizontal).

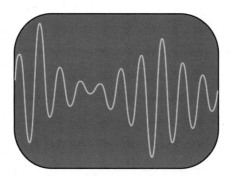

Amplitude modulation is most commonly used by radio and television broadcasters to transmit analog signals. It carries talk and music to your AM radio and the picture to your television set. Engineers also exploit amplitude modulation for digital transmissions. They can, for example, assign one amplitude to indicate a logical 1 and another amplitude to indicate a logical 0.

Pure amplitude modulation has one big weakness. The loudness of a telephone signal is the characteristic most likely to vary during transmission. As the signal travels, the resistance and impedance of the telephone wire tends to reduce the signal's strength; the telephone company's amplifiers attempt to keep the signal at a constant level. Moreover, noise on the telephone line mimics amplitude modulation and might be confused with data. Consequently, pure amplitude modulation is not ordinarily used by modems. Amplitude modulation technology is used by modems as part of a complex modulation system, as discussed later.

The one exception to the rule that modems do not use amplitude modulation is the 56Kbps modem system developed by Rockwell International and now used by the V.90 standard, the highest speed data connection available through local analog telephone lines. The Rockwell system achieves its performance edge by acting unlike a modem. It treats the telephone connection not as point-to-point analog service as it would have been in Alexander Bell's day but as a digital communication system in which one part—the local loop between you and the telephone company central office—is but a poorly performing section. Rockwell considers what the device sends down your local phone line not as modulation but instead as a special form of digital coding, one that encodes the digital signal as 256 levels of a carrier wave matched to the voltage levels used by the analog-to-digital converter at the telephone company central office.

Frequency Modulation

Frequency shift keying is a special case of the more general technology called *frequency modulation*. In the classic frequency modulation system used by FM radio, variations in the loudness of sound modulate a carrier wave by changing its frequency. When music on an FM station gets louder, for example, the radio station's carrier frequency shifts its frequency more. In effect, FM translates changes in modulation amplitude into changes in carrier frequency. The modulation does not alter the level of the carrier wave. As a result, an FM signal electrically looks like a train of wide and narrow waves of constant height, as shown in Figure 22.4.

FIGURE 22.4
Frequency modulation, signal strength (vertical) versus time (horizontal).

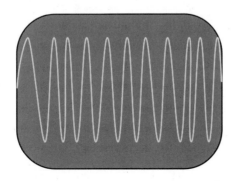

In a pure FM system, the strength or amplitude of the signal is irrelevant. This characteristic makes FM immune to noise. Interference and noise signals add into the desired signal and alter its strength. FM demodulators ignore these amplitude changes. That's why lightning storms and motors don't interfere with FM radios. This same immunity from noise and variations in amplitude makes frequency modulation a more reliable, if more complex, transmission method for modems.

Phase Modulation

Another variation on the theme of frequency modulation is *phase modulation*. This technology works by altering the phase relationship between the waves in the signal. An unmodulated carrier is train waves in a constant phase relationship. That is, the waves follow one after another precisely in step. The peaks and troughs of the train of waves flow in constant intervals. If one wave were delayed for exactly one wavelength, it would fit exactly atop the next one.

By delaying the peak of one wave so that it occurs later than it should, you can break the constant phase relationship between the waves in the train without altering the overall amplitude or frequency of the wave train. In other words, you shift one set of a subsequent waves compared to those that precede it. At the same time, you will create a detectable state change called a *phase shift*. You can then code digital bits as the presence or absence of a phase shift.

Signals are said to be in phase when the peaks and troughs of one align exactly with another. When signals are 180 degrees out of phase, the peaks of one signal align with the troughs of the other. Quadrature modulation can shift the phase of the carrier wave by 180 degrees, moving it from exactly in phase to exactly out of phase with a reference carrier, as shown in Figure 22.5. Note that the two waveforms shown start in phase and then, after a phase shift, end up being 180 degrees out of phase.

FIGURE 22.5

Phase modulation showing 180-degree phase shift.

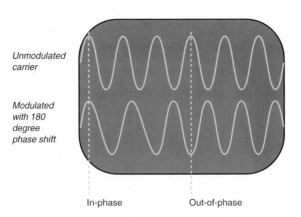

Unmodulated carrier

Modulated with 180 degree phase shift

In-phase   Out-of-phase

If you examine the shapes of waves that result from a phase shift, you'll see that phase modulation is a special case of FM. Delaying a wave lengthens the time between its peak and that of the preceding wave. As a result, the frequency of the signal shifts downward during the change, although over the long term the frequency of the signal appears to remain constant.

One particular type of phase modulation called *quadrature modulation* alters the phase of the signal solely in increments of 90 degrees. That is, the shift between waves occurs at a phase angle of 0, 90, 180, or 270 degrees. The "quad" in the name of this modulation method refers to the four possible phase delays.

Quadrature modulation allows the encoding of data more complex than simple binary bits. Its four possible shifts can specify four different values. For example, a 90-degree shift might specify the value 1, a 180-degree shift the value 2, and a 270-degree shift the value 3. The potential of encoding four states makes systems using quadrature modulation prime candidates for group coding, discussed later. Although quadrature modulation is useful in modem communications, it is most often used in combination with other modulation techniques.

Complex Modulation

The various modulation techniques are not mutually exclusive. Modem makers achieve higher data rates by combining two or more techniques to create *complex modulation* schemes.

In frequency shift keying modems, one bit of data causes one corresponding change of frequency in the carrier wave. Every change of frequency or state carries exactly one bit of information. The unit of measurement used to describe the number of state changes taking in place in the carrier wave in one second is the baud. The term "baud" was named after J.M.E. Baudot, a French telegraphy expert. His full name (Baudot) is used to describe a five-bit digital code used in teletype systems.

In the particular case of the FSK modulation, one change of state per second (one baud) conveys exactly one bit of information per second, and one baud is equal to a transfer of digital information at a one bit-per-second rate. Depending on the number of states used in the communication system, however, a single transition (one baud) can convey less than or more than one bit of information. For example, several different frequencies of tones (that is, several different changes in carrier frequency) might be used to code information. The changing from one frequency to another would take place at one baud, yet because of the different possible changes that could be made, more than one bit of information could be coded by that transition. Hence, strictly speaking, one baud is not the same as one bit per second, although the terms are often incorrectly used interchangeably. Unfortunately for M. Baudot, the confusion between "baud" and "bits-per-second" has become so irremediably confused in common use that communications engineers now often use the term *symbol* instead of baud when speaking of state changes.

The 300 bits-per-second rate using the simple FSK technique requires a bandwidth of 600 Hertz. The two 300 baud carriers, which require a 1,200Hz bandwidth (two times 600Hz), and a wide guard band fit comfortably within the 2,700Hz limit.

Using the same simple modulation technique and exploiting more of the 2,700 Hertz bandwidth of the typical telephone line, modem speeds can be doubled to 600 baud. Beyond that rate, however, lies the immovable bandwidth road block.

Group Coding

A data communications rate of 300 or even 600 bits-per-second is slow, slower than most folks can read text flowing across the screen. Were long-distance communications limited to a 600 bits-per-second rate, the only people who would be happy would be the share-holders of the various telephone companies. Information could, at best, crawl slowly across the continent.

By combining several modulation techniques, modern modems can achieve much higher data rates despite the constraints of ordinary dial-up telephone lines. Instead of merely manipulating the carrier one way, they may modify two (or more) aspects of the constant wave. In this way, every baud carries multiple bits of information.

The relationship between the number of bits that can be coded for each baud and the number of signal states require is geometric. The number of required states skyrockets as you try to code more data in every baud, as shown in Table 22.1.

TABLE 22.1   Signals States Required to Encode Bits

Number of States	Bits per Baud
2	1
4	2
16	4
64	8
256	16

Note, too, that this form of coding makes the transmitted data more vulnerable to error. An error in one bad baud can ripple through multiple bits of data. Because the finer you carve up a baud, the smaller the differences, errors result from smaller disruptions to the signal.

These more complex forms of modulation don't add extra bandwidth to the communications channel; remember, that's a function of the medium, which the modem cannot change. Instead, they take advantage of the possibility of coding digital data as changes between a variety of states of the carrier wave. The carrier wave, for example, can be phase modulated with quadrature modulation so that it assumes one of four states every baud.

Although you might expect these four states to quadruple modem speed, the relationship is not quite that direct. To convert states into digital information, modems use a technique called group coding in which one state encodes a specific pattern of bits. The modem needs a repertoire of unique states wide enough to identify every different pattern possible with a given number of bits. Two digital bits can assume any one of four distinct patterns: 00, 01, 10, and 11. So to encode those two bits into a single baud, a modem needs four different states to uniquely identify each bit pattern. The ultimate speed of a modem on an ideal connection would thus be determined by the number of states that are available for coding.

Group coding is the key to advanced modulation techniques. Instead of dealing with data one bit at a time, bits of digital code are processed as groups. Each group of data bits is encoded as one particular state of the carrier.

As the example illustrates, however, the relationship between states and bits is not linear. As the number of bits in the code increases by a given figure (and thus the potential speed of the modulation technique rises by the same figure), the number of states required increases to the corresponding power of two, the inverse logarithm of the number of available states (tones, voltage, or phases). A 2 bit-for-baud rate requires 4 separate carrier states for encoding; a 4 bit-for-baud rate needs 16 separate carrier states; and an 8 bit-for-baud system require 256 states.

Most 1,200 bits-per-second modems operate at 600 baud with four different carrier states made possible by quadrature modulation. Modems that operate at data rates of 2,400 bps use a modulation method that's even more complex than quadrature modulation and yields 16 discrete states while still operating at 600 baud. Each state encodes one of the 16 different patterns of four digital bits. One baud on the telephone line carries the information of four bits going into the modem.

More complex modulation systems combine two or more modulation methods to cram more bits into every baud. For example, a modem can use a combination of several different frequencies and amplitudes to create distinct states. The group code values can be assigned to each state in a two-dimensional system that arrays one modulation method on one axis and a second modulation method on another. You can then assign a group code value to each discrete coordinate position. Although you could just start in the upper left and list code values in order from left to right, top to bottom, by spacing similar values apart, they are easier for electronic systems to reliably distinguish. The result is a matrix of numbers scattered as if in pigeonholes that, viewed graphically and with enough imagination, looks like a trellis. Consequently, this kind of multiple modulation is called trellis modulation. International modem standards set the arrangement of modulation and code values for the trellis modulation used at each operating speed.

Figure 22.6 shows the constellation of values used by the 2,400 bps V.22bis signaling system. The 16 different points in the constellation allow the coding of 4 bits per baud, allowing the 2,400 bps data rate on a 600 baud signal. Four phase quadrants refer to shifts between the four quadrature phase states, and the four possibilities of shifts allow the encoding of two bits of data in addition to the four possible states in each quadrant. The constellations used by higher-speed modems are similar but more complex (and more confusing to visualize.)

FIGURE 22.6

The V.22bis signal constellation.

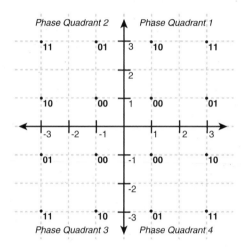

According to the free lunch principle, this system of seemingly getting something for nothing using complex modulation must have a drawback. With high-speed modems, the problem is that the quality of the telephone line becomes increasingly critical as the data rate is increased. Moreover, as modem speeds get faster, each phone line blip (baud) carries more information, and a single error can have devastating effects.

Pulse Modulation

Modulation can also work in the opposite direction and allow a digital system to carry what would otherwise be analog values or to allow direct current systems to transmit alternating current signals. In fact, this reverse form of modulation is the principle underlying digital audio, which was discussed in Chapter 19, "Audio."

Because this technology converts an analog signal into a set of digital pulses, it is often called pulse modulation, although this term is usually reserved for applications that use the resulting digital signal to modulate a carrier wave. Instead of "modulation," the process of creating the raw digital direct current signals is often called *digital coding*.

The simplest form of most pulse modulation uses the number of pulses in a given period to indicate the strength of the underlying analog signal.

Pulse width modulation varies the width of each pulse to correspond to the strength of the underlying analog signal. In other words, pulse width modulation translates the analog voltage level into the duration of the pulses used in the digital signal.

Pulse code modulation is the most complex. It uses a digital number or code to indicate the strength of the underlying analog signal. For example, the voltage of the signal is translated into a number, and the digital signal represents that number in binary code. This form of digital modulation is familiar from its wide application in digital audio equipment such as CD players.

Signal Characteristics

The place to begin a discussion of modems and telecommunications technology is with the problem, getting information—be it digital data or your own dulcet voice—from one place to another. Given a free reign and unlimited budget, and you'd have no problem at all. You could build the biggest transmitter and blast signals to distant corners of the universe. But our budgets aren't unlimited. Nor do you have free access to the pathways of communication. The limited resource would need be split nearly six billion ways to give everyone access.

The underlying problem crops up even in conversation. If everyone talked at once, you'd never be able to make sense of the confusion. Similarly, if everyone tried to send out data at the same time without concern for others trying to do likewise, nothing would likely get through the sea of interference.

To keep order, communications are restricted to channels. The obvious channels are those used by television broadcasters. But even each telephone call you make goes through its channel.

The problem is that channel space is not unlimited. To keep communications economical, telephone companies (for example) severely restrict the size and carrying capacity of each channel so that they can squeeze in more individual channels.

The modulation that's added to the carrier contains information that varies at some rate. Traditional analog signal sources (music or voice signals, for instance) contain a near-random mix of frequencies between 20 and 20,000 Hertz. Although digital signals start off as direct current, which also has no bandwidth, every change in digital state adds a frequency component. The faster the states change (the more information that's squeezed down the digital channel, as measured in its bit rate), the more bandwidth the signal occupies. The on-and-off rate of the digital signal is its frequency, and modulating the carrier with it adds to the frequency range demanded by the carrier-and-modulation combination. In other words, mixing in modulation increases the bandwidth needed by the carrier; the more information that's added, the more bandwidth that's needed.

Channel Limits

Like a great artist, the modem is constrained to work within the limits of its medium, the telephone channel. These limits are imposed by the telephone system. They arise in part from characteristics of analog communications and the communications medium that's used, primarily the unshielded twisted-pair wire that runs between your business or home and the telephone company central office. In long-distance communication, you're also constrained by arbitrary limits imposed by the telephone company that you use. Most long-distance calls get converted to digital signals at your local telephone exchange. Just as an artist must overcome the limitation of his medium, turning its weaknesses into strengths, the modem must struggle within the confines of the telephone connection and turn the ancient technology to its advantage.

Signal Bandwidth

The primary limit on any communications channel is its bandwidth, and bandwidth is the chief constraint on modem speed. Bandwidth merely specifies a range of frequencies from the lowest to the highest that the channel can carry or are present in the signal. It is one way of describing the maximum amount of information that the channel can carry. Bandwidth is expressed differently for analog and digital circuits. In analog technology, the bandwidth of a circuit is the difference between the lowest and highest frequencies that can pass through the channel. Engineers measure analog bandwidth in kilohertz or megahertz. In a digital circuit, the bandwidth is the amount of information that can pass through the channel. Engineers measure digital bandwidth in bits, kilobits, or megabits-per-second. The kilohertz of an analog bandwidth and the kilobits-per-second of digital bandwidth for the same circuit are not necessarily the same and often differ greatly.

When using a modem, the data signals through communications channels are analog. The analog bandwidth of the system consequently constrains the data carrying capacity.

The bandwidth of a simple pair of telephone wires decreases with its length because of physical characteristics of the signals and wires. Scientifically speaking, capacitance in the wires attenuates high frequencies.

The more severe limit comes with the digital conversion process at the telephone central office. Most telephone companies use an 8KHz sampling rate and a bit-depth of 8 bits for their digital long-distance signals. The sampling rate limits the maximum bandwidth of the telephone connection to less than 4KHz. It is this narrow bandwidth that modems and modem designers must contend with.

Channel Bandwidth

The bandwidth of a communications channel defines the frequency limits of the signals that it can carry. This channel bandwidth may be physically limited by the medium used by the channel or artificially limited by communications standards. The bandwidths of radio transmissions, for example, are limited artificially, by law, to allow many different modulated carriers to share the air waves while preventing interference between them.

In wire-based communications channels, bandwidth is often limited by the wires themselves. Certain physical characteristics of wires cause degradations in their high-frequency transmission capabilities. The capacitance between conductors in a cable pair, for instance, increasingly degrades signals as their frequencies rise, finally reaching a point that a high-frequency signal might not be able to traverse more than a few centimeters of wire. Amplifiers or repeaters, which boost signals so that they can travel longer distances, often cannot handle very low or very high frequencies, imposing more limits.

Most telephone channels also have an artificial bandwidth limitation imposed by the telephone company. To get the greatest financial potential from the capacity of their transmissions cables, microwave systems, and satellites, telephone carriers normally limit the bandwidth of telephone signals. One reason bandwidth is limited is so that many separate telephone conversations can be stacked atop of one another through multiplexing techniques, which allow a single pair of wires to carry hundreds of simultaneous conversations.

Although the effects of bandwidth limitation are obvious (it's why your phone doesn't sound as good as your stereo), the telephone company multiplexing equipment works so well that you are generally unaware of all the manipulations made to the voice signals as they are squeezed through wires.

Bandwidth Limitations

One of the consequences of telephone company signal manipulations is a severe limitation in the bandwidth of an ordinary telephone channel. Instead of the full frequency range of a good quality stereo system (from 20 to 20,000 Hertz), a telephone channel will only allow frequencies between 300 and 3,000 Hertz to freely pass. This very narrow bandwidth works well for telephones because frequencies below 300 Hertz contain most of the power of the human voice but little of its intelligibility. Frequencies above 3,000 Hertz increase the crispness of the sound but don't add appreciably to intelligibility.

Although intelligibility is the primary concern with voice communications (most of the time), data transfer is principally oriented to bandwidth. The comparatively narrow bandwidth of the standard telephone channel limits the bandwidth of the modulated signal it can carry, which in turn limits the amount of digital information that can be squeezed down the phone line by a modem.

Try some simple math and you will see the harsh constraints faced by your modem's signals. A telephone channel typically has a useful bandwidth of about 2,700 Hertz (from 300 to 3,000 Hertz). At most, a carrier wave at exactly the center of the telephone channel, 1,650Hz, burdened by two sidebands could carry data that varies at a rate no greater than 1,650Hz. Such a signal would fill the entire bandwidth of the telephone channel without allowing for a safety margin.

Guard Bands

Communications is a two-way street, so most modems are designed with two channels, one in each direction. Putting two channels on a single telephone line does more than cut in half the bandwidth available to each channel. Separating the two channels is a *guard band*, a width of unused frequencies that isolate the active channels and prevent confusion between their separate carriers. The safety margin is, in effect, also a guard between the carriers and the varying limit of the bandwidth.

Once you add in the needs of two communications channels and the guard bands, the practical bandwidth limit for modem communications over real telephone channels that have an innate 2,700 Hertz bandwidth works out to about 2,400 Hertz. That leaves 1,200 Hertz for each of the two duplex channels. Getting the most information through that limited bandwidth is a challenge to the inventiveness of modem designers and modem standards in picking the best possible modulation method.

Shannon's Limit

Fortunately for your modem, it can use modulation technologies that are much more efficient than this simple example. But the modem still faces an ultimate limit on the amount of data that it can squeeze through an analog telephone line. This ultimate limit combines the effects of the bandwidth of the channel and the noise level in the channel. The greater the noise, the more likely that it will be confused with the information that has to compete with it. This theoretical maximum data rate for a communication channel is called *Shannon's Limit*. This fundamental law of data communications states that the maximum number of digital bits that can be transmitted over a given communication path in one second can be determined from the bandwidth (W) and signal-to-noise ratio (S/N, expressed in decibels) by the following formula:

$$\text{Maximum data rate} = W \log (1 + S/N)$$

The analog-to-digital converters used in telephone company central offices contribute the noise that most limits modem bandwidth. In creating the digital pulse-coded modulation (PCM) signal, they create *quantization distortion* that produces an effective signal-to-noise ratio of about 36 dB. Quantization distortion results from the inability of the digital system with a discrete number of voltage steps (256 in the case of telephone company A/D converters) to exactly represent an analog signal that has an infinite number of levels. At this noise level, Shannon's Limit for analog modems is close to the 33.6Kbps of today's quickest products. The V.90 systems sidestep Shannon's Limit to ratchet up to 56Kbps by matching the 256 amplitude modulation levels to the 256 levels of the telephone company A/D converters and thus avoiding the issue of quantization distortion.

Sidebands

In the simplest modulation systems, a modulated carrier requires twice the bandwidth of the modulation signal. Although this doubling sounds anomalous, its the direct result of combining the signals. The carrier and modulation mix together and result in modulation products corresponding to the frequency of the modulation both added to the carrier together with the frequency of the modulation and subtracted from the carrier. The added result often is called the upper sideband, and the subtracted result is correspondingly called the lower sideband.

Because these upper and lower modulation products are essentially redundant (they contain exactly the same information), one or the other can be eliminated without loss of information to reduce the bandwidth of the modulated carrier to that of the modulation. (This form of bandwidth savings, termed single sideband modulation, is commonly used in broadcasting to squeeze more signals into the limited radio spectrum.) Figure 22.7 shows the relationship between the carrier wave and sidebands.

FIGURE 22.7

Display of the carrier wave and lower and upper sidebands.

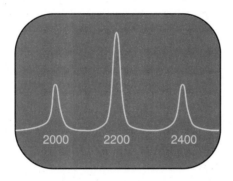

Even with sideband squeezing, the fundamental fact remains that any modulated signal requires a finite range of frequencies to hold its information. The limits of this frequency range define the bandwidth required by the modulated signal.

Most of these technologies rely on the power of Digital Signal Processors to take advantage of novel technologies, such as line probing, multidimensional trellis coding, signal shaping, and protocol spoofing.

Line probing lets a pair of modems determine the optimal transfer method for a given telephone connection. The two modems send a sequence of signals back and forth to probe the limits of the connection and ascertain the higher modulation rate, best carrier frequency, and coding technique that gives the highest throughput.

Multidimensional trellis coding is a way of making modem signals more resistant to errors caused by noise in the telephone connection by carefully selecting the modulation values assigned to the transmitted code.

Signal shaping improves signal-to-noise performance of the modem connection by altering the power of the signal in certain circumstances. Signal points that occur frequently are transmitted at higher power, and less frequent points are transmitted at reduced power.

Protocol spoofing removes the redundant parts of data transfer protocols so that less data needs to be transferred. In effect, it compresses the protocol to speed transmissions much as data compression speeds data transfer. At the receiving end, the protocol is fully recon-structed before being passed along for further processing.

Asynchronous Operation

At lower speeds, most modems are designed to operate asynchronously. That is, the timing of one modem's signals doesn't matter as long as it is within wide limits. More important is the actual bit-pattern that is sent. That pattern is self-defining. Each character frame holds enough data not only to identify the information that it contains but also to define its own beginning and end.

Normally, the time at which a pulse occurs in relation to the ticking of a computer's system clock determines the meaning of a bit in a digital signal, and the pulses must be synchronized to the clock for proper operation. In asynchronous transmissions, however, the digital pulses are not locked to the system clock of either computer. Instead, the meaning of each bit of a digital word is defined by its position in reference to the clearly (and unambiguously) defined start bit. In an asynchronous string, the start bit is followed by seven or eight data bits, an optional parity bit for error detection, and one or two stop bits that define the ends of the frame. (See Chapter 20, "Peripheral Ports.") Because the timing is set within each word in isolation, each word of the asynchronous signal can be independent of any time relations beyond its self-defined bounds.

Synchronous Operation

When speed's the thing (as it almost always is with PCs), asynchronous communication ranks as wasteful. All those start and stop bits eat up time that could be devoted to squeezing in more data bits. Consequently, high-speed modem transmission standards and protocols as well as most leased-line modems do away with most extra overhead bits of asynchronous communication by using synchronous transmission. In this method of transmitting data across phone lines, the two ends of the channel share a common time base, and the communicating modems operate continuously at substantially the same frequency and are continually maintained in the correct phase relationship by circuits that monitor the connection and adjust for the circuit conditions.

In synchronous transmissions, the timing of each bit independently is vital, but framing bits (start and stop bits) are unnecessary, which makes this form of communication two or three bits-per-byte transmitted faster.

Duplex

Communications are supposed to be a two-way street. Information is supposed to flow in both directions. You should learn something from everyone you talk to, and everyone should learn from you. Even if you disregard the potential for success of such two-way communication, one effect is undeniable: It cuts the usable bandwidth of a data communication channel in one direction in half because the data going the other way requires its own share of the bandwidth.

With modems, such a two-way exchange of information is called duplex communications. Often, it is redundantly called full duplex. A full duplex modem is able to simultaneously handle two signals, usually (but not necessarily) going in opposite directions, so it can send and receive information at the same time. Duplex modems use two carriers to simultaneously transmit and receive data, each of which has half the bandwidth available to it and its modulation.

Half-Duplex

The alternative to duplex communications is *half-duplex*. In half-duplex transmission, only one signal is used. To carry on a two-way conversation, a modem must alternately send and receive signals. Half-duplex transmission allows more of the channel bandwidth to be put to use but slows data communications because often a modem must switch between sending and receiving modes after every block of data crawls through the channel.

Echoplex

The term duplex is often mistakenly used by some communications programs for PCs to describe *echoplex* operation. In echoplex mode, a modem sends a character down the phone line, and the distant modem returns the same character, echoing it. The echoed character is then displayed on the originating terminal as confirmation that the character was sent correctly. Without echoplex, the host computer usually writes the transmitted character directly to its monitor screen. Although a duplex modem generates echoplex signals most easily, the two terms are not interchangeable.

With early communications programs, echoplex was a critical setup parameter. Some terminal programs relied on modem echoplex to display your typing on the screen. If you had echoplex off, you wouldn't see what you typed. Other terminal programs, however, displayed every character that went through the modem, so switching echoplex on would display two of every letter you typed, lliikkee tthhiiss. Web browsers don't bother you with the need to select this feature. Most, however, work without echoplex.

Switching Modems

To push more signal through a telephone line, some modems attempt to mimic full-duplex operation while actually running in half-duplex mode. Switching modems are half-duplex modems that reverse the direction of the signal at each end of the line in response to the need to send data. This kind of operation can masquerade as full duplex most of the time communications go only in one direction. You enter commands into a remote access system, and only after the commands are received does the remote system respond with the information that you seek. Although one end is sending, the other end is more than likely to be completely idle.

On the positive side, switching modems are able to achieve a doubling of the data rate without adding any complexity to their modulation. But the switching process itself is time-consuming and inevitably involves a delay because the modems must let each other know that they are switching. Because transmission delays across long-distance lines are often a substantial fraction of a second (most connections take at least one trip up to a satellite and back down, a 50,000-mile journey that takes about a quarter of a second even at the speed of light), the process of switching can eat huge holes into transmission time.

Most software modem protocols require a confirmation for each block of data sent, meaning the modem must switch twice for each block. The smaller the block, the more often the switch must occur. Just one trip to a satellite would limit a switching modem with an infinitely fast data rate using the 128-byte blocks of some early modem protocols to 1,024 bits per second at the two-switches-per-second rate.

Asymmetrical Modems

Because of this weakness of switching modems, *asymmetrical modems* cut the waiting by maintaining a semblance of two-way duplex communications while optimizing speed in one direction only. These modems shoehorn in a lower-speed channel in addition to a higher-speed one, splitting the total bandwidth of the modem channel unequally.

Early asymmetrical modems were able to flip-flop the direction of the high-speed communications, relying on algorithms to determine which way is the best way. The modern asymmetrical technologies have a much simpler algorithm; designed for Internet communications, they assume you need a greater data rate downstream (to you) than upstream (back to the server). This design is effective because most people download blocks of data from the Internet (typically Web pages rife with graphics) while sending only a few commands back to the Web server.

The latest V.90 operate asymmetrically at their highest speed. Cable modems and satellite connections to the Internet also use a variation on asymmetrical modem technology. These systems typically provide you with a wide bandwidth downlink from a satellite or cable system to permit you to quickly browse pages but rely on a narrow-channel telephone link—a conventional modem link—to relay your commands back to the network.

Connection-Enhancing Technologies

Getting the most from your modem requires making the best match between it and the connection it makes to the distant modem with which you want to communicate. Although you have no control over the routing your local phone company and long-distance carrier give to a given call (or even whether the connection remains consistent during a given call), a modem can make the best of what it gets. Using line compensation, it can ameliorate some problems with the connection. Fallback helps the modem get the most from a substandard connection or one that loses quality during the modem link-up.

Data compression helps the modem move more data through any connection, and error correction compensates for transitory problems that would result in minor mistakes in transmissions.

Line Compensation

Although a long-distance telephone connection may sound unchanging to your ear, its electrical characteristics vary by the moment. Everything from a wire swaying in the Wichita wind to the phone company's automatic rerouting of the call through Bangkok when the direct circuits fill up can change the amplitude, frequency, and phase response of the circuit. The modem then faces two challenges: not to interpret such changes as data and to maintain the quality of the line to a high enough standard to support its use for high-speed transmission.

Under modern communications standards, modems compensate for variations in telephone lines by equalizing the telephone line. That is, two modems exchange tones at different frequencies and observe how signal strength and phase shift with frequency changes. The modems then change their signals to behave in the exact opposite way to cancel out the variations in the phone line. The modems compensate for deficiencies in the phone line to make signals behave the way they would have in absence of the problems. If, for example, the modems observe that high frequencies are too weak on the phone line, they will compensate by boosting high frequencies before sending them.

Modern modems also use echo cancellation to eliminate the return of their own signals from the distant end of the telephone line. To achieve this, a modem sends out a tone and listens for its return. Once it determines how long the delay is before the return signal occurs and how strong the return is, the modem can compensate by generating the opposite signal and mixing it into the incoming data stream.

Fallback

Most modems use at most two carriers for duplex communications. These carriers are usually modulated to fill the available bandwidth. Sometimes, however, the quality of the telephone line is not sufficient to allow reliable communications over the full bandwidth expected by the modem even with line compensation. In such cases, most high-speed modems incorporate fallback capabilities. When the top speed does not work, they attempt to communicate at lower speeds that are less critical of telephone line quality. A pair of modems might first try 9,600 bps and be unsuccessful. They next might try 4,800, then 2,400, and so on until reliable communications are established.

Most modems fall back and stick with the slower speed that proves itself reliable. Some modems, however, constantly check the condition of the telephone connection to sense for any deterioration or improvement. If the line improves, these modems can shift back to a higher speed.

Multiple-Carrier Modems

Although most modems rely on a relatively complex form of modulation on one or two carriers to achieve high speed, one clever idea now relegated to a historical footnote by the latest modem standards is the multiple-carrier modem. This type of modem used relatively simple modulation on several simultaneous carrier signals. One of the chief advantages of this system comes into play when the quality of the telephone connection deteriorates. Instead of dropping down to the next incremental communications rate, generally cutting data speed in half, the multiple-carrier modems just stop using the carriers in the doubtful regions of the bandwidth. The communication rate may fall off just a small percentage in the adjustment. (Of course, it could dip by as much as a normal fallback modem as well.)

Data Compression

Although there's no way of increasing the number of bits that can cross a telephone line beyond the capacity of the channel, the information-handling capability of the modem circuit can be increased by making each bit more meaningful. Many of the bits that are sent through the telecommunication channel are meaningless or redundant; they convey no additional information. By eliminating those worthless bits, the information content of the data stream is more intense, and each bit is more meaningful. The process of paring the bits is called data compression.

The effectiveness of compression varies with the type of data that's being transmitted. One of the most prevalent data compression schemes encodes repetitive data. Eight recurrences of the same byte value might be coded as two bytes, one signifying the value and the second the number of repetitions. This form of compression is most effective on graphics, which often have many blocks of repeating pixels. Other compression methods may strip out start, stop, and parity bits.

At one time, many modem manufacturers had their own methods of compressing data so that you needed two matched modems to take advantage of the potential throughput increases. Today, however, most modems follow international compression standards so that any two modems using the same standards can communicate with one another at compressed-data speeds.

These advanced modems perform the data compression on the fly in their own circuitry as you transmit your data. Alternately, you can precompress your data before sending it to your modem. Sort of like dehydrating soup, precompression (also known as file compression) removes the unnecessary or redundant parts of a file yet allows the vital contents to be easily stored and reconstituted when needed. This gives you two advantages: The files you send and receive require less storage space because they are compressed, and your serial port operates at a lower speed for a given data throughput.

Note that once a file is compressed, it usually cannot be further compressed. So modems that use on-the-fly compression standards cannot increase the throughput of precompressed files. In fact, using one on-the-fly modem data compression system (MNP5) actually can increase the transmission time for compressed files as compared to not using modem data compression.

Error Checking and Error Correction

Because all high-speed modems operate closer to the limits of the telephone channel, they are naturally more prone to data errors. To better cope with such problems, nearly all high-speed modems have their own built-in error-checking methods (which detect only transmission errors) and error correction (which detects data errors and corrects the mistakes before they get passed along to your PC). These error-checking and error-correction systems work like communications protocols, grouping bytes into blocks and sending cyclical redundancy checking information. They differ from the protocols used by communications software in that they are implemented in the hardware instead of your computer's software. That means that they don't load down your computer when it's straining at the limits of its serial ports.

It can also mean that software communications protocols are redundant and a waste of time. As mentioned before in the case of switching modems, using a software-based communications protocol can be counterproductive with many high-speed modems, slowing the transfer rate to a crawl. Most makers of modems using built-in error checking advise against using such software protocols.

All modem error-detection and error-correction systems require that both ends of the connection use the same error-handling protocol. So that modems can talk to one another, a number of standards have been developed. Today, the most popular are MNP4 and V.42. You may also see the abbreviations LAPB and LAPM describing error-handling methods.

LAPB stands for Link Access Procedure, Balanced, an error-correction protocol designed for X.25 packet-switched services such as Telebit and Tymnet. Some high-speed modem makers adapted this standard to their dial-up modem products before the V.42 standard (described later) was agreed on. For example, the Hayes Smartmodem 9600 from Hayes Microcomputer Products includes LAPB error-control capabilities.

LAPM is an acronym for Link Access Procedure for Modems and is the error-correction protocol used by the CCITT V.42 standard described later in the chapter.

Combining Voice and Data

Having only a single telephone line can be a problem when you need to talk as well as send data. In the old days, the solution was to switch. You'd type a message to the person at the other end of the connection like, "Go voice," pick up the telephone handset, and tell your modem to switch back to command mode so you could talk without its constant squeal.

In the early 1990s, several manufacturers developed means of squeezing both data and voice down a single telephone line at the same time using special modem hardware. Three technologies—VoiceView, VoiceSpan, and DSVD—vied for market dominance.

Internet technology has made all three irrelevant. Instead of combining data and voice in modem hardware, the modern alternative is to combine them using software inside your PC. Your PC captures your voice with a microphone and digitizes it. Web software packages the voice information into packets that get sent to an ordinary modem exactly like data packets. At the other end of the connection, the receiving PC converts the voice packets back to audio to play through the computer's speakers. The modem connection doesn't care—or even know—whether it's passing along packets of data or digitized audio.

Modem Hardware

A modem is a signal converter that mediates the communications between a computer and the telephone network. In function, a modern PC modem has five elements—interface circuitry for linking with the host PC; circuits to prepare data for transmission by adding the proper start, stop, and parity bits; modulator circuitry that makes the modem compatible with the telephone line; a user interface that gives you command of the modem's operation; and the package that gives the modem its physical embodiment.

PC Interface

For a modem to work with your PC, the modem needs a means to connect to your PC's logic circuits. At one time, all modems used a standard or enhanced serial port to link to your PC. However, because the standard serial port tops out at a data rate that's too slow to handle today's fastest modems—the serial limit is 115,200 bits-per-second but some modems accept data at double that rate—modem makers have developed parallel-interfaced modems.

All modems, whether installed outside your PC, in one of its expansion slots, or in a PCMCIA slot, make use of a serial or parallel communications port. In the case of an internal PC modem, the port is embedded in the circuitry of the modem, and the expansion bus of the PC itself becomes the interface.

With an external modem, this need for an interface (and the use of a port) is obvious. You have to physically plug in the modem PC to a serial, parallel, or USB port. You fill the port's jack with the plug of a cable running off to your modem. With an internal modem, the loss of resources because of the interface requirements is less obvious. You may not even notice that your modem has stolen the ports used by its internal interface until something doesn't work because both your modem and your mouse (or some other peripheral) try to use the same port at the same time.

In the case of serial modems, this interface converts the parallel data of your PC into serial form suitable for transmission down a telephone line. Modern modems operate so fast that the choice of serial port circuitry (particularly the UART) become critical to achieving the best possible performance.

The serial and parallel ports built into internal modems are just like dedicated ports of the same type. They need an input/output address and an interrupt to operate properly. The plug-and-play system assigns these values to the modem during its configuration process. (Older modems required that you select these values with jumpers or switches.)

Ordinarily, you don't need to know or bother with these values. Some communications software, however, may not mesh perfectly with the Windows system. It may demand you tell it the port used by your modem. The Modem Properties sheet lists this value. You can check it under Windows by clicking on the modem icon in Control Panel and then clicking on the Properties tab.

Data Preparation

Modern modem communications require that the data you want to send be properly prepared for transmission. This pre-transmission preparation helps your modem deliver the highest possible data throughput while preventing errors from creeping in.

Most modem standards change the code used by the serial stream of data from the PC interface into code that's more efficient, for example, stripping out data framing information for quicker synchronous transfers. The incoming code stream may also be analyzed and compressed to strip out redundant information. The modem may also add error detection or correction codes to the data stream.

At the receiving end, the modem must debrief the data stream and undo the compression and coding of the transmitting modem. A micro controller inside the modem performs these functions based on the communications standard you choose to use. If you select a modem by the communications standards it uses, you don't have to worry about the details of what this micro controller does.

Modulator

The heart of the modem is the circuitry that actually converts the digital information from your PC into analog-compatible form. Because this circuitry produces a modulated signal, it is called a *modulator*.

User Interface

The fourth element in the modem is what you see and feel. Most modems give you some way of monitoring what they do either audibly with a speaker or visually through a light display. These features don't affect the speed of the modem or how it works but can make one modem easier to use than another. Indicator lights are particularly helpful when you want to troubleshoot communication problems.

Line Interface

Finally, the modem needs circuitry to connect with the telephone system. This line interface circuitry (in telephone terminology, a data access arrangement) boosts the strength of the modem's internal logic-level signals to a level matching that of normal telephone service. At the same time, the line interface circuitry protects your modem and computer from dangerous anomalies on the telephone line (say, a nearby lightning strike), and it protects the telephone company from odd things that may originate from your computer and modem, say a pulse from your PC in its death throes.

From your perspective, the line interface of the modem is the telephone jack on its back panel. Some modems have two jacks so that you can loop through a standard telephone. By convention, the jack marked "Line" connects with your telephone line; the jack marked "Phone" connects to your telephone.

Over the years, this basic five-part modem design has changed little. But the circuits themselves, the signal-processing techniques that they use, and the standards they follow have all evolved to the point that modern modems can move data as fast as the theoretical limits of telephone transmission lines allow.

Packaging

Internal modems plug into an expansion slot in your PC. The connector in the slot provides all the electrical connections that are necessary to link to your PC. To make the modem work, you only need to plug in a telephone line. The internal modem draws power from your PC, so it needs no power supply of its own. Nor does it need a case. Consequently, the internal modem is usually the least expensive at a given speed. Because internal modems plug into a computer's expansion bus, a given model of modem is compatible only with computers using the bus for which it was designed. You cannot put a PC internal modem in a Macintosh or workstation. Similarly you cannot plug an old ISA modem into a PCI slot or a PCI modem into an ISA slot.

External modems are self-contained peripherals that accept signals from your PC through a serial or parallel port and also plug into your telephone line. Most need an external source of power, typically a small transformer that plugs into a wall outlet and—through a short, thin cable—into the modem. At minimum, then, you need a tangle of three cables to make the modem work. You have two incentives to put up with the cable snarl. External modems can work with computers that use any architecture as long as the computer has the right kind of port. In addition, external modems usually give you a full array of indicators, which can facilitate troubleshooting. In addition, you can install an external modem by simply plugging in a cable. Moving the modem to another PC involves nothing more than unplugging it from one and plugging it into another. You never have to open the case of either PC.

Pocket modems are compact external modems designed for use with notebook PCs. They are usually designed to plug directly into a port connector on your PC, eliminating one interface cable. Many eliminate the need for a power supply and cable by running from battery power or drawing power from your PC or the telephone line.

PC Card modems plug into that PCMCIA slots that are typically found in notebook. They combine the cable-free simplicity of internal modems with the interchangeability of external modems. (The PCMCIA interface was designed to work with a variety of computer architectures.) The confines of the PCMCIA slot also forces PC Card modems to be even more compact than pocket modems. This miniaturization takes its toll in higher prices, however, although the ability to quickly move one modem between your desktop and portable PCs can compensate for the extra cost.

The confines of a PCMCIA slot preclude manufacturers from putting a full-size modular telephone jack on PC Card modems. Modem makers use one of two workarounds for this problem. Most PC Card modems use short adapter cables with thin connectors on one end to plug into the modem and a standard modular jack on the other. Other PC Card modems use the X-Jack design, developed and patented by Megahertz Corporation (now part of 3Com). The X-Jack pops out of the modem to provide a skeletal phone connector into which you can plug a modular telephone cable. The X-Jack design is more convenient because you don't have to carry a separate adapter with you when you travel. On the other hand, the X-Jack makes the modem more vulnerable to carelessness. Yank on the phone cable, and it can break the X-Jack and render the modem useless. Yanking on an adapter cable will more likely pull the cable out or damage only the cable. On the other hand, the connectors in the adapter cables are also prone to invisible damage that can lead to unreliable connections.

Indicators

The principal functional difference between external (including pocket) and internal (including PC Card) modems is that the former have indicator lights that allow you to monitor the operation of the modem and the progress of a given call. Internal modems, being locked inside your PC, cannot offer such displays. Some software lets you simulate the lights on your monitor, and Windows will even put a tiny display of two of these indicators on your taskbar. These indicators can be useful in troubleshooting modem communications, so many PC people prefer to have them available (hence they prefer external modems.)

The number and function of these indicators on external modems varies with the particular product and the philosophy of the modem maker. Typically, you'll find from four to eight indicators on the front panel of a modem, as shown in Figure 22.8.

FIGURE 22.8
*Typical indicators on
external modem front
panel.*

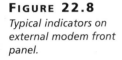

The most active and useful of these indicators are Send Data and Receive Data. These lights flash whenever the modem sends out or receives in data from the telephone line. They let you know what's going on during a communications session. For example, if the lights keep flashing away but nothing appears on your monitor screen, you know you are suffering a local problem, either in your PC, its software, or the hardware connection with your modem. If the Send Data light flashes but the Receive Data light does not flicker in response, you know that the distant host is not responding.

Carrier Detect indicates that your modem is linked to another modem across the telephone connection. It allows you to rule out line trouble if your modem does not seem to be getting a response. This light glows throughout the period your modem is connected.

Off Hook glows whenever your modem opens a connection on your telephone line. It lights up when your modem starts to make a connection and continues to glow through dialing, negotiations, and the entire connection.

Terminal Ready glows when the modem senses that your PC is ready to communicate with it. When this light is lit, it assures you that you've connected your modem to your PC and that your PC's communications software has properly taken control of your serial port.

Modem Ready glows whenever your modem is ready to work. It should be lit whenever your modem is powered up and not in its test state.

High Speed indicates that the modem is operating at its fastest possible speed. Some modems have separate indicators for each speed increment they support. Others forego speed indicators entirely.

Auto Answer lights up to let you know that your modem is in its answer mode. If your telephone rings, your modem will answer the call (at least if it's connected to the line that is ringing.)

Table 22.2 summarizes the mnemonics commonly used for modem indicators and their functions.

TABLE 22.2   Modem Indicator Abbreviations and Definitions

Mnemonic	Spelled Out	Meaning
HS	High Speed	Modem operating at highest speed
AA	Auto Answer	Modem will answer phone
CD	Carrier Detect	Modem in contact with remote system
OH	Off Hook	Modem off hook, using the phone line
RD	Receive Data	Modem is receiving data
SD	Send Data	Modem is transmitting data
TR	Terminal Ready	PC is ready to communicate
MR	Modem Ready	Modem is ready to communicate

Analog Modem Standards

Neither men nor modems are islands. Above all, they must communicate and share their ideas with others. One modem would do the world no good. It would just send data out into the vast analog unknown, never to be seen (or heard) again.

But having two modems isn't automatically enough. Like people, modems must speak the same language for the utterances of one to be understood by the other. Modulation is part of the modem language. In addition, modems must be able to understand the error-correction features and data-compression routines used by one another. Unlike most human beings, who speak any of a million languages and dialects, each somewhat ill-defined, modems are much more precise in the languages they use. They have their own equivalent of the French Academy: standards organizations.

In the United States, the first standards were set long ago by the most powerful force in the telecommunications industry, which was the telephone company. More specifically, the American Telephone and Telegraph Company, the Bell System, which promoted various Bell standards, the most famous being Bell 103 and Bell 212A. After the Bell System was split into AT&T and the seven regional operating companies (RBOCs, also known as the Baby Bells), other long-distance carriers broke into the telephone monopoly. In addition, other nations have become interested in telecommunications.

As a result of these developments, the onus and capability to set standards moved to an international standards organization that's part of the United Nations, the International

Telecommunications Union (ITU) Telecommunications Standards Sector, which was formerly the Comite Consultatif International Telegraphique et Telephoneique (in English, that's International Telegraph and Telephone Consultative Committee). The initials of the latter, CCITT, grace nearly all of the high-speed standards used by modems today, such as V.22bis, V.32, V.32bis, V.42, and V.42bis.

Along the way, a modem and software maker, Microcom, developed a series of modem standards prefixed with the letters MNP, such as MNP4 and MNP5. The letters stand for Microcom Networking Protocol. Some modems boast having MNP modes, but these are falling from favor as the ITU (CCITT) standards take over.

Standards are important when buying a modem because they are your best assurance that a given modem can successfully connect with any other modem in the world. In addition, the standards you choose will determine how fast your modem can transfer data and how reliably it will work. The kind of communications you want to carry out will determine what kind of modem you need. If you're just going to send files electronically between offices, you can buy two non-standard modems and get more speed for your investment. But if you want to communicate with the rest of the world, you will want to get a modem that meets the international standards. The following sections discuss the most popular standards for modems that are connected to PCs.

Bell Standards

Bell 103 comes first in any list of modem standards because it was the first widely adopted standard, and it remains the standard of last resort, the one that will work when all else fails. It allows data transmissions at a very low speed. Bell 103 uses simple FSK modulation, thus it is the only standard in which the baud rate (the rate at which signal changes) is equal to the data rate.

Bell 212A is the next logical step in a standards discussion because it was the next modem standard to find wide application in the United States. It achieves a data transfer rate of 1,200 bits-per-second by adding quadrature modulation to a frequency modulated 600 baud signal. Consequently, a Bell 212A modem operates at 600 baud and transfers information at 1,200 bits-per-second. Although Bell 212A was, at one time, the most widely used communication standard in America, many foreign countries prohibited the use of Bell 212A, preferring instead the similar international standard, V.22.

MNP Standards

Microcom Networking Protocol is an entire hierarchy of standards, starting with MNP Class 1, an out-of-date error-correction protocol, to MNP Class 10, Adverse Channel Enhancements, which is designed to eke the most data transfer performance from poor connections. MNP does not stand alone but works with modems that may conform to other standards. The MNP standards specify technologies rather than speeds. MNP

Classes 2 through 4 deal with error control and are in the public domain. Classes 5 through 10 are licensed by Microcom and deal with a number of modem operating parameters:

MNP Class 1 uses an asynchronous byte-oriented half-duplex method of exchanging data designed to make a minimum demand on the processor in the PC managing the modem. It was originally designed to enable error-free communications with first-generation PCs that had little speed and less storage. Using MNP Class 1 steals about 30 percent of the throughput of a modem, so a 2,400 bits-per-second modem using MNP Class 1 achieves an actual throughput of about 1,690 bps.

MNP Class 2 takes advantage of full-duplex data exchange. As with MNP Class 1, it is designed for asynchronous operation at the byte level. MNP Class 2 achieves somewhat higher efficiency and takes only about a 16 percent toll on throughput.

MNP Class 3 improves on MNP2 by working synchronously instead of asynchronously. Consequently, no start and stop bits are required for each byte, trimming the data transfer overhead by 25 percent or more. Although MNP3 modems exchange data between themselves synchronously, they connect to PCs using asynchronous data links, which means they plug right into RS232 serial ports.

MNP Class 4 is basically an error-correcting protocol but also yields a bit of data compression. It incorporates two innovations. Adaptive Packet Assembly allows the modem to package data in blocks or packets that are sent and error-checked as a unit. The protocol is adaptive because it varies the size of each packet according to the quality of the connection. Data Phase Optimization eliminates repetitive control bits from the data traveling across the connection to streamline transmissions. Together, these techniques can increase the throughput of a modem by 120 percent at a given bit rate. In other words, using MNP4, a 1,200 bits-per-second modem could achieve a 1,450 bits-per-second throughput. Many modems have MNP4 capabilities.

MNP Class 5 is purely a data compression protocol that squeezes some kinds of data into a form that takes less time to transmit. MNP5 can compress some data by a factor up to two, effectively doubling the speed of data transmissions. On some forms of data, such as files that have been already compressed, however, MNP5 may actually increase the time required for transmission.

MNP Class 6 is designed to help modems get the most out of telephone connections independent of data compression. Using a technique called Universal Link Negotiation, modems can start communicating at a low speed and then, after evaluating the capabilities of the telephone line and each modem, switch to a higher speed. MNP6 also includes Statistical Duplexing, which allows a half-duplex modem to simulate full-duplex operation.

MNP Class 7 is a more efficient data compression algorithm (Huffman encoding) than MNP5, which permits increases in data throughput by a factor as high as three with some data.

MNP Class 9 (there is no MNP Class 8) is designed to reduce the transmission overhead required by certain common modem operations. The acknowledgment of each data packet is streamlined by combining the acknowledgment with the next data packet instead of sending a separate confirmation byte. In addition, MNP9 minimizes the amount of information that must be retransmitted when an error is detected by indicating where the error occurred. Although some other error-correction schemes require all information transmitted after an error to be resent, an MNP9 modem needs only the data that was in error to be sent again.

MNP Class 10 is a set of Adverse Channel Enhancements that help modems work better when faced with poor telephone connections. Modems with MNP10 will make multiple attempts to set up a transmission link, adjust the size of data packets they transmit according to what works best over the connection, and adjust the speed at which they operate to the highest rate that can be reliably maintained. One use envisioned for this standard is cellular modem communications (the car phone).

CCITT/ITU Standards

ITU standards are those promulgated by the International Telecommunications Union, part of the United Nations. These standards are used throughout the world:

V.22 is the CCITT equivalent of the Bell 212A standard. It delivers a transfer rate of 1,200 bits-per-second at 600 baud. It actually uses the same form of modulation as Bell 212A, but it is not compatible with the Bell standard because it uses a different protocol to set up the connection. In other words, although Bell 212A and V.22 modems speak the same language, they are unwilling to start a conversation with one another. Some modems support both standards and allow you to switch between them.

V.22bis was the first true world standard, adopted into general use in both the United States and Europe. It allows a transfer rate of 2,400 bits-per-second at 600 baud using a technique called trellis modulation that mixes two simple kinds of modulation, quadrature and amplitude modulation. Each baud has 16 states, enough to code any pattern of four bits. Each state is distinguished both by its phase relationship to the unaltered carrier and its amplitude (or strength) in relation to the carrier. There are four distinct phases and four distinct amplitudes under V.22bis, which, when multiplied together, yield the 16 available states.

V.32 is an international high-speed standard that permits data transfer rates of 4,800 and 9,600 bits-per-second. At its lower speed, it uses quadrature amplitude modulation similar to Bell 212A but at the higher baud rate of 2,400 baud. At 9,600 bits-per-second, it uses trellis modulation similar to V.22bis but at 2,400 baud and with a greater range of phases and amplitudes.

Note that although most current fax machines and modems operate at 9,600 bits-per-second—the primary data rate as V.32—a fax modem with 9,600 bps capability is not necessarily compatible with the V.32 standard. Don't expect a fax modem to communicate with V.32 products.

V.32bis extends the V.32 standard to 14,400 bits-per-second while allowing fallback to intermediary speeds of 7,200 and 12,000 bits-per-second in addition to the 4,800 and 9,600 bits-per-second speeds of V.32. (Note that all these speeds are multiples of a basic 2,400 baud rate.) The additional operating speeds that V.32bis has and V.32 does not are generated by using different ranges of phases and amplitudes in the modulation.

At 14,400 bits-per-second, there are 128 potentially different phase/amplitude states for each baud under V.32bis, enough to encode seven data bits in each baud. Other data rates (including V.32) use similar relationships for their data coding. Because there are so many phase and amplitude differences squeezed together, a small change in the characteristics of a telephone line might mimic such a change and cause transmission errors. Consequently, some way of detecting and eliminating such errors becomes increasingly important as transmission speed goes up.

V.34 is the official designation of the high-speed standard once known as V.fast. Under the V.34 standard, as adopted in June 1994, modems can operate at data rates as high as 28,800 bits-per-second without compression over ordinary dial-up telephone lines. More recently, the standard was amended to permit operation as fast as 33,600 bps. The V.34 standard will also allow lower transmission rates at 24,000 and 19,200 bits-per-second and include backward compatibility with V.32 and V.32bis.

The V.34 standard calls for modems to adapt to telephone line conditions to eke out the greatest usable amount of bandwidth. Although V.32 modems operate at a fixed bandwidth of 2,400Hz, with a perfect connection V.fast modems will be able to push their operating bandwidth to 3,429Hz. V.34 modems will use line-probing techniques to try each connection and then apply advanced equalization to the line. To squeeze in as much signal as possible, V.34 modems use multidimensional trellis coding and signal shaping.

V.34 was immediately preceded by two non-standards, V.32 terbo and V.FC (or V.Fast Class), that were supported by various modem industry groups and chip manufacturers, but which were not formally sanctioned by the ITU. Because technology provided the power to allow higher speeds before the ITU could reach a consensus on a standard, these quasi-standards were widely available until V.34 products became available.

V.32 terbo appeared in June 1993 when AT&T Microelectronics introduced modem chips that operated at 19,200 bits-per-second using an extension of the V.32 modulation scheme. The "terbo" in the name is a poor play on words. "Bis" in modem standards stands for "second"; similarly, "ter" means "third" (as in "tertiary"). "Terbo" means nothing but conjures up the sound of respectability ("ter" for the third iteration of V.32) and speed ("turbo" as in a high-performance automobile with a turbocharger). The technology was originally designed for picture phone technologies. V.32 terbo is backward compatible with V.32bis standards and will connect with older modems at the highest speed at which both can operate. With compression such as MNP5 or V.42bis, V.32 terbo modems can operate at effective data rates as high as 115,200 bits-per-second.

V.FC modems represent the interpretation of some modem makers and a chip maker (Rockwell International) of a preliminary version of the V.34 standard. These V.FC modems deliver true 28,800 bits-per-second speed using V.34 technology, but they don't use the same handshaking to set up communications as V.34. (The V.FC products predate the final V.34 agreements.)

V.34bis has not been officially recognized as a standard. Many of the latest modems that operate at 33.6Kbps refer to themselves with this designation in anticipation of its acceptance.

V.42 is a world-wide error-correction standard that is designed to help make V.32, V.32bis, and other modem communications more reliable. V.42 incorporates MNP4 as an "alternative" protocol. That is, V.42 modems can communicate with MNP4 modems, but a connection between the two won't use the more sophisticated V.42 error-correction protocol. At the beginning of each call, as the connection is being negotiated between modems, a V.42 modem will determine whether MNP4 or full V.42 error correction can be used by the other modem. V.42 is preferred, and MNP4 is the second choice. In other words, a V.42 will first try to set up a V.42 session; failing that, it will try MNP4; and failing that, it will set up a communications session without error correction.

V.42bis is a data-compression protocol endorsed by the CCITT. Different from and incompatible with MNP5 and MNP7, V.42bis is also more efficient. On some forms of data, it can yield compression factors up to four, potentially quadrupling the speed of modem transmissions. (With PCs, the effective maximum communication rate may be slower because of limitations on serial ports, typically 38,400 bits-per-second.) Note that a V.42bis-only modem cannot communicate with a MNP5-only modem. Unlike MNP5, a V.42bis modem never increases the transmission time of "incompressible" data. Worst-case operation is the same speed as would be achieved without compression.

V.90 is the international standard for modem communications at 56,000 bits-per-second (or 56Kbps) across dial-up telephone lines. It is the highest speed modem standard in use today and possibly the highest speed true modems will ever achieve. The modem in any new PC should conform with the ITU V.90 standard.

Despite their 56Kbps rating, most V.90 modems never achieve their highest data rate. All high-speed modems face several challenges, any or all of which may limit their performance. The most important are legal, technical, and practical restrictions.

All of the 56Kbps specifications actually require more from a telephone line than the law allows. Specifically, the voltage swing for 56Kbps communications requires more power than government regulations allow on telephone lines. To keep modems legal, top speed gets limited to the 53Kbps speed you see in the disclaimers in advertisements.

Moreover, the 56Kbps speed requires all the bandwidth of a perfect telephone connection (and more). If your connection is not perfect, then something has to give, and that something is speed. The lower the quality of your connection, the slower your modem will operate. You need a short, high-quality link to your telephone company's central office to get full speed from any 56Kbps modem.

Often, your modem cannot negotiate a full-speed connection with the dial-up service you choose. A 56Kbps modem can only communicate at high speed with a matching modem at the other end of the connection. The typical Internet service provider (particularly small, budget-oriented ISPs) has a raft of modems of different ages. Some allow full 56Kbps operations; others operate only at slower speeds. If you call when the ISP is busy, you're more likely to link with a slower modem.

Note, too, the design of the V.90 system limits your use of its highest speed to communications with service providers with direct digital connections to the Internet. V.90 does not allow 56Kbps communications between individual PCs. One end of a full-speed V.90 connection must have a direct digital link with the telephone network. Most ISPs have the required digital link. The connections between your PCs and their modems are both analog, so the 56Kbps speed cannot be supported.

V.90 evolved out of two competing 56Kbps systems, K56flex and x2, names that you still may have to deal with. *K56flex* is a proprietary technology that was independently developed and initially marketed as two different and incompatible systems by Rockwell and Lucent Technologies. In November 1996, the two companies agreed to combine their work into a single standard. *x2* is a proprietary technology developed by US Robotics. The two systems use the same analog-signal-level digital encoding as V.90 and differ from each other (and the standard) only in the handshaking used to set up the connection. Unfortunately, the handshake is the vital part of getting the systems to work, so K56flex and x2 are not compatible; they cannot talk to each other at their top speeds.

Some Internet service providers support only one of the two V.90 predecessors for their 56Kbps data rate. If your service is unable to negotiate a full 56Kbps connection, it will fall back to a slower standard, typically the 33.6Kbps V.34 rate if the telephone connection can handle the signals.

Digital Services

The V.90 standard is the modem's last stand. It wrings all the speed potential from a dial-up connection. The next step is all-digital communications. After all, nearly all traffic between telephone exchanges throughout the world is digital. The only archaic analog step is the stretch between the exchange and your home or office.

There's no doubt that you'll eventually shift from analog to digital services for your telecommunications needs. The only question is who will provide the connection. Three technologies can provide you with a high-speed all-digital link—telephone, cable, and satellite.

All three work. All three deliver speeds that make modem connections seem like they are—antique. In fact, the most important limiting factor is availability. Only satellite services can promise a link in any part of the United States (and most of the world). The others depend on your local telephone company or cable provider upgrading its facilities to handle digital subscriber services.

Telephone Services

One key player in the supply of digital telecommunications services is quite familiar, the telephone company. Beyond traditional Plain Old Telephone Services (POTS, also used as an acronym for Plain Old Telephone Sets), telephone companies have developed a number of all-digital communication services. Some of these have been around for a while, aimed at business users with heavy data needs. Several new all-digital services are aimed directly at you as an individual consumer.

The range of digital services supplied by telephone companies is wide and spans a range of data rates. Table 22.3 lists many of these and their maximum data rates.

TABLE 22.3   Maximum Data Rates of Digital Telecommunications Standards

Standard	Connection Type	Downstream Rate	Upstream Rate
V.34	Analog	33.6Kbps	33.6Kbps
V.90	Quasi-analog	56Kbps	33.6Kbps
SDS 56	Digital	56Kbps	56Kbps
ISDN	Digital	128Kbps	128Kbps
SDSL	Digital	1.544Mbps	1.544Mbps
T1	Digital	1.544Mbps	1.544Mbps
E1	Digital	2.048Mbps	2.048Mbps
ADSL	Digital	9Mbps	640Kbps
VDSL	Digital	52Mbps	2Mbps

Certainly, you will still talk on the telephone for ages to come (if your other family members give you a chance, of course), but the nature of the connection may finally change. Eventually, digital technology will take over your local telephone connection. In fact, in many parts of America and the rest of the world, you can already order a special digital line from your local telephone company and access all-digital switched systems. You get the equivalent of a telephone line, one that allows you to choose any conversation mate who's connected to the telephone network (with the capability of handling your digital data, of course), as easily as dialing a telephone.

At least three such services are currently or will soon be available in many locations. All are known by their initials: SDS 56, ISDN, and SMDS. Eventually, you will probably plug your PC into one of them or one of their successors.

T1

The basic high-speed service provided by the telephone company is called *T1*, and its roots go back to the first days of digital telephony in the early 1960s. The first systems developed by Bell Labs selected the now-familiar 8KHz rate to sample analog signals and translate them into 8-bit digital values. The result was a 64 kbits/sec digital data stream. To multiplex these digital signals on a single connection, Bell's engineers combined 24 of these voice channels together to create a data frame 193 bits long, the extra bit length to define the beginning of the frame. The result was a data stream with a bit rate of 1.544 mbits/sec. Bell engineers called the resulting 24-line structure DS1. AT&T used this basic structure throughout its system to multiply the voice capacity of its telephone system, primarily trunk lines between exchanges.

As telephone demand and private business exchanges (PBXs) became popular with larger businesses, the telephone company began to offer T1 service directly to businesses. As digital applications grew, T1 became the standard digital business interconnect. Many Web servers tie into the network with a T1 line.

A key feature of the DS1 format was that it was compatible with standard copper telephone lines, although requiring repeaters (booster amplifiers) about every mile. The T1 signal itself is quite unlike normal analog telephone connections, however, and that creates a problem. T1 is based on a signal transmission method called AMI, Alternate Mark Inversion. It is a bipolar system. That is, AMI represents a zero (or space) by the absence of a voltage; a one (or mark) is represented by a positive or negative pulse, depending on whether the preceding one was negative or positive. As a result, marks are inverted on an alternating basis (hence the name). This codegenerates a signal with a bandwidth about equivalent to its data rate, 1.5MHz. At the same time this high-speed signal creates a great deal of interference, so much that two T1 lines cannot safely co-habitate in one of the 50-pair cables used to route normal telephone services to homes.

Outside of the United States, the equivalent of T1 services is called *E1*. Although based on the same technology as T1, E1 combines 30 voice channels with 64 kbits/sec bandwidth to create a 2.048 mbits/sec digital channel.

Serious Web surfers dream of having a dedicated T1 line. The cost, however, is prohibitive. Installation is often thousands of dollars and monthly charges may be a thousand dollars, sometime more. Typically, your Internet service provider has an T1 (or better) connection and divides it up, giving each customer a single modem slice.

T3 is a synonym for DS3 service, which is approximately 45 mbits/sec, and OC-3 is an approximately 155 mbits/sec fiber interface.

HDSL

The primary problem with T1 is the interference-causing modulation system it uses, one based on 1960s technology. Using the latest modulation techniques, the telecommunications industry developed a service called *High data rate Digital Subscriber Line*, or HDSL, that features the same data rate as T1 or E1 but requires a much narrower bandwidth, from 80 to 240KHz. One basic trick to the bandwidth reduction technique is splitting the signal across multiple phone lines. For T1 data rate, the service uses two lines; for E1, three. Besides reducing interference, the lower data rate allows longer links without repeaters, as much as 12,000 feet.

HDSL delivers high-speed data networking up to 1.544Mbps over two copper pairs and up to 2.048Mbps over three pairs at a maximum range of 20,000 feet (about 3.8 miles, or 6.1 km)from a central office. It is similar to SDSL and has symmetrical transmission capabilities. Most T1 lines installed today utilize this technology.

Unfortunately, the "subscriber" in the name of the standard was not meant to correspond to you as an individual. It fits into the phone company scheme of things in the same place as T1—linking businesses and telephone company facilities.

SDSL

Two lines (or three) to carry one service is hardly the epitome of efficiency. By altering the modulation method, however, a single line can carry the same data as the two (or three) of HDSL. The commercial version of this service is termed *Symmetrical Digital Subscriber Line*, or SDSL. Although the definition of the acronym has changed, the technology has not. Originally, it meant *Single-line Digital Subscriber Line* to distinguish it from multi-line systems. The "symmetrical" designation distinguishes it from its more recent asymmetrical competition.

The chief advantage of SDSL over other high-performance services is, as the new designation implies, that it is symmetrical. The data rate is the same in both directions. Web servers and wide-area network connection often require symmetrical operation, making SDSL the choice for them.

The data speed of the SDSL system ranges from 160 kbits/sec up to 1.544 mbits/sec. The maximum usable rate depends on the distance of the subscriber from the central office. The lowest speed occurs at a maximum range of the SDSL system, 24,000 feet (about 4.5 miles, or 7.2 km.)

ADSL

Most of the advanced services aimed at consumer Internet use are asymmetrical. They have a higher downstream data rate from the server compared to their upstream rates, from you back to the server. Telecommunications companies are not ignorant of this situation and shortly after they developed HDSL, they also created a higher speed but asymmetrical alternative that they termed, logically enough, *Asymmetrical Digital Subscriber Line*, or ADSL. To distinguish it from the new G.Lite standard, full-fledged ADSL is sometimes called ADSL Full Rate or G.dmt. Its official designation is G.992.1.

ADSL can move downstream data at speeds up to 8.5 mbits/sec. Upstream, however, the maximum rate is about 640 kbits/sec to 1 mbit/sec. ADSL doesn't operate at a single rate as does T1 or SDSL. Its speed is limited by distance, longer distances imposing greater constraints. It can push data downstream at the T1 rate for up to about 18,000 feet from the central office. At half that distance, its downstream speed potential approaches 8.5 mbits/sec. Table 22.4 summarizes the downstream speeds and maximum distances possible with ADSL technology.

TABLE 22.4   ADSL Downstream Data Rates

Equivalent Service	Downstream Data Rate	Distance
G.Lite	1.544 mbits/sec	18,000 feet
T1	1.544 mbits/sec	18,000 feet
E1	2.048 mbits/sec	16,000 feet
DS1	6.312 mbits/sec	12,000 feet
ADSL	8.448 mbits/sec	9,000 feet

The modulation system used by ADSL operates at frequencies above the baseband used by ordinary telephone service or ISDN. Consequently, an ADSL line can carry high-speed digital signals and ordinary telephone signals simultaneously. In typical ADSL implementations, the ADSL signals start at about 50KHz, leaving the lower frequencies for carrying conventional voice signals.

To divide the signal between voice and data on the subscriber's premises, conventional ADSL systems require the use of a *splitter*. The equivalent of a stereo speaker's cross-over, the splitter combines a high-pass filter to extract a data-only signal and a low-pass filter to extract the voice-only signal. Typically, the splitter gets installed where the phone wires enter the building, and its outputs are routed separately to the telephone system and computer.

G.Lite

One of the major drawbacks with ADSL has been the need to install the splitter to make the system work. The splitter is provided by and installed by the telephone company, and its installation adds a hundred of dollars to the cost of setting up an ADSL connection. To eliminate the need for the splitter and create a common consumer standard for ADSL, several manufacturers in the telecommunications industry banded together to create the *Universal ADSL Working Group*.

In that the "universal" ADSL was to be a specific single application of general ADSL technology, the group gave the standard upon which it was working the name G.Lite. It also bears the formal designation G.992.2. In early 1999, it had completed its work and recommended G.Lite for acceptance as a standard by the ITU. With its single goal achieved, the group planned to disband.

G.Lite allows for a bandwidth downstream of up to 1.544 mbits/sec. Upstream, the asymmetrical system allows for a bandwidth of up to 512Kbps. The maximum length of a G.Lite connection stretching between the central office and your home or business is 18,000 feet.

VDSL

The next step above ADSL is the *Very-high-data-rate Digital Subscriber Line*, or VDSL. A proposal only, the service is designed to initially operate asymmetrically at speeds higher than ADSL but for shorter distances, potentially as high as 51.84 mbits/sec downstream for distances shorter than about 1,000 feet, falling to one-quarter that at about four times the distance (12.86 mbits/sec at 4,500 feet). Proposed upstream rates range from 1.6 mbits/sec to 2.3 mbits/sec. In the long term, developers hope to make the service symmetrical. VDSL is designed to work exclusively in an ATM network architecture. As with ADSL, VDSL can share a pair of wires with an ordinary telephone connection or even ISDN service.

SDS 56

Switched Data Services 56 (sometimes shortened to *Switched-56*) is an archaic connection system that yielded a single digital channel capable of a 56 kbits/sec data rate—the same as with a modem but with true digital signals. The Switched-56 signals traveled through conventional copper twisted-pair wiring (the same old stuff that carries your telephone conversations). For most telephone companies, it was an interim service to bridge the gap between POTS and ISDN service areas.

With Switched-56, you needed special head-end equipment—the equivalent of a modem—to link the wire to your PC. To take advantage of the connection, you also needed to communicate with someone who also had SDS 56 services.

In some locales, SDS 56 was no more expensive than an ordinary business telephone line. Installation costs, however, could be substantially higher (PacBell, for example, at one time charged $500 for installation), and some telephone companies could add extra monthly maintenance charges in addition to the normal dial-up costs. With modern modems promising the same speed with no extra charges, it's little wonder Switched-56 gets discussed in past tense.

ISDN

The initials stand for *Integrated Services Digital Network*, although waggish types will tell you it means "I Still Don't Know" or "It Still Does Nothing." The latter seems most apt because ISDN has been discussed for years with little to show for all the verbiage. Just as it was beginning to catch on, the industry shifted gears to higher performance standards, G.Lite in particular. But ISDN is an internationally supported standard, one that promises eventually to replace your standard analog telephone connection. Sometimes, the name is rendered as *IDSL* to keep it in the DSL family, that name being an compound acronym for *ISDN Digital Subscriber Line*.

IDSL provides symmetric download and upload speeds from 64 to 144Kbps on a single pair of copper wires. IDSL uses 2B1Q line coding, the same kind of line-modulation technique employed in SDSL and ISDN.

History

The first real movement toward getting ISDN rolling occurred in November 1992 when AT&T, MCI, and Sprint embraced a standard they called ISDN-1. Under the new standard, ISDN now has a consistent interface to connect end-user equipment, local telephone companies, and trunk carriers. This common interface now makes coast-to-coast ISDN transmission possible.

Implementations

Today, two versions of ISDN are generally available. The simplest is the Basic Rate Interface (BRI), which takes advantage of the copper twisted-pair wiring that's already in place linking homes and offices to telephone exchanges. Instead of a single analog signal, an ISDN line 2B1Q line is coded to carry three digital channels: two B (for Bearer) channels that can carry any kind of data (digitally encoded voice, fax, text, and numbers) at 64,000bps and a D (or Delta) channel, operating at 16,000bps, that can carry control signals and serve as a third data channel. The three channels can be independently routed to different destinations through the ISDN system.

The maximum distance an ISDN line can stretch from the central office is 18,000 feet (about 3.4 miles, or 5.5 km). To accommodate longer runs, this distance can be doubled by adding a *repeater* in the middle of the line. A repeater is an amplifier that regenerates the digital signals, erasing the signal distortion that arises on long lines.

A single BRI wire enables you to transfer uncompressed data bidirectionally at the 64,000bps rate, exactly like a duplex modem today but with higher speed and error-free transmission thanks to its all-digital nature. Even during such high-speed dual-direction connections, the D channel would still be available for other functions.

The more elaborate form of ISDN service is called the Primary Rate Interface. This service delivers 23 B channels (each operating at 64,000 bits-per-second) and one D channel (at 16,000 bits-per-second). As with normal telephone service, use of ISDN is billed by time in use, not the amount of data transmitted or received.

The strength of BRI service is that it makes do with today's ordinary twisted-pair telephone wiring. Neither you nor the various telephone companies need to invest the billions of dollars required to rewire the nation for digital service. Instead, only the central office switches that route calls between telephones (which today are mostly plug-in printed circuit boards) need to be upgraded.

Of course, this quick fix sounds easier than it is. The principal barriers aren't technological, however, but economic. The change-over is costly and, because telephone switching equipment has long depreciation periods, does not always make business sense for the telephone company.

Once you have access to ISDN, you won't be able to plug your PC directly into your telephone line. You will still need a device to interface your PC to the ISDN line. You will need to match your equipment to the line and prevent one from damaging the other using a device called an ISDN adapter. Such adapters may have analog ports that will allow you to connect your existing telephones into the ISDN network. ISDN adapters are becoming available for use in the limited areas that already have ISDN. Table 22.5 lists the standard wiring for an ISDN jack.

TABLE 22.5   ISDN 8P8C Jack Wiring

Pin	Mnemonic	Signal Name	Polarity	Wire Color
1	PS3	Power Source/Sink 3	Positive	Blue
2	PS3	Power Source/Sink 3	Negative	Orange
3	T/R	Transmit/Receive	Positive	Black
4	R/T	Receive/Transmit	Positive	Red
5	R/T	Receive/Transmit	Negative	Green
6	T/R	Transmit/Receive	Negative	Yellow
7	PS2	Power Sink/Source 2	Negative	Brown
8	PS2	Power Sink/Source 2	Positive	White

ISDN Modems

If you have ISDN service, you need a device to link your PC to the telephone line. Some people call this device an "ISDN modem." In that both your PC and the ISDN connection are complete digital, no modulation is necessary to match the two, so you don't need a modem. You still need a device that matches the data rates and protocols of your PC to the ISDN line and protects the line and your PC from suffering problems from the other. The device that does this magic is called an *ISDN terminal adapter*.

Cable Services

The chief performance limit on telephone service is the twisted-pair wire that runs from the central office to your home or business. Breaking through its performance limits would require stringing an entirely new set of wires throughout the telephone system. Considering the billions of dollars invested in existing twisted-pair telephone wiring, the likelihood of the telephone company moving into a new connection system tomorrow is remote.

Over the past two decades, however, other organizations have been hanging wires from poles and pulling them underground to connect between a third and a half of the homes in the United States—cable companies. The coaxial cables used by most such services have bandwidths a hundred or more times wider than twisted-pair wires. They regularly deliver microwave signals to homes many miles from their distribution center.

Tapping that bandwidth has intrigued cable operators for years, and the explosive growth of the Internet has set them salivating. Most operators foresee the time—already here in a few locations—where you can connect your PC to the Internet through their coaxial cable and incidentally send the check for Internet service to them.

Until recently, the one element lacking has been standardization. On September 24, 1996, however, five major companies with interests in cable modems—Com21, General Instrument, Hewlett-Packard, LANcity, and Motorola—joined together to develop a common data interface specification with the idea of building inter-operable cable modems. Originally known as the Data Over Cable Service Interface Specification or DOCSIS, the standard was governed by Cable Television Laboratories, Inc.—better known as CableLabs—in Louisville, Colorado. In 1999, CableLabs began certifying products to be compatible, labeling them as "CableLabs Certified" for retail sales of equipment. As of June of that year, CableLabs had certified 10 cable modem makers for compliance, including Arris Interactive, Askey Computer Corp., Cisco Systems, General Instrument, Philips Electronics, Samsung Information Systems of America, Sony Corp., 3Com, Thomson Consumer Electronics, Toshiba. The CableLabs technology allows operation at data rates as high as 36 Mbits/sec, although as a practical matter cable modem operate at substantially lower data rates. The basic interface between the cable modem and your PC is an 10Base-T Ethernet link, which in itself constrains speed to 10 Mbits/sec. The cable modem plugs into an Ethernet host adapter in your PC or an internal cable modem emulates an Ethernet adapter. Cable vendors themselves often quote lower speeds, although even the slowest—usually about 2 Mbits/sec—is faster than any other consumer-level connection system.

Grand as the idea of cable modems sounds, it suffers constraints as well. One problem with cable modems is with the current wiring of cable systems themselves. They are designed for program distribution, not for two-way communications. The cable itself does not limit the system to distribution, but many cable companies put amplifiers in their systems to allow their signals to reach for miles beyond their offices. Most of the amplifiers installed in existing cable systems operate in one direction only. To allow two-way data flow, the cable company must replace these amplifiers as well as upgrade the head-end equipment that distributes the signals from their offices.

One expedient exploited by bringing two-way data flow to current cable subscribers in the short run is to use the cable connection solely for downstream data flow and make a second link, usually by an ordinary telephone line, for the upstream data. This kind of asymmetrical operation is exactly suited to Internet use.

In the long term, cable operators suffer a larger problem with their wiring systems. All of the bandwidth on the coaxial cable running to your home is not yours alone. Unlike the telephone company that strings a separate pair of wires to every home, the cable company's coax operates as a bus. The same signals travel to you and your neighbors. The design works well for broadcasting. A similar hardware link-up works well for Ethernet in businesses. A problem arises when you start slicing up bandwidth; as with a pie, the more ways you slice it, the smaller the pieces everyone gets. Divide the bandwidth of a typical cable system by the number of subscribers, and you have less bandwidth available to each than with an advanced telephone service. If everyone attached to a cable system tried to use their modems at once, data transfer would slow to a crawl.

As with local area networks, the overloading of the system can be controlled by slicing the entire system into more manageable sub-units. By limiting each coaxial cable to serving a single neighborhood, bandwidth limits can be sidestepped with a minimum of rewiring of the cable system.

Making the cable modem connection requires both physical and logical installation. The physical part is easy: You simply plug the cable modem into your network adapter. The software installation is more complex. You need driver software to match your modem to your application software and operating system. Most cable companies will provide you with the proper driver and application software. Your primary concern is matching the supplied software to your operating system. In general, you will need Windows 95 or a newer operating system to take advantage of a cable modem. Your cable company should advise you of the exact hardware and software requirements.

Satellite Services

The same technology used by direct-broadcast satellite television, through which you can grab viewable video directly from orbiting satellites, also works for data. Using a small parabolic antenna pointed at a geosynchronous satellite orbiting about 24,000 miles away, you can tap into the Internet at speeds well beyond the capabilities of dial-up telephone connections. Instead of television signals, the satellite simply beams a stream of data down to earth.

The leading satellite service, DirecPC from Hughes Electronics, initiated service in 1997. It bills itself as the fastest Internet service available nationwide. Although slower than either DSL or cable modems, it holds the advantage of availability; anywhere you can see the southern sky, you can make a connection to DirecPC.

Satellite systems are inherently asymmetrical. You don't transmit your needs to the satellite; doing so would require an uplink and a much larger antenna. Instead, you use the satellite connection only for a downlink, to receive data. To send data, your PC connects to the Web through a conventional dial-up modem. The satellite-based downlink operates at 400Kbps, but your phone-based uplink struggles along at modem speed, 14.4 to 56Kbps.

Satellites best fit a broadcast model. That is, they dump out their signals across wide areas for consumption by the multitudes rather than directly targeting individuals. By limiting the downlink bandwidth to 400Kbps, they maximize the number of subscribers that can share the system. In addition, DirecPC attempts to maximize the speed and usefulness of its product using push technology. The system pushes out selected Web and newsgroup information, and your PC captures it as it is sent out, spooling the data to disk. When you want to access one of the pushed Web sites or newsgroups, you can read it almost instantly from the cache. So your PC won't clog up by trying to cache the entire Internet, the system allows you to choose which sites and groups to locally cache.

It uses 21-inch elliptical antennae designed for roof-mounting. The DirecPC antenna is a single purpose device and can be used only for data, not satellite television reception. The system also requires a receiver (sometimes called a "modem"), which may be installed as an expansion board inside a PC or as a standalone external peripheral.

The Internet

The main reason most people buy a modem—or an entire PC, for that matter—is to connect to the Internet. In truth, however, a modem does not connect your PC to the Internet. The modem connects your PC *into* the Internet. More like a weld than glue, the modem makes your PC part of the Internet.

Although the Internet is built using hardware, it is not hardware itself. Similarly, you need hardware to connect to the Internet, but that hardware only serves as a means to access what you really want: the information that the Internet can bring to your PC. Without the right hardware, you could not connect to the Internet, but having the hardware alone won't get you to the World Wide Web.

Despite its unitary name, there is no giant Internet in the sky or some huge office complex somewhere. In fact, the Internet is the classic case of there being "no there there." Like an artichoke, if you slice off individual petals or pieces of the Internet, you'll soon have a pile of pieces and no Internet anywhere, and you won't find it among the pieces. Rather, like the artichoke, the Internet is the overall combination of the pieces.

Those pieces are tied together both physically and logically. The physical aspect is a collection of wires, optical fibers, and microwave radio links that carry digital signals between computers. The combination of connections forms a redundant network. Computers are linked to one another in a Web that provides multiple signal paths between any two machines.

The logical side is a set of standards for the signals that travel through that network. The Internet uses various protocols depending on what kind of data is being transferred. The chief protocol and the defining standard of the Internet is TCP/IP, discussed later.

In truth, the Internet was not designed to link *computers* but to tie together *computer networks*. As its name implies, the Internet allows data to flow between networks. Even if you only have a single PC, when you connect with the Internet you must run a network protocol the same as if you had slung miles of Ethernet cable through your home and office. Whether you like it or not, you end up tangled in the web of networking when you connect to the Internet.

The various protocols that make up the Internet require their own books for proper discussion. We'll just take a moment here to put the Internet in perspective with your PC and its communication hardware.

History

Locating the origins of the Internet depends on how primitive an ancestor you seek. The thread of the development of the Internet stretches all the way back to 1958, if you pull on it hard enough. The Internet's mother—the organization that gave birth to it—was itself born in the contrail of Sputnik. In October 1957, the USSR took the world by surprise by launching the first artificial satellite and made the US suddenly seem technologically backward. In respond, President Dwight D. Eisenhower launch the Advanced Research Project Agency as part of the Department of Defense in January 1958.

Then, as now, ARPA's work involved a lot of data processing, much of it at various university campuses across the country. Each computer, like the college that hosted it, was a world unto itself. To work on the computer, you had to be at the college. To share the results of the work on the computer, you needed a letter carrier with biceps built up from carrying stacks of nine-track tapes from campus to campus. Information flowed no faster between computers than did the mail.

Bob Taylor, working at ARPA in 1967, developed the idea of linking together into a redundant, packet-based network all the computers of major universities participating in the agency's programs. In October 1969, the first bytes crossed what was to become ARPAnet in tests linking the Stanford Research Institute and the University of California at Los Angeles. By December 1969, four nodes of the fledgling inter-networking system were working.

The system began to assume its current identify with the first use of Transmission Control Protocol in a network in July 1977. As a demonstration, TCP was used to link together a packet radio network, SATnet and ARPAnet. Then, in early 1978, TCP was split into a portion that broke messages into packets, reassembled them after transmission, kept order among the packets, and controlled error control, called TCP, and a second protocol that concerned itself with the routing of packets through the linkage of network—Internet Protocol. The two together made TCP/IP, the fundamental protocol of today's Internet.

If the Internet actually has a birthday, it was January 1, 1983, when ARPAnet switched over from Network Control Protocol to TCP/IP. (By that time, ARPAnet was only one of many networks linked by TCP/IP.) To give a friendlier front end to communications with distant computer systems, Tim Berners-Lee, working at CERN in Geneva in 1990, invented the World Wide Web.

The final step in the development of today's Internet came in 1991. In that year, the National Science Foundation, which was overseeing the operation of the Internet, lifted its previous restrictions on its commercial use. The free-market free-for-all began.

Structure

The best view of the Internet comes with following a packet from your PC. When you log into a Web site, you actually send a command to a distant server telling it to download a page of data to your PC. Your Web browser packages that command into a packet labeled with the address of the server storing the page that you want. Your PC sends the packet to your modem (or terminal adapter), which transmits it across your telephone or other connection to your *Internet service provider*, or ISP.

The ISP actually operates as a message forwarder. At the ISP, your message gets combined with those from other PCs and sent through a higher-speed connection (at least you should hope it is a high-speed connection) to yet another concentrator that eventually sends your packet to one of five regional centers (located in New York, Chicago, San Francisco, Los Angeles, and Maryland). There, the major Internet carriers exchange signals, routing the packets from your modem to the carrier that will haul them to their designation based on their Internet address.

One of the weaknesses of today's Internet is its addressing. All of the Internet addresses are global. From the address itself, neither you nor a computer can tell where that address is or, more importantly, how to connect to it. The routers in the Internet regional centers maintain tables to help quickly send packets to the proper address. Without such guidance, packets wander throughout the world looking for the right address. Worse, the current Internet naming convention, which assigns 32-bit addresses, doesn't have the breadth necessary to accommodate all future applications of the Internet. Some experts believe that the Internet will simply run out of available addresses sometime around the turn of the century; although as this is written in mid-1999 no shortage has become apparent.

A new initiative, Internet II, has an improved addressing scheme that sidesteps this shortage, but the developers of Internet II plan to maintain it as a non-commercial link between universities.

Internet addresses are separate and distinct from the domain names used as Uniform Resource Locators (URLs) through which you specify Web pages. The domain names give you a handle with a natural-language look. Internet addresses are, like everything in computing, binary codes.

Even domain names are running short. Finding a clever and meaningful name for a Web site is a challenge that's ever increasing. Believing that one of the problems in the shortage of URLs has been the relatively few suffixes available, one of the coordinating agencies for Internet names, the International Ad Hoc Committee, proposed seven additional suffixes in addition six already in use in the US and the national suffixes used around the world (.US for United States, .CA for Canada, and so on). Table 22.6 lists the present suffixes.

TABLE 22.6 US Internet Domain Name Suffixes

Ending	Application
.arts	Cultural groups
.com	General businesses and individuals
.edu	Schools
.firm	Businesses
.gov	Government
.info	Information services
.mil	Military
.net	Internet service providers
.org	Groups and organizations
.nom	Individuals
.rec	Recreational sites
.store	Retailers
.web	Web-related organizations

Operation

The World Wide Web is the most visually complicated and compelling aspect of the Internet. Despite its appearances, however, the Web is nothing more than another file transfer protocol. When you call up a page from the Web, the remote server simply downloads a file to your PC. Your Web browser then decodes the page, executing commands embedded in it to alter the typeface and to display images at the appropriate place. Most browsers cache several file pages (or even megabytes of them) so that when you step back, you need not wait for the same page to download once again.

The commands for displaying text use their own language called Hypertext Markup Language, or HTML. As exotic and daunting as HTML sounds, it's nothing more than a coding system that combines formatting information in textual form with the readable text of a document. Your browser reads the formatting commands, which are set off by a special prefix so that the browser knows they are commands, and organizes the text in accordance with them, arranging it on the page, selecting the appropriate font and emphasis, and intermixing graphical elements. Writing in HTML is only a matter of knowing the right codes and where to put them. *Web authoring* tools embed the proper commands using menu-driven interfaces so that you don't have to do the memorization.

Performance Limits

Linking to the Internet requires both hardware and software. The hardware runs a wide gamut. Most people connect through standard telephone lines using a modem.

Okay, so your Internet access through your modem or digital connection isn't as fast as you'd like. Welcome to the club. As the Duchess of Windsor never said, "You can never be too rich or thin or have an interconnection that's fast enough." Everyone would like Web pages to download instantly. Barring that, they'd like them to load in a few seconds. Barring that, they'd just like them to load before the next ice age.

The most tempting way to increase your Internet speed is to update your modem—from last year's laggardly 28.8Kbps model to a new 33.6 or 56K model. You may note a surprising difference if you do—little change in your access speed. The small improvement results from two factors: your adding less speed than you think and your adding speed in the wrong place.

With analog modems, high-speed performance depends on the quality of your connection. The added edge of a 33.6K modem requires a near-perfect telephone line. Most long-distance connections strain at squeezing the full bandwidth of a 28.8K modem through. Altering the modem does nothing to improve your connection (and likely your local phone company will do nothing to improve your connection, either). Because 56K modems don't rely on modulation technology, they promise more hope in getting higher speeds, but they come with their own limitations. Their asymmetrical design means any speed boost is only in one direction, toward you (which is not a fatal defect). They are also dependent on line quality; you need the best to get the best. And they require your Internet service provider also provide 56K access.

Any change in your Internet access system—a modem upgrade or switch to a digital service—may reveal the dirty secret: You're working on the wrong bottleneck. I remember the joy of plugging into T1 access to the Internet, only to discover it wasn't any faster than my old, slow 28.8K modem. The slowdown I faced wasn't in the local connection but in the Net itself.

You can easily check your Internet bottleneck and see what you can do about it. Pick a large file and download it at your normal online time. Then, pry yourself out of bed early and try downloading the same file at 6:00 AM EST or earlier when Internet traffic is likely to be low. If you notice an appreciable difference in response and download times, a faster modem won't likely make your online sessions substantially speedier. The constraints aren't in your PC but in the server and network itself.

Security

As originally conceived, the Internet is not just a means for moving messages between PCs. It was designed as a link between computer systems that allowed scientists to share machines. One researcher in Boston could, for example, run programs on a computer system in San Francisco. Commands to computer systems move across wires just as easily as words and images. To the computer and the Internet, they are all data.

Much of the expense businesses put into connecting to the Internet involves undoing the work of the original Internet creators. The first thing they install is a *firewall* that blocks outsiders from taking control of the business's internal computer network. They must remain constantly vigilant that some creative soul doesn't discover yet another flaw in the security systems built into the Internet itself.

Can someone break into your PC through the Internet? It's certainly possible. Truth be known, however, rummaging through someone's PC is about as interesting as burrowing into his sock drawer. Moreover, the number of PCs out there makes it statistically unlikely any given errant James Bond will commandeer your PC, particularly when there's stuff much more interesting (and challenging to break into)—such as the networks of multi-billion dollar companies, colleges, government agencies, and the military.

The one weakness to this argument is that it assumes whoever would break into your PC uses a degree of intelligence. Even as a dull, uninteresting PC loaded with naught but a two-edition-old copy of Office can be the target of the computer terrorist. Generally someone whose thinking process got stalled on issues of morality, the computer terrorist doesn't target you as much as the rest of the world that causes him so much frustration or boredom. His digital equivalent of a bomb is the computer virus.

A computer virus is program code added to your PC without your permission. The name, as a metaphor to human disease, is apt. As with a human virus, a computer virus cannot reproduce by itself; it takes command of your PC and uses its resources to duplicate itself. Computer viruses are contagious in that they can be passed along from one machine to another. And computer viruses vary in their effects, from deadly (wiping out the entire contents of your hard disk) to trivial (posting a message on your screen). But computer viruses are nothing more than digital code, and they are machine-specific. Neither you nor your toaster nor your PDA can catch a computer virus from your PC.

Most computer viruses latch onto your PC and lie in wait. When a specific event occurs—for example, a key date—they swing into action, performing whatever dreadful act their designers got a chuckle from. To continue infecting other PCs, they also clone themselves and copy themselves to whatever disks you use in your PC. In general, viruses add their code to another program in your PC. They can't do anything until the program they attach themselves to begins running. Virus writers like to attach their viruses to parts of the operating system so that the code will load every time you run your PC. Because antivirus programs and operating systems now readily detect such viruses, the virus terrorists have developed other tactics. One of the latest is the macro virus that runs as a macro to a program. In effect, the virus is written in a higher-level language that escapes detection by the antivirus software. Of course, every time a new virus makes the new, the antivirus people update their products. All of the common macro viruses now can be detected, but new ones still pop up.

Viruses get into your PC because you let them. They come through any connection your PC has with the outside world including floppy disks and going online. Browsing Web pages ordinarily won't put you at risk because HTTP doesn't pass along executable programs. Plug-ins may. Whenever you download a file, you run a risk of bringing a virus with it. Software and drivers that you download are the most likely carriers. Most Webmasters do their best to assure that they don't pass along viruses. You should always be wary when you download a program from a less reputable site.

There is no such thing as a sub-band or sub-carrier virus that sneaks into your PC through a "sub-band" of your modem's transmissions. Even were it possible to fiddle with the operation of a modem and add a new, invisible modulation to it, the information encoded on it could never get to your PC. Every byte from an analog modem must go through the UART in the modem or serial port and then be read by your PC's microprocessor. The modem has no facility to link a sideband signal (even if there were such a thing) to that data stream.

Fax

Nearly every high-speed modem sold today has built-in fax capabilities. This bonus results from the huge demand for faxing in the business world coupled with the trivial cost of adding fax capabilities to a modern modem. Everything that's necessary for faxing comes built into the same chipsets that make normal high-speed modem communications possible.

That said, few people take advantage of the fax capabilities of the modern PC modem. Although nearly every modem now offered for PCs is capable of both sending and receiving faxes, a five-year study taken by the Gallup Organization and reported in *The Wall Street Journal* (23 April 1996) indicated that 90 percent of the people in Fortune 500 companies that were surveyed used standalone fax machines rather than PC fax software. In smaller companies where budgets are more an issue, about 80 percent still preferred standalone fax to PC-based fax. On the other hand, the study found that the majority (about 60 percent) of fax users believed that faxing delivers the most reliable communications and quickest responses when compared to email, voice mail, and overnight courier services. Hardly surprisingly, fax machine maker Pitney-Bowes Facsimile Systems sponsored the study.

On the other hand, that leaves millions or tens of millions of people using their PCs to send out faxes. With today's driver fax software that makes sending a fax as easy as printing a letter (if not more so—no ribbons, toner, or paper to deal with), those percentages are sure to shift. Documents already on paper probably will remain the province of the standalone fax machine, but those you create on your PC have their best outlet in your fax modem.

Background

Fax, short for facsimile transmissions, gives the power of *Star Trek's* transporter system (usually without the aliens and pyrotechnics) to anyone who needs to get a document somewhere else in the world at the speed of light. Although a fax doesn't quite dematerialize paper, it does move the images and information a document contains across continents and reconstruct it at the end of its near-instantaneous travels. The recipient gets to hold in his own hands a nearly exact duplicate of the original, the infamous reasonable facsimile.

From that angle, fax is a telecopier—a Xerox machine with a thousand miles of wire between where you slide the original in and the duplicate falls out. In fact, the now aging telecopiers made by Xerox Corporation were the progenitors of today's fax machines.

Today, faxing involves the use of a fax modem, a device that converts page scans into a form compatible with the international telephone system. Or you can use a standalone fax machine, which combines a fax modem with a scanner, printer, and telephone set. In the PC realm, the term "fax modem" also refers to adapter boards that slide into expansion slots to give the host computer the capability to send and receive fax transmissions.

In a classic fax system, you start faxing by dialing up a distant fax system using a touch pad on your fax machine, just as you would any other telephone. You slide a sheet of paper into the fax's scanner, and the page curls around a drum in front of a photodetector. Much as a television picture is broken into numerous scan lines, a fax machine scans images as a series of lines, takes them one at a time, and strings all of the lines scanned from a document into a continuous stream of information. The fax machine converts the data stream into a series of modulated tones for transmission over the telephone line. After making a connection at the receiving end, another fax machine converts the data stream into black and white dots representing the original image much as a television set reconstructs a TV image. A printer puts the results on paper using either thermal or laser printer technology.

PC fax systems can do away with the paper. PC fax software can take the all-electronic images you draw or paint with your graphics software and convert it into the standard format that's used for fax transmissions. A fax modem in your PC can then send that data to a standard fax machine, which converts the data into hard-copy form. Or your PC fax system can receive a transmission from a standard fax machine and capture the image into a graphics file. You can then convert the file into another graphic format using conversion software, edit the image with your favorite painting program, or turn its text contents into ASCII form using optical character recognition (OCR) software. You can even turn your PC into the equivalent of a standard fax machine by adding a scanner to capture images from paper. Your printer will turn fax reception into hard copy, although at a fraction of the speed of a standalone fax machine.

Larger businesses with PC networks incorporate fax servers to allow their employees to share a common facility for sending their PC-based faxes. The fax server eliminates the need for each PC in the network to be equipped with its own fax modem and telephone line.

Reception through fax servers has been problematic, however, because conventional fax messages provide no easy means for electronic routing through a network to the proper recipient. To solve this problem, the fax industry is developing standards for subaddressing capabilities. Subaddresses will be invaluable to businesses with PC networks using fax servers. With current technology, giving each user a private fax mailbox means a separate telephone line for each. Using a subaddress, a single fax server can receive all fax messages and route them to the proper recipient. The fax subaddress will be a mailbox number that's added to your primary telephone number. It will direct the automatic routing of the message through a network fax server to an individual's fax mailbox. The subaddress number will be transmitted during the opening handshake of the fax modems, and it will be independent from the primary telephone number.

PC fax beats standalone fax with its management capabilities. PC fax software can broadcast fax messages to as wide a mailing list as you can accommodate on your hard disk, waiting until early morning hours when long-distance rates are cheapest to make the calls. You can easily manage the mailing list as you would any other PC database.

The concept of facsimile transmissions is not new. As early as 1842, Alexander Bain patented an electro-mechanical device that could translate wire-based signals into marks on paper. Newspaper wire photos, which are based on the same principles, have been used for generations.

The widespread use of fax in business is a more recent phenomenon, however, and its growth parallels that of the PC for much the same underlying reason. Desktop computers did not take off until the industry found a standard to follow, the IBM PC. Similarly, the explosive growth of fax began only after the CCITT adopted standards for the transmission of facsimile data.

Analog Standards

The original system, now termed Group 1, was based on analog technology and used frequency shift keying, much as 300 baud modems do, to transmit a page of information in six minutes. Group 2 improved that analog technology and doubled the speed of transmission, up to three minutes per page.

Group 3

The big break with the past was the CCITT's adoption in 1980 of the Group 3 fax protocol, which is entirely digitally based. Using data compression and modems that operate at up to 14,400 bits-per-second, full-page documents can be transmitted in 20 to 60 seconds using the Group 3 protocol. New transmission standards promise to pump up the basic Group 3 data rate to 28,800 bits per second.

Resolution

Under the original Group 3 standard, two degrees of resolution or on-paper sharpness are possible: standard, which allows 1,728 dots horizontally across the page (about 200 dots per inch) and 100 dots per inch vertically; and fine, which doubles the vertical resolution to achieve 200 by 200 dpi and requires about twice the transmission time. Fine resolution also approximately doubles the time required to transmit a fax page because it doubles the data that must be moved.

Revisions to the Group 3 standard have added more possible resolutions. Two new resolutions compensate for the slight elongation that creeps into fax documents when generated and transmitted in purely electronic form. New fax products may optionally send and receive at a resolutions of 204 x 98 pixels per inch in standard mode or 204 x 196 pixels per inch in fine mode. Two new high-resolution modes of 300 x 300 pixels per inch and 400 x 400 pixels per inch were also established. The 300 x 300 mode enables fax machines, laser printers, and scanners to share the same resolution levels for higher quality when transferring images between them. To take advantage of these resolutions, both sending and receiving fax equipment must support the new modes.

Data Rates

The basic speed of a Group 3 fax transmission depends on the underlying communications standard that the fax product follows. These standards are similar to data modem standards. With the exception of V.34, data and fax modems operate under different standards, even when using the same data rates. Consequently, data and fax modems are not interchangeable, and a modem that provides high-speed fax capabilities (say 9,600 bps) may operate more slowly in data mode (say 2,400 bps.)

The Group 3 protocol does not define a single speed for fax transmissions but allows the use of any of a variety of transmission standards. At data rates of 2,400 and 4,800 bits-per-second, fax modems operate under the V.27 ter standard. At 7,200 and 9,600 bits-per-second, they follow V.29 (or V.17, which incorporates these V.29 modes). At 12,000 and 14,400 bits-per-second, fax modems follow V.17. The V.34 standard will take both fax and data modems up to 28,800 bits-per-second. New standards will allow the use of the Group 3 fax protocol over ISDN and other future digital telephone services.

Fax modems are typically described by the communications standards they support or by the maximum data rate at which they can operate. Most modern fax modems follow the V.17 standard, which incorporates the lower V.29 speeds. Most will also fall back to V.27 ter to accommodate older, slower fax products.

Compression

In a typical fax machine, you slide a page into the machine, place the call, and the machine calls a distant number. Once the connection is negotiated, the fax machine scans the page with a photodetector inside the machine, which detects the black and white patterns on the page one line at a time at a resolution of 200 dots per inch. The result is a series of bits with the digital 1s and 0s corresponding to the black and white samples each 1/200th of an inch. The fax machine compresses this raw data stream to increase the apparent data rate and shorten transmission times.

Data compression makes the true speed of transmitting a page dependent on the amount of detail that each page contains. In operation, the data compression algorithm reduces the amount of data that must be transferred by a factor of 5 to 10. On the other hand, a bad phone connection can slow fax transmissions as fax modems automatically fall back to lower speeds to cope with poor line quality.

Group 3 fax products may use any of three levels of data compression designated as MH, MR, and MMR. The typical Group 3 fax product includes only MH compression. The others are optional, and MMR is particularly rare. To be sure that a given fax products uses MR or MMR, you will need to check its specifications.

MH stands for *Modified Huffman encoding*, which is also known as one-dimensional encoding. MH was built into the Group 3 standard in 1980 so that a fax machine could send a full page in less than one minute using a standard V.27 ter modem that operated at 4,800 bits-per-second. With 9,600 bps modems, that time is cut nearly in half.

MR, or *Modified Read encoding*, was added as an option shortly after MH encoding was adopted. MR starts with standard MH encoding for the first line of the transmission but then encodes the second line as differences from the first line. Because with fine images, line data changes little between adjacent lines, usually little change information is required. To prevent errors from rippling through an entire document, at the third line MR starts over with a plain MH scan. In other words, odd-numbered scan lines are MH and even lines contain only difference information from the previous line. If a full line is lost in transmission, MR limits the damage to, at most, two lines. Overall, the transmission time savings in advancing from MH to MR amounts to 15 to 20 percent, the exact figure depending on message contents.

MMR, or *Modified Modified Read encoding*, foregoes the safety of the MR technique and records the entire page as difference data. Using MMR, the first line serves as a reference and is all white. Every subsequent line is encoded as the difference from the preceding line until the end of a page. However, an error in any one line will repeat in every subsequent line, so losing one line can garble an entire page. To help prevent such problems, MMR can incorporate its own error-correction mode (ECM) through which the receiving fax system can request the retransmission of any lines received in error. Only the bad lines are updated, and the rest of the page is reconstructed from the new data. MMR with ECM is the most efficient scheme used for compressing fax transmissions and can cut the time needed for a page transmission with MH in half.

Instead of individual dots, under MH (and thus MR and MMR) the bit-pattern of each scan line on the page is coded as short line segments, and the code indicates the number of dots in each segment. The fax machine sends this run-length coded data to the remote fax machine. Included in the transmitted signal is a rudimentary form of error protection, but missed bits are not reproduced when the receiving fax machine reconstructs the original page.

The exact code used by MH under Group 3 fax uses four code groups, two for sequences of white dots, two for sequences of black dots. Sequences from 0 to 63 dots long are coded using *terminating codes*, which express the exact number of dots of the given color in the segment. If the segment of like-color dots scanned from the paper is longer than 63 dots, MH codes it as two code groups, a terminating code and a *make-up code*. The make-up code value indicates the number of 64-dot blocks in the single-color segment. You'll find the values used for the terminating and make-up code values for both white and black dots listed on the CD-ROM.

Binary File Transfer

More than just following the same modem standard, the capabilities of fax service is merging with those of standard data communications. New fax modems, for example, incorporate Binary File Transfer capabilities, which enable them to ship BFT files from one fax system to another as easily as document pages. You could, for example, send a file from your PC to a printer for a remote print-out or to a PC where it could be received automatically. The receiving fax modem picks up the line, makes the connection, and records the file as dutifully as it would an ordinary fax page—without anyone standing around to control the modem.

Group 4

In 1984, the CCITT approved a super-performance facsimile standard, Group 4, which allows resolutions of up to 400 x 400 dpi as well as higher-speed transmissions of lower resolutions. Although not quite typeset quality (phototypesetters are capable of resolutions of about 1,200 dpi), the best of Group 4 is about equal to the resolving capability of the human eye at normal reading distance. However, today's Group 4 fax machines require high-speed, dedicated lines and do not operate as dial-up devices. Group 3 equipment using new, higher-resolution standards and coupled to digital services offers a lower-cost alternative to Group 4.

Interface Classes

As with data modems, fax modems must link up with your PC and its software. Unlike data modems, which were blessed with a standard since early on (the Hayes command set), fax modems lacked a single standard. In recent years, however, the Electronics Industry Association and the Telecommunications Industry Association have created a standard that is essentially an extension to the Hayes AT command set. The standard embraces two classes for support of Group 3 fax communications:

> **Class 1** is the earlier standard. Under the Class 1 standard, most of the processing of fax documents is performed by PC software. The resulting fax data is sent to the modem for direct transmission. It includes requirements for autodialing; a GSTN interface; V-series signal conversion; HDLC data framing, transparency, and error detection; control commands and responses; and data commands and reception.

> **Class 2** shifts the work of preparing the fax document for transmission to the fax modem itself. The modem hardware handles the data compression and error control for the transmission. The Class 2 standard also incorporates additional flow-control and station-identification features, including T.30 protocol implementation; session status reporting; phase C data transfer; padding for minimum scan line time; a quality check on received data; and packet protocol for the DTE/DCE interface.

These classes hint at the most significant difference between PC-based fax systems, which is software. Fax modem hardware determines the connections that can be made, but the software determines the ultimate capabilities of the system. A fax modem that adheres to various standards (classes as well as protocols) will open for you the widest selection of software and the widest range of features.

Installation

Installing a modem usually is a two-step process. First, you must prepare the modem hardware by configuring physical switches, sliding it into your PC (or plugging it into an appropriate port), and finally connecting it to your telephone line and, if need be, telephone receiver. To make it work, you also have to perform one or more software installations.

Physical Matters

All modems require physical preparation of some kind before you put them to work; at a minimum, you must connect the modem to a telephone line (or other service). Modem makers have gone to not-so-great lengths to assure that the connection process is easy. They include a cable and mark the jacks on the modem to plug it into. In that most folks have plugged in at least one telephone in their lives, the process isn't difficult. Complications arise when you need to share a jack with other devices or you have an external modem.

Older modem models often require another kind of physical preparation. They have several jumpers or switches that control the interface or operation of the modem. You'll have to properly adjust these switches to get the modem to work.

Some modems have two jacks and are meant to be connected in series with other telephone devices. These two jacks are not identical; one (usually labeled "Line") links the modem to the telephone line, and the other (usually labeled "Phone") is meant for connecting to your telephone set and cuts off the outbound signal when the modem is operating. Reverse the connections, and the modem won't work properly.

If your modem has only one jack and you want to connect your telephone to the same line, you'll need to make a parallel connection with an adapter that plugs into your wall jack and gives two jacks in return. Plug your modem into one and your telephone into the other. Be careful. If you pick up your telephone handset when the modem is operating, you'll blast your ears with a modem modulation and probably introduce errors into the modem's data stream.

Other telephone devices connect similarly. Note, however, some dedicated fax machines may make particular requirements. They may favor being the first or last device in a serial connection. Check the instruction manual accompanying the fax machine to be certain of its preferred kind of connection.

Software

Old operating systems lack internal modem support. They require that you install your modem into each application you want to use it. The installation may be anything from specifying a type of modem to typing in by hand the setup strings and commands your modem uses. Fortunately, most people had only one or two applications that used their modem so the chore was merely bothersome.

Modern operating systems such as Windows have internal modem services. You install the modem once for the operating system, and then all applications that run under the operating system have access to the modem through an API in the operating system. In other words, you confront the modem installation chore only once.

Older operating systems (such as Window 3.1) required manual configuration, and each application often required you to enter proper setup strings. Starting with Windows 95, however, the operating system integrates the modem into its driver structure and application interface. Windows uses the same layered architecture for modem control as it does for other hardware interfaces.

Structure

The Windows family of operating systems separates modem and related communications system into three levels: communication port drivers, a universal modem driver, and the Win32 communication API.

The port driver controls the operation of the port linking to your modem. Typically, it will involve a serial port but also embraces enhanced capabilities ports (ECP) and, in the latest operating systems, Universal Serial Bus.

The Windows universal modem driver, termed UniModem, is the key element that eliminates the need to learn the language of the modem (or, in the case of programmers, all modems). UniModem links to your modem using a mini-driver supplied by the modem maker or, in the case of more common modems, included with the operating system. It sends out the command to make the modem latch onto the telephone line, dial, and connect with a given protocol.

At the other end, the Telephony Application Programming Interface, or TAPI, gives programmers a standard set of calls for modem functions. Instead of issuing hardware commandsdirectly to the modem, the programmer uses a TAPI call to tell the modem what to do. TAPI has another level, the Service Provider Interface, which establishes the connection with the specific telephone network.

Modem Identification

Key to eliminating the hassles involved with properly setting up your modem is identifying your modem to the operating system. Windows provides several means for modem identification, many of which are automatic. In the ideal case, your modem will comply with the Plug and Play specifications, and Windows can automatically determine its capabilities every time your PC boots up. With external modems, this recognition requires the firmware in the modem be cable of responding with Plug and Play identification information.

Without Plug and Play compliance, Windows relies on its hardware configuration process for identifying modems. A primary problem is that the most common command set for modems, the AT commands do not include a function to identify the modem. Consequently, older modems cannot tell your PC what they are, at least directly. To identify older modems, Windows sends commands to the modem, checks the modem's responses, and compares them to a database of known modem information.

This procedure isn't always successful. The results may be ambiguous, so you need to check what Windows determines. In the worst case, you have to tell Windows what you have using the hardware installation procedure or by altering the Modem Properties sheet.

Under Windows, modem installation is part of the hardware installation wizard. You select the wizard (as Add New Hardware) through Control Panel. To install a modem, do not choose to have Windows search for new hardware (unless you want to spend the afternoon while Windows checks all the possible hardware installation options); you'll get to choose the kind of device you want to install. Select Modem, as shown in Figure 22.9.

FIGURE 22.9

The Windows Add New Hardware Wizard.

Windows will again volunteer to automatically detect your modem. Although this process works in most cases, you may prefer to save time by explicitly specifying the brand and model of your modem. To do this, first select the manufacturer of your modem and then the particular model, as shown in Figure 22.10.

FIGURE 22.10

Selecting a modem manufacturer and model under Windows.

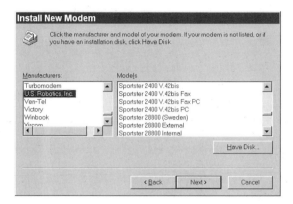

If your modem isn't one of those for which Windows has built-in support, select the Have Disk option and use the driver disk supplied by the modem's manufacturer.

Windows needs to communicate with your modem, so you must specify the port to use. At this point, Windows has not checked to see whether your modem has been installed for a particular port, so you have to tell it. Use the settings you made during the hardware setup of your modem. Specify them by choosing the option Windows offers, as shown in Figure 22.11.

FIGURE 22.11

Selecting a modem port connection under Windows.

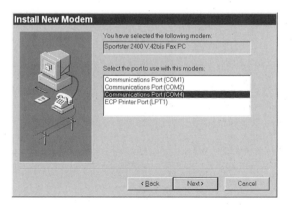

Windows and your applications can take control of all the functions of your modem using the driver software. They can adjust the various settings as their needs require. Sometimes, however, you may want to override their decisions.

You can investigate or set your modems settings in two ways, through Device Manager that you access through the System icon in Control Manager or through the Modem icon.

The Modem Properties sheet will give you access to many of the controls available to you. Figure 22.12 shows the Modem tab of the properties sheet, which allows you to select the maximum speed for your modem to use.

FIGURE 22.12

Adjusting modem speed under Windows.

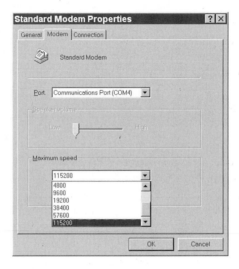

In addition to these global modem properties, each connection requires you make individual settings for it. For example, each service to which you connect will require setting its own telephone number. You make these setting (and adjust other options) through the dialing settings available through the specific application.

Networking

Networks link two to thousands of PCs together, enabling them to share files and resources. In addition, a network can centralize the management of a huge base of PCs, providing one location for coordinated security, backup, upgrades, and control. Networking now is so essential to regular PC operations that it is built into new operating systems and serves both in the home and office.

What you need to know to understand a small PC network

Network feature	In short
Topology	The physical way PCs and servers (if any) are connected together.
Hierarchy	The logical organization of a network—whether all PCs are equal or one or more servers take a dominant role.
Functions	What a network does for you, including sharing files, printer, and other resources.
Standards	Unified specifications that assure you that network components will work together. Today 10Base-T and 100Base-T are most popular.
Components	The hardware that you use to actually build your network, including network interface cards, hubs, and cabling.
Software	A layer cake of programs that make your network actually work, including protocols and services.

By themselves, PCs might never have usurped the role of the mainframe or other large computer systems. Big systems would hold an important business advantage: They are able to link all the workers at a facility. They don't just enable sharing of data; they demand it. The mainframe holds the data (as well as all the computing power) in one centralized location. All workers can have access to the same information and can even work together on projects, communicating with one another through the central computer.

The network provides connectivity that gives the entire web of PCs collective power far beyond that of the mainframe. Anywhere two or more PCs are present, the features and facilities added by a network can make your using PCs easier, more accommodating, and more powerful.

The challenge you face in linking one PC to others is the same as faced by a child growing up with siblings; it has to learn to share. When kids share, you get more quiet, greater peace of mind, and less bloodshed. When PCs share, you get the convenience of sharing files and other resources, centralized management (including the capability to back up all PCs from one location or use one PC to back up others), and improved communication between workers in your business.

The drawback to connectivity is that computer networks are even more difficult to understand and manage than a platoon of teenagers. They have their own rules, their own value system, their own hardware needs, even their own language. Just listening in on a conversation between network pros is enough to make you suspect that an alien invasion from the planet Oxy-10 has succeeded. To get even a glimmer of understanding, you need to know your way around layers of standards, architectures, and protocols. Installing a network operating system can take system managers days; deciphering its idiosyncrasies can keep users and operators puzzled for weeks. Network host adapters often prove incompatible with other PC hardware, their required interrupts and I/O addresses locking horns with SCSI boards, port controllers, and other peripherals. And weaving the wiring for a network is like threading a needle while wearing boxing gloves during a cyclone that has blown out the electricity, the candles, and your last rays of hope.

In fact, no one in his right mind would tangle with a network were not the benefits so great. File sharing across the network alone eliminates a major source of data loss, which is duplication of records and out-of-sync file updates. Better still, a network lets you get organized. You can put all your important files in one central location where they are easier to protect, both from disaster and theft. Instead of worrying about backing up half a dozen PCs individually, you can easily handle the chore with one command. Electronic mail can bring order to the chaos of tracking messages and appointments, even in a small office. With network-based email, you can communicate with your co-workers without scattering memo slips everywhere. Sharing a costly laser printer or large hard disk (with some networks, even modems) can cut your capital cost of a computer's equipment by thousands or tens of thousands of dollars. Instead of buying a flotilla of personal laser printers, for example, you can serve everyone's hard-copy needs with just one machine.

Nearly every aspect of networking has spawned its own literature covered by dozens of books. This single chapter cannot hope to discuss all aspects of network technology. Consequently, we'll restrict ourselves to a practical approach. From a foundation of basic terminology and concepts, we'll work our way to wiring together a small office or home network and setting up the necessary software. In the end, you won't be an expert, but you will have a working network that you can use for exchanging files, sharing printers, and making backups.

Practical Levels

You face four practical levels when configuring your network using your network or operating system software. Under Windows, these levels include the adapter, protocol, service, and client software, as shown in Figure 23.1, the Windows Select Network Component Type menu.

FIGURE 23.1
The Windows Select Network Component menu.

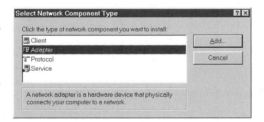

In this model, the network has four components, the client, the adapter, the protocol, and the service. Each has a distinct role to play in making the connection between PCs.

Adapter

The *adapter* is the hardware that connects your PC to the network. The common term *network interface card*, often abbreviated as NIC, is one form of host adapter, a board you slide into an expansion slot. The host adapter function also can be integrated into the circuitry of the motherboard, as it often is in business-oriented PCs.

No matter its form or name, the adapter is the foundation of the physical layer of the network, the actual hardware that makes the network work with your PC. It translates the bus signals of your PC into a form that can skitter through the network wiring. The design and standards that the adapter follows determine the form and speed of the physical side of the network.

From the practical perspective, the network adapter is generally the part of the network that you must buy if you want to add network capabilities to a PC lacking them. You slide a network host adapter or NIC into an expansion slot in your PC to provide a port for plugging in the network wire.

Protocol

The *protocol* is the music of the packets, the lyrics that control the harmony of the data traffic through the network wiring. The protocol dictates not only the logical form of the packet—the arrangement of address, control information, and data among its bytes—but also the rules on how the network deals with the packets. The protocol determines how a packet gets where it is going, what happens when it doesn't, and how to recover when an error appears in the data as it crosses the network.

Support for the most popular and useful protocols for small networks is included with today's operating systems. It takes the form of drivers you install to implement a particular networking system. Windows, for example, includes several protocols in its basic package. The most familiar of these is TCP/IP (Transmission Control Protocol and Internet Protocol), the protocol used for communicating across the Internet. You may also use NetBEUI, which stands for for NetBios Extended User Interface (NetBios stands for Network Basic Input/Output Systems) that lets you directly link PCs. If you need to, you can add others as easily as installing a new software driver.

Service

The *service* of the network is the work the packets perform. The services are often several and always useful. Network services include exchanging files between disk drives (or making a drive far away on the network appear to be local to any or every PC in the network). The service can be the sharing of a printer resource so that all PCs have access to a centralized printer or electronic mail passed from a centralized post office to individual machines.

Most networking software includes the more useful services as part of the basic package. Windows includes file and printer sharing as its primary service. The basic operating system also includes email support. Again, new services are as easy to add as new driver software.

Client

To the network, the client is not you but where the operating system of your PC and the network come together. It's yet another piece of software, the one that brings you the network resources so that you can take advantage of the services. The client software allows the network to recognize your PC and to exchange data packets with it.

Topologies

The topology of a network is the lay of the cables across the land. Most networks involve cables, a lot of them, with at least one leading to every PC. Like the proverbial can of worms, they can crawl off in every direction and create chaos.

If PCs are to talk to one another, however, somehow the cables must come together so that signals can move from one PC to another. If network cables were ordinary wires, you might splice them together with the same abandon as making spaghetti, and the results might have a similar aesthetic. But networks operate at high frequencies and their signals behave like the transmissions of radio stations. The network waves flash down the wires, bounce around, and ricochet from every splice. The waves themselves stretch and bend, losing their shape and their digital purity.

To work reliably, the network cable must be a carefully controlled environment. It must present a constant impedance to the signal, and every connection must be properly made. Any irregularity increases the chance of noise, interference, and error.

Designers have developed several topologies for PC networks. Most can be reduced to one of three basic layouts: linear, ring, and star. The names describe how the cables run throughout an installation.

Linear

The network with linear cabling has a single backbone, one main cable that runs from one end of the system to the other. Along the way, PCs tap into this backbone to send and receive signals. The PCs link to the backbone with a single cable through which they both send and receive, as shown in Figure 23.2. In effect, the network backbone functions as a data bus, and this configuration is often called a bus topology.

FIGURE 23.2
Simple bus network topology.

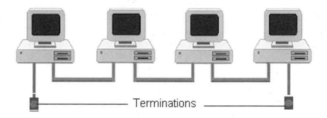

Terminations

In the typical installation, a wire leads from the PC to the backbone, and a T-connector links the two. The network backbone has a definite beginning and end. In most cases, these ends are terminated with a resistor matching the characteristic impedance of the cable in the background. That is, a 61 ohm network cable will have a 61 ohm termination at either end. These terminations prevent signals from reflecting from the ends of the cable, helping assure signal integrity.

Ring

The ring topology looks like a linear network that's biting its own tail. The backbone is a continuous loop, a ring, with no end. But the ring is not a single, continuous wire. Instead, it is made of short segments daisy-chained from one PC to the next, the last connected, in turn, to the first. Each PC thus has two connections. One wire connects a PC to the PC before it in the ring, and a second wire leads to the next PC in the ring. Signals must traverse through one PC to get to the next, and the signals typically are listened to and analyzed along the way.

Star

Both linear and ring topologies sprawl all over creation. The star topology shines a ray of light into tangled installations. Just as rays blast out from the core of a star, in the star topology connecting cables emanate from a centralized location called a hub, and each cable links a single PC into the network, as shown in Figure 23.3. A popular image for star topology is an old-fashioned wagon wheel; the network hub is the hub, the cables are the spokes, and the PCs are ignored in the analogy. Visualize them as clumps of mud clinging to the rim (which, depending on your particular network situation, may be an apt metaphor).

FIGURE 23.3
Simple star network topology.

In the most popular network systems based on the star topology, each cable is actually twofold. Each has two distinct connections, one for sending data from the hub to an individual PC and one for the PC to send data back to the hub. These paired connections are typically packaged into a single cable.

Star-style networks have become popular because their topology matches that of other office wiring. In the typical office building, the most common wiring is used by telephones and telephone wiring converges at the wiring closet in which is the PBX (Private Branch Exchange, the telephone switching equipment for a business). Star-style topologies require only a single cable and connection for each device to link to the central location where all cables converge into the network hub.

As distinct as these three topologies seem, they are really not so different. Cut the ring, for example, and the result is a linear system. Or shrink the ring down to a single point, and the result is a star.

Ethernet, although it started life as a linear bus, is most popular today in the star configuration. Actually, the transformation is a straightforward one, at least in comparison to topologists who try to explain the origins of the universe with 12-dimensional strings. Take the bus and push in to one central point between each node, and soon you'll see the topology transform into a star.

This confluence is hardly coincidental. All networks must perform the same functions, so you should expect all the varieties to be functionally the same.

Hierarchies

Topology describes only one physical aspect of a network. The connections between the various PCs in a network also can fit one of two logical hierarchies. The alternatives form a class system among PCs. Some networks treat all PCs the same; others elevate particular computers to a special, more important role. Although the network serves the same role in either case, these two hierarchical systems enforce a few differences in how the network is used.

Client-Server

Before PC networks, mainframe computers extended their power to individual desks through terminal connections. By necessity, these mainframe systems put all the computer power in one central location that served the needs of everyone using the system. There simply wasn't any other computer power in the system.

In big companies, this kind of computer system organization became an entrenched part of the corporate bureaucracy. Transferring the structure to PCs was natural. At first, the computer managers merely connected PCs to the mainframe as smarter terminals. The connection schemes were called micro-to-mainframe links.

Eventually, however, some managers discovered that PCs provided more power at substantially less cost than the mainframe, and the actual computing was shifted down to the desktop. The powerful mainframe computer was left to do nothing but supply data (and sometimes program) files to the PCs. Managers needed no large amount of enlightenment to see that even a modestly powerful PC could shuffle files around, and the mainframe was replace by a PC that could manage the shared storage required by the system. Because the special PC served the needs of the other PCs, it was called a server. The corresponding term for the desktop PC workstations is client, a carry-over from the mainframe days. This form of network link is consequently called a client-server hierarchy. Note that the special role of the server gives it more importance but also relegates it to the role of a slave that serves the need of many masters, the clients. The server in a client-server network runs special software (the network operating system).

The server need not be a PC. Sometimes, a mainframe still slaves away at the center of a network. Typically, the server is a special PC more powerful than the rest in the network (notwithstanding that the server's work is less computorially intense than that of the clients it serves). Its most important feature is storage. Because its file space is shared by many—perhaps hundreds—of PCs, it requires huge amounts of mass storage. In addition, the server is designed to be more reliable because all the PCs in the network depend on its proper functioning. If it fails, the entire network suffers.

Most modern servers are designed to be fault-tolerant. That is, they will continue to run without interruption despite a fault, such as the failure of a hardware subsystem. Most servers also use the most powerful available microprocessors, not from need but because the price difference is tiny once the additional ruggedness and storage are factored in— and because most managers think that the single most important PC in a network should be the most powerful.

Peer-to-Peer

The client-server is a royalist system, particularly if you view a nation's leader as a servant of the people rather than a profiteer. The opposite is the true democracy in which every PC is equal. PCs share files and other resources (such as printers) among one another. They share equally, each as the peer of the others, so this scheme is called peer-to-peer networking.

Peer-to-peer means that there is no dedicated file server as you would find in big, complex networks. All PCs can have their own, local storage, and each PC is (or can be) granted access to the disk drives and printers connected to the others. In most peer-to-peer schemes, the same DOS commands apply to both the drives local to an individual computer and those accessed remotely through the network. Because most people already know enough about DOS to change drive letters, they can put the network to work almost instantly.

Even in peer-to-peer networks, some PCs are likely to be more powerful than others or have larger disk drives or some such distinction. Some PCs may have only floppy disks and depend on the network to supply the equivalent of hard disk storage. In other words, some PCs are created more equal than others. In fact, it's not unusual for a peer-to-peer network to have a single dominant PC that serves most of the needs of the others. Functionally, the client-server and peer-to-peer architectures are not digitally distinct like black and white but shade into one another.

In a peer-to-peer network, no one PC needs to be particularly endowed with overwhelming mass storage or an incomprehensible network operating system. Each computer connects to the network using simple driver software that makes the resources of the other PCs appear as extra disk drives and printers. There's no monstrous network operating system to deal with, only a few extra entries to each PC's CONFIG.SYS or AUTOEXEC.BAT file. Although someone does have to make decisions in setting up the peer-to-peer network (such as which PCs have access to which drives in other PCs), day-to-day operations usually don't require an administrator.

The peer-to-peer scheme has another advantage: You don't need to buy an expensive file server. Not only will that save cash, but also it can give you the security of redundancy. The failure of a server puts an entire network out of action. The failure of a network peer only eliminates that peer; the rest of the network continues to operate. And if you duplicate vital files on at least two peers, you'll never have to fear losing data from the crash of a single system.

Functions

In the abstract, connectivity sounds more like a friendly rather than practical concept—sort of like holding hands. As with the touch of someone who cares, the contact is not nearly as important as what it leads to. Connecting for the sake of the connection is pointless. Put that connection to work, however, and you can multiply the power of the individual PC.

The two most important functions of the network are communications and resource sharing—abstract and arbitrary distinctions that overlap. The network wire can act as a communications channel to route messages from one machine to another or broadcast to all. Group scheduling programs, online presentations, and email—intra-office, inter-office, and Internet—all put the communication power of the network to work.

Resource sharing uses the power of the PC-to-PC connection to make more from your investment in computer hardware or make your investment go further. Split the price of an expensive piece of hardware several ways, and the cost per user become manageable (although never low enough). It centralizes operation and housekeeping. It can consolidate stock-keeping for consumables; instead of needing to keep on hand ink and paper for a dozen different printers, a single stash of toner suffices. And it gives the network administrator complete control, something that appeals to those who aspire their own banana republics to dictate.

File Sharing

The key benefit of today's simple network systems is that you don't *need* a dedicated file server. Whatever is stored on one machine is fair game for every other PC connected to the network—provided you (acting as the network administrator or owner of the files on your individual computer) give everyone permission to access them.

As networks grow larger and more complex, a centralized server begins to make more sense. After all, you'll quickly run out of drive letters to access co-workers' computers as your web expands beyond the alphabets and basic symbols. A single source for storage also makes management easier; updates made to one centralized database are reflected to all users. Backups are easier (only one drive to worry about). And the network administrator's curiosity is more easily satisfied when there's only one place to snoop to find incriminating evidence.

Along with the power of file sharing comes responsibility. Security becomes an important issue because without suitable restraints, anyone could pry into your most important matters. Consequently file security is a major issue for network managers, and most networks incorporate elaborate security systems that allow the manager to designate different levels of access for individual users. In addition, file sharing lets you distribute both the bad and the good. Just as a kindergarten class lets children pass around the latest diseases, a network lets PCs share the latest computer viruses. System managers must constantly be on guard for intrusions into their networks.

If you *want* a dedicated shared resource—if your network has grown large enough that you need to centralize or if you have the lust for power that marks you as having the heart of an administrator (or the lack of a heart)—you have three primary options.

Server PCs are generally special (usually costly) PCs with high-capacity storage systems and high-reliability designs aimed specifically at file sharing across a network. Adding a server to a small peer-to-peer network to make it into a client-server system involves nothing more than designating one system as the server. As a network becomes more complex, however, the server becomes a more critical issue. It needs large storage resources with fast access (which, for today's networks, usually means a RAID-based disk system). Although the server does not need the power of the latest microprocessors, if you want to move to a true server operating system (such as Windows NT Server), you'll need more power. When an entire organization depends on a single server, making that server *fault-tolerant* means it can ignore simple failures.

Disk servers are hard disks without PCs that plug directly into the network. They give you the advantages of centralized storage without the need for an entire PC. You still need to manage the disk server, but you use one of the clients on the network to control the disk server's functions.

CD servers are more specialized, meant for situations in which you have a need for gigabytes of unchanging storage—for example, putting reams of research online. The CD server links a stack of CD drives to your network so that you have fast access to each disc, about as fast as a local disc connection. Although intriguing, the CD server doesn't work for all applications. Many games require a local CD drive and won't run over any network connection, even to a remote CD drive.

Printer Sharing

Printers are probably the most commonly shared network hardware resource. With today's network software, you can share any printer from the lowliest inkjet to a high-flying color laser. The usefulness of printer sharing has even spawned a new type of hardware, the network printer, a machine optimized for high-speed output and intense use, rated for nearly constant operation.

To turn an ordinary printer into a network printer, all your need to do is connect it to the network. Modern networks and printers give you three options in connecting a printer for sharing through a small PC network:

PC connection. Any printer connected to a PC can operate as a shared resource through simple software setup. The network merely reroutes print commands and data from the printer port (or driver) through the network to the shared printer. The printer remains connected to an individual PC and operates exactly like a local printer to the user of that PC. Other users on the network only have to walk a little farther to get their output. The penalties of this means of connecting a shared printer are a potential slowdown of the printer's PC and the noise and bother of having your printer rattle out someone else's work.

Print server. A *print server* removes the user from the PC to which the printer is connected; it may even remove the PC from the PC. The print server is a separate PC or sub-PC dedicated to collecting print jobs from the network and routing them to the network printer. The typical print server eliminates all the hardware and software not needed for sending signals to the printer—little things such as the display, keyboard, and operating system—to distill the print server into a small box boasting little more than a microprocessor and memory. Available both as a small box or simple cable adapter, a print server turns any printer into a network device. The print server converts network signals into a standard parallel port and gives your printer a network address. Most include buffer memory.

Network printer. A true network printer has a built-in connectivity—typically today a 10Base-T or 100Base-T port—making it ready to accept a cable directly from your hub. Other larger printers often offer slots to plug in their own (usually proprietary) network adapters. Newer printer models have built-in Web-based administration tools. You control your printer by logging onto its built-in Web page. Older models require administration through an associated PC even though the printer doesn't actually connect to a PC. Either form of control works, but the trend is moving to Web-based designs because they offer greater familiarity and versatility.

Internet Sharing

As soon as you have more than one PC, Internet access becomes a problem. Even if you dedicate one telephone line to a modem, you'll soon have two people trying to use the line with different modems at the same time, a situation that only creates frustration. One solution is to give everyone his own modem line, an arrangement that wastes both modems and monthly telephone line charges. When you install high-speed Internet access—a cable modem, an ADSL connection, or a satellite feed—the need to share across your network becomes quickly apparent.

Probably the best way to share Internet access is to set up one of your PCs are a *proxy server.* That is, the designated PC acts as a portal to the Web. Your other PCs see it as being the Internet, and the anointed PC relays their requests to the actual Internet.

The problem with setting up a proxy server is that setting up the software is a maddening chore that usually takes a network expert to get right—and then only after a couple of evenings of trial and error. Consequently, hardware makers have developed hardware solutions to the problem.

A *Remote Access Server* is a special variety of network router that allows all the PCs in your network to access the Internet through a common modem or terminal adapter. Most are offered as all-in-one packages aimed at small businesses. You get a small box that plugs into your network and provides its own link to your Internet service provider.

The link between the remote access server and your ISP may take any of several forms. Most basic is a simple modem connection, which suffers all the limitations of the built-in modem with performance further degraded by shared access; a 56K connection becomes worse than a 14.4 kbits/sec connection when four people try to use it simultaneously. A better choice is a remote access server that allows you to choose your own modem or access device, although you'll still suffer the limitations of the connection between server and modem, be it a serial port, bus connection, or something else.

Advanced networking software (but not that supplied with Windows 95 and 98) allows you to share the Internet connection used by your server—for example, a T1 line. The Internet becomes an extension of your own network. Although this is the best means of linking all your PCs to the Web, it also is the most complex to manage and requires an intimate knowledge of your network operating system.

Standards

A network is a collection of ideas, hardware, and software. The software comprises both the programs that make it work and the protocols that let everything work together. The hardware involves the network adapters, wires, hubs, concentrators, routers, and even more exotic fauna. Getting it all to work together requires standardization.

Because of the layered design of most networks, these standards can appear at any level in the hierarchy, and they do. Some cover a single layer; others span them all to create a cohesive system.

Current technology makes the best small PC network a hub-based peer-to-peer design cabled with twisted-pair wiring and running the software built into your operating system. The big choice you face is the hardware standard. In the last few years, networks have converged on two basic hardware standards, 10Base-T and 100Base-T. Both are specific implementations of Ethernet.

Just as celebrities are people famous principally for being famous, 10Base-T and 100Base-T are popular because they are popular. They are well known and generally understood. Components for either are widely available and inexpensive. Setting them up is easy, and support is widely available.

The original appeal of twisted-pair networking was the wire. Most businesses already had twisted-pair wires stretching to every office and cubicle, installed over the years for tele-phone systems. The twisted-pair networks took advantage of this already-installed wiring. Once networks became part of the corporate infrastructure, however, this argument disap-peared. Telephone wiring no longer is sufficient for a PC network. Special cables must be installed for today's high-speed networks that use twisted-pair. In general, the cost of installation is substantially more than the cost of the wire itself. The higher categories of twisted-pair aren't substantially cheaper than other kinds of wire. There's no good techni-cal argument for using twisted-pair over some other kind of wire. As a practical matter, however, it is today's the best choice for speeds up to 100MHz.

The big decision you face is whether you need 10 or 100MHz speed. There are four pri-mary issues to consider:

Price. As you should expect, slower 10Base-T hardware is cheaper than 100Base-T, although the spread is shrinking. If you want to connect a few PCs together inex-pensively, 10Base-T is all you'll need. You can hedge your bets by selecting dual-speed components. These allow you to link your network together today under 10Base-T and then later upgrade to 100Base-T without buying new hardware.

Cabling. 10Base-T requires less costly, less complicated wiring. Where 100Base-T demands special Category 5 cabling, 10Base-T works with just about any twisted-pair cable, even ordinary telephone wire (but not flat-wire modular cables—the pairs have to be twisted, after all). If you want to make do with old wires you installed years ago, 10Base-T is your choice. If you're adding new wires, opt for 100Base-T. The speed more than makes up for the small price differences.

Performance. 10Base-T is fast enough for printer or Internet sharing and can even let you distribute multiple MP3 files for playback in real-time. (You can even play uncompressed WAV files through a 10Base-T connection without losing any audio.) If you want to move video or multiple stereo audio channels at the same time, how-ever, you'll need the higher performance of 100Base-T. It won't flag with video or any reasonable home or small business load.

Mixing Speeds. Although network components operating at one speed can only communicate with other devices sharing the same speed, you can link together a complex network with portions operating at 10MHz and others at 100MHz. You can make do with 10Base-T for connections that don't require high performance while using 100Base-T for those that do. To make a two-speed network, all you need is a special hub (discussed later) and some careful advance planning.

In your exploration of small networks, you're apt to run into many of these standards. What follows is a brief discussion of some of the more common names you'll encounter.

Ethernet

The progenitor of all of today's networks was the Ethernet system originally developed in the 1970s at Xerox Corporation's Palo Alto Research Center for linking its Alto workstations to laser printers. The invention of Ethernet is usually credited to Robert Metcalf, who later went on to found 3Com Corporation, a early major supplier of PC networking hardware and software. During its first years, Ethernet was proprietary to Xerox, a technology without a purpose in a world in which the PC had not yet been invented.

In September 1980, however, Xerox joined with minicomputer maker Digital Equipment Corporation and semiconductor manufacturer Intel Corporation to publish the first Ethernet specification, which later became known as E.SPEC VER.1. The original specification was followed in November 1982 by a revision that has become today's widely used standard, E.SPEC VER.2.

This specification is not what most people call Ethernet, however. In January 1985, the Institute of Electrical and Electronic Engineers published a networking system derived from Ethernet but not identical with it. The result was the IEEE 802.3 specification. Ethernet and IEEE 802.3 share many characteristics—physically, they use the same wiring and connection schemes—but each uses its own packet structure. Consequently, although you can plug host adapters for true Ethernet and IEEE 802.3 together in the same cabling system, the two standards will not be able to talk to one another. Some PC host adapters, however, know how to speak both languages and can exchange packets with either standard.

The basis of Ethernet is a clever scheme for arbitrating access to the central bus of the system. The protocol, formally described as Carrier Sensing, Multiple Access, with Collision Detection is often described as being like a party line. It's not. It's much more like polite conversation. All the PCs in the network patiently listen to everything that's going on across the network backbone. Only when there is a pause in the conversation will a new PC begin to speak. And if two or more PCs start to talk at the same time, all become quiet. They will wait for a random interval (and because it is random, each will wait a different interval) and, after the wait, attempt to begin speaking again. One will be lucky and win access to the network. The other, unlucky PCs will hear the first PC blabbing away and wait for another pause.

Access to the network line is not guaranteed in any period by the Ethernet protocol. The laws of probability guide the system, and they dictate that eventually every device that desires access will get it. Consequently, Ethernet is described as a probabilistic access system. As a practical matter, when few devices (compared to the bandwidth of the system) attempt to use the Ethernet system, delays are minimal because all of them trying to talk at one time is unlikely. As demand approaches the capacity of the system, however, the efficiency of probability-based protocol plummets. The size limit of an Ethernet system is not set by the number of PCs but by the amount of traffic; the more packets PCs send, the more contention, and the more frustrated attempts.

The Ethernet protocol has many physical embodiments. These can embrace any topology, type of cable, or speed. The IEEE 802.3 specification defines several of these and assigns a code name to each. Today's most popular Ethernet implementations operate at a raw speed of 10MHz. That is, the clock frequency of the signals on the Ethernet (or IEEE 802.3) wire is 10MHz. Actual throughput is lower because packets cannot occupy the full bandwidth of the Ethernet system. Moreover, every packet contains formatting and address data that steals space that could be used for data.

Today's four most popular IEEE 802.3 implementations are 10Base-5, 10Base-2, 10Base-T, and 100Base-T. Although daunting at first look, you can remember the names as codes: The first number indicates the operating speed of the system in megahertz; the central word "Base" indicates that Ethernet protocol is the basis of the system; and the final character designates the wire used for the system. The final digit (when numerical) refers to the distance in hundreds of feet the network can stretch, but as a practical matter also specifies the type of cable used. Coincidentally, the number also describes the diameter of the cable; under the 10MHz 802.3 standard, the "5" stands for a thick coaxial cable that's about one half (five tenths) of an inch in diameter; the "2" refers to a thinner coaxial cable about two-tenths inch in diameter; the "T" indicates twisted-pair wiring like that used by telephone systems.

Other differences besides cable type separate these Ethernet schemes. The 10Base-5 and 10Base-2 use a linear topology; 10Base-T and 100Base-T are built in a star configuration. The three IEEE 802.3 systems with the "10" prefix operate at the same 10MHz speed using the same Ethernet protocol, so a single network can tie together all three technologies without the need for such complications as protocol converters. In typical complex installations, thick coaxial cable links far-flung workgroups, each of which is tied together locally with a 10Base-T hub. This flexibility makes IEEE 802.3 today's leading networking choice.

The 100Base-T system operates at 100MHz, yielding higher performance consistent with transferring multimedia and other data-intensive applications across the network. Its speed has made it the system of choice in most new installations.

Actually, 100Base-T isn't a single system but a family of siblings, each designed for different wiring environments. *100Base-TX* is the purest implementation—and the most demanding. It requires Class 5 wiring, shielded twisted-pair designed for data applications. In return for the cost of the high-class wiring, it permits full-duplex operation so any network node can both send and receive data simultaneously. *100Base-T4* works with shielded or unshielded voice-grade wiring, Classes 3 and 4, but only allows for half-duplex operations. *100Base-FX* uses the same timing and protocol as the 100Base-T systems but operates across fiber-optic cables instead of copper twisted-pair wiring. It also allows full-duplex operation.

The next step in Ethernet is to push the speed up yet another order of magnitude. *Gigabit Ethernet* operates at 1,000MHz, chiefly through fiber optical media, although you can bet labs are working on fitting gigahertz bandwidth on twisted-pair cable. (The twisted-pair cable with the widest bandwidth generally available conks out at about one-third the gigabit speed.)

Token Ring

Another way to handle packets across a network is a concept called token-passing. In this scheme, the token is a coded electronic signal used to control network access. IBM originated the most popular form of this protocol, which after further development, was sanctioned by the IEEE as its 802.5 standard. Because this standard requires a ring topology, it is commonly called Token Ring networking. Although once thought the most formidable competitor to Ethernet, it is now chiefly used only in large corporations. Other networking systems such as FDDI use a similar token-passing protocol.

In a token-passing system, all PCs remain silent until given permission to talk on the network line. They get permission by receiving the token. A single token circulates around the entire network, passed from PC to PC in a closed loop that forms a ring topology. If a PC receives the token and has no packets to give to the network to deliver, it simply passes along the token to the next PC in the ring. If, however, the PC has a packet to send, it links the packet to the token along with the address of the destination PC (or server). All the PCs around the ring then pass this token-and-packet along until it reaches its destination. The receiving PC strips off the data and puts the token back on the network, tagged to indicate that the target PC has received its packet. The remaining PCs in the network pass the token around until it reaches the original sending PC. The originating PC removes the tag and passes the token along the network to enable another PC to send a packet.

This token-passing method offers two chief benefits, reliability and guaranteed access. Because the token circulates back to the sending PC, it gives a confirmation that the packet was properly received by the recipient. The protocol also assures that the PC next in line after the sending PC will always be the next one to get the token to enable communication. As the token circulates, it allows each PC to use the network. The token must go all the way around the ring—and give every other PC a chance to use the network—before it returns to any given PC to enable it to use the network again. Access to the network is guaranteed even when network traffic is heavy. No PC can get locked out of the network because of a run of bad luck in trying to gain access.

The original Token Ring specification called for operation at 4MHz. A revision to the standard allows for operation at 16MHz. The specification originally required the use of a special four-wire shield twisted-pair cabling, but current standards enable for several types of cabling, including unshielded twisted-pair wires.

Asynchronous Transfer Mode

One of the darling technologies of new networking, *Asynchronous Transfer Mode*, or ATM, is fundamentally different from other networking systems. It is a switched technology rather than a shared bus. Instead of broadcasting down a wire, a sending PC sets up a *requested path* to the destination specifying various attributes of the connection, including its speed. The switch need not be physical. In fact, ATM is independent of the underlying physical wiring and works with almost any physical network architecture from twisted-pair to fiber optical. Its performance depends on the underlying physical implementation, but its switched design assures the full bandwidth of the medium for the duration of each connection.

Instead of packets, ATM data takes the form of *cells*. The length of each cell is fixed at 53 bytes. The first five serve as an address. The remaining 48 are the *payload*, the data the packet transfers. The payload can be any kind of data—database entries, audio, video, or whatever. ATM is independent of data types and carries any and all bytes with exactly the same dispatch.

ATM is built from a layered structure. It takes the form of three layers at the bottom of the network implementation—the physical layer, the ATM layer, and the adaptation layer.

> The **physical layer** controls how ATM connects with the overall network wiring. It defines both the electrical characteristic of the connection and the actual network interface.
>
> The **ATM layer** takes care of addressing and routing. It adds the five-byte address header to each data cell to assure that the payload travels to the right destination.
>
> The **adaptation layer** takes the data supplied from higher up the network hierarchy and divides it into the 48-byte payload that will fit into each cell.

ATM is part of a network. Alone, it does not make a network itself. Because of its high-speed potential and versatility, it is becoming popular in large businesses where it neatly sandwiches between other network standards.

FDDI

Although many publications use the acronym FDDI to refer to any network using optical fibers as the transmission medium, it actually refers to an international networking standard sanctioned by the American National Standards Institute and the International Standards Organization. The initials stand for *Fiber Distributed Data Interface*. The standard is based on a dual counter-rotating fiber-optic ring topology operating with a 100MHz data rate. The FDDI standard permits the connection of PCs or other nodes with a distance up to 2 to 3 kilometers between PCs and an entire spread up to 100 kilometers.

AppleTalk

Apple Computer developed its own networking scheme for its Macintosh computers. Called AppleTalk, the network is built around an Apple-developed hardware implementation that Apple called LocalTalk. In operation, LocalTalk is similar to Ethernet in that it uses probabilistic access with Carrier Sensing, Multiple Access technology. Instead of after-the-fact collision detection, however, LocalTalk uses collision avoidance. Originally designed for shielded twisted-pair cable, many LocalTalk networks use unshielded twisted-pair telephone wiring. The LocalTalk system is slow, however, with a communication speed of 230.4KHz (that's about one-quarter megahertz).

Arcnet

Another token-passing network system, Arcnet, predates the IEEE 802.5 Token Ring. Arcnet was developed in 1977 by Datapoint Corporation. In an Arcnet system, each PC is assigned an 8-bit address from 1 to 255. The token is passed from one PC to the next in numerical order. Each PC codes the token signal with the address of the next address in the network, the network automatically configuring itself so that only active address numbers are used. The number is broadcast on the network so that all PCs receive every token, but only the one with the right address can use it. If the PC receiving the token has a packet to send, it is then allowed to send out the packet. When the packet is received, an acknowledgment is sent back to the originating PC. The PC then passes the token to the next highest address. If the PC that receives the token has no packets to send, it simply changes the address in the token to the next higher value and broadcasts the token.

Because the token is broadcast, the Arcnet system does not require a ring. Instead, it uses a simple bus topology that includes star-like hubs. Arcnet hubs are either active or passive. Active hubs amplify the Arcnet signal and act as distribution amplifiers to any number of ports (typically eight). Passive hubs act like simple signal splitters and typically connect up to four PCs. The basic Arcnet system uses coaxial cable. Compared to today's Ethernet systems, it is slow, operating at 2.5MHz.

Zero-Slot LANs

When you need to connect only a few PCs and you don't care about speed, you have an alternative in several proprietary systems that are lumped together as Zero-Slot LANs. These earn their name from their capability to give you a network connection without requiring you to fill an expansion slot in your PC with a network host adapter. Instead of a host adapter, most Zero-Slot LANs use a port already built into most PCs, the serial port.

Protocols and topologies of Zero-Slot LANs vary with each manufacturer's implementation. Some are built as star-like systems with centralized hubs; others are connected as buses. Nearly all use twisted-pair wiring, although some need only three connections and others use up to eight. The former take advantage of a protocol derived from Ethernet; the latter use the handshaking signals in the serial port for hardware arbitration of access to the network.

The one factor shared by all Zero-Slot LANs is low speed. All are constrained by the maximum speed of the basic PC serial port, which is 115,200 bits per second (or about one-tenth megahertz). Lower speeds are often necessary with long reaches of cable because Zero-Slot LAN signals are particularly prone to interference. Serial ports provide only single-ended signals, which are not able to cancel induced noise and interference as is possible with balanced signals.

Components

In building a basic network, you must deal with three different types of components. These include network interface cards, hubs (a small network usually needs only one hub), and the cabling that links it together. Although you must consider specific features of each of these within its category, you also have to know the relationship between them. For example, your network interface cards, hub, and cabling must all conform to the same hardware standard and must be capable of supporting the signalling system you choose (for example, 10Base-T versus 100Base-T.

Network Interface Cards

To become part of a network, each PC requires its own network adapter. On a practical level, the reason is simple. The adapter gives your PC a jack for plugging in the network wire.

A host adapter does exactly what its name implies: It adapts the signals in your host computer to what's needed by the network system. The host adapter takes the form of an expansion board that plugs into a free slot inside your PC. It then provides a jack on its rear panel into which you can plug your network cable.

You need one host adapter for every PC in your network. The adapters do not need to be identical or even from the same manufacturer. However, with less expensive hubs, all must follow the same wiring and signaling standards. That is, you can use any host adapters you want in each PC as long as they all use twisted-pair wiring and 10Base-T.

Some hubs allow you to mix 10Base-T and 100Base-T host adapters. Check whether your hub allows this flexibility before you buy an odd assortment of host adapters.

Host adapters have to make two connections, one with your PC and one with the network. The form of these connections will guide your selection of a host adapter. In general, any host adapter is acceptable, providing it matches your connections and is supported directly by Windows, includes a suitable Windows driver in its box, or emulates another manufacturer's host adapter board that Windows directly supports without external drivers. For example, Novell NE2000 compatibility assures that the board duplicates the Novell product and delivers the features expected by the software.

As with any adapter, a network adapter must match the two things that it is supposed to adapt to one another. In the case of an NIC, it must match the standards and resources of your PC to those of the network hardware and software system.

Network Interface

The network connection used by your host adapter depends on two factors: the wiring you've chosen for your network and the signaling standard.

The wiring choices are two, coaxial cable (typically one of two types) or twisted-pair wiring. For ease in installation, you'll want to use twisted-pair.

You have two chief choices for the signaling standard used by your host adapter, 10Base-T and 100Base-T. Although they are more expensive, the 100Base-T adapters offer greater versatility. Most 100Base-T adapters also work at the slower speed of 10Base-T. You can set your network up as 10Base-T and use the same host adapter for a higher-speed upgrade in the future:

> **Speed.** Your network adapters must match the speed at which your hub operates. Today's choices are two, 10 or 100MHz. The least expensive NICs operate at a single speed, and 10MHz models are the cheapest of all. Two-speed adapters are somewhat more expensive but also more versatile. You can install one in a low-speed network, and if you someday decide to go faster you won't need a new NIC. Most dual-speed hubs are *autosensing*. That is, they detect the speed on the network wire to which they are connected and adjust their own operating speed to match.

Autosensing makes a NIC easier to set up, particularly if you don't know (or care) the speed at which your network operates. You can just plug in the network wire and let your hardware worry about the details. Nearly all two-speed NICs are autosensing, although you might want to check the specs of inexpensive products to be sure the manufacturer hasn't decided to save a nickel by forcing the speed selection back on you.

Wiring. By definition, a 10Base-T or 100Base-T NIC will offer a twisted-pair connection through an RJ-45 jack. If it didn't, it would not meet the standard it purports to follow. Some NICs also give you a coaxial connection. The added jack rings some versatility; you can connect into coaxial as well as twisted-pair Ethernets. If you have no plans to set up a coaxial bus, however, you can consider the coaxial jack the NIC's appendix—a part of the card that's normally innocuous and decidedly useless.

Bus Interface

The connection with your PC is the expansion slot connector inside your system. Most network adapters for desktop computers give you two choices, either the ISA bus or the PCI. Choose ISA only if the sole remaining expansion slot in your PC follows the ISA standard. In any other case, choose the PCI adapter. It will be both faster and easier to configure.

If you have a notebook computer, your choice for the connection with your PC is also twofold. You can get a network adapter that plugs into a parallel port or into a CardBus (or PC Card) slot. The latter is always preferable. The parallel connection is substantially slower and more difficult to set up.

At the other end of the adaptation, your NIC must match your PC, either by fitting into an expansion slot or otherwise linking to it. In general, you should prefer a PCI-based NIC for a modern PC. Although most current systems still have at least one ISA slot, using it for your network connection is rarely a good idea. PCI-based boards are both faster and easier to set up than ISA-based products. If you must use an ISA board, be sure that it connects with the full 16-bit interface. Eight-bit cards are not only slower but also give you fewer setup options. Notebooks computers that lack conventional expansion slots give you two network connection alternatives. CardBus and PC Cards work like PCI or ISA adapters (respectively) in laptop PCs. Slot-saving cards incorporate both network adapters and modems. The convenience of using one board for all your communications needs extracts a price; these cards tend to be costly, often substantially more than their single-function equivalents. Pocket adapters that plug into parallel ports compromise performance; USB external adapters offer higher speed but still top out at about 6 mbits/sec because of bus overhead. They are not in the league of a 100Base-T CardBus card.

Other Features

Some network adapters allow for optional boot ROMs, which allow PCs to boot up using a remote disk drive, but this feature is more applicable to larger businesses with dedicated network servers rather than a home or small business network.

Hubs

Hubs pass signals from one PC to the next. The most basic hub has two functions. It provides a place to plug in the network wire from each PC and it regenerates the signals to ensure against errors.

The design of Ethernet requires for all of the signals in the network loop be shared. Every PC in the loop—that is, every PC connected to a single hub—sees exactly the same signals. The easiest way to do this would be to short all of the wires together. Electrically, such a connection would be an anathema.

The circuitry of the hub prevents such disasters. It mixes all the signals it receives together and then sends out the final mixture in its output.

To make the cabling for the system easy, the jacks on a hub are wired the opposite of the jacks on NICs. That is, the send and receive connections are reserved; the connections the NIC uses for sending, the hub uses for receiving.

Expensive hubs differ from the economic models chiefly by their management capabilities—things such as remote monitoring and reconfiguration, which are mostly irrelevant to a small network.

You'll need at least one hub for your network. A hub is simply a box with circuitry inside and a bunch of jacks for RJ-45 plugs on the back. The circuitry inside links the 10Base-T or 100Base-T cables together.

Some hubs are called *switches*; others have internal switches. A switch divides a network into segments and shifts data between them. A dual-speed hub with a built-in switch can link 10Base-T and 100Base-T devices.

Speed

The hub sets the overall network speed. Dual-speed hubs handle both 10Base-T and 100Base-T. *Autosensing* hubs choose the best speed automatically.

The most important characteristic of hubs to consider is the standard they support. The least expensive hubs only handle 10Base-T signals. The next step up use the 100MHz speed. More expensive hubs use both 10Base-T and 100Base-T signals and are termed two-speed, dual-speed, or 10/100 hubs.

Obviously, you need a hub to match the standard you're going to follow. You may want to start with a 10Base-T network and then later upgrade when the price of 100Base-T equipment comes down. High speed can be a hefty investment today. If you get a 100Base-T hub now, you'll also have to invest in 100MHz network adapters for your PCs. A two-speed hub seems like the perfect compromise because you can use it with 10MHz cards now and not have to discard it when later you upgrade. Then penalty is, of course, higher cost. Figure to pay about $200 more than a basic 10Base-T hub for a dual-speed unit.

Ports

The other critical aspect of hubs you must consider is the number of ports. You need one port on your hub for each PC in your network. You may want to have a few extra ports to allow for growth, but more ports cost more, too. You'll also need ports for Internet sharing devices, print servers, and dedicated shared disk resources. Don't skimp. Five ports will give two PC network growth options; eight is better.

More expensive hubs have additional features. Most have coaxial cable ports for linking multiple hubs together. Others have sophisticated network administration features built in. For a home or small business, you need not bother yourself with such details. A minimal hub likely will be all you need.

Uplinks

Some hubs include a cross-over jack or coaxial connection that serves as an *uplink* to tie additional hubs into your network.

Shop wisely, and you should be able to find inexpensive 10Base-T host adapters for $30 to $40 each. Those suited to 100Base-T may cost $80 to $100. You can always spend more to get brands that are more widely known, a longer warranty, or better support.

Cabling

One of the biggest problems faced by network system designers is keeping radiation and interference under control. All wires act as antenna, sending and receiving signals. As frequencies increase and wire lengths increase, the radiation increases. The pressure is on network designers to increase both the speed (with higher frequencies) and reach of networks (with longer cables) to keep up with the increasing demands of industry.

Two strategies are commonly used to combat interference from network wiring. One is the coaxial cable, so called because it has a central conductor surrounded by one or more shields that may be a continuous braid or metalized plastic film. Each shield amounts to a long thin tube, and each shares the same longitudinal axis: the central conductor. The surrounding shield typically operates at ground potential, which prevents stray signals from leaking out of the central conductor or noise seeping in. Because of its shielding, coaxial cable is naturally resistant to radiation. As a result, coax was the early choice for network wiring.

Coaxial cables generally use single-ended signals. That is, only a single conductor, the central conductor of the coaxial cable, carries information. The outer conductor operates at ground potential to serve as a shield, as shown in Figure 23.4. Any voltage that might be induced in the central conductor (to become noise or interference) first affects the outer conductor. Because the outer conductor is at ground potential, it shorts out the noise before it can affect the central conductor. (Noise signals are voltages in excess of ground potential, so forcing the noise to ground potential reduces its value to zero.)

FIGURE 23.4

Components of a coaxial cable.

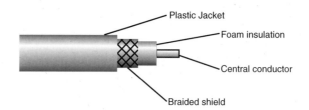

Plastic Jacket

Foam insulation

Central conductor

Braided shield

The primary alternative is twisted-pair wiring, which earns its name from being made of two identical insulated conducting wires that are twisted around one another in a loose double-helix, as shown in Figure 23.3. The most common form of twisted-pair wiring lacks the shield of coaxial cable and is often denoted by the acronym UTP, which stands unshielded twisted-pair.

FIGURE 23.5

Components of a twisted-pair wiring cable.

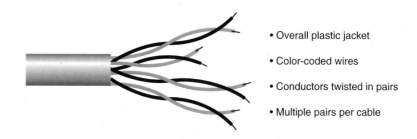

• Overall plastic jacket

• Color-coded wires

• Conductors twisted in pairs

• Multiple pairs per cable

Most UTP wiring is installed in the form of multi-pair cables with up to several hundred pairs inside a single plastic sheath. The most common varieties have 4 to 25 twisted pairs in a single cable. The pairs inside the cable are distinguished from one another by color coding. The body of the wiring is one color alternating with a thinner band of another color. In the two wires of a given pair, the background and banding color are opposites; that is, one wire will have a white background with a blue band and its mate will have a blue background with a white band. Each pair has a different color code (see Table 23.1). The most common type of UTP cable conforms to the AT&T specification for D-Inside Wire (DIW). The same type of wiring also corresponds to IBM's Type 3 cabling specification for Token Ring networking.

the network host adapter. One cable of the network bus plugs into one leg of the T-connector on the host adapter, and another cable plugs into a second T-connector leg and runs to the next host adapter in the network. The network bus consequently comprises multiple short segments. All connections to it are made using BNC connectors. In place of a network cable at the first and last transceivers in a backbone, you plug in a 50 ohm cable terminator instead. You can connect up to 30 transceivers to a single 10Base-2 backbone.

10Base-T

Because of its star topology, 10Base-T networks use point-to-point wiring. Each network cable stretches from one point (a PC or other node) to another at the hub. The hub has a wiring jack for each network node; each PC host adapter has a single connector.

The basic 10Base-T system uses unshielded twisted-pair cable. In most permanently installed networks, wall jacks that conform to the eight-wire RJ-45 design link to standard D-Inside Wire buried in walls and above ceilings. To link between the wall jacks and the jacks on 10Base-T host adapters, you should use special round modular cables. Ordinary flat telephone wires do not twist their leads and are not suitable to high-speed network use.

Although 10Base-T uses eight-wire (four-pair cabling) and eight-pin connectors, only four wires actually carry signals. Normally, the wires between hub and host adapter use straight-through wiring. The PC transmits on pins 2 and 1 and receives on pins 6 and 3 (the first number being the positive side of the connection). Figure 23.6 shows the correct wiring for a hub-to-workstation 10Base-T cable.

FIGURE 23.6
Wiring for a hub-to-workstation 10Base-T cable.

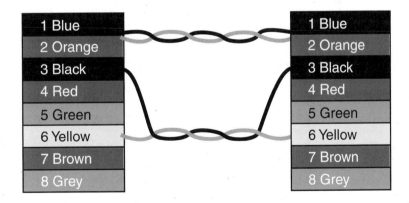

Patching between hubs may require cross-over cables that link pins 1 to 3 and 2 to 6.

The 10Base-T specifications enable the entire cable run between hub and host adapter to be no more than 100 meters (about 325 feet). This distance includes the cable inside the wall as well as the leads between the hub and building wiring and between the node and building wiring. Only one PC or node can be connected to each hub jack, but the number of PCs that can be connected to a single hub is limited only by the number of jacks on the hub. Most 10Base-T hubs provide a thin or thick wire connector for linking to other hubs, concentrators, or repeaters.

Hard Copy

Hard copy is what printers and plotters make, the real paperwork that you can hold in your hand. Despite the dreams in years gone by of the paperless office, paper remains the medium of choice; only mail is in a headlong rush to go electronic, and even that hasn't lightened the load of your letter carrier. Because of the need for putting things on paper, the external peripheral that you're most likely to connect to your PC is the printer. The printer is not singular thing, but rather a creature of many technologies. Each has its own advantages and disadvantages, which themselves vary with what you want to do.

Quick guide to today's most popular printer technologies

Technology	In short	Advantages	Disadvantages
Impact dot-matrix	Inexpensive but becoming hard to find	Makes carbon copies	Noisy, messy, and low quality
Color inkjet	Today's most popular printer	Inexpensive and gives good color	More expensive per page than laser
Phase-change inkjet	Novel technology yields superior color	Bright, deep colors that are excellent for pre-press and presentation applications	More expensive than other inkjets
Monochrome laser	Top quality but one color	Excellent quality text and graphics at the lowest cost per pag	The obvious: only one color
Color laser	The best of both worlds	High print quality in color	Expensive to buy today (but coming down in price—keep an eye on this technology
Thermal wax	Rich, deep colors	High color saturation	High color per page
Dye diffusion	Continuous tone	Best technology for realistic photos	Expensive and falling from favor as inkjet quality catches up

Printing is the art of moving ink from one place to another. Although that definition likely will please only a college instructor lost in his own vagueness, any more precise description fails in the face of a reality laced with printouts of a thousand fonts and far fewer thoughts. A modern computer printer takes ink from a reservoir and deposits it on paper or some other medium in patterns determined by your ideas and PC. In other words, a printer makes your thoughts visible.

Behind this worthy goal is one of the broadest arrays of technology in data processing, including processes akin to hammers, squirt guns, and flashlights. The range of performance is wider than with any other peripheral. Various printers operate at speeds from lethargic to lightning-like, from slower than an arthritic typist with one hand tied behind his back to faster than Speedy Gonzales having just munched tacos laced with amphetamines. They are packaged as everything from one-pound totables to truss-stressing monsters and look like anything from Neolithic bricks to Batman's nightmares. Some dot paper with text quality that rivals that of a professional publisher and chart out graphics with speed and sharpness that puts a plotter to shame. Some make a two-year-old's handiwork look elegant.

The classification of printers runs a similar, wide range. You can distinguish machines by their quality, speed, technology, purpose, weight, color, or any other of their innumerable (and properly pragmatic) design elements.

A definitive discourse on all aspects of printer technology would be a never-ending tale because the field is constantly changing. New technologies often arise and old ones are revived and refined. Innovations are incorporated into old machines. And seemingly obsolete ideas recur.

Printers

Obviously, the term "computer printer" is a general one that refers not to one kind of machine but several. Even in looking at the mechanical aspects of the typical printer's job of smudging paper with ink, you discover that many ways exist to put a computer's output on paper, just as more than one method exists for getting your house cat to part with its pelt.

History

The technology of printing followed the same pattern as display systems; the first devices were character-oriented, but bitmapped quickly evolved as the preferred choice. This pattern should be hardly unexpected. The first PCs were character-oriented. Only when PC hardware assumed enough power and performance could individual bits get manipulated fast and well enough to make bitmapping viable.

Printing is, in fact, far older than display technology—far older, indeed, than the PC, computers, or even electronics. Printing began with stone tablets, clay, and styli and slowly made its way to the papyrus patch and on to the scriptorium.

Printing became publishing with Johannes Gutenberg's 15th century development of movable type. The essence of Gutenberg's invention was to take woodblock printing that made a page-side image as a unit and break it into pieces. Each alphabetic letter became its own woodblock. In effect, Gutenberg invented character-based technology that served the first generation of PC printers so well.

The printing press is, of course, a machine for mass production, but the computer printer is designed for more personal production of hard copy. For four centuries after Gutenberg, personal communications remained exactly where they had been for the millennia before, quill on papyrus or paper.

Personal Printing

The first machine truly designed for personal communications was Christopher Sholes' typewriter. Sholes' goal was not speed but clarity, adding uniformity and legibility of the printing press to individual business papers (the hard copy of the day). Only decades later did the development of touch-typing give the typewriter the speed lead over the quill.

The first generation of PC printers were the direct descendants of the Sholes' original office typewriter. They use exactly the same technology to get ink onto paper—the force of impact. Although an old-fashioned typewriter is a mechanical complexity (as anyone knows who has tried putting one back together after taking it apart), its operating principle is quite simple. Strip away all the cams, levers, and keys, and you see that the essence of the typewriter is its hammers.

Each hammer strikes against an inked ribbon, which is then pressed against a sheet of paper. The impact of the hammer against the ribbon shakes and squeezes ink onto the paper. Absorbed into the paper fibers, the ink leaves a visible mark or image in the shape of the part of the hammer that struck at the ribbon, typically a letter of the alphabet.

In the earliest days of personal computers—before typewriter makers were sure that PCs would catch on and create a personal printer market—a number of companies adapted typewriters to computer output chores. The Bytewriter of 1980 was typical of the result—a slow, plodding computer printer with full typewriter keyboard. It could do double-duty as fast as your fingers could fly, but it was no match for the computer's output.

One device, short-lived on the marketplace, even claimed that you could turn your typewriter into a printer simply by setting a box on the keyboard. The box was filled with dozens of solenoids and enough other mechanical parts to make the space shuttle look simple. The solenoids worked as electronically controlled "fingers," pressing down each key on command from the host computer. Interesting as it sounds, they tread the thin line between the absurd and surreal. More than a little doubt exists as to whether these machines, widely advertised in 1981, were ever actually sold.

Shift to Graphics

All of these machines were, like Gutenberg's printing press, character-oriented, exactly suited to the needs of character-oriented terminal-based early hobbyist computers. The 1982 advent of graphics for the PC shattered character-based technology into bits. That is, instead of working with individual characters, PCs began the inexorable change-over to building the characters and graphics they displayed on screen from bits stored in a memory map. To make hard copy from the rough graphics early PCs showed on their screens, printers too made the transition to bit-image technology.

The result was *dot-matrix printers*, machines that print characters much in the manner they are formed on a monitor screen. With a dot-matrix printer, the raw material for characters on paper is much the same as it is on the video screen—dots. A number of dots can be arranged to resemble any character that you want to print. To make things easier for the printer (and its designer), printers that form their characters from dots usually array those dots in a rectilinear matrix like a crossword puzzle grid.

This kind of printer gets its name because it places each of its dots within a character matrix. Although the dot-matrix as a description clearly applies to any printer that forms text on the fly from individual dots rather than a preset pattern, the term has come to mean one specific printer technology, the impact dot-matrix printer. A more general term for a printer that uses this technology is *bit-image printer*, but that term has fallen into disuse because almost all modern printers use the technology and there's no sense in belaboring the obvious.

The impact dot-matrix printer reflected the movement of personal printing from the mechanical to the information age. It substituted electronic control of each dot for the mechanical complexity of managing several dozen character patterns on individual hammers.

Today, the impact dot-matrix printer survives at the bottom end of the printer range and in specialized applications, the last heir of the hammer-and-ribbon technology of the typewriter. Its days are clearly numbered as newer technologies pound impact printing into oblivion. Modern inkjet printers match the low dot-matrix price but deliver sharper text and graphics, better color, and less noise. Laser printers (and related technologies) outrun dot-matrix printers and improve further on the crispness of text and graphics.

Several other printer technologies play more specialized roles. Near-silent thermal printers are the low-price leaders. Thermal-wax transfer printers brighten graphics with the richest, most saturated colors. Dye-diffusion printers extend the hard-copy color spectrum to the widest printable range.

The native mode of most bit-image printers allows you to decide where to place individual dots on the printed sheet using a technique called *all-points addressable graphics*, or APA graphics. With a knowledge of the appropriate printer instructions, you or your software can draw graphs in great detail or even make pictures resembling the halftone photographs printed in newspapers. The software built into the printer allows every printable dot position to be controlled—specified as printed (black) or not (white). An entire image can be built up like a television picture, scanning lines several dots wide (as wide as the number of wires in the printhead) down the paper.

This graphics printing technique takes other names, too. Because each individual printed dot can be assigned a particular location or "address" on the paper, this feature is often called *dot-addressable graphics*. Sometimes, that title is simplified into dot graphics. Occasionally, it appears as bit-image graphics because each dot is effectively the image of one bit of data. When someone uses the term "graphics" without adorning it with one of these descriptive adjectives or phrases, it means the same thing; again, all printer graphics today are all-points addressable.

Fundamentals

In judging and comparing printers, you have several factors to consider. These include printing speed, on-paper quality, color capabilities, the print engine, media handling, and the cost of various consumables. Although many of these issues seem obvious, even trivial, current printer technologies—and hype—add some strange twists. For example, speed ratings may be given in units that can't quite be compared. Quality is more than a matter of dots per inch. And color can take on an added dimension—black.

Speed

No one wants to wait. When you finish creating a report or editing a picture, you want your hard copy immediately; you've finished, so should your computer. The ideal printer would be one that produces its work as soon as you give the "print command," all 50,000 pages of your monthly report in one big belch.

No printer yet has achieved instantaneous operation. In fact, practical machines span a wide range of printing speeds.

All modern operating systems include print spooling software that let your programs print as quickly as possible and then send the data to your printer at whatever speed it operates, however slowly. You can print a memo or encyclopedia while you use your PC for something else. The speed of your printer becomes an issue only when you need something in a hurry; your publisher's hot breath is pouring down your back for your thousand-page novel while your printer rolls out pages with all the speed and abandon of a medieval scribe. If you have a tight deadline, if you have a lot of printing to do, or if you share your printer with others and you all have a lot of work to do, printer speed becomes an important issue. The speed of your printer—or at least how that speed is measured—depends on the kind of printer you have.

Engineers divide computer printers into two basic types, line printers and page printers. A *line printer*, as its name implies, works on text one line at a time. It usually has a printhead that scans across the paper one line of characters at a time. Most line printers render one line at a time, starting to print each line as soon as it receives all the character data to appear in that line. A *page printer* rasterizes a full-page image in its own internal memory and prints it one line of dots at a time. It must receive all the data for a full page before it begins to print the page.

Line printer and page printers produce equivalent results on paper. For engineers, the chief difference is what gets held in the printer's memory. For you, the chief difference is how the engineers specify the speed of the two kinds of printer.

Measuring Units

The two most common measurements of printer speed are characters per second and pages per minute. Both should be straightforward measures. The first represents the number of characters a printer can peck out every second; the second, the number of completed pages that roll into the output tray every minute. In printer specification sheets, however, both are theoretical measures that may have little bearing on how fast a given job gets printed.

Line printer speed is usually measured in characters per second. Most printer manufacturers derive this figure theoretically. They take the time the printhead requires to move from the left side of a page to the right side and divide it into the number of characters that might print on the line. This speed is consequently dependent on the width of the characters, and manufacturers often choose the most favorable value.

The highest speed does not always result from using the narrowest characters, however. The rate at which the printhead can spray dots of ink (or hammer printwires) is often fixed, so to print narrower characters, the printer slows its printhead.

Characters per second does not directly translate into pages per minute, but you can determine a rough correspondence. On a standard sheet of paper, most line printers render 80 characters per line and 60 lines per page, a total of 4,800 characters per page. Because there are 60 seconds in every minute, each page per minute of speed translates into 80 characters per second. Or you can divide the number of characters per second by 80 to get an approximate page per minute rating.

This conversion can never be exact, particularly on real-world printing chores. Few documents you print will fill every line from left to right with dense text. A line printer uses time only to work on lines that are actually printed. Modern printers have sufficient built-in intelligence to recognize area that will appear blank on the printed sheet and don't bother moving their printheads over the empty spaces. Page printers, on the other hand, must scan an entire page even if it only has a single line of text on it. A line printer, on the other hand, dispenses with a single-line page in a few seconds.

Engine Speed Versus Throughput

Even within a given family of printers, ratings do not reflect real-world performance. The characters per second or pages per minute rating usually given for a printer does not indicate the rate at which you can expect printed sheets to dribble into the output tray. These speed measurements indicate the *engine speed*, the absolute fastest the mechanism of the printer allows paper to flow through its path. A number of outside factors slow the actual *throughput* of a printer to a rate lower—often substantially so—than its engine speed.

With line printers, the speed ratings can come close to actual throughput. The major slowdowns for line printers occur only when lines are short and the printhead changes direction often and when the printhead travels long distances down the sheet without printing.

With page printers, the difference between theory and reality can be dramatic. Because of their high resolutions, line printers require huge amounts of data to make bit-image graphics. The transfer time alone for this information can be substantial. Page printers suffer this penalty most severely when your PC rasterizes the image and sets the entire page as a bit image. On the other hand, if the printer rasterizes the image, the processing time for the rasterization process adds to the print time. In either case, it is rare indeed for pages to be prepared as quickly as the engine can print them when graphics are involved. Instead of pages per minute, throughput may shift to minutes per page.

Modes

Some printers operate in a number of different modes that trade print quality for speed. These modes vary with the technology used by the printer.

Three of the most common modes for impact dot-matrix printers are draft, near letter quality, and letter quality. *Draft mode* delivers the highest speed and the lowest quality. To achieve the highest possible speed, in draft mode the printers move their printheads faster than they can fire to print at each dot position on the paper. Typically in draft mode, these printers can blacken only every other dot. The thinly laid dots give text and graphics a characteristic gray look in draft mode. *Near letter quality mode* slows the printhead so that text characters can be rendered without the machine-gun separated-dots look of draft mode. Because the dot density is higher, characters appear fully black and are easier to read. *Letter quality mode* slows printing further, often using two or more passes to give as much detail as possible to each individual character. The printer concentrates on detail work, adding serifs and variable line weights to characters to make them look more like commercially printed text.

Inkjet printers aren't bothered by the mechanical limitations of impact printers, so you need not worry so much about dot density at higher speeds. Nevertheless, the time required to form each jet of ink they print constrains the speed of the printhead. Most inkjet printers operate at the maximum speed the jet-forming process allows all the time. However, your choice of printing mode still affects output speed. Only the modes are different; typically, you choose between black-and-white and color, and the speed difference between them can be substantial. Most color inkjet designs have fewer nozzles for color ink than they do for black ink. Typically, each of the three primary colors will have one-third the number of nozzles as black. As a result, the printhead must make three times as many passes to render color in the same detail as black, so color mode is often one-third the speed as black-and-white printing.

The speed relationship between color and black-and-white printing varies widely, however. In comparing the speeds of two printers, you must be careful to compare the same mode. The most relevant mode is the one you're likely to use most. If you do mostly text, then black-and-white speed should be the most important measure to you. If you plan to do extensive color printing, compare color speeds.

Although many bit-image printers don't allow you to directly alter their resolution, you can accelerate printing by making judicious choices through software. A lower resolution requires less time for rendering the individual dots, so in graphics mode, choosing a lower resolution can dramatically accelerate print speed. Windows allows you to choose the resolution at which your printer operates as part of the Graphics tab in its Printer Properties menu, as shown in Figure 24.1.

FIGURE 24.1

Selecting printer resolution under Windows.

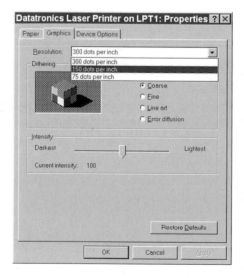

Selecting a lower resolution can dramatically lower the time required to print a page because it reduces rendering time. At low resolutions, graphics printing speed can approach engine speed. The downside is, of course, you might not like the rough look of what you print.

Quality

The look of what you get on paper isn't completely in your control. By selecting the resolution your printer uses, you can raise speed and lower quality. But every printer faces a limit to the maximum quality it can produce. This limit is enforced by the design of the printer and its mechanical construction. The cause and measurement of these constraints vary with the printer technology, whether your machine is a line printer or page printer.

Line Printers

Line printers have two distinct operating modes. They can accept text as ASCII characters, select their bit-patterns from an internal character generator, and print them as a single sequence on each line, one line at a time. Alternately, in their graphics modes, they accept bit-image data from your PC and simply render the bit-patterns chosen by your PC on paper. Those bit-patterns can include both text characters and graphics. Although the printer renders one line at a time in graphics mode, it has no idea what it is printing on each line or how sequential lines relate to one another, even whether tall characters span two or more lines. Your PC keeps track of all of that.

The issues involved in determining the on-paper quality of the printer depend on the operating mode. In text mode, the quality of the characters printed by any line printer is determined by three chief factors—the number of dots in the matrix that makes up each individual character, the size of the dots in the matrix, and the addressability of the printer. The denser the matrix (the more dots in a given area) and the smaller the dots, the better the characters look. Higher addressability allows the printer to place dots on paper with greater precision.

The minimal character matrix of any printer measures 5 by 7 (horizontal by vertical) dots and is just sufficient to render all the uppercase and lowercase letters of the alphabet unambiguously—and not aesthetically. The dots are big and they look disjointed. Worse, the minimal matrix is too small to let descending characters ("g," "j," "p," "q," and "y") droop below the general line of type and makes them look cramped and scrunched up. Rarely do you encounter this minimal level of quality today except in the cheapest, close-out printers and machines designed solely for high-speed printing of drafts.

The minimum matrix used by most commercial impact dot-matrix printers measures 9 by 9 dots, a readable arrangement but still somewhat inelegant in a world accustomed to printed text. Newer 18- and 24-pin impact dot-matrix printers can form characters with 12 by 24 to 24 by 24 matrices. Inkjet printers may form characters in text mode from matrices measuring as large as 72 by 120 dots.

In the shift from character mode to graphics mode, issues of the character matrix disappear. The chief determinants of quality become addressability and resolution.

As with computer displays, the resolution and addressability of any kind of printer are often are confused. Resolution indicates the reality of what you see on paper; addressability indicates the more abstract notion of dot placement. When resolution is mentioned, particularly with impact dot-matrix printers, most of the time addressability is intended. A printer may be able to address any position on the paper with an accuracy of, say, 1/120 inch. If an impact printwire is larger than 1/120 inch in diameter, however, the machine never is able to render detail as small as 1/120 inch. Inkjet printer mechanisms do a good job of matching addressability and resolution, but those efforts easily get undone when you use the wrong printing medium. If inkjet ink gets absorbed into paper fibers, it spreads out and obscures the excellent resolution many of these machines can produce.

Getting addressability to approach resolution is a challenge for the designer of the impact dot-matrix printer (and one of the many reasons this technology has fallen from favor). The big dots made by the wide printwires blurs out the detail. Better quality impact dot-matrix printers have more printwires, and they are smaller. Also, the ribbon that is inserted between the wires and paper blurs each dot hammered out by an impact dot-matrix printer. Mechanical limits also constrain the on-paper resolution of impact machines.

Impact dot-matrix printers use a variety of tricks to improve their often marginal print quality. Often, even bidirectional printers slow down to single-direction operation when quality counts. To increase dot density, they retrace each line two or more times, shifting the paper half the width of a dot vertically, between passes, filling in the space between dots. Unidirectional operation helps ensure accurate placement of each dot in each pass.

Page Printers

With non-impact bit-image printers, resolution and addressability usually are the same, although some use techniques to improve apparent resolution without altering the number of dots they put in a given area.

Resolution Enhancement Technology, or ReT, improves the apparent quality of on-paper printing within the limits of resolution; it can make printing look sharper than would ordinarily be possible. The enhancement technology, introduced by Hewlett-Packard in March 1990 with its LaserJet III line of printers, works by altering the size of toner dots at the edges of characters and diagonal lines to reduce the jagged steps inherent in any matrix bit-image printing technique. Using ReT, the actual on-paper resolution remains at the rated value of the print engine—for example 300 or 600 dpi—but the optimized dot size makes the printing appear sharper.

Increasing resolution is more than a matter of refining the design of print engine mechanics. The printer's electronics must be adapted to match including adding more memory—substantially more. Memory requirements increase as the square of the linear dot density. Doubling the number dots per inch quadruples memory needs. At high resolutions, the memory needs for rasterizing the image can become prodigious—about 14MB for a 1,200 dpi image. Table 24.1 lists the raster needs for common monochrome printer resolutions.

TABLE 24.1   Raster Memory Size for Monochrome Printer Resolutions

Resolution	Dots	Bytes
75 dpi	450,000	56,250
150 dpi	1,800,000	225,000
300 dpi	7,200,000	900,000
360 dpi	10,368,000	1,296,000
600 dpi	28,800,000	3,600,000
720 dpi	41,472,000	5,184,000
1,200 dpi	115,200,000	14,400,000
1,440 dpi	165,888,000	20,736,000

Adding color of course increases the memory requirements. Fortunately, the color bit depth used by common printer technologies doesn't impose the same extreme demands as monitors. A printer has only a few colors corresponding to the hues of its inks, and except for continuous-tone technologies such as dye-diffusion, the range of each color usually is limited to on or off. Thankfully, color resolutions are generally substantially lower than monochrome, defined by the size of the color super-pixels rather than individual dots. In any case, the raster memory requirements of a color printer are substantially higher than monochrome.

Note that when printing text, page printers may operate in a character-mapped mode, so memory usage is not as great. Even with minimal memory, a printer can store a full-page image in ASCII or a similar code, one byte per letter as well as the definitions for the characters of several fonts. In this mode, it generates the individual dots of each character as the page is scanned through the printer.

Moving to higher resolutions makes other demands on a printer as well. For example, in laser printers finer resolutions require improved toner formulations because at high resolutions, the size of toner particles limits sharpness much as the size of printwires limits impact dot-matrix resolution. With higher resolution laser printers, it becomes increasingly important to get the right toner, particularly if you have toner cartridges refilled.

The wrong toner limits resolution just as a fuzzy ribbon limits the quality of impact printer output.

Color

Printers start with the primaries when it comes to color. They start with inks corresponding to the three primary colors—red, yellow, and blue. If you want anything beyond those, the printer must find some way of mixing them together. This mixing can be physical or optical.

The physical mixing of colors requires that two or more colors of ink actually mix together while they are wet. Printer inks are, however, designed to dry rapidly so the colors to be mixed must be applied simultaneously or in quick succession. Few printers rely on the physical mixing of inks to increase the number of colors they produce.

Optical mixing takes place in either of two ways. One color of ink can be applied over another (that has already dried) or the colors can be applied adjacent to one another.

Applying multiple layers of color requires that the inks be to some degree transparent as a truly opaque ink would obscure the first color to be applied. Most modern printer inks are transparent, which allows them to be used on transparencies for overhead projection as well as paper. The exact hue of a transparent ink is, of course, dependent on the color of the medium it is applied to.

Optical mixing also takes place when dots of two or more colors are intermixed. If the dots are so close together that the eye cannot individually resolve each one, their colors blend together on the retina, blending the individual hues together. Most PC color printers take advantage of this kind of optical mixing by dithering.

Three- Versus Four-Color Printers

Color primaries in printing aren't so simple as the familiar threesome. To achieve better color reproduction, printers use a skewed set of primary colors—magenta instead of red, cyan instead of blue, and plain old ordinary yellow. Even this mix is so far from perfect that when all are combined, they yield something that's often far from black. Consequently, better printers include black in their primary colors.

Black, in fact, may play two roles in a color printer. Many inkjet printers allow you to choose between black-and-white and color operation as simply as swapping ink cartridges. In these machines, black is treated as a separate hue that cannot be mixed in blends with the three color primaries. These *three-color printers* render colors only from the three primaries even though some machines can print pure black when using a suitable black-only ink cartridge. The approximation of black made from the three primaries is termed *composite black* and often has a off-color cast. Four color printers put black on the same footing as the three primary hues and mix with all four together. This four-color printing technique gives superior blacks, purer grays, and greater depth to all darker shades.

To further increase the range of pure colors possible with a printer, manufacturers are adding more colors of ink. For example, some new Hewlett-Packard inkjet printers such as the DeskJet 693C offer the option of replacing the black ink cartridge with a second three-color ink cartridge, bringing the total number of primary hues to six. This greater range in primaries translates into more realistic reproduction of photographs with less need for other color-enhancing techniques, such as dithering.

Dithering

Color televisions do an excellent job with their three primaries and paint a nearly infinite spectrum. But the television tube has a luxury most printers lack. The television can modulate its electron beam and change its intensity. Most printers are stuck with a single intensity for each color. As a result, the basic range of most printers is four pure colors and seven when using mixtures, blending magenta and blue to make violet, magenta and yellow for orange, and blue and yellow for green. Count the background color of the paper being printed upon, and the basic range of most color printers is eight hues.

Commercial color printing faces the same problem of trying to render a wide spectrum from four primary colors. To extend the range of printing presses, graphic artists make color halftones. They break an image into dots photographically using a screen. Using special photographic techniques (or more often today, a computer), they can vary the size of the dot with the intensity of the color.

Most computer printers cannot vary the size of their dots. To achieve a halftone effect, they use *dithering*. In dithering, colors beyond the range of pure hues of which a printer is capable are rendered in patterns of primary-colored dots. Instead of each printed dot representing a single pixel of an image, dithering uses a small array of dots to make a single pixel. These multiple-dot pixels are termed *super-pixels*. By varying the number of dots that actually get printed with a given color of ink in the super-pixel matrix, the printer can vary the perceived intensity of the color.

The problem with dithering is that it degrades the perceived resolution of the color image. The resolution is limited by the size of the super-pixels rather than the individual dots. For example, to attempt to render an image in true color (8 bits per primary), the printer must use super-pixels measuring 8 by 8 dots. The resolution falls by an equivalent factor. A printer with 600 dpi resolution yields a color image with 75 dpi resolution.

Drivers

Getting good color with dithering is more art than science. The choice of dithering pattern determines how smooth colors can be rendered. A bad choice of dithering pattern often results in a moiré pattern overlaid on your printed images or wide gaps between super-pixels. Moreover, colors don't mix the same on screen and on paper. The two media often use entirely different color spaces (RGB for your monitor, CYMK for your printer), requiring a translation step between them. Inks only aspire to be pure colors. The primary colors may land far from the mark, and color blended from them may be strange, indeed.

Your printer driver can adjust for all of these issues. How well the programmer charged with writing the driver does his job is the final determinant in the color quality your printer produces. A good driver can create photo-quality images from an inkjet printer, but a bad driver can make deplorable pictures even when using the same underlying print engine. Unfortunately, the quality of a printer's driver isn't quantified on the specifications sheet. You can only judge it by looking at the output of a printer. For highest quality, however, you'll always want driver software written for your particular model of printer, not one that your printer emulates. Moreover, you'll want to get the latest driver. You may want to periodically cruise the Web site of your printer maker to catch driver updates as they come out.

Print Engines

The actual mechanism that forms an image on paper is called the *print engine*. Each uses a somewhat different physical principle to put ink on paper. Although each technology has its strengths, weaknesses, and idiosyncrasies, you might not be able to tell the difference between the pages they print. Careful attention to detail has pushed quality up to a level where the paper rather than the printer is the chief limit on resolution, and color comes close to photographic, falling short only on the depth that only a thick gelatin coating make possible. In making those images, however, the various print engine technologies work differently at different speeds at different noise levels and with different requirements. These differences can make one style of print engine a better choice for your particular application than the others.

Impact Dot-Matrix

The modern minimal printer uses an impact dot-matrix print engine. The heart of the machine is a mechanical printhead that shuttles back and forth across the width of the paper. A number of thin printwires act as the hammers that squeeze ink from a fabric or Mylar ribbon to paper.

In most impact dot-matrix printers, a seemingly complex but efficient mechanism controls each of the printwires. The printwire normally is held away from the ribbon and paper, and against the force of a spring, by a strong permanent magnet. The magnet is wrapped with a coil of wire that forms an electromagnet, wound so that its polarity is the opposite of that of the permanent magnet. To fire the printwire against the ribbon and paper, this electromagnet is energized (under computer control, of course), and its field neutralizes that of the permanent magnet. Without the force of the permanent magnetic holding the printwire back, the spring forcefully jabs the printwire out against ribbon, squeezing ink onto the paper. After the printwire makes its dot, the electromagnet is de-energized and the permanent magnet pulls the printwire back to its idle position, ready to fire again. Figure 24.2 shows a conceptual view of the mechanism associated with one printhead wire.

FIGURE 24.2

Conceptual view of impact dot-matrix printhead mechanism.

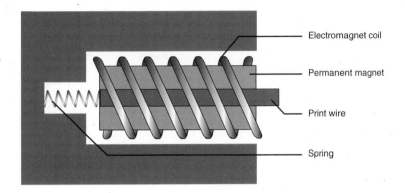

Electromagnet coil

Permanent magnet

Print wire

Spring

The two-magnets-and-spring approach is designed with one primary purpose—to hold the printwire away from the paper (and out of harm's way) when no power is supplied to the printer and the printhead. The complexity is justified by the protection it affords the delicate printwires.

The printhead of a dot-matrix printer is made from a number of these printwire mechanisms. Most first-generation personal computer printers and many current machines use nine wires arrayed in a vertical column. To produce high quality, the second generation of these machines increased the number of printwires to 18 or 24. These often are arranged in parallel rows with the printwires vertically staggered, although some machines use different arrangements. Because the larger number of printwires fit into the same space (and print at the same character height), they can pack more detail into what they print. Because they are often finer than the printwires of lesser endowed machines, the multitude of printwires also promises higher resolution.

No matter the number of printwires, the printhead moves horizontally as a unit across the paper to print a line of characters or graphics. Each wire fires as necessary to form the individual characters or the appropriate dots for the graphic image. The impact of each wire is precisely timed so that it falls on exactly the right position in the matrix. The wires fire on the fly; the printhead never pauses until it reaches the other side of the paper.

A major factor in determining the printing speed of dot-matrix machine is the time required between successive strikes of each printwire. Physical laws of motion limit the acceleration each printwire can achieve in ramming toward the paper and back. Thus, the time needed to retract and re-actuate each printwire puts a physical limit on how rapidly the printhead can travel across the paper. It cannot sweep past the next dot position before each of the printwires inside it is ready to fire. If the printhead travels too fast, dot positioning (and character shapes) would become rather haphazard.

To speed up operation, some impact dot-matrix machines print bidirectionally, rattling out one row from left to right then the next row right to left. This mode of operation saves the time that would ordinarily be wasted when the carriage returns to the left side of the page to start the next line. Of course, the printer must have sufficient memory to store a full line of text so that it can be read out backwards.

Adding color to an impact dot-matrix printer is relatively straightforward. The color the impact printer actually prints is governed by the ink in or on its ribbon. Although some manufacturers build color impact printers using multiple ribbons, the most successful (and least expensive) designs used special multi-colored ribbons lined with three or four bands corresponding to the primary colors. To change colors, the printer shifts the ribbon vertically so a differently hued band lies in front of the printwires. Most of the time, the printer will render a row in one color, shift ribbon colors, and then go across the same row in a different color. The extra mechanism required is simple and inexpensive, costing as little as $50 extra. (Of course, the color ribbon costs more and does not last as long as its monochrome equivalent.)

Although the ribbons used by most of these color printers are soaked with three or four colors of ink, they can achieve seven colors on paper by combining color pairs. For example, laying a layer of blue over a layer of yellow results in an approximation of green.

As with their typewriter progenitors, all impact dot-matrix printers have a number of desirable qualities. Owing to their heritage of more than a century of engineering refinement, they represent a mature technology. Their designs and functions are relatively straightforward and familiar.

Most impact printers can spread their output across any medium that ink has an affinity for, including any paper you might have lying around your home, from onion skin to thin cardstock. Although both impact and non-impact technologies have been developed to the point that either can produce high quality or high speed output, impact technology takes the lead when you share one of the most common business needs, making multi-part forms. Impact printers can hammer an impression not just through a ribbon, but through several sheets of paper as well. Slide a carbon between the sheets or, better yet, treat the paper for non-carbon duplicates, and you get multiple, guaranteed-identical copies with a single pass through the mechanism. For a number of business applications—for example, the generation of charge receipts—exact carbon copies are a necessity and impact printing is an absolute requirement.

Impact printers reveal their typewriter heritage in another way. The hammer bashing against the ribbon and paper makes noise, a sharp staccato rattle that is high in amplitude and rich in high frequency components, penetrating and bothersome as a dental drive or angry horde of giant, hungry mosquitoes. Typically, the impact printer rattles and prattles louder than most normal conversational tones, and it is more obnoxious than an argument. The higher speed the impact printer, the higher the pitch of the noise and the more penetrating it becomes.

Some printer makers have toned down their boisterous scribes admirably; some printers as fast as 780 characters per second are as quiet as 55 dB, about the level of a quiet PC fan. But you still want to leave the room when an inexpensive impact printer (the best-selling of all printers) grinds through its assignment.

Inkjets

Today's most popular personal printers use inkjet print engines. The odd name "inkjet" actually describes the printing technology. If it conjures up images of the Nautilus and giant squid or a B-52 spraying out blue fluid instead of a fluffy white contrail, your mind is on the right track. Inkjet printers are electronic squids that squirt out ink like miniature jet engines fueled in full color. Although this technology sounds unlikely— a printer that sprays droplets of ink onto paper—it works well enough to deliver image sharpness on par with most other output technologies.

In essence, the inkjet printer is a line printer, little more than a dot-matrix printer with the hammer impact removed. Instead of a hammer pounding ink onto paper, the inkjet flings it into place from tiny *nozzles*, each one corresponding to a printwire of the impact dot-matrix printer. The motive force can be an electromagnet or, as is more likely today, a piezoelectric crystal (a thin crystal that bends when electricity is applied across it). A sharp, digital pulse of electricity causes the crystal to twitch and force ink through the nozzle into its flight to paper. The types of inkjet engines are commonplace: thermal, piezoelectric, and phase-change.

At heart, the basic technology of all three kinds of inkjets is the same. The machines rely on the combination of the small orifice in the nozzle and the surface tension of liquid ink to prevent a constant dibble from the jets. Instead of oozing out, the ink puckers around the hole in the inkjet the same way that droplets of water bead up on a waxy surface. The tiny ink droplets scrunch together rather than spread out or flow out the nozzle because the attraction of the molecules in the ink (or water) is stronger than the force of gravity. The inkjet engine needs to apply some force to break the surface tension and force the ink out, and that's where the differences in inkjet technologies arise.

Thermal Inkjets

The most common inkjet technology is called *thermal* because it uses heat inside its printhead to boil a tiny quantity of water-based ink. Boiling produces tiny bubbles of steam that can balloon out from the nozzle orifices of the printhead. The thermal mechanism carefully controls the bubble formation. It can hold the temperature in the nozzle at just the right point to keep the ink bubble from bursting. Then, when it needs to make a dot on the paper, the printhead warms the nozzle, the bubble bursts, and the ink sprays from the nozzle to the paper to make a dot. Because the bubbles are so tiny, little heat or time is required to make and burst the bubbles; the printhead can do it hundreds of times in a second.

This obscure process was discovered by a research specialist at Canon way back in 1977, but developing it into a practical printer took about seven years. The first mass-marketed PC inkjet printer was the Hewlett-Packard ThinkJet, introduced in May 1984, which used the thermal inkjet process (which HP traces back to a 1979 discovery by HP researcher John Vaught). This single-color printer delivered 96 dots per inch resolution at a speed of 150 characters per second, about on par with the impact dot-matrix printers available at the same time. The technology—not to mention speed and resolution—have improved substantially since then. The proprietary name *BubbleJet* used by Canon for its inkjet printer derives from this technology, although thermal-bubble design is also used in printers manufactured by DEC, Hewlett-Packard, Lexmark, and Texas Instruments.

The heat that makes the bubbles is the primary disadvantage of the thermal inkjet system. It slowly wears out the printhead, requiring you to periodically replace it to keep the printer working at its best. Some manufacturers minimize this problem by combining their printers' nozzles with their ink cartridges so that when you add more ink you automatically replace the nozzles. With this design, you never have to replace the nozzles, at least independently, because you do it every time you add more ink.

Because nozzles ordinarily last much longer than the supply in any reasonable inkjet reservoir, other manufacturers make the nozzles a separately replaceable part. The principle difference between these two systems amounts to nothing more than how you do the maintenance. Although the combined nozzles-and-ink approach would seem to be more expensive, the difference in the ultimate cost of using either system is negligible.

Piezo Inkjets

The alternative inkjet design uses the squirtgun approach—mechanical pressure to squeeze the ink from the printhead nozzles. Instead of a plunger pump, however, these printers usually use special nozzles that squash down and squeeze out the ink. These nozzles are made from a *piezoelectric crystal*, a material that bends when a voltage is applied across it. When the printer zaps the piezoelectric nozzle with a voltage jolt, the entire nozzle flexes inward, squeezing the ink from inside and out the nozzle, spraying it out to the paper. This piezoelectric nozzle mechanism is used primarily by Epson in its Stylus line of inkjet printers, except for the Stylus 300.

The chief benefit of this design, according to Epson, is a longer-lived printhead. The company also claims it yields cleaner dots on paper. Bursting bubbles may make halos of ink splatter, but the liquid droplets from the piezo printers form more solid dots.

Phase-Change Inkjets

The third twist on inkjet technology concentrates on the ink more than its motion. Instead of using solvent-based inks that are fixed (that is, that dry) by evaporation or adsorption into the print medium, they use inks that harden, changing phase from liquid to solid. Because of this phase-change, this form of inkjet is often called a *phase-change inkjet.*

Phase-change inkjet printers melt sticks or chunks of wax-based ink into a liquid, which they then spray on to paper or other printing medium. The tiny droplets, no longer heated, rapidly cool on the medium, returning to its solid state. Because of the use of solid ink, this kind of printer is sometimes called a solid inkjet printer.

The first printer to use phase-change technology was the Howtek Pixelmaster in the late 1980s. Marketed mostly as a specialty machine, the Howtek made little impression in the industry. Phase-change technology received its major push from Tektronix with its introduction of its Phaser III PXi in 1991. Tektronix refined phase-change technology to achieve smoother images and operation. Where the Pixelmaster used plastic-based inks that left little lumps on paper and sometimes clogged the printhead, the Phaser III used wax-based inks and a final processing step, a cold fuser, which flattened the cold ink droplets with a steel roller as the paper rolls out of the printer.

No matter the technology, all inkjet printers are able to make sharper images than impact dot-matrix technology because they do not use ribbons, which would blur their images. The on-paper quality of an inkjet can equal and often better that of more expensive laser printers. Even inexpensive models claim resolutions as high or higher than laser printers, say about 720 dots per inch.

Another advantage of the inkjet is color. Adding color is another simple elaboration. Most color impact printers race their printheads across each line several times, shifting between different ribbon colors on each pass, for example, printing a yellow row, then magenta, then cyan, and finally black. Inkjet printers typically handle three or four colors in a single pass of the printhead, although the height of colored columns often is shorter.

The liquid ink of inkjet printers can be a virtue when it comes to color. The inks remain fluid enough even after they have been sprayed on paper to physically blend together. This gives color inkjet printers the ability to actually mix their primary colors together to create intermediary tones. The range of color quality from inkjet printers is wide. The best yield some of the brightest, most saturated colors available from any technology. The vast majority, however, cannot quite produce a true-color palette.

Because inkjets are non-impact printers, they are much quieter than ordinary dot-matrix engines. Without hammers pounding ink paper like a myopic carpenter chasing an elusive nail, inkjet printers sound almost serene in their everyday work. The tiny droplets of ink rustle so little air they make not a whisper. About the only sound you hear from them is the carriage coursing back and forth.

As mechanical line printers, however, inkjet engines have an inherent speed disadvantage when compared to page printers. Although they deliver comparable speeds on text when they use only black ink, color printing slow them considerably, to one-third speed or less.

The underlying reason for this slowdown is that most color inkjets don't treat colors equally and favor black. After all, you'll likely print black more often than any color or blend. A common Lexmark color inkjet printhead illustrates the point. It prints columns of color only 16 dots high, but black columns are 56 dots high (see Figure 24.3). Printing a line of color the same height as one in black requires multiple passes even though the printer can spray all three colors with each pass.

FIGURE 24.3

Printheads from a color inkjet printer showing nozzle placement.

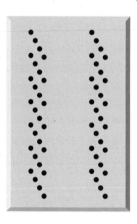 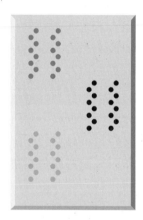

Blank ink nozzle plate　　　　Color ink nozzle plate

Inkjet technology also has disadvantages. Although for general use you can consider them to be plain-paper printers, able to make satisfactory images on any kind of stock that will feed through the mechanism, to yield their highest quality, inkjets require special paper with controlled absorbency. You also have to be careful to print on the correct side of the paper because most paper stocks are treated for absorption only on one side. If you try to get by using cheap paper that is too porous, the inks wick away into a blur. If the paper is too glossy, the wet ink can smudge.

Early inkjet printers also had the reputation, often deserved, of clogging regularly. To avoid such problems, better inkjets have built-in routines that clean the nozzles with each use. These cleaning procedures do, however, waste expensive ink. Most nozzles now are self-sealing so that when they are not used air cannot get to the ink. Some manufacturers even combine the inkjet and ink supply into one easily changeable module. If, however, you pack an inkjet away without properly purging and cleaning it first, it is not likely to work when you resurrect it months later.

Laser

The one revolution that has changed the faces of both offices and forests around the world was the photocopier. Trees plummet by the millions to provide fodder for the duplicate, triplicate, megaplicate. Today's non-impact, bit-image laser printer owes its life to this technology.

At heart, the laser printer principle is simple. Some materials react to light in strange ways. Selenium and some complex organic compounds modify their electrical conductivity in response to exposure to light. Both copiers and laser printers capitalize on this photo-electric effect by focusing an optical image on a photo-conductive drum that has been given a static electrical charge. The charge drains away from the conductive areas that have been struck by light but persist in the dark areas. A special pigment called a *toner* is then spread across the drum, and the toner sticks to the charged areas. A roller squeezes paper against the drum to transfer the pigment to the paper. The pigment gets bonded to the paper by heating or "fusing" it.

The laser printer actually evolved from the photocopier. Rather than the familiar electrostatic Xerox machine, however, the true ancestor of the laser printer was a similar competing process called electro-photography, which used a bright light to capture an image and make it visible with a fine carbon-based toner. The process was developed during the 1960s by Keizo Yamaji at Canon. The first commercial application of the technology, called *New Process* to distinguish it from the old process (xerography), was a Canon photocopier released in 1968.

The first true laser printer was a demonstration unit made by Canon in 1975 based on a modified photocopier. The first commercial PC laser printer came in 1984 when Hewlett-Packard introduced its first LaserJet, which was based on the Canon CX engine. At heart, it and all later lasers use the same process, a kind of heat-set light-inspired offset printing.

The magic in a laser printer is forming the image by making a laser beam scan back and forth across the imaging drum. The trick, well known to stage magicians, is to use mirrors. A small rotating mirror reflect the laser across the drum, tracing each scan line across it. The drum rotates to advance to the next scan line, synchronized to the flying beam of laser light. To make the light-and-dark pattern of the image, the laser beam is modulated on and off. It's rapidly switched on for light areas, off for dark areas, one minuscule dot at a time to form a bit image.

The major variations on laser printing differ only in the light beam and how it is modulated. *LCD-shutter printers*, for example, put an electronic shutter (or an array of them) between a constant light source (which need not be a laser) and the imaging drum to modulate the beam. *LED printers* modulate ordinary light-emitting diodes as their optical source. In any case, these machines rely on the same electro-photographic process as the laser printer to carry out the actual printing process.

The basic laser printer mechanism requires more than just a beam and a drum. In fact, it involves several drums or rollers, as many as six in a single-color printer and more in color machines. Each has a specific role in the printing process. Figure 24.4 shows the layout of the various rollers.

FIGURE 24.4
*Conceptual view of
the laser printer
mechanism.*

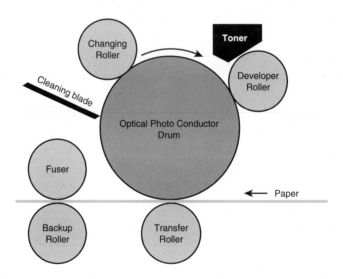

The imaging drum, often termed the OPC for optical photoconductor, first must be charged before it will accept an image. A special roller called the *charging roller* applies the electrostatic charge uniformly across the OPC.

After the full width of an area of the OPC gets its charge, it rotates in front of the modulated light beam. As the beam scans across the OPC drum and the drum turns, the system creates an electrostatic replica of the page to be printed.

To form a visible image, a *developing roller* then dusts the OPC drum with particles of toner. The light-struck areas with an electrostatic charge attract and hold the toner against the drum. The unexposed parts of the drum do not.

The printer rolls the paper between the OPC drum and a *transfer roller*, which has a strong electrostatic charge that attracts the toner off the drum. Because the paper is in between the transfer roller and the OPC drum, the toner collects on the paper in accord with the pattern that was formed by the modulated laser. At this point, only a slight electrostatic charge holds the toner to the paper.

To make the image permanent, the printer squeezes the paper between a *fuser* and *backup roller*. As the paper passes through, the printer heats the fuser to a high temperature—on the order of 350 degrees Fahrenheit (200 degrees Celsius). The heat of the fuser and the pressure from the backup roller melt the toner and stick it permanently on the paper. The completed page rolls out the printer.

Meanwhile, the OPC drum continues to spin, wiping the already-printed area against a *cleaning blade*, which scrapes any leftover toner from it. As the drum rotates around to the charging roller again, the process repeats. Early lasers used OPC drums large enough to hold an entire single-page image. Modern machines use smaller rollers that form the image as a continuous process.

Although individual manufacturers may alter this basic layout to fit a particular package or to refine the process, the technology used by all laser machines is essentially the same. At a given resolution level, the results produced by most mechanisms is about the same, too. You need an eye loupe to see the differences. The major difference is that manufacturers have progressively refined both the mechanism and electronics to produce higher resolutions. Basic laser printer resolution starts at 300 dots per inch. The mainstream is now at the 600 dpi level. The best PC-oriented laser printers boast 1,200 dpi resolution.

In most lasers, the resolution level is fixed primarily by the electronics inside the printer. The most important part of the control circuitry is the *Raster Image Processor*, also known as the RIP. The job of the RIP is to translate the string of characters or other printing commands into the bit image that the printer transfers to paper. In effect, the RIP works like a video board, interpreting drawing commands (a single letter in a print stream is actually a drawing command to print that letter), computing the position of each dot on the page, and pushing the appropriate value into the printer's memory. The memory of the printer is arranged in a raster just like the raster of a video screen, and one memory cell—a single bit in the typical black-and-white laser printer—corresponds to each dot position on paper.

The RIP itself may by design limit a laser printer to a given resolution. Some early laser printers made this constraint into an advantage, allowing resolution upgrades through aftermarket products that replaced the printer's internal RIP and controlled the printer and its laser through a *video input*. The video input earns its name because its signal is applied directly to the light source in the laser in raster scanned form (like a television image), bypassing most of the printer's electronics. The add-in processor can modulate the laser at higher rates to create higher resolutions.

Moving from 300 dpi to 600 dpi and 1,200 dpi means more than changing the RIP and adding memory, however. The higher resolutions also demand improved toner formulations because at high resolutions, the size of toner particles limits sharpness much as the size of printwires limits impact dot-matrix resolution. With higher resolution laser printers, it becomes increasingly important to get the right toner, particularly if you have toner cartridges refilled. The wrong toner limits resolution just as a fuzzy ribbon limits the quality of impact printer output.

Adding color to a laser printer is more than dumping a few more colors of toner. The laser must separately image each of its three or four primary colors and transfer the toner corresponding to each color to the paper. The imaging process for each color requires forming an entire image by passing it past the OPC drum. Forming a complete image consequently requires three or four passes of the drum.

Exactly what constitutes a pass varies among manufacturers. Most color laser printers use three or four distinct passes of each sheet of paper. The paper rolls around the drum and makes four complete turns. Each color gets imaged separately on the drum and then separately transferred to the sheet. The printer wipes the drum clean between passes.

So-called "one-pass" printing, pioneered by Hewlett-Packard, still requires the drum to make four complete passes as each color gets separately scanned on the drum and toner is dusted on the drum separately for each color. The paper, however, only passes once through the machine to accept the full color image at once and then to have all four colors fused together onto the paper. The first three colors merely transfer to the drum. After the last color—black—gets coated on the drum, the printer runs the paper through and transfers the toner to it. The paper thus makes a single pass through the printer, hence the "one-pass" name.

This single-pass laser technology yields no real speed advantage. The photoconductor drum still spins around the same number of times as a four-pass printer. The speed at which the drum turns and the number of turns it makes determines engine speed, so the one-pass process doesn't make a significant performance increase.

The advantage to one-pass color laser printing comes in the registration of the separate color images. With conventional color laser systems, the alignment of the paper must be critically maintained for all four passes for all the colors to properly line up. With the one-pass system, paper alignment is not a problem. Only the drum needs to maintain its alignment, which is easy to do because it is part of the mechanism rather than an interloper from the outside world.

No matter the number of passes, adding color in laser printing subtracts speed. In general, color laser speed falls to one-quarter the monochrome speed of a similar engine because of the requirement of four passes. (With three-pass printing, speed falls to one-third the monochrome rate). For example, a printer rated at 12 pages per minute in monochrome will deliver about 3 ppm in color. Even allowing for this slowdown, however, color lasers are usually faster than other color page printers. They are also often quieter. Compared to thermal-wax transfer printers, a popular high-quality color technology, they are also economical because a laser uses toner only for the actual printed image. Thermal wax machines need a full page of ink for each page printed no matter the density of the image.

Direct Thermal

A printer that works on the same principle as a wood-burning set might seem better for a Boy Scout than an on-the-go executive, but today's easiest-to-tote printers do exactly that—the equivalent of charring an image on paper. Thermal printers use the same electrical heating of the word-burner, a resistance that heats up with the flow of current. In the case of the thermal printer, however, the resistance element is tiny and heats and cools quickly, in a fraction of a second. As with inkjets, the thermal printhead is the equivalent of that of a dot-matrix printer, except that it heats rather than hits.

Thermal printers do not, however, actually char the paper on which they print. Getting paper that hot would be dangerous, precariously close to combustion (although it might let the printer do double-duty as a cigarette lighter). Instead, thermal printers use special, thermally sensitive paper that turns from white to near-black at a moderate temperature.

Thermal technology is ideal for portable printers because few moving parts are involved; only the printhead moves, nothing inside it. No springs and wires means no jamming. The tiny, resistive elements require little power to heat, actually less than is needed to fire a wire in an impact printer. Thermal printers can be lightweight, quiet, and reliable. They can even run on batteries.

The special paper they require is one drawback. Not only is it costly (because it is, after all, special paper), but also it feels funny and is prone to discolor if it is inadvertently heated to too high a temperature. The paper cannot tell the difference between a hot printhead and a cozy corner in the sun.

Gradually, thermal printers are becoming special application machines. Inkjets have many of the same virtues and more reasonable paper; therefore, low-cost inkjets are invading the territory of the thermal machines.

Thermal Transfer

Engineers have made thermal technology more independent of the paper or printing medium by moving the image-forming substance from the paper to a carrier or ribbon. Instead of changing a characteristic of the paper, these machines transfer pigment or dyes from the carrier to the paper. The heat from the printhead melts the binder holding the ink to the carrier, allowing the ink to transfer to the paper. On the cool paper, the binder again binds the ink in place. In that the binder is often a wax, these machines are often called thermal-wax transfer printers.

These machines produce the richest, purest, and most even and saturated color of any color print technology. Because the thermal elements have no moving parts, they can be made almost arbitrarily small to yield high resolutions. Current thermal-wax print engines achieve resolutions similar to those of laser printers. However, due to exigencies of print-head designs, the top resolution of these printers extends only in one dimension (vertical). Top thermal-wax printers achieve 300 dots per inch horizontally and 600 dots per inch vertically.

Compared to other technologies, however, thermal-wax engines are slow and wasteful. They are slow because the thermal printing elements must have a chance to cool off before advancing the 1/300 of an inch to the next line on the paper. And they are wasteful because they use wide ink transfer sheets, pure colors supported in a wax-based medium clinging to a plastic film base—sort of like a Mylar typewriter ribbon with a gland condition. Each of the primary colors to be printed on each page requires a swath of inked transfer sheet as large as the sheet of paper to be printed—that is nearly four feet of transfer sheet for one page. Consequently, printing a full-color page can be expensive, typically measured in dollars rather than cents per page.

Because thermal-wax printers are not a mass market item and each manufacturer uses its own designs for both mechanism and supplies, you usually are restricted to one source for inksheets—the printer manufacturer. Although that helps assure quality (printer makers pride themselves on the color and saturation of their inks), it also keeps prices higher than they might be in a more directly competitive environment.

For color work, some thermal-wax printers give you the choice of three- or four-pass transfer sheets and printing. A three-pass transfer sheet holds the three primary colors of ink—red, yellow, and blue—and a four-color sheet adds black. Although black can be made by overlaying the three primary colors, a separate black ink gives richer, deeper tones. It also imposes a higher cost and extends printing time by one third.

From these three primary colors, thermal-wax printers claim to be able to make anywhere from 7 to nearly 17 million colors. That prestidigitation requires a mixture of transparent inks, dithering, and ingenuity. Because the inks used by thermal-wax printers are transparent, they can be laid one atop another to create simple secondary colors. They do not, however, actually mix.

Expanding the thermal-wax palette further requires pointillistic mixing, laying different color dots next to each other and relying on them to visually blend together in a distant blur. Instead of each dot of ink constituting a picture element, a group of several dots effectively forms a super-pixel of an intermediate color.

The penalty for this wider palette is a loss of resolution. For example, a super-pixel measuring five by five dots would trim the resolution of a thermal-wax printer to 60 dots per inch. Image quality looks like a color halftone—a magazine reproduction—rather than a real photograph. Although the quality is shy of perfection, it is certainly good enough for proofs of what is going to a film recorder or the service bureau to be made into color separations.

A variation of the thermal-wax design combines the sharpness available from the technology with a versatility and cost more in line with ordinary dot-matrix printers. Instead of using a page-wide printhead and equally wide transfer sheets, some thermal wax machines use a line-high printhead and a thin transfer sheet that resembles a Mylar typewriter ribbon. These machines print one, sharp line of text or graphics at a time, usually in one color—black. They are quiet as inkjets but produce sharper, darker images.

Dye-Diffusion

For true photo-quality output from a printer, today's stellar technology is the thermal dye-diffusion process, sometimes called thermal dye-sublimation. Using a mechanism similar to that of the thermal-wax process, dye-diffusion printers are designed to use penetrating dyes rather than inks. Instead of a dot merely being present or absent, as in the case of a thermal-wax printer, diffusion allows the depth of the color of each dot to vary. The diffusion of the dyes can be carefully controlled by the printhead. Because each of the three primary colors can have a huge number of intensities (most makers claim 256), the palette of the dye-diffusion printer is essentially unlimited.

What is limited is the size of the printed area in some printers. The output of most dye-diffusion printers looks like photographs in size, as well as color. Another limit is cost. The newer, more exotic technology pushes dye-diffusion machines into the pricing stratosphere. Dye-diffusions only now are knocking on the $10,000 pricing barrier.

Daisywheels and Tulips

The original typewriter and all such machines made through the 1970s were based on the same character-forming principal as the original creation of Johannes Gutenberg. After laboriously carving individual letters out of wood, daubing them with sticky black ink, and smashing paper against the gooey mess, Gutenberg brought printing to the West by inventing the concept of movable type. Every letter he printed was printed fully formed from a complete, although reversed, image of itself. The character was fully formed in advance of printing. Every part of it, from the boldest stroke to the tiniest serif, was printed in one swipe of the press. Old-fashioned typewriters adapted Gutenberg's individual-character type to an impact mechanism.

In the early days of personal computing, a number of machines used this typewriter technology and were grouped together under the term *fully formed character printers*. Other names for this basic technology were letter-quality printers, daisywheel printers, and a variation called the thimble printer. These more colorful names came from the designs of their print elements, which held the actual character shapes that were pressed against ribbon and paper. Figure 24.5 illustrates a daisywheel, which, if you apply enough imagination, resembles the familiar flower of the family *Compositae* with many petals around a central disk.

FIGURE 24.5
*A fully formed charac-
ter printer daisywheel.*

Nearly all of the fully formed character printers that are likely to be connected to a personal computer use the impact principle to get their ink on paper. Rather than have a separate hammer for each letter, however, the characters are arranged on a single, separate element that is inserted between a single hammer and the ribbon. The hammer, powered by a solenoid that is controlled by the electronics of the printer and your computer, impacts against the element. The element then squeezes the ink off the ribbon and on to the paper. To allow the full range of alphanumeric characters to be printed using this single-hammer technique, the printing element swerves, shakes, or rotates each individual character that is to be formed in front of the hammer as it is needed.

Fully formed character technology produces good-quality output, in line with better typewriters. The chief limitation, in fact, is not the printing technology but the ribbon that is used. Some daisywheel printers equipped with a Mylar film ribbon can give results almost on par with the work of a phototypesetter.

Fully formed character technology, like the typewriter it evolved from, is essentially obsolete, and for several good reasons. The movable-type design limited them solely to text printing and crude graphics. Fully formed character printers also constrained you to a few typefaces. You could only print the typefaces—and font sizes—available on the image-forming daisywheels or thimbles. Worst of all, these machines also were painfully slow;

budget-priced models hammered out text at a lazy 12 to 20 characters per second, and even the most expensive machines struggled to reach 90 characters per second. Other technologies (in particular, laser printers) now equal or exceed the quality of fully formed character printers, run far ahead in speed, and impose little or no price penalty.

Paper Handling

Key to the design of all printers is that their imaging systems operate in only one dimension, one line at a time, be it the text-like line of the line printer or the single raster line of the page printer. To create a full two-dimensional image, all printers require that the printing medium—typically paper—move past the print mechanism. With page printers, this motion must be smooth and continuous. With line printers, the paper must cog forward, hold its position, and then cog forward to the next line. Achieving high resolutions without distortion requires precision paper movement with a tolerance of variation far smaller than the number of dots per inch the printer is to produce.

Adding further complexity, the printer must be able to move paper or other printing media in and out of its mechanism. Most modern printers use sheet feeders that can pull a single page from a stack, route it past the imaging mechanism, and stack it in an output tray. Older printers and some of the highest speed machines use continuous-form paper, which trades a simplified printer mechanism for your trouble in tearing sheets apart. Each paper-handling method has its own complications and refinements.

Sheet Feeders

The basic unit of computer printing is the page, a single sheet of paper, so it is only natural for you to want your printer to work with individual sheets. The computer printing process, however, is one that works with volume—not pages but print jobs, not sheets but reams.

The individual sheet poses problems in printing. To make your ideas, onscreen images, and printed hard copy agree, each sheet must get properly aligned so that its images appear at the proper place and at the proper angle on each sheet. Getting perfect alignment can be vexing for both human and mechanical hands. Getting thousands into alignment is a project that might please only the Master of the Inquisition. Yet every laser printer and most inkjet printers and a variety of other machines face that challenge every time you start a print job.

To cope with this hard-copy torture, the printer requires a complex mechanism called the cut-sheet feeder or simply the sheet feeder. You'll find considerable variation in the designs of the sheet feeders of printers. All are complicated designs involving cogs, gears, rods, and rollers, and every engineer appears to have his own favorite arrangement. The inner complexity of these machines is something to marvel at but not dissect, unless you have too much time on your hands. Differences in the designs of these mechanisms do have a number of practical effects: the capacity of the printer, which relates to how long it can run without your attention; the kinds and sizes of stock that roll through; how sheets are collated and whether you have to spend half an afternoon to get all the pages in order; and duplex printing that automatically covers both sides of each sheet.

No matter the details, however, all sheet feeders can trace their heritage back to one progenitor design, the basic friction feed mechanism.

Friction Feed

When you load a single sheet of paper into a modern inkjet printer, it reverts to *friction feed*, which uses the same technology as yesteryear's mechanical typewriter. It moves paper through its mechanism by squeezing it between the large rubber roller, called a *platen*, and smaller drive rollers. The roller system shifts each sheet through the printer. Friction between the rubber and the paper or other printing medium give the system a positive grip that prevents slipping and assures each sheet gets where it's suppose to. This friction also gives the technology its name.

The name and concept of the platen harks back to the days of impact printing. Its main purpose was as the impact absorber for the pounding hammers of the typewriter or printer. The rubber roller cushioned the hammers while offering sufficient resistance to let the system make a good impression. In typewriters and many printers, the platen did double duty, also serving as the main friction drive roller. Many inkjet and some impact printers now have flat platens that are separate from the drive system. On the other hand, the OPC drum in a laser printer acts like the typewriter's platen in serving as part of the friction-feed mechanism.

Although all sheet-fed printers use a friction mechanism, the term *friction feed* is usually reserved for machines, like the old typewriter, that require you to manually load each page to be printed. The loading process is often complex in itself; you must pull out the bail arm that holds the paper around the platen, insert each individual sheet, line it up to be certain that it is square (so that the printhead does not type diagonally across the sheet), lock it in place, push the bail arm down, and finally signal to the machine that all is well. Easier said than done, of course—and more tedious, too, particularly if you decide to print a computerized version of the *Encyclopedia Britanica*.

On the positive side, however, printers that have these so-called friction feed mechanisms can handle any kind of paper you can load into them, from your own engraved stationery to pre-printed forms, from W-2s to 1040s, envelopes and index cards. They will deal with sheets of any reasonable size—large enough to pass between rollers without slipping out and small enough you don't have to fold over the edge to fit it through.

Better friction-fed printers have accessory mechanisms that automatically load individual sheets. Often termed *cut-sheet feeders* or *bin-feed* mechanisms, these add-ons operate as robotic hands that peel off individual sheets and line them up with the friction-feed rollers. As adapters, they sit atop the printer and often execute a dance akin the jitterbug as they shuffle through their work. You can think of them as mechanical engineering masterpieces, complex band-aids, or simply obsolete but interesting technology.

Modern printers integrate the feed mechanism with the rest of the printer drive system. You load cut sheets into a bin or removable tray, and the printer takes over from there. The mechanism is reduced to a number of rollers chained, belted, or geared together that pull the paper smoothly through the printer. This integrated design reduces complexity, increases reliability, and often trims versatility. Its chief limitations are in the areas of capacity and stock handling.

Capacity

The most obvious difference between sheet-feeding mechanisms of printer is capacity. Some machines are made only for light, personal use and have modestly sized paper bins that hold 50 or fewer sheets. In practical terms, that means that every 10 to 15 minutes, you must attend to the needs of the printer, loading and removing the wads of paper that course through it. Larger trays require less intervention. Printers designed for heavy network use may hold several thousand sheets at a time.

The chief enemy of capacity is size. A compact printer must necessarily devote less space—and thus less capacity—to stocking paper. A tray large enough to accommodate a ream (500 sheets) of paper would double the overall volume of some inkjet printers. In addition, larger tray capacities makes building the feed mechanism more difficult. The printer must deal with a larger overall variation in the height of the paper stack, which can challenge both the mechanism and its designer.

A printer needs at least two trays or bins, one to hold blank stock waiting to be printed and one to hold the results of the printing. These need not and often are not the same size. Most print jobs range from a few to a few dozen sheets, and you will usually want to grab the results as soon as the printing finishes. An output bin large enough to accommodate your typical print job usually is sufficient for a personal printer. The input tray usually holds more so that you need bother loading it less frequently; you certainly don't want to deal with the chore every time you make a printout.

Media Handling

Most printers are designed to handle a range of printing media, from paper stock and cardboard to transparency acetates. Not all printers handle all types of media. Part of the limitation is in the print engine itself. Many constraints arise from the feed mechanism, however.

With any cut-sheet mechanism size is an important issue. All printers impose minimum size requirements on the media you feed them. The length of each sheet must be long enough so that one set of drive rollers can push it to the next. Too short sheets slide between rollers and nothing, save your intervention, can move them out. Similarly, each sheet must be wide enough that the drive rollers can get a proper grip. The maximum width is dictated by the width of the paper path through the printer. The maximum length is enforced by the size of paper trays and the imaging capabilities of the printer engine.

In any case, when selecting a printer you must be certain that it can handle the size of media you want to use. Most modern printers are designed primarily for standard letter-size sheets; some but not all accommodate legal-size sheets. If you want to use other sizes, take a close look at the specifications. Table 24.2 lists the dimensions of common sizes of paper.

TABLE 24.2   Dimensions of Common Paper Sizes

Designation	Height	Width	Height	Width
	Millimeters	Millimeters	Inches	Inches
A9	37	52	1.5	2.1
B9	45	64	1.8	2.5
A8	52	74	2.1	2.9
B8	64	91	2.5	3.6
A7	74	105	2.9	4.1
B7	91	128	3.6	5.0
A6	105	148	4.1	5.8
B6	128	182	5.0	7.2
A5	148	210	5.8	8.3
Octavo	152	229	6	9
B5	182	256	7.2	10.1
Executive	184	267	7.25	10.5
A4	210	297	8.3	11.7
Letter	216	279	8.5	11
Legal	216	356	8.5	14
Quarto	241	309	9.5	12
B4	257	364	10.1	14.3
Tabloid	279	432	11	17

Printers

Designation	Height	Width	Height	Width
	Millimeters	Millimeters	Inches	Inches
A3	297	420	11.7	16.5
Folio	309	508	12	20
Foolscap	343	432	13.5	17
B3	364	515	14.3	20.3
A2	420	594	16.5	23.4
B2	515	728	20.3	28.7
A1	594	841	23.4	33.1
B1	728	1,030	28.7	40.6
A0	841	1,189	33.1	46.8
B0	1,030	1,456	40.6	57.3

Most sheet-fed printers cannot print to the edges of any sheet. The actual image area is smaller because drive mechanisms may reserve a space to grip the medium and the engine may be smaller than the sheet to minimize costs. If you want to print to the edge of a sheet, you often need a printer capable of handling larger media and then trimming each page when it is done. Printing to (and beyond) the edge of a sheet is termed *full-bleed* printing. Only a few sheet-fed printers are capable of managing the task.

Printing media also differ in weight, which roughly corresponds to the thickness of paper. In general, laser printers are the most critical in regard to media weight. The capabilities of a given printer are listed as a range of paper weights the printer can handle, in the case of laser printers, typically from 16 to 24 pounds. (Most business stationery uses 20 pound stock.) If you want to print heavier covers for reports, your printer needs to be able to handle 70 pound paper. Similarly, printer specifications will reveal whether the mechanism can deal with transparency media and label sheets.

Laser printers impose an additional specification on paper stock, moisture content. The moisture content of paper affects its conductivity. The laser printing process is based on carefully controlled static charges, including applying a charge to the paper to make toner stick to it. If paper is too moist or conductive, the charge and the toner may drain away before the image is fused to the sheet. In fact, high humidity around a laser printer can affect the quality of its printouts—pale printouts or those with broken characters can often be traced to paper containing too much moisture or operating the printer in a high humidity environment (which in turn make the paper moist).

Most modern printers readily accommodate envelopes, again with specific enforced size restrictions. As with paper, envelopes come in standard sizes, the most common of which are listed in Table 24.3.

TABLE 24.3   Common Envelope Sizes (Flap Folded)

Designation	Height	Width	Height	Width
	Millimeters	Millimeters	Inches	Inches
6¾	91.4	165	3.6	6.5
Monarch	98.4	190.5	3.875	7.5
Com-10	195	241	4.125	9.5
DL	110	220	4.33	8.66
C5	165	229	6.5	9.01

With a modern computer printer, you should expect to load envelopes in the normal paper tray. Be wary of printers that require some special handling of envelopes; you may find it more vexing than you want to deal with.

Collation

The process of getting the sheets of a multi-page print job in proper order is called *collation*. A printer may take care of the process automatically or leave the chore to you.

When sheet-fed printers disgorge their output, it can fall into the output tray one of two ways—face up or face down. Although it might be nice to see what horrors you have spread on paper immediately rather than save up for one massive heart attack, face down is the better choice. When sheets pile on top of one another, face down means you do not need to sort through the stack to put everything in proper order.

Most printers now automatically collate by stacking sheets face down. A few have selectable paths that give you the choice of face-up or face-down output.

Duplex Operation

A *duplex* printer is one that automatically prints on both sides of each sheet when you want it to. The chief advantage of double-sided printing is, of course, you use half as much paper, although you usually need thicker, more expensive stock so that one side does not show through to the other.

You can easily simulate duplex printing by printing one side, turning each sheet over, and printing the other. When you have a multi-page print job, however, it can be daunting to keep the proper pages together. A single jam can ruin the entire job.

With laser printers, you should *never* try to print on both sides of a sheet except using a duplex printer. When printing the second size, the heat of the second fusing process can melt the toner from the first pass. This toner may stick to the fuser and contaminate later pages. With sufficient build-up, the printer may jam. Duplex printers eliminate the problem by fusing both sides of the sheet at one.

Continuous-Form Feeding

Scrolls went out of fashion for nearly everything except computing printing about 2,000 years ago. Until the advent of laser and inkjet printers, however, most computer printing relied on the same concept as the scrolls stored so carefully by the Dead Sea—continuous-form paper, a single long sheet that was nearly endless. The length was intentional. Printer paper-handling mechanisms were so complex and time-consuming to deal with, akin to threading an old movie projector with film a foot wide, that the only sane thing to do was to minimize the need for loading. The longer the sheet, the longer the printer could run without attention, without your involvement, without paper cuts and cursing.

Although nearly all continuous-form printing systems are based on friction mechanisms, the paper-feeding method they use takes various forms. Each of these requires a particular paper-handling mechanism and, often, a particular kind of paper stock. The choices include roll feeding, pin feeding, and tractor feeding.

Roll Feed

One way to reduce the number of times you must slide a sheet of paper into the friction-feed mechanism is to make the paper longer. In fact, you could use one, long continuous sheet, the classic scroll of Bible fame. Some inexpensive printers do exactly that, wrapping the long sheet around a roll (like toilet paper). The printer just pulls the paper through as it needs it. By rigidly mounting a roll-holder at the back of the printer, the paper can be kept in reasonable alignment and skew can be eliminated. Roll feed is most common for simple narrow-width printers such as those used to generate cash register tapes.

The shortcoming of this system is, of course, that you end up with one long sheet. You have to tear it to pieces or carefully cut it up when you want traditional 8.5 by 11 output. Expensive roll-fed printers such as some thermal-wax transfer printers and even some fax machines incorporate cut-off bars that slice off individual sheets from the paper roll. These add a bit of versatility and frugality. You can make your printouts any length, and when they are short, you can save paper.

Pin-Feed and Tractor-Feed

Although roll-fed paper can be perforated at 11-inch intervals so that you could easily and neatly tear it apart, another problem arises. Most continuous-form friction feeding mechanisms are not perfect. The paper can slip so that, gradually, the page breaks in the image and page breaks at the perforations no longer correspond. In effect, the paper and the image can get out of sync.

By locking perforations in the edge of the paper inside sprockets that prevent slipping, the image and paper breaks can be kept in sync. Two different paper-feeding systems use sprocketed paper to avoid slippage. *Pin-feed* uses drive sprockets that are permanently affixed to the edges of the platen roller. The pin feed mechanism, consequently, can handle only one width of paper, the width corresponding to the sprockets at the edges of the platen. *Tractor-feed* uses adjustable sprockets that can be moved closer together or farther apart to handle nearly any width paper that fits through the printer.

Tractor-feed mechanisms themselves operate either unidirectionally or bidirectionally. As the names imply, a *unidirectional tractor* only pulls (or pushes) the paper through in a single direction (forward). The *bidirectional tractor* allows both forward and backward paper motion, which often is helpful for graphics, special text functions (printing exponents, for instance), and lining up the top of the paper with the top of the printhead.

Push and Pull Tractors

The original tractor mechanism for printers was a two-step affair. One set of sprockets fed paper into the printer and another set pulled it out. For the intended purpose of tractor feeding, however, the two sets of sprockets are one more than necessary. All it takes is one set to lock the printer's image in sync with the paper.

A single set of sprockets can be located in one of two positions, either before or after paper wraps around the platen in front of the printhead. Some printers allow you to use a single set of tractors in either position. In others, the tractors are fixed in one location or the other.

Push tractors are placed in the path of the paper before it enters the printer. They push the paper through the machine, in effect. The platen roller helps to ease paper through the printer while the push tractor provides the principal force and keeps the paper tracking properly. This form of feeding holds a couple of advantages. You can rip off the last sheet of a printout without having to feed an extra sheet through the printer or rethread it. The tractor also acts bidirectionally with relative ease, pulling the paper backward as well as pushing it forward.

Pull tractors are located in the path of the paper after it emerges from the printmaking mechanism. The pull tractor pulls paper across the platen. The paper is held flat against the platen by its friction and the resistance of pulling it up through the mechanism. The pull tractor is simpler and offers less potential hazards than push designs.

Although most pull tractors operate only unidirectionally, they work well in high-speed use on printers with flat, metal (instead of round rubber) platens. Because of their high-speed operation, typically several pages per minute, the machines naturally tend to be used for large print jobs during which the waste of a single sheet is not a major drawback.

Consumables

Consumables are those things that your printer uses up, wears out, or burns through as it does its work. Paper is the primary consumable, and the need for it is obvious with any printer. Other consumables are less obvious, sometimes even devious in the way they can eat into your budget.

You probably think you are familiar with the cost of these consumables. A couple months after the old dot-matrix ribbon starts printing too faintly to read, you finally get around to ordering a new $5 ribbon to hold you through for the rest of the decade. But if you buy one of today's top-quality printers—laser, thermal-wax, and dye-diffusion—you may be in for a surprise. When the toner or transfer sheet runs out, the replacement may cost as much as did your old dot-matrix printer.

The modern trend in printer design and marketing is to follow the "razor blade" principle. The marketers of razors (the non-electric shavers) discovered they could make greater profits selling razor blades by offering the razors that use them at a low price, even a loss. After all, once you sell the razor, you lock in repeat customers for the blades.

Similarly, the prices of many inkjet and laser printers have tumbled while the consumables remain infuriatingly expensive, often a good fraction (such as one third) the cost of the printer itself. This odd situation results from the magic of marketing. By yourself, you can't do anything about it, but you must be aware of it to buy wisely.

If you truly want to make the best buy in getting a new printer, you must consider its overall *cost of ownership*. This total cost includes not only the purchase price but also the cost of consumables and service over the life of the printer. Take this approach and you'll discover a more expensive printer is often less expensive in the long run.

When you have a small budget, however, the initial price of a printer becomes paramount because it dictates what you can afford. Even in this situation, however, you should still take a close look at the price of consumables. Two similarly priced printers may have widely varying consumables costs.

Cartridges

Laser printers use up a bit of their mechanism with every page they print. The organic photoconductor drum on which images are made gradually wears out. (A new drum material, silicon, is supposed to last for the life of the printer, but few printer models currently use silicon drums.) In addition, the charging corona or other parts may also need to be periodically replaced. And of course, you need toner.

Laser printer manufacturers have taken various approaches to replacing these consumables. Hewlett-Packard's LaserJets, for example, are designed with one-piece cartridges that contain both the drum and toner. The whole assembly is replaced as a single unit when the toner runs out. Other laser printers are designed so that the toner, drum, and sometimes the fuser can be replaced individually.

The makers of the latter style of printer contend that the drum lasts for many times more copies than a single shot of toner, so dumping the drum before its time is wasteful. On the other hand, the all-in-one cartridge folks contend that they design their drums to last only as long as the toner.

Surprisingly, from a cost standpoint the choice of technology does not appear to make a difference. (From an ecology standpoint, however, the individual replacement scheme still makes more sense.)

A similar situation reigns among inkjet printers. Some designs incorporate the printhead nozzles into the ink cartridge. Others make the nozzles a separately replaceable item. Although the latter should have a cost advantage and a convenience disadvantage, as a practical matter the differences are not significant.

A more important issue to consider with inkjets is single versus separate cartridges for ink colors. Many printers, typically the less expensive models, use a single cartridge for all three primary ink colors. If you use all three colors equally, this is a convenient arrangement. Most of the time, however, one color will run out before another and force you to scrap a cartridge still holding a supply of two colors of rather expensive ink. If you are frugal or simply appalled at the price of inkjet ink, you'll want a separate cartridge for each ink color.

Refilling

One way to tiptoe around the high cost of laser printer consumables is to get toner or ink cartridges refilled. Most manufacturers do not recommend this; because they have no control over the quality of the toner, they can't guarantee that someone else's replacement works right in their machines. Besides, they miss the profits in selling the toner or ink.

Quality really can be an issue, however. The Resolution Enhancement Technology of the HP's LaserJet III-series, for example, requires toner with a particle size much smaller than that of toner used by other printers. You cannot tell the difference in toner just by looking at it—but you can when blotchy gray pages pour out of the printer. When you get cartridges refilled, you must be sure to get the proper toner quality.

Paper

When comparing the costs of using different printer technologies, do not forget to make allowances for machines that require special paper. In most cases, approved media for such printers is available only from the machine's manufacturer. You must pay the price the manufacturer asks, which, because of the controlled distribution and special formulation, is sure to be substantially higher than buying bond paper at the office supply store.

With inkjet printers, paper is another profit area for machine makers. Getting the highest quality from an inkjet requires special paper. Inkjet ink tends to blur (which reduces both sharpness and color contrast) because it dries at least partly by absorption into paper.

Most inkjet printers work with almost any paper stock but produce the best results—sharpest, most colorful—with specially coated papers that have controlled ink absorption. On non-absorbent media (for example, projection acetates), the ink must dry solely by evaporation, and the output is subject to smudging until the drying process completes. Of course, the treated paper is substantially more expensive, particularly if you restrict yourself to buying paper branded by the printer maker. If you want true 720 dpi quality, however, it is a price you have to pay.

Interfacing

The hardware connection between your PC and printer may be the easiest to manage among all PC peripherals. Most printers—still—use the vintage printer port, as covered in Chapter 21, "Legacy Ports." A few (and soon, more than a few) printers use a USB connection, as covered in Chapter 20, "Peripheral Ports." In either case, you need to do a little more than plug in the printer. All the detail of the link-up are automatically taken care of—or passed off to software.

With the software, the interface gets interesting. The interface doesn't just have to get signals to the printer (the hardware does take care of that), but it must assure that the right signals, those that the printer understands, get there. Modern software considers every dot on the page individually and has to tell the printer what to do with it. Your PC, through its operating system and printer driver, describes what the printer should put on paper using a command language or by sending a bit image of the entire page to print.

At one time, the control language used by a printer determined what applications could take advantage of all the features and quality the printer had to offer. You had to match your software to the *command set* the printer understood.

Modern operating systems have eliminated this concern. Instead, the chief issue is the *printer driver*. The driver matches the printer's native commands to the operating system and *all* of the applications that run under it. Once you install the driver, the printer's command set doesn't matter.

That said, printers usually fit three classes: Windows GDI, PCL, or PostScript.

Windows GDI printers have drivers that directly mate with the Windows Graphic Device Interface. They use proprietary commands for eliciting each printer's features. In most cases, graphics and even the entire page may be send through the GDI to the printer as a bit image. With most printers, the GDI is the fastest way of communicating with a printer; the PC, with its powerful processor, does all the work of rasterizing the image.

PCL is the abbreviation for *Printer Control Language*, a command system originally developed by Hewlett-Packard for its inkjet printers and later adapted to laser machines as well. The commands in PCL tell a specific printer what to do to make an image on a page of paper. PCL thus focuses on *how* to draw the image on the page.

Although PCL is now a common language used by a wide variety of printers, it is a *device-dependent* language. That is, the driver for a printer may send out somewhat different codes for another output device, even if it is another printer.

Through the years, PCL has gone through six distinct versions (four that applied to laser printers), each building on the features of the earlier versions. PCL ships the information to be printed as a combination of characters and graphics commands, relying on a raster image processor in the printer.

PostScript is a *page-description language* developed by Adobe Systems, now in its third major revision (PostScript 3). It describes every dot that appears on a printed page. The language is intended to be device-independent. That is, the PostScript code that yields a printed page will be the same for all devices that understand PostScript and not necessarily only printers. PostScript focuses on the final output, what the image on paper looks like. *How* that image gets drawn doesn't matter to PostScript.

This device independence is a blessing when you need to preview something on a draft-quality machine before sending it out to a production house; both the draft printer and the production house's typesetting equipment work from the same code. At the same time, PostScript attaches a penalty. It requires substantial processing to convert the language commands into a raster image of a page. Using PostScript usually results in slower throughput from a printer.

Printer Sharing

Two printers are not necessarily better than one; they are just more expensive. In a number of business situations, you can save the cost of a second printer by sharing the one with two or more PCs and their users. This strategy works because no one prints all the time; if he did, he would have no time left to create anything worth printing. Because normal office work leaves your printer with idle time, you can put it to work for someone else.

When printers are expensive—as better-quality machines such as lasers and thermal-wax printers—sharing the asset is much more economical than buying a separate printer for everyone and smarter than making someone suffer with a cheap printer while the quality machine lies idle most of the day.

You have your choice of several printer-sharing strategies, including those that use nothing but software and those that are hardware-based.

Hardware Devices

The least expensive—in terms of out-of-pocket cost—is a simple A/B switch box. As the name implies, this device consists of a box of some kind that protects a multi-pole switch. The switch allows you to reroute all 25 connections of a printer cable from one PC to another. For example, in position A, your computer might be connected to the printer; in position B, a co-worker's PC would be connected. It is the equivalent of moving the printer cable with the convenience of a switch.

More expensive active printer-sharing devices automatically make the switch for you. They also add the benefit of arbitrating between print jobs. Arbitration systems determine which PC has priority when two or more try to print at once. The best sharing systems allow you to assign a priority to every PC based upon its need and the corporate pecking order. You should expect to get control software to let you manage the entire printing system to accompany the more versatile sharing devices.

Not all printer-sharing boxes are alike. They differ in the amount of memory they make available and in their arbitration systems. The memory is used to buffer print jobs so that when one PC is printing, others can continue to send printing instructions as if they are running the printer, too. No time is lost by programs waiting for printer access. More memory is generally better, although you might not need a lot if you standardize your office on Windows or UNIX or some other software environment with a built-in software print spooler. With today's graphic printing jobs, you want at least a megabyte in any hardware printer-sharing device.

Sharing devices also differ as to the number and kind of ports that they make available. You need a port for every PC you want to connect. You want parallel ports for easy connections, but serial ports if PCs are located some distance (generally more than 10 to 25 feet) from the sharing device.

Some printer-sharing devices plug into the I/O slots of printers. Although these devices limit the number of available ports because of size constraints, they also minimize costs because no additional case or power supply is required. A few printers are designed to be shared, having multiple or network inputs built in.

Software Sharing

Today, software-based printer sharing has replaced hardware as the favored option. One reason is that it often comes at no cost, for example, when you've installed a small network for another purpose such as file sharing or email. It also simplifies the wiring of the shared printer system and allows you to locate PCs at greater distances from the printer. You also gain greater control and more options. You can even connect more printers with fewer hassles. For example, each PC connected in a simple network can share the printer connected to any other PC (if you want it to, of course).

Appendix T, "Setting Up a Small Network," covers what you need to know to set up a printer-sharing system using the features built into the current versions of the Windows operating system.

Power

PCs require a continuous supply of carefully conditioned low-voltage direct current at several potentials. Batteries provide a direct source of power for portable PCs, but desktop units require power supplies to provide the proper voltages. Similar power supplies charge and substitute for portable PC batteries. Any time you connect any PC to utility power, it stands a chance of damage from power-related problems. Surge suppressors and backup power systems help to ensure that your PC gets the proper electrical diet.

Powerful Abbreviations to Know

Term	What it means	What you should know
W	Watts	Power measurement unit that indicates power supply capacity. If you don't plan to expand your PC, it's a non-issue. If you plan to expand (say a server) you want a power supply that can deliver at least 200 to 250 watts.
VA	Volt-Amperes	Also a measure of power, but one used to make power devices seem heftier than they are. Power in VA is always less than power in watts; the relationship between the two is the *power factor*—typically about 70% for PCs.
Ah	Amp-hours	Measurement of battery capacity. Small batteries may be measured in mAh (milliamp-hours), each equal to one-thousandth amp-hour.
APM	Advanced Power Management	The best way to extend battery capacity by managing power use by eliminating power wasted on circuits not in use.
ACPI	Advanced Configuration and Power Interfac	The standard for hardware and software setup and control for PC power management.
NiCd	Nickel-Cadmium	Battery chemistry losing favor in PCs but notable for its long life and high current capacity (but lower energy density).
NiMH	Nickel-Metal hydride	Common portable computer battery chemistry with higher energy density than NiCd but less than Li-ion. Endures more recharges than Li-ion but fewer than NiCd.
Li-ion	Lithium-ion	Today's most popular (and highest capacity) battery for portable computers. Shorter life than nickel-based batteries but suffers no memory effect. Lithium-polymer batteries use similar technology but different packaging.
UPS	Uninterruptible Power System	A device that supplies emergency power from batteries when utility power fails so that you have time to save files and switch off your PC.

All practical computers made today operate electronically. Moving electrons—electricity—are the media of their thoughts. Electrical pulses course from one circuit to another, switched off or on in an instant by logic chips. Circuits combine the electrical pulses together to make logical decisions and send out other pulses to control peripherals. The computer's signals stay electrical until electrons colliding with phosphors in the monitor tube push out photons toward your eyes or generate the fields that snap your printer into action.

Of course, your computer needs a source for the electricity that runs it. The power does not arise spontaneously in its circuits but must be derived from an outside source. Conveniently, nearly every home in America is equipped with its own electrical supply that the computer can tap into. Such is the wonder of civilization.

But the delicate solid-state semiconductor circuits of today's computers cannot directly use the electricity supplied by your favorite utility company. Commercial power is an electrical brute, designed to have the strength and stamina to withstand the miles of travel between generator and your home. Your PC's circuits want a steady, carefully controlled trickle of power. Raw utility power would fry and melt computer circuits in a quick flash of miniature lightning.

For economic reasons, commercial electrical power is transmitted between you and the utility company as alternating current, the familiar AC found everywhere. AC is preferred by power companies because it is easy to generate and adapts readily between voltages (including very high voltages that make long-distance transmission efficient). It's called alternating because it reverses polarity—swapping positive for negative—dozens of times a second (arbitrarily 60Hz in America, 50Hz in Europe).

The changing or oscillating nature of AC enables transformers to increase or decrease voltage (the measure of driving force of electricity) because transformers only react to electrical changes. Electrical power travels better at higher voltages because waste (as heat generated by the electrical current flowing through the resistance of the long-distance transmission wires) is inversely proportional to voltage. Transformers permit the high voltages used in transmitting commercial power—sometimes hundreds of thousands of volts—to be reduced to a safe level (nominally 117 volts) before it is led into your home.

As wonderful as AC is to power companies, it's an anathema to computer circuits. These circuits form their pulses by switching the flow of electricity tapped from a constant supply. Although computers can be designed that use AC, the constant voltage reversal would complicate the design so that juggling knives while blindfolded and riding a roller coaster would seem tame in comparison. Computers (and most electronic gear) use direct current or DC instead. Direct current is the kind of power that comes directly from a primary source—a battery—a single voltage that stays at a constant level (at least constant as long as the battery has the reserves to produce it). Moreover, even the relatively low voltage that powers your lights and vacuum cleaner would be fatal to semiconductor circuits. Tiny distances separate the elements inside solid state circuits, and high voltages can flash across those distances like lightning, burning and destroying the silicon along the way.

Power Supplies

The intermediary that translates AC from your electrical outlets into the DC that your computer's circuits need is called the power supply. As it operates, the power supply of your PC attempts to make the direct current supplied to your computer as pure as possible, as close to the ideal DC power produced by batteries. The chief goal is regulation, maintaining the voltage as close as possible to the ideal desired by the circuits inside your PC.

Notebook and sub-notebook computers have it easy. They work with battery power, which is generated inside the battery cells in exactly the right form for computer circuits— low voltage DC. However, even notebook computers require built-in voltage regulation because even pure battery power varies in voltage, depending on the state of charge or discharge of the battery. In addition, laptop and notebook computers also must charge their batteries somehow, and their charges must make exactly the same electrical transformations as a desktop computer's power supply.

Technologies

In electronic gear, two kinds of power supplies are commonly used: linear and switching. The former is old technology, dating from the days when the first radios were freed from their need for storage batteries in the 1920s. The latter rates as high technology, requiring the speed and efficiency of solid-state electronic circuitry to achieve the dominant position they hold today in the computer power market. These two power supply technologies are distinguished by the means used to achieve their voltage regulation.

Linear Power Supplies

The design first used for making regulated DC from utility-supplied AC was the linear power supply. At one time, it was the only kind of power supply used for any electronic equipment. When another technology became available, it was given the linear label because it then used standard linear (analog) semiconductor circuits, although a linear power supply need not have any semiconductors in it at all.

In a linear power supply, the raw electricity from the power line is first sent through a transformer that reduces its voltage to a value slightly higher than that required by the computer's circuits. Next, one or several rectifiers, usually semiconductor diodes, convert the now low-voltage AC to DC by permitting the flow of electricity in only one direction, blocking the reversals. Finally, this DC is sent through the linear voltage regulator, which adjusts the voltage created by the power supply to the level required by your computer's circuits.

Most linear voltage regulators work simply by absorbing the excess voltage made by the transformer, turning it into heat. A shunt regulator simply shorts out excess power to drive the voltage down. A series regulator puts an impediment—a resistance—in the flow of electricity, blocking excess voltage. In either case, the regulator requires an input voltage higher than the voltage it supplies to your computer's circuits. This excess power is converted to heat (that is, wasted). The linear power supply achieves its regulation simply by varying the waste.

Switching Power Supplies

The design alternative is the switching power supply. Although more complex, switching power supplies are more efficient and often less expensive than their linear kin. Although designs vary, the typical switching power supply first converts the incoming 60 Hertz utility power to a much higher frequency of pulses (in the range of 20,000Hz, above the range of normal human hearing) by switching it on and off using an electrical component called a triac.

At the same time the switching regulator increases the frequency of the commercial power, it regulates the commercial power using a digital technique called pulse-width modulation. That is, the duration of each power pulse is varied in response to the needs of the computer circuitry being supplied. The width of the pulses is controlled by the electronic switch; shorter pulses result in a lower output voltage. Finally, the switched pulses are reduced in voltage down to the level required by the computer circuits by a transformer and turned into pure direct current by rectification and filtering.

Switching power supplies earn their efficiency and lower cost in two ways. Switching regulation is more efficient because less power is turned into heat. Instead of dissipating energy with a shunt or series regulator, the switching regulator switches all current flow off, albeit briefly. In addition, high frequencies require smaller, less expensive transformers and filtering circuits. For these two very practical reasons, nearly all today's personal computers use switching power supplies.

PC Power Needs

Modern computer logic circuits operate by switching voltages with the two different logic states (true or false, one or zero, for example) coded as two voltage levels—high and low. Every family of logic circuits has its own voltage standards. Most PCs today are built around the requirements of Transistor-Transistor Logic, or TTL. In a TTL design, "high" refers to voltages above about 3.2 volts, and "low" means voltages lower than about

1.8. The middle ground is undefined logically, an electrical guard band that prevents ambiguity between the two meaningful states. Besides the signals, TTL logic circuits also require a constant supply voltage that they use to power their thinking; it provides the electrical force that throws their switches. TTL circuits nominally operate from a 5-volt supply. The power supplies used by all full-size PCs are designed to produce this unvarying 5 volts in great abundance—commonly 20 or more amperes.

PCs often require other voltages as well. The motors of most disk drives (hard and floppy) typically require 12 volts to make their disks spin. Other specialized circuits in PCs sometimes require bipolar electrical supplies. A serial port, for example, signals logic states by varying voltages between positive and negative in relation to ground. Consequently, the mirror image voltages, –5 and –12 volts, must be available inside every PC, at least if it hopes to use any possible expansion boards.

In notebook computers, most of which have no room for generic expansion boards, all these voltages are often unnecessary. For example, many new hard disks designed for notebook computers use 5-volt motors, eliminating the need for the 12-volt supply.

In addition, the latest generation of notebook computer microprocessors and support circuits are designed to operate with a 3.3-volt supply. These lower voltage circuits cut power consumption because—all else being equal—the higher the voltage, the greater the current flow and the larger the power usage. Dropping the circuit operating voltage from 5 to 3.3 volts cuts the consumption of computer power by about half. (The power usage of a circuit is proportional to the square of the current consumed.)

Voltages and Ratings

The power supplies that you are most likely to tangle with are those inside desktop PCs, and these must produce all four common voltages to satisfy the needs of all potential combinations of circuits. In many desktop PC power supplies, the power supply typically produces four voltages (+5, –5, +12, and –12) is delivered in different quantities (amperages) because of the demands associated with each. A separate *voltage regulator* on the motherboard produces the lower voltage in the 3.3-volt range required by Pentium-level microprocessors and their associated circuitry. In some systems, the output voltage of this regulator may be variable to accommodate energy-saving systems (which reduce the speed and voltage of the microprocessor to conserve power and reduce heat dissipation). Newer power supplies, such as those that follow the ATX design standard, sometimes also provide a direct 3.3-volt supply.

The typical PC has much logic circuitry so it needs copious quantities of 5-volt power, often as much as 20 to 25 amperes. Many disk drives use 12-volt power; the typical modern drive uses an ampere or so. Only a few components require the negative voltages, so most power supplies only deliver a few watts of each.

Most power supplies are rated and advertised by the sum of all the power they can make available, as measured in watts. The power rating of any power supply can be calculated by individually multiplying the current rating of each of the four voltages it supplies and summing the results. (Power in watts is equal to the product of voltage times current in amperes.) Most modern full-size computers have power supplies of 150 to 220 watts. Notebook PCs use 10 to 25 watts.

Note that this power rating does not correspond to the wattage that the power supply draws from a wall outlet. All electronic circuits—and power supplies in particular—suffer from inefficiencies, linear designs more so than switching. Consequently, a power supply requires a wattage in excess to that it provides to your computer's circuits—at least when it is producing its full output. PC power supplies, however, rarely operate at their rated output. As a result, efficient switching power supplies typically draw less power than their nominal rating in normal use. For example, a PC with a 220-watt power supply with a typical dosage of memory (say 4MG) and one hard disk drive likely draws less than 100 watts while it is operating.

When selecting a power supply for your PC, the rating you require depends on the boards and peripherals with which you want to fill your computer. Modern PCs are not nearly so power-hungry as their forebears. Nearly all PC components require less power than the equivalents of only half a dozen years ago. The one exception is the microprocessor. Greater performance requires more power. Although Intel's engineers have done a good job at reducing the power needs of the company's products by shifting to lower voltage technologies, the reductions have been matched by increasing demands. Chips need as much power as they ever have, sometimes more.

In a desktop PC, a 200-watt power supply essentially loafs along; most individual PCs (as opposed to servers or workstations) could get along with 120 watts without straining. A system board may require 15 to 25 watts; a floppy disk drive, 3 to 20 (depending on its vintage); a hard disk, 5 to 50 (also depending on its vintage); a memory or multifunction expansion board, 5 to 10. Table 25.1 summarizes the needs of both vintage and modern PC components.

TABLE 25.1 Typical Device Power Demands

Device Class	Device Type	Power	Example
Floppy disk drive	Full-height, 5.25-inch	12.6 watts	IBM PC diskette drive
Floppy disk drive	Half-height, 5.25-inch	12.6 watts	Qume Trak 142
Floppy disk drive	One-inch high, 3.5-inch	1.4 watts	Teac FD-235J

Power Supplies

Device Class	Device Type	Power	Example
Graphics board	Two-board old technology	16.2 watts	IBM 8514/A
Graphics board	High performance, full-length	13.75 watts	Matrox MGA
Graphics board	Accelerated half-card	6.5 watts	ATI VGA Wonder, Graphics Ultra+
Hard disk	Full-height, 5.25-inch	59 watts	IBM 10MB XT hard disk
Hard disk	Half-height, 5.25-inch	25 watts	[estimated]
Hard disk	One-inch high, 3.5-inch	6.5 watts	Quantum ProDrive LPS120S
Hard disk	2.5-inch	2.2 watts	Quantum Go-Drive 120AT
Hard disk	PCMCIA card	3.5 watts	Maxtor MXL-131-III
Hard disk	Full-height, 3.5-inch	12 watts	Quantum ProDrive 210S
Memory	1MB SIMM	4.8 watts	Motorola MCM81000
Memory	4MB SIMM	6.3 watts	Motorola MCM94000
Memory	8MB SIMM	16.8 watts	Motorola MCM36800
Microprocessor	400 MHz	24 watts	Intel Celeron (core logic only)
Microprocessor	550 MHz	40 watts	Intel Pentium III Xeon
Modem	PCMCIA card	3.5 watts	MultiTech MT1432LT
Modem	Internal, half-card	1.2 watts	Boca V.32bis
Motherboard	Mini-ATX	15 watts	Without CPU
Network adapter	Ethernet, half-card	7.9 watts	Artisoft AE-2/T
System board	286, AT-size	25 watts	[estimated]
System board	386, XT-size	12 watts	Monolithic Systems MSC386 XT/AT
System board	486 or Pentium, AT-size	25 watts	[estimated]

Reserve power is always a good thing and with switching power supplies comes without a penalty (except in the cost of making the power supply). In other words, although you could get along with a smaller power supply in your desktop PC, the quasi-standard 200 watts remains a good choice.

Supply Voltage

Most power supplies are designed to operate from a certain line voltage and frequency. In the United States, utility power is supplied at a nominal 115 volts and 60 Hertz. In other nations, the supply voltage and frequency may be different. In Europe, for instance, a 230-volt, 50 Hertz standard prevails.

Most switching power supplies can operate at either frequency, so that shouldn't be a worry when traveling. (Before you travel, however, check the ratings on your power supply to be sure.) Linear power supplies are more sensitive. Because their transformers have less reactance at lower frequencies, 60Hz transformers draw more current than their designers intend when operating on 50Hz power. Consequently, they are liable to overheat and fail, perhaps catastrophically.

Most PC power supplies are either universal or voltage selectable. A universal power supply is design to have a wide tolerance for supply current. If you have a computer with such a power supply, all you need to do is plug the computer in, and it should work properly. Note that some of these universal power supplies accommodate any supply voltage in a wide range and will accept any standard voltage and line frequency available in the world—a voltage range from about 100 to 250 volts and line frequency of 50 to 60Hz. Other so-called universal supplies are actually limited to two narrow ranges, bracketing the two major voltage standards. Because you are unlikely to encounter a province with a 169.35-volt standard, these dual-range supplies are universal enough for worldwide use.

Voltage selectable power supplies have a small switch on the rear panel that selects their operating voltage, usually in two ranges—115 and 230 volts. If your PC has a voltage selectable power supply, make sure that the switch is in the proper position for the available power before you plug in or turn on your computer.

When traveling in a foreign land, always use this power supply switch to adjust for different voltages. Do not use inexpensive voltage converters. Often, these devices are nothing more than rectifiers that clip half the incoming waveform. Although that strategy may work for light bulbs, it can be disastrous to electronic circuitry. Using such a device can destroy your computer. It's not a recommended procedure.

The Power-Good Signal

Besides the voltages and currents the computer needs to operate, PC power supplies also provide another signal called power-good. Its purpose is just to tell the computer that all is well with the power supply and the computer can operate normally. If the power-good signal is not present, the computer shuts down. The power-good signal prevents the computer from attempting to operate on odd-ball voltages (for example, those caused by a brown-out) and damaging itself. A bad connection or failure of the power-good output of the power supply also causes your PC to stop working just as effectively as a complete power supply failure.

Standards

Before Intel introduced its standard motherboard and case designs, two standards dominated among PC power supplies—one to fit into the chassis of the original PC and XT, and another to fit the full-size AT chassis. AT-size power supplies are taller and wider than PC/XT models, measuring 5-7/8 by 8-3/8 by 5-7/8 inches (HWD) with a notch taken out of the inboard bottom corner to allow extra space inside the computer chassis for the system board. PC/XT-size power supplies measure about 4-3/4 by 8-3/8 by 5-1/2 inches.

Although it is obvious that the AT power supply cannot fit into the smaller XT-size chassis, you may be surprised to discover that the smaller XT power supply also cannot fit properly into an AT chassis. The placement of screws and other functional parts is different enough that the little box cannot fit right in the big box.

The ATX standard for motherboards and chassis brought a new power supply design to match. The ATX power supply adds new, lower voltages (relieving some of the voltage regulation needs of the motherboard) and a new combined motherboard connector that makes installation easier and less ambiguous. For systems with lower power needs, Intel also created the SFX power supply design. With a maximum power capacity of 145 watts, the SFX design is more compact than the ATX system. It uses the same combined motherboard power connector (and pinout) but lacks the -5 VDC signal available from ATX units. Appendix Y more fully describes these power supplies and their signals.

Portable Computer Power

As with any PC, electricity is the lifeblood of notebook machines. With these machines, however, emphasis shifts from power production to consumption. To achieve freedom from the need for plugging in, these totable PCs pack their own portable power—batteries. Although they are free from concerns about lightning strikes and utility bill shortfalls, they face a far less merciful taskmaster—gravity. The amount of power they have available is determined by their batteries, and weight constrains battery size to a reasonable value (the reasonableness of which varies inversely with the length of the airport concourse and the time spent traveling). Compared to the almost unlimited electrical supply available at your nearby wall outlet, the power provided by a pound of batteries is minuscule, indeed, with total available energy measuring in the vicinity of five watt-hours.

The power supply in a notebook computer is consequently more concerned with minimizing waste rather than regulating. After all, battery power is close to ideal to begin with—smooth, unchanging DC at a low potential (voltage) that can be tailored to match computer circuitry with the proper battery selection. Regulation needs are minimum: a protection circuit to prevent too much voltage from sneaking in and destroying the computer and a low-voltage detection circuit to warn before the voltage output of the battery supply drops too low to reliably run the machine. Power-wasting shunts or series regulators are unnecessary because battery voltage is entirely predictable; it simply grows a bit weaker as the charge is drained away.

Rather than regulation, management is the principal power issue in a portable PC. Circuitry inside the system monitors which resources are being used and, more importantly, which are not. Anything not being used gets shut off—for example, the backlight on the display screen, the spin of the hard disk, even the microprocessor in some systems.

With but a few exceptions, notebook computers also rely on a battery charger of some kind so that you can use rechargeable batteries for power. In essence and operation, the battery charger is little more than a repackaged power supply. Line voltage AC goes in, and low voltage DC (usually) comes out. The output voltage is close to that of the system's battery output, always a bit higher. (A slightly higher voltage is required so that the batteries are charged to their full capacity.)

Most of the time, the battery charger or power supply is a self-contained unit external to the notebook PC. Although they typically contain more than just a transformer, most people call these external power supplies transformers or power bricks. The name was apt when all external battery chargers used linear designs with heavy transformers, giving the device the size and heft approaching that of an actual clay brick. Modern external power supplies use switching designs, however, and can be surprisingly compact and light.

Manufacturers favor the external power supply design because it moves unnecessary weight out of the machine itself and eliminates high voltages from anywhere inside the computer. The design also gives you something else to carry and leave behind as well as a connection that can fail at an inopportune time.

The brick typically only reduces line voltage to an acceptable level and rectifies it to DC. All the power management functions are contained inside the PC.

No standard exists for the external battery chargers and power supplies of notebook computers. Every manufacturer—and often every model of PC from a given manufacturer—uses its own design. They differ as to output voltage, current, and polarity. You can substitute a generic replacement only if the replacement matches the voltage used by your PC and generates at least as much current. Polarity matching gives you two choices—right and wrong—and the wrong choice is apt to destroy many of the semiconductors inside the system. In other words, make extra certain of power polarity when plugging in a generic replacement power supply. (With most PCs, the issue of polarity reduces to a practical matter of whether the center or outer conductor of the almost-universal coaxial power plug is the positive terminal.) Also available are cigarette lighter adapters that enable you to plug many models of notebook computers into the standard cigarette lighter jack found in most automobiles. Again, you must match these to the exact make and model of the PC you plan to use, being particularly critical of the polarity of the voltage.

Most external power supplies are designed to operate from a single voltage. (A few are universal, but don't count on it.) That means you are restricted to plugging in and charging your portable PC to one hemisphere (or thereabouts) or the other. Moving from 117-volt to 230-volt electrical systems requires a second, expensive external charger. Experienced travelers often pack voltage converters to take care of electrical differences. Two kinds of converters are available: One that works with notebook PC chargers and one that will likely destroy the charger and the computer as well.

Rectifying Power Converters

The simplest, smallest, lightest, and cheapest converter is nothing more than a diode (rectifier) that blocks half the AC wave from getting through, effectively cutting the voltage in half—sort of. The result is an odd-ball half-wave electrical supply apt to wreak both havoc and disaster with critical electronic circuits, such as your PC and its power supply. Although these converters work well with electric razors and hair dryers, never plug your PC into one.

Transformers

The other kind of converter is a simple transformer. Like all transformers, these converters are heavy (making them a joy to pack into an overnight bag). They are also relatively expensive. They are safe for powering your PC because they deliver normal AC at their outputs. Of course, they require that you carry two power adapter bricks with your notebook computer—its power supply and the converter—that together probably weigh more than the machine itself. In the long run—and the long concourse—you are better off buying a second battery charger or power supply for your PC.

Batteries

Think back to elementary school, and you probably remember torturing half a lemon with a strip of copper and one of zinc in another world-relevant experiment meant to introduce you to the mysteries of electricity. Certainly, those memories come in handy if you are stuck on a desert island with a radio, dead batteries, a case of lemons, and strips of zinc and copper, but they probably seem as meaningless in connection with your PC as

DOS 1.1. Think again. That juicy experiment should have served as an introduction to battery technology (and recalling the memories of it makes a good introduction to this section).

Storage Density

The amount of energy that a battery can store is its capacity and is usually measured in watt-hours, abbreviated Wh. The ratio of capacity to the weight (or size) of the battery is called the *storage density* of the battery. The higher the storage density, the more energy that can be stored in a given size or weight of a cell and, hence, the more desirable the battery—at least if you have to carry it and the PC holding it around airports all day long.

Primary and Secondary Cells

Batteries can be divided into two types: primary and secondary or storage. In primary batteries, the creation of electricity is irreversible; one or both of the electrodes is altered and cannot be brought back to its original state except by some complex process (such as re-smelting the metal). Secondary or storage batteries are rechargeable; the chemical reaction is reversible by the application of electricity. The electrons can be coaxed back whence they came. After the battery is discharged, the chemical changes inside can be reversed by pumping electricity into the battery again. The chemicals revert back to their original, charged state and can be discharged to provide electricity once again.

In theory, any chemical reaction is reversible. Clocks can run backwards, too. And pigs can fly, given a tall enough cliff. The problem is that when a battery discharges, the chemical reaction affects the electrodes more in some places than others; recharging does not necessarily reconstitute the places that were depleted. Rechargeable batteries work because the chemical changes inside them alter their electrodes without removing material. For example, an electrode may become plated with an oxide, which can be removed during recharging.

Primary and secondary (storage) batteries see widely different applications, even in PCs. Nearly every modern PC has a primary battery hidden somewhere inside, letting out a tiny electrical trickle that keeps the time-of-day clock running while the PC is not. This same battery also maintains a few bytes or kilobytes of CMOS memory to store system configuration information. Storage batteries are used to power just about every notebook computer in existence. (A few systems use storage batteries for their clocks and configuration memory.)

Technologies

The lemon demonstrates the one way that chemical energy can be put to work, directly producing electricity. The two strips of metal act as electrodes. One gives off electrons through the chemical process of oxidation, and the other takes up electrons through chemical reduction. In other words, electrons move from one electrode, the anode, to another called the cathode. The acid in the lemon serves as an electrolyte, the medium through which the electrons are exchanged in the form of ions. Together, the three elements make an electricity-generating device called a Galvanic cell, named after 18th-century chemist Luigi Galvani. Several such cells connected together comprise a battery.

Connect a wire from cathode to anode, and the electrons have a way to dash back and even up their concentration. That mad race is the flow of electricity. Add something in the middle—say a PC—and that electricity performs work on its way back home.

All batteries work by the same principle. Two dissimilar materials (strictly speaking, they must differ in oxidation potential, commonly abbreviated as E_0 value) serving as anode and cathode are linked by a third material that serves as the electrolyte. The choice of materials is wide and allows for a diversity of battery technologies. It also influences the storage density (the amount of energy that can be stored in a given size or weight of battery) and nominal voltage output. Table 25.2 summarizes the characteristics of common battery chemical systems.

TABLE 25.2   Electrical Characteristics of Common Battery Chemistry Systems

Technology	Cell Voltage (Nominal) Volts	Storage Density Wh/kg	Discharge Curv	Discharge in Storage
Carbon-zinc	1.5	70	Sloping	15% per year
Alkaline	1.5	130	Sloping	4% per year
Lithium	3.2	230	Flat	1% per year
Silver oxide	1.5	120	Flat	6% per year
Nickel-cadmium	1.2	42	Flat	1% per day
Nickel-metal hydride	1.2	64	Flat	1% per day
Zinc-air	1.4	310	Flat	2% per year

Zinc-Carbon

The most common batteries in the world are primary cells based on zinc and carbon electrodes. In these zinc-carbon batteries—formally called a Leclanche dry cell but better known as the flashlight battery—zinc (the case of the battery) serves as the anode; a graphite rod in the center acts as cathode; and the electrolyte is a complex mixture of chemicals (manganese dioxide, zinc chloride, and ammonium chloride). Alkaline batteries change the chemical mix to increase storage density and shelf life. Other materials are used for special purpose batteries, but with the exception of lithium these have not found wide application in PCs.

Alkaline

Ordinarily, alkaline batteries cannot be recharged, but Rayovac Corporation has developed a series of standard-sized alkaline cells called Renewal batteries that accept 25 to 100 recharges. To achieve their reusability, these cells combine novel fabrication techniques and a special microprocessor-controlled charger. The charger pulses power into discharged cells and measures the effect of each pulse. Renewal batteries cannot be charged with conventional battery chargers; in fact, they may explode if you try.

Lead-Acid

The most common storage batteries in the world are the lead-acid batteries used to start automobiles. These have electrodes made from lead (anode) and lead oxide (cathode) soaked in a sulfuric acid electrolyte. Not only are these batteries heavy—they are filled with lead, after all—but they contain a corrosive liquid that can spill where it is not wanted—generally, anywhere. Some lead-acid batteries are sealed to avoid leakage.

Gelled-electrolyte lead-acid batteries, often called simple gel cells, reduce this problem. In these batteries, the electrolyte is converted to a colloidal form like gelatin, so it is less apt to leak out. Unlike most lead-acid batteries, however, gel cells are degraded by the application of continuous low-current charging after they have been completely charged. (Most lead-acid batteries are kept at full capacity by such "trickle" charging methods.) Consequently, gel cells require special chargers that automatically turn off after the cells have been fully charged.

Nickel-Cadmium

In consumer electronic equipment, the most popular storage batteries are nickel-cadmium cells, often called nicads. These batteries use electrodes made from nickel and cadmium, as the name implies. Their most endearing characteristic is the capability to withstand in the range of 500 full charge/discharge cycles. They are also relatively lightweight, have a good energy storage density (although about half that of alkaline cells), and tolerate trickle charging. On the downside, cadmium is toxic.

The output voltage of most chemical cells declines as the cell discharges because the reactions within the cell increase its internal resistance. Nicads have a very low internal resistance—meaning they can create high currents—which changes little as the cell discharges. Consequently, the nicad cell produces a nearly constant voltage until it becomes almost completely discharged, at which point its output voltage falls precipitously. This constant voltage is an advantage to the circuit designer because fewer allowances need to be made for voltage variations. However, the constant voltage also makes determining the state of a nicad's charge nearly impossible. As a result, most battery-powered computers deduce the battery power they have remaining from the time they have been operating rather than by actually checking the battery state.

Nicads are known for another drawback: memory. When some nicads are partly discharged, left in that condition, and then later recharged, they may lose capacity. The cure for the memory problem is deep discharge—discharging the battery to its minimum working level and then charging the battery again. Deep discharge does not mean totally discharging the battery, however. Draining nearly any storage battery absolutely dry will damage it and shorten its life. If you discharge a nicad battery so that it produces less than about one volt (its nominal output is 1.2 volts), it may suffer such damage. Notebook computers are designed to switch off before their batteries are drained too far, and deep discharge utilities do not push any further so you need not worry in using them. But don't try to deeply discharge your system's batteries by shorting them out; you risk damaging the battery and even starting a fire.

According to battery makers, newer nicads are free from memory effects. In any case, to get the longest life from nicads the best strategy is to operate them between extremes; operate the battery through its complete cycle. Charge the battery fully, run it until it is normally discharged, and then fully charge it again.

Nickel-Metal Hydride

A more modern update to nickel-cadmium technology is the nickel-metal hydride cell (abbreviated NiMH). These cells have all the good characteristics of nicads, but lack the cadmium—substituting heavy metals that may also have toxic effects. Their chief strength is the capability to store up to 50 percent more power in a given cell. In addition, they do not appreciably suffer from memory effects.

Both nicads and nickel-metal hydride cells suffer from self-discharge. Even sitting around unused, these cells tend to lose their charge at a high rate in the vicinity of 30 percent per month.

Most PC batteries and battery chargers are designed to be plugged in continuously without any detrimental effects on the battery. In fact, the best strategy is to leave your PC plugged in even after it is fully charged, detaching it from its charger only when you have to take the machine on the road. The trickle charge will not hurt it (in fact, the battery charging circuitry may switch off once the battery is charged), and you will always be ready to roam.

Lithium Ion

Lithium is the most chemically reactive metal and provides the basis for today's most compact energy storage for notebook computer power systems. Lithium-ion cells produce a higher voltage than any other design, nominally 2.2 volts per cell. For this and other reasons, lithium cells are not interchangeable with other technologies, although PCs can be designed to use both.

Lithium batteries offer higher storage densities than even nickel-metal hydride cells, which means you can use your notebook system longer without a recharge. Lithium-ion cells also lack the memory effect that plagued early nickel-based cells, so you don't have to worry about whether you drain your cells completely before recharging.

On the other hand, current lithium cells have a higher internal resistance than nickel-cadmium cells and consequently cannot deliver high currents. The available power is sufficient for a properly designed PC that minimizes surge requirements. Moreover, the life of lithium cells is more limited than that of nickel-based designs. Nickel-cadmium batteries remain the leader for number of charge/discharge cycles you can expect from a battery pack.

Lithium Polymer

Today's brightest new technology is a refinement of familiar lithium chemistry called the *lithium solid polymer* cell. Where conventional lithium ion cells require liquid electrolytes, solid polymer cells integrate the electrolyte into a polymer plastic separator between the anode and cathode of the cell. Because there's no liquid, the solid polymer cell does not require the chunky cylindrical cases of conventional batteries. Instead, the solid polymer cells can be formed into flat sheets or *prismatic* (rectangular) packages better able to fit the nooks and crannies of notebook computers.

Although the energy density of solid polymer cells is similar to ordinary lithium ion cells, PC manufacturers can shape them to better fit the space available in a PC, squeezing more capacity into each machine. For example, simply by filling the empty space that would appear in the corners around a cylindrical cell, a solid polymer battery can fit in about 22 percent more chemistry and energy capacity. In addition, solid polymer batteries are environmentally friendly, lighter because they have no metal shell and safer because they contain no flammable solvent.

Zinc-Air

Of the current battery technologies, the one offering the most dense storage is zinc-air. One reason is that part of its chemical needs is external. Zinc-air batteries use atmospheric oxygen as their cathode reactant, hence the "air" in the name. Small holes in the battery casing allow air in to react with a powered zinc anode through a highly conductive potassium hydroxide electrolyte.

Originally created for use in primary batteries, zinc-air batteries were characterized by long stable storage life, at least when kept sealed from the air and thus inactive. A sealed zinc-air cell loses only about 2 percent of its capacity after a year of storage. Battery makers have adapted zinc-air technology for secondary storage. Zinc-air cells work best when frequently or continuously used in low-drain situations. The chief drawback of zinc-air batteries is, however, a high internal resistance, which means zinc air batteries must be huge to satisfy high current needs; for notebook PCs, that means an auxiliary battery pack about the size of the PC itself.

Zinc-air secondary cells are so new that they have been only crudely adapted to portable PC applications. One of the first products was the PowerSlice XL, developed jointly by Hewlett-Packard and AER Energy Resources for the HP OmniBook 600 notebook PC. The 7.3-pound external battery can power the OmniBook for about 12 hours.

Standards

Contrary to appearances, most rechargeable batteries used by notebook PCs are standard sizes. Computer manufacturers, however, package these standard-size batteries in custom battery packs that may fit only one model of computer. Usually, you cannot change the batteries in the pack but must buy a new replacement if something goes awry.

Attempts at standardizing batteries for notebook PCs have fallen flat, as witnessed by the near extinction of Duracell's "standard" designs. PC makers find proprietary cells more profitable. They can put a few dollars of individual cells in a cheap but odd plastic package and sell the assembly for a hundred dollars or more.

In replacing or repairing the battery pack of your portable PC, you can subvert the manufacturer's efforts to exploit the profits of its proprietary design. The individual batteries in the custom packs used by many notebook computer makers contain several standard-size cells. If you are up to a challenge, you can disassemble the packs, remove the individual cells (they look like ordinary flashlight batteries only smaller and usually lack labels), and replace them with new cells. A couple of warnings are in order: For reliability, these cells are usually soldered together, so you'll need proficiency with a soldering iron to replace batteries. Moreover, you should replace all the cells in a given pack at the same time. Never replace a single cell. Always replace the cells with those of equivalent capacity and technology; more recent battery packs have built-in intelligence that doesn't expect any yahoo is going to monkey with its inner workings, so your change has to be an exact replacement.

Smart Battery Specifications

Rechargeable batteries are fraught with problems. Drain them too much and you kill them. Charge them too much and you kill them. Charge them not enough and you'll wish you were dead when they run dry mid-continent when you have only the rest of the flight to finish your report.

Charging and monitoring the charge of batteries has always been problematic. Both capacity and charge characteristics vary with the battery type and over the life of a given battery.

The smartest conventional battery chargers monitor not the voltage but the temperature of their subjects because a sharp rise in temperature is the best indication available to the charger of the completion of its work. Even this rise varies with battery chemistry, so a nicad and NiMH battery present different—and confusing—temperature characteristics that would lead to a charger mistaking one for the other, possibly damaging the battery.

The Smart Battery system, developed jointly by battery maker Duracell and Intel and first published as the Smart Battery Data Specification, version 1.0, on February 15, 1995, eliminates these problems by endowing batteries with enough brains to tell their condition. When matched to a charger with an equivalent IQ that follows the Smart Charger specification, the Smart Battery gets charged perfectly every time with never a worry about over-charging.

The Smart Battery system defines a standard with several layers that distribute intelligence between battery, charger, and your PC. It provides for an inexpensive communication link between them—System Management Bus, the equivalent of ACCESS.bus, —a protocol for exchanging messages, and message formats themselves.

The Smart Battery Data Specification outlines the information that a battery can convey to its charger and the message format for doing so. Among other data that the battery can relay are its chemistry, its capacity, its voltage, and even its physical packaging. Messages warn not only about the current status of the battery's charge but even how many charge/recharge cycles the battery has endured so the charger can monitor its long-term prognosis. The specification is independent of the chemistry used by the battery and even the circuitry used to implement its functions. What matters is the connection (the System Management Bus) and the messages sent by the battery.

Complementing the battery standard is the Smart Battery Charger specification that, in addition to describing the data exchanged between charger and battery, categorizes the relationship between Smart Batteries and different charger implementations.

Completing the system are a description of its System Management Bus and a matching BIOS interface standard that provides a common control system to link to PC software and operating systems.

Clock Batteries

Nearly every PC since the AT was introduced in 1984 has had a time-of-day clock built into its system board circuitry. To keep proper track of the hours, days, and eons, this clock needs to run continuously even when the computer itself is switched off or unplugged. The source for the needed power is a small battery.

Different manufacturers have taken various approaches to supplying this power. Once, some manufacturers put lithium primary batteries in a plastic holder accessible at the rear of the system unit. Most PC makers put the batteries inside, often hidden if not inaccessible. More recent machines often use integrated clock modules such as those made by Dallas Semiconductor, which have small lithium cells built into molded plastic modules. Some machines make these modules user-replaceable; others solder them in place. In that the modules are rated for a 10-year life, you in theory may never need to replace one during the brief period your PC is actually useful.

Lithium cells have several notable aspects. They offer a high energy density, packing much power for their size. Moreover, they have a very long shelf life. Whereas conventional zinc-carbon dry cells lose potency after a year or so even when no power is being drawn from them, lithium cells keep most of their power for a decade. These qualities make lithium cells suited to providing clock power because today's solid-state clocks draw a minuscule amount of power—so small that when battery and circuit are properly matched, battery life nearly equals shelf life.

The downside of these lithium cells is that they are expensive and often difficult to find. Another shortcoming is that the metals used in them result in an output voltage of three volts per cell. A one-cell lithium battery produces too little voltage to operate standard digital circuits; a two-cell lithium battery produces too much.

Of course, engineers always can regulate away the excess voltage, and that is typically done. Poor regulator design, however, wastes more power than is used, robbing the battery of its life. Some PCs suffer from this design problem and consequently give frightfully short battery life.

Many computer makers avoid the expense and rarity of lithium batteries by adding battery holders for four (or so) type AA cells. Because zinc-carbon and alkaline cells produce 1.5 volts each, a four pack puts out the same six volts as a dual-cell lithium battery and can suffer the same problems in improperly designed PCs—only more so because the cells have shorter lives. A three-pack of AA cells produces 4.5 volts, which is adequate for most clock circuits and need not be hampered by regulation. Special alkaline PC battery modules are available that combine three ordinary cells into one package with the proper connector to match most system boards.

Notebook Power

Portable computers put contradictory requirements on their batteries; they must produce as much power for as long as possible, yet be as small and light as possible. Filling those needs simultaneously is impossible, so notebook computer batteries are always a compromise.

All three of the most popular storage batteries—lead-acid, nicad, and nickel-hydride—are used in notebook and sub-notebook computers. From your perspective as an end user, however, the technology doesn't matter as long as the result is a PC that you can carry without stretching your arms too long and use without getting caught short too often. Odds are, however, you will see nickel-hydride batteries increasing in popularity in notebook computers because of their greater storage density and less hazardous nature.

Notebook computer makers traditionally design the packaging for the batteries of their machines. These custom designs enable them to better integrate the battery with the rest of the notebook package. It also makes you dependent on the computer manufacturer for replacement batteries. (Most packs have standard-size cells inside. You can crack the battery pack open and replace the cells, but the effort is rarely worth the reward.)

This situation is changing. One battery manufacturer (Duracell) has proposed standard sizes for rechargeable batteries for notebook computers.

Rather than battery type or packaging, care is most important with computer batteries. If you take proper care of your PC's batteries, they will deliver power longer—both more time per charge and more time before replacement.

Battery Safety

The maximum current any battery can produce is limited by its internal resistance. Zinc-carbon batteries have a relatively high resistance and produce small currents, on the order of a few hundred milliamperes. Lead-acid, nickel-cadmium, and nickel-hydride batteries have very low internal resistances and can produce prodigious currents. If you short the terminals of one of these batteries, whatever produces the short circuit—wires, a strip of metal, a coin in your pocket—becomes hot because of resistive heating. For example, you can melt a wrench by placing it across the terminals of a fully charged automotive battery. Or you can start a fire with something inadvertently shorting the terminals of the spare nickel-cadmium battery for your notebook or sub-notebook computer. Be careful and never allow anything to touch these battery terminals except the contacts of your notebook PC.

When a battery is charged, a process called electrolysis takes place inside. If you remember your high school science experiments, electrolysis is what you did to break ordinary water into hydrogen and oxygen using electricity. Hydrogen is an explosive gas; oxygen is an oxidizer. Both are produced when charging batteries. Normally, these gases are absorbed by the battery before they can do anything (such as explode), but too great a charging current (as results from applying too high a voltage) can cause them to build up. Trying to charge a primary battery produces the same gas build-up. As a result, the battery can explode from too great an internal pressure or from combustion of the gases. Even if the battery does not catastrophically fail, its life will be greatly reduced. In other words, use only the charger provided with a portable PC battery and never try to hurry things along.

Nearly all batteries contain harmful chemicals of some kind. Even zinc-carbon batteries contain manganese, which is regarded as hazardous. All batteries present some kind of environmental hazard, so be sure to properly dispose of them. Some manufacturers are beginning to provide a means of recycling batteries. Encourage them by taking advantage of their offers.

Desktop PC Power Supplies

Most PCs package their power supplies as a subassembly that's complete in itself and simply screws into the chassis and plugs into the system board and other devices that require its electricity. The power supply itself is ensconced in a metal box perforated with holes that let heat leak out and prevent your fingers from poking in.

In fact, the safety provided by the self-contained and fully armored PC power supply is one of the prime advantages of the original design. All the life-threatening voltages—in particular, line voltage—are contained inside the box of the power supply. Only low, non-threatening voltages are accessible—that is, touchable—on your PC's system board and expansion boards. You can grab a board inside your PC even when the system is turned on and not worry about electrocution (although you might burn yourself on a particularly intemperate semiconductor or jab an ill-cut circuit lead through a finger).

Grabbing a board out of a slot of an operating computer is not safe for the computer's circuits, however. Pulling a board out is apt to bridge together some pins on its slot connector, if but for an instant. As a result, the board (and your PC's motherboard) may find unexpected voltages attacking, possibly destroying, its circuits. These surprises are most likely in EISA systems because of their novel expansion connectors. In other words, never plug in or remove an expansion board from a PC that has its power switched on. Although you may often be successful, the penalty for even one failure should be enough to deter your impatience.

In most PCs, the power supply serves a secondary function. The fan that cools the power supply circuits also provides the airflow that cools the rest of the system. This fan also supplies most of the noise that PCs generate while they are running. In general, the power supply fan operates as an exhaust fan; it blows outward. Air is sucked through the other openings in the power supply from the space inside your system. This gives dust in the air taken into your PC a chance to settle anywhere on your system board before getting blown out through the power supply.

Legacy PCs typically followed one of two standards for their power supplies—XT-size and AT-size supplies. The chief difference was the space available in the case. The ATX specification adds a new design that has become popular in systems following that standard.

Power Management

With few advances in battery storage density expected in the near-term future, PC makers have relied on reducing the power consumption of their notebook PCs to extend the time a machine can operate between battery charges.

Engineers can use two basic strategies to reduce the power consumption of PCs. They can design circuits and components to use less power, and they can manage the power used by the devices. Managing power needs usually means switching off whatever system components aren't being actively used. Although the two design methods can be used separately, they are usually used in tandem to shrink PC power needs as much as possible.

Microprocessors, the most power hungry of PC circuits, were among the first devices to gain built-in power management. System Management Mode endowed processors with the ability to slow down and shut off unnecessary circuits when they were idle. Similarly, makers of hard disk drives added sleep modes to spin down their platters and reduce power needs. Most PCs also incorporated timers to darken their screens to further conserve power.

Although these techniques can be successful in trimming power demands, they lack a unified control system. In response, the industry developed the Advanced Power Management interface to give overall control to the power-savings systems in PCs. More recently, APM has been updated and augmented by the Advanced Configuration and Power Interface specification.

Advanced Power Management

The Advanced Power Management interface specification was jointly developed by Intel and Microsoft to integrate the control of hardware power-saving features with software control. First published in January 1992 as the APM BIOS Interface Specification, the current version, 1.2, was published in February 1996.

Although nominally a BIOS interface, the APM specification describes a layered control system that controls PC devices to reduce power consumption using both BIOS and API interfaces. To be fully functional, APM requires a compatible BIOS and hardware devices that recognize APM control. In addition, hardware devices may have their own built-in automatic power management functions that are not controlled by your PC's software. For example, a hard disk drive may automatically power down after a given period without accesses without a specific command from your PC. The APM specification tolerates but does not affect these built-in functions.

States

APM is an overall system feature. Although it has the ability to individually control the features of each device it manages, the basic design APM controls all devices together to conserve power. It manages system power consumption by shifting the overall operating mode of the PC to *APM states*. APM shifts the operating state of the system based on the needs of the system as determined from a combination of software commands and events. The various APM states provide for power savings in five levels. The APM specification gives each of these levels a specific state name.

The first, *full on state*, means that the system is operating at full power without any management at all. The APM software is not in control, and no power savings can be achieved. A system without APM or with its APM features disabled operates in full on state.

When the APM system is active, all devices run in their normal, full power consumption modes. The system is up and ready to do business, operating in what the specification calls *APM enabled* state.

In *APM standby* state, the microprocessor may stop and many of the system devices are turned off or operate at reduced power. The system usually cannot process data, but its memory is kept alive and the status of all devices is preserved. When your activity or some other event (for example a key press, mouse move, or network command requires system attention, the PC can rapidly shift from standby to enabled state.

In *APM suspend* state, the system shifts to its maximum power savings mode; most devices that following the APM standard are switched off, and the microprocessor switches to its lowest power state with its clock turned off. Your PC becomes a vegetable.

Hibernation is a special implementation of suspend state that allows the system to be switched entirely off and still be restored to the point at which it entered suspend state. When entering suspend state, the system saves all of its operating parameters. In entering hibernation, the system copies memory and other status data to non-volatile storage such as hard disk, allowing you to switch off memory power. A system event can shift back to enabled state from suspend or hibernation, but changing modes from suspend to enabled takes substantially longer than from standby to enabled.

Off state is exactly what the name implies. Power to the system is entirely off. The computer is more a mineral than vegetable. The only event that restores the system is turning it back on. If you enter off state directly—say by switching off your PC—no status information or memory gets saved. The system must run through the entire boot-up process and start with a clean slate.

Structure

APM adds a layered control system to give you, your software, and your hardware a mechanism to shift states manually or automatically.

The bottom layer of the system is the *APM BIOS*, which provides a common software interface for controlling hardware devices under the specification. The APM specifies that the BIOS have at least a real-mode interface that uses interrupt 15(Hex) to implement its functions. In addition, the APM BIOS may also use 16- or 32-bit protected mode using entry points that are returned from the protected-mode connection call using the real-mode interrupt.

The APM BIOS is meant to manage the power of the motherboard. Its code is specific to a given motherboard. Under the APM specification, the APM BIOS can operate independently of other APM layers to effect some degree of power saving in the system by itself. Your PC's operating system can switch off this internal BIOS APM control to manage system power itself, still using the APM BIOS interface functions to control hardware features.

Linking the APM BIOS to your operating system is the APM driver. The driver provides a set of function calls to the operating system, which it translates to BIOS interrupts. The driver is more than a mere translator, however. It is fully interactive with both the BIOS and operating system. For example, the BIOS may generate its own request to power down the system, and the driver then checks with the operating system to determine whether it should permit the power down.

The APM system has a built-in fail-safe. The APM driver must interact with the BIOS at least once per second. If it does not, after a second second, the BIOS assumes the operating system has malfunctioned and takes self-contained control. The driver can regain control by sending the appropriate commands (interrupts) to the BIOS.

Certain system events termed *wake-up calls* tell the APM system to shift modes. Interrupts generated by such events as a press of the resume button, the modem detecting an incoming telephone ring, or an alarm set on the real-time clock can command the APM BIOS to shift the system from suspend to enabled state.

Operation

All real-mode APM interrupt functions require that the AH register of the microprocessor be set at 53(Hex) on entry, identifying that the requested function is for APM. The AL register then defines the function to be carried out. Other registers indicate which devices in the system (which essentially means the microprocessor or everything else) to affect and the parameters of the command. For example, to shift the system from on to APM enable state, your operating system can issue interrupt 15(Hex) with AH set at 53(Hex) and AL set at 08(Hex). The BX register identifies the devices to be affected, and CX tells the

BIOS whether to enable (set at 0001) or disable (set at 0000) power management.
Table 25.3 lists the 17 functions defined for the APM BIOS.

TABLE 25.3   APM Real-Mode Interrupt Functions

AH Value	Function
00(Hex)	APM installation check
01(Hex)	APM real-mode interface connect
02(Hex)	APM protected-mode connect 16 bits
03(Hex)	APM protected-mode connect 32 bits
04(Hex)	APM interface disconnect
05(Hex)	CPU idle
06(Hex)	CPU busy
07(Hex)	Set power state
08(Hex)	Enable/disable power management
09(Hex)	Restore power-on defaults
0A(Hex)	Get power status
0B(Hex)	Get power managed event
0C(Hex)	Get power state
0D(Hex)	Enable/disable device management
0E(Hex)	APM driver version
0F(Hex)	Engage/disengage power management
10(Hex)	Get capabilities
11(Hex)	Get/set/disable resume timer
12(Hex)	Enable/disable resume on ring indicator
13(Hex)	Enable/disable timer-based requests
80(Hex)	OEM APM function

By loading the BX register with an appropriate value, the driver or operating system can
command an individual device, class of devices, or the entire APM system. Device classes
include mass storage, the display system, serial ports, parallel ports, network adapters, and
PC Card sockets.

To determine the state of devices in the system, the APM design requires that the BIOS
be polled at the once-per-second rate. The APM driver monitors the status of power

managed events using the 0B(Hex), and the BIOS responds by sending an event code back to the driver in its BX register. Of course, several events might occur in the second between polls. To accommodate multiple events, the driver repeatedly polls the BIOS. The BIOS reports each event in sequence. The driver ceases its polling when the BIOS runs out of events to report. Table 25.4 lists APM power management events.

TABLE 25.4   APM Power Management Events

BX Value	Event
0001(Hex)	System standby request
0002(Hex)	System suspend request
0003(Hex)	Normal resume system
0004(Hex)	Critical resume system
0005(Hex)	Battery low
0006(Hex)	Power status change
0007(Hex)	Update time
0008(Hex)	Critical system suspend
0009(Hex)	User system standby request
000A(Hex)	User system suspend request
000B(Hex)	System standby resume
000C(Hex)	Capabilities change
000D to 00FF(Hex)	Reserved system events
0100 to 01FF(Hex)	Reserved device events
0200 to 02FF(Hex)	OEM-defined APM events
0300 to FFFF(Hex)	Reserved

The driver can take appropriate action on its own or relay the information it obtains to the operating system, which then makes its own judgment about what to do.

Advanced Configuration and Power Interface

The next generation of power management will integrate PC hardware and operating systems into a cooperative power-saving whole called the *Advanced Configuration and Power Interface*. This new standard, developed jointly by Intel, Microsoft, and Toshiba, builds on the foundation of APM with the goal of putting the operating system into control of the PC power system. Version 1.0 was formally released in December 1996.

ACPI is an integral part of the Microsoft-inspired *OnNow initiative*, which seeks to mini-mize the delays inherent in starting up and shutting down a PC burdened with megabytes of operating system overhead, to let the PC run tasks while it appears to be off, and to lower the overall power requirement of the PC. New operating systems require time to test the host PC, check out plug-and-play devices, and set up their structures. These func-tions take so long that it makes warming up your system seem to start at absolute zero. OnNow seeks to eliminate that wait. At the same time, it promises to integrate the power and configuration interfaces of modern operating systems (meaning Windows) so that programmers can write to a common standard.

To bring these features to life, the OnNow design moves the operating system to the cen-ter of power management using ACPI and builds a new table structure for storing and organizing configuration information.

As a power management system, the ACPI specification can accommodate the needs of any operating system, integrating all the necessary power management features required in a PC from the application software down to the hardware level. It enables the operating system to automatically turn on and off and adjust the power consumption of nearly any peripheral, from hard disk drives to displays to printers. It can reach beyond the PC to other devices that may be connected into a single system some time in the future—televisions, stereos, VCRs, telephones, and even other appliances. Using the Smart Battery specification, under ACPI the operating system takes command of battery charg-ing and monitoring. It also monitors the thermal operation of the system, reducing speed or shutting down a PC that should overheat.

The ACPI standard itself defines the interface for controlling device power and a means of identifying hardware features. The interface uses a set of five hardware registers that are controlled through a higher level application programming interface through the operating system. The descriptive elements identify not only power management but also device features through a nested set of tables. It supplements plug-and-play technology, extending its existing structure with an architecture-independent implementation and replaces the plug-and-play BIOS with a new ACPI BIOS.

Soft Off

The fundamental and most noticeable change made by ACPI is the power button on the front of new PCs. In systems equipped to handle ACPI, this is a soft switch or set of two switches. Although one of these switches may be labeled power and imply that it is an on/off switch, in the ACPI scheme of things the power switch does not actually switch the power to the system on and off. Rather, it sends a command to the system to shut itself off—and not exactly what you think is off.

Using the front panel off button actually puts the PC in a new mode called *soft off*. In this mode, the PC acts like you've shut it off and requires rebooting to restart it. But it doesn't remove all power from the system. A slight bit of power continues to be supplied to the motherboard and expansion boards, enabling them to monitor external events. For example, a network board will still listen to network traffic for packets targeted at it. A modem or fax board may lie in wait of a telephone call. Or you may set a time that starts the tape backup system. When any of these designated external events occurs, the PC automatically switches itself back on to deal with it.

ACPI envisions that some manufacturers will also put a *sleep switch* on the front panel. Pressing it will put the PC in a sleep mode that uses somewhat more power than soft off but allows the system to resume operation more quickly.

States

As with APM, the ACPI design works by shifting modes called *ACPI states*. The states differ substantially from those in APM. Under ACPI, there is a great variety of states, four basic types—global, special sleep, microprocessor, and device—and the last of these is further subdivided. ACPI lets the operating system control all aspects of the power consumption of a PC by shifting the single devices or the entire system between these states.

The ACPI global states most closely correspond to the APM modes:

G0 is a working state in which the PC is operating normally. Programs execute actively. Even in G0 state, however, some devices that are inactive may automatically power down, but they will quickly resume normal operation when they are called upon.

G1 is a sleeping state during which it may appear like your PC has shut down—there's no evidence of operation on the monitor screen—although some internal circuits remain active. The active circuits constantly monitor internal and external events and can switch your PC back to its working state when necessary. Various system events can cause the PC to return to working state, for example an alarm from the system timer or an incoming ring from your modem. In the ACPI definition, G1 has many sub-states that are defined by the devices being managed. The standard allows great flexibility in this state, not only in terms of how (and how quickly) normal operation resumes. Within G1 are several special sleeping states that tradeoff resume speed for reduction in power consumption.

G2 is the new soft-off state.

G3 is complete power off, equivalent to unplugging the PC.

The meaning of the ACPI device modes varies with the device type. The states differ in four chief characteristics—the amount of power that the state saves over normal operation; how long is required to restore the device from the state to normal operation; how much of the operating context of the device is saved in entering the state; and what must be done to return the device back to normal operation. All four device states are designated with names beginning with the letter "D":

D0 designates the fully on state at which the device operates at top speed, is fully responsive, and consumes the most power.

D1 saves power over the D0 state. How it achieves that goal depends on the type of device. In general, the device can quickly shift back to D0 state without needing to reset or losing data.

D2 further saves power over the D1 state and is again device-specific. In general, the device becomes less responsive. It may need to reset itself or go through its power-on sequence to return to the D0 state.

D3 corresponds to the power-off state. Electrical power is removed from the device, and the device does not function. It must go through its power-on sequence to begin operations again. Upon entering D3, none of its operating context gets saved. This achieves the greatest power savings but requires the longest restoration time.

Under ACPI, the microprocessor is a special device that has its own four operating states:

C0 state designates the processor executing at full speed.

C1 state puts the processor in its halt state under command of the ACPI driver without affecting other aspects of its operation.

C2 state shifts the processor to low power state and maintains the integrity of the system's memory caches. In a fully implemented ACPI system, the microprocessor will shift to this state if a bus master takes control of the system.

C3 state pushes the processor down to low power state and does not maintain cache memory.

Sleeping, defined as a global mode of the system (G1, above) is not a single defined state under ACPI but has several variations. PCs may implement one or more of these sleeping states that provide progressively greater power savings. ACPI allows engineers to configure their systems to step down between the supported states to progressive save more power the longer the system remains idle.

S0 state is not sleeping at all but is the fully awake and operating PC.

S1 state shuts down the microprocessor but maintains full system integrity including the memory cache. Most PCs can emerge from S1 state instantly with virtually no delay (latency).

S2 state maintains the microprocessor state as well as that of the rest of the PC except for the memory cache. The PC can wake up quickly with the only loss of a few wasted processor cycles as the cache fills and regains operation.

S3 state saves the microprocessor registers and system device data to memory, shuts down most of the circuitry of the system, then shifts the memory to its low-power mode (in which it is refreshed but cannot be read or written to). Only enough circuitry stays awake to revive the system (including the real-time clock, which may wake up the system at a preset a time). Because all data is held in solid-state memory, waking up is quite quick, typically only a few seconds.

S4 state powers down all devices in the PC. The system hardware no longer maintains memory integrity or device context. The ACPI-compliant operating system is responsible for saving this information, typically spooling the contents of memory and device states to disk. Memory support circuits shut down to save power. Waking up requires shifting all the data save on disk back into memory. With today's systems with 128MB or more of memory, this process can impost a delay that ranges from a few to a few dozen seconds.

S5 state is not G2 sleeping at all but a G3 soft off condition. When shifting into the S5 state, the operating system does not save information about the PC. It must boot up exactly as it would from any other soft off condition.

Configuration

To handle its configuration function, ACPI must manage a tremendous amount of data, describing not only the power needs and management capabilities of the system but also the features available for all of the devices connected to the system. ACPI stores this information in a hierarchy of tables.

The overall master table is called the Root System Description Table. It has no fixed place in memory. Rather, upon booting up, the BIOS locates a pointer to the table during the memory scan that's part of the boot-up process. The Root System Description Table itself is identified in memory because it starts with the signature "RSDT." Following the signature is an array of pointers that tell the operating system the location of other description tables that provide it with the information it needs about the standards defined on the current system and individual devices.

One of these tables is called the *Fixed ACPI Description Table*. In it, the operating system finds the base address of the registers used for controlling the power management system. In addition, the Fixed ACPI Description Table also points to the Differentiated System Description Table, which provides variable information about the design of the base system. Some of the entries in this table are Differentiated Definition Blocks, which can contain data about a device or even a program that sets up other structures and define new attributes. ACPI defines its own languages for programming these functions.

Windows provides a means to control the power features of systems that support APM and ACPI. (Although Windows 98 supports ACPI, Windows NT through version 4.0 does not.)

You can access these control features through the Power Management icon you'll find in the Windows Control Panel. The controls available on various models of PCs differ because of the flexibility afforded engineers in the standards. Typically portable computers—that is, those with battery power—will have more management options than desktop systems.

Power Protection

Normal line voltage is often far from the 115-volt alternating current you pay for. It can be a rather inhospitable mixture of aberrations such as spikes and surges mixed with noise, dips, and interruptions. None of these oddities is desirable, and some can be powerful enough to cause errors to your data or damage to your computer. Although you cannot avoid them, you can protect your PC against their ill effects.

Power Line Irregularities

Power line problems can be broadly classed into three basic categories: overvoltage, undervoltage, and noise. Each problem has its own distinct causes and requires a particular kind of protection.

Overvoltage

The deadliest power line pollution is overvoltage—lightning-like high potential spikes that sneak into your PC and actually melt down its silicon circuitry. Often, the damage is invisible—except for the very visible lack of image on your monitor. Other times, you can actually see charred remains inside your computer as a result of the overvoltage.

As its name implies, an overvoltage gushes more voltage into your PC than the equipment can handle. In general—and in the long run—your utility supplies power that's very close to the ideal, usually within about 10 percent of its rated value. If it always stayed within that range, the internal voltage regulation circuitry of your PC could take its fluctuations in stride.

Short-duration overvoltages larger than that may occur too quickly for your utility's equipment to compensate, however. Moreover, many overvoltages are generated nearby, possibly within your home or office, and your utility has no control over them. Brief peaks as high as 25,000 volts have been measured on normal lines, usually due to nearby lightning strikes. Lightning doesn't have to hit a power line to induce a voltage spike that can damage your PC. When it does hit a wire, however, everything connected to that circuit is likely to take on the characteristics of a flash bulb.

Overvoltages are usually divided into two classes by duration. Short-lived overvoltages are called spikes or transients and last from a nanosecond (billionth of a second) to a microsecond (one millionth of a second). Longer duration overvoltages are usually termed surges and can stretch into milliseconds.

Sometimes, power companies do make errors and send too much voltage down the line, causing your lights to glow brighter and your PC to teeter closer to disaster. The occurrences are simply termed overvoltages.

Most AC-power PCs are designed to withstand moderate overvoltages without damage. Most machines tolerate brief surges in the range of 800 to 2,000 volts. On the other hand, power cords and normal home and office electrical wiring breaks (by arcing over between the wiring conductors) at potentials between about 4,000 and 6,000 volts. In other words, electrical wiring limits the maximum surge potential your PC is likely to face to no more than about 6,000 volts. Higher voltage surges simply can't reach your PC.

Besides intensity and energy, surges also differ in their mode. Modern electrical wiring involves three conductors: hot, neutral, and ground. Hot is the wire that carries the power; neutral provides a return path; and ground provides protection. The ground lead is ostensibly connected directly to the earth.

A surge can occur between any pairing of conductors: hot and neutral, hot and ground, or neutral and ground. The first pairing is termed normal mode. It reflects a voltage difference between the power conductors used by your PC. When a surge arises from a voltage difference between hot or neutral and ground, it is called common mode.

Surges caused by utility switching and natural phenomena—for the most part lightning—occur in the normal mode. They have to. The National Electrical Code requires that the neutral lead and the ground lead be bonded together at the service entrance (where utility power enters a building) as well as at the utility line transformer typically hanging from a telephone pole near your home or office. At that point, neutral and ground must have the same potential. Any external common mode surge becomes normal mode.

Common mode surges can, however, originate within a building because long runs of wire stretch between most outlets and the service entrance, and the resistance of the wire allows the potential on the neutral wire to drift from that of ground. Although opinions differ, recent European studies suggest that common mode surges are the most dangerous to your equipment. (European wiring practice is more likely to result in common mode surges because the bonding of neutral and ground is made only at the transformer.)

Undervoltage

An undervoltage occurs when your equipment gets less voltage than it expects. Undervoltages can range from sags, which are dips of but a few volts, to complete outages or blackouts. Durations vary from nearly instantaneous to hours—or days, if you haven't paid your light bill recently.

Very short dips, sags, and even blackouts are not a problem. As long as they are less than a few dozen milliseconds—about the blink of an eye—your computer should purr along as if nothing happened. The only exceptions are a few old computers that have power supplies with very sensitive power-good signals. A short blackout may switch off the power-good signal, shutting down your computer even though enough electricity is available (See Appendix A, "PC History.")

Most PCs are designed to withstand prolonged voltage dips of about 20 percent without shutting down. Deeper dips or blackouts lasting for more than those few milliseconds result in shutdown. Your PC is forced to cold start, booting up afresh. Any work you have not saved before the undervoltage is lost.

Noise

Noise is a nagging problem in the power supplies of most electronic devices. It comprises all the spurious signals that wires pick up as they run through electromagnetic fields. In many cases, these signals can sneak through the filtering circuitry of the power supply and interfere with the signals inside the electrical device.

For example, the power cord of a tape recorder might act as an antenna and pick up a strong radio signal. The broadcast could then sneak through the circuitry of the recorder and mix with the music it is supposed to be playing. As a result, you might hear a CB radio maven croaking over your Mozart.

In computers, these spurious signals could confuse the digital thought coursing through the circuitry of the machine. As a practical matter, they don't. All better computers are designed to minimize the leakage of their signals from inside their cases into the outside world to minimize your computer's interfering with your radio and television. The same protection against signals getting out works extremely well against other signals getting in. Personal computers are thus well-protected against line noise. You probably won't need a noise filter to protect your computer.

Then again, noise filtering doesn't hurt. Most power-protection devices have noise filtering built into them because it's cheap, and it can be an extra selling point (particularly to people who believe they need it). Think of it as a bonus. You can take advantage of its added protection—but don't go out of your way to get it.

Overvoltage Protection

Surges are dangerous to your PC because the energy they contain can rush through semi-conductor circuits faster than the circuits can dissipate it; the silicon junctions of your PC's integrated circuits fry in microseconds. Spike and surge protectors are designed to prevent most short-duration, high-intensity overvoltages from reaching your PC. They absorb excess voltages before they can travel down the power line and into your computer's power supply. Surge suppressors are typically connected between the various conductors of the wiring leading to your PC. They work by conducting electricity only when the voltage across their leads exceeds a certain level; that is, they conduct and short out the excess voltage in spikes and surges before it can pop into your PC. The voltage at which the varistor starts conducting and clipping spikes and surges is termed its clamping voltage.

The most important characteristics of overvoltage protection devices are how fast they work and how much energy they can dissipate. Generally, a faster response time or clamping speed is better. Response times can be as short as picoseconds—trillionths of a second. The larger the energy-handling capacity of a protection device, the better. Energy-handling capacities are measured in watt-seconds or joules. Devices claiming the capability to handle millions of watts are not unusual.

Four kinds of devices are most often used to protect against surges: metal oxide varistors (MOVs), gas tubes, avalanche diodes, and reactive circuits. Each has its own strengths and weaknesses. Typically, commercial surge protectors use several technologies in combination.

Metal Oxide Varistors

The most popular surge protection devices are based on metal oxide varistors, or MOVs, disc-shaped electronic components typically made from a layer of zinc oxide particles held between two electrodes. The granular zinc oxide offers a high resistance to the flow of electricity until the voltage reaches a breakover point. The electrical current then forms a low-resistance path between the zinc oxide particles that shorts out the electrical flow.

MOVs are the most popular surge protection component because they are inexpensive to manufacture and easy to tailor to a particular application. Their energy-handling capability can be increased simply by enlarging the device. (Typical MOVs are about an inch in diameter; high power MOVs may be twice that.) Figure 25.1 shows a typical MOV.

FIGURE 25.1
A metal oxide varistor.

The downside to MOVs is that they degrade. Surges tend to form preferred paths between the zinc oxide particles, reducing the resistance to electrical flow. Eventually, the MOV shorts out, blowing a fuse or (more likely) overheating the MOV until it destroys itself. The MOV can end its life in flames or with no external change at all—except that it no longer offers surge protection.

Gas Tubes

Gas tubes are self-descriptive: tubes filled with special gases with low dielectric potential designed to arc-over at predictable low voltages. The internal arc short circuits the surge. Gas tubes can conduct a great deal of power—thousands of kilowatts—and react quickly, typically in about a nanosecond.

On the negative side, a gas tube does not start conducting (and suppressing a surge) until the voltage applied it reaches two to four times the tube's rating. The tube itself does not dissipate the energy of the surge; it just shorts it out, allowing your wiring to absorb the energy. Moreover, the discharge voltage of a gas tube can be affected by ambient lighting (hence most manufacturers shield them from light).

Worst of all, when a gas tube starts conducting, it doesn't like to stop. Typically, a gas tube requires a reversal of current flow to quench its internal arc, which means that the power going to your PC could be shorted for up to 8.33 milliseconds. Sometimes, gas tubes continue to conduct for several AC current cycles, perhaps long enough for your PC power supply to shut down. (Many PC power supplies switch off when power interruptions exceed about 18 milliseconds.)

Avalanche Diodes

Avalanche diodes are semiconductor circuits similar to zener diodes that offer a high resistance to electrical flow until the voltage applied to them reaches a breakover potential. At that point, they switch on and act as conductors to short out the applied current. Avalanche diodes operate more quickly than other protection devices but have limited energy capacity, typically from 600 to 1,500 watts.

Reactive Circuits

Although MOVs, gas tubes, and avalanche diodes share the same operating principle—shorting out the surge before it gets to your PC—the reactive surge suppressor is different. The typical reactive surge suppressor uses a large inductance to resist the sharp voltage rise of a surge and spread it out over a longer time. Adding a capacitor tunes the reactance so that it can convert the surge into a semblance of a normal AC waveform. Other noise on the power line is also automatically absorbed.

Unfortunately, this form of reactive network has severe drawbacks. It doesn't eliminate the surge—only spreads out its energy. The size of the inductor determines the spread, and a large inductor is required for effective results. In addition, the device only works on normal mode surges. The reactance also can cause a common mode surge in the wiring leading to the device by raising the neutral line above ground potential.

Most commercial surge suppressors combine several of these technologies along with noise reduction circuitry, and better surge suppressors arrange them in multiple stages, isolated by inductors, to prolong life and improve response time. Heavy-duty components such as gas tubes or large MOVs form the first stage and absorb the brunt of the surge. A second stage with tighter control (more MOVs or avalanche diodes) knocks the surge voltage down further.

Thanks to the laws of thermodynamics, the excess energy in a surge cannot just disappear; it can only change form. With most surge suppression technologies (all except reactive devices), the overvoltage is converted into heat dissipated by the wiring between the device and the origin of the surge as well as inside the surge suppressor itself. The power in a large surge can destroy a surge suppressor so that it yields up its life to protect your PC.

Because they degrade cumulatively with every surge they absorb, MOVs are particularly prone to failure as they age. Eventually, an MOV will fail, sometimes in its own lightning-like burst. Although unlikely this failure will electrically damage the circuits of your computer, it can cause a fire—which can damage not just your PC, but your home, office, or self. Some manufacturers (for example, IBM) forego putting MOVs in their power supplies to preclude the potential for fire, which they see as less desirable than a PC failure.

An MOV-based surge suppressor also can fail more subtly; it just stops sucking up surges. Unbeknownst to you, your PC can be left unprotected. Many commercial surge suppressors have indicators designed to reveal the failure of an internal MOV.

In any case, a good strategy is to replace MOV-based surge suppressors periodically to ensure that they do their job and to lessen the likelihood of their failure. How often you replace them depends on how dirty an electrical diet you feed them. Every few years is generally a sufficient replacement interval.

Three devices help your computer deal with undervoltages. Voltage regulators keep varying voltages within the range that runs your PC but offer no protection against steep sags or blackouts. The standby power system and uninterruptible power system (UPS) fight against blackouts.

Voltage regulators are the same devices your utility uses to try to keep the voltage it supplies at a constant level. These giant regulators consist of large transformers with a number of taps or windings—outputs set at different voltage levels. Motors connected to the regulators move switches that select the taps that supply the voltage most nearly approximating normal line voltage. These mechanical regulators are gargantuan devices. Even the smallest of them is probably big enough to handle an entire office. In addition, they are inherently slow on the electrical time scale, and they may allow voltage dips long enough for data to be lost.

Solid-state voltage regulators use semiconductors to compensate for line voltage variations. They work much like the power supply inside your computer but can compensate over a wider range.

The saturable reactor regulator applies a DC control current to an extra control coil on the transformer, enough to "saturate" the transformer core. When saturation is achieved, no additional power can pass through the transformer. Regulating the DC control current adjusts the output of the transformer. These devices are inherently inefficient because they must throw away power throughout their entire regulating range.

Ferroresonant transformer regulators are "tuned" into saturation much the same as a radio is tuned—using a capacitor in conjunction with an extra winding. This tuning makes the transformer naturally resist any change in the voltage or frequency of its output. In effect, it becomes a big box of electrical inertia that not only regulates, but also suppresses voltage spikes and reduces line noise.

The measure of quality of a voltage regulator is its regulation, which specifies how close to the desired voltage the regulator maintains its output. Regulation is usually expressed as the output variation for a given change in input. The input range of a regulator indicates how wide a voltage variation the regulator can compensate for. This range should exceed whatever variations in voltage you expect to occur at your electrical outlets.

Blackout Protection

Both standby and uninterruptible power systems provide blackout protection in the same manner. They are built around powerful batteries that store substantial current. An inverter converts the direct current from the batteries into alternating current that can be used by your computer. A battery charger built into the system keeps the reserve power supply fully charged at all times.

Because they are so similar, the term UPS is often improperly used to describe both standby and uninterruptible power systems. They differ in one fundamental characteristic: The electricity provided by a standby power system is briefly interrupted in the period during which the device switches from utility power to its own internal reserves. An uninterruptible power system, as its name indicates, avoids any interruption to the electricity supplied to the device it protects. If your PC is sensitive to very short interruptions in its supply of electricity, this difference is critical.

Standby Power Systems

As the name implies, the standby power system constantly stands by, waiting for the power to fail so that it can leap into action. Under normal conditions—that is, when utility power is available—its battery charger draws only a slight current to keep its source of emergency energy topped off. The AC power line from which the standby supply feeds is directly connected to its output and thence to the computer. The batteries are out of the loop.

When the power fails, the standby supply switches into action—switch being the key word. The current-carrying wires inside the standby power supply that lead to the computer are physically switched from the utility line to the current coming from the battery-powered inverter.

The switching process requires a small but measurable amount of time. First, the failure of the electrical supply must be sensed. Even the fastest electronic voltage sensors take a finite time to detect a power failure. Even after a power failure is detected, another slight pause occurs before the computer receives its fresh supply of electricity while the switching action itself takes place. Most standby power systems switch quickly enough that the computer never notices the lapse. A few particularly unfavorable combinations of standby power systems and computers, however, may result in the computer shutting down during the switch.

Most standby power systems available today switch within one half of one cycle of the AC current they are supplied; that's less than 10 milliseconds, quick enough to keep nearly all PCs running as if no interruption occurred. Although the standby power system design does not protect against spikes and surges, most SPSs have other protection devices installed in their circuitry to ensure that your PC gets clean power.

Uninterruptible Power Systems

Traditionally, an uninterruptible power system supplied uninterrupted power because its output did not need to switch from line power to battery. Rather, its battery was constantly and continuously connected to the output of the system through its inverter. This kind of UPS always supplied power from the batteries to the computer. The computer was thus completely isolated from the vagaries of the AC electrical line. New UPS designs are more like standby systems but use clever engineering to bridge over even the briefest switching lulls. They, too, deliver a truly uninterrupted stream of power but can be manufactured for a fraction of the cost of the traditional design.

In an older UPS, the batteries are kept from discharging from the constant current drain of powering your computer by a large built-in charger. When the power fails, the charger stops charging, but the battery—without making the switch—keeps the electricity flowing to the connected computer. In effect, this kind of UPS is the computer's own generating station only inches away from the machine it serves, keeping it safe from the polluting effects of lightning and load transients. Dips and surges can never reach the computer. Instead, the computer gets a genuinely smooth, constant electrical supply exactly like the one for which it was designed.

Newer UPSs connect both the input power and the output of their inverters together through a special transformer, which is then connected to your PC or other equipment to be protected. Although utility power is available, this kind of UPS supplies it through the transformer to your PC. When the utility power fails, the inverter kicks in, typically within half a cycle. The inductance of the transformer, however, acts as a storage system and supplies the missing half-cycle of electricity during the switchover period.

The traditional style of UPS provides an extreme measure of surge and spike protection (as well as eliminates sags) because no direct connection bridges the power line and the protected equipment; spikes and their kin have no pathway to sneak in. Although the transformer in the new style of UPS absorbs many power line irregularities, overall it does not afford the same degree of protection. Consequently, these newer devices usually have other protection devices (such as MOVs) built in.

Specifications

The most important specification to investigate before purchasing any backup power device is its capacity as measured in volt-amperes (VA) or watts. This number should always be greater than the rating of the equipment to which the backup device is to be connected.

In alternating current (AC) systems, watts do not necessarily equal the product of volts and amperes (as they should by the definition that applies in DC systems) because the voltage and current can be out of phase with one another. That is, when the voltage is at a maximum, the current in the circuit can be at an intermediary value. So the peak values of voltage and amperage may occur at different times.

Power requires both voltage and current simultaneously. Consequently, the product of voltage and current (amperage) in an AC circuit is often higher than the actual power in the circuit. The ratio between these two values is called the power factor of the system.

What all this means to you is that volt-amperes and watts are not the same thing. Most backup power systems are rated in VA because it is a higher figure thanks to the power factor. You must make sure that the total VA used by your computer equipment is less than the VA available from the backup power system. Alternatively, you must make sure that the wattage used by your equipment is less than the wattage available from the backup power system. Don't indiscriminately mix the VA and watts in making comparisons.

To convert a VA rating to a watt rating, multiply the VA by the power factor of the backup power supply. To go the other way—watts to VA—divide the wattage rating of the backup power system by its power factor. (You can do the same thing with the equipment you want to plug into the power supply, but you may have a difficult time discovering the power factor of each piece of equipment. For PCs, a safe value to assume is 2/3.)

Standby and uninterruptible power systems also are rated as to how long they can supply battery power. This equates to the total energy (the product of power and time) that they store. Such time ratings vary with the VA the backup device must supply; because of finite battery reserves, it can supply greater currents only for shorter periods. Most manufacturers rate their backup systems for a given time of operation with a load of a particular size instead of in more scientific fashion using units of energy. For example, a backup system may be rated to run a 250 volt-ampere load for 20 minutes.

If you want an idea of the maximum possible time a given backup supply can carry your system, check the ratings of the batteries it uses. Most batteries are rated in ampere-hours, which describes how much current they can deliver for how long. To convert that rating to a genuine energy rating, multiply it by the nominal battery voltage. For example, a 12 volt, 6 amp-hour battery could, in theory, produce 72 watt-hours of electricity. That figure is theoretical rather than realistic because the circuitry that converts the battery DC to AC wastes some of the power and because ratings are only nominal for new batteries. However, the numbers you derive give you a limit. If you have only 72 watt-hours of battery, you can't expect the system to run your 250 VA PC for an hour. At most, you could expect 17 minutes; realistically, you might expect 12 to 15.

You probably will not need much time from a backup power system, however. In most cases, five minutes or less of backup time is sufficient because the point of a backup supply is not to keep a system running forever. Instead, the backup power system is designed to give you a chance to shut down your computer without losing your work. Shutting down shouldn't take more than a minute or two.

UPS makers warn that no matter the rating of your UPS, you should never plug a laser printer into it. The fusers in laser printers are about as power hungry as toasters; both are resistive heaters. The peak power demand when the fuser switches on can overload even larger UPSs and the continuing need for current can quickly drain batteries. Moreover, there's no need to keep a print job running during a power failure. Even if you lose a page, you can reprint it when the power comes back at far less expense than the cost of additional UPS power capable of handling the laser's needs. Some printers, such as inkjets, are friendlier to UPSs and can safely be connected, but you'll still be wasting capacity. The best strategy is to connect only your PC, your monitor, and any external disk drives to the UPS. Plug the rest of your equipment into a surge suppresser.

To handle such situations, many UPSs have both battery-protected outlets and outlets with only surge protection. Be sure to check which outlets you use with your equipment, making sure your PC has battery-backed protection.

Waveform

Different backup power systems also vary as to their output waveform. The perfect waveform is one that matches that the utility company makes—sine wave (or sinusoidal) power in which the voltage and current smoothly alternates between polarities 120 times a second (a frequency of 60Hz). Although the most desirable kind of power, smooth sine waves are difficult to generate. Electronic circuits such as those in a backup power system more easily create square waves, which abruptly switch between polarities. The compromise between the two—called modified square waves or modified sine waves (depending on who's doing the talking)—approximates the power factor of sine waves by modifying the duty cycle of square waves or stepping between two or more voltage levels in each power cycle. Figure 25.2 shows the shapes of these different waveforms.

FIGURE 25.2
*Power supply
waveforms.*

Sine wave   Square wave   Stepped wave

Considerable debate surrounds the issue of whether sine or square waves are better for your equipment. One manufacturer, Compaq, has even gone so far as recommending against the use of square wave power with its computers.

In truth, however, most waveform arguments are irrelevant for PC backup power systems. Although a backup power system should produce square waves most efficiently, commercial products show little correspondence between efficiency and output waveform. On the other hand, square waves are richer in harmonics that can leak into sensitive circuits as noise. But the filters in all PC power supplies effectively eliminate power line noise.

Perhaps the biggest shortcoming attributed to square waves is that they can cause transformers to overheat. All PC power supplies, however, use high-speed switching technology, which breaks the incoming waveform into a series of sharp pulses regardless of whether it is made from sine or square waves. Most monitors also use switching power supplies. Only linear power supplies, now rare in electronic equipment, may be prone to overheating from square waves. Moreover, standby power systems, the inverters of which are designed to operate your equipment for less than 30 minutes, do not provide local power long enough to create a severe overheating problem.

Interfaces

An ordinary UPS works effectively if you're sitting at your PC and the power fails. You can quickly assess whether it looks like the blackout will be short or long. (If the world is blowing away outside your window, you can be pretty sure any outage will be prolonged.) You can save your work, haul down your operating system, and shut off your PC at your leisure. When a PC is connected to a network or is running unattended, however, problems can arise.

During a prolonged outage, a simple UPS only prolongs a disaster with an untended PC; it runs another dozen minutes or so while the power is off, and then the UPS runs out of juice and the PC plummets with it. Of course, if a server crashes without warning, no one is happy, particularly if a number of files were in the queue to be saved.

To avoid these problems, better UPSs include interfaces that let them link to your PC, usually through a serial port. Install an appropriate driver, supplied by the UPS maker, and your PC can monitor the condition of your power line. When the power goes off, the software can send messages down the network warning individual users to save their work. Then, the UPS software can initiate an orderly shut down of the network.

Some UPSs will continue to run even after your network or PC has shut itself down. Better units have an additional feature termed *inverter shutdown* that automatically switches off the UPS after your network shuts down. This preserves some charge in the batteries of the UPS so that it can still offer protection if you put your PC or network back online and another power failure follows shortly thereafter. A fully discharged UPS, on the other hand, might not be ready to take the load for several hours.

Battery Life

The gelled electrolyte batteries most commonly used in uninterruptible power systems have a finite life. The materials from which they are made gradually deteriorate and the overall system loses its ability to store electricity. After several years, a gelled electrolyte battery will no longer be able to operate a UPS even for a short period. The UPS then becomes non-functional. The only way to revive the UPS is to replace the batteries.

Battery failure in a UPS usually comes as a big surprise. The power goes off and your PC goes with it, notwithstanding your investment in the UPS. The characteristics of the batteries themselves almost guarantee this surprise. Gelled electrolyte batteries gradually lose their storage capacity over a period of years, typically between three and five. Then, suddenly, their capacity plummets. They can lose nearly all their total storage ability in a few weeks. Figure 25.3 illustrates this characteristic of typical gelled electrolyte batteries.

Note that the deterioration of gelled electrolyte batteries occurs whether or not they are repeatedly discharged. They deteriorate even when not used, although repeated heavy discharges will further shorten their lives.

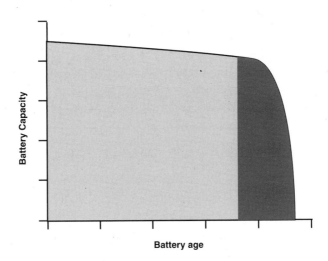

Figure 25.3
*UPS battery capacity
slowly deteriorates
and then suddenly
plummets.*

To guard against the surprise of total battery failure, better UPSs incorporate an automatic testing mechanism that periodically checks battery capacity. A battery failure indication from such a UPS should not be taken lightly.

Phone Line Protection

Spikes and surges affect more than just power lines. Any wire that ventures outside holds the potential for attracting lightning. Any long wiring run is susceptible to induced voltages, including noise and surges. These overvoltages can be transmitted directly into your PC or its peripherals and cause the same damage as a power line surge.

The good news is that several important wiring systems incorporate their own power protection. For example, Ethernet systems (both coaxial and twisted-pair) have sufficient surge protection for its intended application. Apple LocalTalk adapters are designed to withstand surges of 2,000 volts with no damage. Because they are not electrical at all, fiber optical connections are completely immune to power surges.

The bad news is that two common kinds of computer wiring are *not* innately protected by surges. Telephone wiring runs long distances through the same environments as the power distribution system and is consequently susceptible to the same problems. In particular, powerful surges generated by direct lightning hits or induction can travel through telephone wiring through your modem and into the circuitry of your PC. In addition, ordinary serial port circuitry includes no innate surge suppression. A long unshielded serial cable can pick up surges from other cables by induction.

The best protection is avoidance. Keep unshielded serial cable runs short whenever possible. If you must use a long serial connection, use shielded cable. Better still, break up the run with a short haul modem, which will also increase the potential speed of the connection.

Modem connections with the outside world are unavoidable in these days of online connectivity and the Internet. You can, however, protect against phone line surges using special suppressors designed exactly for that purpose. Better power protection devices also have modem connections that provide the necessary safeguards. Standalone telephone surge suppressors are also available. They use the same technologies as power line surge suppressors. Indeed, the voltage that rings your telephone is nearly the same as the 110 to 120 volt utility power used in the United States. Most phone line suppressors are based on MOV devices. Better units combine MOVs with capacitors, inductors, and fuses.

Cases

What holds your whole PC together is its case, but a case is more than a mere box. The case provides secure mountings for circuit boards and mass storage devices. It protects delicate circuitry from all the evils of the outside world—both mechanical and electrical—and it protects the world and you from what's inside the PC—both interference and dangerous voltages. Cases come in various sizes, shapes, and effectiveness at their protective tasks to match your PC and the way you plan to use it.

Style	In short
Tower	Massive case nearly two feet high with room for half a dozen disk drives. Usually reserved for servers.
Midi-tower	Today's most popular package, an upright system with the same storage as a classic desktop: about four drive bays and six expansion slots—exactly what most people want and need.
Mini- or micro-tower	A dwarfed tower meant for those not planning extensive expansion. A top choice when you plan to stick with what you bought and move on to another PC when your current system can't handle the latest incarnation of Windows.
Desktop	The classic case with about four drive bays and six to eight expansion slots that does double-duty as a monitor stand on your desktop. Overly bulky in today's world and losing favor to smaller packages.
Compact	A desktop system with most of the air drained out. Although it may slight on a bay and slot or two, the compact system is substantially smaller than a conventional desktop, usually more attractive and quieter.
Zero Footprint	The latest trend—a notebook-size system anchored down, perhaps hidden inside a flat-panel monitor. Trendiness has its price—these smallest of systems currently cost more and have more limited (and more expensive) expansion options.
Notebook	The traditional laptop package that now holds everything you'd find in a desktop package (along with a battery and monitor) in a 6- to 8-pound package. Both the most powerful and least expensive portable systems fit this package.
Subnotebook	A 3- or 4-pound PC that cuts corners on screen size, keyboard size, disk drives and so on, but is easier to carry. Best suited as a supplemental computer rather than a desktop replacement.
Handheld	Handhelds with keyboards now overlap with subnotebooks but run Windows CE (instant on but not program-compatible with desktop Windows). Those that use pens instead of keyboards are Personal Digital Assistants and serve best as portable appointment books with crude note-taking ability (although new PDAs are remarkable information retrieval and display systems).

The case is the physical embodiment of your PC. In fact, the case is the body of your PC. It's a housing, vessel, and shield that provides the delicate electronics of the computer a secure environment in which to work. It protects against physical dangers—forces that might act against its circuit boards, bending, stressing, even breaking them with deleterious results to their operation. It also prevents electrical short circuits that may be caused by the in-fall of the foreign objects that typically inhabit the office—paper clips, staples, letter openers, beer cans, and errant bridgework. The case also guards against invisible dangers, principally strong electrical fields that could induce noise that would interfere with the data handling of your system, potentially causing errors that would crash your system.

The protective shield of the case works both ways. It also keeps what's inside your PC inside your PC. Among the wonders of the workings of a computer, two in particular pose problems for the outside world. The electrical voltages inside the PC can be a shocking discovery if you accidentally encounter them. And the high-frequency electrical signals that course through the computer's circuits can radiate like radio broadcasts and interfere with the reception of other transmissions—which includes everything from television to aircraft navigational beacons.

Your PC's case also has a more mundane role. Its physical presence gives you a place to put the things that you want to connect to your computer. *Drive bays* allow you to put mass storage devices within ready reach of your PC's logic circuits while affording the case's protection to your peripherals. In addition, your PC's case provides the physical embodiment of the *expansion slot*, affording the boards that slide into the connectors of your PC's expansion bus protection with the same mechanical and electrical shelter as the rest of the system.

The case can play a more mundane role, too. It also can serve as the world's most expensive monitor stand, raising your screen to an appropriate viewing height, elevated high above the clutter and confusion of your desktop. Or a tall, desk-side PC can be an impromptu stand for your coffee or cola cup or a more permanent residence for the papers that spill off your desk. Appropriately chosen, the right notebook PC can be a gimmick pick-up device that can win you dates—providing you hang with the right (or wrong, depending on your perspective) crowd.

Compounding the function of your computer's case is the need to be selective. Some of what's inside your PC needs to get out—heat, for instance. And some of what's outside needs to get in—such as signals from the keyboard and power from your electrical outlets. In addition, the computer case must form a solid foundation upon which your system can be built. It must give disk drives a firm base and hold electrical assemblies out of harm's way. Overall, the simple case may not be as simple as you think.

Physical Construction

When building a PC, two issues are paramount: how the case is put together and how you put together a PC inside it. In the first case, how the case gets constructed—whether with screws, rivets, or welds—is not so important as the size of the finished product. The size of the case determines what it can hold, which in turn limits how much you can expand the system to add all the features you want. How components install inside the case affect how much you want to expand your system. If sliding in an expansion board or just getting at a drive bay to install a new disk makes you think the system was designed by someone in league with the devil (or another employee of Microsoft), you're not going to look on expansion with much favor.

Some PC companies actually sympathize with your plight, knowing the happy customer brings good will and a satisfied customer is less likely to make calls to the support staff that it's so expensive to pay. Over the years, they have developed several schemes to make working on and expanding your PC easier—everything from cases you can open without tools to cases you cannot open at all, relying instead on external expansion.

The obvious function of the case is mechanical; you can see it and touch it as a distinct object. And it steals part of your desktop, floor, or lap when you put it to work. It has a definite size—always too small when you want to add one more thing but too large when you need to find a place to put it (and particularly when that place happens to be inside your carry-on luggage). The case also has a shape, which may be functional to allow you the best access to all those computer accouterments, such as the slot into which you shove your backup tapes. But shape and color also are part of your PC's style, which can set one system apart from the boring sameness of its computer kin.

Modern PCs have wings, waves, and flares—all only aesthetics calculated to make a given manufacturer's machines stand out among the masses, style to make you think it is more modern and capable. The features, like some of the more interesting paint shades with which some manufacturers have started experimenting, are design gimmicks, the tail-fins of the 1990s. There's nothing wrong with a PC that look like you've stolen it from the deck of an aircraft carrier, but there's nothing inherently better about it, either. Beneath the plastic, you'll find that same basic mechanical design and construction of systems built a decade ago.

In computers, form dictates function as much (if not more) than it does for any other type of office equipment. Computers have the shape they have so that they can hold what you want to put inside them—primarily all those expansion options that give your machine power and ability. It has to be large enough to accommodate the expansion boards you want to plug in as well as provide adequate space for all the disk drives your PC and life would not be complete without—hard, floppy, DVD, and the like.

For most manufacturers, the sizes of both boards and drives are preordained—set once long ago and forever invariant. The case must be designed around the needs of each. If you have enough clout, however, you can make the world work to fit your dimensions, a strategy adopted by Compaq that may change the face of PCs and expansion. Although it hasn't yet made a splash on the market, Compaq's *Device Bay* design (discussed later) promises to simplify life—for you, for computer retailers, and for manufacturers.

Beyond allocating space for options, the case also has to provide a place for such mandatory system components as motherboards and power supplies. In addition, everything must be arranged to allow air to freely flow around everything to bring your PC's circuitry, microprocessor, and peripherals a breath of cooling fresh air.

Size

A PC can be any size to carry out its job. Thanks to miniaturization, even the smallest PCs can rival the power of the largest—with one exception. You can stuff more stuff into a big box than you can a small one.

That's the essence of size differences among PCs. Bigger means more expansion, more places to put power-enhancing accessories. As long as you don't need an extraordinary amount of expansion, even the physically smallest PC will suffice.

A number of terms are used to describe the size of PCs, although none approaches being an official designation.

Compact

The basic PC—that is, the smallest with the least future potential—uses a compact device that's sometimes called a *small footprint PC*. In the jargon of the PC industry, the footprint is the space a PC occupies on your desk, so the small footprint steals less desk space, making it an ideal office companion. Compact desktop computers are sometimes called *low-profile PCs* because they are short, usually as short as possible and still hold a whole computer.

To achieve compact size, PC makers must do some serious trimming from the designs of larger computers. The principal loss is in expansion. Compact system have fewer slots and bays than other computers. They have a minimum of extra space for expansion—once filled with standard factory equipment perhaps as little as a single open slot and a single unfilled bay. The underlying philosophy is that the compact PC comes with everything you need already installed, so there's no need to add anything more.

To shave down the height of low-profile cases while conserving the capability of handling tall expansion boards, compact machines move their options on edge. Instead of boards sliding into slots vertically, these tiny PCs align them horizontally. The motherboard boards remain horizontal in the case and have a single master expansion slot. A special expansion board rises vertically with additional slot connectors on one side to allow you to slide in several ordinary expansion boards (typically three) parallel to the system board.

Although the exact assortment of drive possibilities varies with design of compact systems, most small-footprint machines offer similar drive options. They are constrained by what you expect and need in any PC. A floppy disk drive and a CD or DVD drive leer out from the front panel, and a hard disk hides safely inside. If any drive expansion is available inside these systems, it comprises a single bay suitable for an inch-tall hard disk.

The latest trend in compact PC design is to shrink the system unit down to the size of a notebook PC or eliminate it entirely. The cleverest of these squeeze the entire PC including disk drives into a flat-panel monitor. These intriguing systems have garnered much media attention not only because they are technological tours-de-force but also because they provide real benefits. They fit on even the smallest desks, cut the clutter of cables, and even reduce the noise level down to that of a notebook system. On the downside, they suffer all of the limitations of notebook PCs (except for battery concerns). The worst shortcoming is that they severely constrain your expansion options. Of course, if you have no problem with notebook expansion concerns, the expansion limitations of the new miniaturized systems are no big deal.

Desktop

If any size and style of PC could be considered a standard, it is the desktop system. The basic dimensions are patterned after the first official PC, the IBM original. Despite the variety of new computers on the market, the standard desktop survives because of its practical origins. It was sized to fit a pair of big drive bays, an adequate number of expansion slots (at the time, five to eight), and other necessities such as a power supply. The result was a case measuring 21 inches wide by 17 inches deep. Its height, to allow for expansion boards and 3/8-inch feet underneath for airflow (just enough so you could lose a pencil—maybe the designers did have some kind of inspiration!), measured 5.5 inches. Commonly, such systems are termed *XT size* after IBM's most popular early model of this size.

The *mini-AT* size is related—XT in every way but height, gaining an extra inch to accommodate taller expansion boards that at one time were prevalent.

For nearly a decade, the *AT* size case was the reigning standard for desktop PCs. The biggest desktop package in general production, it stretched the XT package by two inches in width and an inch in height (to measure 6.5 by 17 by 23 inches, HWD) to accommodate more circuitry.

Smaller manufacturers—those that buy cases from outside suppliers along with other components to custom-build systems—may still put their products in one of these vintage packages: XT, mini-AT, or AT. Larger manufacturers have abandoned these relics because they are large, expensive to manufacture, and not particularly pretty or friendly. Their custom cases are stylish (which can be good or bad, just like the designer's taste), plastic, and smaller.

Because few people need more than one large (5.25-inch) drive bay, most new machines opt to shrink the other bay area to 3.5-inch size, shaving about two inches of the PC in the process. This intermediate package, measuring about 5.5 by 19 by 17 inches, is today's most popular in desktop systems.

Towers

Stand a conventional PC on edge and you get a tower. At least that's how the tower format evolved. The design has proven so popular that these days, one form of tower or another probably *is* the standard PC.

The upright design actually makes the ultimate small-footprint PC. It steals no space from your desk if you set it next to the furniture. A smaller footprint is hard to imagine.

The AT first brought legitimacy to installing personal computers on edge, using an afterthought mounting scheme—a cocoon to enclose a conventional AT machine on its end. The first mainstream PCs designed from the start for floor-mounting were introduced in 1987.

Freed from restraints required when sharing a desktop, tower computers could expand to suit even the most fanciful dreams. The largest have nearly as many bays as the Eastern seaboard—as many as eight in a single system. On the other hand, they usually do not extend the number of expansion slots over eight. The reason is not a spatial limitation but an economic one. Most towers use standard, off-the-shelf motherboards. Raising the slot could involve expensive redesign (as well as more motherboard, circuitry, and assembly costs).

With modern components, vertically mounting computer components causes no problems. Electronic circuits don't know which way is up. Although mechanical devices such as disk drives may care, the only practical effects with current hardware is really your problem. Putting a CD drive on edge can turn loading a disc into a dash across your office floor and down the hall as you race after the errant disc that dropped and rolled away. Most towers keep bays horizontal to avoid the office chase scene. Compaq even developed a PC transformer; by remounting the drive bay and changing the front panel bezel, you can switch the Deskpro EP series from desktop to tower and back.

The tower design has been so successful, designers have fine-tuned the vertical package to meet a variety of expansion needs. *Mini-tower cases* are the most compact and usually accommodate only mini-AT and smaller motherboards and a few drive options. A microtower shrinks things further, providing only two or three bays and room for a tiny motherboard (for example, mini- or micro-ATX). *Full-size tower cases* hold full-size motherboards and more drive bays than most people know what to do with. Recently, *midi-tower cases*, with accommodation falling in between, have become a popular option. There is no standardization of these terms. One manufacturer's mini is another's midi.

Choose a PC with a tower-style case for its greater physical capacity for internal peripherals and its flexibility of installation wherever there are a few vacant feet of floor space. You also need to be critical about the provisions for physically mounting mass storage devices. Some towers provide only flimsy mounting means or require you to work through a Chinese puzzle of interlocking parts to install a drive. You need a system that provides sufficient drive-mounting options.

Server

With network servers, all bets are off. Although the first PC-based servers were in fact PCs—identical in size, shape, and style—current servers are quite different beasts. Beasts, indeed. Some steal whole equipment racks with shelf upon shelf of disk drive arrays.

Notebook

Back in the days before micro-miniaturization, anything instantly became portable the moment you attached a handle. The first generation of portable televisions, for example, was eminently portable—at least for anyone accustomed to carrying a carboy under each arm. The first generation of PCs had similar pretenses of portability, challenging your wherewithal with a weighty bottle of gas and photons, and a small but hardly lightweight picture tube. The typical weight of a first-generation portable PC was about 40 pounds— about the limit of what the market (or any reasonable human being) would bear.

These portables were essentially nothing more than a repackaging that combined a conventional PC with an integral monitor. Some—for example, IBM's ill-starred PC Portable—used motherboards straight from desktop systems. (The PC Portable was just an XT in schleppable clothing.) Drive bays were moved and slots sacrificed for a package that appealed to the visual senses, no matter the insult to your musculature.

Replacing the bottle with a flat-panel display gave designers a quick way to cut half the weight and repackage systems into lunchbox PCs. The name referred to the slab-sided design with a handle on top reminiscent of what every kid not party to the school lunch program toted to class—but with some weighing in at 20 to 25 pounds, these packages were enough to provide Paul Bunyan with his midday meal. The largest of these did allow the use of conventional motherboards with space for several conventional expansion slots. Overall, however, the design was one that only a mother could love, at least if she advocated an aggressive weight-training program.

The ultimate in computer compression is the notebook PC, machines shrunk as small as possible while allowing your hands a grip on their keyboards (and eyes a good look at the screen) and as thin as componentry allows. Making machines this small means everything has got to give; you can find compromises in nearly every system component.

The fewest of these compromises appear in mass storage. The need for tiny, flyweight drives for both notebook computers and machines of even smaller dimensions has been the principal driving force behind the miniaturization of floppy and hard disks. Drive manufacturers have been amazingly successful at reducing physical size while increasing capacity and improving performance and reliability. Moreover, many notebook system manufacturers are now relegating the hard disk drive to removable status, opting to install drives in PCMCIA Type 3 slots so that your dealer can easily configure a system or you can readily upgrade your own.

Today, the biggest compromises made for the sake of compact size appear in the user interfaces. Making a portable computer portable means making it a burden that a human being can bear, even one that will be willingly borne. And the portable must be something that can be packed rather than needing to be tethered with mooring ropes. Unfortunately, some aspects of the user interface can't be compressed without losing usability; it's unlikely that human hands will be downsized to match the demand for smaller, lighter PCs so the optimal size required for a keyboard won't shrink. But the temptation remains for the manufacturer to trim away what's viewed as excess—a bit around the edges from the function keys or eliminating some keys altogether in favor of key combinations only contortionists can master.

A number of subnotebook machines have been developed with keyboards reduced to 80 percent the standard size. These include the Gateway HandBook series and the Zeos Contenda. Most people adapt to slightly cramped keyboards and continue to touch-type without difficulty. Smaller than that, however, and touch-typing becomes challenging. In other words, handheld PCs are not for extensive data entry.

Besides length and width, notebook computer makers also have trimmed the depth of their keyboards, reducing the height of keytops—not a noticeable change—as well as key travel. The latter can have a dramatic effect on typing feel and usability. Although the feel and travel of a keyboard are mostly user preference, odds favor greater dissatisfaction with the shrunken, truncated keyboards in miniaturized computers compared to full-size machines.

Displays, too, are a matter of compromise. Bulky picture-tube displays are out, replaced with flat screens of size limited by the dimensions of the rest of the notebook package.

Although notebook systems of days gone by have explored a number of variations on the screen-mounting theme, today's most common case is the clamshell. Like the homestead of a good old geoduck, the clamshell case is hinged to open at its rear margin. The top holds the screen. When folded down, it protects the keyboard; when opened, it looms behind the keyboard at an adjustable angle. In general, the hinge is the weakest part of this design.

Physical Construction

To make their systems more ergonomic, some notebook manufacturers try to follow the desktop paradigm by cutting the keyboard, screen, or both free from the main body of the computer. The appeal of these designs is adjustability: You can work the way you want with your hands as close or far from the screen as feels most comfortable. When used in an office, this design works well. When mobile—say in a coach class seat on a commuter plane bounding between less civilized realms in the Midwest—the extra pieces to tangle with (and lose) can be less a blessing than a curse. The worst compromise is the keyboard. Making a machine portable demands the weight of every part be minimized. But lightweight keyboards coupled with cables that are too short and too springing can be frustrating to use—the keys and then the entire keyboard slipping away from under your fingers.

Although a few notebook systems allow the use of ISA expansion boards, the match is less than optimal. Expansion boards designed for desktop use are not built with the idea of conserving power, so a single board may draw as many watts as the rest of a notebook computer, cutting battery life commensurately. Consequently, most notebook PCs and nearly all notebook machines forswear conventional expansion boards in favor of proprietary expansion products or the credit-card size expansion modules that follow the PC Card and CardBus standards.

Access is one major worry with notebook cases. If you plan to expand the memory of your system, you need a notebook that lets you plug in memory modules or memory cards without totally disassembling the PC. The easiest machines to deal with have slots hidden behind access panels that allow you to slide in a memory card as easily as a floppy disk. Others may have access hatches that accommodate the addition of memory modules. The only shortcoming of either of these expansion methods is the amount of additional memory such machines support—notebook machines usually can handle enough memory for the bulkiest of general-purpose applications but have insufficient memory slots for the massive specialized applications programmers stay up nights creating. Many notebook computers, especially the lower-cost models wearing the house brands of mail-order companies, require that you remove the keyboard to access memory module sockets—a tricky job that demands more skill and patience than you may want to devote to such a task. A few even require unbolting the screen for accessing expansion sockets. If you plan on expanding a notebook or notebook system in the future, check both the permitted memory expansion capacity and the method for adding more RAM.

The key design feature of any notebook or subnotebook computer is portability. You need a machine that's packaged to be as compact and light as possible—commensurate with the ergonomic features that you can tolerate. Older notebooks had built-in handles; newer machines have foregone that luxury. With PCs now weighing in under five pounds and sometimes measuring smaller than a stack of legal pads, that lack has become tolerable; you can either wrap your palm around the machine or tuck it into a carrying case.

At one time, the toughest notebook computers had cases crafted from metal, often tough but light magnesium, but nearly all machines today are encased in high-impact plastic. In general, they are tough enough for everyday abuse but won't tolerate a tumble from desktop to floor any more than would a clock, a camera, or other precision device. Inside, you find foil or metal-enclosed subassemblies, but these are added to keep radiation within limits rather than minimize the effects of sudden deceleration after free-fall. In other words, notebook and subnotebook computers are made to be tough, but abuse can be as fatal to them as any other business tool.

Internal Access

Two philosophies surround the issue of access into your PC's case. One school of thought holds that it should be as easy as possible so that you can make upgrades quickly and easily. The other school believes that you can only get yourself into trouble inside your PC. Students of this school believe that the best case is one that's sealed against access. If they had their way, your PC would be embedded in a block of Lucite so you could see its pretty lights but touch not a thing inside.

The curriculum divides roughly on application lines. PCs used at home or in a small business—that is, one small enough that you're responsible for your own PC—are best with open access. Large businesses that have a unified Information Systems department headed by an all-powerful fuehrer want to keep in absolute control—which means keeping you out. The needs of these folks led the move to the Network Computer.

Tool-free entry allows you to open and upgrade your system without special tools or any tools at all. You won't have to steal a knife from the silverware drawer to get into your PC or buy a special screwdriver to pull out an expansion board. In the ideal case, the lid unlatches and slides off your PC with minimum effort. Disk drives snap into place, and knurled posts that you can tighten with your fingers lock expansion boards into place. Some current systems approach this ideal, but few go all the way.

Bays

Bays come in two basic varieties, those with *front panel access* and those without. Front panel access bays are for devices using removable media. You must have access to the front of the drive to slide in a disk or tape cartridge. Floppy disk drives, CD and DVD drives, and tape drives all must be mounted in bays with front panel access.

Internal bays lack front panel access. They may be tucked away inside the computer or just below the bays with front panel access. Internal bays suit devices that require no direct user interaction, those that you don't have to see or touch. The chief occupant of an internal bay is the hard disk drive.

Form Factors

Disk drives come in a variety of heights and widths. The basic unit of measurement of the size of a drive is the form factor. A form factor is simply the volume of a standard drive that handles a particular medium. Several form factors regularly find their way into discussions of personal computers ranging in size from 8 inches to 1.3 inches, most of which allow for one or more device heights.

A full-size drive, one that defines the form factor and occupies all of its volume, is usually a first-generation machine. Its exact dimensions, chosen for whatever particular reason, seemed fitting, perhaps allowing for the mood of the mechanical engineer on the day he was drafting the blueprints. If the drive is a reasonable size and proves particularly successful—successful enough that other manufacturers eagerly want to cash in, too—others follow suit and copy the dimension of the product, making it a standard.

Device Heights

The second generation of any variety of hardware inevitably results in some sort of size reduction. Cost cutting, greater precision, experience in manufacturing, and the inevitable need to put more in less space gang up to shrink things down. The result of the downsizing process is a variety of fractional size devices, particularly in the 5.25-inch and 3.5-inch form factors. At 5.25 inches, devices are measured in subincrements of the original full-height package. Devices that are two-thirds height, half-height, one-third height, or quarter-height have all been manufactured at one time or another.

At the 3.5-inch form factor, sizes are more pragmatic, measured as the actual height in inches. The original 3.5-inch drives may be considered full-height and typically measure about 1.6 inches high. The next most widely used size was an even inch in height (5/8 height, for the fractious folk who prefer fractions). Sub-inch heights have been used for some devices, some as small as 0.6 inches.

However, before 3.5-inch drives had a chance to slim down to two dimensions, smaller form factors came into play—2.5, 1.8, and 1.3 inches. The 2.5-inch devices were designed primarily for notebook computers. Smaller drives fit palmtop computers, even on credit card-size expansion boards. The 1.8-inch size has won particular favor for fitting into Type 3 PC Cards that follow the most recent standards promulgated by PCMCIA.

Note that all of these applications for sub-3.5-inch drives are the type in which the system (or at least its case or other packaging) is designed around the drive. In other words, only the PC manufacturer needs to fret about the exact dimensions of the drive and what fits where.

With the introduction of Device Bay, many PC makers hope that the issue of form factor will disappear from the consumer market. All drives, the Device Bay promoters hope, will eventually be packaged to fit a Device Bay.

Racks

Most drive-mounting schemes are meant for permanent installations. Your hard disk drive is supposed to last for the life of your PC. In certain situations, however, you may want something less permanent.

If you deal in secrets or have valuable information on your PC, you might not want to leave it out on your desk untended all night long. Although packing up and putting your PC away for the evening is more trouble than most people want to bother with, pulling out a disk drive and sliding it into a safe is not.

Although hard disks are quite reliable, every one you add to your system increases the chances that one will fail. Multiple disk drives and the need for reliable operation go hand-in-hand in RAID systems. To speed repairs, most RAID systems have moved to mounting drives for hot-swapping.

In either case, the choice is mounting your drive in a removable *rack*. The typical hot-swap rack allows you to install a 3.5-inch hard disk in a 5.25-inch bay. More than an adapter, it puts the drive on a sub-module that slides into the rack, connects, and locks in place. You can remove a drive for the evening or swap a new drive for an old one at any time. Each rack manufacturer uses its own designs, so there's no intercompatibility among different rack systems.

Slots

All expansion slots are not the same. Put another way, a slot is not a slot is not a slot. Expansion slots differ in two primary ways—the standard followed and length.

The standard followed generally refers to the bus, as discussed in Chapter 7, "The Expansion Bus." In general, today's transitional PCs—that is, those still having ISA slots—class their slots in three ways by standard. PCI, ISA, and combination. Thanks to the clever mechanical design of PCI cards—they put most of their electrical components on the opposite side from ISA cards and mount at the opposite side of each slot—a single physical expansion slot can host both a PCI and an ISA connector. These combination slots allow you to slide in either kind of board. But despite the two connectors, only one board will fit into the slot. You get either PCI or ISA but not both at the same time.

To push up slot totals, many manufacturers also add that their systems (or motherboards) include an Accelerated Graphics Port (AGP) slot. Technically, they are correct. The AGP slot works exactly like an expansion slot. But it is irrelevant when analyzing the availability of expansion. Any PC with an AGP slot likely fills it with an AGP graphics adapter (why else would the slot be there?), so the AGP slot in never available for expansion (although it does allow you to upgrade your video system). Ordinary expansion boards—both PCI and ISA—will **not** fit into the AGP slot in a PC.

Slots also vary in length. A *full-size* slot allows you to install any length of expansion board. A *short slot* cannot hold a full-length expansion board. Although PCI describes the dimensions of a short card, PC makers make short slots of any length that suits their designs. In general, these short slots are more than half the length of a full-size slot and will accommodate most short cards. Most modern expansion boards are short, so you ordinarily won't have problems matching slot length.

Device Bay

Although swapping drives in your PC doesn't hold the same thrills and sense of excitement of, say, giving your cat a bath, it comes close. The scars may be more emotional than epidermal, but the anticipation of the event is rarely fraught with joy. It's a tedious, thankless job that's potentially a source of injury—skinned knuckles, wounded pride, hemorrhaging bank account. To save you from that—and incidentally save the cost of hiring yet another platoon of customer disservice representatives to field your support calls—computer maker Compaq, along with Intel and Microsoft, has been developing a standard for plug-in hard disks and related devices. Called Device Bay, the proposed standard has been gestating for several years and, as this is written, has not yet been approved. Although Device Bay is a recommended feature in all PCs under the Intel/Microsoft PC99 system guidelines, as of early 1999 neither a final standard nor commercial products were available. The specification was still evolving, pegged at version 0.9.

To take Device Bay into full standardization, the work in progress was turned over to the Device Bay Trade Association with an internal working group devoted to finishing the specification. The acting chairman of the working group reported that support for Device Bay will be built into both the second release of Windows 98 and the initial release of Windows 2000, although that support may be limited to Compact Disc, DVD, and non-bootable hard disk drives.

That said, mass storage drives are only one of the targets of Device Bay. The mounting system is designed to be flexible enough to handle communications equipment (for example, modems and network adapters) and security systems.

The options for peripheral manufacturers are several. Device Bay allows for three form factors and two interfaces, USB as well as IEEE 1394. Only the speed of its chosen interfaces limits its ultimate potential; current implementations of the IEEE 1394 connection don't have the performance demanded by modern display systems. Although the speed of IEEE 1394 is slated to rise to 3,200 mbits/sec, it still lags behind the quickest versions of AGP.

The goal of the design is to allow you to swap drives as easily as PC Cards; slide one out and another in regardless of whether your PC is on and running. Device Bay integrates both of its interfaces in a single connector specifically designed for hot-swapping.

Although the physical connections vary from the outline of the interface standards presented in Chapter 20, "Peripheral Ports," electrically and logically the Device Bay implementations follow their respective standards. Each bay under the Device Bay standard supports both interfaces; a device can use either or both interfaces. In addition, the single integrated connector incorporates power connections for the device. Figure 26.1 shows the Device Bay jack found inside compliant PCs.

FIGURE 26.1

The jack used by the Device Bay expansion system.

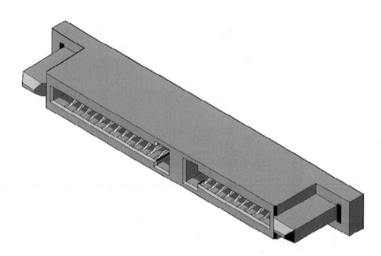

The male plug appears on the back of each Device Bay module. To protect its contacts from damage, the entire connector is recessed behind the plane of the rear panel of the module.

The proposed standard makes allowances for current drive interfaces. It envisions AT Attachment-style drives mounted in a Device Bay module together with circuitry to convert the ATA signals into IEEE 1394. In effect, it makes Device Bay into a hot-swap rack like those used in RAID storage systems but incorporates all the automatic recognition and configuration of the USB and FireWire interfaces.

The three module sizes are denoted by their height in millimeters as DB13, DB20, and DB32. The first two are identical in width and depth, but the last is both wider and longer. In addition, the largest Device Bay is allocated additional power. Table 26.1 lists the dimensions of each Device Bay form factor.

TABLE 26.1   Device Bay Dimensions

Form Factor	Height	Width	Depth	Maximum Weight
	Inches/Millimeters	Inches/Millimeters	Inches/Millimeters	Pounds/Kilograms
DB13	0.512/13.0	5.118/130.0	5.571/141.5	0.77/0.33
DB20	0.787/20.0	5.118/130.0	5.571/141.5	1.10/0.50
DB32	1.260/32.0	5.748/146.0	7.008/178.0	3.08/1.40

The Device Bay itself provides a channel made from top and bottom guides at each side of the bay. A device slides in between the rails. To prevent devices from rattling around in the bay, the specification recommends a small leaf at the top of each guide to hold the device firmly in place.

All device modules must be the same length for the bay size they are to fit. This assures that their connectors will firmly engage while the bezel of the module properly lines up with the front of the host PC. Each bay also has an eject mechanism. In simplest form, an eject button near the bay links to a lever at the rear of the bay. Pushing the button levers the drive module out of the bay. The specification does not preclude motorized implementations that operate like CD or DVD drive trays, interlocked with software controls.

Electrical Operation

The contacts on the Device Bay connector on the rear of each module can be long or short, assuring that the circuits assigned the long contact connect first. All ground contacts are long as is the identification voltage. These mate first.

The IEEE 1394 connection system requires transmitter pins connect with receiver pins. Instead of crossing these connections in the cable, the Device Bay system reverses the definitions of the pins on devices and bays.

Two pins identify the interface used by a Device Bay module, one for USB and one for IEEE 1394. To indicate a module uses an interface, the module grounds the identification pin associated with that interface; otherwise, it makes no connection to the pin.

Although the Device Bay connector provides for all of the data channels used by both IEEE 1394 and USB connections, it does not use connectors that follow those standards. Moreover, it does not provide separate power connectors to meet those specifications. The Device Bay connector does, however, include its own power connections for three different voltage levels to accommodate the widest selection of drives. The voltages provided include 3.3, 5.0, and 12 volts. In addition, Device Bay provides a dedicated connection for indicating device activity, for example, flashing the drive activity indicator on the front panel of your PC.

The Device Bay connector is divided into two parts. The signal section uses 26 connections and the power segment uses 18, for a total of 44 pins arranged in two parallel rows. Table 26.2 lists the pins on the Device Bay connector and their functions.

TABLE 26.2   Device Bay Connector Receptacle Pin-Out

Pin	Signal	Signal	Pin
A1	Gnd	Gnd	A14
A2	TPB	Gnd	A15
A3	TPB#	Gnd	A16
A4	Gnd	Gnd	A17
A5	TPA	Gnd	A18
A6	TPA#	Gnd	A19
A7	Gnd	Gnd	A20
A8	1394PRSN#	Gnd	A21
A9	DEV_ACT#	Gnd	A22
A10	USBPRSN#	Gnd	A23
A11	D+	Gnd	A24
A12	D-	Gnd	A25
A13	V_{id}	Reserved	A26
Gap and keys for signal and power segments			
B1	V_{33}	Gnd	B10
B2	V_{33}	Gnd	B11
B3	V_{33}	Gnd	B12
B4	V_{33}	Gnd	B13
B5	V_{33}	Gnd	B14
B6	V_{33}	Gnd	B15
B7	V_{12}	V_5	B16
B8	V_{12}	V_5	B17
B9	V_{12}	V_5	B18

Motherboard Mounting

A motherboard must somehow be mounted in its cabinet, and PC manufacturers have devised a number of ways of holding motherboards down. This simple-sounding job is more complex than you may think. The motherboard cannot simply be screwed down flat. The projecting cut ends of pin-in-hole components make the bottom uneven, and torquing the board into place is apt to stress it, even crack hidden circuit traces. Moreover, most PC cases are metal and laying the motherboard flat against the bottom panel is apt to result in a severe short circuit. Consequently, the motherboard must not only be held secure, but also it must be spaced a fraction of an inch (typically in the range of 3/8 to 1/2) above the bottom of the case.

IBM originally solved the motherboard-mounting problem ingeniously in its first PC. The motherboards in these machines—and those of later machines from that and many other manufacturers—use a combination of screws and specialized spacers that make manufacture (and board replacement) fast and easy. The design is actually amazingly frugal, using just two (sometimes three) screws.

The balance of the mounting holes in these motherboards is devoted to nylon fasteners, which insulate the boards from the metal chassis while holding them in place. These fasteners have two wings that pop through the hole in the motherboard and snap out to lock themselves in place. The bottom of these fasteners slides into a special channel in the bottom of the PC case.

Mechanically, the two or three screws hold these PC motherboards in place and the nylon fasteners are designed to space the board vertically and fit special channels in the metal work of the case, allowing the boards to slide into place.

In this design, removing the screws allows you to slide the motherboard to the left, freeing the nylon fasteners from their channel. Installing a motherboard requires only setting the board down so that the fasteners engage their mounting channel and then sliding the board to the right until the vacant screw holes line up with the mounting holes in the chassis. Because the number of screws is minimized, so is the labor required to assemble a PC—an important matter when you plan to make hundreds of thousands of machines.

Other personal computer makers developed their own means of mounting motherboards inside their machines. Some of these manufacturers save the cost of welding the fastener mounting channels in place by drilling a few holds in the bottom of the case and supplying you with a number of threaded metal or plastic spacers (usually nothing more than small nylon tubes) and screws. These spacers are meant to hold the system board the same height above the bottom of the chassis as would the standard nylon fasteners.

Many modern system that follow the ATX design have slide-in motherboards. After you remove a few screws, the motherboard slides out the back or side of the case. A good idea, perhaps, but far from perfect. Despite the easy external access, you'll still have to poke around inside your PC to pull out the expansion boards and unplug internal connectors before you can slide the board out.

Today's standardized motherboards (ATX, mini-ATX, micro-ATX, NLX, WTX, and so on) ease the chore of finding the right motherboard. These standards define exactly where all the mounting holes must be. If you match the motherboard standard to your case style (that is, replace your motherboard with one that follows the same standard), everything is guaranteed to fit. You won't have to make holes nor will you have hardware left over when you're done—at least no more than when you work on any other project.

When installing a replacement motherboard in an older, nonstandardized case that forces you to improvise with screws and spacers, you have two choices. You can screw the spacers into the case, put the motherboard atop them, and then screw the motherboard to the spacers. Or you could screw the motherboard to the spacers and then try to get the spacers to fit the holes in the bottom of the case. Neither method is very satisfactory because you're faced with getting 10 or so holes and screws to line up, which, owing to the general lack of precision exercised by cut-rate manufacturers in making these cases, they never do. The best thing to do is compromise. Attach the spacers loosely to the motherboard and then try to get the screws at the bottom of the spacers to line up with the holes in the case. You should be able to wiggle them into the holes.

Sometimes when you want to upgrade or repair a PC by replacing its motherboard, you find that the holes in the case and motherboard are at variance. In such circumstances, the best strategy is to modify your case by drilling holes in it to match the motherboard and then use screws and spacers for mounting. Never modify the motherboard by drilling holes in it. You can damage circuit board traces, some of which are invisible and buried within layers of the motherboard.

Cooling

A case can be confining. It can keep just about everything from escaping, including the heat electronic circuits produced as a by-product performing their normal functions. Some of the electricity in any circuit (except one made from superconductors) is turned into heat by the unavoidable electrical resistance of the circuit. Heat is also generated whenever an element of a computer circuit changes state. In fact, nearly all of the electricity consumed by a computer eventually turns into heat.

Inside the protective (and confining) case of the computer, that heat builds up, thus driving up the temperature. Heat is the worst enemy of semiconductor circuits; it can shorten their lives considerably or even cause their catastrophic failure. Some means of escape must be provided for the excess heat. In truth, the heat build-up in most PCs may not be immediately fatal to semiconductor circuits. For example, most microprocessors shut down (or simply generate errors that shut down your PC) before any permanent damage occurs to them or the rest of the components inside your PC. However, heat can cause circuits to age prematurely and can trim the lives of circuit components.

The design of the case of a PC affects how well the machine deals with its heat build-up. A case that's effective in keeping its internal electronics cool can prolong the life of the system. Better systems incorporate specific means to ensure the hottest components inside (microprocessor, memory, and graphics system) keep cool. They mix passive and active cooling with a combination of fans, heat sinks, and air ducts.

Passive Convection

The obvious way to make a PC run cooler is to punch holes in its case to let the heat out—but to keep the holes small enough so that other things such as mice and milkshakes can't get in. In due time, passive convection—less dense hot air rising with denser cool air flowing in to take its place—lets the excess thermal energy drift out of the case.

Any impediment to the free flow of air slows the passive cooling effect. In general, the more holes in the case, the merrier the PC will be. Remove the lid, and the heat can waft away along with temperature worries.

Unfortunately, your PC's case should be closed. Keeping a lid on it does more than just restrict cooling; it is also the only effective way to deal with interference. It also keeps your PC quieter, prevents foreign objects and liquids from plummeting in, and gives your monitor a lift.

Moreover, passive cooling is often not enough. Only low-power designs (such as notebook and Green PCs) generate little enough heat that convection can be entirely successful. Other systems generate more heat than naturally goes away on its own.

Active Cooling

The alternative to passive cooling is, hardly unexpectedly, active cooling, which uses a force of some kind to move the heat away from the circuits. The force of choice in most PCs is a fan. The high power requirements (and thus heat generation) of Pentium-class microprocessors demands active cooling.

The microprocessor fan is not the only active cooling element in most PCs. Usually tucked inside the power supply, the computer's fan forces air to circulate both inside the power supply and the computer. It sucks cool air in to circulate and blows the heated air out.

The cooling systems of early PCs, however, were particularly ill-conceived for active cooling. The fans were designed mostly to cool off the heat-generating circuitry inside the power supply itself and only incidentally cool the inside of the computer. Moreover, the chance design of the system resulted in most of the cool air getting sucked in through the floppy disk drive slots. Along with the air, in come all the dust and grime floating around in the environment, polluting whatever media you have sitting in the drive. At least enough air coursed through the machine to cool off the small amount of circuitry that the meager power supply of the PC could provide.

Unfortunately, many of the smallest computer manufacturers (sometimes called "third tier" computer makers—meaning an entrepreneur with a few motherboards, a screwdriver, and a shaky business plan) rely on cooling that has not advanced beyond the most basic level. At most, they graft a heatsink-and-fan onto the system microprocessor to keep it running (many microprocessors have integral fans), but may still rely on the fan in the power supply to move the cooling air through the system.

Advanced Cooling

Better computer systems have more carefully thought-out cooling systems, channeling the flow of cooling air to the places it is most needed. The elaborate plastic work inside these PCs ensures that the hottest parts of the PC get the most cooling. In older systems, you can improve the available cooling. Booster fans that clamp on the rear panel of the computer and power supplies with beefed-up fans are available. These do, in fact, increase air circulation through the system unit, potentially lowering the internal temperature and prolonging the lives of components. Note that there is no reliable data on whether this additional cooling increases the life of the components inside your PC. Unless you stuff every conceivable accessory into your machine, however, you're unlikely to need such a device except for the added measure of peace of mind it provides.

On the other hand, blocking the airpath of the cooling system of any PC can be fatal, allowing too much heat to build up inside the chassis. Never locate a PC in cramped quarters that lacks air circulation (such as a desk drawer or a shelf on which it just fits). Never block the cooling slots or holes of a computer case.

Fan Failure

The fan inside a PC power supply is a necessity, not a luxury. If it fails to operate, your computer won't falter—at least not at first. But temperatures build up inside. The machine—the power supply in particular—may even fail catastrophically from overheating.

The symptoms of fan failure are subtle but hard to miss. You hear the difference in the noise your system makes. You may even be able to smell components warming past their safe operating temperature.

Should you detect either symptom, hold your hand near where the air usually emerges from your computer. (On most PCs, that's near the big round opening that the fan peers through.) If you feel no breeze, you can be certain your fan is no longer doing its job.

Microprocessor fan problems are more insidious. You cannot hear the fan above the rest of the din of the PC, so you cannot readily tell whether the microprocessor fan is running. The only way to be sure is to open up your PC and take a look—and even that may be ambiguous. Microprocessor fans (as well as the other fans in your PC) may be thermostatically controlled. That is, they may switch on only when a thermostate detects too high of a temperature. In such systems, not only is a glance at the fan not sufficient to judge failure but also the fan may be working while the thermostat is not.

Many PCs with thermostatic fans allow you to select whether the fan is constantly on, off, or thermostatically controlled. In most systems that allow the choice, you make adjustments through BIOS advanced setup procedure. To check whether the thermostat or fan is the problem, change the BIOS settings to make the fan run constantly. If it does not, the fan is ailing. If the fan then runs and your suspected cooling-related problems subside, then the thermostat is ill.

If you have a thermostatically controlled fan that you cannot test in the above manner, you're better off assuming a fan failure. After all, you can replace the fan but fixing the thermostat will require the efforts of a repair technician. Replacing the fan is a good first move if your PC shuts down periodically or crashes after it warms up.

A fan failure constitutes an emergency. If it happens to your system, immediately save your work and shut the machine off. Although you can safely use it for short periods, the better strategy is to replace the fan or power supply as soon as you possibly can.

Radiation

Besides heat, all electrical circuits radiate something else—electromagnetic fields. Every flow of electrical energy sets up an electromagnetic field that radiates away. Radio and television stations push kilowatts of energy through their antennae so that this energy (accompanied by programming in the form of modulation) radiates over the countryside, eventually to be hauled in by a radio or television set for your enjoyment or disgruntlement.

The electrical circuits inside all computers work the same way but on a smaller scale. The circuit board traces act as antennae and radiate electromagnetic energy whenever the computer is turned on. When the thinking gets intense, so does the radiation.

You can't see, hear, feel, taste, or smell this radiation, just as you can't detect the emissions from a radio station (at least not without a radio), so you would think there would be no reason for concern about the radiation from your PC. But even invisible signals can be dangerous, and their very invisibility makes the more worrisome; you may never know whether they are there. The case of your PC is your primary (often only) line of defense against radiation from its electronic circuitry.

The problems of radiation are twofold: the radiation interfering with other, more desirable signals in the air and the radiation affecting your health.

Radio Frequency Interference

The signals radiated by a PC typically fall in the microwatt range, perhaps a billion times weaker than those emitted by a broadcasting station. You would think that the broadcast signals would easily overwhelm the inadvertent emissions from your PC. But the strength of signals falls off dramatically with distance from the source. They follow the inverse-square law; therefore, a signal from a source a thousand times farther away would be a million times weaker. Radio and television stations are typically miles away, so the emissions from a PC can easily overwhelm nearby broadcast signals, turning transmissions into gibberish.

The radiation from the computer circuitry occurs at a wide variety of frequencies, including not only the range occupied by your favorite radio and television stations but also aviation navigation systems, emergency radio services, and even the eavesdropping equipment some initialed government agency may have buried in your walls. Unchecked, these untamed radiations from within your computer can compete with broadcast signals not only for the ears of your radio but also that of your neighbors. These radio-like signals emitted by the computer generate what is termed radio frequency interference, or RFI, so called because they interfere with other signals in the radio spectrum.

The government agency charged with the chore of managing interference—the Federal Communications Commission—has set strict standards on the radio waves that personal computers can emit. These standards are fully covered in Appendix B, "Regulations." At their hearts, however, the FCC standards enforce a good neighbor policy. They require that the RFI from PCs be so weak that it won't bother your neighbors, although it may garble radio signals in your own home or office.

The FCC sets two standards: Class A and Class B. Computer equipment must be verified to meet the FCC Class A standard to be legally sold for business use. PCs must be certified to conform with the more stringent FCC Class B standard to be sold for home use.

Equipment makers, rather than users, must pass FCC muster. You are responsible, however, for ensuring that your equipment does not interfere with your neighbors. If your PC does interfere, legally you have the responsibility for eliminating the problem. Although you can sneak Class A equipment into your home, you have good reasons not to. The job of interference elimination is easier with Class B-certified equipment because it starts off radiating lower signal levels, so Class B machines give you a head start. Moreover, meeting the Class B standards requires better overall construction, which helps assure that you get a better case and a better PC.

Minimizing Interference

Most television interference takes one of two forms, noise and signal interference.

Noise interference appears on the screen as random lines and dots that jump randomly about. The random appearance of noise reflects its origins. Noise arises from random pulses of electrical energy. The most common source for noise is electric motors. Every spark in the brushes of an electric motor radiates a broad spectrum of radio frequency signals that your television may receive along with its normal signals. Some computer peripherals may also generate such noise.

Signal interference usually appears as a pattern of some sort on your screen—for example, a series of tilted horizontal bars or noise-like snow on the screen that stays in a fixed pattern instead of jumping madly about. Signal interference is caused by regular, periodic electrical signals.

Television interference most commonly occurs when you rely on a "rabbit ear" antenna for your television reception. Such antenna pull signals from the air in the immediate vicinity of the television set, so if your PC is nearby, its signals are more likely to be received. Moving to cable or an external antenna relocates the point your TV picks up its signals to a distant location and will likely minimize or eliminate interference from the PC near the TV set.

You can minimize the interference your PC radiates to improve your television reception by taking several preventive measures.

The first step is to make sure the lid is on your PC's case and that it and all expansion boards are firmly screwed into place. Fill all empty expansion slots with blank panels. Firmly affixing the screws is important because they ground the expansion boards or blank panels that helps them shield your PC. This strategy also helps minimize the already small fire hazard your PC presents.

If the interference persists after you screw everything down in your PC, next check to see whether you can locate where the interference leaks out your PC. The most likely suspects are the various cables that trail out of your PC and link to peripherals such as your monitor, keyboard, and printer. Disconnect cabled peripherals one at a time and observe whether the disconnection reduces the interference.

Because it operates at the highest speed (and thus, highest frequency), external SCSI cables are most prone to radiating interference. All external SCSI cables should be shielded.

Your mouse is the most unlikely part of your PC to cause TV interference. The mouse operates at serial data rates, which are much too low to interfere even with VHF television.

If disconnecting a cable reduces onscreen TV interference, the next step is to get the offending signal out of the cable. The best way is to add a ferrite core around the cable. Many computer cables already have ferrite cores installed. They are the cylindrical lumps in the cable near one or the other connector. Install the ferrite core by putting it around the offending cable near where the cable leaves your PC. You can buy clamp-on ferrite cores from many electronic parts stores. You can also buy inline filters designed for a specific port type. These usually combine ferrites with other kinds of filtering tailored for the frequency at which the port is meant to operate.

Unplugging one cable—your PC's power cable—should completely eliminate the interference radiated by your PC. After all, the PC won't work without power and can't generate or radiate anything. You can reduce the interference traveling on the power line by adding a noise filter between your PC's plug and its power outlet. You can usually obtain noise filters from electronic parts suppliers. Although a noise filter is not the same thing as a surge suppressor, most better surge suppressors also include noise filtering.

Health Concerns

Some radiation emitted by PCs is of such low frequencies that it falls below the range used by any radio station. These Very Low Frequency and Extremely Low Frequency signals (often called VLF and ELF) are thought by some people to cause a variety of health problems (see Appendix B, "Regulations" and Appendix C, "Health and Safety").

Your PC's case is the first line of defense against these signals. A metal case blocks low-frequency magnetic fields, which some epidemiological studies have hinted might be dangerous, and shields against the emission of electrical fields. Plastic cases are less effective. By themselves, they offer no electrical or magnetic shielding. But plain plastic cases would also flunk the FCC tests. Most manufacturers coat plastic cases with a conductive paint to contain interference. However, these coatings are largely ineffective against magnetic fields. Most modern systems now use metal cases or internal metal shielding inside plastic cases to minimize radiation.

No matter the construction of your PC, you can minimize your exposure to radiation from its case by ensuring that it is properly and securely assembled. Minimizing interference means screwing in the retaining brackets of all the expansion boards inside your PC and keeping the lid tightly screwed into the chassis. Keeping a tight PC not only helps keep you safe, but it keeps your system safe and intact as well.

Index

boot volumes

CD-I

cold boot

connectors

depth of sound

disk drives

hard drives

Integrated Services Digital Network (ISDN)

ISA bus

lenses

memory

P

PCI-to-PCI bridge

pixels

refreshing memory

SCSI-1

signals

standards

switch bounce

Thin Film Transistors

Weitek coprocessor

License Agreement

By opening this package, you are agreeing to be bound by the following agreement:

Windows 95/98/NT4 Installation Instructions

1. Insert the CD ROM disc into your CD ROM drive.
2. From the Windows 95 desktop, double-click the My Computer icon.
3. Double-click the icon representing your CD ROM drive.
4. Double-click the icon titled START.EXE to run the installation program.

> **NOTE** If Windows 95 is installed on your computer and you have the AutoPlay feature enabled, the SETUP.EXE program starts automatically when you insert the disc into your CD ROM drive.